FREEDOM

A DOCUMENTARY HISTORY OF EMANCIPATION
1861–1867

SERIES I
VOLUME I
THE DESTRUCTION OF SLAVERY

Fugitive slaves in Virginia, August 1862.
Source: Library of Congress

FREEDOM

A DOCUMENTARY HISTORY OF EMANCIPATION
1861–1867

SELECTED FROM THE HOLDINGS OF THE
NATIONAL ARCHIVES OF THE UNITED STATES

SERIES I
VOLUME I
THE DESTRUCTION OF SLAVERY

IRA BERLIN
BARBARA J. FIELDS
THAVOLIA GLYMPH
JOSEPH P. REIDY
LESLIE S. ROWLAND

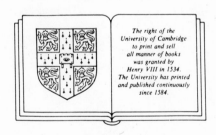

The right of the
University of Cambridge
to print and sell
all manner of books
was granted by
Henry VIII in 1534.
The University has printed
and published continuously
since 1584.

CAMBRIDGE UNIVERSITY PRESS
CAMBRIDGE
NEW YORK   NEW ROCHELLE   MELBOURNE
SYDNEY

Published by the Press Syndicate of the University of Cambridge
The Pitt Building, Trumpington Street, Cambridge CB2 1RP
32 East 57th Street, New York, NY 10022, USA
10 Stamford Road, Oakleigh, Melbourne 3166, Australia

First published 1985
Reprinted 1987 (twice)

Printed in the United States of America

Library of Congress Cataloging in Publication Data
Main entry under title:
The Destruction of slavery.
(Freedom, a documentary history of emancipation,
1861–1867; ser. 1, v. 1)
1. Afro-Americans – History – 1863-1877 – Sources.
2. Slavery – United States – Emancipation – History –
Sources. 3. Freedmen – Biography. 4. United States –
History – Civil War, 1861-1865 – Afro-Americans – Sources.
I. Berlin, Ira, 1941-. II. Fields, Barbara Jeanne.
III. Series.
E185.2.F88 ser. 1, vol. 1   973'.0496   85-6680
ISBN 0 521 22979 0

TO

W. E. B. DuBOIS

PROGENITOR

Previously published

THE BLACK MILITARY EXPERIENCE (1982)

ed. Ira Berlin, Joseph P. Reidy, and Leslie S. Rowland

FREEDMEN AND SOUTHERN SOCIETY PROJECT

IRA BERLIN, DIRECTOR

Contents

Contents

Acknowledgments

THE DESTRUCTION OF SLAVERY, which stands as the first volume of *Freedom*, is the second to reach print. And as the volumes pile up, so do our debts. In the manner of the American exchequer, we cheerfully acknowledge our accumulating obligations with the understanding that they can never be fully repaid.

In *The Black Military Experience*, published in 1982, we recognized the support and assistance of the historians and archivists who enabled us to launch the Freedmen and Southern Society Project. Three years later, we remain no less beholden to them. The assistance of Garrine P. Laney and Gail M. Thomas in the initial research at the National Archives was crucial in preparing the foundation for this and all subsequent volumes. We also reiterate our appreciation for the unflagging support of Frank Burke, Roger Bruns, and, more recently, Richard A. Jacobs, of the National Historical Publications and Records Commission (NHPRC), and Emory G. Evans, chairman of the Department of History at the University of Maryland.

Without continuing financial support, editorial work would wither on the vine. As we began this volume, federal budgetary policy threatened the very existence of NHPRC, which was forced to cut sharply its support for this and other projects. Fortunately, other institutions came to the rescue. In our case, the University of Maryland and the National Endowment for the Humanities were particularly important. We thank Provost Shirley Strum Kenny and Vice-Chancellor William E. Kirwan of the university and George Farr and Kathie Fuller of the endowment for their vote of confidence during our time of crisis. More recently, the Freedmen and Southern Society Project – along with the other members of the Consortium of Afro-American Editorial Projects – has also received support from the Ford Foundation, the Rockefeller Foundation, and the Arco-Richfield Foundation. Knowledgeable and understanding humanists made these grants possible. We would like to thank Sheila Biddle of the Ford Foundation, Lynn Szwaja of the Rockefeller Foundation, and Gerald Secundy and Anna Arrington of the Arco-Richfield Foundation for sympathetic hearings. C. Peter Ripley, editor of the Black Abolitionists Papers, won our lasting gratitude by taking time from his own important work to infuse the consortium with energy and direction.

More direct assistance came from three historians who joined the Freedmen and Southern Society Project while this volume was in progress. Michael Honey, an NHPRC Fellow during the academic year 1981–82, selected most of the documents for chapter 3 and wrote a draft of its introductory essay, while also assisting in numerous research and editorial tasks. As the volume neared completion, two new editors began work on series 3 of *Freedom*. Steven Hahn and Steven F. Miller served as a sounding board for many ideas in this volume and as critical readers of its prose. They also shared in the thankless task of proofreading.

Among the more important contributions of the University of Maryland were numerous student assistants, who brought to the project an energy and resourcefulness that have speeded and improved our work. We would like to acknowledge the hard work and steadfast commitment of the following graduate students, who did research at the National Archives or assisted in editorial chores: Robert Hinton, Greg LaMotta, Joseph Mannard, Edna Medford, Brian Sowers, and Yong Ook Jo. Joseph Mannard and Brian Sowers deserve special commendation for constructing the index with great care. Several undergraduates assisted with clerical tasks and helped keep the word processor humming. For this we thank Beth Bailey, Carla Dickerson, Saira Ghadyali, and Kamla Gupta.

The organization of this sizable task force, and much else as well, fell to the project's secretary, first Susan Bailey and then Lorraine Lee. Susan Bailey left the project in early 1984, taking our shared concerns into another arena. In a real sense, we stand to benefit from her success in the future as much as we have from her work in the past. Lorraine Lee picked up where Susan Bailey left off and mastered with aplomb the complexities of preparing a large manuscript for publication.

As we entered the final stages of the work on this volume, we called upon fellow scholars sympathetic with our interest in emancipation but distant enough to judge our work with objectivity. We knew that their tough criticism would strengthen the volume, and we got what we wanted and then some. Professors Eric Foner, Herbert G. Gutman, James M. McPherson, and Benjamin Quarles gave close and careful readings to a very long manuscript and improved it in countless ways. Herbert Gutman was especially helpful in reminding us to connect this volume with the one that will follow. We also thank Professor Armstead Robinson, director of the Carter G. Woodson Institute for Afro-American and African Studies at the University of Virginia, for taking time out from his own work to make significant comments on chapter 9.

No authors are ever fully satisfied with their publisher. But we are happy to testify that we have one of the best. Steven Fraser (now of Basic

Acknowledgments

Books) and Frank Smith have served as essential guides for this project at Cambridge University Press. In a day when publishers are gutting centuries of tradition in the name of petty economy, Richard Hollick continues to design and produce volumes in which all can delight. Vicky Macintyre, Margaret Willard, and Rhona Johnson – masters of the blue pencil – improved our work as only good editors can. Four hundred years of publishing experience have not been wasted at Cambridge University Press.

As historians, we are taught to remember whence we come. Sara Dunlap Jackson, long an archivist at the National Archives and now a member of the NHPRC research staff, understood before anyone else the importance of the records from which these documents are drawn. She continues to be a source of day-to-day assistance, inspiration, and friendship. The dedication of this book suggests another debt owed by us – and by every student of American history. This small acknowledgment is only partial payment, long overdue.

I.B.
B.J.F.
T.G.
J.P.R.
L.S.R.

College Park, Maryland
March 1985

Introduction

NO EVENT in American history matches the drama of emancipation. More than a century later, it continues to stir the deepest emotions. And properly so. Emancipation accompanied the military defeat of the world's most powerful slaveholding class and freed a larger number of slaves than lived in all other New World slave societies combined. Clothed in the rhetoric of biblical prophecy and national destiny and born of a bloody civil war, it accomplished a profound social revolution. That revolution destroyed forever a way of life based upon the ownership of human beings, restoring to the former slaves proprietorship of their own persons, liquidating without compensation private property valued at billions of dollars, and forcibly substituting the relations of free labor for those of slavery. In designating the former slaves as citizens, emancipation placed citizenship upon new ground, defined in the federal Constitution and removed beyond the jurisdiction of the states. By obliterating the sovereignty of master over slave, it handed a monopoly of sovereignty to the newly consolidated nation-state. The freeing of the slaves simultaneously overturned the old regime of the South and set the entire nation upon a new course.

The death of slavery led to an intense period of social reconstruction, closely supervised by the victorious North, that lasted over a decade in many places. During this period, former slaves challenged the domination of the old masters, demanding land and the right to control their own labor. Former masters, abetted by a complaisant President, defeated the freedpeople's bid for economic independence and imposed on them new legal and extralegal constraints. But whatever the outcome, the struggle itself confirmed the magnitude of the change. Freedpeople confronted their former masters as free laborers in a system predicated upon contractual equality between employers and employees. They gained, if only temporarily, full citizenship rights, including the right to vote and hold public office.

With emancipation in the South, the United States enacted its part in a world-wide drama. Throughout the western world and beyond, the forces unleashed by the American and French revolutions and by the industrial revolution worked to undermine political regimes based upon hereditary privilege and economic systems based upon bound labor. Slavery had already succumbed in the Northern states and in the French and British Caribbean before the American Civil War, and it would shortly do so in its remaining strongholds in Spanish and Portuguese America. Almost simultaneously with the great struggle in the United States, the vestiges of serfdom in central and eastern Europe yielded to the pressure of the age. Only small pockets in Africa and Asia remained immune, and their immunity was temporary. The fateful lightning announced by the victorious Union army was soon to strike, if it had not already struck, wherever men and women remained in bonds of personal servitude.

For all systems of bondage, emancipation represented the acid test, the moment of truth. The upheaval of conventional expectations stripped away the patina of routine, exposing the cross purposes and warring intentions that had simmered—often unnoticed—beneath the surface of the old order. In throwing off habitual restraints, freedpeople redesigned their lives in ways that spoke eloquently of their hidden life in bondage, revealing clandestine institutions, long-cherished beliefs, and deeply held values. In confronting new restraints, they abandoned their usual caution in favor of direct speech and yet more direct action. Lords and serfs, masters and slaves had to survey the new social boundaries without the old etiquette of dominance and subordination as a guide. Their efforts to do so led to confrontations that could be awkward, painful, and frequently violent. The continued force of these encounters awakened men and women caught up in the drama to the realization that their actions no longer ratified old, established ways, but set radically new precedents for themselves and for future generations.

Moments of revolutionary transformation expose as do few human events the foundation upon which societies rest. Although those who enjoy political power and social authority speak their minds and indulge their inclinations freely and often, their subordinates generally cannot. Only in the upheaval of accustomed routine can the lower orders give voice to the assumptions that guide their world as it is and as they wish it to be. Some of them quickly grasp the essence of the new circumstances. Under the tutelage of unprecedented events, ordinary men and women become extraordinarily perceptive and articulate, seizing the moment to challenge the assumptions of the old regime and proclaim a new social order. Even then, few take the initiative. Some—perhaps most—simply try to maintain their balance, to reconstitute a routine, to maximize gains and minimize losses as events swirl around them. But inevitably they too become swept up in the revolutionary process. Barely conscious acts and unacknowledged motives carried over from the past take on a changed significance. Attempts to stand still or turn back only hasten the process forward. At revolutionary moments all actions—those of the timid and reluctant as much as

xvi

those of the bold and eager—expose to view the inner workings of society.

Because they thrust common folk into prominence, moments of revolutionary transformation have long occupied historians seeking to solve the mysteries of human society. Knowledge of the subordinate groups who have formed the majority throughout history has proved essential to an understanding of how the world works. Historians have therefore developed special methods for penetrating the often opaque histories of ordinary people, including peasants, slaves, and wage-workers. Some have viewed them over the *longue durée,* translating glacial demographic and economic changes into an understanding of times past. Others have sought such understanding by focusing on particular events, decoding the fury of *carnaval,* the ritual of a bread riot, the terror of the "theater of death," or the tense confrontation of an industrial strike. Almost all have learned from periods of revolutionary transformation. Whatever the historians' approach, direct testimony by the people involved has usually been a luxury. For this reason, the study of emancipation in the United States promises rich rewards not just to those specifically interested in the question, but to all who seek a fuller view of the human past. Encompassing in full measure the revolutionary implications of all transitions from bondage to freedom, emancipation in the American South has left behind an unparalleled wealth of documentation permitting direct access to the thoughts and actions of the freedpeople themselves. Indeed, it provides the richest known record of any subordinate class at its moment of liberation.

THE RECORDS

As the war for union became a war for liberty, the lives of slaves and freedpeople became increasingly intertwined with the activities of both the Union and Confederate governments. Following the war, federal agents continued to figure prominently in the reconstruction of the South's economy and society. The records created and collected by the agencies of these governments and now housed in the National Archives of the United States provide an unrivaled manuscript source for understanding the passage of black people from slavery to freedom. Such governmental units as the Colored Troops Division of the Adjutant General's Office; the American Freedmen's Inquiry Commission; the Union army at every level of command, from the headquarters in Washington to local army posts; army support organizations in Washington, including the Judge Advocate General's Office, the Provost Marshal General's Office, and the Quartermaster General's Office, and their subordinates in the field; the Civil War Special Agencies of the Treasury Department; individual regiments of U.S. Colored Troops; various branches of the Confederate government (whose records fell into Union hands at the conclusion of the war); the Southern Claims Commission; the Freedman's Bank; and, most important, the Bureau of Refugees, Freedmen, and Abandoned Lands all played a role in the coming of freedom. (See pp. xxxiv–xxxv for a list of record groups drawn upon.)

The missions of these agencies placed them in close contact with a wide variety of ordinary people, and their bureaucratic structure provided a mechanism for the preservation of many records of people generally dismissed as historically mute. The Bureau of Refugees, Freedmen, and Abandoned Lands (Freedmen's Bureau) illustrates the point. Although the bureau often lacked resources to do more than make written note of the abuses of freedpeople brought to its attention, bureau agents scattered across the South conducted censuses, undertook investigations, recorded depositions, filed reports, and accumulated letters authored by ex-slaves and interested whites. Other agencies whose duties focused less directly upon the concerns of former slaves created thousands of similar, though more dispersed, records.

Alongside the official reports in these archival files, hundreds of letters and statements by former slaves give voice to people whose aspirations, beliefs, and behavior have gone largely unrecorded. Not only did extraordinary numbers of ex-slaves, many of them newly literate, put pen to paper in the early years of freedom, but hundreds of others, entirely illiterate, gave depositions to government officials, placed their marks on resolutions passed at mass meetings, testified before courts-martial and Freedmen's Bureau courts, and dictated letters to more literate blacks and to white officials and teachers. The written record thus created constitutes an unparalleled outpouring from people caught up in the emancipation process. Predictably, many of these documents requested official action to redress wrongs committed by powerful former slaveholders who only reluctantly recognized ex-slaves as free, rarely as equal. Others, however, originated in relationships entirely outside the purview of either federal officials or former masters and employers. They include, for example, correspondence between black soldiers and their families and between kinfolk who had been separated during slavery. That such letters fell for various reasons into the bureaucratic net of government agencies (and thus were preserved along with official records) should not obscure their deeply personal origins.

Selected out of the masses of purely administrative records, these documents convey, perhaps as no historian can, the experiences of the liberated: the quiet personal satisfaction of meeting an old master on equal terms, as well as the outrage of ejection from a segregated streetcar; the elation of a fugitive enlisting in the Union army, and the humiliation of a laborer cheated out of hard-earned wages; the joy of a family reunion after years of forced separation, and the distress of having a child involuntarily apprenticed to a former owner; the hope that freedom would bring a new world, and the fear that, in so many ways, life would be much as before. Similar records offer insight into the equally diverse reactions of planters, Union officers, and Southern yeomen — men and women who faced emancipation with different interests and expectations. Taken together, these records provide the fullest documentation of the destruction of a dependent social relationship, the release of a people from their dependent status, and the simultaneous transformation of an entire society. As far as is known, no comparable record exists for the liberation of any group of serfs or slaves or for the transformation of any people into wage-workers.

However valuable, the archival records also have their problems. They are massive, repetitive, and often blandly bureaucratic. Their size alone makes research by individual scholars inevitably incomplete and often haphazard. The Freedmen's Bureau records, for example, extend to more than 700 cubic feet, and they constitute a relatively small record group. The records of U.S. army continental commands for the period spanning the Civil War era fill more than 10,000 cubic feet. In addition to the daunting volume of the archival records, their bureaucratic structure creates obstacles for studies that go beyond the institutional history of particular agencies or the documentation of policy formation to examine underlying social processes. Governmental practice provided the mechanism for preserving these records, but it also fragmented them in ways that can hinder historical reconstruction. Assume, for example, that a group of freedmen petitioned the Secretary of the Treasury complaining of a Confederate raid on a plantation supervised by his department. Their petition might be forwarded to the Secretary of War, since the army protected such plantations. He in turn would pass it on to a military field commander, who would send it down the chain of command. If black soldiers provided the plantation guard, the petition might be forwarded to the adjutant general, who directed the Bureau of Colored Troops, who would then send it to the commander of a black regiment. On the other hand, if the Secretary of the Treasury wished to act himself, he could forward it to a Treasury agent in the field. Augmented by additional information in the form of reports, depositions, or endorsements on the original complaint, the petition might be passed along to still other federal agencies. In the meantime, the Confederate raiders might have made a report to their commander, perhaps noting the effect of their foray on black morale. Rebel planters, anxious to regain their property, could now have their say, addressing the Confederate Secretary of War, his adjutant and inspector general, or a local Confederate commander. At any or all points, additional documents might be added and portions of the original documentation might come to rest. Only a search of the records of all these agencies can make the full story available. In part because of the scope of such an undertaking, individual scholars have been unable to avail themselves of the fullness of the resources of the National Archives. Research has necessarily been piecemeal and limited to one or two record groups or portions of various record groups. Only a large-scale collaborative effort can make these resources available to the public.

THE FREEDMEN AND SOUTHERN SOCIETY PROJECT

In the fall of 1976, with a grant from the National Historical Publications and Records Commission, and under the sponsorship of the University of Maryland, the Freedmen and Southern Society Project launched a systematic search of those records at the National Archives that promised to yield material for a documentary history of emancipation. Over the course of the next three years, the editors selected more than 40,000 items, which represented perhaps 2 percent of the documents they examined. Indexed and cross-referenced topically, chronologically, and geographically, this preliminary selection constitutes the universe from which the documents published as *Freedom: A Documentary History of Emancipation* are selected and annotated, and from which the editors' introductory essays are written.

The editors found it imperative from the outset to be selective. They have focused their attention upon the wartime and postwar experiences of slaves and ex-slaves, but have also sought to illuminate the social, economic, and political setting of the emancipation process. The formation of federal policy, for example, is not central to the project's concerns, except insofar as the preconceptions and actions of policy makers influenced the shape that freedom assumed. Therefore, the volumes published by the Freedmen and Southern Society Project will not undertake a history of the Freedmen's Bureau, the U.S. Army, the Bureau of Colored Troops, or any other governmental agency; nonetheless, documents about the operations of these agencies will be prominent when they describe activities of freedpeople and shed light upon the context in which former slaves struggled to construct their own lives. Throughout the selection process, the editors have labored to reconstruct the history of the freedpeople rather than the institutions that surrounded them.

Above all, the editors have sought to delineate the central elements of the process by which men and women moved from the utter dependence slaveholders demanded but never fully received, to the independence freedpeople desired but seldom attained. This process began with the slow breakdown of slavery on the periphery of the South and extended to the establishment of the social, economic, and political institutions black people hoped would secure their independence. The editors have also sought to recognize the diversity of black life and the emancipation process, by selecting documents that illustrate the varied experiences of former slaves in different parts of the South who labored at diverse tasks and who differed from one another in gender, in age, and in social or economic status. Although former slaves, like other men and women caught in the transition from slavery to freedom, wanted to enlarge their liberty and ensure their independence from their former masters, how they desired to do so and what they meant by freedom were tempered by their previous experiences as well as by the circumstances in which they were enmeshed. At the same time, the editors have been alert to the shared ideas and aspirations that American slaves carried into freedom and to those features of emancipation that were common throughout the South – and more generally still, common to all people escaping bondage. These common characteristics and the regularities of the process of emancipation connect the lives of former slaves across time and space and link them to other dependent people struggling for autonomy.

Reflecting editorial interest in a *social* history of emancipation, *Freedom* is organized thematically, following the process of emancipation. At each step the editors have selected documents that illustrate processes they believe are central to the transition from slavery to freedom. The first two series concentrate primarily on the years of the Civil War. Series 1 documents the destruction of slavery, the diverse circumstances under which slaves claimed their freedom, and the wartime labor arrangements developed as slavery collapsed. Series 2 examines the recruitment of black men into the Union army and the experiences of black soldiers under arms. The remaining series, while drawing in part upon evidence from the war years, explore most fully the transformation of black life that followed the conclusion of armed conflict. They document the struggle for land, the evolution of new labor arrangements, relations with former masters and other whites, law and justice, violence and other extralegal repression, geographical mobility, family relationships, education, religion, the structure and activities of the black community, and black politics in the early years of Reconstruction. The series are organized as follows:

Series 1   The Destruction of Slavery and the Wartime Genesis of
            Free Labor
Series 2   The Black Military Experience

INTRODUCTION

Series 3   Land, Capital, and Labor
Series 4   Race Relations, Violence, Law, and Justice
Series 5   The Black Community: Family, Church, School, and Society

Each series comprises one or more volumes, and topical arrangement continues within the volumes. Each chapter is introduced by an essay that provides background information, outlines government policy, and elaborates the larger themes. The chapters are further subdivided, when relevant, to reflect distinctive historical, economic, and demographic circumstances.

Also in accordance with the editors' predominant concern with social process, the annotation (both the notes to particular documents and the introductory essays) is designed to provide a context for the documents rather than to identify persons or places. The official character of most of the records means that vast quantities of biographical data are available for many of the army officers, Freedmen's Bureau agents, and others who cross the pages of these volumes. The editors have nonetheless decided against the time-consuming extraction of details about individuals, because to do so would divert energy from research into the larger social themes and reduce the number of documents that could be published, while adding little of substance to the business at hand.

In its aim, approach, and editorial universe, the Freedmen and Southern Society Project therefore differs fundamentally from most historical editing enterprises. Rather than searching out the complete manuscript record of an individual man or woman, the project examines the process of social transformation, and rather than seeking all the documentary evidence relevant to that transformation, it confines itself to the resources of the National Archives. *Freedom* endeavors to combine the strengths of the traditional interpretive monograph with the rich diversity of the documentary edition while addressing in one historical setting a central question of the human experience: how men and women strive to enlarge their freedom and secure their independence from those who would dominate their lives.

SERIES I

Series 1 of *Freedom* comprises two complementary volumes. Volume 1, *The Destruction of Slavery,* explicates the process by which slavery collapsed under the pressure of federal arms and the slaves' persistence in placing their own liberty on the wartime agenda. In documenting the

xxii

transformation of the war for the Union into a war against slavery, it shifts the focus from Washington and Richmond to the plantations, farms, and battlefields of the South, and demonstrates how slaves helped accomplish their own emancipation and shape the destiny of the nation.

Volume 2, *The Wartime Genesis of Free Labor,* concerns the evolution of freedom in Union-occupied areas of the South. Among the subjects it addresses are the employment of blacks as military laborers; the experiences of former slaves in contraband camps, on abandoned plantations, and in the employ of loyal planters; federal free-labor policies and practices; and the struggle among black people, Union army officers, Southern planters, Northern teachers and businessmen, and federal officials over the meaning of freedom.

The two volumes of series 1, together with the single volume that makes up series 2 – *The Black Military Experience* – document the death of the old order and the birth of a new one in the crucible of civil war.

Editorial Method

THE RENDITION of nineteenth-century manuscripts into print proceeds at best along a tortuous path. Transcribing handwritten documents into a standardized, more accessible form inevitably sacrifices some of their evocative power. The scrawl penciled by a hard-pressed army commander, the letters painstakingly formed by an ex-slave new to the alphabet, and the practiced script of a professional clerk all reduce to the same uncompromising print. At the same time, simply reading, much less transcribing, idiosyncratic handwriting poses enormous difficulties. The records left by barely literate writers offer special problems, although these are often no more serious than the obstacles created by better-educated but careless clerks, slovenly and hurried military officers, or even the ravages of time upon fragile paper.

The editors have approached the question of transcription with the conviction that readability need not require extensive editorial intervention and, indeed, that modernization (beyond that already imposed by conversion into type) can compromise the historical value of a document. The practical dilemmas of setting precise limits to editorial intervention, once initiated, also suggest the wisdom of restraint. In short, the editors believe that even when documents were written by near illiterates, the desiderata of preserving immediacy and conveying the struggle of ordinary men and women to communicate intensely felt emotions outweigh any inconveniences inflicted by allowing the documents to stand as they were written. Fortunately for the modern reader, a mere passing acquaintance with the primer usually led uneducated writers to spell as they spoke; the resulting documents may appear impenetrable to the eye but are perfectly understandable when read phonetically. In fact, reproduced verbatim, such documents offer intriguing evidence about the spoken language. Other writers, presumably better educated, frequently demonstrated such haphazard adherence to rules of grammar, spelling, and punctuation that their productions rival those of the semiliterate. And careless copyists or telegraph operators further garbled many documents. Both equity and convenience demand, nonetheless, that all writings by the schooled – however incoherent – be transcribed according to the same principles as those applied to the documents of the unschooled. Indeed, a verbatim rendition permits interesting observations about American literacy in the mid-nineteenth century, as well as about the talents or personalities of particular individuals.

Therefore, the textual body of each document in this volume is reproduced – to the extent permitted by modern typography – *exactly* as it appears in the original manuscript. (The few exceptions to this general principle will be noted hereafter.) The editorial *sic* is never employed: All peculiarities of syntax, spelling, capitalization, and punctuation appear in the original manuscript. The same is true of paragraph breaks, missing or incomplete words, words run together, quotation marks or parentheses that are not closed, characters raised above the line, contractions, and abbreviations. When the correct reading of a character is ambiguous (as, for example, a letter "C" written halfway between upper- and lower-case, or a nondescript blotch of punctuation that could be either a comma or a period), modern practice is followed. Illegible or obscured words that can be inferred with confidence from textual evidence are printed in ordinary roman type, enclosed in brackets. If the editors' reading is conjectural or doubtful, a question mark is added. When the editors cannot decipher a word by either inference or conjecture, it is represented by a three-dot ellipsis enclosed in brackets. An undecipherable passage of more than one word is represented in the same way, but a footnote reports the extent of the illegible material. (See p. xxxiii for a summary of editorial symbols.)

Handwritten letters display many characteristics that cannot be exactly reproduced on the printed page or can be printed only at considerable expense. Some adaptations are, therefore, conventional. Words underlined once in the manuscript appear in italics. Words underlined more than once are printed in small capitals. As for printed forms with blanks filled in by hand, the words originally in print are set in small capitals and the handwritten insertions appear in lower-case, with spaces before and after to suggest the blanks in the form. Internally quoted documents that are set off in the manuscript by such devices as extra space or quotation marks on every line are indented and printed in smaller type. Interlineations are simply incorporated into the text at the point marked by the author, without special notation by the editors unless the interlineation represents a substantial alteration. Finally, the beginning of a new paragraph is indicated by indentation, regardless of how the author set apart paragraphs.

The editors deviate from the standard of faithful reproduction of the textual body of the document in only two significant ways. The many documents entirely bereft of punctuation require some editorial intervention for the sake of readability. However, the editors wish to avoid "silent" addition of any material, and supplying punctuation in brackets would be extremely cumbersome, if not pedantic. Therefore, the editors employ the less intrusive device of adding extra spaces at what they take to be unpunctuated sentence breaks. Although most such judgments are unambiguous, there are instances in which the placement of sentence breaks requires an interpretive decision. To prevent the ambiguity that could result if an unpunctuated or unconventionally punctuated sentence' concluded at the end of a line of type, the last word of any such sentence appears at the beginning of the next line.

The second substantial deviation from verbatim reproduction of the text is the occasional publication of excerpted portions of documents. Most documents are printed in their entirety, but excerpts are taken from certain manuscripts, especially long bureaucratic reports, extensive legal proceedings, and other kinds of testimony. Editorial omission of a substantial body of material is indicated by a four-dot ellipsis centered on a separate line. An omission of only one or two sentences is marked by a four-dot ellipsis between the sentences that precede and follow the omission. The endnote identifies each excerpt as such and, when significant, describes the portion of the document not printed. (See the sample document that follows this essay for a guide to the elements of a printed document, including headnote, endnote, and footnote.)

The editors intervene without notation in the text of manuscripts in two minor ways. When the author of a manuscript inadvertently repeated a word, the duplicate is omitted. Similarly, most material canceled by the author is omitted, since it usually represents false starts or ordinary slips of the pen. When, however, the editors judge that the crossed-out material reflects an important alteration of meaning, it is printed as ~~canceled type~~. Apart from these cases, no "silent" additions, corrections, or deletions are made in the textual body of documents. Instead, all editorial insertions are clearly identified by being placed in italics and in brackets. Insertions by the editors may be descriptive interpolations such as [*In the margin*] or [*Endorsement*], the addition of words or letters omitted by the author, or the correction of misspelled words and erroneous dates. Great restraint is exercised, however, in making such editorial additions: The editors intervene only when the document cannot be understood or is seriously misleading as it stands. In particular, no effort is made to correct misspelled personal and place names. When material added by the editors is conjectural, a question mark is placed within the brackets. For printed documents only (of which there are few), "silent" correction is made for jumbled letters, errant punctuation, and transpositions that appear to be typesetting errors.

Although they faithfully reproduce the text of documents with minimal editorial intervention, the editors are less scrupulous with the peripheral parts of manuscripts. To print in full, exactly as in the original document, such elements as the complete return address, the full inside address, and a multiline complimentary closing would drastically reduce the number of documents that could be published. Considerations of space have therefore impelled the editors to adopt the following procedures. The place and date follow original spelling and punctuation, but they are printed on a single line at the beginning of the document regardless of where they appear in the manuscript. The salutation and complimentary closing, although spelled and punctuated as in the manuscript, are run into the text regardless of their positions in the original. Multiple signatures are printed only when there are twelve or fewer names. For documents with more than twelve signatures, including the many petitions bearing dozens or even hundreds of names, the editors indicate only the number of signatures on the signature line, for example, [86 *signatures*], although some information about the signers is always provided in the headnote and sometimes in the endnote as well. The formal legal apparatus accompanying sworn affidavits, including the name and position of the official who administered the oath and the names of witnesses, is omitted; the endnote, however, indicates whether an affidavit was sworn before a military officer, a Freedmen's Bureau agent, or a civil official. Similarly, the names of witnesses are omitted from contracts and other legal documents, but the endnote indicates that the signatures were witnessed.

The inside and return addresses create special complications. The documents in *Freedom* come from bureaucratic, mostly military, files. Therefore both inside and return addresses often include a military rank or other title and a statement of military command and location that may run to three or more lines. Similar details usually accompany the signature as well. Considerations of space alone preclude printing such material verbatim. Furthermore, even if published in full, the addresses would not always provide the reader with enough information to identify fully the sender and recipient. Military etiquette required that a subordinate officer address his superior not directly, but through the latter's adjutant. Thus, a letter destined for a general is ordinarily addressed to a captain or lieutenant, often only by the name of that lesser officer. To bring order out of the chaos that would remain even if all addresses were printed in full, and at the same time to convey all necessary information to the reader, the editors employ a twofold procedure. First, the headnote of each document identifies both sender and recipient – not by name, but by position, command, or other categorical label. For example, a letter from a staff assistant of the Union general in command of the military Department of the Gulf is labeled as originating not from "Lieutenant So-and-So" but from the "Headquarters of the Department of the Gulf." Confederate officials and military units are indicated as such by the addition of the word "Confederate" before their title or command, while those of the Union stand without modification. Most of the time this information for the headnote is apparent in the document itself, but when necessary the editors resort to other documents, published military registers, and service records to supply the proper designations. Second, the citation of each document (in the endnote) reproduces the military rank or other title as well as the name of both sender and recipient exactly as provided in the original document (except that punctuation is added to abbreviations, nonstandard punctuation is modernized, and superscripts are lowered to the line). Thus, the headnote and endnote together communicate the information from the return and inside addresses without printing those addresses in full.

Bureaucratic, and especially military procedures often created document files containing letters with numerous enclosures and endorsements. Although many routine endorsements served merely to transmit letters through the proper military channels, others reported the results of investigations, stated policy decisions, and issued orders. Indeed, enclosures or endorsements themselves are often valuable documents deserving publication. The editors therefore treat the material accompanying a document in one of three ways. First, some or all of such material may be printed in full along with the cover document. Second, accompanying items not published may be summarized in the endnote. Third, any accompanying material neither published nor summarized is noted in the endnote by the words "endorsements," "enclosures," "other enclosures," or "other endorsement." The editors do not, however, attempt to describe the contents or even note the existence of other documents that appear in the same file with the document being published but are not enclosed in it or attached to it. Clerks sometimes consolidated files of related—or even unrelated—correspondence, and many such files are voluminous. The editors draw upon other documents in the same file when necessary for annotation, just as they do upon documents filed elsewhere, but the endnote is normally a guide only to the material actually enclosed in, attached to, or endorsed upon the published document.

A technical description symbol follows each document at the left, usually on the same line as the signature. The symbol describes the physical form of the manuscript, the handwriting, and the signature. (See p. xxxiv for the symbols employed.)

An endnote for each document or group of related documents begins with a full citation that should allow the reader to locate the original among the holdings of the National Archives.[1] The citation refers solely to the document from which the printed transcription is made; the editors have searched out neither other copies in the National

---

[1] Scholars have cited documents from the National Archives in a bewildering variety of forms, many of them entirely inadequate. The editors of *Freedom* have tried to include all the information required to locate a document in the Archives' holdings. They urge similar completeness, if not necessarily their particular form of citation, upon other researchers and publishers.

Archives nor any previously published versions. Because all the documents published in *Freedom* come from the National Archives, no repository name is included in the citation. Record groups are cited only by the abbreviation RG and a number. (See pp. xxxiv–xxxv for a list of record group abbreviations.) For the convenience of researchers, the editors usually provide both series title and series number for each document, but readers should note that series numbers are assigned by the National Archives staff for purposes of control and retrieval, and they are subject to revision. Also for the convenience of researchers, each citation concludes with the Freedmen and Southern Society Project's own file number for that document, enclosed in brackets. In future the editors plan to microfilm all the documents accumulated during the project's search at the National Archives, along with the various geographical and topical indexes created by the staff. The project's file number for each document will thus serve as a guide both to the microfilm copy of the manuscript document and to other related documents in the project's files.

For ease of reference, the documents published in *Freedom* are numbered in sequence. On occasion, the editors have selected for publication several documents that taken together constitute a single episode. These documentary "clusters" are demarked at their beginning and at their conclusion by the project's logo – a broken shackle. The documents within each cluster bear alphabetical designations next to the number of the cluster.

Because *Freedom* focuses upon a subject or a series of questions, the editors consider the function of annotation different from that required in editing the papers of an individual. The editors seek, in the essays that introduce each section, to provide background information and interpretive context that will assist the reader in understanding the documents that follow, but the documents themselves are selected and arranged to tell their own story with relatively little annotation. When the editors judge annotation to be necessary or helpful, it usually appears in the form of further information about the content of a document or about the historical events under consideration, rather than biographical identification of individuals mentioned in the document. Thus, there are few editorial notes to specific items within a document, but the endnote often describes the outcome of the case or discusses other events related to the episode portrayed in the document. Such annotation, as well as the chapter essays, is based primarily on other documents from the National Archives; those documents are cited in full, and their citations provide a guide to related records that could not be published. Quotations that appear without footnotes in a chapter essay, as well as undocumented descriptions of specific incidents, are taken from the documents published in that chapter. When portions of documents are quoted in endnotes and footnotes, they are transcribed by the same procedures as those employed for documents printed in full, except that, for technical reasons, terminal sentence punctuation is modernized. Annotation is also drawn from published primary sources, and, with few exceptions, the editors rely upon primary material rather than the secondary literature.

Headnote*

347: Discharged Maryland Black Soldier to a Freedmen's Bureau Claim Agent

Date and place line (reproduced as in manuscript, except printed on a single line at the top of document regardless of location in manuscript)

Williamsport Washington Co MD oct ^the 8/66

Salutation (reproduced as in manuscript, except run into text regardless of location in manuscript)

Sir   it is With Much Pleser That I seat my self Tu Rit you a few lines Tu Now if you can Git The Bounty That is Cuming Tu us & We hear That The ar Mor for us if The ar Pleas Tu let us Now & if you Can git it With or Discharges if you Can I shod lik for you Tu Du so   sum of The Boys ar Giting on Esey A

Body of document (reproduced as in manuscript, except extra space added at unpunctuated sentence breaks)

Bout Thear Papars & The Monney Tu   The ar so Menney After Them Tu let Them git it for Them & The Tel Them That The Can git it suner   Nomor But I still Reman you abdiant survent

Complimentary closing (reproduced as in manuscript, except run into text regardless of location in manuscript)

Charles. P. Taylor

Signature (reproduced as in manuscript, except titles and identification omitted)

Technical description of the document* (see list of symbols, p. xxxiv)

ALS

Charles P. Taylor to Mr. Wm. Fowler, 8 Oct. 1866, Unregistered Letters Received, ser. 1963, MD & DE Asst. Comr., RG 105^a [A-9641].^b Endorsement.^c Taylor identified himself as a former sergeant in the 4th USCI.^d

Endnote*
a. Full citation of the document: titles and names of sender and recipient exactly as spelled in manuscript; date; and National Archives citation (see list of record group abbreviations, pp. xxxiv–xxxv)
b. Freedmen and Southern Society Project file number
c. Notation of enclosures and/or endorsements that are neither published with the document nor summarized in the endnote text
d. Text of endnote

Footnotes, * if any, follow the endnote
* Elements marked with an asterisk are supplied by the editors.

Symbols and Abbreviations

[roman]   Words or letters in roman type within brackets represent editorial inference or conjecture of parts of manuscripts that are illegible, obscured, or mutilated. A question mark indicates doubt about the conjecture.

[. . .]   A three-dot ellipsis within brackets represents illegible or obscured words that the editors cannot decipher. If there is more than one undecipherable word, a footnote reports the extent of the passage.

. . .⁵   A three-dot ellipsis and a footnote represent words or passages entirely lost because the manuscript is torn or a portion is missing. The footnote reports the approximate amount of material missing.

~~canceled~~   Canceled type represents material written and then crossed out by the author of a manuscript. This device is used only when the editors judge that the crossed-out material reflects an important alteration of meaning. Ordinarily, canceled words are omitted without notation.

[*italic*]   Words or letters in italic type within brackets represent material that has been inserted by the editors and is not part of the original manuscript. A question mark indicates that the insertion is a conjecture.

. . . .   A four-dot ellipsis centered on a separate line represents editorial omission of a substantial body of material. A shorter omission, of only one or two sentences, is indicated by a four-dot ellipsis between two sentences.

Symbols and Abbreviations

SYMBOLS USED TO DESCRIBE MANUSCRIPTS

Symbols used to describe the handwriting, form, and signature of each document appear at the end of each document.

The first capital letter describes the handwriting of the document:

A   autograph (written in the author's hand)
H   handwritten by other than the author (for example, by a clerk)
P   printed
T   typed

The second capital letter, with lower-case modifier when appropriate, describes the form of the document:

L	letter	c	copy
D	document	p	press copy
E	endorsement	d	draft
W	wire (telegram)	f	fragment

The third capital letter describes the signature:

S   signed by the author
Sr   signed with a representation of the author's name
I   initialed by the author
     no signature or representation

For example, among the more common symbols are: ALS (autograph letter, signed by author), HLS (handwritten letter, signed by author), HLSr (handwritten letter, signed with a representation), HLcSr (handwritten copy of a letter, signed with a representation), HD (handwritten document, no signature).

ABBREVIATIONS FOR RECORD GROUPS IN THE NATIONAL ARCHIVES OF THE UNITED STATES

RG 11   General Records of the United States Government

RG 15   Records of the Veterans Administration

RG 21   Records of District Courts of the United States

RG 45   Naval Records Collection of the Office of Naval Records and Library

RG 46   Records of the United States Senate

RG 48   Records of the Office of the Secretary of the Interior

Symbols and Abbreviations

RG 56   General Records of the Department of the Treasury

RG 58   Records of the Internal Revenue Service

RG 59   General Records of the Department of State

RG 60   General Records of the Department of Justice

RG 77   Records of the Office of the Chief of Engineers

RG 92   Records of the Office of the Quartermaster General

RG 94   Records of the Adjutant General's Office, 1780s–1917

RG 99   Records of the Office of the Paymaster General

RG 101   Records of the Office of the Comptroller of the Currency

RG 105   Records of the Bureau of Refugees, Freedmen, and Abandoned Lands

RG 107   Records of the Office of the Secretary of War

RG 108   Records of the Headquarters of the Army

RG 109   War Department Collection of Confederate Records

RG 110   Records of the Provost Marshal General's Bureau (Civil War)

RG 153   Records of the Office of the Judge Advocate General (Army)

RG 217   Records of the United States General Accounting Office

RG 233   Records of the United States House of Representatives

RG 366   Records of Civil War Special Agencies of the Treasury Department

RG 393   Records of United States Army Continental Commands, 1821–1920

SHORT TITLES

Freedom

Freedom: A Documentary History of Emancipation, 1861–1867.

Series 1, volume 1, *The Destruction of Slavery,* ed. Ira Berlin, Barbara J. Fields, Thavolia Glymph, Joseph P. Reidy, and Leslie S. Rowland (Cambridge, 1985).

	Series 1, volume 2, *The Wartime Genesis of Free Labor,* ed. Ira Berlin, Thavolia Glymph, Steven F. Miller, Joseph P. Reidy, Leslie S. Rowland, and Julie Saville (Cambridge, forthcoming).
	Series 2, *The Black Military Experience,* ed. Ira Berlin, Joseph P. Reidy, and Leslie S. Rowland (Cambridge, 1982).
Navy Official Records	U.S. Navy Department, *Official Records of the Union and Confederate Navies in the War of the Rebellion,* 30 vols. (Washington, 1894–1922).
Official Records	U.S. War Department, *The War of the Rebellion: A Compilation of the Official Records of the Union and Confederate Armies,* 128 vols. (Washington, 1880–1901).

MILITARY AND OTHER ABBREVIATIONS THAT APPEAR FREQUENTLY IN THE DOCUMENTS

A.A.A.G.	Acting Assistant Adjutant General
A.A.G.	Assistant Adjutant General
A.C.	Army Corps
A.C.	Assistant Commissioner (Freedmen's Bureau)
Act., Actg.	Acting
A.D.	African Descent
A.D.C.	Aide-de-Camp
Adjt.	Adjutant
Agt.	Agent
A.G.O.	Adjutant General's Office
A.Q.M.	Assistant Quartermaster
Asst.	Assistant
A.S.A.C.	Assistant Subassistant Commissioner (Freedmen's Bureau)
A.S.W.	Assistant Secretary of War
BG	Brigadier General
BGC	Brigadier General Commanding
BBG	Brevet Brigadier General
BGV	Brigadier General of Volunteers
BMG	Brevet Major General

BRFAL	Bureau of Refugees, Freedmen, and Abandoned Lands
Brig.	Brigadier
Bvt.	Brevet
Capt.	Captain
Cav.	Cavalry
C. d'A.	Corps d'Afrique
C.H.	Court House
Co.	Company
Col.	Colonel
col^d, cold., col.	colored
comdg., cmdg.	commanding
Comdr., Commr.	Commander
Comr.	Commissioner (Freedmen's Bureau)
C.S.	Commissary of Subsistence
C.S.	Commissioned Staff
C.S.	Confederate States
c.s.	current series
C.S.A.	Confederate States of America
Dept.	Department
Dist.	District
D.P.M.	Deputy Provost Marshal
E.M.M.	Enrolled Missouri Militia
Freedmen's Bureau	Bureau of Refugees, Freedmen, and Abandoned Lands
G.C.M.	General Court-Martial
Gen., Gen'l	General
G.O.	General Order(s)
HQ, Hd. Qrs., Hdqrs.	Headquarters
Inf.	Infantry
Insp.	Inspector
inst.	*instant* (the current month of the year)
J.A.	Judge Advocate
Lt., Lieut.	Lieutenant
Maj.	Major
MG	Major General
MGC	Major General Commanding
MGV	Major General of Volunteers
M.O.	Mustering Officer
M.S.M.	Missouri State Militia
N.C.O.	Noncommissioned Officer(s)
NCS	Noncommissioned Staff
NG	Native Guard
Obt. Servt.	Obedient Servant

P.M.	Provost Marshal
P.M.	Paymaster
P.M.G.	Provost Marshal General
Priv., Pri.	Private
Pro. Mar., Provo. Mar.	Provost Marshal
prox.	*proximo* (the next month of the year)
Q.M.	Quartermaster
Regt.	Regiment, regimental
RG	Record Group
R.Q.M.	Regimental Quartermaster
S.A.C.	Subassistant Commissioner (Freedmen's Bureau)
Sec. War	Secretary of War
ser.	series
Sergt., Sgt.	Sergeant
S.O.	Special Order(s)
Subasst. Comr.	Subassistant Commissioner (Freedmen's Bureau)
Supt.	Superintendent
ult., ult°	*ultimo* (the preceding month of the year)
USCA Lt	U.S. Colored Artillery (Light)
USCA Hvy	U.S. Colored Artillery (Heavy)
USCC	U.S. Colored Cavalry
USCHA	U.S. Colored Heavy Artillery
USCI	U.S. Colored Infantry
USCLtA	U.S. Colored Light Artillery
USCT	U.S. Colored Troops
U.S.A.	U.S. Army
U.S.S.	U.S. Ship
U.S.V.	U.S. Volunteers
V., Vols.	Volunteers (usually preceded by a state abbreviation)
V.M.	Volunteer Militia (preceded by a state abbreviation)
V.R.C.	Veteran Reserve Corps

The Destruction of Slavery, 1861–1865

THE BEGINNING of the Civil War marked the beginning of the end of slavery in the American South.[1] At first, most white Americans denied what would eventually seem self-evident. With President Abraham Lincoln in the fore, federal authorities insisted that the nascent conflict must be a war to restore the national union, and nothing more. Confederate leaders displayed a fuller comprehension of the importance of slavery, which Vice-President Alexander Stephens characterized as the

---

[1] This essay, like the shorter essays that introduce each chapter, is based primarily upon the documents included in this volume and other documents in the files of the Freedmen and Southern Society Project. In addition, several other primary sources and important secondary sources have served as guides in charting the destruction of slavery in the American South. Since they have been relied upon throughout, they are not cited at every point. Portions of the essays that lack specific footnotes should thus be understood to rest upon the documents reproduced in this volume and upon the following sources. Most significant are U.S., War Department, *The War of the Rebellion: A Compilation of the Official Records of the Union and Confederate Armies*, 128 vols. (Washington, 1880–1901), and U.S., Navy Department, *Official Records of the Union and Confederate Navies in the War of the Rebellion*, 30 vols. (Washington, 1894–1922). Another valuable collection of documents is "The Negro in the Military Service of the United States, 1639–1886," compiled by the Adjutant General's Office between 1885 and 1888. Its eight volumes are among the records of the Bureau of Colored Troops in the National Archives, and they are also available as a National Archives microfilm publication. A convenient compendium of the public record of the period is Edward McPherson, *The Political History of the United States of America during the Great Rebellion*, 2nd ed. (Washington, 1865). General secondary works treating the subject of slavery and emancipation during the Civil War include: Herbert Aptheker, *The Negro in the Civil War* (New York, 1938); W. E. B. DuBois, *Black Reconstruction in America: An Essay toward a History of the Part Which Black Folk Played in the Attempt to Reconstruct Democracy in America, 1860–1880* (New York, 1935); Robert F. Durden, *The Gray and the Black: The Confederate Debate on Emancipation* (Baton Rouge, La., 1972); John Hope Franklin, *The Emancipation Proclamation* (Garden City, N.Y., 1963); Leon F. Litwack, *Been in the Storm So Long: The Aftermath of Slavery* (New York, 1979), chaps. 1–4; James M. McPherson, *The Struggle for Equality: Abolitionists and the Negro in the Civil War and Reconstruction* (Princeton, N.J., 1964), *The Negro's Civil War: How American Negroes Felt and Acted during the War for the Union* (New York, 1965), and *Ordeal by Fire: The Civil War and Reconstruction* (New York, 1982); Allan Nevins, *The War for the Union*, 4 vols. (New York, 1959–71); Benjamin Quarles, *The Negro in the Civil War* (Boston, 1953), and *Lincoln and the Negro* (New York, 1962); James L. Roark, *Masters without Slaves: Southern Planters in the Civil War and Reconstruction* (New York, 1977), chaps. 1–3;

cornerstone of the Southern nation.[2] But if Stephens and others grasped slavery's significance, they assumed that the Confederate struggle for independence would require ño change in the nature of the institution. A Southern victory would transform the political status, not the social life, of the slave states; black people would remain in their familiar place. Despite a vigorous dissent from Northern abolitionists, most whites – North and South – saw no reason to involve slaves in their civil war.

Slaves had a different understanding of the sectional struggle. Unmoved by the public pronouncements and official policies of the federal government, they recognized their centrality to the dispute, and knew that their future depended upon its outcome. With divisions among white Americans erupting into open warfare, slaves watched and waited, alert for ways to turn the military conflict to their own advantage, stubbornly refusing to leave its outcome to the two belligerents. Lacking political standing or public voice, forbidden access to the weapons of war, slaves nonetheless acted resolutely to place their freedom – and that of their posterity – on the wartime agenda. Steadily, as opportunities arose, they demonstrated their readiness to take risks for freedom and to put their loyalty, their labor, and their lives in the service of the Union. In so doing, they gradually rendered untenable every Union policy short of universal emancipation and forced the Confederate government to adopt measures that severely compromised the sovereignty of the master. On both sides of the line of battle, Americans came to know that a war for the Union must be a war for freedom.

The change did not come easily or at once. At first, Union political and military leaders freed slaves only hesitantly, under pressure of military necessity. But, as the war dragged on, their reluctance gave way to an increased willingness and eventually to a firm determination to extirpate chattel bondage. The Emancipation Proclamation of January 1, 1863, and the enlistment of black soldiers into Union ranks in

Armstead L. Robinson, *Bitter Fruits of Bondage: The Demise of Slavery and the Collapse of the Confederacy* (New Haven, Conn., forthcoming); Charles H. Wesley, *The Collapse of the Confederacy* (Washington, 1937); Bell I. Wiley, *Southern Negroes, 1861–1865* (New Haven, Conn., 1938). Useful reference works are: Mark M. Boatner III, *The Civil War Dictionary* (New York, 1959); Frederick H. Dyer, *A Compendium of the War of the Rebellion*, 3 vols. (Des Moines, Iowa, 1908); E. B. Long with Barbara Long, *The Civil War Day by Day: An Almanac, 1861–1865* (Garden City, N.Y., 1971); Raphael P. Thian, comp., *Notes Illustrating the Military Geography of the United States* (Washington, 1881); Ezra J. Warner, *Generals in Blue: Lives of the Union Commanders* (Baton Rouge, La., 1964), and *Generals in Gray: Lives of the Confederate Commanders* (Baton Rouge, La., 1959).
[2] Henry Cleveland, *Alexander H. Stephens, in Public and Private; With Letters and Speeches* (Philadelphia, 1866), pp. 721–23.

the following months signaled the adoption of emancipation as a fundamental Northern war aim, although that commitment availed little until vindicated by military victory. Even after the surrender of the Confederacy, slavery survived in two border states until the Thirteenth Amendment became part of the United States Constitution in December 1865.

While Union policy shifted in favor of emancipation, Confederate leaders remained determined to perpetuate slavery. But the cornerstone of Southern nationality proved to be its weakest point. Slaves resisted attempts to mobilize them on behalf of the slaveholders' republic. Their sullen and sometimes violent opposition to the Confederate regime magnified divisions within Southern society, gnawing at the Confederacy from within. In trying to sustain slavery while fending off the Union army, Confederate leaders unwittingly compromised their own national aspirations and undermined the institution upon which Southern nationality was founded. In the end, the victors celebrated slavery's demise and claimed the title of emancipator. The vanquished understood full well how slavery had helped to seal their doom.[3]

The war provided the occasion for slaves to seize freedom, but three interrelated circumstances determined what opportunities lay open to them and influenced the form that the struggle for liberty assumed: first, the character of slave society; second, the course of the war itself; and third, the policies of the Union and Confederate governments. Although none of these operated independently of the others, each had its own dynamic. All three were shaped by the particularities of Southern geography and the chronology of the war. Together, they made the destruction of slavery a varying, uneven, and frequently tenuous process, whose complex history has been obscured by the apparent certitude and finality of the great documents that announced the end of chattel bondage. Once the evolution of emancipation replaces the absolutism of the Emancipation Proclamation and the Thirteenth Amendment as the focus of study, the story of slavery's demise shifts from the presidential mansion and the halls of Congress to the farms and plantations that became wartime battlefields. And slaves — whose persistence forced federal soldiers, Union and Confederate policy makers, and even their own masters onto terrain they never intended to occupy — become the prime movers in securing their own liberty.

On the eve of the Civil War, the South was a deeply divided society. Although slavery was central to the social order, most Southerners were white and owned no slaves. Apart from their common race and their nonslaveholding status, they lived in widely varying circumstances. A

[3] See Robinson, *Bitter Fruits of Bondage.*

majority of this white majority were farmers, although some earned their livelihood as artisans and small proprietors and many—without property or skill—worked for wages. By residence, by nationality and religion, by education and wealth, by work routine and experience, they differed from each other. A shared desire to live and work on their own drew them together, and most sought an independent social standing by separating themselves ideologically and geographically from the slaveholders' world.[4] A minority, however, struggled to enter the ranks of the masters; aspiration, if not wealth and status, aligned these men and women with the slaveholders. At the margins, some people slid in and out of slaveownership. But even among slaveholders of long standing, the mass stood apart from the grandees—those planters who owned large numbers of slaves, produced staple crops for an international market, and dominated Southern politics and society. Although the great planters differed among themselves, their common concern for their own dominance engendered a strong sense of unity; and their political, economic, and social power extended that unity over the South as a whole.[5]

The lives of Southern blacks were no more at one than those of Southern whites. Black life in bondage assumed distinctive forms as a result of the pattern of the slave trade, the demographic balance of whites and blacks, the size of slaveholdings, and the labor requirements of particular crops, among other circumstances. Many of the nearly four million slaves resided on large plantations among a black majority and answered only to black drivers or white overseers. Those on the largest estates hardly knew their owners. Other slaves lived on small farmsteads, worked alongside their owners, and ate from the same pot, if rarely at the same table. Within the bounds of a single plantation or farm, a handful of slaves occupied special status as drivers, artisans, or house servants and were able to use their positions to gain a variety of prerogatives and a measure of independence; the vast majority never escaped the drudgery of agricultural labor. Differences could also be found among the mass of field hands. Some worked

---

[4] Frank L. Owsley, *Plain Folk of the Old South* (Baton Rouge, La., 1949); Elizabeth Fox-Genovese and Eugene D. Genovese, *Fruits of Merchant Capital: Slavery and Bourgeois Property in the Rise and Expansion of Capitalism* (New York, 1983), chap. 9; Steven Hahn, *The Roots of Southern Populism: Yeoman Farmers and the Transformation of the Georgia Upcountry, 1850–1890* (New York, 1983); Ira Berlin and Herbert G. Gutman, "Natives and Immigrants, Free Men and Slaves: Urban Workingmen in the Antebellum American South," *American Historical Review* 88 (Dec. 1983): 1175–1200.

[5] Eugene D. Genovese, *The Political Economy of Slavery: Studies in the Economy and Society of the Slave South* (New York, 1965), and *The World the Slaveholders Made: Two Essays in Interpretation* (New York, 1969); James Oakes, *The Ruling Race: A History of American Slaveholders* (New York, 1982); Michael P. Johnson, *Toward a Patriarchal Republic: The Secession of Georgia* (Baton Rouge, La., 1977).

in gangs, some by the task, and others by a combination of the two. Work patterns shaped black life in slavery as they would in freedom.[6] Some black people had already achieved that status. In 1860, a quarter of a million Southern blacks enjoyed de jure freedom. Although they labored under constraints that deprived them of citizenship and severely circumscribed their liberty, free blacks still collected their own wages, governed their own family life, and created their own institutions. Just as they stood apart from slaves, free blacks also differed among themselves. Most lived in abject poverty, but some of them climbed off the floor of Southern society, gained an education, and accumulated modest wealth. A handful became slaveholders themselves.[7] The diverse experiences of free blacks, as well as the differences between them and slaves, meant that the same wartime developments would have different meaning for different groups of black people.

In the various theaters of the war, events seldom followed the same course. Military developments multiplied the channels through which blacks might escape from slavery.[8] The prospects for freedom emerged in different ways when a sudden Union invasion forced slaveholders to abandon their slaves, when continual skirmishing gave slaves opportunities to flee to the Union army, when a slowly developing line of battle spurred masters to remove their slaves to the interior, and when the confusion attending removal allowed slaves to flee in the opposite direction from their owners. While some slaves remained on their native ground when their masters turned fugitive, others left family and friends to become fugitives themselves. The establishment of secure federal enclaves on the fringes of the Confederacy created havens from which successful runaways might return to their former homes to guide enslaved loved ones out of slavery. Many such fugitives joined federal forces as guides, laborers, and eventually soldiers, helping to expand the Union's domain. In other parts of the Confederacy, contested territory and shifting military fortunes made escape more uncertain and precarious. Fugitive slaves in these areas followed Union

---

[6] Eugene D. Genovese, *Roll, Jordan, Roll: The World the Slaves Made* (New York, 1974); John W. Blassingame, *The Slave Community: Plantation Life in the Antebellum South*, rev. ed. (New York, 1979); Herbert G. Gutman, *The Black Family in Slavery and Freedom, 1750–1925* (New York, 1976); Nathan I. Huggins, *Black Odyssey: The Afro-American Ordeal in Slavery* (New York, 1977). The spatial diversity and temporal development of slavery in the United States are captured in Willie Lee Rose, ed., *A Documentary History of Slavery in North America* (New York, 1976).

[7] Ira Berlin, *Slaves without Masters: The Free Negro in the Antebellum South* (New York, 1974).

[8] For the pattern of military developments in different regions, see Shelby Foote, *The Civil War: A Narrative*, 3 vols. (New York, 1958–74); Herman Hattaway and Archer Jones, *How the North Won: A Military History of the Civil War* (Urbana, Ill., 1983); Nevins, *War for the Union*; and James McPherson, *Ordeal by Fire*.

soldiers and lived off the land or the meager charity of Northern philanthropists and Union authorities. Eventually, however, the march of federal armies announced the end of slavery throughout the war zone.

Slaves distant from the conflict, with little chance of escape, did not simply wait for freedom to come to them. As news of the war spread – often by recaptured runaways, by slaves impressed for Confederate military labor, or by slaves removed to the interior from areas threatened by Union advances – resistance to slavery stiffened. Confederate slaveholders far from the fighting found that their most trusted servants had turned against them, forcing them to concede new privileges and redefining the relationship between master and slave. The same was true in the border states, whose loyalty to the Union exempted them from military emancipation measures. There, too, slaves seized upon opportunities offered by the war to free themselves, forcing their masters into coercive rearguard actions that steadily undermined their standing in the Union and ultimately required them to accept emancipation.[9] Throughout the South, the character of the war helped determine who would be free, how they would become free, and what freedom would mean.

Amid the diverse responses of slaves to wartime opportunities, both Union and Confederate leaders debated the employment of blacks as military laborers, the recruitment of black men as soldiers, and, in the Union's case, their transformation from slaves to citizens. Decisions in Washington and Richmond, as well as on the field of battle, rested only partly on military exigencies. Political leaders, North and South, formulated policy in response to the demands of diverse constituencies, as well as considerations of world opinion. While merchants and manufacturers in the North and slaveholding planters in the South stood atop their respective societies, others – including farmers, artisans, and unskilled laborers – exercised significant political power in these constitutional democracies and filled the ranks of both armies. Abolitionists in the North and proslavery apologists in the South – propelled by religious zeal and moral righteousness – determined to remake their respective societies. They lobbied those in power and sometimes moved into positions of authority themselves. A complex internal politics developed within both the Union and the Confederate chains of command, creating shifting alliances among state and national officials, members of the executive and legislative branches of government, and

---

[9] On the border states, see Barbara J. Fields, *Slavery and Freedom on the Middle Ground: Maryland during the Nineteenth Century* (New Haven, Conn., 1985); Victor B. Howard, *Black Liberation in Kentucky: Emancipation and Freedom, 1862–1884* (Lexington, Ky., 1983); William E. Parrish, *Turbulent Partnership: Missouri and the Union, 1861–1865* (Columbia, Mo., 1963); Charles L. Wagandt, *The Mighty Revolution: Negro Emancipation in Maryland, 1862–1864* (Baltimore, 1964).

civilian authorities and military commanders. The demands of office, the needs of particular constituents, notions of the general good, and the prejudices and ambitions of individuals also helped determine the course of slavery's demise.[10]

In order to give full consideration to the diversity of Southern society and of the wartime experience, the two volumes that constitute series 1 of *Freedom*—first, *The Destruction of Slavery* and second, *The Wartime Genesis of Free Labor*—follow a geographical organization. Chapters reflect either traditional regional divisions within the South, developing military lines, or political boundaries, depending on which are most useful for understanding the process of emancipation. Some chapters—like that on southern Louisiana—encompass only a fragment of a state; some—like those on lowcountry South Carolina, Georgia, and Florida, and on the Mississippi Valley—cut across state lines; and some—like those on the border states—coincide with state boundaries. During the course of the war, the territory designated by these geographical divisions often changed. In some places, the shifts were small and ephemeral; in others, dramatic and lasting. Though Union lines generally expanded while Confederate lines receded, this was not always the case, especially during the early years of the war.

The Destruction of Slavery follows the chronology by which the liberty of black people gained recognition by the Union. The story begins in tidewater Virginia with the conversion of slaves into contrabands and ends with the liquidation of slavery in Kentucky and in the shrinking Confederacy. Because freedom came to portions of the South early in the war, some chapters—those on tidewater Virginia and North Carolina; on lowcountry South Carolina, Georgia, and Florida; and on southern Louisiana—are relatively brief, reflecting the speed with which emancipation was accomplished. Where it took longer for black people to gain their liberty—as in the border states and the Confederate interior—the chapters are more substantial.[11] Together, they tell the story of the destruction of slavery.

[10] Herman Belz, *Reconstructing the Union: Theory and Policy during the Civil War* (Ithaca, N.Y., 1969); David Montgomery, *Beyond Equality: Labor and the Radical Republicans, 1862–1872* (New York, 1967); Curtis A. Amlund, *Federalism in the Southern Confederacy* (Washington, 1966); Thomas L. Connelly and Archer Jones, *The Politics of Command: Factions and Ideas in Confederate Strategy* (Baton Rouge, La., 1973); Paul D. Escott, *After Secession: Jefferson Davis and the Failure of Confederate Nationalism* (Baton Rouge, La., 1978); May S. Ringold, *The Role of the State Legislatures in the Confederacy* (Athens, Ga., 1966); Emory M. Thomas, *The Confederate Nation, 1861–1865* (New York, 1979).

[11] The reverse is true in *The Wartime Genesis of Free Labor* (forthcoming), which concerns the evolution of freedom within Union lines. There, the chapters on the tidewater, the lowcountry, and southern Louisiana are among the most substantial, because the early arrival of the Union army initiated wartime reconstruction. The

7

The institution of slavery, as it had evolved in the American South, rested on an unequal and uneasy balance of power between master and slave. In law, the slaveholder's authority went almost unchallenged; in practice, it was limited by a variety of constraints. Refusing to be reduced to a mere extension of their owners' will, slaves did not willingly defer or freely relinquish their labor. Although slaveholders rarely hesitated to apply force in exacting deference and extorting labor, they found it both easier and more profitable to achieve these ends by conceding to the slaves some control over their own daily lives. Such hard-won concessions helped mute the conflict inherent in slavery and permitted masters to maintain their dominant place in Southern society.

Slaves also gained from these concessions. Within the tight social space they wrested from their owners, slave men and women created a distinctive culture and a variety of institutions of their own. Masters continually challenged this limited independence, and slaves maintained it only by constant struggle, often at great cost and then sometimes not at all. But whatever the slaves' success in maintaining or expanding their independent realm, it stopped far short of freedom. Ultimately, they accepted their status only because of the superior power of their owners. Despite its seeming flexibility, slavery was a brittle institution. Any change threatened its viability.[12]

Even before sectional discord erupted into war, the debate over slavery was disturbing the delicate balance between master and slave. Slaveholders had long feared that abolitionists or their emissaries would stir bloody insurrection by awakening the slaves to the possibility of liberty. Although a few such emissaries carried the abolitionist message directly to the plantation doorstep, most slaves learned about the deepening sectional dispute from their owners' denunciation of the North and of the Republican Party and its champions, the most threatening of whom was Abraham Lincoln. Indeed, the slaveholders' indiscriminate condemnations exaggerated the antislavery commitment of white Northerners, "Black Republicans," and Lincoln himself. Masters with no doubts about the abolitionist intentions of the North inadvertently persuaded their slaves of the ascendancy and pervasiveness of antislavery sentiment in the free states. The general politicization of Southern

border states, on the other hand, are considered in a single short chapter, since freedom did not come until late in the war or, in the case of Kentucky, until after the war had ended. The brevity of that chapter reflects the fact that the struggle over the meaning of freedom — a struggle already well underway in areas of the Confederacy that had early fallen under Union control — was just beginning in the border states.

12 Genovese, *Roll, Jordan, Roll*; Blassingame, *Slave Community*; Gutman, *Black Family*; Albert J. Raboteau, *Slave Religion: The "Invisible Institution" in the Antebellum South* (New York, 1978); Thomas L. Webber, *Deep like the Rivers: Education in the Slave Quarter Community, 1831–1865* (New York, 1978).

society thus reached deep into the slave community, imparting momentous significance to Lincoln's election, Southern secession, and military mobilization.

Yet the slaves did not immediately accept their owners' assumptions about the intentions of the North. Suspicious of all whites, many slaves doubted that any white man – whatever his provenance – would act in their behalf. Slaveholders fueled this well-founded distrust. Their loud pronouncements that the Yankee devils – horned and tailed – would sell slaves to Cuba, sundering families and friendships, had a sobering effect in the quarters. The slaves debated among themselves the meaning of the onrushing conflict, weighing their masters' claim that the Yankees would reopen the international slave trade against reports that they would abolish slavery. Neither position won immediate or uniform assent, but even before the first shots at Fort Sumter, some slaves had resolved the question and acted upon their convictions. In March 1861, for instance, eight runaways presented themselves at Fort Pickens, a federal installation in Florida, "entertaining the idea" – in the words of the fort's commander – that federal forces "were placed here to protect them and grant them their freedom."[13]

Generally slaves were more circumspect, fearing that any change might be for the worse. Once the fighting began, some of these cautious men and women openly sided with their owners, urging them to whip the Yankees and offering to aid them in doing so. Perhaps they hoped that loyalty would earn them new privileges or feared that disloyalty would bring harsh retribution, especially if the Confederacy triumphed. A few black men, free as well as slave, succumbed to the martial fervor. A chance to escape the stultifying plantation routine and see something of the world may well have animated those who volunteered to accompany their masters into battle as personal servants. Some free blacks, desperate for any opportunity to steady their precarious position in Southern society, offered to take up arms for the Confederacy. In Louisiana and a few other places, free men of color were mustered into Native Guard units.[14]

But most blacks, reasoning that the enemy of their enemy must be their friend, quietly waited for events to turn in their favor. Anxious observers throughout the South described the slaves' unprecedented sense of anticipation that a Union victory would end slavery; an

---

[13] *Official Records*, ser. 2, vol. 1, p. 750. "I did what I could to teach them the contrary," added the commander, who drove the lesson home by delivering the fugitives to the city marshal of Pensacola "to be returned to their owners."

[14] *Freedom*, ser. 2: doc. 11; Mary F. Berry, "Negro Troops in Blue and Gray: The Louisiana Native Guards, 1861–1863," *Louisiana History* 8 (Spring 1967): 165–90; Manoj K. Joshi and Joseph P. Reidy, " 'To Come Forward and Aid in Putting Down this Unholy Rebellion': The Officers of Louisiana's Free Black Native Guard during the Civil War Era," *Southern Studies* 21 (Fall 1982): 326–42.

Alabama farmer characterized them as "very Hiley Hope up that they will soon Be free."[15] Whatever their assessment of the meaning of the war, slaves generally kept their own counsel, in accordance with time-honored practice. Their stolid silence and manifest preoccupation with the extraordinary events that surrounded them worried their owners as much as any formal declaration.

Fears real and imagined induced many slaveholders to slap new restrictions on their slaves, violating the longstanding – if silent – compromises upon which slavery rested. With agricultural productivity increasing in importance, masters pressed slaves hard, thereby imposing a more exacting work regimen. With fear of enemy infiltration escalating, masters restricted travel, thereby denying slaves the chance to visit families and friends. With the possibility of insurrection growing, masters enacted new strictures and enforced old ones, thereby heightening the standards of discipline. Edgy slaveholders answered with the lash violations of plantation etiquette that might once have been overlooked. The imposition of such seemingly arbitrary changes evoked angry and sometimes violent responses from black men and women unwilling to bear additional burdens – especially when their expectations ran in the other direction. Exasperated slaves struck out at their masters, ran away, or turned increasingly sullen. Although most slaves continued to mask their true feelings, the new repression revealed, even to the most cautious, the folly of expecting that loyalty to the old regime would be rewarded. Changes in plantation life magnified the possibilities of the moment.

Those possibilities multiplied as the Confederacy mobilized for war. Long accustomed to political leadership and proud of their military prowess, slaveholders great and small placed their estates in the hands of relatives, overseers, or agents and marched off to confront the Northern enemy. On some estates, the master's absence and the slaves' familiarity with plantation routine allowed the slaves greater control over their daily lives. Elsewhere, supervision by an overseer meant hard driving and arbitrary punishment, without the recourse of an appeal to the master. But as overseers and younger sons followed the master into the army, leaving women and old men in charge, the balance of power gradually shifted in favor of the slaves, undermining slavery on farms and plantations far from the line of battle.

Not all slaves remained at home when their masters marched off to war. In preparing to meet the enemy, slaveholders-turned-warriors almost always took personal manservants with them to tidy their camp and provide for their toilet. Many of these trusted body servants would have an opportunity to trade their owners' faith for their own freedom, leaving their masters to cook and care for themselves.

[15] *Freedom*, ser. 2: doc. 113; see also doc. 114.

Personal servants were only the first slaves directly affected by Confederate mobilization. The defense of the Confederacy demanded thousands, ultimately tens of thousands, of military laborers to wield picks and shovels. Countless others labored as teamsters, stable hands, and boatsmen; butchers, bakers, and cooks; nurses, orderlies, and laundresses; and blacksmiths, coopers, and wagon makers. Slaves had long performed these tasks and, in many places, no other labor force existed. Slaveholders knew this and at first did not have to be asked to volunteer their slaves to the Southern cause. Carried forward by a wave of martial enthusiasm and the belief that their contributions would aid the South in smiting the Yankee invaders, the most patriotic masters gladly sent their slaves to work on Confederate defenses. Some even offered to lead them in battle against the Union army.[16]

But the dislocations that accompanied the employment of slaves in Confederate service eroded the masters' patriotism. Before long, slaveholders began to remove their slaves beyond the reach of either Yankee invaders or Confederate impressment agents. Political uncertainty, particularly in the border states, also caused slave owners to transfer, or (as the process became known) "refugee," their slaves to the Confederate interior. Slaveholders along the exposed periphery of the South soon joined those in the border states in refugeeing the slaves most likely to bolt for the Union lines. Usually they moved suspect slaves to their own or relatives' estates farther from the military action. When this was not possible, they often hired them out or—cutting their losses—sold them for whatever they would bring.

Slaves hated these frightening removals and the resulting separation from family and friends. Many of them fled at the first hint of transfer. Escape itself was difficult enough, even in the confusion of wartime mobilization. But translating escape into freedom was nearly impossible in the absence of a safe harbor. Many slaves hoped that the arrival of the Union army would change that.

In April 1861, within days of Lincoln's call for volunteers to protect the nation's capital and put down the rebellion, the first Northern soldiers arrived in Washington. During the succeeding months, their numbers increased manyfold. As they took up positions around Washington and in the border states, they encountered slaves set in motion by the new disciplinary measures, by the attempts to conscript them into Confederate labor gangs or to refugee them to the interior, and—most importantly—by the desire to be free.

Before long, fugitive slaves began to test their owners' assertions about Yankee abolitionism. Those who ventured into Union army lines early in the war were mostly young men. Camps composed of hundreds of soldiers could be forbidding and dangerous places for women and

[16] See, for example, *Freedom*, ser. 2: doc. 115.

children, and keeping up with an army on the march was nearly impossible for all but young and healthy adults. But fugitive slave men also outnumbered women and children because men generally had greater opportunities to leave the home farm or plantation. Slave artisans, wagoners, and boatsmen often had permission to move about in the course of their work, and sometimes to seek employment on their own; nearly all of them were men. Moreover, where slave hiring was common—as it was throughout the Upper South—seasonal agricultural labor kept hired men on the move between owner and employer. Family arrangements also contributed to the greater mobility of slave men. Because small slaveholdings predominated in the Upper South, members of slave families often had different owners and lived on different farms. Slaveholders customarily permitted men with "broad wives" to visit the farm of their wife's owner, and many a slave man resided away from his master's place on a regular basis, journeying to his wife's home at the end of each day's work. Routinely visible on the public roads in pursuit of such errands and frequently armed with written passes, slave men might turn their steps in the direction of a federal camp without arousing suspicion. No doubt the unmarried and childless found it easiest to leave home. But since children usually shared their mother's residence, even fathers could depart without completely disrupting day-to-day family life. And those slave men who had been mobilized for labor on Confederate defenses and were already separated from home could as easily head in one direction as another.

Whatever their opportunities for flight, these first fugitives took a considerable chance. They understood on good authority that runaway slaves risked severe punishment, even death, and they had no certain knowledge of the truth of their masters' allegations about Northern intentions. Indeed, fugitive slaves found that few Northern soldiers measured up to their owners' worst fears. In the early months of the war, federal commanders hewed close to the Lincoln administration's policy of noninterference with slavery. Eager to reassure wavering slaveholders in the border states and encourage unionism in the Confederacy, Union officers reiterated their determination not to tamper with slavery. Some stumbled over themselves in declaring their readiness to protect slaveholders from their slaves. Benjamin F. Butler, a political general sensitive to the concerns of loyal owners, had no sooner arrived in Maryland in April 1861 than he ostentatiously offered to help suppress a rumored servile rebellion. General William S. Harney, commander of the Department of the West, applauded Butler's offer and gave Missouri slaveholders full assurances of protection for their property. Similar promises not to interfere with slavery and to crush any attempt at slave insurrection were promulgated in May by General Robert Patterson as his forces moved upon Harper's Ferry, and

The Destruction of Slavery

by General George B. McClellan as troops under his command entered western Virginia.[17]

During the summer of 1861, such sentiment received confirmation from federal authority at the highest level. In an Independence Day oration, President Lincoln pointedly omitted any mention of slavery in his discussion of Union war aims and assured the South that he had not altered his views on the rights of the states within the federal government.[18] Congress added its imprimatur by adopting a resolution, introduced by Kentucky's John J. Crittenden, asserting that the North fought only to preserve the Union, and posed no threat to Southern institutions.[19] The President's words and the Congress's resolves stiffened the determination of Union field commanders to honor the claims of slaveholders. They also seemed to unleash racial animosities rampant throughout American society. Instructed to expel fugitive slaves, some Northern soldiers did so with maniacal enthusiasm, turning their overwhelming power on the refugees from slavery.

Not all Union soldiers shared the convictions of those at the top of the chain of command. Although many – perhaps most – held blacks in contempt, some were fierce opponents of slavery and itched for a chance to enact their principles in a practical way. The arrival of fugitive slaves at Union camps – breathless, clothed in tatters, bearing the marks of abuse – gave these antislavery soldiers the opportunity they sought. They offered the fugitives food and protection, and permitted them to share their bivouac or accompany them on the march. Such encounters with runaway slaves intent upon freedom, and their often terrifying aftermath – when slaveholders and their agents dragged frightened men and women back into bondage – moved many soldiers who had previously cared nothing about slavery. What they saw sickened them and sometimes drew them into the antislavery fold. Indeed, as slaves continued to flee to the army camps despite the risk of recapture and punishment, even the most hard-hearted soldiers found it difficult to remain oblivious to the unfolding drama, particularly when the fugitives offered to relieve them of the more onerous aspects of camp life in exchange for a few morsels of food. Many slaves won the protection of Union soldiers by providing bits of useful military information or news of local secessionist activities. In this manner, increasing numbers of black men and women gained residence in and near federal camps as guides, cooks, servants, hostlers, and laundresses.

The protection and employment offered fugitive slaves by individual

---

[17] *Official Records*, ser. 1, vol. 2, pp. 593, 661–62, and ser. 2, vol. 1, p. 753; see below, doc. 153.

[18] Abraham Lincoln, *Collected Works*, ed. Roy P. Basler et al., 9 vols. (New Brunswick, N.J., 1953–55), vol. 4, pp. 421–41.

[19] Edward McPherson, *Political History*, p. 286. Upon approval of Crittenden's resolution in the House, Andrew Johnson of Tennessee secured its passage in the Senate.

13

Northern soldiers, often against the wishes of their superiors, created numerous conflicts between masters and the Union army. Slaveholders, many of them flaunting unionist credentials, demanded that Northern troops return fugitives who had taken refuge within their encampments. When regimental officers would not or could not comply, masters objected loudly and blustered about connections that reached to the highest levels in Washington. Generally the bluster was just that. But often enough, the officers soon felt the weight of high authority, as cabinet members and other federal officials took time out from the business of war to respond to the complaints of slaveholders and their representatives. Federal authorities solemnly reiterated their respect for slavery, and curtly ordered field officers to cooperate with slaveholders and to discipline soldiers who assisted runaways. However, demeaning field commanders before the local citizenry and embarrassing them before their men hardly disposed them to obey with much enthusiasm. Even unionist masters found that they paid a price for their appeals to higher authority. Both regimental officers and soldiers grew contemptuous of slaveholders who seemed more concerned with recapturing slaves than with maintaining the Union.

Confrontations between slaveholders and soldiers multiplied as the number of Union troops in the slave states increased. In late May 1861, when Virginia voters ratified secession, federal forces crossed the Potomac into the northern part of the state, and disputes between masters and military officers became endemic. The conflicts soon made their way into the press, rousing the ire of abolitionists who were outraged by the use of federal soldiers as slave catchers. In July, antislavery congressmen pushed a resolution through the House of Representatives declaring it "no part of the duty of the soldiers of the United States to capture and return fugitive slaves."[20] Although the resolution had no binding effect, it bolstered antislavery sentiment within the Northern army.

The rumblings of congressional radicals were only one indication of the Lincoln administration's difficulty in sustaining a consistent policy regarding slavery. Orders to return fugitive slaves to their owners — designed to preserve the loyalty of the border states and encourage unionism in the Confederacy — lost their rationale once Northern soldiers encountered slaves whose owners were patently disloyal. The change first became apparent under the aegis of General Butler, who in May 1861 took command at Fortress Monroe, in tidewater Virginia.

Antebellum agricultural developments in eastern Virginia had set the stage for wartime events by transforming slaves into a mobile lot. The decline of tobacco monoculture, the concomitant expansion of mixed farming — in which tobacco shared the fields with grains, forage crops, and cattle — and the beginning of truck farming for urban

[20] *Official Records*, ser. 2, vol. 1, p. 759.

markets had shrunk the size of the region's plantations. The new agricultural regimen depended on hiring slaves to satisfy seasonal labor demands. As a result, slaves encountered a variety of masters and employers, worked alongside slaves from other farms and black people who were free, and acquired a familiarity with nearby roads and waterways. Some slaves, permitted to hire their own time, succeeded in buying their way out of bondage, adding to the already substantial free black population. Free blacks lived scattered among the plantations on hardscrabble farms, scratching the soil, fishing and oystering, and hiring themselves to planters for short stints. Shared labor along with ties of kinship and friendship knit free blacks and slaves into a single community.[21]

The pattern of slavery in tidewater Virginia enabled some slaves to turn wartime mobilization to their own advantage. The local Confederate commander unwittingly opened the door by impressing nearly all able-bodied free black and slave men to construct fortifications. Slaveholders objected to this dragnet impressment nearly as much as did their slaves, and by the summer of 1861 had begun to refugee them from the tidewater.[22] Pulled in two directions and unwilling to go in either, many of the slaves struck out on their own, employing their knowledge of the region's geography to head for the federal outpost at Fortress Monroe.

General Butler, who only weeks earlier had volunteered to protect Maryland masters against their slaves, now reversed himself. Realizing that blacks would be used against the Union if not employed for it, he accepted runaway slaves and put the able-bodied men to work on federal fortifications. In carefully drawn letters to General-in-Chief Winfield Scott and Secretary of War Simon Cameron, Butler detailed a policy that he clearly viewed as simple necessity but feared might be interpreted as a radical departure. He had seized the slaves, he argued, just as he seized other contraband of war and would return them, along with compensation for their use, if their owners took an oath of loyalty. Scott and Cameron, weary of conciliating secessionists, required little convincing. They promptly endorsed Butler's policy, and Cameron ordered him not to surrender fugitives to their "alleged masters."[23] Butler's designation of fugitive slaves as "contrabands" captured the Northern imagination, and blacks throughout tidewater Virginia—women and children, as well as men—began fleeing to Fortress Monroe, where they exchanged the status of slave for that of contraband.

---

[21] On the character of black life, slave and free, in tidewater Virginia, see Willard B. Gatewood, Jr., ed., *Free Man of Color: The Autobiography of Willis Augustus Hodges* (Knoxville, Tenn., 1982); Luther Porter Jackson, *Free Negro Labor and Property Holding in Virginia, 1830–1860* (Washington, 1942).

[22] See below, docs. 260A–H.

[23] See below, docs. 1A–B.

Butler's policy also found support in Congress during the summer of 1861. Defeat at Bull Run in July dashed expectations of quick victory over the Confederacy, and the Northern public grew less reluctant to punish traitors. Early in August, just before adjourning its special session, Congress passed and Lincoln signed the First Confiscation Act. Scrupulously following the standard usages of war, the act sought to weaken the Confederate military effort by making all property used in support of the rebellion "subject of prize and capture wherever found." Its provisions specifically included slaves who had been "employed in or upon any fort, navy yard, dock, armory, ship, entrenchment, or in any military or naval service." Although the act did not explicitly declare such slaves free, it nullified all claims by the masters to their labor.[24]

Despite the absence of an unequivocal declaration of freedom, the First Confiscation Act provided the bedrock for future development of federal policy regarding fugitive slaves. Secretary of War Cameron understood the significance of the new departure and pressed upon Butler an expansive reading of the legislation. While accepting the necessity of enforcing all federal laws (including the fugitive slave law) "within States and Territories in which the authority of the Union is fully acknowledged," Cameron admitted no such necessity in insurrectionary states, which, by their treason, had forfeited federal protection. There, according to the confiscation act, the Union could freely accept the services of slaves previously employed on behalf of the Confederacy. Furthermore, Cameron argued, the "substantial rights" of unionist slaveholders in the seceded states would also be served by receiving their fugitive slaves into federal lines, holding out the possibility of compensation to such slaveholders at some future date. Although he explicitly prohibited Butler from interfering with the "servants of peaceful citizens, in house or field," Cameron's instructions worked to the advantage of slaves who came into Union lines, whatever the politics of their owners. With Cameron's blessing, Butler treated all incoming blacks as "if not free born, yet free, manumitted, sent forth from the hand that held them, never to be reclaimed." Butler's successors at Fortress Monroe did the same.[25]

As Cameron and Butler inched beyond the confiscation act, General John C. Frémont leaped. Appointed commander of the Western Department in July 1861, the former Republican presidential candidate arrived in St. Louis determined to give practical application to his antislavery principles. At the end of August, citing civil violence and rampant disloyalty, Frémont proclaimed martial law in Missouri and declared free the slaves of all rebel masters in the state. Local opponents

---

[24] U.S., *Statutes at Large, Treaties, and Proclamations*, vol. 12 (Boston, 1863), p. 319.
[25] See below, doc. 1C; *Official Records*, ser. 2, vol. 1, pp. 770–71.

of slavery rallied to Frémont's side, as did abolitionists in the free states. But unlike Butler's stance in secessionist Virginia, which received wide acclaim, Frémont's proclamation in loyal Missouri met strong opposition. Slaveholding unionists in Missouri and in the other border states lambasted the proclamation, objecting that it would drive masters of wavering loyalty into the waiting arms of the Confederacy. Northern conservatives warned that the allegiance of Kentucky – still hovering in precarious neutrality as Confederate soldiers assembled along its southern border – was hanging in the balance. Convinced of the wisdom of such arguments, Lincoln advised Frémont to modify his proclamation to conform with the far more limited confiscation act, lest the general's action "ruin our rather fair prospect for Kentucky." When Frémont refused, Lincoln ordered him to make the required change, and Frémont complied. That done, the specter of wholesale military emancipation disappeared.[26]

As summer turned into fall and fall into winter, the confiscation act alone dictated the terms by which slaves might legally exit slavery. In most places, it provided but slight access to freedom, assuring slaveholders the return of any fugitive who had not been directly engaged in labor for the Confederacy. After federal troops moved into Kentucky in September 1861, for example, Union generals in the state – including Ulysses S. Grant and William T. Sherman – presumed it their duty to return runaway slaves to their owners. Their conviction was shared by General John A. Dix in Maryland and by General McClellan, now commanding in northern Virginia and the District of Columbia.[27]

The slaves were not deterred. They searched the seams of federal policy looking for ways to expand the fissures opened at Fortress Monroe and enlarged by the confiscation act. In every theater of operation, fugitive slaves moved toward Union army camps. Intimidated by the mass of armed white men and discouraged by reports of rough treatment, many runaways kept a healthy distance, trailing moving columns or camping outside federal bivouacs – just far enough to avoid expulsion by Union commanders, just close enough to discourage Confederate soldiers and slave catchers. Other fugitive slaves marched boldly into Union camps and tried to barter for protection. Some offered useful information – the length and direction of navigable rivers and roads, the movement of Confederate troops, the sighting of some big gun. Others contributed the bounty – pastries, fruit, smoked meat – of their masters' larders or their own. Most declared their willingness to labor at anything from constructing fortifications to cleaning a soldier's tent. Many fugitives were seized and returned to their owners, or simply sent away to fend for themselves. But there

[26] See below, doc. 155.
[27] See below, docs. 46–47, 197, 199; *Official Records*, ser. 2, vol. 1, pp. 763, 765.

always seemed to be some Yankee soldiers willing, for whatever reason, to shelter runaways, and a few who actively encouraged slave flight. The slaves' persistence complicated what at first seemed a simple matter of enforcing the fugitive slave law. When slaveholders pursued fugitives to a Union camp, military officers became embroiled in disagreeable contests whose resolution required considerable time and skill, especially when slaveholders claimed to be loyal and slaves professed to have labored in Confederate service. Masters demanded rendition and slaves begged for protection; Union officers sought a way out of the imbroglio.

Struggling to escape the cross fire of master and slave – to be neither slave stealer nor slave catcher, in the idiom of the day – federal commanders throughout the border states attempted to exclude fugitive slaves from army camps and posts. In the fall of 1861, General Henry W. Halleck, commanding in Missouri and western Kentucky, General Don Carlos Buell in central Kentucky, and General Dix in Maryland all issued orders barring slaves from army lines. All three acted with the encouragement and approval of General McClellan, newly elevated to command as general-in-chief of the Union armies.[28] The architects of exclusion hoped that denying fugitives access to army camps would also make the larger problem of slavery disappear. They expected that, by reducing contact between Union soldiers and both slaves and slaveholders, exclusion would dissipate the growing revulsion in the ranks against returning fugitives to their owners. Without questioning the particular political and military circumstances that made exclusion practicable in the border states, Union military authorities assumed that they had discovered a policy of universal genius, appropriate wherever federal troops encountered slaves. Little did they anticipate the problems that awaited their armies as they advanced into Confederate territory, where the slaveholders were avowed enemies – not wavering friends – and large numbers of slaves had been employed in the Confederate war effort.

Such problems were not long in coming. Through the summer and fall of 1861, as Union officials pondered what to do with slaves, the Confederates were acting with dispatch. They mobilized slave laborers to construct Southern defenses on the Atlantic and Gulf coasts and at strategic points along inland waterways and railroads. When Union troops tested Confederate lines, they encountered slave-built fortifications and often the slaves themselves. In such circumstances, the confiscation act became a veritable emancipation proclamation.

Yet, the First Confiscation Act remained a narrow instrument of liberation. The farther south federal forces advanced, the more appar-

---

[28] See below, docs. 129, 157; *Official Records*, ser. 2, vol. 1, pp. 764–66, 775–77.

ent became its limitations. In November 1861, when Union sailors and soldiers invaded the South Carolina Sea Islands around Port Royal, the inadequacy of the act became transparent. General Thomas W. Sherman and Flag Officer Samuel Du Pont, joint commanders of the expedition, had been furnished copies of Secretary of War Cameron's instructions to General Butler regarding fugitive slaves. Although the War Department explicitly warned Sherman and Du Pont against interfering with the "[s]ocial systems or local institutions" of the islands, it encouraged them to employ captured or fugitive slaves at military labor, much as Butler had done at Fortress Monroe.[29] But the federal forces who stormed ashore at Port Royal, bearing assurances that slave property would be respected, found few slaveholders to assure. The resident planters – many of them leaders of the movement for Southern independence – had fled at the sight of the Union gunboats. Most of the slaves remained behind, having thwarted their owners' frantic attempt to evacuate them to the mainland, some by openly resisting, others by simply escaping in the confusion of the moment. Once their owners had gone, the slaves returned to their homes and celebrated their new freedom – often taking the opportunity to even old scores with their fugitive owners. In the months and years to come, they were joined on the Union-occupied Sea Islands by hundreds of slaves from the mainland.

What the slaves took for granted, neither Sherman nor Du Pont would immediately concede. Although the masters' flight rendered the Port Royal slaves de facto freedpeople, their legal status remained moot, unaffected by the First Confiscation Act since few, if any, had been employed in Confederate service. Sherman and Du Pont put some of them to work for the army and navy, but most blacks remained on the plantations and set about reconstructing their lives, now independent of their former owners.

As in tidewater Virginia, the nature of slavery shaped the struggle for freedom in the Union-occupied Sea Islands. Under the old regime, the slaves – who composed an overwhelming majority of the population – had enjoyed considerable control over their own lives. Many of them had access to gardens or provision grounds, which they cultivated on their own account after finishing each day's plantation task. The produce they raised allowed them to participate in the region's internal economy and to accumulate property – including barnyard fowl, hogs, and small boats – of modest worth. With the flight of their owners, Port Royal slaves turned their backs on cotton, the plantation staple, and devoted their full attention to the provision grounds. Federal officials made no declaration of emancipation, but the actions of the

[29] See below, doc. 18.

slaves and the flight of their owners made such a pronouncement unnecessary.[30]

Still, the absence of a legal foundation for their liberty left Sea Island blacks in a precarious position. The consequences of such insecurity would become evident as federal forces extended their control to other portions of the South Atlantic coast. In coastal Florida, for example, many slaveholders declared themselves loyal to the federal government. Eager to cultivate indigenous unionism, Northern officers honored the masters' claims by paying them when the army employed their slaves and by helping them recapture runaways.[31]

Events in lowcountry Florida and South Carolina paralleled developments in the Upper South. Everywhere, federal policy regarding fugitive slaves moved in two directions: rendition or exclusion where masters remained loyal to the Union; acceptance and employment where slaveholders stood with the Confederacy. When the loyalty of slaveholders was in doubt, the two aspects of federal policy mixed in complex ways. Officers and soldiers of abolitionist bent protected fugitive slaves from their owners; those who believed that respecting slavery would speed restoration of the Union returned fugitives or excluded them from army lines. But slaves, refusing to relinquish their view of the federal army as a refuge from slavery, would not permit exclusion to settle the question. Although national law and federal policy provided only a small opening by which slaves might gain liberty, they struggled to enlarge it. Their determination awakened field officers to the possibility of employing blacks in behalf of the Union, a possibility that seemed increasingly reasonable, if not essential, in the face of the slave-built breastworks and slave-supplied armies of the Confederacy.

By year's end, what had begun to appear as common sense to officers and soldiers in the field seemed even more compelling to Secretary of War Cameron in Washington. In November 1861, Cameron publicly endorsed a proposal to arm slaves to fight for the Union and freedom. He elaborated the idea in his annual report, which he forwarded to the press before it had received Lincoln's endorsement. Condemning as "madness" the practice of leaving the enemy "in peaceful and secure possession of slave property," Cameron proposed that the North free all slaves owned by rebels, employ them in the Union war effort, and arm

[30] Willie Lee Rose, *Rehearsal for Reconstruction: The Port Royal Experiment* (Indianapolis, 1964). On the task system and slave-owned property in lowcountry South Carolina and Georgia, see Philip D. Morgan, "Work and Culture: The Task System and the World of Lowcountry Blacks, 1700 to 1880," *William and Mary Quarterly* 3rd ser., 39 (Oct. 1982): 563–99, and "The Ownership of Property by Slaves in the Mid-Nineteenth-Century Low Country," *Journal of Southern History* 49 (Aug. 1983): 399–420; Thomas F. Armstrong, "From Task Labor to Free Labor: The Transition along Georgia's Rice Coast, 1820–1880," *Georgia Historical Quarterly* 64 (Winter 1980): 432–47.
[31] See below, docs. 22, 26B.

those capable of military service against their masters. His call for emancipation and the enlistment of black soldiers outraged border-state loyalists and Northern conservatives. It also displeased the President, who required Cameron to expunge the offending passage – to the relief of unionist slaveholders and the consternation of the growing antislavery constituency in and out of the army.[32] By the end of January 1862, Cameron had been banished to an ambassadorship in Russia, and the more circumspect Edwin M. Stanton sat as Secretary of War.

Lincoln's suppression of Cameron's recommendation belied the progress of antislavery sentiment in the North. When Congress reconvened in December 1861, its proceedings reflected growing impatience with a policy that protected the property of unrepentant rebels. Northern constituents flooded congressional mailboxes with antislavery petitions and demands for stern punishment of secessionists.[33] Radical congressmen filled the legislative hoppers with measures that urged the confiscation of rebel property, including slaves. Such proposals sat well with those Northerners who had achieved political maturity in the abolitionist movement and who traced the Union's military failures directly to the policy of waging war on the narrowest moral and political grounds. But, in many instances, disenchantment with the course of the war also propelled Northerners of a conservative stripe beyond the bounds of punishing Confederate slaveholders, to a more generalized recognition of slavery as the root cause of secession. An attempt to reaffirm the Crittenden resolution, passed so easily the previous summer, met decisive defeat in the House of Representatives. Instead, the House adopted a resolution calling for emancipation of the slaves of disloyal masters in all military jurisdictions – endorsing, in effect, Frémont's proclamation of the previous August – and defeated by only a narrow margin a resolution censuring General Halleck's order to exclude slaves from army lines.[34]

Apparently unmoved by the flurry of congressional activity, Lincoln

[32] For Cameron's public endorsement of arming blacks, and both the original and modified versions of his annual report, see Edward McPherson, *Political History*, pp. 249, 416.

[33] See, for example, H. P. McChurkin et al. to the Congress of the United States, Dec. 1861, 37A-G21.4, Select Committee on Emancipation, Petitions & Memorials, ser. 467, 37th Congress, RG 233 [D-100]; Calvin Gray et al. to the Congress of the United States, 10 Dec. 1861, 37A-G7.2, House Committee on the Judiciary, Petitions & Memorials, ser. 467, 37th Congress, RG 233 [D-58]; S. D. Taylor et al. to the Congress of the United States, [Dec. 1861], 37A-G7.13, House Committee on the Judiciary, Petitions & Memorials, ser. 467, 37th Congress, RG 233 [D-72]; R. F. Fenton to the Congress of the United States, [Feb. 1862], 37A-G7.13, House Committee on the Judiciary, Petitions & Memorials, ser. 467, 37th Congress, RG 233 [D-101]. The fact that many petitions arrived in multiple copies on printed forms suggests their general and systematic circulation.

[34] Edward McPherson, *Political History*, pp. 253–54, 286–87; Nevins, *War for the Union*, p. 402.

never seemed more out of touch with Northern opinion. But behind the scenes, he was considering various plans for gradual emancipation and compensation to slaveholders – perhaps in the hope of fending off more drastic antislavery measures, certainly with an eye to the special difficulty of slavery in the loyal border states. He began by suggesting that the federal government help Delaware initiate gradual, compensated emancipation. A blow at slavery in Delaware – where fewer than 1,800 blacks remained in bondage – would hardly shake the institution, but Lincoln's proposal did reveal that his position was shifting under the weight of events. Although the Delaware legislature rejected the idea of emancipation in any form, Lincoln persevered. In the following months, he reiterated his support for gradual, compensated emancipation on several occasions, and in April 1862, at his behest, Congress resolved to provide financial assistance to any state that enacted such a measure.[35] Antislavery Northerners, black and white, denounced the resolution as evidence of the President's antiquated preoccupation with the rights of loyal masters. Some abolitionists argued that justice would be better served by compensating slaves for their long years in bondage than by indemnifying slaveholders for their grudging loyalty to the Union. Yet, those same loyal owners discerned the frightening implications of Lincoln's proposal and rejected it out of hand. They understood that Lincoln was edging toward emancipation.

Where Lincoln followed Northern opinion on the question of slavery, others led it. Radical Republicans pressed for a bolder assault on slavery. In March 1862, Congress enacted an additional article of war that prohibited the employment of Union soldiers in returning fugitive slaves to their masters.[36] The new article went beyond the simple expression of opinion offered in the House resolution of the previous summer, for it provided antislavery soldiers with legal grounds to resist the orders of proslavery superiors. Having bolstered the position of their comrades in the army, congressional radicals turned their attention directly to slavery. No target seemed more inviting than the 3,000 slaves in the District of Columbia, where the presence of slavery had long been a source of embarrassment to abolitionists and where federal authority over slavery was certain. Early in the session, Senator Henry Wilson, a Massachusetts Republican, introduced legislation to abolish slavery in the District. Although the measure provided for immediate rather than gradual emancipation, it borrowed in other respects from Lincoln's position, authorizing compensation to slaveholders and urging colonization of the freed slaves outside the limits of

---

[35] Lincoln, *Collected Works*, vol. 5, pp. 29–31, 144–46; *Statutes at Large*, vol. 12, p. 617; Henry Wilson, *History of the Antislavery Measures of the Thirty-Seventh and Thirty-Eighth United-States Congresses, 1861–64* (Boston, 1864), chap. 4.
[36] *Statutes at Large*, vol. 12, p. 354.

the United States. Its passage in April 1862 constituted the first time that the federal government had directly legislated the emancipation of any slave. To be sure, the compensation of slaveholders accorded slavery a legitimacy that abolitionists were loath to concede. Nonetheless, abolition in the national capital put slaveholders in the Union's own slave states on the defensive, and marked a significant step toward placing the federal government on the side of freedom.[37]

As the groundswell of antislavery sentiment in the North began to register in the halls of Congress, the military offensives of early 1862 dramatized the need for a more forthright commitment to emancipation. Shortly after the new year, the Union armies advanced on several fronts. Moving deep into enemy territory, they encountered larger and larger numbers of slaves, some of whom had been in Confederate employ. In such circumstances, most field officers quickly applied the provisions of the First Confiscation Act and put black men (and some black women) to work on the Union side of the line of battle. As they did, federal forces became increasingly dependent on black military laborers.

The army's growing appetite for laborers enlarged its complicity in the slaves' struggle for freedom. Fugitive slaves encouraged this complicity by volunteering important military intelligence and by applying their skill and muscle in the Union cause. Standard usages of war authorized protection in exchange for such assistance, and few Union officers were so lacking in gratitude as to withhold it. But in so doing, they acted against the explicit instructions of their superiors, who had ordered the exclusion and expulsion of fugitive slaves from army lines. Conflicts multiplied within the ranks, sometimes ending in the resignation, court-martial, and even dismissal of officers determined to shield fugitives from recapture.[38] Nevertheless, as the Union army advanced, the utility of black labor – if not the morality of protecting runaway slaves – wore upon the policy of exclusion. Whatever its advantages in the border states, it became increasingly inadequate as the Union army occupied portions of the Confederacy. Federal commanders had believed exclusion to be a panacea for their problems with slavery. It proved to be no solution at all.

General-in-Chief McClellan, whose determination to preserve the war from abolitionist taint had been established in the first months of fighting, directed the federal offensives in the east. Early in 1862, he ordered a joint naval and army expedition to establish a third Union beachhead on the Atlantic coast by invading tidewater North Carolina. In accordance with instructions from McClellan, General Ambrose E. Burnside issued hearty promises to respect slavery as his soldiers

[37] *Statutes at Large*, vol. 12, pp. 376–78; Wilson, *History of Antislavery Measures*, chap. 3.
[38] See below, docs. 63, 85, 87.

smashed Confederate coastal defenses and occupied strategic positions.[39] But slaveholders in tidewater North Carolina, some of whom had already lost slaves to the Union outpost at Fortress Monroe, did not wait to test federal guarantees; they fled before the Northern advance. Federal officers recognized that those who remained did so only from lack of choice. Meanwhile, blacks – moving east as their owners migrated west – flooded into Union lines. As in tidewater Virginia, small farms and extensive slave hiring had familiarized slaves with the geography of the region and given them considerable knowledge of Confederate movements. They volunteered this information and their own labor to Burnside's short-handed command. Their presence in large numbers promised to make a mockery of any attempt at exclusion, and Burnside did not even try. Instead, he employed the fugitives as Butler had at Fortress Monroe, paying them for their labor and elevating them to the status of contrabands.[40]

General McClellan, by contrast, strove to preserve his reputation as the slaveholders' friend. In March 1862, he was relieved as general-in-chief and took personal command of the massive Army of the Potomac for the peninsula campaign in tidewater Virginia. Through the spring and into the summer, McClellan inched cautiously up the peninsula formed by the York and James rivers, waging several costly battles before succumbing to the paralyzing conviction that a superior Southern army threatened to overwhelm him. Confederate forces on the peninsula in fact never equaled the number of Union soldiers, but McClellan's prophecy proved correct, in that the rebel army under General Robert E. Lee rallied to halt the Northern advance. Meanwhile, the turmoil created by the tramping armies allowed large numbers of slaves to escape, including many who had been brought into the area to construct Confederate defenses. Even after fighting his way through a network of slave-built fortifications, McClellan's opinions about slavery remained unchanged. In a letter to President Lincoln, written on the eve of Union withdrawal from the peninsula, McClellan reiterated his belief that "[n]either confiscation of property, political executions of persons, territorial organization of States, or forcible abolition of slavery, should be contemplated for a moment."[41] But slaves in tidewater Virginia attached little importance to McClellan's opinions, preferring instead the precedent established earlier in the war at Fortress Monroe. They simply by-passed McClellan and his subordinates and took refuge at the federal fortress at the tip of the peninsula.

The war followed a different course in the western theater. In the east, both Burnside and McClellan operated within narrow geographical bounds. In the west, the Union offensive stretched from the Ohio

[39] *Official Records*, ser. 1, vol. 9, pp. 363–64.
[40] See below, doc. 6.
[41] Edward McPherson, *Political History*, pp. 385–86.

River deep into the Mississippi Valley. Slavery also differed markedly in the valley. Cotton was the great staple crop and plantations were large, with slaveholdings sometimes extending into the hundreds on the rich bottom lands. Slaves generally worked in gangs and often lived their entire lives within the confines of a single estate. Yet, if large units and the absence of extensive hiring deprived most slaves of knowledge of the region's geography, the community that developed within the slave quarters and the network of communication that radiated outward from each plantation allowed them to mobilize quickly to take advantage of opportunities presented by the war. Not all slaves in the Mississippi Valley resided on plantations. In the interstices between the great river estates and in upcountry districts, small units could be found and slavery exhibited many of the features prevalent on the eastern seaboard.[42] Throughout the Mississippi Valley, slaves quickly became aware of the federal military presence and pushed their way toward Union lines. Wherever Union soldiers entered the Confederacy, the policy of exclusion fell into disrepair.

West of the Mississippi River, military events transformed federal forces into an army of emancipation. In February 1862, General Samuel R. Curtis and his Army of the Southwest advanced upon the Confederate troops who had wintered in southwest Missouri. When they retreated into Arkansas, Curtis followed, winning an important victory at Pea Ridge in early March. He then embarked on a grueling march across the state, emerging at Helena, on the banks of the Mississippi, in July. All along his route, Curtis encountered obstacles constructed by impressed slaves – many of whom escaped in the tumult that accompanied the arrival of Union soldiers. By the time he reached Helena, a considerable number of fugitive slaves followed in his train. A three-term Iowa congressman with solid antislavery credentials, Curtis refused to permit these slaves to be recaptured by their owners and redeployed against his army. Instead, he issued certificates of freedom on the basis of the First Confiscation Act, making the Union-controlled portion of Arkansas a haven for fugitive slaves.[43]

East of the Mississippi River, the transformation of federal policy proceeded at a much slower pace. In February 1862, Union troops from General Halleck's Department of the Missouri (soon expanded and renamed Department of the Mississippi) entered Tennessee. General Ulysses S. Grant advanced up the Cumberland and Tennessee rivers to capture Fort Henry and Fort Donelson, shattering the Confederate line of defense that protected Tennessee and the states farther south. Meanwhile, General John Pope traced the Mississippi, opening the way for

---

[42] Charles S. Sydnor, *Slavery in Mississippi* (New York, 1933); Chase C. Mooney, *Slavery in Tennessee* (Bloomington, Ind., 1957); Orville W. Taylor, *Negro Slavery in Arkansas* (Durham, N.C., 1958).
[43] See below, doc. 95.

federal occupation of Memphis in June. In late February, as his subordinates launched the offensive into the Confederacy, Halleck preached anew the doctrine of noninterference with slavery. "Let us show to our fellow-citizens . . . that we come merely to crush out rebellion . . . [and] that they shall enjoy . . . the same protection of life and property as in former days." Admonishing his troops that "[i]t does not belong to the military to decide upon the relation of master and slave," Halleck ordered that no slaves be admitted into Union lines. As though to leave no doubt about his firmness on the subject, he required that the order be read to every regiment and commanded all officers to enforce it strictly.[44]

Most of Halleck's subordinates executed his exclusion policy scrupulously, a comparatively easy task while they were on the move in areas with few slaves. But as Union forces overran Confederate positions, they inevitably captured slave laborers subject to the provisions of the First Confiscation Act and put them to work for the Union. The blacks labored with the same tools, often in the same ditch, but now enjoyed the protection of federal arms.

Simultaneously with the movement of federal forces into west Tennessee, General Don Carlos Buell's Army of the Ohio advanced into middle Tennessee, occupying Nashville as its new base of operations. Many middle Tennessee slaveholders professed loyalty to the Union, a circumstance that gave Buell added reason to stand by his order to exclude slaves from army lines and, when exclusion failed, to return them to their owners.[45] Conservative Buell remained convinced that respect for slavery on the part of the Union army would disabuse Confederates of mistaken notions about the antislavery intentions of the North, wean them from secession, and foster Southern unionism. Nevertheless, slaves fled to Buell's lines and sought admission. Sympathetic officers and men obliged. Indeed, when one division of the Army of the Ohio pressed into northern Alabama, some of its officers, deeming the slaves "our only friends," promised to protect fugitives who provided military information.[46] These officers did so in direct violation of Buell's orders, and he did his best to force them into line or drum them out of his command. More fully than any other general in the western theater, Buell was determined to protect slave property. But changes in federal policy undercut his commitment to the rights of slaveholders. Much to Buell's dismay, the new article of war in particular gave antislavery officers and soldiers greater latitude to act upon their principles.

The policy of exclusion frayed as federal armies took control of larger

[44] *Official Records*, ser. 1, vol. 8, pp. 563–65. For an order by Grant reiterating Halleck's exclusion policy, see *Official Records*, ser. 1, vol. 7, p. 668.
[45] *Official Records*, ser. 1, vol. 7, pp. 669–70.
[46] See below, doc. 86n.

expanses of Confederate territory. It came completely undone when Union forces reached the plantation South. There, slaves entered Union lines in such numbers that it was nearly impossible to keep them out. Whatever the fugitive-slave policies undertaken – from rendition to unauthorized declarations of freedom – exclusion did not so much as merit a trial. Instead, Union commanders openly debated the question of universal emancipation.

The debate flared first in the lower Mississippi Valley, where General John W. Phelps squared off against the ubiquitous General Butler, under whose command federal forces captured New Orleans in April 1862. Phelps, a Vermont free-soiler who represented the growing commitment to emancipation within the Union army, believed the federal government would do well to abolish slavery as the French had destroyed the *ancien régime*. When his troops occupied Ship Island, Mississippi, in December 1861, Phelps prepared to launch a war against slavery.[47] But before he could act, he became a post commander within Butler's Department of the Gulf.

Unlike Phelps, Butler was no abolitionist. Finding that a good many Louisiana slaveholders professed loyalty to the Union, Butler took them at their word and instructed his troops to assist in maintaining plantation discipline and to return runaway slaves to loyal owners. His orders appeared to violate the additional article of war recently adopted by Congress, but federal authorities neither reprimanded him nor instructed him to do otherwise. The general who had earlier stolen a march by transforming the slaves of disloyal owners into contrabands, now reversed the process for those who fled from loyal owners. Unionism in Louisiana would be built with the support of whites, not blacks; slaveholders, not slaves. For the time being, Butler simply ignored the large number of prosperous, cosmopolitan free people of color, most of whom resided in New Orleans. Nevertheless, free men of color who had previously been mustered into Confederate Native Guard units now proclaimed their loyalty to the Union and declared themselves ready to fight for the federal cause.[48]

Many slave owners, particularly those of Whig pedigree, found Butler's program attractive. Yet federal policy – some of it Butler's own doing – had proceeded too far toward emancipation to reassure all slaveholders in southern Louisiana. Upon federal invasion, many fled the region. Fugitive masters attempted to take their slaves with them to the interior, but – as in the South Carolina Sea Islands – plantation hands refused the passage.

Again, black people drew upon their experience as slaves in struggling for freedom. Slavery in southern Louisiana – with its large

---

[47] See below, doc. 58.
[48] See below, doc. 61. On the Native Guard units, see *Freedom*, ser. 2: doc. 11.

waterfront estates; its dependence on skilled workers, especially in sugar processing; and its connections with the great metropolis of New Orleans – provided slaves with the means to resist their masters.[49] Familiar with the dense network of forests and swamps that surrounded almost every plantation, slaves took to the woods to wait out their owners' evacuation, and then returned to rebuild their lives free of the burdens of bondage. All along the river, in the midst of functioning slave plantations, blacks secured control of abandoned estates. Sometimes under the direction of an old driver, sometimes as groups of independent households, they began to sow subsistence crops while weeds choked the fields of sugar cane and cotton. These settlements of runaways soon attracted other fugitives, and they also affected slaves who remained at home, many of whom now refused to work under the old terms. Confronting their masters directly, they demanded an end to gang labor, the removal of overseers, and the payment of wages. Despite Butler's efforts to sustain unionist masters, the slave regime in southern Louisiana had been shaken beyond repair. Blacks made it known that they would never again accept the old order.

Stationed above New Orleans at Camp Parapet, General Phelps aided their cause. He broadcast his willingness to shelter fugitives, and, before long, slaves from miles around packed their few belongings and headed for his camp. When they appeared in rags, beaten and bloody, the enraged general ordered retributive raids, liberating other slaves and dramatically demonstrating the diminished authority of the master class.

Although not opposed to freeing the slaves of outright rebels, Butler demanded that his subordinates distinguish the slaves of the loyal from those of the disloyal. Phelps knew no such distinction. The two generals warred openly, and each appealed to higher authority in Washington – Butler expecting a restatement of the prevailing policy of honoring the claims of loyal owners, Phelps seeking the articulation of a new commitment to universal emancipation. But Secretary of War Stanton sidestepped their dispute, and it continued into the heat of the Louisiana summer. Meanwhile, Louisiana blacks expanded their liberty inside and outside the old system; slavery languished, even if freedom had not yet arrived.[50]

While Butler and Phelps dueled, General David Hunter, fresh from the Kansas border wars, took command of the South Carolina Sea Islands determined to become the great emancipator. He immediately

---

[49] On slavery in southern Louisiana, see J. Carlyle Sitterson, *Sugar Country: The Cane Sugar Industry in the South, 1753–1950* (Lexington, Ky., 1953); Joe Gray Taylor, *Negro Slavery in Louisiana* (Baton Rouge, La., 1963).
[50] See below, docs. 59–63.

set to work making Port Royal the base for a grand assault against the Confederacy. In April 1862, he sought War Department permission to enlist black men into the Union army, in part to reinforce his short-handed command and in part to strike a blow at slavery. When the department ignored his request, Hunter began recruiting anyway – often dragooning Sea Island blacks into service. In May, he proclaimed martial law throughout South Carolina, Georgia, and Florida, even though he controlled only a few coastal outposts. Then, pronouncing slavery incompatible with martial law, he declared that the slaves in those states were free.[51]

Although they disliked Hunter's recruitment methods, Port Royal blacks cheered his audacious initatives on behalf of freedom. President Lincoln was considerably less impressed, and he promptly reversed them. In acting against slavery, Hunter had moved far beyond the First Confiscation Act, much as Frémont had done the previous August. Although Northern opposition to slavery had increased during the intervening months, Hunter's proclamation nonetheless represented a challenge to the Lincoln administration. The Secretary of War and the President reined the general. Stanton refused to sanction or provision Hunter's black regiment, which, as a result, eventually had to be disbanded. Ten days after Hunter abolished slavery in the Department of the South, Lincoln nullified Hunter's proclamation, reasserting his own authority over the disposition of slavery and restating his commitment to gradual, compensated emancipation.[52]

Although he felt compelled to repudiate Hunter's bold stroke, Lincoln understood that the war was fast eroding his own policy of non-interference with slavery, along with its corollaries – rendition and exclusion. Indicative of the growing strength of antislavery sentiment in the North, Congress prohibited slavery in the territories in June 1862, and soon thereafter took the first steps toward severing West Virginia from Virginia, which paved the way for its admission to the Union as a free state.[53] In a meeting with border-state congressmen in mid-July, Lincoln himself pointedly called attention to the changing circumstances. Warning them that time was running out for slavery, he predicted its inevitable dissolution in their own states "by mere friction and abrasion – by the mere incidents of the war." Lincoln also served notice that he could not continue to contravene the antislavery constituents whom he had offended by abrogating Hunter's proclamation. Once more, he urged that the border states adopt a gradualist plan of

---

[51] See below, doc. 24; *Freedom*, ser. 2: p. 38.
[52] See below, doc. 24; *Freedom*, ser. 2: pp. 38–39.
[53] *Statutes at Large*, vol. 12, p. 432; Richard O. Curry, *A House Divided: A Study of Statehood Politics and the Copperhead Movement in West Virginia* (Pittsburgh, 1964), pp. 100–130.

compensated emancipation.[54] Events were by-passing border-state slaveholders, but Lincoln would not remain behind.

A few days after the border-state meeting, as though to confirm Lincoln's warning, Congress expanded the legal basis for the extinction of slavery. The Second Confiscation Act, approved on July 17, declared slaves owned by disloyal masters "forever free of their servitude" and ordered that they be "not again held as slaves." It thus went far beyond the First Confiscation Act, whose provisions had touched only those slaves employed in Confederate service. Although the new confiscation act assigned to the federal courts ultimate responsibility for determining the loyalty of individual slaveholders, it designated the slaves "captives of war," placing them under the jurisdiction of the Union army. The act also enhanced the antislavery provisions of the additional article of war adopted the previous March. The article had not prevented army officers so disposed from opening their camps to slaveholders in pursuit of runaway slaves, so long as no soldier actually assisted in the capture. The Second Confiscation Act forbade persons in federal service to decide upon the validity of a claim to a slave "under any pretence whatever," or to "surrender up" any slave to a claimant. In effect, the new law deemed free all fugitive slaves who came into army lines professing that their owners were disloyal, as well as those slaves who fell under army control as Union troops occupied enemy territory. Furthermore, it held out a promise of protection from recapture and reenslavement. Bowing to the President's continued interest in removing black people from the United States – a popular idea among many white Northerners – the new confiscation act also encouraged the transfer of freed blacks to some tropical country willing to grant them "the rights and privileges of freemen."[55]

Despite lip service to colonization, Congress contemplated another role for the freed slaves. The Second Confiscation Act authorized the President to employ "persons of African descent" in any capacity to suppress the rebellion. The Militia Act, which became law on the same day, provided for their employment in "any military or naval service for which they may be found competent," and granted freedom to slave men so employed, as well as to their families, if they too were owned by disloyal masters.[56] Together, the Second Confiscation Act and the Militia Act made manifest the North's determination both to punish rebel slaveholders and to employ blacks in the Union war effort.

Five days after signing the two acts, Lincoln issued an executive order translating the new legislation into instructions for the Union

[54] Lincoln, *Collected Works*, vol. 5, pp. 317–19. Two days after their meeting with Lincoln, twenty of the border-state congressmen formally rejected compensated emancipation. A minority of eight approved the President's appeal.

[55] *Statutes at Large*, vol. 12, pp. 589–92.

[56] *Statutes at Large*, vol. 12, pp. 597–600.

army and navy. He authorized military commanders operating in the seceded states to "seize and use any property, real or personal, which may be necessary or convenient for . . . military purposes," and he instructed them to "employ as laborers . . . so many persons of African descent as can be advantageously used for military and naval purposes, giving them reasonable wages for their labor." Although he also reiterated customary injunctions against wanton or malicious destruction of private property, and required that records be kept to permit compensation to slaveholders "in proper cases," there was no mistaking the import of Lincoln's order.[57] Federal army officers understood it as an indication that thereafter no rebel property – slaves included – would escape military appropriation, and that fugitive slaves – at least the able-bodied men – should be welcomed into Union lines and put to work.

The momentous events of July 1862 did not stop with the confiscation and military employment of slaves. On July 22, Lincoln informed the cabinet of his intention to issue a proclamation of general emancipation in the seceded states. While soliciting comments from his advisors, he made clear his determination to act before the new year, regardless of opposition. At the cabinet's recommendation, however, Lincoln agreed to withhold his pronouncement until the occasion of a Union victory at arms, so that emancipation could be presented as an act of strength rather than weakness. The summer dragged on without offering such an opportunity, and in September matters took an even more ominous turn. The Confederates invaded both Maryland and Kentucky, panicking the Northern population, forcing federal troops into defensive retreat, and marking a low point for the Union.

The battle of Antietam, though hardly the hoped-for triumph, halted the Confederate offensive in Maryland and at last provided the occasion for Lincoln's announcement. On September 22, 1862, he issued the preliminary Emancipation Proclamation, serving notice that on January 1 he would declare "then, thenceforward, and forever free" all the slaves in those states still in rebellion. Lincoln pledged that the United States government would protect their freedom and, moreover, would do nothing to repress any actions taken by the slaves themselves to secure their own liberty. While thus – as slaveholders saw it – virtually inviting slave insurrection, Lincoln also renewed his call for voluntary, gradual, and compensated emancipation in the border states, voiced support for colonizing freed slaves "upon this continent or elsewhere," and promised to recommend that all loyal owners be compensated for the loss of their slaves.[58]

The new departures had immediate repercussions in the field. Aboli-

---

[57] Lincoln's executive order, dated July 22, 1862, was promulgated to the armies in the field by a War Department order of August 16. (*Official Records*, ser. 3, vol. 2, p. 397.)

[58] *Statutes at Large*, vol. 12, pp. 1267–68.

tionist officers, who believed that slaveholders were enemies of the Union, whatever their purported loyalty, welcomed the new legislation and presidential pronouncements, and applied them with abandon. Other commanders, less principled than pragmatic, were unconcerned about the fate of slavery but desperate for laborers; they too welcomed the change. General William T. Sherman, whose reluctance to meddle with slavery had become notorious, simply accepted fugitive slaves into his ranks, employed those who could work, and sheltered those unfit for labor.[59] His policy of keeping strict account of the labor performed by fugitive slaves, but withholding wages until the courts should decide upon their owners' loyalty, found wide acceptance among like-minded officers.

The change wrought by legislation and proclamation could be seen even in the actions of military officers who had long deferred to the rights of slaveholders. They too marched to a different beat. General McClellan, stalled on the Virginia peninsula, republished Lincoln's executive order almost upon receipt, adding, with full-throated indignation, "we are engaged in supporting the Constitution and laws of the United States and in suppressing rebellion . . . we are not engaged in a war of rapine, revenge, or subjugation." Despite this petulant restatement of his long-established position, McClellan made haste to implement the President's edict, asserting that black laborers "have always understood that after being received into the military service of the United States in any capacity they could never be reclaimed by their former holders."[60]

By the late summer of 1862, black men in large numbers – as well as some black women – were already laboring for the Union army and navy. Some had been accepted under the First Confiscation Act, others in direct violation of the policy of exclusion. Now their numbers increased rapidly as federal commanders discovered what Confederate officers had known all along: Blacks provided the most readily available – sometimes the only – source of military labor. Nearly every army post, supply depot, and wood yard acquired a contingent of black men to clear camps, build roads, construct fortifications, chop wood, and transport supplies. Few naval vessels lacked a handful of black men who handled the dirty and difficult business of coaling. Union commanders also found that blacks, free and slave, possessed a variety of skills and were knowledgeable wagoners, scouts, and pilots. Whites – Northern and Southern – disdained certain kinds of labor as "nigger work," but blacks stood able and often willing to take up the task – particularly if it would assure their liberty. The generally accepted notion that whites could not labor in tropical climates further increased reliance on black workers as the Union army marched south.

[59] See below, doc. 94.
[60] *Official Records*, ser. 1, vol. 11, pt. 3, pp. 362–64.

Military labor offered thousands of black men an opportunity to escape slavery and gain the protection of the Union army. Still, they found much to criticize in their new position. Federal service frequently took them away from family and friends, and the military and civilian overseers who supervised their work could be as abusive as any master—sometimes more so. Despite the specification of pay and rations in the Militia Act, the federal government often had difficulty meeting its payroll. Black laborers routinely received their wages late, and sometimes not at all—a circumstance that left them at the mercy of sharp traders in the army and out. The burden of work for the Yankee army led some black men to flee military labor as they had fled slavery. When they did, federal officers frequently resorted to impressment, much as had Confederate labor agents. Still, whatever its liabilities, military labor provided fugitive slaves with obvious advantages. Even those who deserted federal labor gangs seldom returned to their erstwhile owners.[61]

The Union army's willingness, indeed its need, to employ able-bodied black men did little to assist the black women, children, and old or infirm men who also made their way into Union lines in increasing numbers. Some women found employment as laundresses, cooks, seamstresses, and hospital attendants, but the demand for such workers paled in comparison with the calls for men to construct fortifications, move supplies, and chop wood. Old people and children had even fewer opportunities to gain a livelihood. Like the women, they generally had to rely upon fathers, husbands, and sons who labored in federal service. But the massive exodus from bondage had disrupted black life, and the reconstitution of families was hindered by the chaos of war. Many of those who escaped slavery had no way to support themselves.

The mass of destitute black refugees posed monumental problems for federal authorities. Anxious to secure their liberty, unattached women, children, and elderly people, along with the families of black laborers, crowded around federal depots and posts. As much as they tried to ingratiate themselves with their liberators, army commanders generally objected to their presence. Officers complained that the former slaves clogged roads and impeded the movement of soldiers and supplies, and that the refugees' squalid quarters and impoverished condition bred disease and vice.

Federal commanders found a variety of ways to deal with the fugitive slaves, all of them makeshift. Some left them to fend for themselves. A few sent them North. Some placed them under the care of civilian superintendents sent to the occupied South by Northern churches and benevolent societies. But as the number of blacks in federal employ swelled, the army itself was forced to accept at least some responsibility

---

[61] On the role of blacks as military laborers, see *Freedom*, ser. 1, vol. 2.

for the refugees within its lines. Indeed, the black men who labored for the army often made it clear that they would not work unless their families were provided with food and shelter. During the fall of 1862, federal commanders began to organize contraband camps, placing sympathetic officers – generally regimental chaplains or other men of humanitarian bent – in charge.[62]

Blacks who labored for the Union army or took refuge in the contraband camps did not remain satisfied with their own escape from slavery. Almost as soon as they reached the safety of federal lines, they began plotting to return home and liberate families and friends. Some traveled hundreds of miles into the Confederate interior, threading their way through enemy lines, eluding Confederate pickets, avoiding former masters, and outrunning the slave catchers hired to track them down. Not all succeeded, but when they did, their courage helped hundreds escape bondage and informed still others of the possibility of freedom. Occasionally, these brave men and women received assistance from sympathetic Union soldiers and commanders, who accompanied former slaves back to the old estates or provided material assistance to those intent upon returning to free others. The bargain seemed mutually beneficial – the Union army gained additional laborers, and the blacks secured the liberty of their loved ones.

The growing importance of black labor increased support for emancipation in the North. Abolitionists publicized the role of black laborers, arguing that their service to the Union made them worthy of freedom, and even of citizenship. Other Northerners, indifferent or even hostile to black advancement, also saw value in the exchange of labor for freedom. Expropriation of the masters' property seemed condign punishment for treason. And they noted that by doing the army's dirty work, black laborers freed white soldiers for the real business of war. Samuel J. Kirkwood, governor of Iowa, was appalled to learn that one of his state's regiments had "*sixty men on extra duty* as teamsters &c. whose places could just as well be filled with *niggers*." He urged the military authorities to employ additional black laborers to do such "*negro work*." Indicating the drift of Northern opinion, Governor Kirkwood added a few words on the subject of enlisting black men as soldiers: "When this war is over & we have summed up the entire loss of life it has imposed on the country I shall not have any regrets if it is found that a part of the dead are *niggers* and that *all* are not white men."[63]

Although hardly inspiring, such sentiments strengthened the hand of abolitionists, white and black, who urged the arming of black men with muskets as well as shovels. They had long maintained that enlisting black soldiers would enhance the military might of the Union,

[62] On the evolution of federal policy regarding the black refugees, see *Freedom*, ser. 1, vol. 2.
[63] *Freedom*, ser. 2: doc. 25.

while also securing emancipation and pushing the nation toward racial equality. Their earlier efforts to introduce black men into military service had been peremptorily dismissed, sometimes with sharp rebuke. But as public opinion turned against slavery, the proponents of black enlistment met with increasing success. In the summer and fall of 1862, the first black soldiers entered Union ranks in the Sea Islands of South Carolina, in southern Louisiana, and in Kansas.[64]

As its advocates had hoped, the enlistment of black soldiers provided a powerful instrument in the war against slavery. Even before they had seen active service, news of the black men in blue uniforms had an electrifying effect on those still in bondage, encouraging many to strike out for the Yankee lines. When the first black regiments took the field, their subversive force increased manyfold. Black soldiers, the vast majority of them former slaves, coveted the liberator's role. Moving from plantation to plantation – up the tidal rivers of the South Atlantic coast and through the bayous and swamps of southern Louisiana – they urged slaves to abandon their owners, and aided them in doing so. Indeed, black soldiers had such a destructive impact on slavery that they sometimes frightened their own commanders. In late 1862, General Godfrey Weitzel, who ended his wartime career at the head of the only all-black army corps, sought to be relieved of his first command of black troops from fear that they would incite a general slave revolt.[65] When officers of steadfast antislavery conviction took command of black regiments, the work of dismantling slavery proceeded apace, transforming the liberated into liberators at dizzying speed. Black soldiers freed slaves and escorted them to the safety of Northern encampments, where recruiting officers inducted the able-bodied men into federal ranks and began drilling them for missions of their own.

The possibility of military service opened the door to freedom for some slaves only to close it for others. As the enlistment of black men and the general increase of federal military activity provoked slaveholders to tighten plantation discipline, escape became more difficult and punishment more severe. Some masters called upon Confederate authorities to execute recaptured fugitive slaves as traitors in time of war, and at least one Confederate commander instituted court-martial proceedings against runaways.[66] Other slaveholders, choosing the risks of removal over the hazards of remaining within reach of federal raids, refugeed their slaves deep into the Confederate interior.

Thus, even with the aid of federal arms, freedom advanced slowly and not always directly. Individual slaveholders could aggravate the difficulties of escape to the Yankees, and Southern armies could recapture black people who had already reached Union lines. Confederate

[64] *Freedom*, ser. 2: chap. 1.
[65] See below, doc. 69.
[66] See below, docs. 318A–B, 320.

military offensives provided harsh reminders that the Northern commitment to emancipation amounted to little without military success. Indeed, any Union retreat could reverse the process of liberation and throw men and women who had tasted freedom back into bondage.

The Confederate invasion of Kentucky in August and September 1862, like other Confederate advances, revealed the full force of what was fast becoming an axiom of emancipation. As the Union army withdrew from northern Alabama and middle Tennessee to counter the rebel threat, thousands of black people fell once again under Confederate control, their title to liberty under the federal confiscation acts rendered valueless. Many found themselves cast back into the hands of their old masters – who had not forgotten how their slaves had turned on them and cooperated with the hated Yankees. Other former slaves, scrambling to retain the protection of the Union army, joined the forced march to Kentucky as pioneers, teamsters, and officers' servants. Still others trailed the retreating federal force – footsore, hungry, and fearful of what lay ahead, but certain of what remained behind. Many fell by the wayside and were captured by guerrillas or jailed by local authorities as runaway slaves. Even those who succeeded in reaching Kentucky learned firsthand of the insecurity of wartime freedom. State and local officials arrested hundreds of them under Kentucky's fugitive slave law, advertised for their masters, and sold them to new owners when no one registered a claim. In the spring of 1863, federal authorities began to intervene in such instances of reenslavement, but many men, women, and children who had escaped bondage in the Confederate states endured the remainder of the war as slaves in Kentucky.[67] Their travail testified to the link between the military success of the Northern armies and the liberty of Southern slaves.

On New Year's day 1863, President Lincoln gave that connection the full weight of federal authority. The Emancipation Proclamation fulfilled his pledge to free all slaves in the states still in rebellion. Differences between the preliminary proclamation of September and the final pronouncement of January 1 suggest the distance Lincoln and other Northerners had traveled in those few months. Gone were references to compensation for loyal slaveholders and colonization of former slaves. In their place stood the determination to incorporate black men into the federal army and navy. As expected, the proclamation applied only to the seceded states, leaving slavery in the loyal border states untouched, and it exempted Tennessee and the Union-occupied portions of Louisiana and Virginia. Nonetheless, its simple, straightforward declaration – "that all persons held as slaves" within the rebellious states "are, and henceforward shall be, free" – had enormous force.[68]

[67] See below, docs. 209–10, 213A–B, 215, 216n., 217B, 218, 223A–B.
[68] *Statutes at Large*, vol. 12, pp. 1268–69.

As Lincoln understood, the message of freedom required no embellishment. However deficient in majesty or grandeur, the President's words echoed across the land. Abolitionists, black and white, marked the occasion with solemn thanksgiving that the nation had recognized its moral responsibility, that the war against slavery had at last been joined, and that human bondage was on the road to extinction. But none could match the slaves' elation. With unrestrained — indeed, unrestrainable — joy, slaves celebrated the Day of Jubilee. Throughout the South — even in areas exempt from the proclamation — black people welcomed the dawn of a new era.[69]

In announcing plans to accept black men into the army and navy, the Emancipation Proclamation specified their assignment "to garrison forts, positions, stations, and other places, and to man vessels" — evidently proposing no active combat role and, in fact, advancing little beyond the already established employment of black men in a variety of quasi-military roles. Nonetheless, blacks and their abolitionist allies — who viewed military service as a lever for racial equality, as well as a weapon against slavery — seized upon the President's words and urged large-scale enlistment. Despite continued opposition from the advocates of a white man's war, the grim reality of mounting casualties convinced many Northerners of the wisdom of flexing the sable arm. Moreover, once the Emancipation Proclamation had made the destruction of slavery a Union war aim, increasing numbers of Northern whites thought it only fitting that black men share the burden of defeating the Confederacy.

Proponents of black enlistment adapted their cause to the new circumstances. They had few scruples about clothing their principled convictions in the rhetoric of military necessity, and such arguments found sympathetic listeners in Washington, where administration officials and legislators had awakened to the implications of protracted warfare and increasing manpower needs. As the number of white volunteers dwindled, Congress prepared legislation (adopted in March 1863) providing for national military conscription. At the same time, the War Department took the first steps toward systematic recruitment of black soldiers. In January, Secretary of War Stanton yielded to the importunities of John A. Andrew, antislavery governor of Massachusetts and long-time advocate of the sable arm, authorizing him to raise a black regiment. Other governors received similar permission, and recruiters — many of them black — fanned out across the free states, politicizing and inspiring black communities as never before. Eventually, nearly three-quarters of the military-age black men in those states enlisted in federal military service.[70]

[69] Franklin, *Emancipation Proclamation*, chaps. 4–5.
[70] *Freedom*, ser. 2: chap. 2, and pp. 9, 12.

The War Department also expanded recruitment of black men in Union-occupied portions of the Confederacy, sending recruiting officers of high rank to tidewater North Carolina and southern Louisiana. In March 1863, the department crowned its new policy by dispatching General Lorenzo Thomas, adjutant general of the army, to the Mississippi Valley, where he propounded its virtues to Union commanders and troops and launched full-scale recruitment of black men. Thomas's appointment signaled a shift from the haphazard recruitment of blacks by interested parties and independent commanders to a centrally coordinated effort under War Department auspices. The Bureau of Colored Troops, established in May 1863, provided bureaucratic embodiment of that shift. From the spring of 1863 to the end of the war, the federal government labored assiduously to maximize the number of black soldiers. The Northern public and officials in Washington came to understand what field commanders had discovered at first hand: Every slave placed in federal military service represented a double gain—one lost to the Confederacy and one added to the Union.[71]

As black soldiers joined white ones in expanding freedom's domain, the Union army became an army of liberation. Although the Emancipation Proclamation implied an auxiliary role, black soldiers would not permit themselves to be reduced to military menials. They longed to confront their former masters on the field of battle, and they soon had their chance. The earliest black regiments acquitted themselves with honor at the battles of Port Hudson, Milliken's Bend, and Fort Wagner in the spring and summer of 1863, and black soldiers thereafter marched against the Confederacy on many fronts. Meanwhile, scores of black regiments served behind Union lines—protecting railroads, bridges, and telegraph lines; manning forts; and fending off guerrillas and rearguard rebel attacks. Their services became increasingly essential to the Union war effort as Northern armies advanced deep into Confederate territory, lengthening the lines of communication and supply. The subversive effect of black soldiers on slavery, first demonstrated on the South Atlantic coast and in southern Louisiana, increased with the number of blacks in federal ranks. By war's end, nearly 179,000 black men—the overwhelming majority slaves—had entered the Union army, and another 10,000 had served in the navy.[72]

Military service provided black men with legal freedom and more. In undeniable ways, it countered the degradation that had undermined black self-esteem. Soldiering gave black men, free as well as slave, a broader knowledge of the world, an acquaintance with the workings of the law, access to some rudimentary formal education, and a chance to demonstrate their commitment to freedom for themselves and their

---

[71] *Freedom*, ser. 2: chap. 3, and pp. 9–10.
[72] *Freedom*, ser. 2: chaps. 10–11, and pp. 12, 14n., 23–26.

people. Battlefield confrontations with the slaveholding enemy exhilarated black soldiers by proving in the most elemental manner the essential equality of men. In their own eyes, in the eyes of the black community, and, however reluctantly, in the eyes of the nation, black men gained new standing by donning the Union blue.[73]

Large-scale enlistment of black soldiers into Union ranks deepened the federal government's commitment to all former slaves. Although black men contributed to the Northern cause both as laborers and as soldiers, it somehow seemed more difficult to deny support to the families of those who shouldered muskets than of those who wielded shovels. When the army mustered black soldiers from the Confederate states, it implicitly—and sometimes explicitly—agreed to protect and provide for their families and friends. Adjutant General Thomas understood the relationship between recruiting soldiers and caring for their families as fully as any federal officer. When he began recruiting black regiments in the Mississippi Valley, he organized contraband camps as he established recruitment stations; often the two were the same. Commanders in other portions of the Union-occupied Confederacy followed a similar course, though their efforts never kept pace with the number of black refugees.[74]

As the population of the contraband camps swelled, the superintendents began settling former slaves on plantations abandoned by their owners, usually as laborers in the employ of Northerners who leased the estates, occasionally as independent farmers. But, at best, the camps and abandoned plantations provided only short-term solutions to the problems created by the growing number of fugitive slaves within Union lines. Indeed, these temporary arrangements merely raised larger questions about the future of black people once slavery was abolished. To address these questions, Secretary of War Stanton appointed the American Freedmen's Inquiry Commission in March 1863, charging the three commissioners to investigate the condition of the refugee slaves and report how they might best defend and support themselves. The creation of the commission signaled that the federal government had come to recognize its necessary role in shaping the future of the slaves freed by the President's proclamation.[75]

Important Union victories in the summer of 1863 marked a turning point in the war and increased the urgency of regularizing federal

---

[73] *Freedom*, ser. 2: chaps. 9, 14, and pp. 26–34.
[74] For Thomas's first thoughts on the problem of refugee blacks, see *Freedom*, ser. 2: doc. 194. On army policy regarding black soldiers' families, see *Freedom*, ser. 2: chap. 16. For a discussion of the contraband camps, see *Freedom*, ser. 1, vol. 2.
[75] For Stanton's instructions to the commissioners, see *Official Records*, ser. 3, vol. 3, pp. 73–74. The commission issued a preliminary report in June 1863, and its final report in May 1864. (*Official Records*, ser. 3, vol. 3, pp. 430–54; ser. 3, vol. 4, pp. 289–382.)

policy respecting former slaves. Northern military success liberated slaves in unprecedented numbers, especially in the Mississippi Valley, where the fall of Vicksburg opened the way to Union control of the great river and severed the Confederacy. Tens of thousands of slaves thereby fell into Union hands, and thousands more fled to Union lines from Confederate territory on both sides of the river. Federal officials, drawing on established policy, promptly enlisted the men into the army and sent the women, children, and old people to safety behind the lines. To accommodate the influx, they established new contraband camps and expanded the plantation-leasing system, with the understanding that Northern lessees would employ the soldiers' families. To defend the plantations and contraband camps against Confederate raids, federal commanders assigned some of the newly enlisted black soldiers to guard duty, making them protectors of their parents, wives, and children.[76]

As the Union army transformed plantations into recruiting stations and contraband camps, the struggle over black manpower escalated. Responding to the federal challenge and the pleas of their own military commanders, Confederate leaders laid greater claim to the South's black labor force. In October 1863, Secretary of War James A. Seddon ordered the implementation of legislation, approved the previous March, that had increased the Confederacy's power to impress black military laborers. But that legislation, the first of a series of enactments expanding authority over slave and free black men, stopped far short of granting unrestricted power to overrule slaveholders and claim the labor of their slaves.[77] Even as the Southern army retreated before the Northern enemy, many slaveholders ignored requests for laborers, refused to hire their slaves to army quartermasters, or raised prices beyond the army's ability to pay. State officials – claiming that the state and not the general government had jurisdiction over slavery – sometimes went so far as to countermand Confederate orders and recall slaves who had been impressed.[78]

Slaveholders resisted impressment in part because it revealed to the slaves the limits of their owners' authority and thereby undermined slavery. Confederate officers, often of junior grade, sometimes rode roughshod over the masters. Observing the derogation of their owners' power – especially the ability to protect their slaves against outsiders – slaves became less willing to accord them the same deference. They worked slower and answered faster – in a tone that chilled their owners. Confederate military commanders fumed at the slaveholders' cupid-

---

[76] On the plantation-leasing system, see *Freedom*, ser. 1, vol. 2.

[77] For the various laws and some of the orders implementing them, see *Official Records*, ser. 4, vol. 2, pp. 469–72, 897–98; ser. 4, vol. 3, pp. 112, 207–9, 897–99, 1082–83.

[78] On Confederate impressment of slaves, see below, especially docs. 260–83.

ity and despaired at the narrow preoccupation of state officials. Some impugned the slaveholders' patriotism, a charge that resonated loudly within the lower ranks of the Southern army. When slave owners ridiculed the accusation and continued to ignore requests for laborers, hard-pressed field officers simply took them, sometimes with the permission of officials in Richmond and sometimes on their own authority. The resulting struggles set off ripples of recrimination. Slaveholders denounced military officers, state officials challenged the general government, small slaveholders condemned large ones, and nonslaveholders rebuked both for their unwillingness to sacrifice their slaves while the yeomanry sacrificed its sons. The widespread conviction that manpower burdens were being borne unequally was reinforced by complaints about inequity in taxation, conscription, and the distribution of food and other scarce commodities.

Slaves studied the divisions in Southern society with great care, dreading the prospect of being dragged into Confederate service. Impressment almost always removed slave men from home and family. Confederate labor superintendents often treated them roughly. Having no interest in impressed slaves as property, they worked them hard with scant concern for their well-being. Often they drove slaves far beyond the usual demands of plantation labor, in spite of protests by their owners. Moreover, as impressment agents and slaveholders debated terms of service and responsibility for rations, clothing, shelter, and medical care, impressed laborers went hungry and cold, fell ill, and died in numbers that appalled even the most hard-hearted. The terrifying possibility of impressment set slaves in motion. Many fled to the woods, but others turned toward Union lines, where federal recruiters waited to fit the men for a Union uniform.

Fearing that they would soon face their slaves on the field of battle if they did not lose them to Confederate labor agents, slaveholders searched for a safe harbor, distant from the dangers of both escape and impressment. During the summer of 1863, refugeeing assumed unprecedented proportions, especially in the Mississippi Valley and in lowcountry Georgia and South Carolina. Slaveholders moved thousands — indeed, tens of thousands — of slaves to the interior and to Texas.[79]

Properly executed, refugeeing effectively slowed the flight from the plantations. But attempted relocation, rather than securing slave property, often became the occasion for its loss. Understanding the diminished opportunities to escape from the interior, and unwilling in any case to leave their homes, slaves resisted removal. Everywhere efforts to refugee slaves spurred flight. Sometimes they escaped to the

[79] On refugeeing slaves to the Confederate interior, see below, especially docs. 307–14.

woods, awaited their owner's departure, and then returned to the old plantation to farm on their own. Despite their vulnerability to rebel raids, these independent colonies served as examples to slaves on neighboring plantations and, before long, as rendezvous for runaways. Even successfully executed refugeeing did not entirely serve the slaveholders' purpose. The swollen slave population of the interior placed enormous burdens on scanty food supplies and disrupted local economies. In effect, refugeeing transferred the disorder of the war zone to areas not yet directly touched by the conflict. With the arrival of refugeed slaves in the interior, the number of runaways surged, as did fear of insurrection.

Insurrection was only one concern of those who governed plantation life.[80] With the impressment and refugeeing of large numbers of ablebodied young men, the burden of plantation labor increasingly devolved upon slave women. Embittered by the enforced absence of their loved ones, and resentful of demands that they do the men's work as well as their own, slave women could not – and would not – continue to labor at the same pace. The motley collection of white women, disabled soldiers, and old men who presided over the great estates seemed incapable of maintaining the old regimen.

The Confederate tax-in-kind and the impressment of draft animals and farm implements further reduced agricultural production.[81] And, with animals and tools in short supply, slaves saw little reason to work beyond their own personal needs. In the early years of the war, planters had been encouraged to switch from staple crops to food production; as the war dragged on, many of them drifted from commercial agriculture to subsistence farming. As the Confederacy shrank, even self-sufficiency became difficult, and inflation increasingly put market purchases out of reach. A subsistence crisis of considerable magnitude gripped the South. For many slaves, the failure of their owners to feed and clothe them severed the last threads of allegiance. When they did not abandon the plantation, they simply raised food crops for their own tables.[82]

The disorder on the home front worried those on the war front. Confederate soldiers petitioned for leave of absence to attend to their families' needs, and, when short-handed commanders rejected their pleas, they deserted in droves. Those who did not desert complained bitterly that their own families went hungry, while slaves fed the

---

[80] On the problem of maintaining slave discipline in the Confederacy, see below, especially docs. 315–31.

[81] Richard C. Todd, *Confederate Finance* (Athens, Ga., 1954), pp. 141–48; James L. Nichols, "The Tax-in-Kind in the Department of the Trans-Mississippi," *Civil War History* 5 (Dec. 1959): 382–89.

[82] On the problem of agricultural production in the Confederacy, see below, especially docs. 292–98.

slaveholders' kin. Disaffection among Southern whites sometimes gave slaves new allies. For a few dollars, deserters and other disaffected whites shepherded runaways to freedom, or they joined slaves in the swamps to form interracial outlaw gangs.[83] As the war dragged on, slaves occasionally found assistance within the ranks of the Confederate army. Soldiers, military overseers, and labor agents sold passes to impressed slaves, allowing them to escape labor and sometimes bondage.[84]

Caught between Confederate impressment officers and Yankee recruiters, reluctant to refugee their slaves for fear of losing them, growing numbers of slaveholders were driven to make new concessions to keep them at home and at work. Negotiations began tentatively and proceeded awkwardly, since slaveholders would not concede their loss of mastery and slaves would not accept the legitimacy of bondage. Often the bargaining assumed an air of unreality, as slaveholders-turned-employers offered a "gift" at harvest time, while slaves-turned-employees demanded more concrete remuneration. Some slaves and their owners bartered labor for a promise of manumission at some future date, others haggled over a portion of the crops, and still others dickered about wages in cash or in kind. Whatever the terms agreed upon, neither party rested satisfied. Slaveholders were sure they conceded too much, slaves convinced they received too little. At the first promising opportunity, each party abandoned concessions and pressed for the ideal — the slaveholders, for reinstatement of the old regime; the slaves, for full independence from it.[85]

The breakdown of these fragile accords sent slaves or slaveholders — and sometimes both — flying to safety. Slaves moved toward Union lines, slaveholders deeper into the shrinking Confederacy. Blacks who remained on the old estates entered an ill-defined world between slavery and freedom. Where their owners abdicated, slaves cultivated food crops on the abandoned land they now considered their own. The presence of these independent black farmers had a ruinous effect on slavery in areas under Confederate control.

Slavery suffered more serious damage in the portions of the Confederacy occupied by the Union army. Slaveholders — even in Tennessee and southern Louisiana, which were exempt from the Emancipation Proclamation — found themselves unable to halt the steady disintegration of their authority. Time and again, unionist masters learned the futility of trying to control their slaves when those owned by rebel masters worked independently upon abandoned land, labored for the

---

[83] For example, see below, doc. 27.
[84] For example, see below, doc. 324.
[85] On the evolution of quasi-free labor arrangements during the war, see *Freedom*, ser. 1, vol. 2.

Union army, or enlisted as Union soldiers. With the slaves' options increasing, the old modes of discipline no longer carried the same force. The wisest slaveholders accepted the demands of the emerging order and did what was necessary to keep their slaves at work. Some welcomed, indeed urged, the establishment of federally sponsored labor systems – like those enacted by General Butler and his successor, General Nathaniel P. Banks, in Louisiana – that required planters to pay wages but pledged Yankee assistance in maintaining plantation discipline.[86] In the absence of federal interference, slaveholders in the Union-occupied South – like their counterparts in the Confederacy – were forced to relinquish old prerogatives if they hoped to retain their labor force.

The federal government's introduction of wage labor formed part of a larger effort to create loyal governments in the occupied states of the Confederacy. Familiar with the sources of Republicanism in the free states, Lincoln hoped to foster similar coalitions in the South by drawing together disaffected yeoman farmers, urban workingmen and shopkeepers, and planters and businessmen of Whig antecedents. Blacks – first, free blacks and soon, former slaves – tried to join these nascent unionist parties, but they were hampered by their exclusion from citizenship. The expansion of the territory under federal control, especially after the fall of Vicksburg in July 1863, gave struggling unionists in Louisiana, Tennessee, and Arkansas an aura of legitimacy they had previously lacked. Meanwhile, the destruction of slavery by federal arms undercut the influence of proslavery unionists in the state coalitions and in Washington, rendering them progressively more isolated and impotent. Feeding upon the debility of proslavery unionism and enjoying the sponsorship of federal military commanders, antislavery unionists pressed their cause and found new adherents as its prospects improved. Their demand for emancipation pushed slavery to the edge in those portions of the Confederacy exempted from Lincoln's proclamation.[87]

The deterioration of slavery in the Union-occupied Confederacy had no immediate effect on the institution in the Union's own slave states. Having stood by the old flag when the other slave states seceded, Delaware, Maryland, Kentucky, and Missouri were not included in the

---

[86] On the wartime labor systems of Butler, Banks, and other Union officials, see *Freedom*, ser. 1, vol. 2.

[87] Peyton McCrary, *Abraham Lincoln and Reconstruction: The Louisiana Experiment* (Princeton, N.J., 1978); Joe Gray Taylor, *Louisiana Reconstructed, 1863–1877* (Baton Rouge, La., 1974), chap. 2; C. Peter Ripley, *Slaves and Freedmen in Civil War Louisiana* (Baton Rouge, La., 1976); James W. Patton, *Unionism and Reconstruction in Tennessee, 1860–1869* (Chapel Hill, N.C., 1934); Thomas S. Staples, *Reconstruction in Arkansas, 1862–1874* (New York, 1923), chaps. 1–2.

Emancipation Proclamation. Insistent upon slavery's full legal standing under the federal constitution, slaveholders in the border states rejected Lincoln's repeated urgings that they adopt some plan of gradual, compensated emancipation. Indeed, their minority position as slaveholders in the Union seemed only to stiffen their resolve. Rather than bend to the winds of change, they deployed old defenses of their right to human property and fashioned new ones. Border-state legislatures bolstered antebellum slave codes, which were rigorously enforced by local officials. State courts not only upheld these laws and sustained the rights of slaveholders, but also entertained suits against anyone who interfered with slavery, including officers of the United States army.

The legality of slavery narrowed the avenues to freedom in the border states, but slaves hazarded them nonetheless. From the earliest months of the war, many of them had found refuge with Northern regiments, and some gained employment as military laborers. In Missouri, especially along the Kansas border, a virtual civil war within the Civil War provided slaves with opportunities to leave their owners, and in Maryland, proximity to the District of Columbia afforded fugitive slaves a safe haven. The slaves' persistence and the receptivity of federal troops and army quartermasters forced border-state slaveholders into rearguard actions that undermined their unionist credentials. By the end of 1863, exasperated army officers and federal officials had tired of feuding with masters who appeared to care more for their property than for the Union. As Lincoln had predicted, the "friction and abrasion" of war were eroding slavery in the border states.

Wartime wear and tear also encouraged indigenous white opponents of slavery in the border states. These men and women felt most at home in the great regional centers of trade and production – Baltimore, Louisville, and St. Louis. White wage-workers – many of them immigrants – had in large measure displaced slaves in these cities. They brought with them notions of the moral and material superiority of free labor, beliefs inimical to slavery. Opposition to slavery could also be found in the countryside, especially among yeoman farmers who had long distanced themselves from both slaveholders and slaves. Many antislavery farmers, like urban employers, depended upon free workers, including free blacks. The active role played by white workers and their employers – urban and rural – in preventing secession had given them an important place in the unionist coalition of each border state, and they battled the slaveholding unionists for leadership. Antislavery unionists enjoyed greatest success in Maryland and Missouri, but even there they failed to gain parity with proslavery unionists until the fall of 1863.

As the federal government enunciated its commitment to emancipation, antislavery partisans in the border states grew bolder. They campaigned openly for an end to slavery, gaining support from nonslave-holding farmers and artisans. Long denied access to black labor by the slaveholders' monopoly, many farmers and tradesmen welcomed the disruption of the old regime. Some of them hired fugitive slaves with few questions asked. When slaveholders threatened prosecution under state codes that prohibited hiring a slave without the owner's permission, employers either had to dismiss their workers or defy the slaveholders. The emergence of a viable antislavery movement made their choice an easier one. As nonslaveholders cast their weight on the side of freedom, the ground shifted beneath the slaveholders.

Still, slavery did not give way in the border states until black men began entering the Union army in large numbers.[88] In the summer of 1863, with the enlistment of black men already proceeding in the North and in the Union-occupied Confederacy, federal authorities inaugurated black recruitment in Maryland and Missouri. Reluctant to offend slaveholding unionists, President Lincoln and the War Department at first authorized the enlistment only of free blacks and of slaves whose owners were disloyal. But black men – including the slaves of loyal owners – volunteered so enthusiastically that it proved nearly impossible to restrict enlistment. This was particularly true once non-slaveholding whites recognized that black recruits reduced conscription quotas that they would otherwise have to fill. Nonslaveholders demanded that slaves be enlisted as well as – and sometimes instead of – free blacks. In Maryland, where nonslaveholding farmers feared that the enlistment of free blacks would diminish their work force while leaving that of the slaveholders intact, this demand reached its highest pitch. In all the border states, antislavery partisans united in urging the elimination of distinctions between slaves of the loyal and those of the disloyal. With the ready compliance of black volunteers, recruiters stepped up enlistment, circumventing regulations regarding the status of the recruits or the politics of their owners.

Recruiters of an abolitionist stamp warmed to the task of dismantling slavery in the border states. In Maryland and Missouri, they raided plantations and farms, offering freedom in exchange for military service. Slaveholders denounced the federal government's betrayal of its promise not to interfere with slavery, but masters who a year earlier could command the full attention of high-ranking cabinet officers now received short shrift from low-ranking bureaucrats. Complaints from slaveholders and their representatives about the recruiters' high-handed tactics brought temporary relief at best. In the fall of 1863, over the opposition of border-state slaveholders, the War Department authorized the systematic enlistment of slave men in Maryland, Missouri, and

---

[88] On the recruitment of black soldiers in the border states, see *Freedom*, ser. 2: chap. 4.

Delaware, including slaves owned by loyal masters. General Order 329 promised freedom to the recruits and compensation to loyal owners.[89] Thousands of black men answered the call.

By the end of 1863, only Kentucky blacks remained forbidden to army recruiters. Many of them took matters into their own hands and fled to neighboring states to enlist, especially after recruitment began in Tennessee. Kentucky slaveholders managed to forestall black enlistment by marshaling the assistance of sympathetic Union commanders – many of them slaveholding natives – and by flexing their still considerable political muscle. But in the spring of 1864, with the demand for soldiers increasing and the success of black recruitment evident, federal authorities ended Kentucky's special standing. Following the earlier pattern in Maryland and Missouri, recruiters began by accepting free blacks, as well as slaves owned by disloyal masters or by loyal masters who consented to their enlistment. Again, slaves flocked to recruiting stations in defiance of their owners' wishes. In the face of such massive volunteering, the restrictions could not hold, and by early summer, federal officials had sanctioned the enlistment of any able-bodied black man who reached a recruitment office, regardless of his owner's loyalty or consent.[90]

The recruitment of black men dealt a death blow to slavery in Delaware, Maryland, and Missouri, and terminally weakened it in Kentucky. Black men in the border states joined the army in staggering proportions: In Delaware, they equaled 25 percent of eligible black men; in Maryland, 28 percent; in Missouri, 39 percent; in Kentucky, 57 percent. Altogether, nearly 42,000 border-state blacks served in the Union army, and 2,400 more – mostly from Delaware and Maryland – enlisted in the navy.[91] What wartime disruption, slave flight, and antislavery agitation had begun, the massive drain of able-bodied black men accomplished in short order.

Border-state black men paid a price for freedom over and above their military service. Slaveholders, understanding the subversive effects of armed service, spared nothing to prevent the transformation of their slaves into soldiers. Unprotected until they reached the safety of a recruitment office, slaves braved arrest, physical assault, even death. Many of them traveled great distances by night to avoid violent en-

---

[89] General Order 329, which provided for black recruitment in Maryland, Missouri, and Tennessee, was issued on October 3, 1863. Its provisions were extended to Delaware on October 26. (*Official Records*, ser. 3, vol. 3., pp. 860–61, 925.)

[90] On black recruitment in Kentucky, see *Freedom*, ser. 2: chap. 4.

[91] *Freedom*, ser. 2: pp. 12, 14n. These figures exclude the numerous border-state black men who fled to free territory before enlisting in the army, notably Maryland slaves who enlisted in the District of Columbia and Missouri slaves who enlisted in Kansas. The District of Columbia, whose black population in 1860 included 1,823 men of military age, was credited with 3,269 black soldiers. Kansas, with a black military-age population of only 126, enlisted 2,080 black soldiers.

counters with slave masters and their hired thugs. Volunteers rejected by recruiters as physically unfit faced similar dangers.[92]

To dissuade slave men from enlisting and to punish those who did, border-state slaveholders turned upon their families. Inveighing against ungrateful servants, some slaveholders drove off the parents, wives, and children of black soldiers, leaving them to fend for themselves. Others avenged the desertion of slave men by whipping and otherwise abusing their families. The soldiers' kin also bore the burden of enlistment in the form of additional chores, including backbreaking work previously reserved for young men. Fearful that this harsh regimen would encourage flight, slaveholders resorted to preventive measures such as locking up the slaves' shoes and clothing at night. But, in the end, even the most ruthless violence could not sustain slavery.[93]

To escape vindictive owners, slave women and children frequently accompanied their husbands, sons, and fathers to the recruitment centers. Others fled on their own and settled near army camps and military posts or squatted on patches of unoccupied land. In the face of relentless harassment by slaveholders whose legal authority was undiminished, black soldiers demanded protection for their families. Their pleas, joined by those of sympathetic white officers, ascended the army chain of command. But Union officials, severely handicapped because the soldiers' families had no legal claim to freedom, could do little to prevent them from being abused or even reenslaved. At times the army itself contributed to their difficulties by evicting them from military posts and nearby shantytowns, thereby exposing them to recapture by their owners or the civil authorities.[94]

Unable to prevent black men from exchanging slavery for military service and freedom, border-state slaveholders executed a series of obstructionist maneuvers to salvage what remained of their eroding power. Some Missouri slaveholders forwarded their slaves to Kentucky, slavery's last sanctuary within the Union. The most optimistic relocated their entire operations, much like the rebel planters who had migrated to the interior of the Confederacy. But many simply sold out, dispatching their slaves to Kentucky slave marts for whatever price they would fetch. This revival of the interstate slave trade evoked a mighty protest from blacks and their allies and eventual military interdiction, but not before many Missouri slaves had been sold from their homes and families.[95]

[92] See below, docs. 146, 188, 190, 227n.; *Freedom*, ser. 2: docs. 74, 88, 90A–B, 100–1, 103, 105.

[93] See below, docs. 191–93, 231, 233, 235, 237; *Freedom*, ser. 2: docs. 74, 79, 83, 90B, 91–94, 106–7, 294, 296–98, 302–4, 312B.

[94] See below, docs. 146, 192, 228A, 233; *Freedom*, ser. 2: docs. 83, 90B, 91, 93, 97, 102A–C, 105, 107, 110–11, 312A–B, 333, 336, 341.

[95] See below, docs. 184A–B, 223A; *Freedom*, ser. 2: docs. 91–94, and pp. 189–90.

While slaveholders lashed out at those blacks still under their control, the new order began to take shape. Increasing numbers of border-state slaveholders—like their counterparts in the Union-occupied Confederacy—were forced to bargain with their slaves, offering inducements in cash or kind to keep them from enlisting in the army or simply running away. Nonslaveholders also began to bid for the services of fugitive slaves. Blacks took advantage of this competition, seeking the most attractive terms of employment. When nonslaveholders became employers of black laborers, they linked arms politically with antislavery unionists, and the momentum of emancipation became irresistible. By January 1865, both Maryland and Missouri had abolished slavery.[96]

As slavery withered in the border states, the war entered its final phase. In a succession of hard-fought Union victories that culminated in the fall of Atlanta in September 1864, General William T. Sherman—now chief commander in the western theater—positioned his army to dismember the Confederacy. After Atlanta, the end came quickly. Sherman's troops swept through Georgia to the sea, taking Savannah in December. He set his sights next on South Carolina, the seedbed of secession, and in early 1865 struck out across the state, his inexorable march cutting a swath of destruction and terror. Areas not scarred by the advancing federal army felt the effects of masters and slaves fleeing desperately for safety. Georgia and South Carolina slaveholders experienced belatedly what had already become common throughout the war zone. Slaves grew impertinent and insubordinate. They refused to be refugeed, and movement at gunpoint bred still greater discontent. Refugeed slaves sought to return to their old homes, especially when their families had been left behind. If they could not do so, they ran toward the Yankees instead of away from them. The reverberations from Sherman's march echoed wherever slavery remained intact. The entire Confederacy shuddered with apprehension.

Slaves not evacuated before Sherman's army followed in its rear. Ragged and frightened, exhausted but determined, they hazarded an uncertain future. Stragglers fell by the wayside, often becoming victims of slave catchers who continued to ply their gruesome trade. But Sherman had no intention of delaying his march to accommodate those who could not maintain the grueling pace. Even slaves who matched Sherman's columns step for step could not count on the sympathy, much less the support, of his army. Sherman had never disguised his

---

[96] Francis N. Thorpe, comp., *The Federal and State Constitutions*, 7 vols. (Washington, 1909), vol. 3, pp. 1741–79, vol. 4, pp. 2191–2219. The Maryland emancipation constitution took effect in November 1864, and the Missouri constitutional convention abolished slavery in January 1865.

contempt for black people, and both officers and men took their cue from him. Moreover, as the commander of an army on the march in enemy territory, living off the land, Sherman felt no obligation to care for those whose lives it crossed and transformed. The thousands of black stalwarts who followed in his train praised Sherman's troops for breaking their shackles, but had precious little else for which to thank them. Union soldiers stripped slave cabins of their meager contents with the same spirit in which they rifled the masters' mansions, often leaving slaves without food or clothing.[97] At the same time, however, the mass of black refugees who crowded upon his ranks provoked Sherman to bestow upon them a gift worthy of their faith in the Union, with far-reaching consequences for postwar reconstruction. In January 1865, after consulting with black leaders in Savannah, Sherman issued Special Field Order 15, which set aside the coastal lands of South Carolina and Georgia, from Charleston southward, for the exclusive occupation of black people and established procedures by which black settlers might acquire "possessory title" to forty-acre plots.[98]

In other theaters of the war, the work of destroying slavery proceeded less dramatically but no less surely. Union troops in the Mississippi Valley steadily extended the territory under their control and maintained the vital supply lines that supported Sherman's Atlanta campaign. In Virginia, enormous federal armies under General-in-Chief Ulysses S. Grant hounded the Confederates into the trenches of Petersburg and Richmond, and then laid seige to the last remnants of General Lee's once mighty Army of Northern Virginia. In all these military operations, black soldiers played conspicuous parts. They manned forts, guarded railroad bridges, protected contraband camps and government plantations, skirmished with guerrillas, and dug and fought in the trenches. The deployment of black soldiers sped the decline of slavery and assured fugitive slaves a friend in the field.[99]

With slavery in shambles and Northern victory increasingly sure, unionists in much of the occupied South concluded the business of emancipation. Federal officials and army commanders turned on their slaveholding allies and made it clear that the liquidation of slavery was prerequisite for readmission to the Union. Antislavery unionists, previously stymied by slaveholding loyalists, took control of the unionist coalitions and pressed for immediate abolition. Early in 1864, Arkansas loyalists enacted constitutional changes ending slavery. Unionists in states partly or wholly exempt from the Emancipation Proclamation followed suit, in Louisiana late in 1864 and in Tennessee early in

[97] See below, docs. 36–38.
[98] *Official Records*, ser. 1, vol. 47, pt. 2, pp. 60–62.
[99] See *Freedom*, ser. 2: chaps. 10–11.

1865.[100] As Lincoln had hoped, these new state constitutions placed emancipation upon firmer ground, beyond the reach of judicial challenge to the confiscation acts or the Emancipation Proclamation.

Union military success also strengthened the North's own commitment to freedom. Sherman's triumph at Atlanta helped Lincoln beat back a challenge for the presidency by George B. McClellan, the former general-in-chief. The previous spring, with his reelection in doubt, congressional support for emancipation had faltered. The Senate had approved a constitutional amendment abolishing slavery, but when it came before the House, the Democratic opposition had denied it the two-thirds majority required for passage. In January 1865, with Lincoln reelected and the Republicans securely in power, the House approved the amendment and forwarded it to the states for ratification.[101] As the state legislatures opened their debates, the President and Congress turned in earnest to the task of postwar reconstruction. In early March, Lincoln signed legislation creating the Bureau of Refugees, Freedmen, and Abandoned Lands (or Freedmen's Bureau, as it became known) to supervise the transition from slavery to freedom. A joint resolution adopted the same day liberated the wives and children of black soldiers, regardless of their owners' loyalty, and thereby provided a claim to freedom for tens of thousands of border-state slaves whose bondage had been impervious to law or presidential edict.[102]

The value of emancipation to the Union did not escape Confederate leaders. They realized that by employing blacks, first as laborers and then as soldiers, and by demonstrating a commitment to black freedom, the North had transmuted the Confederacy's cornerstone into its tombstone. In their last desperate hour, a few Southern leaders tried to reverse that alchemy. They began deliberations on the enlistment of black soldiers into Confederate ranks, with the understanding that freedom would be offered in exchange for military service. In November 1864, President Jefferson Davis asked the Confederate Congress to consider the government's relationship to the slave as person, rather than as property. With the support of General Lee, legislation authorizing black enlistment was finally adopted in March 1865, too late for any slave soldiers to strike a blow for Southern independence. In early

---

[100] Thorpe, *Federal and State Constitutions*, vol. 1, pp. 288–306, vol. 3, pp. 1429–48, vol. 6, p. 3445; LaWanda Cox, *Lincoln and Black Freedom: A Study in Presidential Leadership* (Columbia, S.C., 1981), chap. 2.

[101] Wilson, *History of Antislavery Measures*, chap. 13. See also LaWanda Cox and John H. Cox, *Politics, Principle, and Prejudice, 1865–1866: Dilemma of Reconstruction America* (New York, 1963), chap. 1.

[102] U.S., *Statutes at Large, Treaties, and Proclamations*, vol. 13 (Boston, 1866), pp. 507–9, 571.

April, as Confederate recruiters took to the streets, Lee surrendered at Appomattox.[103]

In the aftermath of Appomattox, word of freedom spread to areas of the Confederacy that had escaped wartime Union occupation. Discharged black soldiers sometimes carried the news. Men who had fled their homes as slaves now returned as liberators, uniformed in Union blue and carrying rifles (which they, like other federal soldiers, could purchase upon muster-out). Along with word of freedom, they also bore the special experience of having been part of the Union's greatest triumph. Black soldiers still in service also traversed the South, forming part of the postwar army of occupation. As representatives of federal power in the former Confederacy, they enjoyed great authority in bringing freedom to fruition and interpreting its meaning.[104] Still, the message did not reach some slaves until well into the summer, or even later. In Texas, where the Confederate surrender came a full two months after Appomattox, blacks celebrated "Juneteenth" as emancipation day. In a few places, slaveholders who were determined to maintain the old order used force to keep their slaves locked in bondage. The liquidation of these vestiges of slavery continued long after the cessation of hostilities, eventually aided by the Thirteenth Amendment. In the concise, clipped language of the law, the new amendment – ratified in December 1865 – summarized the monumental changes wrought by the war: "Neither slavery nor involuntary servitude, except as a punishment for crime whereof the party shall have been duly convicted, shall exist within the United States, or any place subject to their jurisdiction."[105]

The promulgation of freedom followed no set pattern. Sometimes army officers and Freedmen's Bureau agents made the rounds of plantations and farms, armed with the Emancipation Proclamation or an order by the local Union army commander. To hastily called assemblages, they announced the demise of slavery, often appending long disquisitions on the meaning of freedom – the need for freedpeople to work hard, respect rightful authority, and support themselves and their dependents.

Usually, however, word of slavery's death preceded the arrival of federal officers. With rumors of freedom rife and some slaves silently departing their owners' domain, slaveholders understood that if they did not act promptly they would soon face rows of empty slave cabins, if not angry and unruly laborers. In quick order, they called "their people" together to enact a drama for which neither they nor their

---

[103] *Official Records*, ser. 4, vol. 3, pp. 797–99; *Freedom*, ser. 2: docs. 123–26, and pp. 281–82; Durden, *The Gray and the Black*, chap. 7.

[104] See *Freedom*, ser. 2: chaps. 17–18.

[105] *Statutes at Large*, vol. 13, pp. 774–75.

audience was fully prepared. Masters and slaves shifted uneasily, their eyes glued to some formal document or distant object, as they tried desperately to avoid direct confrontation. Struggling to maintain their composure, slaveholders gave deadpan renditions of the proclamation or a military order taken from the local press. Slaves strained to decipher the strange words and peculiar cadence of these official edicts, but the meaning was clear enough from their owners' demeanor. The slaveholders often concluded with words of their own. Some blurted out an oath, cursed their former slaves, and damned their posterity. Others wished the freedpeople well and asked them to remain through the harvest – perhaps agreeing only to feed and clothe them "as usual," perhaps promising a part of the crop, a token payment, or "to do well by them at Christmas." The men and women whose freedom was thus conceded rarely responded directly. Indeed, despite the momentous implications of the occasion, they displayed little emotion. Instead, they returned to the quarters to sort out the meaning of what had transpired, to plan for the future, and to celebrate among themselves. They were slaves no more.

As often as not, however, there was no final confrontation, no moment of truth when master and slave stood eye to eye for the last time. Some blacks, learning of the abolition of slavery, waited for their owners to make amends or offer some better arrangement. Erstwhile slaveholders, unable to conceive of a world without slaves, remained strangely silent – hoping against hope that life would go on as in former times. For a while it might, but then, one morning, the household would be strangely silent, and former masters and mistresses would have to try their hands at unfamiliar tasks. Not all slaveholders let it come to this. As news of freedom spread, they began to bargain with their one-time slaves – much as slaveholders in the Union-occupied Confederacy had been forced to do during the war. Some black men and women accepted these new arrangements; many did not. Although they marched into an uncertain future in either case, they too were slaves no more.[106]

The last chapter of the story of emancipation was not written exclusively in the disloyal South. Through the end of 1865, while Northerners celebrated the triumph of freedom over slavery and army officers and Freedmen's Bureau agents liberated blacks illegally enslaved in the former Confederacy, black people remained legally bound in loyal Delaware and Kentucky. Delaware contained only a handful, but Kentucky slaveholders still held tens of thousands of black people who had no claim to liberty. The end of the war no more deterred these die-hard slaveholders than did congressional passage of the constitutional

---

[106] Litwack, *Been in the Storm So Long*, chap. 4. On the postwar liquidation of slavery, see *Freedom*, ser. 3.

amendment abolishing slavery or its ratification by a steady progression of states. Indeed, the more hopeless their situation, the more adamant they became. They indignantly rejected the amendment and anything else that smacked of abolition, and loudly asserted their right to their slaves. Progressively isolated as emancipation became increasingly inevitable, they held out until the bitter end, making the end as bitter as possible for their slaves.[107]

Until the constitutional amendment was ratified, military enlistment remained the only avenue to freedom for Kentucky slaves. By liberating the wives and children of black soldiers, the congressional joint resolution of March 1865 stimulated a new surge of enlistments. But state courts obligingly declared the resolution unconstitutional, and state and local officials continued to enforce the slave code. Moreover, many Kentucky black soldiers were stationed far from home, in Virginia before Appomattox and in Texas after the Confederate surrender. With the soldiers unable to intervene, would-be slaveholders continued to regard the families of these men as slaves; indeed, they heaped upon them unprecedented abuse. And as discharged black soldiers began returning to Kentucky, they met extraordinary violence. Both slaveholders and nonslaveholders who capitulated to the inevitable end of slavery faced the scorn and judicial persecution of neighbors who still contested emancipation and who remained in control of local government.

Fortunately for Kentucky slaves, the federal commander assigned to their state was an avowed enemy of slavery. General John M. Palmer, himself Kentucky-born, had moved to Illinois as a youth, where he developed a keenly honed hatred of the South's "domestic institution" and participated in the formation of the Republican party. Wartime military service had sharpened his antislavery convictions. Utilizing existing legislation, notably the joint resolution, Palmer undertook the liquidation of slavery in Kentucky. He wielded his military authority to override state laws and to protect black people, and circumvented the slaveholders' power by issuing passes to their slaves. Still, even a commander as determined as Palmer could not overcome all the obstacles created by the continued legality of slavery, especially after martial law was lifted in October. Not until December 1865, when the Thirteenth Amendment was ratified, could slavery be dismantled. In elevating war-won emancipation to constitutional status, the amendment gave many Kentucky slaves their first claim to freedom.

After the war, freedpeople and their allies – some newly minted, some of long standing – gathered periodically to celebrate the abolition of

---

[107] On the postwar struggle for emancipation in Kentucky, see below, docs. 239–56; *Freedom*, ser. 2: docs. 112, 172, 304, 307A–B, 312B, 327.

slavery. They spoke of great deeds and great words, praising the Emancipation Proclamation and the Thirteenth Amendment and venerating their authors. A moment so great needed its icons. But in quieter times, black people told of their own liberation. Then there were as many tales as tellers. Depending upon the circumstances of their enslavement, the events of the war, and the evolution of Union and Confederate policy, some recounted solitary escape; others, mass defections, initiated by themselves or the Yankees. Many depicted their former owners in headlong flight, and themselves left behind to shape a future under Union occupation. Others told of forced removals from home and family to strange neighborhoods and an enslavement made more miserable by food shortages, heightened discipline, and bands of straggling soldiers. Still others limned a struggle against slaveholders whose unionist credentials sustained their power. More than a few black people shared the bitter memory of escaping slavery only to be reenslaved when the Northern army retreated or they ventured into one of the Union's own slave states. Some recalled hearing the news of freedom from an exasperated master who reluctantly acknowledged the end of the old order; others, from returning black veterans, bedecked in blue uniforms with brass buttons. Those who had escaped slavery during the war often had additional stories to relate. They told of serving the Union cause as cooks, nurses, and laundresses; as teamsters and laborers; as spies, scouts, and pilots; and as sailors and soldiers. Even those who had remained under the dominion of their owners until the defeat of the Confederacy and had been forced to labor in its behalf knew that their very presence, and often their actions, had played a part in destroying slavery.

These diverse experiences disclosed the uneven, halting, and often tenuous process by which slaves gained their liberty, and the centrality of their own role in the evolution of emancipation. The Emancipation Proclamation and the Thirteenth Amendment marked, respectively, a turning point and the successful conclusion of a hard-fought struggle. But the milestones of that struggle were not the struggle itself. Neither its origins nor its mainspring could be found in the seats of executive and legislative authority from which the great documents issued. Instead, they resided in the humble quarters of slaves, who were convinced in April 1861 of what would not be fully affirmed until December 1865, and whose actions consistently undermined every settlement short of universal abolition.

Over the course of the the war, the slaves' insistence that their own enslavement was the root of the conflict—and that a war for the Union must necessarily be a war for freedom—strengthened their friends and weakened their enemies. Their willingness to offer their loyalty, their labor, and even their lives pushed Northerners, from common soldiers to leaders of the first rank, to do what had previously seemed unthinkable: to make property into persons, to make slaves into soldiers, and, in time, to make all black people into citizens, the equal of any in the Republic. Southerners could never respond in kind. But they too came to understand the link between national union and universal liberty. And when the deed was done, a new truth prevailed where slavery had reigned: that men and women could never again be owned and that citizenship was the right of all. The destruction of slavery transformed American life forever.

CHAPTER I

Tidewater Virginia and North Carolina

I

Tidewater Virginia and North Carolina

NEWS OF THE WAR spread quickly through the small farms and villages of the Virginia and North Carolina tidewater.[1] But even before the fighting began, Confederate military preparations had disrupted daily life and created openings for slaves to gain their freedom. When Union troops arrived in the tidewater to seal the Confederate coast, black people seized these opportunities for liberty and manufactured additional ones. Thereafter, with each escalation of the conflict, the balance of power between masters and slaves shifted toward the slaves in a region whose black population nearly equaled its white one and included large numbers of free blacks. Many slaves emancipated themselves by crossing into Union-held territory. Moving boldly between the Union's small coastal enclaves and the Confederate interior, black men and women who had only recently escaped from slavery encouraged and aided others to bid for freedom. But even those who remained in bondage exploited the diminution of their masters' power. Still, no matter how wartime circumstances promoted liberty, freedom remained hostage to ultimate Union victory. Not until the Confederacy surrendered was freedom secure in the Virginia and North Carolina tidewater.

Confederate officers inadvertently provoked the first escapes to freedom by requisitioning slave men to build fortifications along Chesapeake Bay, Albemarle and Pamlico sounds, and the rivers near the coast.[2] Angry at being separated from their families and apprehensive of abuse by military overseers or danger from hostile fire, many slaves fled the Confederate works. The dispersion of kinfolk among the region's farms, the long involvement of slaves in the maritime trades, and extensive slave hiring had familiarized tidewater slaves with the geography of the region, making escape in the confusion of wartime mobil-

[1] Published accounts of emancipation in tidewater Virginia and North Carolina include: Robert F. Engs, *Freedom's First Generation: Black Hampton, Virginia, 1861–1890* (Philadelphia, 1979); Louis S. Gerteis, *From Contraband to Freedman: Federal Policy toward Southern Blacks, 1861–1865* (Westport, Conn., 1973), chaps. 1–3. Also useful is John G. Barrett, *The Civil War in North Carolina* (Chapel Hill, N.C., 1963).
[2] See below, docs. 258, 260A–H.

ization relatively easy. The large number of free blacks, many of whom had intermarried with slaves, assured fugitives of some support as they tried to elude capture. But, with Southern soldiers everywhere, maintaining liberty was difficult and dangerous. After a while, most runaways drifted back to their home farms, contending that the harsh conditions of military labor had prompted them to flee.

Slaveholders, anxious for any excuse to reject the increasingly burdensome and disruptive calls for labor, tried to shelter their slaves from military duty. But Confederate commanders would not be denied. When forcible conscription of slave laborers replaced polite invitations, slaveholders – often as fearful of impressment as of successful flight – removed large numbers of slaves from the war zone, separating hundreds of black men and women from families and friends. The inauguration of large-scale refugeeing, a process that intensified as the tidewater became a major battle ground, triggered another round of slave flight. Everywhere the approach of impressment agents and rumors of removal to the interior sent more slaves to the woods.[3] Once having left bondage, some vowed never to return.

Union forces at Fortress Monroe, on the tip of Virginia's lower peninsula (between the James and York rivers), soon faced a flood of fugitives set loose first by the voluntary Confederate mobilization, then by the forcible impressment of slaves into Confederate labor gangs, and finally by slaveholders' attempts to refugee their threatened property. General Benjamin F. Butler, who took command of this remnant of federal authority in May 1861, found his post inundated by slaves fleeing Confederate service and offering their labor to the Union cause. A political general with a sharp tongue and an expansive sense of his own importance, Butler was no abolitionist. At the 1860 Democratic convention, he had voted to nominate Jefferson Davis for the Presidency and subsequently campaigned for John C. Breckinridge. In April 1861, while leading Massachusetts troops through Maryland, he had volunteered to put down a rumored slave insurrection.[4] But the potential impact of the dragnet impressment launched by Confederate commanders in tidewater Virginia – particularly General John B. Magruder, commander of the Army of the Peninsula – evidently gave Butler second thoughts. Realizing that blacks would be put to work against the Union if not employed for it, he accepted the runaways and put the able-bodied men to work on Union fortifications.

Butler acted with great caution and tentativeness, especially for a man who cultivated an image of being forthright and decisive. In reports to General-in-Chief Winfield Scott and Secretary of War Simon

---

[3] On slave flight spurred by Confederate impressment, see, for example, below, doc. 266.

[4] *Official Records*, ser. 1, vol. 2, p. 593.

Cameron, he explained that since rebel slaveholders had left the Union, they could not expect Union officers to enforce the fugitive slave laws. However, Butler did not challenge the legality of slavery, and he offered receipts to slave owners who would apply for them, presumably so that masters could later reclaim their slaves and perhaps compensation for use of their property. In short, fugitive slaves accepted into Union lines remained chattels, and Butler seized them as he would other contraband of war. The designation "contraband" as a name for fugitive slaves given refuge within Union lines quickly gained popularity with federal policy makers and the Northern public, and Butler took credit for it along with the policy he initiated.[5]

Butler had moved cautiously in setting able-bodied slave men to work. Deciding what to do with the women, children, and old people who had fled along with husbands, fathers, and sons posed an even more delicate problem. Butler had no doubt about what he wanted to do, but wished to make sure that the government would sustain him. Referring the matter to his superiors, he in effect told them what their decision should be. The government, he argued, had both a political and a humanitarian obligation to protect the dependents of its newly acquired laborers. Meanwhile, without awaiting a response, he opened his lines to all fugitives, men or women, young or old, healthy or hobbled. The labor of the able-bodied would pay for the army's maintenance of the dependent.

Butler's action received prompt and forceful support from Cameron and Scott. Although the Secretary of War acknowledged the importance of enforcing all federal laws, he affirmed the higher duty of defending the Union and ordered Butler to "refrain from surrendering to alleged masters" the fugitives who entered his lines. With Cameron's encouragement, Butler continued to accept fugitives, and before long slaves all over the region, hearing rumors of freedom, sought out federal protection. By July 1861, some 900 black men, women, and children lived in the shadow of Fortress Monroe.[6]

While some slaves fled to the tiny federal beachhead around Fortress Monroe, others found refuge on board the ships of the Union navy, which had been patrolling Chesapeake Bay since the beginning of the war. From the thousands of inlets that lined the bay, blacks paddled dugouts and dinghies to passing naval vessels. Fully conversant with waterways that they and their forebears had sailed and fished for gen-

---

[5] According to published correspondence, Butler did not use the phrase "contraband of war" in designating fugitives until late July 1861. Benjamin F. Butler, *Private and Official Correspondence of Gen. Benjamin F. Butler during the Period of the Civil War*, 5 vols. (Norwood, Mass., 1917), vol. 1, pp. 185–88.

[6] Col. T. J. Cram et al. to ?, Mar. 1862, enclosed in Major General John E. Wool to Hon. Edwin M. Stanton, 12 Mar. 1862, V-222 1862, Letters Received, ser. 12, RG 94 [K-751].

erations, black watermen brought invaluable topological knowledge to the Union fleet.

Although federal naval officers had no more authority than their army counterparts to offer asylum to fugitives, many did so nonetheless. Some complained that the waterborne fugitives devoured their supplies and disturbed the routine of their small vessels, but most officers welcomed the runaways, particularly after learning that the rebels were mobilizing slaves against the Union. Flag Officer Silas H. Stringham, commander of the North Atlantic Squadron, approved such actions, and his decision was sustained by Secretary of the Navy Gideon Welles.

The general acceptance of fugitives by federal naval officers encouraged other slaves to flee their masters. The islands in the Chesapeake and its tributaries soon sprouted small colonies of runaways. Some of these colonies, like the settlement on James Island, maintained a precarious existence under the protection of the Union fleet. Others became way stations for fugitives headed toward Fortress Monroe, with the Union navy serving as a ferry to freedom.[7] Black men and women beyond the reach of Fortress Monroe, but familiar with the rivers of the Chesapeake and able to commandeer boats, thereby gained their liberty.

Officials in Washington were reluctant to see the war for union transformed into a war against slavery, fearing both that they might offend loyal slaveholders and that they might exceed the bounds of Northern opinion. Nevertheless, the practicality of war sharpened appreciation of the value black labor held for the Confederacy and — potentially — for the Union as well. At the same time, confronted with growing numbers of fugitive slaves, Congress showed an unwillingness to let the army do the masters' dirty work. In July 1861, the House of Representatives resolved that it was not the duty of federal soldiers to capture and return fugitive slaves, and within a month, Congress enacted the First Confiscation Act, declaring that masters who employed or allowed their slaves to be employed in the service of the Confederacy had forfeited all claims to them. Like Butler and Stringham, the federal government would free no slaves, but would confiscate those who had been employed by the Confederacy. Confiscation under the terms of the new act thus provided de facto freedom.

Immediately following passage of the First Confiscation Act, Secretary of War Cameron clarified his earlier instructions to Butler. Reiterating the necessity of enforcing federal law "within States and Territories in which the authority of the Union is fully acknowledged,"

---

[7] Commdr. M. Woodhull to Commodore Charles Wilkes, 19 Aug. 1862 & 22 Aug. 1862, E-63, Letters Sent by Commdr. Maxwell Woodhull, pp. 33–35, Letterbooks of Officers of the U.S. Navy at Sea, RG 45 [T-687, T-688].

Cameron rejected any such necessity in the insurrectionary states, which, by their treasonable conduct, had forfeited any right to military protection. There the federal government could freely accept the services of fugitives whose masters had employed them in the Confederate cause. Equally important, Cameron also believed that "the substantial rights of loyal masters [would] be best protected" by acceptance of their fugitive slaves within federal lines. He instructed Butler to distinguish between loyal and disloyal slaveholders, so that Congress could compensate loyal masters when peace returned. Although Cameron explicitly prohibited Butler from interfering with the "servants of peaceful citizens, in house or field," his instructions clearly benefited slaves who came into Union lines, whatever the loyalties of their masters. Cameron's directives thus expanded the possibilities for liberty beyond those offered by the First Confiscation Act.

But Butler no longer needed any prompting, for his earlier diffidence had been replaced by resolute support for emancipation. He now pronounced the fugitives who reached his lines "[i]f not free born, yet free, manumitted, sent forth from the hand that held them, never to be reclaimed."[8] Following Butler's lead, General John E. Wool, who succeeded him as commander of the Department of Virginia in mid-August, continued to welcome fugitives into Union lines. Moreover, Wool initiated a policy of compensating the contrabands employed at Fortress Monroe, appointing missionary Charles B. Wilder to superintend the newly arrived fugitives.[9]

Despite congressional sanction of Butler's action, and Cameron's amplification of the First Confiscation Act, Union policy remained ambiguous, and that ambiguity allowed individual commanders a great deal of latitude. Not all federal officers welcomed the emancipator's role, and some openly disdained it. Although they often found contraband men a useful and sometimes invaluable source of labor and information, they believed that the enormous number of women, children, and elderly slaves who also flooded into Union territory strained federal resources. Naval officers sympathetic to the claims of loyal slaveholders assumed that runaway slaves taken on board came from Maryland, regardless of how vociferously or desperately the blacks claimed Virginia origins. Not wishing to harbor the slaves of loyal slaveholders from a loyal state, such officers proposed returning them to their masters. Lieutenant Abram D. Harrell, commander of a federal

---

[8] *Correspondence of Gen. Benjamin F. Butler*, vol. 1, p. 187.
[9] General Orders No. 34, Head Quarters Dept. of Va. &c., 1 Nov. 1861, vol. 4 VaNc, pp. 69–70, General Orders Issued, ser. 5078, Dept. of VA & 7th Army Corps, RG 393 Pt. 1 [C-3064]. See also Special Orders No. 72, Head Qrs. Dept. of VA &c., [14 Oct. 1861], Orders & Circulars, ser. 44, RG 94 [DD-14]. For a discussion of federal labor policy in tidewater Virginia and North Carolina, see *Freedom*, ser. 1, vol. 2.

patrol boat in the Potomac River, urged the rendition of fugitives, in order "to put a stop to the whole sale desertion that is now going on and relieve us of a most unpleasant difficulty."

Similarly, army commanders who considered the allegiance of masters more valuable than the labor of slaves tried to curry favor among slaveholders by promising to respect their property rights. In November 1861, as General John A. Dix issued instructions from his Baltimore headquarters to an expedition preparing to occupy Virginia's eastern shore, he sought to reassure slave owners that Union soldiers had no plan to "steal and emancipate their negroes." Dix proclaimed to the people of Accomack and Northampton counties that "[s]pecial directions have been given not to interfere with the conditions of any persons held to domestic service." Thus, through the winter of 1861–1862, policies supporting slavery vied with those favoring freedom in tidewater Virginia.

Dix's policy of safeguarding slaveholders' rights may have worked well on the tip of an isolated peninsula with large numbers of loyal masters, but it would not long serve military officers in the interior. General Ambrose E. Burnside's invasion of tidewater North Carolina in February 1862 soon revealed its limitations. The amphibious expedition under Burnside and Flag Officer Louis M. Goldsborough quickly demolished Confederate coastal defenses and captured Roanoke Island, giving Union forces control of Albemarle and Pamlico sounds and their tributaries. With the sea lanes secure, Burnside laid siege to New Berne. Its surrender in mid-March, and the fall of Beaufort a month later, allowed Union gunships to roam freely in the North Carolina tidewater and contributed to the Confederate evacuation of Norfolk and Portsmouth, Virginia. During the remainder of the war, federal troops conducted raids throughout the coastal area and occupied many of the smaller villages, although they did not gain full control of the region until the spring of 1865.

Like Dix, Burnside began his invasion pledging that slave property would be protected.[10] But the unionist sentiment that Burnside and others had hoped to foster among slaveholders failed to emerge. Meanwhile, the slaves themselves made it hard for him to redeem his pledge. Burnside found the town of New Berne "overrun with fugitives" volunteering their services along with information about the enemy's position, and he observed that, even if he were so disposed, he could not keep them outside Union lines. Masters fumed at the confidence with which some slaves moved back and forth between the federal positions and their former homes, gathering their property, securing their families, and helping others escape. While requesting instructions from Washington, Burnside quietly yielded to the pressure of the

[10] *Official Records*, ser. 1, vol. 9, pp. 363–64.

growing number of fugitives and allowed his earlier assurances regarding slave property to lapse. Following Butler's lead, he put runaway blacks to work for the Union army and, like Wool, paid them for their labor and appointed a Northern missionary, Vincent Colyer, to supervise their reception and employment.[11]

Burnside's policies conflicted with the plans of Edward Stanly, a former North Carolina congressman whom Lincoln had appointed military governor. Stanly hoped to cultivate indigenous unionist sentiment.[12] But congressional enactment in March 1862 of a new article of war forbidding Union soldiers to return fugitives to their masters, as well as the growing importance of black labor to the Union war effort, strengthened Burnside's determination to receive all runaways. Stanly sputtered about the rights of unionist masters, but to little effect. Like Fortress Monroe in Virginia, the Union outposts in tidewater North Carolina became magnets for fugitives.

From its initial footholds, the Union extended its grip on the tidewater slowly and sporadically. Burnside and General John G. Foster, his successor in command of the Department of North Carolina, continued to consolidate their position with a series of raids along the coastal waterways. Their efforts did not, however, significantly enlarge the area under federal control until the closing months of the war. In Virginia, General George B. McClellan moved his ponderous Army of the Potomac to the lower peninsula in the spring of 1862 and began to press toward Richmond, taking Yorktown and Williamsburg in early May. McClellan's tortoise-like advance never reached the Confederate capital, but, like the North Carolina raids, the fighting on the peninsula allowed large numbers of slaves to escape in the midst of the tramping armies. The fierce warfare increased both belligerents' need for laborers, forcing the Confederates to bring slaves into the war zone from all over Virginia and North Carolina, and inducing federal commanders to welcome such slaves when they escaped from the rebels.

Blacks who found employment within federal lines did not rest content with their own freedom. Almost as soon as they arrived, they began plotting to return home and liberate families and friends. The Second Confiscation Act, adopted in July 1862, provided official encouragement, for it guaranteed the freedom of all fugitives who fled Confederate masters and reached Union lines. Some blacks traveled deep into the Confederacy to rescue loved ones. As earlier, the intimate knowledge of tidewater geography they had gained while being hired from farm to farm, or while working as watermen and oysterers, served them well on these dangerous missions. Increasingly they received the

[11] *Official Records*, ser. 1, vol. 9, pp. 399–404. For a full discussion, see *Freedom*, ser. 1, vol. 2.
[12] *Official Records*, ser. 1, vol. 9, pp. 399–404.

support of Union soldiers and commanders who were hard-pressed for laborers and eager to employ blacks as wagoners, pilots, and scouts.

Not all slaves fled to Union lines when the opportunity arose. Some were discouraged by fear of an inhospitable reception. In June 1862, General Dix replaced General Wool as commander of the Department of Virginia. No friend of freedom, Dix had little use for the fugitives who crowded into Union lines, and he openly doubted their ability or desire to work. Instead of seeing contrabands as a source of labor, he schemed to remove them to the North. When that plan failed, he established a contraband camp on Craney Island at the mouth of the Elizabeth River, with an eye toward isolating the fugitive slaves.[13] Dix's actions lent plausibility to slaveholders' warnings that the Yankees would sell fugitive slaves to Cuba and dissuaded many blacks from venturing into Union lines.

While the policies of Dix and like-minded Union commanders encouraged potential fugitives to hesitate before leaving their owners, slave masters created deterrents of their own. Wealthy planters continued to refugee their slaves far from Union lines, eliminating the possibility of escape for thousands. Smaller holders, who generally could not afford the expense of relocation, erected new systems of surveillance, wielded the lash against those caught trying to escape, and abused the families of successful fugitives with new ferocity. Such practices, combined with shortages of food and clothing caused by wartime dislocation and with the ever-present threat of impressment into military labor gangs, burdened blacks in the Confederacy.

At the same time, however, some slaves who remained on the plantations and farms found their prospects enhanced by the federal presence. This was particularly true in the contested zones between Union and Confederate lines. In the face of Union invasion many slaveholders had fled these areas, sometimes leaving their slaves as the sole occupants of the old estates. With the masters gone, life on the plantations and farms had real advantages over labor on Union fortifications and the harsh lot of the contraband. Throughout the war zone, slaves began to reorganize their lives to suit their own needs and aspirations. In the midst of rampaging armies and guerrilla marauders, they took control of abandoned land and tried to establish a stable agricultural routine, sometimes aided by Northern missionaries who had followed the Union army into the Virginia and North Carolina tidewater.[14]

Even when the masters stayed on, the possibility of freedom behind

[13] Maj. Genl. John A. Dix to His Excellency John A. Andrew, 5 Nov. 1862, vol. 3 VaNc, pp. 405–11, Letters Sent, ser. 5046, Dept. of VA & 7th Army Corps, RG 393 Pt. 1 [C-3203]; *Freedom*, ser. 2: doc. 41; Gerteis, *From Contraband to Freedman*, pp. 26–27. For a discussion of the contraband camps, see *Freedom*, ser. 1, vol. 2.
[14] For a discussion of the missionaries' role in the tidewater, see *Freedom*, ser. 1, vol. 2.

Union lines often shifted the balance of power within Confederate territory, allowing slaves to exercise greater control over their labor. If their masters refused to permit greater independence and resisted demands for wages or other compensation, slaves simply fled to the federal enclaves and freedom.[15] The federal presence promoted liberty, in spite of the intentions of unsympathetic commanders. Nearly 3,000 slaves had taken refuge in the vicinity of Fortress Monroe by the end of 1862, while thousands of others had extracted more favorable living and working conditions by the tacit threat that they too might do so.[16]

The de facto freedom achieved by slaves who had reached Union lines in North Carolina acquired new force on January 1, 1863, with promulgation of the Emancipation Proclamation. But Lincoln's edict did little to speed the arrival of universal liberty in tidewater Virginia. Since it exempted certain areas already under Union occupation, the proclamation permitted slavery to survive in several tidewater Virginia counties.[17] As late as the summer of 1863, federal census takers counted nearly 5,000 blacks still held as slaves (presumably by loyal masters) in those counties. The survival of slavery and Dix's well-known sympathy for loyal masters also encouraged some Union soldiers to ignore the strictures of the March 1862 article of war and play slave-catcher, placing the liberty of all black people – free and freed – in jeopardy. As a practical matter, however, masters in the exempted counties found it increasingly difficult to control their slaves, even with Dix's aid. With federal officials anxious to recruit as many laborers as possible, fewer and fewer seemed willing to search out the fine distinctions regarding a master's loyalty. Hounded by Northern missionaries who had converged on the tidewater, Union soldiers who retrieved fugitives for loyal masters faced increasing hostility, although the kidnapping and selling of contrabands continued in some places.

Despite the exemptions, the Emancipation Proclamation swelled the number of fugitives within federal lines. Just as some North Carolina slaves had found their way to Fortress Monroe in 1861, a few slaves from as far west as Alabama reached federal lines in North Carolina in 1863.[18] Moreover, whereas some federal officials had earlier discour-

---

[15] By 1864, slaves in the Confederate-controlled counties of tidewater Virginia were fleeing to Union lines with relative ease. See, for example, below, docs. 313, 328.

[16] Capt. Chas. B. Wilder to Major Geo. J. Carney, 30 Dec. 1864, Annual, Personal, & Special Reports of Quartermaster Officers, ser. 1105, RG 92 [Y-500].

[17] U.S., *Statutes at Large, Treaties, and Proclamations*, vol. 12 (Boston, 1863), pp. 1268–69. The exempted tidewater counties were Elizabeth City, York, Norfolk, and Princess Anne in the Hampton Roads area, and Accomack and Northampton on the eastern shore.

[18] Testimony of Vincent Colyer before the American Freedmen's Inquiry Commission, 25 May 1863, filed with O-328 1863, Letters Received, ser. 12, RG 94 [K-84].

aged black flight, now nearly all encouraged it, for expansion of the war had increased the Union's needs not only for laborers, scouts, and spies, but also for soldiers.

In the spring of 1863, General Edward A. Wild, a Massachusetts abolitionist, began recruiting an "African Brigade" from among North Carolina and Virginia contrabands.[19] Unlike many white soldiers, the new black recruits relished the role of liberator. Assisted by Wild and his antislavery officers, they ventured far into the interior to free families, friends, and other slaves who wanted to leave. Their daring incursions, along with Wild's material and military support, encouraged other contrabands. By October 1863, slaveholders in some areas of the tidewater under Confederate control were reporting that "our slaves have nearly all left us."[20]

During raids in their former neighborhoods, many black liberators took time to even old scores with particularly abusive masters. Wild found grim satisfaction in this "[p]oetical justice" and once personally authorized several recently arrived fugitives to give their former owner a taste of slave discipline at the lash end of the whip. When court-martialed for his participation in this episode and in another relating to the summary execution of a Confederate guerrilla, Wild defiantly declared his readiness to do the same again under similar circumstances. The court decided against Wild, but General Butler, who returned to the tidewater in November 1863 to command the combined Department of Virginia and North Carolina, reversed the decision. Butler's action advertised the determination of federal forces to extend freedom.

More convinced than ever of the importance of putting black labor and black military might at the service of the Union, Butler promulgated policies that would attract additional tidewater blacks into Union lines. He ordered his subordinates to launch raids and expeditions to gather fugitives and enlist the men into federal service. In addition to freedom, he promised protection and subsistence for their families and prompt payment for labor, establishing a Department of Negro Affairs to supervise and assist black refugees.[21] Butler's subordinates, particularly the abolitionist officers who served with Wild, carried far into the interior the promise of rations for the families of men who enlisted in the Union army, thereby disrupting slavery as they recruited additional black soldiers. By war's end, about 8,000 men had enlisted in black regiments in tidewater Virginia and North Carolina,

[19] See *Freedom*, ser. 2: chap. 3.
[20] See below, doc. 303.
[21] General Orders No. 46, Head Quarters Dept. of Va. and North Carolina, 5 Dec. 1863, vol. 52 VaNc, General Orders Issued, ser. 5078, Dept. of VA & NC, RG 393 Pt. 1 [C-3062]. The portion of Butler's order that concerned black soldiers is printed in *Freedom*, ser. 2: doc. 46. For the operations of the Department of Negro Affairs, see *Freedom*, ser. 1, vol. 2.

and most of their families sought refuge and employment at Union contraband camps, army installations, and government-supervised farms.[22] Still, like earlier incursions into the Confederacy, Union raids under Butler also set off new waves of refugeeing, disrupting the lives of slaves removed into the interior and diminishing their chances for liberty.

By mid-1863, the war had transformed the black population of the tidewater. A census taken in July and August indicated the extent of the alterations within Union lines and suggested related developments in the area still under Confederate control. Moving through the Union-occupied portion of Virginia's lower peninsula (the area around Yorktown, and Elizabeth City and Warwick counties) and through the three counties adjoining Norfolk (Nansemond, Norfolk, and Princess Anne), federal officials counted some 26,000 blacks, a total not markedly different from the antebellum enumeration of 29,400, when allowance is made for the partial nature of the wartime count.[23] Of the 26,000, census takers denominated about 5,000 as "free," presumably as a result of their antebellum status; 5,300 as "bond" (these were presumably the slaves of loyal masters in the counties exempted from the Emancipation Proclamation); and 15,600 as "contraband." Viewing tidewater Virginia blacks from the perspective of their geographical origins instead of their legal status, census takers listed 8,500 "transients." The newly arrived doubtless also numbered among the 1,600 blacks living on deserted farms and the 2,000 employed by the government. The possibility of liberty had drawn thousands of blacks to the federal enclave; many blacks from the interior now lived in the tidewater.

Although the federal presence had put freedom within the grasp of some slaves, it had removed freedom beyond the reach of others. Many of the original residents of the area did not fare as well as the newly arrived. Only 17,500 "permanent residents" still lived in the Union-occupied Virginia tidewater, among whom were most of the antebellum free blacks. Thus fewer than half of the more than 29,400 slaves who had resided in the area before the war gained liberty within Union-occupied territory. Others doubtless escaped to freedom outside the region, and still others left once their liberty was secure, but many

[22] Approximately 5,000 black men enlisted in the Union army in North Carolina and 6,000 in Virginia. (*Freedom*, ser. 2: p. 12.) Almost all the North Carolinians enlisted in the state's tidewater counties, but many of the Virginians joined in the area near the District of Columbia rather than in the tidewater counties. Assuming that all the North Carolina black soldiers and half of the Virginia black soldiers enlisted in the tidewater, approximately 8,000 black soldiers derived from that region.

[23] In 1860, the black population of Elizabeth City, Nansemond, Norfolk, Princess Anne, Warwick, and York counties, Virginia, totaled 29,452. Of these, 23,032 were slaves and 6,420 were free blacks. (U.S., Census Office, 8th Census, *Population of the United States in 1860* [Washington, 1864], pp. 516–18.)

more – perhaps a majority – had been removed to continued enslavement in distant parts of the Confederacy. This massive refugeeing of
slaves from the tidewater, where masters had to move hastily before
advancing Union armies, suggests an even more massive removal in
interior regions where time and distance allowed slaveholders to prepare their retreat with greater care. Only the defeat of the Confederacy
could finally stop the see-saw that brought some slaves closer to freedom by casting others farther away.

During the last year of the war, eastern Virginia and North Carolina
became the site of the final confrontations between the great armies of
the North and the South. As the behemoths fought it out from the
trenches surrounding Richmond and Petersburg and General William
T. Sherman pressed into North Carolina from the south, many more
slaves took refuge in the Union-held tidewater. Still, escape was never
easy. Confederate officers, mindful of Butler's determination to transform slaves into soldiers, urged their removal to the interior. Slaveholders organized regular patrols and purchased packs of hounds to
discourage escape and to track down slaves who attempted it. To the
end, unionist masters in the counties exempted from the Emancipation
Proclamation demanded that federal troops protect their property
rights. Slaves who left their owners under such circumstances still
braved numerous dangers. If they failed they faced certain punishment,
and if they succeeded they were frequently forced to abandon family,
friends, and property, knowing that their possessions would be confiscated and their loved ones abused. If liberty remained an irresistible
temptation to some, others – mindful of the dangers – bided their time
and waited for freedom to come to them. Eventually it did, but not
until the spring of 1865, when Confederate Generals Robert E. Lee and
Joseph E. Johnston surrendered their armies.

1A: **Commander of the Department of Virginia to the
General-in-Chief of the Army**

[*Fortress Monroe, Va.*] May 27 /61

Sir

(Duplicate)

. . . .

Since I wrote my last dispatch the question in regard to slave
property is becoming one of very serious magnitude. The

inhabitants of Virginia are using their negroes in the batteries, and are preparing to send the women and children South. The escapes from them are very numerous, and a squad has come in this morning to my pickets bringing their women and children. Of course these cannot be dealt with upon the Theory on which I designed to treat the services of able bodied men and women who might come within my lines and of which I gave you a detailed account in my last dispatch. I am in the utmost doubt what to do with this species of property. Up to this time I have had come within my lines men and women with their children—entire families—each family belonging to the same owner. I have therefore determined to employ, as I can do very profitably, the able-bodied persons in the party, issuing proper food for the support of all, and charging against their services the expense of care and sustenance of the non-laborers, keeping a strict and accurate account as well of the services as of the expenditure having the worth of the services and the cost of the expenditure determined by a board of Survey hereafter to be detailed. I know of no other manner in which to dispose of this subject and the questions connected therewith. As a matter of property to the insurgents it will be of very great moment, the number that I now have amounting as I am informed to what in good times would be of the value of sixty thousand dollars. Twelve of these negroes I am informed have escaped from the erection of the batteries on Sewall's point which this morning fired upon my expedition as it passed by out of range. As a means of offence therefore in the enemy's hands these negroes when able bodied are of the last importance. Without them the batteries could not have been erected at least for many weeks As a military question it would seem to be a measure of necessity to deprive their masters of their services How can this be done? As a political question and a question of humanity can I receive the services of a Father and a Mother and not take the children? Of the humanitarian aspect I have no doubt. Of the political one I have no right to judge. I therefore submit all this to your better judgement, and as these questions have a political aspect, I have ventured—and I trust I am not wrong in so doing—to duplicate the parts of my dispatch relating to this subject and forward them to the Secretary of War.

. . . .

HLcS   Benj. F. Butler

Excerpt from Benj. F. Butler to Lieutenant Genl. Scott, 27 May 1861, B-99 1861, Letters Received Irregular, RG 107 [L-77]. Omitted portions concerned the movement of troops and matériel. Three days earlier, soon after arriving at Fortress Monroe, Butler had reported to General-in-Chief Winfield Scott that three slaves belonging to one Colonel Mallory, commander of Confederate forces in the district, had "delivered themselves up" to his picket guards. Butler had interrogated the fugitives personally and, finding that they were about to be taken south for Confederate service, had determined "as these men were very serviceable, and I had great need of labor in my quartermaster's department, to avail myself of their services." Questioned by another officer concerning his reception of the slaves, Butler had offered to return them if Mallory would take the oath of allegiance. Aware that this was only one instance of many that would soon be before him, Butler had asked Scott for a statement of general policy: "Shall they [the Confederates] be allowed the use of this property against the United States, and we not be allowed its use in aid of the United States?" In endorsements, Scott found "much to praise . . . and nothing to condemn" in Butler's action, and Secretary of War Simon Cameron concurred. (*Official Records*, ser. 1, vol. 2, pp. 648–52.)

1B: Secretary of War to the Commander of the Department of Virginia

Washington May 30, 1861.

Sir: Your action in respect to the negroes who came within your lines from the service of the rebels is approved.

The Department is sensible of the embarrassments which must surround officers, conducting military operations in a State by the laws of which Slavery is sanctioned —

The Government can-not recognize the rejection by any state its Federal obligations, nor can it refuse the performance of the Federal obligations resting upon itself. Among these Federal obligations, however no one can be more important than that of suppressing and dispersing armed combinations formed for the purpose of overthrowing its whole constitutional authority.

While, therefore, you will permit no interference, by the persons under your command, with the relations of persons held to service under the laws of any state, you will, on the other hand, so long as any State, within which your military operations are conducted, is under the control of such armed combinations, refrain from surrendering to alleged masters any persons who may come within your lines. You will employ such persons in the services to which they be best adapted, keeping an account of the labor by them performed, of the value of it, and of the expense of their maintenance. The question of their final disposition will be reserved for future determination.

HLcSr

Simon Cameron

Simon Cameron to Maj. Gen. Butler, 30 May 1861, vol. 44, pp. 205–6, Letters Sent, RG 107 [L-310]. This letter may have been drafted by Assistant Secretary of War Thomas A. Scott. (See below, doc. 18.)

1C: Secretary of War to the Commander of the Department of Virginia

Washington August 8. 1861.

General, The important question of the proper disposition to be made of fugitive slaves from service in States in insurrection against the Federal Government, to which you have again directed my attention in your letter of July 30th has received my most attentive consideration.

It is the desire of the President that all existing rights, in all the States, be fully respected and maintained. The war now prosecuted on the part of the Federal Government, is a war for the Union, and for the preservation of all Constitutional rights of States, and the citizens of the States, in the Union.

Hence, no question can arise as to fugitives from service within States and Territories in which the authority of the Union is fully acknowledged. The ordinary forms of judicial proceeding, which must be respected by military and civil authorities alike, will suffice for the enforcement of all legal claims.

But, in States wholly or partially under insurrectionary control, where the laws of the United States are so far opposed and resisted that they cannot be effectually enforced, it is obvious that rights dependent on the execution of those laws, must, temporarily, fail; and it is equally obvious that rights dependent on the laws of the States within which military operations are conducted, must be necessarily subordinated to the military exigencies created by the insurrection, if not wholly forfeited by the treasonable conduct of parties claiming them.

To this general rule, rights to services can form no exception.

The Act of Congress approved August 6th 1861, declares that if persons held to service shall be employed in hostility to the United States, the right to their services shall be forfeited, and such persons shall be discharged therefrom.

It follows of necessity, that no claim can be recognized by the military authorities of the Union, to the services of such persons when fugitives.

A more difficult question is presented, in respect to persons escaping from the service of loyal masters. It is quite apparent that the laws of the State, under which, only, the services of such fugitives can be claimed, must needs be wholly, or almost wholly suspended, as to remedies, by the insurrection and the military measures necessitated by it. And it is equally apparent that the substitution of military for judicial measures, for the enforcement of such claims, must be attended by great inconveniences, embarrassments and injuries.

Under these circumstances, it seems quite clear that the substantial rights of loyal masters will be best protected by receiving such fugitives, as well as fugitives from disloyal masters, into the service of the United States, and employing them under such organizations, and in such occupations, as circumstances may suggest or require. Of course, a record should be kept, showing the name and description of the fugitives; the name and the character, as loyal or disloyal, of the master; and such facts as may be necessary to a correct understanding of the circumstances of each case, after tranquility shall have been restored. Upon the return of peace, Congress will, doubtless, properly provide for all the persons thus received into the service of the Union, and for just compensation to loyal masters. In this way, only, it would seem, can the duty and safety of the Government, and the just rights of all be fully reconciled and harmonized.

You will, therefore, consider yourself instructed to govern your future action, in respect to fugitives from service, by the principles herein stated; and will report from time to time, and at least twice in each month, your action in the premises to this Department.

You will, however, neither authorize nor permit any interference by the troops under your command, with the servants of peaceful citizens, in house or field; nor will you, in any way, encourage such servants to leave the lawful service of their masters; nor will you, except in cases where the public safety may seem to require, prevent the voluntary return of any fugitive to the service from which he may have escaped. I am, General, Very respectfully, Yr obt. Servt

Simon Cameron

[*In the margin*] Copy

HLcSr

Simon Cameron to Major General B. F. Butler, 8 Aug. 1861, vol. 45, pp. 263–65, Letters Sent, RG 107 [L-309]. This letter may have been drafted by Assistant Secretary of War Thomas A. Scott. (See below, doc. 18.) A search of letters received by the War Department, the generals' papers in the records of the Adjutant General's Office, and the copies of letters sent in the records of the Department of Virginia did not locate the letter of July 30 referred to by Cameron, but a copy appears in Benjamin F. Butler, *Private and Official*

Correspondence of Gen. Benjamin F. Butler during the Period of the Civil War, 5 vols. (Norwood, Mass., 1917), vol. 1, pp. 185–88. In that letter, Butler reviewed his policies respecting slaves who had taken refuge within Union lines and, in a series of rhetorical questions, explained why he had decided to treat them as free: "If property, do they not become the property of salvors? But we, their salvors, do not need and will not hold such property, and will assume no such ownership: has not, therefore, all proprietory relation ceased? Have they not become, thereupon, men, women, and children? No longer under ownership of any kind, the fearful relicts of fugitive masters, have they not by their master's acts, and the state of war, assumed the condition, which we hold to be the normal one, of those made in God's image? Is not every constitutional, legal, and normal requirement, as well to the runaway master as their relinquished slaves, thus answered? I confess that my own mind is compelled by this reasoning to look upon them as men and women. If not free born, yet free, manumitted, sent forth from the hand that held them, never to be reclaimed."

2: Commander of the U.S.S. *Mount Vernon* to the Commander of the North Atlantic Squadron

Copy   Rappahannock [*Va.*] July 15. 1861

Sir   I have to report, that this morning at daylight we observed a boat adrift near Stingaree Light House and soon after discovered a man in the Light house. We manned a boat, armed her, and sent her with an officer to pick up the boat, and to ascertain who was in the Light House

At 8^{h}30^m the boat returned bringing with her six Negroes who had deserted from the shore during the night and taken shelter in the Light House casting their boat adrift to avoid detection

They appear to be very much frightened and state that the people on shore are about arming the Negroes with the intention of placing them in the front of Battle. their taking this course has caused much excitement amongst the negro population, who are deserting in every direction   two other boats made their escape last night in the hope of being picked up by some Vessel passing in the Bay

I have rationed these Negroes on board of this Vessel, until I receive orders from you as to their disposal. They inform me that there is not a Union man near the entrance of the River. A few weeks since they murdered the only Union man near Stingaree Point. His widow Mrs George Wilson, with three little children are yet on the Farm near the Point, they are apparently unmolested.

These negroes further inform me, that amunition is very scarce, and that the five hundred men in Mathews County have not two rounds of Cartridges with them. these men are about ten miles from Stingaree Point and are the nearest armed force in this vicinity

Enclosed I forward you a list of these Slaves together with a list of the names of their owners I am sir very respectfully Your Obedient Servant

O. S. Glisson

List of slaves	Owners
John Hunter Samuel Hunter Miles Hunter	Joseph Moore
Peter Hunter	J Crittenden
Alexander Franklin	Robert R Carter
David Harris	Jeremiah Harron

HLcSr

Comdr. O. S. Glisson to Flag Officer Silas H. Stringham, 15 July 1861, enclosed in Flag Officer S. H. Stringham to Honl. Gideon Welles, 18 July 1861, vol. 121, pp. 166–67, North Atlantic Squadron, Letters from Officers Commanding Squadrons, RG 45 [T-704]. In his covering letter to Secretary of the Navy Gideon Welles, Flag Officer Silas H. Stringham, commander of the North Atlantic Blockading Squadron, approved Glisson's action and added, "If negroes are to be used in this contest, I have no hesitation in saying, they should be used to preserve the Government not to destroy it." Welles agreed with this policy. While noting that it was "not the policy of the Government to invite or encourage this class of desertions," he declared that "under the circumstances no other course than that pursued by Commander Glisson could be adopted without violating every principle of humanity. To return them would be impolitic as well as cruel and as you remark 'they may be made serviceable on board our store ship' you will do well to imploy them." (Gideon Welles to Flag Officer S. H. Stringham, 22 July 1861, vol. 4, p. 483 1/2, Confidential Letters to the Secretary of War & to Officers of the Army, Navy, & Marine Corps, RG 45 [T-825].) In mid-August 1861, General John B. Magruder, commander of the Confederate Army of the Peninsula, observed that "the enemy is in the habit of landing in Mathews County & that from five to eight thousand dollars worth of Negros are decoyed off from that county pr Week." (Br. Genl. J. Bankhead Magruder to Col. Geo. Deas, 18 Aug. 1861, ch. II, vol. 227, p. 75, Letters & Telegrams Sent, Army & Dept. of the Peninsula, Records of Military Commands, RG 109 [F-631].)

3: **Virginia Slaveholder to a Confederate Congressman**

Richmond, Aug. 27" 1861.

Sir: I beg respectfully to submit to you the following statement of facts. You will please give them such direction as to you may seem best.

In certain portions of Virginia all communication between our forces and the Enemy's Army is necessarially by Boats.

In some instances the facility of this communication had led to heavy losses of Slaves.

In the district of country West of Nansemond River (nearly opposite to Newports News.) in the last twenty days, some forty (40) or fifty (50.) have thus escaped.

Several of the fugitives were very intelligent negros – familiar with the country occupied by our forces & with the navigation of the River – such will give valuable information to the Enemy. The labour of all of them is much in demand by the Abolition Army.

In view then of the material aid & of information given the enemy – of loss of property by our own citizens, & of the constant dangers of Treasonable correspondence it is submitted, whether *every means* should be used by our *Forces in the Field* to check these evils?

Among those means, it is apparent that the control of Boats, *liable* to be used in aid of such correspondence, is the most important.

Should they not at once be ordered under the Guns of the Batteries? or *disabled*?

Should not this be done by the Commandant of thé Post?

Is it not the duty of the Military to act promptly for the paramount interest of property in the community where stationed? or rather, is not the protection of property one of the duties of an army in the field?

I have written the foregoing hurriedly having promised, as I informed you at yr. room, several citizens of Isle of Wight Co. to call attention in influential quarters to the matters now submitted to your consideration. Very respectfully Yrs,

ALS

Jas. W. Cook.

Jas. W. Cook to Hon. J. M. Mason, 27 Aug. 1861, #3666 1861, Letters Received, ser. 5, Sec. War, RG 109 [F-38].

4: Commander of the U.S.S. *Union* to the Commander of the Potomac Flotilla

Copy—   off Aquia Creek [*Va.*]— Nov 8, 1861
Sir. I have nothing of importance to communicate in relation to the enemy at this point— I have been down the river and examined Mathias point—found everything still as death— The talk among the negroes however, is, that a battery will be opened there, soon as they can get soldiers—

The Island Belle picked up in the river, the other day, twenty three negroes, men women and children, there are now, some forty or more contrabands on board the different vessels— These people have all to be rationed, and it is becoming very embarrassing to me, short of provisions, as I am— The last party of twenty three have not been employed on any military works, according to their own confessions, and ran away, as they alledge, because their masters did not give them enough to eat, which their appearance, by no means indicate— I think it would be a good stroke of policy to return these negroes to their owners— It would tend to put a stop to the whole sale desertion that is now going on and relieve us of a most unpleasant difficulty— I have no doubt that many of them are from Maryland, notwithstanding they invariably represent themselves as coming from Virginia— Please give me instructions as to the disposition to be made of these, and for my government in future similar cases—

The Ice Boat is becoming more ricketty every day— Her fires are now down, and they are endeavoring to patch her boilers— I fear every day to hear of her breaking entirely down— In that event she would be a source of great trouble to us—

Should you have any vessels above, that you could spare, they could be most usefully employed below— I understand there is communication across the lower part of the river, constantly—

I have the pilot of the Baltimore still in confinement, awaiting your decission   Very Respectfully Your Ob^t Servt
HLcSr   A. D. Harrell

Lt. A. D. Harrell to Capt. T. T. Craven, 8 Nov. 1861, enclosed in Comd. Thos. T. Craven to Honorable Gideon Welles, 9 Nov. 1861, Potomac Flotilla, Letters from Officers Commanding Squadrons, RG 45 [T-601]. In the covering letter, the commander of the Potomac Flotilla noted that he had instructed Harrell to send the contrabands to the Navy Yard in Washington, D.C.

5: Proclamation by the Commander at Baltimore

Baltimore 13th Nov. 1861
PROCLAMATION
To the People of Accomac and Northampton Counties, Va.

The Military Forces of the United States are about to enter your Counties as a part of the Union. They will go among you as friends, and with the earnest hope that they may not by your own acts, be forced to become your enemies. They will invade no rights of person or property. On the contrary, your laws, your institutions, your usages will be scrupulously respected. There need be no fear that the quietude of any fireside will be disturbed, unless the disturbance is caused by yourselves.

Special directions have been given not to interfere with the conditions of any persons held to domestic service; and in order that there may be no ground for mistake or pretext for misrepresentation, commanders of Regiments and Corps have been instructed not to permit any such persons to come within their lines. The command of the expedition is entrusted to Brigadier General Henry H. Lockwood, of Delaware, a State identical, in some of the distinctive features of its social organization, with your own. Portions of his force come from Counties in Maryland, bordering on one of yours. From him, and from them, you may be assured of the sympathy of near neighbors, as well as friends, if you do not repel it by hostile resistance or attack. Their mission is to assert the Authority of the United States; to reopen your intercourse with the loyal States, and especially with Maryland, which has just proclaimed her devotion to the Union by the most triumphant vote in her political annals; to restore to commerce its accustomed guides by re-establishing the lights on your coast; to afford you a free export for the products of your labor, and a free ingress for the necessaries and comforts of life, which you require in exchange; and, in a word to put an end to the embarrassments and restrictions brought upon you by a causeless and unjustifiable rebellion.

If the calamities of intestine war, which are desolating other Districts of Virginia and have already crimsoned her fields with fraternal blood, fall also upon you, it will not be the fault of the Government. It asks only that its authority may be recognised. It sends among you a force too strong to be successfully opposed; a force, which cannot be resisted in any other spirit than that of wantonness and malignity. – If there are any among you, who rejecting all overtures of friendship, thus provoke retaliation, and draw down upon themselves consequences, which the Government is most anxious to avert, to their account must be laid the blood which may be shed, and the desolation, which may be brought upon peaceful homes. — On all who are thus reckless of the obligations of humanity and duty, and on all, who are found in arms, the severest punishment warranted by the Laws of War will be visited.

To those who remain in the quiet pursuit of their domestic occupations, the public authorities assure all they can give — Peace, Freedom from annoyance, Protection from Foreign and Internal Enemies, a guaranty of all Constitutional and Legal Rights and the blessings of a just and parental Government.

HDcSr   (signed) John A. Dix

Proclamation by Major General John A. Dix, 13 Nov. 1861, enclosed in Maj. Genl. John A. Dix to His Excellency A. Lincoln, 15 Nov. 1861, vol. 27 8AC, pp. 452–55, Letters Sent, ser. 2327, Dept. of PA, RG 393 Pt. 1 [C-4167]. In his covering letter to President Lincoln, Dix observed that his proclamation was an attempt to reassure the people of Virginia's eastern shore, who "have got it into their heads that we want to steal and emancipate their negroes." Proper designation of Dix's command is problematic because there was confusion at the time on the part of both Dix and the War Department. A War Department order of August 20, 1861, had merged Maryland and Delaware, formerly in Dix's Department of Pennsylvania, into the Department of the Potomac, commanded by General George B. McClellan. Unaware that his Department of Pennsylvania had thereby been either dissolved or reduced to merely the state of Pennsylvania, Dix had continued to command from Baltimore and to designate his orders and correspondence as issuing from the Department of Pennsylvania. (See *Official Records*, ser. 1, vol. 5, pp. 654–56.)

6: Commander of the Department of North Carolina to the Secretary of War

Newbern [N.C.] Mch 21 /62

I have the honor to report the following movements in my department since my hurrid report of the 16″ inst —

The detailed report of the Engagement on the 14″ is not yet finished, but I hope will be ready to send by the next mail —

As I reported, our forces occupied this city & succeeded in restoring it to comparative quietness by midnight on the 14″, and it is now as quiet as a New England village — I appointed Gen¹ Foster Military Governor of the city & its vicinity, and he has established a most perfect system of guard & police — *nine tenth* of the depredations on the 14″, after the enemy & citizens fled from the town, were

committed by the negroes, before our troops reached the
city— They seemed to be wild with excitement and delight— they
are now a source of very great anxiety to us; the city is being
overrun with fugitives from surrounding towns and
plantations— Two have reported themselves who have been in the
swamps for *five* years— it would be utterly impossible if we were so
disposed to keep them outside of our lines as they find their way to
us through woods & swamps from every side— By my next
dispatch, I hope to report to you a definite policy in reference to
this matter, and in the mean time shall be glad to receive any
instructions upon the subject which you may be disposed to give—

. . . .

I have taken the responsibility as I did at Roanoke of issuing
provision to the poor, who were & have been for some time
suffering for food— In fact I have had to order issues made in some
cases, to persons who have but lately been in affluent circumstances,
but who now have nothing but confederate notes, city shin plasters,
worthless notes of hand and unproductive real estate, and negroes
who refuse to acknowledge any debt of servitude— the suffering
and anxiety is far beyond anything I had anticipated— it seems
strange to me that these people will not percieve that this State of
things has been brought about by their own injudicious & dis-loyal
conduct—

. . . .

HLS   A. E. Burnside

Excerpts from Brig. Genl. A. E. Burnside to Hon. E. M. Stanton, 21 Mar.
1862, vol. 9, Union Battle Reports, ser. 729, War Records Office, RG 94
[HH-14]. Omitted portions detailed military events. On March 27, 1862,
Burnside informed Secretary of War Edwin M. Stanton that the "negroes
continue to come in, and I am employing them to the best possible advantage;
a principle part of them on some earth fortifications in the rear of the city." He
again asked for instructions as to their status and disposition, but by mid-May
had still received none. At that time, he notified Stanton that "In the absence
of definite instructions upon the subject of fugitive slaves I have adopted the
following policy:
  First. To allow all slaves who come to my lines to enter.
  Second. To organize them and enroll them, taking their names, the names
of their masters, and their place of residence.
  Third. To give them employment as far as possible, and to exercise toward
old and young a judicious charity.
  Fourth. To deliver none to their owners under any circumstances, and allow
none of them to leave this department until I receive your definite instructions." (*Official Records*, ser. 1, vol. 9, pp. 373–74, 389–91.)

7: Virginia Slaveholder to the Commander
of the Potomac Flotilla

Lancaster County va April 28″ 1862

Dr Sir   I take the privolede of addressing to you this letter the object of which is to recover my property that has Bin taken from me with out any provocation on my part   Sur on the 7th of April 1862, 7 of my Slaves left me and went on Bord the Ship young Rover then lying in the mouth of the rapahannock river & have sens [S]ent to fortress monro   Sur I am A private & peasable Satersen   I have never Born armes Against the united Stats nor have I any Child or near friend who has   in the Commensment of these troubles I voted for the union Candidate and labord hard for that Caus and made many Enemys By it   the 2 day of April we had some meting And past A resolution unanamus that we wood offer no millitary defence to the northan army   with these Considerations I appeel to you to have my property returned   I am A farmer & have Bin in the Bisness of wood Cutting for 5 years & have A large Contract with Oliver H Booth of new york   At this tim I have 1200 Cords of wood on hand all ready for market But must loose it if my Survants is not returnd   I have Seen the Captin of the Rover Capt John B Studnal   he is A gentleman of fine feelings and I think if this property is returned he is calculated to mak many friends to the union   he is perfectly in posession of my views   the Survants I lost th names are as folows

Sharlott woman	23 years
Isah young man	21
Dennis	18
Emma	16
Laurinda	15
margrett	13
& Charles A blind Boy of 23	

A woman I hired from Aolfin Child & too small Children Isabellar minney moses & A man I hired from mrs Cundif name Mack Kelly   Sur you Compliments will greatly oblige you obedient Surv

B. B. McKenny

PS I think my negroes shold Be returned becaus tha were taken after the order was ishued to take nomore & at the time thear was not A man in lancaster in arms Against the federl Army   I hope Sur if you Can you will return my negroes   if you Cant Pleas forward this to the propper authorites   B. B. McKenny

ALS

B. B. McKenny to Comadore Wyman, 28 Apr. 1862, enclosed in Comdr. R. H. Wyman to Honble. Gideon Welles, 2 May 1862, Potomac Flotilla, Letters from Officers Commanding Squadrons, RG 45 [T-602]. In the same file are several letters from other Lancaster County slaveholders seeking the return of slaves taken on board the *Young Rover* April 6 and 7, 1862, at the mouth of the Rappahannock River.

8: Military Governor of North Carolina to the Secretary of War

New Berne [*N.C.*] June 12th 1862. –

Sir,

. . . .

I do not intend to be guilty of disrespect to the Secretary, nor to betray too much Sensitiveness: and will not therefore comment upon what seems to me to be unusual language, in requesting an "immediate" answer.

My position is one of great responsibility. I am ready to meet it. I hope it is an honorable one. It certainly can bring no profit, and is not unaccompanied with peril. I have great difficulties to overcome – greater than you suppose, and am entitled to all the confidence and support, which I was assured I should have.

I believe the President to be sincere in his various public declarations, and wish to make the people of North Carolina believe him to be sincere and patriotic.

But I am grieved to say, that some of the most eminent and influential of our citizens, from listening to oft-repeated slanders have been persuaded and charge, the Southern country is invaded by "an enemy, who come to rob us, to murder our people, to emancipate our Slaves, & who is now preparing to add a new element to this most atrocious aggression, and involve us in the direful horrors of a servile war. He proposes nothing less than our entire destruction, the total desolation of our country – universal emancipation to crush us, to wipe out the South, to involve us in irredeemable misery, and hopeless ruin."

Though I know all this is the effect of long continued excitement, and not words of truth and Soberness, but of passion, and altogether incorrect in every particular. Still, they are the words of Sincerity, from men of irreproachable lives, who denounced Secession as treason, down to the day, when the North Carolina Convention passed the ordinance of Secession.

If this idea so monstrously incorrect, be in the minds of men of standing and influence, how must the large body of the people regard the action of the General Government?

In view of this most deplorable condition, I avail myself of the privilege I understood from you, I should have, of asking instructions upon the following points. –

1. When Slaves are taken from the possession of their loyal masters, by violence offered by armed men and negroes, what redress shall be afforded to the owners and what protection for the future?

2. When persons connected with the army, prevail on negroes to leave their masters, shall the loyal master or mistress have permission to prevail on them to return, and be protected while so doing?

3. When Steamers and vessels are almost daily leaving this State, and negroes the property of loyal citizens, are taken on board, without the consent of their owners, – who are sometimes widows and orphans – will authority be given, to prevent their being removed?

4. In cases where aged and infirm people who have been always loyal inhabitants – and treated with cruelty, by Secession Soldiers, because of their loyalty – have had their able-bodied slaves taken away, their barns robbed & fences destroyed, themselves unable from age and infirmity to labor – shall any effort be made, either by persuasion, by the civil authority, or otherwise, to have them delivered up?

5. If the Military Governor shall interfere with any action which it is known will violate the long established law of North Carolina, and a person connected with the army on the Sunday following shall make inflammatory appeals to a crowd of several hundred negroes, exhorting them to resort to violence and bloodshed, what action shall be taken by the Governor if any, to prevent the recurrence of such conduct?

6 When the Slaves of loyal citizens – who have never given aid and comfort to the rebellion, and sometimes suffered because they did not – are employed by the authorities of the United States, in various kinds of labor, can any steps be taken to secure a portion of what is due, for their labor, to their owners?

These are not cases of imagination: they have occurred and are most of them, coming before me for action daily. I will not weary or distress you by the details.

I hope I am not exceeding the duties of my place, while I urgently, but most respectfully, request an answer to these questions.

When I receive that answer I shall be able without delay, to inform the Department how far I can be relied upon to carry out its wishes.

Every day's experience impresses more forcibly on my mind the conviction, felt by abler & better men than myself, that some course of policy must be adopted, as to the disposition of Slaves within our lines.

If the army advances, and their numbers, already large, shall be increased, what is to be done with them? Who will support them or their owners, — often loyal & true men, already reduced to want by the rebellion, — who can make no crops without their aid? The expense of feeding the negroes will be enormous. It is estimated that each negro man, employed by Government, will require, in wages and subsistence, forty dollars per month, to support himself and family, who generally accompany him.

It is my heart-felt desire to restore to my native State the countless blessings conferred by the Union. I am ready to make any sacrifice, a gentleman and patriot can make to do so. But if I cannot rely upon the "perfect confidence and full support of the War Department," which was promised me, I desire to know it.

The loss of my humble abilities will not be felt by this great country.

If I am to act without instructions, and not to be supported, when I pursue the deliberate dictates of my judgment and conscience, then I ask — the only favor I ever asked for my personal benefit of any administration — to be allowed to tender my "immediate" resignation, and to be reduced as early as possible, to the honor of a private station. I have the honor to be your Obt: Svt

ALS   Edw. Stanly

Excerpt from Military Govr. Edw. Stanly to Hon. Edwin M. Stanton, 12 June 1862, N-207 1862, Letters Received, RG 107 [L-314]. In the omitted portion, Stanly explained why he had denied a Northern schoolteacher permission to open a school for black children in New Berne. On June 2, 1862, the House of Representatives had requested President Lincoln to inform the House "what powers have been conferred" on Edward Stanly "as Military Governor of North Carolina," and whether Stanly had "interfered to prevent the education of children, white or black" in that state. Secretary of War Edwin M. Stanton referred the House resolution to Stanly, requesting an immediate reply. (Secretary of War Edwin M. Stanton to Hon. Edward Stanley, 3 June 1862, vol. 49b, pp. 317–18, Letters Sent, RG 107 [L-314].) No record of Stanton's response to Stanly's tender of his resignation has been found among the copies of letters sent by the Secretary of War or the adjutant general of the army.

9: North Carolina Slaveholder to the Commander of the Department of North Carolina

Beaufort NC Oct 8th /62

Prompted by the necessity of the case, I have to make on you a requisition quite unpleasant — For the last few months I have supported my Family by the hire of two carpenters. They a few days ago refused to be hired & have gone into the Federal lines — which has left on my hands for support twenty two women & children — *I ask relief*, & refer you to the Provost Marshall or any one else in this place, or any acquaintance in Newbern for satisfaction as to the reasonableness of the case, an order on the proper authority here (if you deem it proper) will be thankfully accepted   Respectfully

ALS   Ja^s H. Taylor

Jas. H. Taylor to Maj. Gen. J. G. Foster, 8 Oct. 1862, enclosed in Maj. A. Zabriskie to Asst. Adjt. Genl. Southard Hoffman, 12 Oct. 1862, Letters Received, ser. 3238, Dept. of NC, RG 393 Pt. 1 [C-3077]. In his covering letter, Major A. Zabriskie, commander of the post of Beaufort, observed that one of the black carpenters had returned to Taylor but bluntly stated his intention of leaving again within the week. Zabriskie reported Taylor to be a "gentleman of respectability and wealth" whose property was outside federal lines. In an endorsement, an adjutant at departmental headquarters reported that Taylor had taken the oath of allegiance; however, it was later discovered that Taylor did not take the oath until after his slaves had left him. See below, doc. 10.

10: Commander of the Post of Beaufort, North Carolina, to the Headquarters of the Department of North Carolina

Beaufort N.C. *[January 14, 1863]*

Major — I am in receipt of two orders dated 12th Jan'y, 1863. The first endorsed upon the letter of James H. Taylor, relating to the taking off of several of his slaves by a *"Government Teamster"* I desire to report that the matter was thoroughly enquired into at the time, that the *Teamster* referred to was a *negro* named York, that Mr Taylor expressly declined to make any formal complaint, saying that the negroes "would have left him at any rate," that under the circumstances the negro driver was reprimanded, that he used the government team very early in the morning & without permission & has been told that in future he must not use it without orders under penalty of severe punishment. In addition I have to say that

Mr Taylor has taken the Oath of Allegiance *since* his slaves left him.

With regard to Mr Davis' case— He is not the owner or rather was not the owner of the negro woman, she belongs to his son-in-law Mr Rieger— Mr Davis & Mr Rieger together tied the woman to a tree her arms over her head & then whipped her severely, the flesh on her arms where the ropes went was badly lacerated & her arms covered with blood when I saw her— She was only released upon the peremptory order of a private of the 9th N. Jersey, who says the treatment was very cruel— Her crime was that she demanded her daughter whom Mr Davis retained in slavery; she is a smart intelligent woman & quite able to support herself & children.

Mr Davis *has not been arrested at all,* but simply informed that the matter was one which I did not understand & about which I should be obliged to ask advice at Headquarters, this seemed especially to alarm Mr Davis, so much so in fact, that I thought the alarm itself sufficient punishment & had therefore not intended to have troubl'd you with the matter.

Lieut Thayer who bears this note can give you any information respecting either of the two cases, or other matters relating to this Post.

The Boat to which you refer is positively necessary for the Hospital Service, the present claimant is not the only claimant of its ownership. Capt Curtiss the former Provost Marshal stated that he had given a receipt to the owner & the matter is now awaiting his return from the East where he has gone on a furlough, rest assured that impartial justice shall be observed. I am very respectfully Your obt serv't

ALS   Wm B. Fowle Jr

Capt. Wm. B. Fowle, Jr., to Major Southard Hoffman, [14 Jan. 1863], F-6 1863, Letters Received, ser. 3238, Dept. of NC, RG 393 Pt. 1 [C-3077]. The letters of Taylor and Davis have not been found among the letters received at the post of Beaufort.

11: **Military Governor of North Carolina to the Commander of the Department of North Carolina**

New Berne [*N.C.*] Jany 20th 1863
General, I have just received a letter from Edenton, of date the 6th Inst. informing that a band of negroes & Soldiers, "*armed,*" visited

the premises of a Mrs Page of that town, and carried away Several negroes, and a parcel of bedding & other furniture: that they were very insolent in their conduct and threatened to have the town shelled if they were interfered with.

My correspondent says that they came, as he heard, from on board the Ocean Wave:

A negro man, formerly living on the plantation of the venerable James C. Johnston, named "Matthew" was the person commanding the party

This negro, is one of desperate character.

The Citizens of Edenton beg your protection from outrages of this Kind: they desire to know whether it can be afforded them, or must they take redress into their own hands?

I have written and informed my correspondent – a gentleman of the highest character – that I would call your attention to this case, & have no doubt you will, as heretofore, take effectual steps to protect peacable citizens and punish such outrages. I have the honor to be &c

ALS   Edw Stanly

Mil. Gov. Edw. Stanly to Major Genl. Foster, 20 Jan. 1863, N-41 1863, Letters Received, ser. 3238, Dept. of NC & 18th Army Corps, RG 393 Pt. 1 [C-3082]. Enclosed is a deposition, undated and unsigned but apparently by one of the black participants in the raid, which indicated that the former slaves who had returned for their families and property were working as stewards on the *Ocean Wave* or as servants for Union officers who approved the raid. Other enclosures. Stanly had earlier complained that Confederate soldiers were seizing and carrying off large numbers of slaves. "This robbery takes civilized beings from their families and homes; it deprives a kind master of his property and punishes slaves for their fidelity to him." "This outrage," he added, "has not the defense attempted for the African Slave trade – that it brought uncivilized beings under the influence of Christianity and Civilization." (Milty. Govnr. Edwd. Stanley to Maj. Genl. Foster, 29 Dec. 1862, F-183 1862, Letters Received, ser. 3238, Dept. of NC, RG 393 Pt. 1 [C-3198].)

12: **Testimony by the Superintendent of Contrabands at Fortress Monroe, Virginia, before the American Freedmen's Inquiry Commission**

[*Fortress Monroe, Va.,*] May 9, 1863.

. . . .

Question How many of the people called contrabands, have come under your observation?

Answer Some 10,000 have come under our control, to be fed in part, and clothed in part, but I cannot speak accurately in regard to the number. This is the rendezvous. They come here from all about, from Richmond and 200 miles off in North Carolina There was one gang that started from Richmond 23 strong and only 3 got through.

. . . .

Q In your opinion, is there any communication between the refugees and the black men still in slavery?

A. Yes Sir, we have had men here who have gone back 200 miles.

Q In your opinion would a change in our policy which would cause them to be treated with fairness, their wages punctually paid and employment furnished them in the army, become known and would it have any effect upon others in slavery?

A Yes – Thousands upon Thousands. I went to Suffolk a short time ago to enquire into the state of things there – for I found I could not get any foot hold to make things work there, through the Commanding General, and I went to the Provost Marshall and all hands – and the colored people actually sent a deputation to me one morning before I was up to know if we put black men in irons and sent them off to Cuba to be sold or set them at work and put balls on their legs and whipped them, just as in slavery; because that was the story up there, and they were frightened and didn't know what to do. When I got at the feelings of these people I found they were not afraid of the slaveholders. They said there was nobody on the plantations but women and they were not afraid of them One woman came through 200 miles in Men's clothes. The most valuable information we recieved in regard to the Merrimack and the operations of the rebels came from the colored people and they got no credit for it. I found hundreds who had left their wives and families behind. I asked them "Why did you come away and leave them there?" and I found they had heard these stories, and wanted to come and see how it was. "I am going back again after my wife" some of them have said "When I have earned a little money" What as far as that?" "Yes" and I have had them come to me to borrow money, or to get their pay, if they had earned a months wages, and to get passes. "I am going for my family" they say. "Are you not afraid to risk it?" "No I know the Way" Colored men will help colored men and they will work along the by paths and get through. In that way I have known quite a number who have gone up from time to time in the neighborhood of Richmond and several have brought back their families; some I have never heard from. As I was saying they do not feel afraid now. The white people have nearly all gone, the blood hounds are not there now to hunt them and they are not afraid, before they were afraid to stir. There are hundreds of negroes at Williamsburgh with their families working for nothing. They would not get pay here and they had rather stay where they are. "We are not afraid of being carried back" a great many have told us and "if we are, we can get away again" Now that they are getting their eyes open they are coming in. Fifty came this morning from Yorktown who followed Stoneman's Cavalry when they returned from their raid. The officers reported to their Quartermaster that they had so many horses and fifty or sixty negroes. "What did you bring them for" "Why they followed us and we could not stop them." I asked one of the men about it and he said they would leave their work in the field as soon as they found the Soldiers were Union men and follow them sometimes without hat or coat. They would take best horse they could get and every where they rode they would take fresh horses, leave the old ones and follow on and so they came in. I have questioned a great many of them and they do not feel much afraid; and there are a great many courageous fellows who have come from long distances in rebeldom. Some men who came here from North Carolina, knew all about the Proclammation and they started on the belief in it; but they had heard these stories and they wanted to know how it was. Well, I gave them the evidence and I have no doubt their friends will hear of it. Within the last two or three months the rebel guards have been doubled on the line and the officers and privates of the 99th New York between Norfolk and Suffolk have caught hundreds of fugitives and got pay for them.

Q Do I understand you to say that a great many who have escaped have been sent back?

A Yes Sir, The masters will come in to Suffolk in the day time and with the help of some of the 99th carry off their fugitives and by and by smuggle them across the lines and the soldier will get his $20. or $50.

. . . .

HD

Excerpts from testimony of Capt. C. B. Wilder before the American Freedmen's Inquiry Commission, 9 May 1863, filed with O-328 1863, Letters Received, ser. 12, RG 94 [K-68]. Topical labels in the margin are omitted.

13: Census of Blacks in the Union-Occupied Virginia Tidewater

[Norfolk, Va. August 20, 1863]

Census Return of Colored Population within the Union Lines, at Yorktown and Vicinity, and in Elizabeth City and Warwick Counties, and the Counties of Norfolk Nansemond and Princess Anne, Virginia, taken between July 1st 1863 and August 20th 1863.

Place.	Total.	Sex.		Age.				Condition.			Permanent Residents	Transient Residents	On Deserted Farms	Otherwise Employed by Government.	Helped by Gov't		Without Employment	Able to Read.	Color.	
		Male.	Female.	Under 10	10 to 20	20 to 45	over 45	Bond.	Free.	Contraband					Wholly.	In Part.			Black.	Mixed.
Yorktown.	2316	1261	1055	578	459	939	268	172	252	1761	1380	732	13	393	518	212	1441	106	1361	782
E.C. & W. Counties,	4811	2475	2336	1174	1102	2107	627	181	606	3999	4475	439	731	726	2681	340	2215	702	3931	872
N.N. and P.A. Counties	18,983	10425	8558	5369	4126	6338	3150	4961	4140	9882	11694	7289	903	965			1800	1323	15,533	3450
Total.	26,110	14,161	11,949	7121	5687	9384	4045	4314 [3314]	4998	15642	17,549	8460	1647	2084			5456	2131	20,825	5104

HD

Census Return, [20 Aug. 1863], enclosed in O. Brown to Col. Hoffman, 24 Aug. 1863, Letters Received, ser. 5063, Dept. of VA & NC, RG 393 Pt. 1 [C-3011]. The full manuscript returns of this census have not been found in the records of either the army commands or the Bureau of Refugees, Freedmen, and Abandoned Lands. Full manuscript returns of censuses taken in York County in 1865 and in Princess Anne County in 1866 have survived. (Census Returns of the Black Population of Princess Anne County, [Mar. 1866], vol. 403, ser. 4232, Princess Anne VA Asst. Subasst. Comr., RG 105 [A-7994]; Census Returns of the Black Population of York County, [Mar. 1865], vol. 511, ser. 4356, Yorktown VA Asst. Subasst Comr., RG 105 [A-7904].) See also a summary of a census taken in Elizabeth City County in the summer of 1867. (E. P. Williams to General S. C. Armstrong, 10 July 1867, W-414 1867, Registered Letters Received, ser. 3798, VA Asst. Comr., RG 105 [A-7774].)

14A: Headquarters of a Black Brigade to the Commander of a North Carolina Black Regiment

(Copy.)   Norfolk Va. Nov, 17, 1863.
Colonel, The Genl. Comd'g directs that you, with two of the companies of your command (100 men,) proceed upon a recruiting expedition, observing the following instructions, viz: —

The men will take with them 3 days rations in haversacks, their arms, overcoats, and blankets. They will be provided also with 40 rounds of ammunition, and will start from camp in season to reach the entrenched Camp at sundown.

The men must do no plundering, but whatever is necessary for food or transportation, may be taken by command, and in presence of the officers.

All Africans, including men, women, and children, who may quit the plantations, and join your train, are not to be driven back, but are to be protected by you. Should they bring any of their masters' property with them, you are to protect that also, as well as themselves, for you are not bound to restore any such property.

You may allow them to take with them axes, scythes, &c., for their defence and horses and wagons for the transportation of their baggage.

Should you be fired upon, you will *at once* hang the man who fired. Should it be from a house, you will also *burn* the house immediately. In case of hanging, you will label the body, according to the nature of the case, as "Assassin's," "Guerrillas" &c.

Guerrillas are not to be taken alive. Should you find firearms, including fowling pieces, in any house, you will bring the owner in as prisoner.

Should you get upon the track of a guerrilla party, you may prolong your stay to pursue them, feeding yourselves from the farms of *disloyal* men. Preserve strict discipline throughout. March in perfect order, so as to make a good impression and attract recruits, keeping good order at night, to guard against surprise.

March out by way of the Intrenched Camp, and warn Capt. C. A. Jones to protect all fugitives, and arrest their pursuers. Warn him also that if he hears firing, he must send out a strong party to your assistance.

Let Capt. Jones pilot such fugitives as come in, to Capt. Croft, who will *enlist* the able-bodied men, and turn over all others to Dr. Brown.[1]

When you return, march slowly, so as to allow the fugitives to keep up with you.

Be careful not to injure crops, and especially not interfere with the farms of Dr. Brown. Upon those farms, you will find guides and allies. Very Respectfully Your Obed't. Serv't.

HLcSr   (Signed) Hiram W. Allen,

1st Lt. Hiram W. Allen to Col. A. G. Draper, 17 Nov. 1863, enclosed in Col. Alonzo G. Draper to Major R. S. Davis, 4 Jan. 1864, D-164 1863, Letters Received, ser. 5063, Dept. of VA & NC, RG 393 Pt. 1 [C-3013].

1 Dr. Orlando Brown, the Department of Negro Affairs superintendent for the portion of Virginia south of the James River, with headquarters at Norfolk.

14B: Commander of the Confederate Department of North Carolina to the Confederate Adjutant and Inspector General

Petersburg, Va., December 15th 1863

General   I have the honor to enclose a dispatch just received from Colonel Griffin. It is impossible with my force to prevent these raids – the section of country that the enemy are now operating in is too far from our line to do more than watch their operations – It is evident from the statements in Mr Lincoln's message concerning the number of Negro troops in the Federal Service, and their boasted Efficiency, that their policy will be to increase that discription of materiel as much as possible, as it strengthens their numbers, and weakens our labor force – General Butler is evidently pursueing a steady couse to effect this object wherever it is in his power – And in a short time all the country that he can overun will be entirely denuded of slaves – Would it not be advisable to cause all the slaves, in the country so exposed to be brought back within our lines? We could send a Cavalry expedition of our own down in such neighborhoods, to collect and bring in the Negroes – Whatever is determined on, should be carried out at once, as every day loses so much valuable property to the Confederacy – In many cases doubtless objections may be made by the owners, but I think the case one of emergency – I enclose copy of Col G's telegram – Respectfully asking a reply   I am General Your Obt Sevt.

ALS   G E Pickett

Maj. Genl. G. E. Pickett to General S. Cooper, 15 Dec. 1863, P-1510 1863, Letters Received, ser. 12, Adj. & Insp. Gen., RG 109 [F-265]. Endorsement. An enclosed telegram from Colonel Joel R. Griffin, Confederate commander at Franklin, North Carolina, also dated December 15, 1863, reported the invasion of southside Virginia and northeastern North Carolina by 1,500 Union soldiers, many of whom were black. In addition to plundering the countryside and "insulting our ladies in the most tantalizing manner," Union soldiers "were gathering up Negroes and carrying them off." Other enclosures. General Pickett, in a second letter of the same date to the Confederate adjutant and inspector general (in the same file), declared that "Butler's plan evidently is to let loose his swarm of *blacks* upon our *ladies* – and defenceless families, plunder and devastate the country. Against such a warfare there is but one recource to hang at once every one captured belonging to the expedition and afterwards any one caught who belongs to Butlers Dept." For the negative response of a leader in the Virginia legislature to the suggestion that slaves be removed from the war zone, see below, doc. 313.

15: North Carolina Slaveholder to the Confederate President

Kenansville N.C. 25th Nov[r] 1863.
His excellency Pres[t] Davis, A perfect stranger presumes to address you in behalf of his Countrymen.

Some time during the past year, the Gov[r] of this State ordered a detail of Patrol guard for this County, amounting to twenty men; and *immediately* thereafter, the Citizens made up a fund & purchased a pack of Hounds at heavy cost to accompany them; and I have *no* fears of contradiction, when I say they have been of *great* service in preventing escapes of Slaves, & also preventing desertions &c.

The Gov[r] issued his order to the Col of the County, and he made his appointments under my advisement (as Chair[n] of Co. C[t]) as also of other Citizens which he relied upon for Counsel: The appointment I think was a *good* one; and (by no means reflecting on our respectable troops in this County,) I must be pardoned for saying that the said Patrol have been "the ounce of preventive in place of the pound of Cure" We are here not far distant from the Yankee lines; and you well Know a good watch should be Kept. Since the organization of this Company, there has been *no* attempt of escapes by the Slaves *but one*, (save in the Raid in July) and the whole number of negroes (save one, & he was shot & killed *near* the Yankee lines) were Captured & returned to their owners through this Company.

I have just heard, that the said Company has been disbanded, and

the members of the Company conscripted. I hope it is not so. But
if such be the order, I hope your Excellency will reverse the order,
& commission the said Company to attend to their former
duties. Ours is almost a defenceless section, and this Guard we
consider a *very valuable* outpost. It secures us from escapes &
deserters; and is also an important Courier establishment to the
army; they quartering & manouvering on or near the line of
separation &.c.

I repeat my request that your Excellency will continue the
protection to this section by Continuing the Patrol Organization
mentioned. With much respect &c. I have the honor to be Your
Obe^t Servt &.c.

Jere Pearsall

Reference,
Hon Wm T. Dortch
  " Geo. Davis
  " O. R. Kenan
ALS

Jere Pearsall to Prest. Davis, 25 Nov. 1863, P-141 1863, Letters Received,
ser. 12, Adjt. & Insp. Gen., RG 109 [F-302]. In an endorsement dated
December 17, 1863, Confederate Secretary of War James A. Seddon disapproved Pearsall's request: "I will not interfere as I can not conceive that a
better use could be made of the men than by conscription to enhance the ranks
of Veteran Companies." Other endorsements.

16: Commander of a Black Brigade to the Headquarters of the Department of Virginia and North Carolina and the 18th Army Corps

Wilson's Wharf, James River [Va.] May 12th 64

Sir— Not being in the habit of accepting rebuke for acts not
committed, and feeling that I can judge of "the qualities becoming
to a man or a Soldier" quite as well as I can be informed by Brig.
Genl. Edwd. W. Hinks in *such a letter* as the *above*, I have the honor
to forward it, together with this, my protest, through Division Hd.
qrs. for the consideration of the Major General Commanding the
Department —

I protest against the whole tone of the above letter, as
unbecoming and unjust; as being full of harsh rebuke, administered
before even making any inquiry; and therefore, as *pre*-judging cases
against me, and taking for granted, that "acts perpetrated" by me

are necessarily "barbarous and cruel" not admitting the possibility of any justification; nor the probability of any excuse —

I have the honor to submit the following statement of facts —

On Friday May 6th I sent a party to surprise a Rebel Signal Station at Sandy Point. The party at the Station numbered 10 men, on being driven from the house they run into a swamp, directly upon one of my detachments, forming part of the trap — after considerable resistance, the Capture was complete, 5 Rebels were Killed, 3 wounded and 2 Caught, the dead were properly buried on the spot, the wounded and Prisoners were brought into camp and afterwards sent down to Fortress Monroe. The 10 guns were brought into camp, according to the nicest discrimination they were classed thus — 8 Soldiers and 2 citizens of whom 1 citizen was killed and 1 wounded. In this affair great credit is due to Capt. Eagle and Lt. Price 1st U.S.C.T. for skillfully carrying out the Plans.

On Monday Morning May 9th before daylight I sent a party to surprise a Squad of Rebel's who had been playing the *Guerrilla*, and attacked us three times, learning that they were passing the night at a Certain house I sent thither to take them; but being misinformed as to the distance, my party did not arrive till day. The Rebels 11 in number, made a stand, in good order under an officer in uniform, (said to be an adjutant) Our mounted advance party consisting only of 5 charged upon the 11 killed one, wounded another, run them into a bit of a swamp, and then waited for the main body to come up, but the rebels had passed through the swamp, and in two Boats crossed the Chicahominy, The Citizen Killed proved luckily to be Wilcox, the owner of the house, and the Enrolling Officer of the District. He was properly buried in the Yard, His house was burned. In this affair Major Cook 22^d U.S.C.T. deserves credit for his boldness, and especially I would mention Henry Harris a Colored Sergeant of Capt. Choate's 2^d U.S.C. Baty. for the daring he displayed, I wish it to be distinctly understood by Brig. Genl. Hinks that I shall continue to Kill *Guerrillas*, and Rebels offering armed resistance Whether they style themselves Citizens or Soldiers —

On Tuesday May 10th William H. Clopton, was brought in by the Pickets. He had been actively disloyal so that I held him as Prisoner of War, and have sent him as such to Fortress Monroe. He has acquired a notoriety as the most cruel Slave Master in this region, but in my presence he put on the character of a Snivelling Saint. I found half a dozen *women* among our refugees, whom he had often whipped unmercifully, even baring their whole persons for the purpose in presence of *Whites and Blacks*. I laid him bare and putting the whip into the hands of the Women, three of Whom took turns in settling some old scores on their masters back. A black Man, whom he had abused finished the administration of Poetical justice, and even in this scene the superior humanity of the Blacks over their white master was manifest in their moderation and backwardness. I wish that his back had been as deeply scarred as those of the women, but I abstained and left it to them— I wish it to be distinctly understood by Brig. Genl. Hinks that I shall do the same thing again under similar circumstances. I forgot to state that this Clopton is a high minded Virginia Gentleman, living for many years next door to the late John Tyler ExPresident of the U.S. and then and still intimate with his family.

And now as this is the second time that Brig. Genl. Hinks, has invoked the rules of Civilized warfare, and enjoined upon us the excercise of magnanimity and forbearance, I would respectfully inquire, for my own information and Guidance, whether it has been definitely arranged that Black Troops shall exchange courtesies with Rebel Soldiers? and if so on which side, such courtesies are expected to commence, and whether any guaranties have been offered on the part of the Rebels calculated to prove satisfactory and reassuring to the African Mind? Very Respectfully Your Obt. Sert

HLcSr   (Signed) Edwd. A. Wild

Brig. Genl. Edwd. A. Wild to Maj. Robert S. Davis, 12 May 1864, copied in endorsement by Brig. Genl. [Edward W. Hinks], 13 May 1864, vol. 34/66 1/4 25AC, pp. 40–42, Endorsements Sent, ser. 1662, 3rd Div. 18th Army Corps, RG 393 Pt. 2 No. 73 [C-3151]. On May 11, 1864, General Edward W. Hinks, commander of the 3rd Division of the 18th Army Corps, had ordered Wild to report the circumstances attending the death of a citizen at the hands of his brigade and the whipping of another citizen prisoner in his camp, averring "the seeming impossibility of any justification for the one, and the extreme improbability of any excuse for the other." Hinks had warned Wild: "I wish it to be distinctly understood that I will not countenance, Sanction or permit any Conduct on the part of my command not in accordance with the principles recognized for . . . modern warfare between Civilized Nations, and for any departure from these rules all officers concerned will be held individually accountable. Barbarism and cruelty to persons in our power are not among the qualities that are becoming to a man or a Soldier." (Vol. 33/66 1/2 25AC, p. 13, Letters Sent, ser. 1659, 3rd Div. 18th Army Corps, RG 393 Pt. 2 No. 73 [C-3151].) Hinks forwarded Wild's response to General Benjamin F. Butler, commander of the 18th Army Corps and the Department of Virginia and North Carolina, requesting in an endorsement that Butler either court-martial Wild or relieve him of command and examine him "to determine and report upon his soundness of mind." The following month, a court-martial found Wild guilty of disobedience of orders and suspended him from rank and pay for six months. During the trial, Wild challenged the legality of the proceedings because the court included no officers who, like himself, commanded black soldiers, and also because some members of the court were his junior in rank. On July 18, 1864, less than a month after judgment was rendered, Butler reversed the conviction, observing that he had "found a prejudice among some officers, now happily dying out, so strong, inveterate, and deep rooted, that in his judgement after mature reflection, such officers would not form an impartial tribunal for the trial of an officer in command of Color'd Troops." Such attitudes had prompted Butler to issue an order in December 1863, requiring that a majority of any court-martial trying an officer in command of black troops be composed of other officers commanding black troops. (Proceedings of general court-martial in the case of Brig. Gen. E. A. Wild, 18th Army Corps, 28 June-30 July 1864, LL-2249, Court-Martial Case Files, ser. 15, RG 153 [H-25].)

17: Commander of a Black Brigade to the Commander of the District of Eastern Virginia

Newport-News, Va. Sept. 1st, 1864.
Sir, I have the honor to report that some Government employees (colored) came up here from Fort Monroe and Hampton Hospitals, having been allowed a short leave of absence for the purpose of getting their families if possible. I told them I had no boats, but would help them with men. They reappeared the next day with sailboats. I sent with them a Captain and 15 men (dismounted Cavalry). The families were in and about Smithfield. I gave them strict instructions to abstain from plundering – to injure no one if possible – to get the women and children merely, and come away as promptly as possible. They were to land in the night. They followed these directions closely: but became delayed by the numbers of women and children anxious to follow, whom they packed in extra boats, picked up there, and towed along. They also had to contend against a head tide, and wind calm. So that their progress down Smithfield Creek in the early morn was exceedingly slow. The inhabitants evidently gathered in from some concerted plan of alarm or signals. For, 3 miles below, the party were intercepted by a force of irregular appearance, numbering about 100 – having horses and dogs with them; – armed variously with shot guns, rifles, &c, and posted behind old breastworks with some hurried additions. They attacked the leading boats, killed a man and woman, and wounded another woman therein. The contrabands then rowed over to the opposite bank and scattered over the marshes. How many more have been slaughtered we know not. Two (2) men have since escaped to us singly. – When the rear boats, containing the soldiers, came up, the Captain landed, with the design of attacking the rebels. But then the firing

revealed their full numbers. He found they outnumbered him, more than 6 to 1, and that the REVOLVERS of our Cavalry, in open boats or on the open beach, would stand no chance against their rifles behind breastworks. He embarked again, and they made their way past the danger, by wading his men behind the boats, having the baggage and bedding piled up like a barricade. They then had a race with 3 boats, which put out from side creeks to cut them off. But for the coolness and ingenuity of Capt. Whiteman, none would have escaped. None of the soldiers are known to have been severely wounded; but 3 are missing in the marshes and woods. We have since learned that there are signal Stations in that neighborhood – which ought to be brooken up. I would also earnestly recommend the burning of a dozen or 20 houses in accordance with *your* General Order No. 23.[1] Very respectfully Your obt. Servant

HLS

Edwd A. Wild

Brig. Gen. Edwd. A. Wild to Brig. Gen. G. F. Shepley, 1 Sept. 1864, Dept. of VA & NC, Records of Other Military Commands, ser. 731, Records of the War Records Office, RG 94 [GG-1].

1 On August 20, 1864, General George F. Shepley, commander of the District of Eastern Virginia, ordered that Confederate guerrillas thereafter captured in North Carolina north of Albemarle Sound and south and east of the Chowan River were to be treated as spies and not prisoners of war, and that citizens who aided the guerrillas would be imprisoned and, with permission from his headquarters, their houses burned. (General Orders No. 23, Head Quarters, District of Eastern Virginia, 20 Aug. 1864, Orders & Circulars, ser. 44, RG 94 [DD-36].)

CHAPTER 2

Lowcountry South Carolina, Georgia, and Florida

2

Lowcountry South Carolina, Georgia, and Florida

THE FEDERAL INVASION of the South Carolina coast in the fall of 1861 struck a powerful blow at slavery in the plantation South.[1] The arrival of Union soldiers in the Sea Islands around Port Royal Sound sent resident slaveholders, among the most prominent and self-conscious representatives of the Southern planter class, scurrying to the mainland. Perforce, it transformed into freedpeople the slaves who remained behind, although their freedom would not gain full standing until affirmed by legislative enactment and executive proclamation, backed by the force of the victorious Union army. The successful invasion created a Union enclave along the South Atlantic coast, and mainland slaves soon availed themselves of the possibility of freedom that the federal presence afforded. It also encouraged federal forces to launch raids up the rivers of the mainland, allowing still other slaves to reach freedom on the Union-held islands. But beyond the reach of occasional expeditions, slavery persisted. Indeed, the prospect of their slaves' escape to Union lines or liberation by Union raiders induced many lowcountry masters to refugee them to the upcountry, far from the possibility of successful flight. Thus, although the collapse of lowcountry slavery began early in the war, its final demise awaited the arrival of General William T. Sherman and his western armies in the final months of the conflict.

In the lowcountry, as in the Virginia and North Carolina tidewater, the evolution of freedom depended on the nature of slavery. Unlike Chesapeake slaves, who resided on small units, hired from farm to farm, and worked closely with free blacks and whites of all classes, slaves in lowcountry South Carolina, Georgia, and Florida lived on large rice and sea-island cotton plantations. They labored by the task under the direction of black drivers. Their overwhelming numerical preponderance and the absence of their owners during much of the year

---

[1] Published accounts of the collapse of slavery in the lowcountry include: Willie Lee Rose, *Rehearsal for Reconstruction: The Port Royal Experiment* (Indianapolis, 1964); Louis S. Gerteis, *From Contraband to Freedman: Federal Policy toward Southern Blacks, 1861–1865* (Westport, Conn., 1973), chap. 3; Clarence L. Mohr, "Before Sherman: Georgia Blacks and the Union War Effort, 1861–1864," *Journal of Southern History* 45 (Aug. 1979): 331–52.

allowed them a large measure of physical and cultural independence. By raising their own crops, poultry, and livestock after completing their tasks, and by selling their produce and stock to their masters, to each other, and to residents of nearby towns and cities, many lowcountry slaves accumulated property of their own. Control over provision grounds and participation in the region's internal economy gave their relative independence a material base. The special character of lowcountry slavery determined the shape of freedom as fully as did the wartime policies of Union and Confederate leaders.

The successful occupation of the islands around Port Royal Sound in November 1861 secured an important base for the federal blockading fleet and provided Union forces with their first beachhead in the plantation South. The Yankees did not come to the lowcountry as liberators. Both General Thomas W. Sherman and Flag Officer Samuel F. Du Pont, joint commanders of the federal expeditionary force, received explicit instructions from the War Department to protect existing property rights and "avoid all interference with the Social systems or local institutions." Although Sherman's orders permitted, even encouraged, him to avail himself of the service of "any persons, whether fugitives from labor or not" (much as General Benjamin F. Butler had done at Fortress Monroe), neither Sherman nor Du Pont showed much interest in the labor of fugitive slaves.

The sailors who came ashore at Beaufort on Port Royal Island bearing assurances that the masters' rights would be respected, found no masters to reassure. Mere rumors of a federal invasion had already driven many resident planters to the mainland. With the actual approach of the federal flotilla, slaveholders on Port Royal and the neighboring islands fled with as much of their movable property as they could carry, including that species of property that could be moved only at gunpoint. Many slaves refused to leave for the mainland, some defying their masters openly, most simply escaping into the marshes and woods in the confusion of the moment. Once their owners had gone, they returned to the plantations and celebrated, refurbishing their wardrobes from the masters' closets and refurnishing their homes from the masters' salons. Although suspicious of the white invaders, they greeted them warmly.

The manifest disloyalty of the fleeing planters and their known attachment to the secessionist cause led some federal commanders to disregard instructions about protecting slavery and instead to aid the slaves, who everywhere pressed for freedom. Patrolling the waters off Port Royal in the days following the invasion, Lieutenant Daniel Ammen, commander of a Union gunboat, found his ship besieged by slaves whose masters had run away. He informed them that the federal government "had not come for the purpose of taking them from their masters," but added that he would not make them "continue in a state of slavery." When he announced that they were "free to go to Beaufort or to Hilton Head," the fugitives promptly headed for the Union-occupied islands.

As Union gunboats extended their patrol, black fugitives darted from hidden inlets to the safety of federal ships. On more distant, outlying islands, naval officers found "abandoned" slaves who had begun to farm on their own. And, in the weeks and months that followed, additional slaves filtered into Union lines, first from assorted hideaways where they had taken refuge, and then from mainland plantations. Such escapes were never easy, especially while Confederate forces remained active on the islands, destroying guns and ginned cotton likely to fall into federal hands and recapturing fugitive and abandoned slaves. Confederate soldiers did not hesitate to shoot blacks who declined the invitation to return to their owners.[2]

During the winter and spring of 1861–1862, the ebb and flow of battle and the seasonal rhythm of lowcountry life provided slaves with new opportunities to gain freedom. On the federal side, amphibious expeditions expanded the Union beachhead beyond Hilton Head, St. Helena, Ladies, and Port Royal, the islands seized in the initial invasion. With the Union navy in firm control of the coastal waters, Union forces took Edisto Island to the north and conducted raids along the Georgia and Florida coast to the south, capturing the coastal town of Fernandina, Florida, in mid-March 1862 and Fort Pulaski, Georgia, at the mouth of the Savannah River, a month later. Union advances put many more blacks within Union lines and allowed slaves to ford the streams and creeks that separated the islands from the mainland. On the Confederate side, slave owners – following their regular seasonal migratory patterns – abandoned their plantations for the health and comfort of Charleston and Savannah at the onset of warm weather. With their masters gone, many lowcountry slaves traced familiar coastal waterways from the Confederate mainland to the Union-held Sea Islands.

A few mainland slaves left bondage with a flourish. In May 1862, Robert Small (later Smalls), along with other Charleston slaves, boarded the steamer *Planter* on which Small had worked as a pilot. Small donned the captain's hat, signaled the countersign to the Confederate harbor master, and cooly steered the ship to the safety of the Union blockade. He won a substantial prize along with his own and his

---

[2] Patrolling the islands north of Hilton Head, the commander of the U.S.S. *Seneca* reported in December 1861 that the "islands of Wadmalaw, John's, and some parts of North Edisto, are infested with gangs of rebel Cavalry, whose principal if not sole object is to drive the negroes into the interior." (Lieut. Danl. Ammen to Flag Officer Saml. F. Du Pont, 29 Dec. 1861, E-49, Correspondence of Comdr. Daniel Ammen, pp. 15–17, Letterbooks of Officers of the U.S. Navy at Sea, RG 45 [T-612].)

comrades' freedom, and he later used the notoriety gained through this exploit to launch a long and successful political career. Most slaves made the trip in considerably less style. Boarding flats or dugouts, often of their own making, they paddled silently past the Confederate sentries, posted – according to one observer – more to keep slaves in than Yankees out. Even when only a short distance separated fugitives from Union lines, Confederate patrols often drove slaves to the swamps, where for days, sometimes weeks, they waited for a safe moment to cross into Union-held territory. They reached federal lines tired and bedraggled, and frequently sick or wounded.

Even after entering Union lines, the fugitives' liberty remained at risk. The relative ease of passage between the mainland and the islands permitted Confederate forces to pass into federal territory no less readily than did runaway slaves. Whether new arrivals or old residents, blacks on the islands lived in constant fear of Confederate patrols, whose lightning raids might drag them back to slavery or destroy their houses and crops.

The Confederates' ability to counterattack revealed the weakness of the federal position in the lowcountry, where a chronic shortage of troops periodically required the abandonment of outlying islands. This recurrent necessity added to the insecurity of the fugitive slaves' life. Even a minor redeployment of Union forces left blacks exposed to Confederate attack; a major reshuffling could spell disaster. In the summer of 1862, as General George B. McClellan's Virginia offensive faltered, the War Department transferred soldiers from the lowcountry to bolster the Army of the Potomac. That forced the evacuation of Edisto Island, where more than 1,500 former slaves had congregated under federal protection, built houses, and planted crops. Union officers tried to relocate them elsewhere within the lines. But even those safely removed had to sacrifice houses and crops, while the less fortunate were left to fend for themselves in the face of now unopposed Confederate raids.[3]

A similar fate befell fugitives on St. Simon's Island, Georgia, which naval officers had established as a refugee settlement during the spring of 1862. The former slaves planted crops, set up a system of self-government, and began an independent life in freedom. The new life came to an abrupt end within a year, however, when the navy, unable to protect the island, had to uproot the settlement.[4]

Union naval superiority allowed federal soldiers and sailors to occupy several of the Georgia and South Carolina Sea Islands temporarily, to expand the federal toeholds around Fernandina and Key West, Florida,

---

[3] Rose, *Rehearsal for Reconstruction*, pp. 182–83.
[4] George A. Heard, "St. Simons Island during the War between the States," *Georgia Historical Quarterly* 22 (Sept. 1938): 249–72.

and to raid the mainland at will. But the attempt to take Charleston during the summer of 1863, and the continuing bombardment of Charleston harbor thereafter, again necessitated the redeployment of federal forces and the abandonment of exposed positions. In sum, the federal beachhead did not consistently extend far beyond Port Royal and the neighboring islands. Instead, much of the coastal plain south of Charleston was a kind of no man's land not effectively secured by either Confederate or Union military forces until after General William T. Sherman's arrival in the closing months of the war. Only at great risk could blacks continue to inhabit island and coastal areas distant from Port Royal.

Even the most secure Union positions did not guarantee a fugitive's liberty unless federal officials recognized it. From the first, not all Union officers welcomed blacks into their lines. Many were suspicious of the abandoned and self-liberated slaves, even those who provided valuable intelligence about Confederate fortifications and movements. Some commanders lacked a forthright commitment to emancipation and placed higher value upon potentially loyal slaveholders than upon demonstrably loyal slaves. This was especially true in Florida, where numerous slaveholders welcomed the arrival of federal forces and proclaimed their loyalty to the Union.[5] But in South Carolina and Georgia, the planters' hasty evacuation, their complete identification with the Confederate cause, and the slaves' demand for freedom sped the evolution of a federal commitment to emancipation. The early arrival of Northern missionaries, teachers, and plantation superintendents, eager to demonstrate the moral and economic superiority of free labor, added force to the claims of resident blacks.[6]

By early 1862, while General Thomas W. Sherman fretted about the growing number of fugitives, most federal officers in the lowcountry were accepting slaves into Union lines with few questions asked.[7] Both the army and the navy gave tacit recognition to the freedom of Sea Island slaves by paying them for their labor and purchasing their produce. Still the status of lowcountry slaves – those who stayed behind when their masters fled, as well as those who had but recently arrived – remained ill-defined. Because their masters had not had the opportunity to employ them in support of the rebellion, lowcountry blacks could not claim the First Confiscation Act as a legal basis for their freedom.

[5] Brig. Genl. H. G. Wright to Capt. L. H. Pelouze, 13 Mar. 1862, Letters Received, ser. 2254, SC Expeditionary Corps, RG 393 Pt. 2 No. 130 [C-1643]; [General David Hunter] to Brig. Gen. H. G. Wright, 18 June 1862, vol. 10 DS, p. 47, Letters Sent, ser. 4088, Dept. of the South, RG 393 Pt. 1 [C-1480].
[6] For a discussion of the role of Northern missionaries and plantation superintendents in the formulation of federal policy in the lowcountry, see *Freedom*, ser. 1, vol. 2.
[7] Brig. Genl. T. W. Sherman to the Adjutant General, 9 Feb. 1862, filed with S-1491 1862, Letters Received, ser. 12, RG 94 [K-126].

Whereas Sherman avoided any taint of emancipationist principles, his successor, General David Hunter, displayed them openly. Hunter assumed command of the new Department of the South (embracing South Carolina, Georgia, and Florida) at the end of March 1862. Taking over just after passage of the new article of war prohibiting the use of federal forces to return fugitives, he saw a chance to smite the slaveholding aristocracy and make his mark as the great emancipator. Shortly after arriving, he sought the War Department's permission to enlist Sea Island black men in the Union army, both to reinforce his short-handed command and to undermine slavery. When the department ignored his proposal, he began recruiting on his own authority.[8] In mid-April, he moved beyond military enlistment and liberated the slaves at recently captured Fort Pulaski, Georgia. In early May, proclaiming slavery incompatible with martial law, he declared "forever free" the slaves of South Carolina, Georgia, and Florida.[9]

Hunter's audacious policies displeased the Lincoln administration as profoundly as they pleased the black people of his department. Secretary of War Edwin M. Stanton overruled Hunter's enlistment policy and eventually forced him to disband his black Zouaves. Because Hunter's emancipation order challenged the administration's policy respecting slavery, it required an even more authoritative rebuke. Ten days after Hunter abolished slavery in the Department of the South, President Lincoln abolished Hunter's abolition, reasserting his own authority over the question of slavery, restating his commitment to gradual, compensated emancipation, and returning lowcountry blacks to their limbo between freedom and slavery.

Unrepentant, even in the face of presidential reprimand, Hunter pressed on. Although his emancipation proclamation was void, he continued to recruit slaves into the army, sometimes by force. This policy brought him into conflict with the former slaves and their missionary allies, who viewed military conscription as enslavement, and with conservative Northerners, who viewed military conscription as emancipation. None of this fazed the indomitable lowcountry commander. When a congressional resolution demanded an explanation for his unauthorized enlistment of fugitive slaves into the Union army, Hunter cited the original instructions to his predecessor as grounds "to employ all loyal persons offering their services in defence of the Union and for the suppression of this Rebellion in any manner I might see fit." He sarcastically reported that he in fact had no fugitive slaves under arms, but had enlisted "a fine regiment of persons whose late masters are 'Fugitive Rebels,'—men who everywhere fly before the

[8] *Freedom*, ser. 2: docs. 1–3.
[9] General Orders No. 7, Headquarters, Department of the South, 13 Apr. 1862, and General Orders No. 11, Head Quarters, Department of the South, 9 May 1862, Orders & Circulars, ser. 44, RG 94 [DD-28].

appearance of the National Flag, leaving their servants behind them to shift as best they can for themselves."[10]

By late summer 1862, Union policy had shifted in the direction espoused by Hunter. In July, Congress passed the Second Confiscation Act, which declared free the slaves of owners who supported the rebellion. Within a month, Captain Rufus Saxton, Hunter's circumspect quartermaster, received permission from the War Department to enlist black men, and Saxton quickly realized Hunter's dream of a slave army of liberation.[11] With the enactment of the Second Confiscation Act, with scores of well-connected Northerners focusing national attention on Port Royal, and with black men entering the Union army, the freedom of blacks in the Union-occupied lowcountry seemed assured.[12]

Spurred by these developments, some of Hunter's subordinates exercised their authority to promote freedom. In August, General Alfred H. Terry, commander of federal forces at Fort Pulaski, Georgia, and Key West, Florida, offered an ingenious interpretation of the March 1862 article of war that prohibited federal forces from returning fugitive slaves. He reasoned that "a slave whom his master cannot compel to remain in his household and render him obedience and service has '*escaped*' . . . and this escape is complete and perfect although the slave may remain in the vicinity of his master." On that basis, Terry forbade the use of military power to restore the authority of masters, ordered that slaves be taken away from masters who abused them, and declared the public use of violence to compel obedience a "disturbance of . . . public order," to be "promptly suppressed" by military force.

But as Terry's action revealed, slavery survived in occupied Florida even after passage of the Second Confiscation Act. Not until the Emancipation Proclamation of January 1, 1863, was the liberty of blacks secure in the Union-held portions of the lowcountry. After the proclamation, the federal government's commitment to freedom was no longer an issue in the region. Lincoln granted no exemption to Union-occupied South Carolina, Georgia, and Florida of the sort stipulated for portions of tidewater Virginia, for southern Louisiana, and for Tennessee. When Hunter left his post as commander of the Department of the South, his successors, including Generals Ormsby M. Mitchel, Quincy A. Gillmore, and John G. Foster, maintained policies aimed at pro-

---

[10] *Freedom*, ser. 2: doc. 3.

[11] *Freedom*, ser. 2: docs. 4–5.

[12] As commander of the Department of the South, Hunter enforced the confiscation acts to the letter. He disciplined subordinates who violated them even in spirit. (Col. Louis Bell to Major Genl. D. Hunter, 2 July 1862, B-331 1862, Letters Received, ser. 4109, Dept. of the South, RG 393 Pt. 1 [C-1302]; Asst. Adjt. Genl. to Col. Louis Bell, 12 July 1862, vol. 10 DS, pp. 148–49, Letters Sent, ser. 4088, Dept. of the South, RG 393 Pt. 1 [C-1302].)

moting freedom, if not for its own sake, then at least to satisfy their ever-expanding need for black soldiers and laborers.

Even after the Emancipation Proclamation clarified the legal status of the former slaves, making good a claim to freedom entailed battling long odds. When threats of punishment and tall tales about the Yankees failed to halt escapes, slaveholders and Confederate authorities substituted deeds for words, increasing surveillance, systematically destroying plantation boats or moving them inland, and taking great pains to capture and punish runaways. Some owners who had resisted pressure to remove their slaves to the interior finally concluded that they could not otherwise stem the drain of their labor force and arrest the deterioration of slavery.[13]

Owners who removed their slaves inland unintentionally seeded the upcountry with dissidents. Refugeed slaves not only broke for freedom themselves when they could, but also demoralized upcountry slaves by their subversive presence. Slaves who had no knowledge of the coast received directions from the newcomers about how to follow inland waterways to the sea and freedom. With determination and luck, they avoided rebel patrols and eventually reached federal lines. Union patrol boats regularly rescued slaves who had wandered in the swamps for weeks or even months. Some blacks safely within Union lines forsook protection and returned to Confederate territory to spirit others to freedom, creating what masters described as "a leaven of corruption in the mass."[14] The mainland thus became crisscrossed with mobile, unfettered blacks: those moving toward the coast in pursuit of freedom and those moving away from the coast in search of relatives and friends. The contagion of liberty spread over onto the mainland from the Union stronghold.

In late 1862 and early 1863, large-scale enlistment of black men into the Union army elevated the struggle for freedom in the lowcountry to a higher plane. Under the command of abolitionist officers, the black regiments organized on the South Carolina Sea Islands brought the war directly to their former masters, launching offensives from the coastal waterways. Colonel Thomas W. Higginson, who led raids along the Georgia coastal islands and up the St. Mary's River in early 1863, reported the "marked effect" produced by black soldiers carrying "the regimental flag and the President's Proclamation far into the interior." Hundreds of black men, women, and children accompanied Union soldiers to freedom in the Sea Islands, and others – learning of the new role they might play in the war against slavery – ran away on

[13] Christopher Flinn et al. to Hon. Jas. A. Seddon, [Mar. 1864], R-301 1864, Letters Received, ser. 12, Adjt. & Insp. Gen., RG 109 [F-332]. South Carolina had earlier passed legislation to enforce the removal of slaves from coastal areas, when removal was "required by the public interest." (*Official Records*, ser. 4, vol. 2, pp. 133–37.)
[14] See below, doc. 320.

their own to join the Union army. Some did not have to await formal enlistment to effect the transition from liberated to liberator. "As soon as we took a slave from his claimant," reported one regimental commander, "we placed a musket in his hand and he began to fight for the freedom of others." The newly liberated slaves made especially good soldiers, and Higginson believed that successful prosecution of the war depended on their rapid enlistment. He thought them far more deeply committed to the Union cause than white recruits, because "[i]nstead of leaving their homes and families to fight, they are fighting for their homes and families; and they show the resolution and the sagacity which a personal purpose gives."[15]

As had happened before, the raids produced a contradictory result, opening the door to freedom for some slaves while closing it for others. For every slave who gained liberty in the riverine raids, several more were consigned to bondage deeper within Confederate territory. But the participation of black recruits added a new dimension. Even when masters succeeded in hustling their slaves out of range of Union expeditions, raiding parties composed of black soldiers tarnished the slave owners' carefully cultivated aura of invulnerability. A number of slaves too far from Union lines to obtain federal protection or assistance took to the woods or swamps of the region, some joining maroon colonies of long standing. Other slaves formed quasi-military organizations of their own. Near the Crystal River on the Gulf coast of Florida, Confederate soldiers chased, captured, and killed several runaways who had been at large for more than nine months; the Confederates identified the leader of the group as a "Captain."[16] Elsewhere in Florida, shaken Confederate officials found black men organizing and drilling a militia company.

Not all blacks—not even all of those within easy reach of Union lines—left slavery on the mainland for freedom on the islands. Many chose to remain on the plantations. Fears sown by slaveholders that the Yankees had "*horns* and *tails*" and that they would abuse them or sell them to Cuba kept some bondsmen and women on the old estates.[17] Although the more extreme stories rapidly lost plausibility, others that fed upon a general suspicion of whites deterred many from flight. The actions of Union quartermasters and enlistment officers, whose meth-

---

[15] *Freedom*, ser. 2: doc. 207, also doc. 208; *Official Records*, ser. 1, vol. 14, pp. 191–92.
[16] See below, doc. 326.
[17] In February 1863, fugitive slaves coming into Union lines informed naval officers that others on the mainland who thought about fleeing to the Union lines "are still very uncertain, as to how they will be treated" and "believe the story of their masters" that the Yankees would sell them to Cuba. One man testified that "he was deterred from running away sooner by this." (Report of Capt. Drayton, 18 Feb. 1863, enclosed in S. F. Du Pont to Gideon Welles, [Feb. 1863], South Atlantic Squadron, Letters from Officers Commanding Squadrons, RG 45 [T-558].)

ods of recruiting laborers and soldiers often stopped little short of kidnapping, convinced some slaves that not much would be gained by exchanging one master for another. The occasional return to the plantation of a disenchanted fugitive reinforced this conviction, along with the master's sense of righteousness.[18]

More than fear and suspicion kept other able-bodied slaves from escaping to Union-held territory. Some stayed because they saw a chance to accomplish more by remaining on their own. With their masters gone, they could translate the limited freedom offered by the task system and possession of property into full-fledged independence. An independent black community on the old plantation had numerous attractions. On their provision grounds, slaves grew garden crops and raised fowl and other farm animals, some of which they sold locally. Many lowcountry slaves owned crops, household goods, and animals whose value totaled in the hundreds and occasionally in the thousands of dollars. Rather than risk the loss of a lifetime's work, some remained on the old estates to guard what was theirs. Indeed, many contended that their long years of labor gave them a proprietary right that went beyond their small personal holdings to embrace the entire plantation and its appurtenances. Not until the war threatened the safety and property of these slaves did the benefits of running away outweigh the risks, and the risks of staying on the old estates outweigh the benefits. When they chose to flee, they struggled to retain what they could of the property they had painstakingly accumulated. Union soldiers, raiding far up the rivers of the region, reported the shore lined with slaves surrounded by piles of household furnishings, herds of animals, and baskets filled with personal goods. The burden of such unwieldy baggage created obvious liabilities for fugitives who needed to travel light and move fast, and it kept many slaves close to home.

In December 1864, when General William T. Sherman's western armies neared Savannah, trailed by a mass of slaves who had joined them as they cut a swath through central Georgia, the faltering slave regime entered its final days in the lowcountry. Confederate troops evacuated Savannah, and most remaining masters and overseers in coastal Georgia fled for their lives, leaving the slaves behind to receive liberty at the hands of Sherman's "bummers." Anxious to disencumber his army of its black followers from the interior, as well as to provide for the newly liberated thousands on the coast, Sherman issued Special Field Order 15 in January 1865, setting aside the Sea Islands and the

[18] Some fugitives, disheartened by abuse at the hands of Union impressment agents and labor superintendents, returned to the mainland and gladly supplied Confederate forces with military intelligence. (See examination of James, 10 Nov. 1863, enclosed in Col. C. J. Colcock to Brig. Genl. Jordan, 11 Nov. 1863, C-570 1863, Letters Received, ser. 72, Dept. of SC, GA, & FL, Records of Military Commands, RG 109 [F-559].)

lowcountry coast between Charleston and the St. Johns River of Florida for the exclusive occupation of the freedpeople. The slaves who followed Sherman's army and the masters who fled at his approach thus pushed Sherman to announce an unprecedented policy of wartime land grants.[19]

Turning attention next to the long-awaited assault upon the heartland of secession, Sherman's army crossed the Savannah River in January 1865 and marched flamboyantly and relentlessly through the South Carolina upcountry, reaching North Carolina in early March with a train of several thousand South Carolina black refugees. As Confederate forces threw their remaining strength into obstructing Sherman's march, federal troops occupied Charleston and other lowcountry areas previously beyond the reach of the Union army. In the early months of 1865, the Union armies thus brought freedom to upcountry slaves and to lowcountry slaves hitherto untouched by the war, liberating as well many blacks who had been refugeed inland from the lowcountry. Upcountry slaveholders petitioned Confederate authorities, desperately trying to halt the massive exodus of their slaves, but, with the Confederacy in shambles, Southern leaders could hardly take notice. Blacks who had long been outside the war zone seized their chance to gain freedom, and the course of war pointed them to the lowcountry.

Sherman's advance radically altered the demography of the lowcountry. Thousands of whites left the region, fleeing at the rumor of his approach. In their place came thousands of upcountry slaves. Many of these blacks had previously resided in the region but had been refugeed to the interior; others were new to the lowcountry. The newcomers settled among the established black population and vied for the land that slaveholders had abandoned and that Sherman had granted to blacks.

While Sherman's arrival provided new opportunities for lowcountry slaves, these often came at a high price. In some areas, his army routed blacks from their homes and stripped them of the property they had painstakingly acquired during slavery and assiduously protected during the war. Union soldiers descended upon the plantations like "bees" or "blackbirds," wasting no time over fine distinctions between the property of the master and that of the slave. Following creation of the Southern Claims Commission in 1871, former slaves, like other Southern unionists, could seek compensation for possessions seized by the Union army for military purposes. Skeptical commissioners required former slaves to present elaborate evidence of their ownership of property taken by the army. Testimony before the commission provided the bittersweet occasion for some lowcountry freedpeople to recall their

---

[19] *Official Records*, ser. 1, vol. 47, pt. 2, pp. 60–62. For a discussion of the results of Sherman's order, see *Freedom*, ser. 3.

wartime service to the Union and to recount how they had gained ownership of themselves but lost their personal estates. As elsewhere in the South, slavery in the lowcountry ended with blacks in possession of their persons and little else but Sherman's pledge of land.

18: Assistant Secretary of War to the Commander of the South Carolina Expeditionary Corps

Copy.   War Department [*Washington*] October 14. 1861. Sir: In conducting military operations within States declared by the Proclamation of the President to lie in a State of insurrection, you will govern yourself, so far as persons held to service under the laws of such States are concerned, by the principles of the letters addressed by me to Major General Butler, on the 30' of May and the 8' of August, copies of which are herewith furnished to you.

Special directions, adapted to special circumstances cannot be given. Much must be referred to your own discretion as Commanding General of the Expedition.

You will, however, in general avail yourself of the services of any persons, whether fugitives from labor or not who may offer them to the National Government. You will employ such persons in such services as they may be fitted for; either as ordinary employees, or, if special circumstances seem to require it, in any other capacity, with such organization, in squads, companies or otherwise, as you may deem most beneficial to the service, this however not being a general arming of them for military services. You will assure all loyal masters that Congress will provide just compensation to them, for the loss of the services of the persons so employed.

It is believed that the course thus indicated will best secure the substantial rights of loyal masters and the proper benefits, to the United States, of the services of all disposed to support the Government, while it will avoid all interference with the Social systems or local institutions of every State, beyond that which insurrection makes unavoidable, and which a restoration of peaceful relations to the Union, under the Constitution will immediately remove. Respectfully

HLcSr   Thomas A. Scott.

Thomas A. Scott to Brigadier General T. W. Sherman, 14 Oct. 1861, filed with W-1290 1861, Letters Received, ser. 12, RG 94 [K-125]. Scott signed as "Acting Sec. of War." The enclosures mentioned are not filed with this copy. For letters of May 30 and August 8, 1861, from Secretary of War Simon Cameron to General Benjamin F. Butler, possibly drafted by Assistant Secretary of War Scott, see above, docs. 1B–C.

19: Commander of a Naval Landing Party to the Commander of the U.S.S. *Seneca*

Beaufort S.C [*November 8, 1861*]

Sir   In obedience to your orders I landed in the town of Beaufort, and found the place deserted by evry inhabitant with the exception of two, one of whom I was conducted to by the Negroes who were rejoiced to see me crowding down in large numbers and cheering the flag.   They told me that their masters had been firing at them and driving them back in the woods to prevent their communicating with the United States Forces, and I judged from their manner that they would commit any act of retaliation that opportunity offered.   They also stated that the Forces, formerly occupying St Phillips Fortifications, with the Beaufort Artillery had retired to Port Royal Ferry, ten miles distant from the town.

Mr Allen an old inhabitant of the place, but Northern by birth, met me at the entrance of his Store, much agitated and holding a flag of truce in his hand.   He Said, and I witnessed its corroboration that the Negroes were perfectly wild, breaking into evry building and destroying or carrying off all portable property, and that the Light Boats had been burned immediately after the Surrender of the Batteries.

Mr Wilcox, an other resident of the place was said to be in the town, but I did not find him, So brought Mr Allen on board –

An intelligent mulato boy dismounted from a horse he was riding and coming towards me said, "the whole County have left sir and all the soldiers gone to Port Royal Ferry," they did not think that you could do it Sir."

On close inquiry I judged that there must be at Port Royal Ferry at this time, or the time of the Negroes departure from there this morning, about a thousand troops and the Beaufort Artillery. Very Respectfully Your obedt Servt

ALS   J Glendy Sproston

Lieut. J. Glendy Sproston to Lieut. D. Ammen, [8 Nov. 1861], enclosed in Flag Officer S. F. Du Pont to Hon. Gideon Welles, 12 Nov. 1861, South Atlantic Squadron, Letters from Officers Commanding Squadrons, RG 45 [T-537]. According to another document in the same file, Flag Officer Samuel F. Du Pont, commander of the South Atlantic Squadron, had on November 8 ordered his officers to use "force in suppressing any excesses on the part of the negroes" and reminded them to "take pains to assure the white inhabitants that there is no intention to disturb them in the exercise of their private rights, or in the enjoyment of their private property." (Flag Officer S. F. Du Pont to Lieut. Napoleon Collins, 10 Nov. 1861.) Despite his order, some naval officers favored liberty. On November 9, 1861, while proceeding up the Beaufort River, the U.S.S. *Seneca*, commanded by Lieutenant Daniel Ammen, was boarded by fugitives fleeing from their masters. Ammen informed them that the federal forces "had not come for the purpose of taking them from their masters, nor of making them continue in a state of slavery; that they were free to go to Beaufort or to Hilton Head." The blacks promptly reboarded their canoes and headed for Beaufort, and Ammen informed his commander that "all of the blacks would come in to avoid being murdered." (Lieut. Danl. Ammen to Flag Officer Saml. F. Du Pont, 9 Nov. 1861, enclosed in Flag Officer S. F. Du Pont to Hon. Gideon Welles, 12 Nov. 1861, South Atlantic Squadron, Letters from Officers Commanding Squadrons, RG 45 [T-537].) Other of Du Pont's officers remained suspicious and thought the former slaves were "quite as likely to act in behalf of the rebels as the United States." (Lt. N. Collins to Flag Officer S. F. Du Pont, 11 Nov. 1861, enclosed in Flag Officer S. F. Du Pont to Hon. Gideon Welles, 12 Nov. 1861, South Atlantic Squadron, Letters from Officers Commanding Squadrons, RG 45 [T-537].)

20: Commander of the U.S.S. *Pawnee* to the Commander of the South Atlantic Squadron

Port Royal Harbour [*S.C.*] Dec[r] 9th 1861
Sir, In obedience to your order of the 4th inst. I proceeded to sea at daylight of the 5th, accompanied by the gun-boat Unadilla, Lt Com'd'g N. Collins, steamer Isaac Smith, L't Com'd'g J. W. A. Nicholson, and coast survey steamer Vixen, Capt. Boutelle, and reached the anchorage off the fort on Otter island, St. Helena sound, at mid-day. In the course of the afternoon, some negroes coming on board, and reporting that there was a body of soldiers at the entrance of Mosquito creek, a place up the Ashepoo, where the inland route to Charleston commences I proceeded as far as that place, when the night coming on, obliged me to return. I saw however, no signs of the presence of white people, excepting that some buildings, which I discovered the next day to have been on Hutchinson's island, were burning. On the morning of the 6th, the U.S.S. Dale, L't Com'd'g W. T. Truxton, appearing off the harbour, I sent the Isaac Smith, to tow her in, a pilot being furnished by Capt. Boutelle.

Unfortunately, however, when half way up, the Dale stuck fast, and as it was then about high water, no exertions could get her afloat until eleven oclock of that night, when she was forced into deep water, without having suffered any apparent injury, and towed the following morning, by Capt. Boutelle in the Vixen, around Morgan island, this having become necessary, owing to her having forced over the shoal which divides that channel from the one she was in originally. So soon as she was safely at her anchorage near us, I proceeded up the Ashepoo, with the Unadilla, Isaac Smith and Vixen, to examine that river further up than I had been able to do on the previous occasion. On approaching Mosquito creek, we saw a picket of soldiers, who took to their horses however, on our approach, and escaped into the woods, hastened perhaps in their flight, by a shot or two which were thrown after them. Continuing up the river, I landed on Hutchinson island, and found that two days before, all the negro-houses, overseer's house, and out-buildings, together with the picked cotton, had been burned. The attempt had at the same time been made to drive off the negroes, but many had escaped, although some of their number, they said, had been shot in attempting to do so. The scene was one of complete desolation; the smoking ruins, and cowering figures, which surrounded them, of those negroes who still instinctively clung to their hearth stones, although there was no longer there shelter for them, presented a most melancholy sight, the impression of which was made even stronger by the piteous wailing of the poor creatures, a large portion of whom, consisted of the old and decrepid. We were not able to leave until sometime after dark, and singular enough the moment we were fairly under way, a bright signal light was burned, on the very plantation we had just quitted, showing that some of the blacks, for there was certainly no white man there, were communicating the fact of our departure. On the following morning, with the same vessels, I started to explore the Coosaw river, but very soon after leaving, the Unadilla, unfortunately was completely disabled, by the breaking of a main cross head, and I was obliged to leave her at anchor, and continue/ on with the other two vessels. When off Fort Heyward, I left the Isaac Smith, it not being quite safe to take so long a vessel higher up, and continued in the Vixen, as far as the entrance of the Beaufort Creek, to a place called the Brick-yards, where I had been told, there was either a fort or a guard of soldiers. Nothing however being seen of either, I anchored off a plantation belonging to Mr. Bythewood close by, for the purpose of getting information, as I saw a great many negroes there.

On landing, I found that a short time previously the cotton house with its contents had been burned, and all of the negroes that could be caught had been taken away. Here were large numbers of those however who had left Hutchinson island after their houses had been burned, and who with their household effects piled up about them, lined the beach; some of them begging to be permitted to go to Otter island, saying that they had neither shelter nor food, were taken back with us.

Late in the afternoon, I returned down the river reaching our anchorage off Fort Otter at sunset, the Unadilla having been towed to the same place by the Isaac Smith. As I did not see that the services of the Pawnee were any longer necessary, in St. Helena Sound, and thinking it important to get the Unadilla as soon as possible to a place where her engines could be repaired, I determined this morning to tow that vessel to Port Royal Harbour, which I have done, reaching here, in company with the Vixen at half-past seven this evening.

In obedience to your instructions, before leaving, I transferred the charge of the fort and adjacent waters to L't Com'd'g Nicholson, who, with the Isaac Smith and Dale, will remain there until he receive further orders from yourself. Very Respy Your Obdt Servt

P. Drayton

As about a hundred and forty negroes, most of them in a very destitute condition, had collected at Otter island before my departure, I directed L't Com'd'g Nicholson to see that they were supplied with food until some disposition could be made of them, or until he heard from you. very Respy

ALS   P. Drayton

Commander P. Drayton to Flag Officer S. F. Du Pont, 9 Dec. 1861, enclosed in Flag Officer S. F. Du Pont to Hon. Gideon Welles, 12 Dec. 1861, South Atlantic Squadron, Letters from Officers Commanding Squadrons, RG 45 [T-540]. In an earlier report, Drayton had observed that Ashepoo River slaveholders had removed most of their slaves to the north side of the river, but that those slaves who remained were "very friendly." "They assisted us voluntarily, whenever we wanted their aid, and sometimes, as at Fort Heyward, worked very hard, and I overheard one of them say, that it was but fair that they should do so for us, as we were working for them." (Commr. P. Drayton to Flag Officer S. F. Du Pont, 28 Nov. 1861, enclosed in Flag Officer S. F. Du Pont to Hon. Gideon Welles, 1 Dec. 1861, South Atlantic Squadron, Letters from Officers Commanding Squadrons, RG 45 [T-539].)

21: Commander of the U.S.S. *Mohican* to the Commander of the South Atlantic Squadron

Copy   St Simons Sound [*Ga.*] March 30th 1862.
Sir   Since my communication of the 16th by the Potomska I have to report, that on the 17th with the Launches and another armed boat I

entered Jekyl Creek and proceeded to Dubignon's place, where I discovered a deserted battery of three guns to command that stream, and the remains of a camp of some two hundred men. A considerable quantity of cattle remained on the Island, but very wild on our approach.

. . . .

On the 22nd the Bibb made her appearance and Capt Boutelle at once commenced placing the Buoys for the Bar and Channel

Since then I have been some distance up the inside passage of St Simons Sound and landed in considerable force at Cooper's place, where we again found a quantity of cattle, but equally wild with those of Jekyl Island.

Contrabands continued to come to us. I sent a number by the Potomska to Fernandina and also several by the Connecticut. On the 26th I started for Brunswick to look to that place, and on my way up the river twenty seven more contrabands came to me. It now became necessary to obtain food for these people, as they mustered over forty men, women, and children, and both my provisions and those of the Pocahontas were getting low.

I was informed that a quantity of corn might be had on Colonel's Island opposite Brunswick, at a Mr Scarlets place. I proceeded there, and with the aid of the Contrabands, who in fact had belonged mostly to this Mr Scarlet, I procured one hundred & fifty bushels of corn, a quantity of peas, and sweet potatoes, with some cotton.

I also brought off tools for working the ground, corn sheller, and a mill for grinding corn; Colonels Island is separated from Fancy Bluff on the main land by a small stream, and at Fancy Bluff, we noticed the Rebel Pickets.

At sundown I threw two shells from the Pocahontas among them

The following morning on landing to finish our work we learned through one of the contrabands that the pickets had been increased to one hundred and fifty soldiers at Fancy Bluff.

We landed our field pieces and a strong force on Colonel's Island, and obtained what we needed, and that night after again firing a shell or two at Fancy Bluff, proceeded to St Simons.

Here I landed all the contrabands with their corn, and provisions, tools, &c and having housed them, have set them to work.

Already they have planted potatoes, tomorrow they begin to prepare the land for corn. They have set up their mill and I have told them they are to plant cotton and thus to become of use to themselves. They seem contented but without a vessel at the other end of the Island, they are in danger of being interfered with by soldiers landing in that direction and approaching them at night. St Simons is a fine rich island, about ten (10) miles long on the north end is a village, Fredrica. It is said to be healthy.

. . . .

A thousand Blacks could be usefully employed here, and made self supporting, such a colony properly managed would do much good. Those that are now here, some forty (40) in number live on T Butler Kings place and under cover of our guns. For the present then you will perceive that I have food such as the contrabands are accustomed to, to last sometime even with increased numbers coming in, but I would earnestly recommend the sending of another small vessel as stated above, at once, to Doboy Island. I do not know what your intentions are in regard to the Blacks, should they be continued here, corn and salt fish should be supplied them, until they can procure their own living from the land they are now tilling I am Very Respectfully

HLcSr   (signed) S W Godon

S. W. Godon to Flag Officer S. F. Du Pont, 30 Mar. 1862, enclosed in Flag Officer S. F. Du Pont to Hon. Gideon Welles, 6 Apr. 1862, South Atlantic Squadron, Letters from Officers Commanding Squadrons, RG 45 [T-542]. Ellipses in manuscript, which is an extract presumably selected by Flag Officer Samuel F. Du Pont.

22: Commander of the U.S.S. *Ottawa* to the Commander of Naval Forces near St. Mary's River, Florida

Off Mayport [*Fla.*] April 13th 1862
My dear Captain Upon consultation with Genl Wright who had orders to evacuate Jacksonville I withdrew the Naval Forces to this place, my reason being to prevent the destruction of property which belonged to Union people rendered probable by a conflict with the land forces of the rebels – of this I have informed the Flag Officer. At the same time when the Ellen returned the day before yesterday to Jacksonville to land Mr Burritt and family who had come on board the Ottawa for protection, I directed Capt Budd to display the white flag, only when appearing off the place, and to haul it down as soon as his mission was fulfiled, – this was done to signify to the enemy that we claimed and intended to hold if desireable posession of the entire River, and at the same time afford protection to the oppressed. It is it appears to me to be the wisest course to pursue for the present, but as the whole condition of

things have been changed by the evacuation of Jacksonville, I shall
go in a day or two with the Ottawa, Ellen and America to Port
Royal to learn the Flag Officers wishes and policy. You are aware
when we first entered the Sr Johns the Flag Officer intended and so
instructed me to make an armed reconnoissance as far as
Jacksonville— this accomplished, I was directed to return leaving a
vessel at the mouth of the River for blockading purposes, with
orders from the Com'dg Officer to report to you whatever
information he might have. These original instructions I shall now
act under and will leave here the Pembina.

This will be handed to you by I. L. Burritt Esqr, a personal
friend of mine and one of the most influential citizens of
Florida. He goes to Fernandina in company with several prominent
citizens all of whom I know have been quite peaceable and
unoffending citizens, who have taken no active part in the rebellion,
to endeavour to secure some property which has escaped from them,
in some of the transports which were at Jacksonville. Capt
Bankhead says he heard Genl Wright give the order, to put all the
negroes on shore before leaving, and that afterward they were
enticed on board by the soldiers, — of course our relations to the
subject are very delicate, but at the same time it appears to me to
be an easy matter for the Com'dg Officer, without taking any active
part in remanding them to allow owners to take them. I can assure
you, and so will Judge Burritt that the policy pursued by us in the
non-interference of property, was rapidly producing a reaction of
feeling which would in a short time have converted a majority of
the citizens of the State to the Union cause and now by refusing to
carry out this policy, I am very well satisfied that the great
advantages gained in securing the confidence of the people and
divesting them of erroneous impressions, will be more than lost, not
only as it effects the union cause here, but throughout the *South*. In
view of this, will you give Judge Burritt whatever assistance you can
in effecting the object of his visit. he has been of great service to
me in the attempt I made, and was doing so well toward effecting
in bringing back people to their senses. I am sorry to trouble you,
but the good of the cause, will I hope as a motive with me, be
Sufficient

I shall leave Bankhead, with an ample supply of provisions and
coal.

If you have any mails for us will you please send them to Port
Royal. A telegraph dispatch lately recv'd at Jacksonville, says
Beauregard after having driven Grant back near Corinth has in turn
retreated. Very truly Yours

HLcSr   T. H. Stevens

Lieut. T. H. Stevens to Commr. P. Drayton, 13 Apr. 1862, E-51, Letters Sent by Comdr. Thomas H. Stevens, pp. 44–46, Letterbooks of Officers of the U.S. Navy at Sea, RG 45 [T-638]. In contrast to Stevens's policy, Commander Percival Drayton, senior officer of Union naval forces at Fernandina, Florida, concluded that in view of the recent enactment of a new article of war prohibiting the use of military forces to return fugitives, "I could not allow a slave, even voluntarily, to return with his master, in a vessel under my control." (Comr. P. Drayton to Flag Offr. S. F. Du Pont, 4 Apr. 1862, E-37, Letters Sent by Comdr. Percival Drayton, pp. 175–77, Letterbooks of Officers of the U.S. Navy at Sea, RG 45 [T-656].) Lieutenant Daniel Ammen, commander of the U.S.S. *Seneca*, patrolling off Jacksonville, Florida, acted upon still another interpretation of the new article of war. Ammen remanded several fugitives to their master when he determined that the slaveholder was too old to fight, although his sons had recently joined the Confederate army – "having satisfied myself that his sons in the rebel service were not minors." But the following day, he gave free passage to eight fugitives whose owners had taken up arms against the Union. (Lieut. Danl. Ammen to Lieut. Comg. Thos. H. Stevens, 2 Apr. 1862, E-49, Correspondence of Comdr. Daniel Ammen, pp. 32–33, Letterbooks of Officers of the U.S. Navy at Sea, RG 45 [T-613].)

23: Commander of the South Atlantic Squadron to the Secretary of the Navy

Port Royal Harbor S.C May 14. 1862

Sir   I enclose a copy of a report from Commander E. G. Parrott, brought here last night by the late rebel Steamtug Planter, in charge of an officer and crew from the Augusta. She was the armed dispatch and transportation Steamer attached to the Engineer Department at Charleston under Brig: Genl: Ripley, whose barge a short time since was brought out to the Blockading Fleet by several contrabands. –

The bringing out of this Steamer under all the circumstances would have done credit to any one. At 4 in the morning, in the absence of the Captain who was on shore, she left her wharf close to the Government office and headquarters, with Palmetto and Confederate flag flying – passed the successive forts saluting as usual by blowing her steam whistle –   After getting beyond the range of the last gun, she quickly hauled down the rebel flags and hoisted a white one.

The Onward was the inside ship of the blockading fleet in the main channel & was preparing to fire when her commander made out the white flag –

The armament of the Steamer is a thirty two pounder on pivot and a few 24 p howitzer. She had beside on her decks four other guns, one 7 inch rifled, which were to be taken, the morning of the escape, to the new fort on the middle ground. One of the 4 belonged to Fort Sumpter and had been struck in the rebel attack on that fort on the muzzle. Robert the intelligent Slave and Pilot of the boat who performed this bold feat so skilfully, informed me of this fact, presuming it would be a matter of interest to us to have possession of this gun.

This man, Robert Small, is superior to any who have yet come into the lines, intelligent as many of them have been — His information has been most interesting and portions of it of the utmost importance —

The steamer is quite a valuable acquisition to the Squadron by her good machinery and very light draft — The officer in charge brought her through St. Helena Sound and by the inland passage down Beaufort river arriving here at 10 last night —

On board the Steamer when she left Charleston were Eight men, five women and three children —

I shall continue to employ Robert as a Pilot on board the Planter for the inland waters with which he appears to be very familiar —

I do not know whether in the views of the Government the vessel will be considered a prize but if so, I respectfully submit to the Department the claims of this man Robert & his associates. Very Respectfully Your Obed. Servt

HLS

S. F. Du Pont

Flag Officer S. F. Du Pont to Hon. Gideon Welles, 14 May 1862, South Atlantic Squadron, Letters from Officers Commanding Squadrons, RG 45 [T-544]. Enclosure. The Navy awarded the blacks who abducted the *Planter* $4,584, half the appraised value of the ship, of which Small received $1,500. (Rear Admiral S. F. Du Pont to Hon. Gideon Welles, 19 Aug. 1862, South Atlantic Squadron, Letters from Officers Commanding Squadrons, RG 45 [T-553].) Small (later, Smalls) continued to serve on the *Planter* to the end of the war, first as pilot at $50 per month, and then as captain at $150 per month. (Alex J. Perry to Hon. Robert Smalls, 3 Jan. 1883, "Planter," Consolidated Correspondence File, ser. 225, RG 92 [Y-48].)

24: Proclamation by the President

Washington this nineteenth day of May, in the year of our Lord
one thousand eight hundred and sixty-two
By the President of the United States of America.
A Proclamation.

Whereas there appears in the public prints, what purports to be a proclamation, of Major General Hunter, in the words and figures following, to wit:

Head Quarters Department of the South,
Hilton Head, S.C. May 9, 1862.
General Orders N° 11. – The three States of Georgia, Florida and
South Carolina, comprising the military department of the south,
having deliberately declared themselves no longer under the
protection of the United States of America, and having taken up
arms against the said United States, it becomes a military necessity
to declare them under martial law. This was accordingly done on
the 25th day of April, 1862. Slavery and martial law in a free
country are altogether incompatible; the persons in these three
States – Georgia, Florida and South Carolina – heretofore held as
slaves, are therefore declared forever free.

(Official) David Hunter,
Major General Commanding.

Ed. W. Smith,
    Acting Assistant Adjutant General.

And whereas the same is producing some excitement, and
misunderstanding; therefore
    I, Abraham Lincoln, President of the United States, proclaim and
declare, that the government of the United States, had no
knowledge, information, or belief, of an intention on the part of
General Hunter to issue such a proclamation; nor has it yet, any
authentic information that the document is genuine – And further,
that neither General Hunter, nor any other commander, or person,
has been authorized by the Government of the United States, to
make proclamations declaring the slaves of any State free; and that
the supposed proclamation, now in question, whether genuine or
false, is altogether void, so far as respects such declaration.
    I further make known that whether it be competent for me, as
Commander-in-Chief of the Army and Navy, to declare the slaves of
any State or States, free, and whether at any time, in any case, it
shall have become a necessity indispensable to the maintenance of
the government, to exercise such supposed power, are questions
which, under my responsibility, I reserve to myself, and which I
cannot feel justified in leaving to the decision of commanders in the
field. These are totally different questions from those of police
regulations in armies and camps.
    On the sixth day of March last, by a special message, I
recommended to Congress the adoption of a joint resolution to be
substantially as follows:
    Resolved, That the United States ought to co-operate with any
State which may adopt a gradual abolishment of slavery, giving to
such State pecuniary aid, to be used by such State in its discretion,
to compensate for the inconveniences, public and private, produced
by such change of system.
    The resolution, in the language above quoted, was adopted by

large majorities in both branches of Congress, and now stands an authentic, definite, and solemn proposal of the nation to the States and people most immediately interested in the subject matter. To the people of those States I now earnestly appeal— I do not argue, I beseech you to make the arguments for yourselves— You can not if you would, be blind to the signs of the times— I beg of you a calm and enlarged consideration of them, ranging, if it may be, far above personal and partizan politics. This proposal makes common cause for a common object, casting no reproaches upon any— It acts not the pharisee. The change it contemplates would come gently as the dews of heaven, not rending or wrecking anything. Will you not embrace it? So much good has not been done, by one effort, in all past time, as, in the providence of God, it is now your high privilege to do. May the vast future not have to lament that you have neglected it.

In witness whereof, I have hereunto set my hand, and caused the seal of the United States to be affixed.

Abraham Lincoln

HDS

Proclamation by Abraham Lincoln, 19 May 1862, #90, Presidential Proclamations, ser. 23, RG 11 [QQ-1].

25A: Commander of the U.S.S. *Dale* to the Commander of the South Atlantic Squadron

St Helena Sound S.C. June 13th 1862

Sir; This morning at 4 o'clock it was reported to me that there was a large fire on Hutchinson's Island, and shortly after that a preconcerted signal that the enemy were in the vicinity had been made from the house of our Pilot. I immediately started in the gig accompanied by the tender "Wild Cat," Boats'n Downs, Launch, Act'g Mid'n Terry, 1ˢᵗ Cutter, Act'g Master Billings, 2ᵈ Cutter, Act'g Master Hawkins, and 3ᵈ Cutter Cox'n Shurtleff, up Horn, or Big River Creek, in the direction of the fire. Soon after leaving the ship a canoe containing three negroes was met, who stated that the rebels, three hundred strong were at Mrs. March's plantation killing all the negroes

As we advanced up the creek we were constantly met by canoes with two or three negroes in them, panic stricken, and making their way to the ship while white flags were to be seen flying from every inhabited point around which were clustered groups of frightened fugitives. When about two and half miles from Mrs March's, I was obliged to anchor the "Wild Cat" from the want of sufficient water in the channel with orders to be ready to cover our retreat if necessary.

On arriving at Mrs. March's the scene was most painful; her dwelling and chapel were in ruins, the air heavy with smoke, while at the landing were assembled over one hundred souls, mostly women and children in the utmost distress. –

Throwing out a picket guard, and taking every proper measure against surprise, I satisfied myself that the enemy were not in our immediate neighborhood, the negroes assuring me that they had left the island and returned to Fort Chapman. –

I then gathered the following particulars: The rebels during the night landed on the island from Fort Chapman with a force of unknown numbers and guided by a negro who for a long time had been on Otter Island in the employ of the army, surrounded the house and chapel in which a large proportion of the negroes were housed, posting a strong guard to oppose our landing.

At early dawn they fired a volley though the house; as the alarmed people sprang nearly naked from their beds and rushed forth frantic with fear, they were shot, arrested or knocked down. The first inquiry of the rebels was for the "d----d Yankees," and at what time we were in the habit of visiting the Islands, mingled with exclamations of "be quick boys the people from the ship will be up," – "Lets burn the houses," – "Not yet, they will see the fire from the ship and come up." –

Having collected most of the chickens and despoiled many of the poor people of their very wretched clothing, and telling them that as they belonged to the estate or others nearly adjoining they would not molest them, they fired the buildings and fled. –

As the people were clamorous to be removed I filled the boats with them and pulled down to the Tender on board of which they were placed. On our return for the remainder they were observed as we approached the landing to be in the utmost confusion, dashing wildly into the marshes and screaming, "the Secesh are coming back;" on investigation however it proved to be that the enemy in full sight about two miles off crossing an open space of ground were in hasty retreat instead of advancing. On our first visit they must have been concealed in a patch of woods not more than half a mile from our pickets. –

Having succeeded in removing or in providing with boats all who wished to remain to collect their little property, I returned to the ship bring with me about seventy, among them one man literally riddled with balls and buck shot; (since dead); another shot through the lungs and struck over the forehead with a clubbed musket laying the bone perfectly bare; one woman shot in the leg, shoulder, and thigh; one, far gone in pregnacy, with dislocation of the hip joint and injury to the womb caused by leaping from a second story window, and another, with displacement of the cap of the knee, and injury of the leg from the same cause. –

It appears that the negro who guided the party had returned to them after the evacuation of this place, told them all the troops had been withdrawn and that the Islands were entirely unprotected except by this ship; I am therefore at a loss to account for their extreme barbarity to negroes, most of whom were living on the plantation where they had been born, peacefully tilling the ground for their support, which their masters by deserting had denied them, and who were not even remotely connected with the hated Yankee. –

I would respectfully request that whenever one of the light draft steamers, such as the Planter, or the Ellen, can be spared for a day or two she may be allowed to visit this place. The Tender is, owing to the prevalence of sea breezes, almost useless in the narrow creeks except in advancing. – The occasional trip of a small steamer up the Ashepoo would make the wooding and watering of this ship less hazardous.

I trust you will approve my sending the contrabands to Hilton Head: had I not been unable to provide for such a large number, and so much embarrassed by the frequent demands made upon me for provisions by new arrivals, I should have waited for your orders in the matter. –

Last Tuesday we had an arrival of thirty from the main-land, and scarce a day passes without one or more arrivals always in a half-starved condition, whose appeals for food I have not yet been able to resist, though trespassing rather largely on the ships stores. All the new arrivals give the same account of the want and scarcity of provisions among the white population, and of their own dangers and sufferings in effecting their escape. –

Though exercising no control over the negroes on the neighboring islands I have, ever since the withdrawal of the troops, urged them to move to Edisto or St. Helena, and warned them that some night they would be visited by the rebels, but the majority insisted on remaining because it was their home while all seemed to have the most perfect faith in the protection of the ship though perhaps as was the case last night, ten or twelve miles distant from her. Very Respectfully Your obdt. servant

HLcSr   (signed) W. T. Truxtun

Lieut. W. T. Truxtun to Flag Officer S. F. Du Pont, 13 June 1862, enclosed in Flag Officer S. F. Du Pont to Hon. Gideon Welles, 16 June 1862, South Atlantic Squadron, Letters from Officers Commanding Squadrons, RG 45 [T-548].

25B: Commander of a Confederate Cavalry Battalion to the Headquarters of the 3rd Military District of the Confederate Department of South Carolina, Georgia, and Florida

Chisholmville [S.C.] June 14th 1862.

Lieut, I beg to report that on the night of 12th, inst. I advanced in three boats with 105 men, – being detachments from Capts Mulligan, Smith and Davis companies – against north end of Hutchinsons Island. From drums heard, I was confident the enemy were there. I approached the settlement and deployed as skirmishers. Before the proper positions assigned had been obtained, the negro watchman gave alarm and a general rush was made to pass the skirmishers, when, after proper halting and warning, entirely disregarded, I ordered men to fire before I discovered they were negroes. Some ten were killed and ten or fifteen wounded. Satisfying myself they were negroes, which from high brush, corn waist high and the darkness of night was very difficult, I ordered the firing ceased. I closed up and found some 125 negroes there, with various kinds of provisions, say corn, bacon, beef &c, doubtless found them by enemy. not being able to procure any transportation, I ordered fire to be applied to houses, which before I left had destroyed about everything. a few muskets found were destroyed. The director or overseer with his wife, the latter teaching the negroes) had left for Beaufort the day before. The enemy some two hundred in number had left the island on Sunday previous. As gunboats were just below and three of them moving up, and my retreat could have been cut off.

I left island so soon as all provisions &c were well destroyed. Three gunboats now lie between Chapman's Fort and Hutchinson's Island, but seem to have no disposition to move up to the mainland, they were engaged some little time yesterday in shelling the island. I noticed planted some 250 acres corn, 25 acres potatoes and 10 acres peanuts and was told cotton was planted in quantity higher up on island. The fine condition of the planted crops indicates conclusively, the direction of the negroes by some white person or persons. I shall make another move in different direction in day or two. I have the honor to be respectfully Your obedient servant.

HLcSr

R. J. Jeffords

Major R. J. Jeffords to Lt. E. H. Barnwell, 14 June 1862, vol. 14, p. 38,
Documents Printed in *The War of the Rebellion*, ser. 4, General Records CSA,
RG 109 [F-1113].

26A: Commander of U.S. Forces at Fort Pulaski, Georgia, and Key West, Florida, to the Commander of the Island of Key West, Florida

Key West, Fla., Aug 14th 1862

Colonel, A considerable number of the inhabitants of Key West are
negroes, who either have been held, or are now held, in slavery. It
is therefore probable that cases involving the relation of master and
slave will from time to time come before you for decision. The
following rules are established for your guidance in such cases.

1st No aid will be given to any master to enable him to compel
his slave to obey him or to labor for him. By the Act of Congress
approved March 13th 1862, "All officers or persons in the military
or naval service of the United States are prohibited from employing
any of the forces under their respective commands for the purpose of
returning fugitives from labor or service, who may have escaped
from any person to whom such labor or service is claimed to be
due." A slave whom his master cannot compel to remain in his
household and render him obedience and service has *"escaped"* from
his master, and this escape is complete and perfect although the
slave may remain in the vicinity of his master If in such cases the
military power compels the labor and obedience of the slave, if it
restores the authority and control of the master it "returns" an
"escaped" slave and violates the law of the land.

2nd Enquiry will be made into all cases of alleged cruel treatment
of slaves, and punishment will be promptly inflicted upon those
who may be guilty of it. The proper punishment of this offense,
and the best precaution against its repetition is to remove the slave
from his master's custody and control. Aggravated cases may
require still further punishment. It is the duty of all Governments
whether civil or military to forbid and punish cruelty and
inhumanity within their jurisdiction.

3rd The slaves of all persons who have fled from Key West for
the purpose of joining in or aiding the rebellion, and of all persons
known to be in arms against the United States, will be regarded as
abandoned by their masters, and no agent or representation of their
masters will be permitted to control or interfere with them, or to

receive in behalf of their principals any portion of the fruit of the labor of such slaves.

4th Violence *publicly* offered by one person to another; whether that other be a slave or freeman, and in the case of a slave, whether it be for the purpose of compelling obedience and enforcing service, or for any other purpose, is a disturbance of that public order which, where Martial Law prevails, it is the duty of the military power to maintain, and it will be promptly suppressed. I have the honor to be Colonel Most Respectfully Your Obt. Servt.

HLcSr   (Signed) Alfred H. Terry

Brig. Genl. Alfred H. Terry to Colonel [James S. Morgan], 14 Aug. 1862, enclosed in Brig. Genl. Alfred H. Terry to Lt. Col. W. P. Prentice, 2 Oct. 1862, T-533 1862, Letters Received, ser. 4109, Dept. of the South, RG 393 Pt. 1 [C-1310].

26B: Commander of the Island of Key West, Florida, to the Commander of U.S. Forces at Fort Pulaski, Georgia, and Key West, Florida

Copy   Island of Key West Fla Sep 12th 1862
General   I have the honor to transmit to you herewith a copy of General Order No "50" issued by me in reference to the employment of Persons of African Descent in the Service of the United States.

Owing to the prevailing Epidemic and the large number of sick, I have been compelled in justice to my command to obtain the services of Persons of African descent for the Hospitals as attendants and nurses – to dig graves – and for the Quartermasters Department.   The colored persons wanted have freely offered themselves for such work as required.   A question has now arisen in connection with this matter on the part of L[t] M[c]Farland of the Eng' Corps in charge of the work on Government Fortifications at this Post.

He has had and still retains many Slaves in his employ whose wages he pays to their masters or agents – as you will see by the communication forwarded in relation to Mr C. Howe.   Among the number are some of Judge Douglas's who is known to be in the Confederate States –   These negroes so employed by Lieut M[c]Farland are constantly coming to Headquarters and endeavoring to obtain employment there –   They state that they will not work for Lieut

MFarland, and I see no authority vested in me to compell them to do so. at the same time I have refused to employ them in the Department before mentioned untill discharged by Lieut MFarland.

I have conferred with Lieut MFarland upon the subject and shown him my orders and those of the President and requested that he should keep an accurate account of the time that such Slaves were employed and not to pay their wages over to masters or agents, if so I would compell such persons of African descent to work in his Department.

Lieut MFarland has declined to act in this manner untill he has received orders from his proper Department—

I respectfully request your instructions, and of such nature as will relieve me from my present embarrasment, as circumstances at this Post call for a large amount of Labor, and entire unity of action on the part of the Officers in charge of the different Departments of this Command—particularly as refers to persons held to bondage—by disloyal residents many of whom having left the Key. I feel fully satisfied the course I am pursuing in the carrying out of the accompanying orders that I shall soon be able to discover who among the residents of this place are Loyal at heart—and who are rebel sympathizers as I have already several arrested and confined in Fort Taylor, for disloyal sentiments expressed since the issuing of this order, who I will release by your kind permission after receiving due punishment. I have the honor to be Sir most respectfully Your Obᵗ Serᵗ

HLcSr

(signed) Jaˢ S. Morgan

Col. Jas. S. Morgan to Brig. Genl. A. H. Terry, 12 Sept. 1862, Letters Received, ser. 4109, Dept. of the South, RG 393 Pt. 1 [C-1312]. General Order 50 provided that blacks employed by the United States government within Morgan's command ("including those held to service or labor under State Laws") "shall receive permanent military protection against any compulsory return to a condition of servitude." (General Order No. 50, Head Quarters, Island of Key West, Fla., 3 Sept. 1862, vol. 66/222 DFla, General Orders, ser. 2271, Island of Key West, RG 393 Pt. 1 [C-375].) A few weeks later, General Alfred H. Terry, commander of Union forces at both Key West, Florida, and Fort Pulaski, Georgia, forwarded a copy of Morgan's letter, along with Morgan's General Order 50, his own earlier instructions to Morgan (doc. 26A, above), and other related material to the headquarters of the Department of the South, requesting guidance in dealing with Lieutenant McFarland's contraband policy. (Brig. Genl. Alfred H. Terry to Lt. Col. W. P. Prentice, 2 Oct. 1862, Letters Received, ser. 4109, Dept. of the South, RG 393, Pt. 1 [C-1310].) No response has been found in the records of Terry's command or among the copies of letters sent in the records of the Department of the South.

27: Headquarters of the Confederate Department of South Carolina, Georgia, and Florida to the Confederate Commander at Adams Run, South Carolina

Charleston Aug 16— 1862

Genl— I am directed by the Maj Genl comdg' to say he desires you should make a reconnaisance (using the "Rebel Troop") up the country around Summerville S.C. He has been informed that much disturbance and alarm is caused by gangs of run away negroes, leagued with deserters, in that neighborhood. the report of such reconnaissance will be made to these H^d Qrs

HLcSr   (Sig) R. W. Memminger

A.A.G. R. W. Memminger to Brig. Gen. Johnson Hagood, 16 Aug. 1862, ch. II, vol. 22, p. 46, Letters Sent, Dept. of SC, GA, & FL, Records of Military Commands, RG 109 [F-159]. No report of the reconnaissance has been found in either the records of the Confederate Department of South Carolina, Georgia, and Florida, or the papers of General James C. Pemberton (department commander at the time) in the Confederate collection of generals' papers.

28: Statement by a Georgia Fugitive Slave

[*Beaufort, S.C.?, September 1862*]

Robert Blake, born in Coosawhatchie S^o C^a about 19 ys of age, waiter—(colored)— I left Savannah on Sunday night Sept 21 /62 at 10 30 P.M., in Company with three others,— We came down Back River into the Main Channel & so on down to Fort Pulaski, which we reached on Monday morng early—

In Savannah there are between five & six thousand troops— At Cranstons Bluff there are three Co^s— At Fort Lee there are about 500 men & eight guns— At Fort Boggs there are about 425 men, & 12 guns— At Fort Jackson one $Comp^y$ and ten guns— At Thunderbolt Battery 3 guns & 1500 men— All the pickets from St Augustine Creek are removed;— About one mile from Fort Lee there is an earthwork thrown up, but no guns mounted, & this is the only obstruction to be met with on the Shell Road until you get clean into the City.—

As soon as the "Fingall" is ready, which will be in about three weeks, she is to come down with the Floating Battery to be used against Ft. Pulaski under the command of Commodore Tatnall; The "Fingall" is pierced for ten guns, & has them all mounted, and the "Floating Battery" six guns mounted, all of the heaviest calibre, two of them being rifled –

I have heard that the "Nashville" lays at "Genesee Point" waiting to go out, but don't know of my own knowledge –

Coffee #2.50 lb– Tea $12. lb Sugar $1. lb Salt $1.50 qrt: Butter $1. lb. Fresh Beef 35¢.

Fort Augustus, mounting six guns, is situate on Fig Island, near the mouth of Back River, which is the only place her guns command –

On the Ogeechee Road, about two miles from the river bank, is two batteries one mile apart, one mounting six & the other five guns, on the first is 200 men & on the other are only 80 – This road is then all clear to the City –

A good point of attack would be to go up the Ogeechee River land at Harbishon's Plantation, strike the White Bluff Road, for about eight miles, when you come to Harrisons Battery, mounting 10 heavy guns & 2 mortars manned by 1100 men, commanded by Col. Harrison, & by walking over this Battery, two miles & a half more, will bring you into the City of Savannah. –

Roads all good, and solid enough for any kind of artillery –

HD

Statement by Robert Blake, [Sept. 1862], Letters Received by the Provost Marshal, ser. 4277, Provost Marshal General, Dept. of the South, RG 393 Pt. 1 [C-1539].

29: Commander of the 3rd Military District of the Confederate Department of South Carolina, Georgia, and Florida to the Headquarters of the Confederate Department of South Carolina, Georgia, and Florida

Official   Pocotaligo [*S.C.*] Nov. 18th 1862
General. Major Jeffords writes me that "he considers the removal of the negroes of Mr Warren, a planter on the Ashepoo River, who are below his pickets, and from incontestable proof in continual intercourse with the enemy, as necessary to the safety of his Videttes." These negroes, he says, are not more than eight in number, and the plantation is to all intents and purposes abandoned.

133

The proprietor has, on a request, refused to remove them. I therefore, respectfully ask authority to do so forcibly, if necessary, since I regard their removal as importantly connected with the safety of that part of my command. Very Respectfully Your obdt Servt
HLcSr   (Signed) W. S. Walker

Brig. Genl. W. S. Walker to Brig. Genl. Thomas Jordan, 18 Nov. 1862 filed with R-1421 1863, Letters Received, ser. 12, Adjt. & Insp. Gen., RG 109 [F-308]. According to other documents in the same file, the department commander promptly approved Walker's request, and Walker's adjutant instructed Major Jeffords to accomplish the forcible removal of the Warren slaves. "Should they return afterwards," he added, "they will be seized, and sent to the jail in Charleston." (Chief of Staff Thomas Jordan to General, 20 Nov. 1862; A.A.A. Genl. Ed. H. Barnwell to Major R. J. Jeffords, 21 Nov. 1862.) A full year later, Walker was still removing blacks from plantations near Union lines, on the grounds that they regularly supplied the enemy with valuable military intelligence. In one instance, he sent a scout "who pretended to be a Yankee" to test "one or two old negroes near the enemy's lines." "They gave him all the information an enemy could desire in regard to the position & strength of my pickets. They were therefore removed." (A.A.I.G. E. W. Fraser to Comdg. Officer of Out Posts, 7 Nov. 1863, in the same file.)

30: Commander of Confederate Forces on Sullivan's Island, South Carolina, to the Commander of the 1st Military District of the Confederate Department of South Carolina, Georgia, and Florida

Sulls Island [*S.C.*] 9^{nth} Jan 1863
General –   In obedience to your orders, I started on Monday 5th inst. to examine the Country and inspect the troops and their positions between Mount Pleasant and South Santee River –
I do not think that any demonstration against Charleston by troops moving through St James Santee and Christ Church Parishes are to be apprehended –   The facilities for defence, against such a movement, are too numerous and conclusive –
There are, however, great facilities for plundering expeditions from the enemy's fleet off the Bar or from forces on Bull's Island; and also for the escape of negroes from both Christ Church and St James Parishes –   I think that these are to mainly guarded against in the disposition of the Troops –
The whole extent of the Country is either penetrated or touched, at short distances, by large creeks running in from the deep water of some one of the various bays which stretch from Charleston to the

Santee River. All of these creeks must be guarded, or Barges and Small Boats can easily approach the land, or go from the land to the adjacent Islands (Bulls, Dewees &c), or to the enemy's fleet. A number of negroes, intimately acquainted with the network of Bays, Inlets, creeks and narrows along the coast, have deserted to the Enemy, and are known to have passed frequently betwean the fleet or the Islands and the Parishes of Christ Church and St James Santee — The defence of the coast against small incursions, or the escape of negroes, is made still more difficult by the fact that, for long distances, a Barge or Small Boat can land any where at high tide —

To patrol and guard the Coast there are three Cavalry Companies (viz, Capts Aiken's Whilder's and Pinckney's) and two infantry Companies from the 26th Regt — The third company is stationed at Ft Warren, high up on the Santee River — There is at McClellanville an artillery Company in addition — This force is greatly inadequate to patrol the Coast but as it is all that probably can be furnished, I looked only to its judicious distribution — Picketts are stationed at Porchers, Toomers, Whitesides, at Palmetto Point, Andersonville, the Grove Grahams creek, at Buck Hall, Seve Hall, Colburn's, DuPree's, Blake's, and McClellanville — I would suggest that a pickett be placed at Rabun's Place, if it be practicable — Capt Aiken discontinued that pickett on account of lack of men — The duty is already very severe — The privates are on duty every alternate night — There should be a day pickett at Buck Hall as well as a night Pickett — There is a section of Artillery at Graham's Creek, I advise its removal to Andersonville, as the latter place is much more exposed, and is also more central — Graham's creek can be covered by a few riflemen, and needs only a few rifle pits —

I would recommend the construction of a fixed Battery on Blake's Place, South Santee River — Two or three 24 pound guns would cover the River, and close it against all but Iron clad Boats — The planters there will gladly furnish the labor — I am well informed — If this were done, and a supporting company sent up, two out of the four pieces of artillery now at McClellanville could easily be spared from that place — A Pickett should be stationed at Venning's place, a few miles from Mt Pleasant, I recommend that a company from Col Wilson's Regiment of reserves be sent there —

I would also suggest the removal of all the small Boats from the Wando River — They can easily be carried from the Wando to the Beach and made available for the escape of negros — The width of land is about three miles, and on most of the plantations there is no white person — Waggons and Teams may readily be used by the negroes to transport boats — I believe that there are continual

135

inducements to the negros to desert to the enemy, and the promptest and most effectual precautions, in my judgement, should be adopted – I have the honor to be – General, Very Respectfully &c

ALS   Lawrence M Keitt

Col. Lawrence M. Keitt to General, 9 Jan. 1863, #61 1863, Letters Received, ser. 72, Dept. of SC, GA, & FL, Records of Military Commands, RG 109 [F-1015]. Endorsements.

31: Florida State Senator to the Commander of the Confederate District of East Florida

East bank St. Johns near Palatka [*Fla.*], April 2^d, 1863. Sir: – On Monday the 23^d ult. a large side-wheel steamer came up the River as far as Palatka, and fired four shells over the town. She then returned to Orange Mill, and lay off that place until 2 o'clock Tuesday evening, and went down the River. Whilst at the Mill the Yankees butchered a Beef, killed several sheep; and took on board a negro man named *John*, belonging to Mr. Frank. Hernandez.

On Thursday morning, a large propeller came up the River, and lay off the Mill, until evening, when she came up opposite Palatka, abreast of the residence of Mr. Antonio Baza. A large force of negroes was landed from the propeller at the residence of Mr. C. Dupont, and also at Orange Mill, which said force marched by land to Mr. Baza's and Mr. Sanchez's place, opposite Palatka, where they joined the force on board the propeller. This force, by land, visited the plantation of Col. Dancy, and caught two of his negroes, one of which afterwards escaped. They cooked and eat at this place, and carried off all the poultry. The Colonels place on the River, was also ransacked by the negroes. They also visited the plantation of Major Balling, destroying all they could, but did not succeed in getting any negroes, as, fortunately, they had been removed a few days previous. This land force, on arriving at the residence of Messrs. Sanchez and Baza, surrounded the places, and took three negroes from Mr. Morris Sanchez, and other things of value from the yard. They did not succeed in catching Mr. Baza's negroes, but took from him three horses and one Cart, all of his poultry, hogs, pots, salt and every thing else they could lay hands upon. They also butchered two Beeves in the yard. The negroes kept the houses surrounded and abused and insulted the women just as they pleased. They camped that night on the banks of the River, in Mr.

Baza's field. On Friday morning, the propeller started and proceeded slowly over to Palatka, and went up to the wharf, landed a number of men on the wharf, and was in the act of landing some artillery, when Capt. J. J. Dickerson and his company, who had been patiently waiting, fired into them. The propeller, then, as fast as steam could carry her, backed out from the wharf, firing shell, grape, canister, and small arms. After they fired for a while, she proceed over the River to Mr. Baza's point, and communicated with a Company of negroes that had been left over there; — the Company of negroes then proceed back by land to Orange Mill, and the propeller went back down the River and took them on board. Every vestige of furniture was taken by the negroes from the residences of Dr R. G. Mays, Major E. C. Simkins, and Major A. H. Cole. Mr. Antonio Baza was taken prisioner by the negroes, but succeeded in making his escape. The Yankees, on the way down the River, again stopped at the residence of Mr. C. Dupont, and demanded the negros, who were hid, stating if the negroes were not immediately delivered they would burn the houses. ˙Mrs. Dupont, who was much alarmed, accordingly delivered up the negroes, against their wish, and urgent appeals.

In a conversation with Col. Montgomery of the negro Regiment (I having been surrounded and taken prisoner, but afterwards released,) he informed me that he had come up for the purpose of permanently occupying Palatka, and that they intended restoring Florida to the Union at all hazards—that he would have a force of some five thousand men at Palatka in a few days—that they had been acting in a mild way all along, but that they intended now to let us feel what *war actually was*—that the U.S. Marshal for Florida was along, and pointed him out to me—that all the negroes were declared free, and he intended to take all he could find.

Thus you will perceive, General, what we are to expect, and had it not been for the brave and gallant conduct of Capt. Dickerson, his officers, and men Palatka would this day have been in possession of the negro enemy. Capt. Dickerson has been one of the most untiring and energetic officers I have ever met with. He is always on the alart, and had he sufficient force, would never let the enemy land on either side of the River, up here. I visited Palatka since the propeller left, and from the great quantity of blood about on the wharf, and pieces of bones picked up, many of the enemy evidently was killed. Every bullet fired by Captain Dickerson's men, must have took effect.

This Company deserves the thanks of the people of Florida and the Government, for I think they have well merited the same.

Allow me, General, to suggest to you the propriety of taking some action in regard to the vast quantity of Cattle on the East side of the St. Johns, as the enemy are continually butchering for the use of their troops: and as the citizens are entirely helpless to defend themselves. All of which is respectfully submitted by your obedt. Servt.

ALS   Thos. T. Russell

Thos. T. Russell to General Finegan, 2 Apr. 1863, R-167 1863, Letters Received, ser. 5, Sec. War, RG 109 [F-132]. Reporting on this raid, Union General Rufus Saxton, superintendent of contrabands in the Department of the South, noted that "the moral effect of the presence of these colored soldiers under arms was very great, and caused a perfect panic among the rebels throughout the State." (*Freedom*, ser. 2: doc. 208.) Speaking of an earlier raid, the Confederate commander of the District of East Florida concurred with Saxton's assessment of the effect of black soldiers: "[T]he entire negro population of East Florida will be lost, and the country ruined . . . unless the means of holding the St. Johns river are immediately supplied." (Brig. Genl. Joseph Finegan to General, 14 Mar. 1863, F-89 1863, Letters Received, ser. 72, Dept. of SC, GA, & FL, Records of Military Commands, RG 109 [F-553].)

32: Testimony by the Commander of a South Carolina Black Regiment before the American Freedmen's Inquiry Commission

[Beaufort, S.C. June 1863]

. . . .

Q. As spies—do you think they [*blacks*] would be apt at that duty and entirely faithful?

A. Yes; they have been spies all their lives. You cannot teach them anything in that respect. I should not attempt to give them instruction; they would be better able to teach me.

Q. Do you think that there might be set on foot any organization of these people simply for penetrating the territory of the enemy and demoralizing the system of labor there and bringing out slaves—inciting the negroes to escape and thus effectually demoralizing the slave system of labor faster than our own forces could penetrate the country of the rebels?

A. I should not have very great faith in such a plan. I should have more faith in military expeditions. The men are willing, however;— I have men who are willing to go on the other side and bring away men. One obstacle to success in that is the system of picketing on the rebel shore. Their pickets are stationed with a view to keeping slaves in rather than others out—they are disposed more with reference to internal than external approaches.

Q. What peculiar characteristics lead you to suppose that their pickets are posted in that manner?

A. It is the universal testimony of the slaves that it is so, and I often find pickets posted up rivers at points where slaves would be likely to come. Then, again, to produce this result of keeping slaves in they deny themselves the use of boats entirely; all their boats are destroyed except a few which are kept on land under a very careful guard. I never spy a boat along the main land anywhere. When a flag of truce is sent we always have to use our boats, and the negroes who escape find great difficulty in getting boats.

. . . .

Q. Do you think any system of recruiting colored regiments can be attained unconnected with the advance of our troops upon rebel territory?

A. I think it is an open question, but I confess that I see no way in which it can be attained. One trouble is that these men distrust their own color as well as whites. They have a great distrust for "secesh negroes." They say that there are a great many slaves who are no more to be trusted than their masters—who will be certain to betray; but I never have doubted that the mass of slaves are eager for freedom and military service.

Q. The truth is then, that wherever our troops can penetrate the mass of the slaves will leave?

A. Yes, sir; but there is one peculiarity respecting it. They have an intense desire to take their property away with them. It is almost provoking to see the way in which they cling to their blankets, feather beds, chickens, pigs, and such like. But this is to be expected—these things represent the net result of all their labors up to this time.

. . . .

HD

Excerpts from testimony of Col. Higginson before the American Freedmen's Inquiry Commission, [June 1863], filed with O-328 1863, Letters Received, ser. 12, RG 94 [K-81]. Topical labels in the margin are omitted. For another excerpt from Higginson's testimony, see *Freedom*, ser. 2: doc. 7.

33: Testimony by a South Carolina Freedman before the Southern Claims Commission

Beaufort S.C. the 20[h] February 1874

I am a free person of color. I was born a slave & became free in 1863. I enlisted in the 34" regiment of US Colored troops at Beaufort South Carolina in 1863 I was in the service about three years My discharge papers are in Washington with the Second Auditor of the Treasury for the purpose of proving my claim for Bounty. I was never in the service of the Confederate States. I never gave or furnished any supplies to the Confederate soldiers. I never worked on the fortifications for the Confederate army. I never took an oath of allegiance to the Confederate Government. I stole away from home & came through the Lines to the Federal army by the first favourable opportunity.

Questions by Special Commissioner.

Q 1 My name is W[m] Drayton. I am Twenty nine years of Age. I reside in Beaufort South Carolina and My Occupation is a laborer

Q 2 I lived on my master's place from the time the war broke out until June 1863 when I came to Beaufort with my mule. I came through the lines with my mule on a dark night, and enlisted in the union Army as before Stated

. . . .

Questions of Ownership of Property by the Special Commissioner

My father died and left me means with which I bought the Jenny mule for which payment is now claimed. William Middleton was my former master. I have not worked for him since I became free. I do not live on his land nor on land bought from him. I am not in any way indebted him. No person has any interest in this claim but myself. I was born in South Carolina.

Questions by Attorney

I was in Beaufort when this mule was taken from me. It was taken by Quarter Master Dickey. I think his first name was William. He was Regimental Quarter master of the 34" regiment. I suppose he was then Acting Post Quarter Master. He gave me no receipt for the mule but told me I would be paid for it. I saw the mule in a government team in the service of the Government for over two years and until my regiment left Beaufort.

My father died & left with his oldest brother my uncle, the means or property he left for his children. I bought the mule by the advice of my uncle who had the means belonging to me. When the mule was taken from me I had already enlisted in the Army but had not been mustered into service. I was living with my Master near Combahee ferry when the mule was purchased by me, and until

140

I left there to join the Union Army. I paid Two hundred dollars for the mule. I made payment at three different times. I paid One hundred dollars in gold and silver at first payment. At second payment I paid Fifty dollars all in silver. At third payment I paid Fifty dollars in State Bank bills. I have never received any pay from the government for the mule. This is the first time I have ever applied for payment.

Questions by Special Commissioner

I do solemnly swear that the mule was mine and that I paid my [Master] the money for the same. Our owner Mr Middletown allowed his slaves to own personal property and raise stock for themselves. I paid the last money for the mule about two years before I run away to join the Union Army.

HDS   William Drayton

Excerpts from testimony of William Drayton, 20 Feb. 1874, claim of William Drayton, Beaufort Co. SC case files, Approved Claims, ser. 732, Southern Claims Commission, 3rd Auditor, RG 217 [I-96]. Sworn before a special commissioner of the Southern Claims Commission. In the manuscript, the question numbers are written in the margin. Other documents in the file indicate that Drayton was awarded $130 of the $170 he claimed for the loss of his mule.

34: Commander of the 4th Brigade of the South Carolina Militia to the Headquarters of the Confederate Department of South Carolina, Georgia, and Florida

Charleston 3 August 1863.

Sir. I beg leave to submit to you, for your consideration the following extract from a letter just received from one of Brig: Genl: Wm S. Walker's staff, dated McPhersonville August 2nd 1863.

"A recent raid was made by order of Genl Walker on Barnwell Island, by some of our troops under command of Capt M. J. Kirk; 31 negroes were captured, 4 of whom are men, the rest women and children; 3 of the men had been drafted for the 2nd So: Ca: Regnt, but had run away; two of them were there a week, and one three weeks. They represent many of the negroes as being very unwilling to be made soldiers of, but say they are forced to be, and are even hunted down in the woods and marshes to be taken; several have been shot in the effort to take them. They say the Fernandina negroes are active soldiers, and are used against them, some of our own negroes volunteer. Most of the negroes are left on the plantations, and plant provisions under a white superintendant; the task they do is about the same they did for us, one half of the produce goes to the Yankees, the rest to the negroes; they are not clothed or fed by the U.S. Govnt; most of them are wearing they say, the clothes their owners gave them, except what they have purchased for themselves; they make a little money by selling eggs, chickens, water melons &c They represent that many of the negroes would be very willing to come back to their owners if they could, but that their boats have all been taken and they are told if they come to us we will shoot them, others are perfectly content to remain.

The negroes from the Combahee raid were all carried to Beaufort, the infirm men, women and children were left there, and the prime men without being allowed to go on shore, were carried to Hilton Head and from there to Folly Island to work on the Batteries; most of them objected to be made soldiers of, or work on the entrenchments but were forced off."

I have the honor to be General, very Respectfully yr obdt. servt.
Wilmot G. DeSaussure

P.S. The above extract is respectfully submitted for consideration, and may or not give information already possessed at Head Quarters But deeming it important that all such matters should be communicated, this is respectfully forwarded.

ALS

Brig. Genl. Wilmot G. DeSaussure to Brigadier Genl. Thomas Jordan, 3 Aug. 1863, S-317 1863, Letters Received, ser. 72, Dept. of SC, GA, & FL, Records of Military Commands, RG 109 [F-1007]. Endorsements. General William S. Walker commanded the 3rd Military District of the Confederate Department of South Carolina, Georgia, and Florida, with headquarters at Pocotaligo, South Carolina.

35: Statement by a Florida Fugitive Slave

Fernandina Fla Nov. 26th /64

Statement of Washington Someroy (Colored.) who came in our lines at Rail Road Drenobridge at this post. Nov. 26" 1864. Says that there are about 800 Rebels at or near Baldwin Fla. taking up Rail Road Iron from the Jacksonville R.R. for the use of making the Pensicola & Ga R.R. further he says that there was four (colored) men hung by the Rebels, for trying to organize a Comp. of (Colored) men. the[y] was to take Lake City, then Baldwin, & then come to Fernandina Fla. reporting themselves for U.S. Service. He himself had to run away for fear of being killed by the

142

Rebels as the[y] tryed to make out he was one of the Comp. to be organized.
HD

Statement of Washington Someroy, 26 Nov. 1864, vol. 238 DS, p. 107, Statements of Escaped Union Prisoners, Refugees, & Confederate Deserters, ser. 4294, Provost Marshal General, Dept. of the South, RG 393 Pt. 1 [C-1552].

36: Testimony by a Georgia Freedman before the Southern Claims Commission

[*Savannah March 12, 1873*]

Charles Jess Testimony   My name is Charles Jess   I was born in South Carolina a slave and was freed when Shermans army came into the County of Chatham   I am 49 years old   I reside on Tweed-side plantation nine miles from the city of Savannah near the Savannah River   I am a farmer.   I am not related to the Claimant at all in any way   it was a common name among the colored people   I have no interest in her claim —   We all belonged to the same master — James Potter —   he owned two large plantations and I think 500 or more slaves   I have known Mary Jess ever since I was a small boy —   I was intimate with her during the war   I lived about 3/4 of a mile from her   I used to see her almost every day   I used to talk with her about the War often —   I was a union man   I was a slave and could not be anything else because I wanted my freedom and I hoped and expected it would give me my freedom as it did   Mary was like all the rest of us in favor of the Yankees   We knew they were our friends   I knew it becaus we heard it from our master   he did not want us to talk about the Yankees at all and would not allow us to   Mary Jess knew I was a Union man   she knew it just as I knew she was a Union woman — by talk and acts —   I dont think she ever did anything for the Union prisoners or for the Union soldiers because she did not have a chance   she lived in the Country — and not near enough to do anything   she never did anything for the Confederate soldiers   she was too sharp for that   she did not like them   I know she was a good Union loyal woman as she could be or as anybody could be —

Second set of Interrogatories by Special Commissioner
1   I was present when Claimants property was taken
2   I saw the soldiers take the property
3   When the soldiers first came to the Plantation they went over

to the mill went to work issuing out the rice   they made the colored people who were there runing the mill continue to pound out Rice for the army —   some went to Marys house and took out all the things they could get   I was not near enough to hear what they said but I could see every thing they did —   the colored people were so frightened they kept out of the way   the white rebs had always said to the slave that the Yankees would carry them off   some said they would burn them —   they said they had *horns* and *tails* and a good many believed it —   We did not know anything   We lived out on the Plantation never went where we could see anything or hear the truth —   We did not beleve it but we were talked to so much we felt afraid

4   The property was taken from Marys house on Potters Plantation taken in Dec 1864   I do not know the day of the month   the Plantation was covered with Soldiers   I have no idea how many soldiers there were   I never saw as many people before in all of my life —   they took the property most of it the day they came there – on to the place

5   I was present, Mary Jess   George Washington   Renty Sheldon & many others

6   I saw officers present I believe Capt & Lieut   I do not know what regiment or command to which they belonged   I do not know whether they ordered the property taken or not   they were about while the property was taken   they did not object or I did not hear them make any objections —

7   The cow was taken on the plantation. They killed her & the yearling there. The hog was taken in the pasture. They shot them down. They just caught the turkeys & fowls. They took the household & kitchen furniture right out of the house. I saw them take the honey – it was over to the plantation. It was in the hives. The syrup was taken & carried right off. They took all these things sugar, tobacco & wine from the store-house.

8   They moved it in wagons & on horses.

9   They carried it right out to the woods where they were encamped. I didn't follow it. I knew where they were camped & they went in that direction

10   I don't know the use they took it for. I didn't see them use any of it.

11   Mrs. Jess complained to an officer that she didn't have any bed covering, & she had nothing to lie on —   He said he was not in time to prevent it. The weather was very cold.

12   I heard no voucher or receipt asked for.

13   The property was taken in the day time —   They took it openly.

14   When they took this property the army was encamped in that

vicinity, about a mile off; but it was on the place. They took the property when they first came in & staid there about 3 w'ks. There had been a skirmish right on the river after the property was taken. I don't know any of the quartermasters or any other officers of the army.

15 The property was in very good condition when taken.

16 *Item No. 1.* The cow was about 4 yrs. old—full-grown. The yearling was not full-grown. It was nearly 2 years old. I don't know how much they would weigh—all I know is that they were in good condition. They were fat & fit for beef.

Item No. 2. These were full-grown hogs—fat—they would weigh about 100 lbs. a piece. I saw them cut their heads off.

Item No. 3. I know she had a great many turkeys. I don't know how many— I saw them take them away.

Item No. 4. She had a great many fowls— I don't know how many— I saw them taken away.

Item No. 5. She had good furniture cooking & household utensils furniture. Her house was well furnished. They took blankets, bedding & everything, didn't leave anything. They took all of their clothing. I cannot tell how much they had; I don't even know how many beds they had; but I know the house was well furnished.

Item No. 6. There were 30 bee-hives. I saw them take this away in boxes. They knocked the hives open. They left the bees there except those that stuck.

Item No. 7. I don't know how much syrup she had. They cleaned this all out at one time.

Item No. 8. The lard was in large stone jars. I don't know how many she had.

Item No. 9. She had one sack of coffee. I don't know how much it would weigh. I saw them take this away.

Item No. 10. She had 2 sacks of flour. 100 lbs. in a sack. They put these across the horse.

Item No. 11. I could not tell how much sugar she had. It was in the barrel. They took this away—

Item No. 12. I think she had about 2 boxes of chewing tobacco. They just scrabbled for that & took it off.

Item No. 13. The wine was in demi-johns. It was Port wine. It was bought.

17. 18. 19. Passed—

This property all belonged to Mrs. Jess. She was a dairy woman. She was allowed privileges that other servants didn't enjoy. She was allowed to raise poultry & stock & cattle. She sold them when she pleased—& she worked a garden. She worked and earned money outside her regular task work—

HDS   Charles Jess

Testimony of Charles Jess, [12 Mar. 1873], claim of Mary Jess, Chatham Co. GA case files, Approved Claims, ser. 732, Southern Claims Commission, 3rd Auditor, RG 217 [I-12]. Sworn before a special commissioner of the Southern Claims Commission. The questions that correspond to the enumerated responses are not in the file. According to other documents in the file, Mary Jess had submitted a claim for $625.50 as compensation for the following property taken by Union soldiers: 1 cow, 10 hogs, 20 turkeys, 60 fowls, 300 pounds honey, 15 gallons syrup, 50 pounds lard, 100 pounds coffee, 1 1/2 sacks flour, 75 pounds sugar, 50 pounds tobacco, 5 gallons wine, and furniture. She was awarded $130.

37: Testimony by a Georgia Freedman before the Southern Claims Commission

[*McIntosh, Ga. July 17, 1873*]

Testimony of Claimant

My name is Samuel Elliott   I was born in Liberty County a Slave and became free when the Army came into the County. I belonged to Maybank Jones. I am 54 years old. I reside at Lauralview in Liberty County. I am a farmer. I am the Claimant in this Case.

2 I resided from the 1st of April 1861 to the 1st of June 1865 where I live now at Lauralview. I worked for my master all the time. I changed my business at one time when I was with my master as a waiter – in the rebel service   I was with him Eleven month. I came home with him. I told my son what was going on –   he with 11 more ran off and joined the Army (the Yankee Army) on St Catherine Island. I dont remember the Year but it was soon after the battle at Williamsburgh Va, and before the 7 days battle near Chickahomony. I mean that was the time I came home with my master. I was with him at Yorktown –   Soon after I came home My son with 11 others ran away & joined the Union Army. My Master had me taken up tied me and tried to make me tell "What made them ran off"   I had to lie about it to keep from getting killed. the 11 slaves belonged to My Master Jones   that stoped the slave owners from sending or taking slave into the Army as waiters or anything else. it stoped it in our neighborhood

3 & 4 Irrelevant

5 I took an oath at Hinesville in this Co after Shermans Army came through   I do not know what the oath was   most all of the people went there and took it   I took another oath at Riceborough before I voted –

6 I never was directly or indirectly so connected except as before stated

7th & 8 Irrelevant

9　I nevr was except as before stated

10　to 24 inclusive having been read over to Claimant　answers no

25　The rebels took all of my turkeys, they did not pay me a cent

26　I was threatened at the time My Master tied me up

27　I was molested as above stated because as my master stated I was the cause of all the slaves leaving the County and joining the Yankees –

28 to 39 Inclusive　to each and every question the Claimant answer no.

40　At the begining of the rebellion I did not know any thing about the war　Mrs Somersall boys told me the War had commenced and we would all be free　that was soon after they fired on Fort Sumpter. they said the South would get whipped that they better not try, it was a sorry day when they fired on Fort Sumpter –　When the boys told we coloured people would all be free I felt happy　I told Mr Somersall "Glory be to God"　I could not feel it would come through　it was so long I began to think it would not come to pass but I felt happy and prayed for the time to come till it did come.

41　I can and do solemnly declare to all of that –

43　At the begining of the war I was a slave and became free when the Yankee Army came through.　I continued farming after I became free and farming now –　When my Father died he had 20 head of cattle about 70 head of hogs – Turkeys Geese Ducks and Chicken a plenty –　he was foreman for his master and had been raising such things for Years　When he died the property was divided among his children and we continued to raise things just as he had been raising.　My Father has been dead about 30 years　I continued to raise stock and that was the way I got the property the Yankees took from me　My Master was Maybank Jones.　My Father belonged to old Mr Elliott.　Mr Jones bought the Elliott Estate out and he allowed us the same priviledge that Mr Elliott did.　I live on the same land yet but it belongs to Suiton Stevens　I do not owe my master any thing not a-red-cent –　I am the only person interested in the claim presented by me against the Government.

2nd set of int[*errogatories*]　1 –　I was present when these things were taken from me.

2　I saw all this property taken,　the hogs pork, rice & ducks, were taken in my own wagon.

3　They asked me where all the rebels were. I told them they gone since day before yesterday gone to meet the Army.　They asked about the horses, I told them they took them all off the place & cary them off too: they asked me where's the money & silver　I told them they carry them all off.　They asked me where the camp was　I told them it was near by Dorchester.　They went right on then shooting chickens. They come right into the house & when they find the meat was there they whoop. They hollered good living boys & began to take out the meat.

4 These things were taken at Laurel-view. this is near by Sunbury on the Seaboard in Liberty Co Ga. This property was taken in Dec between the first & the middle of the month & when the Army came. About 40 or 50 came the first time & then they kept coming & going in gangs as hard as they can. They belonged to Col Bawldin's regiment. When they came there & begun to take my things I asked them "Massa" you going to take all, & leave me nothing to live on, & they said we are obliged to, we come to set you free, & we must have something to eat, but you must go to "*Uncle Sam*" Uncle Sam's pockets drag on the ground. This property was all or pretty much all taken in one day.

5 Clarissa Monroe & Sue, & William, & Crawford, & Augustus Smith & myself were present at the taking of this property.

6 I dont know if there were any officers there or not I dont know them. I didn't hear any orders given for the taking of the property. The Soldier who spoke to me had straps on his shoulder & on his arm, he was on his horse & staid on his horse & looked on while the others took the things.

7 They just drove the cows right out of the yard they were just done milked. They took my wagon & put one of their horses in it, my horse they didn't take because he had fistula on his shoulders. They took my harness. They shoot some of the hogs & those in the pen 2 bacon hogs I left in the pen to kill again they tied them. They took the pork from the table in the house & tied it to their saddles. They tied the ducks to the horse & said they were going to fatten them for me. They took the rice off in the wagon. The rice was in the room clean rice.

8 They drove the cattle off & the other things they moved off in wagon & on horses & in an oxcart.

9 They moved this property to Medway Church. I followed them till I got into the main road they made me go to help drive the cattle about a mile this way, then I came back home & they went on towards the Church.

10 They took this property for the soldiers. They must have taken the things to use I don't believe they would a took em from me & then throw away. I did not see them use anything there except some rice I had cooked when they came, & that they ate.

11 I made no complaint when they took the property but when they took my money I complained to an officer who had Mr Anderson & Rowe, & [Leuck?] & Mr Billy King prisoners. I told him some of the soldiers had taken my money I told them I had $65,00 in old bank bills, this officer spoke to another & sent him

to go & follow the soldiers & see if they could get the money but I never get the money. The day after they took my property I went down to Mr Delegals & on my return some soldiers asked me if I could change some money for them   I told them Yes & took out my pocket-book & they grabbed it out of my hand in the road.

12 I did not ask for any voucher or receipt for the property.

13 They took the property in the day time   they never come about in the night. I would not have felt so bad if they had not took my money but that was the last thing I had in the world.   they took my pants & coat & all   they did not leave me a thing.

14 They were encamped at Medway Church when they took my property & at Sunbury. Midway was 8 or 9 miles from my house & Sunbury 2 or 3 miles. The whole Army was called Sherman's army & Kilpatricks company, & they said it was Col Baldwins company too was there. They took the property the 3rd day after they came there into camp. They staid there about 3 weeks as near as I can tell. They had a little skirmish between Dorchester & Sunbury, they fired & scattered in the woods that was all. I did not know the quartermasters nor any of the other officers.

15 This property was all in good order when taken.

16 *Item No 1.* I had 7 Head of cattle. 2 of these were very fine steers & the rest cows except one calf. I am a poor judge of weight I could not say   2 of the steers were 7 years old. I bought one of the steers from Mr John Mallard; a black steer. I don't know how much they would weigh. They made me go along with them to help drive them a mile out to the big road.

Item No 2. One Jersey Wagon   A bran new wagon only built 3 weeks & a new harness. They took one of their own horses & hitched to the wagon & took it off. I saw them use the wagon to haul poultry & rice away in.

Item No 3. I had 15 head of live hogs all sizes. I had 9 good big ones   the 2 in the pen would weigh 200 lbs   they were very fat & large & 2 ft & a half high. The other 6 were small shoats. They shot some of these & the 2 fat ones in the pen they put in my wagon & took off & they put in the other hogs in this wagon & the oxcart, but the oxcart did not belong to me.

Item No 4. I had 4 hogs salted down   I think one of these would weigh very near 300 lbs & the other 3 – 240 or 250 lbs apiece. I have been used to weighing & selling hogs all the days of my life & am still raising & I own over 200 head of hogs now & a 100 head of sheep.

Item No 5. I had 3 bus & a half of clean rice. I can tell how much it would weigh   I am used to measuring it not to weighing it. (A bus of clean rice weighs 64 lbs)

Item No 6. I had 30 head of ducks & some chickens, the chickens I did not put down at all. I had more things than I have stated here I have only told of those things I saw taken. I had 9 head of cows but I only helped drive away 7. I had 30 head of hogs but only saw 15 of them taken.

17 & 18 passed.

19 They did not pay me a red on this property. This is the first & only account I have ever presented against the Government. I did not see any of this property wasted. they took it all off carefully & they whooped when they see the meat so I think they were glad to get it. They took all my things out of my house, all my clothing they took too. Two men at Thunderbolt who owned a vessel & went out trapping mink named Stokes & Strickland told me it was only a trap to get me into trouble, putting in my claim. I had property left me by my Father in stock. After he died the property was divided between us, the children & I went right on raising & selling. I had been raising ever since my Father died 31 years ago & I continued raising all the time & up to the time the Army came here & since then.

his
Samuel × Elliot
mark

HDSr

Testimony of Samuel Elliot, [17 July 1873], claim of Samuel Elliot, Liberty Co. GA case files, Approved Claims, ser. 732, Southern Claims Commission, 3rd Auditor, RG 217 [I-1]. Sworn before a special commissioner of the Southern Claims Commission. The questions that correspond to the enumerated responses are not in the file. According to other documents in the file, Samuel Elliot had submitted a claim for $436 as compensation for the following property taken by Union soldiers: 800 pounds bacon, 15 stock hogs, 7 cattle, 210 pounds clean rice, 30 ducks, and a wagon and harness. He was awarded $118.50.

38: Testimony by a Georgia Freedwoman before the Southern Claims Commission

[*Savinnah March 22, 1873*]

General Interrogatories by Special Com'r— My name is Nancy Johnson. I was born in Ga. I was a slave and became free when the army came here. My master was David Baggs. I live in Canoochie Creek The claimant is my husband. He was a good Union man during the war. He liked to have lost his life by standing up for the Union party. He was threatened heavy. There was a Yankee prisoner that got away & came to our house at night; we kept him hid in my house a whole day. He sat in my room. White people didn't visit our house then. My husband slipped him over to a man named Joel Hodges & he conveyed him off so that he got home. I saw the man at the time of the raid & I knew him. He said that he tried to keep them from burning my house but he couldn't keep them from taking everything we had. I was sorry for them though a heap. The white people came hunting this man that we kept over night; my old master sent one of his own grandsons & he said if he found it that they must put my husband to death, & I had to tell a story to save life. My old master would have had him killed   He was bitter. This was my master David Baggs. I told him that I had seen nothing of him. I did this to save my husbands life. Some of the rebel soldiers deserted & came to our house & we fed them. They were opposed to the war & didn't own slaves & said they would die rather than fight. Those who were poor white people, who didn't own slaves were some of them Union people. I befriended them because they were on our side. I don't know that he ever did any thing more for the Union; we were way back in the country, but his heart was right & so was mine. I was served mighty mean before the Yankees came here. I was nearly frostbitten: my old Missus made me weave to make clothes for the soldiers till 12 o'clock at night & I was so tired & my own clothes I had to spin over night. She never gave me so much as a bonnet. I had to work hard for the rebels until the very last day when they took us. The old man came to me then & said if you won't go away & will work for us we will work for you; I told him if the other colored people were going to be free that I wanted to be. I went away & then came back & my old Missus asked me if I came back to behave myself & do her work & I told her no that I came to do my own work. I went to my own house & in the morning my old master came to me & asked me if I wouldn't go and milk the cows: I told him that my Missus had driven me off—well said he you go and do it— then my Mistress came out again & asked me if I came back to work for her like a "*nigger*" — I told her no that I was free & she said be off then & called me a stinking bitch. I afterwards wove 40 yds. of dress goods for her that she promised to pay me for; but she never paid me a cent for it. I have asked her for it several times. I have been hard up to live but thank God, I am spared yet. I quit then only did a few jobs for her but she never did anything for me except give me a meal of victuals, you see I was hard up then, I was well to do before the war.

Second Set of Interrogatories by Spec'l Com'r.

1 I was present when this property was taken.

2 I saw it taken.

3 They said that they didn't believe what I had belonged to me & I told them that I would swear that it belonged to me. I had tried to hide things. They found our meat, it was hid under the house & they took a crop of rice. They took it out & I had some cloth under the house too & the dishes & two fine bed-quilts. They took them out. These were all my own labor & night labor. They took the bole of cloth under the house and the next morning they came back with it made into pantaloons. They were starved & naked almost. It was Jan & cold, They were on their way from Savannah. They took all my husbands clothes, except what he had on his back.

4 These things were taken from David Bagg's place in Liberty County. The Yankees took them. I should think there were thousands of them. I could not count them. They were about a day & a night

5 There were present my family, myself & husband & this man Jack Walker. He is way out in Tatnal Co. & we can't get him here

6 There were what we called officers there. I don't know whether they ordered the property taken. I put a pot on and made a pie & they took it to carry out to the head men. I went back where the officers camped & got my oven that I cooked it in back again. They must have ordered them or else they could not have gone so far & they right there. They said that they stood in need of them. They said that we ought not to care what they took for we would get it all back again; that they were obliged to have something to eat. They were mighty fine looking men.

7 They took the mare out of the stable; they took the bacon under the house, the corn was taken out of the crib, & the rice & the lard. Some of the chickens they shot & some they run down; they shot the hogs.

8 They took it by hand   the camp was close by my house.

9 They carried it to their camps; they had lots of wagons there.

10 They took it to eat, bless you: I saw them eating it right there in my house. They were nearly starved.

11 I told one of the officers that we would starve & they said no that we would get it all back again come & go along with us; but I wouldn't go because the old man had my youngest child hid away in Tatnal Co: he took her away because she knew where the gold was hid & he didn't want her to tell. My boy was sent out to the swamp to watch the wagons of provisions & the soldiers took the wagons & the boy, & I never saw him anymore. He was 14 yrs. old. I could have got the child back but I was afraid my master would kill him; he said that he would & I knew that he would or else make his children do it: he made his sons kill 2 men big tall

men like you. The Lord forgive them for the way they have treated me. The child could not help them from taking the horses. He said that Henry (my boy) hallooed for the sake of having the Yankees find him; but the Yankees asked him where he was going & he didn't know they were soldiers & he told them that he was going to Master's mules.

12 I didn't ask for any receipt.

13 It was taken in the day time, not secretly.

14 When they took this property, the army was encamped. Some got there before the camps were up. Some was hung up in the house. Some people told us that if we let some hang up they wouldn't touch the rest, but they did, they were close by. They commenced taking when they first came. They staid there two nights. I heard a heap of shooting, but I don't think that they killed anybody. I didn't know any of the officers or quartermasters.

15 This horse was as fine a creature as ever was & the pork &c were in good order.

16 *Item No. 1.* I don't know how old the mare was. I know she was young. She was medium sized. She was in nice order, we kept a good creature. My husband bought it when it was a colt, about 2 years old. I think he had been using it a year & a little better. Colored people when they would work always had something for themselves, after working for their masters. I most forgot whether he paid cash or swapped cows. He worked & earned money, after he had done his masters work. They bridled & carried her off; I think they jumped right on her back

Item No. 2. We had 7 hogs & we killed them right there. It was pickled away in the barrel: Some was done hung up to smoke, but we took it down & put it into the barrels to keep them from getting it. He raised the hogs. He bought a sow and raised his own pork & that is the way he got this. He did his tasks & after that he worked for himself & he got some money & bought the hogs and then they increased. He worked Sundays too; and that was for ourselves. He always was a hardworking man. I could not tell how much these would weigh; they were monstrous hogs, they were a big breed of hogs. We had them up feeding. The others were some two years old, & some more. It took two men to help hang them up. This was the meat from 7 hogs.

Item No. 3. I had half a barrel of lard. It was in gourds, that would hold half a bushel a piece. We had this hid in the crib. This was lard from the hogs.

Item No. 4 I could not tell exactly how much corn there was but there was a right smart. We had 4 or 5 bushels ground up into meal & they took all the corn besides. They carried it off in bags and my children's undershirts, tied them like bags & filled them up. My husband made baskets and they toted some off in that way. They toted some off in fanners & big blue tubs.

Item No. 5. I don't know exactly how much rice there was; but we made a good deal. They toted it off in bundles, threshed out— It was taken in the sheaf They fed their horses on it. I saw the horses eating it as I passed there. They took my tubs, kettles &c. I didn't get anything back but an oven.

Item No. 7. We had 11 hogs. They were 2 or 3 years old. They were in pretty good order. We were intending to fatten them right next year— they killed them right there.

Item No. 8. I had 30 or 40 head of chickens. They took the last one. They shot them. This property all belonged to me and my husband. None of it belonged to Mr. Baggs I swore to the men so, but they wouldn't believe I could have such things. My girl had a changable silk dress & all had [talanas?] & they took them all— It didn't look like a Yankee person would be so mean. But they said if they didn't take them the whites here would & they did take some of my things from their camps after they left.

her

Nancy ✕ Johnson

mark

HDSr

Testimony of Nancy Johnson, [22 Mar. 1873], claim of Boson Johnson, Liberty Co. GA case files, Approved Claims, ser. 732, Southern Claims Commission, 3rd Auditor, RG 217 [I-5]. Sworn before a special commissioner of the Southern Claims Commission. The questions that correspond to the enumerated responses are not in the file. According to other documents in the file, Boson Johnson, Nancy Johnson's husband, had submitted a claim for $514.50 as compensation for the following property taken by Union soldiers: 1 mare, 625 pounds bacon, 60 pounds lard, 12 bushels corn, 8 bushels rice, 7 meat hogs, 11 stock hogs, and 25 chickens. He was awarded $155.

39: Commander of the District of Wilmington to the Commander of the Department of the South

Wilmington N.C. Mar. 23^{d} 1865.

Sir:— When Maj Gen Sherman's Army reached Fayettsville, it had a column of eight or ten thousand refugees clinging to its skirts. Gen Sherman could carry them no longer, and they were all sent down here. His written orders to Brv't Brig Gen. Dodge, Chief Q.M. Dep't of North Carolina (just now at Newberne) directed that the surplus blacks be sent to the Department of the

South, where the arrangements so long and successfully conducted by Gen. Saxton, would permit the care and protection that we are utterly unable to afford here. Our planting season is passing & we have not the implements, nor the seeds, nor the superintendents; nor are the lands ever yet examined. Could we distribute the colored people, we have not had until now the wagons to carry their rations, a mile away from our wharves.

Therefore, I send herewith, by the "Beaufort," which goes to your Department after troops, three hundred blacks from the column of 6000 which reached here day before yesterday. They are pressing upon us severely, exhausting our resources and threatening pestilence. I have the honor to be Very Respectfully Your Obdt Serv't

Jos. R. Hawley,

P.S. We have no very late news here. Joe Johnston attacked Gen Sherman's left wing, at Bentonsville (between Fayetteville and Goldsboro) four days ago and was repulsed. Gen Scofield was at Kinston and Gen Terry on the W&W. R.R. a short distance from the Neuse at last advices   Latest from the North Mar. 16th J.R.H

HLS

Brig. Gen. Jos. R. Hawley to Maj. Gen. Gillmore, 23 Mar. 1865, Miscellaneous Records, ser. 4171, Dept. of the South, RG 393 Pt. 1 [C-1471].

40: Citizens of Columbia, South Carolina, to the Confederate Secretary of War

Columbia [*S.C.*] March 30, 1865

Sir— By a resolution unanimously adopted, at a meeting of the Ex^e Com^e appointed by his Hon^r the Mayor & Aldermen of this city, we the undersigned were appointed a com^{tte} to lay before you the exposed & threatened condition of our city, and from Columbia to the coast.

We have been informed by Gentlemen that have reached here from Colleton district that the most atrocious acts have been perpetrated by the Slaves from that district, and that they met with no Confed. forces along their route, that could afford protection to the whites. From information wh. has been communicated to his Hon. the Mayor, it is beleived that their are Secret Emisaries in our midst, who are tampering with our Slaves. The negro's leaving for Charleston from here, and the adjacent districts, are increasing daily, and remarks are frequently made by them, that they will soon return & occupy Columbia. His Exc^y Govr. McGrath of the State is ready to do all in his power, but the state force under his control is very small, and all are required to guard our upper line from Raids—the danger there being imminent. There are no Confed. Troops that we know of, between here and Charleston, though we have been informed that a movement is on foot to place a force of mounted men along the line.

Our city is filled with women & children who cannot get away. The more than heroic firmness exhibited by our noble women in the hour of trial deserves all praise: We therefore most respectfully beg to lay before you our exposed condition, and urge the importance of having a force of mounted men between Columbia & Charleston in order to protect our women & children from the worse than Brutal consequences which would result from the ascendence of the negroes, when instigated by the unprincipled yankee   Yours most Respectfully

HLSr

Wm B. Yates   M. C. Mordecai

J. G. Gibbes   H. Leiding

Wm. B. Yates et al. to Hon. J. C. Breckenrige, 30 Mar. 1865, C-584 1865, Letters Received, ser. 12, Adjt. & Insp. Gen., RG 109 [F-335]. The letter and all signatures are in the same handwriting.

CHAPTER 3

The District of Columbia

3

The District of Columbia

IN APRIL 1862, a congressional decree emancipated slaves in the District of Columbia, thereby culminating antislavery agitation that reached back to the time when the District was established as the federal capital.[1] Well before the Civil War, black people in the District had made substantial progress toward freedom. Abolitionists, including antislavery congressmen, angered and embarrassed by the presence of slavery in the shadow of the Capitol, had lashed out at chattel bondage in the District. Although they failed to secure abolition, they had succeeded in prohibiting the importation of slaves for the purpose of sale and, more important, in throwing slaveholders on the defensive. As slavery atrophied during the antebellum years, a large number of black people gained liberty through either self-purchase or direct grants of freedom by masters, and frequently by a combination of the two. The number of slaves declined and the number of free blacks increased, so that by 1860 the District's 11,000 free blacks outnumbered slaves nearly four to one. Moreover, like urban slaves throughout the South, slaves in the District's two urban centers, Washington and Georgetown, secured privileges that drew them closer to freedom. Many hired their own time, lived apart from their masters, and joined together with free blacks to form their own separate community. Maryland and Virginia slaves knew about this world of quasi-freedom. A large number had visited the District or had friends and relatives who had done so, and some had even resided there for a time. When the war came, federal mobilization to defend the capital allowed many of these men and women to escape to the place that they believed offered the best prospect of liberty. The District of Columbia and the federal bastion on the south side of the Potomac River, around the town of Alexandria, became a magnet for fugitive slaves. Emancipation in the District in the spring of 1862 confirmed the fugitives' prescient judg-

[1] Published accounts of emancipation in the District of Columbia include: Constance McLaughlin Green, *The Secret City: A History of Race Relations in the Nation's Capital* (Princeton, N.J., 1967), chap. 4; Michael J. Kurtz, "Emancipation in the Federal City," *Civil War History* 24 (Sept. 1978): 250–67.

ment and made the District and the surrounding area a center for black freedom.

The District of Columbia's special standing and the distinctive development of black life in the city set a unique course for emancipation. Because the District lay on the boundary between the loyal slave state of Maryland and the rebellious slave state of Virginia, President Abraham Lincoln and Congress early confronted the contradictory demands of a war for union in a deeply divided society. At the same time that masters in secessionist Virginia and loyal Maryland demanded enforcement of the fugitive slave act, abolitionists called for its repeal, along with destruction of the rest of the legal apparatus that supported slavery. Because the federal government had sole and undisputed jurisdiction over the District of Columbia, the Lincoln administration could not escape the question of slavery on its home ground. As proponents and opponents of slavery jostled for position, slaves from the District, Maryland, and Virginia entered the debate by deserting their masters and taking refuge in the capital.

Strategic considerations, particularly the determination of each combatant to protect its own capital and capture the other's, made the region between and around Washington and Richmond the focus of intensive military activity. The earliest movements of the contending armies during the spring and summer of 1861 provided the initial opportunity for slaves to make their escape. In April and May, as the Northern regiments that had answered Lincoln's call for three-month volunteers took up positions in the District of Columbia and the surrounding Maryland countryside, slaves moved toward federal army encampments. Abolitionist soldiers, who numbered large among the first volunteer regiments, welcomed these runaways, and others, who cared little about slavery, found the fugitives' offer of personal service and military labor reason enough to accept them into army lines. Resident free blacks and knowledgeable urban slaves, operating out of the District's churches, schools, and benevolent societies, offered food and shelter to fugitives seeking freedom and aided their adjustment to urban life. Antislavery whites also provided assistance. As a result, the black population of the District grew rapidly — to the frustration of slave owners, the delight of abolitionists, the relief of short-handed army quartermasters, and the embarrassment of the Lincoln administration.

Expanded military mobilization further increased the opportunities for slave flight and the administration's problems. In late May, after Virginia voters ratified secession, federal troops crossed the Potomac River en masse to protect the capital's southern approach. Many of the District and Maryland slaves who had found refuge in federal camps accompanied the troops to secessionist Virginia, assuring themselves a modicum of security by increasing the distance from their owners. Virginia slaves, some of whose masters claimed loyalty to the Union, also entered army lines in large numbers. Loyal slaveholders on both sides of the Potomac complained bitterly about the loss of their property and demanded that Lincoln and his advisors live up to their oft-stated pledge of noninterference with slavery. True to their word, administration officials obliged. Armed with authority from cabinet members and other high-ranking officers, masters presented themselves at federal encampments and demanded their slaves. Some regimental commanders readily complied, returning fugitive slaves to loyal and even disloyal slaveholders. Others, offended by charges that their men were slave stealers and by rude assaults on their authority, defied the masters. Perhaps they had learned of the precedent established by General Benjamin F. Butler at Fortress Monroe, Virginia. In any case, slaves would not be put off. They continued to flee from slavery to the camps of Northern regiments, and they always seemed to find soldiers willing to help them elude their pursuers. The confrontations between masters demanding their slaves and soldiers unwilling to surrender fugitives grew more intense and violent.

Constant troop movements through the District aided slaves in escaping and complicated masters' attempts to recover their property. In July 1861, as the first volunteer regiments completed their three-month term of service and headed northward for reorganization or muster-out, they carried numerous District, Maryland, and Virginia slaves with them. Others followed in their train. Masters whose slaves had found refuge in Union ranks now faced the specter of their removal to the free states or some distant point beyond reasonable hope of recovery. They escalated their protests, pressing into service whatever political connections they could muster. As the complaints mounted, army officers bombarded their superiors with requests for instructions on the sensitive issue of the fugitives' status and the masters' rights.

Union policy toward fugitive slaves in the District of Columbia and the surrounding area thus took shape in a hail of pleas from harried field officers. In July, General Joseph K. F. Mansfield, commander of the Department of Washington, directed a District of Columbia justice of the peace not to return Virginia fugitives to their rebel masters, but to put them to work as "[c]ontrabands." Mansfield based his policy on the approval given by Secretary of War Simon Cameron to General Butler's adoption of the same course in tidewater Virginia.[2] Fugitives from the District and Maryland did not fare as well. That same month, as additional regiments prepared to advance across the Potomac into Virginia, General-in-Chief Winfield Scott directed Mansfield to "take

---

[2] For Butler's policy and Cameron's approval of it, see above, docs. 1A–B.

stringent measures to prevent any fugitive slaves from passing over the river particularly as servants with the regiments." Accordingly, Mansfield excluded fugitives from federal camps and prohibited them from accompanying soldiers on the march.[3] But many District and Maryland slaves had already crossed the river and gained freedom in Union-occupied Virginia. Under pressure from loyal slaveholders, President Lincoln proposed to Scott that slaveholders be allowed to "bring back" slaves who had crossed the Potomac with Northern regiments. Scott, requesting that the President's name "not . . . be brought before the public," urged the commander of the Union army in Virginia, General Irvin McDowell, to aid masters in recovering their slaves and thus fulfill the President's "constitutional obligations."[4]

Fugitives paid these orders little mind. They persisted in leaving their owners at every opportunity and appeared at Union picket lines with the expectation that they would be protected. Military activity in northern Virginia in midsummer, which climaxed at Bull Run, allowed many more to escape – including hundreds who had been brought into the region to help supply Confederate armies. In August 1861, the opportunity for such slaves to secure freedom increased markedly when Congress enacted the First Confiscation Act.[5] The act not only permitted federal soldiers to receive slaves who had been employed against the Union, but also meant that blacks could no longer be arrested simply "upon the presumption, arising from color," that they were fugitive slaves. When District police did just that, they felt the heavy hand of official condemnation. Lincoln instructed Secretary of State William H. Seward to remind District officials of their responsibility under the new law.

Using the confiscation act, some federal officials widened the avenues to freedom. The most prominent of these was Secretary of War Simon Cameron, who argued that the spirit of the confiscation act prohibited the return of slaves to masters in rebellious states, regardless of whether the slaves had labored in behalf of the Confederacy and regardless of their masters' loyalty.[6] In October 1861, Cameron went a step further. When a northern Virginia slaveholder protested that a military court had refused his testimony while accepting that of his runaway slave, General William R. Montgomery, the military governor of Alexandria, rejected the proceeding as "not founded in justice." But the Secretary of War blithely turned Montgomery's reasoning inside-out, and the slave's testimony sent the master to jail. These policy changes made it easier for Virginia fugitives to maintain their

[3] *Official Records*, ser. 2, vol. 1, p. 760.
[4] *Official Records*, ser. 2, vol. 1, p. 760.
[5] U.S., *Statutes at Large, Treaties, and Proclamations*, vol. 12 (Boston, 1863), p. 319.
[6] See above, doc. 1C.

liberty in the District, and more Virginia slaves escaped to the capital and the Union-occupied areas immediately south of the Potomac.

While Cameron bent the confiscation act in the slaves' favor, others pushed in the opposite direction. General George B. McClellan, who superseded McDowell after the latter's ignominious defeat at Bull Run, had already established a reputation as the masters' friend.[7] He was determined to keep it. Following the letter of the confiscation act, he allowed his subordinates in the Army of the Potomac to accept fugitive slaves who had been employed against the Union army, but he ordered them to exclude from army lines those who were "simply fugitive from the ordinary condition of labor for their class."

North of the Potomac, the difficulties faced by fugitive slaves also multiplied. Reluctant to offend slaveholding unionists in the border states, President Lincoln continued to lend a sympathetic ear to loyal masters. He repeated his promise of full protection of their property and enforcement of all relevant federal laws, and Maryland's congressional delegation watched carefully to see that he observed his pledge. Congressman Charles Calvert, scion of one of Maryland's oldest slaveholding families, played an especially active part, delivering slaveholders' complaints about runaway slaves to the administration and to military authorities. Along with the seemingly endless laments, Calvert carried a none-too-subtle warning that federal interference with slavery played into the hands of secessionists, who had long claimed that the federal government had designs on slavery. He maintained that by protecting slavery, federal officials would not only secure Maryland for the Union, but also win the allegiance of Union-loving masters throughout the Confederacy. Calvert's reasoning impressed administration leaders. Federal officials stalled for time as the President urged gradual, compensated emancipation upon Maryland and the other border states and pushed his scheme of colonizing freed slaves outside the boundaries of the United States.

While federal authorities fiddled, the question of slavery in the District burned. Slave catchers had a field day, preying upon the fugitives who crowded the streets, alleys, and vacant lots of the city. And with the rural highways dotted with slaves heading for Washington, hard-riding pursuers could often retake them before they reached the District. Maryland masters treated recaptured runaways without mercy. One owner whipped a fugitive to death.[8] Another recaptured two runaways in the District, beat them severely, then clapped them in jail for the duration of the war.[9] While slave catchers plied their grisly trade, city officials and military provost marshals entered into the business by confining alleged fugitives in jail to await

[7] See, for example, *Official Records*, ser. 2, vol. 1, p. 753.
[8] See below, doc. 126.
[9] See below, doc. 136.

the arrival of a plausible owner and then haggling over the price of a slave's return. Complaints of disloyalty among jailors in the District and the vicious abuse of imprisoned blacks were soon confirmed in Senate hearings.[10]

The spectacle of such proceedings in the national capital horrified many Northerners, spreading the anger and indignation previously confined to abolitionists. Those Northerners who for over a decade had questioned the federal government's role as slave catcher were appalled. Increasingly convinced that slavery lay at the heart of the rebellion, they demanded the repeal of all federal laws supporting the peculiar institution. Abolition in the District of Columbia would constitute the first step. During the winter of 1861–1862, petitions poured into the Congress protesting conditions in the District jail and urging emancipation. Slaveholders in the District and in the border states, as well as many Democratic congressmen from the North, vehemently opposed congressional tampering with slavery. But Massachusetts Senator Henry Wilson, chairman of the powerful Committee on Military Affairs and a staunch foe of slavery, introduced legislation to abolish slavery in the District. Wilson's bill reflected the conflicting political currents; while promising an immediate end to slavery, it also proposed to compensate loyal masters for the loss of their property and provided funds to remove the freedpeople from the United States.

As the tide turned against slaveholders, Northern soldiers treated them and their hired slave catchers with still greater contempt, openly protecting pursued slaves. The congressional prohibition of March 1862 against the employment of federal military forces to return fugitives to their claimants deepened the soldiers' resolve. The following month, a series of sharp clashes between Union soldiers and slave catchers led General Abner Doubleday, commander of the federal defenses north of Washington, to declare that blacks coming into Union lines were to be "treated as persons and not as chattels," and were not to be surrendered to pursuing masters under any circumstances. As much as Maryland slaveholders whined about their property rights, they found fewer and fewer officials within military ranks or the federal government willing to listen.[11]

Despite its provisions for compensating masters and colonizing freed slaves, District slaveholders contemplated the likely passage of Wilson's emancipation bill with dismay. They tried every stratagem to stay slavery's demise. Some removed their slaves from the District, hoping to escape the impending legislation.[12] Washington's city council – pleading that emancipation would turn the city "into an asylum for

[10] U.S., Congress, Senate, "Report of the Committee on the District of Columbia," *Senate Reports*, 37th Cong., 2nd sess., No. 60.

[11] See below, chap. 6.

[12] See, for example, *Official Records*, ser. 2, vol. 1, p. 811.

free negroes, a population undesirable in every american community"—tried to frighten Congress from its course. But such diversions
failed. Congress passed Wilson's bill early in April, and on April 16,
1862, Lincoln signed it into law, freeing immediately "all persons held
to service or labor within the District of Columbia by reason of African
descent," and offering compensation to loyal masters for each liberated
slave. The act empaneled a three-member emancipation claims commission to determine eligibility and award compensation. To assess the
value of freed slaves, the commission hired a well-known expert in such
matters—a Baltimore slave trader. In all, the commission awarded
compensation for nearly 3,000 slaves, almost as many as the census of
1860 had enumerated in the District.[13]

Slaveholders made last-ditch efforts to evade congressional emancipation. Recalcitrant masters defied the new law by hiding their slaves
outside the District, confining some 300 at the Baltimore slave pen of
the commission's assessor, and hundreds more in other jails elsewhere
in Maryland. Many remained incarcerated under miserable conditions
until at least the summer of 1863, when Colonel William Birney,
superintendent of black recruitment in Maryland, began systematically
liberating the inmates of Baltimore's city jail and private slave pens.[14]

In the months following emancipation, the national capital in fact
became the "asylum for free negroes" that the city council had feared.
Through the final days of the war, enormous Union and Confederate
armies repeatedly bloodied each other on Virginia battlefields between
Washington and Petersburg, in the Shenandoah Valley, and elsewhere.
As the armies tramped back and forth, gaining territory only to lose it
again, thousands of slaves fled the violence and devastation, and also
their masters. Many found their way to the capital city—some on their
own, others following Union lines of supply. Once in the District and
its environs—the supply center for the entire eastern theater of the
war—able-bodied fugitives found ready employment with army quar-

---

[13] *Statutes at Large*, vol. 12, pp. 376–79. Of 966 petitions filed by former slaveholders
under the emancipation act, the commissioners denied compensation to only 36 and
awarded less than full compensation to only 21 others. The commissioners awarded
compensation for a total of 2,989 slaves. Twenty-three slaveholders received more
than $4,000 each, the largest award going to George Washington Young, who
received nearly $18,000 for sixty-nine slaves. (U.S., Congress, House of Represen-
tatives, "Emancipation in the District of Columbia," *House Executive Documents*,
38th Cong., 1st sess., No. 42.) See also the records of the Board of Commissioners
for the Emancipation of Slaves in the District of Columbia, 1862–1863, RG 217.
[14] For the 300 District of Columbia slaves confined in the Baltimore slave pen of B. M.
Campbell, the assessor for the emancipation claims commission, see testimony of
Geo. E. H. Day, Esq., before the American Freedmen's Inquiry Commission, [Mar.
1863], filed with 0-328 1863, Letters Received, ser. 12, RG 94 [K-67]. For
District slaves who were released by Birney from the Baltimore city jail and from
another private slave pen, see below, doc. 142, and *Freedom*, ser. 2: doc. 70.

termasters, engineers, and commissary agents; with navy suppliers and in the navy yard; and with the government contractors who thronged the city. Beginning in 1863, many of the men enlisted in the Union army. Women, children, and other fugitives not physically fit for government labor took up residence in the numerous contraband camps in and around the District and Alexandria.[15]

Having reached the District, these refugees did not rest content with their own liberty. Aided by friends and relatives, many of whom had been free before the war, runaway and emancipated blacks ventured outside the District to liberate others who remained in bondage.[16] Although the dangers of such forays remained substantial, their prospects of success increased as slavery in Maryland and Virginia grew progressively weaker. By the end of the war, thousands of blacks had gained liberty in the District of Columbia and in the contraband camps just south of the Potomac.

In declaring freedom, the District of Columbia emancipation act gave federal protection to runaway slaves in the capital. Equally important, it provided slaves throughout the South with a convincing sign that the federal government was their friend, further encouraging flight to federal lines. But what pleased the slaves appalled their masters. Slaveholders everywhere saw in these rapidly transpiring events confirmation of their fear that the Lincoln administration fronted for abolition. Even masters in the border states began to doubt that their loyalty to the Union could buy immunity from the oncoming tide of freedom.

As abolitionists had hoped, emancipation in the District represented an all-important first step toward the legal annihilation of slavery. It marked the first time Congress legislated full, uncontested freedom to any slave. In so doing, congressional emancipation in the District served as an important precedent for later legislation. In denying compensation to owners who had given aid or comfort to the enemy, it prefigured the Second Confiscation Act. And in enabling blacks to testify before the emancipation claims commission, it paved the way for supplementary legislation opening all courts in the District of Columbia to blacks – legislation that itself anticipated the 1866 Civil Rights Act.[17] Still, the compensation of loyal masters accorded slavery a degree of legitimacy it would never again receive from the federal government and demonstrated the continuing power of slaveholders within the Union. Abolitionists cheered the advance of freedom but

---

[15] For a discussion of military labor and contraband camps in the District and environs, see *Freedom*, ser. 1, vol. 2.

[16] See, for example, below, docs. 145A–B.

[17] *Statutes at Large,* vol. 12, pp. 538–39; vol. 14 (Boston, 1868), pp. 27–30.

recoiled from the implication that the emancipated slaves had been property legally owned, rather than persons immorally and illegally deprived of their rights. Yet, the compromised victory was a victory nonetheless, and slaves and their allies celebrated even as they resolved to expand the domain of freedom.

41: Commander of a Connecticut Regiment to the Headquarters of the Department of Washington

Washington DC. June 12 /61

Sir: In accordance with a verbal order from General Mansfield I have the honor to report to you that on the 10th inst, six men of color representing themselves to be fugitive slaves from Howard County in the State of Maryland appeared in the Camp of my Regiment and still remain upon my grounds. They also represent that their masters are secessionists in sentiment and opinion and members of secret military organizations hostile to the Government.

ALS   Alfred H. Terry

Col. Alfred H. Terry to Captain Theodore Talbot, 12 June 1861, T-28 1861, Letters Received, ser. 5364, Dept. of Washington, RG 393 Pt. 1 [C-4101]. No response has been found in the records of the Department of Washington or the records of the 2nd Connecticut Infantry, the regiment commanded by Terry.

42: Commander of the Department of Washington to a District of Columbia Justice of the Peace

Washington D.C. July 4 1861

Sir: – Yours of the 2nd of July relative to fugitive Slaves from Virginia is at hand. The decision of the Secretary of War as to Slaves from States in rebellion is, that they Shall not be returned to the rebelious owners but Kept and put at Work   you will therefore consider them as Contrabands, and have them retained, if need be put at work about the jail or for the improvement of public premises, in its neighbourhood, under the charge of some Superintendent   Very Respectfully Your obdt. Servant

HLcSr   (Signed). J. K. F. Mansfield.

J. K. F. Mansfield to Mr. Justice Dunne, 4 July 1861, vol. 19/24 1/2 DW, p. 38, Letters Sent, ser. 5361, Dept. of Washington, RG 393 Pt. 1 [C-4573].

43: Statements of Virginia Freedmen

Alex.ª Va., Aug. 18th 1865.

Edward Parker vs Jonathan Roberts. Complaint of expulsion from his house and charge and appropriation of his property.

Parker states that he was the slave of John A. Washington — that just before the battle of Bulls Run, June 1st 1861. he received orders to go out to Manasses to wait upon Washington and Gen. Lee. But instead of obeying the order, he came to Alexandria, and engaged in cooking for Union soldiers under Capt. Tyler, & then for Williams, Q.M. and from there went to "Capitol Prison" to cook for Mr. Wood. In June of '62 his family — wife & five children — which had been run off, came back to Mt. Vernon, and he returned also; and proceeded by permission of Judge Frees to go to work and take care of his family and three orphan children that belonged on the estate. That while thus employed, Jonathan Roberts, Sheriff of Fairfax County, leased the Mt. Vernon estate to Mr. Geo. Johnson, who sent them away without sufficient opportunity to get a place, though it was snowy cold weather. He had 14 cords of wood which he had cut.

There were others belonging to the estate who were turned away in like manner and who also had wood cut which was left, & join in this complaint

They wish now to know by what authority Mr. Johnson was placed on the estate — whether he had a right to turn them away; and if they are not entitled to compensation for what they had done.

Parker lives at Dr. Lewis Linton's — Sheridan's Point.

Joe and West Ford, vs Jonathan Roberts for expulsion from the Mt-Vernon Estate and the appropriation of their property.

They state that a little while before the war they were taken with their families from the Mt. Vernon Estate to a farm belonging to John A. Washington in Fauquier County. When the War broke out & after the 1st Battle of Bull Run they made their escape through the lines and engaged with the Union Army and was with them on the Peninsula — returning to the Mt Vernon Estate in July of 1862, when there were about 60 colored people on the estate old & young — about 40 of them children — orphans — that the estate at that time was in charge of Thomas Wright, a Quaker, who lives about 4 miles SW. of Mt. Vernon, who told the men to go to work

and take care of the women and children— that it was too late to
make a crop and he told them to cut cord wood which was of oak &
some hickory near the river and little Hunting creek and posts &
rails of cedar— that there were engaged according to their
recollection 13 men who had each his own work by himself   They
state that they, with another brother, two women and 8 children
had according to the best of their judgment off from the place
$250.00 was on the place until Feb. 1863, which was no more than
what was necessary for their families.

HD

Statements of Edward Parker and of Joe and West Ford, 18 Aug. 1865,
Miscellaneous Records, ser. 3878, Alexandria VA Supt., RG 105 [A-10016].
In the same file are statements by two more former slaves from the Mt. Vernon
estate, claiming that Roberts had appropriated crops, cords of wood, and
money belonging to them. One of these claimants had remained on the estate
when the other slaves fled early in the war; the other had "escaped with others
into Union lines, & got back on to the Mt Vernon Estate in July of 62."
(Statements of Gabriel Johnson and James Starks, 9 Sept. 1865.)

44: Two Letters from a Maryland Congressman to the Commander of the Department of Washington

House of Rep. [*Washington*] July 17th 1861

Sir   Since I saw you yesterday I have been called upon by a number
of our Citizens relative to their Slaves being employed and concealed
in the various camps in and around Washington. This has become
a monstrous abuse of our rights and is rightfully causing a great
deal of censure upon the Government for permitting it. I know
from my personal intercourse with you on the Subject that it meets
with your decided disapprobation and that of the Government
because I have received assurances of the kind from the President
and Secretary of War. These encampments not only employ these
Slaves whilst Sojourning here but actually carry them off with them,
as it is well known that many of the Regiments, now in Virginia,
have large numbers of our Slaves concealed in their camps. The
Regiment which left Washington last Sunday week on the cars,
about Sunset for Baltimore, carried off Several & among them one of
my own. As that Regiment passed through a portion of
Pennsylvania I conclude those negroes, who accompanied it, were
turned loose in that State, and are consequently a total loss to their
owners unless the Government can be held responsible for their

abduction. Under these circumstances I conceive I ask nothing unreasonable in behalf of our Citizens when I demand that the Government Shall order the immediate arrest of all Slaves now found in any Camps either in Maryland or Virginia and their confinement in Some place of Safety until their owners can reclaim them and that an order Shall be given to all Commanders and officers not to receive hereafter, on any pretense whatever, Such persons into their Camps or Stations. If Such orders were published in the papers of our State, and properly enforced afterwards, the public feeling, greatly exasperated at this time, would gradually subside and the enemies of the government would be disarmed of one of their most powerful weapons. Again I would suggest that an order be also given and published that no commanders of any forces should permit forays of Soldiers upon the property or persons of private citizens unless upon information from Some reliable Source. When any reliable information is received of the treasonable acts or designs of any party an officer Should be detailed with a Sufficient number of men to make the desired Search and he should be furnished with a written Specification of the charges made against the party which Should be exhibited before making the arrest. Something of this kind would prevent the frequent annoyances which are now Suffered from the roving bands of Soldiers who are committing daily depredation upon innocent citizens under the pretense of searching for arms &c. Trusting that these Suggestions will receive your early attention and that of the government I remain Very respectfully & truly Yr obt Serv[t]

Cha[s] B Calvert

P.S. Since writing the foregoing I have seen your order published on the subject[1] but as that order does not make any provision in relation to those Slaves who have been abducted from our State and carried into Virginia I beg to call your attention to that portion of my communication and ask if the request therein made cannot be complied with as there are a great many of our slaves in the camps and it is impossible to reclaim them unless the government will arrest and confine them. This is being very successfully used by our enemies to prejudice the Union cause and it is asserted that it is a part of the designs of the government. It is very important to us to have it done but it is still more so for the success of the Union cause further South as it would at once open the eyes of those who have been deceived by the Statements of the Disunionists in those States. It is asking nothing that we have not a right to demand under the fugitive slave law and I hope will be complied with. Very respectfully Yr obt serv[t] Cha[s] B Calvert

ALS

House of Rep. [*Washington*] July 27 /61
Dear Sir   It is alledged and known that many slaves have escaped
from their owners with the troops sent North from Washington and
other Stations on the road.   As the three months volunteers are now
being discharged and Sent off in large numbers I Suggest the
propriety of having some one detailed to examine all cars, leaving
Washington and other Stations, to prevent such acts in
future.   Your published orders in regard to receiving Slaves in the
Camps are very satisfactory and, if the officers will only enforce
them properly, will remedy a great evil, but I regret that an order
has not also been published requiring all now in the camps to be
arrested and confined until reclaimed or released according to
law.   With great respect Yr. o'bt. Sev^r

ALS   Chas B Calvert

Chas. B. Calvert to Genl. Mansfield, 17 July 1861, C-28 1861, Letters
Received, ser. 5364, Dept. of Washington, RG 393 Pt. 1 [C-4100]; Chas. B.
Calvert to Genl. Mansfield, 27 July 1861, C-30 1861, Letters Received, ser.
5364, Dept. of Washington, RG 393 Pt. 1 [C-4100]. On July 29, 1861,
Calvert appealed directly to the Secretary of War for assistance in recovering
his own fugitive slave and that of a neighbor. The two slaves had reportedly
left Washington on July 14 with a New York regiment bound for Harper's
Ferry. Convinced that the slaves "are either with that regiment at this time or
were turned loose when they passed through Pennsylvania," Calvert asked for
an order to the Union commander in the Shenandoah Valley "to deliver these
Slaves to our Agent Mr Harrison Wallis provided he finds them . . . and
furthermore to afford him every facility in making a proper Search for them in
his encampment." In compliance with Calvert's request, the War Department
on August 8 instructed the Union commander to "extend to Mr Wallis, every
assistance in your power to accomplish his purpose." (Chas. B. Calvert to
Hon. S. Cameron, 29 July 1861, C-181, Letters Received, RG 107 [L-138];
Thomas A. Scott to General N. P. Banks, 8 Aug. 1861, vol. 45, p. 240,
Letters Sent, RG 107 [L-138].) On August 10 the provost marshal in Washington issued orders regarding railroad travel that were similar to those called
for by Calvert. He instructed the guard at the railroad depot to permit no
blacks to leave Washington by railroad "without sufficient evidence of their
being free or of their right to travel." (*Official Records*, ser. 2, vol. 1, p. 764.)

1 On July 11, 1861, General-in-Chief Winfield Scott had ordered General
Joseph K. F. Mansfield, commander of the Department of Washington (which
included the District of Columbia and portions of Maryland), to "take stringent measures to prevent any fugitive slaves from passing over the river,
particularly as servants with the regiments ordered over." Accordingly, on
July 17 Mansfield issued an order declaring that "[f]ugitive slaves will under
no pretext whatever be permitted to reside or be in any way harbored in the

quarters and camps of the troops serving in this department. Neither will such slaves be allowed to accompany troops on the march." (Asst. Adjt. Genl. E. D. Townsend to Brigadier General Mansfield, 11 July 1861, T-34 1861, Letters Received, ser. 5364, Dept. of Washington, RG 393 Pt. 1 [C-4551]; *Official Records*, ser. 2, vol. 1, p. 760.)

45: Military Governor of Alexandria, Virginia, to the Secretary of War; and the Latter's Reply

Alexandria Va Sept 9. 1861.

Sir— Doubtless you are aware that the undersigned is charged with the duties of Military Governor of this city. In that capacity he has the honor to inform you that he has neither records nor orders to guide or govern him in the discharge of said duties. He would therefore respectfully request to be furnished with such instructions as the Government deem necessary and desire should be inforced and govern in the various cases that may arise.

'Till such instructions be furnished, the undersigned would ask if the local Municipal laws of Virginia have been abrogated in this City. and military authority substituted in lieu thereof, or is the relation of Master and Slave to be interfered with?

The Provost Judge, in this city—has adopted the rule in his court, that any person who declines to take the oath of allegiance to the U. States will not be allowed to take an oath, or give testimony in said Court. — This rule, however apparently right in the abstract does not work well in practice— Under it the following case has arisen.

A negress, at the instance, it is represented, of soldiers, absconded the premises of her master, was apprehended and by her owner's authority confined, and subsequently by the same authority liberated; again She absconded and again apprehended, and subsequently brought before the Provost Judge, before whom she complained of certain bad treatment from her master— His testimony, for the reason stated, was ruled out—whilst hers was admitted—and upon it, she was liberated and her master sentenced to be incarcerated.

Believing the proceedings in the case—erroneous, not founded in justice, and calculated to do injury—they were stayed by the undersigned for the present—till the views and instructions of the Department can be communicated and adopted as the rule of action in all future cases that may arise— Very respectfully Your Ob' Sert

ALS   W. R. Montgomery

Wash Oct 2 /61

Sir   Your letter asking for instructions and general directions with
regard to the duties of your position has been received.

In reply you are respectfully informed that this depart^{mt} is not
disposed to interfere with the decisions of the Provost Judge. In the
particular case referred to, I have no desire to set aside his action in
the premises. I have the honor to be Respectfully

HLdlr   S– C–

Brig. Genl. W. R. Montgomery to Hon. Simon Cameron, 9 Sept. 1861, and
S. C. to Brig. Genl. Montgomery, 2 Oct. 1861, M-740 1861, Letters Received, ser. 12, RG 94 [K-19]. Endorsements.

46: Affidavit of a Maryland Slaveholder

District of Columbia County of Washington [*October 25, 1861*]
On this 25" day of October 1861 Before Thomas C. Donn a
justice of the Peace in and for Said County and District aforesaid
Personally appeared Thomas Martin of St Mary's Co. Md. and Made
oath on the holy Evangely of almighty God, that on the 24" day of
this month, he was in the County of Washington Co. DC, When in
regiment Belonging to the Brigade of Daniel E. Sickles Esqr
Brigadier General, Commanded by Col Dwight and while there he
Seen a Negro Boy Named George Belonging to Dr Jos. F Shaw of
St. Mary's – County Maryland, and that he pointed out Said Negro
to Some of the officers of Said Regiment and asked for the delivery
of said Negro under the order of Genl Sickles as the adjutant
admitted that Such was the orders. the adjutant appeared Willing
to deliver him and told the Lieutenants of the Company he was with
to that effect. No Steps Were taken for His delivery. When he
were taken possession of by the Soldiers, and Removed from the
view of said Deponant, and he was informed and Believe that a
Servant named Daniel Belonging to Mrs. Chandler Shaw of St Marys
Co. is also with Said Regiment   further said Deponant Says that he
was authorised by Dr Shaw verbally that if he Seen or Could hear of
Said Negroes to arrest or Cause to be arrested said negroes and
placed in some secure place, Until he Could have an opportunity to
Prove the ownership of said, negroes And for said purpose he Makes
this affidavit With a Request that Mr Charles Kemble an officer of
the City of Washington Shall be permitted to take into his
possession Said Negroes or Negro, and Carry them or him Before

Justice Donn of Said City, to have the Same Committed to the Gaol of Washington County, for the purpose aforesaid, and that the proper authorities, so direct the Commanding officer or officers as aforesaid or Send them by a Guard detailed for Said Purpose

HDS   Thomas Martin

Affidavit of Thomas Martin, 25 Oct. 1861, M-298 1861, Letters Received, ser. 3976, Dept. & Army of the Potomac, RG 393 Pt. 1 [C-4552]. Endorsement. Martin presented his affidavit to General George B. McClellan, commander of the Army of the Potomac, who immediately directed that General Sickles "institute enquiry for these negroes" and if found in any of the camps of the brigade, "cause them to be returned to Mr. Charles Kemble, an officer of the City of Washington, the agent of their owners." (Lt. Col. to Brigr. Gen. D. E. Sickles, 25 Oct. 1861, vol. 1 AP, pp. 268–69, Letters Sent, ser. 3964, Dept. & Army of the Potomac, RG 393 Pt. 1 [C-4552].)

47: Headquarters of the Army of the Potomac to the Commander of a Division in the Army of the Potomac

Wash^n Dec. 1. 1861.

General. I am directed by Maj: Gen: McClellan to acknowled the rec^t of your communication of the 27th Ult^o. To that portion of it which convey, the inquiry as to what disposition is to be made of the runaway negroes reported to have joined your camp, I am directed to reply. The General commanding desires that you ascertain the nature of the employment of the negroes in question while amongst the enemy. If they or any of them have been employed for military purposes, those so employed will be detained by you for such labor as the public service may offer. Those simply fugitive from the ordinary condition of labor for their class are to be dismissed from your camp. I am, General Very Res^{py} Your obt. Servant

HLc   [*James A. Handie*]

Lt. Col. [James A. Handie] to Brig. Gen. J. Hooker, 1 Dec. 1861, vol. 1/1 AP, p. 425, Letters Sent, ser. 3964, Dept. & Army of the Potomac, RG 393, Pt. 1 [C-4568]. On November 27, 1861, General Joseph Hooker, commander of Hooker's Division in the Army of the Potomac, had reported "sixty or seventy run away negroes in my camp which I would like to dispose of," and had asked of General George B. McClellan, commander of the Army of the Potomac, "What disposition shall I make of them[?]" (Brig. Genl. Joseph Hooker to Brig. General S. Williams, 27 Nov. 1861, H-423 1861, Letters Received, ser. 3976, Dept. & Army of the Potomac, RG 393 Pt. 1 [C-4553].)

After receiving McClellan's reply, Hooker confessed that he had already sent the fugitive slave women to Washington and had placed the men to work "discharging the freight from the public transports." Fugitives who had subsequently arrived had been "disposed of in the same way." Hooker informed McClellan that they had "furnished . . . information concerning the rebels I had not before learned." Nevertheless, Hooker added that he would inquire about "their past employment, and if this is their first experience in military affairs, shall have them discharged agreeably to your directions." (Brig. Genl. Joseph Hooker to Brigadier General S. Williams, 7 Dec. 1861, H-468 1861, Letters Received, ser. 3976, Dept. & Army of the Potomac, RG 393 Pt. 1 [C-4553].)

48: Secretary of State to the Commander of the Army of the Potomac

Washington, 4th. December 1861.

General: I am directed by The President to call your attention to the following subject.

Persons claimed to be held to service or labor under the laws of the State of Virginia and actually employed in hostile service against the government of the United States, frequently escape from the lines of the enemy's forces and are received within the lines of the army of the Potomac. This Department understands that such persons, afterwards coming into the City of Washington, are liable to be arrested by the City Police, upon the presumption, arising from color, that they are fugitives from service or labor. By the 4th Section of the Act of Congress approved August 6th 1861, entitled "An Act to confiscate property used for insurrectionary purposes;" such hostile employment is made a full and sufficient answer to any further claim to service or labor. Persons thus employed and escaping, are received into the military protection of the United States, and their arrest as fugitives from service or labor, should be immediately followed by the military arrest of the parties making the seizure.

Copies of this communication will be sent to the Mayor of the City of Washington and to the Marshal of the District of Columbia, that any collision between the civil and military authorities may be avoided. I am, General, Your very obedient servant,

HLS   William H Seward

William H. Seward to Major General George B. McClellan, 4 Dec. 1861, S-1440 1861, Letters Received, ser. 12, RG 94 [K-123]. Endorsement. At the time of this letter, the commander of the Army of the Potomac, General

George B. McClellan, was also general-in-chief of the army. On the same day, the House of Representatives resolved that its standing committee on the District of Columbia investigate an allegation that "there are confined within the Government jail within the city of Washington fifty-five persons who are not charged with crime but who are suspected of being slaves" and report what legislation was necessary "to relieve said persons from imprisonment and to prevent others from being similarly imprisoned." (*Official Records*, ser. 2, vol. 1, p. 782.)

49: Pennsylvania Citizens to the Congress

West Alexander Pa. Dec. 14th 1861.
To the Honorable Senate and House of Representatives in Congress Assembled. The undersigned Citizens of West Alexander Pa, beg leave to represent to your Honorable body, that we are painfully grieved to learn that men and women, have been, and are now, incarcerated in the jails of Washington City and Alexandria, being denied the comforts of life, to which every prisoner in a civilized land is entitled, they are ragged & almost naked, hungry, have no fire, & not even a pillow, on which to lay their heads, & are filthy & being devoured by vermin,

All this, being in the "land of the free & the home of the brave," We therefore, pray you, not to give sleep to your eyes, or slumber to your eyelids, until you provide means for present relief & future Security, that this disgrace to the civilization of the age Shall be unknown outside of Pandemonium.

HDS   [54 signatures]

Sarah Emery et al. to the Honorable Senate and House of Representatives in Congress Assembled, 14 Dec. 1861, 37A-G7.1, House Judiciary Committee, Petitions & Memorials, ser. 467, 37th Congress, RG 233 [D-13]. Endorsement. The signatures are in columns headed "Mens Names" (twenty-nine signatures) and "Women Names" (twenty-five signatures).

50: Iowa Citizens to the Congress

[*Jefferson County, Iowa February* 1862]
To the Congress of the United States   The undersigned loyal citizens of Jefferson County Iowa, believing that slavery has been the cause of the present rebellion, and is now its main support; that its removal would rapidly hasten the success of our arms; that you in

the exercise of your ordinary legislative functions have the power to
abolish it in the District of Columbia, and that as a war measure it
may be further abolished at least in the rebellious states, do hereby
respectfully ask that you enact a law abolishing slavery in said
District, and that you exert evry power within your control towards
the emancipation of the slaves in the rebellious states, with such
provisions, as to time manner, and compensation to loyal citizens or
exceptions in their favor, as will be the most salutary and effectual

HDS   [*108 signatures*]

Geo. Acheson et al. to the Congress of the United States, [Feb. 1862],
37A-G7.1, House Judiciary Committee, Petitions & Memorials, ser. 467,
37th Congress, RG 233 [D-13]. Endorsement.

51: Affidavit of a Maryland Slaveholder

State of Maryland Montgomery County [*March 3, 1862*]
On this 3^{d} day of March 1862 before me the subscriber one of the
Justices of the peace of the State of Maryland in and for
Montgomery county personally appeared Richard Green of said
county who after being duly sworn made the following deposition
That on or about the 1st day of December 1862 [*1861*] his
Negroe [Iwen] went of and that shortly afterwards he learnt that he
the Negroe was in the camp of the 10th Massachusetts Regiment on
the seventh St road near the district line   that six or seven weeks
ago he went down and saw Col Briggs   that Col Briggs told him to
go into the camp and if he could find his Negroe to take
him   That he went there but was driven out and was not permitted
to look for him   That on 28th of Feby 1862 he went down again
and spoke to Capt Ives about it   that Capt Ives told him to go to
the camp and take his Negroe and that no one would molest
him   that he did so and found him and attempted to take him out
and that a large crowd got around him and knocked him about
throwing small stones and dirt at him and otherwise ill treating him
and finally driveing him out of the camp without allowing him to
take his Negroe

HD

Affidavit of Richard Green, 3 Mar. 1862, enclosed in Jno. H. Bayne et al. to
Hon. E. M. Stanton, 10 Mar. 1862, M-387 1862, Letters Received, RG 107
[L-136]. For the covering letter and other enclosures, see below, doc. 134.

52: Resolution by the Washington City Council

[*Washington April, 1862*]
copy
Council No 59.
In Board of Alderman
Joint Resolution of Instruction
Be it Resolved by the Board of Aldermen and Board of Common Council of the City of Washington, That these councils, disclaiming any desire improperly to interfere with the business of the National Legislature, deem it not impertinent respectfully to express the opinion that the sentiment of a large majority of the people of this community is adverse to the *unqualified* abolition of slavery in this district at the present critical Juncture in our national affairs.

And be it further resolved, That the Joint Committee representing the interests of this Corporation before Congress be and are hereby instructed to urge respectfully upon the members of that honorable body as the constitutional guardians of the interests and rights of the people of this District, the expediency and the Justice of so shaping any legislation affecting the african race here as to provide Just and proper safe-guards against converting this city, located as it is between two Slaveholding States, into an asylum for free negroes, a population undesirable in every american community, and which it has been deemed necessary to exclude altogether from some even of the non-Slaveholding States.

K Richards
HDcSr   W T. Dove

Joint Resolution by the Washington, D.C., City Council, Apr. 1862, 37A-J4, Senate Committee on the District of Columbia, Petitions & Memorials, ser. 547, 37th Congress, RG 46 [E-11]. Richards signed as president of the Board of Common Council; Dove, as president of the Board of Aldermen. Mayor Richard Wallach endorsed the resolution, "Approved." Other endorsements. The resolution was presented on the floor of the U.S. Senate on April 2, 1862.

53: Headquarters of the Defenses North of the Potomac to the Commander of a New York Regiment

Washington April 6th 1862
Sir I am directed by Gen'l Doubleday to say in answer to your letter of the 2^{d} inst. that all negroes coming into the lines of any of

the camps or Forts under his command, are to be treated as persons and not as chattels.

Under no circumstances has the commander of a Fort or camp the power of surrendering persons claimed as fugitive slaves as this cannot be done without determining their character   The additional article of war recently passed by Congress positively prohibits this.

The question has been asked whether it would not be better to exclude negroes altogether from the lines. The General is of opinion that they bring much valuable information which cannot be obtained from any other source. They are acquainted with all the roads, paths fords and other natural features of the country and they make excellent guides   They also Know and frequently, have exposed the haunts of secession spies and traitors and the existance of reble organization. They will not therefore be exclude. The General also directs me to say that civil process cannot be served directly in the camps or Forts of his command without full authority obtained from the commanding officer for that purpose. I am very respectfully your obt Servt.

HLcSr   (Signed) E. P. Halsted

A.A.G. E. P. Halsted to Col. J. D. Shaul, 6 Apr. 1862, vol. 21/240 5AC, p. 35, Letters Sent, ser. 3714, Military Defenses North of the Potomac, RG 393 Pt. 2 No. 235 [C-4575]. The recipient, Colonel J. D. Shaul, commanded the 46th New York Infantry. A notation indicates that a copy of this letter was sent to General James S. Wadsworth, military governor of Washington, and to all the regiments serving under General Abner Doubleday in the military defenses north of the Potomac.

54: District of Columbia Former Slaveholder to the Clerk of the U.S. Circuit Court for the District of Columbia

[Washington May 14, 1862]

In pursuance of the act of Congress entitled "An act for the release of certain persons held to service or labor in the District of Columbia", passed on the 16th April 1862, and in accordance with the 9th section thereof you are hereby authorised and required to file and record in your office the following statement and schedule, under said act, of persons from whom I claimed service as slaves at the time of the passage of said act: viz:

	Age	Name	Sex	Color	Height	Particular description.
1.	65	Peter Jenkins	Male	Black	5.8 1/2	For life – Good farm hand
2.	58	Mary Jenkins	Female	"	5.2	" – Good Cook
3.	60	Ellen Jenkins	"	"	5.7	" "
4.	36	Susan Carroll	"	Dark Mulatto	4.11 7/8	For a term – till 44 years old. 8 years to serve. House servant
5.	7	Dennis Carroll	Male	Light Mulatto	3.10	For life
6.	3	AnaMaria Carroll	Female	"	child	"
7.	2	Wm Carroll	Male	"	"	"
8.	25	Richd Williams	"	Dark Mulatto	5.10 1/2	" Shoemaker, carpenter, good farm hand
9.	45	Chapman Toyer	"	Black	6.	" Good farm hand
10.	59	Sarah Toyer	Female	"	5.1	" Good laundress
11.	54	Mary Young	"	"	5.	" Good Cook
12.	37	Kitty Silass	"	Light Mulatto	5.2 1/2	" Laundress & Cook
13.	8	Gilbert Silass	Male	"	4.2 1/2	
14.	5	Wm Silass	"	"	3.10	
15.	8 months	Philip Silass			Child	
16.	24 y^{rs}	Saml Yates	"	Dark Mulatto	5.2 1/2	" Good house servant
17.	31	Judah Yates	"	"	5.3 1/2	" House servant
18.	41	John Thomas	"	Black	5.8 3/4	" Coachman & farm hand
19.	25	Henry Toyer	"	Dark Mulatto	5.10 1/2	" Farm hand
20.	24	Jos^h Toyer.	"	Black	5.8 1/2	" "
21.	23	Louisa Toyer	Female	"	5.7	" Good Cook
22.	4 months	Danl Toyer	Male		Child	"
23.	18 years	Eliza Toyer	Female	Dark Mulatto	5.1	" Good house servant
24.	36	Jane Yates	"	"	5.1 1/4	" Good Cook
25.	20	Mary Brown	"	Light Mulatto	5.7 1/8	" House Servant
26.	16	Betty Briscoe	"	Dark Mulatto	5.2	" "
27.	11	Milly Briscoe	Female	Dark Mulatto	4.6	For life. House servant
28.	2	Marg^t Briscoe	"	Black		"
29.	34	John Chapman	Male	"	5.9 1/2	" Farm hand
30.	39	Mort^r Briscoe	"	"	5.10	" "
31.	24	Townley Yates	"	Dark Mulatto	6.	" "
32.	33	Resin Yates	"	"	5.9	" Good hostler & farmhand
33.	20	And^w Yates	"	"	5.8 3/4	" Good Currier
34.	14	Wm Cylass	"	"	4.6	"

The persons mentioned in the foregoing schedule were by reason of African descent, and acquired title, my property, and were held by me and in this District, at the time of the approval of the said Act, except the last five on the list, who since the United States troops came here absented themselves and went off, and are believed still to be in some of the Companies and in their service; Mortimer Briscoe, one of the five, was in this District, at the time the act was approved but they, and the others above named, belonged and were held by me as above stated, at the time the said act was approved, and from the whole of them, I claim service and labor, and also compensation for them under said act

HDS   M C Barber –

M. C. Barber to Jno. A. Smith, Esq., [14 May 1862], claim of Margaret C. Barber, Emancipation Papers, ser. 33, Slavery Records, U.S. Circuit Court for the District of Columbia, RG 21 [MM-6]. Check marks appear beside all the names except numbers 29 through 33, and an endorsement indicates that certificates of freedom were issued to all those whose names were so marked. The commissioners appointed to award compensation to slaveholders under the District of Columbia emancipation act reported in January 1863 that they had awarded $9,351.30 to Margaret C. Barber, compensating her for all thirty-four slaves, in amounts ranging from $21.90 for the infant Daniel Toyer to $613.20 each for Henry and Joseph Toyer. Only Samuel Yates was designated as being of "No value," for reasons not specified. (U.S. Congress, House of Representatives, "Emancipation in the District of Columbia," *House Executive Documents*, 38th Cong., 1st sess., No. 42, pp. 37–38.)

55: Statement of Virginia Slaveholders

[*Fredericksburg, Va.*] Sept. 20th 1862 –
We lost from the "Bosedbel" Farm, 4 miles from Fredericksburg in Stafford Coty – the following slaves to wit;
Phil – black about 56 yrs old –
Ben Clomas – black about 21 yrs old
Jacob – one eyed about 55   "   "
Henry – stout black Mulatto about 35 – yrs old
Harry – black man about 40 yrs –
Daniel – Mulatto 35 yrs old said to be working in a paper mill in or near Washington –
Armstead Yancy – black man 40 yrs old in livery stable in Washington –
Tom – small, black, bad teeth – 22 yrs old
Lunsford, black, awkward, &c 23 yrs   "
Roxy Parker – mulatto woman 40 yrs old – cook
Polly Parker – daughter, black thick lipped – 18 yrs –
Nannie   "   14 –
William   "   12 –
Kate   "   10 –
Charles   "   5 –
Edmund   "   3 –
If any one will find Said Slaves in Washington & inform them that if they desire to return to their Home at Said Farm, they may do so & will recieve the same treatment to which they have always been used there, & will not be sold or punished for their desertion – a liberal reward will be paid for Said Servants on their return –

Fitzhugh & Little
[*In the margin, in another handwriting*] Colored boy was to give this to Mr. Rowe.
HDSr

Statement of Fitzhugh & Little, 20 Sept. 1862, Miscellaneous Records of the Provost Marshal, ser. 5457, Records of the Provost Marshal, Defenses of Washington, RG 393 Pt. 1 [C-4782]. Accompanying this statement is a second one of the same date by William A. Little, listing the slaves he had "lost" from his house in Fredericksburg during July and August 1862. They included a 21-year-old woman and her two children, "[s]aid to be living in a rented room in Washington–her husband *George* being waiter in a Hotel there," and a 42-year-old woman with five children. Little offered "a liberal reward" to anyone who would "inform Said negroes that they may return to their Home & will be treated as hertofore & not sold or punished," and who would "facilitate or aid their return so that I can get them again." He added the name of "a mulatto woman" in Georgetown, District of Columbia, who "probably knows most if not all of these 2 lists of negros & may give Some information of their whereabouts." In the same file is a similar statement by another former slaveholder whose slaves had gone to Washington in August 1862, pledging that if, "after trying their new mode of life," they "desire to return to my home and my service, this is to tell them that they will meet the same treatment in all respects, which they have had, throughout their lives." He offered to pay their expenses in returning to him and also offered a reward of $200 to "any person, who shall superintend and arrange for their return, if they desire to come." (Statement of J. L. Mary, Jr., 19 Sept. 1862.)

56: Commander of the Military District of Washington to a Maryland Slaveholder

Washington D.C. Jany 14th 1863

Dr. Sir— I was under the impression that the Post Master General would see you or write to you after the interview I had with him in respect to your case. No action, in any proceeding affecting you, has involved a judgement of disloyalty against you by my authority or with my approval— I have no right to entertain or decide on that question— Whatever detention of fugitives in this District, claimed by you, may have occurred; has been founded on the laws of the United States, which prohibit me from surrendering up such fugitives, on pain of being dismissed from the Service At least, no instructions given by me, go beyond that exposition of the statutes of last winter— I have no right to decide on the validity of your claim; and no right to surrender up the fugitive— And still, in the performance of the duties devolved on me as Military Governor I am required to extend military protection to certain fugitives as Captures of War; In the confusion & disorder incident to a state of war, and the impossibility of ascertaining by evidence the sentiments of the alledged owners of the fugitives it is quite likely to occur that loyal citizens may be deprived of their property under the operation of the laws of Congress referred to— For that reason,

I propose to record your name, if you desire it, in this office, with a statement of the claim made by you, and the disposition made of the fugitives pursued by you; with a view of presenting your case, with others, to the consideration of Congress; so that such proceedings may be had, under the authority of that body, as shall furnish an opportunity to try the question of your loyalty, if it should be disputed, and to compensate you for any loss which you have unjustly sustained by the action taken in relation to your property— Again assuring you that I disclaim all right to decide on the validity of your claim, and therefore on the question of your loyalty; and of my wish to make the performance of my duties consistent with a just regard to the character and rights of a citizen so highly recommended as you are, and of all others similarly situated I am with respect Yr. obt Servt

HLc   [*John H. Martindale*]

Brig. Genl. and Mil. Gov. [John H. Martindale] to Wm. B. Hill, Esq., 14 Jan. 1863, vol. 98 DW, pp. 467–68, Letters Sent, ser. 642, Military Dist. of Washington, Mobile Units in the Dept. of Washington, RG 393 Pt. 2 No. 12 [C-4710]. As commander of the Military District of Washington, General Martindale was also military governor.

57: District of Columbia Freedman to the Congress

[*Washington June 1864*]

To the Senate and House of Representatives of the United States: The Petition of Horace Sprigg a colored citizen of the City of Washington, in the District of Columbia respectfully represents unto your Honorable bodies, that prior to the 16th April 1862 he was the slave of John Parker Esq, of said City of Washington; that he had, through, and in the name of, his brother in law, George Johnson, a free colored man, entered into an agreement with the said John Parker for the purchase of the freedom of his daughter, Martha Ann Sprigg, who was likewise a slave of the said John Parker; and that he had paid to the said John Parker, through his said brother in law, according to said agreement the sum of about Two Hundred dollars–.

That subsequent to the said 16th day of April 1862 he presented his petition to the Emancipation Commissioners according to the provisions of the Act of Congress entitled "An Act for the release of certain persons held to service or labor in the District of Columbia" claiming compensation as the virtual owner of the said Martha Ann

Sprigg; and that his said claim was refused and disallowed by said Commissioners on the ground that, by the law as then in force in said District he could acquire no property in his said daughter prior to said 16th of April 1862, or any other rights of property under said Agreement, he, your Petitioner, being then a slave himself, and your Petitioner was advised by said Commissioners to prefer his claim for compensation to your Honorable bodies –.

Your Petitioner humbly prays that your Honorable bodies will grant him relief in the premises, and compensate him for the money expended by him as above stated And your Petitioner, as in duty bound will ever pray &c.

his
Horace ✕ Spriggs
mark

HDSr

Horace Spriggs to the Senate and House of Representatives, [June 1864], 39A-H4, Senate Committee on the District of Columbia, Petitions & Memorials, ser. 582, 39th Congress, RG 46 [E-54]. Witnessed. Endorsement. Although it was submitted to the first session of the 38th Congress, the petition is filed among the records of the 39th Congress. The 38th Congress passed no law compensating Spriggs.

CHAPTER 4

Southern Louisiana

4

Southern Louisiana

EMANCIPATION CAME to southern Louisiana in fits and starts.[1] Late in 1861, with a federal invasion imminent, the prospects for freedom looked good. In December, an expedition under General John W. Phelps, a Vermont abolitionist, gained a toehold on the islands along the Gulf of Mexico coast. Phelps promptly declared slavery incompatible with free institutions and determined to convince slaveholders of the economic, political, and moral superiority of free labor. But before Phelps could initiate his war on slavery, the incorporation of his command into the federal expedition against New Orleans dulled freedom's sharp edge. Union forces captured the city in April 1862, and Phelps found himself subordinate to General Benjamin F. Butler, commander of the new Department of the Gulf. Unlike Phelps, Butler chose to cultivate the loyalty of Louisiana unionists – immigrant workers and tradesmen in New Orleans and, more importantly, powerful and influential planters in the surrounding sugar parishes – at the expense of black liberty.[2]

During the half-year following the federal invasion, Phelps and

---

[1] This chapter describes the destruction of slavery in the Louisiana parishes near the mouth of the Mississippi River that were occupied by the Union army early in the war. These parishes formed the state's sugar-producing region and included the commercial metropolis of New Orleans. Emancipation in the remainder of the state, which began to fall under Union control only in mid-1863, is considered in chapter 5, as part of developments in the larger Mississippi Valley. Published accounts of the breakdown of slavery in Louisiana include: C. Peter Ripley, *Slaves and Freedmen in Civil War Louisiana* (Baton Rouge, La., 1976); William F. Messner, *Freedmen and the Ideology of Free Labor: Louisiana, 1862–1865* (Lafayette, La., 1978); Peyton McCrary, *Abraham Lincoln and Reconstruction: The Louisiana Experiment* (Princeton, N.J., 1978); John D. Winters, *The Civil War in Louisiana* (Baton Rouge, La., 1963); Louis S. Gerteis, *From Contraband to Freedman: Federal Policy toward Southern Blacks, 1861–1865* (Westport, Conn., 1973), chap. 4. A nineteenth-century account, James Parton, *General Butler in New Orleans. History of the Administration of the Department of the Gulf in the Year 1862. . . .* (New York, 1864), is also useful despite its strong bias in favor of General Benjamin F. Butler.

[2] Butler's plan for bolstering indigenous unionism in New Orleans rested upon distribution of captured rebel stores and upon public employment financed by a heavy tax upon Confederate sympathizers. (*Official Records*, ser. 1, vol. 15, pp. 425–26, 538–42; Maj. Genl. Benj. F. Butler to General Shepley et al., 4 June 1862, vol. 2 DG, pp. 52–53, Letters Sent, ser. 1738, Dept. of the Gulf, RG 393 Pt. 1 [C-611].)

Butler debated the future of slavery. Ignoring both the niceties of that debate and the determination of their masters to keep them in bondage, slaves struck for freedom. Runaways from the great estates of southern Louisiana and the metropolis of New Orleans deepened Phelps's commitment to abolish slavery and, by the end of 1862, had forced Butler to acknowledge the practical demise of chattel bondage. Although President Abraham Lincoln's Emancipation Proclamation exempted the Union-occupied parishes, federal military authorities effectively undermined that exemption by reorganizing plantation labor on the basis of wage payments and by interdicting the forcible apprehension of fugitive slaves. In 1864, a unionist-sponsored constitutional convention declared the formal end of slavery.

Following the capture of New Orleans, federal forces took control of the Mississippi River from the Gulf of Mexico to Baton Rouge, the heartland of Louisiana's antebellum sugar economy.[3] In the low-lying areas near the mouth of the river, rice plantations occupied the alluvial swamps; upriver near Baton Rouge, cotton plantations predominated; and along the Mississippi and the myriad inland waterways west of New Orleans, sugar held undisputed sway. The sugar barons had amassed huge fortunes and owned large, heavily capitalized plantations employing slave forces that numbered in the hundreds. Before the war, the sugar planters had dominated the economy and politics of the parishes south of Baton Rouge, and exerted strong influence on state and national politics as well. Although secession threatened their future, they clung tenaciously to the way of life that had generated their spectacular prosperity.

Upon the arrival of Union forces, planters with fierce Confederate sympathies fled for their lives, taking their slaves and movable property north to the interior of the Confederacy or west to Texas. But in greater proportion than any other segment of the planter class that confronted federal invasion, Louisiana's sugar barons remained on their

[3] In August 1862, Union troops were forced to abandon Baton Rouge, but they retained control of the river parishes of Plaquemines, St. Bernard, Orleans, Jefferson, St. Charles, St. John the Baptist, St. James, and Ascension. Following successful operations west of New Orleans in the fall of 1862, the Union army also occupied Assumption, Lafourche, Terrebonne, St. Mary's, and St. Martin's parishes. After federal troops reoccupied Baton Rouge at the end of the year, Iberville, East Baton Rouge, and West Baton Rouge parishes came into Union hands. Together, the sixteen parishes covered roughly 2,000 square miles. In 1860, the population of Orleans Parish (which included the city of New Orleans) numbered 149,000 whites (40 percent of the state's total); 11,000 free blacks (60 percent of the state's total); and 14,000 slaves. The population of the remaining fifteen parishes comprised 67,000 whites; 3,000 free blacks; and 103,000 slaves (30 percent of the state's total). (U.S., Census Office, 8th Census, *Population of the United States in 1860* [Washington, 1864], p. 194.)

estates. Their antebellum record of proslavery unionism and their reluctant submission to the Confederate regime led them to expect that under Union occupation they could continue to keep their slaves and work the land in the traditional manner. When Butler offered the opportunity, many of these planters quickly swore allegiance to the Union and promised to cooperate with the federal government, expecting the Union army to guarantee the security of their slave property.

Federal military success also spawned other sorts of unionism. Pragmatists bowed to the new military reality while masking their sympathy for the Southern cause; they, too, quickly swore allegiance to the Union. Scattered among these unionist planters (genuine and pragmatic) were numerous died-in-the-wool rebels who by reason of advanced age or physical infirmity could not flee the Union occupation; they tried to appropriate its benefits while maintaining their political loyalties. Their tactics seldom worked, for strong Confederate sympathies were difficult to conceal in wartime Louisiana.

However much planters wanted to preserve the old order, secession and the subsequent Union occupation of lower Louisiana profoundly affected blacks, free as well as slave. Many of Louisiana's free people of color traced their freedom back to pre-Revolutionary times, when French and Spanish colonists occupied the lower Mississippi Valley. Priding themselves on their cultural distinctiveness, they spoke French and worshipped in Roman Catholic churches. The wealthiest among them educated their children in Europe. Although free people of color enjoyed many benefits of freedom, including the right to travel at will and to own property, they were nonetheless debarred from full citizenship, particularly political and civil rights. Notwithstanding these disabilities, free people of color prospered in Louisiana, especially in New Orleans, where they practiced a wide variety of trades and professions. Many enjoyed modest wealth as artisans and urban tradesmen, and a few achieved affluence as slaveholding sugar planters.[4]

In status and often in complexion, the free people of color occupied the middle of Louisiana society, linked by ties of blood to both slaves and masters and relegated to a legal limbo above the position of black slaves but below that of white citizens. Doubting their loyalty, Confederate officials called upon free people of color to affirm their allegiance to the slaveholders' regime. With varying degrees of enthusiasm, free people of color professed their fealty. Some volunteered to serve the Confederacy and were mustered into separate units of the Louisiana militia, denominated the Native Guard. Federal control of southern

---

[4] Herbert E. Sterkx, *The Free Negro in Ante-Bellum Louisiana* (Rutherford, N.J., 1972); Laura Foner, "The Free People of Color in Louisiana and St. Domingue: A Comparative Portrait of Two Three-Caste Slave Societies," *Journal of Social History* 3 (Summer 1970): 406–30.

Louisiana enabled free people of color to strip away the facade of Confederate loyalty. They promptly swore allegiance to the Union and resumed their lives, no longer tainted by the aspersion of treason that had plagued them under Confederate rule. Many were eager to demonstrate their loyalty to the federal government.[5]

Like the free people of color, slaves in southern Louisiana demonstrated support for the Union only guardedly during the early months of the war. Masters who opposed secession did so in the interest of prolonging slavery, not abolishing it, and planters severely punished "sedition" among their slaves. Slaves silently observed the political posturing, understanding that their prospects had changed little; as before the war, refuge in the swamps of the countryside or the back alleys of New Orleans offered the only possibilities of escape. Yet, even within this narrow range, secession and civil war enhanced the slaves' chances for freedom.

The physical geography of southern Louisiana lent itself to the slaves' struggle for freedom. The waterways offered the best routes for moving crops and provisions. As a result, slaves who would have been lost only a few miles from the plantation if traveling by wagon, casually recognized landmarks miles from home when traveling by boat. The waterways brought New Orleans and other more secluded hideaways within striking distance. Perennial flooding determined the physical layout of plantations in southern Louisiana. Virtually every plantation fronted on water, either the Mississippi River or one of the numerous bayous. From the levees, formed naturally over the millennia and maintained more recently by slave laborers, the land sloped gently away to swamps, which provided wood for the sugar mills and also shelter for runaway slaves. Before the war, truant slaves often took temporary refuge in the tangle of vines and stumps to protest cruel treatment or exact concessions from their masters. And some slaves fled there permanently, eluding slave catchers and their hounds and forming small but enduring maroon communities.

The organization of sugar plantation agriculture also aided the slaves' bid for freedom. Gang labor predominated, but some slaves worked by the task. After completing their assigned duties, coopers and other artisans were permitted to work on their own and sell the products of that labor. Woodcutters also labored by the task and sold the extra wood they chopped. The task system in Louisiana, as elsewhere, enabled these slaves to acquire property of their own. The powerful, almost superhuman exertion required during the sugar har-

[5] Mary F. Berry, "Negro Troops in Blue and Gray: The Louisiana Native Guards, 1861–1863," *Louisiana History* 8 (Spring 1967): 165–90; Manoj K. Joshi and Joseph P. Reidy, " 'To Come Forward and Aid in Putting Down this Unholy Rebellion': The Officers of Louisiana's Free Black Native Guard during the Civil War Era," *Southern Studies* 21 (Fall 1982): 326–42. See also *Freedom*, ser. 2: chaps. 1, 6.

vest further broadened the possibilities for property accumulation by slaves. During grinding and boiling, which proceeded round the clock, masters commonly paid their slaves cash for the hours they worked beyond the normal working day. As a result, slaves on sugar plantations had small sums of money to spend, and itinerant peddlers plied a lively trade along the waterways of the lower Mississippi. Slaves thereby gained experience in equating units of labor with units of money and in exchanging cash for commodities in market transactions.

Slaves on the sugar plantations also earned cash from the produce of their garden plots. These plots relieved masters from having to grow or purchase all the food their slaves consumed, and their fresh produce provided a richer and more variegated diet than plantation economics would otherwise have allowed. Moreover, slaves traded and sold the surplus of their gardens to each other, their masters, itinerant peddlers, and the public at large. Most masters also allowed slaves to raise barnyard fowl and swine, for sale as well as for their own consumption. In addition, slaves hunted in the swamps, often with dogs and guns purchased with cash or bartered for produce. Before the war, these customary practices opened to slaves in southern Louisiana a world beyond the plantation and relatively free from the direct control of their masters, even while attaching them more securely to the regime that offered such perquisites. But the war so changed the context of slavery that old patterns of behavior assumed entirely new meaning. Experience with a market economy, access to gardens, and possession of household furniture, tools, and livestock became powerful weapons in the quest for freedom.[6]

Civil war undermined the masters' ability to use unilateral force; hence they could no longer command obedience from their slaves, and instead had to bargain for it. Stripped of its ideological trappings and political underpinnings, the master-slave relationship reduced itself to the slaves' providing labor in exchange for the masters' providing food. Slaves unable to feed themselves remained beholden to a master, because they required access to provision grounds. Slaves able to feed themselves had no use for a master. The flight of rebel masters provided an opening whereby some slaves could terminate their dependence. Runaway slaves could take advantage of the garden plots on abandoned plantations, either by appropriating their fruits or by cultivating them for future harvest. On some abandoned estates, gardens soon overtook fields previously devoted exclusively to sugar or cotton. Independent subsistence established the foundation from which to pursue other measures of freedom.

[6] On slavery in southern Louisiana, see J. Carlyle Sitterson, *Sugar Country: The Cane Sugar Industry in the South, 1753–1950* (Lexington, Ky., 1953); Joe Gray Taylor, *Negro Slavery in Louisiana* (Baton Rouge, La., 1963).

THE DESTRUCTION OF SLAVERY

By appropriating the land on abandoned plantations, some slaves in the southernmost reaches of the Mississippi Valley cut the ties that bound them to the old order. Yet, in doing so they moved onto treacherous terrain. Both former masters and federal military authorities deemed them outlaws — beyond the jurisdiction of either the plantation order or martial law. Rebel guerrillas intent upon terrorizing insubordinate blacks, loyal planters desperate to shield their slaves from seditious influences, and federal authorities anxious to suppress lawlessness all took aim at the self-supporting runaways. Consequently, fugitives preserved their freedom only by remaining on the run. Runaways used the deserted estates as vantage points from which to assess the actions of their masters and of the Union army, waiting to see if either would recognize them as free. When the soldiers under Phelps made their position clear, the runaways hastened to secure federal protection.

The combination of loyal masters and fugitive slaves frustrated Union commander Benjamin F. Butler. During previous service in the loyal state of Maryland and the secessionist state of Virginia, Butler had established two different precedents regarding slavery. Neither, however, seemed precisely applicable to Louisiana. In Maryland, whose allegiance to the Union left no doubt regarding the validity of the laws respecting slavery, Butler had offered to protect the property rights of slaveholders. In secessionist Virginia, however, he had granted sanctuary to fugitive slaves and employed them for military purposes. Secession had severed Louisiana's ties with the Union, thus seeming to liken its situation to that of Virginia. But when Louisiana slaveholders swore loyalty to the Union, Butler felt obliged to support them as he had supported those in Maryland. Pulled in two directions at once, Butler attempted to apply both precedents: employing fugitive slaves as military necessity required, and turning unemployable fugitives out of army lines, preferably into the custody of loyal masters. The second approach appeared to violate the new article of war adopted by Congress in March 1862, but elicited from the Lincoln administration neither rebuke nor alternative instructions. Butler affirmed his belief that "slavery is a curse to a nation," but, in the absence of orders to the contrary, he was willing to "accept the fact of its present existence" and do nothing to destroy it. Ever the pragmatist, Butler took refuge in the undefined area between slavery and freedom.

General Phelps, the purist, occupied a world unblemished by subtle shading. He denounced slavery as "unsuited to the age." Because it depended upon the lash, rather than cash as its "stimulant to labor and effort," slavery destroyed the proper relationship between capital and labor. From Phelps's perspective, free labor was "the granite basis on which free institutions must rest" and slavery a curse on the body politic. Futhermore, slavery violated the "natural rights" of the slaves and compromised the sovereignty of the national government by inter-posing the authority of the master between the nation-state and its "subjects." Given the constitutional obligation to guarantee a republi-can form of government, Phelps called upon President Lincoln to exercise his war powers and proclaim freedom to all slaves. But the Vermont general was too impatient to await the action of his chief. Chafing under the restraints imposed by existing laws and army policy, the sluggish movement of the Lincoln administration, and Butler's accommodation with Louisiana slavery, Phelps began offering sanctu-ary to runaway slaves.

From Camp Parapet, some four miles above New Orleans on the Mississippi River, Phelps broadcast his message of freedom to slaves in the plantation district north of the city. With Butler vowing to secure the slave property of loyal masters, and masters mapping strategies according to their political convictions, slaves quickly cast their lot with Phelps. Requiring "no inducements from me to seek the protec-tion of our flag," contended Phelps, slaves fled to Camp Parapet from the swamps, from abandoned plantations, and even from functioning estates.[7] Plantation hands from as far as a hundred miles upriver piled their humble belongings into boats, navigated the swift and unpredict-able currents, and disembarked at Phelps's camp. Not every attempt to reach the safety of Union lines succeeded, but the possibility of capture failed to discourage blacks from seeking freedom. As word of Phelps's hospitality spread, New Orleans slaves, even those employed at the federally supervised gas works, braved the few miles between the city and Camp Parapet. Phelps welcomed them, and his camp became a beacon of liberty for slaves throughout southern Louisiana.

The ragged condition of the newly arrived fugitives and their reports of barbarous treatment incensed the abolitionist general. Phelps ordered retributive raids on the plantations of the cruelest masters and staunchest rebels. The raids ignited the plantation districts with the spirit of freedom, intensifying the disruptive effects of federal military occupation, the flight of rebel masters, and the de facto freedom of abandoned slaves. Slaves accompanied Phelps's soldiers to safety, fur-ther augmenting the black population at Camp Parapet.

The possibilities opened by Phelps and the slaves' willingness to take advantage of them sped the deterioration of slavery in southern Louisi-ana. Previously loyal field hands defied plantation owners and man-agers. They reformulated the work routine to suit their own priorities, carefully cultivating their garden patches while weeds choked the fields of sugar cane and cotton. Emulating the independence of fugitives who

---

[7] Late Brig. Gen. J. W. Phelps to the Public, 20 Sept. 1862, quoted in J. W. Phelps report of service, 16 Jan. 1873, vol. 6, Generals' Reports of Service, ser. 160, RG 94 [JJ-5].

had seized control of abandoned estates, many plantation hands insisted that they were entitled to move about and work entirely as they pleased. Those willing to labor in the masters' fields demanded wages and the removal of white overseers. Some drove all whites off the estates and declared the plantations their own.

Some masters who tested their slaves' determination met the pent-up fury of years of bondage. Fear of slave insurrection – the perennial insomniac of Southern planters – struck with heightened force. One desperate planter family petitioned General Butler for protection: after having fled to Phelps's camp, four of their slaves returned home boasting "that the General had given them a pass, and an *Order* to the other Negroes, to rise and murder the whole family – and plunder and burn the Plantation."

Neither loyal nor rebel masters could find an antidote for the epidemic of "demoralization." Planters accustomed to ready obedience or at least sullen compliance, found their world turned upside down. The desertion of some slaves and the insubordination of others led masters to despair of slavery's future. Unable to control their slaves, some masters drove them off under the lash, ordering them to "go to the Yankees who are king here now." Phelps waited with open arms.

Such outbursts from allegedly loyal masters, the intended beneficiaries of Union policy, embarrassed Butler, and he moved quickly to eliminate the source of his discomfort. Never reluctant to free the slaves of rebels, Butler declared that planters who cast out their slaves perforce demonstrated their disloyalty. In July 1862, he directed military authorities to treat banished slaves as "manumitted & emancipated." The following month, General Neal Dow, a Maine abolitionist who commanded Fort Jackson and Fort St. Philip, near the mouth of the Mississippi, followed Butler's lead and began issuing certificates of freedom to slaves who reported that their masters had driven them off.

Dow's free papers caused an uproar in the river parishes south of New Orleans. Masters claimed that their slaves obtained free papers under false pretenses, then returned home and disrupted plantation order. Possessing written certification of their freedom, slaves confronted masters and overseers with new demands, threatening to leave if not satisfied. On several plantations, slaves drove off their overseers, and forbade any white person to remain upon the premises. On other estates, they ransacked the big house and sold the booty. One incensed planter declared that Dow's emancipation papers had produced "a state of insurrection" among the slaves; he begged Union authorities to restore order. Some twenty of his slaves had obtained free papers and behaved insolently thereafter, refusing to work and otherwise setting "a bad example to the other negroes." Auguste, one of the "ringleaders," had demanded a gun from the plantation overseer and used "offensive" language: "among other things he said that he wished to go to Virginia, meaning thereby that he wished to enlist." Dow's free papers pitted slaveholders against Union authorities. With the two thus embroiled, slaves played one side against the other to advance the cause of their own freedom.

While Butler undermined the authority of disloyal masters with his left hand, he tried to maintain the authority of loyal masters with his right. Phelps remained a major obstacle. Attempting to win the principled abolitionist to his practical view, Butler asked Phelps to cooperate with slaveholders who sought runaways at Fort Parapet. Citing the new article of war, Phelps peremptorily rejected the suggestion. Butler tried another tack, requesting that Phelps return to their masters slaves who were needed for emergency levee repairs. Butler insisted that the emergency placed the case outside the provisions of the new article of war and might even require soldiers to work on the levee.[8] Again Phelps refused. Stymied, Butler tried to outflank his stubborn subordinate, hoping to check the influx of new fugitives by ordering Phelps to exclude from his lines "all unemployed persons, black and white," but still Phelps held firm.[9] An exasperated Butler at last put the matter bluntly to Secretary of War Edwin M. Stanton, asking formal approval for either his or Phelps's policy. Stanton's noncommittal suggestion that he continue to exercise his "accustomed skill and discretion" could not have pleased General Butler.[10]

Phelps's confidence grew while Butler's doubts multiplied. After passage of the Second Confiscation Act and the Militia Act in July 1862, Phelps anticipated the imminent enlistment of blacks into federal military service. Believing that an army of former slaves would deal a deadly blow to the slaveholders' rebellion, Phelps seized the new opportunity to strike at slavery. He quickly organized 300 black soldiers from among the fugitive men at his camp. At the end of July, he asked Butler to arm and equip them. Butler stalled. Deliberately skirting the question of arming black men, he ordered Phelps to put all able-bodied fugitives to work cutting down the trees surrounding Camp Parapet, as a defense against an expected rebel attack. Confident that Butler had lost touch with Northern public opinion and federal policy, and hopeful that President Lincoln could be forced to take a public stand on one side or the other, Phelps indignantly resigned. He would not serve as a "mere Slave-driver."[11] But Phelps had overextended himself. Lincoln refused to intervene, and after some haggling, Butler accepted the resignation.

Phelps's resignation provided Butler only brief respite. While Butler

[8] *Official Records*, ser. 1, vol. 15, p. 443.
[9] *Official Records*, ser. 1, vol. 15, pp. 443–44.
[10] *Official Records*, ser. 1, vol. 15, pp. 485–86, 515–16.
[11] *Freedom*, ser. 2: docs. 9–10.

could menace the fugitive slaves who had given force to Phelps's aggressive emancipationist policy, he could not avoid the other linchpin of Phelps's program – enlistment of black soldiers. Events forced the issue even before Phelps had loaded his bags aboard the steamer home.

During the summer of 1862, Confederate forces seriously threatened Butler's Department of the Gulf. With Union soldiers in short supply, Phelps's plan to enlist black men no longer seemed outrageous. In August, Butler "called on Africa," incorporating the free colored Native Guard into federal military ranks. Phelps had envisioned an army of emancipated slaves serving as the vanguard of emancipation, but Butler enlisted only free men of color, who he hoped would alleviate his troop shortage without provoking a wholesale assault on slavery. But once Butler had committed himself to arming blacks, it was only a matter of time before slaves would also enter the ranks.[12]

As Phelps had predicted, slave soldiers spread freedom's message far and wide. So too did free black soldiers. After enlisting, recruits returned home on furlough in the Union uniform, visiting relatives and friends and encouraging other men to enlist. Before long, black soldiers traversed the plantation districts and the streets of New Orleans, on official business as guards and recruiters, speaking with the full authority of the federal government and flaunting their power over civilians, former masters not excepted. The enlistment of black soldiers made strikingly clear the monumental changes wrought by the war. Slaves delighted in seeing the tables turned and exulted in a new sense of their own power. Free blacks also shared in the celebration, anticipating new prospects for equality as slavery disintegrated. Whether slave or free, black soldiers accelerated the destruction of chattel bondage, in part by inspiring slaves to act against slavery and in part by making a shambles of the traditional authority of the master.[13]

The subversive force of black men in blue uniforms frightened even Union officials. Some federal officers, fearful that black soldiers would instigate a slave revolt, parroted the charges of the planters. General Godfrey Weitzel, who would later command the Union's only all-black army corps, served his apprenticeship with black troops in Louisiana, plagued with doubts that black soldiers could fight and apprehensive that they would incite a slave insurrection. Late in 1862, in the midst of his successful invasion of the sugar district west of New Orleans, Weitzel begged Butler to remove the three newly organized black regiments from his command. Although Butler hardly wished to instigate wholesale slave revolt, he acknowledged, in the aftermath of the preliminary Emancipation Proclamation, the Union army's official mandate to bring "freedom to this servile race." Fast emerging as a

[12] *Freedom*, ser. 2: pp. 41–44, and docs. 9–11.
[13] For a full consideration of the black military experience, see *Freedom*, ser. 2.

leading advocate of the sable arm, Butler lauded the contribution of black soldiers. Although still determined to preserve order on the plantations of loyal masters and maintain the productivity of the sugar estates, he also sought to punish rebellious masters by depriving them of their slaves. And he intimated that fear and confusion among disloyal citizens might be salutary from a military point of view. When Weitzel requested guidance regarding the large number of fugitives following his army, Butler replied that Congress had declared them free and had forbidden military officers to return them to their masters, but he directed that they be put to work on the plantations "as far as possible." "[U]se every energy to have the sugar crop made and preserved for the owners that are loyal," Butler ordered, "and for the United States where the owners are disloyal."[14] Weitzel's successful military operations at once expanded the federal domain and profoundly aggravated Butler's dilemma. The bifurcated policy that required one rule for fugitive slaves owned by loyal masters and another for those owned by the disloyal, appeared increasingly untenable.

Disregarding the power and influence of their masters, as well as the circuitous policy disputes among federal authorities, southern Louisiana slaves declared their own freedom, forcing the hands of both. Loyal slaveholders had little choice but to compromise. Planters south of New Orleans, who had never regained their authority after the issue of Dow's free papers, capitulated first. In late October 1862, they agreed to pay their laborers wages of $10 per month and to refrain from wielding the lash. To the planters, Butler promised federal assistance in supervising plantation labor; to the freedpeople, he offered military protection against abusive treatment. Following Weitzel's successful military operations west of New Orleans, Butler extended the system to the entire area under Union control.[15]

Late in 1862, as masters in southern Louisiana negotiated the end of slavery, the slaves eagerly awaited its confirmation in President Lincoln's forthcoming emancipation proclamation. Frightened planters reported that slaves—many of them armed—roamed the countryside "[s]hrieking threats, singing and exciting to insurrection." Harvest work virtually halted in anticipation of general emancipation. Slaveholders begged Union officials to reestablish order. New Orleans blacks planned a parade for January 1, 1863, in support of the Union and emancipation, and Butler apparently gave his blessing to the celebration. Anticipating that thousands of plantation hands would attend, whites conjured up the specter of St. Domingue, and urgently

[14] *Official Records*, ser. 1, vol. 15, pp. 162–63.
[15] *Official Records*, ser. 1, vol. 15, pp. 592–95. For a full discussion of the federally sponsored free labor system in wartime Louisiana, see *Freedom*, ser. 1, vol. 2.

requested federal authorities to ban the procession and all similar gatherings. General Nathaniel P. Banks, who succeeded Butler in command of the Department of the Gulf in mid-December, acceded to their wishes. News that Lincoln had exempted the Union-occupied parishes of southern Louisiana from the Emancipation Proclamation compounded the slaves' disappointment.[16]

Still, there could be no turning back the clock. Citing his responsibility to maintain public order, General Banks effectively undercut the exemption. While enjoining blacks to remain on the plantations, upon pain of forced labor on the public works, Banks also forbade military authorities to return slaves to their masters. Moreover, he unabashedly asserted that the total extinction of slavery was merely a matter of time. For a short period after the new year, police officers and provost marshals in New Orleans seized fugitive slaves as vagrants and jailed them, pending return to their masters.[17] A wily provost judge in Lafourche Parish authorized masters to apprehend their slaves by force, as a way around the prohibition against the military's doing so. But, for the most part, only urban masters and a handful of the most powerful and influential planters could take advantage of this "golden moment." At the end of January 1863, in the interest of "the continued peace of the country," Banks issued General Order 12, which forbade the "forcible seizure of fugitives from service or labor by their owners" or by military authorities, threatened black vagrants with forced labor on the public works, and expanded Butler's "voluntary system of labor." Banks solicited from planters suggestions for the establishment of "a yearly system of negro labor, which shall provide for the food, clothing, proper treatment, and just compensation for the negroes, at fixed rates or an equitable proportion of the yearly crop."[18] The order crushed the loyal planters' hope of perpetuating slavery in southern Louisiana and seriously weakened their influence within the fractious politics of Louisiana unionism. Federal victories at Vicksburg and Port Hudson during the summer of 1863 and the President's proclamation of amnesty and

---

[16] The parishes exempted from the proclamation were St. Bernard, Plaquemines, Jefferson, St. John the Baptist, St. Charles, St. James, Ascension, Assumption, Terrebonne, Lafourche, St. Mary's, St. Martin's, and Orleans. (U.S., *Statutes at Large, Treaties, and Proclamations*, vol. 12 [Boston, 1863], pp. 1268–69.)

[17] In addition to the relevant documents included in this chapter, see C. C. Morgan to Maj. Genl. Banks, 19 Jan. 1863, M-6 1863, Letters Received, ser. 1920, Civil Affairs, Dept. of the Gulf, RG 393 Pt. 1 [C-689]; C. C. Morgan to Maj. Genl. Banks, 24 Jan. 1863, M-33 1863, Letters Received, ser. 1920, Civil Affairs, Dept. of the Gulf, RG 393 Pt. 1 [C-689]; Lieut. Col. James Smith to Col. J. H. French, 23 Feb. 1863, filed with C. C. Morgan to Maj. Genl. Banks, 11 Feb. 1863, M-50 1863, Letters Received, ser. 1920, Civil Affairs, Dept. of the Gulf, RG 393 Pt. 1 [C-689].

[18] *Official Records*, ser. 1, vol. 15, pp. 666–67. For the operation of Banks's order, see *Freedom*, ser. 1, vol. 2.

reconstruction the following December infused new life into Louisiana's floundering unionist movement. In 1864, unionists formed a loyal state government and held a consitutional convention that formally ended slavery, ratifying in law the process that slaves in southern Louisiana had set in motion more than two years earlier.[19]

---

[19] For military events and emancipation policy from 1863 to the end of the war, see below, chap 5. On unionist politics in Louisiana, including the state constitutional convention, see McCrary, *Abraham Lincoln and Reconstruction*, chap. 8.

58: Proclamation by the Commander at Ship Island, Mississippi

Ship Island, Miss. December 4th 1861
To the Loyal Citizens of the South-West: Without any desire of my own, but contrary to my private inclinations, I again find myself among you as an officer of the Government.[1] A proper respect for my fellow countrymen renders it not out of place that I should make known to you the motives and principles by which my command will be governed.

We believe that every State that has been admitted as a Slave State into the Union, since the adoption of the Constitution, has been so admitted in direct violation of that Constitution.

We believe that the Slave States which existed, as such, at the adoption of our Constitution, are, by becoming parties to that compact, under the highest obligations of honor and morality to abolish Slavery.

It is our conviction that monopolies are as destructive as competition is conservative of the principles and vitalities of republican government; that slave-labor is a monopoly which excludes free-labor and competition; that slaves are kept in comparative ease and idleness in a fertile half of our arable national territory, while free white laborers, constantly augmenting in numbers from Europe, are confined to the other half, and are often distressed by want; that the free-labor of the North has more need of expansion into the Southern States, from which it is virtually excluded, than Slavery had into Texas in 1846; that free labor is essential to free institutions; that these institutions are better adapted and more congenial to the Anglo-Saxon race than are the despotic tendencies of Slavery; and, finally, that the dominant political principle of this North American Continent, so long as the Caucasian race continues to flow in upon us from Europe, must needs be that of free institutions and free government. Any obstructions to the progress of that form of Government in the United-States must inevitably be attended with discord and war.

Slavery, from the condition of a universally recognised social and moral evil, has become at length a political institution, demanding political recognition. It demands rights, to the exclusion and annihilation of those rights which are insured to us by the Constitution; and we must choose between them, which we will have, for we cannot have both. The Constitution was made for Freemen, not for Slaves. Slavery, as a social evil, might for a time be tolerated and endured; but as a political institution it becomes imperious and exacting, controlling, like a dread necessity, all whom circumstances have compelled to live under its sway, hampering their action, and thus impeding our national progress. As a political institution it could exist as a coordinate part only of two forms of government, viz, the despotic and the free; and it could exist under a free government only where public sentiment, in the most unrestricted exercise of a robust freedom, leading to extravagance and licentiousness, had swayed the thoughts and habits of the people beyond the bounds and limits of their own moderate constitutional provisions. It could exist under a free government only where the people in a period of unreasoning extravagance had permitted popular clamor to overcome public reason, and had attempted the impossibility of setting up, permanently, as a political institution, a social evil which is opposed to moral law.

By reverting to the history of the past, we find that one of the most destructive wars on record, that of the French Revolution, was originated by the attempt to give political character to an institution which was not susceptible of political character. The Church, by being endowed with political power, with its convents, its schools, its immense landed wealth, its associations, secret and open, became the ruling power of the State, and thus occasioned a war of more strife and bloodshed, probably, than any other war which has desolated the earth.

Slavery is still less susceptible of political character than was the Church. It is as fit at this moment for the lumber-room of the past as was in 1793 the monastery, the landed wealth, the exclusive privileges, etc, of the Catholic Church in France. It behooves us to consider, as a self-governing people, bred, and reared, and practiced in the habits of self-government, whether we cannot, whether we *ought* not, to revolutionize Slavery out of existence without the necessity of a conflict of arms like that of the French Revolution.

Indeed, we feel assured that the moment Slavery is abolished, from that moment our Southern brethren, every ten of whom have probably seven relatives in the North, would begin to emerge from a hateful delirium. From that moment, relieved from imaginary terrors, their days become happy and their nights peaceable and free from alarm; the aggregate amount of labor, under the new stimulus of fair competition, becomes greater day by day; property rises in value; invigorating influences succeed to stagnation, degeneracy and decay; and union, harmony, and peace, to which we have so long been strangers, become restored, and bind us again in the bonds of friendship and amity, as when we first began our national career, under our glorious government of 1789.

Why do the leaders of the rebellion seek to change the form of your ancient government? Is it because the growth of the African element of your population has come at length to render a change necessary? Will you permit the free government under which you have thus far lived, and which is so well suited for the developement of true manhood, to be altered to a narrow and belittling despotism, in order to adapt it to the necessities of ignorant slaves, and the requirements of their proud and aristocratic owners? Will the laboring men of the South bend their necks to the same yoke that is suited to the slave? We think not. We may safely answer that the time has not yet arrived when our Southern brethren, for the mere sake of keeping Africans in slavery, will abandon their long cherished free institutions, and enslave themselves. It is the conviction of my command, as a part of the national forces of the United-States that labor – manual labor – is inherently noble; that it cannot be systematically degraded by any nation without ruining its peace, happiness, and power; that free labor is the granite basis on which free institutions must rest; that it is the right, the capital, the inheritance, the hope of the poor man every where; that it is especially the right of five millions of our fellow countrymen in the Slave States as well as of the four millions of Africans there; and all our efforts, therefore, however small or great, whether directed against the interference from governments abroad, or against rebellious combinations at home, shall be for Free labor; our motto and our standard shall be, here, and every where, and on all occasions – FREE LABOR AND WORKING-MEN'S RIGHTS. It is on this basis, and this basis alone, that our munificent government – the asylum of the nations – can be perpetuated and preserved.

ADcS

J. W. Phelps

Proclamation of Brigr. Genl. J. W. Phelps to the Loyal Citizens of the South-West, 4 Dec. 1861, quoted in J. W. Phelps, report of service, 16 Jan. 1873, vol. 6, Generals' Reports of Service, ser. 160, RG 94 [JJ-5]. In his postwar report of service, Phelps indicated that the *New York Times* published the proclamation on December 17, 1861, but "the government never seemed to recognize [it], either to approve or disapprove."

1 Presumably a reference to his earlier service during the Mexican War.

59: Two Letters from the Commander of the Department of the Gulf to the Commander of Camp Parapet, Louisiana

New Orleans May 9th 1862.

General Phelps— Mr J. B. G. Armond says that, a boy by name of Irwin Pardon whose services he claims, has come within your lines. The course which I have adopted in such case is this. If I have any use for the services of such a boy I employ him without any scruple. If I have not, I do not harbor him, as my subsistence would by no means serve for so many extra men that I do not need. If you have any use for him, use him, if not, is he not like any other vagrant about the Camp. Respectfully

HLcSr   (Signed) B. F. Butler

New Orleans. May 10th 1862

Gen Phelps   I commend to you the bearers of this note Peter Saure & P Soniat Gentleman & planters at Jefferson just above your lines. They will make the statement of fact to you which they have made me & which from their characters I am bound to believe. You will see the need of giving them every aid in your power to save and protect the *Levee* even to returning their own Negroes and adding others if need be to their forces. This is out side of the question of returning negroes. You should send your Soldiers let alone allowing the man who are protecting us all from the Mississippi to have these workman who are accustomed to this service. Very Respectfully Your Obt Serv't

HLcSr   Signed Benj. F. Butler

Maj. Gen'l. B. F. Butler to General Phelps, 9 May 1862, and Maj. Gen. Benj. F. Butler to Gen. Phelps, 10 May 1862, vol. 1 DG, pp. 203, 212–13, Letters Sent, ser. 1738, Dept. of the Gulf, RG 393 Pt. 1 [C-1054, C-1055].

60: Louisiana Slaveholder to the Provost Marshal of the District of New Orleans

New Orleans May 19th 1862

Major: On the 9th instant I obtained from you a permit to ascertain the whereabouts of three negroes belonging to me, and to have access to any vessel or spot within your lines, with instructions not to take back the slaves if found, but to report to you.

Having reason to believe that some of my slaves were at Gen Phelps' camp at the fortifications above Carrollton, I approached the General, requested of him permission to search for my fugitive slaves, and was peremptorily refused to do so. I then informed him of the nature of the permit which I had from you, and he declined taking cognizance of the same.

It now remains for me to inform you that I have accidentally seen one of my slaves there, and that I know the other two to be also there.

As I will not approach Gen Phelps any more, he having signified to me that he intended to stop these applications for the recovery of fugitive slaves in his camp, and that he would not return them if there, I will wait that justice be done me by yourself or Major General Butler in the manner that you will judge best & most practicable. your most obedient servant

ALS   Polycarpe Fortier

Polycarpe Fortier to Major Jonas H. French, 19 May 1862, F-69 1862, Letters Received by the Provost Marshal General, ser. 1390, State of LA, Provost Marshal Field Organizations, RG 393 Pt. 4 [C-500]. A search of the surviving records of the provost marshal general of Louisiana and the Department of the Gulf did not reveal a reply.

61: Commander of the Department of the Gulf to the Secretary of War

New Orleans, May 25th *1862.*

Sir, In matters pertaining to the conduct of affairs in my own department which affect that alone, I will trouble you for instructions as little as possible, but in those which affect the administrative policy of the country, I beg leave to refer to Head of the War Department for advice and direction. The question now pressing me is, the state of negro property here and the condition of the negroes as men. It has a gravity as regards both white and black appalling as the mind follows out the logical necessities of different lines of action. Ethnological in its proportions and demands for investigation, it requires active administrative operations immediately upon the individual in his daily life, his social, political and religious status as a human being, while some of the larger deductions of political economy are to be at once worked out by any given course of conduct. It cannot be solved therefore without thought, or discussed by a phrase or a paragraph. The question now comes to me in a different form from that in which it has presented itself to any other Military Commander.

At Fortress Monroe during the last summer, I found the negro deserted by his master; or having been forced by him into the fortification as the builder and thus made to aid in the rebellion. The rights of property under that condition of things could be easily settled. The man was to be treated as a human being wrecked upon a civilized coast; – all his social ties and means of living gone – to be cared for because he was a man. My action thereupon is well known and was approved by the Government.

At Port Royal the same condition of things substantially obtained, and I suppose will be dealt with in like manner. Here however an entirely different state of the question is disclosed.

The General commanding finds himself in possession of a tract of country larger than some States of the Union. This has submitted to the Government of the United States; – a community, with whom by proclamation the President is about opening commercial relation with all the world except for that which is contraband of war, rich in fertile lands, in it a city of the first class wherein its inhabitants by a large majority are attending to their usual avocations and endeavoring in good faith to live quietly under the laws of the Union, and whoever does not do so is speedily punished and his compeers thereby admonished.

To this city and vicinage has been pledged the Governmental protection and inviolability of the rights of property under the laws of the United States, so long as these conditions of peace and quiet shall be preserved; and that pledge has been accepted by the good, loyal, and peaceful, and the power of the Union is respected by the wicked so that they have become peaceful, if not loyal. It is found that a large portion of property held here is in slaves. They till the soil, raise the sugar, corn and cotton, load and unload the ships, they perform every domestic office and are permeated through every branch of industry and peaceful calling.

In a large degree the owners of the soil, planters and farmers, mechanics and small traders, have been passive rather than active in the rebellion. All that had real property at stake, have been the led rather than the leaders in this outbreak against law and order. In the destruction of cotton and sugar, even which has so largely been effected, the owners and producers have not been the destroyers, but in many cases the resistants of destruction.

There is still another class. Those actively in arms and those who for motives of gain, or worse, have aided the rebellion in their several spheres.

The property of these I am hunting out and holding for confiscation under the laws. There is in most cases, no military necessity for its immediate confiscation. Such act if done, would in many instances work injustice to the bona fide loyal creditor, whose interest the Government will doubtless consider. I am only confiscating in fact, in cases where there is a breach of a positive order for the purposes of punishment and example. In all these cases I have no hesitation as to the kinds of property, or rights of property, which shall be confiscated and make no distinctions save that where that property consists in the services of slaves I shall not sell it until so ordered.

Now, many negroes, slaves, have come within my lines. Many have sought to be kept, fed, and to live in the quarters with my troops. Loyal and disloyal masters have lost them alike.

I have caused as many to be employed as I have use for.

I have directed all not employed to be sent out of my lines, leaving them subject to the ordinary laws of the community in that behalf.

I annex all orders and communications to my officers upon this matter up to the date of transmission of this dispatch.

Now what am I to do? Unless all personal property of all rebels is to be confiscated, (of the policy of which a Military Commander has no right to an opinion,) it is manifestly unjust to make a virtual confiscation of this particular species of property. Indeed it makes an actual confiscation of all property, both real and personal, of the Planter, if we take away or allow to run away his negroes as his crop is just growing, it being impossible to supply the labor necessary to preserve it. Again, if a portion of these slaves only are to be taken within my lines, and if to be so taken is a benefit to them, it is unjust to those that are not taken. Those that come early to us are by no means the best men and women. With them as with the whites, it is the worst class that rebel against and evade the laws that govern them. The vicious and unthrifty have felt punishment of their masters as a rule, the exception being where the cruel master abuses the industrious and well behaved slave, and the first to come are those that feel particular grievances.

It is a physical impossibility to take all. I cannot feed the white men within my lines. Women and children are actually starving, in spite of all that I can do. Aye, and they too, without fault on their part. What would be the state of things if I allowed all the slaves from the plantations to quit their employment and come within the lines, is not to be conceived by the imagination.

Am I then, to take of these blacks only the adventurers, the shiftless and wicked to the exclusion of the good and quiet? If coming within our lines is equivalent to freedom, and liberty is a boon, is it to be obtained only by the first that apply?

I had written thus far when by the "Ocean Queen," I received a copy of an order of Maj. Genl. Hunter, upon this subject, in the Department of the South.[1] Whether I assent or dissent from the course of action therein taken, it is not my province to criticise it.

I desire however to call attention to the grounds upon which it seems to be based, and to examine how far they may be applicable here.

The military necessity does not exist here for the employment of negroes in arms, in order that we may have an acclimated force. If the War Department desires and will permit, I can have five thousand able-bodied white citizens enlisted within sixty days, all of whom have lived here many years, and many of them drilled soldiers; to be commanded by intelligent loyal officers. Beside, I hope and believe that this war will be ended before any body of negroes could be organized, armed and drilled so as to be efficient.

The negro here, by long habit and training has acquired a great horror of fire arms, sometimes ludicrous in the extreme when the weapon is in his own hand. I am inclined to the opinion that "John Brown was right," in his idea of arming the negro with a pike or spear instead of a musket, if they are to be armed at all. Of this I say nothing, because a measure of Governmental policy is not to be discussed in the dispatch of a subordinate military officer.

In this connection, it might not be inopportune to call to mind the fact that, a main cause of the failure of the British in their attack on New Orleans, was the employment of a regiment of blacks brought with them from the West Indies. This regiment was charged with the duty of carrying the fascines with which the ditch in front of Jackson's lines was to be filled up, and the ladders for scaleing the embankment. When the attacking column reached the point of assault, the facines and ladders were not there— Upon looking around for them, it was found that their black guardians had very prudently lain themselves down upon the plain, in the rear, and protected their heads from the whistling shot with the fascines which should have been to the front in a different sense.

I am further inclined to believe that, the idea that our men here cannot stand the climate, and therefore the negroes must be freed and armed as an acclimated force, admits of serious debate.

My command has been either here, or on the way here from Ship Island since the first of May – Some of them on shipboard in the river, since the 17th of April. All the deaths in the General Hospital in this city since we have been here, are only 13 from all causes; two of these being accidental, as will appear from Surgeon Smith's report herewith submitted. From diseases at all peculiar to the climate, I do not believe we have lost in the last thirty days, one fifth of one per cent, in the whole command; taking into the account also, the infirm and debilitated who ought never to have passed the Surgeon's examination and come here.

Certain it is, if we admit the proposition that, white men cannot be soldiers in this climate, we go very far toward asserting the dogma that, white men cannot labor here, and therefore establish the necessity for exclusively black labor; which has ever been the corner stone of African Slavery.

We have heard much in the newspapers of the free negro corps of this city, organized for the defence of the South. From this a very erroneous idea may have been derived. The officers of that company called on me the other day upon the question of the continuance of their organization, and to learn what disposition they would be required to make of their arms; and in color, nay, also in conduct they had much more the appearance of white gentlemen, than some of those who have favored me with their presence claiming to be the "Chivalry of the South."

I have satisfied myself, if I have failed to satisfy the department, that no military necessity exists to change the policy of the Government in this respect, within my command.

I have given hurriedly amidst the press of other cares, some of the considerations that seem to me to bear on the question. I only add as a fact, that those well disposed to the Union here, represent that the supposed policy of the Government, as indicated by Genl. Hunter's order, is used by our enemies to paralize all the efforts to cooperate with us.

Reared in the full belief that slavery is a curse to a nation, which my further acquaintance with it only deepens and widens, from its baleful effects upon the master, because, as under it, he cannot lift the negro up in the scale of humanity, therefore the negro drags him down, I have no fear that my views will be anywhere misunderstood. I only accept the fact of its present existence – "the tares among the wheat" – and have asked the direction of the Department, "lest while I gather up the tares, I root up also the wheat with them," or shall I "let both grow together till the harvest"? I have the honor to be Most Respectfully Your obedient Servant.

HLS
Benj. F Butler

Maj. Genl. Benj. F. Butler to Hon. Edward M. Stanton, 25 May 1862, G-810 1862, Letters Received, ser. 12, RG 94 [K-119]. Enclosures.

1 General David Hunter's order, issued May 9, 1862, declared free the slaves in Georgia, Florida, and South Carolina. (*Official Records*, ser. 1, vol. 14, p. 341; see also above, doc. 24.)

62: Headquarters of the Department of the Gulf to the Commander of Camp Parapet, Louisiana

New Orleans, May 28th 1862.
General, I am directed by the Maj. Genl. commanding to call your attention to the following communication and the facts therein set forth.

"Kenner 16 miles above New Orleans
May 27th 1862.
Major Gen¹ Benj. F. Butler
    Commanding Department of the Gulf
Sir, From orders issued to me on May 23rd I understood that I was ordered here to prevent the commission of excesses either on (the) part of soldiers or laborers — This Sir, I shall find impossible to do if soldiers from Camp Parapet are allowed to range the country, insult the Planters and entice negroes away from their plantations, and I regret I must report this conduct on the part of soldiers from that camp. . . .
    If on any of the Plantations here a negro is punished when he most deserves it, the fact becoming known at Genl. Phelp's camp, a party of soldiers are sent immediately to liberate them and with orders to bring them to Camp. A negro convicted of barn-burning and afterwards riotous conduct on the plantation of Mrs. Butler Kannar (a lady who has from you a safeguard and by which all officers and soldiers are commanded to respect her property and to afford her every protection,) was confined in the stocks that he might at the first opportunity be sent to the city for trial, was [*released*] by a company of soldiers, sent by Gen. Phelps, and afterwards taken to the Camp. Yesterday an outbuilding on Mrs. Fendeairs Plantation was broken open by these soldiers and three negroes, confined there over night, taken out and carried to the camp, notwithstanding the presence of the owners, who protested against the act as one contrary to all orders. The soldiers also broke into the house and stole therefrom silver spoons, dresses and other articles. . . .
    While Sir, such acts are permitted it is utterly impossible to call upon the negroes for any labor, as they say they have only to go to the Fort to be free and are therefore very insolent to their masters. If these men could be returned we should need no white men on the

levee and much expense might be saved the Government   I have
now posted sentinels to prevent any more negroes leaving and shall
continue that duty until I receive further orders from you—   There is
much to be done here for over three miles on the levee, and the
planters are willing to take the whole work upon themselves can they
have their own necessary help.   From information received I should
judge there was from One hundred to One hundred and fifty
"Contrabands" at Camp Parapet.   Awaiting Orders I am Sir, Your
most obdt. Servant

(signed) Edward Page Jr.
Capt. 31st Regt.

 Since writing the above Genl. Phelps has sent to me 80
"Contrabands," men, women and children, but I have no provisions
and shall therefore draw upon the Quarter Master for them. . . .
 Having no orders to dismiss the laborers they will continue their
duties.   Respectfully Yours

(Signed) Edward Page Jr.
Capt. 31st Regt. Mass. Vols.

and to say that, by all means and at all hazards, the officers and
men of your Command must be prevented from strolling without
authority and without right, outside of your lines, and from
interfering (under cover of U.S. authority) without right in the
domestic affairs of the people round about you.   I herewith send you
a Copy of General Orders No. 32, which may not have reached you,
wherein this subject is considered.   I have the honor to be Your
most Obediant Servant,

HLcSr   (Signed) P. Haggerty

Capt. P. Haggerty to Brig. Genl. J. W. Phelps, 28 May 1862, vol. 2 DG,
pp. 11–12, Letters Sent, ser. 1738, Dept. of the Gulf, RG 393 Pt. 1
[C-1056]. Ellipses in manuscript. Butler's General Order 32, issued May 27,
1862, prohibited soldiers from taking the property of civilians without special
orders. (*Official Records*, ser. 1, vol. 15, p. 445.)

63: Officer of the Day at Camp Parapet, Louisiana, to the Commander of the Camp; and Commander of Camp Parapet to the Headquarters of the Department of the Gulf

Camp Parapet [*La.*], June 15, 1862

Sir: In addition to the regular "Post Guard Report" of this date
returned to your headquarters, I beg leave to call your attention to
the large and constantly increasing number of blacks who have
congregated near the upper picket station on the River road.

I learn that 24 hours ago they numbered about 75. The Officer of the Guard reports to me this morning that the number has increased to 150 or more.

The first installment were *sent* by a man named La Branche, from the other side of the river, in boats, on the night of the 13th, he giving them the choice, according to their statement, of leaving before sundown or receiving fifty lashes each. Many of these desire to return to their master, but are prevented by fear of harsh treatment. They are of all ages and physical conditions – a number of infants in arms, many young children, robust men and women, and a large number of lame, old, and infirm of both sexes.

The rest of them came in singly, and in small parties from various points up the river within a hundred miles. They brought with them boxes, bedding, and luggage of all sorts, which lie strewn upon the levee and the open spaces around the picket.

The women and children, and some feeble ones who needed shelter, were permitted to occupy a deserted house, just outside the lines. They are quite destitute of provisions, many of them having eaten nothing for days, except what our soldiers have given them from their own rations.

In accordance with orders already issued, the guard was instructed to permit none of them to enter the lines.

As each "Officer of the Day" will be called on successively, to deal with the matter, I take the liberty to suggest whether some farther regulation in reference to these unfortunate persons is not necessary to enable him to do his duty intelligently, as well as for the very apparent additional reasons, that the congregation of such large numbers in our immediate vicinity affords inviting opportunities for mischief to ourselves, and also, that unless supplied with the means of sustaining life, by the benevolence of the military authorities or of the citizens (which is scarcely supposable) they must shortly be reduced to suffering and starvation, in the very sight of the overflowing store-houses of the Government. I am, Sir, your obedient servant.

HLcSr   Frank H. Peck

Camp Parapet, near Carrollton La. June 16th 1862
Sir: I inclose herewith, for the information of the Major General Commanding the Department, a report of Major Peck, officer of the day, concerning a large number of Negroes, of both sexes and all ages, who are lying near our pickets, with bag and baggage, as if they had already commenced an exodus. Many of these Negroes have been sent away from one of the neighboring sugar plantations, by their owner, a Mr. Babillard La Blanche, who tells them, I am

informed, that "the Yankees are King here now, and that they must go to their King for food and shelter."

They are of that 4000.000 of our colored subjects who have no king or chief, nor in fact Government that can secure to them the simplest natural rights. The cannot even be entered into treaty stipulations with and deported to the East as our Indian tribes have been to the West. They have no right to the mediation of a Justice of the Peace or jury between them and chains and lashes. They have no right to wages for their labor; no right to the Sabbath; no right to the institution of marriage; no right to letters or self-defence. A small class of owners, rendered unfeeling, and even unconscious and unreflecting by habit, and a large part of them ignorant and vicious, stand between them and their Government, destroying its sovereignty. This Government has not the power even to regulate the number of lashes that its subjects may receive. It cannot say that they shall receive thirty nine instead of forty. To a large and growing class of its subjects it can secure neither justice, moderation, nor the advantages of the Christian religion; and if it cannot protect *all* its subjects, it can protect none, either white or black.

It is nearly a hundred years since our people first declared to the nations of the world that all men are born free; and still we have not made our declaration good. Highly revolutionary measures have since then been adopted by the admission of Missouri and the annexation of Texas in favor of Slavery by the barest majority of votes, while the highly conservative vote of two thirds has at length been attained against Slavery, and still Slavery exists – even, moreover, altho' two thirds of the blood in the veins of our slaves is fast becoming from our own race. If we wait for a larger vote, or until our slave's blood becomes more consanguined still with our own, the danger of a violent revolution, over which we can have no control, must become more imminent every day. By a course of undecided action, determined by no policy but the vague will of a war-distracted people, we run the risk of precipitating that very revolutionary violence which we seem seeking to avoid.

Let us regard for a moment the elements of such a revolution.

Many of the slaves here have been sold away from the Border States as a punishment, being too refractory to be dealt with there in the face of the civilisation of the North. They come here with a knowledge of the Christian religion, with its germs planted and expanding, as it were, in the dark, rich soil of their African nature, with a feeling of relationship with the families from which they came, and with a sense of unmerited banishment as culprits, all which tends to bring upon them a greater severity of treatment and a corresponding disinclination "to receive punishment." They are far superior beings to their ancestors who were brought from Africa two generations ago, and who occasionally rebelled against comparatively less severe punishment than is inflicted now. While rising in the scale of Christian beings, their treatment is being rendered more severe than ever. The whip, the chains, the stocks, and imprisonment are no mere fancies here; they are used to any extent to which the imagination of civilized man may reach. Many of them are as intelligent as their masters, and far more moral, for while the slave appeals to the moral law as his vindication, clinging to it as to the very horns of the altar of his safety and his hope, the master seldom hesitates to wrest him from it with violence and contempt. The slave, it is true, bears no resentment; he asks for no punishment for his master; he simply claims justice for himself; and it is this feature of his condition that promises more terror to the retribution when it comes. Even now the whites stand accused by their oppression of humanity, being subject to a degree of confusion, chaos, and enslavement to error and wrong, which Northern society could not credit or comprehend.

Added to the four millions of the colored race, whose disaffection is increasing even more rapidly than their numbers, there are at least four millions more of the white race whose growing miseries will naturally seek companionship with those of the blacks. This latter portion of Southern society has its representatives, who swing from the scaffold with the same desperate coolness, though from a directly different cause, as that which was manifested by John Brown. The traitor Mumford,[1] who swung the other day for trampling on the national flag, had been rendered perfectly placid and indifferent in his desperation by a Government that either could not or would not secure to its subjects the blessings of liberty which that flag implies. The South cries for justice from the Government as well as the North, though in a proud and resentful spirit; — and in what manner is that justice to be obtained? Is it to be secured by that wretched resource of a set of profligate politicians, called "reconstruction"? No, it is to be obtained by the Abolition of Slavery, and by no other course.

It is vain to deny that the slave system of labor is giving shape to the government of the society where it exists, and that that government is not republican, either in form or spirit. It was through this system that the leading conspirators have sought to fasten upon the people an aristocracy, or a despotism; and it is not sufficient that they should be merely defeated in their object, and the country be rid of their rebellion; for by our Constitution we are imperatively obliged to sustain the States against the ambition of unprincipalled leaders, and secure to them the republican form of government. We have positive duties to perform, and should hence adopt and pursue a positive, decided policy. We have services to render to certain states which they cannot perform for themselves. We are in an emergency which the framers of the Constitution might easily have forseen, and for which they have amply provided.

It is clear that the public good requires slavery to be abolished; but in what manner is it to be done? The mere quiet operation of Congressional law cannot deal with Slavery as in its former status before the war, because the spirit of law is right reason, and there is no reason in Slavery. A system so unreasonable as Slavery cannot be regulated *by* reason. We can hardly expect the several States to adopt laws or measures against their own immediate interests. We have seen that they will rather find arguments for crime than seek measures for abolishing or modifying slavery. But there is one principle which is fully recognised as a necessity in conditions like ours, and that is that the public safety is the supreme law of the State, and that amidst the clash of arms the laws of peace are silent. It is then for our President, the Commander-in-Chief of our Armies, to declare the abolition of Slavery, leaving it to the wisdom of Congress to adopt measures to meet the consequences. This is the usual course pursued by a General, or by a military power. That power gives orders affecting complicated interests and millions of property, leaving it to the other functions of Government to adjust and regulate the effects produced. Let the President abolish Slavery, and it would be an easy matter, for Congress, through a well regulated system of apprenticeship, to adopt safe measures for effecting a gradual transition from Slavery to Freedom.

The existing system of labor in Louisiana is unsuited to the age; and by the intrusion of the National forces it seems falling to pieces. It is a system of mutual jealousy between the master and the man—a system of violence, immorality, and vice. The fugitive Negro tells us that our presence renders his condition worse with his master than it was before, and that we offer no alleviation in return. The system is impolitic because it offers but one stimulant to labor and effort, viz, the lash, when another, viz, money, might be added with good effect. Fear, and the other low and bad qualities of the slave are appealed to, but never the good. The relation, therefore, between capital and labor, which ought to be generous and confiding, is darkling, suspicious, unkindly, full of reproachful threats, and without concord or peace. This condition of things renders the interest of society a prey to politicians. Politics cease to be practical or useful

The questions that ought to have been discussed in the late extraordinary convention of Louisiana[2] are, *First,*. What ought the

State of Louisiana to do to adapt her ancient system of labor to the present advanced spirit of the age? And *Second*, How can the State be assisted by the General Government in affecting the change? But instead of this, the only question before that body was, how to vindicate slavery by flogging the Yankees!

Compromises hereafter are not to be made with politicians, but with sturdy labor, and the right to work. The interests of political men resent political trifling. Our political education, shaped almost entirely to the interests of Slavery, has been false and vicious in the extreme; and it must be corrected with as much suddenness almost, as that with which Salem witchcraft came to its end. The only question that remains to decide is how the change shall take place.

We are not without examples and precedents in the history of the past. The enfranchisement of the people of Europe has been, and is still going on, through the instrumentality of military service; and by this means our slaves might be raised in the scale of civilisation and prepared for freedom. Fifty Regiments might be raised among them at once, which could be employed in this climate to preserve order, and thus prevent the necessity of retrenching our liberties, as we should do by a large army exclusively of whites. For it is evident that a considerable army of whites would give stringency to our Government, while an army partly of blacks, would naturally operate in favor of freedom, and against those influences which at present most endanger our liberties. At the end of five years they could be sent to Africa, and their places filled with new enlistments.

There is no practical evidence against the effects of immediate abolition, even if there is not in its favor. I have witnessed the sudden abolition of flogging at will in the Army, and of legalised flogging in the Navy, against the prejudice-warped judgements of both, and, from the beneficial effects there, I have nothing to fear from the immediate abolition of Slavery. I fear, rather, the violent consequences from a continuance of the evil. But should such an act devastate the whole State of Louisiana, and render the whole soil there but a mere passage-way for the fruits of the enterprise and industry of the North-West, it would be better for the country at large than it is now as the seat of disaffection and rebellion.

When it is remembered that not a word is found in our Constitution sanctioning the buying and selling of human beings, a shameless act which renders our country the disgrace of Christendom, and worse, in this respect, even than Africa herself, we should have less dread of seeing the degrading traffic stopped at once and forever. Half wages are already virtually paid for slave-labor in the system of tasks, which, in an unwilling spirit of compromise, most of the Slave States have already been compelled to adopt. At the end of a period of five years of apprenticeship, or of fifteen at farthest, full wages could be paid to the enfranchised Negro race, to the double advantage of both master and man. This is just; for we now hold the Slaves of Louisiana by the same tenure that the State can alone claim them, viz, by the original right of conquest. We have so far conquered them that a proclamation setting them free, coupled with offers of protection, would devastate every plantation in the state.

In conclusion, I may state that Mr La Blanche is, as I am informed, a descendant of one of the oldest families of Louisiana. He is wealthy, and a man of standing, and his act in sending away his Negroes to our lines, with their clothes and furniture, appears to indicate the convictions of his own mind as to the proper logical consequences and deductions that should follow from the present relative status of the two contending parties. He seems to be convinced that the proper result of the conflict is the manumission of the Slave; and he may safely be regarded in this respect as a representative man of the State. I so regard him myself, and thus do I interpret his action, although my Camp contains some of the highest symbols of Secessionism, which have been taken by a party of the 7th Vermont Volunteers from his residence.

Meanwhile his slaves, old and young; little ones and all, are suffering from exposure and uncertainty as to their future condition. Driven away by their master, with threats of violence if they return, and with no decided welcome or reception from us, what is to be their lot? Considerations of humanity are pressing for an immediate solution of their difficulties; and they are but a small portion of their race who have sought, and are still seeking, our pickets and our military stations, declaring that they cannot and will not any longer serve their masters, and that all they want is work and protection from us. In such a state of things, the question occurs as to my own action in the case. I cannot return them to their masters, who not unfrequently come in search of them; for I am, fortunately, prohibited by an Article of War, from doing that, even if my own nature did not revolt at it. I cannot receive them, for I have neither work, shelter, nor the means or plan of transporting them to Hayti, or of making suitable arrangements with their masters, until they can be provided for.

It is evident that some plan, some policy, or some system is necessary on the part of the Government, without which the agent can do nothing, and all his efforts are rendered useless and of no effect. This is no new condition in which I find myself; it is my experience during the some twenty five years of my public life as a military officer of the Government. The new Article of War recently adopted by Congress, rendering it criminal in an officer of the Army to return fugitives from injustice, is the first support that I have ever felt from the Government in contending against those slave-influences which are opposed to its character and to its interests. But the mere refusal to return fugitives does not now meet the case. A public agent in the present emergency must be invested with wider and more positive powers than this, or his services will prove as valuless to the country as they are unsatisfactory to himself.

Desiring this communication to be laid before the President, and leaving my commission at his disposal, I have the honor to remain, Sir, Very respectfully, your obedient servant

ALcS   J W. Phelps

Major Frank H. Peck to Gen. J. W. Phelps, 15 June 1862, and Brig. Gen. J. W. Phelps to Capt. R. S. Davis, 16 June 1862, both quoted in J. W. Phelps, report of service, 16 Jan. 1873, vol. 6, Generals' Reports of Service, ser. 160, RG 94 [JJ-5]. On June 18, 1862, General Benjamin F. Butler, commander of the Department of the Gulf, forwarded Phelps's letter to the Secretary of War with the following remarks: "General Phelps, I believe, intends making this a test case for the policy of the Government. I wish it might be so, for the difference of our action upon this subject is a source of trouble. I respect his honest sincerity of opinion, but I am a soldier, bound to carry out the wishes of my Government so long as I hold its commission, and I understand that policy to be the one I am pursuing. I do not feel at liberty to pursue any other. If the policy of the Government is nearly that I sketched in my report upon the subject as that which I had ordered in this department, then the services of General Phelps are worse than useless here. If the views set forth in his report are to obtain, then he is invaluable, for his whole soul is in it, and he is a good soldier, of large experience, and no braver man lives. I beg to leave the whole question with the President, with perhaps the needless assurance that his wishes shall be loyally followed even if not in accordance with my own, as I have now no right to have any upon the subject." (*Official Records*, ser. 1, vol. 15, p. 486.) Secretary of War Edwin M. Stanton replied on June 29, confessing that Butler's views on the question of Louisiana slavery had "strongly impressed" him, but declining to interfere directly in the Louisiana situation: "It has not yet, however, been deemed necessary or wise to fetter your judgment by any specific instructions in this regard." Stanton had referred Butler's and Phelps's letters to the President and, pending Lincoln's consideration of the subject, offered only the following guidance to Butler: "[I]t is confidently hoped that, exercising your accustomed skill and discretion, you will so deal with this question as to avoid any serious embarrassment to the Government or any difficulty with General Phelps." (*Official Records*, ser. 1, vol. 15, p. 516.) There the matter rested until the end of July, when Phelps asked Butler for arms and equipment for the five companies of black fugitives he had organized as soldiers. When Butler ordered Phelps to put the contrabands to work chopping down trees instead, Phelps resigned rather than serve as a "mere Slave-driver." (*Freedom*, ser. 2: docs. 9–10.)

1 William B. Mumford, hanged on June 7, 1862, by order of General Benjamin F. Butler for desecrating a U.S. flag. (*Official Records*, ser. 1, vol. 15, p. 469.)
2 Presumably the Louisiana secession convention, which met in January 1861.

64: Testimony by a Corporal in a Louisiana Black Regiment before the American Freedmen's Inquiry Commission

[*New Orleans February?* 1864]
Deposition of Octave Johnson, Corporal Co. C, 15th Regt. Corps d'Afrique.

I was born in New Orleans; I am 23 years of age; I was raised by Arthur Thiboux of New Orleans; I am by trade a cooper; I was treated pretty well at home; in 1855 master sold my mother, and in 1861 he sold me to S. Contrell of St. James Parish for $2,400; here I worked by task at my trade; one morning the bell was rung for us to go to work so early that I could not see, and I lay still, because I was working by task; for this the overseer was going to have me whipped, and I ran away to the woods, where I remained for a year and a half; I had to steal my food; took turkeys, chickens and pigs; before I left our number had increased to thirty, of whom ten were women; we were four miles in the rear of the plantation house; sometimes we would rope beef cattle and drag them out to our hiding place; we obtained matches from our friends on the plantation; we slept on logs and burned cypress leaves to make a smoke and keep away mosquitoes; Eugene Jardeau, master of hounds, hunted for us for three months; often those at work would betray those in the swamp, for fear of being implicated in their escape; we furnished meat to our fellow-servants in the field, who would return corn meal; one day twenty hounds came after me; I called the party to my assistance and we killed eight of the bloodhounds; then we all jumped into Bayou Faupron; the dogs followed us and the alligators caught six of them; "the alligators preferred dog flesh to personal flesh;" we escaped and came to Camp Parapet, where I was first employed in the Commissary's office, then as a servant to Col. Hanks; then I joined his regiment.

HD

Testimony of Corporal Octave Johnson before the American Freedmen's Inquiry Commission, [Feb.? 1864], filed with O-328 1863, Letters Received, ser. 12, RG 94 [K-219].

65: Commander of the Department of the Gulf
to an Assistant Provost Marshal

New Orleans, La. July 19" 1862.

Sir   The course pursued by certain persons in ordering their slaves "to go to the Yankees" or to join the Federals discribed in your note and like acts, has been brough to my notice from different sources previously to your communication and certainly is a great wrong as well to the Government as to the Negroes.   In order to correct this evil therefore let it been known, that all such declarations by the Owners to their slaves will by the authority here be taken and deemed acts of Voluntary emancipation and slaves sent away by their Masters with such declarations as you described or equivalent ones will be regarded and treated as manumitted & emancipated.   You will see to it, that this necessary police regulation is carried into effect.   Respectfully

HLcSr   Signed. Benj. F. Butler

Maj. Gen. Benj. F. Butler to Capt. Stafford, 19 July 1862, vol. 2 DG, pp. 197–98, Letters Sent, ser. 1738, Dept. of the Gulf, RG 393 Pt. 1 [C-613]. The "communication" referred to has not been found among the letters received by the Department of the Gulf.

66A: **Certificate Issued by the Commander of Fort Jackson and Fort St. Philip, Louisiana**

> Head Quarters
> Fort St. Philip
> Sept . 16 . 1862
>
> Augustus, Colored - and former slave
> to Dr Charles Weatherstrain, having
> been turned off the plantation to shift for
> himself, is *Free*, and at liberty to earn
> for himself and family an honest live-
> lihood. He is a free Man, and has the
> right to Make Contracts for his labor &c
> as any other Man has.
>
> Neal Dow
> Brig. Gen,
> Commanding.

Certificate issued by Brig. Gen. Neal Dow, 16 Sept. 1862, D-37 1862, Letters Received by the Provost Marshal General, ser. 1390, State of LA, Provost Marshal Field Organizations, RG 393 Pt. 4 [C-613].

66B: **Louisiana Slaveholder to the Military Governor of Louisiana**

New Orleans Sept 19. 1862.
Sir   In obedience to an order of Col J N French Provost Marshall, I respectfully submit the following statement —
On Monday last, while on a visit to my plantation, I was startled at the dawn of day by the announcement of my brother in law Mr Smith the manager of the place, that the negroes were in a state of

insurection, some of them refusing to work— Proceeding immediately to the Cabin Yard, I found them gathered in different groups & on enquiry learned, that some of them would not work at all, & others wanted wages, I informed them, I should not pay them wages, & being excited by their ingratitude & not wishing to feed and clothe those who would not work, & to avoid any difficulty, as my sister and her four small children were on the place, I said that it was better to part in peace & go off quietly & that I did not wish to lay eyes on them again, & they went away   I never drove any of them off the plantation, or told them according to the expression of Genl Dow to shift for themselves— So far from it, I sent a written notice to the rice planters below, forbidding them to employ them under the pains & risks of the law, in regard to employment of runaway slaves   about twenty five of them left the plantation, some few of them remained & went to work the next day—

On the 17th ins^t one of the revolted named Auguste, demanded from the overseer his gun, & not being able to find it endeavoured to get possession of the overseer's. In reply to Mr Smith's question, "If he had a pass," he said Genl Dow had given him his free papers which he produced, & said moreover that Genl Dow had told him all the people were free, & that he, (Auguste) had come for what belonged to him— My brother in law, the overseer, and myself, knowing him to be a dangerous man, determined to bring him to the city & have the whole subject properly investigated— I started with him in my buggy, Mr Smith & the overseer on horseback— accompanyed me a short distance and returned— His language was very offensive, among other things he said that he wished to go to Virginia, meaning thereby that he wished to enlist— I succeeded with some assistance in securing him in the jail of St Bernard—

Considering this boy as one of the ring-leaders & a dangerous character on the plantation, I thought it best to remove him, & leave it to the Provost Marshall to dispose of him as it may seem best— There are about twenty negroes with free papers from Genl Dow, a great burthen to the place; a heavy tax on me & a bad example to the other negroes—

Under this anamolous state of affairs, I pray that the Governor & Provost Marshall, will take the necessary steps to examine into this affair, & send an officer to verify this statement. & see into the condition of things on the plantation, that a suitable protection be afforded my sister and her children, that the negroes may be informed how far the emancipation of Genl Dow may be valid, & the future conduct of the place & themselves, may be put upon such a footing & will restore peace & good order— I am very respectfully your ob^t

HLS   John C. P. Wederstrandt

John C. P. Wederstrandt to Brig. Genl. Shepley, 19 Sept. 1862, filed with W-8 1862, Letters Received by the Provost Marshal General, ser. 1390, State of LA, Provost Marshal Field Organizations, RG 393 Pt. 4 [C-613]. Filed with a letter of the same date from Wederstrandt to Jonas H. French, provost marshal general of Louisiana, which reported in part: "I am informed that on the plantation of M^r McManus opposite my place, the negroes have driven the overseer off the plantation and swear they will not allow any white man to put his foot on it, they have also sold every thing off the plantation for their own benefit. On Mr Browns plantation opposite mine, the negroes I am told are masters of the place and that the overseer there is entirely at their mercy. Our family has owned negroes for generations and we never before had any difficulty with them being supported by the government, but now that the government in the parish of Plaquemines, headed by Genl Dow is turned against us, we have no one but yourself and Genls Shepley and Butler to protect us against these negroes in a state of insurrection." In the same file is a statement of September 16, 1862, by J. W. Smith, Wederstrandt's brother-in-law, which characterized Auguste as "a dangerous and violent person."

67A: Commander of Camp Parapet, Louisiana, to the Headquarters of the Department of the Gulf

Camp Parapet La: September 6th 1862

Sir, Three Negro men, Robert Harrison, Robert Morgan and Joe Lewis, now in my camp, are ordered by Provost Marshall Jonas H. French, to be delivered to one Mr. Kincalla, or be sent to him French, "by direction of the Maj Genl."

Mr. Kincalla, it appears, is the day watchman of the New Orleans Gas Company, to which these men belong, and this is the second time that they have sought the protection of the United States, in my camp. This time two of them were loaded with chains and one of them is badly maimed

As the returning of these slaves appears to me wholly incompatible with General Orders No. 91 from the War Department, dated July 29th 1862, Section 10th,[1] I would respectfully ask your attention to that section and request to be informed whether there is not some mistake in the Major General's directions in the case. One of the men is so lamed in consequence of inhuman treatment that he can hardly walk. I am, Sir, Very Respectfully Your Obdt: Servt:

ALS

J. W. Phelps

Brigr. Genl. J. W. Phelps to Captain R. S. Davis, 6 Sept. 1862, #26 1862, Letters Received, ser. 1756, Dept. of the Gulf, RG 393 Pt. 1 [C-508]. Informing Phelps that an investigation into the treatment of slaves at the gas works would be made, the department commander's adjutant nonetheless instructed him to return the runaways to Kincalla, on the grounds that "they do not belong to Mr Kincalla but to the Gas Works which are now under military authority & we need them for public service." (Capt. R. S. Davis to Brig. Gen. J. W. Phelps, 8 Sept. 1862, vol. 2 DG, p. 312, Letters Sent, ser. 1738, Dept. of the Gulf, RG 393 Pt. 1 [C-508].) Phelps's involvement in the case ended on September 8, when he received official acceptance of his resignation, thus sparing him "the unpleasantness of preferring charges against General Butler for this last illegal order, which is directly in opposition to the new article of war." (J. W. Phelps, report of service, 16 Jan. 1873, vol. 6, Generals' Reports of Service, ser. 160, RG 94 [JJ-5].) Apparently the fugitives were returned to the gas works, because one of them later reported having worked as a slave for the company until the end of November 1862. (See below, doc. 67C.)

1 An order publishing several recently adopted laws, including the Second Confiscation Act, section 10 of which required that "no person engaged in the military or naval service of the United States shall, under any pretense whatever, assume to decide on the validity of the claim of any person to the service or labor of any other person, or surrender up any such person to the claimant, on pain of being dismissed from the service." (*Official Records*, ser. 3, vol. 2, p. 276.)

67B: President of the Bank of Louisiana to the Commander of the Department of the Gulf

Canal S^r [*New Orleans*] Sept. 9th [*1862*]
Sir, You may remember that several weeks ago, you placed the Gas Works under the Control of the Provost Marshall, from the insubordination prevailing among the slaves, who formed a large majority of the laborers.

Soon afterwards, four who had run away were arrested at Carrollton & sent back by Colonel French, — whereupon, believing an example indispensable, I directed them to be confined in irons— But a few days having produced the desired effect on two of them, their irons were stricken off, — the other two, who remained contumacious, were kept under punishment. This, as far as I know & believe, is the only corporal punishment inflicted. There are more than 40 slaves at the works, belonging to the Company. They are well clothed & lodged, abundantly fed, and work on an average about 6 hours a day of 24 hours—. The only change made by me is to reduce their allowance of liquor from 3 to 2 gills a day. This in brief, is all that I personally know.

I have directed the superintendant, M^r McCulloch, to make a more detailed statement, which I beg to submit for your information.

In my opinion a decisive policy is necessary. I therefore suggest that a thorough examination be made by some person in whom you have confidence – or what I would greatly prefer, that you permit me to accompany you there, when you can spare half an hour for that purpose. I am with great respect, Sir, Your obed. Servt.

ALS   W. Newton Mercer.

W. Newton Mercer to Genl. Butler, 9 Sept. 1862, #506 1862, Letters Received, ser. 1756, Dept. of the Gulf, RG 393 Pt. 1 [C-508]. The enclosure mentioned is not in the file.

67C: Former Slaves of the New Orleans Gas Works to the Commander of the Department of the Gulf

City Workhouse, New-Orleans, February 23 /1863

Sir   We most respectfully beg leave to represent to your Excellency that we are colored men, having belonged to the Gas-light Company of this city, that the managers of Said Company, being dissatisfied with us, told us to go and look for work elsewhere, as they would have nothing more to do with us, which happened about the end of November; – that we then obtained employment in the Service of the Government, and continued in said employment until the 29th day of January 1863, at which time we were working in a Tobacco ware-house on Magazine-street; and that we were arrested while going from the ware-house to dinner, for no cause, but that we had no passes. We moreover would represent to your Excellency that we were brought to this Workhouse, were we have ever since been held in confinement as prisoners, without having ever been brought before any judge or court. –

We therefore most humbly beg of your Excellency that you grant us a hearing, as we are confident we can show that we were wrongfully arrested, and that there is no cause for keeping us in prison, no crime whatever being laid to our charge. –

Isaac White on his part would most respectfully represent that he has a wife in bad health with a small baby solely dependent upon him for support, and that she is suffering great distress in consequence of the imprisonment of her husband. – Joe Thomas on his part represents that he was cruelly treated by the officers of this prison, – put into the stocks and flogged – for no just cause or provocation.

We confidently trust therefore that your Excellency will cause us to be brought before the Provost-judge for a hearing, and if we are found to be unjustly confined, that we be ordered to be released. –

We furthermore promise that after our release we shall industriously and faithfully work for government or wherever employed and conduct ourselves, as we always did, in a quiet, peaceable manner. We have the honor to be, Your Excellency's most humble & obedt. Servts.

Isaac White	Robert Morgans
Erin Robertson	Edmund King
Joe Thomas	Leonard Williams
John Eldridge	Erin Gitan

HLSr

Isaac White et al. to Major General N. P. Banks, 23 Feb. 1863, W-43 1863, Letters Received, ser. 1920, Civil Affairs, Dept. of the Gulf, RG 393 Pt. 1 [C-508]. Endorsement. The letter and all signatures are in the same handwriting.

68: Louisiana Planter Family to the Commander of the Department of the Gulf

[*Jefferson Parish, La. September 8?, 1862*]
Horerable Sir. The undersigned earnestly petition your powerful. protection for thier lives and property. both of which are threatened by 4 Negroes now in General Phelp's Camp. – Their property in the Parish of Jefferson is threatened with plunder and fire – and their lives are threatened if they resist the destruction of their property – The 4 Negroes. respectively. Len. Peter – Mathias (alias Mat) and Josiah (alias Joe) runaway's – from their Plantation in Parish of Jefferson right Bank. – the said Negroes – have been for – several Week's in General Phelp's Camp – returned to their Plantation a few day's ago – alledging – that the General had given them a pass, and an *Order* to the other Negroes, to rise and murder the whole family – and plunder and burn the Plantation –

General – we humbly petition your protection in our behalf. the undersigned have never. aided nor abetted the rebellion, in any

Way – and have alway's been true and loyal to the Union and who
have all taken the oath of allegiance to the United States.

D. C. Osborn	C. D. Osborn
Winnifred Osborn	P. A. Osborn.
G. C. Osborn	

HLSr

D. C. Osborn et al. to Major General Butler, [8? Sept. 1862], O-4 1862,
Letters Received by the Provost Marshal General, ser. 1390, State of LA,
Provost Marshal Field Organizations, RG 393 Pt. 4 [C-967]. Endorsement.
The letter and all signatures are in the same handwriting.

69: Two Letters from the Commander of the District of the
Teche to the Headquarters of the Department of the Gulf,
and Reply from the Department Headquarters

(Copy)   In Camp near Thibodeaux La Nov. 5th 1862.
Major   I have the honor to report that I have your communication
of the 2nd inst. I think it would be very proper to place a *field work*
at or near Donaldsonville.[1]
A permanent work involving the construction of masonry would
be too slow an operation.
I think you had better send Lieut Palfrey up there to locate it and
construct it. He could carry on Ship Island and that too. A battery
also, I think, would be very appropriate at Berwicks' Bay. I can
direct the position and the construction of this battery. It would
not be proper to build a work near here as the communication with
it can be easily cut off and it could be turned readily.
And now, I desire most respectfully to decline the command of
the District which has been just created, and which, as we have not
yet secured a foot of ground on the Teche, ought properly to be
called the "District of the La Fourche."
The reason I must decline, is because accepting the command
would place me in command of all the troops in the District.
I cannot command those negro regiments.
The Commanding General knows well my private opinions on
this subject. What I stated to him privately whilst on his staff, I
see now before my eyes. Since the arrival of the negro regiments,
symptoms of servile insurrection are becoming apparent. I could
not, without breaking my brigade all up, put a force in every part
of this district to keep down such an insurrection. I cannot assume
the command of such a force, and thus be responsible for its
conduct. I have no confidence in the organization.

Its' moral effect in this community, which is stripped of nearly all its able-bodied men, and will be stripped of a great many of its arms, is terrible. Women and children and even men are in terror. It is heart-rending and I cannot make myself responsible for it.

I will gladly go anywhere with my own brigade, that you see fit to order me.

I beg you therefore to keep the negro brigade directly under your own command or place some one over both mine and it.

I have given instructions to collect as much transportation as possible, so that I can cross Berwicks' Bay with my brigade, and will go down to-morrow in person to hurry up things.

I cannot move my brigade there yet as there is not sufficient drinking water, and this is a better camp. I am, Sir, Very Respectfully Your Ob'd't Servant

HLcSr   (Signed) G. Weitzel

In Camp near Thibodaux La Nov 5th 1862

Major   In still further confirmation of what I wrote you in my despatches of this morning relative to servile insurrection, I have the honor to inform you, that, on the plantation of Mr David Pugh a short distance above here, the negroes, who had returned under the terms fixed upon by Major General Butler, without provocation or cause of any kind, refused, this morning to work, and assaulted the overseer and Mr Pugh, injuring them severely, also a gentleman who came to the assistance of Mrs Pugh.

Upon the plantation, also, of Mr W. J. Miner, on the Terre bonne road, about 16 miles from here, an outbreak has already occured and the entire community there about are in hourly expectation and terror of a general rising   I am, Sir, Very Resply Your Obedt Servt

HLcSr   (Signed) G Weitzel

(Copy)   *New-Orleans*, November 6th *1862*

General: Your despatches of the Fifth of November have been received, as also your Telegram of this evening.

I am directed by the Major General Commanding to reply: Your suggestions as to the *field work* at Donaldsonville will receive consideration. It will be necessary to make a Battery at Brashier City, Berwicks' Bay, or perhaps a field work. Upon this subject he will confer with you.

In establishing the Military District of the Teche he was aware that at the moment you did not occupy it except by your boats; and he gave the name in compliment to your skill and gallantry, as it was not doubted you would soon be in occupation. And in putting the very large force under the command of so young a General, he designed to show a mark of confidence in your discrimination and judgement. If it would be more desirable to yourself he will change the name to the District of the La Fourche.

That you should have declined the command is the occasion of regret, arising most of all from the reasons given for so doing.

As they are comprehended they resolve themselves into two. First, that under your command are put two Regiments of Native Guards (colored); and you say that in "these organizations you have no confidence." As your reading must have made you aware, General Jackson entertained a different opinion upon that subject. It was arranged between the Commanding General and yourself that the Colored Regiments should be employed in guarding the Rail-road. You do not complain in your report that they either failed to do their duty in that respect or that they have acted otherwise than correctly and obediently to the commands of their Officers, or that they have committed any outrage or pillage upon the inhabitants.

The General was aware of your opinion that colored men will not fight. You have failed to show, by the conduct of these free men so far, anything to sustain that opinion; and the General cannot see why you should decline the command, especially as you express a willingness to go forward to meet the only organized enemy, with your own Brigade alone, without further support.

The Commanding General cannot see how the fact that they are guarding your lines of communication by Railroad can weaken your defence. He must therefore look to the other reasons stated by you for an explanation of your declining the command.

You say you "cannot command these negro regiments." Why not? the reason must be found in these sentences of your report:

> "Since the arrival of the negro regiments symptoms of servile insurrection are becoming apparent. I could not, without breaking my brigade all up, put a force in every part of this district to keep down such an insurrection. I cannot assume the command of such a force, and thus be responsible for its conduct. I have no confidence in the organization."
> "Its' moral effect in this community, which is stripped of nearly all its able-bodied men, and will be stripped of a great many of its arms, is terrible. Women and children and even men are in terror. It is heart-rending and I cannot make myself responsible for it."

You say that since the arrival of the negro regiments at that place, you have seen symptoms of a servile insurrection; but, as the only regiment that has arrived there, got there as soon as the rest of your command, of course the appearance of such symptoms is "since their arrival."

Have you not mistaken the cause? Is it the arrival of a negro regiment, or is it the arrival of United States Troops, carrying by the Act of Congress freedom to this servile race? Did you expect to march into that country, drained, as you say it is, by conscription of all its able-bodied white men, without leaving the negroes free to show symptoms of servile insurrection? Does not this state of things arise from the very fact of war itself? You are in a country where now the negroes outnumber the whites ten to one, and these Whites are in rebellion against the Government or in terror seeking its protection.

Upon reflection can you doubt that the same state of things would have arisen without the presence of a colored regiment? Did you not see symptoms of the same thing on the plantations here when we arrived, although under much less favorable circumstances for a revolt. You say that the prospect of such an insurrection is "heart-rending," and that you cannot be responsible for it. You are in no degree responsible for it. The responsibility rests upon those who have begun and carried on this war; who have stopped at no barbarity, no act of outrage, upon the citizens and troops of the United States.

You have forwarded me the records of a pretended Court Martial, showing that seven men of one of your regiments, who enlisted here into the Eight Vermont Regiment, who had surrendered themselves prisoners of war, were in cold blood murdered, and as certain information shows, were required to dig their own graves. You are asked if this is not an occurrence equally as heart-rending as a prospective servile insurrection?

The question is now to be met, whether in a hostile, rebellious part of the State, where this very murder has been committed by the militia you are to stop in the operations of the field to put down servile insurrection because the men and women are terror-stricken? When was it ever heard before that a victorious General in an unsurrendered province, stopped in his course for the purpose of preventing the rebellious inhabitants of that province from destroying each other, and refused to take command of a conquered province lest he should be made responsible for their self-destruction?

As a military question, perhaps the more terror-stricken the inhabitants are that are left in your rear the more safe will be your lines of communication.

You say there have appeared before your eyes the very facts, in terror-stricken women and children and men, which you had before contemplated in theory. Grant it; but is not the remedy to be found in the surrender of the neighbors, fathers, brothers and sons of the terror-stricken women and children, who are now in arms against the Government within twenty miles of you? And when that is done and you have no longer to fear from their organized force, and they have returned peaceably to their homes you will be able to use the full power of your troops to ensure their safety from the so much feared – by them, but not by us – servile insurrection.

If you desire you can send a Flag of Truce to the commander of these forces, embracing these views and placing upon him the responsibility which belongs to him. Even that course will not remove it from you, for upon you it has never rested.

Say to them that if all armed opposition to the Authority of the United States should cease in Louisiana, on the West bank of the river, you are authorized by the Commanding General to say that the same protection against negro or other violence will be afforded that part of Louisiana that has been in the past already in the possession of the troops of the United States. If that is refused, whatever may ensue is upon them and not upon you or upon the United States. You will have done all that is required of a brave, humane man to avert from these deluded people the horrible consequences of their insane war upon the Government.

With or without such a message the Commanding General can see in your reasons nothing which should justly cause you to decline a high and honorable command; nor does he see how the remedy which you propose will aid the matter. And that remedy is that either he or some one of his officers should take command of the negro regiments and relieve you of them. Do you think that change would be less likely to incite a servile insurrection under his command, or that of any of his officers than under your own? Will the horrors be less if they are under the command of an officer not present on the scene to check and allay these horrors, than if they were commmanded by an officer present and ready to adopt proper measures?

If your negro or other regiments commit any outrage upon unoffending and unarmed people quietly attending to their own business, let them be most severely punished. But while operations in the field are going on, I do not see how you can turn aside from an armed enemy before you to protect or defend the wives and children of these armed enemies from the consequences of their own rebellious wickedness.

Consider this case. General Bragg is at liberty to ravage the homes of our brethren of Kentucky because the Union army of Louisiana are protecting his wife and his home against his negroes. Without that protection he would have to come back to

take care of his wife, his home and his negroes. It is understood
that Mrs Bragg is one of those terrified women of whom you speak
in your report.

This subject is not for the first time under the consideration of
the Commanding General. When in command of the Department
of Annapolis in May 1861, he was asked to protect a community
against the consequences of a servile rebellion. He replied that
when that community laid down its arms and called upon him for
protection, he would give it because from that moment between
them and him war would cease. The same principles enunciated
there will govern his and your action now; and you will afford such
protection as soon as the community through its organized rulers
shall ask it.

Your reports, and this reply, I am instructed to say, will be
forwarded by tomorrow's mail to the Commanding General of the
Army.

In the mean time these colored regiments of free men, raised by
the authority of the President and approved by him as the
Commander-in-Chief of the Army, must be commanded by the
officers of the Army of the United States like any other regiments.

The Commanding General does not doubt that everything that
prudence, sagacity, skill and courage can do, will be done by you,
General, to prosecute the campaign you have so successfully
begun. I am General Very Respectfully Your Obt Servant

ALcS   Geo C Strong

Brig. Genl. G. Weitzel to Major Geo. C. Strong, 5 Nov. 1862 (two letters),
and A.A. General Geo. C. Strong to Brig. Genl. Weitzel, 6 Nov. 1862,
enclosed in Major General Benj. F. Butler to Major General H. W. Halleck, 6
Nov. 1862, vol. 15, Union Battle Reports, ser. 729, War Records Office, RG
94 [HH-13]. Weitzel remained in command, but, as he suggested, the district was renamed Lafourche.

1 By direction of General Benjamin F. Butler, commander of the Department
of the Gulf, his chief of staff had advised General Godfrey Weitzel to build a
fort at Donaldsonville. Butler had also instructed Weitzel: "Of course there
will be no more difficult subject for you to deal with than the negroes. By the
act of Congress, independent of the President's proclamation, having come
from rebel masters into our lines in occupation of rebel territory since the
passage of that act they are free. But the question recurs, What shall we do
with them? While we have no right to return them to their masters as such, it
is our duty to take care of them, and that can include employment. Put them
as far as possible upon plantations; use every energy to have the sugar crop
made and preserved for the owners that are loyal, and for the United States
where the owners are disloyal. I am working the plantations along the river

below upon this plan. Let the loyal planters make arrangements to pay their negroes $10 a month for able-bodied men; $3 to be expended in clothing, and so in proportion. Disembarrass your army of them as much as possible. Especially will this be necessary in the case of Colonel Stafford's command." (*Official Records*, ser. 1, vol. 15, pp. 162–63.) Colonel Spencer H. Stafford commanded the 1st Louisiana Native Guard, which was composed of free blacks from New Orleans and vicinity.

70: Louisiana Planter to the Commander of the Department of the Gulf

Parish of St Charles [*La.*] December 20 1862
General   my advanced age, my position as a planter, and my perfect knowledge of the country, make it my duty to present a few remarks which I hope you will receive favorably.   We have suffered greatly during this unfortunate war, and we undoubtedly will have much more to suffer before order is restored and peace smiles again on this country.   So far we have, to regret in most instances, only the ruin and desolation which have extended to crops & farms; but the evil that threatens us is far more terrible than the loss of fortunes; our very lives are at stake!   As far as the memory of man can go, there has existed among the negro population a tradition which has caused us many a sleepless night.   They imagine that they are to be freed by Christmas.   Vague reports are spread about that they intend, taking whatever weapons they can find, to come in vast numbers and force the federal government to give them their freedom.   Having been deceived in their expectation, great crimes might be committed by them.   The negro regiments, in particular, being organized and armed are especially to be feared.   General I have no conduct to dictate to you, but if I were allowed to make a suggestion, I would tell you to disarm the negroes at least for the present and place white men, to see to their behavior   Respectfully Submitted

ALS   P^re Soniat

Pre. Soniat to General, 20 Dec. 1862, S-32 1862, Letters Received, ser. 1956, Field Records – Banks' Expedition, Dept. of the Gulf, RG 393 Pt. 1 [C-827].

71: New Orleans White to the Headquarters of the Department of the Gulf

[*New Orleans*] December 20th 1862

Sir No foresight can tell what may happen in our midst, by the Negroes on the 1st of next month— They, apparently, intend to come in the city then from the Plantations and have a procession:— Doubtless they will apply to the Commanding General for his permission. The citizens apprehend trouble therefrom if it takes place, the Negroes being in a dissatisfied state of mind by the proposed prolongation of term, to 37 years, for their liberty: made by President Lincoln in his Message to Congress;[1] and, you are aware, Colonel, the New orleans community is powerless, having surrenderd all weapons, by order of Gen¹ Butler.[2]

The apprehensions of the People, are, I consider not without cause. Evidently it is a matter of importance; and prevention is better than cure: for any impending harm:—

A Servile outbreak, would be bad enough in the City, but worse on the Plantations. My mind revolts at the idea of the bloodshed and incendiarism that would ensue. All calamities of that Sort, besides the actual loss of life and devastation, have a most pernicious effect for a long length of time afterwards—and, the evil would be incalculable:—

May I be permitted to Suggest, worthy Sir, it would have a beneficial tendency were Male citizens between the ages of 16 and 70, to be invited by the Military authorities to form a "Home Guard" and be supplied with arms:— Unhesitatingly, Col, I believe this matter is worthy the Consideration of the commanding General:— very respectfully Your mo obedᵗ Servant

Thoˢ. D. Hailes

I will to day look for a Dwelling furnished, adapted for 6 Gentlemen, in the location you pointed out. Whenever you wish to see me, please send me written word.

ALS

Thos. D. Hailes to Lieut. Colonel Richd. B. Irwin, 20 Dec. 1862, H-65 1862, Letters Received, ser. 1956, Field Records—Banks' Expedition, Dept. of the Gulf, RG 393 Pt. 1 [C-824]. On the same day, another white resident of New Orleans suggested to General Nathaniel P. Banks, new commander of the Department of the Gulf, that a carver who lived near the general's office could provide "abundant information on the Subject, as he is employ'd to make the Images, Spears, Etc for the procession." The writer cautioned Banks that "we are entirely *without arms* and this the Negroes know too well for the Safety of our families." "[A]lready scenes similar to those (tho of less magni-

tude) that were perpetrated on the Isle of St Domingo have transpired here."
(Edmund M. Ivens to Major Genl. N. P. Banks, 20 Dec. 1862, filed with
H-53 1862, Letters Received, ser. 1956, Field Records – Banks' Expedition,
Dept. of the Gulf, RG 393 Pt. 1 [C-824].) Two anonymous letters voiced
similar fears that blacks intended "to massacre indiscriminately Northerns,
Southerns, women and children!" on the first of January. (Unsigned to the
Honorable Major General Banks, 24 Dec. 1862, and Unsigned to Col. Clark,
24 Dec. 1862, filed with A-54 1862, Letters Received by the Provost Marshal
General, ser. 1390, State of LA, Provost Marshal Field Organizations, RG
393 Pt. 4 [C-824].) To forestall possible violence, the commander of U.S.
forces in New Orleans and Algiers posted sentries to prevent the entry of
blacks from downriver into the city. (Col. Thos. W. Cahill to Lieut. Col. W.
W. Bullock, 24 Dec. 1862, vol. 130 DG, p. 100, Letters Sent, ser. 1884,
U.S. Forces New Orleans & Algiers, RG 393 Pt. 2 No. 97 [C-862].) New
Year's Day passed without incident.

1 Lincoln's message (December 1, 1862) proposed federal compensation to
slave states that agreed to abolish slavery by 1900. (*Official Records*, ser. 3, vol.
2, pp. 892–97.)
2 By an order of August 16, 1862, General Benjamin F. Butler, then commander of the Department of the Gulf, had disarmed the residents of Orleans
Parish, prescribing fines for violators and promising freedom to slaves who
provided information about concealed weapons belonging to their masters.
(Benjamin F. Butler, *Private and Official Correspondence of Gen. Benjamin F.*
Butler during the Period of the Civil War, 5 vols. [Norwood, Mass., 1917], vol.
2, p. 195.)

72: Affidavit of Two Louisiana Planters

[*St. John the Baptist Parish, La.*]
22nd [*21st*] day of December AD 1862.

Be it known, that on this day the Twenty first day of December
AD 1862, before me, P. B. Marmillion, Sheriff of the Parish of S^t
John the Baptist, State of Louisiana, personally came and appeared
Dr Gustave Chabaud and J. Burcard, residing in the Said Parish,
who after being duly sworn depose and Say

That the presence in the lower Parishes of St Charles, St John the
Baptist and St James, of the regiments known as the Second Native
Guards under the Command of Col. N. W. Daniels, is detrimental
to the interests of Said parishes and has had for effect the entire and
effectual demoralisation of the Servile population in Said
parishes – and that the lives of families and inoffensive citizens is in
danger, from the threats and actual misconduct of Said regiments;
that without order or authorisation written – and in Some cases

verbal – they have entered private houses, taken and carried away property, valuables &^{cra} and have at divers and Sundry times Completely robbed and Carried away goods and properties belonging to private persons, inoffensive and loyal – that without authorisation they have disarmed the loyal citizens of Said parishes – have stolen watches from Said citizens, and run about during the night without discipline or order, and incite the quiet Servile population to revolt and cruel treatment toward their masters; that the depredations along the coast are So numerous that it is impossible to enumerate them now, but are of Such a nature as to render the parishes untenable to the inhabitants of Said parishes, who are loyal citizens of the United States, as every person, or very nearly So, from the lower end of St Charles to the upper one of St James, has taken the oath of allegiance required by Gen Butler.

Almost every day acts of violation of domicil & property have taken place and have been committed by the Soldiers of Said regiment, unaccompanied by any white officer; the Same being done on denunciations of Slaves and Sometimes even without any denunciation at all.

Eleven inhabitants of Said Parish, have been illegally arrested by them, taken down in a Cart to the Boutte Station and insulted by the Said Soldiers during the whole distance Say about 20 miles, kept at Said Station for many days

The names of Said persons are J. B. Haydel: Valcour Haydel: [Clarifeux] Faucheux; Octave Borne; Justin Becnel; Prémilieu Becnel, Sévérin Lonpre, Séraphin Lonpre; and two inhabitants of Said parish, fathers of family to wit: Florian Berttolle et Jean Berttolle have been without any Cause and upon the denunciation of one of their own Slave girls, who had previously abandonned the house, been arrested, Sent to New Orleans and are now in the Jail of Said Parish.

Colonel Daniels upholds this monstrous State of things and refuses to listen to the Just demands of the loyal citizens of Said Parish.

This week, three carts loaded with Slaves arrived from Boutte Station, Shrieking threats, singing and exciting to insurrection, and mentioning Christmas as being the time Set for the emancipation of Slaves

Furthermore, that Col Daniels has illegally charged and charges the Sum of $2 for the taking of the Oath to all loyal citizens disposed to return to their allegiance to the United States, and has charged $5 for a permit to carry arms and hunt, and from $5 to $10 for Passes; all of which are in direct violation of the order of the General Commanding this Department.

They therefore would request that the Said regiment of Native Guards be withdrawn from their Said Parish and that their own Sheriff be appointed Provost Marshall, and hereby request him, in the name of all the inhabitants of Said Parish, that this, their demand, be by him transmitted to the Commanding General at New Orleans:

J. Burcard
G. Chabaud

HDS

Affidavit of J. Burcard and G. Chabaud, 21 Dec. 1862, C-90 1862, Letters Received by the Provost Marshal General, ser. 1390, State of LA, Provost Marshal Field Organizations, RG 393 Pt. 4 [C-962]. Sworn before the sheriff of St. John the Baptist Parish. An endorsement ordered the dismissal of Daniels.

73: Officers of a Black Union Association to the Commander of the Department of the Gulf

New orleans Dec 22th 1862

In obedience To Th High chift an Command of Th Head quarters Department of Th Gulf Maggor Gen N P Bank We Th members of Th union association Desir Th & Respectfully ask of you Th privirliges of Salabrating Th first Day of January th 1863 by a Large procesion on that Day & We Wish to pass th Head quarters of th union officers High in a authority that is if it Suit your approbation & We also Wish to Give a Grand union Dinner on th Second Day of Januay that is if it so pleas you & th profit of th Dinner Will Go To th poor people in th Camp th Colour Woman & childeren   Your Most Homble obedien servant

J M Marshall th president of th union association

HLSr   Henry clay th Superintender of th Dinner

J. M. Marshall and Henry Clay to Gen. N. P. Bank, 22 Dec. 1862, M-62 1862, Letters Received, ser. 1956, Field Records – Banks' Expedition, Dept. of the Gulf, RG 393 Pt. 1 [C-824]. The letter and both signatures are in the same handwriting. A search of the copies of letters sent in the records of the Department of the Gulf revealed no reply to the Union Association.

74: Order by the Commander of the Department of the Gulf

New Orleans, December 24, 1862.

GENERAL ORDERS No. 116. The following address of the Commanding General to the People of Louisiana, dated this day, is published to the troops of this Department for the information and government of all concerned:

TO THE PEOPLE OF LOUISIANA:

In order to correct public misapprehension and misrepresentation: for the instruction of the troops of this department, and the information of all parties in interest, official publication is herewith made of the Proclamation by the President of the United States, relating to the subject of Emancipation. In the examination of this document it will be observed:

I. That it is the declaration of a purpose only – the full execution of which is contingent upon an official designation by the President, to be made on the 1st day of January next, of the States and parts of States, if any, which are to be affected by its provisions:

II. That the fact that any State is represented in good faith in the Congress of the United States is conclusive evidence, in the absence of strong countervailing testimony, that such State, and the people thereof, are not in rebellion against the United States:

III. That the State of Louisiana, has not yet been designated by the President as in rebellion, nor any part thereof, as provided in the fourth paragraph of the proclamation annexed, and that, so far as the Government has jurisdiction, it has complied with all the conditions of the proclamation respecting representation:

IV. That pecuniary aid to States not in rebellion, which may hereafter provide for immediate or gradual emancipation; the colonization of persons of African descent elsewhere, and the compensation of all citizens who have remained loyal, "for all losses by acts of the United States, including slaves," are among the chief recommendations of this important paper.

It is manifest that the changes suggested therein, and which may hereafter be established, do not take effect within this State on the first of January proximo, nor at any precise period which can now be designated, and I call upon all persons, of whatever estate, condition or degree, soldiers, citizens or slaves, to observe this material and important fact, and to govern themselves accordingly. All unusual public demonstrations, of whatever character, will be for the present suspended. Provost Marshals, officers and soldiers are enjoined to prevent any disturbance of the public peace. The slaves are advised to remain upon their plantations until their privileges shall have been definitely established. They may rest assured that whatever benefit the Government intends will be secured to them, but no man can be allowed in the present condition of affairs to take the law into his own hands. If they seek the protection of the Government, they should wait its pleasure. Officers invested with command will be vigilant in the discharge of their duties. Leave of absence from camp will not be permitted, except in cases of great emergency. Soldiers enrolled in the regiments of Native Guards, will not be allowed for the present to visit the localities of their enlistment, nor will visitors be received unnecessarily in their camps. These regulations, enforced with all troops of the United States in localities where they are enlisted, are now imperatively necessary. These troops will be confined to the duty specified in general orders, and will not be charged with special authority in making searches, seizures or arrests. It is my purpose to execute faithfully all the orders of the Government, and I assume the responsibility of these instructions as consistent therewith, and require prompt and faithful execution thereof.

Public attention is called to the act of Congress cited in the Proclamation, which forbids the return of fugitives by officers of the army. No encouragement will be given to laborers to desert their employers, but no authority exists to compel them to return. It is suggested to planters that some plan be adopted by which an equitable proportion of the proceeds of the crops of the coming year, to be hereafter determined upon the judgment of honorable men justly representing the different interests involved, be set apart and reserved for the support and compensation of labor.

The war is not waged by the Government for the overthrow of slavery. The President has declared, on the contrary, that it is to restore the "constitutional relations between the United States and each of the States" in which that relation is or may be suspended. The resolutions passed by Congress, before the war, with almost unanimous consent, recognized the rights of the States in this regard. Vermont has recently repealed the statutes supposed to be inconsistent therewith. Massachusetts had done so before. Slavery existed by consent and constitutional guaranty; violence and war will inevitably bring it to an end. It is impossible that any military man, in the event of continued war, should counsel the preservation of slave property in the rebel States. If it is to be preserved, war must cease, and the former constitutional relations be again established.

The first gun at Sumter proclaimed emancipation. The continuance of the contest there commenced will consummate that end, and the history of the age will leave no other permanent trace of the rebellion. Its leaders will have accomplished what other men could not have done. The boldest Abolitionist is a cypher when compared with the leaders of the rebellion. What mystery pervades the works of Providence! We submit to its decrees, but stand confounded at the awful manifestations of its wisdom and power! The great problem of the age, apparently environed with labyrinthic complications, is likely to be suddenly lifted out of human hands. We may control the incidents of the contest, but we cannot circumvent or defeat the end. It will be left us only to assuage the horrors of internecine conflict, and to procrastinate the processes of transition. Local and national interests are therefore alike dependent upon the suppression of the rebellion.

No pecuniary sacrifice can be too great an equivalent for peace. But it should be permanent peace, and embrace all subjects of discontent. It is written on the blue arch above us; the distant voices of the future – the waves that beat our coast – the skeletons that sit at our tables, and fill the vacant places of desolate and mourning firesides, all cry out that this war must not be repeated hereafter.

Contest, in public as in social life, strengthens and consolidates brotherly affection. England, France, Austria, Italy – every land fertile enough to make a history, has had its desolating civil wars. It is a baseless nationality that has not tested its strength against domestic enemies. The success of local interests narrows the destiny of a people, and is followed by secession, starvation and sorrow. A divided country and perpetual war make possession a delusion and life a calamity. The triumph of national interests widens the scope of human history, and is attended with peace, prosperity and power. It is out of such contests that great nations are born.

What hallowed memories float around us! New Orleans is a shrine as sacred as Bunker Hill! On the Aroostook and the Oregon the names of Washington, Jackson and Taylor are breathed with as deep a reverence as on the James or the Mississippi. Let us fulfil the conditions of this last great trial, and become a nation – a grand nation – with sense enough to govern ourselves and strength enough to stand against the world united!

PD

N. P. BANKS,

General Orders No. 116, Headquarters Department of the Gulf, 24 Dec. 1862, Orders & Circulars, ser. 44, RG 94 [DD-34]. Accompanying this order was War Department General Order 139, issued September 24, 1862, which promulgated President Lincoln's preliminary Emancipation Proclamation. In transmitting General Order 116 to the headquarters of the army, General Banks explained his rationale for issuing it: "Great apprehension has been felt here among the planters and others on account of threatened movements by the slaves at Christmas and New Year." (*Official Records*, ser. 1, vol. 15, p. 618.)

75: Louisiana Planter to the Provost Marshal General of Louisiana

New Orleans 7th Jany 1862 [*1863*]

Sir, Having been informed by my friend and neighbour, John Burnside Esqr – that you had authorised the police to arrest and lodge in the prison of this City the runaways from his Estates in S^t

James, I take the liberty to sollicit a similar order from you; as I am continually annoyed by calls of some of my runaway slaves, upon the few remaining servants that have remained faithful to me, to induce them to leave my House— The names of the runaways from my House and from my Estate in Sᵗ James are as follows:

Mulatoe Celestin
Mulatoe Boy Watkins
    〃   Boy Urbain
    〃   Charles
    〃   Girl Sylvania
    〃   Girl Nancy
    〃   Woman Delphine
    〃   Boy Auguste
Negro Francis
    〃 – Mondesir
    〃   Mike
    〃   William
Negro woman Marianne & her 2 children
    〃   Boy Robert
    〃 – 〃 Jack
    〃 – 〃 Auguste
    〃 – 〃 John Mathews
    〃 – 〃 Allen

    An answer at your earliest convenience will oblige Your Obᵗ Servᵗ
ALS   Edm J Forstall

Edm. J. Forstall to Col. Jonas H. French, 7 Jan. 1862 [1863], F-2 1862, Letters Received by the Provost Marshal General, ser. 1390, State of LA, Provost Marshal Field Organizations, RG 393 Pt. 4 [C-963]. A search of the surviving records of the provost marshal general of Louisiana and the Department of the Gulf did not reveal a reply.

76: New Orleans Slave to the Commander of the Department of the Gulf

                        Police Jail New-orleans January 8 1863
General. I take the liberty to adress you this humble request, confiding in your justice. Since the arrival of the federal fleet in New-orleans in april last my mistress put me out door, telling to me to go the Yankee, her husband Mʳ William Converse; being at the time in the rebel army, as a Captain of cavalry, of course I was oblige to go, but finding no occupation a return to my mistress

house accompagnied at my owm request by a police officer, to whom she tell that I could go back where I had been, then I was put in jail Since that time, whitout have commit any offence against any one, or my mistress and master that I have faithfully served all the time   I beg pardon for the liberty that I have take to write thos few lignes to your honor confiding in your kindness and justice even to a poor slave girl who are kept in prison as a criminal   I am whith respect

ALS   Mary Ann. slave of W. Converse

Mary Ann to his honor Mag. gen. N. Banks, 8 Jan. 1863, C-30 1863, Letters Received, ser. 1920, Civil Affairs, Dept. of the Gulf, RG 393 Pt. 1 [C-690]. A search of the retained copies of letters sent by the Department of the Gulf did not reveal a reply.

77: Provost Judge of the District of Lafourche to the Commander of the Department of the Gulf

Thibodeaux [La.] Jany. 25 63

Sir— The first of last week many citizens of the Lafourche District came to me asking what their rights were in reference to their negros, under the late proclamation of the President, saying they wished to be law abiding citizens, Doing nothing to expose themselves to arrest and punishment, desirous of practising nothing but the exercise of their legal rights, if they could but know what they were. So reasonable request I considered entitled to consideration, and at their request I put in writing my understanding of what their legal rights were, in the words following to wit—

"Thibodeaux Jany 1863
Mr   has permission to take his servants by force wherever he finds them, except in the camp of the U.S. Army, or in the employ of the U.S. or an officer thereof, and compel their return to their homes, and their obedience to him, and their quiet application to their business— In case any of his servants are found in the camp of the U.S. Army, not in the employ of any officer, and chooses to return home with their master, they will not be hindered. The master is enjoined to treat his servants justly and kindly, as a judicious man would treat his servants"

I explained to the citizens applicants, that this did not give them any rights more than they in my judgment enjoyed before receiving it, but that it was simply an expression of my understanding of their legal rights, by which I should be governed until I received definite instructions from the Commanding General, the source of Martial law of this District, to which I should cheerfully defer. I have no wish so far as my official duty is concerned, but to vindicate the policy of the Government indicated by yourself—(which I understand to be my official duty) when I know it,—In meantime to do my duty according to the best of my ability, as I am sworn to do.

I respectfully refer the subject of this communication to you for your approval, or that I may receive an indication of your wishes in this behalf, that I may be guided thereby.

I respectfully solicit an early answer, more particularly as Capt. Goodrige, the Provost Martial, has informed me that he shall issue an order forbidding a citizen to use force in returning his estray servant—An order the execution of which I cannot enforce with my present understanding of the rights of the owner of the slave, and it is exceedingly desirable on my part to avoid a collision with a gentleman for whom I entertain so high an esteem as for Capt Goodridge—

I hope General, to be releived from my present position & duties on the moving of Genl. Witsels Brigade, as fighting disloyal citizens is much more to my taste than settling the pecadilloes of negros, creoles, or thorough bred planters. I would like much an interview with you upon these subjects were I not fearful of trepassing upon your time. I am at present in the city at the St Charles & shall return to my duties tomorrow—Monday morng   I am very Respectfully Your Obt Servt.

ALS   O. W. Lull

O. W. Lull to Maj. Genl. N. G. Banks, 25 Jan. 1863, L-30 1863, Letters Received, ser. 1920, Civil Affairs, Dept. of the Gulf, RG 393 Pt. 1 [C-707]. The blank space in the quoted statement appears in the manuscript. Captain Luther Goodrich, provost marshal of the District of Lafourche, meanwhile reported to the provost marshal general of the Department of the Gulf that Lull's order had caused "considerable excitement": "Planters all anxious to retain possession of absent slaves were on the alert to take advantage of the golden moment. Several forcible arrests were made & one man pursued by his master was drowned in the Bayou Laforche." Goodrich countered Lull's order with one of his own, forbidding forcible seizure and return of fugitive slaves to their putative owners, but also providing that "[a]ny negro found idle after eight o'clock on Monday morning next, without any means of support, will be compelled to work on the levees on Bayou Lafourche." Forwarding a copy of his order, Goodrich urged that the department commander "should without delay decide what is the true condition of the slave in this district." (L. Goodrich to Col. Clark, 24 Jan. 1863, enclosing Order No. 1, Provost

Marshal's Office, District of Lafourche, 24 Jan. 1863, Letters Received, ser. 1845, Provost Marshal, Dept. of the Gulf, RG 393 Pt. 1 [C-786].) A search of the surviving records of the provost marshal general of Louisiana and the Department of the Gulf did not reveal a reply to either Lull's or Goodrich's letter, but General Order 12, issued by the commander of the Department of the Gulf on January 29, 1863, forbade forcible seizure of fugitive slaves by would-be masters. (*Official Records*, ser. 1, vol. 15, pp. 666–67.)

78: New Orleans Fugitive Slave to the Commander of the Department of the Gulf

Neworleans Feb th 2 1863
kin Sire   I wash to state to you this morning the hole mattor   I am in truble and like Jacob of old and Can not let the go untill you Comford me   My wife and felloservent was orded to go to yeenkis and they left and went and sence that they hav taken them and put them in prison taken the mother from hire Suckling Child put the mother in and taken the Child home   I and my wife and felloservent am not willing to go Back   we had Rented a house and living in it 20 Days then taken   if you please Sire gave me a premiat to gat my wife out of Prison and my things out off his house the no 262 Cannal St mrs George Ruleff Reseadents   your most obodent Servent
ALS   Nathan mc kinney

Nathan mc kinney to Maj. Genl. Banks, 2 Feb. 1863, M-35 1863, Letters Received, ser. 1920, Civil Affairs, Dept. of the Gulf, RG 393 Pt. 1 [C-709]. Endorsement. No reply has been found among the retained copies of letters sent by the Department of the Gulf.

79: New Orleans Slave to the Commander of the Department of the Gulf

New Orleans Febuary [23] 1863
Sir I Gorgener Roman wright a fue lines to you to ask you if you will be so kind as to send some one to my assistence as soon as posable   I was in prison abut to monts and one of the fideral ofecers paid me a visit and as soon as he came to see me the gail keeper went and informed my master of this visit and he came with a poleace ofecer No 175 and he paid him and a cariage drive name

batteace a black man who was arested once for runing the blocade for the confiderates to kee the secret   I wasent down on borgars pantation to be struck twenty five lashes and then to be put in chaines and I know that I will not be able to endure such cruel treatments   luttenent Beachum and Capten Constock knowes me and can inform you all the perticulars about me and if you will arest the ofece and the carage drive you can fin out where this pantation is   I beg you for God sak pleas to sen some as soo as posable before they kill me   yours respectfully

ALS   Gorgener Roman

Gorgener Roman to Mager General Bankes, 23 Feb. 1863, R-31 1863, Letters Received, ser. 1920, Civil Affairs, Dept. of the Gulf, RG 393 Pt. 1 [C-718]. A search of the surviving records of the Department of the Gulf did not reveal any action in the case.

80: Circular by the Provost Marshal of
St. Martin's Parish, Louisiana

CIRCULAR.

Now Iberia, La., April 24. 1863.

The generally received impression, that the slaves of this Parish, are free, by force of the presence of the Union army, *is erroneous.*

This Parish, (St. Martin) is excepted by name, in the Emancipation Proclamation, of President Lincoln, issued at Washington, D. C., January 1, 1863.

No farther interference, with the institution of slavery will be allowed by the Army Authorities, than may necessarily result from the police regulations.

United States Army Officers, are forbidden, by law of Congress, to use force in the restoration of slaves to masters.

If slaves flee from their masters, they must work on Government works, receiving therefor, full rations, for full day's work.

If slaves voluntarily return to their masters, they will not be molested.

If masters use force, in abducting run-away slaves, the masters will be arrested.

If masters inhumanly punish or whip their slaves, they must be arrested.

No punishment of slaves, will be permitted, except such as are practiced in the Army.

A. B. LONG,
Capt., & Provost Marshal,
Commanding Post,

Circular, 24 Apr. 1863, enclosed in Capt. A. B. Long to Col. Dwight, 30 Apr. 1863, Letters Received, ser. 1845, Provost Marshal, Dept. of the Gulf, RG 393 Pt. 1 [C-791]. In the covering letter to the provost marshal general of Louisiana, Long described blacks in his parish as "a continual source of anxiety and trouble." Before the federal occupation, Confederate authorities had gathered a large number of slave men from the Bayou Lafourche region to work in arsenals and on gunboats, and Long's policy was to grant passes to these blacks to rejoin their families. He also attempted to return to their masters slaves who had run away but were now willing to return. Those unwilling to return he employed in government service. Long also reported "insurrections of armed bodies of negroes" in the vicinity of St. Martinsville that had thrown whites into a state of great "fear and anxiety." On April 23, Long had requested instructions from the provost marshal general of the Department of the Gulf: "I have heretofore encouraged the idea of freedom among slaves not anticipating the exception of this Parish. what policy shall be pursued now towards the hundred who come flocking in here. Are they to be advised to return to their masters or compelled. I am ordered to prosecute govt works that cannot be completed without their aid." (Capt. A. B. Long to Brig. Gen. J. Bowen, 23 Apr. 1863, Letters Received, ser. 1845, Provost Marshal, Dept. of the Gulf, RG 393 Pt. 1 [C-774].) No reply has been found among the surviving records of the provost marshal general of Louisiana and the Department of the Gulf.

CHAPTER 5

The Mississippi Valley

5

The Mississippi Valley

SLAVES IN LARGE NUMBERS worked the plantations and farms of the Mississippi Valley, raising cotton and tobacco for the foreign and Northern markets and hemp, foodstuffs, and livestock for the Southern ones.[1] Some of their masters numbered among the wealthiest in the South. Although many farmers in the upper reaches of the valley – particularly those distant from the great river network – maintained allegiance to the Union, the staple-producing planters almost uniformly embraced secession. Confident that the new Confederate government would sustain the plantation regime and protect its dominant form of labor, they carried on as before, fully expecting their slaves to do the same. The outbreak of war disrupted the old order and with it their fond expectations.

The war in the Mississippi Valley began with federal policy makers committed to restoring the Union without disturbing slavery. But, as elsewhere, wartime exigencies played havoc with that commitment. As Union soldiers moved into Confederate territory, they saw how fully the rebellion depended upon slave labor. With every step south, the number of fugitive slaves increased, for federal invasion invariably disrupted the master-slave relationship. As disloyal masters fled from advancing Union columns, loyal slaves moved toward them. The large number of runaway slaves who besieged federal camps, begging Union soldiers for protection, exposed the folly of federal policy. Under pres-

---

[1] In addition to the Confederate states touching the Mississippi River (Arkansas, Louisiana, Mississippi, and Tennessee), this chapter also deals with northern Alabama, which was occupied by federal forces operating from Tennessee. Published accounts of emancipation in the Mississippi Valley include: John Eaton, *Grant, Lincoln and the Freedmen: Reminiscences of the Civil War* (New York, 1907); Louis S. Gerteis, *From Contraband to Freedman: Federal Policy toward Southern Blacks, 1861–1865* (Westport, Conn., 1973), chaps. 7–10; C. Peter Ripley, *Slaves and Freedmen in Civil War Louisiana* (Baton Rouge, La., 1976); Armstead L. Robinson, *Bitter Fruits of Bondage: The Demise of Slavery and the Collapse of the Confederacy* (New Haven, Conn., forthcoming). Also pertinent are John Vincent Cimprich, Jr., "Slavery amidst Civil War in Tennessee: The Death of an Institution" (Ph.D. diss., Ohio State University, 1977); Stephen V. Ash, "Civil War, Black Freedom, and Social Change in the Upper South: Middle Tennessee, 1860–1870" (Ph.D. diss., University of Tennessee, 1983).

sure from a Northern public determined to punish rebels and from Union soldiers eager to avail themselves of the slaves' proffered assistance, the federal government eventually authorized the army to receive and protect fugitive slaves who could be usefully employed in the war effort.

The federal advance into the Confederacy opened numerous paths by which slaves could escape bondage. Able-bodied men who fled their masters readily found work with the Yankee invaders, first as military laborers with the army, then as field hands in the employ of Northerners who leased captured estates, and, in time, as soldiers in the ranks of the Union army. Some fugitive slave women also labored for the army, usually as laundresses or hospital attendants, but most women — along with children and elderly or infirm fugitives — worked on the leased plantations or were placed in contraband camps established by Union military authorities. Other slaves did not have to leave their homes to gain freedom. Abandoned by fleeing masters, they took over the plantations and lived by their own devices. Even when masters remained at home under federal occupation, slaves gained unprecedented bargaining power — at times translating their new circumstances into a semblance of freedom. Still, no two paths out of slavery followed exactly the same course. Variations in geography, the depth and extent of white unionism, the character of slavery, and — perhaps most important — the progress of military events all gave emancipation a distinctive shape in each subregion and political division of the great valley.

Slavery began to disintegrate first in Tennessee, springboard of the Union advance into the Confederate interior. Early in 1862, federal forces occupied middle and west Tennessee, the state's two plantation regions, and advanced temporarily into northern Alabama. In west Tennessee, many masters fled, and Union commanders wasted little time putting every available slave to work. In the central part of the state, where most masters remained on their plantations and farms and many professed loyalty to the Union, federal commanders promised to respect slavery. But by the end of 1863 — despite Tennessee's exemption from the Emancipation Proclamation — military necessity had diminished the regional differences in the evolution of freedom. The army's demand for military laborers and soldiers, coupled with the deterioration of slave discipline, eroded slavery and promoted freedom.

In July 1863, the Confederate surrender of Vicksburg and Port Hudson gave full control of the Mississippi River to Union forces and enabled federal authorities to redeem the promise of freedom enunciated by the confiscation acts and the Emancipation Proclamation. Union troops occupied strategic points along the entire length of the river, from which they conducted raids and launched full-fledged campaigns into the interior of Arkansas, Louisiana, and Mississippi. By the end of 1863, they had also reoccupied northern Alabama and taken control of east Tennessee. Throughout the valley, federal camps attracted runaway slaves, and army commanders concluded that the deliberate extension of freedom would enhance the security of the river. Federal soldiers – many of them black – brought freedom to hundreds of thousands of slaves in the Mississippi Valley, and in 1864 and 1865, declarations of emancipation by unionist state conventions in Arkansas, Louisiana, and Tennessee confirmed what had been settled by force of arms.

When the Union army invaded Tennessee in February 1862, restoration of the Union, not emancipation of the slaves, was the prevailing Northern policy.[2] Federal commanders uniformly promised to protect the property of peaceable citizens. General Henry W. Halleck, commander of the Department of the Missouri, admonished the troops moving into west Tennessee to show "our fellow-citizens . . . that we come merely to crush out rebellion and to restore to them peace and the benefits of the Constitution and the Union," not "to oppress and to plunder." Halleck insisted that federal forces guarantee "the same protection of life and property as in former days," and he reiterated earlier injunctions against "the stealing and concealment of slaves." "It does not belong to the military to decide upon the relation of master and slave," Halleck pontificated. "Such questions must be settled by the civil courts." In a restatement of his General Order 3, issued the previous November, Halleck explicitly directed that "[n]o fugitive slave . . . be admitted within our lines or camps."[3] Excluding slaves altogether, Halleck hoped, would eliminate the logistical and supply problems created by fugitives, encourage masters to reaffirm allegiance to the Union, and, most important, disentangle the army from disputes about slavery.

Apparently satisfied with their commander's resolution of the vexed fugitive slave problem, most of Halleck's subordinates complied with his policy of exclusion. General Ulysses S. Grant, for instance, operating along the Tennessee River, reiterated Halleck's orders respecting slaves.[4] But when and where the Union army moved bore more heavily

---

[2] In February 1862, federal troops entered Tennessee in a three-pronged assault. Armies from General Henry W. Halleck's Department of the Missouri moved into west Tennessee: General Ulysses S. Grant advanced up the Tennessee River, and General John Pope proceeded down the Mississippi. Meanwhile, General Don Carlos Buell, commander of the Department and Army of the Ohio, moved from Kentucky into middle Tennessee, occupying Nashville shortly after Grant's victories at Fort Henry and Fort Donelson. In March 1862, Halleck assumed command of the newly created Department of the Mississippi, which encompassed Grant's Army of the Tennessee, Pope's Army of the Mississippi, and Buell's Army of the Ohio. Pope was succeeded by General William S. Rosecrans in June.

[3] *Official Records*, ser. 1, vol. 8, pp. 563–64. For Halleck's General Order 3, see below, doc. 157.

[4] *Official Records*, ser. 1, vol. 7, p. 668.

upon the future of slavery than did the intentions of individual federal commanders. The initial Union advance along a sparsely populated stretch of the Tennessee River masked the difficulties inherent in Halleck's policy. But, by the summer of 1862, following victory at Pittsburg Landing in southern Tennessee, the capture of Corinth, Mississippi, and other successes along the Mississippi River, federal armies controlled most of central and western Tennessee and had also advanced into northern Alabama and northern Mississippi. Everywhere they encountered fugitive slaves in large numbers. The arrival of Union troops in areas with heavy concentrations of slaves soon stretched the policy of exclusion to the breaking point.

Some slaveholders fled in panic before the Yankee invasion. Understanding at once how it would compromise plantation discipline and fearing for their property if not their lives, they hurriedly gathered families, movable possessions, and slaves, and trekked to safety in the Confederate interior. Since few had anticipated the sudden collapse of Confederate defenses, the masters' hasty evacuations rarely went as planned. Moving under the gun, many swallowed their losses and transferred only their able-bodied slave men, leaving women, children, and the infirm and aged behind. Refugeeing thus divided slave parents and children and husbands and wives, and it splintered larger kin networks. It also compromised whatever lingering sense of allegiance slaves retained to the old order.

The masters' flight from the Yankees spread discontent throughout the Mississippi Valley. Many slaves refused to cooperate with the relocations, taking cover in the woods instead. Those forced to migrate did not always complete the journey. Although generally unfamiliar with the new terrain, refugeed slaves understood that each step deeper into the Confederacy reduced their chance of rejoining families or achieving liberty. Many attempted to return home at the first opportunity, often with disastrous results. Others headed toward the Yankees. The arrival of these runaways, physically sound though breathless and bruised, exposed the policy of exclusion as self-defeating. Overworked Northern soldiers and short-handed officers sought permission to put able-bodied fugitives to work. The combined demands of Union soldiers and runaway slaves soon proved irresistible.

The federal armies operating in the Mississippi Valley comprised for the most part midwestern regiments, whose officers and men held political views that ranged from Abraham Lincoln's free-soil Republicanism to Stephen A. Douglas's dough-faced Democracy. But whatever their antebellum politics, many soldiers were transformed by the war into determined opponents of slaveholders and slavery – if not into outright abolitionists. Federal legislation, particularly the March 1862 article of war that prohibited soldiers from returning fugitive slaves to their masters, encouraged this transformation. The new article of war subtly shifted the balance in favor of those officers and soldiers who had all along objected to expelling slaves from army encampments. It seemed to legitimate their earlier interventions on behalf of fugitives, and encouraged them to resist orders to have nothing to do with slaves. During the summer of 1862 – as Union troops secured the railroads of middle and west Tennessee, northern Alabama, and northern Mississippi, repairing and reconstructing as they advanced – the enormous labor exacted of the soldiers cast doubt on the wisdom of rejecting slaves who were able, indeed eager, to work for the Union. Many federal officers adopted a pragmatic strategy, welcoming the able-bodied men and turning all others away. However harsh toward the fugitives, such acts subverted the policy of exclusion, rendering it increasingly irrelevant.

The boldest opponents of slavery in the western armies cited the new article of war, as well as high moral principle, and openly violated Halleck's exclusion orders. Union soldiers from Kansas, who had been transferred from the Kansas-Missouri border in the hope of muting their militant opposition to slavery, led the way.[5] The animus of the Kansas "jayhawkers" against Missouri masters was but a specific expression of their general contempt for slaveholders; they viewed Tennessee masters merely as a different species of the same objectionable genus. Kansas soldiers encouraged slaves to run away and harbored fugitives within their lines, inspiring other antislavery soldiers to do the same. The 7th Kansas Cavalry and its commander, Daniel R. Anthony, became especially notorious for aggressive abolitionism. Only weeks after reaching west Tennessee, the regiment was under suspicion for enticing slaves into its camp. Unabashed, Anthony searched for an opportunity to punish slaveholders on a grand scale. A two-day assignment to brigade command in June 1862 offered an opportunity he could not resist. In defiance of his superiors' efforts to mollify loyal slaveholders, Anthony pointedly ordered the arrest of any soldier who helped masters apprehend fugitive slaves. Although his order was generally consonant with the new article of war, Anthony was arrested and charged with allowing his men to harbor runaway slaves and pilfer the property of citizens. High-placed inquiries on Anthony's behalf led to his release, but he resigned soon thereafter when a lower-ranking officer was promoted over him. Anthony's departure from the army curbed the jayhawkers' opposition to slavery but did not end it.[6]

The impassioned pleas of fugitives, combined with the example of

[5] On the activities of Kansas "jayhawkers" against slavery in Missouri, see below, chap. 7.
[6] For a history of the 7th Kansas Cavalry, see Stephen Z. Starr, *Jennison's Jayhawkers: A Civil War Cavalry Regiment and Its Commander* (Baton Rouge, La., 1973), especially chapter 9 on Anthony.

antislavery regiments, convinced other previously unsympathetic soldiers to shelter runaway slaves and obstruct pursuing masters. Northern soldiers who remained unmoved by humanitarian or political considerations also began to relent, if only because they were happy to have blacks do the routine and often back-breaking labor required by the war. From a variety of motives, both soldiers and officers came to understand the hopelessness of trying to subdue the slaveholders' rebellion without turning the slaves against their masters – at least the slaves of disloyal masters. General William S. Rosecrans, commander of the Army of the Mississippi, reflected the mood of the western troops in July 1862, on the eve of the Second Confiscation Act. Although he insisted that "[i]t is not our purpose to admit the slaves of loyal masters within our lines, or use them without compensation, or prevent their recovery when consistent with the interests of the service," Rosecrans proceeded to make clear the growing hostility to protecting the slave property of rebels: "The slaves of our enemies may come or go whenever they please, provided they do not interfere with the rules and orders of camps and discipline. They deserve more at our hands than their masters."[7] The new confiscation act suggested that the United States Congress had reached the same conclusion.

As antagonism toward slavery gained strength in the nation's capital, Union forces cleared west Tennessee of most remaining Confederates. After the federals occupied Memphis in June 1862, slaves from the nearby cotton plantations fled to the city, certain that their masters' enemies would sponsor freedom. At first, they met bitter disappointment. The Memphis police, in league with a cabal of slave catchers, seized incoming fugitives, confined them in the city's "negro yards," and began returning them to their owners. But the army's growing need for laborers soon called a halt to this practice. When General Alvin P. Hovey, the military commander in Memphis, discovered the connivance, he released the runaways and set the able-bodied men to work constructing fortifications around the city. With military protection thus assured and employment provided, Memphis became a refuge for escaped slaves from west Tennessee and the adjoining portions of Arkansas and Mississippi.

General William T. Sherman, a division commander in Grant's army who assumed command at Memphis in late July, almost immediately found himself demonstrating the liberating potential of the Second Confiscation Act without ever having intended to do so. Obeying both Halleck's exclusion orders and the congressional prohibition against returning fugitive slaves to their masters, Sherman had previously resolved "to have nothing to do with the negro." He would

[7] *Official Records*, ser. 1, vol. 17, pt. 2, p. 97.

neither return him to his master nor "smuggle him away."[8] But by the summer of 1862, Sherman could no more evade the problem of slavery than could other Union commanders, though he still had no intention of exceeding the limits imposed by superior orders or national laws. Respectful of the distinction between civil and military authority, Sherman sought only to defeat the rebellion and restore the seceded states to the Union; he declined to address matters that he regarded as more properly within the purview of the President, Congress, or the courts. Indeed, Sherman observed the pronouncements of those bodies with such scrupulous care that some slave owners considered him a malleable pawn. They soon discovered their error.

General Sherman evinced no principled objection to the institution of slavery, and he rarely disguised his contempt for black people. But as a soldier, he subordinated personal feelings to military exigency. "By the simple laws of War we ought to take your effective slaves," he warned a former classmate turned Confederate; "I don't say to free them, but to use their labor & deprive you of it." While refusing to trouble himself about the ultimate status of the slaves—leaving the question to the civil authorities—Sherman maintained that slave-holders had repudiated their rights under the Constitution when they rebelled against the national government; consequently, they could not expect the Union army to protect their slave property. Eventually, Sherman would follow that reasoning to its logical conclusion, and declare secession tantamount to a declaration of emancipation. But for the time being, Sherman contented himself with using the slaves to convince the rebels to lay down their arms. "One of the modes of bringing People to reason," he wryly observed, was "to touch their Interests pecuniary or property." While commanding mobile troops in active military campaigns during the spring of 1862, he had had little occasion to act on these beliefs; in Memphis, where he became commander of an army of occupation, opportunities abounded.

Construction of fortifications required hundreds of laborers, and Sherman preferred not to tax his soldiers with that burden. Instead, he welcomed fugitive slaves to the city, putting the men to work and providing housing for their families, even while instructing his subordinates not to promote wholesale slave liberation. Upon his understanding of the new confiscation act, he ordered that slave men be employed with the armies in the field as well as on the fortifications at Memphis, reserving for future determination by federal courts the ultimate status of such laborers. In the fall of 1862, Sherman ordered that runaway slaves be treated as free, pending final ruling by the

[8] *Official Records*, ser. 1, vol. 17, pt. 2, pp. 15–16.

courts.[9] Sherman thus opened the floodgates of freedom, and the fugitive population grew sharply as a result.

The Second Confiscation Act proved to be a turning point for federal commanders throughout the Mississippi Valley. Only days after Sherman ordered full-scale employment of black men, Grant followed suit. Thereafter Union troops employed steadily larger numbers of fugitive slaves, although forces in the field generally turned away fugitives deemed unsuitable for military labor. Some of these outcasts fared poorly, falling prey to the elements or to hostile whites; others made their way to the outskirts of Union base camps, where they constructed makeshift shelters. Each advance by Union troops extended the lifeline of freedom. In November 1862, Grant appointed John Eaton, Jr., the chaplain of an Ohio regiment, to superintend the fugitive slaves (commonly termed "contrabands") and help relieve their suffering. With the approval of General Halleck, Grant instructed Eaton to employ the former slaves in gathering cotton from abandoned plantations.[10] Eaton and his subordinate superintendents established contraband camps at the major federal posts and supply depots in west Tennessee, northern Mississippi, and eastern Arkansas, and they became centers of refuge for the rest of the war.[11] The official sanction of such camps signaled that the Union army would welcome and protect all fugitive slaves, not just men capable of military labor.

While the armies under Halleck's jurisdiction attacked west Tennessee in February 1862, General Don Carlos Buell, commander of the Army of the Ohio, advanced to Bowling Green, in southern Kentucky, and then into middle Tennessee. Occupying Nashville at the end of the month, Buell echoed a refrain similar to Halleck's: "We are in arms, not for the purpose of invading the rights of our fellow-countrymen anywhere, but to maintain the integrity of the Union and protect the Constitution." Buell insisted that "[p]eaceable citizens are not to be molested in their persons or property."[12] Although Buell instructed his army not to admit slaves into its lines, some fugitives nonetheless found employment as officers' servants or company cooks. When challenged, few soldiers hesitated to bend the truth, often representing all servants, regardless of their actual origins, as Northern free blacks who had accompanied the regiments since organization. Masters were seldom deceived by such subterfuge; instead, they presented their claims

---

[9] The order, issued by Sherman's provost marshal on November 11, 1862, is quoted below in doc. 171.

[10] Ulysses S. Grant, *The Papers of Ulysses S. Grant*, ed. John Y. Simon et al., 11 vols. to date (Carbondale, Ill., 1967–), vol. 6, pp. 315–17n.; Eaton, *Grant, Lincoln and the Freedmen*, chaps. 1–2. See also *Freedom*, ser. 1, vol. 2.

[11] For a full discussion of the contraband camps, see *Freedom*, ser. 1, vol. 2.

[12] *Official Records*, ser. 1, vol. 7, pp. 669–70.

directly to General Buell. Standing by his promises to protect slave property, Buell ordered his division commanders to assist masters in apprehending slaves and to expel all unauthorized blacks. Most of them complied, but resentment mounted, fueled by experiences in the field and by the new signals emanating from Washington. One disgruntled observer protested that Buell "cares more for guarding a rebel cabbage patch, or reenslaving a liberated negro, than he does for gaining a triumph over the enemy." He denounced Buell as "so intensely pro-slavery that . . . he would sacrifice every officer in his District, for the sake of returning to bondage a single slave."

General Ormsby M. Mitchel, a midwestern free-soiler who commanded a division in the Army of the Ohio, eventually became the officer most prominent in opposing Buell's proslavery policy. At first Mitchel himself conformed scrupulously to Buell's orders regarding fugitive slaves. But Mitchel's subordinates did not always endorse such obedience. In March 1862, the commander of an Ohio regiment offered his resignation in protest against Mitchel's order – issued at the express direction of Buell – to expel fugitive slaves from the camps of the division. Terming the order "repugnant to my feelings as a man," the officer insisted that if forced to obey it, he must leave the service. Although only a few other officers and enlisted men took such a principled stand, several faulted Mitchel for "inconsistency in regard to the eternal negro question." Their resentment of Buell's solicitude for the rights of slave-holders, and of Mitchel's subservience to Buell, soon flared openly.

Military events impelled Mitchel to distance himself from Buell's policy. In late March and early April 1862, as the bulk of Buell's army moved southwest from Nashville to join the other western armies at Pittsburg Landing, Mitchel's division marched south toward Huntsville, Alabama, in the heart of the Tennessee Valley plantation district. Deep in enemy territory, attempting to hold several hundred miles of railroad and river, Mitchel depended upon slaves for information about rebel troop concentrations and movements. He declared the blacks "our only friends" and noted that "in two instances I owe my own safety to their faithfulness." In gratitude, Mitchel promised military protection to his slave allies, and Secretary of War Edwin M. Stanton endorsed the pledge. Mitchel's new policy also won the approbation of a Northern public grown impatient with commanders who coddled slave masters.

Mitchel's actions on this and other military matters offended Buell, who felt nothing but relief when Mitchel sought transfer to a more active command. In early July 1862, Mitchel was ordered to Washington to await a new assignment.[13] Buell quickly approved the appoint-

---

[13] On Mitchel's transfer, see *Official Records*, ser. 1, vol. 10, pt. 2, p. 222, and vol. 16, pt. 2, p. 92.

ment of General Lovell H. Rousseau, a Kentuckian known for his sympathy toward slaveholders, to fill Mitchel's place. Rousseau did not disappoint his commander. Ignoring Mitchel's assurance of protection, Rousseau drove blacks from his lines, abandoning them to their masters. Mitchel, in Washington, learned of the betrayal and expressed his outrage to the War Department. Upon investigation by the department, Rousseau justified his abrogation of Mitchel's policy on the ground that it implied a grant of freedom for which army officers lacked authority. There the matter stood: Mitchel and the northern Alabama slaves vanquished; Rousseau and Buell vindicated.

Even though Rousseau and Buell refused to confer freedom, events forced them to modify their practice of remanding slaves to their masters. The Second Confiscation Act went beyond the article of war's prohibition against using federal forces to return fugitive slaves to their owners; it barred military authorities from judging upon the validity of a master's claim "under any pretence whatever" and prohibited the surrender of any escaped slave to any claimant.[14] Many commanders in Buell's army welcomed the new law, and proceeded to employ those fugitives capable of military labor while expelling all others. Purely pragmatic, this approach involved no complicated reasoning about the lofty questions of the day, including the ultimate status of the slaves or how best to nurture loyal sentiment in the seceded states. President Lincoln's executive order of July 1862, which authorized the seizure of private property for military purposes and encouraged full-scale employment of slaves as military laborers, gave this stance still wider currency.[15] The policies enunciated by Congress and the President dissolved most of the lingering opposition in the army to accepting fugitive slaves, particularly able-bodied men.

Despite repeated disclaimers by army commanders about judging upon the ultimate status of fugitive slaves, the admission of slaves into federal lines went far to secure their liberty. It interposed another authority between master and slave, shattering the monolithic power of the master and granting unprecedented options to the slave. Moreover, mobile armies often carried fugitive slaves far from their homes, and distance alone hampered the slaveholders' efforts to reclaim old prerogatives. Nonetheless, the fragility of the freedom enjoyed by military laborers and other fugitive slaves became evident as a result of military events in the late summer and fall of 1862. Confederate invasion of Kentucky forced Buell's army to retreat from northern Alabama and middle Tennessee, so that a federal garrison remained only at Nash-

---

[14] The relevant portion of the Second Confiscation Act is Section 10. (U.S., *Statutes at Large, Treaties, and Proclamations*, vol. 12 [Boston, 1863], p. 591.)

[15] War Department General Order 109, issued on August 16, 1862, promulgated the President's order to the armies in the field. (*Official Records*, ser. 3, vol. 2, p. 397.)

ville. Hundreds of slaves who had taken refuge with Northern regiments found themselves abruptly abandoned to the mercy of their masters. Fearing the worst, many of them accompanied the retreating Union army into Kentucky as personal servants, military laborers, or desperate stragglers. After the rebel advance had been repulsed, state and county authorities in Kentucky jailed hundreds of these blacks as runaway slaves and sold them to Kentucky masters when their Tennessee and Alabama owners failed to claim them—confiscation acts and the Emancipation Proclamation notwithstanding.[16] Both the slaves who remained behind and those who followed the army into Kentucky could testify to the insecurity of wartime freedom in the Mississippi Valley.

Whereas Buell hoped to win the support of Confederate slaveholders by limiting military interference with slavery, General Samuel R. Curtis, operating in Arkansas as commander of the Army of the Southwest, favored the slaves over their masters. During the spring of 1862, after victory at Pea Ridge in northwest Arkansas, Curtis advanced toward Little Rock, the state capital. The likelihood of defeat by a superior Confederate force persuaded him not to confront the enemy directly; instead, he diverted his troops toward the Mississippi River, capturing Helena in July.

All along the way, Curtis encountered military obstacles constructed by slave laborers impressed from plantations near the Arkansas and White rivers. Angered by the Confederates' use of slaves to impede his movement, he vowed to make Arkansas slaveholders suffer for their "attempt to break up the Government and Laws of our Country." Accordingly, Curtis issued certificates on the basis of the First Confiscation Act declaring fugitive slaves who had been employed in support of the rebellion "forever emancipated," and he authorized their removal from Arkansas to the North. As word of Curtis's "free papers" spread, those slaves previously mobilized to halt his progress joined other slaves in seeking freedom certificates, producing what Curtis termed a "general stampede" to Helena.[17] Curtis's policy represented a significant departure from that of commanders operating east of the Mississippi River. Whereas the subordinates of Halleck and Buell turned away slaves unsuitable for military labor, Curtis welcomed them and provided military protection. By the summer of 1863, several thousand Arkansas slaves had taken refuge in Helena, and of that number more than a thousand had emigrated to the Northern states via St.

---

[16] On the reenslavement in Kentucky of former slaves from Alabama, Tennessee, and other Confederate states, see below, docs. 209–11, 213A–B, 215, 216n., 217B, 218, 223A–B.

[17] *Official Records*, ser. 1, vol. 13, p. 525.

Louis.[18] The manifest disloyalty of Arkansas slave owners enabled Curtis's army to become an army of liberation, virtually destroying slavery along the Mississippi and sapping its strength in the interior of the state as well.

Freedom seldom advanced steadily or uniformly in the Mississippi Valley. The tide of federal military success carried freedom forward; military failure saw freedom in retreat and slavery given new life. Grant's setback at Holly Springs, Mississippi, late in December 1862 threatened the numerous advances made earlier in the year.[19] Leaving behind only small outposts of soldiers in northern Mississippi, Grant abandoned his initial plan to assault Vicksburg by land and regrouped his forces in west Tennessee for an attack down the Mississippi River. In a pattern reminiscent of that produced by the Confederate invasion of Kentucky, slavery reasserted itself with the departure of the federal army. As a result, the promise embodied in Lincoln's preliminary emancipation proclamation of September 1862 was seriously compromised. If the confiscation acts and Curtis's free papers were reliable guides, the President's new commitment to freedom counted for little unless the Union armies enjoyed greater military success in 1863 than they had the previous year.

Although the full effect of Lincoln's new emancipation policy remained to be seen, the Confederates felt its repercussions immediately. Word of the final Emancipation Proclamation traveled fast. Early in January 1863, Confederate soldiers apprehended slaves who had been at Corinth, Mississippi, on New Year's Day. The blacks told terrifying tales of Union soldiers assembling slaves, informing them of freedom, arming them, and dispatching them as *"missionaries"* to recruit others of their color. Such reports caused widespread consternation, intensified by Grant's waterborne assault on Vicksburg. With an army of blue-clad abolitionists advancing into the plantation heartland of the Mississippi Valley, rebel partisans moved thousands of slaves away from the river, often under orders from Confederate authorities.[20]

---

[18] On the transfer of Arkansas slaves to the North, see *Freedom*, ser. 1, vol. 2.

[19] Among the booty captured by Confederate General Earl Van Dorn at Holly Springs were some 300 fugitive slaves. (Robinson, *Bitter Fruits of Bondage*.)

[20] On the Confederate removal of slaves from plantations near the river, see Brig. Genl. Jas. S. Wadsworth to the Adjutant General U.S. Army, 16 Dec. 1863, enclosed in S. P. Chase to Wm. P. Mellen, Esq., 17 Dec. 1863, Letters Received from the Secretary of the Treasury, Records of the General Agent, RG 366 [Q-142]. In some cases, the slaves' determination to enjoy the benefits of the proclamation, and their owners' attempts to remove them from the federals, began before the new year. In late November 1862, for example, the commander of a Union gunship operating between Memphis and Helena reported that all the fugitive slaves he had taken aboard "tell me that they are to be free on the 1st of January, but that their owners are getting ready to move them back from the river as soon as possible."

These hastily conceived and haphazardly executed migrations decreased the likelihood of escape for some slaves only to increase it for others. Estates abandoned by slaveholders provided sanctuary for runaway slaves who then set a subversive example for those remaining in bondage. In the vicinity of these plantations, it became nearly impossible for slavery to continue as before. As their authority disintegrated, planters demanded that Confederate officials eliminate these hotbeds of sedition. But Confederate commanders, more preoccupied with columns of disciplined Yankees than with pockets of undisciplined slaves, could pay scant attention to such supplications. Slave patrols, guerrillas, and rebel stragglers gladly took up the task, rendering precarious all efforts by runaway slaves to support themselves. Nonetheless, some colonies survived and thus offered an independent existence to a good many blacks.

Freedom within Union lines also became more secure after the Emancipation Proclamation. Federal troops welcomed all runaway and castaway slaves and even initiated slave-liberating raids, systematically employing the able-bodied men and entrusting the others to the care of Chaplain Eaton and subordinate superintendents of contrabands. With each advance of the Union army, the superintendents established contraband camps and placed fugitive slaves at work on abandoned plantations.

As Grant positioned the noose around Vicksburg during the spring of 1863, the Secretary of War dispatched General Lorenzo Thomas, adjutant general of the army, to the Mississippi Valley and charged him with the task of mobilizing Southern blacks on behalf of the Union. Although his chief responsibility was to launch the enlistment of black soldiers in the valley, Thomas also pursued the larger strategic mission of lining the Mississippi River with a loyal population. To that end, he expanded and consolidated the system of contraband camps and plantation employment initiated by Grant and Eaton in Tennessee, northern Mississippi, and eastern Arkansas, and by Generals Benjamin F. Butler and Nathaniel P. Banks in southern Louisiana. The foundation of Thomas's system (which was extended to include the entire Mississippi Valley after the fall of Vicksburg) was the leasing of abandoned plantations to Northern entrepreneurs. The lessees hired black workers from the contraband camps, which served as labor recruiting stations for the able-bodied and as sanctuaries for those unfit for plantation work. Union soldiers (increasing numbers of whom were black) guarded both the leased plantations and the contraband camps. Promotion of freedom along the river lured slaves

Planters along the Mississippi, he noted, realized "that the slaves had heard of the President's proclamation, and that in spite of all the owners could do they would get to the river." (*Navy Official Records*, ser. 1, vol. 23, pp. 508–10.)

from the interior, sapping both manpower and morale in Confederate territory. Thomas's policy thus affirmed the federal government's commitment to freedom and the incorporation of Southern blacks into the Union war effort.[21]

In all the federal military actions in the Mississippi Valley, army commanders subordinated emancipating slaves to defeating rebels. Still, the pursuit of victory undermined slavery in countless, often unintended ways. As never before, Confederates in the interior feared the active proselytizing of freedom's missionaries, knowing that the slave men they lost to the Yankees might soon face them on the field of battle.[22] But efforts to remove slaves from the danger zone – which wild imagination widened far beyond the actual range of Union raids – often backfired. One Mississippi slaveholder predicted that "every negro on this place will go [to] the Yankees before they would go to the hills." He and other masters found consolation in a conviction that their slaves were unlikely to flee to the enemy if not threatened with removal to the upcountry, having "made up their minds to stay at home and wait the issue of events."[23] Yet the exercise of such discretion by their slaves indicated unmistakably the instability of the old order.

On the basis of their experience in Tennessee, eastern Arkansas, northern Mississippi, and northern Alabama in 1862, federal officials developed policies respecting fugitive slaves, which, after the summer of 1863, embraced the entire Mississippi Valley. For the most part, these policies reflected the problems presented by plantation areas from which most masters had fled and through which contending armies had tramped. In areas where slaveholders remained in residence or the war arrived late, the collapse of slavery followed a different course. East Tennessee and middle Tennessee presented two alternative routes.

In east Tennessee, where the rugged terrain favored small-scale farming rather than plantation agriculture, slavery had never achieved the importance it enjoyed in the rest of the state. The few large slaveholders relied upon the Confederate army, which controlled the region until the end of 1863, to contain potential slave unrest. Repeated promises by President Lincoln to come to the aid of east Tennessee unionists finally bore fruit after Union victory at Vicksburg crippled the Confederate army in the west. In September 1863, a Union

[21] Chaplain John Eaton, Jr., to H. B. Spelman, Esqr., 23 May 1863, vol. 74, pp. 55–58, Letters Sent by John Eaton, ser. 2027, Gen. Supt. of Freedmen, MS Asst. Comr. Pre-Bureau Records, RG 105 [A-4005]. For a full discussion of federal relief and employment of former slaves in the Mississippi Valley during the war, see *Freedom*, ser. 1, vol. 2. On Thomas's role in recruiting black soldiers in the valley, see *Freedom*, ser. 2: chap. 3.

[22] See below, docs. 309–12.

[23] See below, doc. 311.

expedition under General Ambrose E. Burnside advanced from central Kentucky to capture Knoxville. At the same time, General William S. Rosecrans occupied Chattanooga, having forced the Confederates to evacuate. But the rebel troops promptly surrounded and besieged the federal forces at Chattanooga, until General Grant and federal reinforcements rescued their beleaguered comrades. The hard-fought Union victory at Chattanooga in late November forced the Confederates to abandon their simultaneous effort to recapture Knoxville, drove most of the rebel troops from the state, and brought Confederate domination of east Tennessee to an end.

Once Knoxville and Chattanooga were securely in Union hands, the slaves of rebel masters in east Tennessee began fleeing to the two cities to seek freedom and to escape the dangerous guerrilla warfare of the hills and hollows. Slaves of unionist masters did not fare as well. During the two and a half years they controlled east Tennessee, Confederate authorities had suppressed unionist sentiment with a ruthlessness that far exceeded the requirements of securing the region's rich bounty of foodstuffs. Nevertheless, slaves who escaped from oppressed unionists could expect no sympathy from the secessionists. Upon the arrival of federal troops, unionist masters jealously guarded their slaves and expected the federal government to do the same, if only to reward their wartime loyalty. Some slaves owned by east Tennessee unionists managed to escape to Knoxville or Chattanooga, but most saw little change in their status until the closing months of the war.

In middle Tennessee, the collapse of slavery followed yet another path. Unlike west Tennessee, where cotton monoculture fostered strong political ties with the staple-producing states of the Confederacy, middle Tennessee—a mixed-crop region of both plantations and farms—spawned some unionist sentiment that survived the secession crisis. When Union troops moved into the region in 1862, large numbers of slave owners in the Tennessee and Cumberland river valleys remained at home, and some of them welcomed the federal soldiers. But such unionism was hardly unanimous, and Confederate sympathy rivaled the old loyalty throughout the Nashville basin.

The divided loyalties of middle Tennessee masters shaped the demise of slavery in the region. During periods when federal troops occupied the countryside in force, lukewarm rebels kept a low profile or bent with the wind. But committed Confederate partisans fled rather than endure Yankee domination. Before departing, some fugitive masters turned their farms over to their slaves, agreeing to let them claim the products of their labor if they tended the fields and maintained the premises. On these estates, blacks entered a world between slavery and freedom. At first, they subsisted on what remained in storehouses and fields, but before long they planted food crops on the abandoned land they now considered their own, withstanding harassment by neighboring masters, rebel guerrillas, and Union scouting parties.[24] Although their numbers were small, these independent black farmers had a devastating effect on slavery.

Loyal planters in middle Tennessee, hoping that the federal government would sustain the old order, cooperated with the Northern military authorities. But, as in other areas occupied by federal troops, military necessity progressively eroded the Union's commitment to protect slavery, even on behalf of loyal masters. Typically, the army's need for military laborers provided the solvent. Federal commanders impressed slaves to construct fortifications whenever Confederate forces threatened to attack. And as Tennessee became the supply base for campaigns to the south, the number of black military laborers – volunteer and impressed – increased exponentially. Some of them remained in service to the end of the war. Military labor thus subverted slavery in Tennessee, just as it did elsewhere in the Confederacy.[25]

Struggling to reverse the deterioration of slavery, Tennessee masters unwittingly contributed to its further demise. In the face of endemic slave flight, especially in areas close to federal lines, slaveholders offered incentives to keep their slaves at work. Suspending unilateral control over their human property, many found themselves negotiating with their slaves. As one observer explained in early 1864, beleaguered slaveholders had to offer wages in order to secure "the services of there Slaves – or in other words to conciliate & prevent them from running away." Masters who did not adopt new ways often discovered their slave cabins deserted. At times, the arrangements proved so favorable that blacks resented subsequent interference by officious Yankees. But for most masters and slaves, the wartime settlements merely bought time. Both parties entered into them tentatively, and readily violated them when the changing course of the war altered the balance of power. Slave owners might retreat to the interior or slaves might flee to the federals, nullifying months of painstaking negotiation. Regardless of their fragility, such agreements demonstrated how the war had recast relations between masters and slaves, greatly enhancing the possibilities for freedom within the frayed legal framework of slavery.[26]

[24] See, for example, the description of one former master's postwar effort to deprive his former slaves of crops they had grown on the plantation he abandoned in June 1863. (William French to Brig. Genl. Clinton B. Fisk, 8 Aug. 1865, F-55 1865, Registered Letters Received, ser. 3379, TN Asst. Comr., RG 105 [A-6121].)

[25] For a discussion of the military employment of impressed slaves and fugitive slaves, see *Freedom*, ser. 1, vol. 2.

[26] Statement of terms of employment offered by Rutherford County, Tennessee, planters, [Jan. 1864], enclosed in W. Bosson to Maj. Genl. Thomas, 27 Jan. 1864, B-2 1864, Letters Received by Adjutant General L. Thomas, ser. 363, Colored Troops Division, RG 94 [V-81]. For a discussion of the tentative free-labor arrangements negotiated by masters and slaves during the war, see *Freedom*, ser. 1, vol. 2.

The enlistment of black men in the Union army destroyed the remnants of slavery in Tennessee, just as it did in other areas exempted from the Emancipation Proclamation. But recruitment affected each region of the state somewhat differently. In west Tennessee, black recruitment flourished under Adjutant General Thomas from the spring of 1863. Recruiters scoured contraband camps searching for eligible men, whom Thomas organized into regiments and deployed at the forts along the Mississippi River and at the camps and leased plantations where their families lived and worked. In east Tennessee, recruitment could not begin until after federal occupation in late 1863, when fugitive slave men were hastily organized into artillery units for the defense of Knoxville. In middle Tennessee, where Military Governor Andrew Johnson had been granted authority to enlist black troops, recruitment languished until the fall of 1863, when Secretary of War Edwin M. Stanton dispatched abolitionist George L. Stearns to Nashville. To mollify loyal masters and promote recruitment, the War Department promised up to $300 compensation for each slave enlisted. Tennessee slaves gained a fresh reminder of the significance of the state's exemption from the Emancipation Proclamation, as masters tightened restrictions on men of military age, each of whom now represented much-needed money. Masters who had irretrievably lost control over their slaves sought to recoup their investment through enlistment. They begged federal recruiters to take their wayward property, by force if necessary. Some masters rewarded recruiters for the service. But enlistment breathed new life into the master's power only momentarily, because in return for the promise of compensation, they relinquished all claims to enlisted slaves.[27]

The contradictory pressures unleashed by black recruitment eroded slavery in Tennessee in other ways as well. Intractable masters forced the issue. When slave men stole away to recruiting centers to claim freedom and a blue uniform, masters retaliated by punishing the soldiers' families, often by driving them off to fend for themselves. Federal authorities soon recognized the need to protect black men who wished to enlist, as well as the families whom they left behind and volunteers who were rejected as unfit for service. Although slow to move upon this understanding, the government, when it did act, left the slaveholders' strategy in ruins. Military service superseded the state's exemption from the Emancipation Proclamation; out of the struggle over recruitment, freedom emerged on firmer ground by the end of 1863 than it had been at the beginning of the year.

Military enlistment helped clear the path to freedom throughout the Mississippi Valley. More than 70,000 black men from the seceded states of the valley emancipated themselves by enlisting, and, once in

[27] *Freedom*, ser. 2: pp. 122–26 and docs. 63–68.

uniform, they helped liberate other slaves.[28] Along the Mississippi River, black soldiers often served as the advance pickets of the federal army, warding off rebel guerrillas and providing refuge to slaves who escaped from the interior. In middle Tennessee, black soldiers performed similar services. When General William T. Sherman began his bitterly contested advance from Chattanooga to Atlanta early in 1864, his army required thousands of laborers to keep supplies moving to the front and thousands of soldiers to prevent rebel depredations behind his lines. Sherman deemed black men suitable for both purposes, though he pointedly excluded them from his own fighting ranks. Black teamsters and pioneers moved along the roads of central and east Tennessee and northern Georgia, while black soldiers guarded railroads and telegraph lines. Runaway slaves thus never had far to go before encountering friends who could feed them, boost their spirits, and direct them to more secure Union camps.

Once established, this process gained a momentum of its own. Reaching Union base camps, black men enlisted in the army or worked as military laborers. In either capacity, they returned to the roads and bivouacs, where they ushered other fugitives to freedom. White soldiers took the cue from their black comrades. Foraging parties returned from the countryside laden with slaves as well as supplies. Soldiers in the forefront of the advance passed toward the rear the slaves they encountered. But even when turned away, fugitive slaves "skulked back with the train," as one Union commander observed.

Despite slavery's weakness, freedom required the presence of federal forces to be secure.[29] Tennessee slaves who belonged to loyal masters, and therefore lacked protection from the confiscation acts or the Emancipation Proclamation, claimed freedom at great risk. In conceding the practical loss of control over their slaves, some loyal masters drove them ruthlessly away or, on occasion, herded them south for sale in Mississippi, Alabama, or Georgia. Even when they made the compromises required to keep laborers in the fields, the masters retained full

---

[28] The number of black soldiers credited to the Mississippi Valley states were: Alabama, 4,969; Arkansas, 5,526; Louisiana, 24,052; Mississippi, 17,869; Tennessee, 20,133. (*Freedom*, ser. 2: p. 12.)

[29] In November 1863, Governor Andrew Johnson contended that the federal government need not trouble itself about emancipating Tennessee slaves, arguing that the question was "already settled." Nevertheless, recruiter George L. Stearns, who also described slavery's "disintegration," qualified this judgment by noting the unsettled state of the territory outside the federal lines. (Testimony of Gov. Andrew Johnson before the American Freedmen's Inquiry Commission, 23 Nov. 1863, and testimony of Maj. Geo. L. Stearns before the American Freedmen's Inquiry Commission, [23 Nov. 1863], both filed with O-328 1863, Letters Received, ser. 12, RG 94 [K-96, K-98]; George L. Stearns to Hon. James A. Garfield, 4 Mar. 1864, enclosed in George L. Stearns to Major General George H. Thomas, 6 Mar. 1864, S-883 1864, Letters Received, ser. 925, Dept. of the Cumberland, RG 393 Pt. 1 [C-20].)

legal title to their slaves and hoped for an eventual settlement involving compensation. Moreover, many masters refused to abandon old habits of proprietorship. Prominent unionists beat runaway slaves mercilessly, then escaped punishment by garnering testimonials of their good character from other loyalists. Some masters continued to impose barbaric punishments upon those who dared to leave their service. But slaves within striking distance of Union troops did not long tolerate such abuse, and masters who refused to recognize the new reality learned the lesson through the steady attrition of their work forces.

Still, the continued legal standing of slavery in Tennessee jeopardized the full realization of freedom in much the way it did in Kentucky and Missouri.[30] The problem first became apparent in 1862, following passage of the Second Confiscation Act. To obviate it, General Sherman, then in command at Memphis, ordered the civil authorities to regard the federal confiscation acts as superior to the state slave laws. In middle Tennessee, however, neither General Buell nor Governor Johnson issued a similar directive, and civil officers continued to enforce the state's slave code until September 1864, when Johnson ordered that thereafter all blacks be regarded before the law as free persons of color.[31]

With slavery effectively suspended throughout most of the state, Tennessee unionists pressed for legal abolition. The unionist coalition, which had lobbied for exemption from the Emancipation Proclamation in order to enlist support among slaveholders, had long since changed course. As slaves demanded freedom, antislavery unionists grew more vocal, and federal military authorities aided their cause. Loyal masters could not reverse the momentum of events. Some sensed the inevitability of emancipation and joined the assault on slavery. By late 1864, Tennessee unionists were campaigning strongly for abolition, to provide a sound legal basis for a free-labor economy and to defeat the rebellion. In December, Union victory at the battle of Nashville destroyed the Confederates' hope of recapturing the state and cleared the road for the organization of a unionist state government. When Tennessee unionists met shortly after the new year, they resolved themselves into a constitutional convention. Blacks in Nashville, who had played an active though unofficial role in the unionist movement from its inception, petitioned the convention to extend to black men the privileges of voting and of testifying in legal proceedings. They appealed in particular to the role of black soldiers in the recent defense of the city.[32] While ignoring that petition, the convention abolished slavery by constitutional amendment (which took effect on February

---

[30] See below, chaps. 7–8.
[31] Proclamation of Governor Andrew Johnson, 7 Sept. 1864, as printed in *Knoxville Whig and Rebel Ventilator*, 21 Sept. 1864.
[32] *Freedom*, ser. 2: doc. 362.

22, 1865, upon ratification by popular referendum) and called for elections that soon brought about the return of civil rule.[33] Die-hard rebels and unreconstructed unionists clung desperately to slavery, concealing news of emancipation as long as possible. But their days were numbered. By the spring of 1865, few Tennessee blacks were still living as slaves.

Federal victories in the Mississippi Valley also precipitated the legal destruction of slavery in Arkansas and Louisiana. After the fall of Vicksburg, with Confederate armies in disarray and secessionists in flight, federal troops moved into the interior of Arkansas, occupying the state capital and most of the area north of the Arkansas River. Unionists, previously represented by a rump government in exile, quickly seized the reins of power and politicked throughout the occupied portion of the state. Early in 1864, in accordance with President Lincoln's proclamation of amnesty and reconstruction (which outlined the process whereby seceded states might seek readmission to the Union), Arkansas unionists met in Little Rock to reorganize the government and rewrite the constitution, even though much of the state remained in Confederate hands. Understanding full well the federal commitment to abolition, they outlawed slavery, and in March a popular vote approved the new constitution.[34]

In Louisiana, Confederate reverses in the summer of 1863 reinvigorated the unionist movement that had been struggling for over a year to reestablish civil government and gain readmission to the Union. Early in 1864, following a series of bitter and divisive political campaigns that resulted in the election of a governor and a legislature, unionists agreed to call a constitutional convention. The unionist coalition consisted of planters in the countryside and a variety of urban professionals, proprietors, and artisans; its ranks included free people of color as well as native and foreign-born whites. Reflecting this diversity, the unionist movement remained hopelessly deadlocked on many key issues. But despite foot-dragging by loyal slaveholders, Louisiana unionists recognized the necessity of abolition. In the fall of 1864, loyal voters ratified an emancipationist constitution.[35]

---

[33] James Welch Patton, *Unionism and Reconstruction in Tennessee, 1860–1869* (Chapel Hill, N.C., 1934), chap. 2.
[34] Thomas S. Staples, *Reconstruction in Arkansas, 1862–1874* (New York, 1923), chaps. 1–2.
[35] Peyton McCrary, *Abraham Lincoln and Reconstruction: The Louisiana Experiment* (Princeton, N.J., 1978); Joe Gray Taylor, *Louisiana Reconstructed, 1863–1877* (Baton Rouge, La., 1974), chap. 2; Ripley, *Slaves and Freedmen in Civil War Louisiana*, chap. 9; LaWanda Cox, *Lincoln and Black Freedom: A Study in Presidential Leadership* (Columbia, S.C., 1981).

The new state constitutions, of course, had no standing in the portions of the Mississippi Valley that remained under Confederate control, but their significance radiated beyond rebel lines. For both masters and slaves in the shrinking Confederacy, these documents offered incontestable proof of slavery's declining power. Still, many Mississippi Valley slaves had to await the final Confederate surrender to partake of the freedom advanced repeatedly in federal pronouncements, but realized ultimately only through the force of federal arms.

81: Michigan Quaker to the Secretary of War

Battle Creek [*Mich.*] Decr 5th 61

Freind Camron   a Fugitive from Tenesee a few nights Since on his way to Canada Informed me that it is the Settled Intention of the Rebels to Ere Long Arm the Slaves throughout the Entier South put them in the front Ranks to Receive the fier & then Storm the Federal works in all points. he Sais its Talked of in all the Rebel Familys. Declaring that Every Slave Shall first be Butchered before the Rebels will give up   he Sais that Tens of Thousands of Slaves are in the greatest Alarm their masters telling them that our officers & Army will Sell them to Cuba & that 5 Slaves that was Sent over from Kentuckey by our Federal Troops Say that the ware Badly Treated by our officers altho the offered to work or Fight for the Government. but ware told to Clear out that the officers wanted no D----D Niggers about them &c &c & ware actually Driven over to their old Homes. he Sais too that there is not a Slave South but would Take up arms for our Troopes if the Could, but the Treatment the Receive has almost Sett them Crasy. the Expected Friends of us in Stead of Enemys   the are Comeing through here Constantly on their way to Canada. now what a picture is this. is our Relatives to be Butcherd as the Are & we to add fuel to the Flames of the Rebels to Continue the Destruction. oh Can it be that this Government is to Crush 4000000 of Human beings. to uphold the most Blood Thirsty Sett of Tyrants on Earth. your Document[1] is greatly approved of, and if the Administration Dont put a Stop to the Ill Treatment of the Slaves by our Army I greally fear that we will be the Loosers thereby — I think that matter Cannot be Seen to, to Soon for I am Satisfyed that the Rebels will Resort to any Attrocious acts to Carry their points — Very Truly Yours

ALS   H. Willis

THE DESTRUCTION OF SLAVERY

H. Willis to Freind Camron, 5 Dec. 1861, W-443 1861, Letters Received, RG 107 [L-7].

1 Secretary of War Simon Cameron's controversial annual report of December 1, 1861, which advocated employing slaves on behalf of the Union war effort – including arming them for military service – and freeing all those so employed. President Abraham Lincoln forced Cameron to delete the recommendation to arm and free slaves. (Edward McPherson, *The Political History of the United States of America, during the Great Rebellion*, 2nd ed. [Washington, 1865], p. 249.)

82: Order by the Commander of the District of West Tennessee

Fort Donelson [*Tenn.*], Feby. 26, 1862
General Orders No. 14. General Orders No. 3, of the series of 1861, Headquarters Department of the Missouri, are still in force and must be observed.

The number of citizens who are applying for permission to pass through the camps to look for fugitive slaves proves the necessity of the order, and its faithful observance. Such permits cannot be granted; therefore the great necessity of keeping out fugitives.

Such slaves as were within the lines at the time of the capture of Fort Donelson, and such as have been used by the enemy in building fortifications, or in any way hostile to the Government will not be released or permitted to return to their masters but will be employed in the Quartermaster's Department for the benefit of Government.

All officers and companies now keeping slaves so captured, will immediately report them to the District Quartermaster.

Regimental Commanders will be held accountable for all violation of this order within their respective commands. By order of Brig. General U. S. Grant

HD

General Orders No. 14, Headquarters District West Tennessee, 26 Feb. 1862, vol. G3/4 DT, pp. 48–49, General Orders & Circulars Issued, ser. 2733, Army & Dist. of West TN, RG 393 Pt. 2 No. 171 [C-8501].

83: Commander of an Ohio Regiment to the Commander of the 3rd Division of the Army of the Ohio

Camp Andrew Jackson [*near Nashville*], Tenn., March 3, 1862. *General:—* In compliance with your suggestion of yesterday in relation to slaves in Camp of my Regiment, I have the honor to report:—

There are three who came to us at Bowling Green representing that they were the servants of Officers of the Rebel Army, who had been left behind in the fright from that place. Some of them, perhaps all, hid in the woods or by the wayside in the flight and then came to us.

My Officers reported to me the fact, asking what should be done with them. I told them to set them to work if they desired to remain and they wished to employ them, and they did so. They are now in the employ of Officers of the Regiment. I supposed that to be the correct course, and if any wrong has been done in the matter I have been accessory to the wrong. Since we came in Kentucky and also as I am informed by my Officers since the Regiment came into Tennessee, slaves have come to us desiring to remain, but they have been invariably driven from our camp, and there are none now with us except the three above mentioned, and one other which I will state below.

I am informed that on the march here from Bowling Green quite a number came to our lines, but were, by order of Lieut. Col. Given, Commanding, driven away. One boy, however, a lad of perhaps fifteen, it appears, has smuggled himself along by what means I am unable to say. He says his master's name is Stough (or something like that), but I cannot find where he lives except it is beyond Goodlettsville.

I discovered him in Camp yesterday. I do not think any of my Officers or men have been privy to his secession. Were we near his home I should of course turn him out of Camp. Shall I do so here, or shall some other course be adopted?

Permit me here to say that my course on this question since I came into Kentucky, and especially while temporarily in charge under order of Col. Turchin at Bowling Green was to have nothing to do with Slavery. I did, however, give facilities for the capture in every instance of slaves when applied to by proper authority not by using U.S. Soldiers in that capacity, but by upholding the laws of Kentucky, and I know that my course was approved by the citizens of Bowling Green. I did not, however, for a moment suppose that the slaves of masters in arms against us, and those slaves, too, employed in the army were either to be delivered up to their masters or to be driven from our lines when they can be of service to us. If I am mistaken in the policy of the Government I have of course as a soldier only to obey order without question as to their propriety.

Lt. Col. Given, who has been in command of the Regiment since we came to Bowling Green, and in fact for three weeks previous while I was holding Court Martial is making a report which will be submitted to you as to the other matters you spoke of to me. I trust when that report is made you will have no serious cause to be ashamed of us. Very Respectfully, Your Ob^t Servt

HLS   T. R. Stanley

Col. T. R. Stanley to Brig. Gen. Mitchell, 3 Mar. 1862, S-259 1862, Supplemental Letters Received, ser. 882, Dept. of the OH, RG 393 Pt. 1 [C-2046]. Endorsements. Stanley was colonel of the 18th Ohio Infantry. Three days later, General Don Carlos Buell, commander of the Department and Army of the Ohio, acknowledged to the chairman of the Kentucky committee supervising recruitment of federal troops that "slaves sometimes make their way improperly into our lines, and in some instances they may be enticed there," but he insisted that their numbers had been exaggerated. "Several applications have been made to me by persons whose servants have been found in our camps," Buell affirmed, "and in every instance that I know of the master has recovered his servant and taken him away." (*Official Records*, ser. 1, vol. 10, pt. 2, p. 15.) For another episode involving the efforts of a Kentucky slaveholder to reclaim slaves who had accompanied Buell's army on its march from Kentucky to Tennessee, see below, doc. 200.

84: Commander of Fort Donelson, Tennessee, to the Commander of the District of West Tennessee, Enclosing a Letter from a Tennessee Unionist to the Commander of the District of West Tennessee

Fort Donaldson [*Tenn.*] March 30th 1862
(*Confidential*)

General   Inclosed you will find a note to you from Hon^l J. M. Quarles, a member of the 36th Congress & one of my personal friends & highly esteemed by Mg^r Genl McClernand & Brig^r Genl Logan — Every reliance can be placed on his statement of facts — In good truth Genl I have investigated this case carefully, at Clarksville & find that *all* said by Mr. Quarles is *true*. I found a very bad state of feeling at Clarkville — The citizens attributed it all to the administration of Col Wright — (I hope Genl this is not, unmilitary — I wish merely to state facts)   They have lost a large number of slaves — & in consequence of the exasperated state of feeling in & about Clarksville, I am assured that not less than 200 men had gone off in a fit of desperation & joined the Confederate army, who never would have gone, if protection to their property could have been afforded. The two negroes refered to by Mr. Quarles are the property of Mr^s Thomas & her children & I am Satisfied that the return of those two negroes would do more good, & go further to cultivate a union sentiment in & about Clarksville than any other act— a liberal policy, such as you inaugerated here, & instructed me to pursue will be of infinitely more value than a victory with arms— all is quiet here, all Satisfied, commerce & buisness begining to move & I have no doubt but in a short time, a large majority will wish to vote for the "old union" again.

I send you two other memorandums, which are very hard cases indeed— I feel deeply the importence of the step I have ventured to lay before you & *know* the benefits that will result from it.

I have two Companies of my Reg^t stationed at Clarkville by order of Maj. Genl Halleck. upon the subject of negroes, I gave them your instructions to me— The citizens are Satisfied with them & Seem to desire a friendly intercourse with them

With a hope, Genl that I have said nothing out of place I subscribe myself your sincere friend & admirer

ALS
P B Fouke

[*Enclosure*]   Clarksville. Tennessee.   March 27th 1862.
Dear Sir   Mrs R W Thomas had two negro-boys—carried off by Col. wright when his command left this place. by Name James & Stephen— James is about 22 years of age, and very Black and weighs about 150 pounds. Stephen is Liter Complected and inclind to be fat—and is about, 18 years of age. — These negroes are all the property she has. and they were given to her and her Children (eight in number) by her brother in Law—and they are her sole support. Her husband is a cripple—and totally unable to perform physical Labour—but the Editor of a paper at this place and a man of great popularity—and I know the fact to be true, that neither of them were ever employed on any government work of any sort. My information is that they were taken by Col wright as body servants. Mrs Thomas is my Mother in Law and I know every fact that I state— all I ask is that Genl. Grant will send them back to Col Fouke and if these facts are not clearly and conclusively proven then I do not ask their release   It is a great Injustice and should at once be rectified and I trust it will be done—for they have never been used in any way so as to forfeit them to the United States Government— They are stemmers of Tobacco and have always been employed at it—and I appeal to the Gen Commanding to see that the Col here does not violate justice right fair dealing and the

general orders of the Commander— I refer the Gen to Col Fouke Col Logan and Major Genl. McClernand to know who I am and whether my statements are to be relied on Respectfully

ALS   Jas M Quarles.

P. B. Fouke to General, 30 Mar. 1862, enclosing Jas. M. Quarles to Major Genl. Grant, 27 Mar. 1862, Registered & Unregistered Letters & Reports Received, ser. 2732, Army & Dist. of West TN, RG 393 Pt. 2 No. 171 [C-8003]. The two other memoranda mentioned by Fouke are not enclosed.

85: Commander of an Ohio Regiment to the Commander of the Department of the Ohio

[southern Tenn.? April? 1862]

Sir I respectfully tender my resignation as Colonel of the Second Reg't O.V. U.S.A. for the following reasons:

General Order
No 79
    In accordance with orders from Head Quarters of the Department, all fugitive slaves, or negroes suspected of being such, now in Camp of the Third Division, will be at once arrested and held at Brigade Head Quarters and at the Head Quarters of the different Detachments in the Brigade until 12 oclock *M* of to morrow March 12th
    If in that time the owners or the agents shall call for them, the negroes will be delivered up and if necessary the claimant protected from harm or molestation.
    If not called for, the negroes will be released and expeled from the encampment. In future no fugitive Slave will be allowed to enter or remain within the lines of the Division

By Order of
Brig Gen Mitchell.

    Under said Order, negroes were hunted down and (in my temporary absence) imprisoned in the Guard house of the 2^d O.V. U.S.A.
    April 4 1862 I received another Order, as follows—

    The attention of the Officers and Soldiers of the Third Division is recalled to paragraph *III* of General Order No 79.
    The Commanding Officer will be held responsible for the due execution of the Order and the expulsion from Camp lines, of any negro, who has not with him his free papers.

By Order of
Brig Gen Mitchell.

As a Soldier I am compeled to execute an order which is
repugnant to my feelings as a man. If I remain in the Army I have
no alternative but to execute these orders, or resign. I prefer the
latter. I therefore, respectfully tender my resignation as Colonel of
the 2nd Regiment O.V. U.S.A. Very Respectfully,

ALS
                                                      L. A. Harris.

L. A. Harris to Major Gen. Buell, [Apr.? 1862], O. M. Mitchel Papers,
Generals' Papers & Books, ser. 159, RG 94 [V-128]. General Ormsby M.
Mitchel, commander of the Army of the Ohio, had issued
General Order 79 on March 11, 1862, in compliance with instructions of the
same date from General Don Carlos Buell, commander of the Department and
Army of the Ohio. (*Official Records*, ser. 1, vol. 10, pt. 2, p. 31.) According to
an endorsement, Harris's brigade commander forwarded the resignation letter
to Mitchel, who filed it without notation. Harris remained in military service
until December 1862, when he resigned for health reasons. (Col. L. A. Harris
to Major Gen. Rousseau, 11 Dec. 1862, service record of L. A. Harris, 2nd
OH Inf., Carded Records, Volunteer Organizations: Civil War, ser. 519, RG
94 [N-59].)

**86: Commander of the 3rd Division of the Army of the Ohio
to the Secretary of War, and the Latter's Reply**

Huntsville [*Ala.*] May 4 1862
I have this day written you fully embracing three topics of great
importance. The absolute necessity of protecting slaves who furnish
us valuable information—the fact that I am left with out the
command of my line of communications and the importance of
holding Alabama north of the Tennessee. I have promised
protection to the slaves who have given me valuable assistance and
information. My River front is 120 miles long and if the
Government disapprove what I have done I must receive heavy re
enforcements or abandon my position. With the assistance of the
Negroes in watching the River I feel my self sufficiently strong to
defy the enemy.

HWcSr   O. M. Mitchel

Washington 5 May 1862
General O M Mitchel, Your Telegram of the 3d and 4th have been
received   No General in the field has deserved better of his
Government than yourself and the department rejoices to award
credit to one who merits it so well. The Department is advised of

nothing that you have done but what it has approved   The assistance of slaves is an element of military strength which under proper regulations you are fully justified in employing for your security and the success of your operations. It has been freely employed by the enemy: and to abstain from its use when it can be employed with military advantage would be a failure to employ means to suppress the Rebellion and retrieve the authority of the Government. Protection to those who furnish information or other assistance is a high Duty

HWcSr   Edwin M Stanton

Brig. Gen. O. M. Mitchel to E. M. Stanton, 4 May 1862, and Edwin M. Stanton to General O. M. Mitchel, 5 May 1862, vol. 4*, pp. 43–44, 50, Letters Sent by Brig. Gen. O. M. Mitchel, ser. 839, Mobile Units in the Dept. & Armies of the OH, RG 393 Pt. 2 No. 15 [C-8008]. In a letter written the same day as his telegram to the Secretary of War, Mitchel explained at greater length his dependence upon Alabama slaves: "The negroes are our only friends, and in two instances I owe my own safety to their faithfulness. I shall very soon have watchful guards among the slaves on the plantations bordering the river from Bridgeport to Florence, and all who communicate to me valuable information I have promised the protection of my Government. Should my course in this particular be disapproved, it would be impossible for me to hold my position. I must abandon the line of railway, and Northern Alabama falls back into the hands of the enemy." (*Official Records*, ser. 1, vol. 10, pt. 2, p. 162.) Mitchel's telegram of May 3, to which Stanton referred, has not been found, although it may be the dispatch regarding military operations that the War Department received on May 4. (*Official Records*, ser. 1, vol. 10, pt. 2, pp. 161–62.)

87: Order by a Temporary Brigade Commander in the Army of the Mississippi

Camp Etheridge [*near Union City?*], Tenn., June 18th 1862. General Orders No 26

I. The impudence and impertinence of the open and avowed Rebels Traitors, Secessionists and Southern rights men of this section of the state of Tennessee in arrogantly demanding the right to search our camp for their fugitive slaves has become a nuisance and will no longer be tolerated. Officers will see that this class of men who visit our Camp for this purpose are excluded from our lines.

II. Should any such parties be found within the lines they will be arrested and sent to Head Qr[s]

III   Any officer or soldier of this command who shall arrest and deliver to his master a fugitive slave shall be summarily and severely punished according to the laws relative to such crimes.

IV   The strong Union sentiment in this section is most gratifying and all officers and soldiers in their intercourse with the loyal and those favorably disposed are requested to act in their usual kind and courteous manner and protect them to the fullest extent.

By order of Lt. Col Anthony 7th K V Commdg

HDc

General Orders No. 26, Hd. Qrs. Mitchell's Brigade, Advance Column, 1st Brigade, 1st Division, Central Army of the Miss., 18 June 1862, vol. 46 20AC, p. 145, General & Special Orders Issued, ser. 6533, 1st Brig., 1st Div., Army of the MS, RG 393 Pt. 2 No. 444 [C-8850]. This order by Lieutenant Colonel Daniel R. Anthony culminated several weeks of escalating tension between his regiment, the 7th Kansas Cavalry, and superior military authorities. Early in April 1862, soldiers of the regiment had harbored eight slaves whose secessionist master had sent them to work on Confederate fortifications. The master, accompanied by an officer on the staff of General Robert B. Mitchell, commander of the brigade in which the 7th served, made a futile effort to retrieve the slaves. On June 12, Anthony set out to allay the "doubt in the minds of some of the officers and soldiers of the regiment as to their duty in regard to returning Fugitive Slaves": he issued an order directly forbidding them to do so. Meanwhile, General Isaac F. Quinby, commander of the District of Mississippi, ordered Mitchell to enforce the longstanding policy of excluding slaves from army lines. On the eve of a two-day leave of absence, Mitchell ordered Anthony – who would succeed to command of the brigade by virtue of seniority – to read Quinby's exclusion order at dress parade while Mitchell was away. Anthony did so, but also read his own General Order 26. Mitchell reportedly "took no notice" of Anthony's order when he returned to the command of the brigade, permitting it to remain "on the books of the brigade as law." But Mitchell's superiors refused to countenance Anthony's blatant insubordination. They arrested Anthony and charged him with a variety of offenses, which included admitting blacks into his lines in violation of orders, sanctioning depredations by his men, representing "the purpose of the troops to be the freeing of Slaves and taking of all private property," and persuading "4 or more negroes to runaway and to take with them mules, horses and other stock." He was not, however, cited specifically for issuing General Order 26. Upon his arrest, Anthony publicized his predicament widely, and in mid-July, Kansas senator James H. Lane introduced a resolution in the U.S. Senate directing the President to forward information from the War Department regarding the charges against Anthony. Suddenly and without explanation – though presumably as a result of Lane's interest in the case – Anthony was released and ordered to return to his regiment. When he did so, he discovered that a subordinate officer had been promoted to colonel and placed in command of the regiment, and he resigned in protest.

(Charges and specifications preferred by Brig. Gen. Robt. B. Mitchell against Lt. Col. Daniel R. Anthony of the Seventh Regt. Kansas Volunteers, [June? 1862], and Lt. Col. D. R. Anthony to Lieut. F. W. Emery, 7 Aug. 1862, both in service record of Daniel R. Anthony, 7th KA Cav., Carded Records, Volunteer Organizations: Civil War, ser. 519, RG 94 [N-58]; papers forwarded by the President to the clerk of the Senate, 23 Feb. 1863, President 164 1862, Letters Received from the President & Executive Departments, RG 107 [L-176]; Special Order No. 197, Head Quarters 7th Kansas Vols., 12 June 1862, Regimental Books & Papers, 7th KA Cav., RG 94 [OO-11]; General Order No. 16, Headquarters, Dist. of the Miss., 18 June 1862, vol. 101/248A DKy, p. 43, General Orders, ser. 992, Dist. of the MS, RG 393 Pt. 2 No. 24 [C-8852]; *Official Records*, ser. 1, vol. 17, pt. 2, p. 54; Stephen Z. Starr, *Jennison's Jayhawkers: A Civil War Cavalry Regiment and Its Commander* [Baton Rouge, La., 1973], chap. 9.)

88: Order by the Commander of the 5th Division of the Army of the Tennessee

La Grange, Tenn, June 18th 1862.
General Orders, No. 43. The Comm[dg] General must call attention to the duties of Officers and men towards the slaves.

The well settled policy of the whole army is now to have nothing to do with the negro, Exclude them from camp is Gen[l] Halleck's reiterated order. We cannot have our trains encumbered by them, nor can we afford to feed them, and it is deceiving the poor fellows to allow him to start and have him forcibly driven away afterwards. For these and many good reasons the General now especially directs of the Colonels of Regiments, Captains of Companies, and Regimental Quarter Masters to give their personal attention to this matter, to remove all such now in camp, to prevent any more from following our camp or columns of march.

The Laws of Congress command that we do not surrender back to the Master a Fugitive slave, That is not a soldier's business, nor is it his business to smuggle him away. Let the Master and slave look to the Civil authorities and not to us, Also the laws of war make the property of the enemy liable to confiscation if used for warlike purposes, such as horses, wagons hauling stores, slaving making forts &c &c In such cases the Commanding Officer would rightfully appropriate his labor through the Quarter Master, and let the title to freedom be tried as soon as a proper Civil Tribunal can be reached,

If Wagon Masters or Teamsters carry away in their wagons runaway negroes, it is made the duty, first of the Regimental Quartermaster, next of the Brigade Quarter Master, and last of any

Commissioned Officer; who will cause them summarily to be turned
out and the facts reported to Head Quarters, that the actual offender
may be punished by fine and imprisonment as he deserves   By
order of Maj. Gen. W. T. Sherman

HD

General Orders, No. 43, Head Quarters, 5th Division, 18 June 1862,
Orders, W. T. Sherman Papers, Generals' Papers & Books, ser. 159, RG 94
[V-313]. The following month, the adjutant of the 5th Division gave supplementary instructions to the commander of U.S. forces at Lafayette, Tennessee,
authorizing him to employ blacks but urging caution: "If runaway negroes are
encouraged we will be overwhelmed with them. They would soon eat us out,
encumber our march & give ground for the assertion that we come south to
steal negroes. I think policy and our own convenience dictate that we do not
encourage Runaways. If we need Negro labor better call on the Planters &
return them when done." (Asst. Adjt. Gen'l. J. H. Hammond to Col. Worthington, 11 July 1862, Letters Sent, W. T. Sherman Papers, Generals'
Papers & Books, ser. 159, RG 94 [V-301].)

89: Unidentified Northerner to the Editor of the Cincinnati *Gazette*

Huntsville, Alabama, July 6th, '62

(Private)

Dear Sir,   To-day General McCook's Division started on the march
toward Eastern Tennessee, the advance division of General Buell's
army. Singularly enough, they do not go by rail, as was expected,
from here to Stevenson, but have commenced to make the
wearisome journey on foot. As neither they nor their General are
particularly noted for celerity of movement, it is calculated that they
will be about ten days in reaching Bridgeport. General Nelson's
Division is at Athens, and the rest are at Decatur and other points
between here and that place. General Mitchel's Division, now
General Smith's is still considerably scattered. The Second
Eighteenth, and Thirty-third Ohio, five companies of the Fourth
Ohio Cavalry, Edgarton's battery, and the Twenty-fourth Illinois are
at Battle Creek. The Nineteenth Illinois was at Bridgeport but has
been within a day or two ordered back to Huntsville, some say in
disgrace. The Thirty-seventh Indiana is at Stevenson. The
Twenty-first Ohio is at Athens. The Tenth Wisconsin is
performing guard duty along the Line of the railroad between
Huntsville and Stevenson. The Third, and Tenth Ohio, the
Forty-second Indiana, the Fifteenth Kentucky, five companies of the

fourth Ohio Cavalry, and Loomis' and Simonson's batteries are at Huntsville. It may be that that portion of the third division which is still here, will move up to join the remainder at Battle Creek, and still take the advance in the East Tennessee expedition. This it can do, even if it remain here five or six days yet, provided it then goes by rail. It is difficult to say, however, what it will do. There are rumors that it is to be ordered to Corinth, to perform railroad duty in that portion of the country. When General Mitchel left here, he stated privately that, if a command were given him in the east, he would earnestly endeavor to have his old division (at least the Seventeenth Brigade and Loomis' battery) sent to him. In the other two brigades, the Eighth and Ninth, there is a great deal of hostility against Mitchel. The Eighth is probably disorganized, and Colonel Turchin its commander ordered back to his regiment.

As I told you, General Mitchel was growing very unpopular before he left here. He was accused of blowing hot and cold in his treatment of the rebels; of utterly failing to execute the famous proclamation which he issued against guerrilla warfare; of suffering himself to be bamboozled by Mrs. Polk Walker and other secesh women, or milk and water Unionists of both sexes, about Huntsville; of exhibiting gross ingratitude toward his officers and soldiers whose labors had obtained him a Major Generalship, especially toward Colonel Turchin and the Eighth Brigade – of rough and uncourteous treatment of his officers, and insufferably haughty bearing toward them – of inconsistency in regard to the eternal negro question – of the most crushing harshness toward all who differed from him – of weakness, snappishness and irratability – of shameful favoritism toward the members of his own family, making one son Fred., Assistant Adj't. Gen., and another, Ed., Division Quartermaster; both of them, in the opinion of the division, utterly incompetent – and lastly, and worst of all if proven against him, of dabbling in the cotton speculation, and taking pay for carrying cotton in government wagons and on government trains. Col. Norton of the Twenty first Ohio has doubtless gone on to Washington City, in order to prosecute him upon this latter charge.

I have no doubt the malignity and jealousy of Buell toward Mitchel are boundless, and if he can in any way injure him, he will certainly do so. McCook and Nelson would both exult in fiendish glee if General Mitchel could be disgraced. God grant he may yet triumph over his enemies! I was recently inclined to think him indifferent upon the great question of Human Freedom, but I am now certain that all his seeming inconsistency upon that matter arose from the orders of General Buell, who cares more for guarding a rebel cabbage patch, or reenslaving a liberated negro, than he does for gaining a triumph over the enemy. Had General Mitchel been left to himself, he would have pursued a firm, consistent manly and generous course upon this matter, which would have given universal satisfaction. But General Buell is so intensely pro-slavery that I have no doubt he would sacrifice every officer in his District, for the sake of returning to bondage a single slave. As far as he can, he is undoing everything that General Mitchel did here, and the rebels are in a high state of exultation in consequence. The army is really in a paroxysm of terror, each man fearing he may be the next one arrested and punished for having offended some scoundrelly traitor. It is a common remark in the army now, that there is not a traitor in Huntsville or vicinity who would not be received at Buell's headquarters with greater consideration and respect than any Union officer. Is it possible that our noble army is thus to be enslaved by an epauleted, illiberal, narrow-minded hound of slavery? It is enough to wring tears of mortification and anger from every eye. I will furnish you with some facts soon that will astonish you.

Latest. A court-martial has just been summoned for the trial of Colonel Turchin. Genl' Garfield is President, and Colonels Ammon, Munday, Sedgwick, Jones, Pope and Beatty members. It meets to-morrow at Athens. Very Respectfully,

ALS   Wm. S. Furay.

Wm. S. Furay to Richard Smith, Esq., 6 July 1862, G-617 1862, Letters Received, RG 107 [L-141]. A notation at the top of the letter, in another handwriting, reads, "From the Editor of Gazette," and an endorsement indicates that John A. Gurley, congressman from Ohio, forwarded the letter to the War Department.

90: Commander of the 3rd Division of the Army of the Tennessee to the Headquarters of the Army of the Tennessee

[*Memphis*] July 10th 1862

Maj   There are now about 200 runaway negros in the negro yards at Memphis— These men have attempted to reach our works but the "loyal police" for the hope of reward have stopped them— Many of the negros no doubt are from rank rebels in the army and are coming here in hopes that their master's treason will liberate them— Have them sent out under the Escort of the Cavalry

and we will give them work on the fortifications   I have the honor
to be &s

Alvin P Hovey

P.S.   The negroe yard is on Adams Street A & N Delap—

ALS   A. P. H.

Brig. Genl. Alvin P. Hovey to Maj. Rawlins, 10 July 1862, Registered &
Unregistered Letters & Reports Received, ser. 2732, Army & Dist. of West
TN, RG 393 Pt. 2 No. 171 [C-8004]. No reply appears among the copies of
letters sent by the headquarters of the Army of the Tennessee.

91A: **Former Commander of the 3rd Division of the
Army of the Ohio to the Secretary of War**

Washington July 26th 1862

Sir   My attention has just been called to a letter republished in the
Philadelphia Inquirer of this date, presenting some facts and
statements concerning the 3[d] Division of the Army of the Ohio
    From this letter I am led to fear that the Commanding General of
the Army has returned to their masters, Slaves, to whom I promised
the permanent protection of the Government of the United
States.   These Slaves had rendered valuable services, and had
obtained for me most important information, and to these Negros I
offered protection under authority received from you in your
telegram dated May 5th
    I beg your interference in behalf of these Slaves; and I must
further ask if possible, immediate action, for I fear that if they fall
into the hands of their masters, their lives will not be safe   Very
Respectfully Your obed[r] Serv[r]

ALS   O M Mitchel

Maj. Genl. O. M. Mitchel to Hon. E. M. Stanton, 26 July 1862, filed with
M-1743 1862, Letters Received, RG 107 [L-140]. In the same file is a letter
from E. D. Townsend of the Adjutant General's Office to Major General Don
Carlos Buell, commander of the Army of the Ohio, dated July 28, 1862, ordering an investigation of Mitchel's charges: "Wherever the protection of the Government has been duly promised to any person, whatever his color or condition,
the promise must be kept inviolate; and if any one, bond or free, in the insurgent
States, has rendered valuable services, or given important information, he too
must be protected, even though no promise to that effect was made." The telegram of May 5 referred to by Mitchel is printed above as doc. 86.

91B: Commander of the Army of the Ohio to the Adjutant
General of the Army, Enclosing Reports from Division
Commanders to the Headquarters of the Army of the Ohio

Hunsville [*Ala.*] Aug. 15th. *1862.*
Sir. I have the honor to return the letter of Major Genl. Mitchell,
who, from some letter "republished in the Philadelphia Inquirer"
has been led to fear that the Commanding General (of this army)
has returned to their masters, slaves, to whom he (Genl. Mitchell)
promised the permanent protection of the Government of the
United States. I enclose also on the subject, the reports of Genl.
W. S. Smith who temporarily commanded the 3rd Division after
Genl. Mitchell's departure, and of Genl. Rousseau who succeeded
Genl. Smith as the permanent commander. These reports cover the
whole ground as far as I have any knowledge. Genl. Mitchell did
not to my recollection, speak to me of protection promised to any
slaves, certainly he gave me no statement in regard to those who
merited protection for their services. Nevertheless I have no idea
that any such have suffered. It would be contrary to my feelings
and orders if such should have been the case. Very Respectfully
Your Obt. Servt.

HLS   D. C. Buell.

[*Enclosure*]   Tullahoma [*Tenn.*] Aug 6 [*1862*]
There was one slave for whom protection was claimed I think by
Capt Slocum Div Qr Mr and another who brought in information &
was put on duty I believe as a train hand. Neither of them were
given up to my knowledge   these were all the cases of the kind
that came to my knowledge   My instructions from Genl Buell
strictly forbade my giving up slaves who had brought in intelligence
& thus rendered themselves liable to punishment by their masters &
in no case to my knowledge were these so given up

ALS   Wm S. Smith.

[*Enclosure*]   Camp Taylor [*Ala.*] Aug. 7th 1862
Sir: In compliance with the order, of the Major General
Commanding the Army of the Ohio, of yesterday, requiring me to
report touching the subject matter of the letter of Major General O.
M. Mitchel of the 26th ult, to the Secretary of War, I have the
honor to say that I know of no person, black or white, bond or free,
who gave to General Mitchel valuable information, with or without
a promise of protection. All I know as to the subject matter of
General Mitchel's letter is this:

A slave of Mr. Patton, who resides near Huntsville Ala. was about to leave, some days ago, on the cars for Michigan, with Captain Loomis of the 1st Michigan Battery. My attention was attracted to the negro by the suit he had on of a new and handsome uniform of the Artillery Company, and I told Captain Loomis not to take him on the cars. Captain Loomis thereupon replied to me that General Mitchel had set the negro free, and had asserted positively that he should serve no man again. I replied to him that General Mitchel had no power to free slaves, and I should not at all regard any illegal act of the General in that or any other matter; that Patton was a conservative loyal man, entitled to the protection of the Government to which he acknowledged allegiance. That I utterly disputed the right and power of the General, as I did the justice of the act, to transfer the hundreds of horses, mules and other property of loyal as well as disloyal citizens that had been taken by officers and soldiers who were willing to make the seizure, and that loyal citizens were entitled to the protection of the Government in the possession and use of slaves, as well as other property. Captain Loomis said the slave had given valuable information to General Mitchel, and in my presence, he ordered the slave to return to camp, and the slave did so. He is there still, as I understand and was not returned to his master.

This was what occured on that occasion, and it is all I have heard of such information or protection as General Mitchel refers to, and such protection has not been claimed, refused or neglected as far as my information or knowledge extends. I am Very Respectfully Your Obdt Serv't

HLS   Lovell H Rousseau

Maj. Genl. D. C. Buell to Genl. L. Thomas, 15 Aug. 1862, enclosing B. Genl. Wm. S. Smith to Col. Jas. B. Fry, 6 Aug. [1862], and Brig. Genl. Lovell H. Rousseau to Col. J. B. Fry, 7 Aug. 1862, filed with M-1743 1862, Letters Received, RG 107 [L-140]. Endorsement. In the same file is a draft of a subsequent letter from the War Department to General Ormsby M. Mitchel, which simply forwarded without comment copies of the correspondence received relative to his letter of July 26. A crossed-out passage in that draft helps explain the department's unwillingness to press the matter further: "[I]t appears that the statement of the Philadelphia Inquirer, upon which your letter was based, had no sufficient authority to sustain it." (Assist. Secretary of War P. H. W. to Brig. Genl. O. M. Mitchell, 7 Oct. 1862.)

92: Confederate General to a Friend, and Commander of the 5th Division of the Army of the Tennessee to the Confederate General

Oxford Miss. Augst 2^n 1862.

Copy

Dear Sir, The Federal Army at Helena have taken off, by bodies of armed men, all my negroes, men women and children some 400 in number. They have taken off and destroyed everything else I had. They killed one of my overseers, and have the other three in jail. I have been informed that many of the women and children are wandering about Memphis suffering for food. I also understand that there are 85 young men and women in a cotton warehouse or negro mart in Memphis who are also neglected and are suffering for food. It is difficult for me to realize that such conduct is done by the sanction of the Federal Officers of rank, but yet the wholesale robbery which has been carried on below would seem to admit of no other conclusion. My object in this communication is to request of you the favor of ascertaining if the reports I have heard are true, viz: If any of my negroes, men, women, or children are in Memphis, and to inform me of their condition, and if any of them will be restored to me or to my agent. Please see if any gang of the negroes are confined in the Ware house or Negro Mart. I cannot imagine what the Federals want with the women & children.

If you can have access to Genl Grant or Sherman please ascertain if these proceedings have been ordered by them, or meet with their approval. The law of Confiscation does not take effect for some time to come, and my negroes were in no loyal [*legal*] sense liable to seizure.[1] If the Federals intend to seize all the negroes and other property within their power we can only say that the time may come for proper reprisals. My brother James' negroes and L. Long's and Thomas Brown's have all been carried off. Please see if any of these negroes are in Memphis, and what their condition. I have uniformly in Missouri & Kentucky protected the property of Union men, as well as their persons from violence. Genl Crittenden has a plantation and negroes 25 miles below Columbus on the River, which I declined allowing to be interrupted when in command at Columbus though applied to for the purpose.

If you cannot have a personal interview either with Genl Grant or Sherman, you will please transmit my letter to them. Your attention to this matter will be gratefully remembered. Please send me through some channel an answer. Your friend

(signed) Gid. J. Pillow

If any of my negroes are in Helena will you ascertain if Gen[l] Grant
or Sherman will have them restored to me, and all such information
as you can get.

HLcSr   G. J. P.

Memphis. Aug[st] 14th 1862.
Sir, I have received your letter of August 2[d] 1862, at the hands of
S. P. Walker Esq. It is not proper in war, thus to communicate or
to pass letters, but I am willing to admit the extreme difficulty of
applying the harsh rules of War, when but a few days ago all was
peace plenty and free intercourse, and on this ground, not officially,
I am willing that you should know the truth of the matter
concerning which you enquire. It so happens that Gen[l] Curtis was
here yesterday and I enquired of him the truth concerning the
allegations in the first part of your letter, touching the seizure and
confiscation, the killing one overseer, the imprisonment of three
others, and generally the devastation of your entire estate in that
quarter. Gen[l] Curtis answered, no slave was taken by armed men
from your or any other plantation, unless he had proof that such
slaves had been used in war against him. No overseer had been
killed, or none imprisoned, and the damage to plantation was only
such as will attend the armies such as marked the progress of your
and A. Sidney Johnson's column's a year ago in Kentucky.

I understand Gen[l] Curtis has given letters of manumission to
negro applicants who satisfy him they have been used as property to
carry on war.[2] I grant no such papers, as my opinion is, it is the
provision of a Court to pass on the title to all kinds of property. I
simply claim that I have a right to the present labor of slaves who
are fugitives and such labor is regulated and controlled that it may
ultimately be paid for to the Master or slave, according to the
case. I have no control over Gen[l] Curtis who is my superior, but I
take it for granted some just and uniform rule will soon be
established by our common superior to all cases alike.

I certainly never have known, nor do I believe it possible that
your slaves or those of any other person have wandered about the
streets of Memphis in want and destitution. We have abundance of
provisions and no person shall suffer for want here. When we can
provide labor it will be done, and thereby they (laborers or slaves)
earn their provisions, clothing & necessaries but wages are always
held in reserve to answer the order of the rightful party. The worst
you have to apprehend in case you claim the sixty days under the
confiscation law[1] is that your slaves may become scattered. None

are allowed to pass up the River save with written passes, and I understand your negroes are either at your plantation or near Helena, I know of none of them here.

Gen¹ Curtis expressed great surprise at your solicitude for these negroes and at your application that Gen¹ Grant and myself would have them restored to you or your Agent, he says you had sold them all, or had transferred them by some Instrument of writing for a Record to a gentleman near the plantation who is a loyal Citizen of the United States

I will refer your letter to Gen. Grant with a copy of this and have already given a copy to Gen¹ Curtis, now at Helena. If Mr Walker can find any of your negroes here, the men will be put to work; but Mr Walker can keep a watch of them and of the women till such times as rules are Established for ascertaining & determining the right and title to such kind of property. At present I know of none of your negroes in or near Memphis. Certainly none are in the negro pen or any cotton shed here. I am &ᶜ Yr Oᵇᵗ Serᵗ

HLc   [*William T. Sherman*]

Gid. J. Pillow to Saml. P. Walker Esq., 2 Aug. 1862, enclosed in Maj. Genl. W. T. Sherman to Maj. Jno. A. Rawlins, 14 Aug. 1862, and Maj. Genl. [William T. Sherman] to Gen. G. J. Pillow, 14 Aug. 1862, Registered & Unregistered Letters & Reports Received, ser. 2732, Army & Dist. of West TN, RG 393 Pt. 2 No. 171 [C-8006].

1 Section 6 of the Second Confiscation Act threatened to seize the "estate and property, moneys, stocks, and credits" of secessionists who did not cease supporting the rebellion within sixty days of the President's proclamation (of July 25, 1862), warning them to "return to their proper allegiance to the United States." (U.S., *Statutes at Large, Treaties, and Proclamations*, vol. 12 [Boston, 1863], pp. 591, 1266.)
2 See below, doc. 95.

93: Commander of the 6th Division of the Army of the Ohio to the Headquarters of the Army of the Ohio

Decherd, Tenn, Aug't 4, 1862.
Sir: It has been my practice hitherto, without enquiring particularly into the question of the owner's loyalty, to allow citizens to reclaim fugitive negroes. in our lines. My object in this course was, like many other officers, to convince the people it was not our design to interfere with the slaves of the country. But the

passage of the confiscation act has somewhat changed the matter. Is it proper under the spirit of this law to permit the agents of persons known to be in arms against the Government to reclaim fugitives within our lines?[1] or proper to drive the fugitives out of the lines, knowing they will be apprehended for their masters?[2]

A case in point occurs with me. Major Rutledge, of the rebel army, openly known to be such, and so acknowledged by his family, has a plantation in this neighborhood. One of his negroes has escaped from home, and taken shelter, I have no doubt in our lines, though I have never seen him. Mrs Rutledge, a very lady-like person, has called on me for permission for her overseer to reclaim the negro in camp, or to have him driven out of camp that the overseer may arrest him outside. I told her I had doubt, under the late law, whether I had power to grant her request. Her husband is openly in arms against the Government, and it is perfectly certain he will not return to his allegiance in sixty days— Have we the power, or if we had the power, would it be right, to afford such people any assistance? Is it not proper to leave them to their fate? We do not interfere with their negroes, and if they (the negroes) runaway from their masters, who are rebels it is the misfortune of the latter, not our fault. They made the rebellion, not we.

I told Mrs Rutledge I would take her case into consideration, and give her an answer hereafter. She is an old acquaintance of mine, and a daughter of Judge Underwood, of Bowlinggreen Ky—

If contrabands come into our lines to any extent, and to keep them out wholly is impossible, I propose to put them to driving teams, and relieve soldiers from extra duty.[3] I think this course will have a two fold good effect. It will save soldiers to the ranks so far as the contrabands come in; and, secondly, these latter will not be likely to come into an annoying extent when they find out they have to work.

I beg you will submit this communication to the Commanding General for his views. I do not desire to elicit an order on the subject, but simply to learn whether his views and my own coincide. There should be a uniform policy. Respectfully, your obdt Servant,

ALS
                                                        Th: J. Wood

Brig. Genl. Th. J. Wood to Col. J. B. Fry, 4 Aug. 1862, W-146 1862, Letters Received, ser. 880, Dist. of the OH, RG 393 Pt. 1 [C-2044]. The marginal comments printed in the footnotes are in an unidentified handwriting, presumably that of General Don Carlos Buell, commander of the Army of the Ohio, or one of his staff officers. On August 13, 1862, Buell formally approved Wood's plan for employing fugitive slaves, directing that "[t]hey will be turned out of camp only as a measure of necessity when they cannot be made useful to the Government and become a nuisance." (*Official Records*, ser. 1, vol. 16, pt. 2, p. 332.)

1 Marginal notation in another handwriting: "no."
2 Marginal notation in another handwriting: "They will be used for the public service first. It is proper as a measure of discipline to drive them out if they are not useful to the government."
3 Marginal notation in another handwriting: "(*approved*)."

94: Order by the Commander of the 5th Division of the Army of the Tennessee

Memphis, August 8th 1862.
General Orders, No. 67. Inasmuch as by Law of Congress recently enacted, the President of the United States is authorized to receive and employ the labor of slaves, or fugitives from slavery, and such fugitives are coming to our Camps seeking protection, the following rules will be observed at, or near Memphis until the President prescribes others; when these will necesserily be superseded and made to conform to the pleasure of the President.

I. All able-bodied negroes who apply for work at Fort Pickering, will be received and put to work by the Engineer in charge Captain Hoepner, the names of owners and slaves registered, with date of commencement of work, and a general description by which the negroes can be known. Such negroes will be entitled to rations to be drawn on Provision Returns similar to those used for soldiers, and will be supplied with necessary clothing, and tobacco at the rate of one pound per month, An account will be opened with each negro, and his wages will be charged with the value of the clothing and tobacco; but no wages will be paid until the Courts determine whether the negro be slave or free. The negroes employed on the Fort are working as laborers, and will be allowed to return to their masters or mistresses at the close of any week; but masters or mistresses cannot be allowed to enter the Fort in search of their slaves, because it is improper that any one not belonging to the Garrison should enter Fort Pickering, or even follow its lines and ditches on the outside. A list of negroes so employed will be kept at Head Quarters, which may be seen by parties interested.

II. The Post Quarter Master, Captain Fitch will in like manner employ a force of about one hundred negroes out of those who apply to him for work, or he may on occasions, take by force when he thinks it absolutely necessary to have an increased force work on the levee, loading and unloading steamboats, coal boats and such like labor; a list of whom similar to that refered to in Paragraph I., will be kept by the Quartermaster, and a copy sent to Head Quarters for reference. These will in like manner be entitled to rations, necessary clothing and tobacco, but the pay must be reserved until the proper judicial tribunals determine to whom such labor and wages belong.

III. Division Quartermasters may employ fugitives to drive teams, and attend to horses, mules and cattle, keeping accurate accounts under the rules of their Department applicable "to persons and articles employed and hired," and subject to the condition of Paragraph. I. of this Order; this list of persons so employed to be sent to Head Quarters for reference. The number of negroes so hired not to exceed one per team, and one to every six span of animals herded or stabled.

IV. The Commanders of Regiments may cause to be employed as Cooks and Company Teamsters, not to exceed five per Company, and ten per Regiment for extra wagons, and five for staff-wagons, in all sixty-five per Regiment, which negroes shall be borne on the Muster Rolls, and supplied with provisions and clothing as soldiers; but in no case will they bear arms or wear the uniform. The Quartermaster of the Division will supply the Regimental Quartermasters with clothing suitable for such negroes, an account of which will be kept separate and distinct from that of the soldiers — These negroes must be kept to their appropriate duties and place, and the question of wages must remain open and unsettled until the orders of the President are received or until fixed by subsequent regulations.

V. The Commanding General here thinks proper to make known to the people of Memphis the principles by which in the absence of instructions from his Superior Officers, he will be governed in all cases arising under these complicated questions. It is neither his duty, nor his pleasure to disturb the relation of master and slave — that is for the Courts which having been destroyed here by our enemy, are inoperative for the present, but in the due course of events, there must and will be tribunals re-established here that will judge and decide, in cases which have already arisen, or may arise under the Laws and Constitution of the United States. Then loyal masters will recover their slaves and the wages they have earned during their temporary use by the Military authorities; but it is understood that masters who are in open hostility to the Constitution of their Country will lose their slaves, the title to which only exists by force of that very Constitution they seek to destroy.

No influence must be used to entice slaves from their masters; and if fugitives desire to return to their masters, they will be permitted to do so, but on the other hand, no force or undue persuasion will be permitted to recover such fugitive property.

Officers of the Army, from Generals to Lieutenants, must not employ such fugitives for servants. The Government provides to each Officer a distinct pay for his servant, and this is ample for the hire of a free man. Were we to employ such fugitives as servants, our motives would be misconstrued; whereas, their employment by the Government is in pursuance of law, – is clearly within the rules of war, and will increase our effective force by the number of negroes so employed. By order of, Major Gen¹ W. T. Sherman

HDc

General Orders, No. 67, Head Quarters, 5th Division, Army of the Tenn., 8 Aug. 1862, Orders, W. T. Sherman Papers, Generals' Papers & Books, ser. 159, RG 94 [V-313]. Three days later, Sherman's superior, General Ulysses S. Grant, commander of the District of West Tennessee, also authorized army employment of fugitive slaves; at the same time he prohibited officers and soldiers from enticing slaves from their masters and ordered the exclusion of unauthorized blacks from Union lines. Unlike Sherman, Grant permitted officers to employ fugitives as servants. (General Orders No. 72, Head Quarters, District of West Tennessee, 11 Aug. 1862, vol. G3/4 DT, p. 90, General Orders & Circulars Issued, ser. 2733, Army & Dist. of West TN, RG 393 Pt. 2 No. 171 [C-391].) In mid-August, Sherman explained his rationale for issuing General Order 67: "I found about six hundred negroes employed here, and daily others coming into our works. I had knowledge that a Law had passed Congress, for using the Labor of such negroes, approved by the President and sanctioned by Gen¹ Halleck. No instructions had come or could come to guide me, and I was forced to lay down certain rules for my own guidance. Masters and mistresses so thronged my tent as to absorb my whole time and necessity compelled me to adopt some clearly defined rules, and I did so. I think them legal and just. Under this order I must assume to clothe and feed the negroes, but you will observe I make no provisions for any save laboring men. The women and families take refuge here, but I cannot provide for them, but I allow no force or undue persuasion in any case." (Maj. Genl. W. T. Sherman to Major J. A. Rawlins, 14 Aug. 1862, Letters Sent, W. T. Sherman Papers, Generals' Papers & Books, ser. 159, RG 94 [V-303].)

95: Order by the Commander of the Army of the Southwest

Special Orders, No. 1250, Head Quarters Army of the South West, 15 Aug. 1862, Gen. J. R. Chalmers Papers, ser. 117, Collections of Officers' Papers, Records of Military Commands, RG 109 [F-218]. An unidentified confederate, whose penciled endorsement reported that he had "taken several such papers as this from the negroes down here," evidently forwarded the paper to General James R. Chalmers, commander of cavalry forces in the Confederate Army of the Mississippi.

96: Commander of the 5th Division of the Army of the Tennessee to a Tennessee Slaveholder

Memphis Tenn. Aug 24th 1862

My dear Sir, I freely admit that when you recall the times when we were schoolfellows, when we were younger than now, you touch me on a tender point, and cause me to deeply regret that even you should style yourself a Rebel. I cannot believe that Tom Hunton the Companion of Gaither, Rankin, and Irvin and many others long since dead, and of Halleck. Ord, Stevens and others still living can of his own free will admit the anarchical principle of secession or be vain enough to suppose the present Politicions Can frame a Government better than that of Washington Hamilton & Jefferson. We cannot realize this but delude ourselves into the belief that by some strange but successful jugglery the manegers of our Political Machine have raised up the single issue, North or

South, which shall prevail in America? or that you like others have been blown up, and cast into the Mississippi of Secession doubtful if by hard fighting you can reach the shore in safety, or drift out to the Ocean of Death, I know it is no use for us now to discuss this—war is on us. We are Enemies, still private friends. In the one Capacity I will do you all the harm I can, yet on the other if here. you may have as of old my last Cent, my last shirt and pants, You ask of me your negroes. and I will immediately ascertain if they be under my Military Control and I will moreover see that they are one and all told what is true of all— Boys if you want to go to your master, Go— You are free to choose, You must now think for yourselves. Your Master has seceded from his Parent Government and you have seceded from him—both wrong by law—but bothe exercising an undoubted natural Right to rebel, If your boys want to go, I will enable them to go, but I wont advise, persuade or force them— I confess I have not yet seen the "Confiscation Act," but I enclose you my own orders defining my position, I also cut out of a paper Grant's Orders, and I assert that the Action of all our Leading Military Leaders, Halleck, McClellan, Buell, Grant & myself have been more conservative of slavery than the Acts of your own men. The Constitution of the United States is your only legal title to slavery. You have another title, that of posession & Force, but in Law & Logic your title to your Boys lay in the Constitution of the United States. You may say you are for the Constitution of the United States, as it was— You know it is unchanged, not a word not a syllable and I can lay my hand on that Constitution and swear to it without one twang. But your party have made *another* and have another in force How can you say that you would have the old, when you have a new By the new if sucessful you inherit the Right of Slavery, but the new is not law till your Revolution is successful. Therefore we who contend for the old existing Law, Contend that you by your own act take away Your own title to all property save what is restricted by *our* constitution, your slaves included. You know I don't want your slaves; but to bring you to reason I think as a Military Man I have a Right and it is good policy to make *you all* feel that you are but men—that you have all the wants & dependencies of other men, and must eat, be clad &^{c} to which end you must have property & labor, and that by Rebelling you risk both, Even without the Confiscation Act, by the simple laws of War we ought to take your effective slaves. I don't say to free them, but to use their labor & deprive you of it; as Belligerents we ought to seek the hostile Army and fight it and not the people. — We went to Corinth but Beaureguard declined Battle, since which time many are dispersed as Guerillas. We are not bound to follow them, but rightfully make war by any means that will tend to bring about an end and restore Peace. Your people may say it only exasperates, widens the breach and all that, But the longer the war lasts the more you must be convinced that we are no better & no worse than People who have gone before us, and that we are simply reenacting History, and that one of the modes of bringing People to reason is to touch their Interests pecuniary or property.

We never harbor women or children – we give employment to men, under the enclosed order. I find no negroes Registered as belonging to Hunton, some in the name of McGhee of which the Engineer is now making a list – I see McClellan says that the negroes once taken shall never again be restored.[1] I say nothing. My opinion is, we execute not make the Law, be it of Congress or War. But it is Manifest that if you wont go into a United States District Court and sue for the recovery of your slave property You can never Get it, out of adverse hands. No U.S. Court would allow you to sue for the recovery of a slave under the Fugitive Slave Law. unless you acknowledge allegiance. Believing this honesty, so I must act. though personally I feel strong frindship as ever, for very many in the South   With Great Respect Your friend

HLcS   W. T. Sherman

Maj. Genl. W. T. Sherman to Thomas Hunton, Esq., 24 Aug. 1862, vol. 3, pp. 51–53, Letters Sent, W. T. Sherman Papers, Generals' Papers & Books, ser. 159, RG 94 [V-304].

1 On August 9, 1862, General George B. McClellan, commander of the Army of the Potomac, issued an order promulgating President Abraham Lincoln's executive order of July 22, which had instructed the federal armies operating in rebellious states to seize property suitable for military purposes and to employ slaves. McClellan added that slaves employed by the Union army "have always understood that after being received into the military service of the United States in any capacity they could never be reclaimed by their former holders," and he promised such slaves "permanent military protection against any compulsory return to a condition of servitude." (*Official Records*, ser. 1, vol. 11, pt. 3, pp. 362–64.)

97: Commander of the 5th Division of the Army of the Tennessee to the Mayor of Memphis

Memphis Tenn Sep. 23^{d} 1862

Sir, I have given the subject matter of you communication of the   inst my earliest leisure. My opinion is that the simpler the Government the easier it is executed. I have therefore Concluded that the City Recorder must take cognisance of all crimes & misdemeanors here, whether committed inside or outside the City Limits.

In like manner the Major & council of Memphis must control the police of the neighborhood until the State & County Government are reinstalled in power. It is better that you should see that good order prevails not only in Memphis but in the adjoining County. I know that there is full employment for 100 policeman and profitable employment could be given to a party to clean your streets, improve the Levee, Roads & Bridges. The taxes prescribed for the new limits must be collected and properly disbursed. I donot want to meddle with the Civil affairs of your city but the members of the Council must know that in the absence of proper State & County Officers somebody must take their places and in my judgement there is no more suitable substitutes that the Civil authorities of the City. You have a Council to deliberate, an execution to carry out the laws and their resolutions with constables and police to do the work. If you limit the exercise of your power to the new City Limits, of course all the Rogues & thieves of the county will congregate outside your line and Commit their deeds of crime without fear of punishment. This must not be and as Military Commander I have the perfect legal right to supply this glaring defect in your system.

I therefore order that the city authorities extend their police system over the city of Memphis and all the surrounding Country within our Military Lines and to defray the needful Expenses they cause to be collected licenses & taxes heretofor decreed by them within the sphere of two miles of Court Square

If parties refuse to pay such licenses or taxes, the "collectors" may collect the same by the seizure and sale of the personal property of the refusing party or in any manner prescribed by Law for such cases within the City Limits proper

The City Recorder must take cognisance of all cases of violation of Law and good order occuring anywhere, when the police may arrest and procure the accused party with the necessary witnesses

All the City Officers, Mayor & Aldermen included must fufil their whole duties over this enlarged district and in case of refusal or failure will be arrested and punished for the violation of these my military orders

As the County & State authorities gradually resume their proper functions the city authorities can by the same process contract their sphere to the city proper, but in the mean time, of necessity the Peace and Safety of the inhabitants demand that crime in every shape sould be promptly punished and suppressed wherever it may occur

The civil authority is confined to cases when citizens alone are involved. These embrace the negroes who have taken refuge in the city of Memphis. Negroes committing crimes must be punished and vagrants must be confined and put to some work that will entitle them to subsistence. But as the Laws of Congress are the Supreme Law of the land & make it impossible to return the fugitive slaves of even loyal masters until the District Court of the United States is established here, All negroes must be treated as *free* to come and go, but if they steal, get drunk or disorderly or commit any other offense against the laws and ordinances in force here they can and must be punished.

The Military Guard will not interfere unless there be reason to believe that the police are abusing their power, to restore to a Condition of Slavery a negro who has escaped therefrom and who has not been remanded by the only Competant power, viz the Courts of the United States   I have the honor to be Your obt. Sevt

HLcS   W. T. Sherman

Maj. Genl. W. T. Sherman to John Park, Esq., 23 Sept. 1862, vol. 3, pp. 141–42, Letters Sent, W. T. Sherman Papers, Generals' Papers & Books, ser. 159, RG 94 [V-308]. Blank space in manuscript. Several weeks later, Sherman took issue with a Memphis judge who had instructed a grand jury to hold Tennessee's slave code superior to the federal confiscation acts. Sherman advised the judge that the duty of the courts was "to meet and punish crime — that class of crime known all the world over as *malum in se*, common to the codes of all civilized people — and reserve this question of slavery, this dire conflict between National and State authority, to be fought out by the armies now arrayed for that purpose." While denying any personal "hostility to slavery or any of your local laws," Sherman threatened to hold in contempt all civil authorities who attempted to subordinate federal to state law. "For God's Sake," he implored the judge, "don't let this accursed question of slavery blind your mind to the thousand other duties and interests that concern you and the people among whom you live. . . . Do not force me to conclude the conflict to be 'irreconcilable,' as you surely will if you or your grand jury or the officers of your court insist on enforcing the statutes of Tennessee touching negroes at this terrible crisis of our history." (*Official Records*, ser. 1, vol. 17, pt. 2, pp. 863–65.) Meanwhile, the provost marshal at Memphis ordered on November 11 that "any attempt to execute State Laws at variance with the orders of the President and military commanders . . . will be summarily punished." Only the outcome of the war would finally determine "the status of the negro," but "in the mean time, runaway slaves must be treated as free." (Quoted below, in doc. 171.)

98: Commander of the 5th Division of the Army of the Tennessee to the Commander of an Artillery Battery

Memphis Oct. 8. 1862.

Sir. It is reported you sent a party of soldiers to the house of a Mr Curry & caused to be taken therefrom some Clothing & articles belonging to a fugitive negress in Your care

By Genl. Order No   no officer can enter or order the premises of any citizen to be searched except by direction of the Comdg. Genl. The propriety of such orders no one can appreciate better than Yourself

The Clothing & effects of a negro are the property of the master & mistress & whilst we admit the right of a negro to run away we must not sanction theft robbery or violence   If under any mis apprehension you have done as Complained of you will cause the articles to be returned & report fully in writing on the Case. We must not encourage the negroes in their propensity to steal & be impudent   Yours

HLcS   W. T Sherman

Maj. Genl. W. T. Sherman to Capt. Waterhouse, 8 Oct. 1862, vol. 3, p. 192, Letters Sent, W. T. Sherman Papers, Generals' Papers & Books, ser. 159, RG 94 [V-310]. Blank space in manuscript. Federal commanders at every level repeatedly prohibited pillaging and established restrictive procedures for military seizure of private property; the particular order to which Sherman referred may have been General Order 107, issued by the Adjutant General's Office on August 15, 1862. (*Official Records*, ser. 3, vol. 2, p. 388.)

99: Statement by the Commander of an Ohio Regiment

[*Tenn.*]   December 19' 1862.

About the 18th day of June last when I was in command at Fayettsvill Tenna a colored man named Johnston belonging to a man named James Isem residing near that place, come to my pickets in the night and on being brought to my quarters informed me that a party of the enemies Cavelry had suppered at his masters house that evening and that he over-heard them tell his master that they were going to a certain point on the road from Shelbyville to Fayettsville that night and would attack and capture a supply train that was to pass their in the morning. Acting upon this information I sent out two Companies of infantry by diferent roads with the hope of surrounding the enemy and capturing them, but on the approach of the Company in their front they fled from their ambush and scattered into the broken country so that the other company failed to intercept their retreat. Johnston accompanied the party as guide and they reported to me to have found evrything just as he represented, and also that they had returned by way of Isems house & that he admitted his sympathies to be with the rebels. They left Johnston with his master informing him of all that he had don and cautioning Isem not to punish him for it. Soon after they left Johnston overtook them and represented that as soon as they left Isem had ordered him to the stable "to be floged for your last nights work" whereupon he ran of. I found on enquirie that Isem was not only a sympathiser with but an active aider of the enemy. Believing these facts to entitle Johnston to the benefits of the Order giving protection and freedom to all slaves of rebel masters, that migh give valuable information concerning the enemy, I have permitted to remain with the regiment ever since. He has been employed most of the time by Rev J. C. Dillon chaplin to this regiment as a servant. I make this statement that Johnston may avail himself of whatever benefits the facts may entitle him to.

ADS   Josiah Given

Statement of Lieut. Col. Josiah Given, 19 Dec. 1862, G-97 1862, Letters Received, ser. 925, Dept. of the Cumberland, RG 393 Pt. 1 [C-3]. Given commanded the 18th Ohio Infantry. It has been impossible to determine the particular order to which Given referred. In the same file is an undated letter from the regimental chaplain to the commander of the Department of the Cumberland, requesting free papers for the fugitive slave, but no response either to the chaplain or to Given has been found in the records of the department.

100: Statement of a Tennessee Fugitive Slave

Nashville, December 23[d] *1862*

Charlie a black boy belongs to Mrs Elliot, a union woman, who formerly lived in Murfreesboro, but left there last spring when the Federals left there, She has boys grown up who are Union men   Col Ashman knows them well, She left me to take care of myself and wife, who belongs to Mr Bell who is in the Rebel Army. Was working as a blacksmith in the Gov't shops. I can not say how many troops are there but the general opinion and report is that they have altogether about 60000 men. They have no new fortifications, Have not seen any large cannon, They had some small cannon at the Depot, but they have none there now, I have not worked very steady and have gone round in the camps a good deal, They have pleanty of provisions no Sugar and but little Salt. Well clothed, The old troops seem very willing to remain, but the conscripts say they wont fight, The officers are very strict with them   I was told that they shot a man named Gray, whom they had taken prisoner some time since, because he was a Union man and would not join the army, I was arrested last Teusday night by orders of Col Cook of 2nd Tenn Infantry who is a brother in law of young John Bell and confined in jail. They charged me with having tried to leave there which was not true, Their object was to get my wife off south. They did send her away on Wednesday morning, I was brought out with others to work cutting wood at the hospitals and on Thursday evening I broke and run, They shot at me once, I got into a cellar and hid under some rag's till dark, Then I slipped out of town and stayed with some frends until Saturday night then took through the woods and fields going that night about 12 miles. Walked all day sunday generally in the woods, sometimes on bye roads always avoiding the pike for fear of being caught. Came into the Union pickets Monday morning, Got a pass from Genl Crittenden Aide to come into town, Genl Ashman knows me and sent me up here to tell what I knew.

I am a Union darkie, The Rebels keep two days rations ahead all the time, They expect to be driven out of there so I am told. Contraband.

HD

Statement of Charlie, 23 Dec. 1862, T-65 1862, Letters Received, ser. 925, Dept. of the Cumberland, RG 393 Pt. 1 [C-22]. Statement made before the chief of police at Nashville, and forwarded by him to the commander of the Department of the Cumberland.

101: Headquarters of a Confederate Cavalry Battalion to the
Headquarters of the Confederate Department
of Mississippi and East Louisiana

Okolona Miss Jany 8th 1863

You will oblige me by sending instructions in reference to the manner of disposing of negroes – runaways – caught by my scouts and not giving correct statement of the names of their owners and residence. It is difficult by any manner to ascertain where they belong, and the number is increasing beyond convenience.

On yesterday a negro was caught armed and killed two dogs in the attempt to catch him and finally shot himself inflicting a severe wound, after which he stated that he was from Corinth; and that on the night of the 1st inst the negroes (or most of them) were assembled at that place and officers attended making lectures and stating they were free. The negroes after receiving each a pistol (six shooter) were instructed to go to the vicinity of their respective homes and act as *missionaries* (or "in the recruiting service.") I wish to know how to deal with them when caught. Very Respectfully By order of C R Barteau Lt Col Comdg

ALS   Pleas. Smith

Adj't. Pleas. Smith to A.A.G. J. Thompson, 8 Jan. 1863, Gen. J. C. Pemberton Papers, ser. 131, Collections of Officers' Papers, Records of Military Commands, RG 109 [F-231]. In reply, an adjutant at the headquarters of the Confederate Department of Mississippi and East Louisiana instructed Colonel Barteau to remand to the civil authorities all recaptured slaves who withheld the names of their owners or furnished incorrect information. "When you take Negroes with arms evidently coming out from the enemie's camp," the adjutant ordered, "proceed at once to hold a drum head court martial and if found guilty hang them upon the spot." (A.&.I.G. J. Thompson to Lt. Col. Barteau, 14 Jan. 1863, ch. II, vol. 57, p. 307, Letters & Telegrams Sent, Dept. of MS & East LA, RG 109 [F-231].)

102: Certificate of Freedom Issued by a Brigade
Commander in the 13th Army Corps

Helena [*Ark.*] Feby. 23' 1863.
Daniel Webster.

An *"American Citizen of African descent"* bearer of this Declaration by me issued at Helena in the State of Arkansas *in the Federal Union,* formerly held as a slave within a District in rebellion against the United States, has been by a Proclamation of his Excellency

Abraham Lincoln President of the United States declared to be
henceforward and *forever free.*

The freedom of Daniel *Webster* will be *recognized* and *maintained* by
the forces under my command and he is commended to the *Kindness*
and *protection* of other military or naval authorities and to the respect
and esteem of civilians as he journeys northward to the State of
Ohio

HDcSr   (signed) Clinton B. Fisk

Certificate of freedom issued by Brig. Genl. Clinton B. Fisk, 23 Feb. 1863,
vol. 274/632 DMo, p. 85, Letters Sent, ser. 3516, 2d Brigade, 13th Division, 13th Army Corps, RG 393 Pt. 2 No. 225 [C-8739].

103: Chief of Police of Nashville to the Commander of the Department of the Cumberland

Nashville Mar 7th *1863.*

Sir   Leut George Burrughs. Called upon me today. on the Subject.
Securing for labor upon the Fortifycations. a Large Number of
Negroes

There is good many Col^d Laborers can be got in and about the
City. & from the Work Houses & Jails and from the Surrounding
Country —

It is evident General That. Very General efforts is being made by
oweners & drivers. to Run them South and Large Numbers Have
been Taken from the City — Your Officers in Charge of Large
Numbers in Hospitals & on Fortifications have been on more
accassions than one. approched with curupt Propositions. to engage
in the Business of. kidnapping them   If you Should deam it
advisable to Take them from the Holders generally in City &
Country. Large Number Could. be obtained But, in Some instances
would effect the Interest of Persens engaged in Planting — Many
can be got. and at the Same time excercise a Proper Regard. for the
Interest of those who desire to plant — I will aid him with good &
Prudent men — to Secure Such as it will be Proper to
take   Respectfully

ALS   Wm Truedail

Col. Wm. Treudail to Maj. Genl. Rosecrans, 7 Mar. 1863, T-197 1863,
Letters Received, ser. 925, Dept. of the Cumberland, RG 393 Pt. 1 [C-23].
No reply has been found among the records of the Department of the
Cumberland.

104: Statement by a Tennessee Fugitive Slave

Murfreesboro [*Tenn.*] Mar 12th 1863

Statement of Wiley Thompson (colored)   I am a Servant of Newcome Thompson *"the first"*   he lives on the Lewisburg Pike 2 1/4 miles beyon Shelbaville—   I ran away from home on the night of the 2[d] "Inst"   I learned from black persons who were in the camps around Shelbaville that the rebels claim to have about 100,000—troops at and between Shelbaville & Chattanoga—Fortified at Tullahoma—   I was not in the encampments myself but heard that there were a good many troops at Shelbaville, heard there were some troops Encamped at Fall creek and along the road from there to Unionville—   There was a Skirmish at Rover the day I came past (the 4th)   I was in the woods there three days before I could get through the lines—was within hereing of the skirmish,   I heard the Federals get the better of the Rebs & that they cap[d] 50 prisoners—   The Rebels say they are going to fight at Tulahoma,   They have brought a good many troops from Mississippi.   My master is a union man—told me to keep out of the way of the Rebels—but he has 2 sons in the rebel army—   I know he tried to prevent one of them from going,   My design is not to leave my master but want to go back when the Federals go—   Understand their aim is to send a heavy force of cav in rear of Federal Army to neighborhood of Lavergne when Tulahoma is attacked in order to cut off reinforcements—   They intend to Send Wheeler & I think Forrest—   I got the informtion from the Servants of the officers—

HDSr

his
Wiley × Thompson
mark

Statement of Wiley Thompson, 12 Mar. 1863, T 1863, Letters Received, ser. 925, Dept. of the Cumberland, RG 393 Pt. 1 [C-24].

105: Commander of an Iowa Regiment to the Headquarters of the Department of the Tennessee

Biggs plantation [*Miss.*] Mar. 26 /63

Colonel   I send you Seven Contrabands who came over from Vicksburg last night.   The men are bright and inteligent and can give us a great deal of information in regard to the Condition of affairs at Vicksburg.   One of them has been in the Artilery service since the war and can tell you the possition & numbers of almost every gun from Vicksburg down to Warrenton. They seem to be well posted and brought yesterdays Vicksburg & Jackson papers which I have already handed over to Genl Grant. The desire to go North, have money to pay there way I hope that Genl. Grants permission may be obtained for them to do so. You will of course examine them closely as to what they know about matters at Vicksburg, & if approved of by Genl. Grant, I hope you will aid them in leaving for the North I am Colonel Very Respectfuly your obᵗ servt

Charles H Abbott

P.S. Genl. Grant desires that you keep them until he returns Yrs Truly C. H. Abbott Col. &C.

ALS

Col. Charles H. Abbott to Col. Jno. A. Rawlins, 26 Mar. 1863, A-68 1863, Letters Received, ser. 4720, Dept. of the TN, RG 393 Pt. 1 [C-2005].

106: Commander of the 1st Division of the 16th Army Corps to the Headquarters of the 16th Army Corps

Lagrange, Tenn., March 27ᵗʰ *1863*.

Sir I wrote a few days ago asking instructions with regard to the large number of contrabands now finding their way into our Camps— The evil is a most perplexing one. Whole families of them are stampeding and leaving their masters, and I am applied to daily for the return of those belonging to loyal Masters. I know that our General Orders do not permit me to yield to such applications: but something should be done to shield our service from the charge of furnishing an Asylum to the Servants of loyal men living in districts not affected by the emancipation proclamation. Very Respectfully Your obedt Servt.

HLS
Wᵐ Sooy Smith

Brig. Gen. Wm. Sooy Smith to Lieut. Col. Binmore, 27 Mar. 1863, #1581 1863, Letters Received, ser. 391, 16th Army Corps, RG 393 Pt. 2 No. 7 [C-8605]. Smith's earlier letter had reported: "There is a very large number of Contrabands collected here and at Grand Junction subsisting upon Government Stores and not employed for any useful purpose so far as I can learn. The majority of them are unfit for labor, being women and children and super-annuated slaves. Some of them are the property of Citizens of Tennessee and so do not come within the action of the emancipation proclamation, while others are the property of citizens of Alabama and Mississippi. Some belong to loyal and some to disloyal owners. A great many of them are said to be sick and dying. Their presence in the immediate vicinity of our troops is demoralizing in the extreme, giving rise to licentiousness of the lowest and most degrading kind, while it affords an inducement of the strongest character to kidnapping Guerrillas to make dashes at the posts where so many slaves are congregated." (Brig. Gen. Wm. Sooy Smith to Capt. Henry Binmore, 23 Mar. 1863, #1409 1863, Letters Received, ser. 391, 16th Army Corps, RG 393 Pt. 2 No. 7 [C-8605].) No reply to either of Smith's letters has been found in the records of the 16th Army Corps.

107: Commander of the 16th Army Corps to the President

Memphis   March 27. [*1863*]

Sir   I avail myself of the fact that Mr Leatherman a prominent Citizen of Memphis is about to visit Washington – to lay before the Commander in Chief the serious difficulties which enbarrass the Citizens of this region as well as the army in relation to Negroes

There are within the limits of my command about five thousand Negroes male & female & of all ages supported by the Government independent of those regularly organized & employed as teamsters cooks pioneers &c and enrolled as such.

Most of these say from two thirds to three fourths are women & Children incapable of army labor, a weight and incumbrance.

In addition there is a very large number not less in Memphis alone than 2,000 – not supported by the Government crowded into all vacant sheds and houses living by begging or vice the victims and the fruitful source of contagion and pestilence.

Pilfering & small crimes are of daily occurrence among them & I see nothing before them but disease and death.

At the same time many valuable farms and plantations within our lines despoiled of fences from the necessities of a winter campaign – deprived of customary servile labor, stripped of horses & mules either from the needs of regular service or by marauding guerillas lie waste and desolate.   The owners are ready to cultivate but have no labor.   It is Spring – the time to put in crops – either of cotton or of corn or what is not least in a military point of view those garden vegetables the free use of which is so singularly beneficial to the health of an army.

None of these things are done except on the most limited scale

The land is here ready –   The labor is here but I know no authority which I possess to bring them together

There are many here who point out and desire to hire those who were their slaves — I have no power to permit it or rather none to enforce the contract if entered into.

There are no Civil or Criminal Courts and hence the responsibility of the Commanding Officer already heavy enough is enhanced by the want of aid from loyal tribunals.

I believe from careful examination and patient reflection that the condition of the fugitives would be improved in every respect by causing them to be hired either for wages or for clothing subsistence and an equivalent in the crop to such persons as would give bond to take care of them and put them at such work as they can do, and enforcing the contract of hire on both parties.

It is however not to be denied that a very serious risk must be run in so doing. The spirit of marauding and robbery which gave rise to Guerilla parties grows by use & there is danger that they may be seized and run off to some portion of the South as yet not under our Control or it may be that parties obtaining them may misuse their power over them, although I feel less apprehension of the latter.

If the fugitives now lurking about Memphis could return to their homes in the City & vicinity and their former owners would receive them and treat them kindly until the final determination of their status much of the misery and vice which infests the City & vicinage would be removed.

In the present anomalous situation of the State of Tennessee neither exactly loyal nor altogether disloyal, but yet wholly deprived of all the Machinery by which Civil Government operates, it is impossible for any one to say whether the State of Slavery exists or not. The laws of Tennessee recognize and establish it — but the law is in abeyance. No judges to interpret and administer, no sheriff to execute, no posse to enforce.

The State is exempted from the effects of the Proclamation, but the Military authorities both from choice and under orders ignore the condition of Slavery. If they come within our lines we allow them so to do, if they voluntarily go out we allow, and all this works no difficulty when troops are in the field in their limited Camps. But when the lines inclose a vast space of country or fence in as here a great city this incursion of ungoverned persons without employment and subject to no discipline becomes vitally serious, especially where the police and administration of justice are thrust upon Officers of the Army. The evil is pressing, the necessity for prompt action paramount both from feelings of humanity to the people around us and to relieve the Army from this burden.

I have not considered myself at liberty to adopt any course. It is difficult for me to reach my Department Commander and it is doubtful whether his pressing duties would leave him time to decide. It was hoped Congress would adopt some plan of the kind—this has not been done.

The question is one not purely Military and I respectfully submit to the President the Establishment of some general rule by which this difficulty may be overcome   I am very Respy Your Obt Servt

ALS   S. A. Hurlbut

[*Endorsement*] War Department Washington April 16. 1863   The within letter has been referred by the President to this Department with directions to say in answer thereto as follows.

"The within discusses a difficult subject—the most difficult with which we have to deal. The able bodied male contrabands are already employed by the Army. But the rest are in confusion and destitution. They had better be set to digging their subsistence out of the ground. If there are plantations near you on either side of the river, which are abandoned by their owners, first put as many contrabands on such as they will hold—that is, as can draw subsistence from them. If some still remain, get loyal men of character in the vicinity to take them temporarily on wages to be paid to the contrabands themselves—such men obliging themselves to not let the contrabands be kidnapped or forcibly carried away. Of course if any contrabands voluntarily make arrangements to work for their living you will not hinder them. It is thought best to leave details to your discretion subject to the provisions of the Acts of Congress and the orders of the War Department"   By order of the President   Edwin M Stanton Secretary of War

Maj. Genl. S. A. Hurlbut to the President of the U. States, 27 Mar. [1863], enclosed in Edwin M. Stanton to Major General Hurlbut, 18 Apr. 1863, #5333 1863, Letters Received, ser. 391, 16th Army Corps, RG 393 Pt. 2 No. 7 [C-8621]. On April 4, 1863, Adjutant General Lorenzo Thomas informed the Secretary of War that he had just arrived in Memphis and explained to Hurlbut "the policy of the Administration respecting the contrabands." "General Hurlbut," Thomas reported, "is embarrassed with the runaways from their Tennessee masters. They come here in a state of destitution, especially the women and children. He cannot send them back, and I advise their employment as far as possible by the quartermaster, and the general is authorized by General Grant to hire them to citizens who will give proper bonds." (*Official Records*, ser. 3, vol. 3, p. 116.)

108: Commander of a Wisconsin Regiment to the Headquarters of the Department of the Tennessee

Grand Gulf Miss. May 24th 1863

Col. I have recd. to day "Contraband" intelligence from two different sources – that a battle was fought *near* Baton Rouge Miss. on *Thursday* last – in which the *rebels* were *defeated* – I give it for what it is worth – There is over two thousand negroes here women & Children without Shelter – also several hundred Horses & Mules – I desire to know if they could not be sent to Youngs Point – Since Wednesday last, I have sent 41 prisoners to Youngs Point – Stragglers that have come across Black River – Many of the wounded & paroled prisoners at Port Gibson are well and with the paroled nurses there *are* behaving *badly* – they have armed them *selfes* & patrol the Country to prevent the negroes coming here – I send this to *you direct* – as I dont know where Gen. Sherman is   Your Obt Srvt

ALS   G E Bryant

Col. G. E. Bryant to A.A.G. Rawlins, 24 May 1863, B-330 1863, Letters Received, ser. 4720, Dept. of the TN, RG 393 Pt. 1 [C-2160]. Bryant commanded the 12th Wisconsin Infantry.

109: Affidavit of a Tennessee Freedwoman

Memphis Tenn August 10th *1865.*

Personally appeared before me Edward R Beach 1st Lieutenant and Acting Adjutant 88th USC Infy. Mrs Amey Carrington (colored) who after being duly qualified according to law testified as follows.

On or about the 27th day of June 1863, I was driven from home at Germantown Tenn by my master Mr Larodes – without provication. I immediately went to Memphis Tenn where my husband was living at the time. I was in a miserable-destitute condition with hardly enough clothing to cover my nakedness. and have received no mony or clothing from my master since December 1860. I left my children (four in number) with my master who hired them out. and has received compensation for their services since July 1863. I had made several efforts since I was driven from home to get posession of my children but failed in every instance until the 23rd day of July 1865, when I succeeded in finding them and with the assistance of Lieut Col Wedelstandt Asst. Topl Engineer D.W.T. brought them to Memphis Tenn   My children were in a destitute condition with hardly any clothing on them and had ben treated in a brutal manner. My children nor my self have not received mony or clothing as compensation for their services. HD

Affidavit of Amey Carrington, 10 Aug. 1865, Affidavits & Statements, ser. 3545, Memphis TN Provost Marshal of Freedmen, RG 105 [A-6593].

110: **Adjutant General of the Army to the Secretary of War**

Cairo, Illinois, Augt 23. 1863.

Sir,   I arrived at this place this morning with General Grant, and shall return with him to-day or tomorrow to Vicksburg.

I have delayed making a report of the condition of affairs until I visited the several positions on the river. I was disappointed at finding but few negroes at Vicksburg, as they had been either absorbed by the several Departments as laborers, or taken to fill up the regiments previously organized. Of these regiments I get good accounts and some of them are in a high state of discipline. I visited Natchez, which at the present time is the best place for obtaining negroes, and gave orders for the immediate organization of two regiments, one as heavy Artillery to garrison Vicksburg, and also a Cavalry regiment to be mounted on mules. These animals can be obtained in great abundance.

I was fortunate in arriving at Memphis before General Steele left Helena for the interior of Arkansas as I was enabled to have him instructed to bring back all the blacks he could possibly gather, and sent recruiting officers with him. This expedition must give me a large number of men. A force also goes up Red River, and another from Goodrich's Landing back to bayou Macon, and their commanders are also instructed to collect the able bodied men, and in future such will be the standing orders. All the surplus blacks employed by the troops, or hovering round the Camps will be gathered up, General Grant having at my request issued such an order. He gives me every assistance in my work.

On arriving at Lake Providence on my way to Vicksburg, I found upwards of a thousand negroes, nearly all women and children, on the banks of the river, in a most helpless condition, who had left the plantations in consequence of the withdrawal of the troops on account of sickness. They had successfully sustained one attack of guerillas, aided by a gun-boat, but expected another attack. I took them all to Goodrich's Landing where there is a garrison of negro troops. The number of this helpless class in the various camps is very large and daily increasing, and altho' everything is done for their well being, I find that sickness prevails to an alarming extent, and the bills of mortality are very high. This results from their change of life and habits, from daily work to comparative idleness, and also from being congregated in large numbers in camps, which is a matter of necessity. Besides, they will not take care of themselves much less of those who are sick. I have therefore after much reflection and consultation with officers, come to the conclusion that the old men, women and children should be advised to remain on the plantations, especially on those within our lines where we can have an oversight of them. Besides, it is important that the crops on the plantations within our lines should be gathered. A number of those now in our camps express a desire to return to their old homes, and indeed many have already done so. All such will be encouraged to do so, in cases where we are satisfied their former masters will not run them off or sell them. I have conversed with a number of planters, several strong union men at Natchez especially, and they all express the opinion that slavery has received its death blow, and cannot again exist in regions passed over by our armies. They are perfectly willing to hire the negroes and adopt any policy the Government may dictate. Many citizens of Mississippi, Louisiana and Arkansas are desirous that their States should resume their position in the Union with laws providing for the emancipation of slaves in a limited number of years. This feeling is constantly increasing, even among those who were strong advocates of secession. They now see it is vain to resist our arms, and only see utter ruin to themselves as the war goes on.

It is important that woodyards should be established on the river, and General Grant is encouraging the measure. I will permit persons duly authorized to cut wood for steamboats, to hire wood-choppers from those who are unfit for military service, including the women. It will be far more for their benefit to support themselves than to sit in idleness in camps depending on the Government for subsistence.

I have issued an order for general distribution in the armies of Generals Grant and Rosencrans setting forth some of the above points, a copy of which is enclosed – special Order No 45. – [1]

I should be pleased to receive your instructions if my action is in any respect not in accordance with your views. The subject is now assuming vast proportions, and while I will do every thing in my power to carry out the policy of the administration and support the Government, I feel that my responsibilities are great and need the advice of my superiors.

A large amount of clothing will be needed for the women and

children, and as such clothing is not provided by the Government, I propose to appeal to the benevolent for a supply. From this point the government boats can transport it without expence, but I desire your authority to pay the transportation to Cairo from the places where the clothing is provided. I have the honor to be, Very respectfully Your Obed. Svt.

ALcS

L. Thomas

Adjt. General L. Thomas to Hon. Edwin M. Stanton, 23 Aug. 1863, Letters Sent & Orders, L. Thomas Papers, Generals' Papers & Books, ser. 159, RG 94 [V-22].

1 Issued August 18, 1863, the order announced federal plans to enlist able-bodied black men into the army, to employ other contrabands capable of labor on the plantations, and to care for those incapable of labor at contraband camps. (*Official Records*, ser. 3, vol. 3, pp. 686–87.)

111: Freedmen's Bureau Assistant Superintendent at Chattanooga, Tennessee, to the Headquarters of the Tennessee Freedmen's Bureau Assistant Commissioner

Chatta [*Tenn.*], Nov. 10th 1865.
A.A. General: I have the honor to forward the following statement, and respectfully request instructions in the matter, as Jasper is only 25 miles from this Post.

A. L. Griffith, a lawyer, and discharged Union soldier, of Jasper, Tenn., came to this Office and made the following statement: —

"That T. G. Craighead, of Jasper, Tenn., owned many slaves, and, in 1863, at the approach of the Union army, he abandoned his property and fled South, giving his negroes to understand that if thay remained on his farm during the war, they should be entitled to all they could make.

In August last, Craighead returned home, took possession of his farm, and sued the negroes for the rent of his farm for this year, and received judgment against the negroes for $102.50, notwithstanding the testimony of 3 white men of Jasper, (Harmon Cox, H. P. Ramsey, and John Doss) to the effect that the presence and labor of the negroes on the farm during the war, was worth more than the rents of the farm.

The case was tried by John G. Kelley, Justice of Peace, for Marion County, Tenn.

After the decision, no appeal to the Circuit Court would be

granted, and the property of the Freedman has been attached to the amount of $102.50. I have the honor to be, Very Respectfully, Your Obd't Servant,

HLcSr

N. B. Lucas

Capt. N. B. Lucas to Major Jno. H. Cochrane, 10 Nov. 1865, vol. 93, Letters Sent, ser. 3445, Chattanooga TN Supt., RG 105 [A-6427]. Two months later, the Chattanooga Freedmen's Bureau agent adjudicated Craighead's claim against his former slaves, Richard Craighead, John Craighead, and Preston Craighead. Among other testimony taken in the case, Richard Craighead described his former master's unsuccessful effort to remove his slaves from the path of the advancing Union army: "I knew he could not force me to go along the roads from the fact the federals held all the roads at the time, so he would have to take us through the woods. When Mr. Craighead found I would not go, he told me to take my brothers and the rest of the colored families, and go on the farm, and that we might have all that we cold make while we lived on it." John Craighead testified that the slaves had made two crops while on the farm, cleaned up the property, cut trees, and built fences. In the end, Thomas G. Craighead relinquished his claim upon the freedmen's corn in return for their paying court costs. (Testimony in the case of Thos. G. Craighead vs. Richard Craighead, John Craighead, and Preston Craighead, 1 Jan. 1866, and certificate of T. G. Craighead, 3 Jan. 1866, Misc. Records, ser. 3457, Chattanooga TN Supt., RG 105 [A-6427].)

112: Order by the Provost Marshal General of the Department of the Cumberland

Chattanooga Tenn. Oct. 15 1863

Know all men by these Presents   That by reason of Section nine (9) of an act of Congress Entitled an act to make an additional article of War approved July 17th 1862[1] and by reason of satisfactory evidence this day filed in this office that the former owner of a colored man named Frank Wheeton is in rebellion against the Government of the United States and has abandoned the said slave the said Frank Wheeton is hereby declared to be forever free and all officers and Soldiers are commanded to respect him as such.   By Command of &c   Wm M. Wiles Lieut Col and Pro. Mar Genl.

HDc

Free paper issued to Frank Wheeton, 15 Oct. 1863, vol. 118 DC, p. 244, Letters & Telegrams Sent, ser. 1091, Provost Marshal, Dept. of the Cumberland, RG 393 Pt. 1 [C-401].

1 Clearly a reference to the Second Confiscation Act, despite the misleading title.

113: Testimony by a Tennessee Slaveholder before the
American Freedmen's Inquiry Commission

[*Nashville November 23, 1863*]
Testimony of Mrs. DeMoville.
This lady, (who chanced to be at the Governor's room while the
Commission was there,) said she had seven slaves, and would like to
know what was to be done with them. She thought it rather hard
to be obliged to take care of them, and pay their doctor's bills, if
she was not to receive anything in return. They were well clothed
and fed, their rooms nicely carpeted, and their beds comfortable,
and she said she would be willing to pay them wages; but they were
unwilling to stay, because they thought they would not be free
unless they went away. "They are all," said the lady, "devotedly
attached to me; but still, there is the desire for freedom, which you
know is very desirable to all."
HD

Testimony of Mrs. DeMoville before the American Freedmen's Inquiry Commission, [23 Nov. 1863], filed with O-328 1863, Letters Received, ser. 12,
RG 94 [K-97]. Topical labels in the margin are omitted.

114: Statement of a Tennessee Freedman

[*Jonesboro, Tenn. September 1865*]
State ment of asbery Loughlin
Freed man of coulor: who saw his [*Richard Griffin's*] legs cut off by
Dr Williams and Dr Joseph Clark   I know that Richard thomas
Griffin: worked for William. G. Gammon at knoxville and
afterwards at Jonesborough; was most in humanly treated all the
time by gammon; so much so that griffins friends Both white an
coulord told him often to leave gammon and make his way to the
federal army at knoxville if he could   in the month of Dec (63) or
January 64) I donot know precisely which he was sick and gammon
ordered him out with a team   he was not able to drive a team: and
he attempted to get a way to knoxville   But Capt gammon sent
men after him and: he hird of them being after him and he had to
hide out in the freesing cold weather from them till his feet got
frost biten prety Bad; when he came in: finding he could not get

through the lines without being caught he came in: he was
informed by William R Boyed and other that gammon was going to
whip him unmerciful, and he left town a gain and laid out two or
three days in the Biterest cold wether I ever knew in my life they
found him and Braught him in and I saw them cut his feet off in
the Basement story of the court house: they did not try to do any
thing to take the frost out of his feet; But cut them off left him
laying on the floor whear it was done: till the next day myself and
others fixed a Bunk and put him on that I attend to him myself 8
or 10 days [theare] it was cold freesing weather all the time —
the doctor nor gammon never dressed his legs but once after they
ware cut off Williams said to him I thought it would kill you
dick but I believe you will get well; or I believe you will live: after
eight or ten days gammon sent him to Minerva dangerfields and
told her she had to keep him; which She did for fifteen or eighteen
months for which She never got one sent of pay

I do know that gammon was the cause of all his misfortune; or at
least him and Dr. Williams; I have Stated nothing But the truth in
the above: which can be proven by many others

HDSr   asbery loghlin

Statement of asbery loghlin, [Sept. 1865], enclosed in S. E. Griffith to Genl.
Clinton B. Fisk, 18 Sept. 1865, G-47 1865, Registered Letters Received, ser.
3379, TN Asst. Comr., RG 105 [A-6018]. In the handwriting of the Freedmen's Bureau agent at Jonesboro, Tennessee. On October 10, 1865, the
assistant commissioner of the Freedmen's Bureau in Tennessee forwarded
copies of the statements of Loghlin and others to the Freedmen's Bureau
commissioner, with the following appraisal: "I am of the opinion that Griffin
was most cruelly and barbarously treated. It could not have been necessary to
amputate his feet. I am of the opinion that the fiendish outrage was perpetrated in order to terrify and intimidate the colored people thereby preventing
them from making attempts to escape to the Union lines. The villains who
committed the great wrong should be arrested and punished for their crimes."
On January 18, 1866, Joseph Holt, judge advocate general of the army,
recommended to the Secretary of War that the perpetrators be tried by a
military commission. Upon further investigation, however, General Alvan C.
Gillem, commander of the District of East Tennessee, concluded on March 1,
1866, that on the basis of the evidence collected, the physicians "could not be
convicted of mal practice or cruelty" and Gammon now lived beyond the
limits of Gillem's district. Thereupon the proceedings apparently terminated.
(Documents filed with K-15 1865, Letters Received, ser. 15, Washington
Hdqrs., RG 105 [A-6018].)

115A: **Clipping from a Religious Journal**

[*Pittsburgh, Pa. March 1864*]
LETTER FROM REV. JOSIAS STEVENSON.
Camp Holly Springs, Memphis, Tenn., February 18, 1864.
BROTHER KERR: — I had thought the day was past for such a humiliating scene as we witnessed in our camp this morning. The facts, as carefully as I could gather them, are these: A man by the name of Wheaten lives some two miles south of Memphis. I am told by those who had a good opportunity of knowing, that he was a noted secessionist during secesh rule; and that none was more zealous in the cause of rebellion, and did more, according to his ability and means, for the destruction of our Government than this same Wheaton. But when Federal authority was re-established in this part of Tennessee, he professed to be a Union man, and as such obtained a guard of Union soldiers to stand in his yard to keep our soldiers from his hen-roost and smoke-house, and to keep his young slaves from running off. This Wheaten has three slaves, children of John and Pauline Christian, living in this camp. An attempt was made last summer to get the children and bring them into camp, but failed. So, yesterday, the father of these children, knowing that since Brig. Gen. Veatch left there were no soldiers in old Dr. Wheaten's yard, took two black men with him, and watching their opportunity, they caught the children and ran off with them. But as they were getting out of the yard they were discovered.

Wheaton, knowing where the children would be brought, went immediately to see Brig. Gen. Buckland, of Ohio, now commander of this post in the place of Gen. Veatch, who left with Sherman's expedition. The old quondam traitor, but now a very loyal(?) man, doubtless tells a fair story; most likely represents that white men in Holly Springs are at the bottom of it, and should be punished. However this may be, it would seem that he enlisted the General's sympathies in his behalf, for he immediately sent down one of his staff with the doctor, bearing imperative orders for Captain Hay, the commander of the camp, to deliver to Dr. Wheaten the three children belonging to him. The captain could give them no information about the children, but granted them full privilege to go through the camp, and if they could find the children to take them.

What a fine subject for a painter was this! Dr. Wheaten, a slaveholder, and formerly, from the testimony of those who lived with him, a *traitor*, and Brig.-Gen. Buckland's aid-de-camp ride through our camp in a splendid carriage, and attended by three orderlies, in search of three children, aged respectively about ten, eight, and six years, who had been brought home to their father's house. They rode up to John Christian's door, but neither father nor children could be found. After searching through camp awhile, and not finding the children, they return to Captain Hay and command him to get the children or they would report him to Gen. Buckland. The captain replied that he did not know where the children were, had not seen them since they came into camp, and he would not search for them.

In an hour or two another aid-de-camp came down in great haste and style, with an order commanding Captain Hay to report in person forthwith at the headquarters of Brig. General Buckland. Capt. Hay promptly obeyed, and was told by the general, in the presence of Dr. Wheaten, that he would give him to 9 o'clock the next morning to deliver the three children to Wheaten, their owner, or he must report there and be put in close confinement. And had it not been that the captain was thus bound for the sure delivery of the children, they would have been missing this morning too. But the aid-de-camp came down this morning in his carriage and bore off the children from weeping and agonizing parents as triumphantly as was ever done in these States when the whole nation groaned and reeled under the rule of such men as this loyal(?) slaveholder. And you will bear in mind that John Christian, the father of these children, is a soldier in the service of our country.

. . . .

Now, does not this virtually make these contraband camps, authorized, sanctioned and sustained by the general Government, *slave-pens* for collecting and retaining fugitive slaves until their *loyal* masters when they are tired of their mad efforts to destroy our beloved country, can come prove *property*, and carry them off in triumph?

If this is the way these "contraband camps" are going to be managed, what encouragement is there for slaves to run away from their masters, and thus cease producing for rebels in the field? And if the wives and children of black men are liable to be remanded back to slavery, what encouragement is there for them to enlist as soldiers in their country's service, and lay their lives upon their country's altar?

. . . .

PD JOSIAS STEVENSON.

315

Excerpts from clipping from *United Presbyterian*, [Mar. 1864], enclosed in Robert George to Hon. E. M. Stanton, 20 Mar. 1864, G-451 1864, Letters Received, RG 107 [L-44]. Six paragraphs of the clipping have been omitted.

115B: Commander of the District of Memphis to a Tennessee Attorney

Memphis Tenn 23^d Feby 1864

Dear Sir   I am in receipt of your note of yesterday in regard to certain colored children said to have been taken by my order from their father, a colored soldier and restored to a slave owner as his property.   Those children were forcibly taken from the residence of Dr. Wheaton in his absence by armed soldiers and against the wishes of the children, contrary to the written prohibition of Maj. Gen. Hurlbut.   I ordered them returned because they were forcibly taken away in violation of Military discipline and because I was well satisfied from my own knowledge and from information derived from others that it would be for the good of the children.   They are well cared for and kindly treated in the family of Dr. Wheaton.   They were not returned as slaves, nor do I believe they will ever be slaves.   I do not believe that the Government will permit the children of its soldiers to be slaves   I consider slavery as virtually abolished in Tennessee never to be renewed, and I had not the remotest idea of these children being treated as slaves, nor do I believe they will be.   I have never in my life been instrumental in returning a fugitive slave to slavery and no earthly power can compel or induce me to do that act   Yours Truly

HLcSr   R P Buckland

Brig. General R. P. Buckland to M. D. Lauden, Esq., 23 Feb. 1864, vol. 16/25 DWT, pp. 198–99, Letters Sent, ser. 2837, Dist. of Memphis, RG 393 Pt. 2 No. 181 [C-8504].

115C: Superintendent of the Organization of Tennessee Black Troops to the Headquarters of the 16th Army Corps

Memphis   12$''$ April 1864.

Sir: In compliance with request of Maj Genl S. A. Hurlbut made to me in communication dated Memphis Tenn 9$''$ April 1864.

In June or July of last year 1863 – Dr Wheaton a citizen living near Memphis and inside the picket lines sent two of his negro servants one man and one woman (man & wife) to the Freedmans camp with orders not to return under any circumstances – Three Children belongig to th woman one a boy some 10 years of age and two girls 4 and 7 years of age respectivly were kept by Dr Wheaton. For some seven months after this, neither the husband or wife saw the children.

In February last the husband, then a soldier in the US Service in Company with two other solders Colored, went to the house of Dr Wheaton situated about one half mile distant from the camp and during his absence took away the children brought them into camp and concealed them An order was issued by Brig Genl Buckland, Comdg Dist of Memphis to the officer in command of the freedmans camp to return the children forthwith to Dr Wheaton. After some delay the children were found and amid the tears and prostestations of the mother – were returned to Dr Wheaton where they now are. The husband and wife during the past winter lived in a log house or hut and were quite comfortable

The husband is now on duty at Lake St. "Joe," Arkansas, and the wife, who has a child some six months old, is on a plantation near Goodriches Landing working for wages having been sent there by order of the officer in charge of the Freedmen of Dist of Memphis. The children are now as above stated in the custody of Dr Wheaton and as he states held by him subject to the order of the comdg Officer Dist of Memphis. They are in good health – well clothed and well cared for generally.

The mother is charged with abusing her children at times when with Dr Wheaton but while in Camp she is said to have conducted herself with propriety. The foregoing facts I have obtained from Dr Wheaton – Capt Hay (who for some time past has commanded the Freedmans Camp at "Holly Springs") Mrs Hay – his wife Sergt Harrison – now on duty in Camp Holly Springs. – and others.

After carefully investigating this matter I am of the opinion that Capt Hay did not treat General Buckland's order for the return of the children with disrespect but on the contrary, used reasonable diligence in searching for the children.

It is proved that the children were not brought into the Camp immediately by the father but were concealed in the vacinity.

Capt Hay did not see the children until they were brought up and delivered to Dr Wheaton   I have the honor to be Your Obt Serv't.

HLc   [*Augustus L. Chetlain*]

Brig. General [Augustus L. Chetlain] to Lieut. Col. T. H. Harris, 12 Apr. 1864, vol. 34/60 DWT, pp. 38–39, Letters Sent, ser. 2907, Organization of U.S. Colored Troops, Dist. of West TN, RG 393 Pt. 2 No. 183 [C-2208].

116: Provost Marshal at Nashville to the Provost Marshal of the District of Nashville

Nashville Tenn Feby 27 /64

While riding along Cedar St in this city today on the way to my office I overtook a lady riding in a buggy with a Negro girl while behind the buggy with her arms securely tied behind her walked a negro woman with a man beside her apparantly guarding her

This unusual spectacle attracted my attention and I at once accosted the man and demanded to know by what authority this woman was being conducted along the streets in this manner. He immediately produced a written permit or what purported to be such to one Mrs Baker to take the two Negro women to her home mentioned by name and forbidding any civil or military authority to interfere with her in so doing. Said permit was dated "Head Qr^s District Nashville Feby 4th 1864" and signed "By command of Maj Gen Rousseau H Tompkins 1st Lt 19th Mich^n and A Pro Mar"; Although the act of their returning a fugitive from labor (as the man confessed the woman to be) was evidently in contravention of the acts of Congress and a violation of the highest Military authority of the land as set forth in the Proclamation of the President of the United States in as much as it appeared to bear the sanction of superior Military authority I did not interfere but handed back the permit after reading and permitted the party to proceed— Shortly after reaching my office the aforementioned party were brought me by a guard under arrest. The guard informed me that they had been arrested by the officer in charge of the guard at the Bridge at the river for attempting to pass there the Negro women having no passes and the white man insisting upon his right to take them across on his permit which he exhibited to me being the one I had seen before and which was in form and language as follows

"Hd Qr^s District Nashville
Nashville Tenn Feby 4th 1864

"Copy."

Permission is hereby granted to Mrs S. F. Baker of Davidson County Tenn to take to her home the following Negro women Hannah and

Becky (2). Mrs Baker is a good loyal lady and the General
Commanding directs that she will not be interferred with by any
authority either civil or military.

By Command of Maj Gen Rousseau
H Tompkins 1st Lt 19th Mich^{n} and A Pro Mar"

In answer to my interrogations Mr^{s} Baker informed me that
Hannah and Becky were both her servants—that Hannah had run
away about three months before Christmas and came to
Nashville—that Becky was sent to Nashville on an errand Christmas
and had never came back—that they were both unwilling to go back
and that she had to go to Gen Rousseau to get permission to take
them—both the negro women declaring in my pressence their
unwillingness to return— Baker then asked that I would give him a
pass for the two negro women through the lines which I refused to
do informing him that for any officer to assist in any manner
directly or indirectly in returning to slavery fugitives from labor was
a violation of the highest Military authority— I then released the
Entire party from arrest— Baker in committing this outrage has
undoubtedly abused his permit as the General Commanding District
most certainly did not intend to authorize the return and surrender
by force and violence of a fugitive from labor.— I beg that the
attention of the proper authorities may be called to this brutal and
revolting act in order that this fellow Baker may be fitly punished
for subjecting a civilized and Christian city to the humiliating
spectacle of a women chained and pinioned and driven along the
streets. Very Respectfully

HLcS

John W Horner

Major John W. Horner to Maj. W. R. Rowley, 27 Feb. 1864, vol. 239
DMT, pp. 92–94, Letters Sent by the Provost Marshal, ser. 1655, Nashville
TN, Provost Marshal Field Organizations, RG 393 Pt. 4 [C-2063].

117: Tennessee Unionist to the Commander of the District of Nashville

Shelbyville [*Tenn.*] March 16 1864
Dear Sir   The officers Belonging to General Slocum Command
Stationed at this place Seem to Regard the Order Issued by your
adjutant By direction of General Thomas[1] as though It was a Mere
Nullity   having to Forage from this place on the Return of their
Waggons Almost Every Trip a Considered portion of thier Waggon
are Loaden with Negro Women & Children &cr.   One Instance Last
Friday they Compelled by force a Citizen to Lead up his own

Waggon & Take his Negros to a place Near. Petersburg in Lincoln
County   the gentleman from whom they Took th Negroes is by th
name of Robert M^{c}euen and they already have our place crowded
with Negro women who are Strutting about doing Nothing and are
quite a nusance   one of our Citizens Mr Jackson Greer had A negro
man to leave Home on Last Thursday night & Came to this place;
Mr Greer finding the Course of the Negro Came to Town to
Asscertain If he Could Turn the Negro over to the Service and was
anxious to do so but was not permitted to do so & Even Grossely
Insulted & thretened that If he persisted he would have him
arrested   The Policy pursued by these Men toward both Union &
Loyal Men are having a very bad Effect   they pretend on Many
occasions to say such & such Negros are in Govemt Employ   they
Mean practically that Sutlers & officers have them in their use &
Employmt for their own Special use.

ALS   Joseph Ramsy

Joseph Ramsy to General Rousseau, 16 Mar. 1864, Letters & Reports Received, ser. 2922, Dist. of Nashville, RG 393 Pt. 2 No. 184 [C-2034].
Endorsements. In the same file is a report by the commander of the post of
Shelbyville: "The officers of this command have no negroes in their employ for
any purpose whatever, except one or two small boys for boot blacking. On the
contrary they prefer to employ *white* servants." (Maj. L. Baldwin to Lt. Col.
H. C. Rodgers, 26 Mar. 1864.)

1 On February 17, 1864, in accordance with instructions from General
George H. Thomas, commander of the Department of the Cumberland, General Lovell H. Rousseau, commander of the District of Nashville, had issued
an order that admonished federal forces to "have as little to do with slaves as
may be in the discharge of their duties as soldiers, it being considered best to
allow masters & slaves to settle their own affairs without military interference." Rousseau prohibited the soldiers from "taking from their homes old
men and negro women and children," and masters from sending such slaves to
Union authorities "to get rid of their support, and to make them a burden to
the Government." (General Orders No. 8, Head Quarters Dist. of Nashville,
17 Feb. 1864, vol. 9 DMT, pp. 23–24, General Orders Issued, ser. 2923,
Dist. of Nashville, RG 393 Pt. 2 No. 184 [C-2034].)

118: Affidavit of a Tennessee Fugitive Slave

[Knoxville, Tenn. March 30, 1864]
Statement of "Jim" Heiskell

My name is Jim; I have been living on Bull run, with a man by
the name of Pierce; they called him Cromwell Pierce. I run off

320

from him nearly two months ago, because he treated me so mean: he half starved and whipped me. I was whipped three or four times a week, sometimes with a cowhide, and sometimes with a hickory. He put so much work on me, I could not do it; chopping & hauling wood and lumber logs. I am about thirteen years old. I got a pretty good meal at dinner, but he only gave us a half pint of milk for breakfast and supper, with cornbread. I ran away to town; I had a brother "Bob" living in Knoxville, and other boys I knew. I would have staid on the plantation if I had been well used. I wanted also to see some pleasure in town. I hired myself to Capt. Smith as a servant, and went to work as a waiter in Quarter Master Winslow's office as a waiter for the mess. After Capt. Winslow went home, I went to live with Bob, helping him.

Last Friday just after dinner, I saw Pierce Mr. Heiskell's overseer. He caught me on Gay street, he ran after me, and carried me down Cumberland street to Mr. Heiskell's house. Mr. Heiskell, his wife and two sons, and a daughter were in the house. Mr. Heiskell asked me what made me run away; he grabbed me by the back of the ears, and jerked me down on the floor on my face; Mr. Pierce held me & Mr. Heiskell put irons on my legs. Mr. Heiskell took me by the hair of my head, and Mr. Pierce took me around my body, they carried me upstairs, and then Mr. Heiskell dagged me into a room by my hair. They made me stand up, and then they laid me down on my belly & pulled off my breeches as far as they could, and turned my shirt and jacket up over my head. (I heard Mr Heiskell ask for the cowhide before he started with me upstairs.) Mr. Pierce held my legs, and Mr. Heiskell got a straddle of me, and whipped me with the rawhide on my back & legs. Mr. Pierce is a large man, and very strong. Mr. Heiskell rested two or three times, and begun again. I hollowed – "O, Lord" all the time. They whipped me, it seemed to me, half an hour. They then told me to get up and dress, and said if I did'nt behave myself up there they would come up again and whip me again at night. The irons were left on my legs. Mr. Heiskell came up at dark and asked me what that "yellow nigger was talking to me about". He meant my brother Bob, who had been talking to me opposite the house. I was standing up and when he (Mr. Heiskell) asked me about the "yaller nigger", he kicked me with his right foot on my hip and knocked me over on the floor, as the irons were on my feet, I could not catch myself. I knew my brother Bob was around the house trying to get me out. About one hour by sun two soldiers came to the house, one staid & the other went away. I saw them through the window. They had sabres. I thought they had come to guard me to keep Bob from getting me. I heard Bob whisling, and I went to the window and looked through the curtain. Bob told me to hoist the window, put something under it & swing out of the window. I did as my brother told me, and hung by my hands. Bob said "Drop," but I said I was afraid I would hurt myself. Bob said "Wait a minute and I will get a ladder". He brought a ladder and put it against the house, under the window. I got halfway down before they hoisted the window; I fell & Bob caught me and run off with me in his arms. I saw Mr. Pierce sitting at the window, he had a double-barreled gun in his hands. By the time I could count three I heard a gun fired two or three times, quick, I heard Mr. Pierce call "Jim" "Jim" and the guards hollered "halt; halt!" I had no hat or shoes on. We both hid, and laid flat on the ground. I saw the guard, running around there hunting for us. After lying there until the guards had gone away, we got up and Bob carried me to a friend's house. I had the irons on my legs. I got some supper and staid there until next day. My irons were taken off by a colored man, who carried me to the hospital. I am now employed working in the hospital N° 1.

his
−signed− Jim × Heiskell −
mark

HDcSr

Affidavit of Jim Heiskell, [30 Mar. 1864], Records of the General Agent, RG 366 [Q-135]. Sworn before the army post commander. In the same file are a report by the provost marshal general of east Tennessee regarding the arrest of Bob Heiskell for threatening the life of his former master, and a statement by a surgeon in a black regiment describing the nature and extent of Jim Heiskell's injuries. (B.G. S. P. Carter to Maj. J. A. Campbell, 26 Mar. 1864; statement of Surgeon Ralph W. Cummings, 30 Mar. 1864.) Another letter in the file, written by Treasury Department assistant special agent William G. Brownlow, described William Heiskell as "an Honorable man . . . a Slave holder all his days . . . notorious for his kind treatment of his Slaves." According to Brownlow, William Heiskell was worth approximately $100,000 at the beginning of the war "and now he is reduced to poverty and lives alone off of his office, or salary as Local Agent." Brownlow explained the slaveholder's actions thus: "The Boy 'Robert' was walking these Streets with a revolver in hand and threatening the life of Mr Heiskell as he would go to and from his meals. He also planted himself on the Street opposite to Mr Heiskells house, and cursed Mrs Heiskell for a d----d old freckled faced bitch. The community irrespective of parties would have sustained Mr Heiskell if he had put a load of buckshot into him!" (W. G. Brownlow to W. P. Mellen, Esq., 20 May 1864.)

119: Affidavit of a Tennessee Freedman

Memphis, Tenn., Sept 13th *1865.*

Statement of Archy Vaughn. Last spring [*1864*] I was living with *Bartlet Ciles* about 8 miles from Somerville—near McCulloughs and one eving some Confederate soldiers or Guerillas came along and he told me to feed their horses. and I was at the barn gitting corn. and staied longer than he thought I should and when I went back to the house—he told me he was going to whip me in the morning— that night I took an old mare and went to the ferry across Wolf River. I was going to Laffayette Depot to get into the federal lines and Andrew Johnson who lives close to the ferry. took me and kept me until Billy Simons came along and he gave me to him to carry me back to Bartlet Ciles. When he Ciles took me down to the woods. and tied my hands, and pulled them over my knees and put a stick through under my knees. and then took his knife and *castrated* me and then cut off the lop of my left ear, he made a colord man named Dallas help hold me— he drove me off from his plantation some time in June—I think.

HDSr

his

Archy × Vaughn

mark

Affidavit of Archy Vaughn, 13 Sept. 1865, Affidavits & Statements, ser. 3545, Memphis TN Provost Marshal of Freedmen, RG 105 [A-6287]. Sworn before the assistant provost marshal of freedmen. The names of five witnesses to the assault are appended. Endorsements indicate that Freedmen's Bureau authorities in Memphis investigated the case but took no further action at that time. Early in 1866, however, the bureau superintendent at LaGrange, Tennessee, forwarded additional testimony in the case (a portion of which dated the incident as having taken place in January or February 1864) to the Tennessee assistant commissioner's headquarters. A staff officer replied: "One blushes for humanity when he reads the record you give of the case. You should arrest Kyle, fine him heavily, and compel him to pay exemplary damages to the boy. 'Castration' and 'ear cropping' are crimes which ought to call down the vengeance of the civil law, but the consciences of our civil authorities, in matters in which negroes are concerned, appear to be callous." (S. H. Melcher to Lieut. J. F. Alden, 16 Jan. 1866, enclosing testimony in the case of Bureau vs. Bartlett Kyle, 16 Jan. 1866, M-19 1866, Registered Letters Received, ser. 3379, TN Asst. Comr., RG 105 [A-6287]; Bt. Lt. Col. J. E. Jacobs to S. H. Melcher, 28 Jan. 1866, vol. 9, p. 217, Press Copies of Letters Sent, ser. 3373, TN Asst. Comr., RG 105 [A-6287].)

120: Commissioner for the Organization of Black Troops in Middle and East Tennessee to Special Commissioners Appointed by the Secretary of War

Nashville, Tenn. August 15th '64

Gentlemen   I have been informed that a military commission, of which Col. Sipes, 7th Pa. Cavalry was President, sitting at Columbia in this State, called to try several cases of enormous and flagrant abuses, of colored men and women by citizens of that place, has been dissolved leaving several of the cases untried; that in those cases where the accused were found guilty, the findings have been disapproved by the Reviewing Officer upon a legal technicality, while in those cases where the parties were acquitted, they have been approved   The Reviewing Officer is Major General Rousseau and he has all the papers

I earnestly intreat you to investigate them and not only these particular cases but the management of that post—relative to the "contraband" question, under the former Commanders Col. Mizener, 14th Michigan State, and Col Fauthauser, 98 Ill. (Mtd.) Infantry.   I am convinced that an investigation will show that,—

First; Slaves were surrendered to their owners by Col. Mizner in squads.

Second; These whipped and shot to death their slaves, and were not molested.

Third; Extraordinary favors were granted to secessionists.

Fourth; Displays of Loyalty by the blacks were frowned upon.

Fifth, A white man and his wife were banished from the Post, for buying a flag for the negroes to display upon the Fourth of July.

Sixth; The whole economy of the Post Commanders meeting the approval of Major General Rousseau was to discourage Freedom and Nationality

Among the case referred to by me are those of Major Andrews and young Pillow, the banished family is named Hoffman.

Reliable men in Columbia are Colonel Sipes 7th Pa. Cavalry, the Jailor Trewhilt, the Post Commandant Whelaw, or some such name.   I have the honor gentlemen, to be Your Obedient Servant

HLc   [Reuben D. Mussey]

Col. [Reuben D. Mussey] to Messrs. Hood & Bostwick, 15 Aug. 1864, vol. 221 DC, pp. 34–35, Letters Sent by the Commissioner, ser. 1141, Organization of U.S. Colored Troops, Dept. of the Cumberland, RG 393 Pt. 1 [C-43]. The special commissioners, Thomas Hood and S. W. Bostwick, had been appointed in June 1864 to investigate the condition and treatment of "colored refugees" in Tennessee and Kentucky. The commissioners' final report printed a slightly different version of Mussey's letter under the date of August 14 and spelled his name "Massey." On the basis of Mussey's allegations and other evidence, Hood and Bostwick concluded that General Lovell H. Rousseau, commander of the District of Nashville, had "done great injustice to the policy of the government in regard to colored refugees; great injustice to colored refugees themselves, and certainly great injustice to himself as an officer." "[H]is example," the commissioners charged, "is exercising a bad influence over subordinate military officers, of like pro-slavery tendencies, who are scattered all over Kentucky and Tennessee . . . to whom colored refugees must apply for protection and safe conduct to the camps provided for them." Bostwick and Hood condemned Rousseau as "wholly unfit for his present command, or for any command where the care and safety of colored refugees" might "become the subject of his official action." (Order by Edwin M. Stanton, 2 June 1864, W-731 1864, Letters Received, ser. 12, RG 94 [K-570]; U.S., Senate, "Report of the Commissioners of Investigation of Colored Refugees in Kentucky, Tennessee, and Alabama," *Senate Executive Documents*, 38th Cong., 2nd sess., No. 28.) The proceedings of the military commission whose findings were disapproved by Rousseau have not been found among the records of the judge advocate general.

121: Affidavit of a Mississippi Fugitive Slave

Vicksburg Sept 13th /64
Copy

Jack, *Cold* Being sworn, deposes & says— I was the slave of Wylie Boddy who lives 6 miles north of Jackson on the road to Canton. Miss— he owns a plantation & lives upon it, I left my home (at Boddys) Thursday sept 8th—five days ago—intending to make my escape & come to this city. I took my way thrgh the woods & cane brakes. swam Big Black River on Sunday evening (11th Inst) & came to this City yesterday. Before I left home I heard my master (he is a hard rebel) tell my mistress, that Forest was on the other side of Pearl river near or below Jackson with six (6) thousand cavly & right smart of artillery—& that Forest had a lot of boats on wagons (15 I think) & that Forest intended to cross Pearl river way down at some place & attack Natchez & then come up the river and attack Vicksburg on the south side of the city & take it if possible. I heard the son of my masters brother say that there was a right smart lot of cavalry at Livingston (above Yazoo City) He said it was all Cav'ly—no artillery, or Infantry— this son said he was up there & saw them come into Livingston, I did not hear him say who commanded them. I did not see any troops as I came through

325

the woods – only a few rebel scouts   I dodged them through the woods –   I have not been in Jackson for 4 weeks   when there I saw seven peices of artillery which I saw & examined,   the (witness stated that the diameter of the muzzle was about six inches)

his

Signed Jack ✕

mark

HDcSr

Affidavit of Jack, 13 Sept. 1864, V-36 1864, Letters Received, ser. 5515, Military Division of West MS, RG 393 Pt. 1 [C-832]. Sworn before an army provost marshal. Endorsement.

122: Affidavit of a Mississippi Freedman

Memphis, Tenn. October. 9th 1865

Nat. Green, a freedman, being duly sworn, deposes and says as follows, –

My name is Nat. Green, I am 23 years old. I was raised as a slave in the state of Mississippi   I was owned by Miss Betty Jones of De Soto County in that state, but I always worked for her brother Col. Thos. Jones of the same place,   I was working for Col. Jones in the year 1864,   in October of that year all his men servants left him, having been told by Union men that the were freed by Mr. Lincoln,   I was sick the night the others left or I would have left with them.   the next day Col. Jones told me if I would remain with him he would pay me and on this understanding I remained with him eight months, namely from October 1864 till the latter part of May 1865, for which I have never received any pay whatever,

When I left Col. Jones' place I left there a pig which I raised myself two or three months old which was of considerable value,   I could not take any thing with when I left,   Col. Jones having threatened my life I was obliged to leave in the night,

HD

Affidavit of Nat. Green, 9 Oct. 1865, Affidavits & Statements, ser. 3545, Memphis TN Provost Marshal of Freedmen, RG 105 [A-6598]. Sworn before an assistant provost marshal of freedmen. The provost marshal levied a judgment of $160 against Jones, the former owner. Jones countered with a claim for board and clothing against Green, his former slave, and the final outcome is not known. (Thomas B. Jones to Genl. Dudley, [Nov.? 1865], Affidavits & Statements, ser. 3545, Memphis TN Provost Marshal of Freedmen, RG 105 [A-6598].)

123: Affidavit of a Tennessee Freedman

Memphis Tenn. Dec. 12. 1865

Mackley Woods being duly sworn deposes and says as follows –
My name is Makey Woods. I am 43 years old. I have lived with
Mr. William Woods, of Hardaman County, Tennessee for about
twenty years. I was his slave. about three years ago when the
Union Army was in possession of Bolivar Tenn. and when nearly all
the Black people were leaving their Masters and going to the Union
Army Mr. Woods told me and such others as would stay with him
that he would give us *one fourth* of the crop that we would raise
while we stayed with him that he would clothe us and feed us and
pay our doctor's bills. Since which time Mr. Wood has given *me*
nothing but my clothing: about that time and soon after he made
this statement to us he ran off down South into the Rebel lines
fourteen of his slaves among whom were three of my children, Mr.
Woods is now living in Memphis and refus to perform his contract
or fulfil his promises to me in any respect, and when I spoke to him
a few days ago about carrying out his contract he told me that he
was sorry he made such a bargain with us:

There has been raised on Mr. Woods' place this year 48 bales of
Cotton most of which Mr. Wood has taken to Memphis   last year
there were 26 bales raised which Mr. Wood sold   I do not know
exactly how many black people on Mr. Woods' place at
present. Mr. Woods told us that any little patches we might
cultivate at odd hours he would not take into the count but would
let us have it besides the 1/4 of the regular crop

his

HDSr   Mackey × Woods

mark

Affidavit of Mackey Woods, 12 Dec. 1865, Affidavits & Statements, ser.
3545, Memphis TN Provost Marshal of Freedmen, RG 105 [A-6627]. Sworn
before a provost marshal of freedmen.

CHAPTER 6

Maryland

6

Maryland

THE OFFICIAL END of slavery in Maryland on November 1, 1864, completed a process many years in the making.[1] Nearly half of Maryland's 170,000 black people had gained their freedom in the decades following the American Revolution. In the city of Baltimore, free black people outnumbered slaves twelve times over in 1860. By the onset of the Civil War, plantation slavery remained fully at home only within a steadily diminishing portion of the state's southern counties, especially the tobacco-producing counties on the western shore of Chesapeake Bay. The most common slaveholding consisted of only one slave, and more than half consisted of fewer than four. Even substantial owners of slaves had occasional recourse to the hired labor of free black men and women; small-slaveholding and nonslaveholding white farmers depended upon it. Especially was this true of the cereal-producing eastern shore, where black people—more than half of them free—constituted almost 20 percent of the total population in 1860.

Ties of marriage, family, friendship, work, and shared persecution connected the slave and free black populations so intimately that it became impossible to separate one from the other. The defeat of repeated efforts by large slaveholders to expel the free black people demonstrated how entrenched free blacks had become within slave society and economy. Maryland's slave system rested upon a delicate balance of contradictory elements: of slaves and free blacks, of planters and small slaveholders, of slaveholders and nonslaveholders. A small disturbance of any one necessitated a delicate readjustment of all the others; a massive disturbance of any one could call into question the integrity of the whole structure.

The Civil War supplied just such a massive disturbance, which quickly set slavery in Maryland on the road to collapse. Within days of the attack on Fort Sumter, federal troops were moving through Maryland on their way to defend the capital. Despite President Abraham

[1] Published accounts of emancipation in Maryland include: Charles L. Wagandt, *The Mighty Revolution: Negro Emancipation in Maryland, 1862–1864* (Baltimore, 1964); Barbara J. Fields, *Slavery and Freedom on the Middle Ground: Maryland during the Nineteenth Century* (New Haven, Conn., 1985).

Lincoln's repeated professions about fighting for the Union and nothing more, slaves in Maryland concluded at once that the war was about them and moved toward the Northern army, hoping to secure freedom. Once they had set that process in motion, no effort on the part of slaveholders, military officers in the field, or federal officials in Washington could stop it. The emancipation constitution promulgated in 1864 merely recognized at law what had become unavoidable in fact.

When runaway slaves sought refuge with the federal army, they put the Lincoln administration in an awkward position. Maryland, a slave state standing between Washington and the rest of the Union, had to be held at all costs. To do that, Lincoln combined a show of force against open secessionism with assiduous cultivation of unionist sentiment, promising scrupulous respect for the property rights of loyal slaveholders. He and his cabinet paid prompt and respectful attention when Governor Thomas H. Hicks and members of Maryland's delegation in Congress relayed the complaints of their slaveholding constituents about slaves escaping to army encampments. In July 1861, Lincoln confidentially proposed to General-in-Chief Winfield Scott that owners be permitted to retrieve slaves who had crossed the Potomac into Virginia with Union army units.[2]

Commanders whose jurisdiction included portions of Maryland tried to carry out the President's wishes. Shortly before assuming command of the Department of Annapolis in April 1861, General Benjamin F. Butler offered Governor Hicks his aid in putting down a rumored slave insurrection.[3] In July 1861, upon instructions from General Scott, General Joseph K. F. Mansfield, commanding the Department of Washington, barred fugitive slaves from entering federal camps and from accompanying troops on the march.[4] The following month, General John A. Dix, commander of the Department of Pennsylvania (which included large portions of Maryland), adopted the policy with enthusiasm, declaring his wish to keep the Union cause "free from all taint."[5] Dix laid strict injunctions against receiving runaway slaves, directed their surrender to their owners, and offered fulsome reassurances to slaveholders that he wished to "avoid all cause of complaint on the part of the citizens of Maryland, in regard to any interference with their rights of property." Commanders in other departments cooperated, returning Maryland fugitives who had secreted themselves among the troops.[6]

[2] *Official Records*, ser. 2, vol. 1, p. 760.
[3] *Official Records*, ser. 1, vol. 2, p. 593.
[4] *Official Records*, ser. 2, vol. 1, p. 760.
[5] *Official Records*, ser. 2, vol. 1, pp. 764–65.
[6] Col. Henry S. Briggs to Brig. Gen. D. N. Couch, 3 Oct. 1861, Henry S. Briggs to Brig. Gen. Couch, 4 Oct. 1861, and A.A.G. J. M. Wright to Brig. Genl. D. N. Couch, 5 Oct. 1861, Letters Received, ser. 4464, Couch's Brigade, Army of the

Slaves probed the official policy for loopholes and quickly found them. Some offered their services as guides or volunteered information about the enemy's movements. Practical military considerations dictated that these be received and protected.[7] A number of Virginia slaves, claiming that their masters were rebels, sought protection within federal lines in Maryland. Some Maryland runaways found it convenient to represent themselves as slaves of secessionist Virginians.[8] Others claimed asylum on the grounds that their masters intended to send them behind enemy lines to work for the rebel army. Official policy offered some comfort to these slaves, particularly after the House resolution of July and the First Confiscation Act of August 1861. Even so, fugitives risked severe punishment if caught. A master from southern Maryland beat to death a slave whom he recaptured trying to reach federal lines during the summer of 1861. Those who made good their escape usually did so at the cost of leaving behind family, friends, and possessions. A fugitive who escaped to a New York regiment had to console his wife with the promise that "if We dont met on earth We Will Meet in heven Whare Jesas ranes."

Within the ranks of the Union army runaways found valuable allies. The first units to reach Maryland came from Massachusetts and held a number of officers and men spoiling for an occasion to perform their first practical act of abolition. But soldiers of the Pennsylvania, New York, and Ohio regiments that followed also disregarded orders and aided fugitive slaves. Some soldiers lent more than passive assistance. General Charles P. Stone, the federal commander at Poolesville, Maryland, complained in September 1861 that soldiers of his command had "so far forgotten their duty as to excite and encourage insubordination among the colored servants in the neighbourhood of their camps." Various motives were at work. Most Northern soldiers, knowing little of black people, slavery, or abolitionism, gained their first personal acquaintance with slavery as witnesses to the drama of slaves fleeing for their liberty—and often for their lives as well. Just a few such encounters sufficed to make abolitionists of many men who only a short time before had cared little about such things. Others, who never had and never would think in terms of abstract principles, simply reacted instinctively to the events unfolding before them. Still others felt rancor when they contrasted the hardship and privation of camp life with the privileged position of wealthy masters who, in the midst of

Potomac, RG 393 Pt. 2 No. 287 [C-3183]; Capt. L. H. Pelouze to Brig. Genl. Wright, 7 Dec. 1861, vol. 2 DS, p. 138, Capt. [L. H. Pelouze] to Commanding Officer, Fort Monroe, Va., 9 Jan. 1862, vol. 2 DS, p. 223, and Capt. [L. H. Pelouze] to Benj. E. Gerritt, 23 Feb. 1862, vol. 57/111 DS, p. 27, Letters Sent, ser. 2250, SC Expeditionary Corps, RG 393 Pt. 2 No. 130 [C-1648].

[7] See, for example, above, doc. 53.

[8] See above, doc. 4.

war, apparently had no other work to do than chase Negroes. Some resented the slaveholders' arrogant and overbearing manner. And some simply took the opportunity to have servants cook their meals, wash their clothes, and shine their boots.

Slave owners arriving in camp to retrieve runaways met a hostile reception. Enlisted men assailed them with epithets and – not infrequently – missiles. Slaves recently seen in camp could not be found when their owners came to take them, and taunts of "nigger Stealer . . . nigger driver" and exhortations to "bayonet him, kill him, pitch him out" discouraged any protracted search. When slave owners displayed the authority of superior orders, soldiers interposed the authority of superior numbers. Laying the soldiers' misbehavior before their commanders did not always accomplish the desired result. Officers stood on their dignity at the least sign of a slight to themselves, their men, or their home states. During the summer of 1861, General Robert C. Schenck placed the onus of misconduct on the slaveholders themselves and angrily denied that the soldiers of his Ohio brigade had interfered with the recovery of fugitives. If they wished, officers could sabotage the process of recovery by painstakingly literal interpretation of their responsibility to verify ownership and by niggling requests to their superiors for further instructions. In this campaign of attrition, they could rely upon support and encouragement from abolitionists outside the army, ever alert for a chance to turn the war into an antislavery crusade. Late in 1861, a letter from the field describing a slave-catching episode drew the abolitionist governor of Massachusetts, John A. Andrew, into a war of words with the general-in-chief over the use of Massachusetts troops as "hunters of men."

Taking help where they could find it and turning every loophole to their advantage, slaves chipped steadily away at their bondage. They absconded with increasing audacity, almost daring their owners to retake them. Exasperated slaveholders demanded relief from commanders in the field. When that failed to satisfy them, they inspired resolutions of protest in the state legislature and sent delegations to lay their grievances before the administration in Washington. Although official policy sustained the rights of loyal owners, time favored the fugitives over their masters, whether loyal or disloyal. The persistence of the fugitives kept the issue of their status before the administration, while ruling out any resolution of the question that stopped short of freedom.

In April 1862, Maryland slaves received help from an unexpected and perhaps unwitting source. By abolishing slavery in the District of Columbia in the teeth of protest from Maryland slaveholders, Congress opened a new escape route.[9] Gathering up their belongings, sometimes loading them into wagons and carts "borrowed" from their masters,

[9] See above, chap. 3.

slaves made their way to freedom in the District. A number of free blacks seized the opportunity to remove their slave spouses and relatives to freedom. Some of the migrants found employment with the government and managed to establish themselves and their families in new homes. Most probably ended up in the contraband camps that proliferated in the capital and environs.

Slaveholders did their best to discourage fugitives, making flight to the District a risky undertaking for the fugitives and for those who assisted them. In Anne Arundel County, a group of owners sympathetic to the Confederacy formed a pact of mutual assistance, from which they pointedly excluded unionists. Taking a broader view of political loyalties, public and private jailors accommodated both unionist and secessionist slaveholders wishing to place their property in safekeeping. Jailors also offered a helping hand to slaveholders in the District of Columbia hoping to evade the emancipation act. Local sheriffs and constables found profit in the pursuit of refugees along the roads leading to the District, arresting both slaves and free blacks and robbing them of whatever possessions they had taken along in their flight. Professional slave catchers and federal marshals recaptured many who had managed to reach the city. Even nonslaveholding whites could get caught in the cross fire. Two white men landed in a Maryland jail after being hired to retrieve the wives and children of three runaways from Maryland who had found government employment in Washington. Overflowing contraband camps attested, however, to the willingness of slaves and free blacks to brave the risks. The utmost efforts of slave owners could only hinder, not prevent, the escape of Maryland slaves to the District of Columbia.

The abolition of slavery in the nation's capital was only one of the setbacks that the loyal slaveholders of Maryland suffered during the spring of 1862. The events of that busy period confirmed that border-state slaveholders had lost their strategic position in the Union cause. President Lincoln, who had been considering for some time the idea of voluntary, compensated emancipation in the border states, laid such a proposal before Congress in early March. Maryland's congressional delegation, along with other border-state representatives, indignantly rejected Lincoln's plan. Undeterred, Congress passed a resolution of support in April. That same spring, Maryland's delegation watched helplessly as Congress adopted a new article of war forbidding military personnel to return fugitive slaves.

Harried federal officials gradually lost patience with the unending demands that the fugitive-slave problem placed on their time, and the pleas of Maryland slaveholders elicited an increasingly perfunctory response in Washington. In March 1862, the War Department let a delegation from the state legislature twiddle their thumbs for a time, then informed them that the secretary would tend to their complaints

"as soon as he is relieved from more important and pressing duties."
Congressman Charles B. Calvert's demand for the arrest of fugitives the
previous July had started the President and the Secretary of War almost
instantly into motion. Now, in answer to a much more modest request, Calvert received a brusque reminder that the secretary presided
over "more urgent and important business." When Governor Augustus
W. Bradford approached the Attorney General in May concerning
rumors that federal marshals had instructions not to arrest Maryland
fugitives in the District, the Attorney General practically called him
the dupe of "some evil-disposed person" seeking to "frighten the timid
and credulous." The administration had grown weary of appeasing
border-state slaveholders.

Though escape became easier, attempting it remained a difficult
and painful decision. In striking out for freedom, fugitive slaves
generally had to abandon the laboriously accumulated fruits of a
lifetime's work. Still more painfully, they often had to bid farewell to
family and friends with no sure prospect of seeing them again and
with good reason to fear they would suffer reprisals. Such nagging
fear discouraged many a slave from attempting to escape. "If their
families could be cared for or taken with them," a Union army officer
declared, "the whole slave population of Maryland would make its
exodus to Washington."[10]

Against formidable obstacles, Maryland slaves – with the help of free
blacks and sympathetic soldiers – had forced slavery to the defensive by
the summer of 1862. Additional assistance came in July with the
passage of the Second Confiscation Act, the provisions of which made it
illegal for disloyal slave owners and more difficult for loyal ones to
retrieve fugitives across state lines. Thenceforth, Maryland fugitives
stood a better chance of making good an escape to army lines either in
the District of Columbia or in occupied portions of Virginia. News of
changes in federal policy made the rounds quickly, so runaways knew
what they must say in order to gain asylum. Any fugitive slave, when
questioned, was likely to insist that he came from across the state line
and that his owner was disloyal. Much to the chagrin of the civilian and
military officials charged with determining who was who, fugitives
from Maryland and Virginia mingled in both states and in the District.
In September 1862, the commander at Point Lookout, on the southernmost tip of Maryland's western shore, urgently requested instructions from his superiors, explaining that fugitives from Maryland and
Virginia had infiltrated his lines "until the number is greater than we
know what to do with."[11]

[10] *Freedom*, ser. 2: doc. 79.
[11] Capt. H. J. Van Kirk to Capt. R. W. Dawson, 8 Sept. 1862, P-47 1862, Letters
Received, ser. 5063, Dept. of VA & 7th Army Corps, RG 393 Pt. 1 [C-3005].

The maneuvering of armies during the fall military campaign in Maryland afforded the slaves new facilities for escape. Even more important consequences followed the retreat of the Confederates after the battle of Antietam. President Lincoln took the occasion of the Confederate withdrawal from Union territory to issue his preliminary Emancipation Proclamation, with the final proclamation to take effect on New Year's Day 1863. As a loyal state, Maryland did not fall within the purview of either proclamation. But that scarcely mattered to the slaves. At last they had the highest authority for what had seemed obvious to them all along: that the abolition of slavery was the object of the war. Most slaves and free blacks, and a good many Union soldiers as well, neither understood nor respected the technicality that excluded Maryland from Lincoln's proclamation of freedom. With the Union army now officially offering freedom to slaves in the Confederacy, slaves in Maryland fully expected to find sanctuary with the federal army, and soldiers saw no reason to deny it to them.

In vain commanders issued and reissued orders to exclude fugitive slaves from army lines. The army's fugitive policy had collapsed in chaos. No one could any longer state its requirements with precision. In April 1863, General Henry H. Lockwood, commanding at Point Lookout, issued a detailed circular purporting to clarify the army's position. But Lockwood's circular no more resolved the problem than had the various policy decisions the circular summarized. His guidelines required army personnel to determine who was free and who was not; to observe a fine distinction between permitting lawful owners to recover fugitives (legal) and using soldiers to help them do so (illegal); to distinguish between Maryland fugitives (forbidden to enter the lines) and Virginia fugitives (welcomed and protected). The mere setting forth of these contradictory obligations confirmed that the slaves had set in motion a drive toward freedom that no legalities or procedural rules could stem.

Maryland unionists reluctantly learned that lesson. Slavery lost ground daily before their eyes. With federal military might and the prestige of the President now enlisted on behalf of emancipation, influential members of the state's Union party concluded that slavery's time was up in Maryland. During a public meeting in April 1863, they declared the abolition of slavery in Maryland a patriotic duty and proposed that the state immediately seek and accept federal help in accordance with Lincoln's proposal of March 1862.[12] From then on, growing numbers of Maryland politicians lent their support to the movement to end slavery.

The momentum became irresistible in the second half of 1863. Nothing so surely doomed slavery in Maryland as the recruitment of

[12] Wagandt, *Mighty Revolution*, pp. 98-99.

black soldiers by the Union army beginning in July 1863.[13] Slave-holders knew that recruitment would be a fatal blow and bent every effort to prevent it. The Lincoln administration tried to accommodate them at first, ordering that enlistment be confined to free black men. But that restriction angered nonslaveholders, while failing to mollify those who owned slaves. Nonslaveholders feared that, with free blacks gone to the army, they would have to hire slave laborers at a premium. Slaveholders understood that losing control of the free blacks would threaten their control of the slaves as well. Free blacks daring to volunteer therefore came under severe pressure, some of it spitefully directed against their families. "[T]he cornfields of these poor people have been thrown open, their cows have been driven away and some of the families have been mercilessly turned out of their homes," reported the superintendent of black recruitment in August 1863.[14] Civil authorities on the eastern shore, which depended as much upon free black as upon slave labor, devised an ingenious rationale for opposing the enlistment of free blacks. Once a free black hired himself to an employer, they reasoned, he became a slave for the period of his hire and had no legal right to join the army.[15]

In any case, recruiters frequently stretched their orders by taking slaves as well as free blacks. Colonel William Birney, in charge of recruitment in Maryland, made no secret of it, opening jails and slave pens and offering imprisoned men their freedom in return for enlist-ment. Birney's agents in the countryside took a similarly cavalier ap-proach to the distinction between slave and free, provoking hostility and alarm among slaveholders and consternation in Washington. The slaves sized up the situation at once. As soon as they learned of re-cruiters in the vicinity, they found the means to communicate their desire to enlist. Slaves in a Frederick jail made their feelings known by throwing a note attached to a stone into the cell of a recruiter confined elsewhere in the same jail.[16] Singly and in groups, slaves risked recap-ture and punishment and made their way to recruiters. Though they sometimes represented themselves as free, they generally had only to present themselves to recruiting agents, who asked no questions. By November 1863, the War Department had persuaded Lincoln to sanc-tion the recruitment of slaves with, and under prescribed conditions without, their masters' consent. And, according to recurrent allega-tions, recruiters sometimes enlisted both slaves and free blacks without their own consent.

Sensing the end, Maryland slaveholders made their last stand in resisting the recruitment of slaves for the army. They jailed at least one

[13] *Freedom*, ser. 2: chap. 4.
[14] *Freedom*, ser. 2: doc. 74.
[15] *Freedom*, ser. 2: doc. 73n.
[16] *Freedom*, ser. 2: doc. 72.

recruiter, murdered another, and dispatched emissaries to Washington to plead against enlistment of their slaves. They frightened the slaves with warnings that the recruiters planned to sell them to the government for breastworks. They threatened—and frequently carried out—retaliation against the families of men who joined the service. Volunteers rejected as physically unfit became special targets of abuse. Masters would reclaim them as fugitives, then exact vengeance by beating them, working them strenuously, and denying them food and clothing. But all efforts to block the enlistment of blacks proved unavailing. Slaves determined to enlist dared their owners to interfere, brandishing clubs and other makeshift weapons to underline their point. Mobile squads of black soldiers provided shelter from pursuers to slave volunteers. Flaunting their newly-acquired authority, black recruiters marched through rural county seats with fixed bayonets, confronted keepers of slave jails, and defied protesting owners and employers. In June 1864, the Bureau of Colored Troops removed the slaveholders' last lever of control when it directed the superintendent of black recruitment to accept all slave volunteers, assigning the physically disabled to duty in the quartermaster's department.[17]

With the War Department hungry for fresh recruits, the momentum of recruitment overwhelmed slavery in Maryland. More than 8,700 black men from Maryland served in the Union army. Roughly 1,800 others served in the navy, sometimes by escaping directly to naval vessels on the Chesapeake Bay and its tributaries. If no more than half of these men were slaves, they would represent nearly a third of the slave men between the ages of eighteen and forty-five.[18] And a good many others had already escaped slavery—by flight to the Union army or to the District of Columbia—before recruitment began in Maryland. Slavery could not survive a drain of that magnitude on the active work force.

The devastating effect of military enlistment reached beyond those slaves who gained their liberty through military service. Although the most serious fighting within Maryland ended before full-scale recruitment began—sparing slaveholders one of their most horrific night-

---

[17] In addition to the instructions from the Bureau of Colored Troops (below, doc. 146n.), see those from the quartermaster general effecting the new policy. (Quarter Master Genl. M. C. Meigs to Major Gen. Lew. Wallace, 20 June 1864, Q-16 1864, Letters Received, ser. 2343, Middle Dept. & 8th Army Corps, RG 393 Pt. 1 [C-4143].)

[18] *Freedom*, ser. 2: pp. 12, 14n.; David L. Valuska, "The Negro in the Union Navy: 1861–1865," (Ph.D. diss., Lehigh University, 1973). These figures represent conservative estimates. The army figure does not reflect the indeterminable number of Maryland fugitives who enlisted in the District of Columbia and the Northern states, while the navy figure may not include recruits who by-passed the enlistment office in Baltimore and offered their services directly to officers in charge of naval vessels.

mares – the spectacle of black men in uniform and bearing arms seemed the final blow to their social order. Moreover, the departure of the men created upheaval among their families, who, justifiably apprehensive of reprisals by angry masters, sought assurances of their safety. Receiving none, they fled – women, children, old people – either following their fathers, sons, husbands, and brothers into camp or taking the escape routes that had led other refugees to the government works and contraband camps of the District of Columbia.

The delicate balance between slaves and free blacks, which had hitherto helped to sustain slavery, now hastened its collapse. Every move one group made out of its accustomed pattern jarred the other loose as well. Slave wives and families of free black enlistees followed their men and fled slavery. Free black wives and families of slave enlistees lost privileges of residence and employment with their men's owners, or abandoned these voluntarily. Sometimes free blacks took the initiative in spiriting slaves to freedom in the District of Columbia or nearby army posts. Sometimes slave recruits, in their turn, took the initiative in encouraging free blacks to leave their employers and join the army. Where slavery once served as a lever to control the free black population, the disintegration of slavery now placed in question all forms of control over the black population, slave and free.

Slave discipline collapsed in the ensuing turmoil. With their authority eroding, masters had to offer large concessions, according their slaves the de facto status of free blacks. Slaves struck wage or share agreements with their owners or with other employers. Some moved back and forth between government work and employment with farmers and others seeking laborers.[19] As rumors of freedom circulated, slaves tested the limits of their owners' authority, some of them in genuine doubt about where they stood. A slave woman in northern Maryland, taking offense when her mistress denied her permission to visit relatives on the eastern shore during the summer of 1864, wrote directly to President Lincoln asking: "please let me know if we are free."

The manifest decrepitude of the slave system strengthened the position of those in Maryland's Union party who called for immediate emancipation. Recruitment of slaves accomplished what its most ardent sponsors always hoped it would: Isolating slaveholders from support among nonslaveholding whites, it allowed free play to the movement to abolish slavery. With crucial assistance from the federal army, emancipationists flexed their muscles at the polls in the fall of 1863. Encouraged, they determined upon a call for a state constitutional convention to declare the immediate abolition of slavery. By the fol-

---

[19] On the evolution of free-labor arrangements in Maryland during the war, see *Freedom*, ser. 1, vol. 2.

lowing spring, the emancipationists had achieved their goal. Every day further sapped the slaveholders' morale. Their world had suffered so much damage already that the most astute considered further resistance futile. When the convention assembled in April 1864, no one doubted that the delegates would declare an end to slavery in Maryland. On November 1, 1864, the new emancipation constitution took effect.[20]

Nevertheless, the final act of emancipation came as no mere anticlimax. Hard-fought and narrowly won, it left the losers bitter and unwilling to concede that slavery was gone. Former slaveholders still held powerful weapons to constrain the liberty of the newly freed. The most important of these weapons harked back to laws once used to control free black people. A free black apprentice who absconded in 1862 little realized that the status he hoped to exchange for liberty was exactly what former owners would soon be offering their emancipated slaves in lieu of liberty.[21] Freedmen and freedwomen seeking to reunite families and establish households found their way blocked by vengeful former owners who seized their meager property, evicted them from dwellings, and forbade those who left to visit relatives and friends who had stayed behind. Many former owners defiantly refused to pay wages to their ex-slaves and sought to enforce hire arrangements that predated emancipation. Long after the abolition of slavery, ex-masters manipulated the civil law to settle scores with ex-fugitives. In March 1866, a sheriff arrested a freedman in Washington and returned him to Maryland to answer a charge of having used his master's horse and cart while attempting to escape with his family in 1863.[22] The day after emancipation thus found black men and women in the same ambiguous position as on the day before: between slavery and freedom, struggling to define a new free status for themselves. But the struggle proceeded on new terms. Instead of grappling with freedom on the terrain of slavery, they now grappled with slavery on the terrain of freedom.

[20] For an account of the political battle over the constitution of 1864, see Wagandt, *Mighty Revolution*.

[21] For a discussion of the apprenticeship system in Maryland during the war years, see *Freedom*, ser. 1, vol. 2; Fields, *Slavery and Freedom on the Middle Ground*, chap. 6; Richard Paul Fuke, "Black Marylanders, 1864–1868," (Ph.D. diss., University of Chicago, 1973), chaps. 9–10.

[22] Harriette Carter to Col. Rogers, 14 May 1866, #1424, Letters Received, ser. 456, DC Asst. Comr., RG 105 [A-9757].

124A: **Commander of Schenck's Brigade to the Headquarters of the Department of Northeastern Virginia, Enclosing a Letter from the Commander of an Ohio Regiment to the Headquarters of Schenck's Brigade**

Camp Upton V^a July 6th 1861

Sir   I have the honor to acknowledge the receipt of your communication of the 2nd inst, with letters of Mrs Caroline F Noland & John G England referred from the Head Quarters of the Army, in relation to two slaves belonging to persons in Rockville M^d, which slaves are claimed to be in this camp.

I am requested to give my attention to the matter of these slaves & if they are within the limits of my Command to have them returned to their owners when demanded. And I am also reminded that the case of one of them was referred to me some days since, when, as would appear from one of the accompanying letters, the order of the General Commanding was not executed in consequence of the interference of some of the soldiers.

I return now all the letters on the subject and have to make in reply this statement   When the negroes are alleged to have taken refuge, or been first seen, within the limits of the 1st or 2nd Ohio Regiments, I was not in command. That is understood to relate to a time when the troops were encamped within the Department of Washington. Afterwards on the day when certain parties appeared in this Camp with the letter of Ass^t Adjt Genl Townsend, of the 25th of June, referred to me from Head Quarters, I happened to be temporarily absent. Colonel McCook of the 1st Ohio Regmt, the senior officer present, gave his immediate attention to the matter; & I refer to the enclosed statements from himself & Lt Colonel Parrott to show that there was no such evasion of, or refusal to execute, the order of the General Commanding, as is pretended by the persons who came in quest of the slaves. Besides what appears from the reports of those two officers, I have made strict enquiry & do not ascertain, nor believe, that persons seeking the negroes "were harshly dealt with" by any officers or men of my command, that "the object of their visit was denied", or that they "were abused & threatened in person", as they allege— On the contrary, if there was anything offensive in the conduct or condition of any of the parties concerned, it appears to have been only on the part of a drunken policeman or slave-catcher who attended Mr Noland on his first visit to the troops when at Camp Sherman on the other side of the river.

The officers & men of these two Regiments from Ohio, are naturally somewhat excited & indignant at the imputation that they have been "practicing on the abolition system of protecting runaway negroes"— This camp will not be permitted while I have command, to be made a harbor for escaping fugitives: but persons owing labor or service to loyal citizens of loyal states, if they resort to us, shall always be surrendered, when demanded, on proper order or authority, by the lawful owner or his representative—

I will add that in the particular instances in question, I cannot find any negro answering to the name or description of either of the slaves claimed, & I do not beleive that either of them is in the Camp, or concealed by the troops— If the owners or their agents should come again, with evidence of their rights, every facility & assistance will be afforded them to reclaim & secure their property. I am, very respectfully Your obd^t serv^t

HLSr   Robt C. Schenck

[*Endorsement*] Head Quarters Dept. N.E. Va Arlington July 7. 1861 Respectfully forwarded to the Head Quarters of the Army. An officer of the army will be sent to General Schenck's camp with the owners of the slaves whenever it is desired to make further search for them. Irvin McDowell Brig. Gen'l: Comg Dept.

[*Enclosure*]   Camp Upton Virginia July 5th 1861
Capt I have the honor to acknoledge reciept of the letters from the H^d Quarters of the Army relative to a runaway negro from Montgomery County Maryland, purporting to belong to Mrs Caroline Noland of said county Mrs Noland says "by the interference of soldiers which seemed with out control they (my sons) were not permitted to reclaim my negro" this piece of information, as she was not here herself, of course she obtained from her sons. It is absolutely and unqualifiedly false The officer of the day was sent through camp with the Messrs Nolands. No Violence was offered them nor threats uttered save by myself which will be explained further on— The Messrs Noland were especially taken through the company quarters where one of them thought he had seen the negro in question the day before, and then were returned to H^d Quarters and expressed themselves satisfied that thier negro was not in my camp I then sent them with the Officer of the day to the camp of the 2nd Ohio where a like protection was given them.

Mr. Noland, or a man named sergeant Noland a messenger in the war department handed me a letter from Col. E. D. Townsend asst adjt Genl U.S. Army in which Col Townsend states "from Mr

343

Nolands account the Ohio troops have been practising a little of the abolition system in protecting runaway^s." I was very much surprised to hear such sentiments expressed by the Chief of Staff, about my brave men. I then told the Messrs Noland that the man who gave Col. T. – such information stated what was false and that if he was the person, I would have no hesetency in marching him out of camp

Sergeant Noland denied in the presence of my entire staff, that he had ever given Col Townsend any such information, that he Col. T. was in no manner authorized to make such a statement, and more than that had he known what the contents of the letter was he would not have delivered it   I then told Sergt Noland that he might have been mistaken about having seen his Negro in my camp that even if he had, the negro might have been in the camp temporarily –   I then told him to go to the Connecticutt Camps, but he did not go.

The same day Maj Bartholomew of the District Militia accompanied by a friend came into my camp on a similar errand.   I extended to him the same protection. he saw the negro, that was represented to be the property of his friend but said he was mistaken and acknoledged that he had been misinformed and thanked me for my attention, and left the camp.   I do not believe Mrs. Noland has a negro in this camp, and from the lying propensities of her son's I am now in doubt if she ever owned a negro,

I enclose a letter from Lt Col: Parrott on same case –

I know nothing of Mrs: Howard's negro, I am Capt: Respectfully Your obt servant

HLSr   A M^{c}D McCook

Brig. Genl. Robt C. Schenck to Capt. Jas. B. Fry, 6 July 1861, enclosing Col. A. McD. McCook to Capt. Donn Piatt, 5 July 1861, S-1789 1861, Letters Received, ser. 12, RG 94 [K-601]. Along with his letter, Schenck returned Noland's letter and a similar one from another Maryland slaveholder who had written to General-in-Chief Winfield Scott concerning a runaway slave report-edly seen in Schenck's camp. (Caroline F. Noland to Lieut. General Scott, 27 June 1861; John G. England to Lt. Genl. Scott, [27? June] 1861.) Schenck also returned the letter of June 25 from the headquarters of the army to General Irvin McDowell, commander of the Department of Northeastern Virginia, asking that McDowell help one of Noland's sons recover the slave, and commenting that "from *Mr.* Nolan's account [the Ohio soldiers] have been practising a little of the abolition system in protecting the run-away." (E. D. Townsend to Genl. McDowell, 25 June 1861.) Also enclosed is a report from Edward A. Parrott, lieutenant colonel of the 1st Ohio Volunteers, who had been present when No-land's son first attempted to recover the slave. Parrott reported that he had refused admittance to a "drunk and offensive" police officer accompanying Noland and that Noland had been unable to find the slave, but he denied that anyone had made threats or intervened forcibly and moreover declared himself "firmly of the opinion that no such negro was in our camp." (Lt. Col. Ed. A. Parrott to Col. A. McD. McCook, 6 July 1861.)

124B: Adjutant of Schenck's Brigade to the Commander of Schenck's Brigade

Camp Upton Va. July 6th 1861

General. I have the honor to report the following facts in reply to your question touching the claim of Mrs. Caroline F. Noland to a slave said to be either with the 1st or 2d Regiments O.V.M.

Some time about the 20th June last I have forgotten the precise date two gentlemen purporting to be from Maryland called on me at Camp Upton and claimed to be the authorized agents for I believe Mrs. Noland the owner of a negro said to be in our camp. I told them that if such were the case, I was satisfied General Schenck would immediately restore the slave to the own. But I added that to do this properly it was necessary to bring him evidence of their agency, and the fact that Mrs Noland was the owner of the slave claimed. The gentlemen admitted that this would be the proper course, and said on leaving that they would return in a few days with the proofs asked for. There was no ill feeling or harsh conduct on either side — I was therefore much astonished the next day on finding the same gentlemen in camp Upton not with the proofs asked for but a letter evidently based upon their statements in which a grave charge was preferred against the men and officers of our Ohio regiments. This of course created some little excitement but none looking to a concealment of the slave — if any such was in camp. On the contrary Colonel McCook who was then in command during your temporary absence gave these men every facility the could desire. Under his order they searched the camp and returned after a time saying that they could not find the negro.

This is all that I know of, sir in connection with this case, and you will perceive from the facts that the charge preferred that your officers or men in any way harbored a slave, or ill treated his master is unfounded. I have the honor to be sir Your most obt Servt.

HLcSr

Donn Piatt

Asst. Adjt. Gen'l. Donn Piatt to Brig. General Schenck, 6 July 1861, enlosed in Brig. General Robt. C. Schenck to Captain James B. Fry, 8 July 861, filed with S-1789 1861, Letters Received, ser. 12, RG 94 [K-601].

124C: Assistant Adjutant General of the Army to the Commander of the Department of Northeastern Virginia

Washington, July 9, 1861

Sir. I respectfully request you to communicate to General Schenck and Colonel McCook, of the Ohio Volunteers, the following remarks in relation to a passage of a note written by me to you June 25, which has apparently created some dissatisfaction in them. The remark is as follows: "The negro [belonging to Mr. Nolan][1] is with some of the Ohio troops and from Mr. Nolan's account they have been practising a little of the abolition system in protecting the runaway."

I have not time, or inclination, to make an issue with Mr. Nolan and his brother the Sergeant. I will simply state facts to justify my present assertion that the allusion to "protecting the runaway" was their idea, not my own.

The two brothers called on me together the 25th June, and represented clearly and distinctly that one of them, the citizen, had been in the Ohio Camp a day or two before, in search of a negro belonging to his mother; that he had seen then and there another negro belonging to a neighbor of his in Montgomery County, and had endeavored to enter into conversation with him to ascertain where his own negro was; that some of the volunteers standing round had interfered and used language which he considered so threatening, he had feared to look farther for his own boy; and that though he had seen his negro standing somewhere in the camp while he was going away from it, he did not dare attempt to speak to him. Both the men tooks pains to impress me with the idea that the manner of the volunteers was evidently intended to intimidate the one who went among them to recover the negro.

Since I wrote you the note above referred to, I have been told by Sergeant Nolan that he went over with it and when he went into the Ohio camp, the conduct of the men was so violent towards him that he would rather lose his negro than *risk his life* by going among them again.

I trust this brief statement will be sufficient to show my agency in the matter in its proper light. I have no interest in it whatever, and merely give the statement of others to me, without so much as a remark of *my own* upon it. But I must also add that my first note to you (of the 25th June) was not written by authority, expressed or implied of General Scott, but rather as a note of introduction, not intended to be referred beyond yourself. I am, Sir, Very Respectfully, Y^r Ob^t Servt,

E D Townsen

HLS

Asst. Adj't. Genl. E. D. Townsend to Brigadier Genl. McDowell, 9 July 1861, #222 1861, Letters Received, ser. 3694, Dept. of Northeastern VA, RG 393 Pt. 2 No. 234 [C-3224].

1 Brackets in manuscript.

125: Maryland Congressman to the Secretary of War

House of Representatives [*Washington*] July 8 1861
Sir   Various complaints have come to me relative to the difficulties of our Citizens' retaining their Slaves at home, in consequence of the tempting offers made to them by some of the volunteer regiments.   I know that it is not the desire of the Government to encourage the escape of this Species of property from the lawful owner and I would therefore most respectfully ask the Department to issue an order to the Commander of the Maryland Division to exclude from all the camps in his division such Slaves as may be found therein at this time and hereafter to admit none to enter their camp.   If such an order was published at this time and enforced it would at once calm down the Public mind and prevent a great deal of bad feeling which is being engendered by the course at present pursued.   With great respect Yr. Obt. Servt
ALS   Chas B Calvert

Chas. B. Calvert to Hon. Simon Cameron, 8 July 1861, C-137 1861, Letters Received, RG 107 [L-137]. The Secretary of War replied that the subject "has for some time past engaged the consideration of the Department" but "the pressure of business has prevented any definite action in the premises." (Simon Cameron to Hon. Charles B. Calvert, 12 July 1861, vol. 45, pp. 45–46, Letters Sent, RG 107 [L-137].) For further efforts by Calvert to obtain orders to prohibit military interference with slavery and to arrest fugitives who had taken refuge in army camps, see above, doc. 44.

126: District of Columbia Freedmen's Bureau Assistant Commissioner to the Chairman of a Congressional Committee

Washington D.C. [*November 20,*] 1867
Sir– In compliance with request contained in your letter of September 24th 1867, enclosing circular from "Committee on the

treatment of Prisoners of War and Union Citizens"—I have the honor to submit to your Committee the following report of Outrages as shown by the records of this office.

. . . .

On the 28th of May 1866, Henry Seward made affadavit that in December 1861 while in Conversation with Mr. Samuel Cox living five (5) miles South of Port Tobacco, he (Cox) confessed that in August 1861 he had murdered one of his Slaves, Jack Scroggins by whipping him to death—

This statement is corroberrated by affadavits made by John Sims—and William Jackson—(at a different time) who testify that Scroggins was flogged to death for having escaped to the Federal lines, whence he was recaptured— and on the 12th of May 1866—W[m] Hill, col[d] an employee at the Senate Post Office reports this case and states that in whipping Scroggins to death Cox was assisted by Frank Roly his overseer & 2 other men. all these parties are living now at the same place and have never been arrested

. . . .

HLd   [Charles H. Howard]

Excerpts from Bvt. Brig. Gen. [Charles H. Howard] to Hon. John P. C. Shanks, [20 Nov.] 1867, Miscellaneous Reports, ser. 481, DC Asst. Comr., RG 105 [A-9914]. Excerpted from a thirty-four page list of murders, assaults, unjust imprisonments, harassment of black churches and schools, illegal apprenticeships, illegal detention of black children, and violations of the Civil Rights Act in Maryland and the District of Columbia, mostly during 1865–1867.

127: Order by the Commander of the Corps of Observation, Army of the Potomac

Poolesville [Md.] Sept. 23[d] 1861.
General Orders N° 16   The General Commanding has with great concern learned that in several instances soldiers of this Corps have so far forgotten their duty as to excite and encourage insubordination among the colored servants in the neighbourhood of their camps, in direct violation of the laws of the United States, and of the state of Maryland in which they are serving.

The immediate object of raising and supporting this army was the suppression of rebellion, and the putting down by military power of those ambitious and misguided people, who (unwilling to subject themselves to the constitution and laws of the country) preferred the carrying out of their own ideas of right and wrong, to living in peace and good order under the established Government— While, therefore, it should be the pride of Every Army to yield instant and complete obedience to the laws of the land, it is peculiarly the duty of Every officer and Enlisted man in this Army to give an example of subordination and perfect obedience to the laws: and to shew to those in rebellion, that loyal national soldiers sink all private opinions in their devotion to law as it stands. By order of Brig Gen¹ Stone

HDc

General Orders No. 16, Head Quarters, Corps of Observation, 23 Sept. 1861, vol. 44/187 2AC, pp. 39–40, General Orders, ser. 3813, Corps of Observation, Army of the Potomac, RG 393 Pt. 2 No. 242 [C-3223].

128: Commander of a Massachusetts Regiment to the Commander of Couch's Brigade

Camp Brightwood [*near Washington*] Oct 1 1861

Sir— I have this morning received from Capt Buffington A.D.C. a communication directing me by your order to "turn out from my camp any colored servant that may be claimed as a slave"

I beg leave respectfully to enquire whether the direction is to be regarded by me as a positive order, to be obeyed under all circumstances which may arise and come within its terms— If so I pray to be relieved from the order which under some circumstances would not only violate my conscience, but conflict with personal and legal obligations which I have entered into. I have a colored servant, brought with me from Massachusetts, who may be *claimed* as a slave If the alternative presented to me was to deliver him up on the claim of a pretended master, (or what I deem the same thing to turn him out to be seized and imprisoned in a strange and hostile part of the country) or to suffer the consequence of a disobedence of orders and be dismissed from the service in which I have volunteered, I should not hesitate to choose the latter.

Whenever a claimant has made representation to me that his servant was in this camp and has come respectably accredited as a person entitled to confidence, or in company with a police officer, as in two cases in camp while I write, I have protected them in the search, and have assured them that no interference would be permitted in their exercise of any rights of ownership with which the local laws might have invested them. I have informed them as plainly that I shall neither give nor permit those in my command to give *aid* in the rendition of slaves beyond that required under due process of law. When such a requisition comes I shall then determine whether I will comply with the requirements of such a process or choose the penalty of a passive disobedience

The case of my own servant is but one of a class of supposable cases, in all of which I should consider myself under the same moral obligation to protect the rights of other officers and the personal liberty of their free servants as in the individual case supposed — With great respect Your Obt Servt

ALS   Henry S Briggs

Col. Henry S. Briggs to Brig. Gen. D. N. Couch, 1 Oct. 1861, Letters Received, ser. 4464, Couch's Brigade, Army of the Potomac, RG 393 Pt. 2 No. 287 [C-3183].

129: Commander of the Department of Pennsylvania to a Maryland Slaveholder; and Commander of the Department of Pennsylvania to the Commander at Annapolis, Maryland

Fort McHenry [*Md.*] 12. Oct. 1861

Sir. When I took command of this Department, being anxious to avoid all difficulty in regard, to slaves I directed that no negroes should be permitted to enter our encampments except as laborers or servants, and then only with the consent of their masters if they were not free. It was in obeying this order that Col. Morse directed your boy, who had found his way into the Naval School, to be sent out of it. I am Satisfied the Colonel had no other desire but to avoid the very difficulty that has now occurred. The error was originally in permitting the boy to enter the lines at all, and this it seems had been done by the Soldiers before the Colonel was aware of it. —

I have given directions to Colonel Morse, as you request, to ascertain, if possible, by the most Searching examination whether his officers or Soldiers are harboring the boy or have aided in his concealment or escape; I am very desirous to avoid all cause of complaint on the part of the citizens of Maryland, in regard to any interference with their rights of property, especially in Slaves, knowing how sensitive they are on this subject; and I can assure you that no effort will be spared on my part to discover and redress any alleged violation of those, rights. — I am very respectfully Yours

HLc   [*John A. Dix*]

Maryland

Baltimore, Md. 14th Oct. 1861

Colonel   You will please ascertain by the most searching inquiries among your Officers and men whether the colored boy belonging to Mr Richardson has been harbored within your lines since he was sent out by your order, and whether he is still within them. –

My order was not to allow fugitive slaves to come within the encampments at all. – The difficulty in this case arises from his having been allowed to enter yours. The owner now Seeks to hold you responsible for not giving him up when you knew he was a slave. I wish the matter put on such ground as to exonerate us from all responsibility, and it is for this reason that I direct the inquiries above Stated. –

Hereafter no fugitive slave should be allowed to come within your lines at all. But if he comes within them without your knowledge and the owner calls for him while he is actually in your possession or under your control he should be surrendered, on such call or demand. We may decline to receive them, and this is what I wished; but if we do receive them, we cannot decline to surrender. – Respectfully Yours,

HLS

John A. Dix

Maj. Genl. [John A. Dix] to S. R. Richardson Esq., 12 Oct. 1861, vol. 27 8AC, pp. 357–58, Letters Sent, ser. 2327, Dept. of PA, RG 393 Pt. 1 [C-4153]; Maj. Genl. John A. Dix to Col. A. Morse, 14 Oct. 1861, Letters Received, ser. 4882, Post Naval Academy Annapolis, RG 393 Pt. 2 No. 315 [C-4120]. Although a notation on Dix's letter to the post commander at Annapolis indicates that the latter replied on October 15, 1861, no letter of that date appears in the letters-sent volumes of the post. Dix's order has not been found, but in early August 1861 he had informed Secretary of War Simon Cameron of his policy "that we have nothing to do with slaves; that we are neither negro-stealers nor negro-catchers, and that we should send them away if they came to us." Dix believed fugitives in Maryland "should be treated precisely as it would be if we were in the occupation of Virginia. We would not meddle with the slaves even of seccessionists." (*Official Records*, ser. 2, vol. 1, p. 763.) In response, Cameron had referred Dix to his own letter of August 8, 1861, to General Benjamin F. Butler, commander of the Department of Virginia (see above, doc. 1C), in which Cameron had suggested that fugitives from both loyal and secessionist masters be accepted within Union lines. (Simon Cameron to Major General John A. Dix, 3 Sept. 1861, vol. 46, pp. 25–26, Letters Sent, RG 107 [L-315].) Dix issued orders and correspondence regarding Maryland affairs through the fall of 1861, although the Maryland portion of his Department of Pennsylvania had been merged, unbeknownst to him, into another department in late August. (See above, doc. 5n.)

130: Governor of Maryland to the Secretary of War

Annapolis [*Md.*], November 18 *1861*

My Dear Sir   A circumstance occurred at one of the Camps in the vicinity of Annapolis, viz. the Massachusetts 25th Regiment, to day, that, calls forth this communication.

The facts, I briefly, but, correctly narrate. I was called on by a Mr Tucker of this (Anne Arundel) County, who stated that he had a servant, that had left him, and taken refuge in the Encampment of the 25th Regt. from Mass, that he had repaired to the ground so occupied, and that Co^l Upton, Commanding, at first refused, afterward, said to him go through and see if your man is here, He proceeded, but a short distance, when he *Tucker* was surrounded by quite a number, menaced him, and, applied opprobious Epithets; such as Negro stealer, Negro catchers, and that the negro was better than he, the master was &c &c until he was obliged to leave the ground, without looking after his servant. Now whilst in this there is amusement, I must say there was much to provoke, and altho I care little for what becomes of the negroes, yet these things produce bad feeling and bad effect. upon the representation of this case. I wrote to Co^l Upton, and at same time sent for Co^l Morse Commanding the 21st Mass. Regt. and here I discovered the necessity of obtrudeing a little upon your closely occupied time, and patience; Genl Burnside was not here (gone to N.Y)   all here, were then equal in grade (Coln^s) and none to Issue orders, or command supremely.   the result is, the case stands open. Tucker has gone home much fretted, and his servant, at large. now a word as to how these things work; we *all* delighted with Genl Dix, Proclamation, issued for the E. S. of Virginia;[1] rec^d, this morning per mail; but taken quite aback this evening, by the occurrence at Camp Hicks (I understand it is call^d) in regard to this servant and his master, with those offering insult –   Now lest I become tiresome, I make the *Point*. I see the necessity clearly of having some controling officer, permanently located at this Important Point, *who* will be ready at all times to meet Emergencies; and beg to say *Respectfully*, that you cannot in my Humble Judg^t do better for the Gov^t, the Army, for *us* here, and for *all* concerned, than to commission Co^l Morse as Brigadier Genl and let him be permanently fix^d here. If you think it better to send his (the 21st Reg^t away) let him remain, we do not wish his Reg^t to go, but if in your better Judgm^t, that may be deem^d wise, let *him* remain; we know *him*; he understands everything. He has done his duty nobly; all have confidence in him, and I do not believe the Gov^t can be better served by any other man at this Post, –   there is much receiving, as well as Transporting at this point and I have seen enough, to know the disadvantage work^d, by frequent changes here. Co^l M. has been here, say ten weeks. he labors, and discharges his duty. the men, of his Reg^t, are moral and reliable men, but I beg you, do not take the Co^l away, but Promote him for the reasons Indicated and let him remain. If you consult Genl Dix I am sure, he will concur with me, in all I have said in regard to Co^l M. and his Reg^t. (altho they are what the secessionists call Yankees) you are fully aware sir of the difficulty we have had in M^d. things are working right now. let us have no stumbling blocks placed in our way – I care nothing for the Devlish Nigger difficulty, I desire to save the union, and will cooperate with the Administration in everything tending to that important result, that is proper. I know the difficulties surrounding us, and do not wish to mingle and mix up too much with the main design.

I labored to have M^d roll up a majority, that would smother secessionism. We have given them a heavy dose. I hope to strike them another blow by an early convocation of the Legislature of our state, and if we can but keep away outside Issues, and all things foreign from the, one, true, great design of all Patriots, we shall save the union – I will attend early to your Telegram rec^d this evening. I have the Honor to be with great respect y^r ob^t Servant

ALS   Tho. H. Hicks

Tho. H. Hicks to Hon. S. Cameron, 18 Nov. 1861, M-595 1861, Letters Received, RG 107 [L-5].

1 See above, doc. 5.

131A: Governor of Massachusetts to the Secretary of War, Enclosing an Excerpt from a Letter from an Unidentified Correspondent

Boston, Dec 7, *1861*

Dear Sir I wish to call your attention to the enclosed copy of a recent letter from a reliable source, in relation to the use to which Massachusetts soldiers are being put, (as is alleged) by Brigadier General Stone. I cannot for a moment beleive that the War Department will countenance such proceedings, and I invoke your interpostion not only now, but for the future, for the issue of such orders as will secure the soldiers of this Commonwealth from being participators in such dirty and despotic work. Massachusetts does not send her citizens forth to become the hunters of men or to engage in the seizure and return to captivity of persons claimed to be fugitive slaves, without any recognition of even the forms of law & I trust you will save our soldiers and our State from such dishonor, by the exercise of your official authority in such manner as will insure the protection of our men from such outrages in future and humanity itself from such infractions under color of military law and duty. I remain with great respect Your Obedient Servant.

HLS   John A. Andrew

[*Enclosure*]   Poolesville Md Nov 28, 1861
                          (Copy)
                          . . . .

On Saturday last an order came down from General Stone giving a description of two Fugitive Slaves and directing their return (in case they should enter our camp,) to their owners "whoever they might be". This order it appears was handed by Lieut Col Palfrey, to the Officer of the day, Mr Macy of Co I. On Sunday morning several negroes came into Camp as usual for the purpose of selling cakes, pies &c to the Soldiers.

Although having eatables for sale, some of these negroes were themselves almost famished and were treated to a breakfast by the men of one of our German Companies. About the time of guard mounting the vigilant eyes of Lieut Macy espied the negroes as they were disposing of their wares through the Company streets, and, leaving the new guard to be mounted as it might, he beckoned two of the negroes to the Guard house when he ordered them into arrest and then immediately *detailed a file of Soldiers under a sergeant with loaded muskets to escort them to their supposed owners and deliver them up.*

The procedure was therefore unknown to all save the officers who were parties to it and the parties who composed the escort had no knowledge that their prisoners were suspected fugitives.

HDc

John A. Andrew to Hon. Simon Cameron, 7 Dec. 1861, enclosing unsigned excerpt, 28 Nov. 1861, M-1250 1861, Letters Received, ser. 12, RG 94 [K-600]. Ellipses in manuscript. General Charles P. Stone commanded the Corps of Observation at Poolesville, Maryland. In the same file is a copy of a letter in which the Secretary of War suggested to General Nathaniel P. Banks, who commanded a division in the Army of the Potomac and was Stone's superior, that he issue "such directions . . . to the officers of your Division, as may prevent similar complaints for the future, of injustice and oppression to negroes visiting the camps in the exercise of lawful occupations." (Simon Cameron to Major General Nathaniel P. Banks, 12 Dec. 1861.)

Maryland

131B: Office of the Governor of Massachusetts to the
Commander of a Massachusetts Regiment

Boston, December 9 1861
Colonel— His Exellency Governor Andrew directs me to write to
you, that he is informed upon what he deems reliable authority that
an officer of your Regiment, Lieut, (now Captain) Macy has
subjected Massachusetts citizen soldiers to the disgrace of becoming
the kidnappers of their fellow men, and returning them into the
hands of persons claiming to be their owners without any observance
of even the forms of law, either civil or military—

His Excellency is greatly pained that the fame of your gallant
regiment should have been tarnished by an act on the part of one its
officers, the details of which if correctly reported to him, prove him
to be unworthy of any position of honor, trust or responsibility in
her service, or in the service of the Federal Government, and he
earnestly hopes that your influence will be exerted to save and
protect the soldiers of Massachusetts from any such dirty and
despotic work in the future; and humanity itself from such
infractions, under color of military law and duty—

His Excellency also directs me to add, that you will oblige him,
by saying to Captain Macey, that had he been informed of his
discreditable conduct in this affair, after satisfying himself beyond a
doubt that he did seize two colored men in the camp of your
regiment, and order a file of Massachusetts soldiers to guard them,
and to deliver them into the hands of persons claiming their
ownership without investigation and without knowlege that the
claimants were loyal or disloyal he would never have signed his
commission for promotion, which was done, he regrets to say at
about the time this infamous procedure is said to have
happened— With great respect I remain Yours Very Truly
HLcSr   Thomas Drew

Thomas Drew to Lieut. Colonel Palfrey, 9 Dec. 1861, enclosed in Brig. Genl.
Chas. P. Stone to Brig. General S. Williams, 15 Dec. 1861, S-1749 1861,
Letters Received, ser. 12, RG 94 [K-600]. In his covering letter, General
Charles P. Stone, commander of the Corps of Observation at Poolesville,
Maryland, protested the interference of the governor of Massachusetts and
asked that General George B. McClellan, commander of the Army of the
Potomac and general-in-chief of the Union army, take measures to prevent a
recurrence. Accordingly, McClellan brusquely informed Governor John A.
Andrew that state volunteer regiments "when accepted and mustered into the
service of the United States, become a portion of the Federal Army, and are as
entirely removed from the authority of the Governors of the several States as
are the Troops of the regular regiments." Andrew in turn insisted that his

355

authority to appoint and promote the officers of Massachusetts volunteer regiments implied his right to establish and publicize the standards upon which appointments and promotions would be made; that he had not obstructed military discipline; and that the morale and self-respect of the Massachusetts regiments would suffer if the men were required to return fugitive slaves. (Major Genl. [George B. McClellan] to His Excellency John A. Andrews, 20 Dec. 1862 [1861], and John A. Andrew to Major General George B. McClellan, 24 Dec. 1861, filed with S-1749 1861, Letters Received, ser. 12, RG 94 [K-600].)

131C: **General-in-Chief of the Army to the Governor of Massachusetts**

Washington. Dec^r [27] 1861.

Sir. I have received your Excellency's letter of the 24th inst. I regret that you adhere to the opinion expressed in it. I cannot yield mine in a matter of such consequence to the discipline of the army.

You argue, that, because as Governor you appointed a Captain of Volunteers, you may send to him in the service of the United States, through his Colonel, your censures of his military conduct, by way of explaining your motives in making the appointment.

I am of opinion that, as the Governor of the State holds no authority over the Volunteers in the service of the United States, he is not warranted in assuming any such function for any purpose; and that the exercise of it, quite unnecessary in support of the Military authority of the United States, in opposition to it must be very mischeivous.

In this case you inform the officers that certain acts done "*under color of military law and duty*" were "dirty and despotic work"; "disreputable conduct"; "infamous procedure".

The acts your Exellency so warmly and vehemently denounces, were acts under cognizance of the Military authority of the United States; which that authority is competent to order or forbid, to approve or punish; and which, if it approves, it cannot permit any other authority to denounce to the troops, or censure in any way that may tend to excite disobedience or disaffection.

The Volunteer troops from the states must obey, according to the rules and discipline of war, the officers appointed over them by the United States. The regimental commanders must not accept nor convey to the officers or soldiers under them any denunciation, or any advice, opinion or suggestion from the state-authorities in censure of the orders and duty imposed by the United States; and any commander, or other person subject to discipline, so offending, will be liable to answer to a court martial, under the mutiny-articles of war, for inciting mutiny and Sedition.

I trust your Excellency will see that our generals in command of brigades and divisions must find their authority impaired and subverted if Governors may instruct the Colonels on points of duty.

The question is of such magnitude in its consequences that a prompt and energetic settlement of it is indispensable.

I intreat your Excellency to confide to the U.S the conduct of this war, in all its relations, and the government of the troops furnished to it from the state of Mass[ts] — I have the honor to be

HLd   [*George B. McClellan*]

[George B. McClellan] to His Excellency John A. Andrew, [27] Dec. 1861, filed with S-1749 1861, Letters Received, ser. 12, RG 94 [K-600].

132: Maryland Fugitive Slave to His Wife

Upton Hill [*Va.*] January [the] 12 1862
My Dear Wife   it is with grate joy I take this time to let you know Whare I am   i am now in Safety in the 14th Regiment of Brooklyn   this Day i can Adress you thank god as a free man   I had a little truble in giting away But as the lord led the Children of Isrel to the land of Canon So he led me to a land Whare fredom Will rain in spite Of earth and hell   Dear you must make your Self content i am free from al the Slavers Lash   and as you have chose the Wise plan Of Serving the lord i hope you Will pray Much and i Will try by the help of god To Serv him With all my hart   I am With a very nice man and have All that hart Can Wish But My Dear I Cant express my grate desire that i Have to See you   i trust the time Will Come When We Shal meet again   And if We dont met on earth We Will Meet in heven Whare Jesas ranes   Dear Elizabeth tell Mrs Own[ees] That i trust that She Will Continue Her kindness to you and that god Will Bless her on earth and Save her In grate eternity   My Acomplements To Mrs Owens and her Children   may They Prosper through life   I never Shall forgit her kindness to me   Dear Wife i must Close   rest yourself Contented i am free   i Want you to rite To me Soon as you Can Without Delay   Direct your letter to the 14th Reigment New york State malitia Uptons Hill Virginea In Care of M[r] Cranford

Upton Hill January 12th 1862

My Dear Wife it is with grate joy I take this time to let you know whare I am i am now in Safety in the 14th Regiment of Brooklyn this Day i can Adress you thank god as a free man I had a little trubble in giting away But as the lord led the Children of Izrel to the land of Canon So he led me To a land whare fredom will rain in spite Of earth and hell Dear you must make your Self content i am free from al the Slavers Lash and as you have chose the wise plan Of Serving the lord i hope you will pray Much and i will try by the helps of god To Serv him with all my hart I am with a very nice man and have All that hart Can wish But my Dear I Cant express my grate desire that i Have to See you i trust the time will Come when we Shal meet again And if we dont met on earth we will Meet in heven whare Jesus rains

Comary Write my Dear Soon As you C Your Affectionate
Husban Kiss Daniel For me

John Boston

Give my love to Father and Mother

ALS

John Boston to Mrs. Elizabeth Boston, 12 Jan. 1862, enclosed in Maj. Genl. Geo. B. McClellan to Hon. Edwin Stanton, 21 Jan. 1862, A-587 1862, Letters Received, ser. 12, RG 94 [K-23]. The envelope is addressed, in a different handwriting, to "Mrs. Elizabeth Boston Care Mrs. Prescia Owen Owensville Post Office Maryland."

133: Black Former Apprentice to His Former Master, and the Former Master to the Freedmen's Bureau Commissioner

[*Washington*] Oct 7th 1865

Sir   Your humble Servant Thomas Henson writes To you to ask you to tell me what you are going to allow me for my time you kept me over my right time   The Binding of me to you was this   I was to have a [trunk] a new suit of Chlothes and fifty dollars in money   i have never recieved any of These so I wish you to pay me some Reasonabl sum of money and tell me how much you will pay me without me having to apply To the Freedmens Buareu for Justice   I know Exactly how Long I should have staid with you and I know how Long i did stay and I know When i Left

Mr Hill i ought to be Justly Compensated for my time   I know from high aurthority that I can Get my rights   I have a sister Living who have the Exact time set down when I Came to you   she is a Geat deal older than i am

Sir will you Please to answer this and tell me what sum you will give and if it will sattisfey me i will give you no futher Trouble   Signened [&] Respectfuly

Thomas Henson

No. 3.5.1. L St between 15 & 16.

ALS

Upper Marlboro   Prince Georges County [*Md.*] Oct. 16. 1865

Dear Sir   The enclosed note was received some few days since—

I enclose you a certificate from the clerk of our County Court proving the Justice of my claim to his services—Also a certificate from Mr Suit from whom I purchased his unexpired time—

He left me on the 5th Febrrury 1862—   From this statement you will see that his threat of action on your part is groundless—   As to his statement of Clothes money & Trunk I told him when my Son Capt Hill of the Ordinance Dept. might think his services useful to him I would in case of his good Conduct present him withe the articles named & also his term of service due me—   He left me before the Captain wanted him.

I make this statement to you to prevent any trouble hereafter.   With Respect Yours &&c

ALS

Clement Hill

Thomas Henson to Mr. Clement Hill, 7 Oct. 1865, enclosed in Clement Hill to Genl. Howard, 16 Oct. 1865, H-17 1865, Letters Received, ser. 15, Washington Hdqrs., RG 105 [A-9663]. Also enclosed is a statement by the clerk of Prince Georges County, Maryland, certifying that on September 26, 1850, Thomas Henson, then almost nine years old, was apprenticed by the Orphan's Court to Fielder Suit until October 1, 1862, along with a statement by Suit that in 1851 he had transferred his claim to Henson's services to Clement Hill.

134: Maryland Legislators to the Secretary of War, Enclosing Affidavits of Maryland Slaveholders

[*Annapolis, Md.*] March 10, 1862 –

Sir   The Legislature of Maryland in the early part of its Session appointed a committee to proceed to Washington & confer with Major Gen[l] M[c]Clellan in reference to the escapes of fugitive slaves within the lines of the Army.   They presented for his consideration certain resolutions & in response, the Committee have been informed, they were transferred to the Secretary of War for his adjudication –   And not receiving any communication from that Department they felt prompted by the magnitude of the subject to depute D[r] Bayne, one of the members of the committee to solicit an interview with yourself.   He has reported on his return, that the object of the resolutions meet with your concurrence – And we have entertained the belief that Military Orders would be enforced, which would not only prevent the further admission of negroes within the lines of the Army but would have resulted in the expulsion of those already there –   The Committee regret that the Proclamation which has been issued in the Military Department near the seat of Government has still continued to be inoperative –[1]   But they yet hope & believe that some plan will be adopted which will accomplish the object & vindicate the rights of the loyal ctizens of Maryland –

You advised the member of our Committee who had the honor of an interview with you, to consult with the other members on his return & ascertain, if some other suggestions could not be made additional to those contemplated in the resolutions –   In Military matters they defer to your superior judgement, & still believe the plan indicated would be the most successful & practicable one –   In addition they will take the liberty to suggest the organization of a Military Police consisting of a few men, whose specific duty it should be to explore the Camps of every regiment & expel therefrom every negro unless he could furnish indubitable evidence of his freedom –

Gen[l] Halleck has enforced orders prohibiting the admission of fugitives within the lines of his Department— Genl Foster has done the same most effectually at Annapolis— Genl Dix has pursued the same course, & General Burnside has issued a similar proclamation in North Carolina & we believe will have it executed faithfully— He has declared in the most emphatic terms, that it is not the policy of the Government in any way or manner to interfere with the laws of the State constitutionally established, or their property or institutions in any respect— And as we believe Maryland by her loyalty & geographical position has contributed more to the preservation of the Capitol & therby preventing a dismemberment of the Union than other State—We therefore think we have a strong claim upon the Government for its protection of every right guarrantied to us under the Constitution—

The Committee take the liberty to transmit a few affadavits to prove that loyal citizens of Maryland have not only been treated with great indignities, but have been violently contravened in the legitimate pursuit of their property— Hundreds of similar cases could be obtained if necessary— We have the honor to be most respectfully yr obt. servts

Jn°. H. Bayne	E. hammend
John S Sellman	Robert P. Dunlop
Washington Waters	G W Duvall

HLS

[*Enclosure*] State of Maryland Ch^s County 1st Mach 1862

On or about the 14th of november last I proceeded to Camp Fenton near Port Tobacco to get three of my servants viz a man about Twenty four years of age a boy about seventeen years of age and a boy some 13 or 14 years of age who had left their home and taken up their abode with the soldiers at the above named camp Col. Graham who was in command at the time gave me an order to the officer of the day to search the camp for my servants but at the same time intimated I might meet with some difficulty as a portion of his troops were abolitionist I learned by some of the soldiers my servants were in Camp and soon as my mission become general known a large crowd collected and followed me crying shoot him, bayonet him, kill him, pitch him out, the nigger Stealer the nigger driver at first their threats were accompanied with a few stones thrown at me which very soon became an allmost continued shower of stones a number of which struck me, but did me no serious damage. Seeing the officer who accompanied me took no notice of what was going on and fearing that some of the soldiers would put their threats of shooting me into execution I informed him that I would not proceed any farther, about this time

Lieutenant Edmund Harrison came to my assistance and swore he would shoot the first man who threw a stone at me, the soldiers hooted at him and continued throwing. I returned to Co¹ Grahams quarters but was not permitted to see him again. I left the camp without getting my servants and have not been favored to get them yet

HDS   A. J. Smoot

[*Enclosure*]   State of Maryland Charles County Feb. 25th 1862
    Personally appeared before the subscriber a justice of the peace for Charles County aforesaid personally appeared Richard F Nelson & made oath that he is a duly qualified Constable in Charles County and that he recived authority from Charles Jenkins to arrest a runaway slave of said Jenkins who he was informed was in 26 Pennsylvania Col. Small. that on the 5th of Janry he went to the Camp of 26th Pennsylvania & saw the slave there   that as soon as he went into the Camp a large crowd of Soldiers gathered around him & commenced calling out "Bayonet him Drum him out" & such expressions   That a man who he was informed was Col. Small then told him the best thing he could do would be to get on his horse & leave the Camp which this deponent did & did not get the negro   the negro was in Camp a few days ago:

HD

Jno. H. Bayne et al. to Hon. E. M. Stanton, 10 Mar. 1862, enclosing affidavit of A. J. Smoot, 1 Mar. 1862, and affidavit of Richard F. Nelson, 25 Feb. 1862, M-387 1862, Letters Received, RG 107 [L-136]. Affidavits sworn before justices of the peace. Additional affidavits are also enclosed, for one of which see above, doc. 51. A copy of the Assistant Secretary of War's reply is in the same file: "The Secretary of War directs me . . . to state that the alleged harboring of the Slaves of loyal citizens of Maryland within the camps of the Army, will receive his attention as soon as he is relieved from more important and pressing duties." (P. H. Watson to John H. Bayne et al., 17 Mar. 1862.) On December 18, 1861, the Maryland legislature had passed a resolution boasting of the state's loyalty to the Union, asserting that the "present war is waged in no spirit of hostility to the institutions of any of the States," and requesting that the federal government take "specific action" to remedy the problem of slaves escaping "into the lines of the Federal army, thereby causing trouble, and occasionally loss to their owners." A committee of the legislature had presented the resolution to General-in-Chief George B. McClellan, who forwarded it to the Secretary of War noting that these subjects were "political rather than military." (Maj. Genl. Geo. B. McClellan to Hon. Edwin Stanton, 21 Jan. 1862, enclosing excerpt from Journal of Proceedings of the Maryland Senate, 18 Dec. 1861, A-587 1862, Letters Received, ser. 12, RG 94 [K-23].)

1 General Joseph K. Mansfield, commander of the Department of Washington, had ordered on July 17, 1861: "Fugitive slaves will under no pretext whatever be permitted to reside or be in any way harbored in the quarters and camps of the troops serving in this department. Neither will such slaves be allowed to accompany troops on the march." (*Official Records*, ser. 2, vol. 1, p. 760.)

135: Maryland Congressman to the Secretary of War, Enclosing a Letter from a Maryland Slaveholder to the Congressman

Washington City March 31ˢᵗ *1862*
Sir   Enclosed you will find a letter from Mʳ Burgess one of our best Union men in Charles County in relation to a great abuse which is daily practised not only in Charles County but in most parts of Maryland and the District of Columbia.   Genl Mansfield last Summer, under the direction of the President, issued an order that no negro Slaves Should be either permitted to enter the Camps or be transported with the Camps from place to place.¹   I regret to Say this order has never been enforced and hence there are daily complaints against the Government for permitting this great abuse of the rights of our loyal people.   therefore write at the request of Mʳ Burgess and many other loyal citizens to know if this nuisance cannot be abated.   Our people do not ask the army to arrest their Slaves but Simply that they will not entice them away and conceal them in their camps until Such times as they are ordered off and then take them off with the troops.   May I ask a reply to this note at your earliest convenience in order that I may give these gentlemen the information they desire.   Very respectfully Yr obt sevt
ALS   Chaˢ B. Calvert

[*Enclosure*]   Chaˢ Cty [*Md.*], 27″ March /62
Dr Sir   I hope you will pardon the liberty I take in addressing you on the present occasion   As our representative in Congress I have thought you might be enabled to have abated a great grievance which we are suffering at the hands of the Federal Soldiery Stationed among us.   Their camps with but few exceptions have been opened as receptacles for our slaves.   Their emissaries are sent out among the Slaves and all the young negroes are enticed to their camps where they are concealed from recovery by their owners.   Within the last week large numbers have taken refuge in these camps.   I

have lost 3 boys and there is scarce a slave owner in my vicinity who has not lost one or more. I am aware of the recent legislation as to the arrest and delivery of fugitive slaves by the US. troops.[2] Yet while the law inhibits them to be used for that purpose It seems but right that they should be prohibited from giving slaves facilites of escape from their masters as they are now doing. The president has time and again declared in his proclamations that the Federal army was not to interfere with the rights or property of peaceable and loyal citizens, but the rather that they were to be protected in their rights of property by the army if necessary. Now these soldiers in thus robing of us of our slaves are carrying out these views of the executive with a vengeance. I do not mean to charge that these things are done with the consent of General Hooker, but it seems a little remarkable that the General finds himself utterly impotent to enforce his orders among his troops and an order from him authorising one to arrest a fugitive in the camp is baffled and the party seeking the recovery of his slave placed in eminent danger of his life

I visited the camps on Saturday last when I met with no difficulty in obtaining an order authorising me to search for and recapture my boys if they could be found but as soon as my purpose was known they were spirited away and concealed so of course I faild to [get] them though I have since learned they were certainly there. I learn the army is on the eve of crossing the river. General Hooker informed me that he had indirectly learned that an order had, or would be issued forbiding the negroes to be transported over the river with it   I would therefore most respectfully suggest that if you could prevail upon the proper authorities to have such an order promulged before the army moves It might be the means of restoring to us our slaves now in these camps who otherwise will be lost to their owners. With sentiments of the highest consideration I have the honor to remain Yr obt & hum[bl] sevt

F. B. F. Burgess

PS   Please let me hear from you at your convenience –   F B F B –

ALS

Chas. B. Calvert to Hon. E. M. Stanton, 31 Mar. 1862, enclosing F. B. F. Burgess to Honrble. Charles B. Calvert, 27 Mar. 1862, C-545 1862, Letters Received, RG 107 [L-10]. Endorsement. General Joseph Hooker commanded a division of the Army of the Potomac. In the same file is a copy of a reply from the Assistant Secretary of War to Congressman Calvert, dated April 14, 1862: "[B]y reason of the pressure of more urgent and important business connected with the operations of the army, [the Secretary of War] has had no opportunity of considering this subject and determining what is necessary and proper to be done."

1 General Joseph K. Mansfield, commander of the Department of Washington, had ordered on July 17, 1861: "Fugitive slaves will under no pretext whatever be permitted to reside or be in any way harbored in the quarters and camps of the troops serving in this department. Neither will such slaves be allowed to accompany troops on the march." (*Official Records*, ser. 2, vol. 1, p. 760.)
2 The additional article of war, adopted March 13, 1862, which prohibited the use of military forces to return fugitive slaves to their masters. (U.S., *Statutes at Large, Treaties, and Proclamations*, vol. 12 [Boston, 1863], p. 354.)

136: Affidavit of a District of Columbia Freedman

[*Washington*] 6th day of February 1864
Grandison Briskoe being duly sworn says he is about 25 years of age was born in Maryland & has been married to his wife since 1861 Came to reside with his wife in this City in April – 4th day of April 1862 & has resided in said City Since that period of time except a part of the time he has been in the Service of the United States all the time & is now in Said Service in Virginia – That his wife & his mother were taken away from Washington in April (on the 7th day) 1862 & as fugitive Slaves & taken to Piscatawa to Broad Creek to their master's [farm?] whose name is John Hunter & My mothers masters name was & is Robert Hunter – They were both taken to the barn & severely whipped Their clothes were raised & tied over their heads to keep their screams from disturbing the neighborhood & then were tied up & whipped very severely whipped and then taken to Upper Marlborough to jail My wife had a Child about nine month's old which was taken from her & died soon after. Some six or eight months after my wife was imprisoned she had a Child but the inhuman master & mistress though the knew she was soon to be Confined or give birth to a Child made no arrangements provided no Clothing nor anything for the Child or mother I have sent them Clothing & other articles frequently until the first or near the first of January 1864 Since which the new jailor has refused to allow them to receive any thing from me
They have been in prison for the Crime of Coming to Washington to reside, ever since about the fourth of April 1862 now a year & ten months. They are confined in Jail at Upper Marlborough Prince George's County Maryland
HDS   Grandison Briskoe

Affidavit of Grandison Briscoe, 6 Feb. 1864, B-430 1864, Letters Received, RG 107 [L-32]. Sworn before a notary public.

137: Attorney General to the Governor of Maryland

U.S. Attorney General's Office [*Washington*] May 10, 1862
Sir: I am honored with your letter of yesterday, informing me that large numbers of slaves owned in Maryland, are daily making their way into the District of Columbia, from the neighboring Counties of your state, which, you assure me is producing great anxiety and complaint in your community, and that such anxiety is greatly increased, within the last few days, by information received "that the Government has forbidden the Marshal of the District to execute any warrant for the arrest of these slaves, upon the ground, as it is suggested, that the fugitive slave law is not applicable to the District of Columbia.

In these distempered times, I am not at all surprised to hear that Slaves in the border states are using all available means to escape into free territory; but the rumor you speak of; to the effect that the Government has ordered the Marshal of the District not to serve warrants in execution of the fugitive slave law, is to me, new, and unexpected.

I know nothing of any such order, and do not believe any such exists. The Act of Congress of August 2^d 1861, Chapter 37. charges this office with the general superintendence & direction of the District Attornies and Marshals, as to the manner of discharging their respective duties. And hence, I suppose it very probable that, if such an order had been given, I would know it. I think none such was ever given. The rumor I suppose to be a mere fiction, started by some evil-disposed person, to stir up bad feeling and to frighten the timid and credulous. I have the honor to be with great respect Your Obt. Servt.

HLcSr   (Signed) Edwd Bates

Edwd. Bates to Excellency A. W. Bradford, 10 May 1862, vol. B5, p. 92, General Letter Books, ser. 10, Records of the Attorney General's Office, RG 60 [W-58].

138: Commander of the Post of Annapolis, Maryland, to the Commander of the Middle Department

Annapolis Md May 24th 1862
Sir, I have the honor to report that in obedience to your instructions dated, May 20th by "Telegram." I have investigated the report of meetings held at Owensville & other places in this vicinity

and believe the object of Said meetings to be the prevention of negroes running away from their masters.

On Thursday of this week I dispatched Lieut. Tucker of my command dressed in citizens clothes to a place called Annies Bridge one of the points designated for a meeting. At this place he met with a person named Thomas Davison who is represented as a Union Man and who informed Lieut. Tucker that some fifty persons had met there the evening previous to take into consideration the proper course to be pursued to prevent their negroes from escaping, avowing at the same time that no aid should be given to prevent the escape of negroes belonging to persons professing Union Sentiments.

I will keep myself advised of any movements which may be prejudicial to the interests of the service and report accordingly. I am Sir Very Respectfully Your Obdt. Servt.

HLcSr   John F. Staunton

Col. John F. Staunton to Maj. Genl. John A. Dix, 24 May 1862, vol. 145/288 8AC, Letters Sent, ser. 4876, Post of Annapolis, RG 393 Pt. 2 No. 315 [C-4168]. By early June, Staunton concluded that the "armed organizations in this and the adjoining counties . . . are composed entirely of Men professing ultra Southern views, and who openly avow, that should the rebel Army cross the Potomac they would join it." (Col. John F. Staunton to Brig. Genl. Montgomery, 4 June 1862, vol. 145/288 8AC, Letters Sent, ser. 4876, Post of Annapolis, RG 393 Pt. 2 No. 315 [C-4168].)

139: Maryland Legislator to the Secretary of War

Near Washington July 25, 1862

Sir   As chairman of a committee appointed by both branches of the Legislature of Maryland, I had the honor of an interview with you last winter in reference to the admission of fugitive slaves within the lines of the Federal Army — And now in the capacity of private citizen I take the liberty obtruding myself upon your notice —

The partial enforcement of the fugitive slave law in the District of Columbia, has had the effect of forcing all the fugitives from Maryland into Alexandria & its environs: where they receive military protection — The Provost Marshal there, has assumed the prerogative of deciding that no citizen of Maryland shall have the right to arrest any slave within the lines of his Department — This decision is tantamount to issuing an emancipation proclamation in the Counties of Maryland bordering on the Potomac River — Already hundreds and perhaps thousands of servants have absconded from Maryland & now are roaming about the streets of Alexandria & vicinity, & their legitimate claimants dare not interfere with them —

It occurs to me sir, since the Military Authorities have decided that the people of Maryland shall not recover their slave property under any civil process, it would not be unreasonable to ask the Government to place them on at least equal grounds with the people in the rebellious states —

According to the very important order which has just emanated from the War Department — It is required, "that military and naval commanders shall employ persons of African descent for Military & Naval purposes, & that accurate accounts shall be kept to show from whom such persons shall have come, as a basis upon which proper compensation can be made in proper cases" —[1] I believe sir, an order of similar import issued for the benefit of Maryland would be most acceptable to her loyal citizens — But to deprive Union men of their property without affording them any redress, as I have recently seen done in Alexandria is a species of confiscation that I believe many of the extremists have never contemplated —

If the labor of slaves can be made to contribute in any way to the suppression of this iniquitous rebellion: it ought to be the policy of the Government to adopt it — And no patriotic citizen would hesitate to proffer it for that purpose — If in the prosecution of the war for the restoration of the Union the emancipation of slavery should become necessary, I would say let it go — But until then; justice to the loyal men in loyal states demands protection —

The Negro is naturally indolent & unless employed becomes demoralized & utterly worthless — I am sir — most respectfully y^r ob^t sevt

ALS   Jn° H. Bayne

Jno. H. Bayne to Hon. E. M. Stanton, 25 July 1862, B-1394 1862, Letters Received, RG 107 [L-142]. A notation on the outside reads "File," and no reply to Bayne has been found in the records of the War Department. According to a Harford County slaveholder, the northernmost portions of Maryland also suffered from the "recent act of Congress making the District of Columbia *free Soil* and an outlet for all the slave property of Maryland." The Harford County master requested compensation of $1,000 for the loss of his slave, "the lowest estimated value of the services of said colored servant for the period He was bound to serve." (Thos. Hope to the Honorable Senate and House of Representatives, 15 May 1862, 37A-H1.3, Petitions & Memorials Tabled, ser. 468, 37th Congress, RG 233 [D-56].)

1 In an executive order dated July 22, 1862, President Abraham Lincoln ordered military commanders in the seceded states to seize and use any

private property needed for military purposes, and to employ as laborers "so many persons of African descent as can be advantageously used for military and naval purposes, giving them reasonable wages for their labor." The order required that accounts be kept as a basis for compensating unionists whose slaves or other property was thus employed. (*Official Records*, ser. 3, vol. 2, p. 397.)

140: Maryland Unionists to the U.S. Congress

[*Baltimore February 1863*]
To the Congress of the United States of America: The undersigned Loyal Citizens of Maryland being sincerely anxious that Maryland shall cease to tolerate Slavery, and convinced that a grant of ten millions of dollars will suffice to compensate for the inconveniencies, public and private, and to alleviate the shock to the industry of the State, incident to such a change, respectfully petition your Honorable Body for the passage of such an act, subject to such conditions as may be thought reasonable to exclude disloyal persons from taking any benefit under it.

PDS   [*26 signatures*]

Jno. T. Graham et al. to the Congress of the United States of America, [Feb. 1863], enclosed in Jno. T. Graham to Hon. Thos. H. Hicks, 28 Feb. 1863, 37A-J4, Petitions & Memorials, ser. 547, 37th Congress, RG 46 [E-76]. The covering letter noted that the petitioners were "*loyal* citizens" of Baltimore. Among the signatures are those of Judge Hugh L. Bond and Quaker abolitionist John A. Needles. A notation on the wrapper reads "ordered to lie on the Table."

141: Commander of the 1st Separate Brigade of the 8th Army Corps to the Commander of the Middle Department and 8th Army Corps, Enclosing a Clipping from a New York Newspaper and a Circular by the Brigade Commander

Point Lookout. Md, April 1, 1863.
General, Your orders in relation to certain negroes belonging to a Mr Blackstone, a citizen of St Mary's County Md, who were fugitives from justice, were attempted to be executed, but when the Sheriff came for the negroes, they managed by some means to convey themselves away. Mr Blackstone reports to me, that they were secreted by persons within the lines, but after a conference

with the Officers here, who avow their ignorance of any such Secretion, I am confidant that this is not the fact. I enclose a copy of a circular which I have issued in order to carry out your policy with reference to the Slave population of Maryland, You will be kind enough to notify me of your views as to its propriety, Quite a number of negroes—many of whom are Servants of persons, residing in Maryland), had, prior to the assignment of this command to me, been permitted to come within the lines, and were employed in the Quartermasters Department at this Point, as day laborers.

I desire that you will inform me of your interpretation of the Act of Congress of July 17, 1862, as to whether such an employment as this, is the *"employment"* contemplated in the said Act, which constitutes all negroes so employed forever thereafter free.[1]

I enclose a publication—an Extract from the N.Y. Tribune) for your information. I have the honor to be, Very Respectfully Your Obt Servt.

HLS   Henry H. Lockwood

[*Enclosure*]   [*New York   March 1863*]
NEGRO-HUNTING WITHIN OUR LINES.

Letters from the hospitals at Point Lookout, Md., say that the slave-catcher has recently made his appearance there. Months ago persons calling themselves masters claimed as their own negroes who had escaped from Virginia as well as those who had the misfortune to belong to Maryland plantations. But under General Orders issued in conformity with a law of Congress, no officer dared to surrender them. A few weeks since, a detachment of the "Lost Children" regiment stationed at this post was relieved by the "Second Eastern Shore House Guard," under the immediate command of Col. Rogers, and the superior command of Brig.-Gen. Lockwood, who spends a large part of his time at the Point. Soon after the arrival of this regiment a negro-hunter made his appearance in quest, not of a fugitive, but of a "thief," the slaves he sought having taken from their masters a boat in which to make their escape. The officer of the day was sent with a squad of men to hunt up the culprits, but was unable to find them, the law-abiding convalescent soldiers of the hospitals having found means to secrete them. Other so-called masters were more successful: having decoyed their prey beyond the lines, they laid in wait for them, and carried them off. Several instances of this have taken place. We hear that Gen. Lockwood, when remonstrated with on the subject, declared that, in allowing these things to be done, he is acting in strict conformity with general orders from Gen. Schenck, the

commander of the department. Those who know Gen. Schenck, and who remember the campaign of Gen. Lockwood on the eastern shore of Maryland, find it difficult to credit this assertion.
PD

[*Enclosure*]   Pt Lookout, Md   Mch 30, 1863
(Copy)
(Circular)

    The Brigadier General Commanding directs that there shall be no interference with the slave population by the troops within his command except for certain specific purposes hereinafter named. Military Camps shall not be used as places of public resort or for idlers, and All those coming there, except on important business, or to give information, should be denied admittance, Such as have business will be conducted to the proper Officers of the Camp, Information will be sought for from all sources and rewards in money, with protection from danger from giving information may be promised to all, White and Black. Any one suffering from having given information will be protected, without or within the Camp, as may be necessary. Commanding Officers will generally be sustained in the protection afforded by them, but will be held responsible that there be just grounds for such protection. All cases of the kind, should be immediately reported to Head Quarters. All informants – where the information leads to a capture – will be remunerated, and with a view to this, their names should be taken, by the Officer to whom the information is given and reported. Negroes entering the Camps clandestinely, must be placed without the lines, but in no case *delivered* – either *directly* or *indirectly* – to their Masters, Nor should they be placed without the lines, when their masters or others seeking them are in the Neighborhood of the Camps. All vessels lying at the wharves where there are Troops will be considered within the lines. No distinction will be made as to the departure from the Shores of the Potomac of any persons, on account of color, and all orders heretofore issued or Regulations made by any officer making such distinction, either directly or by inference are hereby declared null and void   All negroes coming from the Western Shore of the Potomac will be received and protected. With a view to prevent negroes from being used in the illicit trade, all negroes leaving should be interrogated, as to whether their departure is voluntary. If it shall not appear to be voluntary, they will be detained and protected.
    All Commanding Officers, Quartermasters &c, are cautioned not

371

to employ negroes in the Public Service, unless they be free or refugees from the Western Shore, but when once so employed, they will—in accordance with the act of Congress relating to the subject—be forever thereafter protected   By order of Brigadier Gen'l Lockwood

HDc

Brigdr. Genl. Henry H. Lockwood to General, 1 Apr. 1863, enclosing clipping from *New York Tribune*, [Mar. 1863], and Circular, Head Quarters First Separate Brigade, 8th Army Corps, 30 Mar. 1863, L-93 1863, Letters Received, ser. 2343, Middle Dept. & 8th Army Corps, RG 393 Pt. 1 [C-4130]. A memorandum on the outside of the file, written by General Robert C. Schenck, commander of the Middle Department and 8th Army Corps, noted that he approved Lockwood's circular.

1 Section 11 of the Second Confiscation Act, adopted July 17, 1862, authorized the President "to employ" blacks in any manner for the suppression of the rebellion, but included no explicit provision about the freedom of persons so employed. Section 12 of the Militia Act, adopted the same day, did not use the word "employment" in authorizing the President to receive blacks into U.S. military or labor service, but section 13 provided that the slaves of disloyal masters who rendered such service to the U.S. "shall forever thereafter be free." (U.S., *Statutes at Large, Treaties, and Proclamations*, vol. 12 [Boston, 1863], pp. 592, 599.)

142: Superintendent of Maryland Black Recruitment to the Headquarters of the Middle Department and 8th Army Corps

Baltimore, July 13, 1863.

Sir, I respectfully submit the following facts, for the action of the Major General Commanding.

Twenty four able-bodied colored men, free from diseases and defects which would disqualify them from joining the army, are desirous of enlisting. They are all confined at present in the Baltimore City jail. The facts in regard to each I will briefly state.

1. CHARLES JENNINGS. The jail Record shews that, on the 2^d December, 1861, he was committed by Magistrate *Nalls* as a "Runaway for further hearing". Another entry is "Property of Messrs W^m· J. T. E. & J. H. Stewart; Trustees."

Jennings says he is the property of General J. B. Stewart, of the rebel service, and was placed in prison to be kept there during the war or until the possession of this city by the rebels.

2. JACOB TAYLOR. The jail record shews the same state of facts,

except that he was committed December 3, 1861. Taylor's statement agrees with that of Jennings.

3. PETER KNOX. The jail record shews nothing except that on the 1st June, 1862, he was committed by Magistrate E. R. Sparks, as "a runaway slave." There is no statement of claim or ownership or hearing.

Peter Knox states that he was the slave of a notorious secessionist, Captain John Fulton, of the rebel army, residing in Accomac Co., Va.; that on account of the open display of two secession flags by Captain Fulton, he, Knox, was declared free by General Lockwood, who gave him free papers, that he served for about seven months as waiter to an officer in the 150th N.Y.S.V.; that he lost his papers, was arrested here in Baltimore and thrown into jail where he has been lying ever since. [*In another handwriting*] Was taken out of Slave Pen" by Habeas Corpus by Judge Bond who has his case under consideration

4. JOHN THOMAS. The jail record shews that this man was committed July 30, 1861, by Magistrate Griffin, "for examination, charged with being a runaway slave" – that he was "returned same day & in jail." An entry in pencil is as follows: "Property of G. R. Gaither to be held for him."

Mr. Gaither, I learn, is a wealthy merchant of this city or vicinity, a secessionist whose son is in the rebel army.

5 THOMAS KNOCK. The jail record shews that he was committed May 22, 1863, by Magistrate Hiss, "being a runaway slave, the property of Captain William Knock, of Salisbury, Md. to the order of his master."

This master is now, I understand, and has long been, a captain in the rebel army.

6. BENJAMIN JOHNSON. The jail record shews that he was committed June 29, 1863, by Magistrate Johnson, "Being a slave and the property of GREENLEAF JOHNSON, of Somerset Co., Md."

The slave himself knows nothing of this master but says he belongs to a lady named *Dorsey*, who lives in the country.

7. JOHN NORRIS. The jail record shews that he was committed *June 29, 1863*, by Magistrate *Johnson*, "Being the slave and property of GREENLEAF JOHNSON of Somerset Co. Md"

This man knows nothing whatever of Greenleaf Johnson but says that he belongs to Mr. Noah Worthington, of Baltimore Co.

8 LEWIS AYRES, The jail record shews that he was committed June 29, 1863, by Magistrate Johnson, "being a slave the property of GREENLEAF JOHNSON, of Somerset Co., Md."

Ayres himself has never heard of this master but says he belongs to Mrs. Briscoe, a secessionist lady of Georgetown, D.C., who had him brought here in March, 1862 for fear he would be freed in the

District. At first, he was kept in "Campbell's Slave jail" but afterwards put in the city jail where the expenses are only 30 cents a day.

9. NICHOLAS CROSS. The jail record shews committal of same date, same magistrate, same owner, "GREENLEAF JOHNSON"

Cross never heard of this master but says he belongs to *Noah* *Wor*thington of Watersville, near Baltimore. Mr. W's politics not known.

10. JOHN BOARDLEY same committal, same date, same owner, same entry. owner "GREENLEAF JOHNSON."

The slave says he belongs to Dr. Ristar, who is said to be a secessionist of Baltimore Co.

11. GEORGE BOND. same date, same magistrate, same entry, same owner, "GREENLEAF JOHNSON of Somerset Co. Md.

I did not speak with this man but hear that he knows nothing of Mr. *Greenleaf Johnson*.

12. JAMES GLASCOE. Same date, same magistrate, same entry, same owner, "GREENLEAF JOHNSON, of Somerset Co. Md."

The man Glascoe knows nothing of Greenleaf Johnson, but says he belongs to Dr. Michael Stone, of Prince George's Co., Md. and that he was kept for about one year in the private slave jail known as "*Campbell's*", before he was placed in his present prison.

13. CHARLES JORDAN. Same date, same magistrate, same entry, same owner "GREENLEAF JOHNSON of Somerset Co., Maryland".

Jordan himself says he belongs to *John Dorsey* who is known as a secessionist residing near Ellicott's mills.

14. JOSHUA SCROGGINS. Same date, same magistrate, same entry, same owner "*Greenleaf Johnson* of Somerset Co., Md."

Scroggins himself knows nothing of *Greenleaf Johnson*, but says he belongs to Noah Worthington, of Watersville.

The attention of Major General Schenck is respectfully invited to the fact that not one of these *nine* persons knows anything of Mr. Greenleaf Johnson who claims to be the owner. Without collusion, each one tells a different story, claims to belong to a different master and tells a clear story. I except *George Bond*, with whom I held no conversation on the subject. They were committed on the *same day* by the *same magistrate*, for the same owner & by the same constable, one "F. L. Morrison"

15. FREDERICK ROBINSON. The jail record shews that he was committed Octo. 7, 1861, by Magistrate Hiss as "Runaway Property of Theodore Lanner further hearing" A marginal entry is "Theodore Lamer, 5 miles below Queenstown, Md."

He has been in prison nearly two years without hearing!!

16 JAMES WHITE. The jail record shews that he was committed,

November 29, 1861, by magistrate Nalls, as "Slave property of Harry Kimberly for safe keeping."

Mr. Kimberly is a Union man and James White does not bear a good character at the prison as a peaceable man

17. WILLIAM SHIPLEY. Was committed Feb. 25, 1862, by Magistrate Nalls, as "Runaway from Mrs. *Emily McTavish* for hearing"

I understand that Mrs. McTavish is reputed disloyal.

18 COLUMBUS SHIPLEY. Was committed Feb 25, 1862, by Magistrate Nalls, as "Runaway from Mrs. *Emily McTavish,* for hearing".

19. MOSES SHIPLEY. The jail record shews committal, Feb. 21, 1862, by Magistrate Irving, as "Being about to abscond from his master, Mr. *C. C. McTavish*"

He has been in jail nearly 16 months on this suspicion! Mr. McTavish lives in Howard Co. Politics not known.

20. ISAAC BROWN. The record shews committal, May 6, 1863, by magistrate Hiss, for "Insubordination, Committed subject to the order of his master, A. H. Stump".

The master is reputed to be disloyal.

21. MICHAEL GREEN. The record shews committal May 6, 1863, by Magistrate Spicer, as "a runaway slave the property of W$^{m.}$ D. Clark"

The owner is reputed to be disloyal. His agent is Mr. *Collins McKenzie*, of this city.

22. MATTHEW IBBINS. The record shews committal May 27, 1863, by Magistrate Showacre, as "Being a runaway, the property of N. W. S. Hays, of Harford Co.

The owner is Nathaniel W. S. Hayes, a secessionist, whose son is a surgeon in the rebel army.

The slave has been in jail two years and two months, having been confined for most of that time in one of those private jails known as a "slave pen.

23. AUGUSTUS BADEN. The record shews committal by magistrate *Hiss*, June 3, 1863, as "Being a runaway slave, the property of Catherine Gardiner, of Prince George's Co., Maryland. Subject to the order of his mistress.

Politics of mistress not known.

24. NACE TAYLOR. The record shews committal, June 19, 1863, by Magistrate Johnson, as "Being a runaway slave of Benj. Pembroke, of St Mary's Co., Md. Committed to await the order of his master, Benj. Pembroke."

Another entry directs bill to be sent to B. P. at Robertson & Briscoe's, 149 Pratt St., up stairs.

25. JOHN SHELTON. The record shews committal, May 12, 1863, by Magistrate Forrester, as a "Runaway". Belongs to Francis Dunnington, Doncaster P. O., Charles Co., Md." Another entry is *"Sold Thos. Skinner."*

The first owner, Dunnington is reputed disloyal. The second is not known.

26. MATTHIAS ECLESTON. The record shews committal, May 24, 1863, by Magistrate WELSH, as "Being a runaway slave".

No owner's name is mentioned but the man says he belongs to John Evans, No. 12, Chester St., Baltimore.

Mr. Evans, to say the least, is not known to be a loyal man.

I have the honor to annex hereto literal copies of the jail record and to suggest that these men, with the exception of two, are capable of rendering good service to the country in the field, instead of lying in prison. I trust they will be permitted to enlist in the 4th Regiment, United States Colored Troops, now in process of formation in this city. Your obedient servant,

ALS   William Birney

Colonel William Birney to Assistant Adj. General, 13 July 1863, B-434 1863, Letters Received, ser. 2343, Middle Dept. & 8th Army Corps, RG 393 Pt. 1 [C-4l25]. Two weeks later, Birney liberated fifty-nine other slaves who had been incarcerated in a Baltimore slave pen, enlisting the men in the Union army. (*Freedom*, ser. 2: doc. 70.)

143: Black Woman to the District of Columbia Freedmen's Bureau Assistant Commissioner

Washington, Aug, 16, 1865.
Colonel: I have the honor to state that in Nov. 1863, my husband, Jno. Jones, and Richard Coats, & Caleb Day–(Colored men) were arrested & tried at Port Tobacco, Md, and sentenced to be confined in the Penitentiary at Baltimore, for the term of eleven years & eleven months, for assisting three colored women, & four children, to escape from slavery.

Richard Coats was the slave of Geo. Wm. Carpenter, of Harris Cove, (opposite Acquia Creek); Said Carpenter has several times, been confined in the "Old Capitol" for smuggling goods to the rebels.

Before turning my husband, Jno. Jones–& Richard Coats over to the authorities–Carpenter whipped them so severely with a stave – in which he had bored auger holes, that they suffered severely for over two months. – Caleb Day & my husband – Jno. Jones were free men.

I would earnestly, and respectfully request that you use your influence to procure for the parties named full pardon – & release from imprisonment. – Very Respectfully Your Obt. Servant,

her

HLSr   Dola Ann ✕ Jones

mark

Dola Ann Jones to Col. Jno. Eaton, Jr., 16 Aug. 1865, Unregistered Letters Received, ser. 457, DC Asst. Comr., RG 105 [A-9858]. After learning that Governor Augustus W. Bradford had already requested court records regarding the three men, Colonel John Eaton, the Freedmen's Bureau assistant commissioner for the District of Columbia and adjacent counties of Maryland, asked him to pardon Jones, Coats, and Day, as well as all other "parties held in confinement for violation of the fugitive law, now abrogated & others confined for violation of those statutes of Maryland made to protect & defend slavery and now consequently void." Governor Bradford pardoned the three men in the fall of 1865, upon which Richard Coats, aided by the Freedmen's Bureau, initiated proceedings to reclaim his schooner, valued at $1,500, which had been seized at the time of his arrest. Coats subsequently abandoned prosecution of the case, having made "some arrangement" with the defendants. (G. V. W. Crain to S. N. Clark, 26 Aug. 1865, Unregistered Letters Received, ser. 457, DC Asst. Comr., RG 105 [A-9858]; Col. John Eaton to Hon. A. W. Bradford, 1 Sept. 1865, vol. 6, pp. 62–63, Letters Sent, ser. 449, DC Asst. Comr., RG 105 [A-9858]; Lt. S. N. Clark to James C. Carlisle, 8 Dec. 1865, Unregistered Letters Received, ser. 457, DC Asst. Comr., RG 105 [A-9858].)

144: Affidavit of Two Maryland Freedpeople

District of Columbia, City of Washington
27th day of September 1865.

Humphrey Ware, and Catherine Ware, his wife – being duly sworn, state, that the said Catherine Ware was formerly the slave of one Luke Hawkins, of Charles County, Maryland. – That about eighteen years ago the said Catherine Ware, was married to one Jno. Stone, a free colored man – and that previous to his death (which occurred in 1860) he gave her the following articles – viz: –

(3) Three feather beds, (6) Six sheets, (6) Six Pillow-slips (or cases) (4) Four Pillows – (1) one boulster, (4) Four quilts, (1) one Counterpane (1) one vallance for under skirts, (7) Seven Dresses, (1)

one Shawl, (1) over cloak, (2) Two pieces of white linen, (1) one silver Shield, (1) one Gold ring, – (2) Two Bonnets, (2) Two. pairs of shoes, (1) one pair of stockings – (6) Six tea cups, & saucers, (12) Twelve plates, (1) one wash-bowl & pitcher, (1) one Tea bowl, (1) one cream pitcher, (7) Seven Tumblers, (1) one preserve dish, (1) one butter plate, one (1) Castor, (1) one clock, (1) one bed. stead, (1) one basket, (1) one waterbucket, (2) two tin cans, (2) two sugar dishes, (1) one wooden bowl. – That in the year 1862, she was married to Humphrey Ware, – That in May, 1864 – They left Charles Co. for the purpose of coming to Washington, and that, when within about nine miles of Washington they were overtaken by one Alfred Kirby, a constable of Prince George Co. Md, – who took from them all of the articles above enumerated, as the property of Catherine Ware, also the following articles – (the property of Humphrey and Catherine Ware) viz: (3) Three shirts, one (1) linen Duster, (3) Gold studs, (1/2) One-half pound of yarn, (150) one-hundred & fifty Pounds of Bacon, (1 1/2) one & one-half Gallons of Lard, (3) Three pounds of sugar, also (1) one pair of window curtains, (1) one night gown, – (1) one Revolver, (1) one Silver watch, (1) one hand-saw, and a hatchet. – that the said Alfred Kirby, took them to Marlborough, and their committed them to jail, retaining in his possession all of the property above enumerated, – and to the best of the knowledge and belief of deponents he has made no return of said property to any officer whatever. That the said Alfred Kirby, still holds possession of the same, and although repeatedly called upon to return said property to deponents, refuses to do so. –

his

Humphrey × Ware,

mark

her

Catherine × Ware,

mark

HDSr

Affidavit of Humphrey Ware and Catherine Ware, 27 Sept. 1865, Unregistered Letters Received, ser. 457, DC Asst. Comr., RG 105 [A-9881]. Sworn before a Freedman's Bureau agent.

145A: Statement of a District of Columbia Woman

Washington City May 25th 1864

Mrs Laura A. Moody, of Washington, D.C., applies for the release of her husband Geo. A. Moody, who while attempting to bring from Piscataway, Md some negro women to their husbands, living in this city under Government employ, was arrested and imprisoned in Lower Marlboro Jail. Mr Moody had a pass and had been informed he would not be interfered with, or if he was so interfered with that he would be protected by Government

HD

[Endorsement] Hd. Qrs. First Separate Brigade Relay House *[Md.]* June 1″ 64. Respectfully returned to Depm't. Hd. Qrs. with the information that Detective Wm W. Wood was intrusted with the investigation of this case and reports that Geo A. Moody and a Mr. Jones, were employed by three (3) Negro's (contrabands then in the employ of the U.S. Govm't) to go to Piscataway after the wives and children of these contrabands, who accompanied Moody and Jones on papers purporting to be issued by Cap't Shutz Provost Marshal. In the execution of what they supposed to be authorized by these papers, they, collected the women & children and were on their way to Washington with them, when they were arrested by a Constable, by the name of Kirby (Jones and one colored man eluding the officer) who took Moody, two of the negro men with the women and children before Dr. G. [F]. Harris a justice of the Peace, who ordered them committed to jail. Subsequently Jones who had returned to Washington, at the solicitation of Moody's wife accompanied her to Upper Marlboro Jail to see her husband; On their arrival, Jones was arrested and confined in Jail with Moody.

It appears that Moody and Jones were employed by these colored men because of their having a wagon and horses with which to transport their women and children, and having made their acquaintance while engaged upon the same work for the Govm't near Washington. It appears further that these men (Moody & Jones) are very poor and ignorant, and their families dependent entirely upon their efforts for daily subsistence being brothers in law, they had obtained a team and wagon with which they performed such jobs as they could get from the Govm't and private parties who might require their service.

Being employed occasionally at the [Correll] where these Negroes were at work, and being offered a paying price for this job, they undertook it and fell into the hands of the *Phillistines*.

Their ignorance and utter destitution . . .[1] idea of any intention to commit a crime [. . .] [with] them a Provost Marshals pass would be regarded a passport to the realms of eternal bliss if it was so written. In as much as they supposed they were acting under the authority of proper Military Power, I would recommend if it can be done, that their cases be investigated by a Military commission E. B. Tyler – Brig Genl:

Statement of Mrs. Laura A. Moody, 25 May 1864, M-1590 1864, Letters Received, RG 107 [L-134]. Other endorsements.

1 Approximately two words obscured by an ink blot.

145B: Commander of the 1st Separate Brigade of the 8th Army Corps to the Headquarters of the Middle Department and 8th Army Corps

Relay House [*Md.*] June 15th *1864.*
Colonel, On visiting Port Tobacco on Monday last, I learned that Moody, Jones and two negro men whose cases had been referred to me from the Secretary of War and Secretary of State, were as I had reported, confined in Charles County Jail having been transferred from Prince Georges. Being informed that they were not properly treated I called on the Sheriff and requested an interview with the prisoners; he very politely complied by showing me to a building to all appearances well secured with bars and bolts, at both doors, and windows. After unbolting two doors, I was shown into a medium sized room, where I found the four men heavily chained to the floor with fetters upon their feet, and was told the four were handcuffed together at night. I inquired of the Sheriff by what authority he held the prisoners, and he produced an order from a Prince George' County Magistrate, directed to the Sheriff of Prince George Co. for the commitment of Jones in the Jail of his (Prince George) County, and said the others were charged with running off slaves; but exhibited no authority for holding them and I think he had none. At my suggestion the Irons were taken off.

These men complained very bitterly of the treatment they had received in Prince George and Charles County Jails – and strongly disavowed any intention of committing an offence in what they did, believeing as they did, the pass of Provost Marshal Shutz of Washington all the authority they required. There is evidently a strong prejudice in the minds of a majority of the citizens of Prince George and Charles Counties against these parties and all who sympathize with the slave, and in the death struggle of their cherished institution they appear anxious to vend their spite upon any one that may fall in their power.

Moody Jones and the colored men, claim to have been in the employ of the Government by the Military Authorities, and left that employment temporarily under the sanction and authority of the Military Provost Marshal and now urgently request its protection. I am Colonel, Very Respectfully Your Ob't Serv't

HLS   E. B. Tyler

[*Endorsement*] Referred to Maj. Gen. Wallace, commanding the Middle Department, with instructions to take measures to secure the release of the parties imprisoned. By order of the Sec'y of War   C. A. Dana, Asst Secy of War   War Dept.   June 24, 1864.

Brig. Gen'l. E. B. Tyler to Lieut. Col. S. B. Lawrence, 15 June 1864, T-156 1864, Letters Received, ser. 2343, Middle Dept. & 8th Army Corps, RG 393 Pt. 1 [C-4145]. Other endorsements. On June 29, 1864, General Lewis Wallace, commander of the Middle Department, forwarded the papers regarding the four jailed men to Maryland Governor Augustus W. Bradford, asking that Bradford direct their release from the Charles County jail. While thanking Wallace for this display of respect for civil authority, Bradford evidently concluded that he could not or would not order the release, whereupon Wallace responded that "the endorsement from the War Office entrusting to me the business of procuring the release of the men named, is in language making it my duty absolute; and the parties having been for a long time under close and degrading confinement, it is a duty that will admit of little delay." If the governor would not act, "I have no choice left me but to order Moody, Jones, and the negroes, brought to me, that I may forward them to Washington at once." (Maj. Genl. Lew. Wallace to Hon. A. W. Bradford, 29 June [186]4, and Maj. Gen. Lew. Wallace to His Excellency Gov. A. W. Bradford, 4 July [186]4, vol. 32/35 8AC, pp. 515–16, 549–51, Press Copies of Letters Sent, ser. 2328, Middle Dept. & 8th Army Corps, RG 393 Pt. 1 [C-4169].)

146: Commander of an Ohio Regiment to the Headquarters of the Middle Department and 8th Army Corps

Salisbury, Md, June. 4th 1864.

Captain   Yours of the 2nd I have.   I beg leave to refer a subject to the Brig^r Genl Commanding, that promises me no Small degree of Annoyance.   Many Slaves have been recruited in this district, who upon examination, were rejected and sent home— the masters of these men wish to reclaim them.   They come to me for protection, and refuse to go back to their masters.   Under the Act of Congress and Gen Orders, what Shall I do with them—   The master claims them under the laws of Maryland—   And they claim they are fugitives.   In one instance, and I learn there are many others, Masters have refused to feed and clothe their Slaves, and have beaten and illtreated them.   They come and claim protection   What shall be done.   I do not fully understand to what extent I am to interfere in this matter.   All those who conduct themselves in this manner are openly or covertly sympathisers with the Rebellion.   I want to do my whole duty in this Command, and Shall, if by possibility I can learn what it is.

Lt Fearing of Smiths Ind^t Cavalry has reported, and the telegraph line is Safely Guarded.   I have stationed fifty men on the lower end of the line from this point, and have the remainder of his Command, 49 Men & 2nd Lt with me here—

In the absence of more definite instructions I have notified parties in the negro difficulties to abstain from all *unlawful* practices.   Very Respectfully Your Obd Svt.

ALS   A L Brown

Col. A. L. Brown to Captain, 4 June 1864, enclosed in Maj. Gen. Lew. Wallace to Col. E. D. Townsend, 7 June 1864, M-436 1864, Letters Received, ser. 360, Colored Troops Division, RG 94 [B-567]. Brown commanded the 149th Ohio Volunteers. In a draft letter included in the same file, the Bureau of Colored Troops directed the superintendent of Maryland black recruitment to accept all slaves desiring to enlist, assigning to the Quartermaster's Department any men unfit for active duty. (A.A. Genl. C. W. Foster to Col. S. M. Bowman, 17 June 1864.)

147: Ohio Soldier to the Secretary of War; and Commander of the Post of Annapolis, Maryland, to the Headquarters of the Middle Department and 8th Army Corps

Annapolis M.d. June the 1ˢᵗ 1864

Dear sir Your hunble servant begs leave to address your majesty with a few lines in regard to our Provost returning a slave to his master; A negro about 17 or 18 years old, who came to camp the night of the 28ᵗʰ of may wishing to enlist. He remained in camp until to day about 8 oclock A.M. when he was taken out by the Provost accompanied by a stranger, If he has done justly, please pardon my ignorance and let it drop. It might cause me some trouble. Yours respectfully

J. Morgan

P.S It is very discouraging to white men as well as colored to hinder enlistment

ALS

Annapolis Md, June 13th 1864

Captain, I have the honor to acknowledge the receipt of your endorsement of the 10th instant, referring the accompanying letter from "Sergeant J. Morgan" to the Secretary of War, to me for investigation and report, I beg leave respectfully to report that I have been unable to find such a person as "Sergeant J Morgan" in my command, but that a suitable investigation has fixed the authorship of the above mentioned letter, upon Sergeant J. Brown Co "J" 144ᵗʰ Reg't Ohio National Guard, now on duty at "Camp Parole" near Annapolis Md.. I beg leave also to state that Captain A. W. Briggs 106ᵗʰ New York Vols, Provost Marshal of "Camp Parole," denies having at any time, returned a slave to his owner. Captain Briggs informs me that about two weeks ago, a colored man, in the employ of a Farmer residing in Anne Arundel County, (name not remembered) came within the lines of "Camp Parole," and busied himself in performing various menial offices for the men of the 144th Reg't Ohio "National Guard."

His employer subsequently visited "Camp Parole," and stated to the Provost Marshal that he was in great need of the services of the colored man, and requested that he might be ordered to leave the camp.

Captain Briggs replied that he had no authority to comply with the request, and declined to do so.

Captain Briggs states that subsequently, the Colored man left the camp, in company with his employer.

The subject was not referred to me, and as Sergeant J. Brown, Co

383

"J" 144th Ohio "National Guard" has committed a manifest breach of military propriety in thus addressing the Secretary of War, without the knowledge of his officers, and as Sergeant Brown in so doing, concealed his name, with evident fear that unless he did so, he might be caused "some trouble," I have deemed it proper to avail myself of the opportunity to administer a rebuke to Sergeant Brown, and a warning to his comrades. (all of whom need disciplining) and have accordingly directed Sergeant J. Brown Co "J." 144th Ohio National Guard to be at once reduced to the ranks. I remain Captain With much respect, Your obedient servant,

ALS   Adrian R. Root

Sergeant J. Morgan to Sec. Stanton, 1 June 1864, and Col. Adrian R. Root to Capt. Max Woodhull, 13 June 1864, M-431 1864, Letters Received, ser. 360, Colored Troops Division, RG 94 [B-566]. Endorsements.

148: Maryland Slave to the President

Belair [*Md.*] Aug 25th 1864

Mr president   It is my Desire to be free. to go to see my people on the eastern shore. my mistress wont let me   you will please let me know if we are free. and what i can do. I write to you for advice. please send me word this week. or as soon as possible and oblidge.

ALS   Annie Davis

Annie Davis to Mr. president, 25 Aug. 1864, D-304 1864, Letters Received, ser. 360, Colored Troops Division, RG 94 [B-87]. A Bureau of Colored Troops notation on the outside of the letter reads merely "file," and no response to Annie Davis appears among the copies of letters sent by the bureau or by other offices in the War Department.

Belair Aug 25/[1864]

Mr president —

It is my
Desire to be free to go
to see my people on
the eastern shore. my
Mistress wont let me
you will please let me
know if they are free. and
what I can do. I write
to you for advice please
send me word this
Week. or as soon as possible
and oblidge.

— Annie Davis
Belair Harford
County. Md.

Belair Harford
Co

Document 148: Maryland Slave to the President

149: Maryland Former Slave to the Secretary of War

Boston July 26th 1864

Dear Sir   I am Glad that I have the Honour to Write you afew
line   I have been in troble for about four yars   my Dear wife was
taken from me Nov 19th 1859 and left me with three Children and
I being a Slave At the time Could Not do Anny thing for the poor
little Children for my master it was took me Carry me some forty
mile from them So I Could Not do for them and the man that they
live with half feed them and half Cloth them & beat them like dogs
& when I was admited to go to see them it use to brake my heart &
Now I say agian I am Glad to have the honour to write to you to
see if you Can Do Anny thing for me or for my poor little
Children   I was keap in Slavy untell last Novr 1863. then the
Good lord sent the Cornel borne [*Birney?*] Down their in Marland
in worsester Co   So as I have been recently freed I have but letle to
live on but I am Striveing Dear Sir   but what I went too know of
you Sir is is it possible for me to go & take my Children from those
men that keep them in Savery   if it is possible will you pleas give
me a permit from your hand then I think they would let them
go   I Do Not know what better to Do but I am sure that you
know what is best for me to Do

my two son I left with Mr Josep Ennese & my litle daughter I
left with Mr Iven Spence in worsister Co [. . .] of Snow hill

Hon sir will you please excuse my Miserable writeing & answer
me as soon as you can   I want get the little Children out of
Slavery, I being Criple would like to know of you also if I Cant be
permited to rase a Shool Down there & on what turm I Could be
admited to Do so   No more At present Dear Hon Sir

John Q A Dennis

Hon Sir will you please direct your letter to No 4 1/2 Milton St
Boston mass

ALS

John Q. A. Dennis to Hon. Stan, 26 July 1864, D-1049 1864, Letters
Received, RG 107 [L-51]. No response has been found among the letters sent
by the War Department.

150A: Affidavit of a Maryland Freedman

District of Columbia, City of Washington
12" day of Sept. A.D. 1865.

Jacob Giles, being duly sworn, testifies – that in August, 1864, he went to Prince George Co. Md, to see his family who were living with Mr. Geo. W. Hardisty – that the said Hardisty threatened to "take him into the bush & give him 200 lashes" – that Mr. Richard Hardisty – brother of Geo. W. Hardisty, interfered in his – & that he – (Geo. W. H.) then threatened to cut deponents throat "from ear to ear"; That he was driven away & not allowed to see his family until Mr. Richard Hardisty interfered & procured permission for him to do so.

That in January last said Geo. W. Hardisty, who was in charge of his sister's (Miss Mary Hardisty's) farm, hired his son, Wm. Giles, aged about 19 years, agreeing to pay him 10^{00} per mo, but that they now refuse to pay him, – That in July last, his Son W^m, – in consequence of ill usage. left the said Geo. W. Hardisty, but was arrested & taken before a J.P. & remanded back to the custody of Mr. H. – That while in the presence of the J.P. deponent asked permission to speak in behalf of his son, in regard to the money due him – whereupon the said Geo. W. Hardisty did violently assault & beat him, & deponent verily believes, that had it not been for the interference of Thos. Clark the J.P. who was present, the would have been killed. –

That for attempting to defend himself, he was arrested on the charge of committing an assault on the said Geo. W. Hardisty, & committed to jail & kept in irons for one month – at the expiration of which time he was released on 500^{00} bail.

That Mr. Geo. W. Hardisty has threatened to kill him if he ever comes to his place, & that his wife & two of his children are now at Mr. Richard Hardistys & that the said Richard Hardisty refuses to allow them to come away with him.

HDcSr

his
(Signed) Jacob X Giles
mark

Affidavit of Jacob Giles, 12 Sept. 1865, enclosed in Col. John Eaton, Jr. to Maj. Genl. O. O. Howard, 18 Sept. 1865, Unregistered Letters Received, ser. 16, Washington Hdqrs., RG 105 [A-9674]. Sworn before a Freedmen's Bureau agent.

150B: Maryland Justice of the Peace to the District of Columbia Freedmen's Bureau Assistant Commissioner

Collington Prince George Co Md [*September.? 1865*]
Dear Sir I receved some short time since a letter from washington signed by S. N. Clarke requesting me to see that the Bearer of this Jacob Giles was protected from violence by George. W. Hardisty and also to aid him in his proper efforts to remove his family to washington in this I have done all that I can do under the law here I have called upon Richard Hardisty who has Jacobs wife and two children one of those belonged to him at the time they were liberated and he says he will not give them up that they were hired to him by the year altho he admitted to me that with Lucy Jacob wife he made no positive contract as to price that she came to him and said she would stay with him as long as she lived if he would feed and cloth her but now when called on he says that he will hold on to them for the year and what would be the use of my having him up before a Justice of the Peace when he will swere that the party was hired to him by the year and the laws of this state will not take the black mans oth and theirfore he would retain them and put the cost upon Jacob This is a hard case no doubt and as Jacob has thought proper to go to You I feel it my duty to make you a proper statement of this affair the negroes in this state was declared free on the first of November and Jacob Giles son William a boy of about 18 or 19 was at that time with some others of his family with George W Hardisty and he by some means got him to stay with his Sisters under the promis of $10 pr month Some time in July William was whiped and ran off to his farther & mother this George W Hardisty sent for me and stated that William had ran off & he wished me to give him a writ to arrest him & bring him before me for a breech of contract & I directed the constable of the district to arrest William which he did & had him up the same day I asked of William if he hired to Geor W. H. & he awnsered that he had hired to one of Geo W. H. Sisters at $10 pr month in the presance of G. W. H I then asked him what had been paid him upon his waggers the awnser was two dollars in money and a suit of clothing all this in his Mr Hardistys presance and he did not deny. And I told the boy he must go back & stay the year out as he admitted they had hired him & paid a part of his wages and did not offer any evidence of improper treatment at that time and when I remanded him back this man Jacob in a very polite maner asked my permision to speak which I of course gave him and as soon as he did commence to say somthing in behalf of his Son George W Hardisty commenced beating him in a most violent manner and Jacob runing back some forty feet I supose George

W. H. beating him all the time when Jacob appearantly threw a bottle which he had in his hand all the time over George W. H. sholder and then he was sett upon by four of five and they would have beat him to death if I had not prevented them   they then wanted me to order him a whiping and I declined   they then wished to commit him   I also declined that.   They then carreed him before George A Michill another Justice of the Peace & upon the representtation he committed him and he lay in Jail some four weeks   I went down and baild him out and then made out & acount for Williams hire & gave it to the constable and this Hardesty says he owes him nothing   it is owing to this man Jacobs good conduct and my duty as a Magastrate that I have done as I have   I have made this lenthly statement in order to let you understand & I think Jacob will state you the truth in the matter   I Remain your Respectfuly your

Joshua S Clarke

NB I will state also that those people the Hardisty and my self are not upon very good terms and I have tryed to do all I could to gratify them without going contrary to what I beleved to be my duty   I have the most implict confidence in Jacob or I would not have bailed him out and I want him to be at court in Nov the first week J. S. Clarke

ALS

Joshua S. Clarke to Col. John Eaton, [Sept.? 1865], Miscellaneous Records, ser. 499, DC Asst. Comr., RG 105 [A-9915].

151: Provost Marshal of the 1st District of Maryland to the Commander of the 3rd Separate Brigade of the 8th Army Corps

Easton [*Md.*] Nov. 2 1864.

General: — I take the liberty of writing you relative to the status of affairs in this, (Talbot) County.

Since the adoption of the New Constitution, in this state, there has been a very strong disposition on the part of the disloyal element here, to ignore that instrument, so far as it relates to Slavery and the Elective franchise. Many of the citizens are endeavoring to intimidate the colored, and compel them to bind their children to them, under the old apprenticeship law, and there is no means of preventing them from doing it, without their fears could be dispelled. — Many of them come to me, for advise, & I direct them to file their objections, — but many will be deterred from doing so by fear. — They are in a pitiable condition.

In some localities, the disloyal are determined to pollute the ballot box, by ignoring the law. Chas Key, a son of F. S. Key, says publicly, that he is disfranchised, but intends to vote We need martial law here, if we expect peace— *Very respectfully, Your obt. servt.*

HLS   Andrew Stafford

[*Endorsement*] Head Quarters 3rd Sep Brigade 8th Army Corps Balto Nov 4 1864 Respy referred to Maj Genl Wallace. I have no doubt of the truth of Capt Staffords statement and fear that unless some steps are taken to protect the colored people, of the lower counties the chief object of the new Constitution will be defeated and these people will still be slaves in truth though free in name. I respectfully recommend that a sufficient force be at once placed in these counties to protect the State & military authorities in their just and laudable effort to see that the organic law of the state is not rendered a nullity by chicanery and violence on the part of the disloyal slave-holders of Maryland. If the provisions of the new Constitution are not carried out and these rebels made to respect it it will be worse for the colored man than if it had never been adopted Henry H Lockwood Brig Genl

Captn. Andrew Stafford to General, 2 Nov. 1864, filed with M-1932 1864, Letters Received, ser. 12, RG 94 [K-4].

152: Maryland White Unionist to the Commander of the
Middle Department and 8th Army Corps

Forrest Vill   Prince Georges County [*Md.*]   Dec. 26th 1864
Dear sir   I take the liberty of asking a few Questions for the good
of the Colored People   it does appear from what they tell me that
since they became free they are not cared for by their former masters
and a number of them are women and children that are suffering for
food and raiment   others say they are told that they will be sold
into Bondage again   the poor Creaturs do not know what to
do   they say they are whiped and abused very much   the most of
the young men has left and a number of them are in the
army   those women with their children cannot help them
selfs   they say they are afraid to look for a new home for fear while
doing so their children will be thrown out   this is their statement
to me and I do not doubt it in the least, for, I know what a time
we few Union men have hear for they do not hesitate to say that we
robbed them of their property and such abuse as is hard to
take   you know our vote in the county was very small and we are
few in number but we do not fear them for we think we have stood
the hardist part of the storm and believe it is near to and
end   some information for their good would be thanfully
received   yours Respectfully
ALS   Kelita Suit

Kelita Suit to Genl. Wallace, 26 Dec. 1864, S-574 1864, Letters Received,
ser. 2343, Middle Dept. & 8th Army Corps, RG 393 Pt. 1 [C-4144]. Suit
indicated below his signature that he was a district assistant assessor of internal
revenue.

CHAPTER 7

Missouri

7

Missouri

SITUATED ON THE BORDER between the North and the South, Missouri manifested characteristics of both sections.[1] Like the slave states to the south, it contained a well-developed slave-labor economy, dominated by masters who commanded the best land, owned large numbers of slaves, and enjoyed disproportionate political power and social influence. Although the majority of Missouri slaveholders pursued small-scale commercial agriculture and held just a handful of slaves, they were as dependent on slavery as the more substantial slaveholders who specialized in hemp and tobacco production on the larger farms of the Mississippi and Missouri river valleys. Slavery prospered on big farms and small in the decade before the war. Like the free states to the north, Missouri also contained a vibrant free-labor economy, made up of family farmers, middling entrepreneurs, and wage-workers. During the 1850s, the spectacular rise of St. Louis as a center of manufacture, trade, and transportation attracted thousands of new residents, including many foreign immigrants, and strengthened the free-labor sector of the state's economy. The divergent development of these two economies produced intense social and political conflict. The sectional crisis turned Missouri into a powder keg, and Abraham Lincoln's election touched off the explosion.

The Civil War pitted proponents of free labor against those of slavery in a fierce struggle for supremacy. Pro-Confederate slaveholders pressed for secession, but unionists of both proslavery and antislavery persuasion rallied and established a provisional state government loyal to the United States. Almost immediately, slaveholding and antislavery factions began lobbying well-placed Washington connections to buttress or challenge slavery. By gaining control of the provisional government, proslavery unionists held the upper hand. But antislavery forces steadily grew in strength.

Meanwhile, the war created opportunities for Missouri slaves to seize liberty. Taking advantage of the presence of sympathetic Northern soldiers, the federal confiscation acts, and the renewed hostilities be-

For a history of Missouri during the Civil War years, see William E. Parrish, *Turbulent Partnership: Missouri and the Union, 1861–1865* (Columbia, Mo., 1963).

tween slaveholders in western Missouri and antislavery partisans in eastern Kansas, thousands of blacks escaped slavery during the first two years of the war. The slaves' willingness to risk all for freedom strengthened the antislavery unionists. In the summer of 1863, the state convention that had rejected secession and formed the provisional government enacted an ordinance providing for gradual emancipation. But events, notably the enlistment of black men in the Union army, soon revealed the folly of gradualism in the midst of revolution. Although many slaveholders continued to resist emancipation in any form, their position eroded as slaves and other opponents of slavery pressed for unconditional freedom. In January 1865, following the electoral triumph of the antislavery unionists, a constitutional convention declared the immediate and uncompensated abolition of slavery in Missouri.

Faced with threats of secession in the border states of Maryland, Kentucky, and Missouri, President Abraham Lincoln strove to keep them loyal to the federal government, nurturing all expressions of political fidelity and promoting unionism of every stripe. Lincoln took heart when the Missouri state convention that had been called to consider secession voted against disunion, but he had few illusions about the stability of the loyalist coalition. In July 1861, after federal forces captured the government arsenal at St. Louis from the pro-Confederate state militia, the governor and his chief lieutenants fled the capital, eventually establishing a government-in-exile in the Confederacy. Thereupon, the state convention reassembled, formed a provisional government, and selected a prominent antebellum jurist, Hamilton R. Gamble, as provisional governor.[2] A staunch proponent of unionism throughout the secession crisis, Gamble – like Lincoln – sought to keep Missouri in the Union by restoring order and by assuring slaveholders that the federal government would guarantee the security of slavery.

Slaveholding loyalists applauded Gamble's policy, but secessionists – who included some of the largest slaveholders in the state – remained hostile. Hundreds accompanied absconding state officials into exile, taking their slaves and other movable property with them. As was true elsewhere in the South, such shotgun migrations disrupted slavery and triggered flight – by slaves in transit or about to be moved, by slaves whose relatives on adjacent farms had already been moved, and by slaves who simply observed dispirited parties en route and reasoned that they too would eventually be forced to join the migrant ranks.

[2] After creating the provisional government, the state convention adjourned, subject to recall by Provisional Governor Gamble. In October 1861, again in June 1862, and finally in June 1863, the convention reassembled to address the difficult questions troubling the state, including slavery. (Parrish, *Turbulent Partnership*, chaps. 7–9.)

Runaway slaves entered upon an uncertain future. Federal military authorities in Missouri enunciated widely varying policies regarding slavery, and these were executed in turn by officers and soldiers of divergent intentions. When the fighting commenced, General William S. Harney, commander of the Department of the West (which embraced Missouri), promised federal protection to slaveholders. Although Harney was replaced and Missouri shifted briefly to the Department of the Ohio, his policy remained in effect as President Lincoln searched for the right man to fill the politically sensitive Missouri command. In July 1861, he appointed General John C. Frémont, flamboyant explorer and former Republican presidential candidate, to head the Western Department, with headquarters in St. Louis. Determined to make Confederate slaveholders suffer for their disloyalty, Frémont proclaimed martial law in Missouri at the end of August and declared free the slaves of disloyal masters. His proclamation was the boldest step against slavery taken by any Union commander in the first year of the war. It went far beyond the First Confiscation Act of early August (which freed only those slaves who had labored directly in the Confederate war effort) and anticipated the Second Confiscation Act of the following summer (which freed the slaves of all rebel masters). Frémont's action reverberated through the border states and shook the entire nation. Infuriated unionist masters immediately gained the President's ear.

Although Lincoln "perceived no general objection" to the establishment of martial law, he requested that Frémont modify the proclamation to conform with the more limited emancipation provisions of the First Confiscation Act. When Frémont refused, Lincoln ordered him to do so.[3] Lincoln's repudiation of Frémont's emancipation edict reassured unionist slaveholders in the border states and temporarily revived the shaken border-state strategy. It did not, however, resolve the problem of slavery within the Union, a problem that sooner or later the nation would have to confront directly.

In Missouri, Lincoln's appeasement of loyal masters further divided the unionist camp. Moved by a combination of repugnance to chattel bondage and a desire to secure the state for free labor, antislavery unionists boldly declared immediate emancipation the only solution to the state's and the nation's turmoil. In St. Louis and elsewhere, especially in the state's German communities, they formed antislavery Home Guard units, which enjoyed the favor of General Frémont though not that of Governor Gamble. Frémont refused to disguise either his sympathy for the antislavery radicals or his antipathy toward the defenders of slavery.

Frémont's forthright commitment to emancipation angered Mis-

---

[3] *Official Records*, ser. 1, vol. 3, pp. 469–70, 477–78, 485–86.

souri slaveholders, and they urged his removal. In Washington, Attorney General Edward Bates, Governor Gamble's brother-in-law, championed their cause. Another cabinet member, Postmaster General Montgomery Blair, a long-time friend of Frémont, tried to mute the criticism, but to little avail. Vociferous slaveholding unionists clogged the telegraph wires and the mails with denunciations of Frémont. In addition to charging him with poor generalship, they accused him of slighting Governor Gamble and ignoring the legitimate concerns of slaveholders. They also intimated that Frémont's policies threatened to undermine Missouri's loyalty and, by extension, that of the other border states. In late October 1861, after the failure of numerous attempts to reconcile the general and the proslavery wing of the unionist party, Lincoln capitulated to the critics and relieved Frémont of command.

As the conflict between the provisional government and General Frémont neared a climax, Governor Gamble called the state convention back into session. Among its other actions, the convention mobilized for defense against Confederate partisans by reorganizing and expanding the state militia. Gamble traveled to Washington and laid plans for the Missouri State Militia before the President. Lincoln agreed to arm, equip, feed, transport, and pay the state force and to allow the governor to appoint its officers, on condition that the militia be subordinate to the federal department commander. General John M. Schofield, formerly a St. Louis physics professor, assumed command of the state forces.[4]

Like the provisional government which it served, the Missouri State Militia from its inception displayed the strong influence of slaveholding unionists. Slaveholders dominated the organization, guaranteeing that it would help check insubordinate slaves as well as Confederate insurgents. Antislavery radicals consequently shunned the state militia, and instead enlisted in Missouri regiments of U.S. volunteers, even though the federal army also had its share of proslavery unionists. The composition of military forces in Missouri thus reflected the deepening split among the unionists. Not even the Union uniform could disguise the differences between proslavery militiamen and antislavery volunteers.

In early November 1861, General Henry W. Halleck, a well-

---

[4] For Lincoln's approval of Gamble's proposal and the War Department order of November 7, 1861, authorizing the Missouri State Militia (M.S.M.), see *Official Records*, ser. 1, vol. 3, pp. 565–66, and ser. 1, vol. 8, pp. 454–56. In July and August 1862, faced with increasing guerrilla activity in the state, Schofield further increased the number of citizens under arms by creating the Enrolled Missouri Militia (E.M.M.). (*Official Records*, ser. 1, vol. 13, pp. 506, 508–9, 516, 518–19, 534–35.) For a concise history of both the Missouri State Militia and the Enrolled Missouri Militia, see *Official Records*, ser. 1, vol. 13, pp. 7–12.

schooled officer widely known for his treatises on military science, assumed command of the new Department of the Missouri, which embraced Arkansas, western Kentucky, and several free states, as well as Missouri. Halleck understood that he was walking a tightrope in Missouri and therefore stepped cautiously when events would not permit him to stand still. Annoyed by repeated applications from loyal masters for the return of slaves, he promptly issued General Order 3, which required the unconditional exclusion of all unauthorized persons, particularly fugitive slaves, from army camps. Halleck hoped that his order would relieve military officers from involvement in the "relation between the slave and his master," a subject he preferred to leave with the courts. Like his counterparts, General John A. Dix in Maryland, General George B. McClellan in Virginia, and General Don Carlos Buell in Kentucky, Halleck believed that the federal army had no authority to tamper with the domestic institutions of the states in which it operated. Exclusion seemed a tailor-made guarantee of noninvolvement with slavery and thus pleased slaveholding unionists, especially those in the border states.

Despite Halleck's intentions, General Order 3 did not cover every contingency regarding fugitive slaves. Slaves who had worked on behalf of the Confederate army or provided military intelligence to the Union army could lay claim to federal protection. When, for example, the sheriff of St. Louis attempted to sell several slaves who had accompanied federal troops from southwest Missouri, Halleck intervened and ordered their release. They were entitled to freedom under the First Confiscation Act, he ruled, notwithstanding state laws that required the sale of unclaimed fugitive slaves. Halleck did not intend to "debar any one from enforcing his legal rights to the services of these negroes," but he insisted that "such rights, if any exist, can be enforced through the loyal civil tribunals of this State." Halleck instructed his provost marshal general with respect to such cases: "Military officers cannot decide upon rights of property or claims to service, except so far as may be authorized by the laws of War or the Acts of Congress. When not so authorized, they will avoid all interference with such questions."

Still, federal officers continued to encounter exceptional cases; some, it appears, searched them out. The most scrupulous officers communicated their questions to Halleck, seeking clarification of the exclusion order or permission to keep blacks within army lines. Others dispensed with formality and simply did as they saw fit. Halleck's repeated directives to comply with General Order 3 testified to the reluctance of his subordinates to deny military protection to fugitive slaves.

Military opponents of slavery in Halleck's department came from throughout the midwest. The soldiers' antislavery sentiment ranged along a wide spectrum, from tepid free-soilism to fiery abolitionism. But, whatever their initial ideological commitment, the war nurtured opposition to slavery. Soldiers who witnessed fugitives hounded and abused by masters, slave catchers, and civil authorities began to listen more attentively to the arguments of their abolitionist comrades who favored admitting slaves into army lines. Many commanding officers heard the same message, to which they listened even more closely when it coincided with strategic considerations. Some concluded that it defied the principles of warfare—as well as common sense—to aid the enemy by restoring fugitive slaves to rebel owners. In January 1862, for example, General Ulysses S. Grant, commander of the District of Cairo (which included Missouri's southeastern counties), argued that it was improper for the army "to in any way aid those who in any manner aid the rebellion." Therefore, he ordered, a slave "who is used to support the master, who support[s] the rebellion, is not to be *restored* to the master by military authority." Growing numbers of federal soldiers came to believe that defeating the rebellion required attacking it at its source.

When high principle did not move Yankee soldiers to harbor fugitive slaves, low expediency often did. Officers and enlisted men alike welcomed runaways who assumed the soldiers' burdensome and distasteful camp chores. In time, some soldiers developed genuine affection for the fugitives, but even those who did not grew accustomed to the assistance of the fugitives and had no desire to resume the old regimen. Federal soldiers protected their black servants with a determination fierce enough and, when necessary, violent enough to turn away the most persistent master. Eventually the army employed black laborers in Missouri by the hundreds, as pioneers and teamsters as well as cooks and personal servants. Then federal military authorities at all levels recognized the need to protect the fugitive slaves in their midst.

Meanwhile, the slavery issue further widened divisions within the ranks of Missouri unionists. Free-state soldiers committed to emancipation clashed repeatedly with state militiamen loyal to the old order. The assignment of free-state soldiers to commands headed by proslavery Missourians proved particularly disruptive, especially when the defenders of slavery forced their antislavery comrades to observe the letter of Missouri's slave code. Employing free-state soldiers as the slaveholders' henchmen humiliated and infuriated them and ultimately increased their hostility toward the masters' prerogatives.

The divisions wracking Missouri unionists flared into open violence along the state's troubled western border. During the 1850s, the question of admitting Kansas to the Union had sparked fierce fighting between friends of slavery in Missouri and its adversaries in Kansas. In 1858, when Kansas voters rejected slavery, overt conflict subsided, though not the underlying animosity between the two sides. Missouri's wartime loyalty to the Union transformed former enemies into allies against the Confederacy, but the old passions would not die.

The uneasy alliance shattered over the issue of slavery. Galled by their forced association with slaveholders, Kansas volunteers broke ranks and renewed their war against the baneful institution that had disturbed their peace for nearly a decade. In their view, refusing to protect runaway slaves was tantamount to remanding the fugitives to slavery. Rejecting the Union army's role as slave catcher of last resort, they opened their lines to fugitives and defied orders to desist. At times, they mounted even more aggressive attacks on slavery. Encouraged by Senator James H. Lane, Kansas soldiers pursued rebel guerrillas into Missouri, frequently turning such missions into punitive raids against slaveholders. Lane firmly believed that "the institution would perish with the march of the Federal armies," and he intended that Kansas troops should do their part. He urged retribution against disloyal Missouri slaveholders, arguing that "[c]onfiscation of slaves and other property which can be made useful to the Army should follow treason as the thunder peal follows the lightning flash."[5] The Kansas regiments set the standard of antislavery commitment and activity within Union ranks.

Union soldiers from Kansas did not act alone in their war against Missouri slavery. Antislavery guerrillas from Kansas – known, like the soldiers, as "jayhawkers" – raided western Missouri with the avowed aim of freeing slaves.[6] Organized by Senator Lane (the "great jayhawker" according to General Halleck) and by Charles R. Jennison (a peripatetic physician, seasoned antislavery warrior, and former commander of a Kansas cavalry regiment), the guerrillas spread havoc among Confederate sympathizers and slaveholders of all political persuasions. In retaliation, proslavery partisans from Missouri attacked eastern Kansas. The fighting escalated into a civil war within the Civil War.

Newly liberated Missouri slaves helped sustain Lane's war on slavery. Black women, children, and old people, assisted by the jayhawkers, settled among sympathetic Kansas whites or in refugee camps, and the able-bodied men enlisted in the guerrilla bands. The blacks proved to be invaluable allies. They knew the terrain; they knew the masters; and they knew the slaves. Returning to Missouri, they freed other slaves, spirited them to safety, and recruited the men to their ranks. Kansas became a center for subversion of slavery and a bastion of freedom for slaves in western Missouri.

[5] *Official Records*, ser. 1, vol. 3, p. 516.
[6] *Official Records*, ser. 1, vol. 8, p. 554–55. In terms of opposition to slavery, the guerrilla jayhawkers differed little from their counterparts formally enlisted in federal service. In fact, over the course of the war, some Kansas men served in both roles. The soldiers, however, unlike the guerrillas, were directly beholden to military authority. See Stephen Z. Starr, *Jennison's Jayhawkers: A Civil War Cavalry Regiment and Its Commander* (Baton Rouge, La., 1973).

Slaves elsewhere in Missouri also tailored their escapes to fit the political geography. Along the state's northern and eastern borders, the free states of Iowa and Illinois beckoned, and Missouri slaves took full advantage. In eastern Missouri, St. Louis was a promising destination. St. Louis blacks fed, clothed, and sheltered fugitive slaves, and schooled them in the dangers and opportunities of the city. Military authorities and freedmen's aid societies provided material assistance to newcomers and helped them find employment, often in the free states to the north.[7] But in the central and southern parts of the state, flight proved to be more difficult. Along the Missouri River, where most of the state's slaves resided, masters and slave catchers kept close watch. In the backcountry of southern Missouri, the few slaves lived on small, scattered farms, and vast expanses of territory occupied by hostile whites discouraged escape. Throughout most of the interior, military posts located along rivers and railroads provided the only sanctuaries; even there, refuge depended upon the welcome of free-state soldiers. In these circumstances, the risks of capture and punishment were great, and only the most daring slaves defied the odds.

In the spring of 1862, the vagaries of national politics gave unexpected assistance to runaway slaves. The article of war adopted by Congress in March prohibited the engagement of Union soldiers in returning fugitive slaves to their masters, and it encouraged antislavery officers and enlisted men to protect slaves and repel their pursuers. General Halleck interpreted the new article as further proof of the need to admit no slave into army lines. Nonetheless, slaves found it easier to gain admission after the article was enacted.

But the course of the conflict did not always move in freedom's favor. Although the new article of war aided and encouraged potential fugitives, the war required redeployment of federal troops in the Mississippi Valley in ways that subtly but surely decreased the likelihood of successful escape. In March, the War Department expanded Halleck's authority by consolidating the armies in the western theater into the new Department of the Mississippi, under his command. As federal forces advanced further into Tennessee and Arkansas, and into northern Alabama and Mississippi, Halleck's exclusion policy advanced with them.

The advance of the exclusion policy did not, however, open the way for a welcoming policy to flourish in the rear. When Halleck left his St. Louis headquarters in mid-April to assume field command, he assigned day-to-day administration in Missouri to General Schofield, the state militia commander and a staunch supporter of Governor

---

[7] For a discussion of the efforts of military authorities to transport fugitive slaves in St. Louis — including several hundred who had been brought from Arkansas — to employment in the North, see *Freedom*, ser. 1, vol. 2.

Gamble. Loyal masters had good reason to presume that the man who temporarily filled Halleck's shoes would also follow in his footsteps. Of more immediate significance for Missouri slaves, many of the free-state soldiers who had given the greatest aid to runaway slaves also left Missouri for service elsewhere in the Mississippi Valley. The state militia became the dominant Union force in the state. Fugitives thus found fewer friends within military ranks, a consideration that weighed heavily in calculating the prospects of escape.

The removal of most free-state soldiers granted Missouri slaveholders but short reprieve. In July 1862, Congress enacted the Second Confiscation Act, freeing the fugitive slaves of disloyal masters and escalating the war against slavery. Border-state slaveholders condemned the act as fully as they had denounced Frémont's proclamation. They had castigated Frémont for exceeding federal law; now Frémont's policy was federal law. Moreover, the act signified the steady advance of antislavery sentiment in Washington, a development that frightened all slaveholders, loyal and disloyal alike.

Along the Missouri-Kansas border, the Second Confiscation Act strengthened the avowed enemies of slavery. Both army regulars and jayhawking irregulars cited the act to justify their raids against Missouri slaveholders. Anticipating the imminent enlistment of black men into the Union army, Senator Lane began recruiting a regiment of black soldiers in Leavenworth.[8] Lane's agents derived special pleasure from recruiting escaped Missouri slaves and broadcasting the promise of liberty among their enslaved brethren. Although freedom remained more a promise than a reality to Missouri slaves beyond reach of the Kansas raiders or distant from federal army encampments, that promise intensified the slaves' determination to be free.

General Samuel R. Curtis, appointed in September 1862 to command the reconstituted Department of the Missouri, fully appreciated the liberating power of the Second Confiscation Act and wished to employ it to strengthen the slaves' access to freedom. A former congressman from Iowa who had already seen battlefield service in Missouri and Arkansas, Curtis was a firm ally of antislavery unionists. In the summer of 1862, Curtis provided free papers to Arkansas slaves who had been impressed into rebel service.[9] Upon taking command in Missouri, he extended the policy to his new jurisdiction, and in December he issued General Order 35, which instructed provost marshals to grant certificates to all slaves entitled to freedom under the Second Confiscation Act.

Curtis's order provided Missouri slaves exactly the opportunity they wanted. When fugitive slaves reached army posts and insisted that

[8] On Lane's black regiments, see *Freedom*, ser. 2: chap. 1.
[9] See above, pp. 259–60, and doc. 95.

their masters were "secesh," most federal officers gladly issued them free papers. Some uninformed fugitives may have hesitated before pronouncing their masters disloyal, but the words came readily to most. And few stretched the truth. Throughout the state, only a fine line separated loyal from disloyal. What "loyal" master at one time or another had not displayed "disloyal" sentiments, if not necessarily by joining the Confederate army, then certainly by maligning the Union or at least its actions regarding slavery? And was not slavery the cause of the rebellion, and for that reason every slaveholder an accomplice to treason? Such logic emboldened slaves from all over the state to request free papers with clear conscience and unflinching eyes. It also suppressed lingering inhibitions on the part of the federal officers charged with issuing the papers.

Slavery deteriorated under the impact of the new confiscation act, and colonies of runaway slaves formed near army posts, railway depots, and the larger towns. Army quartermasters, commissary officers, and engineers employed those they needed. But many more slaves crowded into the makeshift camps than were fit for or could find military employment. Hungry, cold, and disease-ridden, the refugees soon exhausted their scant supplies, surviving only by their own ingenuity, the earnings of employed relatives, and occasional relief from federal authorities and Northern freedmen's aid associations. The number of refugees grew but their ultimate status remained uncertain. Because Missouri's loyalty preserved the legality of slavery, the refugees occupied a limbo between slavery and freedom. Only legal abolition would convey unassailable title to the freedom they now claimed by right of seizure.

During the second half of 1862, changing federal policy concerning slavery, both in Washington and in the field, encouraged Missouri's antislavery unionists to press for emancipation. In Washington, they redoubled their efforts to convince the Lincoln administration that they, and not the proslavery unionists, represented the true interests of loyal Missouri. At home, they sought to overturn Governor Gamble's proslavery policies, sponsoring antislavery rallies and running antislavery candidates for political office. Jolted by the electoral success of an assortment of emancipationists, Gamble realized that the slaveholders would have to compromise—even in the loyal border states—if they hoped to maintain slavery. At the end of December, he proposed that the new general assembly enact gradual, compensated emancipation to forestall the immediate, uncompensated abolition advocated by the radicals. Loyal slaveholders broke rank in response to Gamble's initiative. Some dug in their heels, determined to cling to slavery indefinitely; others were willing to support the governor. The division proved unbridgeable, particularly after antislavery unionists rejected gradualism and reasserted their commitment to immediate emancipation. Although a majority in the general assembly favored some form of emancipation, they could not agree on a single plan and adjourned at the end of March 1863 without acting upon the great question of the day.

Missouri's congressional delegation in Washington provided little assistance in breaking the impasse. Although some members of Congress wished to accede to President Lincoln's repeated overtures and negotiate terms of compensated emancipation, hard-liners denounced the whole scheme as unwarranted federal interference in the internal affairs of the state. Others sided with the antislavery radicals, rejecting all proposals that included payment to slaveholders. In December 1862, congressmen from Missouri introduced conflicting measures for compensated emancipation into the House of Representatives and the Senate, and Congress adjourned in early 1863 without adopting legislation regarding emancipation in Missouri. Because Lincoln's Emancipation Proclamation had no standing in the loyal border states, only the state legislature or the U.S. Congress could act against slavery. But the issue had so fractured the unionist coalition that neither could agree on slavery's future.

Irresolution bred factionalism among the unionists and conflict between military and civil authorities. Desperate to reduce the dissension, especially the growing polarization between antislavery radicals and Curtis on the one hand and conservative unionists and Gamble on the other, Lincoln searched for a successor to Curtis who would be free of identification with either extreme. In May 1863, he settled upon General Schofield, formerly commander of the Missouri State Militia and now seasoned by battlefield command in Arkansas and Tennessee. Sending Schofield into the Missouri maelstrom, Lincoln urged him to refrain from taking sides: "If both factions, or neither, shall abuse you, you will, probably, be about right. Beware of being assailed by one and praised by the other."[10]

Heartened by the removal of his nemesis, Governor Gamble took his plan for gradual emancipation to the state convention, which he called back into session in June 1863. Again Gamble stood between the reactionary slaveholding unionists who insisted that slavery remain

---

[10] At the same time, Lincoln elaborated upon his reasons for replacing Curtis: "I did not relieve General Curtis because of any full conviction that he had done wrong by commission or omission. I did it because of a conviction in my mind that the Union men of Missouri, constituting, when united, a vast majority of the whole people, have entered into a pestilent factional quarrel among themselves, General Curtis, perhaps not of choice, being the head of one faction, and Governor Gamble that of the other. After months of labor to reconcile the difficulty, it seemed to grow worse and worse, until I felt it my duty to break it up somehow, and, as I could not remove Governor Gamble, I had to remove General Curtis." (*Official Records*, ser. 1, vol. 22, pt. 2, p. 293.) Curtis was not, however, long removed from involvement in Missouri affairs. In January 1864, he assumed command of the Department of Kansas, including the troubled border between the two states.

inviolate and the radical antislavery unionists who advocated immediate, unconditional emancipation. But the balance of power was shifting steadily toward the radicals, and Gamble realized it. Desperately maneuvering to cushion the fall, Gamble won the convention's approval of a gradual emancipation ordinance on July 1, 1863. The measure would not take effect until 1870, and it stipulated that "all persons emancipated by this ordinance shall remain under the control, and be subject to the authority of their late owners . . . as servants" until 1876. It exempted slaves older than forty in 1870 (who would remain "servants" for life), and provided that slaves younger than twelve at that date would remain "servants" until they reached the age of twenty-three.[11] Gamble believed the ordinance to be a tactical victory for slaveholding loyalists, freeing no slaves for several years to come and guaranteeing that an attenuated form of slavery would linger until the end of the century. Slaveholders, however, knew that the ordinance was a strategic capitulation to the emancipationists. The advance of freedom – sparked by slave flight and sustained by congressional enactments – forced Missouri masters to accept the eventual end of slavery.

Unionist slaveholders hoped that the promise of eventual emancipation would halt the wartime deterioration of slavery, by restoring respect for the rights of loyal masters on the part of soldiers and officers in the Union army. They also expected that gradual emancipation would enable them to control the transition from slave to free labor. Missouri slaveholders, explained one of their number, had given "a cheerful acquiescence" to the emancipation ordinance, "hoping that this might be the occasion of ensuring the possession of their Slaves until free labor could be obtained." But instead of bolstering slavery for several more decades, the enactment of a distant emancipation speeded its downfall. A variety of groups, sharing little but opposition to the gradualist ordinance, turned on the scheme.

Slaves were the first to make their objections known. Although they recognized gradual emancipation as a public admission of the frailty of their masters' authority, they fully appreciated the power still wielded by Missouri slaveholders. Not content with the promise of future freedom, especially since that freedom would be mortgaged to the continued bondage of the oldest and youngest family members, many slaves fled their owners. Some previously successful fugitives returned home to free their families. Those who did not run away acted on an understanding that they would eventually be free. Slaveholders discerned changes in the demeanor of even the most docile slaves. When masters tried to reassert their accustomed control, they met a new and frightening hostility. With freedom in the offing, slaves became increasingly unwilling to submit to the old regime.

[11] The ordinance is printed in Parrish, *Turbulent Partnership*, pp. 223–24.

Many whites, occupying a variety of points on the political spectrum, wanted no more part of gradual emancipation than did the slaves. Antislavery radicals had opposed Gamble from the beginning. When the state convention terminated its existence after adopting the gradual emancipation ordinance, the radicals launched a campaign for constitutional abolition of slavery, immediate and unconditional. They agitated and organized, steadily gaining support among the growing number of Missouri voters who recognized that slavery had become an anachronism. The radicals also appealed to a larger, national audience. They publicized the atrocities committed by Missouri masters, hoping thereby to shield the slaves from ill-treatment and to convince the Northern public of the necessity of immediate emancipation. Recalcitrant masters provided ample grist for the radicals' mill.

Meanwhile, staunch rebel sympathizers severed their silent partnership with the slaveholding unionists, joining the radicals' assault on gradual emancipation from the opposite extreme. Believing they had nothing to lose, they attempted to reinstate the old order by force. Confederate bushwackers, including some of the thousands of prisoners paroled after the fall of Vicksburg in July 1863, lashed out at blacks who dared to claim freedom.[12] Die-hard unionist masters also strove to restore the old prerogatives by employing the state slave code to restrict the liberty of fugitive slaves, even those freed by the confiscation acts. Following antebellum legal procedures for apprehending fugitives, they obtained warrants for the arrest of runaway slaves and, armed with legal writs, brazenly accosted federal officers with demands that fugitives be relinquished. Members of the state militia often did the slaveholders' bidding, sometimes gladly. But most officers in the federal service refused to comply, referring claimants to the federal courts.

Profiting by the continued legality of slavery, slaveholders devised various stratagems for reasserting control over the slaves. They threatened prosecution of any employer who hired a fugitive without the owner's consent. If slaveholders could no longer reap the fruits of the slaves' labor, they would deny them to others and at the same time make it difficult for fugitives to find employment on their own. In another line of attack, masters sued railroad and steamboat companies for transporting slaves without their owners' consent, claiming damages provided under state law — double the monetary value of the slaves. Company officials appealed to military authorities for protection, inasmuch as they had transported many fugitives under army

---

[12] Rebel guerrilla activity increased sharply in Missouri and Kansas during the summer of 1863. Many of the prisoners who had been transported west of the Mississippi River upon their oath not to serve again in the Confederate army became bushwhackers, preying upon federal troops, Union sympathizers, and black people. See *Official Records*, ser. 1, vol. 22, pt. 2, pp. 365–66, 411–13, 428–29, 445–52, 482–84.

orders. Emancipation eventually invalidated all such suits, but in the meantime Missouri slaveholders, aided by the state judiciary, managed to obstruct the progress of freedom. Even legal disputes having no direct connection to the fugitives themselves could threaten their liberty, as when creditors seized them to satisfy defaulted debts of their owners.

The instability of the gradualist compromise emboldened nonslaveholding farmers, who had watched the debacle from the sidelines, to venture onto previously forbidden political terrain. Long deprived of access to black labor by the slaveholders' monopoly and short-handed as a result of wartime mobilization, nonslaveholders hoped to employ fugitive slaves as wage-workers. In 1862, only a few had risked indictment by hiring runaway slaves; a year later many more did so. Nonslaveholders approached runaways wherever they gathered and offered them employment, with few questions regarding the pedigree of their freedom. Each acting for their own reasons, the slaves, antislavery radicals, slaveholding rebels, slaveholding unionists, and nonslaveholders together undermined gradual emancipation and threw slavery into further disarray.

President Lincoln's advice notwithstanding, General Schofield could not remain neutral. Proslavery unionists sought assurances that he would protect their rights. In July 1863, Schofield modified Curtis's mode of dealing with the slaves of disloyal masters. Whereas Curtis had ordered provost marshals to issue free papers to fugitives who were entitled to freedom under the Second Confiscation Act, Schofield enjoined those officers to report each case, with the names of witnesses, to the provost marshal general of the department, "so that the matter may be turned over to the civil authorities."[13]

Loyal slaveholders did not miss the significance of Schofield's order. One such master interpreted it as a signal that the free papers and "other rules of the 'Curtis' administration were now abrogated."[14] Antislavery radicals discerned similar purpose in Schofield's policies. In August, a German newspaper in St. Louis accused Schofield and his provost marshal general of turning that city's jail into a "real 'slave-pen'," filled with blacks "who had believed in the gospel of liberty." The provost marshal general, the editors charged, had assumed the right to "recall and declare null and void the free papers which have been given by his predecessors or by former commanders of this department to the slaves of rebel masters."[15] The radicals demanded Schofield's removal. Badgered by increasingly vociferous critics, the general

---

[13] *Official Records*, ser. 1, vol. 22, pt. 2, pp. 359–60.
[14] Wm. P. Harrison to Hon. J. O. Broadhead, 25 July 1863, Miscellaneous Letters & Reports Received, ser. 2595, Dept. of the MO, RG 393 Pt. 1 [C-170].
[15] *Official Records*, ser. 1, vol. 22, pt. 2, p. 548.

Missouri

asked the War Department for guidance regarding the status of Missouri blacks. The judge advocate general replied that the Union army was obligated to protect slaves freed by federal law and the Emancipation Proclamation, and he recommended that such slaves be issued certificates of freedom. Schofield apparently complied with the recommendation, although he neither modified nor rescinded his order of July. Under Schofield's administration, subordinate officers did not issue free papers with the frequency or enthusiasm of their predecessors under Curtis.

Even Schofield's foot-dragging did little to stem the progress of emancipation. Recruitment of black men into federal military service, which began in Missouri during the summer of 1863, delivered the death-blow to slavery. In early August, General Thomas Ewing, commander of the Kansas-Missouri border district and an ally of Senator (and jayhawker) Lane, proposed raids into western Missouri to escort slaves of disloyal masters to Kansas, where the able-bodied men would be given the chance to enlist and all others offered employment. Schofield approved the operation, although he explicitly warned Ewing against interfering with any slaves owned by loyal masters.[16]

About the same time, black recruitment also began elsewhere in Missouri. In July, Colonel William A. Pile, the antislavery commander of a Missouri regiment, won authorization to recruit in Missouri for a black regiment being organized in Arkansas. Both General Schofield and Governor Gamble consented, provided that Pile enlist only free blacks and slaves who had fled from disloyal masters. Besieged by black volunteers, Pile's recruiters soon paid little heed either to their antebellum status or to their masters' politics. A crescendo of protests from slaveholding unionists prompted Schofield to halt Pile's work in late summer, but the army's need for soldiers and the success of black enlistment elsewhere in the South would not allow the ban to stand. As it became evident that full-scale recruitment of Missouri black men could no longer be deferred, Schofield expanded upon recruitment procedures originally devised by the War Department for Maryland and Tennessee. His General Order 135, issued in November 1863, provided for the enlistment of any able-bodied black man – free or slave – regardless of the loyalty of the slave's master, granted freedom to slaves who enlisted, and promised compensation to loyal masters. Still, Schofield remained a reluctant liberator. While acquiescing to emancipation via military service, he tried to limit the disruptive effects of recruitment upon slavery. His order prohibited mobile recruiting parties, placing recruitment instead in the hands of army provost marshals, many of whom demonstrated little desire to see blacks in military service. As Missouri radicals had feared, Scho-

[6] *Freedom*, ser. 2: doc. 85.

field's system limited the number of slave volunteers and hampered efforts to employ recruitment as a vehicle of wholesale liberation.[17]

Nonetheless, black recruitment offered legitimate access to freedom for the first time to slave men whose owners were loyal. Unionist slaveholders quickly perceived that recruitment doomed gradual emancipation, and they took steps to obstruct the enlistment of their slave men. They begged their slaves not to enter military service. When this failed, they devised a variety of petty deterrents (such as locking up shoes and clothing at night) and threatened violence against both prospective enlistees and their families. Frequently, the masters made good their threats.[18]

Missouri slaves refused to be thwarted by such obstacles. In the end, more than 8,300 served in the Union army – almost 40 percent of the state's black men of military age.[19] Nearly all enlisted in late 1863 and early 1864. Once under arms, these slaves-turned-soldiers assaulted the last bastions of slavery, turning their own freedom and their military service to the cause of universal liberty. From their encampments, they mounted expeditions into the countryside to liberate family members. Black soldiers convalescing at an army hospital near St. Louis threatened to bring the whole force of the Union army down upon masters who refused to free their loved ones.[20]

The entry of some black men into military service provided all Missouri blacks with important new allies, including the white officers of black regiments organized in the state, along with other federal authorities. Sympathetic officers took keen interest in the stories related by their men, particularly regarding the abuse of the soldiers' families. Even when powerless to act directly, the officers, along with the soldiers themselves, protested to Congress, the President, and the War Department the injustice of leaving in slavery the families of the Union's defenders. The efforts of black soldiers and their allies served notice upon Missouri masters that, even though the soldiers' families lacked legal claim to freedom, their mistreatment would not pass uncontested.

Some slave women and children accompanied their husbands, sons, and fathers to military posts, where they gained a precarious de facto liberty. Others left their owners and squatted on patches of unoccupied land or hired themselves to employers who raised no questions about their legal status. Still others moved to neighboring free states. For most, however, the enlistment of black men meant greater uncer-

---

[17] *Official Records*, ser. 3, vol. 3, pp. 860–61, 1009–10, 1034–36; *Freedom*, ser. 2: pp. 187–89, and docs. 84–88.
[18] *Freedom*, ser. 2: pp. 189–90, and docs. 90–92A–B.
[19] *Freedom*, ser. 2: p. 12.
[20] In addition to the relevant documents in this chapter, see *Freedom*, ser 2: docs. 299A–C.

tainty—about the safety of their enlisted husbands, sons, and fathers and about reprisals by their masters. Deeming the soldiers' dependents an unwanted expense, some vindictive slaveholders turned them out to fend for themselves. Other masters required the soldiers' kin to perform unaccustomed chores, including backbreaking work previously reserved for slave men. Others resorted to open terror.[21]

Still, Missouri slave owners could not arrest the march of time. Missouri slaves were determined to be free, and military service provided the surest avenue for the slaves of unionists. The desperate tactics of obstructionist masters ultimately backfired, turning public opinion, both in Missouri and throughout the North, against the loyal slaveholders. Immediate emancipation gained new adherents.

As the world closed in around them, unregenerate Missouri masters searched for a way to salvage their investment in slavery. For a time, Kentucky—where slaveholding unionists still held the upper hand—offered sanctuary. Some Missouri slaveholders moved to Kentucky with their slaves, while others forwarded their slaves for safekeeping, putting them to work with relatives, friends, or hired agents. Still others sold their slaves—often black men contemplating enlistment or the wives and children of Union soldiers—in the Kentucky market or to Missouri traders who then resold them in Kentucky. In November 1863, army officers in Kentucky estimated that some 1,000 Missouri slaves had passed through Louisville's slave marts within a two-month period. By then, the sale of Missouri slaves to Kentucky had created such a scandal that General Schofield enjoined the traffic. But less than one month later, he softened the ban, permitting loyal owners to remove "female Slaves and males not fit for military duty" from Missouri, subject only to the virtually unenforceable restriction that the removal be made *"with their* (the slaves) consent."[22]

As the transfer of "consenting" slaves resumed, so did the protests of the opponents of slavery, black and white. Black soldiers seethed at the ill-treatment of their families. Their white officers, moved by the desperate pleas and violent threats of their men, begged the War Department to intervene. White soldiers also reacted strongly to the masters' attempt to revive the interstate slave trade. In a celebrated case, a squad of Minnesota volunteers liberated Missouri slaves who were on their way to Kentucky, muscling aside state militia officers who attempted to thwart the rescue. Finally, in March 1864, General William S. Rosecrans (who had succeeded Schofield as commander of

[21] *Freedom*, ser. 2: pp. 189–90, and docs. 91–94, 296–98.
[22] Excerpt from Special Orders No. 307, Head Quarters, Department of the Missouri, 10 Nov. 1863, filed with J-445 1864, Letters Received, RG 107 [L-46]; Maj. Genl. J. M. Schofield to Lt. Col. J. O. Broadhead, 9 Dec. 1863, M-927 1863, Letters Received, ser. 2786, Provost Marshal General, Dept. of the MO, RG 393 Pt. 1 [C-198]; *Freedom*, ser. 2: docs. 91–94; and below, docs. 222, 223A.

the Department of the Missouri in January) forbade unconditionally the removal of any slave from the state. Rosecrans appealed to humanity, justice, and Missouri's need to retain "all the slave and other labor she has within her own border."[23]

By the spring of 1864, slavery was virtually dead in Missouri. To prevent their slaves from deserting, masters accorded certain perquisites of freedom, even while seeking to retain title to their human property. Such titular masters offered wages or crop shares and agreed to forego slave-style punishments and other vestiges of the old order. Meanwhile, nonslaveholders were also bidding for the services of black laborers, further speeding the development of free labor.[24] As spring turned to summer, de facto freedom had become so widespread that army recruiters reported the near cessation of all voluntary black enlistments.[25] One provost marshal reported that potential black recruits had "obtained the idea that the service is a dangerous place, and that their freedom is already accomplished." "We are free now," he quoted a typical explanation, "and choose to remain so as long as possible." Masters clamored for forcible enlistment of slaves who had fled to freedom – hoping at least to receive the compensation promised by the government – and, for a time, some provost marshals cooperated. But, like the other efforts by slaveholders to sustain their mastership, dragooning slaves into the army also failed. By August 1864, the War Department conceded the effective end of black enlistment in Missouri.[26]

With slavery all but abolished, antislavery radicals mobilized to purge it from the statute books. The growing popularity of their position – and the exile or disfranchisement of Confederate sympathizers – carried the fall elections for the radicals. At the same time, Missouri voters approved the call for, and elected delegates to, a state constitutional convention whose undisguised purpose was to abolish slavery. In January 1865, the convention assembled and, as its first order of business, declared immediate and unconditional freedom. Constitutional abolition represented a major achievement for the Missouri radicals and reflected their political supremacy. More important, it stood as a monument to the determination of Missouri slaves to be free.

[23] General Orders, No. 35, Headquarters, Department of the Missouri, 1 Mar. 1864, Orders & Circulars, ser. 44, RG 94 [DD-25].
[24] For a discussion of the evolution of free-labor arrangements in Missouri during the war, see *Freedom*, ser. 1, vol. 2.
[25] *Freedom*, ser. 2: p. 190, and doc. 96.
[26] *Freedom*, ser. 2: docs. 95–96.

153: Missouri Unionist to the Commander of the Department of the West, and the Latter's Reply

Saint Louis Mo. May 14, 1861.

Sir: In common with thousands who have perused your admirable proclamation of this morning,[1] I return you the thanks of a citizen of Missouri for its pratriotic tone and tranquilizing assurances.

There is nothing in this paper which is in my opinion needs explanation; yet I wish to be able to answer, with the authority of your name, a question which I have already replied to on my own judgment. Last evening, a gentleman, of the highest respectability, and intelligence, from Greene county, Mo. asked me whether I supposed it was the intention of the United States Government to interfere with the institution of negro slavery in Missouri or any Slave State, or impair the security of that description of property. Of course, my answer was most unqualifiedly, and almost indignantly in the negative. I told him that I had no means of forming an opinion which were not open to every other private citizen; but that I felt certain that the force of the United States, would, if necessary, be exerted for the protection of this, as well as any other kind of property. Will you be good enough to spare from your engrossing military duties so much time as may be required to say whether I answered correctly?

I have the honor to be, with the highest respect, your most obedient Servant.

HLcSr (Sgd) Thomas T. Gantt.

[*St. Louis*] May 14, 1861.

Sir: I have just received your note of this date, inquiring whether, in my opinion, you were correct in replying to a citizen of Southwestern Missouri as to the purpose of the United States Government respecting the protection of negro property.

I must premise my saying that I have no special instructions on this Head from the War Department. But I should as soon expect to hear that the orders of the Government were directed towards the overthrow of any other kind of property as of this in negro slaves.

I entertain no doubt whatever that you answered the question you mention correctly. I should certainly have answered it in the same manner, and I think with the very feelings you describe. I am not a little astonished that such a question could be seriously put. Already since the commencement of these unhappy disturbances, slaves have escaped from their owners, and have sought refuge in the camps of United States troops from Northern states and commanded by a Northern General. They were carefully sent back to their owners. An insurrection of slaves was reported to have taken place in Maryland. A Northern General offered to the Executive of that State the aid of Northern troops under his own command, to suppress it. Incendiaries have asked of the President permission to invade the Southern States, and have been warned that any attempt to do this will be punished as a crime. I repeat it, I have no special means of knowledge on this subject, but what I have cited, and my general acquaintance with the statesmanlike views of the President, makes me confident in expressing the opinion above given. Very respectfully, Your obedt. Servant:

HLc   [William S. Harney]

Thomas T. Gantt to Brig. Genl. W. S. Harney, 14 May 1861, and Brigadier General [William S. Harney] to Thomas T. Gantt, Esq., 14 May 1861, vol. 2/8 DMo, pp. 202–4, Letters Sent, ser. 5481, Dept. of the West, RG 393 Pt. 1 [C-9011].

1 In a proclamation to the people of Missouri on May 14, 1861, General William S. Harney, commander of the Department of the West, criticized the Missouri general assembly, dubbing its recent military bill "an indirect secession ordinance." Warning Missourians that their state "must share the destiny of the Union," he predicted that "the whole power of the Government of the United States, if necessary, will be exerted to maintain Missouri in her present position in the Union" and pledged himself to that end. Regarding the interests of Missouri unionists, he affirmed, "I shall exert my authority to protect their persons and property from violations of every kind." (*Official Records*, ser. 1, vol. 3, pp. 371–72.)

154: Missouri Unionist to the Commander of the Western Department

Saint Louis Augst 9th 1861

D[r] Sir   Three Slaves were taken from Palmyra Mo by Turchin'[s] regiment 19th Ill Vol. The fact that they were thus taken is generally known in Marion & adjoining counties & is now being used by Secessionists greatly to the injury of the government. Justice to parties wrong[d] & especially the interest of the Goverment demand that the slaves be restored to their owners, & that the Conduct of said regiment be repudiated by some prompt & decissive movement of the proper authorities.

I desire that Gen[l] Fremont address such an order to Genl Prentiss

as will if possible secure the property & vindicate the unsullied
honor of the Government.

Mr S. T. Glover informs me that under an authority given by you
he aided in making a search in the arsenal here for said slaves. And
he became satisfied that they left the arsenal with Turchins
regiment. It is almost certain they are not at Norfolk
Mo. Respectfully

ALS   H S Lipscomb

H. S. Lipscomb to Maj. Genl. Fremont, 9 Aug. 1861, L-9 1861, Letters
Received, ser. 5502, Headquarters in the Field, Western Dept., RG 393 Pt.
1 [C-9013]. A search of the records of the Western Department revealed no
evidence of any action in response to Lipscomb's letter. The following month,
soldiers of the same Illinois regiment were accused of absconding with a slave
from Jackson, in southeast Missouri, possibly taking him with them to Washington, D.C. (Brig. Gen. U. S. Grant to Brig. Gen. L. Thomas, 21 Sept.
1861, vol. G2 DT, p. 49, Letters & Telegrams Received & Letters Sent, ser.
2731, Dist. of Southeast MO, RG 393 Pt. 2 No. 171 [C-4806].)

155: Proclamation by the Commander
of the Western Department

Saint Louis,   August 30, 1861.
    Circumstances, in my judgment, of sufficient urgency render it
necessary that the commanding general of this department should
assume the administrative powers of the State. Its disorganized
condition, the helplessness of civil authority, the total insecurity of
life, and the devastation of property by bands of murderers and
marauders, who infest nearly every county of the State, and avail
themselves of the public misfortunes and the vicinity of a hostile
force to gratify private and neighborhood vengeance, and who find
an enemy wherever they find plunder, finally demand the severest
measures to repress the daily-increasing crimes and outrages which
are driving off the inhabitants and ruining the State.

. . . .

The property, real and personal, of all persons in the state of
Missouri who shall take up arms against the United States, or who
shall be directly proven to have taken an active part with their
enemies in the field, is declared to be confiscated to the public use,
and their slaves, if any they have, are hereby declared freemen.

. . . .

TDcSr   J. C. Fremont,

Proclamation, Headquarters Western Department, 30 Aug. 1861, Negro in the Military Service, p. 425, ser. 390, Colored Troops Division, RG 94 [B-620]. Ellipses in manuscript. Upon receiving the proclamation, President Abraham Lincoln expressed "anxiety" about the conflict between its emancipation provision and the more limited confiscation act adopted by Congress in early August. Writing "in a spirit of caution and not of censure," Lincoln asked Frémont to modify the proclamation to conform with the congressional law, so as not to "alarm our Southern Union friends and turn them against us; perhaps ruin our rather fair prospect for Kentucky." But Frémont declined to collaborate in weakening his action against slavery. "If upon reflection your better judgment still decides that I am wrong in the article respecting the liberation of slaves," he replied on September 8, "I have to ask that you will openly direct me to make the correction. The implied censure will be received as a soldier always should the reprimand of his chief. If I were to retract of my own accord, it would imply that I myself thought it wrong, and that I had acted without the reflection which the gravity of the point demanded. But I did not. I acted with full deliberation, and upon the certain conviction that it was a measure right and necessary, and I think so still." Lincoln promptly accepted Frémont's challenge: While professing "no general objection" to the proclamation, he ordered Frémont to modify it as previously directed. (*Official Records*, ser. 1, vol. 3, pp. 469–70, 477–78, 485–86.)

156: Commander of a Brigade in the Army of the West to the Headquarters of the Western Department

Boonville Mo Oct^{br} 6th 61

Sir. I send by the Northerner in charge of Capt Renfro 9th Reg Mo Vol. several slaves who having given important information to Major Eppstein while in command of this post, which saved his command from surprise now seek protection from their masters who threaten to kill them

Major Eppstein can not longer protect them. I therefore send them to Jeff City where they can work on the fortification. [Vy rst]

ALS   Jno C Kelton

Col. Jno. C. Kelton to Asst. Ajt. Genl., 6 Oct. 1861, Letters Received, ser. 5486, Western Dept., RG 393 Pt. 1 [C-9015]. An unsigned endorsement ordered the slaves sent to St. Louis.

157: Order by the Commander of the Department of the Missouri

St. Louis, November 20th, 1861.

GENERAL ORDERS, No. 3.

I. It has been represented that important information respecting the numbers and condition of our forces is conveyed to the enemy by means of fugitive slaves who are admitted within our lines. In order to remedy this evil, it is directed that no such persons be hereafter permitted to enter the lines of any camp, or of any forces on the march, and that any now within such lines be immediately excluded therefrom.

II. The General Commanding wishes to impress upon all officers in command of posts and troops in the field the importance of preventing unauthorized persons of every description from entering and leaving our lines, and of observing the greatest precaution in the employment of agents and clerks in confidential positions. BY ORDER OF MAJOR GENERAL HALLECK.

PD

General Orders, No. 3, Head Quarters, Department of the Missouri, 20 Nov. 1861, vol. 50/77 DMo, p. 2, General Orders, ser. 5488, Western Dept., RG 393 Pt. 1 [C-9010].

158: Missouri Former Soldier to the Secretary of War, and Commander of an Army Camp to the Commander of the Post of Rolla, Missouri

Rolla Missouri De^c 1. 1861

Sir When the army was camped at Springfield a colored man named Kelly was brought into camp. He was formerly a slave of a Mr Vaughn of Christian County. Because of Vaughn's open enmity to the government Gen Fremont refused to return him his slave.

Being in need of a servant Kelly was handed over to me & when part of the army retired to this place he came here with me. On arriving here my connexion with the army being dissolved, I had him at my camp *out side of the lines.* While I was at St Louis last week Col Phelps sent a file of his troops & took Kelly inside the lines & now has him guarded by the army. with the intention as I understand of returning him to his master.

I have no claim whatever to Kelly, but as he was legally in my possession & my servant he is entitled to my protection. I ask you to order that he be returned to me subject to the call of the Government, at which time I shall see whether he is a free man or not.

It is strange any part of the United States army here at Rolla is engaged hunting up & guarding the slaves of traitors while the secessionists are robbing & plundering loyal men in the western part of the state.

Every negro returned to these traitors adds strength to their cause in this state & I hope the policy will be abandoned. In this case I hope you will not permit the army to return Kelly to Greene county & from there be sent south & be sold into perpetual slavery without giving him a *chance* to establish his freedom. In consideration of the fact that I was in possession of the negro & that it is not a legitimate business for the army to be engaged in catching the niggers of traitors, I hope you will grant the order I ask. I am Sir very respectfully Your obdt Servt

ALS   John. M. Richardson

Rolla [*Mo.*], December 2^{d}, 1861.

Colonel   In obedience to your General Order, No. 6,[1] I have the honor to report that there are now in my Camp, and under my control, four fugitive slaves, belonging to citizens of Southwest Missouri, described as follows:

Names of Slaves.	Names of Owners.	Their Residence.
Moses, (Boy)	Geo. W. Andrews	Taney County.
Kelly (Man)	James Vaughn	Christian Co.
Jim (Man)	Samuel Green	Webster Co.
Viney (Woman)	John Wood	Greene Co.

In pursuance of your verbal instructions, subsequently given, I hold them subject to your order. These Slaves came with the Army from Southwest Missouri. One of the owners, (Mr. Green,) I believe to be an Union Man, but in this opinion I may be mistaken.

These Slaves have been obtained by citizens and brought to my Camp for safe keeping, in order to be restored to their owners, and these citizens have acted under my instructions. I am personally acquainted with all of the owners of these Slaves.

A portion of my own Slaves are in my Camp. They came when the people fled from Springfield and vicinity, with a wagon and team, clothing and supplies for their support. They feared they might be stolen by persons in the Army and they fled to me for protection. They will remain with me till I can provide for their comfort and safety. Yrs respectfully

HLS   John S. Phelps

John M. Richardson to Hon. Simon Cameron, 1 Dec. 1861, R-134 1861, Letters Received Irregular, RG 107 [L-84]; Lt. Col. John S. Phelps to Col. G. W. Dodge, 2 Dec. 1861, Unentered Letters Received, ser. 2594, Dept. of the MO, RG 393 Pt. 1 [C-108]. On the outside of Richardson's letter is a War Department notation of December 10, 1861: "Telegraphed the parties to hold the Negro, until his status is determined." On the same day, Governor Hamilton R. Gamble complained to General Henry W. Halleck, commander of the Department of the Missouri, that slaves were being held at the Post of Rolla against the wishes of their loyal masters. (H. R. Gamble to Majr. Genl. Halleck, 10 Dec. 1861, M-79 1861, Letters Received, ser. 2593, Dept. of the MO, RG 393 Pt. 1 [C-394].)

1 The order by Colonel Grenville M. Dodge, commander of the Post of Rolla, required that subordinate officers "immediately deliver to these Head Quarters, All fugitive Slaves" and forbade fugitives "to enter and remain, within the Lines." (Genl. Order No. 6, Head Quarters Post Rolla Mo., 29 Nov. 1861, vol. 446/1135 DMo, General & Special Orders & Post Orders, ser. 1100, Post of Rolla MO, RG 393 Pt. 4 [C-108].)

159: Commander of the Department of the Missouri to the Provost Marshal General of the Department

St Louis December 18th. 1861.

Col. From your verbal statements and the written communication submitted by you yesterday, I am informed that there are some 16 negro men confined in the City prisons in your charge, and advertised for sale under a Statute of this State. You have stated the facts of the case, as you understand them; have called my attention to the Statute of this State on the subject and to the laws of Congress of last Session, and have asked my orders as to how you shall proceed in this matter — whether to release these men from custody and to place them outside of your particular jurisdiction as a military officer in charge of the prisons, in accordance with General Orders No. 3 of this Department, or whether the Sheriff, who, as I understand, is now under your orders, is to proceed and sell the said negro men as he has advertised, and as is directed by the Statute of this State, if said statute has not been modified or changed by the law of the last session of Congress.

As I am informed, most of these negroes came with the forces under Maj General Fremont from Southwestern Missouri, and have either been used in the military service against the United States or are claimed by persons now in arms against the Federal Government, but that none of them have been condemned in accordance with the Act, approved August 6th. 1861, and that no proceedings for such condemnation have ever been instituted.

As I understand the matter, the Statute of this State creates the presumption that these men are slaves, and if not called for within three months of the date of the advertisement of the Sheriff, they are to be sold as slaves. It would seem that the Act of Congress approved Aug. 6th. 1861, if constitutional, over-rules this statute so far as this presumption is concerned. This Act of Congress cannot be regarded as unconstitutional until decided to be so by the U.S. Supreme Court.

It results then, as it seems to me, that these negroes are held in custody without the authority of law and contrary to General Orders No. 3; and you are hereby directed to release them from prison. It appears, however, that they have received from the Quartermasters Department certain articles of clothing required for their immediate and pressing necessities, with the promise that they would pay for the clothing so delivered to them with their labor. They will therefore be turned over to the Chief of the Quartermaster's Department in this city for labor till they have paid the United States for the clothing and other articles so issued to them at the expense of the Government.

This order will in no way debar any one from enforcing his legal rights to the services of these negroes—such rights, if any exist, can be enforced through the loyal civil tribunals of this State, whose mandates will always be duly respected by the Military authorities of this Department. Military officers cannot decide upon rights of property or claims to service, except so far as may be authorized by the laws of War or the Acts of Congress. When not so authorized, they will avoid all interference with such questions. Very respectfully Your obt. servt.

HLcSr   (Sig.) H. W. Halleck

Major Genl. H. W. Halleck to Col. B. G. Farrar, 18 Dec. 1861, vol. 10 DMo, pp. 77–79, Letters Sent by Maj. Gen. Henry W. Halleck, ser. 2576, Dept. of the MO; RG 393 Pt. 1 [C-395].

160A: **Circular by the Commander of the 4th Division of the Department of the Missouri**

Camp Halleck [*near Rolla, Mo.*] Dec 18, 1861
Circular No 2. General Order No. 3, Headquarters Department of Missouri, received on the 20th of November last (current series)

directs that no fugitive slave be permitted to enter the lines of any camp or of any forces on the march, and that all within such lines be immediately excluded therefrom.[1]

It having been represented that in violation of the above order there were still within the lines of the encampment of this Division a number of fugitive slaves; General Order No. 23 was issued from these Headquarters, on the 4th instant. whereby all the Commanders of Regiments and Batteries attached to the Division were directed to exclude immediately all fugitive slaves that might be still found therein, and to adopt the strictest precautions against their admission for the future, – Commanders being held responsible for any violation of this order.

General Halleck Commanding the Deparment of Missouri, directs now under date of Dec. 16 inst. from Headqrs. at St. Louis through Lieut Col. W. Scott Ketchum. Actg Inspector General that the orders above mentioned be strictly enforced by all concerned.

In as much as these orders may not have been complied with up to this time, I once more direct by the publication of this circular all Commanders of Regiments and Batteries composing the 4th Division, to comply fully and immediately with the aforesaid order, and to report tomorrow in writing their compliance therewith, that its injunctions have not been in any manner or by any pretext evaded and that having expelled all fugitive slaves there are none within their camps, – either male or female.

HDS   Asboth

Ac. M. Gl. Asboth, Circular No. 2, Headqrs. 4th Division, 18 Dec. 1861, enclosed in Acting Major Genl. Asboth to Col. W. Scott Ketchum, 18 Dec. 1861, A-69 1861, Letters Received, ser. 2593, Dept. of the MO, RG 393 Pt. 1 [C-390].

1 See above, doc. 157.

160B: Commander of the Frémont Hussars to the Commander of the 4th Division of the Department of the Missouri

Camp Halleck near Rolla Mo. Dec 19th 61

General: In obedience to the order contained in your circular (No. 2), received this day, I beg to report that on the receipt of your order No 23 communicating Gen. Order No. 3, from the Commanding General, ordering fugitive slaves to be excluded from the lines, I caused all negroes in my camp to be examined, and it was reported to me that they all stoutly asserted that they were free.

Since that time a woman employed in my own mess as cook has been claimed by one Captain Holland as the fugitive slave of his father-in-law. In compliance with your order, to that end, which he produced, she was given up to him. Since the receipt of your circular of today, I have again caused an investigation to be thoroughly made which has resulted as in the first instance.

I beg now, General, to ask for your instructions in the matter. These negroes all claim and insist that they are *free*. Some of them, I have no question, are so; others I have as little doubt have been slaves, – but no one is here to prove it, and I hesitate to take so serious a responsibility as to decide, arbitrarily, in the absence of any direct evidence, that they are such.

If I turn them away, I inflict great hardship upon them, as they would be homeless and helpless. Furthermore, such a course would occasion much personal inconvenience and sincere regret, to other officers no less than to myself. These people are mainly our servants, and we can get no others. They have been employed in this capacity for some time – long enough for us to like them as servants, to find them useful and trustworthy, and to feel an interest in their welfare.

The Commanding General, in his letter to Col. Blair, (as published in the Missouri Democrat of the 16th inst), says – in explanation of General order No 3. – "Unauthorized persons, black or white, free or slave, must be kept out of our camps." The negroes in my camp are employed, in accordance with the Army Regulations, as officers servants, teamsters, and hospital attendants, and, with the exception of one little child are such as we are authorized to have in the camp. It seems to me that they are without the pale of the order and the *intention* of the Commanding General, and I trust that I may be excused for awaiting more explicit instructions before doing what may be an extra-official act – at which my private feelings revolt.

I recognize the fact that obedience to Gen. Orders No. 3 is a part of my military duty, and I shall unflinchingly comply with it in the consciousness that I am in no way responsible therefore; but I *am* personally responsible for my decision, when it is to affect the happiness and security of others.

May I ask you, General, to relieve me of this responsibility by giving me your final decision at your earliest convenience. Very Respectfully Your Obedient Servant

ALS

Geo. E. Waring, Jr.

Major Geo. E. Waring, Jr. to Acting Maj. Gen. Asboth, 19 Dec. 1861, enclosed in Actg. Maj. Gen. Asboth to Colonel W. Scott Ketchum, 23 Dec.

1861, A-68 1861, Letters Received, ser. 2593, Dept. of the MO, RG 393 Pt. 1 [C-390]. Enclosed alongside Waring's report are reports by the other nine subordinate commanders in the 4th Division. Most of them simply stated that there were no fugitive slaves in their camps, but the commander of the 2nd Ohio Battery took the occasion to deny emphatically any involvement with slaves: "I am not a Nigger man have had no fugitives in my Battery nor have none now and dont intend to have." (Capt. [T.] J. Carlin to Acting Brig. Genl. Carr, 20 Dec. 1861.) In his covering letter, General Alexander S. Asboth, commander of the division, declared that, with the exception of those in Major Waring's unit, "there are no fugitive slaves in the Division nor any negroes to whom a suspicion of being so can attach." Asboth requested instructions to meet the circumstances described by Waring.

160C: Commander of the Department of the Missouri to the Commander of the 4th Division of the Department

St Louis Dec. 26th 1861.

General. It would seem from the report of Major Waring to you (referred to these Head Quarters) that he had, in compliance with your instructions, delivered to a Capt. Holland a fugitive in his camp claimed by Capt H. as the property of his father-in law.

This is contrary to the intent of General Orders No. 3. The object of those orders is to prevent any person in the Army from acting in the capacity of negro catcher, or negro stealer. The relation between the slave and his master, or pretended master, is not a matter to be determined by military officers, except in the single case provided for by Congress. This matter in all other cases must be decided by the civil authorities. One object in keeping fugitive slaves out of our camps is to keep clear of all such questions. Masters or pretended masters, must establish the rights of property to the negroes as best they may, without our assistance or interference, except where the law authorizes such interference.

Orders No. 3 do not apply to the authorized private servants of officers, nor to negroes employed by proper authority in camps; it applies only to "fugitive slaves. The prohibition to admit them within our lines does not prevent the exercise of all proper offices of humanity in giving them food and clothing outside, where such offices are necessary to prevent suffering. Very respectfully Your obt. servt.

HLcSr   (Sig.) H. W. Halleck

Major Genl. H. W. Halleck to General Asboth, 26 Dec. 1861, vol. 10 DMo, pp. 109–10, Letters Sent by Maj. Gen. Henry W. Halleck, ser. 2576, Dept.

of the MO, RG 393 Pt. 1 [C-395]. Two weeks later, General Halleck wrote in the same vein to the commander at Ironton, Missouri: "I do not consider it any part of the duty of the military to decide upon the rights of master & slave. It is our duty to leave that question for the action of the loyal civil authorities of the state. This is accomplished by keeping all such fugitives out of our camps. This is the object of orders No 3. Those orders should in all cases be enforced, and we shall then be freed from these vexatious questions." (Major Genl. H. W. Halleck to Col. Carlin, 9 Jan. 1862, Unentered Letters Received, ser. 2594, Dept. of the MO, RG 393 Pt. 1 [C-111].)

161: Headquarters of the District of Cairo to the Commander of U.S. Forces at Cape Girardeau, Missouri

Cairo [*Ill.*], January, 5, 1862.
I am instructed by Gen. Grant to say to you that he has carefully read your communication with reference to the slave of Dr. Henderson, and fully concurs in your views of the case. While it is not the policy of the Military Arm of the Government to ignore or in any manner interfere with the constitutional rights of loyal citizens, except when a military necessity makes individuals subservient to the public interest, it certainly is not the policy of our army to in any manner aid those who in any manner aid the rebellion. The slave, who is used to support the master, who supported the rebellion, is not to be *restored* to the master by military authority. If such a master has a civil right to reclaim such property he must resort to the civil authorities to enforce that right. The Gen'l Commdg, does not feel it his duty to feed the foe, or in any manner contribute to their comfort, If Dr. Henderson has given aid and comfort to the enemy, neither he nor his agents have any right to come within our lines, much less to invoke our aid and assistance for any purpose whatever.
Official
HLcSr

(Sgd) W. S. Hillyer

Aid de Camp W. S. Hillyer to Col. L. F. Ross, 5 Jan. 1862, vol. G1 DT, p. 175, Letters Sent, ser. 2730, Dist. of Cairo, RG 393 Pt. 2 No. 171 [C-4804]. On December 31, 1861, Colonel Leonard F. Ross, commander of U.S. forces at Cape Girardeau, Missouri, had written to General Ulysses S. Grant, commander of the District of Cairo, for instructions regarding Dr. Henderson's slave. Ross had reported his observance of orders requiring the exclusion of blacks from his lines, affirming his intention "to offer no obstacle to the recovery of all fugitives at the same time affording no assistance to those who come for the avowed purpose of such recovery." With respect to Henderson's slave, Ross had expressed the opinion "that duty as an officer would dictate that so far from sending the black boy back to support the family" while the master had left home to aid the Confederacy, "that I should rather retain him in some useful employment for the Government." (*Official Records*, ser. 2, vol. 1, pp. 797–98.)

162: Provost Marshal General of the Department of the Missouri to the Commander of the Department, Enclosing an Opinion by a U.S. District Attorney

St. Louis, Feb 4th *1862.*

General   There are a number of Negroes at the military prison at M'Dowells College who, were captured with the rebels taken at Blackwater. They have frequently applied to me to be released from the prison. They were employed in hostile service against the Government of the United States contrary to the provisions of the Act of Congress of 6 July [*August*] 1861. before preferring their request, I asked the opinion of the U.S. Dist Attorney as to the rights of such slaves; enclosed is his reply   Very respectfully Your Obt sert

ALS   Bernard G Farrar

[*Enclosure*]   St Louis Feb: 2. 1862 —

My opinion has been asked as to whether; in case of slaves taken by the military authorities on account of their having been employed in the service of the rebellion, there is any necessity of enquiry into the facts or of condemnation by any tribunal —

Of course I can only speak of the act of Congress — for what the military authorities may do under the operation of martial law is another question —

The act of Congress of August 6th 1861 — is very plain and explicit —

That act provides "That whenever during the present insurrection, any person claimed to be held to labor or service under the law of any state, shall be required or permitted by the person to whom such labor or service is claimed to be due, or by the lawful agent of such person, to take up arms against the United States, or shall be required or permitted by the person to whom such labor or service is claimed to be due, or his lawful agent to work or to be employed in or upon any fort, navy-yard, dock, armory, ship,

425

entrenchment, or in any military or naval service whatsoever, against the Government and lawful authority of the United States, then and in every such case, the person to whom such labor or service is claimed to be due, shall *forfeit* his claim to such labor."

And the same section provides further that "whenever thereafter, the person claiming such labor or service, shall seek to enforce his claim, it shall be a full and sufficient answer to such claim, that the person whose service or labor is claimed, had been employed in hostile service against the Government of the United States contrary to the provisions of this act" –

It needs no argument to show that the evident intention of the act was to make the slave *eo instanti* free, whenever he had been employed in hostile service against the Government – The act of the owner, or agent of the owner in compelling the slave to such hostile service or in permitting him to engage in it – is his deed of emancipation –

The last clause of the section above cited shows it clearly – for whenever an effort is made to enforce the claim to service or labor – the full answer to such claim is – not a decree of any tribunal under the act – but that he had been employed in hostile service against the Government contrary to the provisions of the act –

It may be further remarked that while the act of Congress provides a mode of proceeding in all other cases of forfeiture under the act, and declares how the property forfeited may be condemned – it makes no provision for the case of slaves whose services have been forfeited by reason of their being employed in hostile service against the Government –

There is no occasion therefore for the military authorities to hold slaves thus seized, for the purpose of instituting or having instituted by the civil authorities, – any enquiry into the matter – Respectfully yours

ALS   Ja⁵ O. Broadhead

Prov. Mar. Genl. Bernard G. Farrar to Maj. Gen. Halleck, 4 Feb. 1862, enclosing Jas. O. Broadhead to Col. B. G. Farrar, 2 Feb. 1862, F-71 1862, Letters Received, ser. 2593, Dept. of the MO, RG 393 Pt. 1 [C-100]. Another enclosure.

163: Missouri Slaveholder to the Commander of the
Department of the Missouri, and Commander of an Iowa
Regiment to the Headquarters of the Department

Fulton [*Mo.*] Feb 12th 1862

Sir; Your admirable order, excluding all fugitive slaves from your
lines, was hailed by the union men of this portion of the state with
delight, for it furnished them with a complete practical refutation of
the incipient cry of the rebels that the war was for the liberation of
the negro, but, sir, I am sorry to inform you that many of your
subordinates have wholy refused and neglected to put your order in
execution, to the serious detriment of the growing Union sentiment
here; I have just witnessed a breach of that order which is too
flagrant to be permitted to pass unnoticed. Two days since, several
slaves, the property of union men who under all circumstances have
been loyal to their government, escaped from near Columbia in
Boone County and took refuge with a brigade, marching through
that county, commanded by Col Worthington of the 5th Iowa
regiment   The owner of one of the negroes, a Mr Garth, appealed
to Col W for permission to recover his negro; but this was rudely
refused, although Mr G's loyalty was endorsed by some of the best
known, Union men of Columbia. On the passage of the brigade
through this place, I saw Mr G's negro with several other
fugitives marching in ranks. A gentleman present also recognized
the negro and tried to get possession of him but was repulsed by an
officer who threatened to shoot him if he persisted. I afterwards
obtained letters from a leading union man and Maj Caldwell, 3rd
Iowa cavalry vouching for my loyalty and respectability and essayed
to obtain the negro, but was refused all aid by Col W and forbidden
to come within his lines for that purpose. Now, sir, I ask you for
the sake of our common country, for the sake of the loyal citizens of
Mo. and for the sake of your consistency as an officer and your
unimpeachable integrity as a man, to give force and efficency to
your excellent order respecting fugitives, Your enforcement of it
will be a moral victory for us as effective as if won on the field of
battle. This complaint is not prompted by a captious disposition,
but by a desire to see our cause, maintained in its integrity. I
know, in some measure at least, the difficulties which surround
you. I know the exigencies of the service, but I feel assured that
you will do all in your power to secure us in our persons and
property I write in haste. If necessary I can get the endorsement
of every union man in this county and also of the US officers which
have been stationed here during the winter. Will you give me an

order directing Col W upon proper proof to give up the
negroes? Very Respectfully

ALS   T A Russell

St. Charles Mo Feby 17th 1862

Captain   The enclosed communication from T A Russell was found
upon my arrival at this place. The facts are as follows— the
morning after passing through Collumbia a Mr Garth rode up as the
column was moving out and informed me he had lost a negro the
evening before and supposed he was in my lines— he stated that he
had passed the wagons and that he did not see the negro. I then
told him to pass along the lines and if he saw him I would order
him out but that I would not have anything to do with catching
him, as that was against orders I had received from my superior
officer. he declined going with me to look for him. Two nights
after this (on the 12th) three men came into my camp after dark and
stated they had come for Mr Garth's negro. I again repeated to
them that I should order the commanders of the different regiments
to put all such persons out of the camp, but that I neither could
catch the negro's myself nor permit any one to search my camp for
that purpose. One of the party turned off muttering the name of
Genl. Halleck. I then told him that it was against the orders of
Genl. Pope, under whose command I was for me to hunt up negroes
or permit Strangers, or in fact any one to go through camp for that
purpose and gave him the reasons assigned by Genl. Pope for such
orders. Immediately after they left I had the inclosed order dated
Feby 12th 1862 issued. I would also refer to the enclosed order of
the 5th inst. issued at Boonville before crossing the river. I have
taken every precaution to prevent negroes coming into my lines on
this march but owing to the length of the line some have come in
and have been harbored by parties belonging to the command.

You are well aware that I have no sympathy with any interference
by the army with private property of any kind and in this case have
acted strictly in obedience to the orders from Genl. Pope. I shall
try to prevent any fugitives from leaving this place with my
command   I am Very Respectfully Yours

HLS   W H Worthington

T. A. Russell to Maj. Genl. Halleck, 12 Feb. 1862, enclosed in Col. W. H.
Worthington to Captain, 17 Feb. 1862, W-151 1862, Letters Received, ser.
2593, Dept. of the MO, RG 393 Pt. 1 [C-102]. Worthington, who commanded the 5th Iowa Infantry, also signed as commander of the column. Also
enclosed in his letter are two orders issued by him, one on February 5, 1862,

calling for compliance with Halleck's General Order 3 (see above, doc. 157), and the other on February 12, 1862, instructing commanders of the regiments and battery in his brigade to clear their camps of "alleged fugitive slaves" and thereafter keep them outside their lines.

164: Commander of the Missouri State Militia to the Headquarters of the Department of the Missouri

St. Louis, March 3, *1862*

Colonel, There are in the camp at Fulton two Slaves, and at Columbia one, who have been used as guides to conduct our troops to places where rebels and military stores were secreted, and who have given much valuable information which could not be obtained from white men. To drive them from the camp would subject them to severe punishment, perhaps death. I have therefore directed that they be permitted to remain under the protection of our troops, not doubting but this course would meet with the approval of the Commanding General. I am, Colonel Very Respectfully Your obt. Servt.

HLS   J. M. Schofield

Brig. Genl. J. M. Schofield to Col. J. O. Kelton, 3 Mar. 1862, S-271 1862, Letters Received, ser. 2593, Dept. of the MO, RG 393 Pt. 1 [C-101]. A penciled notation on the outside of the letter reads: "Inform Genl S that his course is approved."

165: Missouri Slaveholder to the Secretary of War

Syracuse Morgan County Missouri April 5th 1862

I feel great delicacy my dear Sir, in taking the liberty, of addressing you, on a matter entirely personal; being unknown to you and to fame: But having been reared under our glorious representative government, I have ever rejoiced in the fact, that the humblest individual might respectfully present himself before our Rulers. On the 25th of Janry as Genl Davis command passed through our town on its march to Springfield two of my most valuable Negro Boys joined the Regiment of Col Julius White   The command camped for the night near Tipton – I saw Genl Davis that night: and was assured by him that they should be excluded from the lines   He had the kindness to give me a letter to Col

Cummings: The next morning finding that my Boys were in Co^l Whites command I saw him & introduced myself to him & stated my business & at the same time placed in his hands Genl Davis' letter: He Co^l White told me positively he would have nothing to do with it: I said surely he would comply with the order of Genl Halleck: when he again stated positively he would have nothing to do with it: The army then being on the march I rode on with my Son: as we passed one of the Boys was in a wagon: when we reached the head of the column I found the other Boy with knapsack & Gun: I asked for the Capt of the advance guard & stated to him my business: The man came forward and took his property, & I ordered the Boy to follow us: we had gone but a few paces before we met Co^l White: I stopped & most respectfully told the Co^l There was one of my Boys, the other behind in a wagon: The Co^l stopped gave me a stern. defiant look but said not a word: seeing that, I passed on: my Son made the Boy get up behind him: we had passed but a few paces from Co^l White until a yell was raised, behind us where we left the Co^l sitting on his horse   we were instantly surrounded by several hundred armed men, threatening us with instant death; two of them seized the Boy pulled him from the Horse & ran him back to where we had left Co^l White: They then commenced stoning us, & stoned us so long as we were in reach of their Stones: We got out of their reach as soon as practicable but were pursued by two Officers on horse back with drawn Swords forced back & put under a guard of Soldiers & ropes were called for to hang us. Now Sir as the army was here to meet men in arms & for the protection of loyal citizens in life liberty & property: I felt that the onus of recovering my Negroes rested upon me, and proceeded with all due respect to every one to do so: But was glad to escape with my life from Co^l White: The facts were forthwith reported by me to Genl Halleck & I urged my prayrer that my Boys might be ordered back into my hands: I have written him repeatedly & have never had a direct reply: I have just received a letter from my friend in St Louis who has been urging my claim: He says Genl Halleck refuses to act in the case: says it does not come under his jurisdiction: I have written to the Honble Garret Davis & to Genl T. L. Price begging that a request or an order, if need be, might issue from the President himself the head of all power, to Genl Halleck that my Boys might be ordered back into my hands   I have stated that I ask it as a constitutional right, & as a rebuke to the outrage upon my person & property: I ask it farther because a large part of the hard earnings of my laborious life, is in my Negro property, to all of which a death blow has been struck & lastly I ask it because I raised those Boys am greatly attached to

them, and consider that they have entered upon a career of ruin as
they are very young, & know nothing of the world: I am dear Sir
respectfully & most truly yours

John R. Moore

If my dear Sir you will give me your kind assistance you will confer
a favour, never to be forgotten. I have just received a letter from
Gen[l] Price telling me that he could not make the application to the
President requested by me Now my dear Sir what am I to do,
unless I can get redress through you: I had thought of addressing a
copy of this application to the Pres[nt] also; but think that will be
unnecessary as you will if need be do me the favour to confer with
him: I think the case so aggravated that you will do me the
kindness to order my Boys back into my hands, or to my
Agent: One of those Boys is the eldest son of a family of
thirteen: The Parents are old and if thrown upon the world could
not sustain themselves: the Boy was just now of an age to aid in
the support of his large family

I have been greatly distressed at the conduct of Co[l] White, as I
ardently desire the restoration of our glorious Union as we received
it from our Fathers: His conduct has had its influence for evil; is a
strong reason why I wish that my Boys may be restored to
me: Please let me hear from you immediately, as they have now
been gone upwards of two months: Co[l] White is under the
command of Gen[l] Curtis: you will ever have my fervant prayrer,
that your efforts may be crowned with success, in the reastablisment
of peace, and that we may soon again, be a united happy
people most respectfully yours John R Moore

ALS

John R. Moore to Honble. E. M. Stanton, 5 Apr. 1862, M-455 1862, Letters
Received, RG 107 [L-13]. A "File" notation on the outside suggests that the
War Department did not reply to Moore's letter. An accompanying letter
from an acquaintance of the Secretary of War described Moore as pious and
benevolent, a master whose "25 servants who yet remain . . . are instructed
and treated more as children than merely as slaves." (Mary Demuth to Hon.
Edwin M. Stanton, 5 Apr. 1862.)

166: Indiana Congressman to the Secretary of War, Enclosing a Letter from the Commander of an Indiana Regiment to the Congressman

H.R. Wash. May 17. 1862.

Dear Sir, I enclose you papers & offical orders that speak for themselves. My constituent, Lt Co^l Cameron, who has served honorably in our Legislative Halls, dislikes to be converted into a Slavecatcher instead of a soldier; & Senator Lane of Ind & I both hope that such orders may issue as may relieve him & other officers from this degradation. Respy Yrs

ALS   Schuyler Colfax

[*Enclosure*]   Fort Thompson New Madrid Mo May 11th 1862

Dear Friend I am in a world of trouble with Col. Ryan in regard to the Contraband question, and wish you to give me some information

We are posted here and it seems as if he intended to make us Slave Catchers, instead of Soldiers. if we are to be the former, I shall resign immediately, if the latter, I will wait the event of the war

Enclosed I send you copies of his orders No 1 and No 2. giving permission to remove, by force if need be, Contrabands from our lines. No 3 is an order, prohibiting the 7th Wisconsin Battery from taking their Servants with them to "Island No 10", where they are ordered, and are being shipped to-day.

In the first order you will see that I was not only ordered to allow the nameless man to take Contrabands from our lines, but he asks me to take a receipt for the pretended property. I did nothing of the kind. In the case of the second, order, I told Mr Lewis I should have nothing to do with it, he could see them and if they wished to go with him, they could do so, but that I would furnish no force, nor protect him in any effort to take them away by force.

In the 3^d case, I know nothing about the Contrabands in question, but I do know that there are men in the employ of the Officers of the Army, who worked for their masters on rebel Fortifications, some of whom have been taken from our lines and are now chained in the Swamps, waiting the first opportunity to be shipped South

I wish you would ascertain from lawful authority, what I can be obliged to do, and if you write me that I must give my time to such purposes, I go home as soon as possible

I have also written to Senator Lane on the same subject

Let me hear from you as soon as possible while I remain Your
Obedient Servant

HLS   R. A. Cameron.

[*Endorsement*] This letter is sent for Mr. Stanton's inspection & to
explain the official orders; but not to be sent West to cause any
difficulty to my constituent, its writer. S. Colfax

Schuyler Colfax to Hon. E. M. Stanton, 17 May 1862, enclosing Lieut. Col.
R. A. Cameron to Hon. S. Colfax, 11 May 1862, C-484 1862, Letters
Received, ser. 12, RG 94 [K-25]. Cameron commanded the 34th Indiana
Infantry. The three orders noted in his letter are enclosed. Issued by Colonel J.
Ryan, commander of the post of New Madrid, the first two were dated April
26, 1862, and the third, May 10, 1862. In the same file is a draft of the War
Department's reply to Congressman Colfax: "[I]t is impossible for this Dep't.
to give instructions as to the *limits* of an officer's obedience to the orders of his
superiors. The additional article of war prescribes the duties of officers in
relation to negroes and a violation of this article will be good cause for a
court-martial." (Brig. Genl. C. P. Buckingham to Hon. S. Colfax, 24 May
1862.)

167: Commander of an Iowa Regiment
to the Governor of Iowa

Camp Totten Sedalia Mo Aug 28. 1862
Copy

Sir I know you entertain a deep interest in relation to the welfare
of the troops you have ordered into the field hence I feel it to be my
duty to advise you as often as I can in relation to the movements
and condition of the 18th Regt

I have now on sick list about 200 men principally with measles
and diarrhoea. many are debilitated I have today only about 450
men fit for duty and expect to be ordered tomorrow to march to
Springfield 120 miles

I very much regret I was ordered to this State for the reasons
there are no other Iowa Infantry in this state and I beleive none
from other states therefore I cannot become brigaded. I have been
thrown among the Missouri Militia Cavelry all the time and under
the commands, of Missouri Milita officers. I have been very much
imposed upon in consequence, double duties are imposed upon me
to screen their own troops. They have the command of the posts

and the comisary department, so you can conjecture our treatment. They heap upon us the vilest Epithets and endeavour to predjudice the citizens against us. They issue orders to me to drive out of my lines fujutive slaves without discrimination between loyalty and disloyalty in their owners and require my men to do camp drudgery when I could usefully releive them by the Employment of Contrabands and then impose upon me Extra duty. Many of these officers I fear who command me, are not more loyal than they should be.

Why cannot Missouri troops who are fed armed and paid by the General Government protect this state, There is a screw loose somwhere. I hope you will use your influence to get me out of this dilema, and sent where there are other Iowa troops, and where I can have my regiment brigaded Having friends in our midst   Your obt Svt

HLcSr   Jno Edwards

[*Endorsement*] Respectfully referred to the Secretary of War. It does seem to me the loyal men of Missouri armed & paid by the U.S. should be able to protect the State against the guerrillas or if they cannot do it should treat decently the troops from other States sent to protect them —

I am sure it will not work well to require of the new regiments from this state much work in the way of driving contrabands away from our lines into the hands of rebel masters — It was understood when our new regiments were formed this kind of work was about done and to require it will certainly cause trouble. Col. Edwards is an excellent man and from my knowledge of him I have no doubt of the correctness of his statements. Cannot his wishes be complied with? Very Respectfully   Samuel J Kirkwood

Col. Jno. Edwards to Gov. S. J. Kirkwood, 28 Aug. 1862, I-65 1862, Letters Received, ser. 12, RG 94 [K-35]. Several weeks later, Governor Kirkwood asked the Secretary of War to remove Iowa troops from the command of Missouri officers. Kirkwood complained that the Missourians "not only hold opinions, but act with reference to the vexed and ever-recurring contraband question directly in opposition to the convictions of our officers and men." He denounced the policy whereby Iowans were "compelled to drive away from our lines and back into the hands of rebel masters slaves who are willing to render service to the country, and who, as they and I understand the laws of Congress, are free men." (*Official Records*, ser. 1, vol. 13, p. 643.)

168: Missouri Slaveholders to the President, Enclosing a Statement by One of the Slaveholders

Saint Louis Missouri Sep 8 1862

Sir: There is on the border of our State an armed band of negroes threatening an invasion of the state, and particularly the Counties of Clay and Jackson. In view of the uneasiness felt by our citizens, and to secure peace between Kansas and Missouri the undersigned have come to this City to confer with the Governor of the state in reference to this matter, and now beg leave, also, to address your Excellency, and, respectfully and earnestly, to ask of you an order to have these negroes disbanded, and their arms taken from them, and a further order to put a stop to such things in future. We are loyal, Union men, determined, at all hazards, to uphold the integrity of the Union, and to oppose all its enemies, and Can assure you that, were it not for the threats of Lane, Jennison and others to invade us; to despoil us of our property, to burn our Towns and dwellings, murder our Citizens, and run off our negroes, We would be comparatively at peace. At this time We know of no bands of Confederate Guerilla^s in any part of the state in larger squads than 50 to 100 men, and there are but few of these; none, as we believe, in either Clay or Jackson Counties; whilst our loyal militia are organizing in sufficient numbers to drive them all out of the state, or kill them, and to keep the state Clear of Rebels. We greatly fear, Mr President, that unless these negroe Brigades and Regiments are disbanded and disarmed, and those men who have been instrumental in organizing them are severely dealt with by the Govt the most serious difficulties will take place between Missouri and Kanzas — two loyal states — the end of which no man can see. The Officer in Command of the Department of Kansas should be instructed not to suffer the arming or enrollment of Negroes for any such purpose, and if he is not willing to execute such an order a *new* Commander should be put in his place. We are aware that it is Contrary to your orders, as we believe it is against your wishes, to arm negroes, and have them clothed in the uniform of soldiers, and we beg to assure you that, whilst our people are fast returning to their loyalty, such irritating causes as we have alluded to, are a terrible burden upon the loyal men. We pray you, Mr President, to give these matters your instant attention, and assure you of our very high regard.

Edward. M. Samuel.   Francis Foster
M. [J]. Payne.   E. R. Threlkeld
HLS   Patrick Shannon.   Joseph O Boggs

[*Enclosure*]   St Louis M° Sep 8 1862
Statement of Edward. M. Samuel, of Liberty Clay Co Mo.

About 15 days ago some 15 persons from the state of Kansas — white men — under the Command of a man calling himself "Jeff Davis," but whose real name is said to be Swain, and who is reported as a desperately bad man, came into the County of Clay, as Swain said, to *"recruit* negroes for Genl Lanes negro Brigade" — They took *forcible* possession of some 25 negro men, and about 40 Horses from persons, indiscriminately, and started to cross the Missouri River with them over into Kansas — Hearing of it, Capt Johnson of the MSM — then in Command at Liberty — sent out about 50 men to Capture or shoot the men and retake the negroes and Horses. This Company of Militia succeeded in Capturing 8 of the "Jayhawkers", and recovered *all* the negroes and Horses. The "Jayhawkers" were lodged in the Jail at Liberty, where they were when I left home on the 4th — A day or two afterwards a white man presented to the Officer at Liberty a *written* demand for the release of these 8 Jayhawkers signed by "Col Jennison", with a *threat* that he "would hold the County responsible if they were not released and given up". The demand, of Course was refused — The "Enrolled Militia" of Clay County are *sworn* into the service of the state, and sworn to fight all the *enemies* of the state, domestic or foreign". and surely these "Jayhawkers" are *enemies*. Our people desire to live in peace with the people of Kansas, and I am sure that good feelings and peace between the two states would soon be universal if it were not for these "raids", by unauthorized bands, upon the persons and property of citizens of Missouri, and especially if the Govt of the US would put an effectual stop to the career of "negro stealers", and those who threaten to *arm* them and come into Missouri to steal other negroes, and to lay waste our property and take our lives.

ADS   Edward. M. Samuel.

Edward M. Samuel et al. to His Excellency Abraham Lincoln, 8 Sept. 1862, enclosing statement of Edward M. Samuel, 8 Sept. 1862, President 197 1862, Letters Received from the President & Executive Departments, RG 107 [L-175]. Endorsement. Adjoining their signatures on the petition, Shannon indicated that he was a captain in the Missouri State Militia in Jackson County, Foster that he was provost marshal of Jackson County, Samuel that he was from Clay County, and Payne and Threlkeld that they were from Jackson County.

169: Commander of the Post of Lamine Cantonment, Missouri, to the Headquarters of the Central Division of Missouri

Lamine Cantonment [*Mo.*] Oct 1st 1862
To A A Gen¹ Central Division   I beg leave to report fourteen (14) contrabands at this post and as we have no Provost Marshall to take charge of them, ask directions as to their disposition. The horses and saddles they bring I return to owners on proof – without any regard to their loyalty   Would be glad to receive orders on this head also   Respectfully

ALS   W^m R Butler

[*Endorsement*]   H^d Qrs., Dep^t of the Mo. St. Louis, Oct. 3. 1862   Slaves, the property of persons in the rebel service, or the property of men giving aid, &c., *are forfeited and free,* and their rebel masters should be prevented from having the benefit of their Labor.

The military should see that such negroes are cared for, if they come into our lines. Let them be employed by Quartermasters as teamsters, or in companies, as cooks, and paid $10 a month & rations.

But the fact of their being the property of a rebel should be carefully ascertained, and the negro should have a paper to show that he is ascertained to be such a contraband. By order of Maj. Gen¹. Curtis, H. Z. Curtis Asst. Adjt. Genl.

Capt. Wm. R. Butler to A.A. Genl. Central Division, 1 Oct. 1862, B-18 1862, Letters Received, ser. 2593, Dept. of the MO, RG 393 Pt. 1 [C-103]. Another endorsement.

170: St. Louis Custom House Official to the Commander of the Department of the Missouri

St. Louis, Oct 10. *1862.*
Dear Sir: A few weeks since I called on Provost Marshal Gantt for the purpose of procureing free papers for four Slaves, belonging to Joe Wright, (son of Maj Uriel Wright) who is now in active service in the rebel army endeavoring to subvert the laws, by virtue of which he claims to hold his slaves,

Col Gantt is of opinion that slaves can be made free only by proceedings in the U.S. Court. i.e. on information and &

libel, Martial law having been declared, I think there can be no doubt that you, as Military Commandant of this district have ample power to declare the slaves of ever rebel, engaged in the attempt to subvert the institutions of our country, free. If you agree with me in this opinion I shall be most happy to furnish you evidence substantiating the above facts. Very resply,

ALS   R J. Howard

R. J. Howard to Maj. Genl. Curtis, 10 Oct. 1862, H-55 1862, Letters Received, ser. 2593, Dept. of the MO, RG 393 Pt. 1 [C-105]. Three weeks earlier, a military officer in St. Louis had sought advice about what to do with blacks who claimed their masters were disloyal, and with masters who bore warrants issued by civil officers authorizing them to apprehend their runaway slaves. In an endorsement, Colonel Thomas T. Gantt, provost marshal general of Missouri, had condemned the interference in such cases by military officers as usurpation of authority belonging to the federal courts. "The only mode in which the property of persons violating the act of 17″ July 1862, (commonly called the Confiscation act) can be forfeited, is by sentence of a court of the U.S. of competent jurisdiction." (Col. John F. Tyler to Capt. Griffing, 20 Sept. 1862, and endorsement by Col. Thos. T. Gantt, 20 Sept. 1862, Letters Received, ser. 3285, St. Louis Division, RG 393 Pt. 2 No. 211 [C-222].)

171: Missouri Unionist to the Commander of the Department of the Missouri; and Provost Marshal at Hermann, Missouri, to the Commander of the Department

Hermann, Mo. Novbr 19, 1862.
General, A case occurred to-day in this town, which may give rise to a conflict between *State*-laws and *Federal* authority; for this reason we refer at once to the highest tribunal, to you General, for your decision or order on the subject.

A stampede of slaves had taken place from beyond the river, Loutre Island, Montgomery County, some of whom had crossed the river and had been in this town. To-day several of the respective owners, for the most part *avowed* secessionists and *enrolled sympathizers*, came across and demanded of John B. Miché, Justice of the Peace, a warrant, according to the Statutes of the State. We advised him to refuse it on the ground that the matter belonged before the *Federal* authorities under the order declaring martial law over Missouri and under subsequent orders from the President and Department Commanders. We just find the following parallel case in the papers:

"Provost Marshal's office,
Memphis, Novbr 11, 1862
The judge of the Criminal Court having charged the Grand Jury on
certain points, where a conflict of authority might arise, all persons
will take notice, that any attempt to execute State Laws at variance
with the orders of the President and military commanders will be
construed as a contempt of the authority of the United States, and
will be summarily punished. The status of the negro is involved in
the war now existing, and will in its progress be clearly
determined. – In the mean time, runaway slaves must be treated as
free, and people encouraged to give them employment as such. So
far as the court confines itself to punishing murder, arson, burglary,
and crimes *mala in se,* the provost guard is required to co-operate
D. C. Anthony
Prov. Marsh. Memphis"

The disappointed owners now threaten to prosecute the above named
Justice. The act of congress, confiscating rebel property and
liberating their slaves, now in full force, places it clearly beyond the
power of a Justice of the peace to decide, who is a loyal owner and
who not, and in consequence they cannot be required to issue
warrants to *any* of them. It is to be expected, that *many similar*
cases will arise within the next days, and in order to protect the
unconditional *supporters* of the Government against mischief from the
hands of its avowed *enemies,* we would respectfully request an
authorative order or re-publication of orders already existing
touching the subject.

If a few *loyal* owners shall suffer under the circumstances, it
cannot be avoided, as little as the injury done by a battle to
thousands of loyal families; besides, if the loyal owners, would
emancipate their slaves voluntarily under the condition that the thus
liberated hands would remain with them in the condition of *hired
laborers,* they would neither lose their services, nor the compensation
which our legislature certainly will afford them.

If our honored friend, Mr. Henry T. Blow was not absent from St
Louis, we should have asked him, to lay the matter before you; but
as *delay* is inadmissible in this instance, we take the liberty of
addressing you immediately. Most respectfully
ALS
F. A. Nitchy.

Herman [*Mo.*] Nov 26ᵗʰ 1862.
Sir   My Appointment as Provost Marshal was received last
night   there was immense excitement here in regard to four
Negroes confined in the Jail here   their owners had taken out a
writ before a Justice of the Peace under the old civil law of the state

and would taken or would have attempted to take them acrost the river   the citizens had turned out and would have broken open the Jail and freed the Negroes but for your timely dispatch   I upon the receipt of the dispatch issued an order and they were turned loose by the Dept Sheriff   they are here in the immediate Neighborhood will in all probability go to work for Union men by the month   I will state my reasons for turning them loose

I They the Negroes had come within the lines of the United States Army a comp of the 4th Reg Mo Vol stationed at Gasconade bridge & placed themselves under the protection of Capt Mundweller Comdg Post   he Capt Mundweller not having rations enough to feed them and no work for them ordered them to go into the county and get work that no one could interfere with them   Their having placed themselves under the Protection of United States army officers were entitled to such protection   that is (if I understand the law of Congress) that no US Officer can return fugitives to their owners unless the fugitives so claimed are willing to go of their own free will   Such was not the case   they were unwilling to go   I have questioned them myself, and upon these facts I ordered their release.

The owners of said Slaves are to the best of my knowledge are first Hale Talbot who owns two of them has always classed as Secession and upon the ordering of the Militia to enroll he left and went to Canada or Europe; Mr Martin who claims to own one of them is represented to me as being Secession Sympathizer and the other belongs to Mrs Clark who is accused of being in the same class as the last one but of that I have no certain knowledge only the opinions of good Union men.   these are some of the reasons governing me and also your letter to Mr F A Nitchy   please inform me if I will be sustained in what I have done and can there be anything done to give those fugitives from slavery that belong to disloyal men.   with high sentiments of regard I remain your obedent servt

C C Manwaring

PS   Please excuse all errors in writing and poorness of same as I am suffering under severe cold and Neuralgia in head   C C Manwaring

ALS

F. A. Nitchy to Major General Curtis, 19 Nov. 1862, N-25 1862, Letters Received, ser. 2593, Dept. of the MO, RG 393 Pt. 1 [C-107]; Capt. C. C. Manwaring to Maj. Gen. Curtiss, 26 Nov. 1862, M-178 1862, Letters Received, ser. 2593, Dept. of the MO, RG 393 Pt. 1 [C-106]. General Samuel R. Curtis, commander of the Department of the Missouri, penciled on Nitchy's letter a notation to his clerks, instructing them to inform Nitchy "that the Justice has done right in witholding his warrant" from the slave-holders who sought the return of their fugitive slaves. On Manwaring's letter, Curtis noted that "[t]he Justice who got up this trouble" by issuing the warrants should be arrested, along with all others connected with the disturbance. Neither a reply to Nitchy or Manwaring, nor Curtis's earlier "dispatch" to Manwaring, has been found in the records of the Department of the Missouri.

172: Order by the Commander of the Department of the Missouri

St. Louis, December 24th, 1862.

GENERAL ORDERS, NO. 35.

. . . .

XIII   On the 4th of December, 1861, Major General HALLECK, commanding this Department, in General Orders relating to Provost Marshals, declared that it was the province of the military authorities to execute the act of Congress that had then been passed, confiscating the slaves of rebels which had been used in aiding the rebellion, and he forewarned disloyal slave owners in these words, that "should Congress extend this penalty to the property of all rebels in arms, or giving aid, assistance or encouragement to the enemy, such provisions will be strictly enforced."

On the 5th of December, 1862, an order was issued by the War Department, directing that the Provost Marshal General should proceed to carry out the provisions of the Act of Congress of July 17th, 1862, below mentioned.

And on the 24th of September, 1862, in General Orders No. 139 of the War Department, a proclamation by the President of the United States was published for the information and government of the army, and all concerned, in which the 9th and 10th sections of said Act of Congress were set out as follows:

SEC. 9. *And be it further enacted:* That all slaves of persons who shall hereafter be engaged in rebellion against the government of the United States, or who shall in any way give aid or comfort thereto, escaping from such persons, and taking refuge within the lines of the army; and all slaves captured from such persons, or deserted by them, and coming under the control of the Government of the United States; and all slaves of such persons found *on* (or) being within any place occupied by rebel forces, and afterwards occupied by the forces of the United States, shall be deemed captives of war, and shall be forever free of their servitude, and not again held as slaves.

SEC. 10. *And be it further enacted,* That no slave escaping into any State, Territory, or the District of Columbia, from any other State, shall be delivered up, or in any way impeded or hindered of his liberty, except for crime, or some offense against the laws, unless the person claiming said fugitive shall first make oath that the person to whom the labor or service of such fugitive is alleged to be due, is his lawful owner, and has not borne arms against the United States in the present rebellion, nor in any way given aid and comfort thereto; and no person engaged in the military or naval service of the United States shall, under any pretence whatever, assume to decide on the validity of the claim of any person to the service or labor of any other person, or surrender up any person to the claimant, on pain of being dismissed from the service.

By which order of the War Department, it was published to the army, and all concerned, that the President did enjoin upon, and order all persons engaged in the military and naval service of the United States, to observe, obey and enforce, within their respective spheres of service, the act and sections above recited.

And whereas there are large numbers of slaves in this Department that belonged to rebels in arms, and disloyal men who have given them aid and countenance by such acts and conduct as are above specified; and also a large number of men who defy said Act of Congress and order of the War Department, by pursuing and attempting to hold as slaves those who, by said Act of Congress, are declared to be free of their servitude, and captives of war: and as captives are entitled to full protection to their persons from all enemies of the government and opposers of the law:

XIV   Now, all Provost Marshals within this Department are hereby commanded to protect the freedom and persons of all such captives or emancipated slaves, against all persons interfering with or molesting them; and they will arrest all persons guilty of such conduct.

XV   And whereas it is represented to the Major General Commanding, that the slaves of disloyal men, emancipated by said Act of Congress, are kept imprisoned and confined in both the public and private jails, but not upon criminal charges, it is hereby made the duty of Provost Marshals to examine into all such cases, and report the facts to the Provost Marshal General.

XVI   And all persons disobeying any proper order of a Provost Marshal, in relation to emancipated slaves, will be arrested, the evidence taken against them, and tried for violation of military orders.

XVII   And that loyal men may not be interfered with in their rights, whenever slaves seek protection, under circumstances provided for in said Act of Congress, it shall be the duty of all Provost Marshals to take evidence as to the facts; and upon ascertaining that the slave is one of the class emancipated and

protected by said 9th and 10th sections of said law, the Provost
Marshal will give to such slave a paper, signed by himself, in the
following form:

> In pursuance to General Order No. 35, Department of the
> Missouri, dated St. Louis, Dec. 24, 1862, and in obedience to the
> order of the War Department, made 24th September, 1862, I have
> ascertained that   a negro,   color,   size, aged
> about   years, is to be considered and treated as a captive of war,
> and as such is entitled to the protection of all officers of the United
> States.
>   Given by me at   in the County of   State
> of   the   day of   186

The blanks in said paper to be carefully filled up, so as to state
the name, sex, color, size and age of the negro, and the place where
given. It shall be signed by the officer executing the same, and
delivered to such negro, and upon the paper, or annexed to it,
should be stated the names of the witness, or witnesses, upon whose
testimony such paper is granted, and the place of residence; and no
negro holding such paper shall be deprived of it against his will.
Said Act of Congress provides as follows:

> Sec 9th. 1st, As to persons hereafter engaged in rebellion against
> the United States.
>   2d, And as to persons who shall in any way give aid or comfort
> to the rebellion.
>   Their slaves shall be deemed captives of war, and shall be forever
> free of their servitude, and not again held as slaves, under the
> following circumstances:
>   1st, Slaves escaping from *such persons,* and taking refuge within
> the lines of the Army.
>   2d, Slaves captured from *such persons.*
>   3d, Slaves deserted by *such persons,* and coming under the control
> of the Government of the United States.
>   4th, Slaves of such persons, found or being within any place
> occupied by rebel forces, and afterwards occupied by the forces of the
> United States.

XVIII   Any negro designated in such writing given by a Provost
Marshal, will, by persons in the military service of the government,
be regarded as emancipated by said Act of Congress: but no person
in military service will regard such paper as justifying him to decide
on the validity of the claim of any slaveholder to the services or
labor of his slave.   .

XIX   By said order of the War Department, attention was called
to an Act of Congress, entitled "An Act to make an additional
article of war," approved March 13th, 1862, as follows:

Be it enacted by the Senate and House of Representatives of the United States of America, in Congress assembled: That hereafter the following shall be promulgated as an additional article of war for the government of the Army of the United States, and shall be obeyed and observed as such

Article – All officers or persons in the military or naval service of the United States are prohibited from employing any of the forces under their respective commands, for the purpose of returning fugitives from service or labor, who may have escaped from any persons to whom such service or labor is claimed to be due; and any officer who shall be found guilty by a Court-Martial of violating this article, shall be dismissed from the service.

SEC. 2. *And be it further enacted:* That this act shall take effect from and after its passage.

This, and all other rules and articles of war, should be sustained by Provost Marshals, who are specially assigned to duty for the purpose of maintaining the laws of war and the peace of society.

The foregoing rules and regulations are made, BY COMMAND OF MAJOR GENERAL CURTIS,

PD

Excerpt from General Orders, No. 35, Head Quarters, Department of the Missouri, 24 Dec. 1862, Orders & Circulars, ser. 44, RG 94 [DD-35]. Blank spaces in manuscript.

173: **Provost Marshal at Linn Creek, Missouri, to the Provost Marshal General of the Central District of Missouri**

Linn Creek Mo Jan 29 /63
copy

Captain Dear. Sir, I wish to become in possession of the following information

If a Negro who belongs to a Rebel, and are to be deemed Captives of War, under, The act of Congress – and applyes for such Papers, and Such Papers be granted, to such Slaves and afterwards If Such Slaves are subject to be taken and sold, for Debt.

As we have a Case of that Charater at this Post. A Slave which belonged to one George W Twink, formerly a Citizen of this Post, who is and has been in the Rebel army over Twelve months and has not returned. The said Negro applied to me for such Papers and was granted, and since that time, Has been Levied upon and is locked up at this time in our County Jail

444

Hoping to be furnished with the necessary information I am Captain Your Obdt Servt

HLcSr
[H. H.] Green

[*Endorsement*] Office Pro. Mar″ Jeff City [*Mo.*] Feb 3 /63   Lieut [N. N.] Green   Pro. Mar″ Linn Creek Mo.   You will order the release of said negro *immeeditly* and see that your order is *promptly obeyed* —

You will further order all parties implicated in the *arrest* and *imprisonment* of said negro, to report in Person, at these. H^d Qurs, or if necessary you will send them here under Guard.

Also send an Offical Copy of "Paper issued to said negro and the *Evidence* in the case upon which said Paper was issued. Jno. S. Minick   Capt   Pro. Mar″ Cent Dist of Mo

Lieut. [H. H.] Green to Captain Minnick, 29 Jan. 1863, Unentered Letters Received, ser. 2594, Dept. of the MO, RG 393 Pt. 1 [C-128].

174: **Assistant Provost Marshal of Audrain County, Missouri, to the Commander of the Department of the Missouri**

Mexico, Mo., Feby 16th *1863.*

General, I desire to get some instruction about slaves who are emancipated by Act of Congress of July 17th 1862. Many of these slaves have applied to me for protection and in cases where they were badly treated by their masters I have given them protection and found places for them to work, but inasmuch as I could not find employment for all, and there being no United States forces here now, I advised such as were humanely treated to remain with their masters until there was a prospect for them to better their condition by leaving their masters.

Many of these blacks could get employment in the country and would, no doubt, work faithfully but they are not safe to go out of town. The seceshionists have threatened to shoot every black who gives us any information and have already made way with several in this and adjoining counties. I have a case now in hand. Last week I sent a squad of men into the country in the night and when they got into the neighborhood the commander pressed a slave for guide. When the slave returned next morning the master gave him 150 lashes and since then has used inhumane severity on the black mans family. Many blacks have been taken into government service from here and are now in Southern Mo and some are Arkansas. The families of these blacks are subjected to violence now if they are found sending any word to or receiving any news from these parties.

Great constertation prevails among the slaves in the country owing to the horible falsehoods of the rebels.

The time of the year is coming when these slaves can be of profit to the rebels, and it seems to me that we should *vigourously enforce* the law as a punishment for rebellion, but while we do this it is necessary that we guard well against the rebels taking any advantage or wreaking vengence on the blacks who are freed by the acts of their masters.

Are there any orders against parties interfering with slaves who have rendered assistance to Gov't?

An answer, with instructions about this matter, is desired at your early convenience. Very Respy your obt servt

ALS   O. A. A. Gardner

Asst. Pro. Mar. O. A. A. Gardner to Maj. Genl. Curtis, 16 Feb. 1863, G-34 1863, Letters Received, ser. 2593, Dept. of the MO, RG 393 Pt. 1 [C-125]. General Samuel R. Curtis, commander of the Department of the Missouri, forwarded the letter to Washington for instructions. Henry W. Halleck, general-in-chief of the army, returned it on March 8 with an evasive endorsement: "It is the duty of the Comg Genl of the Dept to take measures to enforce the laws in regard to colored men as well as whites." Another endorsement.

175: Missouri Unionist to the Chairman of the Senate Committee on Military Affairs

Paris   Monroe Co. Mo.   Feb 16" /63

Sir   As an old Republican and unconditional Union man I take the liberty of writing you a few lines. I have read the debates in the senate on the Missouri emancipation bill, and must say the views expressed by you are the correct ones. living in the country and having no political axe to grind, will give you the true state of affairs in this county. in the first place am of Mr Pomeroy opinion, that within thirteen years from this the negroes will take leave of their masters and Congress need not make any appropriation to pay for the blacks, if the policy is to put of[f] there freedom untill 1876, In this county we have about 3000 negroes, and about 780 owners. out of that number I dont believe there can be found ten (10) unconditional union men, although at this time a great many

call themselves constitutional union men (two thirds of them are
under bonds and oath to the government) and want the South to
succeed and then form a treaty leaving the Eastern states out, this
is there great dependance at this time, they are watching Illinois
and should rebellion break out there, this state will be in a blaze
soon after, owing to the lenity of the government the gurilla and
bushwackers, are coming home again to get readdy to start again in
the summer, men that have plundered me of every moveable article
they could take, are now sent home this winter and making
preperation to commence another raid of plundering and murders
next summer. If Noell bill[1] as it passed the house was applied to
this county, with the clause excepting all those that had given aid
or comfort to the enemy, from any benefit of the act, there would
not be 300 negro to pay for, for among all the slave holders that I
can hear of I dont know of over two or three but have given aid or
comfort. To give you a correct ide of the rebellious feeling in this
county over 1100 men joined Porter last summer out of a voting
population of about 2100. if the wish of the true loyal men could
be made known they would not pay the disloyal one cent. there is
but few that will come under the confiscation act for they have been
to cunning for while they have sent their sons, and hired poor men
to join the rebels, those of property have staid home and circulated
stories to bring the government in bad repute. another thing a
negro cannot give testimony against a white man. they have
employed their blacks carring aid to gurrilas or thieves, because they
knew their evidence would not be received against them. and this
is the way they all expect to get pay for their negroes. I dont think
that negro would sell for over $175 on the average at this
time   one likely man a miller was sold short time since here for
$305   he has been hired out by the year for $300 two or three
years ago. the hiring of negro at this time is no criterion for what
he would sell for   some people wanting help would give almost as
much for the servasis for one year as they would for life for should
the hand runaway they only pay for the time he was with
them. there is a strong feeling that the negros will stampede in the
spring   one word in behalf of those that want to rid the state of
slavery   either abolish it at once say 1864 or let it die out of
itself, if made gradual as by the senate amendment we will be
cursed with it for a long time, but if left alone I think it will die
out before the time mentioned in Mr Henderson bill.[2] I give M. H
due praise for his loyalty and devotion to the Union. I think he is
not quite posted up to the feelings of the people about this section
of country. there may be loyal slave owners about his locality, but I
defy him to find them in Monroe Co. and why should those men be
paid for their negros after doing all they could to distroy the

government, and waiting and watching for a chance to begin again. I may be called radical in my views I have some cause to be. I am the only living Republican in Monroe Co that voted for Mr Lincoln (the orthe seven left soon after the rebellion commenced) and dearly have I paid for the privilege. my stock all taken my crops distroyed my family draged from there beds there clothes and bedding all taken myself shot at, attemps made to hang me, and keeping my house over my head only by the commanding officer holding certain neigbours responsible. my object is not to complain but to ask for immediate emmancipation and that those who have aided this rebellion shall not be paid for there slaves

To help the cause would like to have authority to raise a regiment of blacks in North East Missouri. I have been attached to the military for over twenty five years in New York before removeing to this county and know it would help the emancipation along to have two or three regiments of blacks in this state. Dont put to much faith in Gov Gamble   Yours Respectfully

ALS   J H Holdsworth

J. H. Holdsworth to Mr. H. Wilson, 16 Feb. 1863, 37A-E7, Senate Committee on Military Affairs, Committee Papers, ser. 544, 37th Congress, RG 46 [E-62].

1 Introduced in the U.S. House of Representatives in December 1862 by John W. Noell of Missouri, and passed by the House on January 6, 1863, the bill pledged $10 million in U.S. bonds to compensate Missouri slave owners if the state legislature passed an act of immediate emancipation by January 1, 1864. It also denied compensation to "persons who have, at any time engaged in or in any manner aided in the rebellion, or held office under the Confederate States," and enjoined the federal government to "employ all reasonable means" to colonize the emancipated slaves (with their consent) outside the United States. (Edward McPherson, *The Political History of the United States of America, during the Great Rebellion*, 2nd ed. [Washington, 1865], pp. 224–25; Henry Wilson, *History of the Antislavery Measures of the Thirty-Seventh and Thirty-Eighth United-States Congresses, 1861–1864* [Boston, 1864], pp. 227–29.)
2 In December 1862, John B. Henderson of Missouri introduced in the U.S. Senate a bill offering financial assistance to Missouri if the state provided for gradual emancipation. The Senate postponed indefinitely consideration of that bill but, with Henderson's support, considered instead a committee bill proposed as an amendment or substitute for the bill regarding compensated emancipation in Missouri that had been passed by the House of Representatives. The Senate bill, adopted by the Senate on February 12, 1863, provided $20 million in U.S. bonds to be used by Missouri "to compensate for the inconveniences" produced by emancipation if the state adopted emancipation legislation within one year. Unlike the House bill, the Senate bill permitted either gradual or immediate emancipation, requiring only that slavery end by

July 4, 1876. The House of Representatives later considered but did not pass the Senate bill, and in the end Congress adopted no law providing for compensated emancipation in Missouri. (McPherson, *Political History*, pp. 225–26; Wilson, *History of the Antislavery Measures*, pp. 227, 230–48.)

176: Missouri Slaveholder to the Commander of the Department of the Missouri

Jackson Missouri February 24 1863

Sir The Federal military by an Act of Congress are prohibited from returning to their owners, slaves escapeing from them and seeking refuge in the Federal lines. Hundreds from this and the adjoining Counties have escaped and sought protection, within the Federal lines at the Post at Cape Girardeau – A great many of those thus escapeing are yet there. Whenever they wish to release a relative from bondage, they issue out from that place, as I understand, armed, and by menace take property of that description from the owners – Many instances of that kind have occurred. About two weeks since, five were taken from an aged citizen of this County, resideing about five miles from this place – On last night, I have heard, six negroes, four armed, about 12 oclock rescued some three or four, from the residence of a citizen about two & a half miles from here – On the same night about nine oclock my residence was visited by two negroes, entrance demanded and the delivery up of a small girl (the only one I have) on my refusal, the threat was made, that the soldiers would come & take her – On my replying I would go and see the Colonel (Lieut. Col. Sayear commanding a detached portion of the Mo S.M. stationed at this place) they left. So long as that Regiment remains here, I do not believe such conduct will be tolerated. If they are removed, the citizens of town have no more surety for their lives and property, than those of the country – Surely, the Act of Congress never contemplated or intended to sanction the abstracting of property in this way.

Under this belief, I would respectfully call the attention of the Commander in Chief of this Division, to the facts, that a number of escaped negroes are at the Post at Cape Girardeau – that they come out of the lines of that Post armed, – that the inhabitants of the County, generally are unarmed. and that those escaped negroes, can not only take by force or menace, negroes from their owners; but, if so disposed, may rob and plunder *ad libitem*. I do not know that the Commander of the Post at Capt Girardeau has knowledge of these things; and under the circumstances, I would respectfully submit, if you as Commander in Chief, could not put a stop to this state of affairs, by issueing an order, prohibitting negroes carrying arms or leaving the lines of the Post either armed or unarmed unless on lawful business and by a special permit from the Provost Martial, or could not those escaped negroes be removed to some point, where their services are needed by the Goverment. My opinion is, if something is not done to arrest this evil, the consequences cannot be predicted without a shudder.

I can with the more confidence appeal to the military authorities for redress, as we have no Sheriff in this County to execute civil process.

I respectfully ask for myself and other citizens of this County that the Commander in chief, give this subject his immediate attention and afford such relief, as in his opinion our situation demands. By permission, I refer to Lieut. Col. Sayeare for my character   I am Sir Very Respectfully Your Obedient Servant

ALS   Greer W Davis

[*Endorsement*] St Louis Mar 7. 1863   Referred to Brig Gnl Davidson commanding District. The matter may deserve special attention. Slaves of loyal men should not be enticed away by our troops and our lines should not be made a fort for negroes to operate from in carrying on their contraband affairs

Beyond this I do not know that we have much to do in the premises   S R Curtis Maj Gen[1]

Greer W. Davis to Major General Curtis, 24 Feb. 1863, D-83 1863, Letters Received, ser. 2593, Dept. of the MO, RG 393 Pt. 1 [C-121].

177A: **Missouri Slaveholder to the President**

St. Louis March 24 *1863*

My Dear Sir,   You are aware that I have written to you several letters heretofore & in which I have shewn you that I have approved of your measures & especially do I refer to your suggestion or proposition to aid Missouri in emancipating slaves (which I fully indorse). That I have always been a loyal man faithful to the Union and the constitution of the U. States, & know not how to be any thing but a devoted Union man. To be any thing else I would of course have to stultify myself.

Having more fully stated all these things to you in my previous
communications, to you, & having more fully given my views., I
now proceed to the matter for which this communication is more
especially addressed. I live in Franklin County Mo, which I think
is as loyal a county as perhaps any in the U. States, & most so of
any in our State. It is the banner county for Loyalty & devotion to
the Union. We were all getting along prosperously & unitedly
until a few months ago, when by some construction of some order,
the officers assigned us in our County came to the conclusion that
all negroes who came into the camp then, & ever afterwards were
free from their owners., & that no one could take them afterwards
in the county without such person being arrested. Such being the
case, the poor negro thought that he had nothing to do but to go to
the camp & there be fed & clothed & do nothing & be free.

For a very long time under the operation of this construction of
the order, my negroes remained quiet, until nearly evry other negro
had left his owners & gone to Washington in Franklin County &
took what they call free or Protection papers —

Mine having wives among some of those having free papers, of
course would naturally become affected by it, & finally in my
abscence at the hour of midnight when my wife & children were
solitary & alone, nearly all of my negroes started off to Washington
taking with them whatever they saw proper & are there now
claiming to have free papers.

Even the nurse, that assisted in attending to my smallest child
went off, a girl about 12 years old, leaving us without any one there
to attend to the farm, or stock or any thing else. I have just passed
through Washington & saw my negroes in a brick House, & they
showed me what they call their free papers. The Capt intimated
that he was sorry he could not do any thing — That he was under
orders & would be removed, if he disobeyed. I told him that I did
not wish him to disobey any order! but that I thought he was
wrong in his construction of it. He said further that I could not
get them, & that he would resist any & evry effort to retake them.

Evil by civil process. Now to be brief. Nearly all my negroes
are there young & old, & nearly all of my best hands. My farm will
go uncultivated, for there are no white men to get here. Is it right
that I should be broken up. Last summer for being a Union man
my horses were stolen from me & the only man in the
neighborhood, who lost any thing that way was myself.

I have a large family, of helpless little children to support, &
have got a farm to support them on, & if I cant cultivate it, it will
be valueless to me. I make my appeal to you to grant me relief &
that those professing to be agents of the Gov. should not destroy
me.

Why cant Franklin Co be treated as well as Saline or Lafyette, where there are Southern sympathisers. Why cant the State Militia of Franklin Co attend to Franklin. Franklin is loyal to the backbone. Nearly all the slaves of Franklin County are now congregated at Washington. We can do nothing. And yet here there is no other earthly trouble. What shall I do? Were I a single man, & no family, I would not care, if my property was destroyed, And now if it was necessary to serve the interests of my country that I should sacrifice my property, I would submit without a murmur. I as a loyal man intending to stand by the Union & the Govermt of U. States, through evil as well as good report, I ask you to extend protection to me. My negroes are well treated well taken care of, & do less labor than any others in my county— A family of them that I purchased five or 6 years ago, who came to me to save them from being sold South, & whom I purchased more from sympathy than any other consideration, & who have never been taken to my residence, but lived on a farm near the County seat to themselves with evry comfort of life, they have taken up their abode in Washington.

I will not trouble you longer, but do again appeal to you to render me such assistance as may be proper; and command me for the Governmt in any way that I can be useful & I will give you any guantee that I will serve my country & Govt in any way in my power— I wish my rights to be protected in an open & substantial manner, that the people may see that there is property in being a loyal man, extending even to the protection of his property. I wish it to be effectual   I tell my slaves, that I know they are misled, and if they return not a hair of their heads shall be Hurt & no violence used. And such shall be the case— I want protection that in the open day, like an honest transaction I can have my rights redressed. If it cant be done effectually & substantially I dont care to have it done. For as an honest man, making my living honestly & fairly in evry way, I desire protection as my Governmt always has protected her citizens fully, effectually & substantially. *I am a Loyal American Citizen.* Now having said this much, I deem it unnecessary to say more, but as we are now in a ruinous condition unable to cultivate our farms, implore your intervention, & you can accomplish it at once—

Permit me, My Dear Sir, to say that sinking or swimming, surviving or perishing, I will be found to the last man standing if necessary solitary & alone *for the Union & the Constitution of the U. States.* With Sentiments of the very highest Consideration, I am Yours Most Truly

Charles Jones

I write hastily & hope you will excuse.

I again refer you to Hon Ed. Bates, Att. Gen Our most excellent & worthy Gov. H. R. Gamble. Sam T. Glover, & John R. Shiply. Esqr. Our whole delegation in Congress, & to the County at large —
ALS

Charles Jones to His Excellency Abraham Lincoln, 24 Mar. 1863, J-198 1863, Letters Received, RG 107 [L-26]. On the same day, Jones also complained to the army district commander at St. Louis that twelve of his slaves had fled to the Union army at Washington, Missouri, and he feared that he would have difficulty reclaiming them. "You must imagine my situation," pleaded Jones, "when my house servants down to the nurse of my little children . . . have all left to go to Washington on the ground that they are to be free to do nothing." (Charles Jones to Gen. Davidson, 24 Mar. 1863, Unentered Letters Received, ser. 2594, Dept. of the MO, RG 393 Pt. 1 [C-175].) Jones had written President Lincoln earlier that month, when the first of his slaves fled to the army camp "because his wife belonging to another man went thither." Jones had pursued the "remedy" provided by civil law, sending the sheriff to the camp with a writ for the arrest of the fugitive slave, but "[t]he Sheriff was interferred with by the soldiers & prevented from executing the writ." (Charles Jones to His Excellency A. Lincoln, [Mar. 1863], President 64 1863, Letters Received from the President & Executive Depts., RG 107 [L-168].)

177B: **Headquarters of the District of Western Kentucky to the Provost Marshal General of the Department of the Missouri**

Louisville, April 15th *1863.*
About a week ago James Huey, and John Newcum having in their possession seven (7) negroes, namely, Polly and her five (5) children to wit: Alice, Evaline, Sarah, Martha and Benjamine, also one negro man named Sam, were arrested by Capt, Cutts one of Genl. Burnside's Staff under the suspicion that the negroes were free and that the parties above named were wrongfully attempting to carry them into Slavery. Huey and Newcum state that the negroes above described are the property of one A. Weiesman and were bought by said Weiesman of Charles Jones of Franklin Co. Mo. They farther state that Charles Jones the original owner and A. Weiesman, the present claimant are both loyal Union men, and that the negroes are slaves for life and were brought to Kentucky to evade no law civil or Military. Weiesman Newcum and Huey being residents of St Louis. Mo. are ordered by Brig. Genl. Wright comdg. to report in person to you and he requests that you examine into the case and report to him in writing as to the loyalty of

453

Charles Jones and A. Weiesman and also as to whether the negroes above described are slaves or free   By Order of Brig Genl Wright
ALS   Stephen E. Jones.

[*Endorsement*] Office of the Provost Marshal Genl. Dpt. of the Mo. St. Louis Apl 21. 1863. Respectfully returned to Brig. Genl. Wright with this information. Charles Jones is a loyal man— his sale to Wiseman was in good faith— his title to the negroes in question was good— Wiseman is also believed by me from evidence adduced, to be loyal— Jones I have known for many years— he is a responsible Citizen of good standing— Halligan, a witness mentioned in the [within] enclosure, I know to be a credible man. F. A. Dick Lt. Col. Prov. Mar. Genl

[*Endorsement*] Hd Qrs West Dist of Ky Louisville April 24th /63   Respectfully forwarded to Lt. Col. Richmond A.A.G. for his information   On the report of Lt. Col. Dick, Pro. Mrshl. St Louis Huey & Newcome, have been discharged and the negroes turned out of the Mil. Pris. By order of Brig Genl Boyle   Stephen E. Jones Capt & A.D.C.

Capt. Stephen E. Jones to Col. Dick, 15 Apr. 1863, B-128 1863, Letters Received, ser. 3514, Dept. of the OH, RG 393 Pt. 1 [C-4605]. The enclosure referred to in Colonel Dick's endorsement is not in the file.

178: Commander of a Regiment of the Enrolled Missouri Militia to the Commander of the District of Northeast Missouri

Troy Mo. March 26th 1863.
General, It is from a serious apprehension of results greatly detrimental to the laboring interests of the loyal citizens of Lincoln County that I again call your attention to the absolute necessity of some immediate action on the part of the Military Authorities in Missouri to stop the running away of negroes from their owners. If steps are not taken very soon to exclude negroes from the lines of military camps & to prohibit them from taking refuge amongst them we make no other calculation but that we will be deprived of slave labor in a great measure & for the scarcity of free or white

labor, our people must inevitably suffer materially in agricultural interests, Since I reported through you to Dep^r H^d Quarters concerning this matter, some twelve or fifteen negroes have left our County & the adjoining County (Pike) and have taken refuge within the lines of the camp at Warrenton. I have been informed that some of those negroes took horses from their masters & now have them in their possession under the protection of the soldiers. Application has been made for the property taken by the negroes, without success. General have not the loyal people of Missouri the right to demand redress for these grievances, may they not expect that a good & just Government will extend to them the protection of their property, that is guaranteed to us in our Constitution & which Mr. Lincoln as our Chief Executive has repeatedly pledged himself should be done. We have confidence in the pledges of the Administration & feel that all that is necessary for us to do to have redress for our wrongs is to make them known through the proper source. Hoping General that you will lay our complaint before the proper Authorities & that you will ask for us that something be done for our grievances, I remain Very Respty Your Ob^t Servt

ALS   C. W. Parker

Col. C. W. Parker to Brig. Genl. T. J. McKean, 26 Mar. 1863, Unentered Letters Received, ser. 2594, Dept. of the MO, RG 393 Pt. 1 [C-177]. Parker commanded the 37th Regiment, Enrolled Missouri Militia. He had written in the same vein to the commander of the District of Northeast Missouri on February 23 and again on March 14, 1863. In reply to Parker's charges, the commander of the regiment stationed at Warrenton, Major John Y. Clopper, explained that claimants who made application "for the rendition of fugitives . . . [had] been informed in every instance, that no obstructions would or should be placed in their way to prevent them from inducing the negro to return home; that the negro should be left to the exercise of his own wishes with regard to remaining in employment in Camp, or returning to his claimant; & that no force would be allowed to compel the negro to go or stay." "This policy," Clopper asserted, "is in conformity with the law which forbids the employment of the military in the rendition of fugitive slaves; while it is evident that it would be incompatible with the good order of Camp & the dignity & authority of the government to permit the exercise of outside force." He further pointed out that the law referred to (the March 1862 article of war) "makes no distinction between the slaves of loyal men & those whose disloyalty is established; but expressly states those 'who may have escaped from ANY persons.' " In an endorsement dated April 1, 1863, General Samuel R. Curtis, commander of the Department of the Missouri, approved Clopper's policy, except for the prohibition against the use of force to reclaim fugitives: "In this state slavery actually exists and it exists by force of state laws. The state authorities must not be prevented from exercising force if they do not disturb the peace of Camp. Let alone is our duty. We cannot 'deliver up' and have no legal right to restrain. It is a personal matter between the master & slave which we have nothing to do with." (Col. C. W. Parker to Brig. Genl. T. J. McKean, 14 Mar. 1863, and Major John Y. Clopper to Major Geo. Merrill, 21 Mar. 1863, both filed with Col. C. W. Parker to Brig. Genl. Thos. J. McKean, 23 Feb. 1863, P-95 1863, Letters Received, ser. 2593, Dept. of the MO, RG 393 Pt. 1 [C-134].)

179: Missouri Unionist to the Attorney General

Orleans Missouri   May 25 /63

Sir   I want you To furnish me with all the Confiscation Lawes passed By Congress Concerning Rebel property   I want you To give as much instruction as you Can in this matter for there is a great many Rebels in this Country that their property is subject to Confiscation and I intend it Shal be done tho the government will have To be verry Cautious who is Apointed Marshals and Attornyes for that purpose for the Enrolled Malitia of this State generaly protects Rebels better than Loyal men   this I blame governor gamble for appointing so many Conservative Officers   tha Looks up to Slave holders Too much   we that advocates the Cause of Immediate amansipation of Slaves from the State has but Little Shoing with the Conservative Officers of the E.M.M. but still we Intend that the Negroes Shal Leave M.O. and be free   the most of those officers pretend to be the best of union men and tha want the negro with it and If govenor gamble has the Appointing of those Marshals and Attorneys you will find but Little property Confiscated (for tha will favor the Rebels and rebel Simpathizers all tha can   tha is one thing that I want you to tel me that is whare a Rebel owes a union man by Note on account will Such debts be paid To Loyal men before Confiscated for the use of the goverment   any Information you ma desire of me Concerning the Rebels iwil give or any duties you may wish me to perform I will attend to   I Can Satisfy you at any time of my Loyalty to the govermen and all wayes have bin   Let me hear from you Soon   Yours Truley

L. V. Hollyfield

PS   the rebels and Simpathizers or Buying up all the Stock and Driving North

ALS

L. V. Hollyfield to Hon. Edward Bates, 25 May 1863, Letters Received: MO Private Citizens, Attorney General's Records, RG 60 [W-13].

180: Missouri Slaveholders to the Governor of Missouri

Lexington [*Mo.*] June 4. 1863

Dear Sir   We the undersigned Union men Citizens of Lafayette County in the State of Missouri, would earnestly state to your Excellency, that under the order of F. A. Dick Lt. Col. & Provost Marshall General Department of the Missouri, purporting to be "By command of Major General Curtis, dated St Louis 24th December 1862 and numbered General Orders N° 35,[1] we have been made to suffer great inconvenience as well as loss of property—

Our servants have been induced to run away and come to the Post at Lexington; and we have in vain endeavored to get them— We go to the Post Commander and though our loyalty is unquestioned, we have been unable to reclaim our negroes— We see them in camp or around the Camp, the Commander will not do anything: but his soldiers in many cases are standing by, ready to aid the negroes in resisting their masters; These negroes are most of them armed; they have been furnished with tents and with rations— It is no matter what proof the master offers, the negroes say that they be long to secessionists, and the officers believe them— We suppose that there are now or were on yesterday at least 150 negroes at the College and around it at Lexington—and not one can be obtained by the owner, no matter how loyal he may be— Apply by force of legal process and the soldiers will pay no regard to civil officers or civil process— Now Governor, what can we do?— The Military will obey Dick's order; but have no respect for the advice or orders of the President and the Attorney General— These self-constituted Judges, Military Judges, will decide and confiscate our slaves and little subordinate Provost Marshalls under the order of Mr. Dick will gravely confiscate the best Union man's servant; give him a pass and imprison his master, if he resent this injury by retaking his servant. Such has been the practice at this Post heretofore— We ask your Excellency since we have a new Commander here, and a new Provost Marshall, that you will see Major General Schofield & have so much of said order N° 35 above mentioned rescinded or abrogated as relates to the confiscation of our negroes & other property by the mere Military arbitrament of Provost Marshalls— Have articles or paragraphs XIII, XIV up to XVIII either rescinded or altered, so that we may be safe in our . property— We ask nothing for the disloyal men of our Country— Still we think the Courts & not the Military should confiscate the property, after trial & hearing in open Court—

The President's Proclamation of 1st Jany '63 does not embrace Missouri. Why should the radicals enforce it here—at the point of the bayonet? This is grievous, a crying evil and calls loudly for redress— We therefore desire you as our Chief Magistrate to do something for us in this business— Gen¹ Schofield will do what is right, we doubt not, especially if you Governor will call his attention to it— We ask a repeal of this abolition order; this military license to steal our negroes— We will not be understood to cast censure on the present Provost Marshall & the Commander now at this Post, they but obey Dick's order & Gen¹ Loan's instructions as we beleive— Very respectfully your obt servts

John F. Ryland   Henry C Chiles

HLS   Eldridge Burden   L W Smallwood

[Endorsement] Lexington *[Mo.]* May *[June]* 5ᵗʰ 1863. I fully endorse the above letter, and in addition beg to say that when negroes steal horses & come into the camp at Lexington, they sell them to the soldiers & when applied for by their owners, (loyal men) they are not listened to by the commander of the post, nor any facilities granted for the recovery of their property, while the soldiers are freely licensed to insult them & threaten their lives. One of the Companies sent from this place are now at Marshall Saline Co. & I take the liberty of inclosing a letter just received from Mʳ Estill one of the best citizens of that County relative to the outrages which they are committing there   I am Sir most resply. R. C. Vaughan

John F. Ryland et al. to His Excellency Governor Gamble, 4 June 1863, R-44 1863, Letters Received, ser. 2786, Provost Marshal General, Dept. of the MO, RG 393 Pt. 1 [C-188]. Another endorsement. In an enclosed letter, John H. Estill, a slaveholder in Miami, Missouri, complained that "redlegs" from Kansas "pass my house almost every day & go into my fields & order my negroes to take my teams & go to Kansas & if they dont they will kill them." He also reported that "negroes are going off by scores to Marshall & other places & if this state of affairs exist much longer we will be destitute of stock labor & every thing else." (John H. Estill to Genl. Vaughan, 30 May 1863.) On July 2, 1863, the governor referred both letters, without comment, to the provost marshal general of the Department of the Missouri, Colonel James O. Broadhead, who in turn referred them to General John M. Schofield, commander of the department.

1 See above, doc. 172.

181A: Missouri Unionist to a Delegate in the Missouri State Convention

Farmington Mo June 16. 1863
Dr sir   Unless you work rapidly your labors so far as this part of the Country is concerned – will be useless, as the work of emancipation is going on finely here in the last fiew days   yesterday over 75 negroes were forcibly taken from their homes in Cook Settlement, with waggons and teams sufficient to carry them off and I am credibly informd that the work in Madison County has been Completd – Sebastian Coffman the Harries – Clark & others are the sufferers –   I can see no use of action by the Convention in regard to this species of property, and would advised for the interest of the state that if they have no other business before them to adjourn immediately and return home – and leave this matter with the radicals of the St Charles Democrat school and the thing will be acomplished in Short order.   we expect every day a raid in upon us from this band of outlaws and Jayhawkers –   I cannot think this thing is sanctioned by authority yet it Saviors Strongly of it – or why the necessity of the order of the Adjutant General requiring the RR to Carry over them this Class of persons when the law makes the rail Road responsible to the owener for carrying them,   It seems to me that the thing is understood fully by those in power, and to evade this law this order is published –
Where are we drifting   Respectfly
ALS   W R Taylor

W. R. Taylor to Honr. M. P. Cayce, 16 June 1863, T-112 1863, Letters Received, ser. 2593, Dept. of the MO, RG 393 Pt. 1 [C-145]. The order referred to has not been found among either the orders issued by the Department of the Missouri or those issued by the Adjutant General's Office of the War Department. A son of the convention delegate addressed by Taylor informed his father a few days later that slaves in the Farmington area had been liberated by recruiting parties from the 3rd Missouri Cavalry, whose activities had "about stripped Cooks Settlement & Fredericktown of negroes," leaving the wheat and other grain crops "rotting in the Fields for want of Harvest hands." (*Freedom*, ser. 2: doc. 84.)

181B: Delegate in the Missouri State Convention to the Commander of the Department of the Missouri

Farmington M° July 31. 1863

Sir. Since the adjournment of the State Convention I have been frequently questioned by Loyal owners of Slaves, respecting the probability of their being able to reclaim fugitives from labor now at the various Military Posts; and also, whether the services of those they still retain possession of will not be rendered more secure by our Government during the term of years granted by the Convention. I have understood, & have hazarded the opinion that a gradual scheme of Emancipation, similar to ours, would meet with favor from President Lincoln, & that as soon as feasible, as much security would be granted to loyal owners, in the possession of their property—as the present condition of Affairs will admit of.

So far as my knowledge extends, the Slave owners of this district gave a cheerful acquiescence to the Emancipation Act, hoping that this might be the occasion of ensuring the possession of their Slaves until free labor could be obtained, which cannot now be done. They, however, continue to lose their slaves as rapidly as before this act was passed. In this vicinity several Negro Men have left their owners, and the Women & Children are preparing to go also: Indeed, it is expected that in a short time there will be an extensive stampede among them.

It would not be proper in me, Sir, to offer advice in the management of the affairs of our State. But I would venture to express the belief that if our Government could with propriety exclude Slaves from entering military Posts or Camps, & forbid their passage on Rail Roads, that it would give confidence to many loyal & law abiding Citizens, and also serve to induce a greater respect for the Emancipation ordnance, from those whom it most narrowly concerns. With high consideration & respect I am your obedient Servant

ALS   M. P. Cayce

M. P. Cayce to Maj. Gen. Schofield, 31 July 1863, C-655 1863, Letters Received, ser. 2593, Dept. of the MO, RG 393 Pt. 1 [C-118]. No reply has been found in the records of the Department of the Missouri.

182: Commander of the Department of the Missouri to the
Secretary of War, and Judge Advocate General
to the Secretary of War

St. Louis, July 17th *1863.*

The State of Missouri having adopted an ordinance of
Emancipation, the civil tribunals being in operation in the greater
part of the State, the Federal Courts never having suspended their
functions and the Presidents proclamation of Freedom never having
been extended to Missouri—some serious questions arise as to the
powers and duties of the Military Authorities in this Department so
far as they affect the people of Missouri:—and I would be pleased to
have your views and instructions in regard to them, and particularly
as to what authority if any, the military may assume in respect to
the slaves of loyal men—and also, in respect to negroes made free by
operation of the several acts of Congress.

First, Are the Military Authorities to determine the question of
freedom or slavery under the provisions of Acts of August 6^h 1861,
and of July 17th 1862—and to give Certificates of freedom to the
slaves of disloyal persons?

The 14th section of the act of July 17th 1862 provides that "The
Courts of the United States shall have full power to institute
proceedings, make orders and decrees, issue process, and do all other
things necessary to carry this act into effect."

The 16th [*10th*] Section provides that ". . . no person engaged in
the military or naval service of the United States shall under any
pretence whatever assume to decide on the validity of the claim of
any person to the service or labor of any other person, or to
surrender up any such person, to the claimant on pain of being
dismissed from the service."

This last clause, though general in its terms would seem from the
context to refer to cases of fugitive slaves escaping from one State to
another.

The new article of war, adopted by act of March 13th 1862
forbids the use of any military force to return fugitives from labor
under penalty of dismissal from the service.

The question arises whether in a loyal state, or at least those parts
of it where the civil tribunals perform their regular functions, the
whole matter is to be left subject to their jurisdiction, or whether
the military may interfere and undertake to execute the provisions of
the acts of Congress in this respect.

You are aware, perhaps, that the President has required the
Attorney General to prepare instruc- to the Marshalls and District
Attorneys to institute proceedings under the act of July 17th 1862
and Aug. 6 1861, but nothing is said about Slaves.

It is very clear to my mind that those persons declared free by the 4th section of the act of August 6th 1861 and by the 9th Section of the act of July 17th 1862 are free by the operation of the law and the disloyal acts of their owners, and that no judicial decree is necessary to perfect their freedom. Is it any part of the duty of the Military authorities to furnish evidence of such freedom or must they be left to plead the acts either in suit for freedom, or in defence against the person claiming their services or labor.?

These questions of course do not apply to the proclamation of the President of January 1st 1863. Under that proclamation the Military and Naval authorities are expressly required to enforce its provisions and to give protection to the persons liberated by it—

2^{d}. Another question arises, as to how far the Military Authorities under the terms of the Article of War of March 13^{h} 1862 may protect a civil officer from violence if he undertakes to arrest a fugitive from labor, when found in a military camp, either on account of any criminal offence committed by such fugitive, or because his service or labor is claimed by the person who sues out the writ.

In the present condition of affairs in Missouri, it is important to have the views of the head of the Department on these subjects. As I do not desire to contravene the policy of the Government or to do anything which may create any unnecessary disturbance in the public mind or prevent the restoration of peace in Missouri.

Military authority is still needed in this state for, although there is no enemy in force within its borders, the disorders necessarily resulting from a state of war, still in many parts of the state require something stronger than the civil law to repress them. I have the honor to be Very Respectfully Your Obdt Servant

HLS   J. M. Schofield

Judge Advocate General's Office [*Washington*] August 17th 1863. Sir. The letter of Major General J. M. Schofield, addressed to yourself under date of 17th July, and referred to this office, has been carefully considered.

The object of the communication, is to ask from the Secretary of War, instructions as to the line of conduct to be pursued by the Military authorites in Missouri, in reference to the population of African descent found in that state, which being loyal was not embraced in the President's proclamation of the 1st January 1863. The points to which the inquiries and suggestions of Genl. Schofield are mainly directed, may be resolved into three. viz: The status: First of the persons held to service or labor in Missouri, as growing out of the 4. Sec. of the "Act to confiscate property used for insurrectionary purposes" approved 6th August 1861: Second of those enumerated in the 9th Section of the "Act to suppress insurrection, to punish treason and rebellion" &c, approved 17th July 1862: and Thirdly of those referred to in the 10th Section of the last mentioned act; together with the rights and duties of the Military authorities in regard to persons belonging to each of these classes.

The emancipation of the persons held to service or labor named in the first class viz: Such as have been required or permitted by those to whom such service or labor is due to take up arms against the United States, or to work or be employed in or upon any Fort, Navy Yard, dock, armory, ship, entrenchment, or in any naval or military service whatever against the government of the United States, results *ipso facto*, from the performance of the acts mentioned; and should thereafter any attempt be made to enforce such claim to labor or service against the person thus manumitted, is is declared by the act of Congress that "it shall be a full and sufficient answer to such claim, that the person whose service or labor is claimed, had been employed in hostile service against the government of the United States." The statute evidently contemplates that this defence or assertion of a right to freedom, shall be made before the Courts, and I am not aware of any grounds, on which the military authorities in the state of Missouri, where the Courts are open, can intervene, in the settlement of any questions arrising under this act— Should the party claimed to be held to service be seized for the purpose of enforcing the claim, he would only have to sue out a writ of Habeas Corpus, and make proof of the facts, to secure his discharge.

The persons described in the second class stand upon an entirely different footing. The language of the act in reference to them is as follows:

> "And be it further enacted, that all slaves of persons who shall hereafter be engaged in rebellion against the government of the United States, or who shall in any way give aid or comfort thereto, escaping from such persons and taking refuge within the lines of the army; and all slaves captured from such persons, or deserted by them and coming under the control of the government of the United States; and all slaves of such persons found or being within place occupied by rebel forces, and afterwards occupied by the forces of the United States, shall be deemed captures of War, and shall be forever free of their servitude, and not again held as slaves."

The slaves thus enumerated, being made and declared to be "Captives of War," as well as freedmen, are necessarily under the military control and protection of the government of the United

States. This protection should, in good faith, be fully extended to them against all efforts made to re-enslave them, or to deprive them of the freedom which this act bestows upon them. That their condition and the rights belonging to it may be known and respected, it is recommended that through the Departmental or other Military commanders, certificates shall, upon a proper ascertainment of the facts, be issued to these persons, defining distinctly their status, and declaring them to be as "captives of War" under the military protection of the government. These certificates should state briefly, but distinctly the facts on which the party's right to freedom rests, in order that it may appear, the legal conclusion reached is warrented by the law as cited.

The 10th Section relates to fugitive slaves of loyal masters; and they constitute the Third class: The section is in these words:

> "And be it further enacted, that no slave escaping into any state territory or the District of Columbia, from any other state, shall be delivered up or in any way impeded or hindered, of his liberty, except for crime, or some offense against the laws, unless the person claiming said fugitive shall first make oath that the person to whom the labor or service of such fugitive is alleged to be due, is his lawful owner, and has not borne arms against the United States in the present rebellion, nor in any way given aid and comfort thereto; and no person engaged in the military or naval service of the United States shall, under any pretence whatever, assume to decide on the validity of the claim of any person to the service or labor of any other person or surrender up any such person to the claimant, on pain of being dismissed from the service."

The duty of the military authorities in reference to this class of fugitives from labor, is that of absolute non intervention. This follows alike from the prohibition to surrender the fugitive, and from the prohibition to decide on the validity of the claim made to his service. As the military cannot primarily exert any power in behalf of the claimant, neither can it be done in a secondary or subordinate capacity—as a posse comitaties to the civil authorities or otherwise. If therefore a loyal claimant or his agent acting in person or through a civil officer, shall attempt to arrest one of these fugitives from labor, in the presence of the military authorities, he must do so on his own responsibility, and cannot claim from such authorities, nor can they extend to him, any support or protection whatever.

It is believed that these suggestions meet all the points presented by the letter of Major General Schofield. Very respectfully Your Obedient Servt.

HLS

J Holt

Maj. Genl. J. M. Schofield to Hon. E. M. Stanton, 17 July 1863, and Judge Advocate Genl. J. Holt to Hon. E. M. Stanton, 17 Aug. 1863, M-1499 1863, Letters Received, ser. 12, RG 94 [K-573]. Endorsement. The ellipses in Schofield's letter appear in the manuscript.

183: **Railroad President to the Commander of the Department of the Missouri, Enclosing a Letter from Missouri Slaveholders to the Railroad President**

St. Louis, Sept. 9 *1863*

Sir   I beg leave to call your attention to the enclosed letter, which I can assure you is only one out of a large number daily received by me, and which I need hardly add gives me much annoyance. If the statute of the State is enforced against the Company, by the owners, the funds in the treasury of the Co received from all sources would hardly suffice to satisfy the demands –

I enclose you this communication to exhibit clearly the disabilities we labor under, and the embarrassments that are increasing from day to day, which meet us in our efforts to do justice to all and to protect the interests which have been confided to my trust   Yours truly

HLcSr   I. H. Sturgeon

[*Enclosure*]   Montgomery Co. Mo. Aug. 31ˢᵗ 1863
Dear Sir   We had five negroes transported on the N.M.R.R. from Florence, in this county, on Wednesday 26ᵗʰ Inst. to St. Louis Mᵒ   This we can prove, and we intend to hold the No. Mo. R.R. Company responsible for them,

There were also several other negroes from this section of County, and we understand that the parties to whom they belong will do as we intend doing, The negroes first above alluded to, belong to W. Graves O. F. D. Hampton and O C MᶜKay   Three to W Graves viz: Jonah, Carr, and Burwell one to Hampton viz – Ralph, and one to MᶜKay viz – Simon,

We intend to make demand for the above mentioned negroes and should they not be returned we will have pay for them, If you should wish to write to us on the subject address either of us at High Hill Mᵒ   Very Respectfully &C
(Copy)   Washington Graves
                                                             O F. D. Hampton
HLcSr   O. C. MᶜKay

I. H. Sturgeon to Maj. Genl. Schofield, 9 Sept. 1863, enclosing Washington Graves et al. to I. H. Sturgeon, 31 Aug. 1863, S-706 1863, Letters Received, ser. 2593, Dept. of the MO, RG 393 Pt. 1 [C-141]. Sturgeon was president of the North Missouri Railroad. An executive officer of another Missouri railroad also reported that his company was being threatened with suits by slaveholders for transporting slaves "without the written permission of the owner." The president of the Pacific Railroad noted that his company had been named in more than ten such legal actions. (G. R. Taylor to Major General Schofield, 10 June 1863, T-110 1863, Letters Received, ser. 2593, Dept. of the MO, RG 393 Pt. 1 [C-144]; G. R. Taylor to Major General Schofield, 5 Aug. 1863, enclosing W. N. Grover to Geo. R. Taylor, Esq., 3 Aug. 1863, T-163 1863, Letters Received, ser. 2593, Dept. of the MO, RG 393 Pt. 1 [C-144].) In April 1864, after months of official indecision on the part of both his predecessor and himself, General William S. Rosecrans, commander of the Department of the Missouri, instructed his provost marshal general that "Rail Road Companies in this Dept are authorized to transport colored persons having free papers, good under the laws of the State, or issued by competent Military authority, on the same terms and conditions as other free persons." Rosecrans also ordered provost marshals "to give official security" to the railroad companies "for passing any contrabands for which the U.S. is to be responsible." (Major H. M. Dunn to Major General Rosecrans, 13 Apr. 1864; Maj. Genl. Rosecrans, 19 Apr. 1864, endorsement on Isaac H. Sturgeon to Maj. O. D. Greene, 7 Apr. 1864, S-793 1864, Letters Received, ser. 2786, Provost Marshal General, Dept. of the MO, RG 393 Pt. 1 [C-141].) The issue was finally resolved on January 31, 1865, when the Missouri legislature repealed the antebellum statute concerning transportation of slaves by railroad companies, annulled fines and penalties incurred under the old law, suspended legal proceedings pending under that law, and prohibited future suits against railroads for transporting slaves. (Missouri, *Laws of the State of Missouri Passed at the Adjourned Session of the Twenty-Third General Assembly.* . . . [Jefferson City, 1866], pp. 128–29.)

184A: **Commander of a Subdistrict of the Central District of Missouri to the Headquarters of the Central District**

Tipton Missouri   November 11" 1863

Captain   I have the honor of submitting to you the following report of a high handed outrage committed on the Cars of the Pacific. R.R. this Morning by a detachment of about 40 men of the 9th Minnesota Volunteer Infantry

At Smithtown Mr C. W. C Walker living 2 miles from Sedalia, came on board with 11 of his negroes en route for Kentucky, having a permit to ship the same from W B Davis Lieut and Asst Provost Marshall at Sedalia. On the cars reaching Otterville they were boarded by several soldiers of the 9" Minn Vol Inft. who ordered the negroes out, And upon Mr Charles White the Conductor of the Train asking them by whose authority they were acting, replied they had orders   I then went up to the appearent ringleaders, and asked them if they had an officer with them to, which, they replied they had. I told them who I was, and some of them remarked "they didn't care a damn" for the Commanding Officer of the District they had their orders and were going to obey them. The Conductor and myself then tried to prevail upon them, to leave the Negroes where, they were untill we got to the bridge and saw Capt Wellman   One of them was disposed to do this, but the others overruled him and marched the negroes out of the cars. On arriving at Lamine Capt Pritchard the Inspecting Officer of the District who was on board and witnessed the whole proceedings, came with me to Capt Wellman who disclaimed all knowledge of the whole proceedings, said the men acted without orders and entirely on their own responsibility, and seemed much put out at their conduct. We returned to near Otterville, where we met the detachment coming down towards the bridge. The negroes were not with them and they told Capt Wellman they had left them in town. (Otterville) where they said they could take care of themselves. This the conductor says is the first instance of the kind which ever took place on the road. Comment is unnecessary   I remain Captain Very Respectfully Your Obt Servant

(Signed) Oscar. B. Queens

HLcSr

Capt. Oscar B. Queens to Capt. James H. Steger, 11 Nov. 1863, filed with J-445 1864, Letters Received, RG 107 [L-46]. In the same file is a similar report by Captain Levi Pritchard, inspector of the Central District of Missouri, who added that when questioned regarding the whereabouts of their officers, the Minnesota soldiers replied that "they were all officers." He also reported that the soldiers had cocked their guns at the conductor and engineer of the train. Pritchard included in his letter a copy of the permit issued to C. W. C. Walker by the assistant provost marshal at Sedalia, Missouri, on November 11, 1863, "to ship from Sedalia to St Louis en route to Kentucky the following blacks Emily 25 her five Children. John aged 23, Rachel 21 with 2 Children, Anna 14, Patsey 12 Billey 23." (Capt. Levi Pritchard to Brig. Genl. E. B. Brown, 11 Nov. 1863.) Also in the file is an excerpt from Special Order 307, issued November 10, 1863, by General John M. Schofield, commander of the Department of the Missouri: "Hereafter, no Provost Marshal nor other officer in the Military service in Missouri will give any *pass or permit* to any person, authorizing him to take *Slaves* from Mo. to any other State." In the same file is a letter from an adjutant at the Department of the Missouri headquarters, pointing out that this order was issued one day prior to the provost marshal's permit for the removal of the slaves to Kentucky, "although it may not have been recd by him at the time." (Maj. J. A. Campbell to Maj. Genl. J. M. Schofield, 13 Jan. 1864.) The file also includes copies of correspondence regarding the arrest and confinement, while awaiting trial, of thirty-five enlisted men of the 9th Minnesota Infantry.

184B: **Members of the Missouri Legislature to the Commander of the Central District of Missouri, and the Latter's Reply**

[*Jefferson City, Mo. December 1863*]
Dear. Sir— The undersigned, Members of the Genl Assembly of the State of Missouri, respectfully desire herewith to transmit a synopsis of a letter received by one of your petitioners—signed—"Private Co. C. 9th. Regt. Minn. Vols. substantially embodying the following representations:—

On Novem. 11th. information was brought into Camp that a family of Negro Slaves, numbering eleven in all, and owned by a rebel now in arms against the Govt. of the U.S., were being brought down upon the Mailtrain, in view of removing them to the State of Kentucky; said negroes being then in charge of a Son of the Rebel by whom the—*property*(?)—was owned. That upon receiving the above information a volunteer party consisting of members of companies C. & K., numbering in all about forty, in command of a Sergeant, proceeded to Otterville a Station on the P.R.R., and as the train came to a stand for the reception of passengers, entered the cars and informed the slaves that they were at liberty to go their own way if they chose. That several gentlemen on the train, "whom we supposed to be private citizens demanded of us by what authority we had permitted the slaves to leave the train?" 'We replied'—"We have authority." That they had since been informed that the aforesaid gentlemen were officers having authority, a fact of which they were entirely ignorant, as no insignia or badge of office was visible upon their persons. That the train was not stopped or detained by them beyond its usual time, as had been represented in an article published in the "Mo. Republican." And that the Soldiers engaged in freeing those slaves—though not acting under regular orders at the time, had the sanction of at least, some of their superior officers.

The foregoing embraces the most of the leading points in the letter referred to; and your petitioners—having signed a petition recommending your promotion—beg leave to ask of you a favorable consideration of the following facts which we hope may to some extent mitigate the offence for which these men are held under arrest:

1$^{st.}$ That their Regt. having been but recently organized it is hardly to be expected, that the strict orderly bearing and dicipline wich characterizes the old soldier should have been fully acquired.

2$^{d.}$ That they are men of high moral stand- in the community in which they resided previous to enlisting in the cause of our Government, and are at all times ready to sacrifice their lives in its defence and maintenance.

3$^{d.}$ That they are soldiers from a free State and it is but natural that they should hate slavery—the cause of the Rebellion—as it should be hated!

In view of these representations which are, in accordance with the best information at our command, founded on facts, your petitioners would respectfully pray—that if not derogatory to your high duties as a Soldier, occupying the important position occupied by you—that our prayer in behalf these men may meet with your approval, and that they be liberated. Respectfully submitted

HLS   [59 *signatures*]

"*Copy*"   *Jefferson City, Mo.* Decr 7th *1863.*
Gentlemen, I have the honor to acknowledge the receipt of your petition in behalf of a number of members of the 9th Minnesota Regiment of Volunteers who are under arrest for mutiny,—in which you state the Circumstances, as related to you by a Soldier, one of the mutineers. As a citizen from a free state, I hold in Common with all the army, an abhorrence of the institution of Slavery, and fully appreciate and participate with others in the belief, that Slavery is the Cause of the war, yet I do not see the necessity of setting at defiance the Rules made for the government of the army, in order to give expression to my individual views, nor can I

recognize the right to do so by Soldiers under my Command. I would respectfully Correct the statement which you say, you received from a Soldier. The 9th Regiment Minn. Volunteers has been in service over a year, and its soldierly appearance, and strict discipline, as well as General reputation shews that it has been Commanded by Officers who Knew and have done their duty, So, that the plea of ignorance would not be received in their Case. The statement that persons who they believed were Citizens, commanded them to desist from their interference in the Case referred to, and that they wore nothing that indicated their rank in the service, is not true. Capt Queen of the 7th M.S.M. and Capt Pritchett of the 4th M.S.M. who were present were both in full uniform The former announced his rank, and that he was in the Command of the Troops in the 2nd Sub. District of which this detachment of the 9th Minnesota was a part, and the latter as Inspector General for the District of Central Missouri, both of whom vainly used all the authority and force in their power to stop the Mutinous Conduct of these men. These men are not under arrest for their participation in the release of Slaves, for, the Army is engaged in doing that duty, as one of the means of conquering a peace, but for their violation of the 6th 7th 8th & 9th Articles of War.[1]

The offences with which they are charged are of so grave a character, and are so clearly set out in the reports of the officers who witnessed them, that I do not feel authorized to order their release, but will refer the question with your petition for the decision of the Secretary of War. I am Gentlemen Very Respectfully Your obed^t Servt

HLcSr   E B Brown

[*Endorsement*] Washington D.C. Jan 17 1863 [*1864*] The enclosed petition from members of the Missouri Legislature asking the release of certain soldiers of the 9th Minnesota Infantry, and accompanying papers showing the offence which said soldiers had committed, are respectfully forwarded to the Hon. Secretary of War. They were received by me only a short time before I left St. Louis and had not been acted upon in consequence of my being suddenly called away. Upon learning that the Senate had passed a resolution of enquiry on the subject of the arrest and confinement of these soldiers, I telegraphed for all the papers in the case. They are respectfully submitted with a view to enable the War Department to give the information desired by the Senate or for such other action as the Hon Secretary of War may be pleased to take in the premises   J M Schofield Maj Genl

E. H. E. Jameson et al. to Brig. Genl. E. B. Brown, [Dec. 1863], and Brig. Genl. E. B. Brown to E. H. E. Jameson et al., 7 Dec. 1863, J-455 1864, Letters Received, RG 107 [L-46]. On January 21, 1864, General Brown reported to the headquarters of the Department of the Missouri "that the men were good soldiers, and had cheerfully performed their duty, and obeyed all orders except in this case, and that they acknowledged the fault they had committed, believing that the punishment they had received would prevent future offenses of this character; and as the case had been referred to the Secretary of War, I ordered them to duty with their regiment, and discharged them from arrest to await his decision." On February 1, General William S. Rosecrans, new commander of the Department of the Missouri, forwarded Brown's report and other papers in the case to the Secretary of War with the opinion that "the interests of the service do not require any further steps to be taken in the matter." On February 27, in transmitting the papers to the U.S. Senate, Secretary of War Edwin M. Stanton concurred with Rosecrans's judgment. (U.S., Congress, Senate, *Senate Executive Documents*, 38th Cong., 1st sess., No. 24, pp. 1, 6–8.)

1 Articles 6, 7, 8, and 9 defined the following as offenses punishable by death: contempt or disrespect for a commanding officer, mutiny, failure to suppress mutiny, and violence against a superior officer. (U.S., War Department, *Revised United States Army Regulations* [Washington, 1863], appendix, p. 486.)

185: Testimony of a U.S. Senator from Missouri before the American Freedmen's Inquiry Commission

ST. LOUIS, Nov. 30, 1863.

Testimony of Hon. B. Gratz Brown.

For a time, fugitives from the insurgent States, taking refuge here, were arrested and imprisoned, and sold for jail fees, but that has been entirely broken up, and I do not believe that it now occurs in a single instance. The more severe laws enacted against negroes (which, however, were never carried so far here as in Kentucky) are practically broken up, and may be said to be no longer in force. There is an order from headquarters providing that no slaves are to be sent out of the State; if, therefore, any slaves reach Kentucky, it is in disobedience of that order.

M. Brown expressed the opinion that, in a general way, the slaves of Missouri, if emancipated, can take good care of themselves, & he considers them very much more intelligent and self-reliant than the slaves of the cotton States; yet he believes that it would be proper and necessary that a portion of the system of organization proposed by the Commission should be extended over the Border States;

especially the system of registration, in connection with a record of what becomes of the negroes – whether sent to the Quartermaster's Department, enlisted, or otherwise disposed of; and also a temporary supervision of the fugitives who come hither from the insurgent States. Any supervision for the negroes of Missouri themselves he considers unnecessary. He believes that the plan of enlistment incorporated in Gen. Schofield's order will practically effect emancipation in Missouri, if it be carried out in the proper spirit, with zeal and industry; but so far from this being the case at present, the most of those entrusted with the execution of the order put every possible difficulty in the way. He believes that, if properly carried out, in 90 or 120 days, 30,000 negroes could be enlisted in Missouri.

M. B. says that many of the colored people in St. Louis are wealthy and respectable, and, in a general way, that they manage very well for themselves.

At this moment, according to Mr. Brow's statement, there is a small majority in the Legislature in favor of a popular Convention, which popular Convention would, beyond all possible doubt, make arrangements for immediate emancipation; but they are withheld from taking action in the matter by the doubt whether the Governor is earnest in the matter. Their doubts arise from the character of the persons appointed by the Governor to carry out the measures of the gov't in Missouri. The opponents of the system of enlistment went at one time so far as to prevent the negro regiments from having any arms put into their hands until they left the State; but representations in regard to this were made to the proper authorities, & the evil has been corrected.

HD

Testimony of Hon. B. Gratz Brown before the American Freedmen's Inquiry Commission, 30 Nov. 1863, filed with O-328 1863, Letters Received, ser. 12, RG 94 [K-205]. Topical labels in the margin are omitted.

186: Testimony by the Former Provost Marshal General of the Department of the Missouri before the American Freedmen's Inquiry Commission

[*St. Louis December 1, 1863*]
Testimony of Franklin A. Dick, Esq.
Q   What is your idea in reference to slave-stealing in this State at the present time?

A   My impression is, that there is not much of it in this State.   There is an old order of Gen. Curtis, which stands as words, if nothing more, and I believe has had a negative effect, at least, even during the present administration.   It stands somewhat *in terrorem* over the believers in slavery.

Q   You think they are not seized now?

A   I don't hear of it at all.   The anti-slavery men in this State have been so active, they have taken so much courage, and they have so much hope, that I believe any abuses of that kind would have found their way into the newspapers.   I have not heard any thing of the kind.   I have been absent for some time until within the last two weeks, but during all the time I was away, I had the papers on both sides sent to me, and if there had been anything of that sort reported, I should certainly have noticed it, and probably should have called the attention of the Provost Marshal General to it, who is really a strong anti-slavery man.

Matters here have assumed a most remarkable shape.   Men are placed in false positions more by personal feeling than any thing else.   I cannot say I belong to either branch of the party here, for the reason that there are Union men on both sides, and hostile to each other.   I am a radical, without belonging to the radical paty.   I don't want to feel unkindly towards men that I know to be earnest, loyal Union men, and anti-slavery men, too, even though they may do some things that I strongly disapprove.

Q   Do you think that order 135, in regard to negro enlistments will be carried out in good faith?

A   I feel this way about that.   When I read that order, I wished very much that there was a radical anti-slavery man at the head of this department.   I do not at all concur in a great deal that is said against Gen. Schofield, because I know that there are good men who differ essentially with me in opinion.   Unfortunately, there is so much bitterness of feeling here, that if you differ from a man in opinion, you are almost bound to impute his motives, or his principles.   Now, I do not attribute bad motives or bad principles to Gen. Schofield, but I think that his policy is so wrong, that it might almost be called vicious, so far as the interests of this State are concerned.   Hamilton Gamble, I can't help believing, is an honest man; but he is so much influenced by prejudice against anti-slavery men, and his partialities for the opposite are so great, that he cannot see straight or feel right; and Gen. Schofield is greatly under his influence.   I regard the General as one hand of the Governor.

Q   Is Gov. Gamble pro-slavery in his feeling?

A   Indeed he is.   If a fellow stops you in the highway, and says, 'Give me your money, or I will blow out your brains," you surrender your purse, but not out of kindness. You do from fear, what another man, under other circumstances, would do from kindness. Gov. Gamble has made great concessions to the anti-slavery feeling, for the same reason that you would give up your purse to a man when you couldn't help yourself. I regard Gen. Schofield as opposed to anti-slavery men, and very much under the influence of the Governor; and therefore I say, it is very important that under this order, there should be good anti-slavery men to carry it out.

Q Do you think the slaves would go if they were reached?

A They will go. You will find that all sorts of terrorism and desperate things are resorted to intimidate the negroes, and make them say they don't want to go, unless protection precedes the invitation. Of course, the right men should be put in to do this work. There has been a great deal of difficulty here from local feeling. If an officer having power exercises it, and injures the persons against whom he exercises it, it is said his motives are personal, that he is vindictive, &c. Now, if good men, who are not interested in this State, could be placed here to exercise that power, they would do better; they would accomplish more than many of our own people. If some good man, sufficiently acquainted with affairs here in Missouri to act intelligently and yet disinterestedly, could be put at the head of this matter, it could be made a complete success. Unless Missouri is saved during this rebellion, it will be lost to the North for generations. It sometimes makes me almost tremble to think of the war stopping, though of course I would stop it this moment, if I could, with the success of the government. The Northern people know nothing of the iniquities of slavery, nor of its effects. It is dark at a distance, but it is intensely black when you get close to it. I have lived in this State twenty-one years, and have been acquainted with the operation of the system during all that time. I regard it as absolutely indispensable that we should eradicate it, in order that we may have a country such as we should have.

Q What do you consider the capacity of the slaves of Missouri to take care of themselves, supposing they were emancipated tomorrow?

A I think it would be judicious in the Legislature, if they had the power to pass an emancipation law, or in a Convention, if one should be held to authorize the Legislature to pass such a law, to enable a commission or board in each county to take the slaves and hire them out, in case they won't work. I am rather speaking first impressions, than anything that is the result of mature thought upon the subject; but I think that would probably be a judicious thing, though I don't regard it as an indispensable thing.

Q   You believe that, if let alone, they would get along?

A   Yes, I have not a doubt of it. They know this – that they cannot live by stealing; all men know that who have been raised in a civilized community; and they would have to starve and go naked, or else go to work. Well, they are actuated by the same motives as the free negroes in the Northern States, and the same motives as other laboring men. They are actuated by the same motives that you and I are.

Q   How have the free negroes got on here?

A   The free negroes get on here splendidly. They show very great capacity for financiering. They can get more money for the same amount of work than white man, all the time. If I could only do it by the [breath] of my mouth, I would make every slave in the State a freeman at this moment, because I believe it would be for the benefit of the people. Many of these negroes would not work for their present masters, because of some particular personal reason; but they would not go far; they would take up with the first man who would pay them fair wages and treat them like men. I should not be afraid of emancipating the negro suddenly. And then I am perhaps a little ultra on another point. I do not believe in compensating the owner. No doubt, it might work some hardship in certain cases, as, for instance, single ladies and old people, and perhaps exception should be made in their favor, because their means have been put into this property; but in the case of men able to make their own living, young men, I would not have them compensated, because I feel in this way, – that they hold property which has become a public injury, that a necessity for its destruction has arisen, & the general welfare requires that it should be destroyed, and along with that necessity (for this is not like the use of ordinary property, that has to be destroyed, which there is no injury in holding) is connected this consideration, that it is a personal wrong to hold that property. I would not say that it is a personal wrong for the aged person, who has no other property, but for the young person, just starting in life, it is. I have no patience with these men who have held on to their slaves. They have brought ruin on our State, and I have no patience with them.

There is one thing I have observed: all these negroes want to learn to read and write. They are capable of taking care of themselves; they are amiable and honest, and if you will only give them a chance to rise, they will certainly avail themselves of it. If we can only spread the spirit of freedom throughout the State, we will turn it upside down. What I dread is, to have the slave element continue in this State. It makes life unendurable. It is just fighting the devil all the time.

HD

Testimony of Franklin A. Dick before the American Freedmen's Inquiry Commission, [1 Dec. 1863], filed with O-328 1863, Letters Received, ser. 12, RG 94 [K-206]. Topical labels in the margin are omitted.

187: Missouri Slaveholder to the President

[*St. Louis? December 1863*]

To the President of the U. States. I dont know what to do in present troubles but apply to your excellency for assistance, all the property I held consisted of seven negroes, who living with me, we were able to make comfortable support. My two men went with the soldiers, one with an Iowa regiment & the other is at Camp Edwards near the city— He say an Iowa Col. gave him free papers & told him to stay within the lines of the camp. My two women & girls have left & gone to Chicago because they say that as the husband of one was in the army a year waiting on officers they are entitled to their freedom. I am now 50 years old & this takes from me & my two daughters our all, which we sadly need— The Provost Marshal here will attest my loyalty at any time, as he knows me well & his wife is a relation of mine— I hope you will in your goodness Do something for our relief, either, have thier value given to us or let us have them returned. They were well cared for & seemed perfectly happy, untill the soldiers persuaded them off Y^rs repy.

Mrs E. Stewart.

care of Provost Marshal St Louis

ALS

Mrs. E. Stewart to the President of U. States, [Dec. 1863], S-340 1863, Letters Received, ser. 360, Colored Troops Division, RG 94 [B-12]. A notation on the letter reads "file."

188: Missouri Unionist to a St. Louis Friend

Copy   Mexico Mo Dec 28th 1863

Dear Friend   Thank God I am up again and at my Post— Matters are not right, Doctor and I know it is connived at by officers whose duty it is to see the orders enforced— Eleven men came in from Munroe on Saturday— they were halted on the road and ordered back   The negroes being resolute and about to show fight the rebel Patrole backed down and they came on. It appears that on

Christmas Eve Ebenezer Queary, Simpson Mitchel and John Glen whom I know to be active Rebels made a speach on the platform in Madison and declared this colored enrollment was a d-mb-d abolition Scheme to steal negroes and that they and others were going to arm and put it down. Their language became so violant that at length some union men of the place stoped them   On Christmas night the negroes assembled at Madison to have a party intending to Start in the morning for Mexico

Queary and Michell were there, also a man named Dry—   They were arranging a plan to prevent the negroes from leaving—   Mitchell and Dry Started their negroes back home   Mitchell remained at the party and Quairy left about two hours before day, to arrange his Patrole—   Aaron one of the negroes was cautioned by his master (a good Union man) not to start before daylight   at daylight the Negroes began to leave when Mitchell posted himself in the door and asked the Negro (Aaron) what he ment   The man replied we are going to Mexico, Mitchel then pulled out his revolver and threatened to shoot him   The Negro told him he was not scared   Michell seeing the mans master present put his Pistol up and Eleven of them came on—   They were stoped as I have stated by the party on the road under Ebenezer Queary and finaly came on   I have ampl Evidence of all the matter here stated except the Patrole on the road   that Statement I have from four of the men and I have no doubt the others will coroberate it   The names of the Patrole are John Dry Wesley Dry Tom Dry and Ebenezer Quary all rebels   the two last were Bush Whackers   I have hunted for them   These men were armed with Rifles   The same may be said of nearly every Rebel in Munroe County   Who permits them to carry arms? Cap Richie our Pro Mar   He has been notified time and again of the fact   He received a writen notice from Capt Fowles of Paris that Sheriff MͨNautt of Monroe was distributing a large number of Contraband arms to the worst Rebels in that County   he has never heeded. And why   because he has been doing the same thing himself   Armed Rebels are a common thing in this town and Wilkins (the Gun Smith) has Stacks of Arms that have been hid in the Brush by Rebels now in his shop and is working day and night repairing them   they all appear in a hurry to have their arms

Dr Myers who swore so solemnly that he had no Gun when he was visited by the soldiers his gun is now repairing at his Shop   There is a constant demand for Powder and in a word a General determination to be on a war footing again—   Why dont the officers here attend to it   because the Rebels are oure officers associates   The Commandant of this Post plays billiards and eats oyesters Suppers with rebels who have been banished the state and

477

accused of Horse Stealing and the Pro Marshals Head Quarters is the common Rendezvous of Rebels   He is spoken of by the Rebels here as being a good Southerner man   Why the Chief Auctioneer of Contraband Sales is a Captain of Bushwackers and Bridge burners and a companion of our officers here   Oh my Friend this is no libel   I can produce evidence for all I assert and more   a Negro (belonging to Lt Arnolds Father) came up from St Louis last Monday   the Lt marches him off to his boarding house and gave him his breakfast   Shortly after the Negro was in town with a humble tale of the Suffring by Cold Starvation and death the poor darky endured who Enrolled   He had seen them lay in piles like Hogs   They died at the rate of 27 per day   They were treated worse than dogs and advised all Darkeys to Keep from there if they wanted to live   I learn the Lieut gave him a pass to go home   Now Lieut Arnold is very much opposed to the Enrollment and with all very much of a *Provisional Pet*

You can make your own comments   I believe I wrote you in a former letter about Five armed rebels going to the house of one David Woolrige (a notorious Rebel) to assist him in carrying off his Negros   They were confined in the Paris Jail   The woman was taken out and sold to a Slave holder to carry to Kentucky   The men they tried to smuggel across to Quincy but were sent back   I informed Capt Richie and Col Miller of the transaction and tried to get them to do something about it   They informed me it was none of thier business and further that if any man should pass through town with fifty Negroes on their way to Kentuckey they had no right to stop them   They appear to have no right and certainly no inclination to prevent armed Rebels from violating the laws of Congress   My God! how long are we to be cursed with this mockery   how long will this outrageous imposter last   Loyal men are daily humiliated by the acts of these imposters who grin deridingly when our goverment issues an Edict   And Why! because they Know their men wearing the uniform of that Goverment will not obey the orders if possible to avoid them   Their men feel this and their shame is vented in execrations deep and bitter over the abuse they are unable to redress   I want you to see Col Pile— let him Know all about this Enrolling business and if there is not some arrests made the Enrolling will be arrested   Write me how the Cols health is   My Respects to the Major   And believe Ever Truly Yours

(Signed) W A Poillon

PS. Tuesday Twelve oclock

Dear Doctor

I was to late yesterday for the mail   I have learned since that there was in Paris on Christmas day 45 Negro men in town who

had determined to be in Mexico on Monday   They have not come
yet   I know the men were there but if they have not gone to
Hannible they have been stoped   The last is most probable   I hear
of another party form Calloway that have been stoped
   There is no doubt about these Patroles
   I must close   As Ever yours   (Signed) W A Poillon
HLcSr

W. A. Poillon to Dr. Martine, 28 Dec. 1863, enclosed in Surg. Ira Russell to
A.A. General O. D. Greene, 13 Jan. 1864, R-14 1864, Letters Received, ser.
2593, Dept. of the MO, RG 393 Pt. 1 [C-162]. Poillon had earlier written
directly to Colonel William A. Pile, superintendent of the organization of
Missouri black troops, reporting that armed patrols prevented slaves from
reaching the enlistment office and that Captain Richie, the local provost
marshal, was unsympathetic to black recruitment. Richie refused to enlist
slaves without certificates from their masters and actively discouraged black
volunteers – telling one slave, for instance, that "he was a fool to leave a good
home, that if he went in the army they would put him in the front rank and
make breastworks of him." (Wm. A. Poillon to Col. Wm. A. Pile, 28 Nov.
1863, Miscellaneous Letters & Reports Received, ser. 2595, Dept. of the MO,
RG 393 Pt. 1 [C-173].)

189: **Headquarters of the District of North Missouri to the
Commander of the District of Central Missouri**

Macon [Mo.],   March 6th *1864*.
General. In the absence of Genl. Guitar, I send you the following
telegram just received from Glasgow.

"Glasglow, March 6, '64"
   "Some negroes who were enlisted in this county and sent to St.
Louis, have come back to Booneville and crossed into Howard
County with some white soldiers and are hauling off tobacco from
their former masters and owners and taking their wives and children.
   Is this to be allowed."
                                   (Signed) "J. P. Lewis
                                     Asst Prov. Ml."

   I have sent a copy of this dispatch to the Commanding Officer at
Boonville in case the party may attempt to recross at Booneville.
   There are no troops in Howard to send after this party. There is
one company of the 9th M.S.M. at Mexico, but this would be too
far. Who the white soldiers are I do not Know, they must be

however stationed in the Central District   Very respectfully Your
obdt servt

ALS   J. Rainsford

Asst. Adjt. Genl. J. Rainsford to Brig. Genl. E. B. Brown, 6 Mar. 1864,
Unentered Letters Received, ser. 2594, Dept. of the MO, RG 393 Pt. 1
[C-181]. Endorsements. Several weeks earlier, other northern Missouri whites
had lodged a similar complaint, accusing two black men (discharged from the
army for physical disability) of visiting the homes of "a number of our best
citizens" during the night and taking away "by violence, not only their
families, but a large quantity of household property" and "a regular caravan of
other negroes." The blacks reportedly also threatened to return, "with a larger
crowd, to burn some houses, of citizens." (John B. Hale and Capt. D. A.
Calvert to Genl. O. Guitar, 21 Feb. 1864, enclosing Lt. Wm. McIlwrath[?]
to Asst. Provost Marshal Carroll Co., 11 Feb. 1864, H-3 1864, Letters
Received, ser. 3537, Dist. of North MO, RG 393 Pt. 2 No. 226 [C-215].)

190: Commander of the Department of Kansas to the Commander of the Department of the Missouri

Fort Leavenworth [Kans.],   Mar 13 1864
General   A negro "Sam Marshall" who resides in Leavenworth,
reports to me that yesterday he went over to Platte City Missouri,
to get his children, who he was told would be allowed to come
away free.   The children were at a Mr Greens.   Sam went in day
light, with a team, driven by a white man, and made no
demonstration of insolance or disrespect to any body.   He was
arrested by the Military, Commanded by one Captain David
Johnson of the Mo Militia, who talked to him about the
impropriety of his conduct.   The Sheriff one Jesse Morris also
lectured him, and told him the Captain would send a guard to take
him away, as it was a wonder he was not killed.   About a dozen of
the soldiers did escort him about half a mile out of Platte City,
where they tied him to a tree, and stripping him to the waste
lacerated his back with a cow skin the marks of which Sam will
carry to his grave.   They told him they were "introducing him to
the Pawpaw Militia" and that if Col Jennison would come to Platte
City, they would treat him in the same way.
    The Militia were dressed in Federal uniform, and armed with
revolvers
    Two of them Sam knew.   They are young – "Chinn", and a young
"Cockeril".

Sam is a quiet well behaved negro, whose tears and sorely lacerated back, seem to attest the truth of his statement.

The white man that drove the wagon, was arrested, but had sufficient influence (as formerly a citizen of the County) to get off without being harmed.

I call your attention to the use made of Federal troops, or troops clothed, fed, and foraged if not paid by the Federal Government.

I most respectfully suggest General, that on both sides, it is far better that troops unconnected with old border difficulties, and negro katching and negro whipping, should be substituted for such miserable wretches as those who disgrace their uniforms, and humanity, by acts of cruelty and baseness.

I hope General you will not suppose I hold you accountable for such transactions in a Command to which you have so recently been assigned; but I know a Sense of duty and disgust must be awakened by any loyal Citizen acquainted with such brutality, and I report Such matters to you, for early correction. –

They called "Sam" a Jayhawker, and pretended that he had run off horses; but all this was no doubt a mere subterfuge; as probably the only real offense "Sam" has been guilty of, was to run himself off, with a son who has entered the Federal Army. –

Platte City, is only about 6 miles from my lines and Such treatment of men from here going into that place, is well Calculated to induce fierce resentments from this Side, which of course I shall restrain; Conscious of your own desire to correct such outrages. I remain General Very Respectfully Yours

ALS   S. R. Curtis

Maj. Gen. S. R. Curtis to General, 13 Mar. 1864, Unentered Letters Received, ser. 2594, Dept. of the MO, RG 393 Pt. 1 [C-182]. No reply has been found in the records of the Department of the Missouri.

191: Provost Marshal at Sedalia, Missouri, to the Superintendent of the Organization of Missouri Black Troops

Sedalia Mo   March 21st 1864

Sir   I have the honour to inform you that we have a large number, of Black women and Children,   manny of them are the wives of soldiers, that have been enlisted in my District,   Manny of them will of Nesesity, come to a state suffering as they have been (manny of them) driven from their masters homes, after their husbands enlisted   humanity Demands that somthing should be done in their behalf, with a little assistance they will be able, to take care of themselves. I have been informed that, there is a move on foot for the benifit of the Destitute contrabands, General you will confere a favour by giving me information, what can be done for their benifit, I Remain most Respectfully your most obt servant

ALS   Wm Argo

[*Endorsement*] Hd Qrs Org Cold Troops Benton Bks Mo March 24th 1864   Respectfully refered to Dep^t *Commander* with the request that these Women and children be ordered to contraband camp at this place— All the able bodied can be provided with good homes at fair wages, and the helpless and infirm taken care of and children sent to School   W^m A Pile Brig Genl

Lt. Wm. Argo to Brigadiear General Wm. A. Pyle, 21 Mar. 1864, A-111 1864, Letters Received, ser. 2593, Dept. of the MO, RG 393 Pt. 1 [C-164].

192: Provost Marshal at Troy, Missouri, to the Provost Marshal General of the Department of the Missouri

                              Troy Lincoln County Mo April 5" 1864
Cololnel   I have the honor to report that several colored women have come to this Post and state that since their husbands and Sons have volunteered in the United States service their Masters say they do not want them about and are not willing to *feed them*— In most cases they are not only able to make a living for themselves and children but if permission were given would command considerable wages for their labor— I am of the opinion that this action is taken by their Masters in order to discourage further enlistments and vent their spleen against the Government for authorizing the recruiting of Negroes. I have said to them, that if your Masters will not allow you to stay at home you must hire yourselves out the best you can until I can get some instructions on the subject from H^d Quarters at St Louis. Will you please advise me as to what action if any I shall take in cases of this kind   I am Very Respectfully Your Obt. Servt

ALS   A. C. Marsh

Maj. A. C. Marsh to Col. J. P. Sanderson, 5 Apr. 1864, M-454 1864, Letters Received, ser. 2786, Provost Marshal General, Dept. of the MO, RG 393 Pt. 1 [C-197]. According to an endorsement, the provost marshal general referred the letter to the commander of the Department of the Missouri, but no instructions to Marsh have been located among the records of either the provost marshal general or the department headquarters.

193A: Missouri Black Soldier to His Wife and Her Owner

Benton Barracks Post Hospital Mo St Louis May the 10, 1864
Dear Wife   It is with pleasure that I am allowed this morning to write to you and inform you that by the tender mercies of that God who has been my Protector and keeper thus far and still watches over me with parental care & Love – and it is my prayer that when this comes to you it may find You in the enjoyment of good health

and in the Love of God— I want you to write to me as soon as this comes to you. I am well and here in the Post Hospital and doing well—in ward 4, I have orders from General Piles & Major Russell to take you at any time. General Piles has given orders if I want you to come here that it shall be granted & determined by the Provost at Tipton So it lays to your own choice to stay or come. Now I want You to consider with Your own mind which You will do.— If You donot want to stay tell Mr Wilson in a decent manner, that You do not and General Pile says if You Mr Wilson is as a good a Union man as Sam Hannah recommends you to be you will let her come on good terms and give her a piece of writing to shew that You are what you profess to be, and if you do not this, we will shew You what we intend to do.— We are not expecting that this will insult a Union man. You know that a Soldiers wife is free read this letter to her and let her return her own answer I will find out whether this has been read to her in afull understanding with her or not, and if I should find out that she has never heard her deliverance I will undoubedly punish you Caroline William & Hopson & Ellen I am determined that they shall be taken care of and supported by the government under the Stars & Stripes. recollect I am writing to Your interest if You look at it right You can See I have power and You know that on the 10, day of May I write to You with this dertermination that by the 20th day of May this matter must & will be closed so you can rest till Then or doit sooner as it will be better for You I expect between now & then to send Sam after his family and I shall give him power to take 10—or 20. Soldiers from Tipton with him according with the Provost Marshall^s orders at Tipton also and Howard & Dixon may remember their behaviour to their neighbors & families— Dixon I expect to be taken from his home and never return again I have heard from You Sir from good authors your carrying on and the way You are doing shall remain under the Black flag— I want you to understand that we hav labourd in the field to Subdue Slavery and now we mean to protect them this is all to Howard & Dixon John Howard mind how you walk be very particular you are in closer quarters than you have any idea— Your neighbors see you if I dont fair warning watch— Dixon had the assurance to write to John which has been his own Servant at Headquarters and [oppose?] to say that John knew that he is upright as much as to say he was a union man But we dont believe that was never will. I will close by saying write immediately—

Sam Bowmen

Post Hospital Benton Barrack ward 4, St Louis Mo— to Mr Wilson—

P.S. please read this to my wife and then if you please answer it Immediately so I may know what Steps to take   Yours Friend Sam Bowmen

[*In the margins*] I herein send you one dollar   accept cash in hand   I could sent you more But I was afraid
    I have got all my pay for 4 months
    If you want more money send me word —

ALS

Sam Bowmen to Dear Wife, 10 May 1864, filed with W-497 1864, Letters Received, ser. 2593, Dept. of the MO, RG 393 Pt. 1 [C-168]. In the same file is a letter dated May 17, 1864, from G. Wilson, owner of Bowmen's wife, and from A. Dixon, presumably the "Dixon" mentioned in Bowmen's letter, to the commander of the Department of the Missouri, which quoted passages from Bowmen's letter and appealed for protection from "meditated violence on the part of the Soldiers."

193B: **Provost Marshal at Tipton, Missouri, to the Provost Marshal of the District of Central Missouri, Enclosing a Letter from an Officer in a Missouri Black Regiment to a Missouri Slaveholder**

Tipton Mo, June 16th /64

Col — I have investigated the within case & obtained the original letter which I enclose — Mr Goodridge Wilson to whoom the letter was addressed says that the negro previous to his enlistment always bore a good character — that in fact his conduct was unexceptionable & as the negro can neither read or write he thinks that the letter was written by some designing person & that the negro was ignorant of its contents   the woman refered to as the wife of the soldier informed me that she was not mistreated that she was furnished with sufficient food & clothing though of a very coarse quality & only complained that she & her children were compelled to work beyond their strength — the enclosed letter is the only one received that contains any threatining language or any allusion to the matters contained in this letter — I saw one received on the 14th ult. by the wife of this soldier & written by the same hand. it contained no allusion to the enclosed letter or to the subject — Mr Wilson claims to be a loyal man but I am credibly informed that he is to say the least a rebel Sympathizer
    I also enclose you a letter received by Mr. A. Dixon, purporting to be from Capt. McMakin Co. C. 62" U.S. Inft — Mr. Dixon informs me that the woman in question dose not belong to him she

as well as his entire property having been taken for debt   the woman is however in his possesion & he expresses himself (so far as he is concerned) perfectly willing that she shall go to St. Louis   Mr. Dixon has the reputation of being a very kind & humane Master & a Gentleman – but of rather doubtfull loyalty   Very Respectfully Your Obt – Sevt –

ALS   Franklin Swap

[*Enclosure*]   Benton Barracks St Louis Mo. June 1" 1864. Sir, John Ray, a member of my company informs me that you have his wife & will not permit her to come here to him. Mr Dixon, I would say to you as a friend to avoid much trouble & expense you will immediately consent for Johns wife to come here to him.

For I tell you I *will* have her brought away if by armed force. A Soldier who vollunteers to go & peril his life for his country will not be imposed upon nor any one of his family, & we are authorised not to allow such to pass unattended to. I understand you have worked her verry hard & have not clothed her nor compensated her in the leaste for the labor.

Now Sir I inform you this will not be tollerated long.

As I am going to be away from this place a fiew days on buisiness you will confer a favor & save your Selfe, much time & expense to immediately write to John Ray, Ward 4 Benton Barracks Post hospital St Louis Mo. & inform him as to this matter.

Hoping you will immediately attend to this I will close. I remain verry Respectfully

ALS   Capt. McMackin

Lt. Franklin Swap to Lt. Col. T. A. Switzler, 16 June 1864, enclosing Capt. McMackin to Mr. Dixen, 1 June 1864, filed with W-497 1864, Letters Received, ser. 2593, Dept. of the MO, RG 393 Pt. l [C-168]. Endorsements.

194: Missouri Unionist to the Commander of the Department of the Missouri

                                         Clarksville Mo June 23^d 1864
Dear Sir   I desire to call your attention to abuses of General orders in this County of Pike –   There are recruiting officers at Louisiana recruiting Negroes and taking them to Quincy generally the old men – whilst the Younger ones are recruited & sent to St Louis –   as

I understand the former is contrary to orders & unjust to Missouri – Then again an order from You – stating Mo requires her labor &C prohibiting the taking out of the State Negroes.

There exhists at Louisiana a Band that has & continues to run off Negroes – men & women & children to Illinois as a compensation generally take their all – thereby depriving Farmers &C from carrying on their business – the result is farmers do not know what to do in the way of cropping as long as this Band exhists for once in Louisiana – no one feels safe to apply for them – all this is applicable to & is applied to such as are not fit for Military Service – I will state also that Negroes go to Louisiana & Refuse to enlist & hire themselves out & their master cannot & dare not reclaim them – same with women & Boys   so long as it is allowed it does the Government harm as many will collect in Small Towns if it continues & will not go into the US Service   many of our Farmers have a good harvest & partly from the above causes no Hands to save it   I will also state that the class of Negroes that remain about the towns contrary to the will of their owners – do entice (& are used for that purpose by Bad men) away those that would labor if permitted – There is no use applying to the civil or military authorities at Louisiana for redress hence this letter to you –   I refer you to Col^n James O Broadhead – Respectfully Yours
ALS   Henry. V. P. Block

Henry V. P. Block to Maj. Genl. W. S. Rosencrans, 23 June 1864, enclosed in A. J. Reid to Maj. Genl. Rosencrans, 29 June 1864, R-322 1864, Letters Received, ser. 2593, Dept. of the MO, RG 393 Pt. 1 [C-166]. An endorsement ordered an investigation of the allegations, but no subsequent report has been found in the records of the Department of the Missouri.

195: **Assistant Provost Marshal of the 4th Subdistrict of the District of Central Missouri to the Provost Marshal of the District**

Kansas City, Mo., July 22^d 1864.

Colonel, I have the honor to state that there are in this vicinity numbers of ablebodied Negro men who are to all appearance engaged in no regular employment and apparently without visible means of support.

Many of them are almost daily applying to this office for passes to different Counties in Mo and Kansas, having left their Masters, and while I am using every means in my power to enlist these men I find that not one out of twenty of them are willing to enter the

Service, giving for their reasons, "We have served long enough and it will be time enough when we are pressed in the Service. We are free now and choose to remain so as long as possible."

These men have obtained the idea that the service is a dangerous place, and that their freedom is already accomplished and in this portion of the state, with hardly an exception, refuse to enlist. I have used every means allowed, to persuade these men to join us, but with very poor success and I feal as though they should be *required* to enter the Service.

I would therefore respectfully recomend that the proper officers be made acquainted with the difficulties connected with recruiting these men and that measures be at once taken, authorizing the various recruiting officers in this Department to press all ablebodied Colored men into the Service of the Government, in all cases when they refuse volunterely to enlist.

Believing that the interests of the service, as well as the present and future welfare of the negro requires and justifies such a course, I trust the subject may receive due and favorable consideration by the proper Military Authoritys. I have the honor to be Very respectfully Your obd Servant

ALS   J. C. W. Hall

[*Endorsement*] Hd Qrs. Dept of the Mo St Louis Aug 2 /64   Respectfully returned to Maj Genl A Pleasanton Comdg Dist of Central M^o with instructions to have all able bodied male contrabands who are fit for the military service, collected & forwarded with their immediate families to the Contraband Camp at Benton Barracks for inlistment into the service   By order of Maj Genl Rosecrans J. F. Bennett A.A.G.

Capt. J. C. W. Hall to Col. T. A. Switzler, 22 July 1864, H-176 1864, Letters Received, ser. 3379, Dist. of Central MO, RG 393 Pt. 2 No. 217 [C-8726]. Other endorsements. As early as February 1864, Missouri legislators had complained "that, a large number of negros have left their masters or owners, and are now wandering about: many of them out of employment, and in a destitute condition: and likely to become a nuisance to the neighborhoods in which they have located." The legislators recommended compulsory enlistment of those fit for military service. (*Freedom*, ser. 2: doc. 95.) Cooperative provost marshals enlisted black men by force, but others hesitated to compel enlistment. The provost marshal at Lexington, Missouri, reported in August 1864, "[T]here is a great many here that have left their masters and they are either loafering about town or at work for themselves." Noting that he had made every appeal except force to induce black men to enlist, he explained his lack of success: "Wages is high and demand for hands keep the negroes out of the Army." (*Freedom*, ser. 2: doc. 96.)

196: Commander of the District of North Missouri to the President of the Western Sanitary Commission

Macon Mo. Mch 25 /65.
Dear Sir, I have yours of the 22nd inst & will cheerfully do all I can to restore the family Circle of the Munroe Co Freedwomen —. Slavery dies hard I hear its expiring agonies & witness its contortions in death in every quarter of my Dist. In Boone, Howard, Randolph & Callaway the emmancipation ordinance has caused disruption of society equal to anything I saw in Arkansas or Mississippi in the year /63. I blush for my race when I discover the wicked barbarity of the late Masters & Mistresses of the recently freed persons of the counties heretofore named. I have no doubt but that the monster Jim Jackson is instigated by the late slave owners to hang or shoot every negro he can find absent from the old plantation. Some few have driven their black people away from them with nothing to eat or scarcely wear. The consequence is between Jim Jackson & his co-laborers, among the first families — the poor blacks are rapidly concentrating in the towns & especially at garrisoned places. My hands & heart are full. I am finding homes for them in North West Missouri, Kansas, Illinois & Iowa. There is much sickness & suffering among them, many need help. Is there any fund that you can appropriate a small sum from to aid me in the deportation of the families I cant provide for in Missouri I am retaining all in Mo that I can get work for in quiet localities We ought not to spare a single pound of our industrial element. We need to import rather than deport manuel labor. I hope the waters will soon grow still & Missouri in peace be permitted to pursue her way in the golden path of freedom & empire. It looks well all around the rapidly contracting lines. Shermans conquering legions are marching on." Redemption draweth nigh — All hail the Republic. Very Respectfully Your Obt Servt,

HLcSr

Clinton B. Fisk.

Brig. Genl. Clinton B. Fisk to Jas. E. Yeatman, Esq., 25 Mar. 1865, vol. 284 DMo, p. 276, Letters Sent, ser. 3530, Dist. of North MO, RG 393 Pt. 2 No. 226 [C-8848]. The Western Sanitary Commission was headquartered in St. Louis, with James E. Yeatman as its president. Neither Yeatman's letter of March 22 nor any subsequent letters from him have been found in the records of the District of North Missouri.

CHAPTER 8
Kentucky

8

Kentucky

SLAVERY LASTED LONGER in Kentucky than in any other state except Delaware. Not until the ratification of the Thirteenth Amendment in December 1865 – without Kentucky's concurrence – did slavery officially end.[1] Nevertheless, the work of destroying slavery began in the first year of the war. It gathered momentum as the federal army settled in for a long stay, became irresistible once the army began unrestricted enlistment of black men, and by the end of the war had been all but accomplished. Slaveholders fought a bitter rearguard action, whose ferocity grew with its hopelessness. But in Kentucky, as elsewhere, the first shots fired upon Fort Sumter portended the end of slavery.

The pattern of slavery's collapse arose from the nature of the institution as well as the state's political allegiance and wartime experience. More numerous and more widely dispersed than in the other border states, Kentucky's 225,000 slaves constituted 20 percent of the state's population in 1860. The 39,000 slaveholders – outnumbered only in Virginia and Georgia – generally owned these slaves in small units. Only seventy were master to fifty or more. Still, one-fifth of Kentucky slaves lived and worked on large farms and plantations with twenty or more slaves, principally in the bluegrass region surrounding Lexington and in a few tobacco counties on the Tennessee border. Elsewhere, they were scattered throughout the countryside, and in crossroad county seats and river ports, the largest of which was Louisville. Only a few slaves lived in the mountainous, sparsely populated counties of east and southeast Kentucky, but regional concentration of slaveholders or nonslaveholders was otherwise far less pronounced than in the other border states.

Extensive ownership enhanced the viability of slavery in Kentucky, and the institution flourished through the antebellum decades. The

---

[1] Published accounts of emancipation in Kentucky include: E. Merton Coulter, *The Civil War and Readjustment in Kentucky* (Chapel Hill, N.C., 1926); Victor B. Howard, *Black Liberation in Kentucky: Emancipation and Freedom, 1862–1884* (Lexington, Ky., 1983). Delaware, like Kentucky, refused to end slavery by state action and also declined to ratify the Thirteenth Amendment. But Delaware, unlike Kentucky, had a tiny slave population at the beginning of the Civil War (fewer than 1,800) and a relatively large population of blacks who were already free (nearly 20,000).

slaveholders' prosperity rested upon the sale of market staples, notably tobacco and hemp, with cereals and livestock increasingly important. Kentucky was a major supplier of grain and hogs for its neighbors to the south and nearly monopolized the production of mules for the plantation market; the famed horses and cattle of the bluegrass region found ready purchasers both north and south. Kentucky slaves thus worked at a variety of tasks, and fluctuating demand induced many owners to hire them out to other slaveholders and to nonslaveholders, sometimes for short stints but usually for a year at a time. Widespread slave hiring supplemented widespread ownership, giving Kentucky whites a strong vested interest in black bondage. The slaveholders also profited handsomely in the interstate slave trade, which directly linked their own concerns with those of lower-South planters. They stood shoulder to shoulder in the struggle against Northern abolitionists, while smothering internal dissent. In 1850 a new state constitution enshrined slavery as never before, and subsequent legislation all but eliminated the possibility of manumission. Most slaves who gained freedom before the Civil War promptly crossed the Ohio River. In 1860 fewer than 11,000 free blacks lived in the state, a number hardly large enough to challenge dominant notions about the proper status of black people. When the war came, Kentucky's stand with the Union reflected no attenuation in commitment to slavery.

The decision against secession was not taken without dissent. Although many Kentucky slaveholders believed that the Union offered the best prospect for perpetuating the institution that underlay their prosperity, others had their doubts. Some doubters cast their fortunes with the slaveholding Confederacy. Others, convinced that secession itself threatened slavery, nonetheless feared that a war for the Union would be equally subversive, that a Northern army of reunification might become an army of liberation. During the electoral campaign of 1860 and the crisis that followed Republican victory, slaveholders broadcast their fears in courthouse speeches and in the press, on the hustings and around the dinner table. By the time the fighting began, most Kentucky slaves knew that slavery was at issue in the war, and that their masters did not trust the Republicans to honor the promise of noninterference. They eagerly awaited the advent of the Yankees whom their masters had so roundly denounced as abolitionists.

For several months they had to bide their time. While federal troops rushed to secure the other border states and the District of Columbia in the spring and summer of 1861, Kentucky's legislature declared the state neutral and forbade both Union and Confederate armies to cross its borders. At first, the belligerents honored Kentucky's anomalous stance, and some slaveholders used this interval to remove their slaves to plantations deep in the Confederacy. But the state's strategic location guaranteed that Kentucky could not evade the conflict for long. In early September 1861, Confederate forces abrogated neutrality by occupying Columbus, on the Mississippi River. Union General Ulysses S. Grant, commander of the District of Southeast Missouri, immediately responded by seizing Paducah, at the mouth of the Tennessee River, and Smithland, at the mouth of the Cumberland. Neutrality was at an end, and the war was on.

Competing for Kentucky's territory and allegiance, Confederate and Union officials outdid each other in claiming to be the true guardians of slavery. Nevertheless, the presence of the contending armies almost immediately had a subversive effect. Confederate troops controlled Kentucky's southernmost counties for nearly six months, during which time they steadily fortified the chief positions in their line of defense — Columbus, Forts Henry and Donelson, Bowling Green, and Cumberland Gap. Often they used slave laborers hired from secessionists and impressed from unionists. Slaveholders of every political persuasion dreaded the unsettling effects and physical danger of military labor, and many of them resisted Confederate claims upon their able-bodied slave men. The creation of a Confederate-sponsored state government in November 1861 lent some legitimacy to these requisitions by rebel military authorities, but Kentucky masters still hesitated to risk their slaves in the Confederate cause.

They found equally abhorrent any interference with slavery on the part of the Union army. Through the fall of 1861, Northern troops from the Department of the Cumberland staked out positions south and east of the bluegrass region to guard the mountain passes, and occupied Louisville, from which they advanced hesitantly along the Louisville and Nashville Railroad. Meanwhile, Union troops from the Department of the Missouri established posts in western Kentucky, and federal gunboats patrolled the rivers. No sooner had these federal forces taken up positions to secure Kentucky's loyalty than runaway slaves sought refuge in their ranks, testing their masters' suspicion about the antislavery inclinations of Northern soldiers.

The first fugitives were nearly all young men, the slaves who were most mobile and least likely to have family responsibilities, and who could most readily find places in the Union camps as guides, servants, or laborers. Some soldiers were happy to accept them and put them to work. Because Northern troops were not yet stationed in the areas of largest slave population, the number of fugitives remained small for several months. Nonetheless, young slave men were mainstays of agricultural production, and their owners promptly entered a protest at Union headquarters.

Neither the President nor federal military commanders took these complaints lightly. Eager to demonstrate that they fought only to restore the Union, not to abolish slavery, officials in Washington and commanders in the field called for strict observance of local laws, especially the slave code. Kentucky's strategic importance dictated the utmost effort to appease wavering unionists. To reassure them, President Lincoln often assigned army commands within the state to Kentucky officers who would be sensitive to local custom and opinion. Field commanders at the highest level demonstrated similar respect for the slaveholders' sensibilities. In October 1861, General William T. Sherman, commander of the Department of the Cumberland, reminded a subordinate that the laws of Kentucky were binding on federal troops and ordered that fugitives "be delivered up on claim of the owner or agent."[2]

In this, Sherman adhered closely to the line laid down by his superiors. Military circumstances might warrant stern measures against rebel masters, but political prudence called for solicitude toward professedly loyal ones. In November 1861, upon placing General Don Carlos Buell in command of the Department of the Ohio (newly reorganized to include most of Kentucky), General-in-Chief George B. McClellan advised him of the delicacy of his position: "It is possible that the conduct of our political affairs in Kentucky is more important than that of our military operations." The state's "domestic institutions," McClellan emphasized, should "in no manner be interfered with," but should "receive at our hands every constitutional protection." These views, he assured Buell, reflected the "feelings and opinions" of the President.[3] Later that same month, General Henry W. Halleck, whose Department of the Missouri included western Kentucky, ordered that all fugitive slaves be refused admission into army camps and posts.[4] General Grant, Halleck's chief subordinate in Kentucky, conformed scrupulously to the exclusion directive. He ordered both that fugitive slaves be turned away and that Northern soldiers be punished for harboring them.

The deceptively simple solution of having nothing to do with fugitive slaves proved to be no solution at all. Events overtook it almost at once, placing slavery in question despite the efforts of the Lincoln administration and the higher echelons of the army. The presence of rebel units in the state, impressing slave men to construct fortifications, encouraged masters – loyal and rebel alike – to send their slaves into hiding, and forced Union commanders, as a simple matter of military necessity, to recognize some fugitives' claim to freedom under the First Confiscation Act. Slaveholders smelled danger even while the number of slaves involved remained small. They reacted with fear and anger to General John C. Frémont's proclamation of August 1861 that

[2] *Official Records*, ser. 2, vol. 1, p. 774.
[3] *Official Records*, ser. 1, vol. 4, p. 342.
[4] See above, doc. 157.

freed Missouri slaves owned by disloyal masters.[5] They panicked again in December when Secretary of War Simon Cameron indiscreetly suggested that confiscated slaves should fight in the Union army.[6] Lincoln immediately repudiated both initiatives, but the damage was done. For a time Confederate leaders hoped that by playing on doubts about the federal government's intentions and by offering suitable inducements, they might persuade Kentucky regiments in the Northern army to desert en masse to the Southern ranks.[7]

Confederate hopes for Kentucky came to naught, because military developments in February and March of 1862 drew both Union and rebel soldiers out of the state, furnishing respite to edgy slaveholders. Union troops under General Grant advanced up the Tennessee and Cumberland rivers to capture Forts Henry and Donelson, fracturing the Confederate line of defense and forcing the rebels to evacuate Kentucky. As the Confederates retreated into Tennessee, the federal army followed. Some Kentucky slaves took advantage of these military movements to fall into rank with Northern regiments exiting the state, as did a number of slaves who escaped from the retreating Confederates. Kentucky masters followed at their heels. When General Buell's Army of the Ohio reached the Nashville district and settled in for a stay, regimental officers soon discovered that responding to the demands of slaveholders was among the most exigent of their duties.

Buell left his subordinates in no doubt about their responsibility when a slaveholder came to call. He issued strict orders requiring them to assist in recapturing fugitives, and set deadlines for ejecting all slaves from the camps of his army. Not a few of Buell's officers and enlisted men found compliance with these orders both annoying and distasteful. Their encounters with overbearing masters and desperate fugitive slaves eventually turned many against slavery.[8] But for the time being, Buell's army offered little to Kentucky slaves. Many of those who had accompanied the Union soldiers to Tennessee were returned to bondage, and the scanty federal forces left in Kentucky provided few opportunities for escape. In the spring of 1862, as the locus of military activity shifted still further south, Kentucky's congressional delegation persuaded President Lincoln to appoint General Jeremiah T. Boyle, a native slaveholder and prominent unionist, to supervise the federal troops in his home state.[9] Boyle's sentiments with respect to slavery accorded squarely with those of Buell. "I want men of

[5] See above, doc. 155.
[6] Edward McPherson, *The Political History of the United States of America, during the Great Rebellion*, 2nd ed. (Washington, 1865), p. 249.
[7] *Official Records*, ser. 1, vol. 7, pp. 801–2.
[8] In addition to documents in this chapter, see above, docs. 83, 85.
[9] *Official Records*, ser. 1, vol. 10, pt. 2, pp. 218, 266, 285.

my command to have nothing whatever to do with negroes," he instructed one subordinate. "This must be understood."[10]

With General Boyle in charge and all but a few Northern regiments
removed from the state, Kentucky slaveholders felt few repercussions
from the federal antislavery legislation of 1862. Neither the new article
of war nor the Second Confiscation Act posed a threat to slavery if
slaves lacked opportunities to reach army lines. In July, President
Lincoln warned border-state congressmen that the war would inevitably wear away slavery in their states, but its erosion in Kentucky
awaited the return in force of the Union army.

Within weeks of Lincoln's warning, the rebel army opened the way.
Confederate strategists, struggling to recover lost ground, gambled on
a daring invasion of Kentucky. In late August of 1862, Confederate
General E. Kirby Smith moved swiftly into the bluegrass region,
where his forces collected grain, cattle, and horses to supply the rebel
army, and recruited soldiers to increase its ranks. Confederate General
Braxton Bragg invaded by a route further west, hotly pursued by
Buell's Army of the Ohio, which abandoned northern Alabama and
middle Tennessee to counter the rebel threat. Bragg came close to
capturing Louisville, and Smith threatened the defenses of Cincinnati.
They occupied Frankfort, the state capital, long enough to inaugurate
the governor of Kentucky's Confederate government.

But the rebels missed the mark. Though Kentucky's reputedly pro-
Southern populace did not resist the invasion with much enthusiasm,
neither did it rise in support of the invaders. Meanwhile, the threat
galvanized the midwest. Fearing that a Confederate Kentucky would
endanger the safety of their own homes, thousands of midwestern
recruits rushed to repel the rebels. In Kentucky, they joined the soldiers of Buell's army, whose months in Tennessee and Alabama had
taught them the usefulness of slaves to the Union cause and made them
reluctant to defer to slaveholders or proslavery military commanders.[11]
Instead of gaining a rich prize for the Confederacy, the invasion boom-

[10] Brig. Gen. J. T. Boyle to Col. Dent, 13 June 1862, Letters Received, ser. 1636,
Louisville KY, Provost Marshal Field Organizations, RG 393 Pt. 4 [C-5000]. In the
portion of Kentucky west of the Tennessee River – which lay outside Buell's jurisdiction – army commanders issued similar instructions to exclude fugitive slaves from
army lines. However, following the policy that prevailed in western Tennessee, they
generally recognized the freedom of slaves whose masters were disloyal. For example,
in June 1862, General Isaac F. Quinby, commander of the District of the Mississippi
(with headquarters at Columbus, Kentucky), prohibited the admission into army
lines of "colored persons . . . who are not free, or who, by the acts or consent of their
masters have not become clearly contraband." (General Order No. 16, Headquarters,
Dist. of the Miss., 18 June 1862, vol. 101/248A DKy, p. 43, General Orders, ser.
992, Dist. of the MS, RG 393 Pt. 2 No. 24 [C-8852].)
[11] See above, chap. 5.

eranged against Kentucky slaveholders by increasing the number of troublesome Union soldiers in their midst.

In early October, after what seemed to the frantic Northern public an unconscionable delay, General Buell engaged the invaders. Although poorly managed, militarily indecisive, and extremely costly, the battle of Perryville stemmed the rebel offensive. The Confederates withdrew from Kentucky, their wagons and cattle droves filled with the spoils of war. Buell's desultory pursuit of the retreating army added fuel to complaints of his military ineptitude and excessive solicitude for the rights of slaveholders. At the end of October, he was removed from command. Most of his army—augmented by new midwestern troops, given a new name, and placed under a new commander—left Kentucky the following month.

Kentucky slaveholders were not thereby relieved of the presence of Union troops. Raw midwestern regiments, hurriedly mustered to rescue Kentucky from the invasion, joined a handful of the state's own regiments to form the Army of Kentucky, which occupied the bluegrass region as the Confederates evacuated. Scattered amid the state's largest slave population, the camps of the midwestern regiments proved to be irresistible magnets for fugitives. With the state rid of Confederate soldiers, Kentucky slaveholders and midwestern soldiers turned upon each other, forced into confrontation by the slaves' determination to be free.

Repeated complaints implicated soldiers of Ohio, Indiana, Illinois, Michigan, and Wisconsin regiments in the escape of slaves from self-proclaimed unionists, and sometimes even from slave-owning Union soldiers. In November 1862, a Kentucky and an Illinois regiment crossed swords when the Kentucky soldiers, joining local citizens, attempted to seize fugitive slaves from the Illinois ranks. Few of the midwestern soldiers were outright abolitionists, but many held free-soil views. None had a personal stake in slavery. All had cause to regard with suspicion the very Kentucky slaveholders whose vacillation had seemed to place their own home states in jeopardy. Suspicion deepened to grievance when bluegrass slaveholders pointedly refused to furnish supplies at a reasonable price.

In that hostile mood, midwestern soldiers got their first view of what slavery meant and, for the most part, were disgusted by what they saw. Obliged to stand by while pursuers threatened frightened fugitives with deadly violence, many of them came to resent orders to exclude runaway slaves from their camps. Some soldiers recognized a chance to acquire servants who could ease the burdens of army life. Others genuinely wished to extend protection to the fugitive slaves and had no other way to do so. Whether from high motives or low, midwestern soldiers defied orders and welcomed runaway slaves into their camps, setting them to work at various menial tasks. When the masters followed in pursuit, the soldiers jeered, threatened them with bodily harm, and helped the slaves elude recapture.

Many officers of the midwestern regiments felt as little enthusiasm as their men for the chore of apprehending slaves and appeasing slaveholders, or even standing aside while others did so. They accepted – according to some complaints, enticed – slaves into their camps and resisted demands, even by commanders of the highest rank, to surrender or expel them. The Kentucky generals appointed to reassure local slaveholders had the opposite effect on these midwestern officers. Unpopular orders to assist slaveholders received contempt precisely because Kentucky generals issued them. When the cautious, temporizing measures of their commanders did not suit the midwesterners, they seized the initiative. Brushing aside military etiquette and by-passing their immediate superiors, they laid their dissatisfaction before higher military authorities, the War Department, and the President. Frequently, they sought support from their home-state congressional delegations and press.

Some midwestern officers challenged their superiors directly. In November 1862, Colonel William L. Utley and Colonel Smith D. Atkins (commanders of, respectively, Wisconsin and Illinois regiments) refused direct orders to turn fugitive slaves out of their camps. Lectured by a superior that slavery enjoyed the same rights in Kentucky as though the army were not there, Colonel Utley retorted that the army ought to enjoy the same rights in Kentucky as though slavery were not there. To his commander's face, he refused either to surrender fugitives to their owners, to expel them from his regiment, or to place them at his commander's disposal. He had had nothing to do with their coming into his lines, and he would have nothing to do with sending them out. After learning that citizens of Georgetown planned to take the slaves from his regiment by force, Utley paraded his men through its streets with loaded muskets and fixed bayonets and vowed to "lay [the] town in ashes" should any "hostile demonstrations" interrupt his march. Colonel Atkins bluntly warned slaveholders in the vicinity of his camp at Mt. Sterling to keep their slaves at home if they wished to keep them at all, because he and his men did not intend to return runaways. Advised by a superior officer to cooperate with a civil summons regarding a slave, Atkins replied that he was too busy putting down the rebellion "to piddle away my time in hunting up niggers or in replying to bills in chancery filed against me." The midwestern press followed both colonels' insubordination with enthusiastic approval. So did their men.

The midwestern soldiers who assisted slaves and defied slaveholders acted upon more than their personal convictions, for the Union army that met the rebels in Kentucky in the fall of 1862 marched under new orders. The additional article of war, adopted the previous March, prohibited the employment of Union troops to return fugitive slaves to their owners, and it included no exemption on behalf of loyal slave-holders. The Second Confiscation Act of July, although it granted freedom only to slaves whose owners were disloyal, encouraged soldiers to view slaveholding and disloyalty as virtually synonymous. Lincoln's preliminary Emancipation Proclamation of September, which some soldiers mistakenly took to include Kentucky, quickened their anti-slavery enthusiasm. Union commanders might defer to loyal masters and enjoin their subordinates from interfering with either slaves or slaveholders, but officers and enlisted men had wide latitude to indulge their antislavery inclinations.

For that reason, frontal challenges embarrassed those holding command in Kentucky. Loyal slaveholders demanded protection from army interference with their slaves, but overt interference on their behalf could easily appear to violate the new article of war. Federal commanders thus had to walk a narrow line between offending unionist masters and contravening the law of the land. Most, like General Gordon Granger, commander of the Army of Kentucky, resorted to some version of the shopworn exclusion policy, in the futile hope that barring slaves from army lines would eliminate contact between Northern soldiers and Kentucky slaves.[12] Some, like General Boyle (now in command of the District of Western Kentucky[13]), took exclusion one step further – and came closer to violating the article of war – by requiring that slaves who had taken refuge in Union camps be put outside the lines. Subordinates who saw excluding and expelling fugitive slaves as the equivalent of returning them to their owners could make a public point of refusing to cooperate, forcing their superiors to perform a difficult balancing act under unwonted public scrutiny.

Higher authorities in Washington intervened only when left no

---

[12] For Granger's order, see below, doc. 202Dn. President Lincoln himself still considered exclusion a viable and appropriate policy in the loyal border states. In January 1863, he recommended Granger's order – which simply excluded all non-combatants from military camps – to General Samuel R. Curtis as a solution to "difficulties in Missouri." Curtis, who commanded the Department of the Missouri, rejected the order out of hand, denouncing it as nothing but "General Halleck's Orders, No. 3, in different words." It "would not do in my command, where we are taking the 'bull by the horns.'" In fact, Curtis gratuitously advised the President, the military commanders in Kentucky should themselves follow his lead and adopt a forthright antislavery policy. "A few snarling officers and rebel slaveholders oppose, but the great mass demand that the acts of Congress and your proclamation shall appear a living reality." (*Official Records*, ser. 1, vol. 22, pt. 2, pp. 88–89.)

[13] Despite its misleading name, Boyle's district was not the western region of the state, but rather the westernmost one-third of that portion of Kentucky included in the Department of the Ohio. Until August 1864, the counties west of the Tennessee River – which might more logically be denominated "western Kentucky" – were in the Department of the Tennessee.

choice: as when the colonel of a Wisconsin regiment reported his commanding general (a Kentucky slaveholder) to the War Department for arresting and returning a fugitive slave in violation of the additional article of war; or when the colonel of a Kentucky regiment issued an order, in brazen contempt of the article, that called for the delivery of fugitive slaves to their owners, "whether the owner be *loyal* or a *rebel*."[14] By and large, Washington officials preferred to keep their distance from the embarrassing dilemma, leaving field commanders to sort the situation out for themselves. General Boyle telegraphed both the President and the War Department for instructions in November 1862, but received no reply. That same month, General Horatio G. Wright, commander of the Department of the Ohio, asked General-in-Chief Henry W. Halleck for advice, following a plea for guidance from General Granger. Halleck evaded direct reply, referring Wright without further elaboration to "the law of Congress of last session, the President's proclamation, and the printed orders of the War Department." Amid the rapidly shifting currents of national politics, officials at the highest level had little to gain and much to lose by any pronouncement upon the status of slavery in the border states. Their evasion of the question encouraged each contending local party to claim legal sanction and moral righteousness for his own position, further intensifying the daily confrontations between slaveholders and the army, between military and civil officials, and among army officers.

Heedless of the discomfiture of federal policy makers, Kentucky slaves seized every opportunity for liberty. Neither slaveholders nor military authorities seemed able to prevent runaways from reaching army lines. Expulsion from one camp did not preclude a bid for refuge at another. Flight was never easy, and the pattern of slavery increased the difficulties. Small holdings and widespread hiring meant that slave families often lived apart – a husband with one owner, a wife with another, perhaps children and grandparents in the hands of still others. While escape from a single vigilant owner posed problems, simultaneous flight from several compounded the risk. Moreover, it remained far more difficult for slave women, children, and elderly people to receive

---

[14] The Kentucky general reported by the Wisconsin officer was Stephen G. Burbridge, who contended that he had merely ordered the exclusion of slaves from army lines. Burbridge added indignantly that the slaves in question "belonged to firm and staunch Union men," one of them a federal army officer. The Wisconsin officer later withdrew his charges, after witnessing Burbridge's bravery in the battle of Arkansas Post. (Lieut. Colonel Edmund Jussen to the Secretary of War, [Dec. 1862], endorsement of Brig. Gen. S. G. Burbridge, 26 Jan. 1863, and Lt. Col. Edmund Jussen to the Secretary of War, 26 Jan. 1863, all filed as J-292 1862, Letters Received, ser. 12, RG 94 [K-36].) The Kentucky colonel who ordered that fugitive slaves be delivered to their owners was John H. McHenry, Jr., commander of the 17th Kentucky Infantry. The War Department cashiered him for violating the article of war. (See below, doc. 202Fn.)

protection than it was for able-bodied men. Federal authorities established no contraband camps in loyal Kentucky like those created in Union-occupied areas of the Confederacy to receive fugitive slaves unsuited to life with an army regiment.[15] And outside the protection of a Union regiment, fugitives were vulnerable to arrest and return to bondage. The legal standing of slavery in loyal Kentucky continued to impede the path to freedom.

Kentucky slaves were not the only victims of the instruments of state authority that served slaveholders. The rebel invasion in the fall of 1862 indirectly drew black people from the Confederacy into Kentucky, where the existence of slavery jeopardized the freedom to which they were entitled under federal legislation. Hundreds of slave men accompanied the invaders as body servants to their masters and as military laborers. When the rebels retreated, many of these involuntary Confederates made their escape and claimed freedom under the confiscation acts. Their numbers paled in comparison with the black men, women, and children—several thousand by some estimates—who marched north into Kentucky with the Union troops withdrawn from Tennessee and Alabama. Some of these former slaves had worked for the Union army. Others had simply fallen into Union hands when the army occupied their region of the Confederacy. Still others had fled their owners and taken refuge near federal camps. All faced reenslavement and reprisals if they remained behind after the Northern evacuation. To escape that fate, they followed Buell's army as servants or military laborers and as desperate camp-followers. After reaching Kentucky, most of them fell away from the Union ranks or were ejected. With the exception of those whose owners were Tennessee unionists, these black refugees could all claim freedom under the terms of the Second Confiscation Act (many of them, under the Militia Act as well). Lincoln's preliminary Emancipation Proclamation in late September 1862 announced a still broader foundation for their liberty. But legislation and proclamation notwithstanding, Kentucky whites intervened to extinguish their claims.

With the connivance of the civil authorities, unscrupulous entrepreneurs disregarded the freedom of the former slaves, jailed them as runaways, advertised for their owners to claim them and pay the requisite reward, or simply sold them outright. Policemen and sheriffs often acted the part of slave catcher. The private citizens and local officials who enforced the fugitive-slave laws with abandon also deployed other provisions of the state slave code to nullify the freedom promised by

---

[15] In western Kentucky, administered as part of the Department of the Tennessee, a somewhat different policy prevailed. There, Union army officers generally recognized the freedom of slaves whose owners were disloyal and tolerated the growth of fugitive-slave settlements on the outskirts of military camps and posts. Even in western Kentucky, however, the army established no formal contraband camps.

federal legislation. Citing state laws against transporting a slave without the owner's permission, railroad conductors and boat operators refused black people passage through or out of the state, forcing them into the hands of slave dealers or sheriffs. Laws against hiring a slave without the owner's permission made it nearly impossible for former slaves to find employment, as did laws against trading with slaves. The influx of newly liberated blacks would not be allowed to endanger slavery in Kentucky.

On January 1, 1863, when the Emancipation Proclamation declared freedom for all slaves from the states still in rebellion, Kentucky's jails and slave pens overflowed with black people entitled to liberty under its provisions. They had escaped slavery in the Confederacy only to be reenslaved in the Union. Kentucky whites – who opposed Lincoln's proclamation overwhelmingly, even though it did not touch slavery in the border states – took additional steps to ensure that the freedom it proclaimed should have no standing in their state. The legislature denounced the proclamation as "unwise, unconstitutional and void," and only the most recent of many "unconstitutional acts of Congress, and startling usurpations of power by the Executive."[16] A variety of still more drastic resolutions were entertained, some of which virtually called for overthrowing federal authority. For a time, anxious military commanders feared that Kentucky would secede and join the Confederacy, and field officers worried about the loyalty of regiments from the state.[17]

Though the prospect of overt resistance soon subsided, the state legislature commanded considerable resources to obstruct federal emancipation. Expanding upon antebellum measures that prohibited free blacks from entering the state, a new law made it illegal for blacks freed by the Emancipation Proclamation to migrate to, or reside in Kentucky, on pain of being "arrested, dealt with, and disposed of as runaways."[18] Since the jails already bulged with captured blacks, the legislators streamlined the disposition of runaways. They reduced to one month the period during which a jailor was required to advertise for the owner of a captured black and after which the "runaway," if

---

[16] "Resolutions concerning National Affairs," No. 98, approved 2 Mar. 1863, *Acts of the General Assembly of the Commonwealth of Kentucky, 1861–63* (Frankfort, Ky., 1863), pp. 391–93.

[17] Col. S. A. Gilbert to Brig. Gen. Q. A. Gillmore, 30 Jan. 1863, and resolutions introduced by Mr. Bush, Kentucky House of Representatives, 19 Jan. 1863, both enclosed in S. Draper to Maj. Genl. Wright, 11 Feb. 1863, D-20 1863, Letters Received, ser. 3514, Dept. of the OH, RG 393 Pt. 1 [C-4606]; *Official Records*, ser. 1, vol. 20, pt. 2, pp. 282, 287, 308.

[18] "An Act to prevent certain negroes and mulattoes from migrating to or remaining in this State," Chapter 983, approved 2 Mar. 1863, *Acts of Kentucky, 1861–63*, p. 366.

unclaimed, would be sold to the highest bidder. To protect the rights of former owners – most of whom lived in the Confederacy and were thus unlikely to respond to an advertisement in a Kentucky newspaper – the law made such sales conditional and provided for a full refund to the Kentucky purchaser if the previous owner redeemed his "slave" within a year.[19]

Few Confederate masters ever reclaimed freed slaves who had found their way to Kentucky, but hundreds of Kentucky whites purchased them in courthouse sales across the state, consigning them once again to bondage and frequently dismembering families in the process. These sales diminished the threatening presence of black people freed under Lincoln's proclamation. At the same time, they enlarged the ranks of Kentucky whites who had a direct interest in perpetuating slavery.

As both legal and extralegal measures shored up slavery in Kentucky, still other black people fell under its sway. In neighboring Missouri, the growing strength of antislavery sentiment and the state convention's approval of gradual emancipation induced some disheartened owners to transfer or sell their slaves to the greater security of Kentucky.[20] The state also ensnared black people from throughout the Mississippi Valley who attempted to secure their freedom by migrating to the North. Often these emancipated slaves carried passes from Union military officers. Sometimes they traveled in the employ of discharged or furloughed soldiers, or in the company of Northern women who had been visiting relatives in the army. Frequently they headed north on their own. Kentucky blocked their route to liberty. At Louisville, terminus of the railroad line from the front, state authorities ignored personal patrons and military passes, prevented the former slaves from crossing the Ohio River, and jailed them as runaways or permitted private slave catchers to do so. Kentucky's defense of slavery thus not only subjugated the state's own slaves, but also entrapped black people from other parts of the nation.

However indulgent of loyal slaveholders, federal authorities could not countenance such blatant disregard of the Emancipation Proclamation and the confiscation acts, and some Kentucky whites themselves objected to the reenslavement of freed blacks and the transformation of their state into the nation's slave mart. General Boyle declared "wicked" the practice of confining runaways in private slave pens for the purpose of sale. Nonetheless, rather than liberate them, he instructed the Louisville provost marshal to seize the inmates of such pens and place them at military labor, unless the county court had

---

[19] "An Act concerning runaway slaves," Chapter 965, approved 2 Mar. 1863, *Acts of Kentucky, 1861–63*, pp. 362–64.

[20] In addition to documents in this chapter, see above, docs. 177B, 184A–B.

explicitly authorized the jailors' activities. Boyle shared the determination of the civil authorities to prevent any unsettling presence of black people controlled neither by their owners nor by the army.

Others reacted more strongly to the effrontery of Kentucky slaveholders in violating federal law. Dismayed citizens and appalled army officers conveyed their outrage to authorities in Washington and to General Ambrose E. Burnside, who became commander of the Department of the Ohio in March 1863. Matters came to a head in April, after a Michigan officer halted the sale – from the steps of the Louisville courthouse – of a black man entitled to freedom under the Emancipation Proclamation. Stunned by a newspaper notice of the affair, President Lincoln ordered that Burnside "take immediate measures" to prevent the return to bondage of persons "entitled to protection from the Government." Secretary of War Stanton instructed Burnside to accomplish this while avoiding "any forcible collision with State authority." Burnside accordingly issued an order that tried to serve both ends. He insisted that "slaves made free by the war measures of the President of the United States, by Congress, or by capture during the war, are entitled to their freedom," and declared "void" any sale of such persons. At the same time, he forbade army personnel to "aid or abet" the escape of Kentucky slaves from their owners, or to "impede the operation of any civil process . . . having in view the recovery of slaves of citizens of the State."

Burnside's injunction against military interference with slavery proved no more successful than similar previous efforts. Midwestern soldiers continued to harbor fugitive slaves, employ them, and resist their return to pursuing slaveholders. Relatively few midwestern regiments now served in the state, however, and these usually not for long. With the military front far in advance, a small Union force sufficed to occupy Kentucky and protect the vital railroad supply line. Moreover, much of this force consisted of Kentucky troops, who scrupulously accommodated the slaveholders' claims, as did the Kentucky generals and colonels who held most district and post commands. Still, the state remained a thoroughfare for Northern regiments moving to and from the front, and for individual officers and soldiers who had been discharged, furloughed, or hospitalized. In transit, a good many of them spirited away slaves. Disputes about slaves continued to flare up between midwestern soldiers and Kentucky citizens and soldiers.

Burnside's order to protect freedom in the midst of slavery enjoyed equally meager success. In those towns and cities occupied by Union soldiers, the sale of black people entitled to liberty under the Emancipation Proclamation generally ceased. But untold hundreds remained in jails across the state, pending public sale to new owners. On a single day in May, the sheriffs of Oldham and Bullitt counties sold into slavery at least seventeen blacks from Tennessee, Mississippi, and Ala bama. Both sales transpired within twenty-five miles of Louisville, General Boyle's headquarters and the largest army installation in the state. Elsewhere, at greater distance from Union troops, there was even less likelihood that Burnside's order would be enforced. At the end of 1863, military authorities estimated that more than a thousand blacks from the Confederate states had been reenslaved.

Unable – indeed, unwilling – to launch a sweeping campaign to liberate these blacks, Boyle enforced Burnside's order in a manner less threatening to the sensibilities of Kentucky slaveholders. He ordered his subordinates in Louisville to seize jailed ex-slaves and put them to work for the army – the men on construction gangs and the women in military hospitals. Former slaves thus exchanged liability to reenslavement for liability to military labor. Boyle refrained from explicitly recognizing the freedom of these people. He simply designated them "contraband negroes" and "captives of war," and ordered them held for labor. The Louisville labor dragnet also swept up freedmen and women employed as servants by Northern soldiers, those halted at the Ohio River when they tried to cross into the free states, and others from the Confederacy. All were denominated "contrabands" and carefully distinguished from Kentucky slaves, who were left in the jails or, if found at large, arrested as runaways. Boyle, whose jurisdiction expanded when he became commander of the District of Kentucky at the end of May,[21] admonished subordinates throughout the state to be discreet in enforcing the release of jailed contrabands. Kentucky officers, he suggested, could best handle the job.

In Louisville, Boyle appointed a three-man "contraband commission" to take charge of blacks who came into the city and to permit freedom of movement only to those holding passes from Union officers of the highest rank. The commission examined all others, including officers' servants, and, at its discretion, furnished them passes to cross the Ohio River or assigned them to labor on public works. In Louisville itself, the commissioners forcibly released jailed contrabands, but in the surrounding counties – theoretically also under their jurisdiction – they could do little more than issue ineffectual notices to private citizens and sheriffs. At the end of the year, they testified that hundreds of freedpeople were still held as slaves and that civil officials flouted orders from the commission. On occasion, the commissioners employed armed force to release blacks from county jails. In a few instances, they returned fugitive slaves to their owners, apparently untroubled by the March 1862 article of war. Usually, they assigned their charges to army quartermasters or engineers.

[21] *Official Records*, ser. 1, vol. 23, pt. 2, p. 357. The District of Kentucky encompassed the portion of the state included in the Department of the Ohio, that is, the portion east of the Tennessee River.

THE DESTRUCTION OF SLAVERY

The appropriation of contrabands for military labor mollified Kentucky slaveholders who, fearing that an uncontrolled influx of freed black people would undermine the discipline and morale of their slaves, welcomed their confinement under military restraint. Army officials encouraged slaveholders to interpret the policy in this light. Colonel Marcellus Mundy, the post commander at Louisville and himself a Kentucky slaveholder, explained to a judge of the Jefferson County Court that the army's seizure of contrabands preserved both the spirit and the letter of the state law that required the capture and sale of free or runaway blacks. A few weeks earlier, Mundy had complained that Northern officers who brought contrabands into Louisville were debasing the army "into a mere negro freeing machine." Like other masters, he hoped that military control would eliminate the danger that freed blacks posed for slavery in Kentucky.

But both slaveholders and the army eventually learned what slaves and former slaves understood at once: Military labor, however restrictive, still meant an irrevocable break with slavery. Kentucky slaves – sometimes claiming to be contrabands from the Confederacy – began offering their services, and army engineers and quartermasters raised few questions concerning their provenance. Indeed, many Kentucky slaves first set foot on free soil when army employers assigned them to labor in Jeffersonville, Indiana, just across the Ohio River from Louisville. As military laborers, they mingled with contrabands freed by the Emancipation Proclamation, collected wages, savored their new freedom, and sometimes returned home to rescue relatives from bondage.

Union officers became the slaves' accomplices in spite of themselves, as the army became the primary agent of emancipation. Even Kentucky officers who had been the staunchest defenders of the slaveholders' rights became unwitting accessories to their destruction. Colonel Mundy, who had complained directly to President Lincoln when his own slaves found refuge in a Michigan regiment in late 1862, now found himself superseding state law in the interest of military necessity. Entrusted by General Boyle with the task of releasing incarcerated contrabands, Mundy confessed to having no means of ascertaining whether or not the jailed blacks were in fact subject to the provisions of the Emancipation Proclamation or the confiscation acts "except by the statements of the negroes themselves, which would not properly be evidence in the Courts of Ky." Federal power overruled the state's regulation of its domestic institutions, and, once set in motion, the process gained momentum.

In time, the army's unintentional complicity in the deterioration of slavery became more direct. As federal troops advanced deeper into the Confederacy, they required an endless reservoir of laborers to construct and maintain their lengthening supply lines. When the number of contrabands failed to equal the demand, military authorities set their sights on Kentucky slaves. In August 1863, General Boyle (under General Burnside's authority) ordered the impressment of 6,000 slave men from selected counties for work on military roads. Boyle's order limited the number to be taken from each owner, provided payment to the owners for their slaves' services, and directed that the laborers be collected at Camp Nelson (near Lexington) under the supervision of General Speed Smith Fry, another Kentucky native. Within weeks, Burnside ordered an additional impressment of 8,000 slave men for railroad construction. Subsequent commanders called for still more slave laborers.[22] In addition, a shortage of teamsters induced Boyle to propose enlisting slave men in a special teamster corps, freeing each enlistee and paying his owner $300. Although the scheme came to nothing, it revealed Boyle's new willingness – under pressure of military necessity – to interfere with slavery in his own home state.[23]

Once slave men became the target of labor impressment, the most scrupulous care on the part of army commanders could not prevent the further disintegration of slavery. Military laborers acquired unprecedented experience living and working outside the control of their owners, usually alongside slaves from farms beyond the immediate neighborhood, and sometimes alongside black men who were already free. Many impressed slaves returned home quarrelsome, demanding, and insubordinate. Even if they managed to complete their service uncontaminated by subversive habits, they still might return so depleted in health as to be of little further use to their owners. Some slaves neither returned home nor labored long for the army, but fled the labor camps after receiving clothing and rations. No doubt many found employment with sympathetic soldiers or with quartermasters too desperate to ask awkward questions. On occasion, through accidental or deliberate confusion of orders, the army shipped slave laborers out of the state, contrary to assurances given their owners. Once beyond reach of Kentucky authorities, the slaves drew their own wages and passed silently into the ranks of the freed.

Nonetheless, Kentucky slaveholders soon had more than adequate incentive to swallow their objections to military labor, weighing the prospect of receiving compensation for their slaves' work against the growing possibility of losing the slaves altogether. By the summer of

---

[22] The number of slaves actually impressed, however, never approached what had been authorized.

[23] For Boyle's proposal to enlist black teamsters and the War Department's enthusiastic approval, see *Official Records*, ser. 1, vol. 31, pt. 3, pp. 150–51, 284; ser. 3, vol. 3, pp. 1077, 1085, 1104–5. Boyle had difficulty securing the cooperation of the governor of Kentucky and eventually hired additional black teamsters rather than enlist them.

1863, the enlistment of black soldiers had become a central component of federal war policy, with recruitment under way in the free states and in the Union-occupied Confederacy.[24] Attention turned next to the border states, and in October the War Department approved plans for enlisting free blacks and slaves in Maryland, Missouri, Tennessee, and Delaware.[25] Kentucky temporarily escaped inclusion and even served Missouri slaveholders as a haven for slaves likely to enlist.[26] But state lines could not insulate Kentucky slavery from the corrosive effects of recruitment. Recruiting stations in neighboring states, especially Tennessee, attracted a steady exodus of slave men who hoped to obtain freedom by enlisting in the Union army. Women, children, and old people often accompanied them.[27] Fear lest others run away to enlist so agitated slaveholders in southern Kentucky that in December 1863 an army officer reported them "not only willing, but . . . exceedingly anxious" to hire their slaves for railroad construction work.

The change of heart came too late. By February 1864, military authorities had concluded that the railroads under construction could not be completed in time to be of use in the spring campaign. General Ulysses S. Grant, chief commander of the western armies, ordered the cessation of government work on railroads in Kentucky and the revocation of impressment orders.[28] In the meantime, a greater menace to slavery hove into view. In the portion of Kentucky west of the Tennessee River – part of the Department of the Tennessee – enlistment of slaves into the Union army began in January 1864.[29]

Recruiting centers at Paducah and Columbus provided a beacon to slaves in western Kentucky, and to slaveholders throughout the state a grim forecast of what lay in store. In February, Congress made slave

---

[24] See *Freedom*, ser. 2: chaps. 1–3.

[25] *Freedom*, ser. 2: doc. 77, and pp. 123–24, 185, 188; *Official Records*, ser. 3, vol. 3, pp. 860–61, 1162.

[26] The War Department ruled out black recruitment in Kentucky on the grounds that the army was already laying claim to the state's slave men by impressing them for work on military roads. Secretary of War Stanton argued that, with no enemy activity in Kentucky, "it is not essential that they [black men] should be enlisted as troops in that State, as they should be employed in labor for the supply of other troops." (*Official Records*, ser. 3, vol. 3, pp. 855–56.) On the transfer of Missouri slaves to Kentucky to evade enlistment, and the sale in Kentucky of the families of Missouri black soldiers, see above, doc. 188; *Freedom*, ser. 2: docs. 91–94.

[27] In addition to documents in this chapter, see *Freedom*, ser. 2: docs. 97–98, and pp. 191–92.

[28] *Official Records*, ser. 1, vol. 32, pt. 2, pp. 126–27, 497–98. In early March 1864, in accordance with Grant's instructions, General John M. Schofield, the new commander of the Department of the Ohio, revoked all orders authorizing the impressment of Kentucky blacks for railroad work. (Special Orders No. 67, Headquarters Dept. of the Ohio, 7 Mar. 1864, Orders & Circulars, ser. 44, RG 94 [DD-32].)

[29] *Freedom*, ser. 2: docs. 98–99, and p. 193.

men in the border states liable to conscription, and promised compensation to loyal owners of up to $300 for each slave who volunteered. The following month, in the face of heated opposition, provost marshals in Kentucky began adding the names of slaves to the draft rolls. So threatening was the slaveholders' resistance to this enrollment that federal and state authorities only narrowly averted open conflict, by agreeing that slaves would not be drafted as long as white soldiers filled the state's quota. Nonslaveholding whites protested that the exemption of slaves increased their own likelihood of conscription. What is more, the enrollment crisis encouraged slaves to believe that recruitment was about to begin. Some slave men sought out provost marshals and pressed to be enlisted. Their enthusiasm frightened slaveholders and further eroded bondage.

In April 1864, as white enlistment languished, the commander of the District of Kentucky issued an order authorizing limited recruitment of black men. General Stephen G. Burbridge, a native slaveholder who had assumed command in February, at first confined enlistment to free blacks and to slaves whose owners consented. But the eagerness of slaves to volunteer, the nearly universal opposition of their owners, and the vicious assaults upon those who tried to enlist prompted the removal of all restrictions by early June.[30]

Black volunteers streamed into recruitment offices faster than the provost marshals could enlist them. Camp Nelson, convenient to the large black population of the bluegrass, teemed with slave men awaiting enlistment. The overwhelming numbers forced the army to abandon its effort to appease slaveholders by sending black recruits out of the state for organization and training.[31] Some whites charged that slaves pretended to enlist only long enough to get passes allowing them to escape from Kentucky, or that they idled about the recruitment stations, living on government rations and refusing either to work or to fight. Well-founded accusations revealed a flourishing trade in black substitutes, kidnapped by dealers who could realize a quick profit by selling them either in Kentucky or in states to the north.[32] The army itself resorted to forcible impressment when the flow of volunteers began to subside. But, by any standard, Kentucky blacks gave massive

---

[30] *Freedom*, ser. 2: docs. 99–100, and pp. 192–93. For the law requiring enrollment and draft of slave men and authorizing compensation to loyal owners of slave volunteers, see U.S., *Statutes at Large, Treaties, and Proclamations*, vol. 13 (Boston, 1866), pp. 6–11.

[31] *Freedom*, ser. 2: pp. 194–95.

[32] On the trade in black substitutes, see Geo. W. Culver to Col. Hammond, 3 Oct. 1864, Letters Received, ser. 734, Post of Louisville KY, RG 393 Pt. 4 [C-6051]; affidavit of Chas. Smith, 3 Dec. 1864, Letters Received, ser. 1636, Louisville KY, Provost Marshal Field Organizations, RG 393 Pt. 4 [C-5005].

support to the Union cause. Fourteen thousand men volunteered during the summer of 1864, and by the end of May 1865, nearly 24,000 — more than half the black men of military age in the state – had taken up Union arms.[33]

Full-scale military enlistment doomed slavery in Kentucky, and both slaves and masters knew it. The slaveholders reacted with indignation, adding black enlistment to their expanding catalogue of depredations by the Lincoln administration. Their anger reached such a pitch that President Lincoln placed the state under martial law in July 1864.[34] Despite their owners' violent opposition, slaves continued to avail themselves of the opportunities created by enlistment. Moreover, the departure of thousands of black men, and the probability that others would follow, gave slaves who could not or did not enlist leverage to exact more favorable working arrangements. Some agreed to remain with their owners under the promise of compensation in cash or kind. Others left home and obtained employment with the army, with nonslaveholders, or with erstwhile slaveholders whose laborers had deserted them.[35]

General Lorenzo Thomas, adjutant general of the army, proposed to turn this situation to the army's advantage by authorizing the forcible enlistment of slaves who had left their owners "without intending to enter the service of the United States."[36] Nonslaveholders, seeing black enlistments as a means of reducing their own liability for the draft, abandoned the slaveholders and urged the recruitment of slaves.[37] By the end of 1864, some slaveholders themselves had joined what was now all but a *fait accompli*, hoping at least to collect the compensation promised by Congress. Just as they had earlier switched from opposing to inviting military labor, they now asked the army to enlist slaves whom they themselves could no longer control. One master requested that federal authorities enlist a forty-nine-year-old "boy" who "has refused to serve me any longer, and affirms that he is as free as I am."

[33] For a full discussion of black recruitment in Kentucky, see *Freedom*, ser. 2: chap. 4. Adjutant General Lorenzo Thomas reported in September 1864 that 14,000 Kentucky black men had been enlisted to date. (*Official Records*, ser. 3, vol. 4, p. 733.) For the total number of black soldiers from Kentucky and their proportion of the state's black men, see *Freedom*, ser. 2: p. 12.

[34] He also suspended the writ of habeas corpus. (*Official Records*, ser. 1, vol. 39, pt. 2, pp. 180–82.)

[35] On the evolution of free-labor arrangements during the war, see *Freedom*, ser. 1, vol. 2.

[36] *Official Records*, ser. 3, vol. 4, p. 543. The order was issued on July 25, 1864. As commander of the District of Kentucky, General Burbridge enforced Thomas's policy enthusiastically. For instance, he instructed one subordinate officer to seize and enlist "all negroes in your command who have left their masters." (Asst. Adjt. Genl. J. H. Hammond to Brig. Genl. Hugh Ewing, 14 Aug. 1864, Letters Received, ser. 734, Post of Louisville KY, RG 393 Pt. 4 [C-6049].)

[37] *Freedom*, ser. 2: docs. 100, 108.

Still, some slaveholders resisted. Forced to surrender much of their ground, they dug in hard to preserve what remained. Many of them attempted to deter enlistment by threatening to abuse the families of volunteers. Failing to stop the men from enlisting, they made good their threats, punishing the families with brutal reprisals.[38] Some black soldiers resorted to direct, armed action to secure the release of family members held in bondage. More frequently, they took their families with them to the camps and recruiting centers. Hundreds of black civilians gathered at Camp Nelson, which had earlier served as a holding center for military laborers and now served the same purpose for army recruits. Makeshift villages sprang up near army posts and encampments as families sought protection by remaining near their soldier husbands, fathers, brothers, and sons. Volunteers rejected as physically unfit and slaves who were "simple runaways, or castaways" added to the numbers of camp-followers.

Unable to distinguish the families of soldiers from the mass of black refugees, and unwilling in any case to provide for slaves ineligible for army service, military authorities in Kentucky ordered the expulsion of noncombatants. Black soldiers fumed at the forcible removal of their families, as did some of their white officers. In late 1864 the horrific spectacle of ill-clad women and children, invalid and old people turned out of Camp Nelson into the November cold appalled many Northerners. The resulting outcry eventually forced the army to readmit black refugees to the camp, though not before many suffered and some died. The War Department satisfied no one with its effort to dodge the question of the soldiers' families by deferring to the "sound discretion" of local commanders.[39]

In March 1865, by joint resolution, Congress at last provided freedom for the wives and children of black soldiers, even those owned by loyal masters.[40] Additional thousands of Kentucky black men rushed to recruiters in order to liberate their families, but their enlistment did not stop the slaveholders. They mobilized the legal apparatus of the state government to sustain their claims to the soldiers' families, and on occasion even recaptured former slaves duly enlisted in the Union army.[41]

[38] In addition to documents in this chapter, see *Freedom*, ser. 2: docs. 106, 301–4, 307A–B, and pp. 195, 657–58.
[39] On the families who accompanied slave men to recruiting centers, and the army's treatment of them, see, in addition to documents in this chapter, *Freedom*, ser. 2: docs. 102A–C (quotation from 102C), 105, 107, 172, 294, 312A–B, and pp. 195–96, 658–59.
[40] *Statutes at Large*, vol. 13, p. 571. The Militia Act of 1862 had declared "forever free" the mothers, wives, and children of black men who served the Union army as soldiers or military laborers, but only if they were owned by disloyal masters – effectively excluding the families of most border-state black soldiers. (*Statutes at Large*, vol. 12, p. 599.)
[41] In addition to documents in this chapter, see *Freedom*, ser. 2: docs. 111–12, 327.

As slaveholders mounted the last defense of their crumbling institution, General John M. Palmer, an Illinois Republican, took command of the new Department of Kentucky.[42] The first military commander in the state to welcome wholeheartedly the destruction of slavery, Palmer delighted in the chance to speed it faster toward its doom. Among his first official acts, he extended military protection to the women and children freed by the joint resolution of Congress, and interposed his authority when a state court declared the resolution unconstitutional and ordered a soldier's wife returned to slavery. Even as the war drew to a close, he continued to encourage slave men "to coin freedom for themselves and posterity" by enlisting.[43]

Trained as a lawyer, Palmer took special pleasure in belaboring slaveholders with detailed legal arguments, one of their own favorite weapons. In June 1865, he learned of a slave confined in the Louisville workhouse under the law that required slave owners to prevent slaves from hiring their own time. Palmer observed that the man's owner could no longer control him and hence had no interest in giving the bond required to free him from confinement, while the slave could do nothing to effect his own release. Lecturing the judge of the city court upon the principle, "[w]hen the reason of the law ceases, the law itself ceases," Palmer ordered the man's release. Later he offered an elaborate legal rationale calling – unsuccessfully – for authority to declare slavery defunct in Kentucky. He dabbled unabashedly in state politics, hoping to promote "a true Union party." But he saw himself first and foremost as a military commander, in whose judgment a "revolution adverse to the system" of slavery had caused it to perish.

Nevertheless, so long as slavery retained legal standing, General Palmer and other federal authorities could merely cripple, not destroy it. In 1865, Kentucky blacks found themselves in a nightmare world between slavery and freedom, and their owners gave no sign of submitting gracefully to the passing away of slavery. Indeed, the defeat of the Confederacy – and, with it, the end of slavery everywhere in the nation but Kentucky and Delaware – seemed only to render Kentucky slaveholders more vindictive in asserting their claims. Through the remainder of the year, they enforced the state's slave code with a vengeance.

Although the law could not restore the slaveholders' disintegrating authority, it afforded ample means to obstruct and harass their nominal slaves. Public conveyances were forbidden to transport slaves without their owners' permission, and the rule was enforced even against slaves whose owners had cast them out. Slaveholders had the right to whip

---

[42] The department was organized in February 1865, with Palmer as its first commander. Its boundaries coincided with those of the state.

[43] *Freedom*, ser. 2: docs. 110, 112.

and otherwise punish slaves, and they exercised their power freely, even upon the soldiers' wives and children freed by Congress. The law permitted slave owners to sue individuals who entered into wage contracts with their slaves and to claim the slaves' earnings for themselves, and many owners thereby seized the proceeds of the labor of men and women they had neither the intention nor the means of employing themselves. Clever employers could extort literally free labor, withholding wages from black employees on the plea that they feared a lawsuit by their owners, but also declining to pay the owners since, after all, they had contracted with the slaves themselves.[44]

The slaveholders' intransigence found political expression in the August 1865 elections for Congress and the state legislature. Candidates who acknowledged the death of slavery failed to muster a majority, despite the assistance of a state law disfranchising Confederate voters and a military order excluding rebel sympathizers. The victors, by a narrow margin, stood firmly opposed to ratifying the federal constitutional amendment abolishing slavery, and to acting against slavery by state measures. Thousands of blacks in Kentucky who were entitled to freedom under federal law continued to face judicial denial of their liberty, difficulty in obtaining employment, and murderous violence. Moreover, at Palmer's conservative estimate, at least 65,000 Kentucky blacks remained slaves in the eyes of the law. While the rest of the nation celebrated the end of the war and the destruction of chattel bondage, black people in Kentucky struggled against the constraints imposed by slavery's continued legality.

The federal military presence constituted the only limit upon the slaveholders' determination to preserve slavery and punish freedpeople. Fearful that federal authority might be withdrawn now that the war had ended, a delegation representing Kentucky blacks traveled to Washington in June 1865 to confront President Andrew Johnson with their dismal future if left at the mercy of their would-be owners. In a petition that appealed both to justice and to the patriotism of thousands of Kentucky black soldiers, the delegates recounted the suffering engendered by the anomalous survival of slavery and the merciless enforcement of the slave code. Only the retention of martial law and General Palmer, they insisted, offered hope to Kentucky blacks. And as if to offer evidence in support of the petition, slaves in search of military protection congregated at army posts across Kentucky, especially at Louisville.

Black soldiers sometimes afforded security against the slaveholders' violence. An officer at Paducah reported in October 1865 that the replacement of white troops at that post by black ones had discouraged

[44] For a discussion of the evolution during 1865 of free-labor arrangements amid continuing legal slavery, see *Freedom*, ser. 1, vol. 2.

attacks upon black people.[45] But most of the black regiments recruited in Kentucky served far from its borders, and in June 1865 many of these were sent even farther from home, transferred from Virginia to Texas to secure the Mexican border. There they seethed with helpless anger and frustration over the treatment of their families.[46] Because virtually all of Kentucky's black soldiers enlisted during the last year of the war, they were among the last to be discharged. Thus the concluding struggle to destroy slavery was waged in the absence of half the able-bodied black men, and the burden weighed heavily upon black women and children.

Seeing slavery staggered, Kentucky blacks pressed for the kill. Thousands of those who remained in bondage claimed their own freedom by leaving their owners or demanding wages or simply refusing to perform customary duties. Nonslaveholders grew increasingly bold about hiring nominal slaves who had fled their owners. Though he lacked the authority to destroy slavery outright, General Palmer acted deliberately to expand the slaves' maneuvering room. In May 1865, complaining about the large number of runaway slaves who had taken shelter in Louisville, the city authorities tried to manipulate Palmer into enforcing the vagrancy ordinances and the laws that prohibited slaves from hiring themselves as free people. But Palmer saw through their ruse and, turning their complaint against them, used it as an excuse to loosen the bonds sustaining slavery. His General Order 32 authorized the provost marshal of the Post of Louisville to issue to "any colored person who may report him or herself as unable to find sufficient employment in the city" a pass permitting freedom of movement to any other point. The pass covered the applicant and family, and – in defiance of state law – required railroads, steamboats, ferryboats, and other public conveyances to transport black passengers.

Palmer's pass system was not what the mayor and his colleagues had in mind. Though strictly applicable only to blacks without gainful employment, the passes effectively released slaves who obtained them from further restraint by their owners. Quickly grasping their meaning, slaves put Palmer's passes to service in the cause of freedom. By late July, more than 5,000 black people had crossed the Ohio River from Louisville under the authority of General Order 32.

As the rearguard defense of slavery continued unabated into the summer of 1865, slaves in ever larger numbers fled their owners and collected at army posts throughout the state. General Palmer blamed the slaveholders themselves for their predicament. Their refusal to

---

[45] Lt. Col. A. M. York to Brig. Gen'l C. B. Fisk, 2 Oct. 1865, Y-7 1865, Registered Letters Received, ser. 3379, TN Asst. Comr., RG 105 [A-6219].

[46] See, for example, *Freedom*, ser. 2: docs. 333, 341. On the postwar military service of black soldiers, including a great number from Kentucky, see *Freedom*, ser. 2: chap. 17.

accept the end of slavery, and their intemperate denunciations of federal policy, gave the slaves extravagant expectations that the government would free them, furnish them with food and clothing, and place them on an equal footing with white people. During the secession crisis of 1860–1861, the masters' charge of Yankee abolitionism had encouraged the slaves to assume that Northern soldiers were their friends; now the masters' contumacy quickened the slaves' faith in the purposes of the federal government. In July 1865, as the population of fugitive slaves swelled, Palmer issued General Order 49, extending the Louisville pass system to all places in the state occupied by federal troops and urging "colored persons congregated about posts" to apply for military passes to search for employment.

Slaves needed little prompting to seize the benefits of Palmer's passes. They poured into army posts and provost marshals' offices to receive what they insisted were "free papers." When questioned upon what grounds they had concluded they were free, slaves still in the custody of their owners retorted, "General Palmer told them so." Additional thousands joined the exodus out of the state, stirring Palmer to ask sarcastically of the slaveholders "whether it is a paying policy to give the adjoining states all of the most valuable portion of your colored population." Other blacks, including many of the families who awaited the return of husbands and fathers from the army, used passes issued under the two orders not to leave the state, but to move elsewhere in Kentucky, beyond their owners' reach. Still others obtained passes but chose to remain at their homes, as one slaveholder charged, "not . . . with the view of living in harmony with their old Master, but to taunt him with their free papers and threaten him with military power." Even slaves who did not apply for passes found their bargaining power enhanced, for both masters and slaves knew that a slave who remained at home did so only of his or her own volition. The pass system ended what remained of slaveholders' practical control over their slaves, leaving little behind except a legal technicality.

In the months between Palmer's issuance of General Orders 32 and 49 and the ratification of the Thirteenth Amendment, Kentucky slaveholders vented their anger and frustration in brutal attacks against the symbols of their defeat. Erstwhile unionists and ex-Confederates joined forces to attack returning black veterans. Civil authorities, as well as roving bands of toughs, took special pains to seize weapons from black people, including discharged soldiers who had purchased their guns as they were mustered out.[47] Slaveholders defied the congressional resolution that freed black soldiers' families, hunting them down, confiscating their wages and possessions, and reenslaving their children. The slaves' participation in bringing slavery to its knees – especially the

[47] For attacks on discharged black soldiers, see *Freedom*, ser. 2: docs. 356, 360.

prominence of black soldiers – and the slaveholders' intransigence en-
sured that racial violence would continue in Kentucky long after the
sectional hostilities had ceased.

Martial law, which remained in effect until October 1865, gave
General Palmer some leverage against the abuse of black people. He
vetoed local ordinances designed to expel destitute blacks or to prevent
wives and children of black soldiers from renting living quarters. He
also announced his intention to enforce wage contracts made with
blacks, whatever their legal status. Welcome reinforcement arrived in
the summer of 1865, when General Clinton B. Fisk became assistant
commissioner of the Freedmen's Bureau for Tennessee and Kentucky.
From his Nashville headquarters, Fisk appointed a handful of subordinate agents in Kentucky, but the continued legality of slavery ham-
strung his plans to enforce a free-labor system and protect blacks from
violence. Fisk, like Palmer, had little patience with the tenacious
attachment of "loyal" Kentucky whites to the tattered remnants of
slavery. Complaining that he could not "run a *Freed*mens Bureau for
Slaves," Fisk instructed his agents to compel the payment of wages
promised to blacks, " 'vi et armis' if necessary." In reality, however,
the bureau remained nearly powerless in Kentucky until slavery was
legally ended.

The lifting of martial law by President Johnson in October and the
steady reduction of federal troops gave Kentucky slaveholders one last
wind. They used the state courts to prosecute Union army officers who
had acted against slavery, including provost marshals who had enlisted
slaves. Grand juries indicted General Palmer, construing the issuance of
passes under his authority as "aiding slaves to escape," an offense punishable by imprisonment. Individual slaveholders, including a U.S. senator
and a former congressman, sued him for damages in the tens of thousands of dollars. When Palmer reported the indictments to the Attorney
General, he noted ruefully that, if guilty of helping one slave to escape,
he must plead guilty to helping 20,000. Congress, Palmer suggested,
would have to pass a law extending his lifetime a few thousand years if
the state meant to hold him answerable in each case.

Kentucky slaveholders refused to accept defeat and, with the end of
martial law, exercised wider latitude in indulging their rancor and taking revenge upon blacks and Union officers. But they could no longer
hold freedom at bay. On December 7, 1865, anticipating the official
announcement that the Thirteenth Amendment had been ratified, General Palmer issued a circular declaring slavery at an end. No sudden
dawning of acceptance or good will overcame the former slaveholders
and, in many respects, Kentucky blacks had barely begun their struggle.
Nevertheless, they had won the opening battle, however belatedly. Kentucky had at last reached the goal quietly but confidently announced by
the first runaways who sought Union army lines in 1861.

197: Commander at Camp Nevin, Kentucky, to the Commander of the Department of the Cumberland; and the Latter's Reply

Camp Nevin Kentucky November 5th 1861

General: The subject of Contraband negros is one that is looked to, by the Citizens of Kentucky of vital importance   Ten have come into my Camp within as many hours, and from what they say, there will be a general Stampeed of slaves from the other side of Green River —   They have already become a source of annoyance to me, and I have great reason to belive that this annoyance will increase the longer we stay —   They state the reasons of their running away — there masters are rank Secessionists, in some cases are in the rebel army — and that Slaves of union men are pressed into service to drive teams &&c

I would respectfully suggest that if they be allowed to remain here, that our cause in Kentucky may be injured —   I have no faith in Kentucky's loyalty, there-for have no great desire to protect her pet institution Slavery —   As a matter of policy, how would it do, for me to send for their master's and diliver the negro's — to them on the out-side of our lines, or send them to the other side of Green River and deliver them up —   What effect would it have on our cause south of the River —   I am satisfied they bolster themselves up, by making the uninformed believe that this is a war upon African slavery —   I merely make these suggestions, for I am very far from wishing these recreant masters in possession of any of their property — for I think slaves no better than horses in that respect —

I have put the negro's to work —   They will be handy with teams, and generally useful.   I consider the subject embarrassing and must defer to your better judgement

The ammunition we have for our Guns is not servicible.   I have been trying it to day —   The powder is old, lost its strength by exposure and frequent transportation —   The fuzes in the spherical case are not made properly or else the graduation is very imperfect.   You have been telegraphed to on the subject —   All quiet below, Miller came back from Green River to day,   He states that he has it from reliable sources that there never has been more than 8000 armed Infantry in all of Buckner's army —

They have without doubt pressed the wagons into service —   Where they are going time will determine —

The negros that came to me to day state that their master's had notified them to be ready to go south with them on Monday Morning, and they left Sunday night —

My command is improving each day and you need have no fears for us —   I will be timely apprised of their movements and will

move to please you— Bear in mind also that they cannot insult a
force of 12,000 with impunity, particularly when my movements
can be more rapid than theirs—

Please send the Fist Ohio to me at your earliest convenience and
very much oblige   Your obt servant

ALS   A. M^cD. McCook

Louisville Kenty Nov 8, 1861
Sir   I have no instructions from Government on the subject of
Negroes, my opinion is that the laws of the state of Kentucky are
in full force and that negroes must be surrendered on application of
their masters or agents or delivered over to the sheriff of the
County. We have nothing to do with them at all and you should
not let them take refuge in Camp. It forms a source of
misrepresentation by which Union men are estranged from our
Cause

I know it is almost impossible for you to ascertain in any case the
owner of the negro, but so it is, his word is not taken in evidence
and you will send them away   I am yours

HLcS   W. T. Sherman

Brig. Genl. A. McD. McCook to Genl. W. T. Sherman, 5 Nov. 1861,
Miscellaneous Records, ser. 3534, Dept. of the Ohio, RG 393 Pt. 1 [C-1];
Brig. Genl. W. T. Sherman to Brig. Genl. McCook, 8 Nov. 1861, vol. 2
DO, p. 91, Letters Sent, ser. 866, Dept. of the Cumberland, RG 393 Pt. 1
[C-1]. A few weeks earlier, General Sherman had informed Colonel John B.
Turchin, commander of an Illinois regiment, of a complaint by two Kentucky
slaveholders that their slaves had "taken refuge in your camp and are there
sheltered." Sherman had reminded Turchin that "[t]he laws of the United
States and of Kentucky all of which are binding on us compel us to surrender a
runaway negro on application of negro's owner or agent." He recommended,
however, that such difficulties be avoided by keeping blacks out of the regiment's camp altogether, except for those who had been brought from Illinois
as servants. (*Official Records*, ser. 2, vol. 1, p. 774.)

198: **Commander of U.S.S. *Conestoga* to the Commander
of Naval Forces in the Western Rivers**

Paducah. K^y Decr 10th 1861.
Sir. On the night of the 8th inst: I proceeded with this vessel up
the Cumberland river to near the fortifications below Dover,
Tennessee. General Smith had received information that there were

a number of union people, near Linton, Ky; – just below the line of Tennessee – who wished to join the Union forces, or were refugees, driven from their homes by rebel marauders, and were unable to escape through the rebel lines. On arriving at Linton two signal guns were fired as requested by these people, and we afterwards returned to that place to remain over night, and about Sixty persons came in during the night from the back country in small parties and were taken on board & brought down either to Smithland or to this place. Previous to anchoring at Linton I had dropped down to the lower end of Line Island, intending to remain there, but learning in the evening that persons had collected about the woods with the intent of cutting off all parties attempting to escape, I moved up to Linton itself, where the people succeeded in reaching the vessel. Just before dark a negro ran down to the river bank, near the boat, chased by blood hounds in full cry after him, and begged to be taken on board. I sent a boat to his rescue, and learning by his statement confirmed by Kentuckians on board, that he was being chased by rebel cavalry – he had run 18 miles – with the intent of seizing him and taking him to Dover to work upon the fortifications at that point, I received him on board and brought him away. His master is a Secessionist. The cavalry did not show themselves and the hounds were taken from the track; but we saw three of them. No demonstration against us was anywhere made and we could hear of no outrages being committed near the river, no doubt owing to the assurance we have given that the secessionists of the Cumberland will be held to answer for the Security of their Union neighbors. –

The greatest efforts are being made by the Secessionists to fortify the Cumberland below Dover, and a panic prevails; they being confident that an attack on Nashville is preparing. Under the "Authority" of Govr Johnson, elected Govr of Ky: by the secession convention held at Russelville in that State, the rebels are calling out Kentucky troops and are drafting men, impressing them into the rebel service; and, under the same "Authority", are seizing the negros of Kentuckians, carrying them to Dover to work upon the fortifications. Thus it happens that Union men and secessionists alike are telling their slaves to escape to the woods to avoid the rebel cavalry engaged in seizing them. I am informed that union men have been seized and carried off to work in place of their escaped Slaves. It appears that the sons of the owner of the negro taken on board this boat, gave him warning to escape, notwithstanding these sons themselves, had been active in assiting rebel troops to find Government arms, &c, in their neighborhood.

. . . .

ALS

S. L. Phelps.

Excerpt from Lt. Comdg. S. L. Phelps to Flag Officer A. H. Foote, 10 Dec. 1861, Area 5, Area File, RG 45 [T-1]. The remainder of the letter described Confederate fortification of the Cumberland and Tennessee rivers and offered recommendations regarding possible action by Union forces.

199: Commander of the District of Cairo to the Commander at Fort Holt, Kentucky

Cairo [*Ill.*], Dec. 25. 1861

Your communication in relation to Mr. Mercer, is received. I will see that he does not trouble your camp in future so frequently as formerly. I am satisfied however from other evidence than his own of his loyalty, and regret that he should have come so much under your suspicion. Whilst we wish to keep everything from the enemy, it is our duty to alleviate the hardships consequent upon a state of war, of our union friends in the border States as far as practicable. I gave permission for a man to go into your camp for the purpose of recovering his fugitive slaves. If Gen. Order, No. 3, from Headquarters Dept. of the Mo.,[1] had been complied with, this would not have been necessary. Mr. Mercer now reports to me that these negroes were found concealed in one of the huts at Fort Holt, and that the owner was forcibly prevented from recovering his property. If true this is treating law, the orders of the Comdr. of the Dept. and my orders with contempt. Mr. Mercer does not charge that this was by your order, but after your attention was called to the fact that fugitive slaves were in your camp as the pass over my signature informed you was probably the fact, an investigation should have been had and the negroes driven out. I do not want the army used as negro catchers, but still less do I want to see it used as a cloak to cover their escape. No matter what our private views may be on this subject there are in this Department positive orders on the subject, and these orders must be obeyed. I direct therefore that you have a search made and if you find these or any other fugitive slaves in camp at Fort Holt you have them expelled from camp, and if hereafter you find any have been concealed or detained, you bring the party so detaining them to punishment.

HLcSr

(Sgd) U. S. Grant

Brig. Gen'l. U. S. Grant to Col. J. Cook, 25 Dec. 1861, vol. G1 DT, pp. 164–65, Letters Sent, ser. 2730, Dist. of Cairo, RG 393 Pt. 2 No. 171 [C-4802]. Although this letterbook copy is headed District of Southeast Missouri, General Grant's command had been designated District of Cairo since

December 23, having been enlarged to include that part of Kentucky west of the Cumberland River, as well as southern Illinois and southeast Missouri. (*Official Records*, ser. 1, vol. 7, p. 515.) Mercer, the Kentucky slaveholder, had made earlier protests to Grant that the soldiers at Fort Holt (opposite Cairo) had interfered with slaves. Colonel John Cook, commander of the fort, had responded on November 23, 1861, with assurances of full compliance with Grant's orders respecting slaves: "[N]o portion of the command has either aided or assisted in any manner the enticing or holding of any slave owing service under the laws of any slave State in or out of the Union, and when such have asked protection they have only temporarily obtained it, and I still hold as under previous orders from you any such . . . in readiness to be instantly turned over either to the lawful owner or any identified agent of said owner." On the same day, Cook had issued an order declaring that "[n]o officer or soldier shall be allowed to arrest, secrete or harbor or in any way interfere with persons held to service (negroes), property of citizens of slaveholding States." (*Official Records*, ser. 2, vol. 1, pp. 778–79.) After receiving Grant's letter of December 25, Colonel Cook complied promptly with its instructions to search Fort Holt for fugitive slaves, issuing orders that required the expulsion of any fugitives thereby discovered. He also ordered that soldiers who concealed fugitives be punished. Cook reported his action to Grant, at the same time reminding the general of "the vast length of line" his troops had to guard, and the consequent difficulty of preventing blacks from passing through the lines – a difficulty further complicated by the fact that free blacks from Illinois were employed as servants by almost all the officers. (*Official Records*, ser. 2, vol. 1, pp. 794–95.) Only a few days later, Grant issued instructions to another subordinate officer that made a sharper distinction between loyal and disloyal slaveholders, this time ordering that the army should neither restore a fugitive slave to a master who had aided the enemy nor allow the master to come into army lines to reclaim the slave. (See above, doc. 161.)

1 See above, doc. 157.

200: Commander of a Brigade in the Army of the Ohio to the Commander of the Department and Army of the Ohio

Camp Andy Johnson [*near Nashville, Tenn.*] March 9 1862
Sir: – To remove the impression indicated in your letter of the   inst That I had refused to deliver Mr Garrisons negroes permit me to offer an explanation of the facts– Mr Garrisons negroes ran off at his own request. "Allison" was placed in my care at Mumfordville through the Kindness of Genl M{c}Cook– the other two came voluntarily and were supported by my Staff out of Charity
At Bowling Green Genl M{c}Cook in the presence of Mr Garrison requested the negroes to be given up. – I directed Mr Garrison to my Head Quarters where he went and had an hours interview with

his slaves – No opposition was made to his taking them with him

During that night the negroes instead of going home, as Mr Garrison said they promised to do – Secreted themselves untill they could follow the Troops and get back to my camp

At Edgefield, an order from Genl McCook was handed to me requiring the delivery of the negroes to Mr Garrison – I confess being surprised at the orders, having virtually delivered them before, and having offered no opposition to his taking them, I immediately placed the order in the hands of Capt Lowrie Asst Adj^t Genl and directed him to accompany Mr Garrison, and the three Citizens who were with him – to my Camp and see that no opposition was made to his removing his negroes, – Mr Garrison then requested a Guard of Soldiers to take his negroes to a place he would designate, This request I refused in the absence of an order to do so and because I deemed it predjudicial to the harmony and discipline of the Troops – to require them to perform what they would all consider an obnoxious duty. During the interview with Mr Garrison the negroes again fled beyond the lines of my Camp. Upon the return of two of them yesterday information was given by my order to the Provost Guard of the Division who secured them – I am informed that "Allison" is concealed somewhere in Nashville –

In order to avoid this very vexatious question and to avoid being subjected to the unmilitary conduct of the Provost Guard who have been in the habit of visiting my Camp – have forced the Guards – have arrested a sentinel on his post and have insulted officers who were in the proper discharge of their duties – I have deemed it necessary to issue a General order – a copy of which I respectfully enclose and refer to. I have the honor To Remain

HL   [*James S. Negley*]

[Brig. Genl. James S. Negley] to Genl. Buell, 9 Mar. 1862, N-75 1862, Supplemental Letters Received, ser. 882, Dept. of the OH, RG 393 Pt. 1 [C-2046]. The blank space in the first sentence appears in the manuscript. The signature has been cut out, but a notation on the outside of the letter indicates the name of its author. The order issued by Negley is not enclosed but was presumably his General Order 17 of March 8, 1862, which prohibited the admission of slaves into the camps of the brigade; ordered the expulsion of any slaves employed as officers' servants; and threatened to punish "to the extreme limit of military rigor" any officer or soldier who employed or harbored a slave, or failed to report the presence of a slave in camp. (General Order No. 17, Head Quarters 7th Brigade, 8 Mar. 1862, L-96 1862, Supplemental Letters Received, ser. 882, Dept. of the OH, RG 393 Pt. 1 [C-2046].) For another report regarding Kentucky slaves who accompanied the Army of the Ohio when it advanced into Tennessee in February 1862, and Kentucky masters who followed in pursuit, see above, doc. 83. On March 6, General Don Carlos Buell, commander of the Army of the Ohio, acknowledged that "slaves sometimes make their way improperly into our lines, and in some instances they may be enticed there; but I think the number has been magnified by report." Buell assured Kentucky masters that his subordinates would cooperate in returning such slaves to their owners: "Several applications have been made to me by persons whose servants have been found in our camps, and in every instance that I know of the master has recovered his servant and taken him away." (*Official Records*, ser. 1, vol. 10, pt. 2, p. 15.)

201: Hospital Steward of an Illinois Regiment to the President, and a Report by the Former Commander of the District of the Mississippi to the Headquarters of the Department of the Tennessee

Columbus K.Y. Sept' 26th 1862

Dear Sir   Inclosed You will find an exact coppy of an order issued from Gen Quinby, in persuence of which, one Negro man caled Bob was forcebley deliverd to his reputed master. Bob was a sober industrious and intelegent man, imployed as cook in Co E (Capt Irvins) 76 Reg Ill vol"

I would State that Such transactions are common here, and are Susseptible of the plainest and most posative proof. And negro hunters too, are searching, sometimes in gangs, almost daily our camp for fugetive Slaves in persuence of written permits from the aforesaid Gen". The Regemet feel indignut about it. the most of us enterd the service with the understanding that there was to be an end to such dirty work, We think we understand the law that protects us from it. And we appeal to the Goverment to See to it so far as it is posable, that the late laws touching this subject be executed.

I am 53 years old and joined the army in good faith, to help in putting down the rebelion   The goverment is welcom to me. all there is of me to the end, in any way that I can serve it to the best advantage. Also to my two sons one of which has alredey given his life to the cause, but as a citizen of this great Republic I do most earnestly entreat Your exelency to Shield us from this infernal business, of negro catching, or of witnesing it in our camps.

The foregoing facts may be substanated by application to Capt Irvin & Leut, Williams and a detachment of men under ther command, Company E, 76 Reg Ill vol" and to Col" A W Mack, and Maj" Dubois. I am also creditabley informd that a case equily

525

as attrocious was enacted in the 72^d Reg″ in this place on last
Saboth. Respectfuly Yours

ALS   Wm Thirds

Corinth, Miss October 27th 1862.
Major I have read with much pain the letter of Wm Thirds,
Hospital Steward 76th Ills. Vols, addressed direct to his Excellency,
President Lincoln. The animus of that letter is calculated to do me
great injustice by holding me up in a false light before the
President, and also before the public, for I am told that similar
charges have been made against me in some of our northern
news-papers.

As instructed by the Major General Commanding, I proceed to
make a full report on this and other like transactions charged upon
me.

During the time that I was honored with the command of the
District of the Mississippi I am conscious of having violated, neither
in letter, nor in spirit, either the orders of my military superiors, or
the laws of Congress; but have striven faithfully to carry them out
according to their fair interpretation. Within my limited sphere, I
hope that my efforts have not been altogether unsucessful in
disarming hostility against our government and in exposing the fatal
errors by which the minds of the Southern people have been blinded
to the real character of this contest. My object has been not only to
punish traitors, but, also to protect, in both person and property,
the grieveously persecuted union men within the borders of this
rebellion, so far as this could be done, under existing laws and
orders, and the means at my disposal would permit. Numerous cases
have been reported to me, in which the Negro servants of loyal
masters have been enticed away by officers and soldiers, thereby
giving foundation to the false assertion, that the great object of the
North in the prosecution of this war, was the abolition of Slavery,
and paralysing the efforts of union men in the south to check the
wave of treason that seemed to be sweeping all before it. Until
quite recently the President himself, and I doubt not wisely,
abstained from any distinct declaration of principle on the Subject of
Slavery. The conservative union-loving men of the North, thought
they understood the object of the President in thus holding himself
in reserve and admired him for it. Even before the passage of the
law of Congress prohibiting the employment of military force in
returning negroes to their masters,[1] no force under my command
was ever to my knowledge, thus employed, and since the
publication of that law, which I heartily approve I have carefully

avoided doing anything, which by forced construction, would justify the charge made against me by Hospital Steward Thirds.

The facts in the case he refers to, are, as nearly as I can recall them, as follows:

A few days before the date of the transaction complained of, Mr. R. R. Taylor, a confirmed and almost helpless invalid, a resident of Ballard County, Ky. whose loyalty to the federal goverment is, and has been throughout, above suspicion, applied to me for permission to look for a negro man who had recently left him. I gave him the desired permit, assuring him that if he found his negro, and could pursuade him to go home, no obstacles should be thrown in his way, that unless he employed force, no force would be opposed to him. After the lapse of about an hour Mr. Taylor returned to my office, and reported that he had found his man, but that the Soldiers, incited, I have reason to beleive by a commissioned officer, would not permit the negro, though willing to leave, to accompany his master, and threatened Mr. Taylor with violence if he attempted to take him. I advised him to go home for a few days to allow the excitement to subside which he did. On his return several days afterwards, he was referred to Lt. Col. Duff 2^d Ill. Arty, who did issue the order of which a copy was sent the President, though it was neither dictated by, nor submitted to me. Still as he acted in accordance with my understood wishes I assume all criminality, if any, which attaches thereto. The object of Col. Duff was Simply to place the negro beyond the reach of force and improper influence, so that the latter might be free to act.

Capt. Irvine reported to me with the negro, and on asking the latter if he belonged to Mr. Taylor and his replying in the affirmative, I told him to go to the Columbus House, near by, and see his master then there. Whether he did so or not I am unable to say. No force or threat was employed by me, and with my knowledge or sanction none was employed by others. This ended my connection with this transaction. In conclusion permit me to say that I too have made sacrifices neither few nor small to aid in crushing this rebellion, and am willing to make still greater, rather than submit to any compromise with the traitors who have brought these evil times, upon my beloved country.

If his Excellency the President will take the trouble to inquire into my circumstances from Senator Harris and others from the State of New York, acquainted with them he will beleive at least that I am anxious to co-operate with him in his efforts to restore our Union and give peace to a suffering nation. I am very respectfully Your obt. servt

HLS   I. F. Quinby

[*Endorsement*] Judge Advocate General'[s] Office June 9th 1863, In view of the explanation offerred by Brig Gen Quinby, it is suggested that this complaint against him should not be further considered. The object of his action was doubtless in good faith, not to restrain the freedom of the negro named but to prevent it from being restrained by others. If his course was misconceived it was certainly free from all taint of insubordination, & it is not believed that it calls for the formal rebuke of the government— J Holt— Judge Adv Gen[1]

Hospital Steward Wm. Thirds to his Exelency Abraham Lincoln, 26 Sept. 1862, and Brig. Genl. I. F. Quinby to Major J. A. Rawlins, 27 Oct. 1862, T-600 1862, Letters Received, ser. 12, RG 94 [K-46]. Other endorsements. The order mentioned by Thirds and Quinby is not enclosed. Although a notation indicates that Quinby's report and the other papers had been received in Washington by November 8, 1862, there is no indication of any further action in the case until the endorsement by the judge advocate general. While in command of the District of the Mississippi, with headquarters at Columbus, Kentucky, General Quinby had "strictly prohibited" the admission into army camps and posts of "colored persons . . . who are not free, or who, by the acts or consent of their masters have not become clearly contraband," and he had threatened to dismiss any commissioned officer and court-martial any enlisted man who violated the exclusion order. (General Order No. 16, Headquarters, Dist. of the Miss., 18 June 1862, vol. 101/248A DKy, p. 43, General Orders, ser. 992, Dist. of the MS, RG 393 Pt. 2 No. 24 [C-8852].)

1 The additional article of war, adopted on March 13, 1862.

202A: **Commander of an Illinois Regiment to a Chicago Friend**

Mt. Sterling, Ky. Nov. 2[d] 1862.
Dear Miller: I got your letter from Chicago, but until today I have not thought I had anything of interest to write you. I arrived safely at Covington, & have had a pleasent march out, & am now, as you will see, by my order, in Command of this Post. I am in the 3[d] Brigade of the 3[d] Division of Grangers. Army, under Genl Baird. Col. Cochran of the 14th Ky. Vol. commands the Demibrigade in which I am. & his regiment is at Winchester. Here I am, one regiment of Infantry, all alone, 20 miles from any support, just in the edge of the Cumberland Mountains, & they are full of Guerrilla Bands. One of 300 strong

has its headquarters at Hazel-Green. Humphrey Marshall with his Division 4000 strong is at Prestonburgh 60 miles distant by a good turnpike. He has 400 cavalry & ten pieces of artilery. If he attacks us we are "gone up" but we are not apprehending an attack. We are evidently doomed, to a winter of *ination* in tents where snow falls 2 feet deep *guarding* a little sesesh hole that is too *cowardly* to guard itself, and our principle business is, expected to be returning niggers. The old policy, is to prevail of cutting up the union forces to guard rebel property & let regiment after regiment fall by the enimies concentrationg, & then the loyal North must have a draft for a new army. My superior Commanders order me to give up the niggers. Ought I to do it? I love my country, Miller; I have risked my life in its battles and am willing to do so again & again. I am deeply anxious to do my whole duty. But under the Presidents proclamation of Sept 22$^{\rm d}$ 62. I cannot conscientiously force my boys to become the slavehounds of Kentuckians & I am determined I will not. You see my order. Doubtless before you get this I will under arrest, & undergoing Court Martial, but I want my friends in Northern Illinois to know that it is not for cowardice or disquallification but Simply because I will not make myself & my regiment a machine to enforce the slave laws of Kentucky & return slaves to rebel masters. If I go down in disgrace it will be with a clean conscience; if I am *right* my friends must not let me go down. Let me hear from you: Truly Thine

ALS

S. D. Atkins

S. D. Atkins to Miller, 2 Nov. 1862, enclosed in James Miller to Hon. Abraham Lincoln, 10 Nov. 1862, M-2041 1862, Letters Received, RG 107 [L-19]. The order referred to by Atkins is printed immediately below as document 202B. Atkins commanded the 92nd Illinois Infantry. For an example of orders to Atkins to give up fugitive slaves who had taken refuge in his regiment, see below, doc. 202Fn.

202B: Order by the Commander of an Illinois Regiment

Head Quarters Camp Dick Yates,
MT. STERLING, KY., NOV. 2D, 1862.

GENERAL ORDER NO. 1,

In compliance with General Orders No. 1, issued from the Head Quarters of Demi Brigade, I hereby assume command of the post of Mt. Sterling and vicinity.

Loyal citizens will be protected as such, and the civil authorities assisted in the enforcement of the Laws.

All loyal citizens and soldiers in Mt. Sterling and vicinity are commanded to give information of the whereabouts of any one who is now, or has been in any capacity in the confederate service, and to arrest all such parties found in Mt. Sterling or vicinity and report them in custody to the commander of the post for further proceedings.

All loyal citizens are commanded to give information to the commander of the post, of the whereabouts of any citizen who has at any time during hostilities given any aid or comfort to the common enemy.

Farmers are invited to bring their marketable products to the town and camp for sale, and will be granted protection in so doing.

Dealers in intoxicating liquors are commanded not to sell, or in any way to dispose of any intoxicating liquor to any soldier. Any one doing so, will, for the first offence have his stock in trade destroyed; and for the second offence be severely punished and confined.

Loyal citizens who are the owners of slaves, are respectfully notified to keep them at home, as no part of my command will in any way be used for the purpose of returning fugitive slaves. It is not necessary for Illinois soldiers to become slave-hounds to demonstrate their loyalty—their loyalty has been proven upon too many bloody battle fields to require new proof.

By command of

SMITH D. ATKINS,
Col. 92nd Ill. Vol. Com. Post.

I. C. LAWVER, Adj't.

General Order No. 1, Head Quarters, Camp Dick Yates, 2 Nov. 1862, enclosed in James Miller to Hon. Abraham Lincoln, 10 Nov. 1862, M-2041 1862, Letters Received, RG 107 [L-19]. The covering letter called the attention of President Lincoln to the last paragraph of Colonel Atkins's order, which was said to reflect "the sentiments of the *true men* of the west those who stand by you and your proclamation of Sep 22 1862."

202C: Summary of a Speech by the Commander of an Illinois Regiment

[*Mt. Sterling, Ky. early November, 1862*]

Co¹ Atkins said:— That the question as to what disposition to make of negroes coming within his lines had given him considerable trouble at first, but that he had now no difficulty whatever. — He made up his mind to return none within his lines, or that may come within his lines, to either loyal or disloyal master's. — That

he would not obey any order from Co¹ Cockran in conflict with his
expressed opinion upon this Subject. — He reminded his officers
and men that they were now in an enemy'ˢ Country &c. In his
order's read upon dress parade, he said that his men had not come
here for the purpose of "hunting Negroes" &c — that loyal men must
keep their negroes at home if they wish to keep them as Slaves. —
HD

Summary of a speech by Col. Atkins, [early Nov. 1862], enclosed in Brig.
Genl. J. T. Boyle to Maj. Gen. Wright, 13 Nov. 1862, B-245 1862, Letters
Received, ser. 3514, Dept. of the OH, RG 393 Pt. 1 [C-4644]. In his
covering letter, General Jeremiah T. Boyle, commander of the District of
Louisville, complained to the commander of the Department of the Ohio that
Atkins's regiment, the 92d Illinois Infantry, was "stealing negroes & com-
mitting other depredations." "If something can not be done," Boyle warned,
"I fear trouble — Such villainous conduct should be stopped, and I am asked to
call your attention to it and beg your interference — "

202D: Article from an Ohio Newspaper

[*Cleveland, Ohio November?* 1862]
COL. SMITH D. ATKINS.

Since the publication of a letter in the Cincinnati *Commercial*,
from Mt. Sterling, Kentucky, (which letter was copied,
thoughtlessly as we believe, into several Illinois papers) containing
charges of depredations on loyal citizens of Kentucky by the 92d
Illinois regiment, Col. Smith D. Atkins, we have been at some
pains to ascertain the facts in the case, and we believe they will be
found to possess a considerable degree of public interest. The
charge against Col. Atkins and his regiment is the old one of
"nigger stealing" — a phrase which signifies giving a black man his
liberty. We were told, in the letter referred to, that this practice
was "having a most injurious effect upon the loyal sentiment here;"
also that it was "heart-rending to a Union man;" likewise that this
Illinois regiment "should be sent somewhere where they cannot ruin
the loyal sentiment of the people."
Remarking first that the 92d Illinois regiment and its gallant
colonel desire no earthly boon, so much as an order sending them
out of Kentucky and into the presence of an enemy with bayonets
and batteries, instead of bailiff's writs and bills in chancery, we
proceed to the narration. The regiment has been brigaded with
certain Kentucky regiments, under Colonel Cochrane of the 14th
Kentucky, acting brigadier general. They were stationed for a short

time at Mt. Sterling, Kentucky. While there, fifteen negroes owned by notorious and avowed rebels came into Col. Atkins' camp. They were employed as servants by commissioned officers of the regiment. They were free by the terms of the confiscation act, and their employment by the officers of the 92d gave practical force and effect to the law – nothing more. The claimants of the negroes applied to Gen. Gordon Granger for an order directing Col. Atkins to deliver them up. General Granger, being mindful probably that the law forbade that method of determining the status of negroes, issued an order to Col. Atkins, directing him not to let any one, white or black, come within his lines.[1] This did not answer the case of the rebel owners, and accordingly they procured an order from Gen. G., most acceptable to the 92d, sending the regiment away from Mt. Sterling. At Winchester, on the road to Lexington, the citizens threatened, with the aid of the 14th Kentucky to "clean out," the Illinois boys. Col. Atkins accordingly marched through the town with fixed bayonets and loaded guns, and an excellent stomach for the fight. At Lexington the rabble came into the ranks of the 92d and tried to take one of the negroes, belonging to one of the worst secessionists in Kentucky. Col. Atkins went to the rear where the fracas was going on and told them that if they dared to interfere with his march he would fire a volley into them, so help him God! Whereupon they fell back in disorder. The regiment then continued its march toward Nicholasville.

But the negro hunters persevered. Two miles south of Lexington they came into the camp of the 92d with a hat full of documents, of which the following are samples:

ORDER FOR DELIVERY OF PROPERTY – SECTION 231.
Fayette Circuit Court – Order of Delivery,
Emily G. Hood, Plaintiff, *agt.* Smith D. Atkins, Defendant.
The Commonwealth of Kentucky, to the Sheriff of Fayette county: You are commanded to take the slave Henry, of black complexion and 18 years old, in the petition of affidavit mentioned and of the value of $500, from the possession of the defendant, Smith D. Atkins, and deliver him to the plaintiff, Emily G. Hood, upon her giving the bond required by law: and you will make due return of this order on the 1st day of the next February term of the Fayette Circuit Court.
Witness: John B. Norton, Clerk of said Court, this 18th day of November, 1862.
JOHN B. NORTON, C.F.C.C.

SUMMONS – ORDINARY.
The Commonwealth of Kentucky – To the Sheriff of Fayette County, greeting: You are commanded to summon Smith D. Atkins

to answer, on the first day of the next February term of the Fayette Circuit Court, a petition filed against him in said Court, by Emily G. Hood, and warn him that, upon his failure to answer, the petition will be taken for confessed, or he will be proceeded against for contempt, and you will make due return of this summons, on the first day of the next February term of said Court.

Witness: John B. Norton, Clerk of said Court, this 18th day of November, 1862.

JOHN B. NORTON, C.F.C.C.

LEXINGTON, Ky, Nov. 18, 1862.

COLONEL: It is reported to me that a civil process is to be served in your camp, and Judge Robertson requests me to drop you a line, intimating the course I pursue in such cases.

I invariably recognize the civil law in all its operations, as martial law does not exist here in Kentucky.

We have no right to resist the execution of any civil process, and an attempt to do so would render us amenable to the severe laws of this State. I can give you no order, but would, for the good of the cause recommend that the civil authorities be respected always. Your ob't servant.

Q. A. GILLMORE, Brig. Gen.

Col. ATKINS, Present.

To the latter document Col. Atkins made the following satisfactory and sensible reply:

IN CAMP TWO MILES SOUTH OF ⎱
LEXINGTON, Nov. 19th, 1862. ⎰

GENERAL: I have your note. I beg to state that I am under orders to proceed southward with my command, and I do not know at what moment I may find the enemy, and I cannot afford to piddle away my time in hunting up niggers or in replying to bills in chancery filed against me. When the war is over, and I am at leisure, I will answer any civil process, but I beg to assure you, General, that I am now altogether too busy with a terrible rebellion and bloody war, to be fooling away my time in writing answers to bills in chancery filed by secession sympathizers. I have not resisted and do not expect to, for I have not a single nigger in my possession at all, but I cannot stop to answer formally in court. Your ob't serv't.

SMITH D. ATKINS, Colonel.

Q. A. GILLMORE, Brigadier General.

Col. Atkins and the 92d need no defense at our hands. Their services can be had to fight rebels anywhere and at all times, but to return negroes, to rebel masters, never! All they ask is to be put into an Illinois brigade and sent out of Kentucky, where they can see the white of the enemy's eyes. Is it an unreasonable demand?

PD

THE DESTRUCTION OF SLAVERY

Clipping from an unidentified Cleveland, Ohio, newspaper, [Nov.? 1862], enclosed in Brig. Genl. Q. A. Gillmore to Major Gen. Gordon Granger, 11 Dec. 1862, G-1321 1862, Letters Received Relating to Military Discipline & Control, ser. 22, RG 108 [S-47]. General Gordon Granger commanded the Army of Kentucky, and General Quincy A. Gillmore commanded its 2nd division. Because the 92nd Illinois Infantry was in the 3rd division, General Gillmore could merely recommend, not order, Atkins's compliance with the civil process. On November 24, 1862, General Absalom Baird, commander of the 3rd division, informed the lieutenant colonel of the 14th Kentucky Infantry that, according to reports from several citizens, officers of the Kentucky regiment had "combined together in the preparation of a paper commenting upon the official conduct of another officer; that this paper was exhibited to Citizens, and was, from its character, calculated to produce prejudice, if not hostility, on the part of the community, against that regiment [the 92nd Illinois Infantry]; that certain of your officers and men have made, in the hearing of citizens, threats against the other regiment, or its members, and that they have gone into the ranks of this other regiment with arms in their possession, attempting, by violence, or otherwise, to take negros therefrom." Baird denounced these actions as "a military offense second only to mutiny" and ordered the immediate arrest of one Kentucky officer, whose letter to a citizen had come into Baird's hands. (Capt. B. H. Polk to Lt. Col. Geo. W. Gallup, 24 Nov. 1862, vol. 61/79 DMT, pp. 33–34, Letters Sent, ser. 840, 3d Division, Army of Kentucky, Dept. of the OH, RG 393 Pt. 2 No. 15 [C-7000].) The officer was apparently not brought to trial.

1 On November 4, 1862, General Gordon Granger, commander of the Army of Kentucky, had issued a general order that included the following provision: "No citizen nor non-combatant will be permitted within the camps or lines of this army, without special authority to that effect." (General Orders, No. 15, Headquarters Army of Kentucky, 4 Nov. 1862, Orders & Circulars, ser. 44, RG 94 [DD-37].)

202E: Officer in a Kentucky Regiment to the Commander of the Army of Kentucky, and Commander of an Illinois Regiment to the Headquarters of the 3rd Division of the Army of Kentucky

("Paper") [*bluegrass area, Ky. November 24?, 1862*]
I respectfully state to Major General Gordon Granger, that 3 negroes, namely, Lyrus Moley & Henry, belonging to Chas Gilkey (an uncle to the undersigned) were enticed from their owner at Mt Sterling Ky. by soldiers of the 92^d Illinois Regiment also Henry, slave of Mrs B. White, and Charles slave of James McGowan. These negroes and about 30 more are now harbored in said regiment, and the Colonel says he will not give them up, unless, his Captains & Co. agree, as they are entitled to servants. There was also 2 other

negroes belonging to Thos Hill & James Hill's estate, who came back to their Homes— This Regiment is Commanded by Col Smith D. Atkins, and is now within 8 or 10 miles of Lexington, on Winchester Pike. I can give to Genl Granger any reference he may desire as to veracity of statement, and respectfully ask of him if there is anything he can do for owners of said slaves, it will be appreciated, and we soldiers of Kentucky, can have some assurance, that our property is being protected at home, while we are away battling for our loved Country. The above is respectfully submitted to General Granger.

HLcSr

Charles S. Rogers

Nicholasville Ky. Nov. 25 /62.

Sir: In reply to your note of the 24th inst and paper enclosed, I have to report.

That I am not aware that any of the slaves mentioned in the paper, are within my lines at all, but presume they are. There are now I am told fifteen colored persons employed by my Commissioned officers, as servants; no more, I am certain. The McGowan mentioned refused to take a U.S. voucher for oats he had for sale, and I do not think myself nor any of my officers, will spend much time in hunting up a slave for him, without specific orders. I tried at Mt Sterling to adopt a conciliatory course, and on receiving, Maj Genl" Gordon Grangers Genl" order No. 15,[1] turned out of Camp all that were not properly employed as soldiers or servants— no others are now within my regimental lines— Five to Eight hundred colored persons were sent to my regiment on the 8th of November, evidently for the purpose of creating trouble on this .question. At Winchester I was threatened by a mob, and some of the 14th Ky. Infy. tried to take by force, servants from my lines, while marching along. We were compelled to march through the town with bayonets fixed and guns loaded. At Lexington a similar affair took place, and a riot nearly occassioned. I am sued in the civil courts of Kentucky, for part of the slaves mentioned in the paper, although I have not had a thing to do with any of them, since I came into the State. Kentucky soldiers are no more willing to fight for our beloved Country, than the sons, of Illinois, as the History of this war has already demonstrated. Illinois is loyal without conditions, She imposes no "ifs" in her devotion to the Union. Illinois loves the Union, and her volunteer soldiers are in the field to fight for it as Commanded by the Commander In Chief of the Armies of the United States. I have the honor to be Captain Your Very Obt Sevt.

HLcS

Smith D. Atkins

535

Captain Charles S. Rogers to General Granger, [24? Nov. 1862], and Col. Smith D. Atkins to Capt. B. H. Polk, 25 Nov. 1862, both enclosed in Col. Smith D. Atkins to Hon. Owen Lovejoy, 11 Dec. 1862, 37A-E10.4, Committee on Military Affairs, Committee Papers, ser. 465, 37th Congress, RG 233 [D-11]. Endorsements. Rogers served in the 10th Kentucky Cavalry. Atkins commanded the 92nd Illinois Infantry.

1 Issued on November 4, 1862, by General Gordon Granger, commander of the Army of Kentucky, the order required that no non-combatants be permitted within army lines. (See document 202Dn., immediately above.)

202F: Commander of an Illinois Regiment to an Illinois Congressman

Danville, Ky. Dec. 11th 1862.

Sir: I take the liberty of enclosing you copies of [these] interesting documents, and when you are quite at liberty beg a moity of your attention for them

The First in relation to Buzz, a negro boy, who was born free in Ogle County Illinois, and with proper passes started home with a Lieutenant living in Ogle County, who had resigned. On the Cov. & Lex. R.R. he was twice put off, and not at all permitted to go home, and is now within my regiment, and compelled to remain within the regimental lines for fear of a Kentucky jail. This road was repaired and is now run by the U.S. troops, and by them guarded its whole length. Is it right? Must we loyal volunteers submit? Illinois soldiers open and guard the road but her free sons dare not pass over it with the Commanding General's pass.

The Second paper is a complaint on the part of somebody claiming to be a Kentucky soldier made to Genl Granger, because we have as servants the former slaves of Secessionists, and by him refered to Genl Baird, and by him refered to me, and my report on it.

The third is a copy of an "Order" from Col Cochran to me to deliver up a fugitive Slave. I have more of them, but only inclose the one copy. Because I would not obey, his regiment, stationed at Winchester, threatened to fire on my regiment in passing through, and his officers actually did draw revolvers, and bloodshed was only avoided by our bold front and firm determination. I see that Col of the 17th Ky has been dismissed for giving such an order.¹ Why not Col Cochoran?

The third is a copy of proceedings, or rather the original, for I have abundance of them, of a suit against me for negroes employed as servants by my officers. Can I, as a loyal Colonel, stop from the pusuit of rebels to answer formally in court? If not, and defaulted, and Kentucky juries & judges give virdicts, what defense have I when sued on the judgments in Illinois courts? As I understand it *"nul tiel record"* is the only allowable plea, and that would be unavailing. Must then my property in Illinois go to sale to pay for the freedom of these men that the law has made free, and the Presidents order and article of war forbid my sending back to bondage? If so, hard lot for loyal Colonels that have and are offering their lives in the battles of the Union. Bear in mind that if the Illinois boys were not here not a court could be held – our bayonets alone make it possible to hold court, and then we ourselves to become the victims, and that for only obeying the Articles of war, the Orders of the President, and our consciences as men.

I have consulted military men and am told I violate no military rule in writing you such a letter. If Gov ranger will not protect, and refuses to take action, where else am I, as a *citizen soldier* to apply, but to the *people*, through their representatives!

Trusting that I do not trouble you too much, and assuring you that come weal or woe, I am for my country, and hereafter, as heretofore, ready to fight for it, I am Very Respectfully Your Obt Servant

ALS   Smith D. Atkins

Col. Smith D. Atkins to Hon. Owen Lovejoy, 11 Dec. 1862, 37A-E10.4, Committee on Military Affairs, Committee Papers, ser. 465, 37th Congress, RG 233 [D-11]. Enclosed are papers relating to the refusal of a Kentucky railroad to transport John Helms ("Buzz"), an Illinois free black who had been employed as a servant to an officer in Atkins's regiment. The second enclosure, the complaint of a Kentucky soldier to General Gordon Granger, is printed above as document 202E. The third enclosure is a copy of an order from J. C. Cochran, colonel of the 14th Kentucky Infantry and commander of the brigade that included Atkins's 92nd Illinois Infantry. Cochran had instructed Atkins to put outside the lines of his regiment a fugitive slave owned by James Bullard, "a good Union man." Atkins noted on the order that Cochran's regiment "with loaded arms tried to take servants from my lines at Winchester."

1 Colonel John H. McHenry, Jr., commander of the 17th Kentucky Infantry, announced on October 27, 1862, near Newmarket, Kentucky, that any fugitive slave in his regiment "will be delivered to his owner or agent . . ., whether that owner be *loyal* or a *rebel*." When McHenry's order came to the attention of the War Department, General-in-Chief Henry W. Halleck recommended his dismissal from service for violating the article of war that prohibited the use of U.S. forces to return slaves to their masters. McHenry was cashiered on December 4, 1862. (Genl. in Chf. H. W. Halleck to Major Genl. H. G. Wright, 11 Nov.

1862, with endorsements, First Lieut. George W. Gist to Major C. Goddard, 21 Nov. 1862, and General Orders No. 199, War Department Adjutant General's Office, 4 Dec. 1862, all filed as Y-107 1863, Letters Received, ser. 496, Volunteer Service Division, RG 94 [BB-10].)

202G: Commander of an Illinois Regiment to the Secretary of War

Danville, Ky. Dec. 23[d] 1862.

Sir: Some days since I forwarded through regular channel of my superiors statement required by paragraph 1433 army regulations in regard to civil suits.[1] As I am now addressing you direct in obedience to your communication of the 13th inst, I beg also to add a new feature relative to suits against me in Kentucky. The Grand Jury of Montgomery County have found several indictments against me for stealing negroes – Grand Larceny. These negroes came into my camp, said they belonged to the enemies of our country, claimed protection, were employed by Captains & Lieutenants as servants; Col J. C. Cochrain 14th Ky Vols commanding Brigade ordered me to deliver them up – I declined to do so – and find myself proceeded against as a "criminal" in these Kentucky Courts that a few weeks ago could not hold a sitting, and could not now, were it not for the protection of the bayonets the union soldiers wield. I have acted in good faith throughout, trying to do only my duty as a loyal colonel, and I will, of course, expect the government I serve to protect and shield me from these oppressive suits I have the Honor to be Very Resy Your Obt Sert

ALS   Smith D. Atkins

Col. Smith D. Atkins to Hon. E. M. Stanton, 23 Dec. 1862, filed with M-2041 1862, Letters Received, RG 107 [L-19]. No letter to Atkins of December 13 has been found in the records of the Secretary of War.

1 Paragraph 1433 provided: "When an officer is made a party to any action or proceeding in a civil court which may involve the interest of the United States; or when, by the performance of his public duty, he is involved in any action or proceeding in which he claims protection or indemnity from the United States, he shall promptly report the case to the Adjutant-General, to be laid before the Secretary of War." (U.S., War Department, *Revised Regulations for the Army of the United States, 1861* [Philadelphia, 1861], p. 474.)

Kentucky

203: Article from an Ohio Newspaper, Reprinting Letters from a Wisconsin Soldier

[*Cleveland, Ohio late November?, 1862*]

More of Brig. Gen. Gilmore's Doings.

We gave extracts lately from Brig. Gen. Gilmore's orders in Kentucky, by which he made the Union Army under his command slave-catchers.[1] By a letter we find in the Milwaukee Sentinel, which letter is dated, "In Camp Near Nickolsville, Ky., Nov. 14th," we see the General is determined to carry out his inhuman mandate, and that officers under him who refuse to turn nigger drivers and slave catchers are made to suffer.

Brig. Gen. Gilmore was appointed to West Point from Lorain County, where his relatives still reside.

But to the letter, which in speaking of the Wisconsin 22d, says:

Col. Utley is a jewel. He is the first and only Colonel who has met the great Ethiopion Lion boldly in his own den, confronted and bearded him. You will remember it was he who refused to obey the order of Gen. Gilmore, requiring him to give up certain slaves to their owner, who had taken refuge in his camp. When the brigade was about to leave Georgetown, Gen. Gilmore, aware that an intense feeling had been excited against the 22d in consequence of Col. Utley's refusal to render up the fugitives, ordered his regiment to remain behind, as if he desired that whatever wrath was to be showered upon the brigade, should be centered where it belonged — upon the 22d Wisconsin. As the brigade was passing through Georgetown, the mob assailed it with revolvers, stones, and whatever missiles they could lay their hands to, demanding the negroes they had with them. Like whipped dogs they cowed and yielded to the mob those human beings who had sought protection within their lines. When Col. Utley started the next day the citizens told him he never would be permitted to leave the city with the negroes he had with him. He ordered his regiment to load their guns and fix bayonets, then advised the citizens that if they intended any hostile demonstrations upon him, as was shown to the other regiments the day previous, to clear the city of women and children, for, as sure as there was a God above, he would shoot down every man who interfered with him, and lay their town in ashes. The result was, as might be expected, he marched through the city with flying colors, led by that splendid regimental band of his, and no man dared to oppose him. So much for being a *man*, God bless him!

About ten days ago, during the recent snow storm that visited this region, a little dwarf negro came into Col. Utley's camp, who said he had concealed himself in the woods and lived on acorns for a week; that he had sought protection in other regiments, but they told him that the Generals had ordered them to return all negroes who came to them, and they could not take him. At last he found his way to this regiment, where he has since remained.

To-day Judge Robinson visited the camp, riding in a fine carriage, and called for the Colonel. He informed the Colonel that he had a slave in his camp, and inquired if he would deliver him up. The Colonel replied: "No, sir, I will not deliver him up, but if he is your boy, and is willing to return to you, I will not oppose it." They then proceeded to Company A, in whose charge the boy was. The Colonel found the boy secreted in one of the tents. He asked him if he ran away from Judge Robinson, and if so, what for? He replied that he was the Judge's boy; that the Judge had been in the habit of hiring him out ever since he was five years old; that for the last year he had hired him to an Irishman for fifty dollars, who had beat, bruised and maltreated him in a shameful manner, until he had rather die than endure it any longer. The Irishman's excuse was, that the Judge had cheated him, in representing that the boy was larger than he was, and he swore he would have the value of his money if he had to take his blood. The boy further stated that he had repeatedly told his master that he could not endure the treatment he was receiving – whose only reply was, "go back, you dog."

Col. Utley returned to the Judge and related the boy's story, and asked him if he supposed he was going to deliver that little innocent boy, who had been dwarfed in body and mind, to an inhuman aristocratic bloat, who has grown fat on the labors and sweat he had robbed from him.

The Judge said:

"You can't believe him; 'niggers will lie.' "

The boy was then brought out, who manfully met the tyrant with "good mornin', massa," and shook hands with him. He then confronted him with the same story he had told the Colonel, and added: "Massa, you know it is so."

The Judge did not deny it, but said:

"Yes, but didn't I tell you I would take you away?"

"Yes, massa," said the boy *"but you never did."*

The Judge then inquired of the Colonel if he would deliver him up.

"No," the Colonel replied, "but if he is willing to go he may."

When asked if he was willing to go back with his master, the boy said "no."

The Judge then threw himself back on his dignity, and informed Col. Utley that he (the Judge) was "some punkins;" that he was the only man living who voted for the Missouri compromise; that he had written able and eloquent articles on the subject of emancipation, which Abe Lincoln had sent for; that he didn't like slavery, but if this is the way the Union army and the administration are going to trample their rights under their feet, there would not be a Union man left in Kentucky, and the Union never could be restored.

Col. Utley told him "he never had much confidence in the loyalty of Kentucky, but he and thousands of his fellow countrymen had left their families, their homes and their business, and periled their lives and their happiness to protect him and his neighbors from the lawless ravages of robbers and murderers. That but a few days since the county was overrun by Kirby Smith and Morgan, who stole in this immediate vicinity over $160,000 worth of horses, without pay or reward; they robbed your cornfields and your granaries, they drove off your cattle and your hogs, and helped themselves without stint to everything a hungry, ragged and destitute horde of barbarians could desire, and you howled and groaned with patriotic loyalty and unfeigned Unionism, until you induced the government to send us here to protect you. And what is our reward? Have we lived upon you? Yes, at the rate of two dollars per bushel for potatoes, seventy-five cents for a chicken, half a dollar a pound for butter, under Kentucky Generals, who have issued orders that we shall be severely punished for taking a mouthful of food from a citizen when presented to us, and even I was ordered to march two of my boys in front of my regiment, to the tune of the Rogue's March, for taking a few apples from an orchard with the consent of the owner, and to cap the climax, have ordered us, in violation of the proclamation of the President, to act as nigger-catchers for you. Judge Robinson, we from Wisconsin did not leave our happy homes for any such purpose. You talk to us about being 'nigger-stealers!' Look at that boy! Is he your *slave?* Havn't you grown fat, rich and aristocratic upon the sweat and labor you have stolen from him? The same God made him that made you, and endowed him with the same natural rights to life, liberty and the pursuit of happiness that you possess, and if Kentucky's loyalty and unionism depends upon my willingness to be converted into a negro hunter for her bloated, aristocratic Union hypocrites, she may go to hell, with all the nations that forget God. That little boy, whose life blood you have fattened upon, dwarfed by your inhumanity, looms up before me, in my estimation, and I believe in the estimation of God and angels, as much above his master as heaven is above hell."

If that old tyrant had not become brutalized, he could never have stood up under the withering looks of the officers and men who witnessed this scene.

"Sir," said the Colonel, "do you think you will take that boy?"

The shout that went up from a thousand soldiers, told him plainly that it would not be safe for him to undertake it. Such a scene is seldom witnessed on earth. No person can describe it, – no painter can do it justice. That poor little dwarfed slave rose to the dignity of a man and overwhelmed his rapacious master with his native eloquence. I cannot do justice to Col. Utley in attempting to repeat his truly eloquent and scathing speech. It was high-toned, eloquent, and from the heart, so low down that every word was a minnie ball to the old tyrant's feelings. In about two hours after this scene transpired, Col. Utley was ordered to report himself forthwith to Gen. Coburn, commanding the Brigade. Gen. C. told him that the

Army of Kentucky was peculiarly situated among a people well disposed but jealous of their rights, and for the sake of peace and harmony, he had better obey the order of Gen. Gilmore, and return the fugitives. That notwithstanding the proclamation of the President, he regarded the status of slavery in Kentucky the same, and entitled to the same rights and privileges as though no army was here.

Col. Utley replied "that although an inferior officer, he begged to differ with him, and that he regarded the status of the *army* the same in Kentucky, and entitled to the same rights and privileges as though no slavery existed here." He further said, "Sir, I am aware that Kentucky has resorted to the most powerful means to seduce the officers of the Union Army, to adopt her policy of ignoring the laws of Congress and the order of the Commander-in-Chief. All that handsome women, fine carriages, sumptuous dinners, virgin wine, and great men could do, has been done to lay me under obligations to their policy, but my honor as a gentleman and a soldier, has so far deterred me from yielding. I stand alone. Every other officer has yielded, and it reminds me of a speech once made in Congress by Senator Sumner, when he said that slavery reminded him of the fabled mountain in Arabia, whose attraction was so great that it drew all the bolts out of every ship that sailed by, and the vessel went to pieces. So it is here. Slavery in Kentucky has, by her wily machinations, drawn the bolts out of every commanding officer, and in the estimation of every true man, he has gone to pieces. But I want you to understand, General and Judge Robinson, that God Almighty has put heads on both ends of the bolt that holds me together, which slavery can never draw out as long as soul and body hang together."

When he had finished, the Judge took him by the hand, and with tears in his eyes, he said:

"Colonel, don't regard this as a personal matter. I admire you for your frankness and honesty. It is a momentous question that is bound to shake Kentucky to the centre, and must be settled. I have two remedies, one civil and the other military. Which I shall resort to, I cannot tell."

I have given nearly the exact conversation as it occurred. Col. Utley has been threatened with assassination, and as he is resolved to adhere to the Proclamation, and his Kentucky Generals as firmly resolved to ignore it, I apprehend trouble ahead.

CAMP NEAR NICKOLSVILLE, KY.,⎱
November 18, 1862.⎰

Messrs. Editors:— Since I wrote you last, Col. Utley has been indicted on complaint of Judge Robeinson, and a warrant issued for his arrest, the letters of instructions to the Sheriff of Jessamine Co., accompanying the warrant, ordering him to arrest the Colonel and hold him to bail in the sum of $2,000, in defaulting which, to lodge him in the Lexington jail. Also, take the writ of replevin

Kentucky

accompanying the warrant and serve it on the Colonel, and if he refused to deliver up the boy, go to General Baird, and demand a *posse comitatus* to go and take him forcibly, which demand the General would not dare to disobey. These papers were shown to Gen. Baird last evening, and he immediately notified Col. Utley of the fact. I designed to leave for Frankfort this morning, but remained at the request of the Colonel, to see the end of the matter. The camp this morning is all excitement. The guard have been instructed to admit no citizen unless their business is known, and then only one at a time.

I think Judge Robeinson will have a happy time in getting his boy from the Twenty-second, or in arresting the Colonel. The boys came here to fight, and they will not meet a foe during the whole campaign they will fight with a better relish than these Kentucky Union hypocrites. I see this trouble is brought upon Colonel Utley by pretended Union men, by Judge Robeinson, Chief Justice, who declares he is the most loyal man in Kentucky, and at the same time says the President's proclamation is unconstitutional and not binding, and never will, or can be enforced in Kentucky. To this policy General Wright, Gen. Gilmore, and, in fact, all the Kentucky Generals, are firmly committed. No man who has not been here, and seen, felt and heard, has the least idea what Kentucky loyalty is. It is just this: they are loyal, not from motives of patriotism or because they love the Union, but because loyalty, in their estimation, will protect their property. The most loyal men in Kentucky will tell you, that if the President's proclamation and the laws of Congress are enforced, there will not be found a loyal man in the State. We are in the heart of the State, in the old Blue Grass region; the home of Daniel Boone, Henry Clay, John C. Breckinridge, and John Morgan. Still you may travel a whole day and not find one man in one hundred who has ever been beyond the limits of his township or county. Daily papers are seldom if ever seen. No schools – and no intercourse with the world or other parts of the nation. How can we expect such a people to be patriotic beyond the narrow confines of their own selfish interests?

PD

Clipping from the Cleveland *Daily Herald* [late Nov.?, 1862], enclosed in Brig. Genl. Q. A. Gillmore to Major Gen. Gordon Granger, 11 Dec. 1862, G-1321 1862, Letters Received Relating to Military Discipline & Control, ser. 22, RG 108 [S-47]. George Robertson, the slaveholder whose name was variously misspelled, had been chief justice of the Kentucky Court of Appeals from 1829 to 1843, and in 1864 would assume that office again. Colonel Utley and Judge Robertson both submitted their cases to President Lincoln. On November 17, 1862, Utley summarized the facts as he saw them and appealed for protection against legal harassment for "simply standing by the Constitution, obeying the laws of Congress and honoring the Proclamation . . . issued on the 23d day of

September last." (Abraham Lincoln, *Collected Works*, ed. Roy P. Basler et al., 9 vols. [New Brunswick, N.J., 1953–1955], vol. 5, pp. 512–13n.) Two days later, Robertson warned Lincoln by telegraph that "[t]he Conduct of a few of the Officers of the army in forcibly detaining the Slaves of union Kentuckians may provoke a conflict between Citizens & Soldiers," while failing to mention his personal involvement in the matter. Robertson asked Lincoln "to prevent such a Catastrophy" by ordering "that military force will not be permitted for the detention any more than for the restoration of such property, & especially in resistance & contempt of the legal process of a Civil tribunal." (G. Robertson to President Lincoln, 19 Nov. 1862, Telegrams Addressed to the President, Telegrams Collected by the Office of the Secretary of War [Bound], RG 107 [L-217].) In a reply to Robertson dated November 20, which was evidently never sent, Lincoln indicated his growing impatience with the constant bawling of unionist slaveholders. After suggesting a comparison between Robertson and a suspected Revolutionary War Tory, Lincoln crisply refused to issue any order that would return fugitive slaves: "Do you not know that I may as well surrender this contest, directly, as to make any order, the obvious purpose of which would be to return fugitive slaves?" Perhaps deeming his initial reaction injudicious, Lincoln penned a less indicting response on November 26. There remained, however, a hint of exasperation in Lincoln's proposal to settle the whole affair by personally paying Robertson up to $500 as compensation for freeing the slave in Utley's camp. Robertson indignantly rejected the President's offer, contending that his object in suing Utley was "far from mercenary – it was solely to try the question whether the civil or the military power is Constitutionally supreme in Kentucky," but also boasting that he could easily obtain judgment for at least $1,000 in the civil suit he had initiated against Utley. Robertson proved nearly correct. In 1871, he obtained judgment against Utley in the U.S. Circuit Court for the Eastern District of Wisconsin in the amount of $908.06, plus costs. Congress came to Utley's relief in 1873, adopting legislation that provided for payment of the judgment from the federal treasury. (Lincoln, *Collected Works*, vol. 5, pp. 502, 512, 514n.)

1 For the order regarding fugitive slaves issued by General Quincy A. Gillmore on October 22, 1862, see below, doc. 207.

204: Commander of the Army of Kentucky to the Commander of the Department of the Ohio

Lexington Ky. Nov. 18th 1862.

General; I am daily annoyed and harassed by the many complaints made to me by Union men of this part of Kentucky, of the abduction of their negroes, by officers and men in this army. There is no doubt but that it has been carried on to a very great extent. We have officers in some of the regiments now stationed near this city, who have so far forgotten their duties as soldiers, as to confine their exertions almost entirely to seducing negroes from their homes into their camps; nor are they particular as to whom these negroes belong; the friends of the Government suffer such losses as much, if not more, than others. It was but this morning that complaints were made by men of the 10th Ky. Cavalry, to the effect that while they were fighting to protect their property, under the constitution and laws of the country, some of the men in other regiments of their own Army, were taking and secreting such property from them. Many of the camps are being crowded with worthless negroes, interfering with the proper exercise of military duty, and, in fact, greatly demoralizing the men. Already a Colonel of one of our Regiments has been indicted under the laws of Kentucky, for abduction of negroes. In some cases where loyal citizens, who have had proper permission to do so, have endeavored to look for their negroes, they have been disgracefully treated by officers and men, who had secreted their negroes, and directly refused to put them out of their camps. Such action of officers of our army, not only tends greatly to demoralize it, but gives the greatest discouragement to our friends and supporters, many of whom had most of their negroes stolen by the armies of Kirby Smith and Bragg — I am very desirous that you will lay down some policy by which I may be guided in this matter. Something ought to be done immediately. Very respctly yours,

HLS

G Granger

Maj. Gen. G. Granger to General, 18 Nov. 1862, G-93 1862, Letters Received, ser. 3514, Dept. of the OH, RG 393 Pt. 1 [C-4601]. General Horatio G. Wright, commander of the Department of the Ohio, was unwilling to venture onto the treacherous terrain of Kentucky slavery without first seeking the advice of his superiors. On November 23, he telegraphed General-in-Chief Henry W. Halleck, summarizing Granger's report "that he is much harassed by complaints of Union men in Kentucky of the abduction of their slaves by officers and men of his army [and] that many of the camps are crowded with worthless negroes, to the great demoralization of the troops," and forwarding Granger's request "that some definite policy be laid down for his guidance." Wright, who considered the army's involvement with fugitive slaves in a loyal state "embarrassing," proposed "an order prohibiting the residence within camp or garrison limits of persons not belonging to the military service, and that all authorized civil processes shall be served within such limits, without obstruction on the part of the officers and men." If Wright hoped for either explicit instructions or a general indication of whether his proposed order met with the approval of the War Department, he was no doubt disappointed by Halleck's evasive telegram of the following day: "In regard to treatment of fugitive slaves, I respectfully refer you to the law of Congress of last session, the President's proclamation, and the printed orders of the War Department." (*Official Records*, ser. 1, vol. 20, pt. 2, p. 91.) For an example of complaints by members of the 10th Kentucky Cavalry that their slaves were being harbored by soldiers in Northern regiments, see above, doc. 202E.

205: Commander of a Kentucky Regiment to the President

Louisville, Nov 27th *1862*

Mr President. I deem it my privilege as a Citizen to make the following Complaint directly to you. While I have been absent from my home serving our Country in the field to the utmost of my humble ability, I have not only suffered large pecuniary loss from rebel depredations but worse still, federal officers, particularly those of the 18th Michigan Infantry Volunteers have taken within their lines and hold the negroes of my loyal neighbours and myself. That regiment has now not less than twenty five negroes in Camp at Lexington Ky, who belong to loyal union men who have been masters for loyalty's sake, and among the rest one of mine. I called upon the officer Commanding the regiment and mildly remonstrated against this injustice, particularly to myself, and requested him to have my negro turned out of his lines, which he flatly refused to do, justifying his detention by virtue of Your proclamation and the new article of war. My father-in-law, Col E. N. Offutt had in the mean time, during my absence, as the best means of recovering my slave which they refused him permission to take, issued a writ of replevin for the negro which was duly served by the Sheriff of Fayette County – but was disobeyed by the officer and the Civil authorities defied. Another fact I should mention in this Connection, which is, that our negroes are being taught by the abolition officers from Michigan and other northern states now serving in Kentucky, that on the first day of January next, they are all to be free, and will have a right even to kill their masters who may attempt to restrain them, which has aroused a lively apprehension in the minds of Citizens in Central Kentucky of a servile insurrection at that time unless prevented by such orders as will check the evil – This is neither slander upon those officers or idle rumor; but a fact for which I and hundreds of citizens can vouch. Mr President I deem it unnecessary to resort to argument to show to you the magnitude of the injustice in this case to me – When I became a soldier I sacrifised a large and lucrative practice as an attorney in Philadelphia and placed my property in this state at the mercy of our enemies – who have revenged themselves largely upon me – and now my utter ruin is to be Completed by our own officers to promote a fanatical partizan theory – which not only ignores gratitude as a principle; but does me and many loyal men of my state bold wrong for a supposed benefit to another race. Mr President is this right and will you sanction it? While in opinion I must dissent from your policy of *freeing* the slaves of rebels, which would result in great wrong to loyal slave owners, as well as to all loyal men burthened with this immense war debt – I approve of the *Confiscation* of the slaves and all property of rebels to weaken the resources of our enemy and relieve the tax burthen of our friends. Being a soldier whether palatable or impalatable, I am always ready to execute the orders of the President as my Commander in Chief; but Mr President were I Commander in Chief I would never trample upon the Constitutional rights of a loyal people in a loyal state whereby our friends would be estranged and our enemies advantaged   I need not reassure you sir of my abiding faith in your goodness, integrity of purpose and sense of justice of which this appeal is the evidence   I have the Honor to be Your Ob^t Servt

ALS   M Mundy

Col. M. Mundy to His Excellency Abraham Lincoln, 27 Nov. 1862, M-2159 1862, Letters Received, RG 107 [L-135]. On letterhead stationery of the District of Western Kentucky. Mundy commanded the 23rd Kentucky Infantry. File notations suggest that President Lincoln or an assistant referred Mundy's letter to the Secretary of War, but no indication of a reply has been located in the index of letters sent by the secretary.

206: New York Republican to the Secretary of State, Enclosing a Letter and an Order from the Commander of the District of Western Kentucky

Syracuse [N.Y.] Dec 5. 1862

My Dear Sir   I have just returned from a visit of about two weeks to the west, a part of which time I spent in Kentucky.

In this State (Ky) I found every thing very much unsettled. Designing men on both sides have attempted to create a false impression among the ignorant people as to the real effect of the Presidents Proclamation, and except in intelligent circles it is represeted as bringing freedom to every slave there on the 1st day of January next.

Gen Boyle at Louisville says that some of our Union officers & men from Indiana & Michigan have behaved very improperly on the negro question by enticing away the property slaves of loyal men, which course has produced a great deal of irritation as a natural result. Loyal men have been forbidden to seek their slaves in camps & some times collisions between citizens & soldiers have been most

imminet   Boyle telegraphed twice to Washington, to the Prest &
Secy of War for instructions & in the absence of any answer issued
an order a copy of which I have just recd from him & enclose you.

He says that under this order all slaves are sent to the rear of our
lines, but that some of our northern officers will not obey orders &
will not abstain from an active interferece with slaves.

When I left Louisville he very much feared that armed collision
might arise.

I am convinced as matters now stand that the preservation of
Kentucky demands a consiliatory course toward her loyal
citizens   They are willing to suffer for the cause of the Union, but
they do not wish to be injured by those who should protect them.

I see difficulty on every hand, but I think the wise course is to
receive counsel from the true men of that State.

Boyle is a loyal & true man, ready to sacrifice his slaves & all else
for his country, but he must be sustained by or at least advised by
the authorities at Washington.

I think him one of the best men in Kentucky.

You will find also enclosed one of his letters in which his views
are stated.

If they can be of service please use the letter or its statements as
you may deem best   I pray that the wisest counsels may prevail to
save our country & the civilization which has grown up under its
glorious institutions from the disasters which menace their
being   Very Truly Yours

Tho⁵ T Davis

Gen Boyle will be very grateful for any advice you may give him or
any which you can furnish him from the other departments.
T. T D.

ALS

[*Enclosure*]   *Louisville,* Dec 1ˢᵗ *1862*
My Mʳ Davis   I recd your kind note written on your departure and
regretted I did not have pleasure of seeing you again.   I was "*sorry*"
too that you hurried off so that you missed my present –   Mʳ
Crocker promised to take it, and I forgot to send it to him in
time.   I will endeavor to contrive to Syracuse some way –

I enclose you the General Order No 2 issued by me –   You will
see that it does no conflict with or infringe the new Article of
War –   I wish you would examine the Article of War and the order
and give me your opinion on the subject –

I regard this order as most important to Kentucky just now –   If
I can enforce it, or rather if it, could be enforced, throughout the

state, it will give us peace and order   Troubles threaten in Ky by reason of the interference of troops with the slaves— In my opinion this interference is doing us great harm, and doing the cause of emancipation real harm— If this matter were left to me I could manage it, and accomplish more toward peaceable and just emancipation, than can possibly be accomplished by any other policy— There is danger of bringing the state, unwilling as she is to be placed in such position, into collision with the federal troops and the federal Government— Such a calamity would be disastrous, and in [. . .] would cost the government more than the value of all the slaves. I trust to heaven that wise counsels and a wise and prudent policy will be adopted for action in Kentucky. I trust the Government will not do anything "to alienate a loyalty that has proved true amid fire and blood" Kentucky has vindicated her loyalty in the fiery ordeal of battle— I would make no invidious comparisons, but I am sure that no state in the Union contributed more to the national glory on the field of Shiloh than Kentucky— I am most anxious that a just and prudent policy may prevail in administration of affairs in Kentucky and knowing how conservative you have always been, though a Republican I invoke your influence with your friends for a conservative and just policy, and especially for such policy as will not result in collision of state and federal forces and authority. I shall do my whole duty as I understand it, and shall be satisfied with approval my own [conscience] and judgment—

I will be glad to hear from you in reply to this hurried note. I am Sincerely & Truly Your Friend

ALS   J. T. Boyle

[*Enclosure*]   LOUISVILLE, November 27, 1862.
GENERAL ORDERS NO. 2.

I. All commanding officers serving in this District are ordered not to permit negro slaves to enter the camps; and all officers and privates are forbidden to interfere or intermeddle with slaves in any way.

II. All slaves within camps will be placed beyond the guard lines, and not be permitted to return.

III. All officers neglecting to enforce these orders and all enlisted men violating them are required to be reported to these Head-Quarters, that they may be dealt with and reported to the proper authorities.

By command of BRIGADIER GENERAL BOYLE.

PD

Thos. T. Davis to Hon. Wm. H. Seward, 5 Dec. 1862, enclosing J. T. Boyle to T. T. Davis, Esq., 1 Dec. 1862, and General Orders No. 2, Head-Quarters District of Western Kentucky, 27 Nov. 1862, D-1128 1862, Letters Received, RG 107 [L-24]. One of the complaints received by General Boyle about the interference of Northern troops with Kentucky slaves had been that of John D. Brent, a slaveholder and former captain in the Louisville Legion. Brent had written on November 28, 1862, "in the midst of excitement" at Munfordville, Kentucky, charging that "our citazens have been plundered and the laws of our State are dayly trampled under foot." In a recent "outrage," Northern soldiers had released "at the point of the Bayonett" three slaves who had been jailed as fugitives in accordance with state law. In addition, Brent protested, loyal Kentuckians who tried to recapture their fugitive slaves were refused admission into the camps of the Northern regiments, even when they cited the provisions of Boyle's newly issued order. "There is not So far as I know a single union man in all this country," concluded Brent, "but would prefer having the Rebals here to having the men that are now here." Brent's letter was referred to the commanders of the Illinois, Indiana, and Michigan units whose conduct he had maligned. By then stationed in Tennessee, they denied Brent's charges of plundering and outrage, and denounced him as "one of these gentlemen" whose "loyalty is conditioned upon the 'Negro', and who is now actively plotting a counter Revolution upon the Negro issue." They noted that the blacks arrested by the sheriff and subsequently released from jail were officers' servants who "had been taken up . . . at or near Perryville and had been steadily in their employ since the battle." (John D. Brent to Friend Semple, 28 Nov. 1862, B-57 1862, Letters Received, ser. 925, Dept. of the Cumberland, RG 393 Pt. 1 [C-2]; Col. A. S. Hall to Lieut. Alex A. Rice, 12 Dec. [1862], Colonel Thos. G. Allen to Col. A. S. Hall, 13 Dec. 1862, Col. James Monroe to Col. A. S. Hall, 13 Dec. [1862], Col. Wm. Garver to Col. A. S. Hall, 13 Dec. 1862, Capt. S. J. Harris to Col. A. S. Hall, 13 Dec. 1862, and Capt. B. P. Wells to Col. A. S. Hall, 14 Dec. 1862, all filed with B-36 1862, Letters Received, ser. 925, Dept. of the Cumberland, RG 393 Pt. 1 [C-2].)

207: Commander of the 2nd Division of the Army of Kentucky to the Commander of the Army of Kentucky, Enclosing an Order by the Former and a Letter to a Citizen of Ohio

near Lexington Ky. Dec 11th 1862

Sir I have never, until now, felt disposed to take notice of attacks in the public press, upon my offical conduct.

My course in regard to "Contrabands", which no dispassionate man can regard otherwise than as mild, just to the soldier, eminently politic, and strictly in conformity to law and orders as well as custom, and which has not only received your reiterated verbal approval, but is simply the enforcement of your positive orders on the subject, has been made the object of the most infamous misrepresentation and abuse, which have culminated, I am informed, in unscrupulous efforts to injure me with the authorities at Washington. The volumes of falsehood contained in the newspaper articles which I enclose, are releived only by a very few stinted grains of truth. The charges against me of nigger catching, and of returning slaves to their owners or agents, have not the slightest foundation in fact, as the writers must or might have known at the time.

I have never, that I know of, by any order of mine, hindered any slave of his liberty in any way shape or form, and do not remember to have ordered but one to be sent beyond the lines.

I have advocated and recommended no resistance to the civil authorities, in the exercise of their legitimate functions, within the loyal State of Kentucky, for the reason that martial Law, except in its limited application in arresting disloyal persons, does not exist here.

The object of my contraband order, herewith enclosed, is shown upon its face. It was to avoid any further accession of that class of persons, male or female, and to provide suitable employment, under proper restraints, for those "now within the lines or that may hereafter in any way gain access thereto."

I am most happy to be able to assure you that the order works admirably, that there are very few in my command who do not cordially endorse, although quite a number originally opposed it, that the colored people are leaving daily, either voluntarily or by reason of being thrown out of employment, and that I anticipate no trouble, and but a few individual cases of difference of opinion on this subject.

I enclose duplicate of the only letter I have written in reply to the newspaper misrepresentations of my course, and request that this communication with all its enclosures be forwarded to the General-in-Chief through the Department Commander. I have the honor to be Very Respectfully Your Obt. Servant

HLS   Q. A. Gillmore

[*Enclosure*]   GEORGETOWN, KY., October 22d, 1862.
GENERAL ORDERS, No. 9. The practice indulged in by some of the officers and men of this Division, of enticing colored people within the lines, is becoming an evil of such magnitude as to demand the immediate and rigorous application of a remedy.

It is demoralizing to an army to be encumbered with

non-combatant hangers-on of any kind or class, and they will not be allowed in this Division, except under such restrictions as will place them within direct and entire control from these Head Quarters.

It is especially made the duty of guards and pickets, and of brigade and regimental commanders to refuse admission within the lines to that class of people known as "contrabands."

All those now within the lines or that may hereafter in any way gain access thereto, will at once be taken in charge by the division Quartermaster and reported to these Head Quarters, for such action thereon as may be deemed expedient. By order of BRIGADIER GENERAL Q. A. GILLMORE,

PD

[*Enclosure*]   Lexington Ky. Dec' 2nd 1862
My Dear Sir   I am in receipt of your note of the 26th ulto: enclosing Sundry slips from Cleveland news-papers, in which the writers condemn in unmeasured terms my course, as they understand it, in regard to "contrabands". I am certain they do not fully appreciate the subject. I am convinced, and one weeks sojourn here would thoroughly convince them, that the policy which they condemn, slightly modified perhaps, is the only one adapted to the loyal state of Kentucky.

The writers seem to forget that Kentucky *is* loyal, that she has now, and always has had a full representation in Congress, that consequently we are not in the enemy's country, that martial law does not exist here, and that the civil authorities are in the full exercise and enjoyment of their legitimate functions, the same as they are in the state of Ohio, or any other loyal state.

They contrast, unfavorably to myself, my order and Gen: Grant's on this subject, ignoring the fact which contains the gist of the whole matter, that Mississippi and Tennessee where Gen: Grant is operating, are in persistent rebelion by their own deliberate acts while Kentucky is true to her allegiance.

Force of circumstances has made me an unwilling and reluctant actor on this question; my education and profession make me, I trust, an unprejudiced one. – While I regret that a course which is demanded of me by the positive orders of my military Superiors, and which my own judgement dictates as eminently proper, should not meet the approval of my former friends, I congratulate myself that I am not yet, and never have been, placed in a position where I could be swerved from a plain and evident line of duty, by any political party or organization sitting in judgement on my actions. – As a soldier I have schooled myself to ignore such things. – My desire in these trying times is, to serve my country to the best of my ability, obeying the orders of my military superiors according to the rules and articles of war. –

I have never returned a slave to any claimant loyal or disloyal, and never will. – I will not even turn them out of my lines if I know or suspect the owners or their agents are in waiting to seize them. – Such a course would be not only a violation of the spirit of the law, but repugnant to my own feelings. – But while I am unwilling that any of my troops should become *slave catchers*, I consider it my sworn duty to see that they do not contract the demoralizing habit of indiscriminate appropriation of private property, particularly slave property, in the loyal state and among the loyal people of Kentucky. They are not here for that purpose. –

I claim the right, under existing laws and orders, and the usage and custom of war, to exercise entire military control over all non-combatants within my lines, whether clerks, teamsters, or servants, regardless of their color or social position. – Any compulsory restriction of that right in the field would ruin any army, but especially a union army in a slave state, and convert it into an ungovernable and licentious mob. – If I have no right to keep contrabands beyond my lines it is my duty to harbor them; and if bound to receive one, I am equally bound to receive thousands without regard to sex, until every soldier, restrained only by individual caprice or lust, would have with him a negro man or a negro woman, and this colossal and debauching abuse would find its only practical limit in satiety. – What honor could such an army expect to reap on the field of battle! – What punishment would be too severe for the commander who would prostitute it to such ignoble ends.

Aside from considerations of professional utility and propriety, I have no feeling in this matter. It is not my aim to harm the negro, or specially to serve the master, but to serve and save from debasing vices the gallant soldiers intrusted to my care, and prepare them for the honors and dangers of the day of battle. – I claim to be a philanthropist, and shall rejoice to see every slave free in a legal and constitutional way, at the proper time and in the proper manner. – But it is not my duty in Kentucky to free them, and would not be if I held supreme command here, and I do not intend to become their custodian, to the demoralization of my command. When ordered to do so I will discharge the duty to the best of my ability. – Until then I shall exercise at my discretion, under restrictions from superior authority, the right to send them away whenever they become a serious impediment to the discipline and efficiency of my command. – Nothing short of this would satisfy my convictions of the duty I owe my country, or free me from the charge of incompetency and neglect.

Please excuse the blunt and unfinished manner in which, for want of time, I am compelled to express my opinions and believe me— Respectfully Your obdt. Servant

HLcS   Q. A. Gillmore

[*Endorsement*] Head Q^{rs} Army of Ky Lexington [*Ky.*] Dec 11th 1862 Resp^y forwarded. I regard Genl Gillmore's order a proper one, demanded by the Circumstances, mild in its application to the Negroes, just & protective to Soldiers, eminently politic & fully justified by law orders & the usages of war. It & his course thereon not only met & now meets my fullest approval, but was required by my positive orders to him on the Subject. G Granger Maj Genl Comd'g

[*Endorsement*] Head Q^{rs} Dept of the Ohio Cin. O. Dec 12th 1862 Respectfully forwarded to the Genl-in Chief of the Army, as desired by Brig Genl Gillmore with my full approval of the course of the latter in the delicate matter involved.

It is but just to Genl Gillmore as well as myself that I should say that on learning that there were apprehensions of serious troubles between our troops and the citizens of Ky in consequence of the camps becoming asylums for negroes belonging to loyal citizens in their neighborhoods, I visited Lexington partly in reference to this matter, with the intention of issuing an order prohibiting the remaining in camps in Ky of persons not connected with the military service; thus freeing the mil^y authorities from all connection with the slavery question, and what was equally important, preventing our camps from being overrun with worthless persons to the great detriment of the discipline and instruction of the troops Such an order I believed not to be in violation of the letter or spirit of any law of Congress, to be demanded by the best interests of the service, and to be in accordance with sound policy toward a recognized and professedly loyal state. Finding on my arrival, however, that such orders had been issued already by commanders of troops, I took no action in the matter. I believe the policy indicated in such orders to have been thusfar successful, and that in a short time both the people of Ky and the troops will be entirely satisfied of its propriety and justice. H. G. Wright Maj Genl Com^{dg}

Brig. Genl. Q. A. Gillmore to Major Gen. Gordon Granger, 11 Dec. 1862, enclosing General Orders, No. 9, Head Quarters 2d Division, Army of Kentucky, 22 Oct. 1862, and Brig. Genl. Q. A. Gillmore to M. R. Keith, Esqr., 2 Dec. 1862, G-1321 1862, Letters Received Relating to Military Discipline & Control, ser. 22, RG 108 [S-47]. Also enclosed are six articles clipped from Cleveland, Ohio, newspapers, which described conflicts between Northern regiments and Kentucky soldiers and citizens on the question of fugitive slaves. One of the articles, dated November 21, 1862, quoted with outrage a Lexington, Kentucky, newspaper that had praised Gillmore's policy and assured slaveholders "of WHATEVER PERSUASION" that under Gillmore's orders, *"Negroes will be driven from the lines of Union armies whenever they may enter them."* Another (undated) labeled Gillmore a "pro-slavery blood-hound" whose orders violated the law prohibiting the use of Union forces to return fugitive slaves to their masters. For two more of the enclosed clippings, see above, docs. 202D and 203. Well before the appearance of these newspaper articles, General Gillmore had defended his fugitive slave policy in terms similar to those employed in his letter to the Ohio citizen. At the end of October 1862, the commander of a Michigan regiment had objected to Gillmore's order, protesting that he could not allow himself or his men "to be degraded to the level of slave catchers." In reply, Gillmore had agreed that it was both illegal and distasteful "to return fugitives . . . to persons claiming to be their owners, or [to put] them outside the lines when I knew the claimants were waiting there to seize them." "But," Gillmore had insisted, "I would spurn as equally abhorrent and repulsive the idea of having any portion of my command degraded to the level of slave stealers in the loyal State, and surrounded by the loyal people of Kentucky." (Brig. Gen. Q. A. Gillmore to Col. M. Wisner, 3 Nov. 1862, vol. 91/209 DKy, Letters Sent, ser. 1130, 2nd Division, Army of Kentucky, RG 393 Pt. 2 No. 30 [C-4356].)

208: Commander of the Department of the Ohio to the Commander of the Army of Kentucky

Cincinnati Ohio Dec 14th 1862

General: I have the honor to acknowledge the receipt of your letter of the 12th inst, enclosing a communication from Messrs Wm Bryant Esqr, Hon D. C. Wickliffe, and J. B Johnson Esqr to you, transmitting a certain resolution also herewith enclosed, which was passed at a popular meeting of the citizens of Fayette County, held at Lexington Ky on the 8th inst.

This resolution, which you have referred to me for action, contains certain interrogatories addressed to you, which are in substance as follows Viz: "does the military claim or intend to assert supremacy over the Civil power in the Union State of Kentucky? if so, why? and to what extent? whether the forcible detention of certain slaves belonging to Union Citizens of Kentucky within the lines of Regiments under your command was authorized, and whether the same will be hereafter sanctioned or authorized, and if so under what law? and for what purpose? also requesting you to furnish the names of slaves, so detained, and the Regiments in which each is detained." If I have been correctly informed in regard to the matters mentioned in said resolution, I must say, that I think there was little occasion for the meeting of the citizens of Fayette County called to give public expression to their supposed grievances. Yet I am ready to believe that their object was peaceful and patriotic: prompted solely as they aver, by a desire to prevent possible collision between citizens and the military in matters in which strong antagonistic feelings are supposed to exist. Admitting this I can assure the citizens of Fayette County, that the forces which are now in Kentucky for its protection, and for the defence of the Union against the assaults of the rebels, shall be, as far as its officers are concerned, the conservators of the Civil power. I may confidently point to the general conduct of our forces as proof of this disposition on the part of both officers and men, Every assurance to this effect has been given, and the admission in the resolution, that the complaints apply to only "A few of the regiments" is good evidence of this fact.

While admitting without hesitation the purity of the motives, which prompted the Citizens of Fayette County to adopt this resolution, I am very anxious to learn, "Under what law and for what purpose" they called upon you to furnish them the names of the slaves in each Regiment, and the Regiment in which each is detained.

You may assure the Committee of the popular assemblage, that so far as I am concerned, no law of Kentucky, not in contravention of the laws of Congress, shall be violated: that any force at my command shall be ready to serve to preserve law, and order, at the call of the executive of Kentucky, but that no Regiment or officers of my command shall be required by my orders, to hunt up run away negroes. The "sober second thought" will show our friends in Kentucky that this is not to be expected or desired from us, You can further assure them on my part, should this be necessary – that so long as the civil power is in operation, the military shall be subservient to it. This is not only in accordance with the spirit of our Institutions, but is in obedience to the doctrines taught us in the Military Code. The Civil Power is supreme. Very Respectfully Your Obedt. Servt

HLcSr

(Signed) H G Wright

Maj. Gen'l. H. G. Wright to Maj. Gen'l. Gordon Granger, 14 Dec. 1862, vol. 4 DO, pp. 409–11, Letters Sent, ser. 3482, Dept. of the OH, RG 393 Pt. 1 [C-4620]. Although the "interrogatories" in the resolution passed by the

Fayette County meeting had been addressed to General Gordon Granger, commander of the Army of Kentucky, he had referred them to his superior officer, General Wright, whose department included most of the state of Kentucky. At the same time, however, Granger informed the committee appointed at that meeting of his surprise at their complaint that the military authorities "had to some extent, usurped, or attempted to usurp, the civil power"; he contended that, to the contrary, he had always recognized and upheld the civil authorities. Granger argued that "we, officers and soldiers in the U.S. Army, while in your State, are subject to the civil laws thereof in the same manner as other non-residents; but we are also, at the same time, subject to the supreme civil and military laws of Congress. Between these, there is no conflict, and so long as there is not, it is my intention scrupulously to observe and obey both." Granger also indicated his disappointment that "the supposed conflict of civil and military authority . . . was made the subject of a public meeting" before any effort had been made to seek redress through military channels. "Such meetings," he argued, "can be easily influenced and controled by a few designing and bad men . . . to the great damage of our cause. Heretofore, many, who were once honest and loyal Citizens, have been so led astray by the machinations and duplicity of disloyal men at such, that they have joined hands with them in their traitorous designs against the Government. For this reason such meetings are much to be regretted." Moreover, Granger scolded, "[p]ublic rehearsals of idle and unfounded stories of outrages committed by soldiers excite the Citizens, without cause, to condemn the soldier; and the soldier finding himself misrepresented, to condemn the Citizens." (Maj. Genl. G. Granger to Hon. D. C. Wickliffe et al., 11 Dec. 1862, G-99 1862, Letters Received, ser. 3514, Dept. of the OH, RG 393 Pt. 1 [C-4600].) The resolution adopted by the citizens' meeting is not filed in the records of the Department of the Ohio with the copy of Granger's letter to the committee; a file notation indicates that it and other related papers were returned to Granger, the records of whose headquarters do not survive.

209: Former Tennessee Slave to the Commander of the District of Ohio, and Officers of the Louisville Contraband Commission to the Provost Marshal General of the Department of the Ohio

Cincinnati [*Ohio*] November 12th 1863.
Sir: I most respectfully present for your consideration, the following statement of the facts relative to a gross outrage perpetrated upon me and my family, by the police authorities of Louisville Ky; and I most humbly but earnestly pray that you will use influence or power as you may possess to have justice done me.

At the time of the capture of Memphis Tenn., I belonged to a certain Geo. M. Gill, who had served as a private in General Pillows bodyguard, but had been discharged because of ill

health. The day preceding the one on which Memphis was
captured, he left for the South, leaving me to shift for myself. In
the autumn of 1862 he came within the union lines to Memphis,
and directed his agent, one C. M. Widrig, to give me free papers or
a pass, I being at that time in the city of Nashville. This pass, I
now have. The said Geo. M. Gill, then returned within the rebel
lines, declaring his intention of remaing there until the Confederacy
is recognized.

Five of my children belonged at the same time to one Byrd
Douglass of Nashville Tenn. This Byrd Douglass has four sons
regularly enlisted in the rebel army, and a fifth engaged in guerrilla
warfare in the state of Tenn. He (Byrd Douglass) declared at the
outset of the war, that he would give thirty thousand dollars to aid
the rebel cause, and he has in all ways in his power aided the
rebellion. Gov. Johnson of Tenn. to whom I applied for a pass,
informed me that Douglass was a declared traitor, and that his
property will certainly be confiscated and his slaves freed.

You will see by this that I and my children are free, our owners
being rebels.

In July 1862 I engaged myself as a servant to Captain A. Clark
Denson, a resident of Memphis, and connected with Col. Stoke's
Tennessee Cavalry, whom I served until December 1862, when
because of ill health he obtained a furlough. We started to go
home by way of Louisville Ky, he procuring a pass, from General
Rosecrans, for himself, me and my two daughters who belonged to
the said Byrd Douglass. At Louisville he met certain other officers
who were on their way to Washington, he, having business there,
was persuaded by them to go there, before returning home. He
gave me the pass, and directed me to apply at the Provost Marshal's
office for a pass for myself and daughters to Memphis. I was
informed that Capt. Denson must apply in person for the
pass. This he could not do, for he was already departed for
Washington. By the advice of a Capt. Jackson, of the artillery
service, I applied to General Boyle's headquarters, and was granted a
pass by his adjutant the General being absent from the city. Not
being able to secure an immediate passage, I remained in Louisville
until the next night, when I was waited upon by two policemen,
who informed me that General Boyle was desirous of seeing the pass
which had been issued to me. They took me and my daughters to
the Galt House, one of them took my pass and went into the
building. He soon returned, and informed me that General Boyle
had torn up my pass, being determined that none of that character
should be issued. We were then taken to the jail, the keeper of
which, at first refused to admit us, but after some words consented
to admit the girls, I remaining outside. The girls while confined in

the jail became sick, when the jailer permitted me to move them to a small building in a corner of the jail yard, where I could nurse them. While nursing them I found that one of my sons who had belonged to Byrd Douglass was confined in the work house as a runaway; which had occurred in this manner. After the capture of Nashville by the Union forces, my son was employed as a servant by the quartermaster of an Indiana regiment belonginging to General Buell's command. He accompanied the army to Pittsburgh Landing and Corinth; then in the march after Bragg, until the regiment was encamped in the suburbs of Louisville. Here was seized by a policeman, although at the moment he was in sight of the encampment. He remained in the work-house until taken out as I shall now relate.

While my children were kept in jail I remained in Louisville endeavoring to secure their release. We came under the notice of Mr Eugene Underwood of Louisville, formerly of Nashville, who desired to purchase me and my family. I informed him that we were free and could not be purchased, but he persisted and wrote to Byrd Douglass concerning us. In a few, days one Bryce Grubbs, an agent of Byrd Douglass came to Louisville and took my daughters and son to Glenville M⁤ᶜLain Co. Ky., where they were informed they were sold to one William Jewell. I do not believe they are sold, because this William Jewell is the overseer of Archibald Wilson who was a brother in law of Byrd Douglass. They have been placed there to be easily reached by Byrd Douglass should the fortune of war give him a chance to run them into the Confederacy.

I trust I have shown that both Geo. M. Gill, and Byrd Douglass are rebels and that I and my children are free in consequence; also that we were wrongfully arrested in Louisville. If there is any power in your hands by which relief can be afforded, you will earn the thanks of a father bereaved of his children, and the reward of heaven, by exerting it.

ALS   Solomon Meek.

[*Endorsement*] Head Qrs. Dist. of. O. Cinti. Dec. 4, 1863 Resp'y. referred to Head Qrs. Depᵗ of the Ohio with recommendation that some action be taken in this case —

From investigation I am satisfied that is only one of a large number of similar case   J. D. Cox B.G. Comd'g.

Louisville, Ky., Dec. 15ᵗʰ *1863*

General, I have the honor to report that in compliance with your instructions, I have examined the records of the County Jail of

Jefferson County Ky. and find that upon the 19th day of November 1862 policeman Alexander Gilmore, committed to said Jail three (3) Negroes, Solomon, Maria and Mary Jane, as the property of George Gill of Memphis Tenn. Mary Jane and Maria were released December 16th 1862. Opposite Solomon's name is entered without date "escaped". – H. K. Thomas Ass't Jailor, (the Jailor being absent) being examined as to his knowledge of the case, testified that said Negroes were regularly committed to Jail as runaway Slaves in accordance with the laws of the State of Kentucky, by policeman Alex. Gilmore on the day above mentioned   That Solomon, on account of his good conduct, and the trust reposed in him was not long confined to the Jail, but was allowed to go at large through the City seeking work, which he did until the day he ran off. The daughters were kept in Jail until they were taken sick, when their Father was permitted to take them out, and keep them until their recovery. On the 16th day of December 1862 they were delivered to one Bryce Grubb, he having the required legal evidence of being the Agent of their owner.

Alexander Gilmore being examined testified substantially the same as the Ass[t] Jailor.

They both assert that their proceedings were strictly in accordance with the laws of Kentucky, that the whole thing occurred previous to the issuing of the Presidents Emancipation proclamation, and when no law or enactment, conflicted with the laws of Kentucky on the subject of the treatment of Slaves: that there was nothing before them to show that the owner of said Slaves was a Seccessionist; much less that he had ever been connected with the rebel army, or had used said Solomon in the Military Service of the rebel Gov[t]. Believing said Statements to be true in the main, substantiated as they are in part by the records of the Jefferson County Jail, and that no enactment of Congress or Proclamation of the President was violated, since none effecting the case, had then been issued. I shall before taking any further steps in the matter, await further instructions. Very Respectfully Your Ob[t] Serv[t]

D. C. Fitch

HLS   M. H. Jouett

Solomon Meek to General J. D. Cox, 12 Nov. 1863, and Maj. D. C. Fitch and Capt. M. H. Jouett to Brigd. Genl. N. H. McLean, 15 Dec. 1863, the former filed with and the latter enclosed in Brig. Genl. N. C. McLean to Capt. W. P. Anderson, 22 Jan. 1864, M-10 1864, Letters Received, ser. 3514, Dept. of the OH, RG 393 Pt. 1 [C-4631]. A second endorsement on Meek's letter, by General Ambrose E. Burnside, commander of the Department of the Ohio, (6 Dec. 1863) ordered General N. C. McLean, the department's provost marshal general, to go to Louisville and investigate the case. McLean's report, enclosing that of Fitch and Jouett, concluded that "Maria and Mary Jane, daughters of Solomon Meek, were not entitled to their freedom by virtue of the Presidents Proclamation of freedom of January 1st 1863. They having been arrested and confined as runaway slaves, by the civil authorities of Louisville Kentucky, and by the Jailor of Jefferson County Ky. delivered to a legally authorized agent of their owner (in accordance with the laws of the State of Kentucky) in December 1862, before the Presidents Proclamation was issued." McLean did not address the question of whether they were entitled to freedom under the confiscation act of July 1862. On the Louisville contraband commission, of which Fitch was president and Jouett a member, see below, docs. 217An., 223A–B.

210: Citizen of Ohio to an Indiana Congressman, and Commander of the District of Western Kentucky to the Secretary of War

Eaton O. Dec 16 /62

Copy

Dear Sir   On the 2^d day of December, 1862, a colored boy about 18, years old was arrested in the City of Louisville, Kt, to be dealt with as a fugitive slave by the laws of Kt.

The history of the case is this.   He came within the lines of the 35th Regt. O.V.I. near Tuscumbia, Alabama, was the slave of one widow Akin, so I was informed.   He was employed by Capt Gans as a servant about nine months ago, and served during that time faithfully, as such servant, in pursuance *of the army regulation, and so reported by him on the rolls & drew his rations.*

He was in company with me on his way to Ohio, & had some articles of clothing for the Captain's men he was taking to their friends in Ohio, when arrested by one Galleger who claimed to be controlled in his actions by Genl Boyl.   I interceded in behalf of the boy, by informing him he was no slave, but nothing short of Genl Boyl's release would do, so I appealed to Genl Boyl, who refused to act.

I telegraphed on the same day from Jeffersonville Ind. to Stanton Sec War, the following –

"Jeffersonville, Ind: Dec 2 /'62"

"Hon Edward M. Stanton"

"Sec of War"

"Is a slave entitled to his freedom who has been in the service of the United States army as a servant of a Capt over nine months"?

"This servant was a citizen of Alabama, before he entered the service"

"He has charge of some private property, of soldiers of the 35th Regt O.V.I he is to deliver to their friends in Ohio"
"He is deprived of his liberty in Louisville on the presumption he is still a slave"
"I await your answer at Jeffersonville."

"G. W. Gans."

Will you obtain an answer to this question of the Sec of War. I had not time to stay long in Jeffersonville, it may have been answered, but I think not.

I wish Sec Stanton to direct Genl Boyl to release the negro, whose name is Joseph Alexander, alias Joseph Wright, who has a written discharge from Capt Gans 35th Regt. O.V.I.

Genl Boyl is responsible for this and *others daily of the same kind in that city.* It must be corrected. This Gallegher boasted to me he had daily against the consent and advice, and orders of Col^s Maj^s & Capt^s taken their servants from them. I followed the scoundrel to the pen where he had his hundreds locked up, three fourths of whom had on the habiliments of soldiers of the U.S. Army. *You have no idea the injury it is doing our cause with the army,* they see it & you dont   Yours truly

HLcSr

G. W. Gans

Louisville January 7th 1863.

Sir,   The letter of G. W. Gans to Hon Geo W. Julian, in reference to a negro man named Joseph Alexander, alias Joseph Wright and refered to me by order endorsed 29th Dec 1862, has just been received.

In reply I have to say I do not know G. W. Gans and have no recollection of the matter refered to in his letter. I know nothing of the negro man— I have refused to give passes to negroes to go to Indiana or Ohio, unless I was satisfied they were free, and the officers of boats refuse to take them. The laws of Kentucky inflict a heavy penalty on any one passing negroes, not free, over the river— In my whole action I have had regard to the laws of the state. I have passed a large number of negroes but in every case I was satisfied they were residents of the states north or free men— If Mr Gans had made his statements to me as contained in his letter to Mr Julian I would not have felt authorized to have given him a pass for the negro. In case of the negroes captured with the 3rd Georgia Cavalry in September, I asked instructions of General Buell, and failing to receive any, I asked instructions of the Secretary of War as to what disposition to make of the captured negroes, and not receiving instructions, acting on my own judgement I ordered the negroes to be turned loose, free to go where they pleased, without molestation or hindrance from military or civil officers or any person whatever. All of these negroes, voluntarially went off with the prisoners, when they were sent except one. I beleive one or two of them were free men residents of Georgia, and all of them had families in that state except the one that remained.

It is not true that refusals to pass negroes is of daily occurrance, though it has been frequent and the refusal based on the ground that it would be a violation of the laws of the State, and subject owners of boats and others to heavy penalties, and involve a colision that would be prejudicial to the country— In my opinion the evil resulting from indiscriminate passes over the river to negroes with officers or persons claiming to be agents of officers, would prove to be much more injurious than the dissatisfaction of the few officers asking such permits. —

I know nothing of what may have taken place between the policeman and Mr Gans. I do not interfere with the civil authorities of the city or state— I have on one or two occasions notified the cival authorities that I was satisfied negroes were free and ought to be released and it was done. I confidently beleive that it is not true that Mr Gans followed the policeman "to the pen where he had his hundreds locked up, three fourths of whom had on the habilaments of soldiers of the U.S. Army." I am informed that there are now confined in the jail of Jefferson County in this city less than one hundred negroes, most of them slaves of this state and some of them belonging to citizens of Tennessee. There was a negro pen in this city in which there were confined about thirty four or five runaway negroes, and on receiving information that the negro dealer was selling them or selling what he called his claim to them, I ordered all the negroes to be turned out, excepting six negroes that he had possession of by the authority of their owners— I placed the negroes at work at the military prison, then at the Cave Hill Cemetary to fill the rifle pits dug on the grounds and which I was ordered to have filled, and I have directed the Provost Marshal to retain these negroes as long as there was Government work to do, and when through to turn them loose to go where they please. — This negro pen was a private jail and not authorized by law, and beleiving it worse to steal a negro to sell him into slavery than to steal him to secure his freedom, I deemed it proper to take the negroes from the pen and put them at Government work. —

I do not beleive the refusal to pass negroes over the river is doing any injury to the cause of the country— The officer whose patriotism is measured by his success in such matter, is scarcely

THE DESTRUCTION OF SLAVERY

above a class amongst us who care more for their negroes or poultry, than they do for their Government.

In this whole matter I have acted according to the measure of my ability, having reference to the laws, to justice to the negro, and to the rights of the citizens. I am very Respectfully Your Obdᵗ Servᵗ

HLc   [*Jeremiah T. Boyle*]

G. W. Gans to Hon. Geo. W. Julian, 16 Dec. 1862, enclosed in Geo. W. Julian to Hon. E. M. Stanton, 24 Dec. 1862, and Brig. Genl. [Jeremiah T. Boyle] to Hon. E. M. Stanton, 7 Jan. 1863, B-21 1863, Letters Received Irregular, RG 107 [L-94]. Endorsement. General Boyle had learned in early December 1862 that John Clark, "a negro trader and keeper of a private negro jail," had in custody a number of runaway slaves, whom he held "with view of selling on his own account, depriving their rightful owners of their property." On December 9, Boyle had informed the Louisville provost marshal that it was illegal for anyone to seize runaway slaves and confine them in private jails, except by their owners' authority. "If it is wrong and wicked for an abolitionist to steal negroes to secure them their freedom, it is worse and more wicked for a negro buyer to steal them to sell into slavery." Boyle had therefore ordered the provost marshal to remove the slaves from Clark's jail and put them to work at military labor, keeping an account of the time they worked. In a concluding sentence – which he characterized in his letter to the Secretary of War as instructions "to turn [the blacks] loose to go where they please" when no longer needed for government work – Boyle had issued the following direction: "When you are through with the negroes in doing this work you will allow their owners to take them or allow the negroes to go to their masters." When the provost marshal executed Boyle's order on December 10, he discovered twenty-six blacks in the jail, most of whom had been the slaves of Tennessee and Alabama owners. He assigned the able-bodied men, twenty-one in number, to military labor at the cemetery. Later that month, the provost marshal again removed black men from Clark's jail, assigning them to the quartermaster. And as late as February 1863, Clark still held slaves in his private jail and refused, despite threats of military arrest and imprisonment, to obey orders from the provost marshal not to receive any more "unless placed in his pen by their masters." (Brig. Gen. J. T. Boyle to Maj. Selby Harney, 9 Dec. 1862, Letters Received, ser. 1636, Louisville KY, Provost Marshal Field Organizations, RG 393 Pt. 4 [C-5002]; Maj. Selby Harney to Brig. Genl. Boyle, 10 Dec. 1862, Maj. Selby Harney to Lt. Col. Ferrell, 18 Dec. 1862, Maj. Selby Harney to Lt. Col. Ferrell, 30 Dec. 1862, and Lt. Col. Selby Harney to Col. Henry Dent, 26 Feb. 1863, vol. 220/524 DKy, pp. 3, 7, 13, & 28, Letters Sent by the Provost Marshal, ser. 1632, Louisville KY, Provost Marshal Field Organizations, RG 393 Pt. 4 [C-6014, C-6015, C-6013, C-6017].)

211: Kentucky Unionist to the Secretary of State

M⁺ Vernon Ky Jan: 6 /'63
D⁺ Sir: When Bragg, and Smith and Marshal invaded Ky a large
number of slaves from all the rebel states came with them in the
character of servants. When Bragg retreated many of the slaves left,
hoping to find protection among the Union party. The would be
rebels among us to make money arrested them as runaways and put
them in our Jails under state authority. The reward for each is
large. I am and was opposed to it – giving protection to rebel
property. They should now be turned loose. I think they can be
relieved by Habeas Corpus. I would write Honᶫ Mʳ Bates for an
opinion as to the modus operandi, but a Plebian as I am I fear he
would not give me an answer. Their condition deserves attention
by some person. The rebel states would not protect Ky slaves for
the owner. Respectfully

ALS   E. Smith

E. Smith to Honl. W. H. Seward, 6 Jan. 1863, Letters Received: KY Private
Citizens, ser. 9, Attorney General's Records, RG 60 [W-6]. The State Department referred Smith's letter to Attorney General Edward Bates, but,
according to later correspondence, Bates replied neither to this nor to two
subsequent letters from Smith. (E. Smith to U.S. Attorney Genl., 6 Feb.
1863, E. Smith to Honl. Mr. Bates, 18 Apr. 1863, and E. Smith to Honl.
Wm. H. Seward, 21 July 1863, Letters Received: KY Private Citizens, ser. 9,
Attorney General's Records, RG 60 [W-8].)

212: Chief of Police of Louisville, Kentucky, to the Provost Marshal at Louisville

Louisville, Ky., Jany 7th *1862* [*1863*].
D⁺ Sir I ought sooner, perhaps to have explained to you the
method and manner of treating runaway negroes which are found
running at large in the City. The Jail has been full for several
months and the County Court has made no further provision for
them. My orders to the Police have been, to commit them
according to law as far as possable by taking them before a
Magistrate, and take the Mittimus and negro to the Jailor, and if
refused admittance by him, to do the best they can by placing them
in a place of security until their owners can be heard from. In every
instance the owner is written to, immediately. This course has very
generally been persued and many have been returned to their owners
by this plan. The evil of permitting them to prowl about the City

can hardly be tolerated, the Civil law making no provision for such cases, and there being quite a number turned loose recently that had been secured in the manner above stated I thought it advisable to get your opinion as to the disposition to be made of them hereafter, if any   Hoping to hear from you on the subject I am Very Respectfully Your Obt Svt

ALS   Cha⁵ L. Stancliff

Chas. L. Stancliff to Major Harney, 7 Jan. 1862 [1863], Letters Received, ser. 1636, Louisville KY, Provost Marshal Field Organizations, RG 393 Pt. 4 [C-5003]. The provost marshal assumed that Stancliff was objecting to the recent seizure of slaves from "negro pens" for military labor and on the same day replied curtly that he had acted in accordance with orders from his commanding officer, who alone could answer questions about future policy. The next day Stancliff clarified his purpose: "The information and advise which I intended to ask for was this, Shall we arrest runaway negroes at all, and if so, shall we commit them as far as we can under the State law, and do the best we can to keep them for the owners, or shall we deliver them to the Pro Marshal or to Genl Boyle or to whom." "They ought not," the police chief warned, "to be permitted to run at large in the City." The provost marshal replied that it was not the policy of General Jeremiah T. Boyle, commander of the District of Western Kentucky, to interfere with the civil law, "unless the necessity be to perform some military work of importance." Therefore, the provost marshal presumed, "you should execute the Civil Law, as you under-stand it." He added that he had no use "at present" for any more black laborers than were already under his control. (Major Selby Harney to Captain Chas. Stancliff, 7 Jan. 1863, and Maj. Selby Harney to Capt. Chas. Stancliffe, 8 Jan. 1863, vol. 220/524 DKy, pp. 14–15, Letters Sent by the Provost Marshal, ser. 1632, Louisville KY, Provost Marshal Field Organizations, RG 393 Pt. 4 [C-5003]; Chas. L. Stancliff to Major Harney, 8 Jan. 1862, Letters Received, ser. 1636, Louisville KY, Provost Marshal Field Organizations, RG 393 Pt. 4 [C-5004].)

213A: Former Alabama Slave to the Freedmen's Bureau Superintendent of the Subdistrict of Louisville, Enclosing the Former Slave's Affidavit

Louisville Ky August 14ᵗʰ 1865

Col   I have the honor to forward the enclosed affidavit and ask the assistance of the military authorities in procuring my own and my mothers and Sisters Freedom Papers under the Presidents Proclamation of Sept. 22ⁿᵈ 1862. We claim protection under that

Proclamation from the fact of our living in one of the States
mentioned in Said Proclamation. We further ask your assistance in
procuring our wages for the time we have labored for these parties
as slaves since we have been actually free   Respectfully

her

Amy ✕ Moore

mark

HLSr

[*Enclosure*]   [*Louisville, Ky. August 14?, 1865*]
    Amy Moore Colored, being duly Sworn deposeth and Says, that
in the Summer of 1863 [*1862*] the United States Soldiers under
command of Major McMillen came to her masters house in
Huntsville Alabama, (her master and his family having left them)
and carried away deponent together with her mother and three
Sisters, that they brought us all to Nashville Tenn where we were
put on board of a transport and Started for Cincinnati Ohio   that
when we arrived at Louisville Ky we were arrested by a man who
Said he was a watchman and taken to the Slave pen on Second Street
Louisville Ky and kept there two or three days when we were taken
to the Depot of the Louisville and Nashville Rail Road and there
another watchman took charge of us and took us to Shepherdsville
Ky and kept us confined several weeks when we were sold at auction
by the Sherriff of Bullett County Ky. Dr. McKay bought deponent
and paid for her the sum of Five Hundred (500) dollars   *James Funk*
bought deponents mother and youngest Sister paying Six Hundred
(600) dollars for the two, and Soon after Sold her mother to *Judge
Hoegner* who now holds her as a Slave   *James Shepherd* bought my
Sister Nora and *Richard Deets* bought my sister Ann, and further
deponent saith that she and her mother and Sisters have been held
as Slaves Since the above Sale and Still continue to be so held.

her

Amy ✕ Moore

mark

HDSr

[*Endorsement*]   Bureau Refugees Freedmen &c Sub Dist Louisville
Louisville Ky. Aug 15″ /65 Respectfully referred to Capt Harlan
Asst. Adjt. Genl. Dept. of Ky. with the request that all the parties
concerned in abducting, returning to and holding in Slavery these
Freed people be arrested. H A McCaleb Lt. Col. and Supt

Amy Moore to Col., 14 Aug. 1865, enclosing affidavit of Amy Moore, [14?
Aug. 1865], Unregistered Letters Received, ser. 1209, Louisville KY Supt.,

RG 105 [A-4515]. Both letter and affidavit are in the same handwriting, the affidavit undated but subsequently sworn and signed before a justice of the peace on August 15, 1865. Other endorsements indicate that the affidavit was referred to the military commander of the Post of Louisville, and by him to the provost marshal, who reported on August 24, 1865, that Dr. McKay had already responded to a summons and had been sent to the Louisville Freedmen's Bureau superintendent, and that the other purchasers of members of the Moore family would report on August 25. There is no indication of the outcome.

213B: Legal Papers from the Jefferson County and Bullitt County, Kentucky, Courts

The State of Kentucky County of Jefferson Feb 17th 1863
D. Z. Bligh. J. S. Gallagher of Louisville Ky. brought before me a runaway slave woman who calls her name Margaret Moore, is about thirty three or four years old, black color weighs about 125 pounds and was arrested in the city of Louisville Ky. Says she belongs to Sam Moore of Huntsville Alabama.

Also one female runaway slave the daughter of the said Margaret – mulatti color – twelve years old was arrested in the city of Louisville Ky. belongs to the same person. calls her name Anna

Also a runaway slave child who calls her name "Marah" – Brown color – about eight years old. child of the said Margaret and belongs to the same person and was arrested in the City of Louisville Ky.

Also a runaway slave girl who calls her name "Redley." Brown color – about six years old. Child of the said Margaret, was arrested in the city of Louisville Ky. and belongs to the same person as the above.

Also a runaway slave girl who calls her name Caroline. Black color, about two years old. child of the said Margaret was arrested in the city of Louisville Ky. and belongs to the same person as the above.

Attest (signed) Jo^s Clement J.P.N.

D. Z. Bligh and James S Gallagher is commanded to deliver the above named runaway Slaves "Margaret Moore", "Anna", "Norah", "Ridly", and "Caroline" into the custody of the Jailor of Bullett County for safe keeping as the Jail of Jefferson County Kentucky is full and no more runaway slaves can be received therein, and it being represented to me that there is room in the said Jail of Bullett county so that the said slaves can be taken care of in said Jail.

HDc

[*Endorsement*] Committed to the Bullett County Jail Feb'y 18th 1863. Margaret Moore, Anna, Norah, Ridley, and Caroline Runaway Slaves, the properity of Huntsville Alabama were arrested in the city of Louisville Jefferson county Ky. finding no room in said Jail they were transmitted to this Jail. (signed) B. F. Troutman.

        Kentucky, Bullitt County Court 13th April 1863
   "B. F. Troutman Jailor of Bullitt County having this day filed a report showing the number and ages with discription of negroes now in the County Jail that have been advertised according to law in the Frankfort Commonwealth, It is now ordered that the sheriff shall on County Court day in May next expose to public sale to the highest bidders the following named negroes unless they shall, before that time be legally reclaimed by their owners or agents, viz;

Negro	woman	Margaret
"	Girl	Anna
"	"	Norah
"	"	Bidley
"	"	Caroline
"	Man	Henry
"	"	Steve —

The woman Margaret and her child Caroline 2 years old to be sold together. The said slaves to be sold on a credit of 12 months, the purchaser to give bond with security, payable to the Commonwealth of Kentucky, and having the force and effect of a replevien bond for and with the condition that the sale is to be vacated in case said slaves or any of them are legally reclaimed by their owners or agents within 12 months from the day of sale — in which case the purchasers are to pay no hire for the time they have had the services of the Negroes and the sale is made upon this Condition — Sale to be made after advertising the time, place and terms and Conditions of sale for at least 20 days in the Louisville Journal and in 3 public places in the County — Said Sheriff is directed to have each of said slaves valued in like manner as lands sold under Execution are now directed to be — Said slaves not to be sold unless they bring one Third of their value —

                    W^m R Thompson.
                    P.J.B.C.C.
18th May 1863, We S. A. McKay & R H. Field having been first sworn to value the within- (by the sheriff of Bullett County, Ky,) described slaves value the same as follows — Margaret Moore and her child 2 years old named Caroline valued at $700. — Amy 11

years old $600. – Norah 8 years old $450   Ridley 6 years old
$350 –   attest –   R. H. Field
W Phelps, S B.C.   S. A. McKay

After advertising as directed in the within orders I sold the within
named slaves at the Courthouse door in Shepherdsville, County
Court day, as follows, James Funk being the highest and best
bidder bought Margaret and child for $535 – paid cash; – James
Shepherd bought Norah for $380 – gave bond with Orleans Lee
security, R. W. Deats bought Ridley for $326 – gave bond with
John Mooney security, S. A. McKay bought Anna for $405 – &
gave bond with James Y. Pope security, J. W. Gleen bought
Henry Brown for $436. gave bond with Orleans Lee
security, Robert Hall bought Steve for $475, gave bond with
Nathan Hall security, this 18th day of May 1863.
                                                    W. Phelps S.B.C

. . . .

HDc

Mittimus by a Jefferson County justice of the peace, 17 Feb. 1863, and
excerpt from Bullitt County Court records of sale of slaves, 13 Apr. & 18 May
1863, filed with Amy Moore to Col., 14 Aug. 1865, Unregistered Letters
Received, ser. 1209, Louisville KY Supt., RG 105 [A-4515]. The remainder
of the Bullitt County Court papers consist of the bonds of the purchasers of the
"slaves," dated May 18, 1863, and receipts for payment of balances outstanding on the purchases, on dates between November 1863 and May 1864.

214: Commander of the Louisville Barracks to the Headquarters of the District of Western Kentucky

Louisville, Ky., April 4th 1863.
Captain   Another discharged Michigan officer applied to me for a
pass to carry a slave that he admitted belonged to a man near
Franklin Tennessee, to Michigan. He says two of the mans sons are
in the rebel army and that Gen. Stanley gave him permission to
carry the negro away. As a matter of course I could not give him a
pass and this matter has become an unbarable nuisance in filling up
the City with roving worthless negroes. I truly wish some means
could be adopted to turn the patriotism of these officers into another
channel. I am ashamed to find so many officers disposed to debase
the noble principle for which we are battleing and degenerate it into
a mere negro freeing machine. I would respectfully suggest that the

evil might be remedied in a large degree if Gen Boyle would have a guard at the nearest station to the southern line of his department instructed to stop all negroes there who were not free. Respectfully
ALS   M Mundy

Col. M. Mundy to Capt. A. C. Semple, 4 Apr. 1863, Letters Received, ser. 2173, Dist. of Western KY, RG 393 Pt. 1 [C-4301].

215: Judge Advocate General to the Secretary of War

Judge Advocate General's Office [*Washington*] April 24th 1863. Sir, It appears from the letter of Major General Negly, under date of the 7th inst, that while his forces were engaged in an expedition into East Tennessee, in the summer of the past year, two negro slaves, escaped from their masters and joined his command, where they were employed as servants. That one of them belonged to a methodist clergyman, an active guerilla – and persecutor of citizens in Sweeden's Cove, and who was with Adams' cavalry, at the time they were driven out from that place. The other belonged to a noted rebel residing near Fayettevill. It further appears that the latter negro had previously rendered valuable services to General Mitchell's command, as he afterwards did to Major General Negley – by furnishing them secret information, of which fact he held a certificate from General Mitchell. It is further shown that during the last fall when General Buell's army entered Kentucky, these negros, whose names are *Sandy* and *George*, accompanied it, having under the direction of the Wagon Master of General Negley's Division, charge of some of the animals he was taking to Louisville Ky – . While en route, they were seized as fugitive slaves, by the civil authorities at Hardinsburg, Breckenridge County, in that state, where they have remained in jail until the present time, and, as stated by the jailor of the county, are advertised to be sold as slaves, under the local laws of Kentucky, on the 3[d] Monday in May.

These negroes were under the 60th Article of War, virtually in the military service, of the United States, as "retainers to the camp,"[1] though, at the moment of their arrest they may have been seperated from the main body of the army – Being in such service, they were not liable to be seized by the civil authorities.

But they have a more decided character assigned to them by the 9th sec of the act of 17th July 1862, chap 195: Having been the property of men known to be in open rebellion against the government of the United States, and taking refuge within the lines of our army, – which was their status at the time of their arrest – they are declared by the section of the act referred to, to be "captives of war and forever free of their servitude." This act is a part of the supreme law of the land, to which the local legislation of the states must give way. The civil authorities have no more right to seize and detain in prison, negroes falling within the purview of the section quoted, than they have to seize and imprison other captives of war taken by the armies of the United States.

It is understood that the disgraceful practice of kidnapping negroes declared to be "captives of War and free" under the act of Congress, with a view to their sale into slavery under local laws, extensively prevails, and it should be repressed with a vigorous and decided hand. The supreme law, and the right it gives to the military custody and control of the victims of these shameless oppressions, should be enforced with the whole power of the government if necessary. It should be added that the important services voluntarily and so loyally rendered by one of these negroes to the Union cause, appeal strongly to the government to interpose for his protection.

The claim of $250, for expenses, set up against each of these negroes, should not be recognized or regarded. Those who have incurred these expenses – if indeed they have been incurred to the amount named – have done so in their own wrong and in violation of law, and they have no right to look either to the government, or to their victims, the negroes, for redress. Very respectfully Your Obedient Servt.

HLS

J Holt.

Judge Advocate General J. Holt to Hon. E. M. Stanton, 24 Apr. 1863, filed with N-106 1863, Letters Received, RG 107 [L-143]. In the same file is General James S. Negley's letter of April 7 to the Secretary of War, reporting the jailing of the two former slaves. On April 29, Secretary of War Edwin M. Stanton forwarded a copy of Holt's opinion to General Ambrose E. Burnside, commander of the Department of the Ohio, noting in a covering letter that "many other cases have arisen, or are arising, within your Department, presenting the same questions as the case before the Judge Advocate General." Stanton instructed Burnside "to prevent any person or persons, whomsoever, whether civil or military officers, from transgressing the Act of Congress, and the President's Proclamation in respect to persons of African descent," but "to avoid, as far as possible, any forcible collision with State authority." "It is obviously the desire of the enemies of the Government in Kentucky," concluded Stanton, "to defy the government upon this point, and to nullify its authority, and this only renders it more necessary firmly, but with prudence, to enforce the law." (Edwin M. Stanton to Major General A. E. Burnside, 29 Apr. 1863, A. E. Burnside Papers, Generals' Papers & Books, ser. 159, RG

94 [V-152].) Earlier that same day, Stanton had telegraphed Burnside at the behest of President Lincoln, who had read with dismay a newspaper item regarding the sale in Louisville of blacks who were entitled to freedom under the Emancipation Proclamation. Lincoln had ordered that Burnside "take immediate measures to prevent any persons who . . . are entitled to protection from the Government . . . from being returned to bondage." (*Official Records*, ser. 1, vol. 23, pt. 2, p. 291.) General-in-Chief Henry W. Halleck also wrote Burnside on April 29, informing him that "[t]he same game was attempted last year in Missouri under the local laws of that State to sell back into slavery those who by the law of Congress were made free." "There can be no doubt, general," argued Halleck, "that the law of Congress on this subject overrides any State law. Negroes freed by the operations of the war and taken into our service are under the protection of the military, and I have always considered it my duty to thwart and defeat the operations of negro stealers to have them resold into slavery." (*Official Records*, ser. 2, vol. 5, p. 536.) Under the date of April 28, Burnside issued an order voiding the sale of blacks who were entitled to freedom under the war measures of the President and the Congress, while at the same time requiring the army not to interfere with Kentucky slaves. (See document 216, immediately below.) The commander of the District of Western Kentucky later reported that he had ordered the release from the Breckinridge County jail of the black men whose reenslavement had led to the opinion of the judge advocate general. (Brig. Genl. J. T. Boyle to Capt. D. R. Larned, 12 May 1863, A. E. Burnside Papers, Generals' Papers & Books, ser. 159, RG 94 [V-160].)

1 "ART. 60. All sutlers and retainers to the camp, and all persons whatsoever, serving with the armies of the United States in the field, though not enlisted soldiers, are to be subject to orders, according to the rules and discipline of war." (U.S., War Department, *Revised United States Army Regulations* [Washington, 1863], appendix, p. 494.)

216: Order by the Commander of the Department of the Ohio

Cincinnati, O., April 28, 1863.

GENERAL ORDERS, No. 53.

I. In accordance with the spirit of the proclamation of the President of the United States, dated January 1, 1863, it is ordered that all persons belonging to, or following the Army in this Department, are forbidden to inferfere with, or impede the operation of any civil process in the State of Kentucky, having in view the recovery of slaves of citizens of the State, and they are likewise forbidden to aid or abet in their escape from their homes, or to employ such persons against the consent of their owners, except in cases where military necessity requires their impressment, which impressment must be made in accordance with regulations governing such cases.

II. All slaves made free by the war measures of the President of the United States, by Congress, or by capture during the war, are entitled to their freedom, and no one in this Department has a right to interfere with that freedom. Any sale of such persons in this Department is void. The rights of citizens must be respected by the army, and the war measures of the Government must be sustained.

III. Any person wilfully violating this order will be at once arrested, and reported to the Headquarters of General Boyle, at Louisville, for trial.

Regulations to prevent confusion and injustice in the execution of this order will be published.

By command of Major General Burnside.

PD

General Orders, No. 53, Headquarters, Department of the Ohio, 28 Apr. 1863, vol. 39 DO, Printed Copies of General Orders, ser. 3519, Dept. of the OH, RG 393 Pt. 1 [C-4639]. General Ambrose E. Burnside, who had become commander of the Department of the Ohio in late March 1863, had received several reports that blacks entitled to freedom under the Second Confiscation Act and the Emancipation Proclamation were being reenslaved in Kentucky. On April 21, for example, a resident of LaGrange, Kentucky, had informed him that some fifteen or twenty blacks were in that town's jail, "two of whom claim to be free, and all the others claim to be persons whom the U. States army captured from Rebels." Jailed since the previous December, they had been appraised and were scheduled to be sold into slavery in a few days. (W. F. Parker to Maj. Gen. Burnside, 21 Apr. 1863, A. E. Burnside Papers, Generals' Papers & Books, ser. 159, RG 94 [V-156].) Burnside's General Order 53 did not halt all such sales. The sheriff of Oldham County, Kentucky, sold between ten and fifteen fugitives from Tennessee and Mississippi on May 18, 1863. (M. W. Lodwick to ?, [May 1863], A. E. Burnside Papers, Generals' Papers & Books, ser. 159, RG 94 [V-161].) Seven freedpeople were sold into slavery by the sheriff of Bullitt County on the same day. (See above, docs. 213A–B.) In late 1863, it was estimated that 1,000 blacks brought into Kentucky with the Union army from states further south had been similarly reenslaved. (See below, docs. 223A–B.)

217A: **Headquarters of the District of Western Kentucky to the Commander of the Post of Louisville**

"Copy"   *Louisville,* May 3rd *1863.*

Colonel:, The following instructions in regard to contraband negroes in this District will be strictly complied with.

All negroes coming into this District from states south of Tennessee and all negroes who have been employed in the rebel service, coming within the lines are captives of war and will be held as such and placed on the redoubts and fortifications in process of construction and retained, until the Major General Com^{d}g the Department directs other disposition of them and orders the mode of their release. All officers civil, and military, Jailers and others, will deliver all such negroes to the custody of such officers as the Commandant of the Post of Louisville shall designate, to be sent to the public works now being constructed and the Commandant of the Post will demand such captives, and use such force as may be necessary to reclaim such captives of War and place them on the fortifications and other works, according to instructions to be furnished him.

This order is made in pursuance of instructions from the Major Genl Com^{d}g the Department of the Ohio, and Col Marc Mundy is charged with the execution of it. He will make application to Jailers and other civil officers for the delivery of these captives, and he will use only such force as may be necessary to secure the custody of all such captives.

He will not interfere with negroes belonging to citizens of Kentucky and Tennessee, excepting where the negro has been in the service of rebels in arms.

The military authorities of the United States claim the costody and control of all captives until released by the proper authority of the Government   By command of Brig Genl Boyle

HLcSr   (Signed)   A. C. Semple

A.A.G. A. C. Semple to Col. Marc Mundy, 3 May 1863, filed as B-142 1863, Letters Received, ser. 3514, Dept. of the OH, RG 393 Pt. 1 [C-4604]. Endorsement. Nine days later, General Jeremiah T. Boyle, commander of the District of Western Kentucky, extended these orders to other areas of Kentucky, giving General Henry M. Judah, the commander at Bowling Green, similar responsibilities in Warren, Allen, Simpson, Logan, Todd, Christian, Trigg, Muhlenberg, and Butler counties. Boyle's adjutant forwarded to Judah a copy of the orders to the Louisville post commander, adding the following instructions: "To execute this order, you will select from your command a discreet and reliable officer, (a Kentuckian if practicable). . . . In taking negroes from jails, the Jailers must be furnished with certificates that the negroes were taken by the Military authorities, in order that the Jailers will not be held responsible for the negroes thus taken. All 'contrabands' thus taken in the above named counties will be collected at Bowling Green, furnished with quarters and subsistence, and held subject to the order of the District Commander." (A.A.G. A. C. Semple to Brig. Genl. H. M. Judah, 12 May 1863, quoted in General Orders No. 34, Head Quarters U.S. Forces,

15 May 1863, vol. 123/294 DKy, p. 105, General Orders, ser. 1073, U.S. Forces at Bowling Green KY, RG 393 Pt. 2 No. 27 [C-4347].) On May 13, 1863, General Boyle created a special commission in Louisville, composed of a Michigan officer and two Kentucky officers, to "examine all cases of contra-bands or captured negroes, coming to this city, and give them certified declarations of the fact of their freedom under the War measures of the Government." Boyle instructed the commission to examine all blacks claimed as servants by army officers, as well as other blacks traveling through the city, and to honor only those passes signed by generals who commanded at the level of military districts or divisions, or higher. "Any others at the discretion of the Commission will be placed on the public works or allowed to pass." Boyle also authorized the commission to order the release of contrabands confined in jails or held by individuals. (Special Orders No. 117, Head Quarters District of Western Kentucky, 13 May 1863, vol. 15 DKy, pp. 216–17, Special Orders Issued, ser. 2178, Dist. of Western KY, RG 393 Pt. 1 [C-4631].) For the operation of the commission, see below, docs. 223A–B.

217B: Commander of the Post of Louisville to a Judge of the Jefferson County Court

Louisville Ky. May 7, 1863

With an abiding loyalty for the Law and respect for the Courts that administer it, in obedience to your request I submit the annexed statement of the Contrabands I have seized from the Sheriff of Jefferson County. Under my orders (a copy of which I have furnished to the Sheriff and which have been filed in your Court) you will perceive by reference to them that I am ordered to take all negroes coming from south of Tenn. and from Tennessee and Ky. who have been in the Rebel service. I had no means of determining those facts, except by the statements of the negroes themselves, which would not properly be evidence in the Courts of Ky. but are sufficient to determine me in the execution of my orders, coupled as they are with the facts of the negroes' presence here without lawful owners or claimants. It is perhaps, unfortunate that many or all of these have been brought by officers and soldiers serving in the Federal Army; who have thus disregarded the laws of Kentucky; but when so brought neither the spirit or letter of the act providing for the capture & sale of free or runaway negroes is violated by the their seizure by the Military for service upon public works. As contrabands or captives of war, for whether or not they are proper or lawful captives, need not be discussed to disprove the presumption that they are either free or runaway negroes, such as the case contemplates. Many free negroes have found their way to this city, some coming from the North with Officers as servants in the army,

nd I respectfully suggest that some order ought to be made by the
Court, not only to permit them to cross the river, and quit the
tate, but to compel them to do so, in obedience to the laws of
Ky. The boy, Julius, who represents himself as a free boy from
New Orleans, I have had redelivered to the Sheriff for such
lisposition as the law may make of him, being free he is neither
ontraband nor captive of war and does not fall within the perview
of my orders, Assuming as I do that he claims his freedom by birth
or manumission and not by virtue of the President's
Proclamation. I have the honor to be Your Obt Servant

HLcSr   M. Mundy

Col. M. Mundy to Hon. Andrew Monroe, 7 May 1863, vol. 142/330 DKy,
Letters Sent, ser. 729, Post of Louisville KY, RG 393 Pt. 4 [C-6002]. Copied
n the same volume is a list of the "contrabands" Mundy had taken from the
efferson County sheriff, comprising twenty-three men and six women, formerly the slaves of owners in Tennessee, Alabama, Mississippi, South Caro-
ina, and Virginia. Eleven of the men had been servants in the Confederate
rmy; fourteen men and women were owned by masters who were themselves
Confederate soldiers or had relatives serving in that army; two men belonged
o Alabama masters listed as not in the Confederate army or as having "taken
no part in the Rebellion"; and one man belonged to "a good loyal man" in
Alabama. Julius, the free black from New Orleans, was listed as "sold in this
ity last Monday." On May 4, Colonel Mundy had instructed an officer to
collect from the different jails and work houses in the Military District of
Western Kentucky all negroes to be found therein, who have come or been
brought into the state from states south of Tennessee, and all negroes who
ave been in employed in the rebel service," turning them over to the commander of the military prison in Louisville for assignment to "government
vork." He also ordered the seizure of "all contrabands found in private
nands," adding that "[n]o Officer has the right to appropriate negro slaves as
ervants, and all such will be taken and turned over upon Government works."
Special Orders No. 100, Head Quartes Post Commandant, 4 May 1863, vol.
49/353 DKy, Special Orders Issued, ser. 739, Post of Louisville KY, RG
93 Pt. 4 [C-6002].)

218: Michigan Congressman to the Commander of the Department of the Ohio

St Louis   May 4th /63
General   I was in Louisville K'y lately on my return from Nashville
nd wish to call your attention to the manner in which Contrabands
re treated in that City— Colored men from Arkansas Tennessee

Miss and other Rebel States who have Certificates of their freedom
signed by Generals in the field are siezed – imprisoned, and sold for
costs &c – The temptation to kidnap them is very great as the man
who takes them up gets $75″ each & the Jailor is well paid also and
these poor fellows have no friends to help them   The Ferry Boat
which crosses the Ohio will not let a Contraband cross no matter
tho' Gen'l Rosecrans should certify in writing that he is a free
man   Many – yes a great many colored men who have rendered
great service to the army & secured the good will of officers, who
wished to send them to Ohio or Michigan have been siezed in spite
of all these papers or Certificates & sold into slavery – sent no one
knows where –   This infernal treatment of such men ought to call
down the vengeance of Heaven on all who permit it

Let me state a case   I was in Franklin Tennessee in Maj Gen'l
Grangers Camp – the last Sunday in April – when a very intelligent
Contraband came in & told us his master was a Mississi Officer &
he had run away   He told Gen Granger how to surprise two Camps
& Gen G – did capture all in one of them the same night without
the loss of a man – & would have taken the other but for an
accident –   This fugitive did all he could for us – & would do more
& yet if I wished to take him to Michigan & Gen'l Rosecrans
certified to all these facts & that he was legally free I could not get
him over the Ohio River   A Louisville kidnapper can sieze &
imprison him & unless I will stay & see to it he must be sold –

Kentucky is called a loyal State & is exempted by the Pres't from
the operation of the Proclamation   Protect them then & enforce the
return of *their* fugitive slaves but devise some way by which Officers
of a certain rank can certify to the freedom – of any colored man *not*
a resident of K'y who wishes to go North & compel these Ferry men
to respect them

Orders should be issued regulating the passage of these men over
the River & Officers app'ted who should see these orders
enforced   I believe Col Moore does all he dare do without your
orders[1] & I hope you will adopt some course to remedy this grivious
wrong –   You must pardon me for writing at such length for I
cannot see *humble* & poor men – who have done us often great service
treated so inhumanely –   I met you several times in Washington &
you may remember me   Perhaps too you have this subject under
consideration now & I cannot help feeling you will do what is
necssary & right   I have the honor to be Your Obt Serv't

ALS   F W Kellogg

F. W. Kellogg to Maj. Gen'l. Burnside, 4 May 1863, K-99 1863, Letters
Received, ser. 3514, Dept. of the OH, RG 393 Pt. 1 [C-4609]. Kellogg

signed himself "MC. 4th Dis't Michigan." General Ambrose E. Burnside, commander of the Department of the Ohio, referred Kellogg's letter to General Jeremiah T. Boyle, commander of the District of Western Kentucky, for action under Burnside's General Order 53 regarding contrabands. In the same file is Boyle's response that, so far as he could ascertain, Kellogg's statements were not true. "These politicians," Boyle complained, "look at these matters from a different point of view from other folks and do not see straight on this subject." Boyle asserted that since Burnside's order, "the contrabands . . . are treated better and more justly in Ky than in any part of the nation." (Brig. Genl. J. T. Boyle to Maj. Gen. Burnside, 20 May 1863.) For Burnside's order, see above, doc. 216.

1 Orlando H. Moore, colonel of the 25th Michigan Infantry, was provost marshal in Louisville. On May 1, 1863, he issued an order prohibiting "all unlawful interference with the authorized negro servants of officers of the United States Army and negroes legally entitled to their freedom, passing from Kentucky to Indiana," but it was immediately countermanded by Colonel Marcellus Mundy, a Kentucky slaveholder and the commander of the Post of Louisville: "Any unlawful interference with the Serv[t] of officers or others can be properly redressed by the Courts of Justice . . . We would have no more right to impose military authority in such cases here than we would have in New York or Mishigan." (Special Order, No. 12, Hd. Qrs. Pro. Marl., 1 May 1863, vol. 161/381 DKy, p. 19, Miscellaneous Records, ser. 1644, Louisville KY, Provost Marshal Field Organizations, RG 393 Pt. 4 [C-7002]; Col. M. Mundy to Col. O. H. Moore, 2 May 1863, vol. 142/330 DKy, Letters Sent, ser. 729, Post of Louisville KY, RG 393 Pt. 4 [C-6000].)

219A: Chaplain of an Illinois Regiment to the Commander of the Post of Louisville

near Murfreesboro Tenn May 9" 1863.
Col, I have today received a letter informing me that my colored servant "Billy" was taken from my wife in Louisville by the guards & informed he would go no further & after fruitless efforts on the part of wife to obtain permission for him to proceed, She left him with yourself receiving a promise that you would try to send him back to me here. As I have heard nothing from the "Boy" and have no notice from the Post whatever concerning him. I wish to make a few statements & also a few Enquiries, before proceeding farther in the matter, As Mrs R was not accustomed to travel alone and needed some one to look after her baggages – Sent my Private Servant to accompany her & to avoid vexation on the way & Especially at Louisville, I procured a pass from Gen'l Rosecrans

Head Quarters, in these-words, "Pass Mrs Mary B. Raymond & Colored Servant "Billy" from Murfreesboro to Peoria Ill, &c"— Having learned also that there had been much "unlawful influence" with colored men, whether born free or made free by the Government, by the Provost "guards" & Louisville Police, and having heard from R Road-men; & officers of the army who were Knowing the facts, that many after they were arrested were "Spirited away & sold by Villainous Kidnappers into Slavery." I took the further precaution to make a "certificate" over my own signature & one over the signature of one of the 19″ Ill Vols, with which Regiment he first served as "Cook" in the army, from March 1862 till Oct last, since which time he has been with me. The certificate in substance was this, "Billy" was born & raised as the slave of "Ruff Gamble" two miles from Morresville Alabama & 15 miles from Athens of the same state. His master early in the war joined the Rebel Army & was made a Lieut, In March 1862. In March 1862, while our army lay near Decatur "Billy" of his own accord made his way to the lines & hired out to cook in the 19″ Ill Vols, & thus secured his freedom, by the decision of Congress, "That the Slaves of Rebels in arms against the Government should not be returned to Slavery, after serving in the Gov't employ, but should be forever free— He was free then as a *"contraband"* He is also free under the Proclamation of the President, coming from Alabama. He never was in the State of Kentucky in his life, until the day your guards arrested him (23rd of April) & Kentucky has nothing to do with him. And as a "Freedman" Provided with a legitimate pass and proper information no one has a *Just right* to take him from my wife or prevent his Proceeding on his journey. (I am aware Col that "Orders" may have made it necessary—for you to stop him—therefore do not say where the blame is, But I know something is wrong. Now Col what has been done with the boy? I shall look to you, for him, so far at least as to what the military authorities have done, and I wish to make a few more Enquiries in order to intelligent action in the future. *And 1st* are we to understand that the authorities at Louisville do not & will not respect the passes of General Rosecrans.

2nd Is it taken for granted that every colored man is a fugitive slave & owned by Kentucky? 3rd What amount of evidence & of what Kind must the Officers of the US army furnish to get our Colored Servants allowed the privilege of peaceably pursuing their journey beyond Louisville? 4$^{″}$ Do the guards after arresting these strangers (& some of them *Orphan Boys* of 14 or 15 years of age like mine) when released, leave them unprotected, where these Kidnapping villains—can take them away & send them into Slavery again? I do not by these statements & Enquiries charge the blame on yourself, as do not know who is to blame. *But somebody is Responsible*, & I wish to place to the right account, the daily wrongs that are justly complained of at that Post. No place in the United States takes the liberty to interfere with the Servants or plans of Officers & their just pledges to those employed by them as the Post of Louisville, unless in those parts under Rebel Rule. I send this by Major Joel Morse Surgeon 52nd Ohio Vols. If "Billy" is in Louisville, will you give him a pass & put him in charge of Major Morse who will forward him to Mrs Raymond, who ought not to have been deprived of him. I shall be much obliged to you if you will allow Major Morse to send him forward. *If you will not do that* will you secure his return to me, at Murfreesboro without delay. Should you incur any necessary expense forward to me your Bill & I will honor it.

Pardon this long letter. I have wished to give you all the facts and my views of the Right of the case. All I wish is to have *Right* done, & if you notice any remark that seems wanting in respect in this hasty letter I wish to say it is unintentional. I beleive what I have said about the complaint made of things at Louisville. I plainly and honestly represent the feeling in the "Army of the Cumberland" on that point.

I beleive also we are fully sustained by the Commander of the Department of the Ohio. "See" General Order No 53 Department of the Ohio April 28″ 1863," to which I beg leave to refer you.[1]

I am in Earnest, in this matter, and if all is set right, It will save the Trouble of appealing to Major Gen'l Burnsides. Hoping to hear from you soon I am Respectfully Yours,

HLcSr   Lewis Raymond

Chaplain Lewis Raymond to Col. Mundy, 9 May 1863, vol. 142/330 DKy, Letters Sent, ser. 729, Post of Louisville KY, RG 393 Pt. 4 [C-6004]. Raymond was chaplain of the 51st Illinois Infantry.

1 See above, doc. 216.

219B: Commander of the Post of Louisville to the Chaplain of an Illinois Regiment

Louisville Ky May 24 1863.

Sir Yours of the 9″ inst is received and permit me to inform you that your colored servant "Billy" was not taken from your wife in Louisville by the guard, nor did the Military Authorities here interfere to prevent his crossing the Ohio river with your wife. Let me assure you that the Provost Guard at Louisville does not make lawful or unlawful interference with free or bond negroes at Louisville as you seem to have been informed, their time being fully occupied in executing their proper duties under my orders. I will add further in reply to your enquiry, that the orders of General Rosecrans will be cheerfully and promptly obeyed at this Post, when not in conflict with the direct orders of the General Commanding this Department (a most unlikely exception) And to give you full information upon the matter in which you have concern. I will state that the Statute laws of Kentucky affix a penalty of 1200$ besides forfeiture of the wherry against any ferryman who shall transport a negro slave across the Ohio river into free territory By statute law the State of Indiana and also Illinois from whose Authorities you receive your Commission, forbid the imigration or bringing of free negroes into their territories, and as all of these states are supposed to be loyal, and by the Constitution of the United States are entitled to arrange their internal polity, I did not feel authorized in disobedience of orders I had received from District H^{d} Q^{rs} to the contrary, to violate the [laws] of those states and shift the responsibilites of the ferryman upon my own shoulders by interposing my Military Authority, to secure the passage of "Billy" across the Ohio river although he may be an "orphan." I informed your wife of the orders I had regarding negroes and she left "Billy" with my Provost Marshal Colonel Moore of the 25th Michigan who would never permit the "villainous kidnappers" you allude to, to sell him into slavery. My orders referred to forbid me to give passes to negroes and required me to detail an Officer to seize all contrabands in the District of Western Kentucky who had come into the state from south of Tennessee, and all those from Tennessee & Kentucky who had used by their owners in the rebel service as Captives of War and place them to work on Government fortifications being constructed in this Department which I have done and "Billy" is no doubt serving the government now, which is much better than to have him serving a mistress or idling his time in your state contrary to her laws You say "Billy" came from Alabama, if so the Presidents Proclamation frees him and under a liberal construction of that instrument, neither you nor I as individuals have the right to appropriate or control him but as our government exercises the power to press her citizens into [service] when needed and has published no edict exempting either free or bond negroes from such contingencies I logically conclude that she [has the] right not only to require the services of Billy but to precedence over your claims notwithstanding you are entitled to a servant by army regulations. You quote the Certificate of an officer in the 19″ Ill Infty who though he entered Alabama less than two years ago attests to the birthplace of "Billy" which happened some sixteen years since. Such evidence would not be important, nor would it bring Billy within the Act of Congress to which you alluded. If as you state he was received within the federal lines and harboured in our camps it was in direct violation of the orders of the General Commanding the Department and reflects more upon the act than advantages "Billy." If he belonged to a citizen resident in Tennessee or Kentucky who had employed him in the rebellion against the government, by the provisions of the Act of Congress his Owner will have forfeited the right to his services, and a proper Court of record can upon such proof render judgement to that effect; but the Constitution nor government have Commissioned neither you or me to decide such issues nor has she transferred her claim to such forfeited services to us and therefore I conclude as you perceive, under any circumstances that "Billy" is very properly disposed of. Your inquiry as to whether Kentuckians claim all colored persons coming within state, needs no answer Your assertion that Kentuckians are villainously kidnapping and selling free and Contraband is a gratuitous slander upon a people who have a record for pride, valor & virtue and let me assure Mr Chaplain that I as one of those traduced people, believing that slavery is right and proper and therefore ready to use all lawful means to protect my neighbors unforfeited rights to that species of property would not only willingly free my own; but actively aid in freeing every negro in Kentucky, rather than aid or countenance the selling of one free negro into slavery. And this I proudly assert because of my respect for individual rights under the Constitution and laws for all persons, whether a poor freed negro or a proud and lordly citizen. Can you who would traduce Kentucky say as much? I have been greatly surprised at the extraordinary zeal displayed by some of our Commissioned Officers from the north western states in capturing the slaves of citizens of the United States appropriating them as servants and sending them into free territory. I have had the good fortune to have two of my own negroes thus disposed of by my brother officers in the 18″ Michigan Infantry and I have yet to discover how the *great & glorious cause* in which we are battling has been served thereby. I might add that I have known of a great many houses much silver-ware clothing and other personal property being appropriated in the same way, and I suppose for a like purpose of weakening the enemy and hastening this war to a conclusion; but I confess to being too stupid to see how private plundering either honors or assists our cause. Enlightened men who are risking their lives and shedding their brothers blood to maintain Constitutional government law and order, should not set examples of disregard for laws and private rights, nor complain so bitterly against their brothers in arms who conscientiously respect them. I cannot believe what you assert that the Army of the Cumberland denounces the Military Authorities in Kentucky who respect her laws and those of her sister states, who are obedient to the Constitution of the United States and refuse to aid those less scrupulous who would inflict private wrongs, appropriate private property and contemn the laws of their own states   Allow me to suggest to you Mr Chaplain in conclusion that all war is Contrary to the teachings of the good book, your profession implies that you should have studied, and that civil war, most horrible of all in its features can only be justified among us the laity, by the grand purpose we had in view of maintaining our good and tried Constitutional Government. If the great aim of the loyal American people shall dwindle into the mere purpose of freeing negroes; that justification which now nerves the arm to strike even a brother dead in this calamitous war will have passed away.   Respectfully

HLcSr   M Mundy

Col. M. Mundy to Dr. Lewis Raymond, 24 May 1863, vol. 142/330 DKy, Letters Sent, ser. 729, Post of Louisville KY, RG 393 Pt. 4 [C-6005]. The previous November, Colonel Mundy had protested to President Lincoln about the refusal of the commander of the 18th Michigan Infantry to turn out of his regiment a fugitive slave claimed by Mundy. (See above, doc. 205.)

220: West Kentucky Slaveholder to the Commander of the 16th Army Corps

Paducah [Ky.], June *1863*.

Dear Sir   At a meeting held this evening on the part of a number of the most respectable citizens of this county for the purpose of adopting some measures to arrest the almost daily departure of slaves from their owners, in this portion of Ky. west of the Tenn River, under your control, attended with the most ruinous consequences to them in the total loss of their crops, now in cultivation, aside from the discouraging uncertainty existing throughout the whole community from apprehension of the loss of the labor necessary to complete and secure their crops, A committee of three To Wit Judge Trimble Col Turman and myself were appointed to visit you in person at your head quarters and present all the facts connected with our grievances to you for the purpose of obtaining such relief as may be in your power to give, and in fact as far as possible to remedy a serious wrong and prevent a public calamity A continuance of this state of things can certainly result in no good to the great cause in which our deepest feelings are involved. As a member of the Board of Enrolment for this Con. District my duties render it impracticable for me to accompany the other members of the committee who will doubtless represent the facts to you as they really exist

Let me most ernestly and respectfully ask your favorable consideration of the subject of their mission. Very Respectfully Your Obedient Servant

ALS   A. Bradshaw

A. Bradshaw to Brigadier Genl Hurlbutt, June 1863, Miscellaneous Records of the District of Jackson, ser. 6209, 3d Division 16th Army Corps, RG 393 Pt. 2 No. 410 [C-2149]. On letterhead stationery of the provost marshal of the first congressional district of Kentucky. Colonel James S. Martin, commander of the Post of Paducah, had already indicated a willingness to prevent military interference with the recapture of fugitive slaves. "As some misunderstanding exists at this Post in regard to the recovery of slave property," he had announced on May 19, 1863, "it is ordered that hereafter all loyal slave owners . . . will be allowed to recover their slaves by civil process, the Military not interfering, neither aiding the capture, or preventing the escape." (General Order No. 7, Headquarters U.S. Forces, Paducah, Ky., 19 May 1863, Miscellaneous Records of the District of Jackson, ser. 6209, 3d Division 16th Army Corps, RG 393 Pt. 2 No. 410 [C-2148].)

221: **Order by the Commander of the District of Kentucky**

Louisville Ky.,   August 10, 1863.

General Orders No 41.

I. The construction of military roads in the State being a necessity, by the order of the Major General commanding the Department, six thousand laborers from the negro population of the country though which the roads pass will be impressed.

II. The negro laborers will be impressed first from the following counties: Harrison, Bourbon, Scott, Clarke, Fayette, Woodford, Jessamine, Mercer, Boyle, Garrard, Lincoln, Marion, Washington, and Nelson.

III. Male negroes from the ages of sixteen to forty-five both inclusive, are subject to this impressment.

IV. In order that the impressment may not hinder and materially injure the cultivation of and the harvesting and gathering the crops for the subsistence of the country, it is ordered that when a citizen has but one male negro laborer he will not be impressed under this order. In case a person has more than one and less than four, one is to be impressed. In case a person has four male laborers and over, one-third of them are impressed by this order.

V. Brig. Gen. S. S. Fry is charged with the execution of this order, and is directed to appoint officers from the 1st Division of the 23^{d} Army Corps to assist him, and to employ citizens to take charge of said negro laborers.

VI. The negroes hereby impressed are required to be delivered by the owners at the points to be designated by the 20th August inst., or at such time thereafter as Brig. Gen. S. S. Fry shall appoint officers or persons to take charge of them. Persons failing to comply with this order will have taken all their negroes of the ages designated.

VII. He will concentrate the negroes impressed by this order at Camp. Nelson, or such other place as may be directed, and have them subsisted as laborers in the Quartermaster's Department; requiring complete rolls to be kept, with the names of the negroes, their owners, and place of residence.

VIII. All owners will be paid for the services of the laborers, and at the expiration of each month proper vouchers will be furnished to the persons entitled thereto. The negroes taken under this order will be delivered to their owners after the expiration of the time for which they are impressed.

IX Brig. Gen. Fry is ordered to take immediate action for the execution of this order, and report to these Head Quarters the number of laborers collected, for information, that further orders may be issued to secure the quota of laborers required, and to distribute the impressment as equitably as practicable over the country to be mainly benefited by the proposed improvement. By order of Brig. Gen. Boyle

HD

General Orders No. 41, Head Quarters District of Kentucky, 10 Aug. 1863, vol. 14 DKy, pp. 206–7, General Orders Issued, ser. 2177, Dist. of KY, RG 393 Pt. 1 [C-7004]. General Boyle issued General Order 41 under instructions from the commander of the Department of the Ohio, General Ambrose E. Burnside, who subsequently, on August 20, ordered him to make a further impressment of slaves – to the number of 8,000 – to construct a railroad leading toward east Tennessee. (*Official Records*, ser. 1, vol. 30, pt. 3, pp. 92–93.) In early September, when work began on the railroad, Boyle reported that "[s]ince the negroes have been impressed and part of them collected, it is not so popular, and there is more signs of dissatisfaction." He informed General

Burnside that "many of the best men in the country" urged that the work be discontinued. (Brg. Genl. J. T. Boyle to Maj. Gen. Burnside, 8 Sept. 1863, A. E. Burnside Papers, Generals' Papers & Books, ser. 159, RG 94 [V-164].) By the end of September, when about 2,300 slaves were employed on the railroad, the War Department was expressing doubts about its completion in time to be militarily useful and about the legality of public expenditures for its construction. (*Official Records*, ser. 1, vol. 30, pt. 3, pp. 786–87, 810, 942.) The chief engineer of the Department of the Ohio reported in mid-October that 3,000 slaves at most had been impressed, and the prospect for obtaining a large labor force was not promising: "My opinion is that we shall come far short of the 8000, & that the number will not reach 5000." (Major J. H. Simpson to Major Gen'l A. E. Burnside, 15 Oct. 1863, A. E. Burnside Papers, Generals' Papers & Books, ser. 159, RG 94 [V-168].) In December 1863, General John G. Foster, Burnside's successor, suspended the employment of impressed slaves on the railroad, assigning them instead to work on the wagon roads through south Kentucky into east Tennessee. (See George MacLeod to Brig. Genl. Ammen, 1 Feb. 1864, Letters Received, ser. 1636, Louisville KY, Provost Marshal Field Organizations, RG 393 Pt. 4 [C-5012].) Subsequently, in February 1864, General Stephen G. Burbridge, the new commander of the District of Kentucky, extended to still more counties the impressment of slaves ordered by Boyle the previous August. (*Official Records*, ser. 1, vol. 32, pt. 2, p. 479.)

222: **Affidavit of a Kentucky Freedwoman; Affidavit of a Kentucky White; and Extract from Records of the Coroner of Jefferson County, Kentucky**

State of Kentucky County of Jefferson 7th of Mch. 1866
Fanny Ann Flood, colored, being duly sworn, declares
I am 35 years of age. I reside on Jefferson St, at Dr Hughes's, between 1st and 2nd. I am a widow.
My husbands name was Peter Flood. I married him in Shelby Co. Ky, about eleven years since   We then belonged, both of us, to Jason Chamberlin a farmer, near Middletown. My Owner carried us to Georgetown, in Pettus Co, Missouri; Immediately after reaching there he hired us out to James Mitchel, a preacher in Saline Co—about thirty miles from Georgetown. We remained about two years with Mr Michel— Mr Chamberlin then carried us to Pettus Co and sold us, by private bargain, to one George Rothwell a surgeon. Dr Rothwell kept us eight years. He then lived in Longwood, Pettus Co, He is now in Booneville, M^o.
One day the D^r came to me and said "Fanny, I want you & Peter to stay here, and take care of my family, I cannot stay here, constant, He talked as if he was afraid of the soldiers killing him, if they Caught him. He said he would come now and then to see

us & how things were getting on. We lived twelve miles from Mr Chamberlin. I only saw him once during these eight years after he sold us. I on that occasion went to see him. The Doctor was a widower. He had four children. I did the work inside, had full charge of it— My husband did the whole outside work.

One morning Mr Chamberlin came to the Doctor's house. He told me & my husband, that we had to go with him to Kentucky; that he had not been paid for us by the D^r. My husband objected to leaving so suddenly—and without the consent of the doctor—but Chamberlin forced us to come off at once— He would not give me time to pack or take my own few personal things. He said he was in a great hurry, and would pay me for them—but he has not done so yet.

We left Sedalia on a Wednesday and arrived here next Friday. He took us at once to Middletown. We remained with him until next Tuesday when he took us to Mrs Chamberlins on the Bardstown pike & about three miles from Louisville. This was in May two years ago. We remained with the widow Chamberlin until next October, (1863,)

While we were at the widow Chamberlin's my husband was wishful to return to Missouri. He told me so often. One day he left me, he did not tell me whereto. In about a month afts he came to see me. On a Sunday. He told me he had been across the river, and was working for the Gov^t He came about ten AM and left about 3 P.M. He told me he would come to see me in about two or three weeks again. He gave me $5.

Next day, Monday, Mr Chamberlin heard of my husband having been to see me, and also where he was working.

Next Wednesday, a gent^n who boarded with Mrs Chamberlin, named Major Kemp, read from a newspaper, that my husband was dead, that he had been put in gaol, and that Mr Chamberlin had whipped him to death in the jail. Major Kemp told myself so. He said "Fanny I have bad news to tell you, Your husband was whipped to death"— That Chamberlin had went, or sent, and got him. Mrs Chamberlin told me that Chamberlin allowed he did not wish to punish him to death, but only to give him a severe whipping.

About a week before Christmas Mr. Chamberlin came to the widow's He sent for me. I found him in his buggy, at the front of the house. He asked me how I was, & then went into the house. While he was in the house I went to him and asked him for help The widow, & her aunt Mrs Hall, were present. He asked me what help I wanted. I told him all the other servants in the house received help from their owners & I asked him to give me some. He said I had good clothes & he reckoned I got plenty to eat

& he did not see what more I wanted. He told me if I was "not satisfied, to pick up my duds, and leave", – and he would "get me and serve me as he "did Peter." After he left Mrs Chamberlin (the widow) came to me and said she would give me something as my owner would not.

Mr Chamberlin was rough to us, after he took us from Missouri.

My husband was a man of good health. I never knew him to be sick a moment, except when we lived in Missouri I saw him have a chill once or twice there. He had none after we returned to Kentucky He was a strong, very strong man. He was rather younger than me We had five children: four of them are living. Three of them are now with me. My oldest, a boy, works out.

her

Fanny Ann × Flood

mark

HDSr

State of Kentucky County of Jefferson [*March 1866*]
John E: Van Sant, being duly sworn, declares
I am   years of age. I reside in the City of Louisville
There resides in Middletown in Jefferson Co Ky a man of the name of Jason Chamberlin, a refugee from Missouri. While in Mo. he had certain slaves which were freed by the Mo State Emancipation Act. Shortly after the emancipation in Mo said Chamberlin came to Ky. and brought ~~slaves~~ freedmen with him here. One of them was named   I am informed and believe he, said freedman, was arrested in this City of Louisville, as a runaway slave, and committed to the County jail. and while so imprisoned was flogged and beat by said Jason Chamberlain and a son in law of his named English?[1] until he died
A coroner's inquest was held on the body at Wash Wyatts office and found the man had come to his death at the hands of Chamberlain and others.
[*In the margin*] Robt Seay care Jack Johnson _
Certain parties not satisfied with this finding as being a reflection on the fair fame of Ky – applied for & obtained a second inquest Two surgeons were present, named Knight and Seeley. These gent^n certified that the deceased had died from congestion of the lungs (or brain)?[2]
I am credibly informed, by one John Martin, that Dr Knight said He be damned if the whipping ever caused this man's death.
The whole story was then hushed up. The parties seemed very anxious to prevent the military coming to learn of the facts.
Capt Thomas, the Keeper of the jail, pronounced the occurrence a

"damned outrage". That they had the negro in the whipping room of the jail – that he thought they were only talking to the negro – that he had no idea they were whipping the man – that he heard nothing of what transpired in the whipping room as it is thickwalled, double doored and rather apart from the other buildings. A negro employed in the jail as cook said the injured man could hardly walk when they took him out of the whipping room

HD

[*Louisville*] September 30 1863

Inquest No 147 was held this morning, at W Wyatts office, cor 7th and Jeff^n Streets, on the body of "Peter" slave of Jason Chamberlain

Mr Chamberlain had sold the negro to a man in Missouri – the man failing – Mr Chamberlain took the negro back, and sent him to this place with a drove of cattle.

When the negro got here he reported to the Provo Marshal as a contraband, and was sent to Jeffersonville to work in the government bakery.

Last Monday he came to this side of the river to get his clothes His master seen and took him to General Boyel, who gave him permission to take him. His master put him in jail

On Tuesday his master whipped him, and in six hours after the negro died.

I summoned a jury, & held an inquest on the body – The verdict of the jury was that the negro came to his death from injuries received at the hands of his master.

I did not believe the verdict was a just one, as I could not see that the negro had received an unmerciful whiping. I therefore summoned another jury and held another inquest on the body. I got Drs Knight and Seely to examine the body. They boath said that the whiping could not cause his death. They made a Poste Mortom on the body – but could not determin the real cause of death

HDcSr   (signed) James C. Gill

Affidavit of Fanny Ann Flood, 7 Mar. 1866, affidavit of John E. Van Sant, [Mar. 1866], and extract from Jefferson County coroner's record book, 30 Sept. 1863, Affidavits & Records Relating to Complaints, ser. 1218, Louisville KY Supt., RG 105 [A-4538]. The two affidavits are filed under "F" and the coroner's records under "C." Affidavits sworn before a Freedmen's Bureau agent. The blank spaces in the Van Sant affidavit appear in the manuscript. Filed with the extract from the coroner's book are the findings of Coroner's Inquest No. 147 and Coroner's Inquest No. 148, both dated September 30, 1863, upon the body of "Peter, slave of Jason Chamberlain." No. 147 concluded that Peter "came to his death at the Jail of Jeff. Cty on or about 5 o'clock P.M. Tuesday Sept. 29, 1863 from injuries inflicted (at the place above cited, viz. the jail) by his master Chamberlain." No. 148 put the death at the same time and place, "from some cause unknown to the Jury."

1 The name "English?" has been penciled into what was originally a blank space, in the same handwriting as the body of the affidavit.
2 The words "of the lungs (or brain)?" have been penciled into what was originally a blank space, in the same handwriting as the body of the affidavit.

223A: **Testimony by Members of the Louisville Contraband Commission before the American Freedmen's Inquiry Commission**

[*Louisville, November 1863*]

Testimony of Maj. D. C. Fitch & Capt. M. H Jewett, Commissioners appointed by authority of Gen. Burnside to examine the cases of contraband or captured negroes coming into Louisville.

We will state, as a Commission, that when Gen. Buell's army left here, in the fall of 1862, there were undoubtedly one thousand negroes picked up and sold, at prices ranging from $4.50 to $200 apiece. These men came here with the army. The greater portion of them have been recovered by this Commission, and have been placed on the public works, and are now receiving $10.20 a month from the Government; and we are still continuing the work. We have eleven counties in our district.

Q   You think that evil has now been eradicated?
A   Yes, Sir, entirely.
Q   Do you know of any other part of the State where it still exists?
A   We think Bowling Green is one point, and that there is more or less of it at all points in Kentucky. The men that were taken here were picked up by the State law and thrown into jail, like brutes. The State law says that if they are not claimed within a certain time, they shall be sold for jail fees. Thirty-one were sold in one day, and we arrested the Sheriff the next day, & got every one of them back, set them at work on the public works, and there they are now, and are well satisfied.

Q   Do you or not think there has been a great change in public feeling within the last few months?

A   We think there has been a great change. There are negroes in our own district which we have not been able to get hold of; but we have used all the exertion we could. We issue notices occasionally calling upon all persons who hold contrabands to report them to this office. We wrote to the Sheriffs of the eleven counties in our district, calling upon them to obey that order, but not one of them has paid any attention to it. We mean to make some of those men suffer. The difficulty is, that the State officers won't obey the order. There is one man who thinks he can get from fifty to a hundred contrabands in four counties, and another who thinks he can get a hundred from two counties. Men in the lower counties are holding them, working them, and don't give them a thing. They are so ragged that they are half frozen. The region about Henderson & Owensboro', in the lower part of the State, is the worst part of the State in this respect; and there is a great deal of it in Hopkinsville. The only way we can get hold of these negroes is by private parties, whom we can get interested. We have no means of sending for these men. If we had a company of cavalry, it would help us a great deal. We sent some cavalry – ten or eleven men – down into Breckinridge County, and they were driven off. We then sent down forty men, and they brought off some sixteen that they took out of jails there, some of whom were freemen. We sent to Lagrange, and brought off nine, that were taken out of jail there. A great many are brought here from Missouri and sold. We had six of those people here this morning.

Q   What number do you suppose has been brought here from Missouri?

A   There have been thousands sent here and sold. We will venture to say there have been a thousand sent here within the last two months. The order of Gen. Schofield at St. Louis [for the recruitment of colored soldiers, free or slave][1] brought the Missouri negroes here. Within a month, we have sent down 150 to the military road that is being built from Lebanon to Knoxville. It is called the Lebanon Extension Road. We have got good homes for fifty or sixty little girls and boys, the persons taking them agreeing to take good care of them, feed and clothe them well, and hold them subject to our order

HD

Testimony of Maj. D. C. Fitch & Capt. M. H. Jewett, [Nov. 1863], filed with O-328 1863, Letters Received, ser. 12, RG 94 [K-92]. Topical labels in the margin are omitted.

1 Brackets in manuscript. The order, issued on November 14, 1863, by General John M. Schofield, commander of the Department of the Missouri, authorized the enlistment of black men in Missouri, whether freemen or slaves and regardless of the loyalty or consent of their owners. (*Official Records*, ser. 3, vol. 3, pp. 1034–36; *Freedom*, ser. 2: pp. 188–89.)

223B: President of the Louisville Contraband Commission to the Provost Marshal General of the Department of the Ohio

Louisville, Ky., Decr 9th 1863

Genl I have the honor to inclose a copy of the order appointing a Military Commission (of which I am President) to investigate the cases of all Contrabands at or arriving at this Post.

I report that in the case of "Solomon Meeks" and his family, having been interfered with, happened previous to the appointment of this commission, and that we have never heard of it until now.[1]

When the Commission was first appointed we found that the City of Louisville had many Contrabands in it and we immediately issued an order for the parties holding same to produce them and have done so from time to time ever since.

The Males we have placed upon public works – such as fortifications then being built in this District – latterly we have sent them to the Chief Enjineer of the military Rail Road now building from Kentucky to Tennessee – in each case taking recpt for said Negroes which Recpts we now hold.

The Females we have placed in Hospitals where they recieve good wages for thier services.

All Negroes from Mississippi & Alabama who arrive here without the pass of a Genl Officer we take and place upon the public works. We have also notified Captains of Steamboats and Ferry Boats to allow no Negroes to pass north of the Ohio River without a pass signed by us.

I inclose herewith a copy of said pass used by us also one of our Notice's published in the daily papers. We also frequently call the keepers of Slave Pens before us with the negroes they may have on hand and examine & see if there are any Contrabands among them.

We have within the last two months sent forward to Lebanon Ky about 100 Contrabands (picked up here) to be employed on the military Rail Road. Very Respectfully Your Ob^t Servt

ALS   D. C. Fitch

Maj. D. C. Fitch to Brigd. Genl. N. H. McLean, 9 Dec. 1863, enclosed in Brig. Genl. N. C. McLean to Capt. W. P. Anderson, 22 Jan. 1864, M-10

1864, Letters Received, ser. 3514, Dept. of the OH, RG 393 Pt. 1 [C-4631].
Enclosed is a copy of the order of May 13, 1863, creating the commission. (See
above, doc. 217An.) Also enclosed is a sample printed certificate, stating that
the bearer was free under the Emancipation Proclamation and "entitled to pass
North of the Ohio River into free territory." Two newspaper clippings are also
enclosed, one a notice from the commission dated October 5, 1863, instructing "[a]ll persons having contraband negroes in the counties of Jefferson,
Oldham, Shelby, Spencer, Bullitt, Nelson, Washington, Meade, Hardin,
Larue, and Breckinridge" to report them to the provost marshal's office at
Louisville. "Any one having them in their possession after the 20th of October, 1863, . . . will be arrested and punished for the violation of this
order." The second clipping urged citizens to cooperate in reporting contrabands to the commission, because "there is an urgent necessity for working
hands."

1 See above, doc. 209.

224: **Commander of U.S. Forces in Southwestern Kentucky
to the Commander of the District of Kentucky**

Bowling-Green Ky December 5th. 1863

General:

. . . .

The slaves in southern Kentucky are running away in great
numbers, and are either enlisted in the army, or seized by the
military authorities in Tennessee and placed at work on the
North-Western Railroad   The citizens of that section of our State,
are not only willing, but, as I am informed, exceedingly anxious
that their negroes should be put to work on the unfinished
Henderson & Nashville Railroad in their own State, and intelligent
men from there say that if notice were given that hands were
wanted to complete the road, the owners in several counties, the
disloyal as well as the loyal, would in a week's time cheerfully
furnish negroes enough to complete the road from the State line to
Henderson in a month, and without any more cost to the
Government than the rations and clothes of the negroes while at
work and the material used on the road
    While Speaking of the Slaves in Southern Kentucky, I would
remark, General, that Something ought to be done to protect the
loyal Slaveholders at least against the consequences of having
recruiting stations for negroes in Tennessee close to the border   I
am told no distinction is made between the loyal and disloyal

owner, but I do not know what to suggest, though it does seem to me an outrage that the Slaveholder who has been true and loyal through all the troubles of Southern Kentucky, should receive no more consideration than the traitorous sympathizer with the causeless, wicked Rebellion, and who has actively given it aid and encouragement   Very respectfully,

ALS   C. Maxwell

Excerpt from Col. C. Maxwell to General J. T. Boyle, 5 Dec. 1863, Letters Received, ser. 2173, Dist. of KY, RG 393 Pt. 1 [C-4303]. Endorsement. The first half of the letter detailed the condition and projected route of the Henderson and Nashville Railroad. Maxwell was colonel of the 26th Kentucky Volunteers.

225A: Governor of Kentucky to the Commander of the District of Kentucky, Enclosing a Letter from Kentucky Slaveholders to the Governor

Frankfort [*Ky.*],   Feby 26th, *1864.*

Genl— I enclose you herewith Communication from some citizens of Marion County which demands attention. Our Government should see that faith be kept with the citizen, and that the Contracts of its authorized agents be Complied with. I trust you will take all proper steps to have this matter set right. — Respectfully

ALS   Tho E Bramlette

[*Enclosure*]   Lebanon Ky   Febry 24th 1864
To his Excellency Gov. Bramlette   The undersigned citizens of Marion County respectfully state to your Excelancy that on the last days of December they hired to James Wright of Lebanon Several of their Slaves as Teamsters for the Government servace with the distinct understanding and agreement that they were to be engaged at the Post of Lebanon Ky and in no case to be taken out of the state of Ky   Said Hiring was made after an Advertisement calling for Teamsters by Capt Geaubert Quartermaster at this place promising $30. per month to them or their masters if slaves. Under these circumstances they hired their slaves to Mr Wright who had the promise of the position of wagon master in the

Train, He had had at this post that position hertofore and had some of our Servants ane we were pleased with his management. They would further state that on the 26 day of January 1864 all the Teamsters hired by Wright and ours with them were transfered to Nashville Tenn. and taken there with Mr Wright as wagon master and with them was transfered the 26 days they were employed here. Since they arrived at Nashville Said negroes have been paid themselves, the Quartermaster Donalson there ignoring our claims and refusing to make any difference with teamsters Black or white. They also understand that said negroes will not be returned to us at the end of the time for which they were hired which will be the 1st April next, unless the negroes are willing to return The undersigned would respectfully state to your Excellancy, that they think they are entitled to have the hire of their slaves and to have them returned to them on the 1st April next and that the United States Authorities on a proper statement of the case would give the necessary orders to secure us justice we earnestly request your aid and assistance in the pemasises Whatever may be done for our benefit we desire to go also for the benefit of our neighbours who had Slaves to go off with Mr Wright. Mr Wright is now Devision Quartermaster 1st Brig. 1st Devision 11. A.C.

Hervey. McElrey   John Lancaster

HLS   Sam. Spalding   R M. Spalding

Tho. E. Bramlette to Brigdr. Genl. Burbridge, 26 Feb. 1864, enclosing Hervey McElrey et al. to his Excellency Gov. Bramlette, 24 Feb. 1864, filed with K-323 1864, Letters Received, RG 107 [L-47]. On March 1, 1864, General Stephen G. Burbridge, commander of the District of Kentucky, forwarded the petition to the commander of the Military Division of the Mississippi, noting that all the petitioners were "truly loyal men." From there, the petition was referred to the supervising quartermaster of the Department of the Cumberland, whose report is printed immediately below.

225B: Supervising Quartermaster of the Department of the Cumberland to the Headquarters of the Military Division of the Mississippi

Nashville, Tenn., March 9th 1864.

Colonel: I have the to return communication from the Governor of Kentucky on the subject of the Slaves of loyal persons being ordered from Lebanon Ky. to Nashville Tenn. These slaves were ordered by me to Nashville under the following circumstances: At

Chattanooga, Capt. Dickinson Chief Quartermaster, Genl. Foster's army informed me he had nine hundred Mules and four hundred Teamsters at Lebanon Ky. which I might have if I desired. I replied that I should want them, and on my return to Nashville telegraphed Capt. Gaubert to hold the mules, and send me two hundred Teamsters at once, not Knowing at the time that a portion of them were slaves. He sent me a number, and the transfer list said nothing of the contract that they were to be retained in Kentucky, or that a portion were Slaves; and on their arrival, in good faith, and in ignorance of their Status, I authorized their transfer to the 1st Division, 11th Army Corps, commanded by Genl. Ward of Kentucky.

This is my connection with the subject, and the first intimation I received that a number of the teamsters transferred to this Depot were slaves, was a letter addressed to Maj. Genl. L. H. Rosseau by Mr. R. M. Spalding which he referred to me with the following endorsment:

> "H'd Qr's District of Nashville
> "Nashville Feby. 5th 1864.
>
> "Respectfully referred to Lt. Col. J. L. Donaldson C.Q.M. who will please say what Mr. Spaulding may expect in the premises. Mr. Spaulding is a most estimable gentleman, a brother of Bishop Spalulding of Louisville Ky.
>
> (signed) "L. H. Rosseau
> "Maj. Genl. Comd'g"

To which endorsment I replied as follows:

> "Office Senior & Sup. quartermaster
> "Nashville Feby. 5th 1864.
>
> "Respectfully returned. I cannot make any distinction between these teamsters and others that may be hired for the Quartermaster's Department, white or black. I ordered the teamsters from Lebanon Ky. by the authority of the Chief Qr. Mr. of Genl. Foster's Army & until they arrived did not Know how and under what circumstances they were engaged; now that they are here however, I must regard them as I regard all other teamsters.
>
> (Signed) "J. L. Donaldson
> "Senior & Sup. Quartermaster"

I am, Colonel, Very Respectfully Your obdt. Servt.

HLS

J L Donaldson

[*Endorsement*] Hd. Qrs. Mil. Div. of the Miss. Nashville Tenn. April 4, 64 This is a matter for the War Dept. and not for a military officer, who deals with men and not Constitutional or legal questions. W. T Sherman Maj G Comdg.

Senior & Sup. Quartermaster J. L. Donaldson to Lt. Col. T. S. Bowers, 9 Mar. 1864, filed with K-323 1864, Letters Received, RG 107 [L-47].

225C: Governor of Kentucky to the Secretary of War

Frankfort [Ky.], Ap^l 12th, 1864.

Sir: I transmit to you for final action the enclosed documents.

These citizens of Ky certainly have just cause of complaint and demand for redress. An Officer in the regular line of his official duties & under orders employed by contract of these Citizens their slaves—was to pay them $30. per month—not to remove them from Ky and to return them at the expiration of the service.— Every promise has been violated. Their slaves are sent off to Tennessee—put in the Army service—without any compensation to the owner—no voucher given—pay for the hire as per contract refused and no return of the slaves, nor hope thereof.

Surely this will not be permitted to pass without some fair and just compensation to men who trusting to their Government and the obligations incurred by its accredited organs now through me appeal for justice to the last resort—the War Dept— Respectfully

ALS   Thos E Bramlette

Thos. E. Bramlette to Hon. E. M. Stanton, 12 Apr. 1864, K-323 1864, Letters Received, RG 107 [L-47]. A War Department notation of April 27 stated: "No action at present."

226: Provost Marshal General of the 1st Division of the District of Kentucky to the Headquarters of the Department of the Ohio

Lexington [Ky.] April 14 1864

Captain, I have the honor to submit the following Statement in reference to the impressment of Slave labor in the state of Kentucky

August 10th 1863 Brig General Boyle Commanding Dist of Ky. by the order of Major General Burnside Commanding Dept of the Ohio, issued an order (a copy of which is enclosed) for the impressment of Slave labor in Central Kentucky for the purpose of constructing Military roads, which order with very few exceptions was promptly responded to by the owners of Slaves and at a time when these hands were needed for farming purposes. These negroes were employed on the road until the 5th of March 1864 when by order of Brig General Burbridge Commanding District of Ky they were returned to their owners   Many of the Counties have never received pay for this labor or remunerated in any way.   Many of the owners have lost their Slaves, Some by accidents, some by death from diseases contracted while employed and a large number are physically disabled for life caused by exposure in the severe cold and inclement weather.   All this has a tendency to creat dissitsfaction among those interested and inasmuch as the books and papers pertaining to the impressment have been placed in my hands for adjustment, and many letters of inquiry received daily, I deem it my duty to make these representations to the Assistant Adjutant Gen'l for the consideration of the General Commanding hoping that an early action will be had and steps taken to satisfy these claims or such disposition of them as may seem proper and just   I am Captain Very Resply Your Obt Servt

ALS   W. W. Woodward

[*Endorsement*]   H^d Qrs. Dist. of Kenty Louisville, April 21. 1864   Respectfully referred to Department Head Quarters.   The Impressment was made under orders of Maj. Genl. Burnside and with assurances that the owners of the slaves would be paid for their services.   Justice demands that the remuneration should be made, and it is respectfully and Earnestly recommended. S. G. Burbridge Brig Genl Cmdg

Capt. W. W. Woodward to Capt. R. Morrow, 14 Apr. 1864, W-297 1864, Letters Received, ser. 3514, Dept. of the OH, RG 393 Pt. 1 [C-4634]. Other endorsements. A copy of General Boyle's August 1863 impressment order is enclosed. (See above, doc. 221.) No reply to Woodward has been found among the records of the Department of the Ohio. The claims of many slaveholders remained outstanding at the end of the war. According to one claim agent, those masters who did collect usually received payments that "did not amount to much, as the gov't had charged the negroes with blankets &c to allmost the full amount due them, and in some cases they were indebted to the Gov't." Moreover, many of the impressed slave laborers had run away while in government service. (W. F. Rice to Bvt. Col. R. E. Johnston, 5 July 1866, enclosing statement by L. S. McFarland, [July 1866], Unregistered Letters Received, ser. 1186, Lexington KY Chief Supt., RG 105 [A-4441].)

227: Provost Marshal of the 4th District of Kentucky to the
Assistant Provost Marshal General for Kentucky

Lebanon, *Ky.*, June 2 *1864*

Sir: I have the honor to make the following statement of facts for
your action: —

It has come to my knowledge that a number of the negroes who
apply to Dpty. Pro Marˢ to enlist, only do so in order to obtain
passes to aid them to escape from Ky— The representative of
Hardin Co., J. B. Thomas, represents to me that some ten or more
negroes who applied to my deputy and obtained proper papers made
for the ohio river and crossed into Ind. This mode of procedure
deprives the master of the work of the slave, and the state of its
proper recruits. Certainly this should be remedied in some way. I
can see but one remedy, and that remedy is, to furnish
transportation to my Hd-Qrs for recruits; or an escort— It could be
remedied, perhaps by establishing recruiting offices with surgeons at
several points in the district— I may say in this connection that at
the present time I believe that there are parties from other states
running slaves off. I have no evidence of this fact, further than the
success with which slaves escape— Awaiting your orders I am Your
obt sevᵗ

ALS   Jamˢ M. Fidler

Capt. Jams. M. Fidler to Maj. W. H. Sidell, 2 June 1864, Letters Received,
ser. 3967, KY Actg. Asst. Pro. Mar. Gen., RG 110 [R-8]. In reply, the
assistant provost marshal general asked for details about particular instances in
which Kentucky slaves had fled the state using deputy provost marshals'
passes, observing that the slaves might simply have traveled to a different
Kentucky enlistment office: "There is no intention to make the passes given
by the Deputies free transportation passes but only protective passes to secure
them from molestation on their way." Enlistment procedures required that a
slave who volunteered for army service at the office of a deputy provost marshal
proceed to the headquarters of the district provost marshal for medical examination and completion of enlistment. The system of providing passes to such
slaves had been instituted in Kentucky after several slave recruits were arrested
as runaways while en route to the district provost marshal's office. (Maj. W.
H. Sidell to Capt. J. M. Fidler, 3 June 1864, vol. 3, p. 158, Letters Sent, ser.
3962, KY Actg. Asst. Pro. Mar. Gen., RG 110 [R-8]; see also *Freedom*, ser.
2: doc. 100.)

228A: Kentucky Slaveholders to the
Adjutant General of the Army

[Todd County, Ky., early August, 1864]

The undersigned loyal Citizen of Todd County in the State of
Kentucky respectfully represent: that they reside on the borders of
the State of Tennessee and about twenty five miles from Clarksville
Tennessee

That within twelve months past several hundred slaves have left
their owners in this Co and gone to Clarksville where a part of them
have enlisted as Soldiers in the Army of the United States. but a
large number are still lounging about Clarksville in idleness or are
on the river engaged at intervals on trade boats. The owners have
received no compensation for the slaves and the State no credit for
such as have been enlisted in the army. The owners cannot recover
them nor can they enlist them because the slaves object

They are still going in large numbers. Some to avoid the draft &
others we suppose to live in idleness. They will not enlist while
they know they can so easily avoid Military duty & labor at home:

These facts result in great hardships to Our people. are prejudicial
to the interest of the Government: We therefore Respectfully
request that you will publish an order or extend order N° 25¹ so as
to direct that such slaves be seized by the provo. Marshals in
Tennessee at the requst of the owner. & deliver to the proper
authorities in Kentucky to be enlisted. that Kentucky may receive
her proper credits for those remaining to be enlisted

H. G. Petree	S. Black
J. G. Hollingsworth	E. B. Edwards
J. H. Lowry	J. G. Roach
	J. R. Penick

HLS

[Endorsement] I fully indorse and approve the suggestions made in
the foregoing petition, and in addition would respectfully add, that
it is and will continue to be impossible to recruit any considerable
number of negroes in this part of Ky, while they are allowed not
only to loiter & idle about Clarksville themselves, but can take their
wives & children with them and have them subsisted by the
Govmt. Able-bodied negroes in this County will conceal themselves
and run to Clarksville on this account, whenever efforts are made to
enlist them in Ky. In other words so long as the present condition
of affairs at Clarksville continues, the Govmt is thereby furnishing

the able bodied negroes of Ky, not only means of avoiding enlistment in the army but is absolutely offering them an inducement to avail themselves of the means. B. H. Bristow

H. G. Petree et al. to Adjutant General L. Thomas, [early Aug. 1864], B-992 1864, Letters Received, ser. 360, Colored Troops Division, RG 94 [B-94]. Black indicated after his signature that he was deputy provost marshal for Todd County. The petition was forwarded through General Stephen G. Burbridge, commander of the District of Kentucky, who endorsed it on August 12, 1864, "with the request that measures may be adopted to put a stop to the evils mentioned within and secure for the Government the services of able bodied negroes now at Clarksville and vicinity." After passing through the headquarters of the Department of the Ohio, the Military Division of the Mississippi, and the Bureau of Colored Troops, the petition reached Adjutant General Lorenzo Thomas, who, on October 8, 1864, referred it to Colonel Reuben D. Mussey, commissioner of black recruitment in middle and east Tennessee, with instructions that "[a]ll able bodied negroes from Kentucky found at Clarksville Tenn, or anywhere else in Tennessee should be put in service." Mussey returned the petition on October 13, with an endorsement stating that measures had already been taken "to put these men into Service." He insisted that there were fewer than eighteen able-bodied black men at Clarksville who had not already been enlisted. For earlier complaints by southern Kentucky slaveholders about the flight of their slaves to Clarksville after black recruitment began in Tennessee, see J. S. Golladay to Genl. J. T. Boyle, 20 Nov. 1863, G-103 1863, Letters Received, ser. 360, Colored Troops Division, RG 94 [B-423]; *Freedom*, ser. 2: doc. 97; and Sarg. J. M. Bailey to Hon. E. M. Stanton, 27 June 1864, B-732 1864, Letters Received, ser. 360, Colored Troops Division, RG 94 [B-550].

1 Order 25, issued by Adjutant General Lorenzo Thomas on July 25, 1864, authorized the arrest and forcible enlistment of Kentucky slaves who had escaped from their masters but had not joined the army. It also instructed military officials to seize Kentucky slaves who attempted to cross the Ohio River and enlist in the free states. Thomas justified the order on the grounds that "many slaves in Kentucky have left their owners without intending to enter the service of the United States, and . . . have resorted to the towns, or are roving around the country." (*Official Records*, ser. 3, vol. 4, p. 543.)

228B: Assistant Provost Marshal General for Kentucky to the Commissioner for the Organization of Black Troops in Middle and East Tennessee, and the Latter's Reply

Louisville Ky. August 18" 186.

My Dear Colonel— I am informed that Christian County one of th. largest slaveholding counties in this State has given no negro recruits here or very few although the recruiting of slaves is active elsewhere.

The reason stated is that they go from Christian County to Clarksville instead of coming to a Pro. Marshal or recruiting officer here and thus the State loses the credit it is entitled to and we lose the force which might be organized out of them to suppress guerillas and disloyal persons. It is desirable to correct this if possible for the very reasons stated. But another very strong reason is this (if the information be correct) that at Clarksville the refugee slaves refuse to enlist considering the act to be at their option but are nevertheless received by Capt. Smith commandant at Clarksville and fed at cost of U.S. they and their women and children.

The first question is as to the fact, the second the remedy. Until I hear from you I assume the fact stating that my informant is Col. Bristow one of the firmest, bravest, most uncompromising and clearest headed and eloquent unconditional Union patriots of the State.

I think that these slaves should be conscripted at once and forced to serve the same as drafted men if they or theirs have fed on a single ration of the U.S. or even if they be rambling at large without masters or even at work by hire unless hired through their masters and even then they may volunteer.

This is just what they are doing here

It is estimated that not less than 2000 have gone to Tennessee by flight from Kentucky and that 500 are in and about Clarksville (some of them kept and fed in Camp) who are lost to the U.S. by the simple process on their part of refusing to go in.

They should be forced to serve and be credited to the County of Ky that they have fled from.

An officer would be sent from here to recruit them if permitted (by whom?) Military Commander? and sustained.

One remedy is if a mulish negro refuses to enlist to press him for hard work on fortifications or elsewhere without pay & other supplies than food   When willing to enlist then enlist him.

I would be glad to hear from you soon on this matter   Truly Yours

HLcS

W H Sidell

Nashville   Sept 3ᵈ *1864*

My dear Major,   Some time since you wrote me about the large number of able-bodied idle negroes fugitive from Kentucky and at Clarksville. I wrote to Col. Smith Commandant of the Post about it—   He writes under date of Sept 1ˢᵗ—

"I have picked up and got the names of all the male negroes of *all ages* at this place from Kentucky. They number One hundred twenty five (125) They are the cullings of all the troops raised at this place I do not think there is more than 15 or so of this number *able bodied* The statement made to you is absurd. The Recruiting Officers are on the streets every day picking up these negroes."

I am Major Very Truly Yrs

ALS   R D Mussey

Maj. W. H. Sidell to Col. R. D. Mussey, 18 Aug. 1864, vol. 3, pp. 365–66, Letters Sent & Circulars Issued, ser. 3962, KY Actg. Asst. Pro. Mar. Gen., RG 110 [R-35]; Col. R. D. Mussey to Major W. H. Sidell, 3 Sept. 1864, Letters Received, ser. 3967, KY Actg. Asst. Pro. Mar. Gen., RG 110 [R-13]. At Mussey's request, Colonel A. A. Smith, commander at Clarksville, issued an order on August 26, 1864, requiring all able-bodied black men from Kentucky who were neither enlisted as soldiers nor employed by the government as laborers to report to his headquarters within five days. The enumeration that resulted included 125 men, nearly all described as employed, too old for service to the government, or physically disabled. (General Orders No. 25, Head Quarters United States Forces Clarksville and Ft. Donelson, 26 Aug. 1864, vol. 171/208 DMT, General Orders Issued, ser. 3031, RG 393 Pt. 2 No. 192 [C-2071]; List of Colored Refugees from the State of Kentucky Not in the Army or Employed by the Government as Laborers, [Aug.–Sept. 1864], vol. -/213 DMT, ser. 3035, U.S. Forces Clarksville & Ft. Donelson TN, RG 393 Pt. 2 No. 192 [C-2072]).

229: Governor of Kentucky to the President

Frankfort [Ky.] Sept 3rd 1864

Sir: Kentucky is and ever has been loyal as a State and people. Her people have triumphantly passed through the severest ordeal, and borne without yielding the severest tests ever applied to the loyalty of any people. Yet we are dealt with as though Kentucky was a rebellious and conquered province, instead of being as they are a brave and loyal people. –

Without any occasion for such measures the State has by special Executive edict been declared under Martial law; and this just preceding the elections.

Without rebuke the Military Commandant issued an order directly interfering with the most important election then depending; and in open Conflict with the Constitution and laws of the State, and in dereliction of the most sacred rights of a free and loyal people.

The ordinary and necessary trade of the State is now by Military trade regulations subjected to restrictions, which harrass the citizen without any compensating public good; and which wear more the phase of subjecting the citizens to odious political tests, than looking to the public good. I send herewith a copy of a permit, with the test questions as appended, the original I retain as a specimen and memorial of the military follies and harrassments to which Kentuckians are subjected.

The citizens of Western Kentucky have for a long while been the subjects of insult, oppression, and plunder by officers who have been placed to defend and protect them.

Having on yesterday stated the conduct of Genl Payne & his accomplices & heretofore Communicated in reference to Cunningham who is now overshadowed by Genl Payne, I will not again state it. —

The Military Authorities throughout the State assume at pleasure to make assessments upon the citizens and enforce the payment of heavy fines without a hearing. And yet the laws of Kentucky are ample and the Courts open for redress of every just grievance, without any such military judgements.

I send herewith a copy of one of those orders assessing a citizen—merely as a specimen of what is of daily occurrence.

That these measures with others of kindred nature have been urged by the Counsels of a class of men who represent the *evil genius* of loyalty, I am well assured

No one who has a love for our Country and a desire to preserve our Government, if possessed of ordinary intellect and a common inteligence with a knowledge of our people, would advise such measures. My hope is that in the multifarious affairs of State, your attention has not been caught to these matters, and that by my drawing your attention to them your sense of justice and what is due to a loyal people will prompt you to order a revocation of those orders and a correction of these evils. The course pursued by many of those entrusted with Federal authority in Kentucky, has made to your Administration and re-election, thousands of bitter and irreconcileable opponents, where a wise and just policy and action would more easily have made friends.

Extreme measures by which they sought to break the just pride and subdue the free spirit of the people; and which would only have fitted them for enslavement, have aroused the determined opposition to your re-election of at least three fourths of the people of Kentucky; when a different and just policy might have made them friends. You will pardon me for speaking thus plainly, for I assure you it is done in the kindest spirit; although I am opposed to your re-election, and regard a change of policy as essential to the salvation of our Country.

In common with the loyal masses of Kentucky *my Unionism is unconditional.* We are for preserving the rights and liberties of our own race—and upholding the character and dignity of our position. We are not willing to sacrifice a single life, or imperil the smallest right of free white men for the sake of the negro. We repudiate the Counsels of those who say the Government must be restored *with Slavery,* or that it must be restored *without Slavery, as a condition of their Unionism.* We are for the restoration of our Government throughout our entire limits regardless of what may happen to the negro. We reject as spurious, the Unionism of all who make the Status of the negro a sine qua non to peace and unity. We are not willing to imperil the life liberty and happiness of our own race and people for the freedom or enslavement of the negro. To permit the question of the freedom or slavery of the negro, to obstruct the restoration of National authority and unity is a blood stained sin. Those whose sons are involved in this strife demand, as they have the right to do, *that the negro be ignored in all questions of settlement, and not make his condition*—whether it shall be free or slave, *an obstacle to the restoration of national unity & peace.* Such are the sentiments of the loyal masses of Kentucky. Why therefore are unequal burdens laid upon the people of Kentucky? Is it not unwise, not to say unjust that this is done. Surely the appealing blood of her sons, which crimsons the battlefields, sufficiently attests the loyalty of Kentucky and her people, to entitle the State to be freed from those Military manacles, which fetter her noble limbs, and chafe the free spirit of her loyal people.

It cannot surely be the purpose of any to ascertain by actual experiment how much a brave and manly people will bear rather than revolt against their Government.

And yet some of the measures adopted wear much the aspect of such an experiment.

May the God of our Fathers speedily give to us deliverance, by a restoration of our Government in unity and peace Respectfully
ALS Thos E Bramlette

Thos. E. Bramlette to His Excellency A. Lincoln, 3 Sept. 1864, P-61 1864, Letters Received Irregular, RG 107 [L-129]. Enclosures. President Lincoln's secretary referred the letter to the Secretary of War on September 12. No reply to Governor Bramlette has been found among the copies of letters sent by the Secretary of War.

230: Agent for Madison County, Kentucky, Slaveholders to the Mustering Officer at Camp Nelson, Kentucky; and Statement by the Deputy Provost Marshal of Lincoln County, Kentucky

Camp Nelson [*Ky*.] Oct 1ˢᵗ 1864

Dʳ Sir   There are a number of Colored persons probably from 50 to 100 in and around Camp Nelson, without the consent or approval of their Masters who live in Madison County Ky, and it is the desire of their owners (expressed in a Public Meeting held in Richmond Ky) That said persons be enlisted as soldiers in the United States Service, that the County have the proper credit.

My object is to get your assistance Capt in having all such persons properly enlisted as above intimated   Very Respectfully &c

John Bennett

P.S.   I understand that there are a number of sᵈ persons, in one Capt Dayˢ Employ preparatory to starting South with stock or a train. And there some employed by other persons.   Jno Bennett Agt

ALS

Camp Nelson Ky Oct 1ˢᵗ 1864

I hereby state that a number of Colored persons have left their owners in Lincoln County Ky and gone to Garrard County Ky near Lancaster without the consent of their owners and are aiming to hire themselves to attend to government stock in that vicinity and as I learn expect to go south with said stock and it is the desire of their owners so far as I have heard them express themselves that they shall be enlisted in the United States service as soldiers

ADS   Robert [S] Barrow

John Bennett to Capt. Kinney, 1 Oct. 1864, and statement of Robert S.[?] Barrow, 1 Oct. 1864, both enclosed in Capt. N. C. Kinney to Major W. H. Sidell, 3 Oct. 1864, Letters Received, ser. 3994, KY Chief Mustering & Disbursing Officer, RG 110 [R-24]. In the same file is a similar statement by the deputy provost marshal of Garrard County, Kentucky. The mustering officer at Camp Nelson forwarded the statements to Major William H. Sidell, assistant provost marshal general for Kentucky, who reported to the headquarters of the military District of Kentucky that "[f]requent just complaints are made . . . that many slaves leave their masters and are employed by U.S. officers without having been enlisted." Sidell noted that most of the complaints concerned Captain Day, the quartermaster in charge of collecting and driving cattle from Kentucky to the Union army in north Georgia. The owners of the fugitive slaves, argued Sidell, "are willing and anxious that [their slaves] should enlist" and thus provide credits against their counties' draft quotas. Sidell therefore suggested an order to army officers "forbidding the employment of runaway slaves who are not enlisted." (Major W. H. Sidell to Capt. J. Bates Dickson, 8 Oct. 1864, Letters Received, ser. 734, Post of Louisville KY, RG 393 Pt. 4 [C-6050].) General Stephen G. Burbridge, commander of the District of Kentucky, had already indicated his determination to enlist – by force if necessary – all fugitive slaves at large in Kentucky. On August 14, 1864, for example, he had ordered a subordinate officer to seize and enlist "all negroes in your command who have left their masters in Ky. & all refugee negroes from the disloyal states who are loose on the public." (Asst. Adjt. Genl. J. H. Hammond to Brig. Genl. Hugh Ewing, 14 Aug. 1864, Letters Received, ser. 734, Post of Louisville KY, RG 393 Pt. 4 [C-6049].)

231: Kentucky Black Soldier to the President

Taylors Barrecks [*Louisville*] December 4th 1864
Mr Abrham Lincoln   I have one recest to make to you that is I ask you to dis Charge me for I have a wife and she has four
Children   thay have a hard master one that loves the South hangs with it   he dos not giv them a rage nor havnot for too yars   I have found all   he says let old Abe Giv them Close   if I had them I raise them up but I am here and if you will free me and hir and heir Children with me I Can take Cair of them
   She lives with David Sparks in Oldham Co Ky
   My Woman is named Malindia Jann my daughter Adline Clyte and Malindia Eler and Cleman Tine and Natthanel Washington and my name is George Washington   heir in Taylors Barrecks and my famaly suferring   I have sent forty dollars worth to them cence I have bin heir and that is all I have and I have not drawn any thing cence I have bin heir   I am forty eight years   my woman thirty three   I ask this to your oner to a blige yours &c   your un Grateful Servent
ALS   George Washington

George Washington to Mr. Abrham Lincoln, 4 Dec. 1864, W-953 1864, Letters Received, ser. 360, Colored Troops Division, RG 94 [B-190]. Washington served in Company B, 123rd USCI. A notation on the wrapper indicates that his letter was simply filed by the Bureau of Colored Troops.

232: Kentucky Slaveholder to a Kentucky Congressman

Owensborough [*Ky.*] 6 Dec. 1864
Dr Sir   Enclosed I send your Order N° 25 of the Sec. War. The
Authorities of Indiana Say they have no Authority to act under
it   The Consequence is that Indiana is Now Swarming with Ky.
able Bodied negro men who are Skuling from their owners as well as
from Military duty. I have two in the Neighborhood of Evansville
and Ridley Ewing one who have 5 or 6 months been hiding and
have not even been Enrolled in Indiana. I went down last week for
the purpose of Enlisting them in the Army but was informed that it
Could Not be done unless I could induce them to Come back to
Ky. this of Course I Could not do unless aided by the Military
power. which they refused. to give   Will you please lay this matter
before the Secty of War. and If possible get him to modify or
amend his order N° 25. so as to Compell the Military authorities of
Indiana on the application of a Loyal Kentuckian at least to
apprehend his fugitive slave and Send him to the nearest recruiting
station in Ky. So that he Can be Enlisted and Ky get her Credit
upon the quota to be furnished, or Enlisted in Indiana & reported to
the nearest Provo Marshal in Ky. Verry Respectfully yrs
ALS   John S McFarland

[*Endorsement*] [*Washington December 14.?, 1864*] Respectfully
referred to the Secty of War — M^r M^{c}farland is a member of the Ky
Legislature, a leading union man of the state, and I know the case
he mentions is only one of *thousands* in that state — The negroes
have it in their heads that they will be free without either *work* or
fight — and are becoming of no account to the people or the *govt*
 Some more stringent orders to show them they *will not* benefit
themselves by leaving the state, and enabling masters promptly to
enlist all such, either in or out of Kentucky will *greatly* benefit the
service. Geo H Yeaman

John S. McFarland to Hon. G. H. Yeaman, 6 Dec. 1864, M-2 1865, Letters
Received, ser. 15, Washington Hdqrs., RG 105 [A-6009]. Enclosed is a copy
of Order 25, issued by Adjutant General Lorenzo Thomas in Lexington,
Kentucky, on July 24, 1864, "[b]y order of the Secretary of War." Stating
that "many slaves in Kentucky have left their owners without intending to
enter the service of the United States, and . . . have resorted to the towns, or
are roving about the country," the order provided that "it is only necessary for
the owners of such refugees to report to the Provost Marshal, and make known
their wish for their slaves to be placed in the service, and it will be the duty of
the Provost Marshals to arrest such refugees and deliver them for enlistment."

233: Assistant Provost Marshal General for Kentucky to the Commander of the District of Kentucky

Louisville Ky, December 15" 1864

General: I observe today, (15" Decbr) in the correspondence of the Louisville Union Press a letter dated Camp Nelson; 7" Decbr, 1864, which discusses the policy by which the families of enlisted negroes were deprived of U.S. protection. I do not propose to discuss that policy, but merely to call your attention to a passage in the letter which states that *the masters* of men who have enlisted turn away their families to shift for themselves and that they thereby become paupers and take refuge at U.S. posts. The letter writer says further, that masters *deter* the men *from enlisting* by making a threat to treat their families thus.

I add to this statement an extract from the tri monthly report of the Pro. Mar. of 4th District: viz. "Colored Men are willing to enlist and, if possible, a thousand men in this District would go to the army — *Attend to their wives* and *families* and they would immediately rush to arms."

This matter involves consideration of large importance and the case merits the attention of the highest authority, and there may be partial remedies within the power of the Commanding General.

In cases known to be like those stated above, the masters might be either required to keep the female and young members of the families of enlisted men and treat them well, or in case they did not, might be assessed for their support—and in case of threats of the kind made to deter men from enlisting there is already an adequate military remedy.

All women and children thus turned out by their masters and compelled to be supported by the U.S. should be thereby made free.

An incidental difficulty is that all thus seeking to be supported by the U.S. are *not* the wives and children of *enlisted* men but are often simple runaways, or castaways, or are the families of runaways or of unenlisted employees of U.S. Officers, &c, &c.

It may thus be seen that though the whole subject is complicated and from its importance worthy of adjustment by the highest authority, yet that a partial remedy in regard to some points may be applied by the Military Commander, so far at least as regards the families of undoubted enlisted men, and of those desiring to enlist and therefore I make this communication. I am, General, Respy Your Obdt Servt

HLcS

W H Sidell

Lieut. Col. W. H. Sidell to Bvt. Maj. Genl. S. G. Burbridge, 15 Dec. 1864, vol. 4, pp. 117–18, Letters Sent & Circulars Issued, ser. 3962, KY Actg. Asst. Pro. Mar. Gen., RG 110 [R-38]. On the ejection of black soldiers' families from Camp Nelson in late November 1864, see *Freedom*, ser. 2: docs. 107, 312A–B. On the abuse of black soldiers' families by Kentucky slaveholders, and the use of threats of such abuse to deter slave men from enlisting, see below, doc. 237; *Freedom*, ser. 2: pp. 195–97, 657–58, and docs. 106, 294, 302–4.

234: Commander of a Kentucky Black Regiment to the Superintendent of the Organization of Kentucky Black Troops

Maysville [Ky.]. Feb. 4 1865

Sir   I have the honor to acknowledge the receipt, of your communication of the 31st ult. and to report as follows.

No *Slave* or *black* has ever been *pressed* into the service by myself or any officer of my command.

No one, except those connected with recruiting, can form any idea of the strategy used by their masters to keep their slaves from us. For it is a notorious fact that nine tenths of the slaves whom we can get to *talk* to in *camp* for an hour will enlist. The masters know this and so hide their slaves from us, and keep them out of any town that any recruiting force may be at. They tell the poor slave that the cold. soldiers do not get sufficient to eat. That we have the small pox in camp and that hundreds have already died. That the mean *white* officers have shot numbers of the soldiers simply for being awkard on drill.

That we treat them like dogs. That their wives and children are Kicked out of camp when they come on a visit, any many more such things even more ridiculous. always closing by saying to the slave "If you want to enlist, go." Of course the slave says no.

They tell him to run if he sees any darky soldiers coming, or they will press him. The result of this education is that we cannot see more than one tenth of the slave population. For instance, I have seen for the last three months but five able bodied slaves on the several pikes leading to Maysville, and each one I have insisted on coming to camp, and seeing the "boys". A little reluctantly they have come in, but of the five four enlisted in my Regt. within sixty min. after they came in, and the other enlisted a few weeks afterwards.

Adopting this policy I have sent out and brought in all the able bodied slaves and let them see that soldiering was not the auful and dreadful thing they had been lead to believe. and as the result of this policy recruiting has become much more lively. and about %90 voluntarily enlist, While those who still dislike to enlist are forthwith discharged.

I have not a man in my Regt. who will say he was either scared or forced to sign any papers, or who would today accept a discharge and go back to slavery. I wish you would send an officer here to examine into each and every charge made against myself or my officers. As well as to learn of the deep toned disloyal sentiment which rankles through almost this entire community. The very men who make these complaints speak of Maj. Genl. Burbridge always, as the "Brute Burbridge" There is more real disloyalty here today than I ever saw in Va. in 1862 & 1863 I am Col. Very Respct. Your Obdt Servt.

ALS   W. A. Gage

Lieut. Col. W. A. Gage to Lieut. Col. A. Cotes, 4 Feb. 1865, Letters Received, ser. 734, Post of Louisville KY, RG 393 Pt. 4 [C-6053]. Gage commanded the 121st USCI. Enclosed is the letter of January 31 that had ordered a written response to charges that Gage and other officers of his regiment "have been pressing into the U.S. Service slaves of persons living in the vicinity of Maysville." Complaints by residents of Augusta, Kentucky, about a recruiting party from the same regiment had also been forwarded to Gage for investigation, and in a second letter of February 4, he denied the truth of those charges, asserting that during his four years of army service he had "never known better diciplind troops than those I have the honor to command." When the detachment first arrived in Augusta, the citizens had told its commander that General Stephen G. Burbridge, commander of the District of Kentucky, "did not allow any Colored recruiting done in that Co." "The truth is," Gage asserted, "that the People there were *determined* to have us ordered away, and so represented outrageous conduct on the part of my troops. The whole community here is determined to save their slaves and keep them out of the army, and resort to every subterfuge to accomplish the end." Nevertheless, Gage was sure he would enlist between fifty and seventy-five black men in that part of Bracken County. (Lieut. Col. W. A. Gage to Lieut. Col. A. Coates, 4 Feb. 1865, Letters Received, ser. 734, Post of Louisville KY, RG 393 Pt. 4 [C-6054].) In endorsements on the two letters, General James S. Brisbin, superintendent of the organization of Kentucky black troops, reported that he found no fault with Gage's recruitment procedures, aside from his having overzealously forced a few black men into camp "to show them that the colored service had been mispresented to them by their masters." Brisbin ordered that practice discontinued.

235: Commander of a Kentucky Black Regiment to the Headquarters of a Brigade in the 25th Army Corps

In the Field—Va. February 6th 1865.

Sir:

. . . .

In behalf of the enlisted men of the Regiment and their families, it is my duty to inform you of the peculiar circumstances under which they are placed, with the hope that it will sooner or later be brought to the notice of the Government, and such action be taken as will remedy the evil.

All the men of the Regiment were recruited in Kentucky. A large proportion of them were slaves previous to entering the service. A large number of them have families still remaining in servitude, who are most shamefully and inhumanly treated by their masters in consequence of their husbands having enlisted in the union army. It is the highest ambition of a large number to mitigate and relieve their wants by remittances whereby some of the necessary wants and comforts of life may be given them.

A moment's reflection will prove to any one that it is impossible under the existing circumstances to alleviate their wants in the slightest degree. Unable to read or write they are entirely dependent upon their masters for any information they may receive from husbands and friends who are in the service. In a great many instances, letters have been returned with some miserable, contemptible expression written by a miserable southern sympathizer in regard to the service they have entered, probably stating that their families do not require relief, or information from such contemptible "trash."

Under such circumstances, it would be extremely unsafe to forward money to their families, for the reason that it will fall into the hands of those who are wholly unprincipled and would benefit no one.

From my knowledge of Kentucky slave owners, gained while recruiting in the state, I can safely state that the above illustration is the rule and not the exception. Men who plead with their lives in their hands are certainly worthy of consideration, without regard to color. I have to request in behalf of the enlisted men of the Regiment, that some plan be adopted whereby such portion of their pay as they may see fit to set apart, may be placed in the hands of their families for their own use.

. . . .

HLcS

D. M. Sells

THE DESTRUCTION OF SLAVERY

Excerpt from Lieut. Col. D. M. Sells to Capt. F. W. Draper, 6 Feb. 1865, Letters Sent, 107th USCI, Regimental Books & Papers USCT, RG 94 [G-145]. The omitted portions reported that Sells's regiment, the 107th USCI, had been organized in the summer of 1864 but neither officers nor men had ever been paid.

236: Officer in a Kentucky Black Regiment to the Headquarters of the District of Tennessee

Clarksville, Tenn. March 9th 1865

Major: I have the honor to make the following statement of facts, and ask therefor the consideration of the General Commanding:

Nov. 12. 1864, a Recruiting party from this place enlisted from Todd Co. Ky., among others, John & Matthew Randall.

Nov. 18th — as Co. Comd^r I gave them a pass to visit friends and make arrangement for their families; they to return Nov 21st. On the evening of the 20th of Nov. they had, on returning pursuant to their passes, reached within 3 miles of this post, when they were overtaken by their former master and 6 others and compelled to return.

Since that time they have twice sent me word that they could not return on account of their "master's" opposition. But that if I would send out a force, they would come in with the squad

On the 7th inst. a portion of this Command found them at their home; and without any opposition or apparent desire to escape, they voluntarily came in, and are now in arrest.

I do not believe they intended the commission of any crime; but do think they will become good and faithful soldiers. They never drew any clothing and have never been mustered.

In view of the above facts, I have the honor to earnestly request that you reinstate and place them in their former Status, excepting as to their pay which till now is equitably forfeited, that I may avoid placing them upon their trial before a G.C.M. or in Lieu thereof that they be permitted to enlist from this date; their former absence working no prejudice.

I am only induced by a strict sense of duty & right to ask this at your hands

Earnestly soliciting an *early* response to this request reluctantly written I have the honor to remain Major Very Respectfully Your Obt Servt

J. Jay Buck

ALS

1st Lieut. J. Jay Buck to Major B. H. Polk, 9 Mar. 1865, Letters Received, 101st USCI, Regimental Books & Papers USCT, RG 94 [G-139]. Endorsement. Two months earlier, the commander of the same regiment, the 101st USCI, had requested a squad of mounted men to arrest twenty-four black soldiers who were listed as deserters because they had returned to their Kentucky homes (in this case, without an officer's permission) and had been forcibly detained by their former masters. (Lieut. Col. H. G. Davis to Col. A. A. Smith, 12 Jan. 1865, Letters Received, 101st USCI, Regimental Books & Papers USCT, RG 94 [G-140].)

237: Affidavit of a Kentucky Black Soldier's Wife

Camp Nelson Ky 27th of March 1865

Personally appeared before me J M Kelley Notary Public in and for the County of Jessamine State of Kentucky Clarissa Burdett a woman of color who being duly sworn according to law doth despose and say

I am a married woman and have four children. My husband Elijah Burdett is a soldier in the 12″ U.S.C.H. Arty. I and my children belonged to Smith Alford Garrard County Ky. When my husband enlisted my master beat me over the head with an axe handle saying as he did so that he beat me for letting Ely Burdett go off. He bruised my head so that I could not lay it against a pillow without the greatest pain. Last week my niece who lived with me went to Camp Nelson. This made my master very angry and last monday March 20″ 1865 he asked me where the girl had gone. I could not tell him   He then whipped me over the head and said he would give me two hundred lashes if I did not get the girl back before the next day. On Wednesday last March 22″ he said that he had not time to beat me on Tuesday but now he had time and he would give it to me. He then tied my hands threw the rope over a joist stripped me entirely naked and gave me about three hundred lashes. I cried out. He then caught me by the throat and almost choked me then continued to lash me with switches until my back was all cut up. The marks of the switches are now very visible and my back is still very sore. My master was a very cruel man and strongly sympathizes with the rebels. He went with the Rebel General Bragg when the latter retreated from the State. He took me and my children to Beans Station and send the parents and two sisters of my niece to Knoxville where he sold them. After he whipped me on Wednesday last he said he would give me until next morning to bring the girl back, and if I did not get her back by that time he would give me as much more. I knew that I would be whipped so I ran away. My master frequently said that he would be jailed before one of his niggers woulg go to Camp. I therefore knew he would not permit any of my children to come with me. So when I ran away I had to leave my children with my master. I have four children there at present and I want to get them but I cannot go there for them knowing that master who would whip me would not let any of my children go nor would he suffer me to get away

her
(Signed) Clarissa Burdett
mark

HDcSr

Affidavit of Clarissa Burdett, 27 Mar. 1865, filed with H-8 1865, Registered Letters Received, ser. 3379, TN Asst. Comr., RG 105 [A-6148].

238: Kentucky Slaveholder to the Superintendent of the Organization of Kentucky Black Troops

Lexington [Ky.] April 1st 1865

Kind Sir: I have a black Boy, or rather, a mulatto, who has refused to serve me any longer, and affirms that he is as free as I am. Said Boy has done me only one days work since Christmas. He is 49 years old, about five feet ten in., high; and a very stout, able bodied Boy. I wish to enlist him into the service; and being some distance from home, and anxious to join my family, I will be under lasting obligations to you; if you will instruct your recruting officer, Porteus P. Bielby (at Lexington) immediately to have him arrested and enlisted.

Said Boy is in the vicinity of Hutchison's station nine miles from Lexington on the Covington R.R.   Yours very Respectfully,

ALS

I. N. Steele

I. N. Steele to Bt. Brig. Gen. J. S. Brisbin, 1 Apr. 1865, Letters Received, 119th USCI, Regimental Books & Papers USCT, RG 94 [G-173]. General James S. Brisbin, superintendent of the organization of black troops in the Department of Kentucky, referred Steele's letter to the commander of the 119th USCI, at Camp Nelson, Kentucky, "for his information and action."

239: Article from an Ohio Newspaper, and Commander of the Department of Kentucky to the Secretary of War

[*Cincinnati, Ohio early April, 1865*]
[For the Cincinnati Enquirer.][1]
Important Judicial Decisions in Kentucky – The Act Liberating the Wives and Children of Negro Soldiers Declared Unconstitutional – Military Impressment of Private Property Illegal.

MESSRS. EDITORS: Two highly important judicial decisions, involving the Constitutional rights of the people of this State, in regard to property, have just been made by the Hon. L. W. Andrews, the Judge presiding in this judicial circuit. The first of these cases arose under the late Act of Congress, providing for the freedom of the wives and children of the slaves who have been taken into the military service of the Government.[2] The plaintiff, B. B. Marsh, owned the wife of a negro man who had enlisted in the army, and upon the passage of the late law the negro soldier took his wife from the house of her master and placed her in the possession of the defendant, B. F. Corbin, claiming her to be free. The plaintiff brought his suit against the defendant to recover the possession of the woman, and if not to be had, then her value. The defendant pleaded the freedom of the woman under the Act of Congress, set up the facts by which he came into possession, denied the right of the plaintiff to recover, and claimed judgment accordingly. To this answer the plaintiff interposed a demurrer, on the grounds that if the facts stated are true, they constituted no defense to the action. The demurrer was argued by the Hon. Garrett Davis for the plaintiff, and by Colonel William Norvell for the defendant, and sustained by the Court. The defendant failing to answer further, proof was taken as to the value of the woman, and judgment rendered for the restitution of the slave, and if she was not to be had, then for her value, five hundred dollars, and the costs of the suit. Judge Andrews, in sustaining the demurrer to the defendant's answer, decided that Congress had no power to liberate slaves in Kentucky, and that the act of Congress relied on, and the military orders under it, were illegal, unconstitutional and void.

. . . .

LYNDON.

CARLISLE, NICHOLAS Co., Ky., March 27.
PD

Louisville, Ky., April 3[d] *1865.*
Sir: I have the honor to enclose for your consideration a slip cut from the Cincinnati Enquirer, which contains according to my

information a substantially correct statement of decisions of Judge *Andrews* of this State in two causes tried in the Nicholas Circuit Court.

I also have the honor to forward a copy of my General Orders, No. 10, issued with reference to the general subject of the first of the cases.

I am extremely anxious to understand the views and wishes of the department on what it is apparent to me will soon be a matter of sharp controversy in this State.

I am informed that with the exception of three, the Circuit Judges of this State, will agree with Judge Andrews and that probably the Court of Appeals will decide the same way.

This case may have been made with a view to its effect upon enlistments and the elections, and similar cases will probably be decided by other courts of the State very soon and in the same way, while I am ordering the arrest of all persons who forcibly restrain the wives and children of enlisted men of their liberty.

Indeed I have gone further, I have two masters in confinement charged with beating women who claim freedom under this law, and have ordered their trial by a Military Commission and if found guilty and sentenced as they will be propose to punnish them.

I will see that the particular woman adjudged by Judge *Andrews* to be a slave is put beyond his control and respectfully ask the approval of the Department and such instructions as may be thought necessary.

The decision in the second case is quite as important as if acquessed in it puts an end to all efforts to keep troops mounted at remote points in the State.

I present these cases thus early because I regret to say that there are strong indications of a purpose on the part of the enemies of the administration to create and foment difficulties between themselves and the federal authorities and forces, to make capital for the approaching canvass.

The evidence is found partly in these decisions, in the frequent declarations made by leading men, that the State Courts will declare the law of the 3^{d} of March unconstitional and especially in the language and conduct of the Hon. Mr. *Powell*. and Mr. *Mallory*. in the presence of, and in reference to the soldiers language and conduct which I need not repeat or describe but irritating and offensive as reported to me.

My theory is to desregard every thing but real opposition but to suppress that, not by "General Orders," but by the direct and quiet application of force. I have the honor to be, Very Respectfully

HLS   John M Palmer

Excerpt from clipping from *Cincinnati Enquirer*, [early Apr. 1865], enclosed in Maj. Genl. John M. Palmer to Hon. E. M. Stanton, 3 Apr. 1865, K-44 1866, Letters Received, ser. 360, Colored Troops Division, RG 94 [B-263]. Garret Davis, the attorney for the purported owner of the black soldier's wife, was a U.S. senator from Kentucky. The omitted portion of the newspaper article described Judge Andrews's decision declaring illegal the military impressment of a citizen's horse, and assessing damages against the army lieutenant who had seized the animal. Also enclosed in General Palmer's letter is a copy of General Order 10, Department of Kentucky, issued by him on March 12, 1865. It announced the joint resolution of Congress freeing the wives and children of black soldiers, encouraged Kentucky slave men "to coin freedom for themselves and posterity" by enlisting, and pledged that military authorities in the Department of Kentucky would enforce that freedom. (See *Freedom*, ser. 2: doc. 110.) No reply to Palmer's request for instructions has been found among the records of the War Department. At the end of April, he nevertheless issued a circular denouncing the abuse of black men and women who claimed freedom under the confiscation acts, executive proclamations, military orders, or the joint resolution of Congress. "All such persons are under the protection of the Government," Palmer proclaimed. "Colored persons within the laws, proclamations, and orders refered to are free, and whether free or not, are to be protected from cruelty and oppression." (Circular No. 3, Head Quarters Department of Kentucky, 29 Apr. 1865, vol. 10/11 DKy, p. 21, General Orders Issued, ser. 2177, Dept. of KY, RG 393 Pt. 1 [C-7003].)

1 Brackets in newspaper article.
2 By a joint resolution approved March 3, 1865, Congress provided that the wife and children "of any person that has been, or may be, mustered into the military or naval service of the United States, shall . . . be forever free." The resolution further stated that in determining who was entitled to freedom under its provisions, evidence that the soldier had cohabited with the woman claimed to be his wife, or that they "associated as husband and wife" should be sufficient proof of marriage, whether or not their union was recognized by law. (U.S., *Statutes at Large, Treaties, and Proclamations*, vol. 13 [Boston, 1866], p. 571.)

240: Order by the Commander of the Department of Kentucky

Louisville, Ky., May 11, 1865.

GENERAL ORDERS, No. 32. Whereas, it has been represented to the General Commanding the Department of Kentucky, in an official communication from the Hon. Philip Tomppert, Mayor of the city of Louisville, and Henry Dent, S. A. Hartwell, John S. Hubbard, and John G. Baxter, Esqrs., a committee of the General Council of said city, that "large numbers of negroes, most of them women and children (and the numbers are increasing daily), have flocked to said city, claiming to be free, and looking to the military authorities for protection and assistance," and that such colored persons "have been compelled to seek shelter where they could find a place, and that by reason of the crowded state of the city and the scarcity of houses, they have crowded together in numbers so great at each place as to render disease almost certain, and that small pox is now, from the cause aforesaid, prevailing in several localities in the city among these people," and the said Mayor of the city of Louisville, and the committee of the General Council, have requested the cooperation of the General Commanding to remove said evil from the city.

As an effectual method of co-operation with the city authorities, and to prevent the spread of disease among the people, all colored persons in the city of Louisville are advised at once to seek employment, and such as are unable to find sufficient employment for the support of their families in the city, are advised to seek it elsewhere.

To enable them to do so, it is ordered that the Provost Marshal of the Post of Louisville, upon the application of any colored person who may report him or herself as unable to find sufficient employment in the city of Louisville, will issue a pass to such colored person and for his or her family, specifying the number of persons to be passed, and their names, and the point to which they wish to go, to engage in or in search of employment.

Conductors and managers of all railroads, steamboats, ferryboats, and other means of travel out of and from the city of Louisville, will, upon the presentation of such pass and the payment of the usual fare, transport the persons named therein.

Any conductor or manager of any railroad, steamboat, ferryboat, or other means of travel who shall refuse, upon the tender of the legal fare, to sell to any person named in any such pass the usual transportation ticket, or shall refuse to transport any such person on their said railroad, steamboat, ferryboat, or other means of travel, will be at once arrested, and sent out of the Department or punished as a military court may adjudge.

The commanding officer of the post of Louisville will adopt the necessary measures for carrying into effect the provisions of the above order. By Command of Major General J. M. Palmer: PD

General Orders No. 32, Head-Quarters Department of Kentucky, 11 May 1865, Orders & Circulars, ser. 44, RG 94 [DD-19]. Two months later, Palmer issued General Order 49, extending the provisions of General Order 32 to all Kentucky points occupied by federal troops, and urging "colored persons congregated about posts" to obtain military passes to allow them to travel freely in search of employment. (General Orders No. 49, Head-Quarters Department of Kentucky, 10 July 1865, Orders & Circulars, ser. 44, RG 94 [DD-19].) For a discussion of the circumstances that led Palmer to issue General Orders 32 and 49, see below, doc. 246.

241: Assistant Provost Marshal General for Kentucky to the Headquarters of the Department of Kentucky

Louisville, 17th May, 1865

Captain: Permit me to introduce my friend W. H. Churchill, Esq. and if necessary, request that you will present him to Genl. Palmer whom however he has met in society here already.

I think however that you can give to Mr. Churchill all the advice he needs in the case he has in hand.

His house servants, all women and unmarried and therefore not free under any law or regulation, still believe themselves free or say that they do and that "General Palmer told them so." They of course do not tell the truth or made false representations to General Palmer. I explained the case to Mr. Churchill and also the whole purpose and effect of the recent order of the general (No. 32)[1] and told him that if the women should go to the Provost Marshal of the Post and *say* that they wanted a pass in order to seek for work, he would probably give it to them without much inquiry.

But Mr. Churchill says that they do not want to go away but to get the pass and stay around the city. Moreover they do not need work being now in full employment at Mr. Churchill's house.

This is the whole case and Mr. C. wants to know what practical steps to take to comply with orders and yet not be subjected to annoyance through false representations. I am Capn. Respy Your Obt. Servt.

HLcS   W H Sidell

Bvt. Col. W. H. Sidell to Capt. J. Bates Dickson, 17 May 1865, vol. 4, pp. 430–31, Letters Sent & Circulars Issued, ser. 3962, KY Actg. Asst. Pro. Mar. Gen., RG 110 [R-39].

1 See above, doc. 240.

242: Commander of the Department of Kentucky to the Judge of the Louisville City Court

Louisville. Ky. June 3. 1865.

Sir: Your letter of yesterday's date, addressed to Capt. E. B. Harlan. Assistant Adjutant General, in which you state that "Jacob Hardin, represented to the court to be a slave, was committed to the workhouse until his master should give bail that he would not be suffered to go at large and hire himself out as a free man," was this morning laid before me.

It is no part of the duty of the military authorities, under ordinary circumstances, to interfere with the action of the courts of the State, or to obstruct the operations of the local laws, but it is their clear and positive duty to protect the people from forcible wrongs, whether inflicted under the forms of law or otherwise.

I beg to assure you that I do not question the integrity of the Judge whose sentence is under consideration, though I express the opinion that it is wholly without and unsupported by any existing law. "When the reason of the law ceases, the law itself ceases," is a rule founded in reason, and is recognized by all courts.

The particular law, which must be referred to to support this order, was enacted by the Legislature of Kentucky in support of slavery. According to the policy of the State, then recognized as correct, it was the duty and it was then in the power of masters to prevent their slaves from going at large and hiring themselves as free persons, while the slave himself had no interest in the question.

This state of things has, however, ceased. During the last four years, from causes familiar to every one, masters were not, in a majority of cases, able to give protection to their slaves. It was not their duty, then, even according to the theory of the law itself, to restrain them; and now, when the bonds of slavery are relaxed, if not totally broken, it is not in the power of masters to prevent slaves from going at large and hiring themselves as free men.

This highly penal law, which demands impossible acts from the owners of slaves, must, therefore, be held to have ceased to exist, as much as if repealed by Legislative authority.

There is, however, another thing to be said, which demonstrates the correctness of that conclusion. Masters have ceased to provide for or control those who are nominally their slaves. According to the theory of this obsolete law, these were his duties. He has neglected them, yet, by a strange perversion of justice, the slave is selected as the object of punishment. This man Hardin, now before me, has upon his limbs marks made by iron fetters placed upon him only because his master has failed to obey this law. Nor is this the only enormity presented by the case. Hardin is ordered to be kept in the workhouse, as you inform me, not for a period so fixed as to terminate, not until he does some act, but until the master, over whom he can have no influence or control, and who has, now that slaves are valueless, no interest in him, shall voluntairly give bail that he shall never again go at large or hire himself as a free man.

For anything Hardin himself can do, his confinement must be perpetual.

I forward you herewith my order made upon a consideration of the whole case. Very Respectfully,

HLcS

John M Palmer

Major General John M. Palmer to Judge Geo. W. Johnston, 3 June 1865, vol. 1 DKy, pp. 116–17, Letters Sent, ser. 2164, Dept. of KY, RG 393 Pt. 1 [C-4309]. Palmer's order to the judge was not copied into the letterbook along with the letter, and it has not been found in the volumes of orders issued from the Department of Kentucky.

243: Affidavit of a Kentucky Black Soldier's Wife

Camp Nelson Jessamine Co Ky. June 17th 1865

The affiant Mary Wilson of the County of Fayette State of Kentucky being first duly sworn states that she is the lawful wife of Lewis Wilson 119 U.S.C.I. and that under the laws of Congress she is entitled to her freedom. That on or about the 31st day of May 1865 Sap Mason and _____ Downey policemen of the City of Lexington Ky. came to her house in that City, where she was then living in an orderly and quiet manner and without just cause or provocation arrested her and forcibly and against her will took her to the residence of her former master William Adams living about three miles from Lexington Ky. on the Newtown Pike and there in the presence of the said Sap Mason and William Adams the said Downey tied her in a Slaughter house to a rafter or beam and with a leathern buggy trace inflicted upon her naked body a severe beating and bruising. That the said beating and bruising was done in pursuance of instructions from her former master who himself inflicted several stripes upon her naked body. That again on or about the Sixth (6) day of June 1865 the said Downey arrested her in the City of Lexington Ky, without just cause or provocation and had her confined in the watch house or City prison of Lexington Ky, against her will and that on the same day the said Downey took her to the residence of her former master William Adams and there in the presence of the said Adams the said Downey did tie her as aforesaid in a slaughter house and beat and bruised her person by inflicting blows upon her naked body with a leathern buggy trace. That this second beating and bruising was inflicted by the directions of the said Adams. That the said Adams has the unlawful custody of her son Richard which he refuses to surrender much against her will. That these facts as occurred in respect to the said first beating and bruising on or about the 31st of May 1865 and the unlawful detention of her child by the said Adams were promptly laid before the Military Authorities in the City of Lexington Ky. on the same day of the said first beating and bruising and that up to this time she has been unable to have any redress for the said wrongs and outrages inflicted upon her body as aforesaid and further affiant saieth not.

HDcSr

her
(Signed) Mary Wilson
mark

Affidavit of Mary Wilson, 17 June 1865, filed with H-8 1865, Registered Letters Received, ser. 3379, TN Asst. Comr., RG 105 [A-6148]. Sworn before a notary public.

244: Delegation of Kentucky Blacks to the President

[*Washington, late June, 1865*]

Mr President   Haveing been delegated by the Colored People of Kentuckey to wait upon you and State their greiveances and the terrible uncertainty of their future, we beg to do so in as respectfull and concise a manner as Posible—

First then, we would call your attention to the fact that Kentuckey is the only Spot within all the bounds of these United States, where the People of colour Have No rights *whatever* Either in Law or in fact—and were the Strong arm of Millitary Power no longer to curb her—Her Jails and workhouses would Groan with the Numbers of our people immured within their walls—

Her Stattutes are disgraced by laws in regard to us, too barbarous Even for a community of Savages to Have Perpetrated. Not one of those laws have Even yet become obsolete, all Have been Executed Promptly and Rigoursly up to the time the government intervened—and will be again Executed in the Most remorseless Manner and with four fold the Venom and Malignanty they were

Ever Heretofore Enforced – the Very Moment the Government ceases to Shield us with the broad aegeis of her Power –

Not only that – but the brutal instincts of the Mob So Long restrained will Set no bounds to its ferocity but like an uncaged wild beast will rage fiercely among us – Evidence of which is the fact that a member of the present common council of the city of Louisville who when formerly Provost Marshall of that city caused his guards to carry bull whips and upon meeting colored men, women or children in the Public High ways any time after dark to surround them and flay them alive in the public Streets) is allready a petitioner to Gen¹ Palmer to remove the Millitary Restrictions that he and others May again renew the brutaleties that Shocked Humanity during that Sad Period – therefore to Prevent all the Horrible calamities that would befall us and to shut out all the terrors that So fiercely Menace us in the immediate future – we Most Humbly Petition and Pray you that you will Not Remove Marshall Law from the State of Kentuckey Nor her Noble Millitary commander under whose Protection we have allmost learned to Realise the Blessings of a Home under the Safeguard and Sanction of law for in him and him alone do we find our Safety – we would Most Respectfully call your attention to a few of the laws that bear Most cruelly upon us –

1ˢᵗ we have No Oath
2ⁿᵈ we have no right of domicil
3ʳᵈ we have no right of Locomotion
4ᵗʰ we have no right of Self defence
5ᵗʰ a Stattute law of Kentuckey makes it a penal crime with imprisonment in the Penitentiary for one year for any free man of colour under any Sircumstances whatever to pass into a free State Even although but for a Moment any free man Not a Native found within her Borders is Subject to the Same penalty and for the Second offence Shall be sold a slave for life –

the State of Kentuckey Has contributed of her colored Sons over thirty thousand Soldiers who have illustrated their courage and devotion on Many battle fields and Have Poured out their blood Lavishly in defence of their Country and their Country's flag and we confidently hope this Blood will be carried to our credit in any Political Settlement of our Native State – yet if the government Should give up the State to the control of her civil authorities there is not one of these Soldiers who will Not Suffer all the grinding oppression of her most inhuman laws if not in their own persons yet in the persons of their wives their children and their mothers –

Therefore your Excellency We Most Earnestly Petition and pray you that you will give us Some security for the future or if that be impracticable at least give us timely warning that we may fly to other States where law and Christian Sentiment will Protect us and our little ones from Violence and wrong.

Chas A Roxborough	Jerre Meninettee
R M Johnson	Henry H. White
Thomas James	Wm F. Butler

HLS

Chas. A. Roxborough et al. to Mr. President, [late June, 1865], President 1957 1865, Letters Received from the President & Executive Departments, RG 107 [L-170]. Endorsement. The petition and Roxborough's signature are in the same handwriting; each of the other signatures is in a different handwriting. Roxborough signed as chairman and Butler as secretary of the delegation. Martial law was continued in Kentucky until October 12, 1865. (*Official Records*, ser. 1, vol. 49, pt. 2, p. 1116.)

245: Kentucky Slaveholder to the President

Craborchard [*Ky.*], July 24th 1865.

My Dear Sir; As you are at the head of a Government that admits of petitions and grievances, you will excuse this letter, which is intended more for your own good, for the honor of the nation, and for the harmony of the people and their good will towards yourself, than from anything I can expect from it. And now the simple question whether, (under the constitution of the U. States, the laws of Congress which authorized us to take our property from any state in the union, and under the constitution and the laws of Kentucky), my Tom belongs to me or to some unknown power under your individual influence; will bring my grievance and the complaint of Kentucky fairly and squarely up before your mind. Tom and I have lived together as mutual friends for fifty years, without a hard thought or a harsh word passing. I gave him a good home, boarded him free of charge, nursed him when sick, clothed and fed his family and paid his debts, while Tom, on his part, seeing his family healthy and happy and protected from the wants of the world by a kind Master, Guardien, Friend or whatever you may see proper to call it, did his duty cheerfully. But now Tom comes to me with what he calls free papers from Camp Nelson and a pass to go where he pleases and to do what he pleases; and yet he is unhinged and unhappy, feeling that he is by his new master turned out upon the world with all its cares and troubles, without a home and without a protector He has seen those I myself set free, call upon me in times of distress, to help them to pay thier debts and to bury them, and knwing that his acceptance of those papers divorced him from

626

me, he under no circumstancs would ever again have a right to call upon me. Thousands of such cases occur daily and hourly throughout Kentucky, where whole families, even sucking infants are taken off and exposed by thier mothers, and I only mention Tom's case, that like the Dred-Scot case, may represent all others. Tom was worth nothing to me, and in his case I have no feeling but pitty for him, but have a deep and abiding sense of feeling for the insecurity of all property, for if our constitutional rights can be invaded with impunity in one case or in one species of property, it may in all. Had I a pet-bird, worth nothing, taken from me and kept by force of arms, it would involve a principle alarming to every man in the community If the signeture of Tom Dick and Harry can free every man woman and child in Kentucky, as it is now doing, why disturb the nation and spend the people's money in a struggle for a Constitutional Amendment?

We profess before foreign nations to be living under a written Constitution, a Divine and sacred instrument which protects life liberty and property, and it cannot then be by your approbation that the best of its citizens are, by arbitrary arrests and consequent death, with other acts, as above named, deprived of life liberty and property, and that in the face of Heaven and in open day! I then though an humble citizen, hold it as my privilege and feel it my duty to appeal to you, as our *Legitimate* (and I say) *Good* President, to save our count[r]y from the charge of infamy and the reccords of eternal disgrace. Did I believe that you knew of what is now going on in Kentucky, I certainly would not write you, for though we poor fellows in the west, have as good a right to humbly and respectfully address you, as the imperious and dogmatic down easters have to call upon you by committees; yet I view them both, when seeking office or aiming at party preponderance, as insolent and anoying to one already over taxed with the cares of the nation. And Honored Sir, let me here impress it upon you, that I have no object aside from the honor of the Administration and the well being of our common country. I know that you have fought too hard against rebellion to now place yourself in rebellion against the Government of the united states; for, you know, the Administration is not the Government, as in that case, we should have no stable Government, but every four years a new one, and the dictation of a single man would overrule the constitution and make it a misnomer and a rediculous farce. Then I again, most respectfully assure you, that being unwilling for millions of your subjects to secretly feel in thier hearts that our Administration is in rebellion against the Government and laws of the land, as a friend, I will do all in my power to correct such unfortunate impression. I know there is a party, at Wasington, who would be willing to see

the Administration take from the states who created it, all their
inherent and reserved rights, and thus place it as certainly in
rebellion against its Maker, as is the man who defies Heaven, a
rebel against the God who made him, Thus with my views of the
limited powers of the Administration, I have looked on with alarm
and disgust at the scenes now acting in Kentucky. Though the
Constitution of Kentucky forbids free blacks remaining in the state,
they are bid, by Camp Nelson papers, to remain in it: and again,
the laws of the State orders that no public conveyance shall take a
slave off, without the consent of the Master, yet those papers order
all conveyances to take them off. And now, if this is not a violation
of the laws of Kentucky, a grievous wrong to her people and a gross
insult to her National dignity; we may next strip our backs for the
lash and sink in contempt with all mankind, who *like yourself*, have
a high sense of personal honor and of state rights   You would
not—you could not respect craven and degraded Kentucky, were she
too recreant to make her wrongs known to you.

I, this moment, hear that this high-handed and sudden breaking
up of all our domestic relations and leaving our crops to perish for
want of help, has been checked by your kind and just order, and
were it sure, I would throw my pen down and cry long live Andrew
Johnson, and long live the Government which he has cemented by
just and kindly acts, but I fear you have not yet known our
condition. Not having had time to supply the place of the blacks,
we are forced to suffer   On yesterday morning, there was hardly a
servant to be found in our town. The man with a sickly wife had
his cow to milk and the breakfast to get, while many an old and
infirm widow, whose only son has fallen in the federal service, has
now had the servant she reared with tenderness and care to be a
support in her old days, taken from her, by that government she has
given her all to support, and she left sadly and alone a begger upon
the world. A fanatic and radical brute might say this is all right,
for people should do their own work; but if by the order of any man
or set of men, Washington should be suddenly deprived of all help,
and Mr S. or any other member of your Cabinet had to get up and
milk the cow and get their breakfast; circumstances would as
quickly alter the case as they did with the farmer and the lawyer in
the Fable of the ox and the cow. We feel that we as certainly own
our slave property as any other, and any power which may rench it
from us without consent or compensation is unjust; and be assured
that he who submits to it, submits as does the traviller his purse to
the highway robber, because the knife is across his throat—as has
been beautifully expressed by my Friend Joseph Holt, your able
Judge advocate, when speaking upon this very subject of state rights
and domestic institutions. I am, myself, an emancipationist, and

have written a work upon that subject, but my moral sense and my judgement of right have led all my efforts to do justice to the Master and to better the condition of the Slave. By the destinies of Providence and the original action of the Northern states, the blacks have been placed amongst us, and we cannot help it, nor can they help it; but all who know human nature know this—that an unprepared for and violent breaking up of all domestic control and turning loose four millions of beings upon the world, who never thought or acted for themselves any more than children have done under the guidance of their parents, is not a remedy, but a grievous evil to both black and white. Were you to witness the scenes I have, you would shudder at the sight— Old and young, blind and lame, with heavy packs, crowd the highways and the by ways, rushing on through heat and dust for free papers and as certainly to ultimate distruction, as presses the Pilgrim Hindoo on his path to perish by the hand of the god he worships. The unrestrained Abolitionist, whose only feeling is envy and malice to the whites and whose selfish heart would not give a dime for the purchase or freedom of a slave, is to be the death of the African race in America

But as I set out to give you some idea of the state of things in Kentucky I will on with the work. The servants being seduced from their happy homes by the pledge of free papers at Camp Nelson, assemble in such numbers as to render their condition uncomfortable and unhealthy; so much so that the fatality amongst those deluded creaturs has been sadly and notoriously great. Mothers becoming wearied with the toil of their children and scarce of food often neglect them till they perish, while others throw them into the ponds around camp Nelson, from which many have been taken Disease of every kind, *Private* and public, seems to be rife in thier ranks, and the time is fast coming when, if not checked, the loafing vagrants and filthy lepers will die off like sheep with the rot. The worst feature about this Camp Nelson business is, that the blacks have taken up the idea that their free papers is to enable them to live the remainder of their lives without work, and that the Government will support them, at the expense and labor of the white man: in short, they feel that by the aid of the military, they can defy the decrees of Heaven itself which bid them get their living in the sweat of their face— Yes and there is another unfortunate sequel of this pass manufactory; those servants who return home, do not do it with the view of living in harmony with their old Master, but to taunt him with their free papers and threaten him with military power; a thing illy calculated to reconcile our people with the Administration or gain friends to the Constitutional amendment, as you will find, by the result of the Kentucky election.

629

THE DESTRUCTION OF SLAVERY

I have lived long (75 years) and been much through the world and found that an open hand and kind heart was worth all the weapons I could buckle about me, and in your case you are safer and more beloved than a million of bayonets would make you. A Government sustained by standing armies and ruinous taxation is not worth the cost, and cannot last, while one governed by even handed justice and cemented by fraternal love will last through ceaseless ages. It is now in your power to do more than any man on earth can do, and to immortalize your name in the pages of history. Clamor as much as the present, but short lived faction may, for standing armies, for office and for blood, heed them not, but rise manfully above their din like the towering mountain above the thunders brawl, and show to them and to the world that you are without envy malice or revenge against your erring subjects, but that you are the Saviour of your country and like the Saviour of the world have a heart for those who cry for mercy, even his persecurtors and the thief upon the cross. Such endearing loveliness such Divine forgiveness will command the respect of all mankind and make friends of enemies. The foulest fanatic in the radical ranks knows that he could not whip a wife a ~~child~~ man of honor or neighbour into a love for him, and in spite of his vengeful heart and sorded grasp, would have more respect for a conciliatory than a cruel course   Therefore heed not their Moloch howl, but gain the hearts of the people, discharge your armies, tell the idle negroes they must support themselves, pay our myriad debt, redeem the currency and sustain the credit and the honor of the nation —

I have done, and now if there be anything offensive or unbecoming in my hurried address, I shall be exceedingly sorry, and as a good subject ask for pardon. I am a Quaker and had intended to address you Brother Andrew, for we are all Brothers and should not be offended at any familiarity intended for the good of all so I have made free to advise with you upon some subjects, I will farther say to you, that I am one who would be unwilling to see our poor black Breathern driven from their native land; but think they should remain amongst us, where the climate suits them, where their labor is wanted and where they can get good wages and feel at home. There is, *at present*, much bad feeling between the races in Kentucky, owing mainly to the premature and daring interference, as before related, with our domestic institutions. The blacks are not to blame, but the whites who *seduce* them from home *in more ways than one*, and make them insolent and refractory. Your authority however will soon settle all things down satisfactorily. A captain in your servic stationed at Camp Nelson, told us here, a few days ago, that the authorities there were giving seventy-five dollars a head for cows to give milk to the idle blacks who would not work— This he did not approbate, nor will the people of the U. States, *who pay the tax*, approbate it. Just proclaim to the blacks and to your Agents, that they must go to work and support themselves, and all will soon go like clock work, for the blacks will then want a home and the whites want their services. This would be humanity to the tender infants many of whom are daily dieing for want of care, and it would give to the infirm a home, where they might again be taken into favor and receive the blessings of friendship and kindness in their dieing moments. I do not wish to bore you, but while on this subject will say, that I recogniz the white man, the black man and the red man, and all human beings on earth, as of the one great family, and for the brute force of one over the other, I have a deeply abiding and religious abhorrence; consequently feel more rational kindness for our coloured breathern than any abolitionist in the north, for their envious and levelling spirit seems to be against their white breathern and spending nothing and careing nothing of what becomes of the blacks. Thousands of dollars may be taken out of the pocket of a white brother in Kentucky, and they will chuckle over it – ah, and take but one dollar out of theirs by the same authority, and they would cry robbery. robbery!

Thus you will see that I am not promted by any designing or party spirit, but that my efforts are for peace peace and prosperity to all; and now knowing God to be my judge, who will approbate what I have said, I have a hope that you will forgive any seeming impropriety in this my appeal to you. Most respectfully and sincerely, your adviser well wisher and Friend

C. Graham, M.D.

Should you amongst the ten thousand letters daily placed upon your table, break the seal of mine, you will say to yourself, who is this Doct. Graham who thus addresses me, and hence I refer you to the Hon. Joseph Holt, to my Cousin John A. Graham, in the Treasury Department, to Genl. Martin D. Harden, in command in your city, also my relation, who married my Grand Daughter. Also Genl. Scott, Genl. Wool, your Attorney General Speed, who is also a relation, and in fact to almost any body and every body in the U. States – Yes and could the dead speak, I would refer you to President Monroe, President Jackson, President Harrison and President Taylor, with all of whom I was a personal Friend. I never sought office or was willing to accept of it, or I might have been well known to you I fought through the war of 12, again in the Black Hock war, have lived 76 years, and seen all the great west grow up from a wilderness. I have studied well the rise and fall of all nations, have written a work on Moral and Mental Philosophy, and on the character man from his cradle to his grave. You cannot then think from my past history that I could become a trifler or

631

anoy you for nothing— I must then again say, in all sincerety, and with as much attachment to yourself as any subject you have in the U.S., look into the abuses in Kentucky, for I want our people to love you and to aid you through your laborious term— Excuse my writing—it is that of an old man whose hand must give—

ALS

C. Graham, M.D. to Hon. Andrew Johnson, 24 July 1865, Letters Received by President Andrew Johnson Relating to Bureau Affairs, ser. 17, Washington Hdqrs., RG 105 [A-35]. A notation on the wrapper reads merely "File."

246: Commander of the Department of Kentucky to the President

Louisville, Kentucky. July 29, 1865.

Sir: I have already by telegram, acknowledged your despatch of yesterday containing copy of despatch of Mr Price which states that Provost Marshals issue "Free Papers" to negroes indiscriminately. I refer you to my despatch in which I say no "free papers" are issued by any officer in this Department, which, though literally true, does not quite meet the facts as they are.

I forward you my General Orders Nos 32 and 49. Under these orders many passes have been issued by Provost Marshals &c to negroes who hold them; and, I am told in many cases they regard and act upon them as "free papers."

The reasons for issuing Order No. 32 will be found on the face of the order, but the reasons which influenced the Mayor and his friends to apply to me do not. Large numbers of negroes were then in Louisville from the surrounding country, who had escaped, from, or repudiated the authority of their masters.

The Mayor and others desired my approval of a plan they had arranged for the general enforcement of the laws against vagrancy, and the law which forbids slaves to go at large and hire themselves out as free persons. To have enforced these laws would have produced great misery and alarm amongst the blacks. To leave the negroes in the city would have alarmed the fears of the citizens who were before hand taught to think their presence would cause a pestilence. They sought to make me responsible for either consequence.

To avoid both, I issued order No. 32. Under it over five thousand negroes have crossed the Ohio river at this place alone.

Before the 4th of July, an impression got abroad amongst the negroes throughout the state, that on that day they were all to be made free. Inflamed by this, belief, thousands of them left their masters houses and came into our posts at different points in the state. Every nook and hiding place at such places as Camp Nelson, Lexington, Frankfort, Bowling Green, Munfordville &c, was filled with them. They were without work or means; and the greater the number, and the more destitute they were, the more the people resisted employing them. I was compelled, from these causes, to issue General Orders No. 49, and the "free papers" referred to in the telegram of Mr Price, are merely passes issued under that order.

I have been greatly embarassed in respect to the colored people by the acts and declarations of politicians and presses in the Anti Administration interest. They have given the negroes extravagant ideas of the purposes of the government by announcing in their speeches and columns that it was the intention of the government to free them all, furnish them with food and clothing, and put them upon an equality with whites. Invariably, a conservative gathering in a neighborhood is followed by a stampede of negroes.

I think and respectfully submit that it is impossible, under the existing state of facts here, to recognize the laws of the state in reference to slaves and slavery.

At the beginning of the war, Kentucky had about two hundred and thirty thousand slaves.

say	230,000
Our reports show number of negro enlistments	28,818.

Estimated number of women and children freed by resolution of Congress of March 3, 1865. 2 1/2 for each man   72,045–100,863.

Ballance	129,137.

One half of this residue are presumed to have belonged to rebels, and are, therefore, free.

64,569
64,568.

From this small number ought still to be taken a percentage for the thousands who have escaped from the state.

For the sake of keeping the small number in subjection to masters, the whole race in the state are most cruelly oppressed and outraged under color of laws which renders freedom to a negro in Kentucky impossible.

I have felt it my duty to give protection to this large free population as far as possible, but in doing so I have been, on occasions, compelled to do acts which, in effect greatly impair the tenure of the small number of persons who are still technically masters of slaves. Indeed it must be admitted that many slaves have left the state under Orders No. 32 and 49, which are enclosed, and every decision I make in favor of a negro, seems to start a host of individual cases which come within the same principle.

In short, slavery has no actual existence in Kentucky, and if the Constitutional Amendment is defeated at the election, the whole active colored population will fly unless I employ the troops to prevent it, and you have not, and will not be likely to order that to be done.

To illustrate the effect of any fair rule upon the status of slavery in Kentucky I will advert to the effect of one rule which I am compelled to recognize and observe.

By the laws of Kentucky—laws once when all were slaves, just enough in their application, all negroes were presumed to be slaves. Now a large majority are certainly free. To presume slavery from color alone is contrary to justice; to presume freedom without regard to color and give protection accordingly is to end slavery.

I am often called upon to afford protection where there is no proof at hand, and am compelled to presume one way or the other.

I submit these difficulties to meet some of the complaints which will probably reach you from the *loyal people* of Kentucky. I have the honor. to be Very Respectfully

HLcS

John M Palmer

Major General John M. Palmer to His Excellency Andrew Johnson, 29 July 1865, vol. 1 DKy, pp. 188–90, Letters Sent, ser. 2164, Dept. of KY, RG 393 Pt. 1 [C-4343]. For General Orders 32 and 49, see above, doc. 240.

247: Kentucky Slaveholder to the President, Enclosing a Pass Issued by the Provost Marshal at Louisville and a Letter from a State Agent

Shepherdsville Ky 4 Augst 1865.

Sir. Enclosed you will find copy of a pass issued to one of my servants by the Military authorities at Louisville, together with a note from Maj Van Armon, who owing to my absence from home, at the time, volunteered to see Genl Palmer on the subject—

This Girl, if she went to Jeffersonville at all, remained but a few minutes and returned to Louisville where she now is—claiming to be free—working when and for whom she pleases—

The gentleman who procured the enclosed copy for me and with whom the girl is living, refuses to pay hire and intimates, he is admonished by the Military not to do so and has assurances of protection &c.—

She was hired in Louisville on the 1st Janry last and had a good home— Has no relation in the army nor color of right, by law, to freedom— The laws of Ky furnish me ample remedy for this violation of my rights, but an apprehension is very generally felt here, that an attempt to enforce the legal remedy, would be followed by a violation of a more sacred right.

If assured of protection, I could ask nothing more than the laws afford me—

I very reluctantly ask to call your Excellency's attention to a private greivance of such small moment, but was determined as soon as the copy was procured to submit it to you.

You will notice that the paper declares the girl *free*.

I am personally known to Mr James Speed, to whom I ask to refer you as to my position socially and politically   With great esteem

ALS   R. H. Field.

[*Enclosure*]   Louisville Ky   May 27 1865
No 8801

Guard will pass bearer Lucy Scott to Jeffersonville until further orders

Description   Black Complexion   Black Eyes   Black hair   5 ft 3 in high

Free   By order of Geo. L. Swope   Capt & PV Marshal
[*In the margin*] Approved
J M Carter
  C & PV Marshal

HDcSr

[*Endorsement*]   Given me by Bainroth who says he will not be responsible for hire of negro woman— Dupuy

[*Enclosure*]   *Louisville, Ky*. June 4th *1865*
Dr Sir   I have just had a long conversation with Genl Palmer about your matter   he said he would give no order for your girls return   I then asked will you permit Mr Field to take his girl— he answered that he would give protection to all black people in the limits of his department and I gathered generally from his remarks that he would never tolerate any return to Slavery of anyone who had at one time left the Service of his or her Master

it is unsatisfactory but all I could get from him   I am Sir Very Respectfuly Your Obedient Sevant

ALS   N Van Arman

[*Endorsement*] H^d Qrs Dept of Ky Louisville Aug. 21 /65 Respectfully returned to the Adjutant General USA with the remark that if Mr Field who resides near Louisville had called upon me he could have obtained much more accurate information than he has through Van Arman I have not at any time to my knowledge confered with any one about Mr Fields slave and I am sure have decided nothing in his case beyond this – that I would not aid in returning the woman to slavery I may have said in reference to that case as I know I have in many others that men *who make contract with slaves for wages shall keep the contract* but have not in any manner committed – myself either for or against the claim of Mr Field

The "pass" of which a copy is furnished is of a class of papers issued by the Provost Marshals to Colored persons who report themselves as out of employment and is designed only as a means of compelling carriers of passengers to convey the person described in the same upon the paym^t of the usual fare I enclose a copy of Genl Order No 32 under the authorty of which the "pass" was issued John M Palmer Maj Genl Comdg

R. H. Field to His Excellency Andrew Johnson, 4 Aug. 1865, enclosing Pass No. 8801, Provost Marshal's Office, 27 May 1865, and N. Van Arman to Mr. Field, 4 June 1865, F-577 1865, Letters Received, ser. 12, RG 94 [K-507]. Other endorsements. Van Arman's letter is written on stationery headed "Head-Quarters Military Agent, Western Department." In the same file is a copy of Palmer's General Order 32. (See above, doc. 240.) Also in the same file is a draft of the War Department's reply to Field, which simply transmitted a copy of Palmer's endorsement. (Thos. T. Eckert to R. H. Field, Esq., 29 Aug. 1865.) At about the same time, "several Loyal Citizens" of Lexington, Kentucky, complained that the provost marshal at that post was issuing passes to their slaves to leave the state, "and it is producing a bad state of things here [because] farmers cannot obtain help to save their Crop." (John M. Lee to Major Genl. G. H. Thomas, 26 July 1865, Letters Received, ser. 2173, Dept. of KY, RG 393 Pt. 1 [C-4330].)

248: Kentucky Former Slave to the Freedmen's Bureau Superintendent of the Subdistrict of Louisville, Kentucky

Louisville Ky Aug 10th 1865

Colonel I have the honor to make the following statement. I was formerly the slave of Mr Morris of Louisville Ky. On the 5th day of July 1865 I contracted with the Steward of the National Hotel, to work for Mr Kean the proprietor of said hotel for the sum of

Twenty Dollars per month— that I commenced working for said Mr Kean in accordance with said contract, On the 5th day of July 1865 and continued so to work without loss of time until the 5th day of August 1865— that on the 5th day of August 1865 I demanded of said Mr Kean the amount of my wages under the aforesaid contract— that the said Mr Kean refused to pay me and still refuses to pay me the amont of my wages giving as a reason that I cannot show my Freedom Papers, nor the written consent of my former master to entitle me to draw my wages. My former master Mr Morris told me repeatedly that he wanted me to leave his place—that if I did not he would drive me off and he has never attempted to take me back home since I left him. I have the honor to be Very Respectfully Your Most Obt Servt

his
Willis × Stillman
mark

HLSr

Willis Stillman to Col. H. A. McCaleb, 10 Aug. 1865, Unregistered Letters Received, ser. 1209, Louisville KY Supt., RG 105 [A-4514]. The Freedmen's Bureau superintendent referred Stillman's statement to the headquarters of the Department of Kentucky, "for information as to whether this class of Freedmen come within the jurisdiction of this Bureau." On August 14, it was returned to the superintendent with an endorsement reporting that the case had already been considered by General John M. Palmer, the department commander, in personal discussion with Kean. The endorsement did not report Palmer's decision. On a previous occasion, Palmer had taken Kean to task for refusing to pay "[s]everal colored boys lately in [his] service" after they made complaints about him at the general's office. (Maj. Genl. John M. Palmer to Charles Kean, Esq., 5 July 1865, vol. 1 DKy, p. 147, Letters Sent, ser. 2164, Dept. of KY, RG 393 Pt. 1 [C-4310].)

249: Freedmen's Bureau Superintendent of the Subdistrict of Louisville, Kentucky, to the Headquarters of the Tennessee and Kentucky Freedmen's Bureau Assistant Commissioner

Louisville Ky. Aug 14" 1865

Major: There are three classes of cases within this District which do not come within any of the Proclamations, Acts of Congress, Circulars, General or Special Orders, from the War Dept.

1st Those slaves who are driven from their homes by their masters.

2nd Those slaves who leave their masters contrary to the masters wish.

3rd Those slaves who leave their masters by the mutual consent of both parties.

Under all three of the above classes the former owner can collect the wages of his or her *slave* from the employer under the State laws of Kentucky, if the party employing such slave lives within the State of Kentucky. The legal status of these people under the State laws of Kentucky, is in no wise changed the State having been considered loyal throughout the rebellion.

Is there no way by which payment to these people can be enforced, and the employer be relieved from liability to the former owner under the State law?

In considering this question please do not forget that Slavery exists in the State of Kentucky by virtue of State law, as much to day, as it did prior to the rebellion, and that the class referred to are not Freedmen under any of the Acts of Congress.

I truly desire that some way may be devised whereby this class of people may be able to collect their wages for their labor, but I do not feel safe in enforcing payment to these people while the present State laws of Kentucky are in force

I hold myself ready to carry out any instructions which you may give. I have the honor to be Very Respectfully Your Obdt. Servt.

HLS   H A McCaleb

Lt. Col. H. A. McCaleb to Major Jno. H. Cochrane, 14 Aug. 1865, M-70 1865, Registered Letters Received, ser. 3379, TN Asst. Comr., RG 105 [A-6176]. No reply to this letter has been found, but in response to an earlier request from McCaleb for guidance about cases involving nonpayment of wages to "Freed people," General Clinton B. Fisk, the Freedmen's Bureau assistant commissioner for Tennessee and Kentucky, wrote the following endorsement: "See that strict and prompt *justice* is done – enforce the Contracts upon both parties – Compel the immediate payment of all sums justly due the Freedmen 'vi et armis' if necessary – " (Endorsement by Bg. Genl. Clinton B. Fisk, 15 Aug. 1865, on Lt. Col. H. A. McCaleb to Capt. E. B. Harlan, 9 Aug. 1865, Unregistered Letters Received, ser. 1209, Louisville KY Supt., RG 105 [A-6176].) McCaleb then sought – and received – permission to publish in the Louisville newspapers Fisk's "endorsements on communications affecting 'Freedmen' and their Employers so that all concerned may understand their obligations." (Lt. Col. H. A. McCaleb to Major, 17 Aug. 1865, M-51 1865, Registered Letters Received, ser. 3379, TN Asst. Comr., RG 105 [A-6176].)

250: Commander of the Department of Kentucky to the Mayor of Paris, Kentucky

Louisville. Ky., August 22, 1865.
Sir: I reply to your letter of the 19″ inst which reached me to day.

I cannot sympathize with the citizens of Paris if you correctly represent them when you say, "The great desideratum is to rid ourselves of a population that will not labor but simply exist as a nuisance — Where they go or to whom they are sent is a matter of little moment to us, so that they be constrained to active honest labor and we relieved of a burden." Such views and feelings of and toward a race born in your midst with just such habits of industry and morals as you have taught them are not very creditable to your humanity, or to the system to which these people have been subjected.

I trust however that you do the good people of the rich and refined city of Paris an unintentional injustice, and that they will be found willing to endure their share of the burdens of a system which they have supported with so much zeal and which has created the vagrancy and vice from which they now suffer.

I assure you that I would be glad to be able to suggest some speedy and effectual remedy for the evils you describe which would meet your approbation, but I am certain that no such remedy is possible. Your people expect or desire what can never be accomplished. They seem to hope that after enjoying the unpaid and extorted labor of the colored people for generations, after having denied them all means of mental and moral elevation and improvement, enforced them to that condition that their earnings are in the hands of their late masters, and the negroes for that reason utterly destitute, some one or some people will be found who are willing to "relieve them of a burden" and eagerly accept a population which you say "Will not labor but simply exist as a nuisance." Any such expectation is chimerical. The people of Paris will be compelled in a great measure to bear this evil themselves, and if they care as little for the welfare and happiness of their late bondmen, as might be inferred from your language, but few persons can be found who will much care how heavily it presses them.

I do not think that any plan can be devised which will realize all you desire.

Under present circumstances there is but one course which can rid the people of Paris of their present embarrassment, and in that alone can they have the cooperation of the Military Authorities of Kentucky. This plan includes several distinct things to be done.

1st The colored people to whom you allude must be relieved of all doubts and anxieties with respect to their status. They must be assured of freedom. They cannot and will not understand that they are free as long as men who have heretofore owned them deny it. My assurances which are sincerely given to them that all are in fact free though fortified and strengthened by the declared opinion of the present able and patriotic Governor of the Commonwealth, and by many of the most distinguished citizens are neutralized by the claims of men once their masters, and whom they have been accustomed to fear and obey. The clear, precise and unreserved admission of the fact of freedom is one indispensable preliminary condition to the success of any plan which may be presented for the relief of the races from the evils they inflict upon each other.

2^d You must abandon the scheme of expelling them from the state. The idea of expulsion is morally unjust, and politically tyranical and in the highest degree oppressive. These furnish sufficient reasons for abandoning it, but what will have more weight with many is that it is impracticable. You may by injustice which will degrade and injure you and by the petty oppressions which are now possible compel a few negroes to leave the state of Kentucky; You may in this way compel the most sensative and intelligent to abandon their birth place and seek homes in other states amongst strangers, but the old and helpless, the stolid and worthless will endure all and stay with you and burden you. The political economists of Kentucky will begin to enquire soon whether it is a paying policy to give to the adjoining states all of the most valuable portion of your colored population, retaining for yourselves only the aged, the maimed the halt and the blind. The policy of persecution will result in this, as certain as it is persisted in.

3^d You must gain or regain, if that form of expression is preferred, the confidence of the colored people. You have not that confidence now. whether you desire it or not, need not be discussed. The unreserved admission of their right to freedom and of their right to live where they were born and have toiled will go far toward reassuring them of your purpose to be just, and if to this you will add that perfect protection in life, liberty and property which you demand for yourselves, and which is secured to you by the laws, the work will be complete. A few years of unrestrained industry will give to the largest portion of the colored population improved habits of industry, morality and usefullness and put them in possession of the material results which are sure to follow industry and thrift.

To cling to the shadow of slavery and that is all they left, is to hug vagrancy amongst the negroes and discontent and disappointment to your bosoms. Slavery never can be reestablished: To struggle for its reestablishment, is injurious to both races. the weakest suffers most now, but "time makes all things even."

In conclusion I will gladly cooperate with the authorities of the city of Paris in every effort to rid the people of the burdens of which you complain, which is based upon the following leading principles.

1st The free admission of the right of the colored people to the enjoyment of their personal freedom.

2^{d} Their perfect right to remain in Kentucky, or to emigrate if they prefer emigration, and I will render such assistance to those who are able to support themselves, and desire to go to some other state as may be in my power. I will not encourage or aid the helpless to go out of the state; their support is properly the duty of your own people; I will not assist in throwing it upon others. I have the honor, to be, Very Respectfully,

HLcS

John M Palmer

Major General John M. Palmer to B. F. Bullen, 22 Aug. 1865, vol. 1 DKy, pp. 229–32, Letters Sent, ser. 2164, Dept. of KY, RG 393 Pt. 1 [C-4315]. The mayor's letter of August 19 has not been found among the letters received by the Department of Kentucky. Palmer's reply was evidently intended to be a public statement. One newspaper published it under the headline, "CAUSTIC LETTER FROM GEN. PALMER. The Mayor of Paris, Ky., Goes for Wool and Gets Sheared," printing the mayor's name as B. F. Pullen. (Unidentified clipping, inserted in vol. 229/551 DKy, Letters Sent, ser. 1012, Provost Marshal, Dist. of Western KY, RG 393 Pt. 2 No. 24 [C-8673].)

251: Commander of the Department of Kentucky to a U.S. Senator from Tennessee

Louisville, Ky., September 4. 1865

Dear Sir: It has occurred to me since our interview at Louisville, that you would pardon me for asking you to read my reasons for entertaining the opinion which I then expressed to you that "Slavery has ceased to exist as a legal institution in Kentucky," and for the further opinion that "it is competent for the government of the United States to recognize the fact that it has ceased and protect the late subjects of the slave system as free people."

I will not attempt to disguise the fact from you that all of the political party in this state, opposed to the Administration, and perhaps a majority of the Union party differ with me. They regard slavery as yet in full *legal existence* as one of the "institutions" of the state, only disturbed or obstructed in its operation by causes which some admit to be inevitable and legitimate, but which others denounce as avoidable, unnecessary and unjust; but they agree that these supposed obstructions and disturbances may cease without totally destroying slavery, while I without enquiry as to the legitimacy of the attacks upon slavery, or whether it has been assailed or disturbed by inevitable or avoidable causes, maintain that it is overthrown and destroyed; and that as a legal system it has ceased to exist. I also have to observe that I find much difficulty in securing a hearing for my reasons, and the adoption of my conclusions from the force of old habits of thought, old political formulas, and in a general unwillingness amongst even intelligent politicians to commit themselves to any principle, or theory, which in application may advantageously affect the status of the black race, until it has been endorsed by official authority; or announced as an article of faith in the creed of a party.

I wish if possible to avoid all these difficulties, and submit my arguments and conclusions to you for your candid, deliberate consideration and judgement.

Slavery is now a Federal, and not a State question; hence it is within the power of the United States government to determine whether it has ceased or not.

It will be objected to this view, that it is opposed by the current of authorities, political and legal, and I am ready to admit, that until the great changes produced by the late civil war, and by the political and military acts of the United States government, it was conceded that the government of the population of African descent belonged to the state in which they resided, and that they were not subject to the interference of the United States. That opinion was predicated upon the concession to the slave states that they were property. The legal personality of negroes was not generally claimed, and the right of the states to govern them as property was not disputed. But the United States government is now committed to the doctrine, that negroes are not property, or if property only so in an exceptional and modified sense. This political change may be easily traced. President Lincoln in his inaugural address delivered on the   day of March 1861, disclaimed for himself and for the general government, all power to interfere with slavery in the states in which it then existed, and his disclaimer was approved by men of all parties in the country.

Without noting particularly the acts of the government, or the expressions of public bodies or individuals, indicative of the change in the public mind which commenced about this time, on this subject and the more important one of the relation of the people of african descent to the government, it will be observed that on the 22d day of September 1862, the President of the United States issued his proclamation in which he announced that on the first day of January 1863, all persons held as slaves within any state, or designated part of a state, "the people whereof shall then be in rebellion against the United States," shall be then, thenceforward forever free, and the executive government of the United States, including the Military and Naval authority thereof, will recognize and maintain the freedom of all such persons. This proclamation also referrs to certain laws enacted by Congress in reference to slavery, and clearly indicates the changed opinion of the President, and the adoption of new theories in respect to the powers of the United States. On the first day of January 1863, in pursuance of the purpose already declared the President issued that proclamation which has become historical, and will survive all his other public acts; In that paper he designated certain states and parts of states, wherein the people thereof respectively were on that day in rebellion against the United States – and did order and declare that all persons held as slaves within said designated states and parts of states, are, and from henceforward shall be free, and pledged the government to maintain their freedom.

These proclamations assert the principle, that the question of slavery has ceased to be of state, but had become to be one of federal control, that it had ceased to be a mere legal property question, but had become one of high policy, affecting not individual rights alone, but the perpetuity of the government.

I will not do more than advert to other executive and legislative acts of the President and Congress, of the United States which though of far less historical importance are quite as conclusive proof that the political Departments of the government had even before Sept. 1862, adopted the opinion that slavery had become a national question. On the 6th day of March 1862, the President recommended, and both branches of Congress by large majorities adopted a resolution which declared that "the United States ought cooperate with any state which may adopt a gradual abolishment of slavery, giving to such states pecuniary aid; to be used by such state in its discretion to compensate for the inconvieniences, public and private, produced by such change of system.

On the 13th day of March 1862, Congress adopted an additional article of war, by which officers of the Army and Navy were forbidden to employ any part of the forces under their respective command, for the purpose of returning fugitives from service or labor, and by the 9th section of the act of July 9th 1862, provided that all the slaves of persons who should thereafter engage in rebellion, should under the circumstances therein mentioned be forever free.

In addition to the force of the foregoing facts, it must be observed that the Federal constitution provides that the United

States shall guarantee to each state in the Union a republican form of government. Sec. 4 Art. 4. Reduced to its simplest terms the clear meaning of the constitution is, that the United States shall guarantee to each state a government and that the form of government shall be republican. This obligation of the United States extends, not only to maintaining in the states governmental forms, but goes to the extent of demanding for them an effective government – one which shall be capable of affording protection to the lives, liberty and property of all the inhabitants of the state. If from any cause the government of a state shall totally cease to exist, the duty of creating a government for the state devolves upon the United States In framing such a government for a state, there is no other limitation upon the powers of the United States than that the government thus framed, shall be "republican in form."

Prudence, wise statemanship and a proper respect for the feelings and prejudices of the people will suggest that the government thus formed and maintained for a state, shall conform as nearly as possible to that to which the people are accustomed, but all that the Federal constitution demands is that it be republican in form.

The existing policy of the government in respect to states in which their governments have been subverted by the treason and rebellion of their officers and people is based upon this theory. In respect to those states, the United States is under no constitutional obligation to revive or again set in motion the constitution in force immediately before the subversion of the state government, nor does the plan of reconstruction adopted by the President do so. That plan as I understand it, is based upon the idea that state governments do not originate in written constitutions – they spring directly from the people and constitutions are but limitations upon the powers of the people. The United States animated by a proper respect for the principles of free government, may select for the people of a state, the government of which is subverted, that constitution which contains the latest expression of their will, and without modification, or without only necessary alterations put it in force and maintain it, until the state shall be in a condition to maintain itself independent of the Federal guarantee.

The government of the United States in the execution of this constitutional duty of giving a republican form of government to states of the Union, in which government is subverted, must temporarily deposit the powers of the government with agents of its own selection. Those agents may be military or civil officers appointed by the President or, may be the people acting under the immediate protection of the federal government, or the powers of the government may be divided at the discretion of the federal government and certain of them entrusted to the military, and others to civil functionaries and others devolved upon the people or a part of the people.

These agents, military and civil officers, derive their authority to act, from the President; and the people are limited in their action to the sphere assigned them by him. If any of them disregard his views of policy, or fall short of the end he has in view, he may overrule and disregard their acts.

A state government may be partially subverted, or certain of its essential powers may be destroyed to a degree which deprives it of the essential quality of a republican form. The duty of the United States to interfere to supply the absent or deficient powers, would be as clear in such case of partial subversion, as in case of the total overthrow of the government. A state government exists but it may have lost its effective republican quality; then the interposition of the Federal government is demanded to restore the essential quality of all American state governments.

Again, a state government may be so far deprived of its power by rebellion or otherwise, or there may be such radical changes in the condition of a portion of the people that the powers of the government do not extend to, or comprehend that portion of its population, whose condition is so changed. It then becomes incapable of affording to them the protection which is involved in the most rudimentary ideas of government.

In that case the general government may, and ought do for the state and for the protection of the lives and liberties of that portion of its people whose interests are not secured, that which it may and ought do for a state whose powers are totally subverted for the benefit of all its people – guarantee an effective republican government. This principle, and the right of the federal government to interfere for the protection and advantage of a portion of the inhabitants of a state who are not within its general system of government and laws, is vindicated and illustrated in the acts of Congress establishing the Freedmans Bureau, and in similar legislation.

But another case may be supposed. The controling forces of a state of the Union, a majority if you will, might obtain complete control over all the Departments of the state government, and pervert and misdirect them, so as to permanently defeat all the objects of government with respect to a portion of the inhabitants of the state.

The executive, legislative, and judicial Departments of the state government become alike deaf to the demands of justice and law. It would be the clear duty of the Federal government, through some or all of its departments to interfere and guarantee to the outraged people, the benefits of a republican form of government.

I am conscious of some obscurity in the application of this clause of the Federal constitution to the existing state of things, and will endeavor to remove it by a brief summary.

I mean to maintain that it is the duty of the United States to guarantee a republican form of government to all the states in the Union. That in case of the total subversion of a state government, the United States may organize, and maintain in the state, whose government is subverted, an *adinterim* government and invest all its powers in agents of its own selection.

2^{d} That in case of a partial subversion of a state government, the United States may rightfully interfere to supply the subverted powers.

3d. That in case the condition of the whole or any part of the people of any state becomes so changed that they are not in their new relations comprehended within the existing government it is within scope of the powers of the United States to furnish to such people a government adapted to existing facts, and maintain that government for them, until the state shall properly comprehend them in its own system.

The government of the state of Kentucky, so far as relates to its population of the African and mixed races, is subverted and overthrown. The white people of the state for their own government, "adopted" a constitution, under which laws have been enacted for the protection of their own lives, liberty and property. They did not embrace the negroes within that system, but referred the government of that whole class to such individuals of the white race, as accident might select with the designation of masters. They gave to those masters with but few limitations, and restrictions, full power over the persons of their subjects, and in turn held them responsible for their health, morals and conduct. The master was Governor to control them, lawgiver to furnish them rules of civil conduct, priest if he chose to be so, to prescribe the faith to be believed, and the code of morals to be observed, Chancellor to dissolve or prohibit marriage, control their domestic relations, and settle all controversies amongst them.

Under this system of government, they were so far placed under the protection of the master, that injuries inflicted upon their persons were wrongs to him, and he alone could demand redress.

The master as incident to this government received the proceeds of their labor, and was held responsible to the government for their share of all public burdens and duties, including taxes and civil and military services, or because of their paramount duties to the master, they were relieved of these burdens altogether. Their political existence was merged in him and they were only known to the general political system through him, and then only for the support of his authority over them, the protection of his rights, and the definition of his duties

The system of slavery was therefore a part of the state government of Kentucky, and of all the late slave states and is subverted. If slavery was a part of the political system of states, it does not come within the general rule, that mere property rights are not affected by political changes; a rule which is often invoked to maintain its present existence. On the contrary, like other political forms it may be weakened or gain strength from either peaceful or forcible revolutions. A revolution adverse to the system has taken place and as I maintain, it has perished. Before the commencement of the late civil war, the current of political opinions, and to a very great extent of judicial decisions consigned the colored race to the system of slavery as their normal condition. It is true, this theory was not everywhere assented to, but its practicable application was scarcely opposed anywhere. Their actual capacity for a state of freedom was gently hinted at, by a few, but the opinion was not urged with great confidence. It was either yielded, or entertained in silence under the pressure of an almost universal denial, coupled with the fierce denunciations sanctioned by the habits of the times. The United States government through many successions of high functionaries were committed to it, and it either expressly or by implication formed a part of the creed of all "safe" political organizations.

The subversion of the system commenced in the change of the government.

Important as were the acts of Congress, and the proclamations of President Lincoln already referred to in emancipating the colored race from slavery, they are equally so in recognizing their new status – their changed relations to the people of the United States. In the proclamation of the 1st of January 1863, the President assuming that the words already written had accomplished the fact of emancipation, addressed the people thus made free, in language only proper to be used to those who were, or had become subject to his executive authority.

For the first time in our history men of the colored race were addressed directly by the chief magistrate of the United States. He warns them as citizens to abstain from all violence, unless in necessary self defence. He urges them to industry, and intimates to them the new duties to which they have become subject. He informs them that such of them as are of suitable condition will be received into the military service of the United States.

Since that marked event, all Departments of the United States

government have recognized the new status of the colored
race. Persons of the African race have been commissioned by the
President as officers of the army, (surgeons) one of them has been
admitted to the bar of the Supreme Court of the United
States. Congress has by repeated acts, removed many of the
disabilities to which they were subjected, while former opinions
prevailed, and finaly under the authority of Federal laws, colored
men have been made competent witnesses in all federal courts, and
are enrolled as a part of the national forces and made subject to
military duties precisely as are all others.

I think I may pause here long enough to say that in my opinion
the law which requires colored men to be enrolled, and subjects
them to responsibilities to the government for military services, of
itself as a mere act of legislation without reference to the principles
upon which it is provided upon the narrowest view renders all the
enrolled free.

By the law, they were directly responsible to the government for
military services. They were permitted to volunteer in disregard of
the authority of masters. They were subjected to the draft like the
master, but as slaves they could not legally acquire even by gift, the
amount of money which might be required to pay the commutation
which certain classes of persons were at one time alowed to do, nor
to procure a substitute as was permitted to all other persons. The
money which benevolence might furnish him for either of these
purposes, the moment it touched his hands, became the property of
his master, and if he should at last engage in the military service of
his government and die in battle bravely doing his duty, or from
sickness contracted in fatigueing marches, or in pestilentios camps,
the pension to wives and children or aged parents unless they too
were free, would be intercepted by the legal claims of a master. I
know a mother of two sons, who died in the military service of the
United States. One was killed in battle at Saltville, Virginia, she
is claimed as a slave, and is one if any are. If she is a slave, to what
end will government pay her a pension.

By, and as the effect of these acts of the executive, legislative,
and judicial departments of the United States government, the
status of the colored race is fixed and defined to be that of
inhabitants with a natural and political capacity to become freemen
and citizens; that with respect to them, slavery is an accident; a
mere relation or condition imposed upon them and from which they
may rightfully escape; that in this new relation they became directly
responsible to the government, for the performance of duties which
are paramount to, and inconsistent with the claims of masters upon
them. It is also true, that this is the status of the race, and from it
the most important results necessarily follow. All laws and customs

adverse to their freedom, must according to just rules of interpretation be construed strictly and the most liberal interpretation and effect must be allowed to all acts, whether of an executive, legislative or judicial character which favor their freedom. So also public events which affect institutions and relations are to be allowed their widest reasonable scope for the attainment of the same result. Tested by these principles we may now preceed to enquire into the effect of all the public acts, and political events already referred to and mention others which interpreted rightly, do completely subvert and destroy slavery.

At the commencement of the late civil war, slavery existed in nearly half the states of the Union, and comprehended nearly four millions of slaves. It was so nearly universal in its operation upon the African race within the limits of the United States, that slavery was considered to be the rule with respect to them, and freedom the exception. It was a condition judged applicable to that race and no other. The policy of enforcing slavery with respect to this race was considered so far proper and judicious that the liberty and interests of the exceptionally free were entirely subordinated to it. The free colored men were odious in almost all communities; their very presence in slave states was an offence, and they were expelled whenever it was possible to do so. But note the actual changes the events of five years have produced in their condition Of the four millions of slaves within the limits of the United States at the beginning of the civil disturbances, all are now admitted to be free, except those in two states – Deleware and Kentucky – Deleware may be disregarded – her insignificance in nothing is more remarkable than in the smallness of the number of her slaves, and the tenacity with which she clings to them.

Kentucky had two hundred and thirty thousand slaves, some thing less than one seventeenth of the whole number in the United States. As all outside of Kentucky are made free, (sixteen seventeenth's of the whole number.) it might be fair to argue that such an extensive change in its political consequences, destroy slavery in this state, but in that view, the case can be made far stronger. Of the whole number of slaves in Kentucky, twenty eight thousand eight hundred and eighteen, have been freed by the terms of their enlistment in the military service of the United States. Seventy two thousand and forty five are shown by reliable official reports to be free as the wives and children of colored men, who have enlisted in the military service of the government.

Total number,		230,000
" "	free as above	100,863
Whole number whose freedom is disputed		129,137

Only one thirtieth of the number who were slaves at the beginning of the war. But the proportions may be still farther reduced.

It is correct as a legal proposition to assert that the slaves of all persons who were engaged in the late rebellion against the authority of the United States are free. One half of the number given above whose freedom is in dispute are upon sufficient data presumed to have belonged to persons compromised by their connection with the rebellion. Sixty four thousand five hundred and sixty nine is the highest number of slaves in Kentucky, admitting what is not true that the number of colored persons in the state remains unchanged, and that no other causes have operated for the overthrow of slavery than those already mentioned.

According to this view, fifty nine sixtieth's of all the four millions of slaves once in the United States are now free. Have been made so by executive and legislative acts the operative force of which are now scarcely controverted and by great national events which have affected every political, social and material interests of the country. Will it be seriously said that the whole effect of the emancipation of nearly the entire colored race in the United States, is simply the loss of the market value of Three millions nine hundred and thirty five thousand four hundred and thirty one slaves to their former owners while the tenure of the claimants of the sixty four thousand five hundred and sixty nine who are not embraced in that larger number the mode of whose emancipation is pointed out and all of whom are in a single state, is unimpaired. The most conclusive refutation of that opinion is found in the fact that all of the persons, claimed to be slaves in Kentucky, could scarcely be sold to day for as many dollars.

This effect is apparent: it is not denied by any one. I insist upon another that these changes have legitimately resulted in overthrowing the whole system of slavery and all are now free. That the value of slaves is destroyed, is admitted. From these facts and arguments it cannot be denied that the system of slavery is overthrown and subverted — and if the system is subverted, it is not easy to understand how it has sufficient vitality and force to compel persons to slavery.

But what answer is there to this, that such is the actual demoralization of the slave system in Kentucky, that it is no longer effective for the control of the slaves. as a rule they are in fact free. It is true, their freedom is not perfect, for the master has from the state of the local laws, and from the aid which he derives for that purpose from the habits and opinions of the white people of the state the power to harass and annoy his late bondmen, but the power of annoyance falls very far short of the actual complete dominion which is of the essence of slavery, and in the pursuit of any scheme of annoyance, he confessedly renounces the duty of protection and support, which is implied in the very nature of the system. In fact, in this view of the case, a state of war exists between the races. The late master employs in many cases actual force to compel submission; the slaves fly and take refuge where they can, or avail themselves of such expedients for resistance as the state of the country affords., While the return of peace and order to the country is hindered and every interest industrial and moral suffers from the conflict.

Notwithstanding the great length of this argument, there is one additional consideration which demands attention. I assume that none will question the right and duty of the United States to give protection to the free colored people of the state, nor its power to determine who of them are free, and for that reason entitled to demand protection. Without entering into the question whether any of the two hundred and thirty thousand slaves in the state five years ago are free, other than enlisted soldiers, their wives and children and slaves once the property of rebels, it may be said that there is an aggregate number of free blacks in the state of one hundred and sixty five thousand, four hundred and thirty two, against a slave population of sixty four thousand five hundred and sixty eight. Now I affirm with the greatest confidence that the free people of the state cannot have the protection they have a right to demand; they cannot have the benefit of just laws, nor the support of an enlightened liberal public opinion if this remnant of slavery is to be preserved. This free people have no voice in the enactment or execution of the laws; their freedom is an offence to those who have. For years to come the prevailing effort will be to strengthen slavery, and discourage freedom.

The existing antagonism of races which has its only foundation in slavery, will go on. No considerable improvement in the condition of the free will be possible. Oppression, injustice, discouragement and misery will be their condition until long after the struggle ceases.

I maintain as a final conclusion that slavery is a political system, is subverted. That it is within the powers, and is clearly the duty of the President to declare that fact.

To authorize such a recognition, the aid of no other Department of the government is needed. No law is to be enacted, and none repealed.

Such a declaration, supported by the authority of the United States, would close the great controversy forever; would give confidence to the blacks, and peace to the white population of the country. It would disarm faction and strengthen the loyal, and would give the President a new claim upon the confidence of the country. Very Respectfully Your Obt. servant

HLcS   John M Palmer

Major General John M. Palmer to Hon. Joseph C. Fowler, 4 Sept. 1865, vol. 1 DKy, pp. 260–75, Letters Sent, ser. 2164, Dept. of KY, RG 393 Pt. 1 [C-4343]. The blank space in the date of Lincoln's inaugural address appears in the manuscript. In a second letter, written to accompany this lengthy argument, General Palmer proposed that the Tennessee senator "lay [the argument] before the President and Secretary of War." Convinced that "success" in Kentucky "can be reached only by aggression," Palmer complained that "[t]he Union Party here is distinguished by its timidity . . . Certain of its leaders . . . are temporising with the hope of conciliating the Conservatives. My hope of the success of a true Union party is to destroy the platform upon which they hope to meet. They will agree this winter in the support of Slavery in Kentucky without any other motive than temporary personal advantage. 'I want to burn their ships.' " After offering this proposal "as a politician," Palmer added that he "could furnish a volume of outrages committed upon the colored persons in the name of the 'Speck' of Slavery which is still nursed in Kentucky." "No power on earth," he concluded, "can prevent or punish these outrages as long as the existence of Slavery is admitted. I only ask permission to say officially 'there is no Slavery in Kentucky.' " (John M. Palmer to Hon. J. C. Fowler, 7 Sept. 1865, vol. 1 DKy, p. 279, Letters Sent, ser. 2164, Dept. of KY, RG 393 Pt. 1 [C-4343].)

252: Anonymous Letter to a Louisville Newspaper

Lebanon, Ky., Sept. 10, 1865.
(Communicated)

The Grand Jury of Marion County at the late term of the Circuit Court, thought it necessary to indict Capt. Fidler, Provost Marshal 4th District of Kentucky, for giving a pass to a negro not his own property. An examination of the papers in the case shows that the pass was given in the words of General Order No. 49, C.S. Dept. Ky.,[1] and given to a negro woman who claimed to be drove from home, and out of employment. This same Grand Jury failed to indict a single returned rebel for stealing horses, or a single guerrilla for robbery and murdering. In the case of Capt. Fidler it was actually known that he obeyed the legitimate order of a legitimate superior. And yet he was indicted for an offense that if a *crime* entitles him to ___ years in the State penitentiary. In this case the Grand Jury announces that an inferior is not shielded by the orders of a superior. Yet when rebels are sued for horses stolen, or for crimes committed, they are freed if they can show that they obeyed orders.

The fact of the business is just this: Kentucky slaveholders – fanatics as they are – are determined to drive from Kentucky, if possible, loyal men. My attention has been called to the efforts of rebels and slaveholders in this direction by more than a dozen prominent men. The Commonwealth's Attorney for this district called my attention to the fact that rebels are now bringing up and vehemently prosecuting every minor offense committed by Union men that occurred during the war. Others have pointed out to me instances where blatant rebels have gone free for committing misdemeanors because committed in the name of the rebellion, while Union men have been thoroughly prosecuted.

If martial law is withdrawn from Kentucky loyal men must suffer immensely. To have martial law withdrawn all rebels are now working. God forbid that they succeed. Respectfully

HDc   (Signed) Loyalist.

Loyalist to the *Louisville Daily Journal*, 10 Sept. 1865, filed with P-39 1865, Letters Received, ser. 15, Washington Hdqrs., RG 105 [A-6010]. The Provost Marshal General's Bureau made this copy of the letter and forwarded it to the commissioner of the Freedmen's Bureau, along with other documents about Kentucky. In the same file is an excerpt from a report by Captain Fidler to the provost marshal general about his indictment for issuing a pass to a slave without the consent of her owner. "There can be no doubt in my mind," Fidler warned, "that a Kentucky Jury of slave holders will find me guilty not only of a fact, but of the crime charged. It has long since become apparent to me that those men who have been connected with the Administration in any manner will be persecuted constantly by the slave holders of this State hereafter. In truth this is the case now. Those officers who have been connected with the Pro' Mars Bureau must expect to be driven out of the State or to submit to all manner of indignities. My former deputies are threatened with suits for slaves enlisted in many counties. Several of these officers have found it best to leave the State. If Martial Law is removed rebel juries will make Kentucky too warm for any man of loyalty." (Capt. James M. Fidler to Brig. Genl. Jas. B. Fry, 10 Sept. 1865.) President Andrew Johnson ended martial law in Kentucky on October 12, 1865. (*Official Records*, ser. 1, vol. 49, pt. 2, p. 1116.)

1 See above, doc. 240n.

253: Affidavit of a Kentucky Freedwoman, and a Tennessee Attorney to the Tennessee and Kentucky Freedmen's Bureau Assistant Commissioner

State of Tennessee Montgomery County 19" day of September 1865

I Minerva Banks (at one time called Minerva Summers) on oath say that I am the mother of Charles Banks Co. "H" 101st U.S.C. Inf who died Dec. 5. 1864.

That since Christmas 1863 I have made Tennessee my home and since my said son – Charles enlisted as a soldier I have regarded myself as free & have been so informed and believe it to be true. I worked as Cook in the Engineer Dept at Nashville and received a discharge in these words:

> "Engineer Department Nashville Tenn. May 4 1865
> Minerva Sommers (colored) in the employ of this Department owing to General Orders is hereby discharged
> (Signed) J. W. Barton Capt U.S. Eng^{rs} In Charge of Defences"

1st June 1865 Lawyer Davis at Cadiz Trigg Co Ky hired me, but his wife was always unkind to me & abused me so that I was compelled to leave and I then hired to Mr W. H. Martin who lives 3 miles North from Cadiz and received from him a writing in these words

> "I will give Mary Banks seven Dollars & 50 cents per month for the ballance of the year and pay her at the end of each month – she to clothe herself
> June 12 1865   (signed) W. H. Martin"

I had been to work there but a few days when Edward Sommers my former master who lives about 2 miles from Hopkinsville – came to Mrs Martin's with Dr Russell who brought a gun & threatened to shoot me if I offered to resist or run, Sommers at first being hid. Somers then came up with a large whip & accosted me saying he was afraid he would have to die before seeing me as he wanted to live to give me one good thrashing – Sommers then took me off from the house about 1/2 mile into the woods. He then took the bridle rein from his buggy & hung me up by the neck for some time & then took me down & compelled me by force to strip *naked* & then tied my hands to a limb of the tree so that my feet but just touched the ground. then cut limbs from the trees with which he scourged me for a long time whipping me from my head to my feet cutting some severe gashes & among some of the injuries inflicted he broke one of my fingures with the but end of his heavy whip –

I worked for said Martins until about Sept 1st when he informed that he would not pay me any thing as he was obliged to pay my wages to Mr Sommers –

I have the original papers the copies whereof are above recited –

654

The above has been carefully read over to me & before God I solemnly swear that it is true & that I left that Country for fear of my life— All my things such as bed Clothes &c are or were left at Mr Martins—

her
Minerva × Banks
mark

HDSr

Clarksville, Tenn., Decr 18" 1865

General: We have the honor to trouble you again— Some time since we drew up a sworn statement of Minerva Banks (Somers) of an outrageous treatment she had rec'd from Edward Sommers living near Hopkinsville Ky. which statement arrived at your office in your absence—& after your return was referred to your agent D. S. Hays at Hopkinsville, with instructions— We have before us letter from Hays of 13" inst— He would be glad to do something but cannot. He says: "If Major Bond (Supt at Clarksville) will give a peremptory order requiring Sommers to report to him (Bond) he (Hays) will serve it— That he is powerless to do any thing without Troops, that his hands are tied completely—" He further says: "We have a set of infernal returned Rebels in our County (Christian Ky) who are going the rounds & robbing the Darkeys of their guns & pistols & when they come across one who has been in our service, they beat him unmecifully & threaten his life if he does not leave— They go undisguised— If I had some colored Soldiers I would soon settle matters with them— We need soldiers here now & shall particularly about the end of the year— Our County Judge refuses to issue peace Warrants upon the oath of a colored free man—"

The above quotations show how Gen Hays is situated, and the necessity for hanging a few of the many "Loyal Kentuckins" who disgrace any Country—

As regard Minerva Sommers the man who stripped & flogged her ought to be dealt with—

Were I commanding the Co I once did I could be under no necessity of *writing* but would *right* some matters summarily— as it is I again appeal to you   Respy Your Obt Servts

Buck & McMullen
pr J. Jay Buck

ALS

Affidavit of Minerva Banks, 19 Sept. 1865, enclosed in Buck & McMullen to Brig. Gen. C. B. Fisk, 19 Sept. 1865, B-128 1865, Registered Letters Received, ser. 3379, TN Asst. Comr., RG 105 [A-6084]; J. Jay Buck to

Brig. Gen. C. B. Fisk, 18 Dec. 1865, B-202 1865, Registered Letters Received, ser. 3379, TN Asst. Comr., RG 105 [A-6084]. Affidavit sworn before a Freedmen's Bureau agent. J. Jay Buck had been an officer in the 101st USCI, a regiment of Kentucky blacks organized at Clarksville, Tennessee. (See above, doc. 236.) Evidently displeased by Buck's implication that Freedmen's Bureau efforts in this case had been inadequate, General Clinton B. Fisk, the bureau assistant commissioner, endorsed on Buck's letter the following instructions to an adjutant: "Advise the writer that we understand Kentucky matters pretty well – and know all the difficulties and shall overcome them as rapidly as possible." It is not clear whether Edward Sommers was ever brought to justice. In October 1865, when presented with a letter from attorneys Buck and McMullen, endorsed by General Fisk, Sommers had retorted "that if [they] wanted any thing with him to come on or Come to him." As late as March 1866, D. S. Hays (who had by then been relieved as Freedmen's Bureau agent at Hopkinsville, Kentucky) forwarded papers in the case to Buck and McMullen, no action apparently having yet been taken. (Buck & McMullen to Capt. W. T. Clark, 18 Oct. 1865, enclosing Saml. Feland to Messrs. Buck & McMullen, [Oct. 1865]; D. S. Hays to Major Genl. C. B. Fisk, 5 Mar. 1866, B-142 1865 and H-110 1866, Registered Letters Received, ser. 3379, TN Asst. Comr., RG 105 [A-6084].)

254: Freedmen's Bureau Superintendent of the Subdistrict of Louisville, Kentucky, to the Tennessee and Kentucky Freedmen's Bureau Assistant Commissioner; and the Latter's Reply

Louisville Ky Oct 9 1865

General: I have the honor to request a definite answer to the following questions

Am I to consider slaves who leave their masters under General Order, No 32. Head Quarters Dept of Ky[1] and General Order No 109 A.G.O.(CS)[2] as "freedmen"? and shall I enforce payment to them for their labor?

This question is becoming more annoying every day and I wish to have authority to cover my action in these cases   Very Respectfully Your Obdt Servant

H A M⁽c⁾Caleb

PS Please return this without delay with your answer as I have a number of cases awaiting it   H. A. M.

ALS

Nashville Tenn Oct 11th 1865

Col. In acknowledgment and reply to yours of 9" inst would say that I have submitted the *Kentucky* questions to Washington for

definite instructions— I am daily expecting a reply— I can not see
how I can run a *Freed*mens Bureau for *Slaves*—

I expect to visit Louisville and Frankfort within a very few
days—when I hope to be able to adopt and enforce a *free*
policy— wait action until you hear further from me— Very
Respectfully Yr. Obᵗ Servant

ALS   Clinton B. Fisk

Col. H. A. McCaleb to Brig. Genl. C. B. Fisk, 9 Oct. 1865, M-104 1865,
Registered Letters Received, ser. 3379, TN Asst. Comr., RG 105 [A-6176];
Brig. Genl. Clinton B. Fisk to Col. H. A. McCaleb, 11 Oct. 1865, Unregis-
tered Letters Received, ser. 1209, Louisville KY Supt., RG 105 [A-6176].

1 See above, doc. 240.
2 Presumably General Order 129, issued by the Adjutant General's Office in
July 1865. It prohibited military restrictions upon the ex-slaves' freedom of
movement, as well as any special punishments not imposed on "other classes."
The order further provided: "Neither whites nor blacks will be restrained from
seeking employment elsewhere when they cannot obtain it at a just compensation at their homes, and when not bound by voluntary agreement; nor will
they be hindered from traveling from place to place on proper and legitimate
business." (General Orders No. 129, War Department, Adjutant General's
Office, 25 July 1865, Orders & Circulars, ser. 44, RG 94 [DD-31].)

255: Commander of the Department of Kentucky to the Attorney General

Louisville, Kentucky, Nov 28ᵗʰ *1865*.

The Grand Jury of Jefferson County have prefered two
Indictments against me for the Offence of "aiding slaves to escape"
as they regard the giving of a pass by one of my Subordinates to a
negro as a felony in me   I dont know how many more they will
present   If the giving of a pass to a negro is an Offence there are
twenty thousand crimes for which I am punishable and Congress
will have to pass a law extending my life—to lengthen it out a few
thousand years that I may meet the punishment   Perhaps the
President can do it under the War power.

Brutus Clay has sued me for the price of

Forty negroes @ $1000 each	$ 40 000
Garret Davis for ten negroes at $1000	" 10,000
these are in the [Bourbon] Circuit Court	
Samˡ A Hall has sued me for damages	" 10,000

in Harrison for false imprisonment though I have no knowledge of the facts beyond this that he says I commanded the Negro troops

These prosecutions and suits are against for Official acts so far as they proceed for acts done by me

I would have been entirely willing to encounter a few suits on account of the negroes but this is more *practice* than I want   they promise to make me an involuntary citizen of the State

I have the honor to request that you direct the District Atty to defend them   I am very respectfully

John M Palmer

PS I would under ordinary circumstances have reported these cases to the Adjutant General and asked the attention of the War Department to the cases but my personal acquaintance with you induces a direct application   J M P

ALS

Maj. Genl. John M. Palmer to Hon. James Speed, 28 Nov. 1865, Letters Received: KY Other Federal Officials, ser. 9, Attorney General's Records, RG 60 [W-2]. Endorsements. Garret Davis was a U.S. senator, and Brutus Clay, a former U.S. representative. Within two months a fourth suit, claiming $10,000 damages, was brought against Palmer. The Attorney General directed the U.S. district attorney in Kentucky to defend Palmer in the suits, advising their removal to the federal courts. (James Speed to Genl. John M. Palmer, 1 Dec. 1865, vol. E, p. 330, Letters Sent: General Letter Books, ser. 10, Attorney General's Records, RG 60 [W-2]; Maj. Genl. John M. Palmer to the Adjutant General, 26 Jan. 1866, with endorsement by Judge Advocate General J. Holt, 3 Feb. 1866, and Thos. T. Eckert to James Speed, 15 Feb. 1866, with unsigned endorsement, 19 Feb. 1866, both in Letters Received: War Department, ser. 9, Attorney General's Records, RG 60 [W-54].)

256: Circular by the Commander of the Department of Kentucky

Louisville, Ky. Dec. 7. 1865.

CIRCULAR, No. 6. The General Commanding announces that, though the fact has not been officially announced, enough is known to warrant the statement that the amendment to the Constitution of the United States prohibiting slavery has been ratified by the Legislatures of three fourths of the states and is, to all intents and purposes, a part of said Constitution.

Whatever doubts may have heretofore existed on the subject, Slavery has now ceased to exist in Kentucky and with it fall all the laws of the state heretofore in force intended for its support.

General Orders Number Thirty two (32) and Forty nine (49)[1] and all other orders from these Head-Quarters relating to the issuing of passes to Colored people, having become unnecessary, are therefore rescinded. From henceforth Colored people will be under the protection of the general laws of the land, and if the owners or operators of Boats or Rail Roads shall disregard their undoubted right to travel at pleasure, upon conforming to reasonable regulations, they are advised to apply promptly to the Courts for redress. BY COMMAND OF MAJOR GENERAL J. M. PALMER: PD

Circular No. 6, Head-Quarters Department of Kentucky, 7 Dec. 1865, Orders & Circulars, ser. 44, RG 94 [DD-27]. On December 18, the Secretary of State officially proclaimed that the 13th Amendment prohibiting slavery had been ratified. (U.S., *Statutes at Large, Treaties, and Proclamations*, vol. 13 [Boston, 1866], pp. 774–75.)

1 See above, doc. 240.

CHAPTER 9

The Confederacy

9

The Confederacy

I F NORTHERN political leaders and the Northern public began the war divided over the relationship of slavery to the great struggle for the Union, Southerners had no doubt about its centrality.[1] Southern nationalists had long predicated the existence of a distinctive Southern culture on slavery, and the South's claim to independence and the prospect of war with the North magnified slavery's importance. Slaves, it was thought, would be relied upon to construct fortifications, manufacture ordnance, and move the supplies required by the armies in the field. Slaves would also grow food for soldiers and civilians alike, and produce the cash crops that would finance the war and bring European powers to the aid of the Confederacy. Finally, in serving as the mudsill upon which all whites could stand, slaves would assure the unity of white society in a time of crisis.

But, as the war proceeded, Southern whites suffered a sad disappointment. On the war front, slaves proved to be undependable laborers. By deserting at every opportunity, they simultaneously weakened the Southern cause and strengthened the Northern one. On the home front, slaves were equally unreliable. When they did not flee, they shirked their duties and became increasingly suspect servants and intractable workers. Their sullen and sometimes violent resistance to customary discipline reduced Southern agricultural and industrial productivity, creating morale problems among civilians that soon per-

---

[1] Published accounts that discuss slavery in the Confederacy include: Frank L. Owsley, *State Rights in the Confederacy* (Chicago, 1925); Charles H. Wesley, *The Collapse of the Confederacy* (Washington, 1937); Bell I. Wiley, *Southern Negroes, 1861–1865* (New Haven, Conn., 1938); James H. Brewer, *The Confederate Negro: Virginia's Craftsmen and Military Laborers, 1861–1865* (Durham, N.C., 1969); Paul D. Escott, *After Secession: Jefferson Davis and the Failure of Confederate Nationalism* (Baton Rouge, La., 1978); Armstead L. Robinson, *Bitter Fruits of Bondage: The Demise of Slavery and the Collapse of the Confederacy* (New Haven, Conn., forthcoming); Harrison A. Trexler, "The Opposition of Planters to the Employment of Slaves as Laborers by the Confederacy," *Mississippi Valley Historical Review* 27 (Sept. 1940): 211–24; Bernard H. Nelson, "Legislative Control of the Southern Free Negro, 1861–1865," *Catholic Historical Review* 32 (Apr. 1946): 28–46, and "Confederate Slave Impressment Legislation, 1861–1865," *Journal of Negro History* 31 (Oct. 1946): 392–410; Tinsley L. Spraggins, "Mobilization of Negro Labor for the Department of Virginia and North Carolina, 1861–1865," *North Carolina Historical Review* 24 (Apr. 1947): 160–97.

meated the ranks of the Confederate army. And far from unifying Southern whites, slavery divided them, exacerbating conflicts that pitted state officials against national officials, national officials against army officers, army officers against slaveholders, and slaveholders against nonslaveholders. To their horror, Confederate partisans found their great asset transmuted into an enormous liability. Slaves, by their presence and by their actions, gnawed at the Confederacy from within, while Northern armies pounded it from without. Together, they brought the Confederacy down and severed the chains that bound black people.

Understanding the importance of slavery to their new nation, slaveholders at first responded generously to the Confederacy's call for labor. During the first months of the war, as they rushed to meet the enemy, some slaveholders volunteered their slaves to assist the Confederate army or even to fight the Yankee invaders.[2] Confederate leaders declined the offers to make slaves into soldiers, but they welcomed donations of slave laborers. Though they had soldiers aplenty, they needed all the laborers they could get. Many Southern soldiers, at least early in the war, disdained the menial labor necessary to keep the Confederate army moving. Most officers, particularly at the higher ranks, took their own slaves with them to minister to their persons and to groom their horses. Occasionally, common soldiers also marched off to war with personal servants. These slaves, more familiar with the routine of the house than the field, were seldom of much help with the heavy work war entailed. Moreover, their owners showed little interest in sharing their services – particularly when that sharing posed a danger to valuable property. The removal of hundreds of such slaves from the home front thus did little to aid the Confederate war effort.

In time, Confederate soldiers learned that warfare necessitated digging as well as fighting, and before long they took up the shovel as well as the sword. But, as the war progressed, they proved unable to battle the Yankees and at the same time satisfy the army's growing need for laborers. Confederate engineers needed laborers to construct fortifications, trenches, and roads; quartermasters required teamsters, stable hands, boatmen, and laundresses; commissary officers wanted butchers, bakers, and cooks; and medical officers demanded nurses, orderlies and, inevitably, grave diggers. For all these tasks, slaves and free blacks appeared to be the surest source of labor.

Confederate labor requirements quickly outpaced the slaveholders' generosity, and the free black population was too small to be relied upon. At the end of 1861 and the beginning of 1862, when Union forces began to occupy the periphery of the South, Confederate officers

[2] See, for example, *Freedom*, ser. 2: docs. 114–15.

tried to revive the earlier spirit. As they rallied their troops, commanders issued numerous pleas for able-bodied slave men, appealing alternately to the slaveholders' patriotism and to their self-interest. However, even the best calculated and most fervent proclamations failed to move a majority of masters.

Masters resisted the calls of Confederate commanders because they feared for the security of their property. Slaves who left their owners for military service frequently did not return. At the approach of Union forces, the most vigilant and well-meaning Confederate officers had difficulty preventing slave laborers from escaping to the woods and perhaps to freedom. But even if the slaves did not abscond, masters understood that forwarding them for Confederate labor details disrupted plantation routine. Slave men resented being separated from their families, and their families – who had to shoulder additional duties – objected to their absence. All viewed military labor as a violation of the carefully contrived protocol between master and slaves, a violation that placed the entire system in jeopardy.

Military labor posed manifold dangers to slave property. More concerned about the exigencies of war than about the lives of slaves or the investment of owners, Confederate commanders sometimes put slaves to work in positions exposed to enemy fire, where they numbered among the first casualties. Even when slaves worked far from the line of battle, engineers, quartermasters, and medical officers drove them hard, assigning demanding tasks to men (and, occasionally, women) whose age and condition had long disqualified them from physical labor on plantations. The necessities of war caused officers otherwise sensitive to the needs of black laborers and the rights of masters to push their charges beyond the limits of their endurance. The strongest slaves sometimes suffered injury as a result. Of those who did not break under the harsh regimen, many fled at the first opportunity. Slaveholders found to their dismay that service in support of the Confederacy often drove their slaves to the woods and swamps, if not to Union lines.

Losses due to desertion and death were only the first of the slaveholders' apprehensions. Even when slave laborers returned physically unscathed, military service left its mark. Work on Confederate fortifications and service among Confederate troops imperiled the discipline of plantation life by broadening the slaves' knowledge of the world. It awakened slaves to the full meaning of the war and to the new opportunities for freedom. For the most part, these subversive ideas originated with other black laborers, some of whom were free and many of whom had been dragooned into Confederate service. But white soldiers and civilians who were employed as overseers and impressment agents also inculcated notions that ran counter to the good order of the plantation. If only by their studied disregard for the slaveholders' authority, military overseers advertised to slaves the limitations of their masters' power.

Slave laborers also returned from military employment with a good deal of practical information about how to escape bondage – familiarity with roads and rivers, the location of federal encampments, and the pattern of troop movements. Such knowledge bolstered their confidence and provided a valuable commodity that might be traded to the enemy of their enemy. Thus, for a variety of reasons, slaves returned from Confederate service different in demeanor from when they left. They no longer deferred as quickly or worked as readily. Many returned just long enough to gather their families and their belongings and, perhaps, to raid their master's larder before striking out for Union lines.

The loss of slaves and erosion of discipline that resulted from military labor made owners increasingly reluctant to hire their slaves to the Confederacy. Guarantees of prompt payment for the services of slave laborers and compensation for losses by flight, injury, or death failed to diminish the opposition. The masters' recalcitrance did not reduce military need, however, and when slaveholders refused to provide slave laborers voluntarily, army commanders simply took them. Impressment put Confederate military authorities on a collision course with the first principle of Southern society: the authority of the master and the sanctity of slave property. Whether slaves were marched into Confederate labor gangs under the aegis of high-ranking state and national officials or at the peremptory command of hard-pressed field officers, impressment revealed that the owners' power had been abridged. Slaves sensed this breach of authority and, much to their owners' distress, acted accordingly. As slaveholders came to understand that impressment compromised their sovereignty, they addressed bitter complaints to state and Confederate officials about the violation of their rights.

Confederate leaders, slaveholders to a man, had no desire to challenge the master's power and prerogatives. Although they considered some of the complaints short-sighted if not unpatriotic, they shared the fear that impressing slaves would reduce Southern agricultural and industrial output. Moreover, until the third year of the war, they lacked authority to order impressment directly (except perhaps in dire emergencies) and had to rely upon state legislatures and governors to impress slave laborers when requested by army commanders.[3] Confederate officials therefore moved slowly, trying to balance the needs of the army against the needs of the master. Access to slave labor became a three-sided struggle, with army field commanders and slaveholders vying for control and Confederate officials trying to mediate the differences. At times state officials also entered the fray, further complicating the dispute.

---

[3] Even the Confederate legislation of March 1863 that did provide direct authority to impress slaves applied only in those states that had not adopted their own impressment laws or procedures. (*Official Records*, ser. 4, vol. 2, pp. 469–72.)

General John B. Magruder, commander of the Confederate Army of the Peninsula in tidewater Virginia, was among the first to be caught between military necessity and slaveholders' prerogatives. At the start of the war, Magruder mobilized free blacks and slaves to construct fortifications on the peninsula between the York and James rivers. His efforts assumed greater urgency when, in late May 1861, General Benjamin F. Butler took command at Fortress Monroe, the Union outpost at the tip of the peninsula. When rumors circulated that they would soon be assigned to Confederate labor gangs, slaves absconded to Fortress Monroe, where General Butler welcomed them, declared them contraband of war, and put them to work in the Union cause.[4] The slaves' flight and Butler's ready reception increased Magruder's need for laborers and heightened the conflict between the army and the slaveholders. The more slaves Magruder lost, the more he needed. Indeed, he not only had to replace those who had fled, but also to create a still larger force to confront the growing federal menace. Magruder called again and again for local farmers to forward their slaves. Receiving neither free blacks nor slaves in requisite numbers, Magruder ordered impressment on an unprecedented scale, calling for all the free black men and as many as half the slave men in the tidewater counties under his command, and even in some piedmont counties outside his jurisdiction.

Magruder's actions troubled slaveholders almost as much as Butler's presence. Impressment especially worried those masters out of the range of Butler's guns but within easy reach of Magruder's agents. In areas yet untouched by the war, rumors of the approach of Confederate press gangs sent slaves fleeing to the woods, often with the blessing of their masters. Some slaves did not stop there, but steered a course for Union lines. Slaveholders throughout the Virginia tidewater peppered Confederate officials in Richmond with petitions, challenging Magruder's legal authority, questioning the propriety of his actions, bemoaning the abuse of their slaves, and predicting grave consequences from their slaves' absence during periods of peak agricultural demand. Official sanction of Magruder's impressment hardly satisfied their queries.

When Union General George B. McClellan transferred his formidable Army of the Potomac from northern Virginia to the York and James rivers in the spring of 1862 and began advancing up the peninsula, Magruder issued new calls for laborers. Many slaveholders simply refused to comply, and others removed their slaves, or at least the able-bodied men, to the interior. A few openly resisted Magruder's

---

[4] Benjamin F. Butler, *Private and Official Correspondence of Gen. Benjamin F. Butler during the Period of the Civil War*, 5 vols. (Norwood, Mass., 1917), vol. 1, pp. 185–88. See also above, doc. 1A.

impressment agents, making it appear at times that Confederate soldiers spent more time chasing impressed slaves than confronting the enemy. Magruder appealed anew to Southern patriotism and, bowing to the opposition, devised new procedures to assure slaveholders that they would be promptly paid and their property well treated. He also tried to distribute the burden of impressment more equitably among the counties under his command. In the end, Magruder succeeded only in spreading the opposition beyond his immediate jurisdiction and provoking still more masters to transport their slaves beyond his reach.

The problem confronting Magruder in the first year of the war soon plagued other Confederate commanders as they scrambled to meet the enemy. The more white soldiers the Confederates put under arms, the more black laborers they needed as well. Skilled workers were particularly in demand, for not only did fortifications have to be built, trenches dug, and supplies delivered, but horses had to be shod, wagons repaired, saddles mended, and caissons constructed. Confederate armories, foundries, tanneries, mines, and railyards relied upon slave (as well as free black) artisans. As in tidewater Virginia, so throughout the South, Confederate officers called for slaves; and when their calls produced meager results, they impressed every able-bodied man within reach. Commanders in various theaters were taught in their turn the lesson Magruder had learned early in the war: Slave owners could not be relied upon to volunteer their slaves.

Impressment drew anguished howls from masters, who lamented the loss of numerous slaves through death or desertion and the demoralization of many others. The complaints of other aggrieved citizens joined those of the slaveholders, for the war increased the demand for laborers even faster among civilians than within the military. Those who depended upon the labor of slaves and free blacks resented the army's claims, particularly when so many black men accompanied the troops as personal servants. Losses to the South's agricultural and industrial work force consisted, moreover, not only of black military laborers and fugitives, but also of white volunteers and conscripts. Southern manufacturers confronted the shortage first, because they had long depended on a mixture of slave and free artisans, factory hands, teamsters, and laborers. But before long planters and farmers also felt the pinch, as overseers, rural artisans, and farm hands disappeared into the army.

The struggle over control of slave labor escalated with the war. But as the fighting extended into a second year, Confederate officials grew impatient with recalcitrant slaveholders and their endless complaints about military impressment. Occasionally, they set aside their deference to the masters' power and awarded Confederate army commanders full authority to impress slave laborers. In October 1862, comparing an army officer's right to impress slaves in order to save the state with a

668

captain's right to destroy the cargo in order to save his ship, the assistant secretary of war empowered one hard-pressed field commander to take whatever slaves he needed.[5] As the war continued, similar decisions slowly but steadily shifted authority over slaves from the master to the Confederate state.

Although wartime necessity hardened officials in Richmond against the complaints of masters, state authorities were more sympathetic. The solicitude of state officials derived in part from their proximity to the slaveholding electorate and in part from an abiding fear that massive impressment of slaves would disrupt agricultural production; as the governor of Florida observed, it was as important to till as it was to fight. Invoking another axiom of Southern politics – that slavery was a state, not a national institution – state officials tried to retain control of impressment. In some states, antebellum regulations requiring the public to participate in road maintenance provided a basis for impressing slaves. In most states, however, no legislative precedent existed and none was enacted during the early years of the war. Moving into the vacuum, some governors acted by executive fiat. Elsewhere, state legislatures debated the issue, establishing quasi-independent agencies to impress, transport, and supervise slaves for military labor. Not every state had acted by the end of the war; but where they had, state officials sought to limit slave impressment.

Whatever the system adopted, impressment depended in large measure on the course of the war and on relations between authorities in the various state capitals and those in Richmond. As long as Union troops remained a distant threat, state officials generally held the reins of power tight; once the federals attacked, the politicians usually yielded to the generals. But not always: Officials in some states refused to cooperate with the army even in the face of enemy invasion. While locked in battle, Confederate commanders still had to beg for authorization to impress slaves, and, despite continuing perils, field officers sometimes watched helplessly as state officials discharged labor gangs that had been painstakingly assembled. Several governors recalled military laborers at planting and harvest time. State sovereignty thus compromised efforts to muster an adequate labor force.

As Union commanders put more and more fugitive slaves into federal service, making the war, in part, a contest over which side could best mobilize black manpower, Confederate leaders attempted to assert greater control over impressment. In March 1863, the Confederate Congress authorized the army to impress slaves in accordance with state laws where appropriate legislation had been adopted, and in accordance with regulations to be promulgated by the Confederate Secretary of

[5] A.S.W. J. A. Campbell to Brig. Genl. W. N. R. Beall, 23 Oct. 1862, ch. IX, vol. 8, pp. 151–52, Letters Sent, Sec. War, RG 109 [F-987].

War where it had not.[6] But Secretary of War James A. Seddon moved slowly in using his new power. While he delayed, Confederate manpower problems multiplied, and the fortunes of battle turned against the South. In July 1863, following defeats at Gettysburg and Vicksburg, the assistant secretary of war admitted that "the sacrosanctity of slave property . . . has operated most injuriously to the Confederacy." President Jefferson Davis heartily endorsed a suggestion that the Confederacy augment its armies with regularly organized units of black laborers, in order to "release a large force of white men to do the fighting." Pressed from above and below, Seddon finally acted. War Department regulations issued in October specified which slave men could be impressed, in what proportion, for what length of time, and under what circumstances – exempting until December, for instance, slaves engaged in food production, and guaranteeing payment to the masters of those impressed.[7] Notwithstanding assorted genuflections to slaveholders' rights and state sovereignty, the regulations expressly empowered Confederate military commanders to decide when impressment had become necessary – which, to many, meant whenever they needed laborers. In the months to come, the Confederate government extended its impressment powers and regularized the process.[8] But because the legislation authorized Confederate authorities to act only in states that lacked impressment laws of their own, army commanders often remained answerable to local officials. State authorities continued to wield considerable power, and military officers continued to see impressed slaves returned to their owners regardless of military emergencies.[9]

The conflict engendered in this division of authority rent Southern society and weakened the Confederacy. It made everyone suspect. State and national officials fought one another, while military authorities and masters battled both, even as they too fought each other. All cast aspersions on the others' honesty, competence, and patriotism. No attempt to resolve these conflicts fully satisfied anyone. On the one hand, the army never had enough laborers, and commanders felt that owners withheld their slaves for selfish reasons. They complained that slaveholders acted only when subject to force, that they forwarded their least able slaves, and that often they sent these both late and ill-equipped for the task at hand. Planters and manufacturers, on the other hand, maintained that military commanders requisitioned slaves with-

---

[6] The Confederate law required, however, that no impressment be made if slaves could be "hired or procured by the consent of the owner." (*Official Records*, ser. 4, vol. 2, pp. 469–72.)

[7] *Official Records*, ser. 4, vol. 2, pp. 897–98.

[8] *Official Records*, ser. 4, vol. 3, pp. 112, 207–9, 897–99, 1082–83.

[9] For a survey of state regulations concerning slave impressment, see Nelson, "Confederate Slave Impressment Legislation," pp. 394–98, 408–10.

out regard to the problems of wartime agriculture and industry, taking those most needed on plantations and in factories. Slaveholding farmers and artisans shared the planters' alarm about the army's appetite for slave laborers, but also grumbled about having to contribute as large a proportion of their slaves as the great planters. Meanwhile, the largest planters insisted that Confederate agents squeezed them harder than they did neighboring farmers. All slaveholders, great and small, worried that impressment might erode their dominion over their human property.

Even when masters willingly answered Confederate labor requisitions, for reasons of patriotism or profit, the needs of the Confederate army created new conflicts and aggravated old ones. In areas where slave hiring had been customary before the war, some slaveholders gladly rented their slaves to army quartermasters, seeing the Confederacy as simply another employer who could pay the fee and then some. They may have benefited from the higher rates that the Confederacy frequently paid, as well as from the government's guarantees for the safe return of their property. But the enormous demand generated by military employers played havoc with the market for slave hirelings. Army quartermasters pushed prices beyond the means of many farmers and manufacturers. And when civilian employers could afford the higher rates, other problems complicated the once routine process of slave hire. Those who relied on seasonal labor found themselves especially hard-pressed, since the army's need for laborers generally bore little relation to the accustomed rhythm of labor demands. The intervention of Confederate authorities to ensure some private employers – particularly railroads – a ready supply of labor brought bitter complaints from those not so favored.

These conflicts resonated in both courthouse and statehouse. When slaveless and small slaveholding farmers discovered that conscripting white men as soldiers and impressing black men as laborers reduced their work force far more sharply than that of the great planters, they and their representatives petitioned for relief, demanding that the Confederate government exempt either their sons or their slaves. The planters objected, and the battle was on. It raged through state legislatures and found its way to the floor of the Confederate Congress. Those who accepted in principle the necessity of impressment and the utility of a particular plan, still bemoaned the inequities. Complaints about the fairness of slave impressment joined with complaints about injustice in conscription and taxation, compounding and magnifying them and being compounded and magnified by them. "We must have equality in this confederacy or it will blow up," warned one Georgia slaveholder.

The complex struggle among authorities in Richmond, elected officials in various statehouses, military commanders in the field, and slaveholders throughout the Confederacy placed a heavy burden upon slaves and free blacks. In some places, impressment policies sent black men to work far from their homes and kept them in service for the duration of the war. Such assignments separated families and disrupted the slave community much as had slave trading and slave hiring before the war. Impressment also weighed heavily on slaves who remained at home, especially the women who inherited the duties of men requisitioned for Confederate labor. Attempts to equalize the burden of impressment among owners by shuttling slaves between plantation and fortification hardly lightened the burden on the slaves. The separation from family and friends might be shorter, but the movement back and forth through the countryside could be dangerous, because straggling soldiers, rebel guerrillas, and local bullies frequently assaulted slaves unaccompanied by their owners or overseers.

Amidst the suffering and dangers, opportunities occasionally appeared. Although slaves lamented the disruption of family life that usually accompanied being hired out, many thereby gained their first experience of travel from the home plantation. They generally welcomed a chance to escape the owner's proprietary eye, as well as the prospect of learning new skills and practicing new trades. Slave hirelings often enjoyed considerable control over their own lives; some won the right to sell their own time, to collect "overwork" payments, and to live on their own. On occasion, impressed slaves also benefited from the prerogatives granted to hirelings. Mindful of both the difficulty of acquiring skilled laborers and the ease of escape, some military employers relaxed the constraints of bondage in small but significant ways.

Most impressed slaves received none of these advantages. Instead, they faced numerous new dangers to life and limb. The officers in charge of Confederate fortifications, armories, and hospitals, who showed scant consideration for their charges at the beginning of the war, showed less as the war dragged on. Quartermasters and commissary officers, having no direct interest in slave property and laboring under urgent wartime demands, had no hesitancy about resorting to the stocks and whipping post to increase productivity. They freely assigned impressed slaves to work deemed too dangerous for anyone else, placing them in smallpox hospitals, malarial swamps, and salt mines. In spite of promises to the contrary, the food, clothing, shelter, and medical care supplied to impressed slaves commonly fell below the standard provided by their masters. Ranking low on the Confederate list of priorities, slaves lived in moth-eaten tents and rudely constructed shacks near fortifications, in overcrowded dormitories at ordnance works, and in back rooms and closets at hospitals. They rarely received more than the basic ration, no matter how hard they worked. With good reason, masters charged that their slaves returned from Confederate service much the worse for wear.

As the number of impressed slaves grew, their condition deteriorated. At the outset, Confederate commanders expected slaveholders to supply slave laborers with shoes, clothing, blankets, and even food.[10] Some did, but others balked at losing their slaves and having to support them too. This conflict between the masters and the army left many slaves ragged, footsore, and hungry at day's end. As the war progressed and impressment increased, masters and military commanders clarified their particular responsibilities in law, if not always in practice. But by then shortages of all sorts prevented either army officers or slaveholders from fulfilling their obligations. With Confederate soldiers marching in rags and Confederate civilians living close to subsistence, slaves could hardly expect better treatment. In the closing months of the war, Southern commanders had to beg for rations to keep slave laborers strong enough to work.

Military labor exerted a subversive influence upon slavery, an influence that touched more and more slaves as the conflict proceeded. Knowledge of the Confederacy's declining fortunes and of the Union's increasing commitment to freedom became common coin among those forced to labor in the Southern cause, as they listened in on the conversations of their overseers, read scraps of newspapers, and watched the long faces of battle-scarred Confederate veterans. When military laborers returned to their homes, they broadcast that knowledge. News of the war gained through labor on behalf of the Confederacy and amplified by countless other sources reverberated on plantations and farms far from the front. Even slaves who accompanied their masters into the army as personal servants carried home word of the Union's promise of freedom, inspiring fellow slaves to flee to the Yankees.[11]

The upsurge in the number of fugitives prompted slaveholders to take precautions to secure their property. They locked slaves up at night, redoubled patrols, and punished recaptured runaways with special ferocity. When these actions failed to stem the "stampede" to the enemy, some masters urged even more severe measures. Characterizing runaway slaves – particularly those carrying valuable information and skills to the enemy – as traitors, several planters in lowcountry Georgia proposed that the Confederate government punish recaptured fugitives in a manner befitting those who give aid and comfort to the enemy in time of war.

Although the Confederate commander at Savannah did not share their enthusiasm for capital punishment, other officers did. Colonel Thomas M. Jones, commander of the Confederate Army of Pensacola,

---

[10] The timing of impressment often placed slaves in jeopardy. Slaves impressed for terms that spanned seasonal change inevitably seemed to be incorrectly clothed when the weather turned.

[11] See, for example, above, doc. 37.

court-martialed as traitors several slaves captured while attempting to reach federal lines. His superior, General Samuel Jones, commander of the Department of Alabama and West Florida, approved his course and believed, along with the masters in lowcountry Georgia, that only the summary punishment of a few would halt an exodus of many. Colonel Jones's action found little support in the Confederate high command, where the court-martial of those deemed property seemed a ludicrous waste of time. It also raised objections from slaveholders, who, even in a most desperate moment, refused to surrender power over their slaves to outsiders. Many doubted that such military punishment would help to secure their property.

Although proportionately few slaves immediately broke for Union lines and many continued to labor as before, slaveholders – particularly those near the federal line of advance – sensed a new mood of defiance even among ordinarily meek slaves. Plantation hands worked at a more leisurely pace and spent more time tending their own garden plots than laboring in their owners' fields. The departure to the army of young white men, formerly the mainstay of plantation discipline, licensed unruliness among the slaves. Many Southerners blamed the collapse of discipline for a noticeable falling off in agricultural production. The white women and elderly white men who remained on the plantations flooded Confederate and state officials with pleas for the discharge of husbands, sons, overseers, and managers.

Before long, the Confederate Congress acted on these pleas. In October 1862, it exempted from conscription one white man on each plantation with twenty or more slaves, to ensure proper supervision on the largest estates.[12] As military campaigns resumed the following spring, the baleful effect of the new legislation became manifest. The "twenty-nigger law" did little to stem unrest on the plantations, but it intensified disaffection among small slaveholders and nonslaveholders, who objected to the class bias of the enactment. In May 1863, the Confederate Congress repealed the offensive provision, replacing it with a far more restrictive exemption for overseers.[13] But the damage was already done. The alienation of nonslaveholders from the Southern cause increased sharply during the last years of the war.

Disaffected whites, some of whom had been unionist in sentiment from the outset, made their own contribution toward the demoralization of slave laborers. In some places, labor shortages forced the Con-

---

[12] *Official Records*, ser. 4, vol. 2, pp. 160–62.

[13] The new legislation exempted one overseer for each plantation with twenty or more slaves, but only when it was owned by a minor, a widow, or a man serving in the Confederate army. The law required, moreover, that the overseer himself not be liable for military service. (*Official Records*, ser. 4, vol. 2, pp. 553–54.) For a full discussion, see Albert B. Moore, *Conscription and Conflict in the Confederacy* (New York, 1924).

federate army to use disaffected whites – upcountry yeomen, foreign immigrants, and transplanted Northerners – as military laborers, and when they worked alongside slaves, insubordination increased markedly. During the summer of 1864, Confederate authorities assigned interned members of the "Heroes of America," a unionist organization in western North Carolina, to labor in the Wilmington salt works; not long thereafter, the slave salt workers fled to Union lines.[14] Avowed unionists were not the only problem. Many Confederate soldiers, tiring of the rich man's war, felt no compunction about selling passes to slave military laborers, allowing them to leave government employment, return home, make for Union lines, or simply remain at large. Occasionally, Confederate soldiers put fugitive slaves to work in their own service. The prospect of having servants to cook and clean for them, much as personal attendants did for their officers, was attractive to the lower ranks of the Confederate army. Like Billy Yank, Johnny Reb sometimes developed a strong attachment and even affection for the slaves who took refuge in army encampments. If Southern soldiers evinced no desire to free "their" slaves (indeed, some sold them when given the chance), they showed little interest in returning them to the sure punishment of vengeful owners.

As the master's declining power encouraged thousands of slaves to flee to Union lines, so did the federal government's deepening commitment to freedom. The Second Confiscation Act in the summer of 1862, the Emancipation Proclamation of January 1, 1863, and the systematic recruitment of black men into the Union army that began the following spring signaled a decisive shift in federal policy; and Union advances on the battlefield put freedom within reach of ever greater numbers of slaves. The enlistment of black soldiers, while swelling the federal ranks, imposed new and frightening limitations on the ability of slaveholders to control their slaves. "Every sound male black left for the enemy becomes a soldier whom we have afterwards to fight," observed General E. Kirby Smith, commander of the Confederate Trans-Mississippi Department. To prevent the transformation of plantations into federal recruiting stations, Confederate commanders ordered able-bodied black men removed deep into the interior of the South or to Texas. But attempts to tear black men from their families, rather than ending unrest, further stimulated flight.

Slave owners searching for a safe harbor, distant from the dangers of escape and impressment, moved frenetically about the South. The removal of slaves that began as a trickle in the first year of the war

---

[14] Maj. Genl. W. H. C. Whiting to Hon. James A. Seddon, 7 June 1864, Maj. Genl. W. H. C. Whiting to Hon. James A. Seddon, 28 July 1864, and Maj. Genl. W. H. C. Whiting to His Excellency Govr. Vance, 28 July 1864, ch. II, vol. 336, pp. 327–28, 374–75, Letters Sent, Gen. W. H. C. Whiting's Command, Dept. of NC & Southern VA, Records of Military Commands, RG 109 [F-662, F-668].

turned into a flood in the second half of 1863. Many slaveholders along the eastern seaboard from Virginia to Florida had already refugeed their slaves inland, and those along the northern borders of the Confederacy headed south. After Union forces gained control of the Mississippi River, masters refugeed their slaves from the valley – those on the east bank generally moving to Alabama and Georgia, those on the west going to Texas. The movement uprooted thousands, indeed hundreds of thousands, of slaves. According to one estimate, some 150,000 slaves were forcibly moved from the Mississippi Valley to Texas in the year following the federal capture of Vicksburg.[15] Wartime refugeeing altered the geography of black life and, contrary to its design, added momentum to slavery's decline.

Rather than secure slave property, relocation frequently became the occasion for its loss. Slaves resisted removal by their masters just as they resisted removal by military authorities. They resented being taken from familiar neighborhoods. They worried that they would be stripped of their possessions and that their new circumstances would be inferior to the old. They recognized the reduced chances of escaping to freedom from the interior. But, most of all, they feared the destruction of their family life. Young men and women, who were usually the first selected for removal, proved particularly resistant to their masters' plans. Many fled at the mere rumor of possible transfer. Masters planning to refugee their slaves tried to keep the proposed migration as quiet as possible, but there could be few secrets in households dependent upon slave labor. In the end, to ensure the orderly movement of their slaves, some planters had to shackle them together in advance of migration and guard them at gunpoint as they marched. Even then, some refugeed slaves escaped and returned to the old plantation, struck out for Union lines, or simply hid in the woods. Those left behind sometimes took advantage of the master's absence and began to farm on their own, establishing independent communities that, despite vulnerability to rebel assault, served as rendezvous for runaways and sources of information for Union scouts.[16] Such plantations became so notorious that Confederate commanders required planters to remove all their slaves if they planned to remove any, an order masters generally construed as yet another unwarranted infringement of their authority.

Slaveholders hoped that transfer to the interior would insulate their slaves from the disruptive effects of the war. Instead, from the first, refugeeing disrupted the plantation order and transferred the disorder of the war zone to areas yet untouched by the conflict. Slaves familiar

---

[15] Asst. Engr. Theo. Herman to Captain E. A. Warren, 4 Dec. 1864, ch. II, vol. 201, p. 300, Letters Sent, Dist. of AR, Trans-MS Dept., Records of Military Commands, RG 109 [F-900].

[16] See, for example, above, docs. 12, 123.

with the shifting balance of power between Union and Confederate forces informed slaves distant from the war front about the course of the struggle, the presence of black men in blue uniforms, and the promise of freedom within federal lines. Following the arrival in the interior of refugeed slaves from the battle zone, the number of runaways surged upward, as did the incidence of other forms of resistance that slaveholders denominated collectively as "demoralization."

As refugeeing swelled the black population in the interior of the Confederacy, wholesale conscription into the Confederate army simultaneously removed white men. In some places, even in areas of the upland South that had never before known a substantial number of slaves, blacks came to compose a large proportion of the population, placing additional burdens on already scanty food resources. This demographic shift, along with the removal of white men from all areas of the South, created a new sense of power among blacks and a new sense of insecurity among whites, slaveholders and nonslaveholders alike. The slaveholding women, old men, disabled soldiers, and exempted overseers who managed the farms and plantations had difficulty controlling unruly slaves and making them work. Fears evinced since the beginning of the war—that "the slaves [will] become our masters"—multiplied rapidly as the racial balance shifted in various parts of the South.

Insurrection was only one concern of whites left on the plantations. Many planters had already switched from staple crops to food production; as the war went on, they seemed to be retreating from commercial to subsistence farming. Indeed, with slaves unwilling to work, some plantations became centers of consumption more than sources of production. The motley collection of whites left to run the great estates searched for some means to control their black laborers, who carefully tended their own gardens and paid little attention to their erstwhile superiors. Unable to wield the lash without risking wholesale flight or violent retaliation, frustrated plantation managers resorted to previously unthinkable measures to get their slaves to work. Some bartered future freedom; others promised a part of the crop; still others offered wages of unspecified amount. Sensing their owners' loss of mastery, slaves rarely accepted the first offer or, if they did, rarely remained satisfied with it. Before long, they were back with a new list of demands: shorter hours, no overseers, and an end to corporal punishment.[17] While some owners were struggling to preserve the old routine, others—unable to endure the impudence of their slaves—abandoned their estates. Petitions decrying plantation disorder and urging the return of white men able to discipline slaves or muster a pack of

[17] On the wartime evolution of free and quasi-free labor arrangements, see *Freedom*, ser. 1, vol. 2.

"negro dogs" poured in to Confederate officials in Richmond and state governors throughout the South.

Without the force to sustain the old order, the slave regime disintegrated at an ever accelerating rate. The fabric of allegiance that had been frayed by impressment and refugeeing and weakened by military failure and economic chaos unraveled entirely when slaveholders could no longer provide subsistence for their slaves. Moreover, hungry men and women made desperate slaves. Some broke into plantation storehouses or expropriated food from the cupboards of the big house to feed their families. Others roamed the countryside foraging wherever they could. Nothing so frightened those whites left to fend for themselves as the specter of roving gangs of slaves. The "demoralization" of slaves in turn demoralized Southern whites, thus compromising the Confederate war effort.

The dual fear of slave uprising and of starvation spread from those at home growing the crops to those away fighting the Yankees. Bread riots – designated "[w]omen riots" in one Alabama county – sent shock waves through Southern society. Learning of the frightful conditions at home, nonslaveholding Confederate soldiers complained bitterly that, while slaves continued to produce food for the families of slaveholders, no one was left to feed the families of nonslaveholders. They petitioned for leave to return home and assist their families. When short-handed commanders rejected their pleas, they deserted in droves.

Amid the general disintegration of Southern society, slaveholders still resisted inroads upon their sovereignty over their slaves. But the more they resisted, the harder Confederate authorities pressed. Military commanders, brandishing new legal authority, impressed slaves with even greater rigor. In December 1863, General John B. Magruder, by then commanding the District of Texas, Arizona, and New Mexico, attempted to take nearly every able-bodied slave man in Texas for military labor. Fearing for the safety of slaves sent to the war front and desperately needing labor on the home front, Texas slaveholders protested and demanded that Confederate and state authorities protect them from Magruder's emissaries. Magruder's superiors saw the logic of the slaveholders' appeal. With little prompting, they modified Magruder's dragnet impressment in Texas, much as they had circumscribed his earlier orders in the Virginia tidewater.

Although masters tried to protect their slaves from impressment, free blacks had few powerful friends. Slaveholders who objected vociferously to military claims upon their slaves demanded just as vociferously that black freemen be inducted into Confederate service. Impressing free black men, they insisted, would at once transform a socially valueless caste into useful laborers and prevent an incorrigibly subversive element from infecting slaves with the virus of liberty. Besides, should impressed free blacks flee to the enemy, their defection would entail no loss of property. Nonslaveholding whites, including white workingmen who had long complained of competition from black freemen, added their voices to this call. And state officials, who balked at slave impressment, readily assented to a draft of free blacks. Beginning with Magruder's first large-scale impressment in the summer of 1861, free black men were forcibly placed in Confederate service, generally for longer terms than impressed slaves. Indeed, because free blacks enjoyed a higher level of skill than slaves, Confederate impressment officers frequently singled them out, especially as white artisans lost their exemption from conscription into the army. Beginning in the first months of the war, state legislatures and governors provided for the systematic enrollment and impressment of free black men, and both state and national impressment regulations stipulated that military commanders take free blacks before laying claim to slaves. Finally, in February 1864, the Confederate Congress cast aside all pretense of equalizing the burden, declaring free black men between eighteen and fifty universally liable to impressment.[18]

The war and the deterioration of slavery subjected free blacks to intense scrutiny. To maintain their position, some publicly pledged their allegiance to the Confederacy and offered to take up arms in the Southern cause.[19] But no assurances seemed to satisfy Southern whites. Instead, their deep-rooted belief that *"Free Negroes* will cause an insurrection among the Slaves" only grew stronger as slavery tottered. Free blacks tried to gain a measure of protection by strengthening their ties with powerful white patrons. But, lacking the protection of masters, they frequently found themselves treated "worse than slaves" by local authorities, who seized their property, and by impressment officers, who seized their persons. Some free blacks spent the war eluding Confederate agents; others simply abandoned their homes and fled to the protection of the Union army.

Nevertheless, free blacks at times found unexpected supporters among those formerly hostile to their very existence. With labor in great demand, some free blacks found new markets for their services and a host of white defenders. Urban manufacturers and merchants, who depended on free black artisans, draymen, and laborers, complained that impressment disrupted their trade and petitioned the Confederate government for exemptions. Before long, nonslaveholding farmers, particularly in those border regions with large free black populations, joined the appeal. Moreover, as slaves fled to Union lines,

---

[18] *Official Records*, ser. 4, vol. 3, pp. 207–9. For wartime state legislation regarding free blacks, see Nelson, "Legislative Control of the Southern Free Negro." For an example of state regulations, see Circular, Medical Director's Office, 24 Aug. 1863, ch. IV, vol. 302, Letters Sent & Letters, Orders & Circulars Received, Chimborazo Hospital No. 4, Records of Chimborazo Hospital, Medical Dept., RG 109 [F-30].
[19] See, for example, *Freedom*, ser. 2: docs. 11, 127.

slaveholders also came to rely upon the labor of free blacks, "the only means in our reach of getting our wood cut, rails mawled, or any other labor whatever performed." Planters who had earlier urged the impressment of free blacks now begged Confederate authorities to exempt them.

The intensifying struggle for control of black labor enhanced the bargaining position of those slaves who remained at home. Rather than pawns in the multisided struggle among masters, the army, and the state (both national and state governments), black men and women became increasingly active participants in the conflict, alternately joining with one side and then the other in pursuit of their own interest. These alliances took a variety of forms. Slaves unwilling to leave home to labor on Confederate fortifications and masters unwilling to have them leave conspired to subvert labor drafts. Masters sent slaves into hiding at the approach of impressment agents. They armed impressed slaves with passes that could be used to return home at the first opportunity. Impressment officers denounced this unseemly union of masters and slaves to subvert Confederate authority, but could do little to end it. Indeed, to keep slaves at work in Confederate service, quartermasters were not above offering additional rations, furloughs, and even small payments. Slaveholders denounced this unseemly union of Confederate officers and slaves to subvert the master's authority, but could do little to end it, either.

Everywhere slaves took advantage of the possibilities created by the war to unbind their shackles. Although extralegal arrangements with Confederate masters, hirers, or impressment officers fell far short of the freedom and regular wages promised to black laborers and soldiers with the Northern army, such arrangements appealed to slaves who were far from Union military lines, eager to remain near their families, wary of abusive Yankee quartermasters and recruiters, or fearful of death on a distant battlefield. Moreover, a furlough from a Confederate quartermaster, like a pass from a master, could sometimes be used to travel freely through the countryside and, despite the dangers, enjoy a measure of liberty far beyond anything previously known.

The increased independence of many slaves angered Southern whites, in the army and out. Tempers flared as masters and military commanders exchanged charges and countercharges. Because the respective positions oscillated so wildly, Confederate authorities found it increasingly difficult to referee the disputes. The competing interests seemed to move in all directions at once as they restated old positions, exchanged them, and finally formulated new ones in a hopeless effort to sustain a failing cause. As the Union army closed in on the last Confederate strongholds, Southern military commanders who had previously opposed the slaveholders' practice of refugeeing slaves from contested territory now wanted to hustle slaves off before federal recruiters mustered them into the Union army. In some areas, however, Confederate commanders still opposed removal. General E. Kirby Smith, commander of Confederate forces west of the Mississippi River, feared that the departure of slaveholders and their slaves from the Red River Valley of Arkansas would forfeit one of the Confederacy's last productive agricultural districts. He blocked their exodus to Texas, first by appeals to Confederate patriotism and then by force.

Slaveholders also reversed their positions. In the trans-Mississippi west, planters who had previously ignored military pleas to transfer their slaves from contested ground now smuggled them to distant points, hoping to avoid both impressment by the Confederacy and capture by the Union. In the east, however, where planters had initiated the earlier evacuations and the army was now urging the removal of slaves, many slaveholders came to oppose refugeeing. Experience had taught them that slaves would flee for freedom at the mere threat of relocation. Rather than risk moving to safe ground – which was becoming scarce in any case – they petitioned for exemption from removal orders, citing the growing fear of agricultural disaster if military authorities continued to tamper with their slaves.

Persuaded by the combined effect of Union victories and the steady disintegration of slavery, many masters displayed a new willingness to donate their slaves to the defense of the Confederacy. Black-belt planters who had previously maintained that upcountry soldiers would gladly do the work of impressed slaves for a small increment in pay now searched for ways in which slaves could augment the Confederate force. Some slaveholders argued for the creation of a black labor corps to be assigned to each Confederate regiment. A few urged the enlistment of black soldiers into Southern ranks.[20]

This readiness to enlist slaves in Confederate service did not, however, originate solely from a revival of patriotism. Slaveholders seemed to view military service – with shovel or musket – as a form of protective custody; the Confederacy had become the overseer of last resort. Confederate officials hastened to take advantage of shifting opinion by enlarging their authority still further at the masters' expense. In November 1864, Confederate President Jefferson Davis spoke openly about the slave as "person" rather than as "property." Preparing the way for an exchange of freedom for military service, he suggested that the Confederate Congress consider emancipating slaves as a means of assuring their allegiance to the Southern nation.[21]

During the last months of the war, some Confederate commanders shared the slaveholders' concern that massive starvation would follow any further disruption of Southern agriculture. They also realized that

---

[20] *Freedom*, ser. 2: docs. 116–22.
[21] *Official Records*, ser. 4, vol. 3, pp. 797–99.

the depredations of their own troops did as much to alienate the planters and farmers as did the ravages of the Yankees. Moved by these considerations to yet another reversal of policy, a few commanders acceded to the planters' wishes and began replacing slave military laborers with soldiers during planting and harvesting seasons. But most field officers kept battlefront considerations paramount, reasoning that every slave man not kept under close watch might soon be wearing Union blue. They impressed slave laborers with increasing vigor, and some, echoing the pleas of the nearly hopeless planters, advocated the enlistment of black men as soldiers.[22]

As the Confederacy made its last stand, slavery had become a shambles over large portions of the South. Although Confederate leaders strove to balance the rights of the bickering competitors for slave labor, the infighting continued between state and national officials, national officials and army officers, army officers and slaveholders, and slaveholders and nonslaveholders; if anything, it grew more intense. Slaves seized the moment and pressed for concessions that increasingly smacked of freedom. Those who tried to maintain the old order soon found their slaves on the federal side of the battle line, sometimes wielding a musket. In a final desperate gamble to forestall defeat, the Confederate Congress, at the urging of President Davis and General Robert E. Lee, authorized the enlistment of black soldiers in the Confederate army. Davis's order implementing enlistment promised freedom to slave volunteers.[23] Before any blacks could act upon this invitation, the war ended and with it the Confederacy.

The collapse of slavery in the Confederate interior proceeded neither uniformly nor completely. Some masters successfully moved their slaves beyond the possibility of escape, deprived them of any knowledge of the war, and, through guile and force, kept the old system intact. At the end of the war, the last remnants of the Confederate heartland – crowded with refugeed slaves – contained a considerable portion of the South's antebellum slave population. The liquidation of bondage in these areas would await the postwar arrival of the Union army of occupation and the agents of the newly established Freedmen's Bureau.[24] But even before the fighting ceased, wartime events had abolished slavery in all but name in much of the Confederacy.

[22] *Freedom*, ser. 2: docs. 123–26.
[23] *Official Records*, ser. 4, vol. 3, pp. 1161–62; *Freedom*, ser. 2: pp. 279–82.
[24] On the eradication of the last vestiges of slavery in the former Confederacy, see *Freedom*, ser. 3.

SUPPORTING THE ARMY IN THE FIELD

257: Alabama Mechanics to the Confederate Secretary of War

Montgomery [*Ala.*] Apl. 26th 1861.

Sir:— The undersigned Contractors & master mechanics, believing that the present crisis demands that all the effective force needed by our Government in maintaining our Independence should with alacrity be furnished by its citizens, would hereby most respectfully inform you that they have twenty able bodied negro fellows, well disposed and easily governed, many of whom are good mechanics, and six wagons and twelve horses, and mules, the use and services of all which they hereby cheerfully tender to the Confederate States, to go anywhere and perform any duty which the Government may assign, suggesting merely that they be kept as near together as may consist with the public service. We have the honor to be with much regard your Ob^t Ser^{ts}

ALS

John P. Figh &
G. M. Figh

John P. Figh & G. M. Figh to Hon. L. P. Walker, 26 Apr. 1861, #477 1861, Letters Received, ser. 5, Sec. War, RG 109 [F-31]. The Secretary of War promptly accepted the Fighs' offer, and they thanked him for the opportunity to "render service to our beloved confederacy." (J. P. Figh and Geo. M. Figh to Honbl. L. P. Walker, 1 May 1861, #553 1861, Letters Received, ser. 5, Sec. War, RG 109 [F-31].)

258: Proclamation by the Commander of the Confederate Coast Defenses of North Carolina

Steamer Fairfield [*off the coast of* N.C.], June 9— 1861.

General Gwynn appeals to the county of currituck to assist in the coast defences.

The citizens of currituck should be up and doing in the cruel war that is upon the south. We are called on to defend our firesides and families against a stealthily encroaching and unscrupulous foe. Their obvious aim is to take all they can and to hold all they take. Then let all patriots do what they can to resist and repel such a foe. The commanding General wants men and implements for constructing fortifications. If men and implements for labor be furnished, the coast of N° Carolina can be and shall be promptly prepared for a successful resistance.

This appeal is to the citizens of currituck county to send laborers, slaves or free-negroes, to be put in charge of *Maj D. S. Walton at Roanoke Island.* Send them on at once. Delay is dangerous. It will be made known when he has enough. Let the laborers be furnished with as many tools as can be spared from the farms of their owners. They shall be taken care of and returned when the work is done.

To prevent any mistake or want of knowledge where the laborers are required, the commanding General repeats the direction that it is designed that they will report to Maj D. S. Walton at Roanoke Island. The tools required are axes, spades, shovels, Picks, Grubbing Hoes and the like. The hands should bring blankets and cooking utensils with them. A strict account of the time will be kept, for which the State of N° Carolina will pay a fair price.

HDcSr   Walter Gwynn

Proclamation by Brigr. Genl. Walter Gwynn, 9 June 1861, ch. II, vol. 259 1/2, pp. 8–9, Letters Sent, Coast Defenses of NC, Dept. of NC, Records of Military Commands, RG 109 [F-655]. Later that month, Gwynn extended his call for laborers to other coastal counties, offering to pay free black men $11 a month. (Circular, Headquarters, 20 June 1861, ch. II, vol. 259 1/2, p. 12, Letters Sent, Coast Defenses of NC, Dept. of NC, Records of Military Commands, RG 109 [F-657].)

259: Commander of a Confederate Alabama Regiment to the Commander of the Confederate Post of Yorktown, Virginia; and the Latter's Reply

Yorktown [*Va.*] June 19, 1861

Sir   The order to report Twenty Men & a commission[d] Officer to Cap[t] Bloomfield is I suppose for the purpose of laboring in the unloading of Ships,   I conceive such a requisition a diversion from the legitimate duties of a Volunteer Soldier, and protest against it,   While we are ready to work on Military roads and defences, I think there are Negros & hirelings enough to do the menial labor of unloading transports.   Respectfully

HLcSr   Jno A Winston

Yorktown [*Va.*] June 19th 1861

In reply to your note, I would simply state that in all services, French, English, American &C working details are constantly made, It is often impossible to carry a corps of labourers with an army, My own Regiment has done two thirds of the unloading at this point without a murmur though a very large portion of the men had never labored a day in their lives, The Quarter Master here has found it impossible to procure Negros, I sent out armed parties Saturday Sunday & Tuesday to scour the Country and only five Negros could be got; They have been seized by the Enemy or run into the interior, Under such circumstances, the wants of the service ought not to be embarrassed by points of etiquette, *See Article* 890[1] Men of my Regiment have been detailed for unloading schooners as lacksmiths, nurses, teamsters, brick masons, well Diggers and so on., No objections has been raised by either officers or men

If C^l Winston declines sending the men he must take the consequences of disobedience of orders & the referance of the matter to the Gen^{'l} Commanding Very Respectfully

D H Hill

HLcSr

Col. Jno A. Winston to Col. Hill, 19 June 1861, and Col. D. H. Hill to Col. Winston, 19 June 1861, ch. II, vol. 27, pp. 21–22, Letters & Telegrams Sent, Army & Dept. of the Peninsula, Records of Military Commands, RG 109 [F-627]. Southern soldiers were also unwilling or unable to provide other services that warfare necessitated. In July 1861, General John B. Magruder, commander of the Confederate Army of the Peninsula, petitioned the Confederate Secretary of War for permission to hire black women "at very cheap rates" to work in military hospitals in the place of soldiers detailed from the ranks. "The troops here being Volunteers and unused to such duties as are required from Hospital attendants and nurses, cooks &c, the sick in the Hospitals suffer greatly if left to their care." (Brig. Genl. J. B. Magruder to Sir, 18 July 1861, #2686 1861, Letters Received, ser. 5, Sec. War, RG 109 [F-37].)

1 Article 39, paragraph 890, of the Confederate army regulations provided: "Although the necessities of the service may require soldiers to be ordered on working-parties as a duty, commanding officers are to bear in mind that fitness for military service by instruction and discipline is the object for which the army is kept on foot, and that they are not to employ the troops when not in the field, and especially the mounted troops, in labors that interfere with their military duties and exercises, except in cases of immediate necessity, which shall be forthwith reported for the orders of the War Department." (C.S.A., War Department, *Army Regulations Adopted for the Use of the Army of the Confederate States* [New Orleans, 1861], p. 111.)

685

260A: Headquarters of the Confederate Army of the Peninsula to the Confederate Commander at Gloucester Point, Virginia

W^{ms}burg [*Va.*] July 28th 1861.
Sir   Genl Magruder directs that you will make a call upon the citizens of Gloucester, Middlesex and Mathews counties for one half of their male force of slaves to finish the works around Gloucester Point— They will be allowed fifty cents a day and a ration for each negro man during the time he is at work. You will send out agents to collect & bring in these negroes and detail some one to take down the names of the slaves, of their ower & the date of their arrival, & to give a certificate of the number of days they have worked. The free negroes will be impressed if they refuse to come and a force will be sent to bring them in— The Genl directs that the work be made if possible impregnable which he thinks can be done by deepening the ditches & thickening the parapets & putting up traverses— 600 negroes could effect this in ten days or perhaps in five. nerely 800 hands have been procured here in a very short time— You will consult with Capt Page & Capt Meade in regard to the best method of strengthening the lines & batteries at Gloucester— You will enforce if it should be necessary the above call—though it is hoped it will not be— I enclose the call— I am sir Respy—

HLcSr   G. B. Cosby

A.A.A.G. G. B. Cosby to Col. Crump, 28 July 1861, ch. II, vol. 227, pp. 68–69, Letters & Telegrams Sent, Army & Dept. of the Peninsula, Records of Military Commands, RG 109 [F-630]. Magruder's call for laborers was not copied with this letter, and it has not been located elsewhere.

260B: Confederate Secretary of War to the Commander of the Confederate Army of the Peninsula

Richmond, August 28th 1861.
General: The subjoined extract from a letter written by the Hon. John Tyler of the Confederate Congress and Col. Hill Carter of the 52nd Reg^t of V^a Militia to this Department on the 26 August, and the reply of the Department thereto, is furnished for your information:

"Some six weeks ago Genl Magruder, commanding in the Peninsula, made a requisition on the slave holders of the County of Charles City and New Kent, for one half of their farm operatives to throw up entrenchments at W^{ms}burg. The requisition was promptly complied with. The much longer detention of the slaves, which has delayed the threshing of the wheat crop, has engendered some little feeling of discontent among some of our people, who begin to question the legal authority of the proceeding – nor has this disquietude been allayed by the fact, that many of the slaves have returned to their masters, which has been followed by a posse to recover the fugitives. To allay all discontent we ask to be informed, not for ourselves, so much as for others, of your opinion of the legality of this proceeding on the part of the General: your opinion being entirely sufficient to quiet all further uneasiness."

"We also submit, whether it would not be altogether proper, that the officer having charge of the laborers should give a certificate for the negroes of each proprietor so as to protect the master against possible contingencies of loss."

"We are, Sir, Truly & resp^{ly} yrs,
"John Tyler   M.C.C.
"Hill Carter   Col. of 52^d Reg^t V^a Militia"

"To Secretary of War."

(Reply)

"Confederate States of America
"War Department.
"Richmond, Aug 26th 1861."

"Sir":

"Your letter of this date, in relation to the impressment of slave-labor on the Peninsula, has just been received: and I proceed, at once to express the opinion of the Department on the subject."

"In times of war, the necessities of the public service often demand departures from the ordinary rules of administration, and the cases you suggest can be justified only by such necessities. Of this the Generals in command must, *ex necessitate rei*, be the sole judges, in the first instance, and should, therefore, exercise this power with caution and discretion. But, however urgent and obvious the necessity, the power should be exercised only in subordination to the ultimate rights of owners: And, therefore, certificates should, in all cases, be given to the owners, not only for the return of the negroes, but for reasonable hire."

"The Department will embody these suggestions in an official communication to the Commanding Generals in the Peninsula, where the impressments referred to seem to have been made."

"With high regard, &c. &c,
"L. P. Walker,
"Secretary of War."

"Hon. John Tyler,"
"Congress."

Your attention is asked to the foregoing correspondence. Very respectfully,

HLcSr

L. P. Walker

L. P. Walker to Brig. Genl. J. B. Magruder, 28 Aug. 1861, ch. IX, vol. 2, pp. 136–37, Letters Sent, Sec. War, RG 109 [F-601]. Tyler, who had been President of the United States, 1841–1845, was a member of the provisional Confederate congress in 1861.

260C: Commander of the Confederate Army of the Peninsula to the Confederate Adjutant and Inspector General

Williamsburg [Va.] Sept 20. 1861

Sir, Some wealthy men of Gloucester County, & a Mr Underwood, of Surry, have refused to send their slaves on requisition signed by myself, to work on the Fortifications – They are very incomplete, & my troops have worked until they are too sick to work any longer – I ordered detachments of Dragoons to bring them, – They have done & will do it – If these gentlemen are sustained in their refusal no negroes can be had when wanted – The laws of V^a do not specify negroes – but it is a necessity of war – If sustained, I will carry out my plans. I have already the sanction in writing of the Secy of War to this Course – but will use the free negroes as far as possible – I have never call'd for more than one half of the male working hands – I enclose one of my proclamations on this subject – I am sir very Respctfully Y^r obt Ser

ALS

J Bankhead Magruder –

Brig. Genl. J. Bankhead Magruder to Genl. S. Cooper, 20 Sept. 1861, M-549 1861, Letters Received, ser. 12, Adjt. & Insp. Gen., RG 109 [F-634]. Endorsement. Enclosed is a printed circular dated September 7, 1861, in which Magruder called upon slaveholders to send half their slave men to work on the fortifications, along with "the necessary implements of labor, Spades, Shovels, Picks, Grubbing-hoes and Axes." He offered to pay slaveholders fifty cents a day for each slave and to provide the laborers with "plenty of provisions." The circular also announced that "[a]ll free negroes who are capable of labor" would be employed at the same rate. Magruder warned the slaveholders that he had received authority from the Confederate Secretary of War "to press into service all the slaves of the country, if necessary" but preferred "to rely upon the patriotism of his fellow citizens for the needful supply of labor" and hence called for voluntary compliance. In response to Magruder's plea that his impressment policy be sustained, the Confederate Secretary of War decided that the general's "course in impressing labor for work upon fortifications, in cases of absolute necessity, and for a fair price, is fully approved." (A. T. Bledsoe to Genl. J. B. Magruder, 24 Sept. 1861, enclosed in Maj. Genl. J. Bankhead Magruder to Genl. S. Cooper, 23 Jan. 1862, M-167 1862, Letters Received, ser. 12, Adjt. & Insp. Gen., RG 109 [F-1021].) On September 17, William P. Underwood—apparently the same Surry County slaveholder who defied Magruder's requisition for slaves—had asked the Confederate Secretary of War whether Congress had authorized Magruder's impressment. (Wm. P. Underwood to Secretary of War, 17 Sept. 1861, #5515 1861, Letters Received, ser. 5, Sec. War, RG 109 [F-42].) No response to Underwood has been found in the records of the secretary.

260D: Commander of the Confederate Army of the Peninsula to the Confederate Adjutant and Inspector General

Yorktown [*Va.*] January 22^d 1862

Sir   Under the sanction of the War Department, granted by Mr Walker, I have called from time to time upon the inhabitants of the neighboring counties for their servants to work upon the fortifications which were deemed necessary here by the Engineers and by myself. By far the most important and extensive of these works were projected, located, and laid out by the Engineers then employed in the service of the State of Virginia and were ordered to be executed by Genl Lee, whether with or without the authority of the Federal Government I was not informed nor did I deem it proper for me to enquire.

My instructions from General Lee, when I arrived here, were among other things, to prosecute the works at Yorktown, Gloucester Point & Williamsburg, and subsequently I received orders from him to furnish the labor necessary to build the work at Mulberry Island Point—which work was likewise located by Col Talcott. I kept the troops employed in executing these orders at most of the places named, but found that it was necessary to employ additional labor which could not be hired, I therefore called upon the people to furnish their slaves and the magistrates, the free negroes and employd them when furnished. When the sickly season came and the Army could no longer work, I substituted negro labor almost entirely for that of the Soldiers. In the meantime questions as to the legality of pressing the slaves having arisen, the subject was refered to the War Department and my course was sanctioned by the then Secretary of War Mr. Walker. This practice continued until some time in the latter part of Dcb, when I was informed that the Government could hire slaves in January. I therefore asked for authority to hire, what, after consultation with the Engineers and the Quarter Master General of this Department, was supposed to be, the proper number. I obtained this authority and sent agents in various directions to hire the negroes. They found however that it was a very difficult matter to do so, and required more time than I expected. I discharged almost all of the slaves who had been employed in this Department for six or eight weeks and the remaining number being totally inadequate for the requisitions of the Engineer Department, I called upon several other Counties for one third of their working male force and for the male free negroes to be employed here, until the regular hiring of laborers could be accomplished. The laborers previously obtained have been almost exclusively employed in executing the works ordered from Richmond—Such field works as were required by the troops being exclusively done by themselves. I have just been informed representations have been made from the County of Chesterfield to the War Department and the President protesting against this latter call. I have to state that this is the only call that has ever been made upon that County by me for labor of any sort, or upon either of the Counties embraced in the last call. The counties previously called upon having done even more than the proper proportions of this work, I thought it right to release them from further call and to ask the assistance of their neighbors a little further removed— I was aware from the commencement, of the odium which would be attached to me from this course and that the Engineer Department should furnish this labor itself, but as the work had to be done, and done promptly, and the Engineer Department at Richmond neither would not or could not furnish the labor, I did not shrink from the performance of an odius duty, believing that the community, when they could sleep in peace and cultivate in safety, would look upon their contributions of labor as well bestowed, taking care however in the meantime to ascertain if my course met the Sanction of the War Department, which it did. I have already written to Capt Rives, understood to be in temporary charge of the Engineer Department of the Confederate States, requesting him to take charge of the labor necessary for the executions of such fortifications as may have been or may be ordered from Richmond, and I shall proceed no further in this matter except to obey any fresh orders which I may receive from the Goverment or to afford any facilities that may be in my power, whether the duty be agreeable or disagreeable, in carrying out the views of the Goverment for the public safety— I have the honor to be Sir Very Respectfully Yr Obt Sev^t

J Bankhead Magruder

I should have stated that I commenced procuring those negroes without refering to the War Dept. but that sanction of the Dept was given afterwards & authority at the same time granted to give a fair compensation for negroes so obtained *J B M*

HLS

Mjr. Genl. J. Bankhead Magruder to Genl. S. Cooper, 22 Jan. 1862, M-128 1862, Letters Received, ser. 12, Adjt. & Insp. Genl., RG 109 [F-272]. The postscript is in Magruder's handwriting. The following day, after receiving a letter from the Confederate Secretary of War that directed him to countermand his impressment order in Chesterfield County, Magruder forwarded another lengthy defense of his impressment policy. He had planned, he claimed, to use impressed slave labor only "until the exercise of the authority, granted me by the Government, to hire slaves, should be successful in procuring the requisite labor." The order to the slaveholders of Chesterfield and Dinwiddie counties "was intended to be my last call." Magruder enclosed copies of instructions from General Robert E. Lee to push work on the fortifications, and a copy of the War Department's approval of his "course in impressing labor for work upon fortifications, in cases of absolute necessity." (Maj. Genl. J. Bankhead Magruder to Genl. S. Cooper, 23 Jan. 1862, enclosing Major Genl. R. E. Lee to Col. Jno. B. Magruder, 25 May 1861, Gen'l. R. E. Lee to Col. J. B. Magruder, 10 June 1861, and A. T. Bledsoe to Genl. J. B. Magruder, 24 Sept. 1861, M-167 1862, Letters Received, ser. 12, Adjt. & Insp. Gen., RG 109 [F-1021].) In reply, the Secretary of War assured Magruder that he had no desire to interfere with Magruder's "impressing whatever may be necessary for the public defence" within his own department. "The point of difficulty was that *you went out of your district into the district of another General*." (J. P. Benjamin to Maj. Genl. J. B. Magruder, 27 Jan. 1862, ch. IX, vol. 4, p. 244, Letters Sent, Sec. War, RG 109 [F-1021].)

260E: Commander of the Confederate Army of the Peninsula to the Confederate Adjutant and Inspector General

Lee's Mill [*Va.*]— March 1ˢᵗ 1862

Sir I recᵈ your letter directing me so to arrange my forces as to send reinforcements when I recᵈ orders to Suffolk. You do not state what reinforcements you intend to send; hence it is impossible to know what arrangements to make. I immediately however gave preliminary orders. I can send but one Regᵗ & one field battery & that with great risk here. The reason why I cannot do more, is that notwithstanding all my efforts to procure negroes I have recᵈ but eleven from the Counties in my district. The Presiding Magistrate referring the call in some cases to the District Attorney who decided that it is illegal & in other cases no response is made. Two months fully have already been lost in consequence of the War Dept disapproving of my arrangements & countermanding my orders. I fear that it will be a fortnight before the evil flowing from these causes will have ceased if ever. The people have got an idea that the influence of the Government will be cast against my efforts. Whilst I was in Richmond 135 slaves from the Co of Greenville were discharged, I am informed, by order of the Sec of

War & without my knowledge   I had expected to have employed these negroes & others some 800 [ready in Henry?] in fortifying the 2nd line of my position whilst my troops were occupying & fortifying the front line where I prefer to fight but may be forced to leave as the flanks may be turned by the operations of ships of the enemy.   I supposed that by this time I would have had negroes enough to have fortified my positions sufficiently to have enabled me to spare temporarily & for a short distance 2000 men.   As I have not had the negro I cannot spare more troop than I have stated & for the militia ought at once to be substituted —   I am sir Very Resp^{ly} your ob^r serv^t

J Bankhead Magruder

P.S.   I have to request that this communication be laid thro the Sec of War, before the President —   Very Respectfully

ALS   J B Magruder

Maj. Genl. J. Bankhead Magruder to Genl. S. Cooper, 1 Mar. 1862, M-72 1862, Letters Received, ser. 5, Sec. War, RG 109 [F-1020]. In response, the Confederate Secretary of War assured Magruder that his impressment orders had not been countermanded and that he retained the full confidence of the War Department. The department insisted, however, that Magruder confine his impressment to the counties under his command: "The slaves from Greenville Co. were in no sense under your control or authority and the Secretary was forced on appeal to decide that you had no right to retain them." (J. P. Benjamin to Maj. Genl. J. B. Magruder, 4 Mar. 1862, ch. IX, vol. 7, pp. 75–76, Letters Sent, Sec. War, RG 109 [F-1125].)

260F: **Virginia Legislator to the Confederate Secretary of War**

Crimea   Dinwiddie Co [*Va.*]   April [8.?] 1862

Dear Sir   I beg leave to submit to you in behalf of a portion of my constituents the following facts —   that a large portion of the effective male slaves in a portion of my district has been drafted to work on the forts in the Peninsular — that the said slaves have been kept there for the past six weeks — that in consequence of their absence, the crops must necessarily be materially diminished — that from great exposure, being worked in mud & water & badly sheltered, several have died, and many now in the hospitals must, in my opinion die by such endurance — that none have been drafted from the county of Brunswick, a portion of my district, which bears unequally; nor from the counties of Nottoway, Mecklenburg & Lunenburg — that by a recent act of the Legislature, to which I call your attention & which I have submitted to Capt Rives for your &

692

his consideration, the free negroes of the state are subjected to a draft for one hundred & eighty days, which act has not been enforced— Therefore I respectfully submit to you that these slaves be remanded, and their places supplied either by the slaves from the counties not yet drafted, or by the slaves from the invaded portions of the state, which slaves, I presume, would be readily furnished by their owners, if applied to—or by the enforcement of the Act which the Legislature contemplated would furnish an ample force for all the demands of the Government, without abstracting from the plantations the labour indispensably necessary for the support of the population and the army— Yours respectfully

ALS   W^m F Thompson

Wm. F. Thompson to Hon. Geo. Randolph, [8?] Apr. 1862, T-110 1862, Letters Received, ser. 5, Sec. War, RG 109 [F-63]. Enclosure. A War Department endorsement declined to dismiss the slave laborers, noting that their withdrawal from the fortifications "might cause great dissaster." Similar complaints about the equity of impressment, suggesting that slaves be impressed from "adjoining counties," had reached the Confederate Secretary of War from other parts of central and eastern Virginia. (See, for example, Carter W. Wormeley to Hon. J. P. Benjamin, 12 Nov. 1861, #7513 1861, Letters Received, ser. 5, Sec. War, RG 109 [F-44].)

260G: Proclamation by the Commander of the Confederate Army of the Peninsula

Lee's Farm, near Lee's Mill [*Va.*] Ap^l 11th 1862.
Proclamation
To the citizens of the Peninsula and South side of James River:
McClellan at the head of one hundred thousand men is threatening our whole line. To meet the force sucessfully, our main reliance is to be placed upon brestworks. Soldiers cannot be expected to work night and day, and fight besides

Our negro force now at work on fortifications is too small to accomplish this object before the enemy may attempt to carry us by assault, when it will be beyond the power of all the force in the country to remedy that which, earlier, could have been effected with a slight additional assistance. Under these circumstances, I am sure that no patriotic citizen, with the issue truly at heart, would hesitate to respond, most cheerfully, to the call which I now make (viz) "One negro man with his axe, or spade, to be furnished at once, by each proprietor" Without the most liberal assistance in axes, spades and hands to work, we cannot hope to succeed, and the

Northern Army, will be in possession of your farms in a few days. Mr Julius Lamb is my authorized agent to receive the negroes— Send them at once: under overseers, to Co^l Ewell at Williamsburg.

HDcSr   J. B. Magruder.

Proclamation, Head Quarters Army of Pens., Asst. Adjt. Genls. Office, 11 Apr. 1862, ch. II, vol. 69, pp. 112–13, Letters & Telegrams Sent, Army & Dept. of the Peninsula, Records of Military Commands, RG 109 [F-622].

260H: Commander of the Right Wing of the Confederate Army of Virginia to the Confederate Secretary of War

Lee's Farm [*Va.*] April 29. 1862

Sir, I have learned that complaints have been made to you of the treatment of the slaves employed in this army—

It is quite true that much hardship has been endured by the negroes in the recent prosecution of the defensive works on our lines— But this has been unavoidable owing to the constant and long continued wet weather.

Every precaution has been adopted to secure their health and Safety as far as circumstances would allow— The soldiers, however, have been more exposed and have suffered far more than the slaves. The latter have always slept under cover and have had fires to make them comfortable, whilst the men have been working in the rain, have stood in the trenches & rifle pits in mud and water almost knee-deep, without shelter, fire or sufficient food— There has been sickness among the soldiers and the slaves, but far more among the former than the latter—

I write this for your information, supposing that you might not know the facts. Very respectfully Yr ob^t ser^t

ALS   J. B Magruder

Maj. Genl. J. B. Magruder to Hon. G. W. Randolph, 29 Apr. 1862, M-449 1862, Letters Received, ser. 5, Sec. War, RG 109 [F-1020].

261: South Carolina Planter to the Confederate President

Private.   Charleston S° Cᵃ 8ᵗʰ August 1863 [*1861*]
My Dear Sir: I respectfully place before you, a Plan I have long
entertained, of ATTACHING to each Regiment in the Service, 100, say
One Hundred Blacks, more or less, as experience might determine, to
be used, as follows, viz. –   1ˢᵗ *To Cook and Wash for our
men.* –   2ⁿᵈ To *act* as a *Police, especially when the Army is in Camp*, AS
AT MANASSAS. –   3ʳᵈ To take charge of the Waggons, and Horses,
used for Transportation. –   4ᵗʰ To aid in Fortifying our Camp at
night. –   The *hardest*, and *most painful duty* of the *young Volunteers*, is
to *learn how* to *Cook*, and *Wash* – and we must never lose *sight* of the
great fact, that *our Battles*, must *mainly* be *fought* by *our Brave
Volunteers*, and my long experience in this Service has taught me,
that if the *Food, especially*, be *hastily* and *badly prepared*, – the *health*
and *efficiency* of our *Troops* will be *greatly impaired*, and *must most
assuredly develop itself during* the *Autumn Months*. –   At *home*, the
young Soldier, has his *Food Cooked* for *him*, by his *Mother, Sister's or* by
our Slaves – but not *so* in the *Field of Battle*. –   At New-Orleans
General Jackson used *Free Blacks*, and they *fought at our side* – and *he*
used *Slaves largely* on our *Fortifications*, and it worked well – *Morally*,
in *keeping our men Fresh*, and *good spirits* for the *Battle Field* – *physically*
in *giving* them *better health*, and *endurance under hardships* –   I hazard
nothing in saying, in the hour of trial, in will be found, that the
South will *beat* the *North, Middle & Western* States, in *every
Battle* – but to do so *effectually*, we should *avail ourselves of our peculiar
population* not only to *Till* the *Earth* – Manufacture &. & – but also
use them as our Father's did, before the Revolution of "76" – also in
the *War of 1812*, with *England* – and as the *Greeks, Spartans*, and
Romans did – and on *all occasions*, they *proved true & faithful* to *their
Masters* –   You can work this great proposition better than I can,
and I pray you to do so – commencing with *Food properly prepared* – &
the *luxury* of a *clean shirt once* a *week* – *for our brave men* – and to which
I would *add* – a *rigid Police, especially when* in *Camp* – as at
Manassas. –
     Your Masterly Movement, upon Richmond – saved *Virginia*, and *gave*
us *North Carolina* – and *her gallant son, Tennessee* – Thus, in a *moment*,
as *it were, doubling* the *Moral, Physical*, and *Financial power* for *War*,
and all *other purposes*, of our dear Confederate States of America – and
as *I believe securing beyond* all *doubt, our separate independence,
forever* – from the *grasp of a Brutal enemy*. –
     I congratulate you, with my *whole heart*, on the *Great Battle*, and
great, and *most decisive Victory achieved by our men*, at *Manassas* – and
the *cheering fact*, of *your being present*, on that *great occasion*. –   *O! that
I could have been at your side, & why shd I not be with you?* –

Our *cause* is the *cause* of our *God* & *Father* in *Heaven* — *and you are his Right hand Man* — Take *care* of your *health*. — *We cannot afford to lose you.* — With respectful salutations, *from* & *to all* — *as ever, your friend*:

ALS

A. P. Hayne

A. P. Hayne to His Excellency Jefferson Davis, 8 Aug. 1863 [1861], #5460 1861, Letters Received, ser. 5, Sec. War, RG 109 [F-41].

262: Chief Engineer of the Confederate Western Department to the Governor of Tennessee, and a Call for Laborers by the Engineer

Nashville Tenn December 11th 1861

Sir   The agents heretofore employed to procure a laboring force for building fortifications for defending the approaches to this city, have failed to get any more than a few Negroes — A Number quite insignificant, when compared with the work to be undertaken.

With a hope that a large force of Negroes may yet be obtained, by an appeal to the citizens of the vicinity and neighboring counties; I have prepared the form for the call upon them, which I submit for your endorsement.

Having your endorsement I have thought it might be advisable, to have a Number of coppies printed and placed in the hands of some officers Say sheriffs and constables — with instructions to apply to every citizen within reach and urge the Necessity of a prompt compliance with the call   I am Sir Very Respectfully Your Ob't Serv't

HLcSr

J. F. Gilmer.

Nashville. Dec 11th 1861

It has been decided by the General-commanding the Western Department to fortify the approaches to the city of Nashville, the better to protect your capital and state, against the contingency of invasion by our relentless enemy. To this end a call is now made upon all citizens, to contribute a part of the labor which they control, to aid in the erection of the Necessary works.

It is necessary that each negro sent from a distance, be furnished by his master, with blankets or other bed clothing sufficient to make him comfortable also with cooking and messing utensils. It is essential that the lumber be assembled, with the least practicable delay, at "Cockrills Hill" and "Fosters Hill", near and north of the town of Edgefield on the Goodlettsville Turnpike.

The force employed will be lodged at night either in tents or frame huts in the vicinity of the work, and as a care, more satisfactory to the owners may be secured to their hands by placing them under the charge of some person or persons known in the neighborhood or county, from which the negros are sent, it is desired that this place, by agreement among the citizens, be adopted

If subsistance be furnished by the owner, one dollar per day for each hand, will be paid by the Confederate States   if supplied by the Government, then seventy cents per day.

Nothing but a great necessity causes this additional call upon the patriotism of the citizens and a promt response will the better ensure protection to your property and your homes.

By direction and authority of Gen: A. S. Johnston, Commanding the Western Department. J. F. Gilmer.

HDc

Maj. J. F. Gilmer to His Excellency Isham G. Harris, 11 Dec. 1861, and proclamation, C.S. Engineer Office, 11 Dec. 1861, ch. III, vol. 8, pp. 31–33, Letters Sent, Chief Engineer, Western Dept., Records of Military Commands, RG 109 [F-798].

263: Commander of a Confederate Artillery Company to the Chief of Artillery of the Confederate Army of Northern Virginia

Camp Pendleton [*Va.*] Feby. 22^d 1862.

Col. Pendleton   During last fall, finding I could not enlist blacksmiths, as artificers in my company, I addressed a letter to the adjutant General asking permission to hire the labor needed. I received the enclosed letter in reply, granting permission to hire *a smith* provided the hire should not exceed the pay of an enlisted blacksmith."– In accordance with the spirit of that letter, I have hired, *by the year* a smith and a striker for my company– for the former the annual hire is $150, for the latter $120. I deem myself very fortunate to have procured two such excellent artificers upon such favorable terms–less indeed than I was authorized to pay. The hands employed are now discharging their duties satisfactorily.– As there is some difference between the authority granted me by the Adjutant General & the bargain I have

made – growing out of the fact that I was forced to hire these smiths
by the year – instead of by the month, on the usual terms of enlisted
smiths, I beg that you will submit this matter to the proper
authorities and ascertain whether the bargain I have made will be
ratified by the Government or not. It is proper to add that these
smiths are slaves & hired on the usual terms – they to be clothed &
fed by the hirer. I have been offered $20 a month for each of these
smiths by the Quarter Master, but I would prefer that contract of
hire as stated above, may be assumed by the Confederate states – it
being in my opinion clearly to their advantage to do so. Very
respectfully Your Obt. svt

ALS   Tho J. Kirkpatrick

Capt. Tho. J. Kirkpatrick to Col. Pendleton, 22 Feb. 1862, K-65 1862,
Letters Received, ser. 12, Adjt. & Insp. Gen., RG 109 [F-251]. Endorsements. The enclosure mentioned is not in the file. The Confederate Adjutant
and Inspector General's Office promptly authorized hiring the blacksmith for
$150 a year and the striker for $120 a year. (A. & I. Genl. R. H. Chilton to
Col. W. N. Pendleton, 27 Feb. 1862, ch. I, vol. 36, p. 495, Letters &
Telegrams Sent, Adjt. & Insp. Gen., RG 109 [F-251].)

264: Virginia Slaveholder to the Confederate Secretary of War

                              Etna P.O. Hanover [Va.] May 2 [1862]
Dear Sir   Many farmers in Virginia are injured by a practice which
has become habitual and extensive among the soldiers of our own
army. The soldiers employ runaway negroes to cook for the mess,
clean their horses, and so forth. The consequence is that negroes are
encouraged to run away, finding a safe harbour in the army. Two
of my neighbours have each recovered runaway negroes within the
last few weeks; who were actually found in the employment of the
soldiers on the Peninsula and these negroes had been runaway many
months. I therefore write to ask you to issue a general order
forbidding this practice and anexing a penalty sufficiently severe to
break it up.
    All that is necessary is to forbid the employment of any coloured
person unless he can show free papers or a pass from his master; and
hold the soldier responsible, for the genuineness of the free papers or
pass.
    In this section of country a heavy draught has been made upon
the farmers (half of our available working force) to work on the
fortifications. I, for one, rendered this tribute cheerfully to a cause

which is dear to my heart, though that, together with the excessive rains will materially shorten my crop. I think however, we ought to be protected by the army authorities from the abuses above mentioned. Yours &c

L. H. Minor

I can scarcely see to sign my name

One of my negro men has been runaway for many months and I have reason to believe that he is in the service of the soldiers.

ALS

L. H. Minor to Sir, 2 May [1862], M-458 1862, Letters Received, ser. 5, Sec. War, RG 109 [F-68]. The problem of Confederate soldiers' harboring fugitive slaves was not confined to Virginia. More than a year later, upon learning that soldiers under his command were guilty of "acts of pillage & destruction upon the private property of our own citizens," a Confederate cavalry commander in Mississippi ordered: "No negroes will be permitted to remain with this command, except such as are allowed by the Regulations viz one servant for each officer – one teamster for each wagon or ambulance, & four cooks & four washermen for each company – Each negro will be provided with a pass to be approved by the Reg^{tal} or Battalion Comd^r & by the Inspector Genl of the Brigade, & which shall be renewed monthly – showing the name of the negro – the position he occupies & the Reg^t & Co to which he is attached, or the officer whom he is serving – All other negroes will be sent out of camp at once – " (General Order No. 65, Hd. Qrs., Chalmers Cav. Brigade, 12 Sept. 1863, ch. II, vol. 299, pp. 363–65, Orders & Circulars Received, Papers of Gen. J. R. Chalmers, ser. 117, Collections of Officers' Papers, Records of Military Commands, RG 109 [F-859].) Confederate authorities repeatedly ordered regimental commanders to report those slaves who were working for the troops "without written authority from their masters." (*Official Records*, ser. 4, vol. 2, pp. 86, 551–52.)

265: Georgia Slaveholder to the Confederate Secretary of War

Laurens Hill, Georgia– Sep 8th 1862

Sir, Perhaps you will think it presumptuous in me to write you, but, as an humble & I trust loyal citizen of this confederacy I feel that I have the right to appeal to you for redress when I think myself imposed upon by the military authorities of the day; a government that does not protect its subjects in the enjoyment of their property, so far as lies in its power, is not the kind of government to command respect, or encourage the feelings of patriotism – do you think it is? I allude to the late order of Gen. Mercer for the impressment of slaves in Geo. he has sent his agents into our country & without notice or ceremony impressed & taken 20 pr ct of the slaves away from their owners, under penalty of arresting every man who refused, & he still holds them against their wishes when they think it is time for their hands to be sent home, & other counties be called on to bear their part of the risque & labor necessary to make the city of Sav^h impregnable. – The people of Laurens county I believe are patriotic, & are ever ready to do their full share in any work calculated to promote the welfare of our country, – in this case, our patriotism has not been appealed to at all, the *ipse dixit* of a military commander was the first intimation we had of the matter, & with but few exceptions our county people responded forthwith & without a murmur, – other counties refused, and telegraphed to you on the subject, & your answer stopt the further impressment of slaves, those counties that refused to obey the order, were the most able to send slaves, & have sent none. – Is it right for a few poor counties to risk their slaves & do all the work, while the wealthier counties stand aloof & do nothing at all – ? nor do we complain at helping, we are willing to help, but we do complain at having to do more than our share – I am sorry you interfered, for it has been the means of exposing a degree of selfishness among our people, that is both shameful & alarming, and has convinced me that Gen Mercer was right in ordering the impressment – Please be kind enough to tell me if Gen. Mercer can keep our impressed slaves as long as he pleases, his agent said they would be needed about a month, the month is now out. & I hear no talk of the hands coming home. have we any way to get them back? if so, please tell me how – If you deny his right to impress hands, you ought certainly to make him give up those he has impressed, will you allow him to take property from some men, & not others, & then keep it as long as he pleases? we must have equality in this confederacy or it will blow up – If this is to be a free-will offering upon the altar of our country, I wish to be placed on an equal footing with the people of other counties, so that when I send my hands, no one can deny but that a motive of patriotism & not the order of Genl Mercer has prompted me to do it – you can readily perceive the distinction   Very respectfully

ALS   Joseph. M. White

Joseph M. White to Hon. Geo. W. Randolph, 8 Sept. 1862, W-857 1862, Letters Received, ser. 5, Sec. War, RG 109 [F-67].

266: Virginia Legislator to the Confederate Secretary of War

Senate Chamber Richmond Va Oct 2nd 1862

Sir I write to request you respectfully, if it be consistent with the public good, not to impress the slaves in the County of Southampton to work on the defences about Richmond — I will briefly state my reasons for this request. They have every facility for runing to the enemy in the adjoining counties of Isle of Wight & Nansemond & they have a perfect horror of working on entrenchments, & I feel certain that if they hear of another impressment, we will lose nearly all of our men — When the General commdg, at Petersburg called for labourers some two months ago, about 200 left the county in 3 days — We furnished all required of us to work on the defences of Yorktown & Ptersburg, & I hope you will not think me or my constituents wanting in patriotism from this request — The general assembly will pass a bill giving you power to impress as many you want & as I am compelled to leave today I write before the bill is passed — I am resply yr obt Servt

ALS   Thos H. Urquhart

Senator Thos. H. Urquhart to Hon. G. W. Randolph, 2 Oct. 1862, U-22 1862, Letters Received, ser. 12, Adjt. & Insp. Gen., RG 109 [F-276]. Urquhart signed as "Senator from Sussex Va." General Samuel G. French, the Confederate commander at Petersburg, Virginia, reported in an endorsement of October 30 that blacks had earlier been impressed for work on the defenses, but there was no new impressment planned. Furthermore, French added, "[i]t appears those that ran away were those that were not impressed. Of *all those at work* I know of but *one* negro that has not reached his master." On November 4, General G. W. Smith, the Confederate commander at Richmond, disposed of the complaint in an even briefer endorsement: "The whole subject is old. Action has been taken long ago." Other endorsements.

267: Confederate Commander at Columbus, Mississippi, to the Headquarters of the Confederate Department of Mississippi and East Louisiana, Enclosing a Broadside Issued by the Former

Columbus Miss Nov 4th /62

Major By directives from Dep Head Q^{rs} hand bills were struck up & circulated calling upon planters for negroes (a copy of hand bill is enclosed) Once before I called upon Owners for their negroes — but in both cases met with but little success thus far only about one dozen negroes have reported to Lt Topp— the only way that appears practicable is from the *"Tax* List" to call upon each Planter for his proportion of negroes and force them to furnish— This might require the concurrence of the Governor of this state— it was the method pursued by my predecessor— Unless some plan of this kind is followed the planters will not send their negroes—

They perhaps fear that in case the federals got possession, those who have furnished the Govt—labor will suffer. therefore they desire the Confd States to *press* or demand the negroes   I am Major [very Resp your ob sv]

ALS   John Adams

[*Enclosure*]   [*Columbus, Miss. October 1862*]

WANTED!

200 NEGROES.

By direction of Lieut. Gen. Pemberton, Commanding Department of Mississippi and East Louisiana, I call upon the Planters of Lowndes and adjacent counties for Negroes to complete the fortifications.

For every negro furnished, including cooks, the Quartermaster's department will pay $1 25 per day—owners to feed their negroes. Tents or other shelter will be provided by the Government.

Good and experienced overseers will be employed to stay with and take charge of the laborers.

Report on Monday morning, 3rd Nov. in front of Court House.

JNO. ADAMS,
Col. C. S. Army.

Col. John Adams to Major Waddy, 4 Nov. 1862, enclosing broadside by Col. Jno. Adams, [Oct. 1862], Gen. J. C. Pemberton Papers, ser. 131, Collections of Officers' Papers, Records of Military Commands, RG 109 [F-234]. Endorsements.

268: Surgeon in Charge of a Confederate Army Hospital to the Medical Director of the Confederate Defenses of Richmond

G. H. Howard's Grove Richmond Dec. 13th 62

Sir, The owners of negroes, hired in this Hospital by the month, are demanding their release, inasmuch as, the Hospital has been appropriated for the reception of cases of smallpox. I have refused to give them up, contending that, as I hired them by the month, I am entitled to their services, Several have taken them away without my consent— Would I be justifiable in arresting them & bringing back to Hospital?

If they are permitted to leave the patients will suffer greatly— Many of the negroes, (some of whom are free) were impressed into the service, by order, Brig. Gen. J. H. Winder in July last. Very Respectfully Yr. obt. Serv't

ALS   C. D. Rice

Surg. C. D. Rice to E. S. Gaillard, 13 Dec. 1862, R-705 1862, Letters Received, ser. 5, Sec. War, RG 109 [F-62]. In an undated endorsement, the Confederate Secretary of War declared that "[t]he negroes hired by the month, if hired for attendance on Hospital must take their chance of the diseases there & sh^d be retained or compelled to stay. The negroes impressed sh^d be retained only in case others to attend cannot be hired." Other endorsements.

269: Chief Engineer of the Confederate Army of Mississippi to the Commander of the Confederate Department of Mississippi and East Louisiana

Grenada [*Miss.*] Jan. 4 /63

General   My fortifications are progressing slowly, my negro force diminishing rapidly. Of 972 negroes received at this point I had by the Musterroll of Dec. 31st only about 380 fit for duty. Most of them have run away—many are sick—and some are dead. I think the remainder had better be discharged for the following reasons:

1st: It has now been raining steadily for nearly 30 hours—the streams are rapidly swelling, and there is consequently no possibility of the enemy's advancing to attack this point during the winter.

2nd: The negroes are in a bad condition—sick and badly clothed. We ought to pay if we keep them at least $20⁰⁰ p^r month, and the work they will be likely to do at this season will not be worth the expenditure.

3rd. The want of system in the impressment of negroes causes the burthen to fall very unequally on the owners of that species of property, some sending all & others none, and I do not think there is any present emergency to justify the continuance of this unequal pressure.

I would therefore respectfully suggest that the negro force now on hand be disbanded and that arrangements be made by which the owners of slaves may be required & compelled to furnish a proportionable share of their laborers for work on fortification otherwise that the soldiers be detailed to do the work during favorable weather, which I dare say would be the best plan, as the work can now be carried on leisurely so as not to occasion them any undue hardships or exposure.

In the meantime I should be glad to put my whole Corps in the field to make topographical Surveys of the most important sections of the State. Very respectfully your ob^t Servt

HLS   P. Robinson

Capt. P. Robinson to Lt. Genl. Pemberton, 4 Jan. 1863, Gen. J. C. Pemberton Papers, ser. 131, Collections of Officers' Papers, Records of Military Commands, RG 109 [F-232]. Endorsement.

270: **Alabama Slaveholder to the Confederate Secretary of War**

Montgomery Ala July 23 /63
Dear Sir   Permit me to make a suggestion, which seems to me will strengthen our military arm and enable us to strike a more effective blow in the cause of our country— I understand that it requires about one fourth of the men in the army to *wait* on the others, in attending upon wagons, and other things necessary for the movements of the main body. I think this could be supplied by negroes and thereby release a large force of white men to do the fighting. It would require a small number of whites to act as superintendents & directors, but the number would be comparitively small, whilst the work would be as effectively done   I am willing as a slaveholder to contribute one fourth or more of my fellow force for this purpose, & I think it would be generally responded to. Some might grumble but the majority would prefer any sacrifice rather than subjugation— By drafting the requisite number of negroes promptly & placing them in the army as teamsters, nurses & for bringing the wounded to the rear, such a number of men may be released as would enable us to keep back the enemy

from ravaging the country and *possibly* to drive him beyond our limits — If you do not do this, they are taken by the enemy and placed not only in similar positions but also armed and placed in their ranks as fighting men — Negroes are easily influenced by those around them and when placed in our army would make it a matter of pride to remain loyal & true to our cause, but when left in contact with the enemy they are imposed upon by their teachings and are enticed away by them, As an evidence of the truth of my position, see how few of those who have been carried as servants into the army have deserted, and they too come from a class which would be most likely to do so — I hope you will excuse me for making these suggestions. I am actuated solely by a desire to benefit my country — Very Respectfully

W C Bibb

[In the margin] The negroes, refugees, would supply the deficit of labour if any, necessary to produce food for the country

ALS

[Endorsement] There is a good deal of force in the suggestion. Negro teamsters have been found hard to get. They are better than detailed men for the purpose, and would put back into the ranks some thousand of good soldiers — The same thing is true of Company *cooks*.

[Endorsement] *Secy of War* The sacrosanctity of slave property in this war has operated most injuriously to the Confederacy

If there had been organised at the beginning of the war, bands of slaves to attend the army to perform its heavy work & they had been employed on all the fortifications, the condition of things would have been better — The government has obtained with great difficulty this labor & has been required to insure its safety when obtained — J A C.

[Endorsement] Respectfully submitted to the President for consideration   I have always thought negroes might be used with advantage on many duties connected with the Army and organized companies of workers, similar to the Navies (so called) of the English service would be found eminently useful   Such employment and organization however could only be obtained by additional Legislation, unless by the voluntary action of slave owners, which I fear is not to be expected   J A Seddon Secy of War July 29th 63

[*Endorsement*] Secty of War, accept the offer and require Qr. Masters to procure when practicable slaves for teamsters and ostlers   They are preferable also for company & Hospital cooks –   J. D.

[*Endorsement*] Referred to the QMG who will note & comply with the suggestion of the Presidents endorsement   11 Augt 63
J A S sy

[*Endorsement*] Q^r Mr G. Office Aug 15. 1863   Respectfully returned to the Secretary of War.
    It is very desirable to substitute negroes for the duties referred to – and general instructions to that effect have been given heretofore. It is suggested that a Gen: Order from the A & I. Genl's Office will be more effective than an order from this office – as the latter will only bind officers of the Q.M. Dep^t   The co-operation of commanding officers is required. A R Lawton Q^rM^rG

W. C. Bibb to Hon. James A. Seddon, 23 July 1863, B-1700 1863, Letters Received, ser. 12, Adjt. & Insp. Gen., RG 109 [F-291]. The first endorsement was evidently a Confederate War Department memorandum. John A. Campbell, author of the second endorsement, was assistant secretary of war. Other endorsements indicate that Secretary of War James A. Seddon instructed the adjutant and inspector general to issue an order in accordance with the quartermaster general's suggestion. Meanwhile, Seddon informed Bibb that his suggestion had been "to some extent adopted" and his offer to contribute slaves "thankfully accepted." "The employment of slaves would not be as armed soldiers but for collateral duties required in an army as teamsters cooks nurses &c." (James A. Seddon to W. C. Bibb Esq., 12 Aug. 1863, ch. IX, vol. 12, p. 351, Letters Sent, Sec. War, RG 109 [F-291].)

271: Paymaster of the Confederate Engineer Bureau to the Chief of Construction of the Confederate Department of Northern Virginia

                    Richmond August 24th 1863
Col. I have the honour to return, herewith, the enclosed communication of the 16th of June last from Maj. Genl J. B. Magruder in relation to the impressment of negroes, which was referred by you to this office on the 22^d inst for examination and report and with the request that "a rule should be suggested for impressing slaves when no State law obtains".

The 9th and 10th Sections of the Act of Congress concerning impressments,[1] to the former of which Gen[l] Magruder refers in his letter, are in the words following. to wit:

> Section 9. "Where slaves are impressed by the Confederate Government to labour on fortifications or other public works the impressment shall be made by said Government according to the rules and regulations provided in the laws of the State wherein they are impressed; and in the absence of such law, in accordance with such rules and regulations, not inconsistent with the provisions of this Act, as the Secretary of War shall from time to time prescribe; Provided that no impressment of slaves shall be made when they can be hired or procured by the consent of the owner or agent".
>
> Section 10. "That previous to the 1st day of December next (1863) no slave labouring on a farm or plantation exclusively devoted to the production of grain and provisions shall be taken for the public use without the consent of the owner, except in case of urgent necessity".

Upon an examination of such of the Statutes as are accessible I find that they contain nothing respecting the "*impressments*" of slaves — the laws of most of the Southern States merely defining what shall constitute offences committed by them or their owners and the punishments inflicted for a violation thereof. So far as I am advised, Virginia appears to be the only state which has legislated specially upon the subject, and this legislation is contained in her Acts of Assembly (passed at a called session,) of October 3[d] 1862 and March 13th 1863, the latter being an Act to amend and re-enact the former Act.

The necessity of such special legislation seems only to have arisen since the commencement of the present war, so far as *this* state is concerned. I find, however, in the revised statutes of Georgia of 1849, an Act of her Legislature to provide for the purchase of a certain number of slaves to work on river and harbour improvements.

It would seem that where no state law obtains the 9th Section of the Act of Congress referred to, makes it the duty of the Secretary of War to prescribe such rules and regulations, not inconsistent with the provisions of the Act, as to him may seem proper.

In the absence of any information as to the views of the Hon[l] Secretary and also of any State law upon the subject, it is difficult to suggest a rule that would be uniform in its operation and meet with his approval. Under these circumstances I respectfully submit a synopsis of the present Virginia law, which is so stringent upon the Government, and jealous of the rights of its citizens that I presume it will be acceptable in those states where no law now obtains.

1st That the Governor of a state whenever thereto requested by the President of the Confederate States, call into the service of the Confederate States for labour on fortifications or other works for the public defence within said state from time to time for a period not exceeding sixty days a number of male slaves between the ages of 18 and 55 years not exceeding 5 per cent at any one time of the entire slave population of any County, City or town in said State of the ages specified. Such requisition shall be apportioned rateably among all the slave-owners in the several Counties, Cities and towns on which the requisition shall be made so as to charge each slave holder with the same proportion of his male slaves between the ages specified capable of performing ordinary labour which may be demanded from his County, City or town

2^d The Governor of a State in his discretion to exempt wholly or partially such counties cities or towns in his State as may have lost so large a portion of their slaves in consequence of their escape to the public enemy as will materially affect the agricultural products of said counties or which from their geographical position or contiguity to the public enemy he may deem expedient

3^d The sum of   Dollars per month for each slave shall be paid by the Confederate States to the person entitled to his services and soldier's rations medicines and medical attendance furnished; and the value of all such slaves as may die during their term of service or thereafter from injuries received or of diseases contracted in such service or not be returned to their owners shall be paid by the Confederate States to the owners of such slaves. Compensation shall also be made for all injuries to slaves arising from the act of the public enemy or for any injury arising from a want of due diligence on the part of the Authorities of the Confederate States

4th The Confederate States shall not be liable for any slave not returned by reason of fraud or collusion on the part of the owner or his agent nor if his death should be caused by the act of God or by disease of such slave existing when received by the Confederate authorities

5th When a requisition is made by the President of the Confederate States upon the Governor of a State; – the latter to give notice thereof to the several counties, cities and towns upon which he may make the call in such manner and form as he may deem best.

6th After the proper apportionment of slaves shall be made among the slave holders of any county city or town in each state each slave-holder shall be required under such rules and regulations as the proper state or other authorities may prescribe to deliver on a day and at a place appointed his quota of slaves to the Sheriff or Sargeant as the case may be to be delivered by such Sheriff or

Sargeant to an agent or officer of the Confederate States duly authorized to receive and receipt for them at the expense of the Confederate States   In case of failure of said owners to deliver their slaves as above unless good and sufficient cause be shown therefor to the proper State authorities it is recommended that the Confederate States be authorized to hold said slaves for the period of Ninety days and the expenses attending said delivery be paid by the owners and moreover that such fines and penalties be imposed upon them by the State authorities as in their judgment may seem proper to enforce a compliance with the requisition

7th In making a requisition upon a State the Governor thereof is requested to equalize the burden as near as may be among the several Counties Cities and towns and amongst its citizens having when practicable due regard to the number of slaves furnished under any call heretofore made by the President or Secretary of War or any officer of the Confederate army.

8th Slaves furnished under a requisition shall be placed when practicable and desired by the owners in charge of an agent or overseer (if a suitable person) selected by themselves during the period of said slaves impressments and such agent or overseer shall not be discharged by any officer of the Confederate Government except for good cause to be approved by Chief of Engineers in charge of the works where they are employed

9th Subsistence and provisions furnished slaves by their owners shall be commuted for in money equal to the commutation allowed soldiers in the service

10th All slaves sent voluntarily by their owners to the Confederate authorities and accepted by them shall stand on the same footing as impressed slaves.

11th No slave shall be received and accepted by the Confederate authorities for labour on public defences without having first been examined as to his physical fitness by a competent medical officer.   Very Respectfully Your obt servt

ALS

J B. Stanard

1st Lt. J. B. Stanard to Col. W. H. Stevens, 24 Aug. 1863, filed with M-1440 1863, Letters Received, ser. 12, Adjt. & Insp. Gen., RG 109 [F-297]. Endorsement. The blank space appears in the manuscript. In the same file is the letter of June 16 from General John B. Magruder, commander of the Confederate District of Texas, New Mexico, and Arizona, to the head-quarters of the Confederate Trans-Mississippi Department, in which Ma-gruder had requested authority to impress slaves for labor on the coastal fortifications of Texas, labor "now absolutely required." Magruder had pointed out that the impressment act adopted by the Confederate Congress provided "no direct right to impress slaves" and the Secretary of War had issued no regulations regarding impressment in those states that lacked legislation on the subject. Magruder's letter had been forwarded to the Confederate War Department, which instructed the chief of the Engineer Bureau to "make a draft of suitable regulations for impressment of slaves to work on fortifications, or to do other work." The bureau chief had in turn directed that Lieutenant Stanard "examine the laws of Va. & such other states as may be accessible on the subject of impressing slave labor, with a view to drawing up the regulations requested." (Maj. Genl. J. Bankhead Magruder to Brig. Gen. Boggs, 16 June 1863, and endorsements.)

1 The "Act to Regulate Impressments," adopted March 26, 1863, was reprinted in General Order 37, issued by the Confederate Adjutant and Inspector General's Office on April 6, 1863. The order also included instructions implementing the legislation. (*Official Records*, ser. 4, vol. 2, pp. 469–72.)

272: Chief-of-Staff of the Confederate Department of South Carolina, Georgia, and Florida, to a Labor Agent at Kingstree, South Carolina

Charleston S.C., September 1ˢᵗ 1863.

Sir, I regret that you have found planters so ready with excuses for not furnishing labor to defend *Charleston* — May God grant that, in seeking to avoid furnishing a fourth of their labor, at this momentous juncture, they do not materially contribute to the loss of the whole.

If unable to find Road Commissioners who will loyally assist you in your duties, call on the planters to give you, in good faith, a list of their able-bodied male negroes between ages of 18 & 45, and, also, a statement of what amount of labor they have severally furnished on the works in South-Carolina. Every man in the District must be required to send one fourth, including that already furnished. Should you find, after trial, that this does not work, take one-fourth, irrespective of former contributions, except from those who voluntarily furnished labor at my call, last February and March.

Working on Rail Roads cannot be taken as ground of exemption.

Negroes found in your District refugees, of course must fare the same with others.

Send back all negroes who have run away from the works.

I repeat, as far as practicable, impress the slaves of those who, hitherto, have not furnished labor. Respectfully, Your obᵈᵗ Servᵗ

HLcSr   Thomas Jordan

Chief of Staff Thomas Jordan to Jno. S. McDaniel, 1 Sept. 1863, ch. II, vol. 31, pp. 519–20, Letters Sent, Dept. of SC, GA, & FL, Records of Military Commands, RG 109 [F-605]. Jordan had long complained about the unwillingness of South Carolina planters to furnish slave labor upon the requisition of military authorities. In February 1863, he informed leading members of the South Carolina legislature that "[d]espite repeated requisitions made on the State authorities during the past sixty days for at least 2500 negroes to work on the fortifications for the defence of the harbor and the several land approaches to the city, there are now not more than four hundred & fifty hands available to the Engineers." The legislature, it was true, had recently authorized the governor to impress slaves, but Jordan feared that delay in implementing the legislation would "deprive us of the labor essential for the completion of the defences of Charleston, within the time at which an attack seems inevitable:—that is, negroes manifestly will be furnished too late under the system as yet to be inaugurated at this late day by Governor Bonham." (Chief of Staff Thomas Jordan to Hon. A. G. Magrath et al., 20 Feb. 1863, #216 1863, Letters Sent, ser. 71, Dept. of SC, GA & FL, Records of Military Commands, RG 109 [F-180].)

273: Broadside by the Chief Quartermaster of the Confederate Trans-Mississippi Department

TO THE PEOPLE
OF THE
TRANS-MISS. DEPARTMENT.

Office Chief Quartermaster, Trans-Miss. Department.
Shreveport, La., September 15th, 1863.

In this struggle for all that makes life desirable; as a band of brothers we must stand shoulder to shoulder, be true to ourselves, sacrifice freely, and never give up.

Do this, and we are, and will remain freemen; decline to do it, and we will be subjugated, our property wrested from us, and our country lost. Nothing can be gained by submission. By Lincoln's law you are told your property is confiscated, yourselves are rebels, and that "rebels have no rights."

Your country needs labor, as well as men to fight. The negro men our enemies would arm against us, can be well employed as teamsters, cooks, mechanics and laborers; better then, far better to let the Government have them than the enemy. They will be well cared for, and a fair compensation paid for their services. You cheerfully yield your children to your country, how can you refuse to hire your servants?

We appeal to the slave holders of the Trans-Mississippi Department generally, and particularly to that portion of the Department likely to be visited by the enemy in any raid he may make, to let the Government have their able-bodied men, thereby saving them from falling into the hands of our enemies, and enabling the Lieut. Gen'l Commanding, to place in the ranks thousands of men now employed as teamsters, laborers, etc., for want of other labor for that service.

The Government requires from two to three thousand laborers. and the Chief Quartermasters of the Districts of Arkansas, Louisiana and Texas will receive them; any one person or neighborhood furnishing twenty able-bodied men, can designate a person to take charge of them, who will be employed by the Government for that purpose.

The Government will pay for any servants that may be killed by the enemy, but will not be responsible for those that die from disease, or run away. Any person wishing to furnish hands under this call, will please address the Chief Quartermasters of the Districts of Arkansas, Louisiana or Texas, or the undersigned, setting forth the number he will furnish, and steps will be taken at once to receive them. None but able-bodied men received.

J. F. MINTER,
Major and Chief Quartermaster, Trans-Miss. Dept.

Caddo Gazette Print.)

Broadside, Office Chief Quartermaster, Trans-Miss. Department, 15 Sept. 1863, Orders & Circulars, ser. 107, Trans-MS Dept., Records of Military Commands, RG 109 [F-902]. Earlier in September, the commander of the Trans-Mississippi Department had instructed his subordinates to assist planters in removing able-bodied male slaves from areas exposed to enemy raids, in order to prevent their being recruited into the Union army. (See below, doc. 309.)

274A: **Confederate Assistant Superintendent of Labor for Christ Church Parish, South Carolina, to the Confederate General Superintendent of Labor for South Carolina**

Mount Pleasant [*S.C.*] December 5" 1863. Sir Yours of the 4" Ins^t is received, enclosing Copy of a letter to you from Co^l Harris of the Same date, in which he says— "I am informed that there is a general conviction throughout the State that the negroes impressed for Labor on the defences, are not Sufficiently and judiciously cared for." A plain Statement of facts will show that there is no just Cause for this Impression.

The hands employed in this Division, receive 1 1/4 ^{lb} of meal 1/2 ^{lb} Rice— 1 ^{lb} Beef. or 1/3 ^{lb} of Bacon, per day, & 4 1/2 ^{lb} Salt. 4^{lb} Soap is allowed to 100 hands per week; and when they are at work in Mud or Water two rations of Whiskey per day. In my Division I have three Camps: two on the Mount Pleasant Side in which are encamped all the hands working in Christ Church Parish, and at and from Battery Beauregard, to the Bridge. At one of these Camps there are 50 fine Shanties — the camp-ground is high and dry, — convenient to wood, and the best water in the neighbourhood The other camp in Said Parish, is near Kinlochs landing. it is a very good one; and I have no hesitation in Saying that these two will compare favourably with the Camp of any Regiment in the Confederacy. The third Camp on Sullivans Island is not a good one, in fact it can hardly be called one. Still the Soldiers camped near them were not much better off— those hands I would have removed every night to the Mount Pleasant Side where they could use the new camps, but the objection to this is, they would have to walk 7 or 8 miles in going to, and returning from work. I have been unable to furnish them with better quarters for want of necessary material for building Shanties. I am however pleased to State that this difficulty is about being removed by a supply of Lumber, — In a Short time I hope to have finished comfortable quarters for all the hands on the Island. Each of the Camps are visited daily by a Surgeon, and an Ambulance or wagon Sent daily to convey the Sick to Hospital. The Hospital is as good and as well conducted, under the circumstances, as could possibly be expected. It is in charge of one Surgeon and two Stewarts, all of whom are attentive. It is kept in a church, — has in it two good Stoves, Bunks, Pallots, Comforts &c to meet all the wants of the patience. It is well supplied with Wood. New Straw is always used and pallets washed as they are required for the use of new patience.

I am disposed to think the dissatisfaction that exists is owing to the hands being detained in Service longer than the owners expected they would be. Much neglect and indifference is exhibited on the part of Some of the owners in Sending their Slaves badly provided with clothes and Shoes— Many are in great want of both. Besides this, many Send hands unfit for work at home or on the fortifications light as the work on the latter is— The hand in no respect are ill treated by those having charge of them, so far as my knowledge Extends. Very Respectfully

ALS   J. J. Ryan

J. J. Ryan to R. L. Singletary, 5 Dec. 1863, enclosed in R. L. Singletary to Col. D. B. Harris, 5 Dec. 1863, filed with E-463 1863, Letters Received, ser. 72, Dept. of SC, GA, & FL, Records of Military Commands, RG 109 [F-1013]. The letter of December 4 from the general superintendent of labor, which had enclosed a letter from Colonel D. B. Harris (chief engineer of the Confederate Department of South Carolina, Georgia, and Florida), has not been located. Evidently Harris had passed on a complaint about the treatment of impressed slaves originally made by William H. Trescot, member of a South Carolina legislative committee that was exploring the question of slave impressment.

274B: Commander of the Confederate Department of South Carolina, Georgia, and Florida, to the Chairman of a South Carolina Legislative Committee

Charleston S.C., Decr 10th 1863.

My Dear Sir, Your letter of the 1st instant was duly received, referred at once to the proper staff officers for their reports upon the several matters necessary for an intelligent consideration of the subject matter and due reply to your several inquiries, and, at the earliest moment practicable I hasten to make those replies:

1. The "minimum effective force" of negroes which I desire to have at the disposition of the Engineers, is 3,500; but to make up for casualties, from sickness and run-aways, I place the number at 4.000. Estimating the number of hands liable to road-service at 85.000, this will be less than 5 percent of the male negro-labor of the State, leaving out of view the large number of negro women available for and actually employed in field labor.

2. All things considered, less inconvenience will result from fixing the term of service of these negroes at 60 days, with an

arrangement in the outset by which not more than one third of the
force shall be changed at one time.

3. It is impossible to determine for what time the necessity for
this supply of labor will continue. That must depend entirely on
the operations of the enemy, which it will be our task to meet and
foil if possible: and to that end I must rely on the good sense and
patriotism of the people of South Carolina to furnish me, if
necessary, at least five per cent of their labor resources. Surely the
demand is not large.

The suggestion on the part of those gentlemen "familiar with the
habits and disposition of the troops recruited from the upper
Districts of this State," that they would "cheerfully volunteer to do
the work now conducted almost entirely by slave labor, if they were
paid for, such work the extra per-diem now paid for the service of
the negro," is not feasible and must be based on a want of
knowledge of the smallness of the force at my command – which is
barely sufficient for mere military and police duties, causing guard
duty to fall heavily on the troops. The only possible merit of such a
plan would be the sum thus added to their meagre monthly pay of
the men thus employed, but the exigencies of the service will not
admit of that. It is impracticable in every military point of view.

Indeed, My dear Sir, in consequence of the extraordinary and
culpable difficulties experienced in getting negroes for government
service, too many soldiers are already diverted from their legitimate
duties, whose places should be filled by negroes – that is, teamsters,
company-cooks and hospital nurses. We want men at this critical
hour in the fortunes of our Country; and slave owners, instead of
holding back, should come forward with their negroes to place them
freely in every possible position by means of which a soldier may be
restored to the ranks. A radical change of the policy of our people
in this particular is essential.

It is not my province to discuss the causes which have made the
State authorities unable, especially since the first of July '63, to
furnish me more than 6.250 negroes – or a monthly average of but
1,250 – that is less than a half of what I asked for, or less than 1 &
a half per cent of the male negro labor of the State. But I must be
permitted to deny the soundness of the alleged "conviction
throughout the State, that these negroes are not sufficiently or
judiciously cared for especially in sickness," as I have taken pains to
ascertain the facts and they do not warrant such a belief. The truth
is, this indisposition to furnishing negroes for military labor began
before there was the least possible grounds for the germination, or
time for the spreading of such a conviction. These negroes, you
may rest assured, as a rule, are as well fed and sheltered as our brave
soldiers, and, moreover, have as good medical attention. Of course

there have been exceptional cases of hardship and criminal
negligence, but not even as many instances of these, in proportion,
as in connexion with our troops. Can their masters ask more? —

I should prefer that some stringent and comprehensive State law
should be passed, providing for effective local organizations by
means of which all the negroes I may want shall be supplied
promptly, and thus obviate the necessity of any resort on my part to
impressments to make up deficiencies in the labor furnished by the
State officials.

I beg to suggest further, that by enactment, it should be made
the duty of *Road Commissioners*, or of other local functionaries, to
assist *Enrolling* or other Confederate *officers* or agents, if in any
sudden emergency the Commanding General of the Department
should feel obliged to resort to impressments. Some such legislation
would seem called for in view of the apparent indisposition on the
part of these local officials to render any assistance — which, I regret
to say, is reported.

I must earnestly invoke the assistance of the Legislature of the
State of South Carolina, with some means better than any which
now exist, for giving me the labor I need — and shall continue to
need so long as the enemy confronts me with such great offensive
resources. Recent exigencies elsewhere have induced the withdrawal
of a portion of my force — A still greater reduction may be
necessary for a time, in the execution of a great effort to strike our
enemies a crushing blow in some vulnerable quarter. This might
make an additional force of negroes indispensable for the safety of
Charleston. I have the honor to be, With high respect, Your Ob^{dt}
Servt

HLc   [P. G. T. Beauregard]

[General P. G. T. Beauregard] to Wm. Henry Trescott, Esqr., 10 Dec. 1863,
ch. II, vol. 32, pp. 393–95, Letters Sent, Dept. of SC, GA, & FL, Records of
Military Commands, RG 109 [F-167]. The letter is addressed to William H.
Trescot as "Chairman of House Committee for Supplying Labor for coast
defence." According to Trescot's letter of December 1, the committee had
been appointed by the South Carolina House of Representatives "to devise
some scheme which will supply the Military necessities of Coast Defence with
as little injury to the agricultural wants and as little injustice to the Farmers
and Planters, as is consistent with the proper discharge of what they consider
an imperative duty." The committee had offered the following suggestion to
General Beauregard: "In the opinion of those gentlemen most familiar with
the habits and dispositions of the troops recruited from the upper districts of
this State, it is considered certain that most of them would cheerfully volunteer to do the work now conducted almost entirely by slave labour if they were

paid for such work the extra per diem (one dollar or one dollar and a half I believe) now paid for the service of the negro. They think that the soldiers from the farming districts who are generally accustomed to manual labour would regard it as a privilege to be allowed thus to make the additional pay for the benefit of their families and that from this source a supply might be obtained which would to an appreciable extent diminish the amount of slave labour required. The Committee desire to know whether in your opinion such an experiment is practicable and if so whether there exists any Military reasons why it should not be attempted." (Wm. Henry Trescot to General Beauregard, 1 Dec. 1863, T-258 1863, Letters Received, ser. 72, Dept. of SC, GA, & FL, Records of Military Commands, RG 109 [F-983].) Beauregard based his reply to the committee upon a report by the chief engineer of the department, who had sought reports from subordinate labor superintendents. (Colonel D. B. Harris to Brig. Gen. Thomas Jordan, 5 Dec. 1865, filed with E-463 1863, Letters Received, ser. 72, Dept. of SC, GA, & FL, Records of Military Commands, RG 109 [F-1013].) For the report of one of the subordinate superintendents, see above, doc. 274A.

275: **Chief Engineer of the Confederate Department of the Gulf to a Confederate Senator from Alabama**

Mobile, Ala., Dec. 29th 1863.
Sir, In a letter to Hon. H. M. Bruce the undersigned found an opportunity to mention the advantages, that might be derived from the organization of a sufficient number of negroes into a corps of engineer-laborers to serve during the war; advantages, which must appear the more striking when compared to the system of impressment adhered to at present.

My views are based on the experience which I have gained at different periods in your own state, and as they are endorsed by Maj. Genl. Maury, the safety committee of Mobile and His Excellency Gov. Watts I cannot hesitate to lay them respectfully before you:

Negroes are generally impressed for 60 days; they arrive but seldom provided with the necessary clothes and shoes to last them for that period, much less to make the changes required by cleanliness and hygienic laws; one out of ten is unfit for work and has to be discharged at once, others will be taken sick a few days after their arrival and have to be discharged because their is no prospect of their being able to resume work during the limited period for which they are impressed, all have to undergo the process of acclimatisation to which all persons are subject who change their place of domicile and their accustomed mood of living; they have to be taught the work they have to do, when hardly beginning to understand their work they are discharged and a new gang of unexperienced hands is taking their place requiring to be taught again, and causing a more serious loss of time than any one not familiar with the construction of military works would suppose; the sums paid by the Government for transportation and for the hire of impressed negroes are enormous; the paying off of planters the amount due them for hire of negroes requires the employment of ~~an unnecessary~~ number of agents and clerks which causes in itself a considerable outlay of public money; and the payment for negroes deceased on the works will yet be the cause of much dispute   the overseers sent by planters from the several counties with their negroes are but seldom efficient and reliable men, very often not even an overseer can be obtained to escort the negroes from the counties to the point at which they have to work; the strictest vigilance is not sufficient to make these men do fully their duty; impressment agents will show partiality and show not the energy required in their position; there is an odium yet attached to the whole system and an engineer is never able to count on any given number at any given time and for any given period with a certainty.

The best plans of the most talented engineer cannot be carried out unless materials, tools and laborers be furnished to him. Materials can be found almost anywhere, tools can be manufactured and procured by purchase or temporary impressment, but laborers have been and are wanting yet. Many of the places now lost to us have been lost because they had not been properly fortified, they could not be properly fortified because laborers were wanting, an unfortunate circumstance which for instance during the late campaign in East Tennessee had very serious consequences.

The organization of a corps of Engineer-laborers in the different states would:

1. Enable the Chief Engineer of an Army or a Dept. to carry out with certainty the plans he has determined upon.

2. Render these laborers much more efficient then any number of impressed negroes will ever be

3. Save to the Government a very considerable expense

4. Do away with the defects and the odium of the impressment system. –

Could this plan be extended to teamsters and hospital-nurses many more able to bear arms would be redeemed from an inactive, unsoldierlike service. I have the honor to be Very respectfully, your obd^t ser^t.

HLcSr

V. Sheliha

V. Sheliha to Hon. C. C. Clay, 29 Dec. 1863, ch. III, vol. 12, inserted between pp. 525 and 526, Letters Sent, Engineer Office, Dept. of the Gulf, Records of Military Commands, RG 109 [F-967].

276: Headquarters of the Confederate District of West Louisiana to a Louisiana Planter

[*Alexandria, La.*] February 2nd 1864

General   By direction of the Maj Genl Comdg, I have the honor, to acknowledge receipt of your communication of 31st ult to him, and to reply thereto as follows.   As the works at Fort DeRussy, and below there on the river, are designed chiefly for the immediate, and direct protection of the Valley of Red River, It is certainly not asking too much of the planters living in that Valley to aid in the construction of said works, particularly as the aid asked for, is asked under a law of the state, which provides remuneration for such labor as the planters are called upon to furnish.   Nor was it unreasonable to expect, after negroes were called out, and sent to the works, or started there, & runaway without cause and went to their homes, that their owners would have taken steps without delay to have had them sent back,   unfortunately however, tho. the number of negroes that have runaway from Fort DeRussy, & Sabine point, and on the way to those places, has been large, in no instance have any of the negroes, been sent back by their owners, notwithstanding it is well known that in most instances the runaway negroes have gone directly home.   Under the circumstances however unpleasant it might be to the Maj Genl Comdg he had no other alternative but to send cavalry with orders, to gather up the runaway negroes, and bring them back if they could be found. Or if the identical negroes that had runaway could not be obtained to take from their respective owners, other negroes in their stead.   In individual instances as appears from your communication to be the case with you the order to take other negroes in place of the runaways may bear hardly.   But as the order was issued in a case of emergency for the public good, under the conviction that an order of any other character would not answer the purpose, the Maj Genl Comdg trusts it will be acquiesced in by all.

Every arrangement has been made at the works below, to secure the comfort & well being of negroes, that can be made.   temporary huts have been erected for their Shelter, bountiful rations are issued to them—and a skillful, Surgeon has been sent there, provided with medicines to attend them if taken sick—   Last year the rations allowed to negroes at Fort DeRussy were larger than the rations allowed to Soldiers, and this winter there has been an increase in the rations to negroes at Fort DeRussy &c over the allowance of last year. As the necessity for more labor at the works below, is urgent, and as the return to you of these three negroes which you say, Lt West took on the 31st ult. would weaken the force of an order necessary for the collection of the runaway negroes, they cannot be returned to you at present. Among the three negroes however, you represent one, as being a young fellow, of mechanical genius—and particularly useful to you on that account, and further that in consequence of having been raised about the house, he is unfitted for such work, as would be required of him at Fort DeRussy, this negro will be given up to you at any time. when you choose to substitute another in his place— I am General. Very Respectfully Your obt Servt.

HLcSr

A. H. May

A.A.A. Genl. A. H. May to Genl. G. Mason Graham, 2 Feb. 1864, ch. II, vol. 75, pp. 167–70, Letters Sent, Dist. of West LA, Trans-MS Dept., Records of Military Commands, RG 109 [F-880]. The planter's letter of January 31 has not been found in the records of the District of West Louisiana or those of the Trans-Mississippi Department.

277: Commander of the Confederate Department of Cape Fear to the Adjutant General of North Carolina

Wilmington [N.C.] 1st March 1864—

General. Yours of the 27 Ulto concerning negroes & labor has been received— I will endeavor to carry out the wishes of the Governor as far as in my power; but I must regard them as subordinate to the public necessity— I have hitherto refrained from exercising the power of impressment from an understanding with the Governor that he would furnish the details for labor upon requisition, while I would regularly cause them to be discharged at the expiration of a limited time— The supply has in no case equalled the requisition, nor in general have the relief parties been punctual— Were I to discharge all hands at the expiration of their term of service without a corresponding punctuality in the reliefs, it is manifest not only that the public safety is impaired but that the work will be indefinitely protracted—

I will endeavor to discharge by April all the negroes here by order of the Governor; but request an early answer to this letter with the views of his Excellency on this important matter the supply of labor— Should it be likely to fail, I must make arrangements accordingly and especially before that date— I am fully aware of the importance of the coming crops and the importance of this work— It is equally clear to me that of the 300000 negroes in N.C. one thousand may be spared, at whatever inconvenience to individuals for labor here— Very Respectfully

HLcSr   Sgd W. H. C. Whiting

Maj. Genl. W. H. C. Whiting to Genl. Gatlin, 1 Mar. 1864, ch. II, vol. 336, p. 207, Letters Sent, Gen. W. H. C. Whiting's Command, Dept. of NC & Southern VA, Records of Military Commands, RG 109 [F-663]. No file of letters received by Whiting survives, and the letter of February 27 from the adjutant general of North Carolina has not been found elsewhere. On March 18, Whiting wrote directly to the governor of North Carolina, lamenting the governor's "inability" to furnish additional slave laborers after April 1, but promising nevertheless to return on that date the slaves previously furnished under the governor's order. Whiting planned to apply to the Confederate War Department and the governor of Virginia for replacements, but he warned that if laborers were not forthcoming from Virginia, "I shall be compelled to resort to the power of impressment conferred on the Comdg Generals of Departments by act of Congress, though I shall do so with great reluctance and with the endeavor to burden this people as little as possible." (Maj. Genl. W. H. C. Whiting to his Excellency Gov. Vance, 18 Mar. 1864, ch. II, vol. 336, p. 222, Letters Sent, Gen. W. H. C. Whiting's Command, Dept. of NC & Southern VA, Records of Military Commands, RG 109 [F-663].) Whiting evidently did not exercise his power to impress slaves at this time and as late as January 1865 was still unwilling to do so, although he was eager to impress free blacks. (See below, doc. 283.)

278: Circular from the Headquarters of the
Confederate District of Florida

Camp Milton [*Fla.*] Ap^l 13th 1864

Circular Letter

The following instructions for Agents impressing Negroes in Marion and Alachua Counties and vicinity, will be strictly carried out.

1st The Agents will proceed with a guard to the plantations &c of any owners who, having been notified to send in their quota, have failed to do so, and will impress and take with them every suitable working hand on the place.

2nd— In all cases where impressed negroes have been run off from the officer in whose charge they were placed, the Agent will call on the owner to return the slave, or an equivalent hand, and should the owner fail to do so within a reasonable time, the Impressing Agent will proceed to impress and remove every working hand, suitable for labor on fortifications, that may be on such delinquents place.

3^d Any white person who may give passes to negroes to leave, after being impressed, will be at once arrested, and sent under charge of a guard to these H'd Q'r's—and should the party be a holder of slave property, every suitable working hand he may have will be at once impressed and removed—

Impressing Agents will report to these H'd. Q'r's. through the Chf. Qr. Master, all cases in which they act under these orders—and will exhibit them as their authority to act, to all holders of slave property concerned. The Major Genl Comd'g. deeply regrets that his fellow citizens should have been so blind to their own interests, now gravely threatened; and so deficient in a sense of duty to their country, as to necessitate the issue of the foregoing orders.

HD

Circular Letter, H'd. Q'r's. Milty. Dist. of Florida, 13 Apr. 1864, ch. II, vol. 1 1/2, pp. 131–32, Letters Sent, Dist. of FL, Dept. of SC, GA, & FL, Records of Military Commands, RG 109 [F-170]. General Patton Anderson was the commander of the district.

279: Headquarters of the Confederate Department of Alabama, Mississippi, and East Louisiana to the Chief Impressment Agent of the Department

Meridian Miss June 16 /64.

Sir. Gen Lee directs me to say that he coincides in your view with regard to the Selma Wharf & authorizes you to withdraw the laborers heretofore furnished for it. In regard to the absconding of slaves, he is of the opinion that it is largely carried by the encouragement given by owners of slaves and directs that for everyone so leaving you impress from the same owner two in his place. Respy. your ob^t Servt

HLcI   P. E. Jr

A.A.G. P. E. Jr. to F. S. Blount, 16 June 1864, ch. II, vol. 14, p. 24, Letters Sent, Dept. of AL, MS, & East LA, Records of Military Commands, RG 109 [F-211].

280: Commander of the Confederate Army of Northern Virginia to the Confederate Secretary of War

[*Petersburg, Va.*] 20th Sept. 1864

Sir, I have the honor to acknowledge the receipt of your letter of yesterday with reference to the impressment of negroes for work on fortifications &c, and thank you for the prompt measures you have taken in the premises.[1]

I think that the time has arrived when the public safety requires that we shall employ negro labor with the army in all cases where it can be used to relieve able bodied white men. The teamsters and other laborers employed in the QM department, the laborers engaged in cutting wood for mines and factories, machine shops &c and all doing mere manual labor in connection with supplying the armies, can be well taken from this class, and the white men now detailed for that purpose put in the ranks. The accession to our numbers by this means would be great, and I need not repeat what I have said as to the necessity of recruiting our armies. I understood the act of Congress of 17th Feby last as designed to clothe the Department with this authority, as its title and preamble indicate.[2] The slaves called for in my last letter for 30 days, as I understand the subject, are to be impressed in accordance with a former law passed to regulate temporary impressments of negro labor.[3] This former law is referred to in the law of the 17th February to regulate the *manner* of impressment, but not as I understand it, to limit or alter the powers conferred by the latter act. If I am correct in this view, I respectfully urge the exercise of this power by the Department without delay to the extent of replacing all detailed men in service with negroes where the latter can be used with advantage, and all white laborers in gov^t employ whose work can be done by slaves or free negroes. In addition to thus substituting negroes for whites, I recommend the impressment to be extended far enough to provide a corps of laborers for the army, to prevent the necessity of many of those temporary details that are now made, to cut wood, work on roads &c. I shall require a large force to build roads, cut & transport wood, and make other preparations for the supply & comfort of the troops at this place during the winter months. These preparations are absolutely necessary, or the health and efficiency of the army will be greatly impaired by exposure and accumulated labor. It is impossible also, owing to the proximity of the enemy to take the troops from the lines as was done last winter on the Rapidan, to do this work. Among other things that will have to be done, in order to save our animals and procure adequate supplies of fuel, a short railroad will have to be constructed to connect us with suitable wood for fuel, the green pine around us being unfit for that purpose.

I trust you will find means to give effect to these suggestions, if I am correct in my interpretation of the law. I enclose a copy of an order said to have been issued by Gen Kirby Smith, which seems to me to be in accordance with the law in the main, and would recommend that something of the same kind be done at once here.

I am informed that there is some legislation by the State on the subject of obtaining negro labor, and the Governor may, if applied to, lend us material assistance.

I beg to assure you that in my judgment it is necessary for us to use our negroes in this war, if we would maintain ourselves, and prevent them from being employed against us. I am confident that our people will contribute this species of property with as much willingness as they have all others, and no time should be lost in procuring the great addition to our resources which the use of our negroes can afford us. With great respect Your ob^t serv^t

HLS   R E Lee

Genl. R. E. Lee to Hon. Secty. of War, 20 Sept. 1864, ser. 1, vol. 42, pt. 2, p. 1260, Documents Printed in *The War of the Rebellion*, ser. 4, General Records of the Government of the CSA, RG 109 [F-1011]. Endorsements. Enclosed is an order issued in July 1864 by General E. Kirby Smith, commander of Confederate forces west of the Mississippi River. Formulated in accordance with the Confederate impressment law of February 17, 1864, Smith's order instructed officers of the Bureau of Conscription to enroll immediately all free black men between the ages of eighteen and fifty, and one-fifth of the male slaves between eighteen and forty-five, forwarding them to state rendezvous for assignment to military labor. (General Orders – No. 55, Headquarters Department Trans-Mississippi, 20 July 1864, printed in unidentified, undated newspaper clipping.) James A. Seddon, Confederate Secretary of War, replied on September 22, 1864, to General Lee's suggestion that a general impressment of blacks be conducted under the Confederate law of the previous February, to replace white men detailed for government employment and to create a permanent corps of laborers instead of the short-term impressments hitherto relied upon. Seddon informed Lee that he would proceed at once to impress, as the law authorized, up to 20,000 slave men and all the free black men, the latter "to be employed mainly in localities most exposed and where there is the greatest danger of slaves running away." He proposed that the impressed black men, free and slave, be "organized into something like companies, battalions, and regiments, after the plan adopted by the English, with reference to what they call navvies, or laborers, with superintendents and overseers in lieu of officers." (*Official Records*, ser. 1, vol. 42, pt. 2, pp. 1269–70.) Neither the thirty-day impressment of 5,000 slaves for the Army of Northern Virginia, nor Seddon's more general impressment under the law of February 1864, obtained laborers enough to meet General Lee's requirements.

On December 11, 1864, Lee reported that no more than 2,000 slaves had been forwarded, even though the thirty-day term had been extended to sixty days; moreover, many had deserted, leaving only 1,200 still at work. "Of the negroes called for under the act of February 17, 1864," Lee added, "I have not yet received enough to replace the white teamsters . . . [and] Not one has yet been received for laboring purposes." (*Official Records*, ser. 1, vol. 42, pt. 3, p. 1267.)

1 On September 17, 1864, General Robert E. Lee had informed James A. Seddon, Confederate Secretary of War, of the "immediate necessity for the services of 5,000 negroes for thirty days" to construct fortifications around Richmond and Petersburg, on the James River, at Danville, and on the South Side and Danville railroads. Lee understood that he, as a commanding general, possessed the power to impress even those slaves engaged in food production, which Seddon could not do; but he asked that the War Department's Bureau of Conscription be ordered to execute the impressment. Seddon had replied on September 19 that he concurred in Lee's understanding of their respective powers and promised to act immediately upon his request. In an order dated September 21, Seddon directed the Bureau of Conscription to impress 5,000 slaves for military labor with the Army of Northern Virginia, in accordance with a schedule of county quotas published with the order. (*Official Records*, ser. 1, vol. 42, pt. 2, pp. 1256–57, 1260, 1268–69.)
2 The act was titled "An Act to increase the efficiency of the Army by the employment of free negroes and slaves in certain capacities," and its preamble explained that "the efficiency of the Army is greatly diminished by the withdrawal from the ranks of able-bodied soldiers to act as teamsters, and in various other capacities in which free negroes and slaves might be advantageously employed." It made all free black men between the ages of eighteen and fifty liable to military labor; authorized the Confederate Secretary of War to hire as many as 20,000 slave men from their masters; and further authorized him to impress up to 20,000 slave men if military laborers were still needed after impressing the free blacks and hiring slaves. (*Official Records*, ser. 4, vol. 3, p. 208.)
3 General Order 138, issued by the Confederate Adjutant and Inspector General's Office on October 24, 1863, published instructions to execute the section of a law of March 26, 1863, that related to the impressment of slave laborers. The order stated that commanding generals had the power to decide when impressment was necessary, and specified which slaves could be impressed and for how long – prohibiting the impressment of slaves employed as domestic servants or (until December) slaves engaged exclusively in food production; limiting impressment to 5 percent of a county's slave population; and naming sixty days as the usual period of impressment. (*Official Records*, ser. 4, vol. 2, pp. 897–98.)

281: Chief Surgeon of a Confederate Hospital for Black Military Laborers to the Chief Engineer of the Confederate Department of Northern Virginia

Engineer Hospital Richmond Decr 16th 1864

Sir I beg leave to make the following report in reference to Some statements in a communication addressed by Mr W[m] F Macklin to the Hon: Robt: Whitfield M.C., in which it is said that he learns "through servants returned from the fortifications at Richmond that his man Dudly is very ill in the Hospital & that he has very little attention, & also that the sick in the Hospital are very much neglected & almost starved"

I am aware that you know there is *no truth* in thes statements, but in order to satisfy other parties, you will pardon me for giving the following details

Dudly Slave of W[m] F Macklin was received into the Hospital on the 27th day of Nov:, Suffering from an Epidemic disease of the Brain & Spinal cord of a terribly fatal character, & died on the 2nd day of Decr.,

This man soon sunk into stupor & though he received every attention from the attending Surgeon & nurses he died on the 6th day of his admission in a state of profound coma I mentioned to you in a former report the great fatality of this disease, & that many writers on the disease, of the most extensive experience had never seen a case recover under any circumstances, or treatment. I am glad to state that the disease has been arrested by abandoning the camp at which it occured

I wish to say a few words in regard to the general charge of neglect at this Hospital

The wards are visited every day by the attending Surgeon, as often as the necessities of the sick require, & every patient is carefully examined & prescribed for; every prescription is written in a book kept for the purpose, & the medicines are prepared by a practical & skillful Druggist. The medicines are then distributed to two ward masters, (intelligent & competent white men), & by them given to the patients according to their respective prescriptions. The ward masters, assited by a Sufficient number of trained coloured nurses, are under the immediate controul of the steward, (who has a general Supervision of the Hospital), & remain constantly in the building day & night & give all necessary attention to the patients —

Particular attention is paid to the diet of the patients. Fresh beef, & beef soup chickens & chicken soup, eggs, milk, Rice, stewed fruit, apples & Peaches, Potatoes, molasses Tea & Sugar are furnished them in such quantities as the nature of the disease & the

circumstances of the patients require. It is often necessary to
restrict the diet of the patient – hence possibly the charge of
starvation. Brandy or whiskey is always given them when
prescribed

The Wards are kept clean & neat, well lighted, well heated &
ventilated   The mortality of this Hospital will compare favourably
with any in the Confederacy.

It is regreted that Mr Macklin did not visit the Hospital to see
the condition of the patients & the attention they receive, instead of
relying upon the statements of servants who are proverbially prone
to give false testimony   The Hospital is always open to the
inspection of the public, & thos interested are invited to visit it &
satisfy themselves that their Slaves receive proper attention –   Very
Respectfully Yr obt: Servt:

ALS   R. S. Vest

[*Endorsement*]   Head qtrs Eng[r] Dept: D.N.V Richmond. 16th Decr.
1864   Respectfully forwarded to Eng[r] Bureau – And I endorse the
statements of D[r] Vest, fully as to the unvarying good treatment and
care bestowed on all sick negroes at the Hospital of this Dept: The
orders of Gen[l] Stevens have been to spare no expense in procuring
food suitable for sick, medicines or whatever would add to their
well being or comfort. Since I have been in charge of the Dept: my
orders have been similar and I have no reason to believe that they
have been departed from in a single instance –

The building used is one of the best in the city for Hospital
purposes, is kept *clean*, well heated (temperature regulated by
Thermometer) and is well ventilated

As to the treatment of the particular diseases, that is a
professional matter on which I can give no opinion – But will state
that I have every confidence in the skill of D[r] Vest and know him to
be prompt & constant in his attendance –   The pr cent of mortality
at this Hospital will compare favorably with that of any Hospital in
the confederacy. Capt Snead, the Adj[t] of the Dept lives in the
building and has immediate supervision and no Officer in the
Confederate service would more certainly check all cruelty or with
more promptness report the official neglect of the officers and
employees in the discharge of their duties –

The statement of negroes are generally unreliable. They will
invent any statement of hard usage & starvation to justify their
owners in keeping them from their duty, very many having run
off. I believe there is a disinclination on the part of the slaves to
labor on the defensive works, resulting not from hard usage or
starvation but from a disinclination to do labor that will thwart the

Federals, who they look upon as fighting for their freedom and to which all are looking forward as being near at hand—

As to the reliable gentleman from So hampton Co, who avouches for the negroes statements—He must have drawn on his imagination for his knowledge For there has been no slave from that county on the Ric^d defences since the organization of this Dept: in July 1862.

The invariable plea from that county, when the various impressments have been made, was that if attempted to be enforced in that *county* that the negroes would run to the Yankees, showing the utter demorelazation of the slaves & showing that the owners regarded their right & authority over their slaves was so frail as to preclude all attempts at controll or discipline—

Letter of Mr Maclin, herewith— W. G. Turpin Capt Eng^r & acting Chief Cons^n D.N.V

Surg. in chg. R. S. Vest to Capt. W. G. Turpin, 16 Dec. 1864, V-110 1864, Letters Received, ser. 5, Sec. War, RG 109 [F-98]. Another endorsement referred to Dr. Vest as the surgeon in charge of "the negro Hospital." In the margin alongside the second paragraph of Vest's letter, but in a different handwriting, is the notation "omit." In the same file is the letter from William T. Maclin of Hicksford, Virginia, to a Confederate congressman, in which Maclin had reported rumors about the ill-treatment of his slave Dudley. Maclin noted that "these reports of starvation & neglect are causing the negro men to run to the Yankees in great numbers, so as to avoid the draft." "Neglect of our negroes," warned the slaveholder, "will certainly recruit the Yanke army most effectually." (Wm. T. Maclin to Hon. Robt. Whitfield, 4 Dec. 1864.)

282: Virginia Farmer to the Confederate Secretary of War

Keysville V^a Dec 17th 1864.

Sir   About the 10th of October a number of slaves were by your order and authority impressed in Charlotte County Virginia to labor on the fortifications near Richmond for *30 days.* This is earlier than farmers in this County are generally ready to supply their slaves with winter clothing shoes &c and as they had only two or three days notice (on account of the urgency of the call) many of them went off but poorly equpped even for a period of 30 days when the weather was comparatively mild.   More than 60 days have now elapsed and although we have made dilligent inquiry we have been unable to hear any thing from our negros.   We know from past experience and observation that negros impressed for the fortifications are generally badly treated and suffer much. We know too that the overseers detailed from the army to attend to them regardless of the good of the service as of the welfare of the slaves often keep them as long as possible in order to prolong their own detail from the army.

It is therefore to be feared that these negros unexpectedly detained and poorly provided have suffered greatly and are still suffering. Many of them have run away and are now at home thus leaving the labor the hardship and exposure of these winter months to the faithful few who have chosen to stay and obey orders.

It is then no longer a question of property and value but of justice and humanity and I respectfully submit it to your Honor whether it would not be fairer and better to discharge each levy at the end of the 30 days and order a new one. If you will be so kind as to inform me or refer me to the proper person who can inform me where those slaves are under whose care and to whom a communication with regard to them may be addressed you will very greatly oblige Your humble Serv'

ALS   Horace P Lacy

Horace P. Lacy to Hon. James A. Seddon, 17 Dec. 1864, L-361 1864, Letters Received, ser. 5, Sec. War, RG 109 [F-89]. In an endorsement dated December 26, 1864, the Secretary of War noted: "There is much force in these views. New call has been made." Another endorsement.

283: Commander of the 3rd Military District of the Confederate Department of North Carolina and Southern Virginia to the Governor of North Carolina

                                    Wilmington [*N.C.*] Jany: 4 1864 [*1865*]
Sir, While our recollection of Christmas day & Fort Fisher is fresh, let me beg your aid & cooperation in getting immediately as large a force of free negroes as possible.

I need labor always now especially. We must not let our last place go for want of work, still less because we have foiled the enemy's first effort must we fold our arms and say enough has been done. In every department, I need force, laboring force. I am earnestly desirous of releasing all slaves, especially in view of the complaints I learn relative to clothing them. That is not my fault. I have done all in my power to provide Clothing for negroes; even to overstepping the limits of my authority. It has been

729

literally due to want of money & material. Still, the reports are greatly exaggerated, for many negroes have been sent here totally unprovided in the first instance by their masters.

But at all times I am unwilling to impress. The act provides for the conscription of free negroes before impressing the slaves[1] & I hope with your aid & that of your militia organization to obtain a sufficient number of free negroes & to get back those that have deserted.

An enrolled corps of 1200 to 1500 free negroes properly organized into companies according to regulation, entitled to furlough at proper times, fed, clad and paid and retained in service, would relieve the people of the state of all use of their slaves for the defence here. With my works so well advanced, I can preserve their condition & provide all I want of new constructions with such a force.

If we can get it in the state, I will guarantee the exemption of the slave labor as far as we are concerned here. Please to let me hear from you.

I have written to Col. Mallett   Very Respfy

HLcSr   (Sgd) W. H. C. Whiting

Maj. General W. H. C. Whiting to His Excellency Gov. Vance, 4 Jan. 1864 [1865], ch. II, vol. 338, Letters Sent, Gen. W. H. C. Whiting's Command, Dept. of NC & Southern VA, Records of Military Commands, RG 109 [F-690]. As the war entered its final months, other Confederate commanders also had difficulty feeding and clothing slave and free black military laborers. In March 1865, the commander of the Post of Danville, Virginia, requested additional rations for laborers on the fortifications at that post. The food then being issued to them was, he argued, "inadequate to maintain their physical strength to a degree sufficient for them to perform the labour required – (1/3) one third of a pound of meat, & 2 gills of sorghum, alternately, and 1 lb of *unsifted* corn meal – being the maximum amt: of issue authorized by orders from the subsistence Dept: – " As a result, he reported, "it is *impossible* with any means at my disposal to retain the hands at work – they *will* run off, & their owners knowing that they have not a sufficiency of food rather encourage them in deserting – " He concluded that the cost of increased rations would be of less consequence than further delay in constructing the defenses. (Col. R. E. Withers to Gen. J. C. Breckenridge, 29 Mar. 1865, W-72 1865, Letters Received, ser. 5, Sec. War, RG 109 [F-101].)

1 Presumably the act adopted by the Confederate Congress on February 17, 1864, which declared all free black men liable to impressment and authorized military authorities to impress slave men only after first impressing free blacks. (*Official Records*, ser. 4, vol. 3, pp. 207–9.)

MAINTAINING SOUTHERN INDUSTRY AND TRANSPORT

284: Virginia Millers to the Confederate Secretary of War

Lynchburg [*Va.*] Sept. 25 1861

We have this minute recd your Telegram saying "I understand from Gov Letcher that, the impressment is made from an order of Court under the law of Virginia & I therefore decline to interfere.

By reference to Co[l] Northrop you will find that we are manufacturing Flour for the Government. These negroes are a part of our milling force and are essential to the fulfillment of our contract. The order only requires 30 men & there are in the County over 150 able bodied free negroe men. This we learn from the Sheriff of the County. The committee appointed to collect the negroes have taken 1/5 of the whole amount required from us, (Coopers) which leaves our force intirely inadequate to fill our contract. If these hands could be replaced we would make no effort to reclaim them, But so great is the demand for coopers, that thay are not to be had any where. It seems there was a committee appointed by our City Court to collect 20 for the same purpose. Our Mayor, readily released all Mechanics, especially those engaged upon work for the Government   If after considering the above facts, you think it right to interfere, we would be pleased for you to do so immediately in as much as our supply of Barrels is cut short by some 80 or 100 Barrels per Day.

We would farther state that we deem these hands as much essential to our operations, as millers, who are released by the Gov'[s] Proclamation.   Very Respctfully Your Obt Sevts

Langhorne & Scott

The names of the Negroes we wish released are
Lorenzo Harris
Lorenzo Scott
Jno M Steuart
Elihu [Buintes]
W[m] Henry Steuart
Tom Scott

HLS

Langhorne & Scott to Hon. J. P. Benjamin, 25 Sept. 1861, #5910 1861, Letters Received, ser. 5, Sec. War, RG 109 [F-43]. Earlier the same day, the

Confederate Secretary of War had telegraphed his refusal to interfere with the impressment ordered by the governor of Virginia. (J. P. Benjamin to Messrs. Langhorne & Scott, 25 Sept. 1861, ch. IX, vol. 34, p. 16, Telegrams Sent, Sec. War, RG 109 [F-43].) No further response to Langhorne and Scott has been found in the records of the Confederate Secretary of War.

285: Agent for a Virginia Coal Mine to the Confederate Secretary of War

Richmond Mar 14 1862

Sir   The Carbon Hill Mines in this county are operated by a working force of about one hundred Slaves; and the product of their labor, in Natural Coke, presents the only substitute yet discovered in this region of country for anthracite Coal. Early in the fall I came under engagement with Thos. T. Giles esq Supt Public Buildings, and Capt Whitfield of the Qr Masters Department to supply the War, Post Office & Treasury Departments, and all of the Hospitals in Richmond & Manchester with this fuel. In addition to this I have continued to furnish the Laboratory & various workshops in the employment of the Government

In consideration of the engagement with the Government, it was promised me at the time that any miners serving in the army who might be essential to my operations would be detailed upon application. This privilege I have thus far managed to dispense with. The action of our state Government, however, has deprived me of the services of the only two overseers I had left; and without whom it will not be possible to continue operations. It is indispensable to the safety of the negro operatives, as well as to the preservation of the works, that intelligent and experienced white men should constantly supervise and control their labor. It is of the greatest importance that our work should be unremittingly pressed forward during spring, summer & autumn, as the only possible means of supplying the wants even of the Government during the next winter.

I therefore am constrained to ask that you will grant discharges for John Houston and W^m M Wade (Recruiting Station Richmond) Courtney^s Artillery 7th Brigade Army of Potomac

These men have been induced to muster into the service of the Confederacy to avoid the call upon the militia; and will cheerfully return to my service if simply discharged, without involving the Department in the trouble incident upon a detail. They have not drawn and will not receive the bounty if discharged or if it must be received I will contribute the amount to the fund for the benefit of the soldiers fund. Very Respy & faithfully

ALS

Jno. J. Werth

Jno. J. Werth to the Hon. J. P. Benjamin, 14 Mar. 1862, W-383 1862, Letters Received, ser. 12, Adjt. & Insp. Gen., RG 109 [F-277]. Endorsements indicate that the overseers were discharged as requested.

286: South Carolina Engineer to the Confederate Secretary of War

Charleston September 6th 1862

Dear Sir   Allow me the liberty of asking a question and that is weather you or Goverment allow Negroes to Run Steam Boats as Engineers in the Confederate States. at the time the Planter was Stolen they had a negro Engineer on Board   he was the one carrid her out   I think myself and i speak for others it is hard that they Should put an Negro Engineer, in a Boat where they Should put a white man, and more over, look at the lives men woman and children which is on Board. now sir let me say a word to you in Relation to Engineers   I am one my self and it is hard that after we have serve our time at the Business, and for the owners of Steam Boats to put negro Engineers, before us   the owner Mr Ferguson of all the Boats which Runs here has negros as Engineers   I ask you is it right or not, white men Should be in the Boats and not Black ones, please Let me hear from you on this Question. Most Respectfully. most obt Servt

ALS

D. W. Davis

D. W. Davis to Secty. of War, 6 Sept. 1862, D-485 1862, Letters Received, ser. 5, Sec. War, RG 109 [F-53]. No reply has been found in the records of the Confederate Secretary of War. See above, doc. 23, for the liberation of the *Planter* by Robert Smalls.

287: Railroad President to the Confederate Secretary of War

Richmond, July 9th: *1863.*

Sir   I have received a communication from G. W. Lay Lt Col. A.A.G. acting Chief of Bureau, stating that the Governor of North

Carolina objects to the Government of the Confederate States calling out the free negroes in that State, to work on the Piedmont Railroad. May I ask if any steps have been taken to procure the use of those negroes and with what success? without those negroes but little progress can be made on the work during the current year. Indeed if the Company is left (unaided by the Government) to procure labor I very much apprehend that no reliance can be placed on the use of the Road for through transportation for some time to come. I can only promise that no effort will be left untried hereafter as none has been left untried heretofore to prosecute the work with energy and expedition. I have thought proper to make this statement in order to prevent the Government from making erroneous calculations upon the early completion of the work   Respectfully

ALS   Lewis E Harvie

Lewis E. Harvie to Hon. James A. Seddon, 9 July 1863, H-468 1863, Letters Received, ser. 5, Sec. War, RG 109 [F-77]. Endorsement. Harvie was president of both the Richmond and Danville Railroad and the Piedmont Railroad. Confederate officials had urged the impressment of half the free black men of North Carolina to speed completion of the Piedmont Railroad. (Col. J. F. Gilmer to Hon. James A. Seddon, 9 June 1863, G-285 1863, Letters Received, ser. 5, Sec. War, RG 109 [F-77].) No reply to Harvie's letter has been found in the records of the Confederate Secretary of War.

288: Railroad Director to the Confederate Secretary of War

Selma Ala: 15 – February 1864

Sir; Some facts of a character so important, as in my estimation to be worthy of the most earnest consideration, have come to my knowledge by information deemed reliable. These facts I feel constrained to communicate to you, although you may have derived information of them from other sources. Among the greatest needs of the Government, (to say nothing of the imperitive wants of the agricultural community) maybe reconed a proper supply of iron for the construction of war vessels, and materials of war, such as shot and shell. But you are much better informed on this subject than I am. Equally important are the means for transportation, principally by rail road. Being a director of two important roads, I can speak from personal knowledge in relation to them. I refer to the Alabama and Mississippi rivers, and the Alabama and Tennessee river roads. The iron on both of these roads is good, and will last for years; but there is a scarcity of rolling stock; and it is of the utmost importance to keep what they have in proper repair, and to replace such as may be worn out by constant usage. For this purpose, two things are indispensible; a supply of iron, (now wanting) and a sufficient number of competent mechanics and workmen. There is probably no portion of the world, where the natural facilities for making iron on a large scale, and of superior quality, are greater than in the region intersected by the Alabama and Tennessee road, where inexhaustible quantities of coal suitable for making iron (either in the raw state or as coak) are in convenient proximity to equally inexhaustible deposites of suprior iron ore. The only serious obstacles in the way of the production of an abundant supply of iron, are a sufficiency of laborers to supply fuel for the blast furnaces for making pig iron, and workmen skilled in the business of converting the pig into wrought iron; and there is now a defficiency of both. Unfortunately nearly all of these workmen are foreigners from Europe, or natives of the Northern states, the majority being foreigners. These men do not feel identified in any great degree with the South, and are not imbued with sentiments and feelings calculated to impress them so strongly in favor of our cause, as to induce them to make any great sacrifices of interest or feeling in its behalf. They are generally without families; at least many of them have no families or family ties here. So far, those of them who have remained, have been induced to do so by the very high wages paid them. They are deprived of what have become luxuries here, but before the war were regarded as necessaries from their general use; while absolute necessaries are so dear as to require the greater portion, not to say the whole of their wages for support. It is understood that wages of this class of workmen have become high in the United States, where the necessaries of life and goods of all kinds are comparatively very cheap. If these men were left to draw their own conclusions from these facts, uninfluenced by other causes, it is but reasonable to conclude that more or less of them would be induced to leave this country. But in addition to the causes mentioned above, powerful, and no doubt systematic influences are at work to entice them away; and unless these influences are speedily counteracted, there is great danger that a large portion of those who remain (a good many have left heretofore) will be drawn away. I am informed that a secret circular from Gen[l] Grant has got among the workmen in this region, offering them strong inducements to go to the United States. It is stated and believed, that he offers them a bounty of $600, with liberty to go where they please, and with exemption from military service. There is reason to believe, that he does not rely on secret circulars, but that emissaries have been sent into the country to entice these men away. I am informed that a

735

considerable number of them have recently been induced to leave Georgia. By avoiding the public routes, and places where our scouts and cavalry are stationed, they can easily get within the lines of the enemy, or across the borders into Tennessee. Other influences having the same tendency, are in operation. I allude to the course pursued by some of the conscript officers. Recently, a considerable number of the workmen employed at one of the principal iron works, were summoned to a conscript camp, contrary to express orders which had been issued by Gen[l] Pillow, who had prohibited interference with men employed in the iron establishments. After being detained at camp for a time, they were permitted to return to their work. These men without knowing or enquiring into the reason for such proceedings, are apt to regard their position as insecure, and to conclude that if they can be thus summarily taken from their work to a conscript camp, they may some day be suddenly summoned into the field. On another occasion, a body of cavalry was sent to the same works to surround them for the purpose of catching one of the workmen who had been detailed, but about whose detail there was some alledged irregularity. He succeeded in eluding the cavalry, and quit the employment of the company, and may have left the country. The effect of such proceedings is unfortunate, and any thing but assuring to these workmen. They are as a class, very clanish, and what they regard as harsh treatment of any one of their number, is resented by all. True policy would I think dictate the most liberal and assuring course toward men so indispensible to our cause, and who at best are held by so insecure a tenure. Having alluded to the iron, coal and rail road interests, I beg leave at the risk of trespassing beyond reasonable measure on your valuable time, to refer to another matter of great importance, in connection with them. From some cause or other, it is much more difficult now to procure laborers than it was a year ago, even at double the prices usual then. There is a great deficiency of laborers on the two rail roads with which I am connected, so that the roads cannot be kept in proper repair; and both of these roads are mainly occupied in transporting for the Government; one in transporting iron and coal to Selma; the other in transporting supplies of various kinds, including shot and shell, and not unfrequently, troops, for the army of Mississippi   Both these roads require a considerable amount of work to put and keep them in proper condition.

With the requisite number of laborers, the production of coal and iron could be very largely increased. Most of the iron furnaces in this state have been out of blast since the first of this year, being short of fuel. Being run exclusively with charcoal, the laborers they have been able to command are insufficient to keep up a supply of fuel; and this difficulty is becoming greater, as the forests near the furnaces are consumed. Unless some means can be devised for increasing the number of laborers, it will I fear be impossible to furnish the government with any thing like a competent supply of iron; leaving [out] of view the necessities of the planting community, a large portion of whom are almost entirely destitute of iron, and in a great measure of proper implements needed in preparing for and cultivating their crops. One plan suggests itself to me by which it is probable that a competent number of negro laborers for the purpose above refered to, may be obtained. It is supposed that Congress has passed or will pass an act rendering a certain proportion of negroes liable to conscription for certain kinds of military service. Should there be such an act, it would probably be competent for you or the president to make a regulation in connection with the act, by which those owners who shall furnish by hiring or otherwise, a portion of their negroes to work on rail roads, and in making iron, and mining coal, shall have credit therefor in any call for negroes under the act, as if they were in military service. Uless this is done, or unless a portion of the negroes who may be called into service, can be detailed in these employments, the difficulties of procuring laborers will be greatly enhansed by such an act. As rail roads, iron establishments, and coal mining are so indispensible to the military service, they may be fairly regarded as a portion of it, so as to render details for them under any military law, legitimate and proper. Unless an increase of laborers can be obtained by some such means as this, it will probably become indispensible to resort directly to impressments. The first plan suggested would be far more satisfactory, and better in every respect. I hope the importance of the subjects refered to, if not the value of the suggestions I have taken the liberty to offer, will be deemed a fair apology for this, I fear, too great trespass. Most Respectfully yours

ALS

J. W. Lapsley

J. W. Lapsley to Honl. J. A. Seddon, 15 Feb. 1864, L-68 1864, Letters Received, ser. 5, Sec. War, RG 109 [F-88]. In an endorsement dated February 27, the Confederate Secretary of War noted: "The Law of Congress does this to a Limited extent & will be executed." Approved on February 17, the new law made all free black men liable to impressment; authorized Confederate military authorities to hire as many as 20,000 slave men; and provided that, when unable to hire enough slave laborers and after having impressed all free black men, military authorities might impress as many as 20,000 slave men. Neither the law nor the enforcement procedures announced by the Confederate War Department included regulations resembling those proposed by Lapsley. (*Official Records*, ser. 4, vol. 3, pp. 207–9.)

289: Commander of the 3rd Military District of the Confederate Department of North Carolina and Southern Virginia to the Confederate Adjutant and Inspector General

Wilmington [N.C.] June 16th 1864.

Gen'l: I beg leave to call your attention to the fact that the R.R. Bureau or some other bureau in Richmond have lately commenced the practice of sending here to work in the shops a number of Yankee mechanics who have either been taken prisoners & refused to be exchanged or are deserters or have left the enemies lines to avoid the war. I protest against these men being sent here. They have the worst possible effect upon the negroes with whom they constantly associate. I cannot regard them in any other light than spies or incendiaries. My troops have taken many in the act of making their way to the enemy's lines. Please to inform me whether I shall send those taken up as alien enemys to Salisbury N.C or to the Georgia prison. Very respectfully

HLcSr   signed W. H. C. Whiting

Maj. Gen'l. W. H. C. Whiting to Gen'l. S. Cooper, 16 June 1864, ch. II, vol. 336, p. 338, Letters Sent, Gen. W. H. C. Whiting's Command, Dept. of NC & Southern VA, Records of Military Commands, RG 109 [F-665].

290: Chief Impressment Agent of the Confederate Department of Alabama, Mississippi, and East Louisiana to the Headquarters of the Department

Mobile June 23rd 1864.

Major, The letter of M. B Prichard Chief Engineer & Supt of Rail Road from Demopolis to McDowell's Landing, with its reference to me for vigorous and prompt action, and for report, is received this morning

Referring to my letter to you of 6th inst, and to the accompany papers numbered from 1 to 6 inclusive, you will perceive that several causes have conspired to delay the furnishing of the entire number of hands required by the orders of Genl Polk, and repeated by Genl Lee, for the completion of the Road. –

The lettes to Mr Nevill, Impressing Agent for Sumter County, in its northern division, show that the planters of that county resisted an impressment of their negroes upon the ground, that there was no authority conferred on the Secretary of War, or Genl Polk, to order an impressment of their slaves to work for the benefit of a *private* corporation, and the same [idea] prevails in Greene County as you

738

will perceive from Genl Kerr's letter N° 7. – Counsel [were] employed, who gave it as [their] opinion that the [Act] of Congress of 17th Feb 1864 did not warrant any order for impressment unless for work on "fortifications, or in government works for the production or preparation of materials of war, or in military hospitals" – and that an impressing agent would render himself liable to prosecution under an act of the Legislature of the State of Alabama, which inflicted severe penalties for its violation. –

Acting under this impression, Wm H. Nevill Esq the agent of this office, resigned his commission – feeling unwilling to encounter the hostility of the planters who had refused to permit their slaves to be impressed for work on the Rail Road. – I returned Mr Nevill his commission, and urged upon him the necessity of still aiding the Government – his position and influence as a citizen, giving him deservedly a high position in the estimation of the people of Sumter. – Judge Reavis of Sumter came to the city during the progress of this correspondence, and being interested himself in this question, and having concurred in the opinion that the negroes could not be impressed under the act of 17th Feby 1864 – I called his attention to the act of 26th March 1863 – the 9th section of which provided labor [for all] "public works" in which the Government was engaged – He agreed in [the? opinion] with me that the negroes could be impressed for any public [work] under this law, and Mr Nevill was advised accordingly, and I presume that he is now diligently engaged in procuring them – See copy of my letter to him of 16th June. –

On 7th of June I sent one of my special agents, Vernon H. Linderberger, to Sumter and Marengo Counties, to have these negroes furnished to the full number required. – He was met on his arrival at Gainesville by the condition of affairs as stated in the preceding paragraph, and brought me a letter from Mr Nevill informing me of their existence, and that the negroes could not be procured. – The first instructions to Mr Lindenburger No. 3. are dated 7th June; the second N° 5. on the 16th. – The first were prepared, and Mr Lindenberger despatched on the next day after the receipt of Genl Lee's telegram on the [subject.] Mr Lindenberger *is now* in Sumter and Marengo, urging the collection of the entire number of negroes required. –

Mr Sherrol, the Superintendant of labor on the road, was in my office this morning, and informs me, that of One Hundred and fifteen negroes at work on the road, all but forty five ran off, and that as at present organized, it is difficult to keep them at their work. – My sub-agents have all along been instructed to take two negroes for every one, who runaway from the public works, where they have any reason to think their owners connive at their escape. –

I have had three seperate calls made upon me to re-furnish the 43
hands required for the telegraph line between Selma and Rome,
Georgia. — On each occasion after the hands were replaced, they
escaped to their homes within a very short period after they were so
returned to the Superintendant. — On the last occasion the Special
agent sent by me reached Mobile on the 7th of June by boat from
Selma, [and] reported that the full number required by Mr Roche
had been [delivered] to him — yet within an hour afterwards, M^r
Roche telegraphed [me] that all but fifteen had run off again. — I
at once sent a special messenger to return them for the fourth time,
with instructions as before given, to take two for one, where the
negro was retained by the owner and not sent back, or knowingly
receiving the negro on his escape. — The Special Agent is now
engaged in returning these negroes. —

In order to obviate as much as possible, the objections of many
planters to their negroes being sent to the fortifications at and near
Mobile, when public works requiring labor were being constructed
in their own, and adjoining counties, I have directed impressing
agents in such counties, to deliver the negroes impressed by them,
to the Superintendants [at?] the nearest public works. — I am
satisfied that the whole thing was [wrong?], and that negroes should
not be put to work, in or near the [counties] of their owners
residence, but as far off as possible. — They are more easily
controlled, and their chances of running away successfully very
much decreased. — I shall therefore, so soon as the crops of wheat
rye, and oats, are gathered, and negroes from the extreme eastern
portion of the state reach here, send a sufficient number of them to
relieve the negroes at work on the Demopolis & McDowell's landing
Rail Road, and bring the negroes there to Mobile, and place them
on the fortifications here. — I know no other means by which this
stampeding of negroes can be prevented, unless a large military
patrol is kept up wherever public works are carried on by slave
labor. —

I send herewith a letter received from John W. DuBose Esq this
morning explaining the causes why the One Hundred and Sixty five
negroes from Marengo have not been forthcoming. —

The difficulty of procuring military assistance to hasten the tardy
patriotism of some of our planters has to a very great extent retarded
the operations of Messrs Houston & DuBose, and the unprincipled
conduct of some owners in furnishing their negroes with passes on
the eve of leaving, with instructions to return home on the first
favorable opportunity, accounts for the spirit of absenteeism with
which nearly all the negroes seem imbued. —

You have in the foregoing remarks, and the correspondence and
orders to Sub-agents, the facts furnished for a distinct appreciation

of the efforts made by me to supply the labor required for the
public works at Demopolis and Selma, for the Rail Road and
telegraph line. –

*The difficulty principally lies in retaining the labor when furnished, and
I here call your attention to the peculiar phraseology of the reports to Head
Quarters, which merely state that the writer has only so many hands for the
work, without stating that he has permitted the slaves furnished him to
escape, leaving the inference (which is a very natural one) that the number
they [have] were* ALL *the hands that were furnished to them.* –

I express the hope that the military assistance which has been
furnished to Mʳ DuBose may, whenever there is any need of it, be
promptly called out to aid my sub-agents in keeping up the number
of hands necessary to complete a road so vitally important to the
protection of the very individuals, whose highest patriotic impulses
never ascend above their own petty and [. . .] schemes for the
accumulation of wealth. – I am very respectfully &c

F. S. Blount

P.S. June 24ᵗʰ Since the foregoing was written, Genl Lee's
despatch of this date is received. –

I have ordered by telegraph, V. H. Linderberger Esq. Special
Agent, to report to him, and obtain if necessary, military
assistance. – The gathering of the crops *now*, and the planting of
them in the *first instance*, to some extent accounts for the tardiness
of well disposed persons to send forward their negroes. –

ALS

F. S. Blount to Major P. Ellis, Jr., 23 June 1864, #1134 1864, Letters &
Telegrams Received, ser. 93, Dept. of AL, MS, & East LA, Records of Military
Commands, RG 109 [F-1001]. The enclosures mentioned are in the file. Also
in the same file is the letter from M. B. Prichard, chief engineer of the Alabama
and Mississippi Rivers Railroad, that had been forwarded to Blount for report.
Prichard had complained that "the requisitions of this Road for Negroes have
not been complied with," that no more than forty-five impressed blacks were
then at work on the railroad, and that it would be impossible to complete the
Tombigbee connection by the end of the year unless 350 men were furnished
immediately. "The negroes," Prichard had concluded, "runaway to their
owners and are not returned to the work by them." (M. B. Prichard to Maj.
Thos. Peters, 18 June 1864.) In one of the documents enclosed in Blount's
report, William Kerr, the impressment agent for Greene County, Alabama,
reported that "[t]he Planters in this Section are very much averse to sending
their hands to work on the R.R. from Demopolis to MᶜDowels Landing – They
say that . . . it is an advantage taken of the Planters & in this way they [the
railroad stockholders] get their road finished for nothing – They make the
farmer do the work & the Gov't. pay for it – " Kerr also reported that the slaves
previously sent to Demopolis for work on the railroad had run away, returning
to their masters with complaints that "their provisions were all taken away from

them, and that they had been inhumanely treated." (Wm. Kerr to Col. F. S. Blount, 20 June 1864.) Soon thereafter, Blount told another of his subordinate agents that completion of the Demopolis & McDowells Landing Railroad "depends on the Keeping of the negro laborers." "The road is too important to the Government to have its completion delayed by the cause of their absconding, either voluntarily, or by the agency, and connivance of their owners." Blount ordered the agent to obtain from the railroad superintendent the names of impressed slaves who had "absconded from said works" and the names and residences of their owners, then to arrest all such slaves and return them to the railroad. (F. S. Blount to Vernon H. Lindenberger, Esq., 2 July 1864, enclosed in F. S. Blount to Maj. William Elliot, 6 July 1864, #1228 1864, Letters & Telegrams Received, ser. 93, Dept. of AL, MS, & East LA, Records of Military Commands, RG 109 [F-200].)

291: Superintendent of a Confederate Armory to the Confederate Chief of Ordnance

Macon Ga. November 15th 1864

Colonel, The question of negro labor required at this Armory during the ensuing year should now be considered, with reference to the best means of securing it – and I therefore respectfully direct your attention to the subject, in the hope that some more satisfactory arrangement will be made for the supply of negro labor generally in Ordnance Establishments than that which has heretofore pertained –

Reference to my letters on the subject of negro labor addressed to you during the past year will show how very difficult it has been to *hire* negroes in numbers sufficient to meet the requirements of this Armory – As a means of overcoming the difficulty Col. Mallet and myself received the Secty. of War, – through you – authority to impress the negro labor required, but this authority was barren of results, for the reason that no means were provided, or at our command, by which the impressment could be made – After much effort I succeeded in hiring – late in the season – about one-half the number of negroes I required – The greater portion of these, and the most useful, were taken from this Armory early in August and were sent to Atlanta – by order of Genl Hood, to work on fortifications – Of these only about one half have been returned to me within the past month – The rest have been assigned to other work – some as cooks, others as teamsters with the Army of Tenn. – and some have ran away, I know not where – The building operations at this Armory have been greatly retarded in consequence of all these difficulties in connection with negro labor, and it would seem to be politic in the Govt. to provide a means by which they may be overcome in future— Most of the negroes hired to this Armory were hired on contracts providing that the negroes should be employed only on work pertaining to this Armory— Owners claim that their contracts are void by reason of their negroes being ordered to the front without their consent. The effect of this diversion of negroes from their employment at this Armory is that owners are hesitating to hire their negroes to Govt Establishment generally, and I forsee that the difficulties attending the hiring of negro labor next year will be greater than ever before.

I notice the recommendation of the President in his late message, to organize a force of 40000 negroes, for the purpose of supplying the War Dept. generally with all the labor required—[1] This I think an excellent idea, and one which, if carried into effect, would greatly promote the interests of the War Dept. and of the country at large—

Is it probable that some such measure will be adopted?

I respectfully request to be informed at your earliest convenience, what course to pursue with reference to securing negro labor for the ensuing year—inasmuch as if they are to be hired as heretofore—Steps should be taken at once to that end— It is important also that I should know how the negroes are to be furnished rations next year— Those at this Armory have been rationed with provision purchased and provided by me. If this is to be the case again next year I should know it soon, in order that I may be early in the market for Bacon &c— That the Ord. Dept. should be required to perform this Commissary duty I think is all wrong— I respectfully recommend the organization of a regular force of negro laborers for the Service of the War Dept. generally—the assignment to each manufacturing Establishment of such numbers as may be required by each:—and the clothing & feeding of the negroes by Q.M. & Commissary Depts—

I have consulted with Cols. Mallet & Cuyler and we all agree in the opinion that some such measure as is referred to above is required to meet the interests of the Bureau, and War Dept generally—

An early reply will oblige, Colonel   Respectfully Your obdt. svt.
HLcSr   Jas. H. Burton

Jas. H. Burton to Col. J. Gorgas, 15 Nov. 1864, chap. IV, vol. 29, pp. 146–47, Letters Sent by the Superintendent of the Macon GA Armory, Records of the Ordnance Dept., RG 109 [F-2].

1 On November 7, 1864, President Jefferson Davis proposed that the Confederate Congress increase from 20,000 to 40,000 the number of slaves that

might be impressed into Confederate service and suggested that the Confederacy obtain such slave laborers by purchasing them from their owners, rather than by impressing their labor for a limited term. He further proposed that the Confederacy promise emancipation "as a reward for faithful service." (*Official Records*, ser. 4, vol. 3, pp. 797–99.)

FEEDING THE CONFEDERACY

292: Attorney General of Virginia to the Confederate Secretary of War

Richmond Aug. 27, 1861 –

Dear Sir. I am requested by some of the Citizens of the Valley Counties to make a representation to you of the facts bearing upon the Call of the Militia in that region.

It is the most fertile part of Virginia, and for wheat and corn growing. It has no other staple of consequence.

The Call of the Militia was at a time when the harvest was scarcely over – and the Farmer left his crop standing in the field unhoused.

No plough has been put into the ground for the fall seeding of wheat.

See then the sacrifice, which our people in that region are called on to make – To imperil the crop of the past year, and to prevent the raising a crop for the coming year –

I know it is supposed, the same rule of 10 per cent being applicable elsewhere, must be applied to the Valley, & with no worse results. But one fact will show the Contrary.

In Shenandoah County, there is a white population of 12.800. and a total population of 13.800, showing only 1000 blacks, free & slave, 10 per cent of the whites makes a call of 1280 for Militia Service – drafted from the laborers, the tillers of the soil, and not leaving sufficient Slaves at home to work while the master is abroad to fight.

Nansemond County near Norfolk has a total population of 13.700 – nearly the same as Shenandoah – of which 5.700 are white – & 8000 black, free & slave – The draft of 10 per cent draws 570 whites, but leaves the negro to the farm labour –

This is an evil, which calls for a remedy if one can be had –

Of the Militia at Winchester, numbering say 5000, perhaps one half are unarmed — Might not furloughs be allowed – or a part be disbanded, who are unarmed, upon call to be summoned again, if needed?

Especially since report says the Column of Gen[l] Banks has fallen back from the Valley towards Baltimore —

If any thing can be done for as true and patriotic a people as there are in the South, I appeal to you to do it — When I tell you, that Shenandoah County which cast 2500 votes for the Secession Ordinance & only 5 against it, where there are only 700 Slaves, I think I may vouch for the integrity of her people upon the great crisis of the South — I am with high respect Yours

J. R. Tucker

Shenandoah has furnished about 950 volunteers — Could not enough of her Militia be retained to make up her quota, & release the residue on furlough. As it is now, she has largely more than her quota in the field, counting her Volunteers and her militia. J. R. Tucker

ALS

J. R. Tucker to Hon. L. P. Walker, 27 Aug. 1861, #3584 1861, Letters Received, ser. 5, Sec. War, RG 109 [F-561]. Endorsements. Secretary of War Leroy P. Walker referred Tucker's letter to General Joseph E. Johnston, commander of the Confederate Department of the Potomac, under whose authority the militia had been mobilized in the Shenandoah Valley. Walker observed that Tucker had made a strong case for the valley farmers, "but the Department must rely upon the judgment of its commanding generals as to the exigencies originally requiring this force to be called into the field, and which may still render it necessary to be retained in service." In response, Johnston suggested "reduction of the militia force in the valley of the Shenandoah to the number of 2,500, and that the proper authorities of Virginia be requested to select the portion to be disbanded." (*Official Records*, ser. 1, vol. 5, pp. 816–17, 826.)

293: Virginia Slaveholder to the Confederate Secretary of War

Brunswick Va June 13th 1862

Sir, Allow Me to Make an appeal in behalf of the people of Brunswick for their Negroes Now at Work on fortifications Near Richmond. If you Could know the situation of our crops I am Confident you would send them to us. We planted full Crops of Corn for all our hands our determination being to raise grain and meat. We have planted all our best lands in Corn, (no tobacco is planted with us) Never before have we known as much rain at this season. the consequence is, we are so in grass that to do all possible with all our hands the crop must be injured. if not worked in a very short time I fear a large portion ruined. in such an event the opportunity to help to feed our Soldiers will be lost. The enemy has so much of our best grain growing region, – that we should use every effort to prevent famine which may be added to the rest of our troubles   in a very few days harvest will begin when the Corn must be left to ruin, if nothing is done before that time. that too will require our full force. the hands from Brunswick were divided, many of them being left in Petersburg; the last named have been sent home. had all been Kept together some of us would have suffered less as all would have been sent home sooner. I do not make this appeal through selfish motives,   our cause demands it   None will more willingly submit to any sacrifice than the people of Brunswick   We desire to help feed our noble army   we will do all we can for the achievement of our independence   it is as necessary to till the land as to fight the battles. With the help of God we are resolved to do our part. we ask of you the help which you can give we hope without detriment to the Military operations of the Country   With very great respt

ALS   J. B. Lundy

J. B. Lundy to Sir, 13 June 1862, L-316 1862, Letters Received, ser. 5, Sec. War, RG 109 [F-56]. According to an endorsement, the Confederate War Department replied that calls for slaves had been made on other counties "for the purpose of relieving" those from Brunswick County.

294: Governor of Florida to the Confederate Secretary of War

Tallahassee. Fla: February 17th. 1863.

Sir   The maintenance of our armies in the field – of the families of those in Military Service – of the civil Government of the Confederate States and the States seperately – in a word, not only the liberty, but the lives of the people of the State, depend upon Agricultural labor. The advocates of Slavery, in our National Councils and throughout the various forms of arguments to sustain it, have contended forcibly and truthfully, that negroes had not the inclination or ability to labor successfully, without the superior skill of the White man to direct and enforce their labor.

Upon slave labor, the Agriculture of the Southern States is mainly dependent, and consequently overseers for the management and direction of the Slaves should be exempt from Military Service. I say *overseers*, not owners of slaves, because as a general rule, slaves

746

have been managed by overseers; and but few owners have manifested the industry, skill and energy, necessary to successful Agriculture.

The safety of the Confederate States demands the exemption of overseers, for two important reasons. First, because without them slaves will not labor in a manner to secure subsistence for the armies in the field, the support of families at home, and to ensure the revenue necessary to the Confederate and State Governments. Secondly, If left without the control of overseers to whom they have been accustomed to yield obedience, the result will probably be, insubordination and insurrection.

A more effectual auxiliary to the Emancipation Scheme of Lincoln, and for the subjugation of the South, could not, in my humble judgment be devised, than an Act of Congress (if it shall be respected by the States) which would entrust the Agriculture, and the lives of families, to the slaves unrestrained by the presence, authority and skill of overseers.

As a matter of policy, owners and overseers on plantations where cotton shall be planted, might be subjected to military service; but, on plantations where labor is exclusively directed to the raising of grain, meat &c for subsistence, overseers should be exempt from Military Service.

In a time of profound peace, when not the slightest anticipation of war could have reasonably existed, the General Assembly of this State in its wisdom (the result of experience) enacted a law requiring a white person (either the owner or an overseer) to reside on the plantation where slaves lived, for their proper control and management. A copy of the last act on the subject is herewith enclosed. If the Slaves are left without proper management, they will not only fail to make the crops, but will destroy the Stock, necessary to the very existence of the country.

Convinced of the truth of the allegations herein made, as the Governor of the State, in the maintenance of its laws and for the General Welfare of the Confederate States, I feel it my duty to protest against the enforcement of the Conscript Act in its application to overseers, where necessary to the management and direction of Slaves; and more especially on plantations where the labor is devoted to securing the means of subsistence necessary to maintain our armies and protect our people from starvation. I have the honor to be Very Respectfully

HLS
John Milton

Governor John Milton to Hon. James A. Seddon, 17 Feb. 1863, M-156 1863, Letters Received, ser. 5, Sec. War, RG 109 [F-80]. Enclosed is an

1851 Florida law that mandated the presence of a white person, either owner or overseer, on slave plantations. Governor Milton wrote a similar letter to General Joseph Finegan, commander of the Confederate District of East Florida, who referred it to the commander of the Confederate Department of South Carolina, Georgia, and Florida. (Govr. John Milton to Brigr. Genl. Joseph Finegan, 17 Feb. 1863, #219 1863, Letters Received, ser. 72, Dept. of SC, GA, & FL, Records of Military Commands, RG 109 [F-102].) No reply to Milton's letters has been found in the records of the Confederate Secretary of War or the Department of South Carolina, Georgia, and Florida.

295: Former Governor of Virginia to the Confederate Secretary of War

Charles City Court house [*Va.*] Mar: 7th 1863.
My dear Sir, As I told you in a previous letter, I intended to write to you, I will proceed to redeem my promise. You will I am sure pardon me for old acquaintance and old friendships sake, even if you should not approve of the views I present to you.

In the begining of this war, I thought, unless our rulers were discreet beyond what I feared they would be that, the suffering and injury to the Southern confederacy would be incalculably greater than the necessities of the war would require or demand. This impression arose from my knowledge of the Character and habits of the Southern people and my knowledge of the Yankees. I never doubted but that the object of the Yankees in bringing on the war was to abolish slavery entirely, or to render it valueless to us. Entertertaining this view, I deprecated the use of negro slaves in our army for any purpose whatever. But my warnings were unheeded and very early in the war the commander on the peninsular, ordered one half of all the slaves (male) in the tide water counties to be sent to his camps Immediately after the order was issued, I communicated with that officer; urging him to rescind it — The reasons which prompted me to this course were numerous and some of them to the following effect. That the field labor of the south, the slaves, not being subject to military duty was one of its most potent elements of strength; that it ought to be left on the plantations to produce supplies for the army; that if negroes were employed by us to do such work as soldiers ought to do, the Yankees would use that as a pretext to interfere with them and to emancipate them. I also urged that the negro was a timid animal not used to being with large bodies of white men and never having gone amongst large numbers of armed white men; that if they were carried into our camps, they would become used to these things and being thus changed they would with less fear try to get to the

Yankee army. All I could say had no effect — The negroes were sent to work on the fortifications, the runingaway commenced with those who had been sent or who had become familiarised to armies from their proximity to them. The Yankees denounced negroes as contraband of war and offered them protection in their camps. This was as far as the Yankees dared venture to go at that time. Seeing it was useless to argue with a Military Commander, I wrote to the Honbl J. P. Benjamin then the Secretary of War, expressing the views which I had presented to the military commandant, and also told him that I knew of no law authorising the calling out of slaves from their homes to work in camps, and requesting him if he knew of any such to refer me to it; stating to him that by his doing so, much difficulty might possibly be avoided; after waiting sometime to hear from Mr Benjamin and not doing so, I addressed him a second letter upon the same subject; he never replied to either of my letters; tho I know he received the last of them if not both.

Concluding from Mr Benjamin's silence that nothing was to be expected from him I wrote to the Honb^{ls} Wm Ballard Preston and James Lyons presenting to them all the objections which I had before urged against the legality of ordering slaves into our camps to labor as well as against the policy of the passage of any law to authorise its being done. Those gentlemen acted *Mum*   neither answered my letters and as far as I know or believe neither of them ever did or said anything. During all this time very few slaves had left their homes and gone to the Yankees, and I verily believe if they had never been ordered to the camps to labor not one tenth of those who went would have gone. But those things are past and gone. My object now is to invite your attention to the present state of things and to point out to you what I fear will be the dreadful condition of our people and army, unless there be immediate and thorough change in the present state of affairs. Then to the point.

What is the condition of our army and of those not subject to Military duty the old men, women and children? Judging from what I know, as also from what I hear I conclude there is a very great scarcity of all the necessaries of live. One of two propositions is true. Either our currency has been made nearly worthless, by our public men, for they alone have had the control of it, or bread and meat are very scarce in the Southern Confederacy. I do know that there is less bread and meat in eastern Virginia than there ever was before for many years. I know less grain was saved in tide water Virginia in 1861 than there had been in any of the forty years before. I know that in the same section of country there was less, far less land seeded in wheat than had been for many years before, consequently there was but a very short crop gathered in 1862. I know that less ground was planted in corn in the spring of 1862 than had been for many years before. I know that less wheat was seeded in the fall of 1862 than was in the fall of 1861. I do not believe, if, all the wheat seeded last fall in tide water Virginia, comes well and should be saved that it will be more than enough to seed the usual breadth of land seeded in wheat before this war. I presume all agree that there is a very great scarcity of grain at this time in all of the Southern Confederacy accessible to our armies. These being the facts. What has produced the present scarcity of provisions for the army and the people and of feed for the horses? It is true that Virginia has been converted almost into one entire Camp a very large portion of it has been occupied by the enemy. It is true that the enemy have taken from the plantations or induced a large number of the field laborers to leave and go with them, this of itself would have caused a considerable diminution in the production of grain, but there are many laborers left. – Where are they? A few are yet on the farms, a great many in the camps, at work on the fortifications and acting as servants to our officers and soldiers. I think it a very moderate estimate, to put the number of negroes now in our camps at 40,000. In the camps the negroes are mere consumers, they must live and they can only do so upon what should be for the soldiers; if these negroes were sent from the camps now they would become producers, and would produce grain enough to supply our army, at least they would make a large quantity of grain; each man would make at least five hundred bushels of grain, that is three hundred bushels of corn, one hundred bushels of wheat and one hundred bushels of oats. In the aggregate they would produce (20,000000) twenty millions of bushels of grain, allowing fifteen bushels of grain to a man per year, that quantity would feed 133.333 soldiers a year, and this would be in addition to what will be produced. Let these negroes be sent at once, from the camps and they may make this year some crops, if they are not sent immediately, it will be too late to plant corn or sew oats, and they will be mere consumers the balance of the year. If the government had not interfered with the negroes, if it had never ordered them to work on public works, or allowed them to be carried into our camps, we should now have a plenty of food for every body – Keep them in the camps and starvation will result in less than three years or the army will be disbanded. Instead of government looking to and husbanding all of the sources of supply for the army and people, instead of its encouraging and stimulating in every proper manner the production of food; it has from the begining of the war to the present day pursued a course, which has discouraged as far it could farming. The government has been from the begining of the war taking the negroes slave and free from the farms to work in the

camps and do the work which the soldiers ought to have
done. From the begining – The government has been offering
higher wages for negroes than farmers could afford to pay. Negro
men hired for from seventy five to one hundred dollars to work on
farms in 1861. corn was only worth then three dollars per
barrel. The government gave fifty cents a day for hands rather over
one hundred & fifty dollars per year. If the negroes had not been
taken by force or threatened force very few would have been sent to
the camps even for the high price; the negroes in the begining were
very much opposed to going into the camps: The commandant on
the peninsular sent his soldiers for them. some of the negroes
ranaway to keep from going, that officer actually threatened to send
his New Orleans, Zouaves, a body of soldiers notorious on the
peninsular for their destructive propensities, and quarter them on
the owners of the slaves who had runaway, if they were not
sent. Thus the farmers were forced to send their negroes to the
camps. The consequence was that the crops of 1861 were short and
badly gathered – There was not labor to cultivate well or gather
cleanly what grain was made owing to the same scarcity of labor
on the farms a less breadth of land was seeded in wheat in the fall of
1861 than had been the fall before and than had been for several
previous years. Yet tolerable crops were made and corn and wheat
did not rise much in price. In the winter of 1861–1862, corn was
worth from three to four dollars per barrel in the latter part of
that winter it got up to about four dollars to four and a half dollars
per barrel and wheat rose some fifty or sixty cents per bushel In
the spring of 1862 less land was planted in corn than usual owing
entirely or nearly so to the negroes being in our camps – very few
negroes had up to this time gone to the Yankees; in that spring in
the month of April, I think, the Confederate army evacuated the
peninsular. Then the exodus of the negroes commenced and now
the best informed and most reliable gentlemen estimate the loss of
negroes to this county at from fifty to seventy per cent of the entire
slave population. I am confident it must be at least seventy per
cent of the young able bodied men. In consequence of this great
loss of labor very little grain was raised last year, and less will be
raised this year. This county which before the war had raised a
large surplus, for its population, cannot under the present state of
things raise more than enough for its own consumption. Tide water
Virginia is very generally in the same condition. The condition of
Virginia heretofore, during this war has been bad enough; I do not
now refer to the ravages of the enemy which have been savage,
wasteful and evil beyond all precedent, but of the prospect of
getting something to eat. There is an abundance of labor in this
state yet to produce not only enough of bread and meat but a large

surplus. Where is it? In the camps. Our legislature has directed
the Governor upon the request of the president of the confederate
states to detail from the several counties and towns a number of
male slaves between the ages of 18 and 45 years, not to exceed
10,000 at any one time. If these slaves are not sent as the law
directs they are to be taken and carried to work on the fortifications
and other public works, if they go the owners are to have sixteen
dollars a month for each slave and the government to provide the
slave with food and medicine, and if he is injured or dies or escapes
to the enemy by the neglect of the officers of the Confederate
government, the owners are to receive the full value of all
such. Since the first of January last the Governor has called for a
large number of slaves under this law and they are, I presume, now
at work on the public works; this will in a great measure curtail the
grain crops of the present year. Starvation is now looking every
body full in the face, and all are awaiting in dreadful consternation
that direful calamity. How is it to be averted? My opinion is that
the government of the confederate states should immediately send
from their camps and armies every negro in them, and for the
government to announce that no more negroes should be carried or
sent into the camps or armies to labor or act as servants— Let our
soldiers build all necessary field works, as the soldiers of every other
nation have always done from the begining of war. This would be
hard very hard upon our soldiers at first but in a very short time
they would become accustomed to labor and be more healthy and
contented than they would otherwise ever be. Let our soldiers but
know the truth that, if the negroes are kept in the camps or armies
as mere consumers they are rendering more efficient aid to the
Yankees than are those negroes in the Yankee lines with arms in
their hands, and my life upon it you will never hear a word of
murmur or discontent from any true patriot or any single member
of our patriotic and gallant army. Unless the negroes be sent
speedily from the camps and armies at once, they had as well
remain their all the year, or at least until harvest, as it will be too
late for them to plant a crop this year. But I may be told the
negroes cannot be discharged from the armies and camps now; that
the fortifications are indispensible and must be completed at once;
that active operations with the armies are just about to begin and
the men cannot be spared from the lines to labor. We were told all
this and much more by the officers on the peninsular; but now we
all know that, the peninsular fortifications, numerous and costly as
they were have turned out to be worse than useless to us, for they
are all now in the possession of the enemy and ready to be used
against us. If Richmond should ever be surrounded by the enemy
and our armies driven in the fortifications, with all the avenues of

supplies closed? In other words, if Richmond should ever be thoroughly and completely besieged. How long is it thought it could hold out with its present supplies of provisions? Of course I do not know what supplies there are in Richmond, but judging from what I know of the citizens, from the great scarcity of provisions in the country, and the exorbitantly high prices every article of food bears in that market, I fear the supply is small If the fortifications must be completed and the soldiers cannot be taken from the lines to do the work, call out more men, more white men, call all up to forty five, if that will not be enough call all up to fifty or even sixty years old and let the fortifications, these mere hobbies and toys of our Engineers and military leaders be completed as soon as possible. But in the name of all that is sacred and dear to us, do not let us do for the Yankees what they can never do for themselves, even with the aid of Great Britain subdue and conquer our gallant and heroic army. So far from using negroes to work on fortifications or other public works or allowing them to be with our armies, I very much believe it would be wise to order that all of them suitable to farm labor should be employed *only* in raising grain during the continuance of this war; but, I would not issue such an order now, as I do not believe there is at this time any necessity for it. Let the government cease to employ negroes, let it cease to offer, as it has done from the begining of this war, a bounty to the owners of slaves not to work them on farms, and possibly we shall by the end of the next year have enough produced for the army and people too to eat. I am entirely willing that everything shall be done except the surrender of my liberties and the independence of the country to carry through this war to a successful end if it be necessary to attain that end let the government take every dollars worth of property of every description and use and consume it. But pray spare our army our brave men. Stop short the course heretofore pursued or the army will be starved into subjection and the country conquered.

I have written a great deal more than I thought I should when I began, I have not expressed very clearly many of the ideas I entertain, but I am sure you will readily comprehend all I have said or meant to say. I regret that I have deemed it my duty to inflict upon you such a paper as this, but you are the only person I could address with even a hope that if you approve of the suggestions made by me, some good may come of my labor. I am nearly three score and infirm so I ought not to go to the field but I am very willing and ready to go there and do what I can. My health has been bad lately, I am now hardly able to write but I could not forbear to send you these my views. I hope your health is better than when I saw you and that it may continue to improve, you are yet a comparatively young man and I trust you may live and enjoy good health for many years to come. This is intended as a private letter to you, but use it as you chose. I have written very hurriedly because I was afraid my health would give out before I got through. If you should ever have time to write me a line I shall be glad to hear how your health is, if no more Believe me to be very Truly y^r friend

ALS   Jno M. Gregory

Jno. M. Gregory to Honbl. James A. Seddon, 7 Mar. 1863, G-142 1863, Letters Received, ser. 5, Sec. War, RG 109 [F-76]. Endorsement. No response has been found in the records of the Confederate Secretary of War. Gregory had complained to a previous Secretary of War about the impressment of slaves by General John B. Magruder, commander of the Confederate Army of the Peninsula, and had expressed the fear that a Confederate commander given the power to impress might use it to abolish slavery. (Jno. M. Gregory to Honbl. J. P. Benjamin, 12 Mar. 1862, G-87 1862, Letters Received, ser. 5, Sec. War, RG 109 [F-76].) For Magruder's impressment of slaves during the first year of the war, see above, docs. 260A–H.

296: Headquarters of the Confederate Trans-Mississippi Department to the Commander of the Confederate District of Texas, New Mexico, and Arizona

Shreveport La Jan 7th 1864

General, The attention of the Lt Genl. Comd'^{g} has been called to your circular "To the Planters and Farmers of Texas" dated Rugelys 7th Dec /63 a copy of which is enclosed. In reference to this subject, he instructs me to call your attention to Gen Orders No 138 A.&.I.G.O Richmond Va. 1863 Oct 24th. By a comparison of your circular with this order, you will see that it conflicts with its second, third and fourth paragraphs.[1] In calling for labor on fortifications, this order should as nearly as possible be followed, and except in a great emergency not more than one fifth per cent of the male slave population between the ages of seventeen and fifty, should ever be called for. The wisdom of calling for a larger proportion than one fifth per cent, scattered over a wide extended territory is greatly to be doubted. They can but rarely be all needed, or used judiciously, and when thus called out are necessarily withdrawn from their labors upon the farms and plantations, and as a consequence, there must be a corresponding decrease in the grain and other productions which are essential to the subsistence both of the army and the citizens; thus lessening the power of endurance, which must now be one of the main elements of our success, and nursing the spirit of disaffection that may be amongst us. For these and other obvious reasons, such a call for labor as the one enclosed, unlimited in its duration, sweeping in its provisions, and drawing upon so large a proportion of the slave population, and over such an extent of country, for the defense of points so distant from each other, seems to be injudicious, and if still necessary should at least be modified so as to conform to Gen Ord No. 138 above referred to, and relaxed even more if it can be safely done. Such portion of the circular as embraces the counties of Red River, Lamar, Bowie, Davis, Marion, Harrison, Titus and Upshur, will be revoked as these counties have already been called on for their full quota to complete the defences of upper Red River   I am very respectfully Your most obt servt

HLcSr

C. S. West

Capt. C. S. West to Maj. Gen. Magruder, 7 Jan. 1864, ch. II, vol. 70, pp. 698–99, Letters Sent, Trans-MS Dept., Records of Military Commands, RG 109 [F-832]. The circular "To the Planters and Farmers of Texas" was not copied into the volume of letters sent, nor does a copy appear in the volume of orders and circulars issued from the Confederate District of Texas, New Mexico, and Arizona. In another circular issued the same day, probably similar to the missing circular, General John B. Magruder, commander of the district, called upon the planters of Brazoria, Matagorda, and Fort Bend counties, Texas, "to place all their able-bodied male slaves between the ages of 16 and 50 years, except one for each proprietor, at the disposal of the Government, to work upon the Fortifications." (Circular, Head Quarters, District Texas, New Mexico, and Arizona, 7 Dec. 1863, ch. 2, vol. 114, p. 57, General Orders, Dist. of TX, NM & AZ, Trans-MS Dept., Records of Military Commands, RG 109 [F-712].)

1 Following enactment of legislation by the Confederate Congress in March 1863, General Order 138, issued by the Confederate adjutant and inspector general in October, regulated the impressment of slaves in states that had not legislated on the subject. Paragraph 2 prohibited impressment of slaves from "plantations exclusively devoted to the production of grain and provisions . . . except in cases of urgent necessity." Paragraph 3 barred impressment of slaves employed in domestic service or upon farms where there were three or fewer adult male slaves, and limited the total number of slaves impressed to 5 percent of the slave population of a county, "unless the necessity is very great." Paragraph 4 provided that the ordinary term of impressment be sixty days and recommended that slaves be impressed in consultation with state authorities. (*Official Records*, ser. 4, vol. 2, pp. 469–72, 897–98.)

297: Order by the Commander of the Confederate District of Georgia

Copy   Savannah March 23. 1864
General Orders No 9

In consequence of the great necessity for retaining for the present, on the farms and plantations, as much labor as possible, for agricultural purposes, that necessary for constructing, and repairing Fortifications or defensive works, must be performed in part for a time by details from the Troops.

The safety and protection of our Coast demand continued labor on the works for defence, now but partially completed, and the efficiency of our armies depends upon an ample supply of food from the Interior for future use. The latter can be had only from the work of our Slaves at home; the former can be accomplished by the efforts of the Soldiery. Cheerful and willing labor will soon secure the desired end. With a view therefore, to the performance of the necessary work on the fortifications in this vicinity, Commanding Officers of Districts will report to these Head Quarters, without delay, the number of Troops that can be furnished for daily labor by details from the respective Commands, and Garrisons within their Districts; the other duties required from each being duly considered. By Order of Maj. Gen. Gilmer

HDc

General Orders No. 9, Head Quarters, 23 Mar. 1864, Orders & Circulars, ser. 82, Dist. of GA, Records of Military Commands, RG 109 [F-624]. Other Confederate commanders also gave thought to how they might best employ slaves as the Union army advanced and the Confederacy's food supply shrank. In April 1864, an adjutant at the headquarters of the Trans-Mississippi Department telegraphed the department's chief-of-staff: "Do you not think making corn at this time more important than constructing defenses around Shreveport, if so, had not all the hands employed in that way best be discharged and returned to their owners." (Asst. Adjt. Gen. S. S. Anderson to Gen. Boggs, 28 Apr. 1864, ch. II, vol. 73 1/2, p. 205, Letters Sent, Trans-MS Dept., Records of Military Commands, RG 109 [F-846].)

298A: Alabama Farmers to the Confederate President

Wesabulga Randolph Co Ala May 6th 1864
To his Excellency Jefferson Davis The undersigned citizens & Slaveholders of the county of Randolph & State of Alabama would

respectfully represent to your Excellency That Col Blount impressing agt of Slaves Stationed at Mobile Ala; has recently ordered an impressment of 33 1/3 per cent of the able bodied Slaves of this County; when in adjoining counties where the Slave population is greater only from 5 to 10 per cent have been taken— This we think to be unjust, & *not* in accordance with the intentions of the act. We think that an uniform rate should be levied in the whole State; or so much of it as is now within our lines; So that the burden Should fall uniformly on all; But he appears to order an arbitrary number from each county without refferance to the number of Slaves in the County. He thus levies a percentage which is uniform in the county, but does not bear any proportion to the levies in adjoining Counties— He also counts *in* all the women that are within the ages of 17 to 50 & takes one third of the *total number in men* between the ages of 17 to 50.

Randolph is a poor & mountainous County with the largest population of any in the State. There are only 300 negroes (women & men) within the prescribed ages in the county & he takes one Hundred Seventy five per cent of the White Males are now in the Service; leaving the great majority of their wives & children to be Supported by the remainder There are numbers of widows & orphans of the Soldiers who have perished by the casualities of war to be also Supported by public funds—

The County does not in ordinary times produce more than a Sufficiency of food for its population; last year there was a deficit of over 40000 bushels; of corn about one half of which has been provided from the tax in Kind; the ballance has to be purchased in the Canebrake; transported a distance of 125 miles on R.R, & hauled thence in waggons from 30 to 50 miles to reach the various points of distribution in the county—

There are now on the rolls of the Probate court, 1600 indigent families to be Supported; they average 5 to each family; making a grand total of 8000 persons Deaths from Starvation have absolutely occurred; notwithstanding the utmost efforts that we have been able to make; & now many of the women & children are seeking & feeding upon the bran from the mills

Women riots have taken place in Several parts of the County in which Govt wheat & corn has been seized to prevent Starvation of themselves & families; Where it will end unless relief is afforded we cannot tell

We have entered into these details that your Excellency may See the deplorable condition of things in this County, & aid us if in your power & the exigencies of the Service permit—

To take the Negroes *now* from the fields when the crop is just planted & ready for cultivation would inevitably cause the loss of a portion of the crops So essential to feed the County   we have appealed to Col Blount asking that the impressment be delayed or abandoned; but without effect & we now appeal to your Excellency as our last resource under God to give us Such measure of assistance as you can.   If you refuse us – we must Submit & take our [chance] – do our duty & trust to Almighty Providence for the result   under all the circumstances we therefore pray your Excellency.

That Randolph County be exempt from the operations of the impressment act.   If, however the Case is so urgent & the hands are so essential to save Mobile; then we ask that the impressment be delayed until fall when the crops are gathered;   In case neither of these prayers can be granted we pray that the rate be made uniform in the Whole State – & that *we* be not punished for our poverty –   we would Humbly Suggest to your Excellency that there are large numbers of negroes about our towns & cities (used for the pleasure of their owners; or idling about; a curse to the community – *consumers not producers*) that we think might be exhausted before the agricultural labour of the county is interfered with.

Hoping that your Excellency may favourably consider our humble prayer – we remain as ever your Excellencies devoted Servants
HLS   [46 *signatures*]

Wm. N. Harris et al. to his Excellency Jefferson Davis, 6 May 1864, H-1518 1864, Letters Received, ser. 12, Adjt. & Insp. Gen., RG 109 [F-328]. Endorsements.

298B: Impressment Agent for Randolph County, Alabama, to the Chief Impressment Agent of the Confederate Department of Alabama, Mississippi, and East Louisiana

Wedowee   Randolph Co   Ala   June 1st 64
Sir   Yours of the 14th Ult. has just come to hand with a requisition for fifty negroes from this county to serve until 20th Decr next.   I have examined into the subject and will to the best of my ability obey your instructions but from my investigations I find that there is but *five men* in this county that own five male Slaves between the ages of Eighteen and forty five years, so that the number required cannot be obtained if your instructions IV is followed.

The persons in this county who own Slaves at all own but few most of them not more than two or three Slaves or a family of Slaves. You may not be fully informed as to the condition of this county   I therefore take the liberty to say that the county is generally poor and has a large poor population most of them owning no Slaves at all

Last year in consequence of so many men having gone to the Army there was not enough of provision raised in the county for support by about one half the quantity necessary, and it is the opinion of well informed men in various parts of the county that the crop raised the present year will not last the population beyond the 1st of January next

The wheat will be ready to commence harvesting about the 10th or 15th of this month and on very many of the little farms there is no one but a woman and a parcel of children (the wife and children of some soldier) who are not able themselves to cut the wheat and are dependant on the few men that are left to cut it for them — if therefore this county could be exempted from furnishing negroes to the Government I think that the interests of the whole country would be Subserved.

As I stated to you on a former occasion there is less than two thousand slaves in the county and there are now between 1800 and 1900 families of Soldiers dependant on the County and are actually drawing their provisions from the Probate Judge

All of the corn, received as Tax in kind raised in the county was purchased by the Court of County Commissioners for the use of the families of Soldiers and then a large amount of money say $11.000. has already been used by the Court in addition for the same purpose and the corn is now being shipped from Dallas Marengo and other counties in South Ala. to supply the destitution and will still have to be kept up during the existence of the present war and all the labor taken from the county will make the deficit still greater

It may be thought by persons at a distance that this is because the people do not work but this is a mistake. I have seen in many places in the county and indeed it is a common thing to see the women and children industriously engaged on their farms, and I am satisfied that the people as a general thing are doing all they can to supply themselves, I therefore very respectfully ask that this county may be exempted from the requisition, and if this cannot be done consistently with the public service I then ask for further instructions as to how I shall make the apportionment, for taking one Slave from each man in the county who owns five male Slaves between the ages of 18 and 45 years will only furnish five Slaves to the service and one of those is a refugee from the State of Mississippi.

759

Under the circumstances I shall wait further instructions from
you   Your obt. servt.
HLcSr   (Signed) H. M. Gay

H. M. Gay to Col. F. S. Blount, 1 June 1864, enclosed in F. S. Blount to Lt.
Genl. S. D. Lee, July 1864, filed with H-1518 1864, Letters Received, ser.
12, Adjt. & Insp. Gen., RG 109 [F-328]. Another enclosure in the same file
indicates that Randolph County was exempted from the general impressment.
(F. S. Blount to H. M. Gay, Esq., 8 June 1864.)

MOBILIZING FREE BLACKS

299: Virginia Mechanic to the Confederate President

Lynchburg [*Va.*] July 15th 1861.
Dear Sir   There is a large number of Free Negroes in this City a
great portion of which are Mechanicks of various trades
viz: Carpenters Bricklayers Stone masons, & Blacksmiths a large
portion of which are now liveing on the honest industry of our
Volunteers already in service by stealing and robing their families
out of the provisions stored to them before their enlistment in the
Confederate army. I want to know if that degraded and worse than
useless race could not do something in the way of defending the
south such as throwing up Breat works Building tents or any thing
els that would be of advantage to us. and take the hard portion of
the labor off of the Soldiers who has to drill 6 or 8 hours every day
besides work. I think I Could if I had the proper authority furnish
the state with about 100 or 150 from this place alone. if such a
course is compatable with your views and the interest of the state
demand it by giveing such an order would greatly relieve this
Community of a class who instead of being a benefit, is more than
useless. Very Respectfully your Obedient Servt
ALS   John Lenahan

John Lenahan to Hon. Jeff. Davis, 15 July 1861, #2275 1861, Letters
Received, ser. 5, Sec. War, RG 109 [F-36]. Endorsement. From a different

perspective, Confederate General Roger A. Pryor – who in the 1850s had led the movement in Virginia to reenslave free blacks – reached a similar conclusion. In October 1862, he proposed "that Free Negroes be impressed to replace the soldiers who are employed as teamsters. A Waggon Master from each Regiment would suffice to insure proper attention to their duties. By this arrangement you will realize the following desirable results

1st You will restore to the ranks several thousand able-bodied and effective Soldiers

2nd You will enable masters to employ their slaves exclusively in the Cultivation of the soil

3rd You will relieve the community of a thriftless and vicious class and compel them to labor for the public advantage

Another Consideration; slave teamsters often escape into the United States; Free-negroes are not apt to run away, and if they do there is no loss of property." (Roger A. Pryor to Hon. G. W. Randolph, 29 Oct. 1862, P-681 1862, Letters Received, ser. 5, Sec. War, RG 109 [F-60].)

300: Virginia Manufacturer to the Confederate Secretary of War

Richmond, Va. April 23^d *1862*
Sir A free black man, by name James Robinson, has four Waggon Teams working on the Street – They are the only public teams now left, all others having been taken some time ago by Government. I am informed by Robinson that Genl Winder has notified him to deliver up his tomorrow. As we are dependant on them for pursuing our business, I deemed it my duty to inform you that without them we cannot go on with our Contracts with Government to furnish Boiler Plates, shovel Iron & Nails – and we will be compelled to close the Works. If the exigencies of the occasion in another direction require these Teams & Waggons, of course I do not complain, my sole object being to lay the case before you. Most Respectfully Yr obdt: Servt:

ALS   Wm S. Triplett.

[*Endorsement*] [*Confederate War Department, Richmond*] Send copy to Genl Winder & say That the business of the City being almost exclusively confined to maters in which the Gov^t is interested should be interrupted as little as possible   That the teamsters should not be interfered with nor private business interrupted except in cases of absolute necessity   The object of Martial Law is principally to preserve order and but little should be done beyond the maintenance of police

Wm. S. Triplett to Hon. Geo. W. Randolph, 23 Apr. 1862, T-113 1862,
Letters Received, ser. 5, Sec. War, RG 109 [F-64]. On letterhead stationery
of the Old Dominion Iron & Nail Works Company, of which Triplett was
president. Petitions from rural areas also revealed dependence upon the labor
of free blacks. In April 1863, for example, the county officers of New Kent
County, Virginia, reported that many free blacks were employed by "[f]arm-
ers who have been deprived of their slaves" or by "the families of soldiers now
in the service of the Confederate States," and that "to deprive them of the
services of the Free population would bring much distress upon the County
and diminish the chances or prospects of raising Crops." (Jno. D. Christian et
al. to the Secretary of War, 16 Apr. 1863, C-302 1863, Letters Received, ser.
5, Sec. War, RG 109 [F-75].)

301: Virginia Justice of the Peace to the Confederate Secretary of War

Farmville [*Va.*] Apr 2^d 1863.
To the Secretary of War. I have rec^d two orders for free negroes,
one from Genl Lee for 52 negroes to work on fortifications and the
other for ten, from the Nitre and Mining Bureau— on recpt. the
orders the Sheriff of the County was directed to summon the
number required   After scouring the County only twenty five or six
could be found within the ages required by the act of the V^a
Legislature.[1] Some of them are employed by the Hospitals and
Commissary of this place, Some of the others are in the
employment of individuals who alledge that they have Government
Contracts &c and a few are sick leaving very few to send. The State
law excepts none from these calls but those in the service of Officers
or Soldiers in active service & in the army.
I have therefore concluded, to inform the Department of these
facts and wait for instructions. There are more than one hundred
free negroes belonging to this County subject to these calls, but
after the requisition made for free negroes in 61. & 62 — they
scattered in every direction some leaving the County & others
seeking employment that they supposed would exempt them from
the work contemplated by these orders, some few [as] have been in
the habit of going off and returning as soon as they thought they
could do so safely — these last I think should be arrested and sent to
some public works if it were worth the trouble & expense it would
be to the Government. My Authority is derived entirely from State
law   The orders & expense belong to the Genl Goverment, If the
Department is of opinion that the matter is worth the trouble to

give me any instructions in relation to these negroes – I will
Cheerfully do any thing that may be desired – Very Respectfully
ALS   C A Morton

C. A. Morton to the Secretary of War, 2 Apr. 1863, M-271 1863, Letters
Received, ser. 5, Sec. War, RG 109 [F-79]. Morton signed as presiding
justice of Prince Edward County, Virginia. According to a Confederate War
Department endorsement, Morton was instructed to send to General Robert
E. Lee all the free Negroes "within his reach or that can be readily obtained,"
and to verify that those who professed to be employed on government work
were actually so employed. Morton was not, however, "to incur any extraordinary expense in . . . recovering the fugitives." "The demands of Gen Lee are
of much importance," concluded the endorsement, "& should be answered."

1 An ordinance adopted by the Virginia state convention in July 1861, and
reenacted with amendments by the state legislature in February 1862, authorized (and, later, ordered) county courts to enroll all free black men between
the ages of eighteen and fifty and, upon requisition by a Confederate army
commander, to impress from the enrollment list the number of free blacks
requested "for labor in erecting batteries, entrenchments, or other necessities
of the military service." (*Acts of the General Assembly of the State of Virginia
Passed in 1861* [Richmond, 1861], appendix: *Ordinances Adopted by the Convention . . . June and July 1861*, pp. 67–68; *Acts of the General Assembly of the State
of Virginia Passed in 1861–2* [Richmond, 1862], pp. 61–63.)

302: Confederate Tax Collector to the Confederate Secretary of War

Marion, N.C. August 4$^{th'}$ /63.
Hon. Mr. Benjamin: Your Honor will pardon the intrusion of a
communication from an inferior source, upon your time and
patience.

I am the District Collector of the Confederate Taxes, for
McDowell, Mitchell and Yancy Counties in Northcarolina, and I
have discovered that the people here apprehend great fears, that
when the Conscripts all are called out, the *Free Negroes* will cause an
insurrection among the Slaves. There are, probably, nearly or quite
as many Free Negroes in some of the Western Counties of N.
Carolina as slaves; and already have some of these Free Negroes
made their boast, that when the Conscripts were all gone, they
would be Cols. and Captains in these localities.

One Free boy has gone so far as to say that he already had 50
negroes at his command, who could be called out at any hour.

Is there no law or authority lodged in your hands, that can call these Free Negroes into camps and make them *fight* for the country? If it is not Constititional to do so, could not the Congress of the Confederate States so change the Constitution as to make these people liable to Conscription as well as the whites?

I trust Sir, if anything can be done, it will be done speedily.

The Union men and deserters have united in portions of my District, and every pass upon the Blue Ridge from Virginia to S.C. are guarded by the tories; and here are hundreds of strong, well-developed Free Negroes lounging about and endeavoring to poison the minds of the slaves.

I believe several Regiments of Free Negroes could be mustered in N.C; and if the whole South were *raked* for these people, an army little inferior in numbers at least, to that afforded by any *two* States, could be collected.

Again, I must ask your Honor's pardon for *presuming* even to address you upon this subject. But being a *true* Southern man, amidst many *tories*, I could not refrain.

I remain, Honored Sir, Your obedient servant,

R. L. Abernethy

P.S. This is intended for the Hon. Secretary of War, but I fear I have addressed the wrong man. R. L. Abernethy

ALS

R. L. Abernethy to Hon. Mr. Benjamin, 4 Aug. 1863, A-258 1863, Letters Received, ser. 5, Sec. War, RG 109 [F-72]. Abernethy signed as "Dist Collector of Con. Taxes." In writing to Judah P. Benjamin, Abernethy had indeed addressed the wrong man: Benjamin, who had earlier served as Confederate Secretary of War, was now the Secretary of State. Abernethy's letter was nevertheless delivered to the Confederate War Department, where it received a notation suggesting that it was filed without reply.

303: Citizens of Isle of Wight and Nansemond Counties, Virginia, to the Commander of the Confederate Department of North Carolina

[*Isle of Wight and Nansemond counties, Va. October 1863*]

We the undersigned citizens of the counties of Isle of Wight & Nansemond, having heard from reliable authority that there is a probability of the government at Richmond, having the Free Negroes removed from these counties, (through a misrepresentation that it is the wish of the people of these counties) beg leave to assure the authorities, that so far from its being the case, we are *decidedly* and *strongly* opposed to any attempt of the sort, for two importantat population, (the disloyal having gone to the enemy), and furnish the only means in our reach of getting our wood cut, rails mawled, or any other labor whatever, performed— 2nd such an action would create such an excitement amongst our *few* remaining slaves as to cause them all to run off—

Under all the circumstances, we are urged to petiton most respectfully, that no such action should be taken, as it would greatly augment our already, very great sufferings—

The above is very respectfully, and *earnestly* submitted,

HDS   [77 *signatures*]

Petition of Jas. Eley et al., [Oct. 1863], enclosed in Maj. Genl. G. E. Pickett to Genl. S. Cooper, 24 Oct. 1863, P-1306 1863, Letters Received, ser. 12, Adjt. & Insp. Gen., RG 109 [F-305]. An endorsement by James Eley, whose name appears first on the petition, reads: "This petition has been hurriedly gotten up, and a very limited time for its circulation, or the sheet would have been full of names." Other endorsements.

304: North Carolina Congressman to the Confederate Secretary of War, Enclosing a Letter from a North Carolina Farmer to the Congressman

Richmond Feb 12 1864

Dear Sir   I beg to present for your consideration the matter suggested in the communications enclosed. They are from citizens of my own County of high respectability

The County of Hertford lies upon the southern side of the Chowan river over whose waters the enemy's boats often pass, and furnish facilities for the escape of slaves. Several invasions have been made of its soil with the troops landed from their transports, and hundreds of its slaves have been carried off and the country pillaged and robbed. Some of the farmers are now wholly dependent on free negro labor, and it is of the deepest importance that the agricultural operations of the present year should not be interrupted by impressments. In view of its peculiar situation I do most respectfully ask that no free negroes who are industriously engaged in cultivating the soil and raising crops, may be taken from their labor during the season, and I commend the suggestions of the writers Messrs Daniel and Valentine   Most respectfully &c

ALS   W. N. H. Smith

[*Enclosure*]   Pitch Landing NC Feby 9th 64

My Dear Sir   Your favour of the 3rd inst is just to hand and
contents noted.   I am sorry to see from the papers that the bill
conscripting all free negroes from 18 to 50 has passed the House
and will if it has not already pass the Senate   I think the law will
have a very bad effect in this County and it is the opinion of every
one that I have herd express an opinion on it, (and I have herd a
good many.)   from the time it was known that such a law was
under consideration by Congress they commenced leaveing for the
Yankee lines and such as are left have generally very large families
and to put them in the service at Eleven dolls per month the county
will have to support their families and at the present high price and
scarcity of Provision. it will entail an expence on the county with
that we already have that will make our Taxes almost
unbearable.   besides it takes away the only surplus labor we
have   as I said before many persons are entirely dependant on them
for the hope of raiseing any crops the present year.   cannot you get
the Secretary of War to exempt such as are engaged by the year by
Farmers — whose slaves are gone and who are dependant on their
labor for raiseing a support from the operation of the law in the
Border Counties,   in the, interior of the country there is a large
amount of Slave labor. and they can spare considerable but here we
have almost none   I can not get a load of wood cut but by a free
negro. Col Starky Sharp has only a cook & three or four children
left on his premises   Mr Pruden is in the same box. also Mr
Valentine and a number of others.   I hope you will make a trial for
if I can not keep the free negroes I have employed I shall have to
abandon all Idea of trying to raise a crop & so it will be with
others.   Harrelsville was not all burnt. only five Houses, Stores &
offices no private dweling,
     nothing new   let me here from you.   Yours Truly
                                                            W L Daniel
P.S.   I recd the draft from Lane   he kept it nearly 12 mo.
ALS

W. N. H. Smith to Hon. Secretary of War, 12 Feb. 1864, enclosing W. L.
Daniel to Hon. W. N. H. Smith, 9 Feb. 1864, S-215 1864, Letters Received, ser. 5, Sec. War, RG 109 [F-92]. Another enclosure, endorsement.
On February 17, 1864, the Confederate Congress enacted legislation making
all free black men subject to impressment. The law provided, however, that
the Secretary of War could exempt "such free negroes as the interests of the
country may require should be exempted, or such as he may think proper to
exempt, on grounds of justice, equity, or necessity." (*Official Records*, ser. 4,
vol. 3, pp. 207–9.) On February 25, the citizens of Hertford again petitioned, this time requesting that neither slaves nor free blacks "employed on

farms or useful mechanical pursuits" be impressed under the new legislation, because they were "indispensable to the well-being if not subsistence" of the county. Congressman Smith forwarded the petition to President Jefferson Davis, noting that "[t]o some extent free negro labor has been secured in place of that of slaves enticed and carried off by the enemy, and it is of deep importance to the agricultural interest that, so far as thus employed, this class should be left to make the crops." Davis referred the petition to the War Department, and in late March, Secretary of War James A. Seddon assured Congressman Smith that both the law and the department's enforcement regulations provided that "slaves employed in agriculture are the last to be impressed." Seddon did not, however, address the question of free blacks. (W. W. Mitchell et al. to the President of the Confederate States, 25 Feb. 1864, enclosed in W. N. H. Smith to His Excellency President Davis, 5 Mar. 1864, S-177 1864, Letters Received, ser. 5, Sec. War, RG 109 {F-92}; James A. Seddon to Hon. W. N. H. Smith, 21 Mar. 1864, ch. IX, vol. 17, p. 274, Letters Sent, Sec. War., RG 109 {F-92}.) Two months later, Seddon responded to renewed complaints from Smith about the execution of impressment in North Carolina: "Mechanics useful to a community and free negroes permanently employed in agricultural labor should as far as practicable be permitted to remain." (James A. Seddon to Hon. W. N. H. Smith, 30 May 1864, ch. IX, vol. 17, p. 462, Letters Sent, Sec. War., RG 109 {F-92}.) A year earlier, the escape of a large number of slaves to the enemy had caused Confederate officials to exempt free blacks in New Kent County, Virginia, from impressment. (Endorsements on petition of Jno. D. Christian et al., 16 Apr. 1863, C-302 1863, Letters Received, ser. 5, Sec. War, RG 109 {F-75}.)

305: Superintendent of a Confederate Ordnance Harness Shop to an Officer at the Richmond Arsenal

Clarksville [*Va.*] Octr 15th 1864

Sir, Your communication relative to the pay of negroes is at hand.

I am satisfied you do not fully understand the class of free-negroes we have employed here when you say "seventy to seventy-five dollars pr month would be enough at Clarksville" we have been paying near those rates for *labourers* but the negroes to whom I refer are almost altogether carpenters, blacksmiths or blacksmiths helpers, and selected as the best of that class of mechanics to be found in the neighbourhood, some of them in fact superior workmen to many white men.

We have one boy, although a slave, and whom we are now paying 182$ p month who is as a general workman, the best blacksmith in the shops; on piece work at harness; this boy excells in industry any of the workmen; if the rule is applied in this case, we most certainly will loose one of our *best hands* so will it be with the others, although compelled by the Conscript law to remain where detailed; still they will soon desert us to find employment with some Quartermaster who is at present paying labourers $40 pr month and rations

Rations cannot be bought here as you are no doubt aware, for less than $90 p month (viz 10^{lb} bacon & 30^{lb} flour)

The quartermaster informs me he is drawing rations for the same class of men who were detailed under the same law as those employed by us are, certainly the Quartermasters dep^t has a decided advantage over the Ord^c dept in this respect.

Considering our negroes (free) were entitled to the benefit equaly as much as those employed by the Quartermaster, I have heretofore drawn their rations from the commissary as I can not do so hereafter some arrangement should be made for them else we will soon loose their services by desertion.

I have taken the liberty of writing fully on this subject for the reason that I have experienced a great deal of trouble in my endeavours to procure a competent sett of blacksmiths and their helpers, and to loose them now, would in my opinion be a serious loss to this establishment. Already we have lost two white men from this shop by the enforcement of Genl Order No 77[1]

As the majority of the free negroes in our employment are mechanics and of the best class of negroe mechanics I think it would be fair to allow them a proportionate pay to that which is given to other employees it might be a cheaper plan for the shops to buy for and sell to them, by this means save the time that each and all of them require to search up provisions through the county as it is well known free negroes are a most improvident sett

As employees they are very useful and have given much more satisfaction than slaves either in the shops or elsewhere doing work that slaves cannot do, and which white men would be of little use at, besides it is an impossiblity for me to hire slaves without coming into competition with the publick on the 1st of Jany and hiring on the same terms. Very respety Your obd^t serv^t

ALS   John Kane

Capt. John Kane to Capt. Jas. Dinwiddie, 15 Oct. 1864, chap. IV, vol. 93, #153, Letters Received at the Richmond VA Arsenal, Records of the Ordnance Dept., RG 109 [F-16].

1 General Order 77, issued by the Confederate Adjutant and Inspector General's Office on October 8, 1864, revoked most details granted by the War Department to men between the ages of eighteen and forty-five, and ordered their assignment to active service in the army. (*Official Records*, ser. 4, vol. 3, p. 715.)

306: Testimony of Two South Carolina Former Free Blacks before the Southern Claims Commission

Blountville South Carolina 18th *day of* September, *1877*

1. My name is John Cochran, 50 years old. I live at Blountville S.C. I was born and raised here. Have lived here all my life. I am a carpenter and farmer. I am a free born colored man, my parent were free before me. I own a farm of 12 acres here at Blountville. I inherited the land from my parents. no other person has any interest in this claim.

4. I lived right here before and during the war carried on my trade and farmed.

5. My symphaties were always for the Union from the beginning to the end. We free born colored people were very much oppressed before the war. We had high personal taxes to pay and could not move, not go any where without a ticket from our white guardian. In fact during the war the slaves were better off then we, for they had a master to protect them, while we were continually harrassed and made to work for the rebel quartermaster or the Engineer Department.

6. Never done any thing against the Union except what we were forced to do as stated.

7. I was willing to do whatever I could in aid of the Union

8. As soon as the Union forces came to the main land I went to the Union Army and stayed with them. I helped to pilot them on the roads to the up country.

. . . .

17. Nearly all the free born colored people were for the Union. The Wilcox boys did not belong to our settlement. If there were white Union men here I did not know it. I believe there were, but they did not dare to let their sentiments be known, for fear of maltreatment. The same was the case with the free born colored people, they did not dare to open their mouth. I have known some to be beaten for speaking for the Union. My own uncle, Peter Jackson, was beaten in his own house and so was my brothers wife.

. . . .

his
John X Cochran
mark

. . . .

1. My name is Charles J. Williamson, 34 years old. I live at Blountville S.C. Have lived here all my life – was born and raised here. I am a farmer and Carpenter.

11. I am a free born colored man, my parent were free

people. Am not in claimants employ or service—not in his
debt—do not live on his land—have a farm of my own. Am not in
any way to share in his claim if allowed.

. . . .

56. Conversed with him much during the war and as he
belonged to one of our crowd we could trust each other to talk
freely. He was always like myself in favor of the Union and hoped
for the Yankee army to be successful. Remember nothing
particular, but was satisfied from his talk and his actions that he
was for the Union.

57. I know that he piloted the Union troops through the
Salkehatchie swamp to where the rebels had their works— he was
soon after captured by the rebels and put into Charleston Jail.

58 Never know him to anything against the Union of his own
free will. He was like myself forced to work on the rebel
fortifications and on bridges and they had always guards around us
to prevent us from escaping. I know this because I was with him
all the time. I came home on an account of sickness shortly before
the Union army came It was sometime in December 1864 and I
was at home when the Union Army came and took all our stock and
provisions.

. . . .

HDS   Charles J. Williamson

Excerpts from testimony of John Cochran and Charles J. Williamson, 18 Sept.
1877, claim of John Cochran, Beaufort Co. SC case files, Approved Claims,
ser. 732, Southern Claims Commission, 3rd Auditor, RG 217 [I-102]. Sworn
before a special commissioner of the Southern Claims Commission. The questions that correspond to the enumerated responses are not in the file. According to other documents in the file, Cochran had submitted a claim for $418 as
compensation for the cattle, grain, tools, and a cart taken by Union soldiers.
He was awarded $133. Thomas Jackson, another former free black from the
same settlement, testified before the commission that he too had been "compelled to work on the fortification." The "free colored men were in every way
worse of[f] than the slaves," he recalled. "The slaves had masters to protect
them from violence, but we had to submit to the abuse of every mean white
man who chose to take advantage of us. We had no redress because our
testimony was not allowed in the Courts." Jackson himself was "nearly killed
in 1863 by some Rebel Soldiers in protecting my family from violence. I
receive five cuts with a knife. Having no white witnesses I had no redress."
(Testimony of Thomas Jackson, 22 Mar. 1875, claim of Thomas Jackson,
Beaufort Co. SC case files, Approved Claims, ser. 732, Southern Claims
Commission, 3rd Auditor, RG 217 [I-103].)

REMOVING SLAVES TO SAFETY

307: Commander of a Confederate Mississippi Artillery Company to the Commander of Pettigrew's Brigade

Camp French [*Va.*] Decr 13th 1862.

General, I have the honor to ask for thirty days leave of absence, to visit the Town of Pontotoc in the State of Mississippi, for the following reasons: viz,

I I reside at Pontotoc Miss, and have just been informed by letters from my family that the enemy is encamped within 18 miles of that place, and is expected to take possession of it, in a Short time, and that most of the citizens have removed their families, and property, in order to avoid their being captured; leaving that Section of Country, almost entirely to the mercy of Runaway Slaves, and reckless Straglers from our army, and that the enemy is devastating the country where ever they go, taking all of the male slaves by force, if they do not accompany them willingly. All of the above Statements are *true* or they would not have been made to me, for they are the first words of complaint, that I have heard from my home since I last saw it, (on the 26th day of August 1861).

My family is a helpless one, (consisting of a mother, and five little children) and has now, to rely *alone*, on the labor of fifteen or twenty Slaves for its support, without any person (except my wife, *who* is *entirely unaccustomed* to *such things*) to controll them; (My overseer having volunteered in the army long since). I have no relatives, to whom my wife can apply for advice or assistance, as they are all in the army, or too distant to render aid. If the enemy takes the place; they will certainly, *Rob* me of all I have, and riase the very foundation of my house, for *many* of them *know me.* I have been in the Service, since the 26th day of August 1861. and have not visited, my home, or been absent one single day from my command, except on special duty by orders from my Superiors.

II I require Fifty two (52) privates to fill the ranks of my company, and if permitted to go home I think, perhaps, I may get some if not all of them. Very Respectfully Your ob^t Servt

ALS   W D. Bradford

Capt. W. D. Bradford to Brig. Genl. J. J. Pettigrew, 13 Dec. 1862, B-2932 1862, Letters Received, ser. 12, Adjt. & Insp. Gen., RG 109 [F-258]. Bradford signed as captain of the "Confederate Guard Artillery," Mississippi Volunteers. According to endorsements, General James J. Pettigrew, the brigade commander, approved Bradford's request, and the Confederate War Department granted a thirty-day leave.

308: Headquarters of the Confederate Department of South Carolina, Georgia, and Florida to the Confederate Commander at Adams Run, South Carolina

Charleston, March 23ᵈ *1863.*

Gen'l   It is the wish of the Comd'g Gen'l, that you advise all planters and owners of Negroes in your Military District to remove their negroes as far as practicable into the interior of the State, as otherwise they are liable to be lost at any moment. Very Respectfully Your Obd't Servt.

ALcS

Jno. F. O'Brien

Capt. Jno. F. O'Brien to Brig. Genl. Hagood, 23 Mar. 1863, Letters Sent, ser. 71, Dept. of SC, GA & FL, Records of Military Commands, RG 109 [F-181]. A notation indicates that an identical letter was sent to General William S. Walker, Confederate commander at Pocotaligo, South Carolina.

309: Commander of the Confederate Trans-Mississippi Department to the Commander of the Confederate Army of the West

Shreveport La Sept 4ᵗʰ 1863

General, The policy of our enemy in arming and organizing negro regiments, is being pushed to formidable proportions. Our plantations are made his recruiting stations, and unless some check can be devised, a strong and powerful force will be formed which will receive large additions as he advances on our territory

More than 1000 recruits, in some cases organized on the plantations and forced into the ranks, were made in the recent raid on Monroe. When we fall back, as little as possible should be left for the enemy. Able bodied male negroes and transportation should be carried back in advance of our troops. Facilities should be given, and our friends and planters instructed, in positions exposed to the enemy, that it is the wish of the Dept Commander that, without awaiting his approval they remove to safe localities, their able bodied slaves and transportation

Every sound male black left for the enemy becomes a soldier whom we have afterwards to fight. This is a difficult subject and must be handled cautiously, but I believe it will be wisdom to carry out the above policy to the extent of our abilities   I am General respectfully Your obt servt

HLcSr

(signed) E Kirby Smith

Lt. Gen. E. Kirby Smith to Maj. Genl. Price, 4 Sept. 1863, ch. II, vol. 70, p. 328, Letters Sent, Trans-MS Dept., Records of Military Commands, RG 109 [F-995]. A notation indicates that an identical letter was sent to General Richard Taylor, commander of the Confederate District of West Louisiana. Later in the month, General Smith's chief quartermaster proposed to slave-holders in areas exposed to enemy raids that they hire their able-bodied male slaves to the Confederate army rather than permit them to fall into enemy hands. (See above, doc. 273.) Beginning in the summer of 1863, when Union forces gained control of the entire length of the Mississippi River, federal authorities systematically expanded the recruitment of black soldiers into adjacent territory still under Confederate control. Union expeditions moved from the river into the interior of Arkansas and Louisiana, under orders to push back rebel troops who might otherwise attempt to join their comrades east of the river, and to bring back all able-bodied black men suitable for enlistment. (See, for example, above, doc. 110.)

310: Headquarters of the Confederate District of West Louisiana to the Headquarters of the Confederate Trans-Mississippi Department

Alexandria [*La.*], Sept 29th *1863*

Colonel: In the absence of Maj Genl Taylor who has gone below I ask respectfully to make the following statement for the consideration of the Lieut Genl Comdg.

A few weeks since General Taylor received instructions from your H^d Qrs to render every assistance to planters removing their negroes, and to promote such action where negroes were at all liable to fall into the hands of the Enemy. These instructions have been obeyed but planters complained bitterly that one fourth of their negroes was taken from them after crossing the Sabine.

It is now reported by persons returning from Texas that *one half* is taken, in consequence of which many planters will not move, and some even who have started are, I am informed, returning, preferring to risk the chances with the Enemy. These reports may be much exaggerated — or altogether false, and as I am frequently called upon by planters in relation to them I would respectfully ask for such information as you may deem proper or have it in your power to give. I have the honor to be Colonel Very Respectfully Yr obt Sert

ALS   E. Surget

[*Endorsement*] Hd Qrs D.T.M Shreveport [*La.*] 6" Oct '63 Respectfully referred to Maj Gen Magruder Comdg Dist of

Texas &c. I am directed by the Lt Gen'l Comdg to say that persons driven from their homes and seeking an asylum elsewhere should not have their negroes disturbed until they become settled, when they should and would come under the same rule as other residents— this is due alike to the Government to the master and the negro, for if they are taken away before a home is selected they will certainly run off and not knowing where to go will be lost both to the Government and their masters. Respectfully Y^r Most Ob^{dt} Servt S. S. Anderson Asst Adjt Gen'l

[*Endorsement*] Hd. Qrs. District. [*Houston, Tex.*] Oct 9. 1863 This subject has received my fullest reflexion—& I am convinced that the Texan owners of negroes, will not send their slaves so willingly, if the same rule be not adopted in regard to the people of L^a as to themselves. Few or no negroes have been lost in the manner stated—& few have been so impressed, *if any*—but if the suggestion of Lt Genl Smith be carried out, the masters will *never find* a *home* for their slaves— It will produce great confusion to make this change now & I hope the endorsement of Col. Anderson is not considered an order— Should be ordered by the Lt Genl Comdg that I should discharge all the negroes I have impressed from the people of L^a in Texas who have not *settled themselves*, I would have to discharge all I have— The business of the Negro Bureau works well now for the first time & I do hope, the Lt Genl will not permit the representations of interested parties (planters from La or elsewhere to interfere) with it— I am sir J. B. Magruder Maj. Genl.

A.A. Genl. E. Surget to Col. S. S. Anderson, 29 Sept. 1863, Letters & Telegrams Received by Trans-MS Dept., ser. 106, Trans-MS Dept., Records of Military Commands, RG 109 [F-1010]. In July 1863, the chief of the Labor Bureau in the Confederate District of Texas had authorized the impressment of "one in every four [slaves] who may be passing into the State." (B. T. Carter to Col. C. G. Forshey, 29 July 1863, ch. II, vol. 132, p. 140, Letters Sent, Dist. of TX, NM, & AZ, Trans-MS Dept., Records of Military Commands, RG 109 [F-957].) And in early September, General E. Kirby Smith, commander of all Confederate territory west of the Mississippi River, had authorized his subordinates (including General John B. Magruder, commander of the Confederate District of Texas, New Mexico, and Arizona) to resort to impressment if planters had not volunteered their male slaves in sufficient numbers. (See below, doc. 325.) But in mid-October, Smith ordered Magruder to stop impressing slaves "while in transitu, their masters seeking a home." Smith added, however, that "any attempt to violate the spirit of such an order by the owners of slaves, by continual moving under pretense of not being able to find a home, and where it was apparent it was

made a cover to shield their negroes from impressment, would not be toler-
ated." (Asst. Adj. Genl. S. S. Anderson to Major Genl. J. B. Magruder, 15
Oct. 1863, ch. II, vol. 251, p. 138, Letters Received, Dist. of TX, NM, &
AZ, Trans-MS Dept., Records of Military Commands, RG 109 [F-915].)

311: Mississippi Planter to the Confederate Secretary of War

Washington County Miss November 3^d 1863

Dear Sir   I was told to day that you had commissioned A. M.
Paxton Esq as Major for the express purpose of coming into the
Island formed by the Yazoo and Miss Rivers, to remove all of the
able bodied men and women, mules and stock of every description,
leaving only the old decrepid men and women and the
children— The reason assigned by you was, that by doing so, it
would prevent the Yankees from getting them and thus weaken
them to that extent— If you were here upon the spot you would
see the utter impracticability of accomplishing it— Instead of
weakening the Yankees the very first lot of negroes taken by
surrounding the quarters, which would be the only way to secure
even one lot, there would be a stampede of all the balance, who
would take every mule with them to the Yankees— Some three
months since Mr J. W. Vick had his quarter surrounded and his
men all taken to the hills— Since that time the negroes have been
very shy of our Soldiers and only within the last month all the
negro men on the Creek laid out for about ten days while they were
in here collecting cattle— The report came before them that they
were taking all the men for the army and the consequence was all
the men laid out for over a week and many were scared off entirely
to the Yankees— There are over one hundred and ninety negroes on
this place, I have never thought or talked about moving them, and
had not lost one by running off until the scare about a month ago
when four men and a woman left— I am the only one as far as my
acquaintance extends who had not either attempted to or were
preparing to move and every one who did so lost nearly if not all of
the men and many of the women and children— I believe every
negro on this place will go the Yankees before they would go to the
hills, and at same time think they have made up their minds to stay
at home and wait the issue of events if they are permitted to do
so— I believe it utterly impossible for major Paxton to be
successful in such a measure, but the result will be the running off
the negroes now on the plantations and the mules they would steal
and the making of bad citizens of good ones, who will view the
measure as intolerable oppression— There were many persons who

ran with the residue of their negroes to the hills, who found it impossible to live and either have or are returning to their homes— I write to you because I can make myself known to you, when I tell you, that I am the brother of Mrs Martha Stanard the widow of Robt C. Stanard both of whom I know esteemed you as a friend— I have not the value of one dollar interested in the measure and if you want disinterested testimony I have given it to you and you can take it for what it is worth   Yours truly

ALS   Jon'a Pearce

[*Endorsement*] [*Confederate War Department, Richmond*]   30 Nov 63   It has been my conviction that when there was a probability that the enemy would either seduce or force the able bodied male negroes into their Armies they should be removed by our Forces as a matter of plain Military Authority.   Beyond that I have not gone and that I thought ought only to be attempted with a considerable force so as to prevent the negroes from taking the alarm   I gave no express instructions to remove negroes (except that I authorised him, if he could to remove men) but I expressed to him the view. I have stated and directed him to confer with Genl Johnston and if they met his sanction, to concert proper action on the subject.   On the theory of this writer, it is palpable, if the negroes remain on the estates, they will be subject to Yankey control and the males may at any time be Drafted into their Armies— Is it not the duty of the Confederate Gov^t to prevent this and instead of allowing the male slave to be converted into armed soldiers agst us to preserve them as useful laborers for their owners & the Confederacy   J A S   secy

Jon'a. Pearce to Honl. Jas. A. Seddon, 3 Nov. 1863, P-366 1863, Letters Received, ser. 5, Sec. War, RG 109 [F-81]. The substance of the endorsement was forwarded to Pearce on December 1, 1863. (James A. Seddon to J. Pearce, Esq., 1 Dec. 1863, ch. IX, vol. 15, pp. 271–72, Letters Sent, Sec. War., RG 109 [F-81].)

312: Order by the Commander of Confederate Cavalry in North Mississippi

Oxford [*Miss.*] Novr 7 1863

General Orders N° 70—

I   In obedience to the Orders of Genl Johnston Comd'g &c detachments will be sent from each Brigade into the Dist of

Country adjacent to the enemies lines to arrest and remove within our lines all able bodied negroe men who are liable to be Captured by the enemy   The object being to remove such negroes as the enemy would be likely to persuade or force into their service as Soldiers no others than those Capable of performing Military duty will be taken.   Those most exposed to Capture will be first removed.   The Negroes thus taken will be sent to Head Qrs at Meridian to be employed on Gov^t work

II   The Comd'g Officer of each detachment will give to the owner of each negroe taken a receipt showing the name age description and value of the negroe and the date when he was taken. He will also forward a similar descriptive list of the negroes arrested by him together with the names and residences of the owners with the negroes to H^d Qrs at Meridian

III   All negroes arrested under this order by detachments from Richardsons Brigade will be sent with their descriptive lists direct to Genl Johnstons H^d Qrs at Meridian   Those arrested by other detachments will be sent to these H^d Qrs

IV   The Attention of Brigade & Regimental Comdrs is called to the evident lack of the proper drill and discipline in their respective Commands.   The Orders from these H^d Qrs in regard to daily drills and strict discipline will at once be put in force and rigidly executed   By Order of Brig Genl Chalmers

HD

General Orders No. 70, Head Qrs. Cav. in N. Miss., 7 Nov. 1863, ch. II, vol. 299, p. 372, Orders & Circulars, Gen. James R. Chalmers's Brigade, Commands of Individual Officers, Records of Military Commands, RG 109 [F-860]. On October 20, 1863, General Joseph E. Johnston, commander of the Confederate Department of the West, had ordered Chalmers to send all black men within his field of operations to Meridian, Mississippi, "for Gov^t work." "The principal reason for the order," noted Johnston's adjutant, "is to be found in the fact that every negroe fit to be made a soldier of is put by the enemy in his ranks [and] it is important and necessary to check this in every possible way." He added that "[o]ld men women & children will be allowed to remain." (A.A.G. B. S. Ewell to Brig. Genl. Chalmers, 20 Oct. 1863, ch. II, vol. 293, p. 30, Letters, Telegrams, Orders & Circulars Received by Gen. James R. Chalmers, Commands of Individual Officers, Records of Military Commands, RG 109 [F-865].)

THE DESTRUCTION OF SLAVERY

313: Virginia Legislator to the Confederate Secretary of War

[*Richmond*] January 13 1864

Sir   Your communication, to me, of the   inviting attention of the Legislature to the policy of withdrawing all able bodied male slaves from within the enemies' lines, and without our own, liable to seizure by them, through the intervention of our own forces, was referred to the Committee of Confederate Relations, and has received from them the attention its importance demands.   They have considered the subject in both the aspects in which you presented it viz: The saving the property of our citizens, and the defeating of the enemy's design of recruiting a black force within the limits indicated, and have invited and obtained the expression of the views of a large number of the member[s] of the House, representing the counties more immediately interested, as to the effects likely to be produced by the adoption of the policy suggested.   They concur, I believe without exception in believing it would be attended with very serious mischiefs, and with very partial compensating good.   They represent that within the enemies lines the number of slaves left at their homes, fit for military service, is now very limited – forcibly or voluntarily the great bulk of them of that description having already gone to the enemy: That the few remaining are retained, generally, by strong local, or family, attachments, but none by any motive which would not yield to the aversion they entertain to be forced away from their homes within our lines, and employed on our public works.   That they are so scattered, that but a very small proportion could be captured, if any, by a military raiding party before they would fly to the woods, or to the enemy, soon to be followed by their families, whose labor and assistance is now so invaluable to the loyal whites (chiefly females and children) still remaining in the enemies lines would be attended with the most deplorable consequences.   That many of those citizens would be left in great extremity for support if they remained, or exposed to great loss and suffering, if they removed, besides, by coming further into the interior, increasing the existing pressure on our already overtaxed means of subsistence.   The fear was also expressed by some of the gentlemen who favored the Committee with their views, that the loss of their still remaining slaves, occasioned by such an intervention of the Government, might lead, however injustifiably, to alienating from our cause persons now friendly to it.   The effects, on the slaves of the interior, of bringing amongst them, so far as the measure should prove successful, those who had become imbued by the enemy with ideas and habits, but little consistent with the obedience and subordination proper to their condition, and necessary to the peace and safety of the whites, was strongly urged as dissuading from the adoption of the policy under consideration. In respect to the consequences of such a measure as applied to the district's, between our lines, and those of the enemy, the gentlemen representing them thought the effects would be similar to those above presented. While in them a plan might be adopted, no doubt, attended with more success for getting possession of the slaves than in the other case, yet they believe large numbers would attempt successfully to escape to the enemy, while it would be the signal for the immediate stampede into the enemys camps of all the slaves within their lines. There was no difference of opinion as to the general opposition of the owners to the plan, nor as to its resulting in a greater loss of slave property to the state than would ensue by leaving the owners to pursue the best measures in their power to save them as exigencies might recommend. Not considering that the communication received from you was intended so much to indicate a line of policy determined on, as to invite a conference, and comparison of views, with those most interested in it, in regard to its expediency, the committee have instructed me to lay before you the facts and views herein communicated for your consideration, before adopting any conclusions, or taking any definite action, on the subject. They should probably say, however, that they so far feel the force of them as to be disinclined to recommend to the favor of the House the policy of a forcible withdrawal of the slaves from the Quarters of the state embraced by your suggestion, by the military intervention of the Confederate Government. But they trust there will be found no room or occasion for any conflict to arise between the authorities respectively of the two Governments, at least in the conclusions they shall arrive at. They are pursuaded that the Confederate Gov^t even, if not concuring entirely in the views above set forth, would yet readily refrain, in a matter of so much delicacy, and so vitally affecting our citizens, unless from the clearest conviction of an overruling necessity, from exercising a power which any state might deem seriously objectionable and prejudicial to her most important interests. Hoping to learn from your reply that the Confederate Government does not, in view of all the circumstances, propose to pursue the policy to which you invited the attention of the Legislature of Virginia, unless with their concurrence. I am Very Respectfully.

ALS   Wyndham Robertson

Wyndham Robertson to Hon. James A. Seddon, 13 Jan. 1864, R-22 1864, Letters Received, ser. 5, Sec. War, RG 109 [F-1006]. The blank space in the opening sentence appears in the manuscript. Robertson was chairman of the

Committee on Confederate Relations of the Virginia House of Delegates. In reply, the Confederate Secretary of War concurred in the committee's sympathetic understanding of the "repugnance and apprehension entertained by owners" who feared the effects upon their slaves of removal into the interior; and he promised that the Confederate government would not order such removal except in the event of an emergency. (James A. Seddon to Wyndham Robertson, Esq., 24 Jan. 1864, ch. IX, vol. 17, pp. 10–11, Letters Sent, Sec. War, RG 109 [F-1006].) For a plea by Confederate military commanders in southside Virginia and northeastern North Carolina that slaves be removed from the area to prevent their enlistment in the Union army, see above, doc. 14B.

314: Commander of the Confederate Trans-Mississippi Department to Planters in the Red River Valley of Arkansas

Shreveport [*La.*] Nov 23rd 1864.

Gentlemen. I have learned with much regret that you are preparing to remove with your labor to Txs, leaving your present plantations uncultivated. Setting aside all patriotic considerations urging the importance of producing crops in localities where they are accessible and therefore of increased value for subsistence to our troops, I am induced to submit other reasons which should cause you to abandon a course detrimental as I believe to your personal interests. Owing to the exhausted condition of the intervening country it will be impossible for the enemy to campaign successfully from the Arkansas to the Red River. An Experience of fourteen years in the state of Texas has taught me, that except in the region near the coast and in the lower vallies of the Brazos and Colorado, no dependence can be placed upon the grain crop, more than one year in four, or a sufficiency raised even for the support of your family and slaves. There, while the difficulty of providing for your families would be increased, you would gain little in point of security. The country near the coast and west of the Colorado, being at any time liable to hostile attempts of the enemy. I trust therefore that you will reconsider your resolution to remove, and most earnestly appeal to you to remain at home and cultivate your plantations. If the valley of Red River is abandoned by its planters, and that great granary of the Dept goes to waste from the absence of labor, our armies must be withdrawn and your slaves reduced to starvation, searching in Mexico that security which you sacrifice on abandoning your homes   I am Gentlemen, With great respect Your most obdt Servt

HLc   [*E. Kirby Smith*]

General [E. Kirby Smith] to Mr. R. C. Cummings and other Planters on Red River, 23 Nov. 1864, ch. II, vol. 71, p. 228, Letters Sent, Trans-MS Dept., Records of Military Commands, RG 109 [F-837]. The planters had informed General Smith that they were moving to Texas not "from fear of the enemy, but because of the depredations of our own troops, and from the belief that their produce will be taken by the Government without leaving them sufficient for a support." Smith urged his subordinate commanders to offer the planters assurances that would allay these fears. (General [E. Kirby Smith] to Maj. Gen. J. B. Magruder, 29 Nov. 1864, and General [E. Kirby Smith] to Col. Leonidas Johnson, 29 Nov. 1864, ch. II, vol. 71, pp. 241–42, Letters Sent, Trans-MS Dept., Records of Military Commands, RG 109 [F-837].) At the same time, however, Smith prepared to use force to prevent their exodus. (S. S. Anderson to Col. E. G. Randolph, 29 Nov. 1864, and General [E. Kirby Smith] to Mrs. Elizabeth R. Wright, 10 Dec. 1864, ch. II, vol. 71, pp. 243, 280, Letters Sent, Trans-MS Dept., Records of Military Commands, RG 109 [F-837]; Brig. Genl. W. R. Boggs to Col. B. F. Danley, 19 Dec. 1864, ch. II, vol. 71, p. 303, Letters Sent, Trans-MS Dept., Records of Military Commands, RG 109 [F-843].)

MAINTAINING SLAVE DISCIPLINE ON THE HOME FRONT

315: Alabama Lawyer to the Confederate President

Cahaba, Ala. 22[d] *May 1861*

Dear Sir: Under a late act of the Congress of the Confederate States, military Companies can present themselves to the War Department, and be recieved, without a call from you or the Governor of the Confederate States. This may be right; but, there should be a watchfulness in the reception of troops, in too large numbers from different localities?

In behalf of the women & children of our County (Dallas), I beg you to instruct the War Department to recieve no more of our troops, for the following reasons:

1. Dallas is the largest slaveholding County in the Southern Confederacy, and needs a *home support:*

2. Dallas has 1600 voters and has over 500. of them now in the field:

3. We need the remainder of them to keep the slaves down, and save ourselves from the horrors of insurrection, which may be an incident of the war.

Our County will thank you to consult Gov. Moore on this subject, whose views are known to them.

If no check is interposed, by some one in power, our whole white population will volunteer (men, women & children, I believe) and *anarchy* will prevail and the slaves become our masters, if they can. For Heaven's Sake, bring this popular madness, if you can, into discipline, or we will ruin ourselves by the *recklessness* of our patriotism. With distinguished regard, Yr. Obt. Servt

ALS   G. W. Gayle

G. W. Gayle to Hon. Jeff. Davis, 22 May 1861, #1229 1861, Letters Received, ser. 5, Sec. War, RG 109 [F-35]. Earlier in May, similar fears led a farmer in Monroe County, Alabama, to suggest that Confederate authorities remove black men — "Ether fort them up or put them in the army" — to prevent insurrection. (*Freedom*, ser. 2: doc. 113.)

316: Virginia Slaveholder to the Confederate Attorney General

                                        Albemarle county [*Va.*]   December 4th 1861

Dr. Sir, Although a stranger to you, yet in consequence of the excitement and distress in this section of country, in reference to a certain matter; I am constrained to address you, not merely on my own account; but on behalf of a large number of most respectable citizens; with the hope entertained on our part, that you will not refuse to respond to our inquiries, contained in this communication. –

A practice has prevailed for some considerable time in *this* section of the country of impressing into the service of the confederate army, the horses wagons and *slaves* belonging to the people

The "Press masters" will go to their houses, and drag of their property to Just Such an extent as they choose; until it has not only created great excitement and distress; but bids fair to produce wide spread ruin. And I am told that these "Press masters" are paid by the Government the enormous price of *two dollars and fifty cents for each team which they impress*: – hence their anxiety and untiring exertions to increase the number: – thus making thirty or forty dollars pr day –

Whilst I do not controvert the right of the Government to impress into its service *wagons and teams*; yet I do controvert the right to impress *Slaves*: – It does seem to me that no one can be impress'd into military service of any kind, unless he is subject to military duty: because this whole business is relating to the Army, and is purely a military matter. –

The Confederacy

The people in this section of the country are much attached to their slaves, and treat them in a humane manner – consequently they are exceedingly pained at having them dragged off at this inclement season of the year, and exposed to the severe weather in the mountains of north western Virginia – (halling from Staunton, through the Alleghany and other mountains to Greenbrier River.) – Some have already died, and others have returned home afflicted with Typhoid fever, which has spread through the family to a most fatal and alarming extent. –

I am a practicing lawyer myself, but these "Press masters" will hear nothing from any one residing amongst the people –

Therefore Sir, in consequence of the distress produced by the causes before mentioned, I am constrained to write to you; requesting you if you please, to give your opinion upon the questions involved.

To wit – If a man's wagon and team should be impress'd into Service, can his slave be impress'd to drive the said team –

Secondly – If a man has neither wagon or team can his slave be impress'd to drive some other team (*some* of the "Press masters" yield this *last* point, whilst others do not, and contend that they can impress just as many slaves as they choose from any plantation, taking all the negro men if they think proper.) –

Some few of the people have not been able to sow their grain this fall: – and there is a deep dissatisfaction amongst the people – therefore I deem it proper and expedient that the authorities should know it –

In reference to the questions herein before presented to you I beg leave to invite your attention to the Code of Virginia – (of 1860) – page 176 – Chap 32nd Section the 1st [1] by which it seems there is no power to impress Slaves: and I presume there is no act of Congress, of the Confederate states, giving the power – or that such a thing was ever thought of –

There is also a serious evil in impressing slaves for the service in North western Virginia: – whilst there they get to talking with *Union men* in disguise, and by that means learn the original cause of the difficulty between the North & South: then return home and inform other negroes: – not long since one of my neighbors negro men went to his master, and desired to let him go again to the north western army – adding "I wish you to let me go further than I went before – I have the honor to be most respectfully your Obt Servt.

John B. Spiece

Please direct your answer to Greenwood Albemarle

ALS

783

John B. Spiece to Attorney General of the Confederate States, 4 Dec. 1861, enclosed in Wade Keyes to Hon. Judah P. Benjamin, 6 Dec. 1861, #8230 1861, Letters Received, ser. 5, Sec. War, RG 109 [F-46].

1 "Any officer in command of any corps or detachment of the militia, or other troops, . . . when unable to procure supplies by contract in due time, may impress such transportation, fuel, forage, rations, camp equipage and horses for artillery service, as may be required for the use of said corps or detachment." (*The Code of Virginia, Second Edition*, [Richmond, 1860], p. 176.)

317: Commander of the Confederate Department of North Carolina to the Commander of the Confederate District of Pamlico

Goldsboro [*N.C.*], Feb. 18th, 1862.
General, Your letter of the 16th inst. has just reached me.

I approve of Major Hall's evacuation of Hyde County under your orders, and I also approve of the disposition you propose to make of the force, unless on after consideration you should deem it advisable to keep a small force, say the two companies of the 17th Regmt., at Leaksville, to give some sort of protection to the people of Hyde against their slaves. I suppose they could safely retire upon the approach of a large force of the enemy.

I am under the impression that Lt. Col. Johnson was ordered to proceed to Washington and collect the fragments of his Regmt. If I am in error please give him the necessary orders to do so and to report by letter to his Col. – Martin. Very Respectfully Your Obt Sert

(Signed) R. C. Gatlin
Note. I think a company was raised in Hyde for special service and local defense. That company ought either to be disbanded, or left in the County or elsewhere according to the terms of its original muster.

HLcSr   R. C. G.

Brig. Genl. R. C. Gatlin to Brig. Genl. L. O'B. Branch, 18 Feb. 1862, ch. II, vol. 262 1/2, pp. 125–26, Letters & Telegrams Sent, Dept. of NC, Records of Military Commands, RG 109 [F-659].

318A: Charges and Testimony in the Confederate Court-Martial of Five Florida Slaves

[*Pensacola, Fla.*] Sunday April 6, 1862
Was arrayned and tried George Robert Stephen Peter &
William – Slaves the property of Jackson Morton of Santa Rosa
County Florida on the following charge and specifications
charge –
Attempt to violate 57 article of War.[1]
Specification first
In this that the said Slaves George Robert Stephen Peter and
William did attempt to escape to the Island of Santa Rosa and was
caght in the act.
Specification Second
That the Said Slaves possessed information well calculated to aid
the enemy.
specification third
That the said slaves are inteligent beings possesing the faculties of
Conveying information which would prove useful to the enemy and
detrimental to the Confederate states – all this in and near the City
and harbour of Pensacola on or about the 2nd day of april 1862.

. . . .

Leut J A Foster of 4th Bat Ala Vols on part of Prosecution was
duly sworn
By Judge Advocate
What is your rank company & Regiment
First Leutenent Co G 4th Battalion Alabama Volenteers
Do you know the accused.
I have seen them   I saw them at Deer point first
Will you state to the Court the circumstances under which you
met the accused.
about daylight I think about the 3^d or 4th of this month I was
awaken by the sentinel who had two of the boys in charge – they
were William & Peter – Several of the Sentinels were standing with
him when I saw them
Will you state to the Court how the slaves came in charge of the
Sentinels?
I can only say what they say about it. on being called by the
sentinels Capt Wagnor and myself, went out to them and
ascertained that the Slaves had been questioned by the Sentinels –   I
asked one the boys I think Peter if was runaway   he said he was,
that he belonged to General Morton – & that he was trying to get to

Santa Rosa Island. — I had very little conversation with them before the other three Came up but Peter said that he and Williams were the only ones & that they had crossed over; on a raft, but while he was speaking the other three came up. — recognises the slaves present as being the ones who came up while Peter was talking — it was fifty yards from where we were standing to where we first saw the other three Negroes — some one remarked that they were hands belonging to the boat and no attention was paid to them until they got up to where we were talking to Peter and William — the first that attracted my attention was Capt Wagnor turning to Robert and asking him if he was runaway. he answered he was & that he belonged to the same Crowd or something to that effect. I do not recollect the exact words. — upon ascertaining that they had a boat I sent a Seargent & one or two men with the slave, Robert after the boat, & I took Peter & stephen off to question them — I then took Peter off and sit down on a log, and asked him every question I thought would elicit the truth from him he Peter said he had been induced to beleive that if he could get to Santa Rosa Island or Ft Pickens that he would be free — he stated that he had a Kind master and had always been treated well, but that never the less he desired to be a free man. — he Stated that although his master had always fed him Very well — that of late he his Master had not had it in his power to get provisions Meat particularly, and that he expected to get a plenty on the Island — that there was no disposition on the part of his master not to give it to him but that he his master Could not get it he referred to the burning of the mills and the general excitement of the people in the Country above here — he stated that the people were very much excited, and moving away & carrying their slaves with them and that he had heard his Master say, that he had an idea of moving his slaves away from home. — he gave this as a reason that he came away, that he did not want to be carried into Alabama he stated that he was influenced by Mr Chance and Mr Mayo to runaway. — he sid that Mayo told him if he could get away, that he Could go to new York or Cuba or Havannah and enjoy himself as he pleased as a free man. — He told me that in one Conversation he had with Mayo that Robert was present — this is about all I remember of importance he said — He also said that he Knew that a great many of our best troops had been sent off — and that the troops that are here now are not armed, or diciplined — When I asked him how he Knew these things — he said that he had heard people talk — but could not call any names. I then questioned stephen he said that he had heard a good deal about black people being free if they Could get, to Santa Rosa Island — and that he agread with the other boys to try to go over there — there was nothing that Conflicted

786

with what Peter said and as he was not as Communicative as Peter I
did not examine him as thouroughly. the Conversation was
short— In the close of my conversation with Stephen he said if he
had a chance he would still go to Pickens—that he was not changed,
in desire or object in getting there

Peter said he would like very much if he Could to get home and
stay there

I asked stephen if I were to give him the boat and turn him
loose, whether he would go home or to the Island   he said to the
Island   about the time I had finished talking with stephen Robert
and the Sergent came with the boat & Capt Wagnor and myself
talked with him Robert—   his tale corresponded with Peters except
in one particular   Peter had stated that Robert was with him when
he had the Conversation with Mayo, but Robert denied any
Knowledge of if—   he said he had been talked to on the subject by
a white man whose name was Garrett—   this is about all I recollect
of the Conversation—   with the other two boys I had but very little
Conversation—but they both told Me that it was their object to get
over, to the Island and be free

. . . .

Monday 7th april /62

. . . .

Capt John F Wagnor on part of prosecution was duly sworn.

Do you recognise the slaves present as being the Same Captured
on Deer point

I do.

Will You state to the Court all you Know of, their Capture and
all you heard them say of their intended escaspe

The first I knew of their Capture was in the Morning soon on the
2nd instant I think   I ordered them tied and a guard placed over
them—that they should not be questioned   learned soon after that
they had been questioned by the pickett   after a short while I asked
them where they had started—   they replied that they had runaway
from their Master Genl Morton—   I asked the reason. they replied
because they had not been fed well recently and that they did not
want to be sent into Alabama—   in the meantime the other three
Came up, & upon being questioned as to who they were the boy
Robert replied that they belonged to Genl Morton and made the
same answers to the same enquiries as the others

I had a guard placed over them with instructions that they should
not be allowed to hold Conversations with each other—   Leut Foster
took one and I took another (names not recollected or cant identify
them)   the one I took denied upon being questioned his intention
to go to Pickens   I then told him that he was in my power that he
must answer the truth to the following questions   Were you going

787

to Pickens or did you start   he confessed that he was. gave as his
reason for denial before that it would implicate white Men. I then
pressed him for the names of the men who had instigated him to
leave. — he gave them as Mayo a Grogshopkeeper or whisky seller
in Millton — Arthur Chance a man who had been in the employ of
his master and a Mr Garrett a man who gets shingles: all
implicated — Mayo and Chance had at different times from the
election of Lincoln during the year 1861 advised these boys to go to
Pickens — stating that by Lincoln^s election they were as free as he was
and that they were fools if they did not go to Pickens as it was
easily done. they also at different times told them of the benefits of
freedom, and every thing pertaining to it — as inducements to do
what they proposed. Garrett told Robert and Eli that they the
(negroes) were as free as he (Garrett) is if they had a mind to go to
Pickins they Could do so easily — Robert admitted that his master
had raised him and his mother and that he had Consented to desert
his master his home & family to go to Pickens but said that he was
Sorry then that he had been induced by white men to do so.

Stephen said he was persuaded to go by, William & Peter and
that the project had been on foot for some time — he hesitated
whether or not to accept the proposition not Knowing what would
come of it but William and Peter upbraided him until he Consented
to go. — the time was appointed — William and Peter Conducted
them to a boat Which was locked — and after the boat was broken
loose he (stephen) still hesitated — thought of his Wife his home his
master & put one foot in the boat and took it out again   the other
boys told him he was foolish to come on with them and go to the
Island and be free. he stepped in and the boat was shoved off. — I
think he said William sat in the stern of the boat to guide
it — either William or Peter I cant say which claiming to Know the
way. — they went on and landed at 75 points on tuesday
night — William & Peter were sent on ahead   the other thee staid
with the boat. William Robert & Peter all Said that Mr Chance Mr
Mayo (I do not recollect whether all mentioned Garrett or not) had
at different times advised them to leave for Pickens — they all five
acknowledged [to] distinct understanding & premeditated intention
to escape to the Island

I do not recollect hearing any of them say that whether they
Knew any thing about our Army or not.

Stephen admitted in my hearing that he thought when he landed
that night he was on Santa Rosa Island — Peter said he thought
that they were on live oak Island

I was unable to learn from any of the Negroes that any two white
men talked to them at the same time but that all implicated the
same men

Cross Exd by accused.

Did you in your Conversation with these slaves elicit any
information then in their possesion which would aid the enemy if
Communicated to Said enemy?

The Negroes were well aware, that the mills and Gunboats had
been burned, & the reasons why they were of the general stampede
& moving Negro property & the reasons for moving I will also
state that either Peter or William claimed to be familiar with the
County from his masters home to Pickens and the other three
Robert stephen & George would never have Consented as stated by
them had they not been well assured, by Peter and William that
one or both knew the route as one of them stated that one or the
other of the boys, Peter or William I cant say which had some time
in the past been to the Navy Yard or Pickens I cant say which in a
lumber boat.

George never admitted of having been talked to by any white
persons, on the subject of leaving and stephen claims not to have
Known as much, of the Conversation as the others and Robert
claims not to have Know as much as the other two. – The negroes
had in their possesion clothes boots hats &c in large quantities for
slaves.

By the Court.

Will you designate the Ringleaders

It was generaly Conceded that William & Peter were.

Hon Jackson Morton was sworn on part of prosecution

Do you Know the accused

I do.

Are they your Slaves.

they are.

Will you state to the Court the general character of them

Peter is the most inteligent of the five has been considered by me
as a very trust worthy Servant. Not what is considered an Eye
servant. send him to do a peice of Work, & he will perform it
without the suprintendence of a white person. I would have as soon
suspected any negro I owned as him to lead a stampede I had
confidence in his fidelity

William is less inteligent than Peter fine servant for
Work. disliked being controlled by any white person except
myself. – Not at all surprised at his being one of the principal
movers in the stampede as my overseer had intimated to me that
since the enemy were in possesion of Ft Pickens he judged from his
deportment and general Conduct he would be willing at any time to
form one of a party to go to Ft Pickens or the enemy.

Robert is still less inteligent than William he is a self willed
perverse Negro. though in the general a good labourer, easily

controlled by myself but not by an overseer or suprintendant. I am not surprised at his being induced to Join a party or stampede but would never originate a movement of the Kind

Stephen is quite an ignorant boy a petty theif and very much of an Eye servant and requires some one to overlook him constantly   Could be lead or induced by a Negro of superior inteligence to do most anything

George is young boy about 18 or 19 not inteligent but has been a remarkable fine boy for work, honest and trust worthy but like stephen Could be persuaded by a Negro of inteligence to join a party of the Kind — Withal he is a very timid boy.

When did the Negroes leave your place?

Monday night about 8 oclock 31st Mar.

Can either of the Negroes read or write?

I think not

Were you in the habit of Keeping your Negroes strictly about your plantation?

I was not   I have been too indulgent

. . . .

HD

Excerpts from proceedings of a general court-martial in the case of George, Robert, Stephen, Peter, & William, 6–8 Apr. 1862, enclosed in Maj. Genl. Saml. Jones to Genl. S. Cooper, 22 Apr. 1862, J-79 1863, Letters Received, ser. 5, Sec. War, RG 109 [F-69]. The defendants' counsel argued that they had not violated the 57th article of war, because they had not communicated with or given aid to the enemy. He characterized the fugitives as merely "slaves who during these troublous times were ill fed on account of the scarcity of provisions, and were about to be taken to the state of Alabama, and who were at the same time receiving assurances from traitrous persons with white skins, that by deserting their master and fleeing, they would not only be well fed and cared for, but would also be invested with the inestimable blessing of freedom, and placed upon the basis of a white man — to escape the misery which the future foreshadowed and to grasp the ease and happiness promised, was a picture and an allurement too tempting to be resisted by human beings occupying the degraded position of these accused, — to attain which they fled and attempted to reach this modern Canaan, this land of refuge to their longing desires. —" The court found the five slaves guilty. Peter and William were sentenced to be hanged; George, Robert, and Stephen, to be whipped for four days in succession, receiving each morning twenty-five, thirty, and thirty-nine lashes, respectively, and then to be removed outside the lines of the Army of Pensacola by their master. The court acknowledged that strict construction of the regulations governing courts-martial would not sustain its decision, but claimed the justification of "high Military Necessity." "[T]he peculiar Condition of this division of the Army and this portion of the Country demand that this Sumary and irregular proceedings be Carried out as the only safe means to protect the lives and interest of this portion of the Confederacy. – " Colonel Thomas M. Jones, commander of the Army of Pensacola, approved the death sentences of Peter and William, but reduced the punishment of George, Robert, and Stephen to "fifty lashes Each, well laid on with a rawhide." He confessed that he was reducing the latter sentences only because the articles of war permitted no more than fifty lashes, "for these negroes have all deserved death."

1 "Whosoever shall be convicted of holding correspondence with, or giving intelligence to, the enemy, either directly or indirectly, shall suffer death, or such other punishment as shall be ordered by the sentence of a court-martial." (C.S.A., War Department, *Army Regulations Adopted for the Use of the Army of the Confederate States* [New Orleans, 1861], p. 414.)

318B: Commander of the Confederate Army of Pensacola to the Confederate Adjutant and Inspector General

[*Pensacola, Fla.*] April 12th 1862
Sir   I have the honor respectfully to fow^d the proceedings in the cases lately tried by a Genl Court Martial, assembled in Pensacola Fla – by my order, as directed in a dispatch from the Hon. Secy. of War, received Yesterday.

There were six negroes cought in the act of escaping to the enemy, and in order to make a distinction, if possible, in the cases, I directed the court, not as a regular Court Martial, but rather as an "Investigating Committee" to determine whether these slaves could be held longer as property without danger to the public, or whether they should be destroyed.   Consequently the proceedings are not altogether as regular as they would have been under ordinary circumstances.

I enclose a copy of my order, and a "Proclamation" previously published which the urgency of the case, in my opinion, required; and the necessity of prompt and energetic action, and summary punishment, is not only shown by the tone and wording of my order, but is evident to all persons here, who have the good of the country at heart.   I am confident the Genl Comd^g the Dept. will testify, that he, not only deemed such a course necessary, but sanctioned the steps taken by me, to prevent the frequent desertions to the enemy that were almost daily taking place, and the consequent transmission of information, rendering the condition of my little army exceedingly critical, and dangerous.

I am very much pained to perceive that Mr Jackson Morton to whom five of these Slaves belonged, and were lost to him, until captured by my troops, beyond all reasonable chance of recovery

Should have found grounds of complaint against my judgements in these cases, and which I had made less severe on him in consideration of the losses he has already sustained in this vicinity; and that he should have made use of his influence & position to cripple me, in an hour of danger & difficulty, and at a time when prompt and energetic steps were absolutely necessary, not only for the greatest security of this kind of property, but for the protection & safety of the troops under my command.

The infliction of the punishment, in these cases, hereafter, will be of little or no consequence, and had, in my opinion, as well be dispensed with entirely. The execution of a few bad negroes. unquestionably guilty, would, perhaps have rendered my position comparativly safe, and would have, at once, put an end to the greatest trouble at this place, that is, the absconding of negroes & the transmission of information respecting our defences, strength &c.

As an evidence, others have escaped, since it became known, that strong influences had been interposed to protect & shield those who have been detected and apprehended. Since this citizen is unwilling to make a sacrafice of his personal interests to the public welfare, and has had the power to interfere with the interior of my command, & with what I conceive to be, the proper execution of my duties, I beg that I may not be held responsible for the difficulties & escapes which will most certainly follow.

It is impossible for me to execute the Slave of Mr R. L. Campbell, sentenced under similar circumstances. Mr Campbell being a true and patriotic citizen, has cheerfully come forward and given me all the assistance, his splendid talents and high moral character, were so well calculated to render effective, in this community – surrendering, without a murmur his slave, into the hands of the high toned & concientious Southern gentlemen and officers, who, I took good care, should compose the court.

In making the above statements, I have no desire to make personal references, either offensive or agreeable to individuals, but I simply wish to state facts, that have controlled me, and should I think controll those, who, having an undoubted right to to so – have thought proper to question my judgment, upon the statements of an individual outside of my command. Not, that I so much object to such scrutiny, for the Department has relieved me from a responsibility, for which I am truly thankful, as it was a case about the strict legality of which I had some doubt, but the punishment of which, at the same time, I knew full well, the exigencies of the Service, imperitively demanded. I am sir Very Respectfully Your Obt Svt.

HLS

Tho⁵ M. Jones

[*Endorsement*] H^d Q^{rs} Dep^t A & W. Fla. Mobile [*Ala.*] Apl. 22. /62 Respectfully forwarded. I believed that so much information had been conveyed to the enemy on Santa Rosa, and so much mischief done in the Community by the tampering of bad white men with negroes and the escape of the latter to the enemy, that I advised Col. Jones it would be necessary to make examples of some of them & suggested that the one who was detected in conveying news papers and other documents to Fort Pickens should be the first. Col. Jones was left at Pensacola under very trying circumstances and strong measures were needed to prevent spy^s whether white or black conveying information of his true condition to the enemy A few examples such as Col. Jones undertook to make would I think have produced a good effect in the Community & not only tended to prevent the Conveying of information to the enemy but would have prevented the loss of much valuable property. If negroes are given to understand that when they attempt to escape and Convey information to the enemy & fail to do so their Masters will interpose & shield them from the severest punishment, the enemy will have constant information of our condition & much valuable property will be lost. Saml Jones. Maj Genl

Col. Thos. M. Jones to S. Cooper, 12 Apr. 1862, enclosed in Maj. Genl. Saml. Jones to Genl. S. Cooper, 22 Apr. 1862, J-79 1863, Letters Received, ser. 5, Sec. War, RG 109 [F-69]. Colonel Thomas Jones's order and proclamation are not in the file. The court-martial proceedings against the five slaves of Jackson Morton are enclosed; for excerpts see document 318A, above. Also enclosed are the court-martial proceedings (5–6 Apr. 1862) in the case of Ebenezer, a slave of R. L. Campbell, who had been captured while escaping to Santa Rosa Island with newspapers in his possession; he was found guilty of attempting to convey information to the enemy and was sentenced to be hanged. In his covering letter to the Confederate War Department, General Samuel Jones, commander of the Confederate Department of Alabama and West Florida, argued that if recaptured fugitive slaves were "suffered to go at large with only the punishment of the lash, many will escape and Convey information to the Enemy who would be deterred from attempting it if a few were punished with death." Jackson Morton, who owned two of the slaves condemned to be hanged, had petitioned the Confederate Secretary of War to suspend the sentences and examine the record of the trial; and the secretary had complied, ordering Colonel Thomas M. Jones to forward a copy of the proceedings. Morton denounced the court's procedures as "vulgar and improper," believing that his rights as master had been controvened: "[T]he negroes should have been delivered to me when apprehended, I should have had them properly punished and removed to a place of perfect safety." A month after the court-martial Morton had received no response from the War Department, and he was still angry. He denounced Colonel Jones as a "cox-

comb and fool" who was playing "the Autocrat of Pensacola." "Who ever
heard before of a negro slave being arregned before a court martial for a
violation of the Articles of War?" protested Morton. "The idea is absurd and
the very consummation of folly." (Jackson Morton to Hon. A. E. Maxwell, 17
Apr. 1862, and Jackson Morton to Capt. E. Farrand, 6 May 1862, M-602
1862, Letters Received, ser. 5, Sec. War, RG 109 [F-69].) Seven months after
the court-martial, the condemned slaves had not yet been executed, and
doubts remained about the legality of the proceedings. In an endorsement
dated November 11, 1862, the Confederate adjutant and inspector general
summarized the questions about the case for the Secretary of War. In the first
place, the 57th article of war required that the accused be convicted of " 'holding correspondence with, or giving intelligence to, the enemy'. A conviction
of an *attempt* to do this does not meet the terms of the article, & would not
justify the punishment of death under it." Secondly, since the convicted
parties were slaves, "can they be guilty of a violation of the Military code, even
when extended to the civil community by the proclamation of Martial law."
(Endorsement by S. Cooper, 11 Nov. 1862, filed with J-79 1863, Letters
Received, ser. 5, Sec. War, RG 109 [F-69].) No further record of the case has
been found, and it is not known whether the slaves were executed.

319: Order by the Commander of the 1st District of Confederate Department No. 1

Tangipahoa La July 4th 1862.

General Orders No 4.

I   The passing of negroes, slaves or free, towards or into the
enemys lines is positively prohibited without a pass from the master
(if a slave) countersigned and approved by the provost marshal or
highest military authority of the Parish to which he belongs. If
free, in addition to the permission of the local authorities, the
approval of the provost marshal general at these headquarters will be
required.

Every negro, slave or free, who shall violate this order, will be
shot, in the attempt, unless he or she shall immediately submit to
arrest when making the attempt to pass the lines, or beyond the
prescribed limits indicated by our advanced pickets or guards.

All negroes, slave or free, who come from the enemy within our
lines will be taken immediately under charge, by our pickets and
guards, and delivered to the nearest provost marshal for examination
and detention who will report each case without delay to these
headquarters. By command of Brig Gen'l Ruggles

HDc

The Confederacy

General Orders No. 4, Hd. Qrs. 1st District, Dep't. No. 1, 4 July 1862, enclosed in Brig. General Daniel Ruggles to General S. Cooper, 22 Oct. 1862, R-1249 1862, Letters Received, ser. 12, Adjt. & Insp. Gen., RG 109 {F-1022}.

320: Georgia Slaveholders to the Commander of the 3rd Division of the Confederate District of Georgia

[Liberty County, Ga. August 1, 1862]
General: The undersigned Citizens of Liberty County of the
Fifteenth District, would respectfully present for your consideration
a subject of grave moment, not to themselves only but to their
fellow Citizens of the Confederate States, who occupy not only our
territory immediately bordering on that of the old United States,
but the whole line of our sea coast from Virginia to Texas. We
allude to the escape of our Slaves across the border lines landward,
and out to the vessels of the enemy Seaward, & to their being also
enticed off by those who having made their escape, return for that
purpose, and not unfrequently, attended by the enemy. The injury
inflicted upon the interests of the citizens of the Confederate States
by this now constant drain is immense; independent of the forcible
seizure of Slaves by the enemy whenever it lies in his power; and to
which we now make no allusion, as the indemnity for this loss, will
in due time occupy the attention of our Government. — From
ascertained losses on certain parts of our Coast, we may set down as
a low estimate, the number of Slaves absconded & enticed off from
our Seaboard as 20,000 & their value as from $12 to 15 millions of
Dollars, to which loss — may be added the insecurity of the property
along our borders & the demoralization of the negroes that remain,
which increases with the continuance of the evil & may finally result
in perfect disorganization and rebellion. —
 The absconding Negroes hold the position of Traitors, since they
go over to the enemy & afford him aid & comfort, by revealing the
condition of the districts and cities from which they come, & aiding
him in erecting fortifications & raising provisions for his support:
and now that the United States have allowed their introduction into
their Army &, Navy, aiding the enemy by enlisting under his
branners & increasing his resources in men, for our annoyance &
destruction. Negroes occupy the position of Spies also, since they
are employed in secret expeditions for obtaining information, by
transmission of newspapers & by other modes; and act as guides to
expeditions on the land & as pilots to their vessels on the waters of
our inlets and rivers. —

795

They have proved of great value, thus far, to the Coast operations of the enemy, & without their assistance, he could not have accomplished as much for our injury & annoyance as he has done; and unless some measures shall be adopted to prevent the escape of the negroes to the enemy, the threat of an Army of trained Africans for the coming fall & winter's campaigns may become a reality. Meanwhile the counties along the Seaboard will become exhausted of the Slave population, which should be retained as far as possible for the raising of provisions & supplies for our forces on the Coast. –

In the absence of penalties of such a nature as to ensure respect and dread, the temptations which are spread before the negroes are very strong, and when we consider their condition, their ignorance and credulity & love of change, must prove in too many cases decidedly successful. No effectual check being interposed to their escape, the desire increases among them in proportion to the extent of its successful gratification, & will spread inland until it will draw Negroes from Counties, far in the interior of the State; & Negroes will congregate from every quarter, in the counties immediately bordering on the Sea and become a lawless set of runaways, corrupting the Negroes that remain faithful, depredating on property of all kinds & resorting it may be to deeds of violence; which demonstrates that the whole State is interested in the effort to stop this evil: & already have Negroes from middle Georgia made their escape to the Seaboard Counties, and through Savannah itself to the enemy. –

After consulting the Laws of the State we can discover none that meet the case & allow of that prompt execution of a befitting penalty, which its urgency demands. The infliction of capital punishment is now confined to the Superior Court; & any indictment before that Court, would involve incarceration of the Negroes for months with the prospect of postponement of trial – long litigation – large expense & doubtful conviction; and moreover, should the Negroes be caught escaping in any numbers, there would not be room in all our Jails to receive them. The Civil Law therefore as it now stands cannot come to our protection.

Can we find protection under Military Law? This is the question we submit to the General in Command – Under Military Law the severest penalties are prescribed for furnishing the enemy with aid & comfort, & for acting as Spies and Traitors; all which the Negroes can do as effectually as white men, as facts prove and as we have already suggested. There can be but little doubt, that if Negroes are detected in the act of exciting their fellow slaves to escape; or of taking them off; or of returning after having gone to the enemy, to induce & aid others to escape: – they may in each of these cases be summarily punished under military authority. But may not the case of Negroes *taken in the act of absconding*, singly, ~~(or in families)~~ or in parties, without being directly incited so to do by one or more others, be also summarily dealt with by Military Authority? – Were our white population to act in the same way, would it not be necessary to make a summary example of them, in order to cure the evil or put it under some salutary control? If it be argued, that in case of the Negroes, it would be hard to meet out a similar punishment under similar circumstances, because of their ignorance pliability, credulity, desire of change, the absence of the political ties of allegiance & the peculiar status of the Race; – it may be replied – that the Negroes, constitute a part of the Body politic, *in fact*; and should be made to know their duty; that they are perfectly aware that the Act which they commit is one of rebellion against the power & authority of their owners & the Government under which they live; they are perfectly aware that they go over to the protection & aid of the enemy who are on the Coast for the purpose of killing their owners & of destroying their property; & they know further, that if they themselves are found with the enemy that they will be treated as the enemy – namely shot & destroyed: – To apprehend such transgressors, to confine & punish them privately by owners or publicly by the Citizens of the County by confinement and whipping & then return them to the plantations will not abate the evil; for the disaffected will not thereby be reformed, but will remain a leaven of corruption in the mass & stand ready to make any other attempts that may promise success. It is indeed a monstrous evil that we suffer. – Our Negroes our property – the agracultural class of the Confederacy, upon whose order & continuance so much depends, may go off, (inflicting a great pecuniary loss both private & public) to the enemy – convey any amount of valuable information – and aid him by building his fortifications: by raising supplies for his armies – by enlisting as Soldiers – by acting as Spies & as guides & pilots on his expiditions on land & water & bringing in the foe upon us to kill & devastate; and yet if we catch them in the act of going to the enemy we are powerless for the infliction of any punishment adequate to their crime & adequate to fill them with salutary fear of its commission! Surely some remedy should be applied & that speedily for the protection of the Country, aside from all other considerations. A few executions of leading transgressors among them by hanging or shooting would dissipate the ignorance which may be supposed to possess their minds and which may be pleaded in arrest of judgement. –

We do not pray the General in Command to issue any order for the government of the Citizens in the matter, which of course is no part of his duty; but the promulgation of an order to the military for the execution of ring-leaders who are detected in stirring up the people to escape – for the execution of all who return having once escaped & for the execution of all who are caught in the act of escaping; will speedily be known & understood by the entire slave population, and will do away with all excuses of ignorance, & go very far towards an entire arrest of the evil. While it will enable the Citizens to act efficiently in there own sphere – whenever circumstances – require them to act at all –   In an adjoining County which has lost some 200 since the shooting of two detected in the act of escaping not another attempt has been made & it has been several weeks since the two were shot. –

As Law abiding men we do not desire Committees of Vigalence, clothed with plenary powers; nor meetings of the body of our Citazens, to take the Law into their own hands, however justifiable it may be under the peculiar circumstances, & therefore in the failure of the Civil Courts to meet the emergency, we refer the Subject to the General in Command, believing that he has the power to issue the necessary order to the forces under him, covering the whole ground, and knowing that by so doing he will recieve the commendation and cordial support of the intelligent & Law abiding citizens inhabiting the military department over which he presides.   All which is Respectfully submited by Your friends & fellow citizens. –

R. Q. Mallard.

T. W. Fleming.

E. Stacy

HDS

R. Q. Mallard et al. to Brigadier General Mercer, [1 Aug. 1862], enclosed in Brig. Genl. H. W. Mercer to Hon. Geo. W. Randolph, 5 Aug. 1862, M-1867 1862, Letters Received, ser. 5, Sec. War, RG 109 [F-1000]. Alongside the signatures appears the designation "Committee of citizens of 15 Dis. Lib County." In his covering letter to the Confederate Secretary of War, General Hugh W. Mercer, commander of the 3rd Division of the Confederate District of Georgia, sympathized with the planters' plight and predicted that the "evil & danger alluded to may grow into frightful proportions, unless checked," but he argued that "the responsibility of life & death, so liable to be abused, is obviously too great to be entrusted to the hands of every officer, whose duties may bring him face to face with this question." Mercer recommended that the Confederate Congress act on the matter.

321: Tennessee Planter to the Commander of a Tennessee Confederate Regiment

Clarksville Tenn. 1 December 1862

Dear Sir   I am very desirous, that my son Thomas D Johnson should if possible be released from the public service. I have become so infirm that I can seldom leave my room in this place, whilst I own a plantation near New York, upon which I have sixty four negroes, besides four taken off by the Federals & which is only Twenty miles above Fort Donelson— hundreds of negroes have been taken off by them from my immediate neighborhood and I am apprehensive that the balance of mine may unless some of my family could be present to protect them— I have only three sons— The oldest commands company G in your Regiment, was wounded at the battle of Cedar Run in the foot & not now able to walk & will join his company as soon as he is— my youngest son just now entered upon 18 years old—was one of the prisoners at Chicago & is now with the Southern Army— My second son Tho⁵ D. is now with you— my son in law Col Forbes was killed at the battle of Manassas, leaving his widdow, two step daughters & a son only seven or eight years old & no one of the family to manage their affairs but myself— my son Tho⁵ D. will be twenty one in January next and is the most able to give me assistance in the management of my negroes & other business thrown upon my hands as above stated

It is with great reluctance that I ask for the discharge of my son, when I know the Confederacy needs the aid of every one of her sons but it seems to me under the circumstances stated and at a time when such efforts are making by the Federal Government to excite insurrection & seduce the slaves from their masters, that some indulgence might be shown to owners, who are in danger of loosing everything from such an unprincipled enemy— I have had an overseer for the last year or two & who will probably enter the service after the 1ˢᵗ of January, when I shall have no white man on the place but he if he should remain cannot secure the confidence of the servants & afford them the proper protection like one of my sons

May I hope under these circumstances that you will use your influence to get my son sent home by the 1ˢᵗ of January if possible— I suppose under the Law of the Confederacy I would be entitled to his discharge   yʳ friend

ALS   C Johnson

C. Johnson to Col. McComb, 1 Dec. 1862, J-1147 1862, Letters Received, ser. 12, Adjt. & Insp. Gen., RG 109 [F-263]. Johnson's son served in the

14th Tennessee (Confederate) Volunteers. There are no endorsements or file notations that indicate whether the discharge was granted.

322: Order by the Commander of Confederate Camp Finegan, Florida

Camp Finegan E F[*la.*] April 2ʺ, 1863

Special Orders No. 18 Captain Wᵐ E Chambers will proceed with a detachment of twelve (12) men of his company to the neighborhood known as the Echoniah Scrub in Putnam County, where he will make diligent and careful examination & investigation, as to the truth & extent of certain revelations made by the Slave Toby recently arrested at Jacksonville, conserning alledged conspiracies of the negros in that section, to leave their owners and go to the Enemy. Capt Chamber will arrest such negro's as may be implicated and should he have reasonable ground for suspecting that any white person are also implicated, he will not hesitate to arrest them. Much discretion is necessarily given to Captain Chambers as to the measures necessary to arrive at the facts in this matter He will however act coolly & temperately and not use any unnecessary harshness to not afterward to be justified –

After completing his investigations he will return with his detachment and report result to the officer in command. Capt G. W May being familiar with the localities in that section, will accompany Detachment and render all aid and whatever information he can necessary to Capt. Chamber careful investigations.

HDcSr   T. W. Brevard

Special Orders No. 18, Camp Finegan E. F., 2 Apr. 1863, ch. II, vol. 38, p. 12, Special Orders of the Dist. of East FL, Dept. of SC, GA, & FL, Records of Military Commands, RG 109 [F-602].

323: Mississippi Planter to the Headquarters of the Confederate Department of Mississippi and East Louisiana

Jackson Miss – July 5 /63

The officers of the Institute Hospital near this place several weeks ago called at the plantations in this vicinity jointly owned by Bourbon Shotwell my son & my self for negroes to act as nurses for the sick & I willingly consented they should take one man & three women with which number they professed to be satisfied &

promised to return them as early as others could be had to replace
them— We thought this a fair number for our place to contribute
out of about 30 avrage hands on it.

A few .days ago & in my absence from home they sent out & took
about ten more of the most efficient men & women on the premises,
stating to our manager they heard we were about to Send them to
the salt works & they supposed the negroes would prefer work at
the Hospital— The manager on the place called up all the negroes
on the premises & asked them to select others as those on their list,
they brought with them, were mostly those I had arranged to send
in a day or two at farthest to the salt works— This they refused
swearing they would have none others— They also refused to call
on other plantations in the same vicinity for a fair quota & thus
releive us from such onorous exactions— They also have stated they
had learned from the negroes themselves that they would not go to
the salt works. thus fostering & encouraging this spirit of
insubordination now so dangerous & general in our country.

I will here state that my said son & myself have three plantations
in Miss—one on Yazoo & one on Cassidays byeau in Tallehatchie
Cty, from all of which we have been continually furnishing aid for
the fortications at Vicksburg Fort Pemberton & Yazo City &
Jackson & the Yazoo Pass & we now have hands at Yazoo City &
have in every case responded to every call for labourers. I will also
state that the arrangement to send hands to the salt works I had
made with Dr Grant for the government works & had promised to
send 30 or forty hands, & I had just been to our Yazoo place &
started 20 hands who left on yesterday morning & now to meet
those impressed here at Enterprise— In making this arrangement I
have been prompted by a desire to get out of the country my negro .
men (with a few women) who would not be controuled should
Vicksburg fall & I am now in constant fear they will run away &
giv me trouble & nearly all of them (the men) would be dangerous
persons for the enemy to controul as they would no doubt shoulder
the musket willingly & be dangrous negroes in that capacity.— By
getting clear of these negroes I have selected for that [view]—I could
at any time controul the ballance & it is clear our government
should take such measurs as would prevent such negro men from
falling under the controul of the enemy—

Dr Mirable seems to have obtained a list of the very negroes
intended to be thus sent off for the reasons aforsaid from as I think
two of those first sent to him who are deep in the conspiracy & has
thus (without design as I think certainly) produced such a state of
insubordination as will render it doubtful if I can again controul
them at all without the severest measurs. One of the negroes takin
is our blacksmith, a valuable workman I intended to take to the

801

government shop at Enterprise— He is a dangerous negro if he should rebel & I understand swears he will not be taken off—

I respectfully ask that Dr Mirable shall be compelled to call on other plantations for nurses & relieve us of all but a fair contribution & that in justice to us untill this is done he be directed to return those last taken— Let our qota justly due be assertained & they shall be sent without impressment— We also ask that the number we should furnish be assertained by the medical board or others appointed for that purpose so that we may be released from oppression now practised on us, & that for obvious reasons our redress be as speedy as possible   Respectfully

R. & B Shotwell
By Robert Shotwell

The writer of this would also state that he has only three children—all sons & in the army now in active service   the one named within is now in the trenches in Vicksburg—One in Port Hudson, & one in the army in V^a That he is nearly 60 years of age & afflicted with Rheumatism so he gets about with difficulty & cant ride much on horseback, & has to attend to the intrest of all the family which he is really unable to do as it should be & the present proceedings of Dr Mireable are thus peculiarly oppressive at this time—

ALS   Rbt. R. Shotwell

Rbt. R. Shotwell to Lieut. Coln. T. B. Lamar, 5 July 1863, #806 1863, Letters & Telegrams Received, ser. 93, Dept. of MS & East LA, Records of Military Commands, RG 109 [F-198]. In an undated endorsement, the assistant medical director of the Confederate Department of Mississippi and East Louisiana ordered that the slaves be returned to the Shotwells, except for two men and three women. He also instructed the surgeon in charge of the hospital to make more equitable impressments in the future. Other endorsements.

324: Confederate Engineer to the Headquarters of the Confederate Department of South Carolina, Georgia, and Florida, Enclosing a Letter from Two South Carolina Slaveholders to the Engineer

Charleston Augt 25th 1863

Genl According to instructions to discharge the negroes only on demand, I have required it generally to be made positive, which are very freely made and some of the owners even venting themselves to charge "breaches of faith and contract on the part of the Gov. State &c." demands are becoming very numerous. together with the runaways will soon materially reduce the present force in numbers, and large parties of them have been caught and returned, in possession of passes of all descriptions. many, the negroes state are given them by Soldiers, for pay and other considerations. And no doubt some of them come down with their owners passes to return home in their pockets. as they have been found with them in their possession. The boats also permit perfect freedom of transportation to the negroes, with or without passes. I enclose a sample. Total received since 10″ July about 3900, effective force 2500. I have the honor to be very respectfully Your obt svt.

ALS   Wm H. Echols

[*Enclosure*]   Mayesville [*S.C.*] August 24th 1863
Dear Sir   We have good reason to believe that you have some traitor in your camp on Sulivans Island, who are giving our negroes forged Tickets or at least Such is the testimony of the negroes, that have returned   they report that Tickets are given by one of the guard with instructions to tare it up as soon as they past over the bridge   they report that they pay 75 cents for each ticket which goes to shew that the object in part is to make money & no doubt another object is to leave the fortification in an unfinished State, the precident is a very bad one, and will no doubt cause dissatisfaction amongst those that are still in your employ   it is reported that there is at least 30 hands that have returned in this clandestin manner contrary to the wishes of their owners)   You will please do as good a part by those who remain with you as the nature of your Situation will Admit   I hope will be able to keep the enemy at bay until you get such ordinance in your possession as will batter down the Iron Clads of the enemy   We remain yours Truly

                                                                  Wm Harris
HLSr   C. T. Rembert

Maj. Wm. H. Echols to Brigr. Genl. Thomas Jordan, 25 Aug. 1863, enclosing Wm. Harris and C. T. Rembert to Sir, 24 Aug. 1863, E-294 1863,
Letters Received, ser. 72, Dept. of SC, GA, & FL, Records of Military
Commands, RG 109 [F-110]. The enclosure and both signatures are in the
same handwriting. Other enclosures, endorsements. Among the other enclosures is a barely literate, undated pass to "Permit Boy to pass home." In
response to this and similar complaints that Confederate soldiers were selling
passes to slave laborers, General P. G. T. Beauregard, commander of the
Confederate Department of South Carolina, Georgia, and Florida, issued an
order prohibiting "trafic of any kind whatsoever between enlisted men and
slaves engaged at work on fortifications." "It is unlawful, pernicious, and
demoralizing and all persons found engaged in it hereafter will be held to a

strict accountability." (General Orders No. 104, Head Quarters, Dept. of S.C. Ga & Fla., 20 Oct. 1863, ch. II, vol. 41, pp. 187–88, General Orders, Dept. of SC, GA, & FL, Records of Military Commands, RG 109 [F-168].)

325: Commander of the Confederate Trans-Mississippi Department to the Commander of the Confederate District of Texas, New Mexico, and Arizona

Shreveport La   Sept 5th 1863

General,   The necessity of increasing our effective force, and the policy of employing negro labor in the place of detailed soldiers, forces itself so strongly on my mind, that I will call your attention to my letter of x x x

I know not what success you have met with, nor how far the people in their patriotism may have responded to your call –   The urgency is immediate –   If your expectations have not been realized you must resort to impressment.

The temper of the people is now favorable for such a step: there is a feeling of distrust in the loyalty of their slaves, and an anxiety to have the able bodied males in the service of the Government.   Especially is this the case in the exposed portions of the Country, and I think there, large numbers could be obtained without difficulty.

Estimates should be made of the wants in the several Departments, including the Hospital Department, and Cotton Bureau, and immediate steps be taken, for procuring by impressment, if necessary, the requisite negro force.   I believe a large number of men would by this measure be added to the effective force in your District.

Your own judgement will suggest the best method of carrying out this measure –   I would suggest, however, that having made your estimates and determined the pro rata call in each County, a well Known citizen of the County be appointed as Agent, or to accompany the Agent, for the purpose of fairly and impartially carrying it into effect.   I am General Your obt servt

HLcSr   (signed) E. Kirby Smith

Lt. Gen. E. Kirby Smith to Maj. Genl. J. B. Magruder, 5 Sept. 1863, ch. II, vol. 70, p. 331, Letters Sent, Trans-MS Dept., Records of Military Commands, RG 109 [F-994]. A notation indicates that identical letters were sent to General Richard Taylor, commander of the Confederate District of West Louisiana, and to General Sterling Price, commander of the Confederate Army of the West. The growing distrust of the slaves noted by General Smith was no doubt a response to the greatly increased recruitment of slave men into the Union army that followed federal occupation of Vicksburg in the summer of 1863. On September 4, Smith had warned General Price that the plantations were becoming "recruiting stations" for the enemy, and later in the month Smith's chief quartermaster appealed to slaveholders to hire their able-bodied slave men to the Confederate army, "thereby saving them from falling into the hands of our enemies." (See above, docs. 273, 309.) Confederate impressment and refugeeing policies, along with planters' complaints, suggest the increasing fragility of slavery in northern Louisiana after mid-1863. By early 1864, General Taylor had become reluctant to impress slaves for fear "there will be a general stampede" to Union lines, "and we will be held to be the cause of it." He thought, however, that Louisiana planters would readily hire their slaves to the Confederate government: "Along the banks of the Miss. negroes are worthless as property, and I suppose their nominal owners would be glad to place them in Govt service, if the necessary means to remove the negroes could be secured." (Maj. Genl. R. Taylor to Major Genl. Walker, 3 Feb. 1864, ch. II, vol. 75, pp. 178–80, Letters Sent, Dist. of West LA, Trans-MS Dept., Records of Military Commands, RG 109 [F-884].)

326: Confederate Officer at Crystal River, Florida, to the Headquarters of the Confederate District of East Florida

                    Christal River Flor[ida]. September 8" 1863
   In my report to you of 1ˢᵗ inst I stated that I had suceeded in capturing the boat and had the negroes cut off so as there would not be much doubt in my getting the negroes . . .¹ raid on Mr Kings plantation. on the morning of the second day I took their trail from where I fired on them the evening previous. they led off towards the mouth of Withlacoochee River, edgeing the Coast as near as they could for tide creeks &c. about 4 ock in the evening we discovered one in a cedar tree looking out, on an Island they discovered us about the same time, we being in the open marsh. here they seem to have seperated only two being together. after chasing them about two miles through the saw Grass we came up in gun shot of them. we began to fire at them, and they returned the fire very cool and deliberately but we soon got in close range of them and killed them. one of these negroes was recognized by some of my men as belonging to Mr. Everett, who lives near hear, which ran away from him about nine months ago. he was styled Captain of the party, as I learned from the negroes recaptured of Mr Kings. myself and men being completely tired down for the want of water, we had to go back and camp until next morning when we took the trail and followed on the third

day. about the same time in the eveing of the third day, we came up with two more, and after a Similar chase of the second day, we succeeded in Killing both of them. from here I never could strike the trail of any more of them, but I am under the impression that we killed or wounded the other three the first day. I could not get any information from either of the four that was killed, as they were killed dead.

The only information that I have been able to get is from an old negro man of Mr Kings who ran away from them the first day and came back home. he says that [they] . . .² [left] Sea Horse Key at the same time [that] boat did destined for Homasassa, but as yet they have not reached there. he also states that a Gun-boat had gone up the Suwanee River and as soon as it returned it was to come up this River.

Night before last my picket Guard heard several guns down the River in the direction of shell Island. it may be them, but I think if they go up either River their destiny will be as these has been. I am Captain Very Respectfully Your obt Sevt

ALS   Samuel E. Hope

Capt. Samuel E. Hope to Capt. W. Call, 8 Sept. 1863, Letters Received, ser. 72, Dept. of SC, GA, & FL, Records of Military Commands, RG 109 [F-187]. Endorsement.

1 Letter torn at fold; two or three words missing.
2 Letter torn at fold; approximately three words missing.

327: South Carolina Slaveholders to the Confederate Secretary of War

Darlington District S.C [*March 1864*]

We the undersigned citizens of Swift Creek and the surrounding Country Darlington Disᵗ S.C. do hereby most respectfully lay before you a very serious grievance which is this, the male population is so small and the few left are so infirm that they are not able to remedy the evil We and the soldiers families are continually annoyed by the depredations Committed on us by the black population such as breaking open dwelling houses under[min]ing meat houses, robbing hen houses, Killing Cattle Hogs &c and stealing everything the can lay their hands on knowing we are not able to help ourselves. What we ask is this, Mʳ Jnᵒ B. Rhodes of this district is at present in the 21st S.C Reg^t C^o H, is a man well acquainted with Creeks bays & swamps in this part of the Country where the negroes hide themselves, he has likewise a excellent trained pack of dogs for that purpose which no person with any success manage but himself, we therefore ask you to have him discharged, detailed or otherwise as you think best, so as he could give us the necessary assistance in the case   We have not the least doubt but he would do more real good in this case to us and the soldiers families than ten other men   We lay the matter before you hoping you will give it your serious and necessary attention and by so doing you will confer on us and the soldiers families a lasting obligation

HLS   [*22 signatures*]

Christopher Flinn et al. to Hon. Jas. A. Seddon, [Mar. 1864], R-301 1864, Letters Received, ser. 12, Adjt. & Insp. Gen., RG 109 [F-332]. Referred through the chain of command, the petitioners' request received an endorsement of disapproval at every level, from the captain commanding Rhodes's company to the general commanding the Confederate Department of South Carolina, Georgia, and Florida. For a similar request from a North Carolina slaveholder that was also disapproved by Confederate authorities, see above, doc. 15.

328: Virginia Slaveholders to the Confederate President

Coman's Well   Sussex Coty   V^a October 13   1864
Dear Sir   A report has reached us that the Government is about to make another requisition on this County for Slaves for the Publick works, We most respectfully represent to your Excellency the State of things in this County   The County of Sussex adjoins that of Prince George which last County you are aware is occupied by the enemy, There is no barier to prevent the escape of our Slavs who choose to go to the enemy, they may pass directly into Prince George Coty, or cross the Blk water, they are going constantly, Any attempt of the Gov^t to enforce a draft of negroes in this county or even a report to that effect (if it reaches the negroes) will have the effect in our deliberate opinion to cause a stampede among those of the men who are not now disposed to go or are hesitating to do so, We believe that for every man the Gov^t would obtain by such a measure the Enemy would add ten or twenty to his ranks to Say nothing of the imposibility of gathering the crops &

seeding wheat, Some of us will find it almost imposible to Save our Crops by the Small force left and all of us have suffered more or less,

We hope the Gov^t will at least Suspend the requisition (if any was intended for this County) until it can obtain information as to the truth of our Statement, we are personally unknown to you, but well known to Hon John R Chambliss, Hon Robert Whitfield & Hon Thos S Gholson, none of these Gentlemen are in the County at this time

We Submit that the County of Sussex has on three or four occasions promptly responded to the requisitions of the Gov^t for hands for the publick works, but in the present ticklish Situation of things, such a requisition would be of no benefit to the Gov^t, but tend to Strenghten the enemy, and bring disaster and ruin to many of the Citizens, With the best wishes for the triumph of the Cause in which you are so ardently and industriously engaged, we ask your attention to this and remain Your obedient Servants

Wm D. Taylor   James. D. Howle
Nathaniel. R. Peebles   Henry Harrison
J. B. Freeman

HLS

Wm. D. Taylor et al. to His Excellency Jefferson Davis, 13 Oct. 1864, T-206 1864, Letters Received, ser. 5, Sec. War, RG 109 [F-94]. An endorsement indicates that the Confederate President forwarded the letter to the Secretary of War, but no response has been found in the records of the secretary. The deterioration of discipline that allowed slaves to leave their masters whenever they felt threatened was not confined to Sussex County, but was common wherever Union lines abutted the Confederacy. In December 1864, a state legislator from neighboring Southampton County observed that "experience has shown for the last two years, that any attempt on the part of the Government, to arrest these slaves for the purpose of working them on fortifications or any other Government work, results simply in driving them across the lines to the enemy, and almost a total failure to secure them for the Government, thus depriving the Citizens of their slaves and labor, and nothing accruing to the Government." He took issue with the argument that the county's remaining slaves would run away even if not threatened with impressment, contending that "they are not disposed to leave, and . . . have been orderly and worked as well as I have ever known." However, he warned, "always having a great dread of any Government work, they now have added to it, the fear of being put into army, which has caused the greatest alarm in their midst." Thus far the new attempt to impress slaves in the county had been "altogether futile." "Only two or three have been arrested, whilst nearly two hundred have escaped to enemy." (Wm. H. Pretlow to Hon. James A. Seddon, 14 Dec. 1864, P-269 1864, Letters Received, ser. 5, Sec. War, RG 109 [F-91].)

329: Escaped Union Prisoners of War to the Provost Marshal
General of the Department of the South

Hilton Head S.C. December 7th 1864

Sir   Agreably to your request the undersigned have the honor to
present to you the following brief summary of their observations in
and escape from the Southern States

On the 5th October, the officers confined in Roper Hospital
Charleston S.C. received orders to prepare for a removal, we,
together with Lieut Millward A.D.C to Gen[l] Scammon, having
provided ourselves with rebel uniforms (while in route to the dept,
walked deliberately out of the ranks.   Knowing no one in the city
we relied upon the negroes & the same day, we related to one Tho[s]
Brown (Col'd Barber) who we were, & asked assistance –   Said
Brown, who seemed proud of speaking of his being a Black
Republican – placed us in charge of his son who the same night
procured for us a hiding place among some friends of his (colored)
where we remained at least one month.   We, a short time after our
escape, heard of one Mr. Riels (German) who was hiding away the
other officers –   This gentleman provided us with money & used all
endeavors to get us away.   Having procured 5 negroes and about on
the 2[7]" Oct. we made the attempt to run out of the harbor, from
the foot of Hazel St.   As we were about starting, a Lieut with 7
men – suddenly appeared and without speaking fired at the men
collected on the wharf wounding the Lieut. in charge and capturing
the negroes –   We, in the obscurity of the night, crawled away and
hid in an empty building –   Being compelled to leave our quarters
we got separated from Lt. Milward who we have since learned was
recaptured on Sullivans Islan

Being introduced to a Mr. Christmen (German) we in conjunction
with Capt. Telford & a private made an attempt together with a Mr
O'Conner (Citizen) to leave by the route by which we subsequently
escaped.

But Capt[n] Telford whilst presenting his pass at the bridge in the
Ashley river was recognized by the guard (who had previously
guarded us) & he Mr O'Connor, & private Sweeney were lodged in
Charleston jail after being stripped of watches & all money in their
purses. Mr O'Connor though a British Subject being heavily ironed

Becoming acquainted with a Mr. N. Sherhumer, formerly a U.S.
soldier who took us to his house gave us clothes, money &c. Here
in the room of a Mr. Whittaker, we stayed till Nov. 29"   On that
day passes being procured for us by Mr Whittaker & Mr. Riels, we
under the guidance of Towles priv. 32nd Ga. arrived by the cars at
his (Towles) house & with Mr. Whittaker & 5 deserters from Castle
Pinckney arrived via Toogoods creek & the Edisto river in our lines

landing on board the U.S. Sloop o War, the "St. Lewis". This route, leaving the cars at New Road, distant from Charleston 22 miles & marching easterly to Towles' house by the Toogoods Crk, has been open a long time. Its known to the Union men in Charleston & to some officers & men of the 32nd Ga. who are paid by Towles for their connivance. We stayed in Charleston two months, relying all that time on the negroes for safety – who we found remarkably intelligent, thoroughly comprehending their own *Status* in the Rebellion. The Germans also rendered us every assistance. Indeed without them we could not have escaped. As a general rule the foreign born population (Chiefly Germans) are loyal. They have a Union Association to which 1400 belong who, as a member told us, carry one of these – suiting the action to the word and showing a revolver. They say they're ready at any time with security of protection to co-operate with our forces upon an attack.

They have about 5000, troops in & around Charleston – The yellow fever carried off several officers & men whilst hid away in the City. We both of us had it.

There's a general depression prevailing among the soldiers and civilians, they move about like melancholy shadows, [&] there's no doubt that if the middle & poor classes dare express their sentiments, that they would declare themselves ready to return to their proper allegiance. All that has been said about the sufferings of our prisoners, particularly enlisted men, does not, cannot depict their sufferings – Let one fact suffice. A negro told us that when they were on the race course – they actually allayed their thirst with *urine* We have the honor to be sir, in haste Very Respectfully Your Obdt. Servant

(Signed) Alured Larke

HLcSr   (Signed) R. H. Day

Capt. Alured Larke and Capt. R. H. Day to the Provost Marshal, 7 Dec. 1864, vol. 238 DS, pp. 103–6, Statements of Escaped Union Prisoners, Refugees, & Confederate Deserters, ser. 4294, Provost Marshal General, Dept. of the South, RG 393 Pt. 1 [C-1551]. Larke and Day were captains in the 2nd Wisconsin Infantry and the 56th Pennsylvania Infantry, respectively.

330: Testimony by a South Carolina Freedman before the Southern Claims Commission

State of South Carolina Charleston County Charleston.
August 24th 1872 —

. . . .

To question 1, he says — "My name is Mack Duff Williams — I was born a slave, in the state of South Carolina, and am 46, years of age — I live in said state 29 miles from Charleston, at a settlement called "Wassamsaw" on the state road from Charleston to Columbia — I hire 25 acres of land there, which I cultivate on my own account — I have no other occupation except farming — To question 2, he says — I lived all the time on the farm of Mr Louis Seel, in said state, five miles from Charleston — except 6. months during the second year of the war, when I went from Mr Seel's farm to my masters plantation at "Wassamasaw" in said state, where I now live — My master during the war was Mr John Wilson — All the time during the war, until the evacuation, I belonged to Mr John Wilson, and hired my time from him — working on my own account — I hired all my time during the war, except when I was sick during said 6 months — I paid him for my time out of money paid me by Mr Seel — I did no work during the war except for Mr Seel, as a farm laborer and wood chopper — To question 3, he says. I staid all the time in South Carolina, inside the rebels line, until the Union Army came to Charleston —

. . . .

To question 24, he says About 2 months before the evacuation some rebel soldiers took me from Mr Seels farm and locked me up in a building in Charleston, with some other colored men, the soldiers said we had to work on the breastworks on James Island — I was locked in building about 2 hours, at night, I broke out and ran away to Mr Seels house in the city where he took care of me one night & day, after which I went to work again on his farm. I was never arrested at any other time by the Confederates. . . . To question 28, he says about 6 months before the evacuation 6 or 7 union soldiers came to my house on Mr Seels farm I kept them in my house one day and one night so that they might not be caught by the rebels — I gave them vegetables from my own little garden patch around my house — I gave 3 pairs of my pantaloons so that they might make their escape without being known — They had on uniform pantaloons when they came to my house, The soldiers asked me to let them come in my house for shelter — They said they belonged to the Union army and had been taken prisoners — but escaped — I told them I was glad to have them do so — I did nothing else for any Union soldiers or for the Union cause — I did not ask or receive anything from any Union soldiers or prisoners — They did not give anything to my wife or children —. . . . To question 40, he says, I sympathized with the Union cause, because that was the party I believed would give me my liberty — "I told my friends that the war was a good cause — I said I believed every man would be made free" — I remained all the time in favor of the United States — To question 41, he says, My sympathies were all the time with the United States — I wanted the Union army to succeed over the rebels so I and all colored men would be free, I knew we could never be free if the Confederates were victorious — I always prayed for the Union army to succeed — I was a preacher during the war and am now, I led the meetings of the colored people very often during the war — We made a great deal of noise sometimes praying for the success of the Union cause, The rebels forbid me to hold such meetings and suspected we had been saying something in favor of the Yankees — We did continue to hold our meetings and once during the war some rebel soldiers locked me and my congregation in the house where we had our meeting, and would not let us out for several hours, Some of the rebel soldiers then questioned me about our meeting, what we had been saying &c — I was very polite and humble to them and they let us out — I did not deny having prayed for the Union cause — They did not ask me if I had done so, they only asked me what we said, I told them "we met to pray for the whole word". I never gave or did anything to help the Confederacy or for any of its officers or soldiers, and never wished for its success — I never refused to help or do anything for Union people, and was always ready and willing to do what I could for them — To question 43, he says, I was a slave when the war began, I belonged to Mr John Wilson — I became free when the Union Army came to Charleston, in 1865. I always worked on a farm I remained at Mr Seels farm employed by him after the evacuation for about one year, when I went to Wassamasaw (where I now live) and rented a farm — I bought the mule, for which I now make claim, about 6 months before the evacuation out of money received from Mr Seel for my work on his farm — I paid my master $20 — pr month for my time, all the time during the war — Mr Seel paid me $35. or $40. pr month when I worked as a laborer on his farm, and $5. pr cord (!) (in Confederate money) for cutting wood on the farm — In this way I made from $15. or $30 — pr month after paying my master for my time —

. . . .

HDS   Mack. Duff. Williams

Excerpts from testimony of Mack Duff Williams, 24 Aug. 1872, claim of Mack Duff Williams, Charleston Co. SC case files, Approved Claims, ser. 732, Southern Claims Commission, 3rd Auditor, RG 217 [I-100]. Sworn before a special commissioner of the Southern Claims Commission. The questions that correspond to the enumerated responses are not in the file. According to other documents in the file, Williams had submitted a claim for $200 as compensation for a mule taken by Union soldiers, and he was awarded $130.

331: Testimony by a South Carolina Freedman before the Southern Claims Commission

State of South Carolina Georgetown County Georgetown
March 17th 1873 –

. . . .

To question 1, he says – "My name is Alonzo Jackson – I was born a slave, in the state of Virginia – and am 64 years of age – I reside at Georgetown state of South Carolina and am a Livery stable keeper by occupation – To question 2 he says – I have lived all the time at Georgetown since 1823 – and from that time was a slave until made free by the war when the US. Forces came to Georgetown in February 1865 – When the war began in 1861, I belonged to Mr Joseph B. Pyatt who lived on his own plantation about 2 miles from Georgetown (he lives there now) For 18. years just before the war I hired all my time from my master and continued to do so all the time I was a slave – I paid every year $140 – for my time and supported myself and family from my own earnings – working only for whom I chose – When the war began I was employed as "hostler" (in the same livery stable which I now keep on my own account) I was then receiving $25. pr month for my wages – and had been receiving the same wages at same place for about 18. years continuously I had in 1861 – a wife – one child and 2 nieces to support – My wife earned money as pastry cook & Laundress – My child and 2 nieces were small children – I remained, employed as stated, until February 1864 – when I hired a flat boat at Georgetown and did freighting business on the "SamPitt" "Black" "Pee dee" & "Waccamaw" rivers – I continued about a year in this business, all the time on my own account, until the US. Soldiers came to Georgetown in Feby 1865 when I left the flat boat and was employed as a laborer at Georgetown by citizens until the end of the war – I received all my wages from the livery stable except during the last year I worked there – The rebel

soldiers plundered the stable so that we could not do
business— The last year I was at the stable during the war I
divided the earnings of the stable with my employer— my share
was only enough to feed my family— I had 2 horses of my own at
the stable, all the time during, and for about 4 or 5 years before the
war, while I was employed there— I received extra pay whenever
my horses were used and earned some money in this way— I owned
a house and lot at Georgetown when the war began— I have lived
in the house all the time since then— The property is worth about
$800— I never owned any other real estate— When I left the
livery stable to do freighting business on the rivers during the war I
had 2-horses about $6.000 or $8.000 in Confederate money and
about $500— state money— I did not own or have in my
possession any other property of any kind at that time, except my
house & lot, as stated— I earned about $300 (in Confederate
money) every month, besides the support of my family—while I was
in the freighting business— I had no other occupation or business
during the war— I was not away from Georgetown during the war
except when driving for persons who hired carriages from the stable
and while I was doing freight business on the rivers— I went 4
times to Charleston during the 1st & 2nd years of the war only to
take people there who had hired me to do so— I went several times
to Kingstree (40, miles from Georgetown on N. Eastern R.R.) and
to other places nearer for same purpose only— I was never absent
from Georgetown on such business longer than 3 days at a time— I
was sometimes absent on my flat boat for 2 weeks at a time and
never went further than 60. miles from Georgetown in any boat— I
only went up the rivers—except on several occasions when I went to
"Hesterville" about 7 miles from Georgetown towards the
coast— To question 3. he says— Yes I went twice to "North
Island" in "Winyaw bay" (about 10 miles from Georgetown) during
the 3rd year of the war with Union soldiers who had escaped from
the rebel "stockade" at Florence— I went with them to show them
the way to the gun boats— I went out of the rebel lines to do so,
and returned without being discovered— I took the soldiers in a
boat and landed them on "North Island" which was then in
possession only of Union forces— About one month after
Georgetown was occupied by Union forces during the last year of
the war I went about 10. miles out of the Union lines, to a
plantation on "Black river" for a boat load of rice—with a flat
boat— I was hired to do so by a citizen of Georgetown, I had a
permit from the US. Provost Marshal to do so— I got the rice and
brought it to Georgetown— The rebels came very near catching
me, they fired at me, and I heard them threaten me— They said
they would "kill me for taking provisions to the yankees." They

were separated from me by the river and did not catch me— I
never went through either lines at any other times during the war
. . . .

To question 26, he says Yes— About 6 months after the war
began—a constable at Georgetown named "Gasquay" (a white man)
came one day to the livery stable where I was employed and told me
he had been sent to me by the Confederate Provost Marshal (Dr
Parker) to order me to assist in hanging 3 colored men at the jail in
Georgetown— I knew at the time that the 3 men were to be hung
for attempting to escape to the blockading fleet—but did not know
either of the 3 men— I had not had anything to do with their
attempt to escape and had not been accused of knowing anything
about it— I believed that I had been ordered to assist in the
hanging because I was suspected of being on the side of the
Yankees— (The rebels tried colored people very often in this way,
to frighten them) I replied to the constable that I was busy and
could not go— The constable was angry and said I must go— I
insisted that I was busy and could not go— I gave no other reason
for refusing to assist in the hanging, and did not say anything about
the hanging— I deceived the constable by saying that I had to go
to Gen'l Trapiers plantation (2 miles distant) for Gen'l Trapier—and
in order to make him believe me, I got on my horse and went
there— The Constable said "if you don't look pretty sharp, you will
be hung next"— At the time I went to Black river for rice in the
flat boat, (after Union Army came to Georgetown) with permission
and pass from US. Provost Marshal—(as stated) The rebels who fired
at and tried to catch me told me they would sink my boat and hang
me because I was taking provisions to Georgetown for the
Yankees. I do not know of any other threats that were made to me
in person, on account of my Union sentiments. To question 27. he
says No. except when I was at the livery stable during the war— I
was employed by a free colored man named Augustus Carr—who
owned the livery stable— The rebel soldiers came so often to the
stable with their horses and treated us so badly that as stated we
had to give up the business— They used to feed their horses
without paying anything and if we asked for any pay they would
sometimes draw pistols on us, threatening to shoot us— They
behaved so unkindly towards us that we could not do
business— My employer lost a great deal of money by their conduct
and for this reason could not pay me my last years wages at the
stable—and has never done so— I am now renting the same stable
from him and what he owes me for back wages will be deducted
from the rent I pay him— I have already had the stable for one year
at $200— and have paid no rent— I expect to pay rent after I have
occupied the stable long enough to get my back wages— He owed

me about $500. one year ago— I was not injured in any other way
on account of my Union sentiments— To question 28. he
says— No. except giving food to Union soldiers when they came to
my house— They sometimes asked for food and sometimes took it
without asking I never refused them— To question 29. he says.
Yes— About 8 months before Georgetown was occupied by Union
soldiers—while I was in the freighting business on my flat boat on
"Mingo creek" (up "Black river") about 30 or 40 miles from
Georgetown by water, 3 white men came near the boat which was
at the bank of the river— I was on the boat with only one person a
colored man (in my employ named "Henry") As soon as the 3
white men saw we were colored men they came to the boat and said
"we are Yankee soldiers, and have escaped from the rebel "stockade"
at Florence, we are your friends can't you do something for
us we are nearly perished" As soon as I saw them, before they
spoke, I knew they were Yankee soldiers—by their clothing. They
were all private soldiers—so they told me— I invited them to come
on the boat and told them I would hurry and cook food for them,
which I did and gave it to them in my boat— As soon as they
entered the boat I shoved off from land and anchored in the creek
about 60. ft from shore— I was loading cord wood in my boat
when the soldiers came and had completed my load within about 4.
cords— I did not wait to take it all—fearing that, some one else
might come and catch the Yankees— Neither of the 3 soldiers
ordered me to take them in the boat, or made any threats— They
did not go in the boat or secure it in any way so that I could not
leave in it— They only entered the boat after they had told me who
they were (as stated) and when I invited them— They were very
weak—and had no weapons— They had no shoes on— It was then
winter weather, and cold— The 3 Yankees did not suggest
anything for me to do for them except to feed them—and wanted to
get to the gun boats— They did not know where the gun boats
were— I did—and I told them I would take them where they could
get to the gun boats unmolested. The soldiers did not pay or give
me anything—or promise anything to me at any time—and I have
never received anything for any service rendered to any Union
soldiers— They did not threaten me or use any violence— they
were very friendly and glad to get into such good hands— They
showed that they felt very grateful— I hid the 3 soldiers in my flat
boat and started at once down the river towards Georgetown as soon
as the tide allowed— In about 3 days time we came to "North
Island" (about 12 miles from Georgetown) which I then knew was
in possession of the Union forces— I did not pass Georgetown by
day light for fear of being stopped by the rebels who had "pickets"
all along the shore to stop all boats from going below— In the

night I floated with the ebb tide (without being seen) to "North Island" — I got there in the night and landed the 3 soldiers in my small boat — I showed them the direction to cross the Island so as to get to the gun boats — I knew there were many of the gun boat people on the shore there at that time — I saw the 3 soldiers go as I directed — I never saw or heard from any of the 3 soldiers afterwards — but through a colored man named "Miller" (who was on the shore near the gunboats) learned that the 3 soldiers had got to the fleet — "Miller" told me this about 2 weeks after I took the 3 soldiers — he saw them and described them so that I was certain he had seen the same 3 soldiers safe in the protection of the gun boats — About 2 Months after this occurrence — I brought 2 other Yankee soldiers (one a corporal) to "North Island" from the same place in "Mingo creek" The circumstances were nearly the same except that when I saw the soldiers I called to them saying there was "no danger" — for they were running away in a swamp — They came nearer and asked me if I was a friend to them that, they were Yankee soldiers who had escaped from rebel prison — I replied that "I was as good a friend as ever they had in their lives"! Then they came on my boat where I fed and delivered them (as before described) on "North Island" In February 1865 while I was at "Mingo creek" as before I found 4. other Yankee soldiers there who also said they had escaped from Florence — I fed and took them towards "North Island" but told them it might not be necessary as the Yankees were then probably at Georgetown — When we came near Georgetown I found out that this was true — and landed the 4 soldiers there — I never asked or received anything or the promise of anything for what I gave or did for any Yankee soldiers during the war — While they were in my boat I kept them hidden away — I know I would have been killed if the rebels had found out that I had Yankees on my boat — I cannot remember that I ever did anything else to aid any Union soldiers — I never had a chance to do anything else — or I would have done it!

. . . .

To question 40. he says — I sympathized with the Union cause — "I knew what I needed most and looked that way certain"! I wanted to be free — and wanted my race to be free — I knew this could not be if the rebels had a government of their own — All the time during, and before the war, I felt as I do now that, the Union people were the best friends of the colored people — I always rejoiced over Union victories — I talked with a few white men at Georgetown and with such colored men as I could trust, in favor of the Union all the time during the war, but I knew my life would be taken if it was known how I really felt about the war — To question 41. he says. Yes. I was all the time anxious for

817

the success of the Yankees— I never did or said anything to help the rebels and never wished for the success of any rebel soldiers— I did what I could for the Yankees and wanted to do more! I was always ready and willing to do what I could even at the risk of my own life— I could every time have avoided bringing the Yankee soldiers to "North Island" and could have caused their arrest if I had wished to do so, on my way to "North Island"—

. . . .

HDS   Alonzo Jackson

Excerpts from testimony of Alonzo Jackson, 17 Mar. 1873, claim of F. Alonzo Jackson, Georgetown Co. SC case files, Approved Claims, ser. 732, Southern Claims Commission, 3rd Auditor, RG 217 [I-99]. Sworn before a special commissioner of the Southern Claims Commission. The questions that correspond to the enumerated responses are not in the file. According to other documents in the file, Jackson had submitted a claim of $1,925 as compensation for property taken by Union soldiers, including two mules, a gun, and twenty tierces of rice. He was awarded only $250, the commissioners having disallowed entirely the $1,500 he claimed for the rice.

Index

Index

Fort Wagner SC: battle 38
Fortier, Polycarpe: leter from, 203
Fortress Monroe VA: 15–16, 27, 60–61, 63, 70–72, 88–90, 161, 667
Foster, Charles W.: 382n.
Foster, Francis: letter from, 435
Foster, John G.: 65, 80; fugitive slave policy, 109–10, 361; letter to, 86–88; military labor policy, 587n.
Fouke, Philip B.: fugitive slave policy, 272–73; letter from, 272–74
Fowle, William B., Jr.: letter from, 86–87
Fowler, Joseph C.: letter to, 641–52
Frankfort KY: 498
Fraser, E. W.: 133–34
Frederick MD: 338
Free blacks: 5, 44; Confederate impressment, 15, 666–67, 671–72, 678, 686, 734, 737n., 750–51, 760–63, 765–66, 770; Confederate military laborers, 664–65, 667, 683–84, 686, 688n., 689, 703, 729–30, 760–63, 767–68, 770; as Confederate soldiers, 9, 27, 189, 207; Delaware, 493n.; District of Columbia, 159–60, 183–84; enlistment, 38, 46, 196, 207, 338, 409, 511; and fugitive slaves, 60, 160, 402; Illinois, 523n., 536; imprisonment, 376–77; Kentucky, 494, 651; as liberators, 376–77; Louisiana, 9, 27, 188n., 189–90, 196–98, 207, 230–31n., 268, 576–77, 794; Maryland, 331, 335, 337, 340, 359, 376–77; Missouri, 402, 472, 475; Native Guard, 9, 27, 189, 196, 207, 231n.; and nonslaveholders, 331, 679; North Carolina, 683–84, 763–66; property compensation, 770n.; skilled, 668, 697–98, 760–61, 767–68; slaveholders, 189; and slaveholders, 331, 679; and slaves, 331, 340; South Carolina, 769–70; Virginia, 15, 69, 731, 760–63, 767–68; Union informants, 770; Union military laborers, 349–50, 523n., 536–37; as Union soldiers, 27, 37, 195–96, 207, 231n.; unionists, 189–90, 268, 769
Freedmen's Bureau: 51, 637n., 653n., 682; Kentucky, 518, 655; letter to, 359; Maryland, 377n.; Tennessee, 313n., 323n., 518

Freedmen's Bureau, Chattanooga TN: letter from, 310–11
Freedmen's Bureau Commissioner: letter to, 359
Freedmen's Bureau, District of Columbia: letter from, 347–48; letter to, 376–77, 387–89
Freedmen's Bureau, Subdistrict of Louisville KY: letter to, 566–67
Freedmen's Bureau, Tennessee: letter to, 310–11
Freedmen's Bureau, Tennessee and Kentucky: letter to, 655
Freeman, J. B.: letter from, 807–8
Frémont, John C.: 397–98, 403, 417–18; emancipation policy, 16, 397, 415, 496–97; letter to, 414–15; proclamation, 415, 496–97
Frémont's Hussars: letter from, 421–22
French, Jonas H.: 198n., 220n.; letter to, 203, 238–39
French, Samuel G.: impressment policy, 701n.
French, William: 264n.
Fry, James B.: 653n.; letter to, 283–84, 287–88, 342–43
Fry, Speed Smith: 509
Fugitive slaves: 12; abused by Confederate soldiers, 105–6, 116–18, 125–26, 128, 142–43; abused by Missouri militia, 480–81; abused by slaveholders, 86–87, 110, 163, 267, 312–13, 320–23, 347–48, 376–77, 588–90, 618, 623–24, 673; Alabama, 36, 67, 257–59, 275–76, 283, 303–4n., 503, 507, 561–64, 566–70, 577n., 580, 593; Arkansas, 25, 254, 259, 403, 577–78; attempts to recapture, 14, 18, 67, 70, 82–83, 86, 93–95, 105–6, 161, 163, 169, 173–74, 177, 181–83, 198, 202–3, 217, 238–43, 256–57, 273–74, 277n., 285–88, 312, 314–15, 318, 334–35, 342–46, 352–53, 361–62, 364, 369–71, 382, 399, 407–8, 417–18, 424, 427–31, 438–40, 457–58, 476, 500, 523–24, 527, 532–33, 540, 550n., 698–99, 805–6; and Confederate deserters, 43, 132; and Confederate guerrillas, 308–9; Confederate informants, 112n., 417; Confederate policy, 134–36, 300, 699n., 794n.; Con-

829

Index

Speed, James: letter to, 657–58; *see also* Attorney General's Office
Spelman, H. B.: 262n.
Spiece, John B.: letter from, 782–83
Spriggs, Horace: petition from, 183–84
Sproston, J. Glendy: letter from, 115
Stacy, Ezra: letter from, 795–98
Stafford, Andrew: letter from, 390
Stafford (Capt.): letter to, 218
Stafford, Spencer H.: 231n.
Stanard, J. B.: letter from, 706–9
Stancliff, Charles L.: letter from, 565–66
Stanley, Timothy R.: fugitive slave policy, 271–72; letter from, 271–72
Stanly, Edward: 65; letter from, 83–85, 87–88
Stanton, Edwin M.: 21, 28, 325n., 362n., 434n., 471n., 602n.; American Freedmen's Inquiry Commission, 39; black enlistment policy, 29, 38, 108, 510n.; emancipation policy, 29; fugitive slave policy, 195, 216n., 257, 306, 506, 572n.; letter from, 275–76; letter to, 80–81, 83–85, 203–7, 275, 282, 308–10, 360–64, 367–68, 383–84, 386, 429–33, 461–65, 538, 562–64, 571–72, 598, 617–18; military labor policy, 510n.; telegram to, 561–62; *see also* War Department
Starks, James: 169n.
State Department: 659n.; letter from, 175; letter to, 547–49, 565
State Department (Confederate): 764n.
Staunton, John F.: letter from, 366–67
Stearns, George L.: 266n.; black enlistment policy, 265
Steele, I. N.: letter from, 616
Steger, James H.: letter to, 467
Stephen: 273–74
Stephen: court-martial, 785–90
Stephens, Alexander: 1–2
Stevens, Thomas H.: fugitive slave policy, 121; letter from, 120–21
Stevens, Walter H.: letter to, 706–9; military labor policy, 727–28
Stevenson, Josias: letter from, 314–15
Stewart, E.: letter from, 476
Stillman, Willis: letter from, 636–37
Stone, Charles P.: 333, 355n.; order by, 348–49; slavery policy, 348–49
Stringham, Silas H.: fugitive slave policy, 62, 76n.; letter to, 75–76

Strong, George C.: letter from, 226–30; letter to, 225–26
Sturgeon, Isaac H.: letter from, 465; letter to, 465–66
Suit, Fielder: 360n.
Suit, Kelita: letter from, 391
Sullivan's Island SC: 134–36
Surget, Eustace: letter from, 773–74
Swap, Franklin: letter from, 485–86
Switzler, Theodore A.: letter to, 485–88
Swope, George L.: order by, 635

Talbot, Theodore: letter to, 167
Taylor, George R.: 466n.
Taylor, James H.: letter from, 86
Taylor, Richard: 773n.; impressment policy, 804–5n.; military labor policy, 804–5n.
Taylor, S. D.: 21n.
Taylor, W. R.: letter from, 459
Taylor, William D.: letter from, 807–8
Tennessee: 249n., 495, 498, 524–25n., 550n.; black enlistment, 47, 265, 510; black soldiers, 266n., 655; Confederate military laborers, 26, 696–97; constitutional convention, 50, 251, 267–68; contraband camps, 256, 314–15; emancipation constitution, 50, 251, 267–68; emancipation politics, 50, 267; Emancipation Proclamation, 36, 260n.; evolution of free labor, 264, 310–12, 320n., 326–27; families of black soldiers, 265, 314–17; families of fugitive slaves, 303, 307–8, 311; Freedmen's Bureau, 310–11, 313n., 323n., 518; fugitive slaves, 26, 36, 253, 258–59, 260n., 263, 266, 270–72, 274–77, 279n., 281–82, 289–99, 302–8, 312–13, 318–24, 503, 507, 557–60, 564n., 570–71, 574n., 577–78; independent settlements, 263–64, 310–11; military governor, 696; military operations, 25–26, 250n., 253, 257, 262–63, 402, 497; Organization of Black Troops, 316–17, 324; refugeeing, 327; slave catchers, 254; slave-owned property, 297, 326; slaveholders, 250, 256–57, 263–67, 272–74, 312, 314–15, 318–23, 799; slavery, 262–63, 305; slaves, 265–66, 297–98, 503;

847